# Dictionary of Literary Biography

1 *The American Renaissance in New England*, edited by Joel Myerson (1978)

2 *American Novelists Since World War II*, edited by Jeffrey Helterman and Richard Layman (1978)

3 *Antebellum Writers in New York and the South*, edited by Joel Myerson (1979)

4 *American Writers in Paris, 1920-1939*, edited by Karen Lane Rood (1980)

5 *American Poets Since World War II*, 2 parts, edited by Donald J. Greiner (1980)

6 *American Novelists Since World War II, Second Series*, edited by James E. Kibler Jr. (1980)

7 *Twentieth-Century American Dramatists*, 2 parts, edited by John MacNicholas (1981)

8 *Twentieth-Century American Science-Fiction Writers*, 2 parts, edited by David Cowart and Thomas L. Wymer (1981)

9 *American Novelists, 1910-1945*, 3 parts, edited by James J. Martine (1981)

10 *Modern British Dramatists, 1900-1945*, 2 parts, edited by Stanley Weintraub (1982)

11 *American Humorists, 1800-1950*, 2 parts, edited by Stanley Trachtenberg (1982)

12 *American Realists and Naturalists*, edited by Donald Pizer and Earl N. Harbert (1982)

13 *British Dramatists Since World War II*, 2 parts, edited by Stanley Weintraub (1982)

14 *British Novelists Since 1960*, 2 parts, edited by Jay L. Halio (1983)

15 *British Novelists, 1930-1959*, 2 parts, edited by Bernard Oldsey (1983)

16 *The Beats: Literary Bohemians in Postwar America*, 2 parts, edited by Ann Charters (1983)

17 *Twentieth-Century American Historians*, edited by Clyde N. Wilson (1983)

18 *Victorian Novelists After 1885*, edited by Ira B. Nadel and William E. Fredeman (1983)

19 *British Poets, 1880-1914*, edited by Donald E. Stanford (1983)

20 *British Poets, 1914-1945*, edited by Donald E. Stanford (1983)

21 *Victorian Novelists Before 1885*, edited by Ira B. Nadel and William E. Fredeman (1983)

22 *American Writers for Children, 1900-1960*, edited by John Cech (1983)

23 *American Newspaper Journalists, 1873-1900*, edited by Perry J. Ashley (1983)

24 *American Colonial Writers, 1606-1734*, edited by Emory Elliott (1984)

25 *American Newspaper Journalists, 1901-1925*, edited by Perry J. Ashley (1984)

26 *American Screenwriters*, edited by Robert E. Morsberger, Stephen O. Lesser, and Randall Clark (1984)

27 *Poets of Great Britain and Ireland, 1945-1960*, edited by Vincent B. Sherry Jr. (1984)

28 *Twentieth-Century American-Jewish Fiction Writers*, edited by Daniel Walden (1984)

29 *American Newspaper Journalists, 1926-1950*, edited by Perry J. Ashley (1984)

30 *American Historians, 1607-1865*, edited by Clyde N. Wilson (1984)

31 *American Colonial Writers, 1735-1781*, edited by Emory Elliott (1984)

32 *Victorian Poets Before 1850*, edited by William E. Fredeman and Ira B. Nadel (1984)

33 *Afro-American Fiction Writers After 1955*, edited by Thadious M. Davis and Trudier Harris (1984)

34 *British Novelists, 1890-1929: Traditionalists*, edited by Thomas F. Staley (1985)

35 *Victorian Poets After 1850*, edited by William E. Fredeman and Ira B. Nadel (1985)

36 *British Novelists, 1890-1929: Modernists*, edited by Thomas F. Staley (1985)

37 *American Writers of the Early Republic*, edited by Emory Elliott (1985)

38 *Afro-American Writers After 1955: Dramatists and Prose Writers*, edited by Thadious M. Davis and Trudier Harris (1985)

39 *British Novelists, 1660-1800*, 2 parts, edited by Martin C. Battestin (1985)

40 *Poets of Great Britain and Ireland Since 1960*, 2 parts, edited by Vincent B. Sherry Jr. (1985)

41 *Afro-American Poets Since 1955*, edited by Trudier Harris and Thadious M. Davis (1985)

42 *American Writers for Children Before 1900*, edited by Glenn E. Estes (1985)

43 *American Newspaper Journalists, 1690-1872*, edited by Perry J. Ashley (1986)

44 *American Screenwriters, Second Series*, edited by Randall Clark, Robert E. Morsberger, and Stephen O. Lesser (1986)

45 *American Poets, 1880-1945, First Series*, edited by Peter Quartermain (1986)

46 *American Literary Publishing Houses, 1900-1980: Trade and Paperback*, edited by Peter Dzwonkoski (1986)

47 *American Historians, 1866-1912*, edited by Clyde N. Wilson (1986)

48 *American Poets, 1880-1945, Second Series*, edited by Peter Quartermain (1986)

49 *American Literary Publishing Houses, 1638-1899*, 2 parts, edited by Peter Dzwonkoski (1986)

50 *Afro-American Writers Before the Harlem Renaissance*, edited by Trudier Harris (1986)

51 *Afro-American Writers from the Harlem Renaissance to 1940*, edited by Trudier Harris (1987)

52 *American Writers for Children Since 1960: Fiction*, edited by Glenn E. Estes (1986)

53 *Canadian Writers Since 1960, First Series*, edited by W. H. New (1986)

54 *American Poets, 1880-1945, Third Series*, 2 parts, edited by Peter Quartermain (1987)

55 *Victorian Prose Writers Before 1867*, edited by William B. Thesing (1987)

56 *German Fiction Writers, 1914-1945*, edited by James Hardin (1987)

57 *Victorian Prose Writers After 1867*, edited by William B. Thesing (1987)

58 *Jacobean and Caroline Dramatists*, edited by Fredson Bowers (1987)

59 *American Literary Critics and Scholars, 1800-1850*, edited by John W. Rathbun and Monica M. Grecu (1987)

60 *Canadian Writers Since 1960, Second Series*, edited by W. H. New (1987)

61 *American Writers for Children Since 1960: Poets, Illustrators, and Nonfiction Authors*, edited by Glenn E. Estes (1987)

62 *Elizabethan Dramatists*, edited by Fredson Bowers (1987)

63 *Modern American Critics, 1920-1955*, edited by Gregory S. Jay (1988)

64 *American Literary Critics and Scholars, 1850-1880*, edited by John W. Rathbun and Monica M. Grecu (1988)

65 *French Novelists, 1900-1930*, edited by Catharine Savage Brosman (1988)

66 *German Fiction Writers, 1885-1913*, 2 parts, edited by James Hardin (1988)

67 *Modern American Critics Since 1955*, edited by Gregory S. Jay (1988)

68 *Canadian Writers, 1920-1959, First Series*, edited by W. H. New (1988)

69 *Contemporary German Fiction Writers, First Series*, edited by Wolfgang D. Elfe and James Hardin (1988)

70 *British Mystery Writers, 1860-1919*, edited by Bernard Benstock and Thomas F. Staley (1988)

71 *American Literary Critics and Scholars, 1880-1900*, edited by John W. Rathbun and Monica M. Grecu (1988)

72 *French Novelists, 1930-1960*, edited by Catharine Savage Brosman (1988)

73 *American Magazine Journalists, 1741-1850*, edited by Sam G. Riley (1988)

74 *American Short-Story Writers Before 1880*, edited by Bobby Ellen Kimbel, with the assistance of William E. Grant (1988)

75 *Contemporary German Fiction Writers, Second Series*, edited by Wolfgang D. Elfe and James Hardin (1988)

76 *Afro-American Writers, 1940-1955*, edited by Trudier Harris (1988)

77 *British Mystery Writers, 1920–1939,* edited by Bernard Benstock and Thomas F. Staley (1988)

78 *American Short-Story Writers, 1880–1910,* edited by Bobby Ellen Kimbel, with the assistance of William E. Grant (1988)

79 *American Magazine Journalists, 1850–1900,* edited by Sam G. Riley (1988)

80 *Restoration and Eighteenth-Century Dramatists, First Series,* edited by Paula R. Backscheider (1989)

81 *Austrian Fiction Writers, 1875–1913,* edited by James Hardin and Donald G. Daviau (1989)

82 *Chicano Writers, First Series,* edited by Francisco A. Lomelí and Carl R. Shirley (1989)

83 *French Novelists Since 1960,* edited by Catharine Savage Brosman (1989)

84 *Restoration and Eighteenth-Century Dramatists, Second Series,* edited by Paula R. Backscheider (1989)

85 *Austrian Fiction Writers After 1914,* edited by James Hardin and Donald G. Daviau (1989)

86 *American Short-Story Writers, 1910–1945, First Series,* edited by Bobby Ellen Kimbel (1989)

87 *British Mystery and Thriller Writers Since 1940, First Series,* edited by Bernard Benstock and Thomas F. Staley (1989)

88 *Canadian Writers, 1920–1959, Second Series,* edited by W. H. New (1989)

89 *Restoration and Eighteenth-Century Dramatists, Third Series,* edited by Paula R. Backscheider (1989)

90 *German Writers in the Age of Goethe, 1789–1832,* edited by James Hardin and Christoph E. Schweitzer (1989)

91 *American Magazine Journalists, 1900–1960, First Series,* edited by Sam G. Riley (1990)

92 *Canadian Writers, 1890–1920,* edited by W. H. New (1990)

93 *British Romantic Poets, 1789–1832, First Series,* edited by John R. Greenfield (1990)

94 *German Writers in the Age of Goethe: Sturm und Drang to Classicism,* edited by James Hardin and Christoph E. Schweitzer (1990)

95 *Eighteenth-Century British Poets, First Series,* edited by John Sitter (1990)

96 *British Romantic Poets, 1789–1832, Second Series,* edited by John R. Greenfield (1990)

97 *German Writers from the Enlightenment to Sturm und Drang, 1720–1764,* edited by James Hardin and Christoph E. Schweitzer (1990)

98 *Modern British Essayists, First Series,* edited by Robert Beum (1990)

99 *Canadian Writers Before 1890,* edited by W. H. New (1990)

100 *Modern British Essayists, Second Series,* edited by Robert Beum (1990)

101 *British Prose Writers, 1660–1800, First Series,* edited by Donald T. Siebert (1991)

102 *American Short-Story Writers, 1910–1945, Second Series,* edited by Bobby Ellen Kimbel (1991)

103 *American Literary Biographers, First Series,* edited by Steven Serafin (1991)

104 *British Prose Writers, 1660–1800, Second Series,* edited by Donald T. Siebert (1991)

105 *American Poets Since World War II, Second Series,* edited by R. S. Gwynn (1991)

106 *British Literary Publishing Houses, 1820–1880,* edited by Patricia J. Anderson and Jonathan Rose (1991)

107 *British Romantic Prose Writers, 1789–1832, First Series,* edited by John R. Greenfield (1991)

108 *Twentieth-Century Spanish Poets, First Series,* edited by Michael L. Perna (1991)

109 *Eighteenth-Century British Poets, Second Series,* edited by John Sitter (1991)

110 *British Romantic Prose Writers, 1789–1832, Second Series,* edited by John R. Greenfield (1991)

111 *American Literary Biographers, Second Series,* edited by Steven Serafin (1991)

112 *British Literary Publishing Houses, 1881–1965,* edited by Jonathan Rose and Patricia J. Anderson (1991)

113 *Modern Latin-American Fiction Writers, First Series,* edited by William Luis (1992)

114 *Twentieth-Century Italian Poets, First Series,* edited by Giovanna Wedel De Stasio, Glauco Cambon, and Antonio Illiano (1992)

115 *Medieval Philosophers,* edited by Jeremiah Hackett (1992)

116 *British Romantic Novelists, 1789–1832,* edited by Bradford K. Mudge (1992)

117 *Twentieth-Century Caribbean and Black African Writers, First Series,* edited by Bernth Lindfors and Reinhard Sander (1992)

118 *Twentieth-Century German Dramatists, 1889–1918,* edited by Wolfgang D. Elfe and James Hardin (1992)

119 *Nineteenth-Century French Fiction Writers: Romanticism and Realism, 1800–1860,* edited by Catharine Savage Brosman (1992)

120 *American Poets Since World War II, Third Series,* edited by R. S. Gwynn (1992)

121 *Seventeenth-Century British Nondramatic Poets, First Series,* edited by M. Thomas Hester (1992)

122 *Chicano Writers, Second Series,* edited by Francisco A. Lomelí and Carl R. Shirley (1992)

123 *Nineteenth-Century French Fiction Writers: Naturalism and Beyond, 1860–1900,* edited by Catharine Savage Brosman (1992)

124 *Twentieth-Century German Dramatists, 1919–1992,* edited by Wolfgang D. Elfe and James Hardin (1992)

125 *Twentieth-Century Caribbean and Black African Writers, Second Series,* edited by Bernth Lindfors and Reinhard Sander (1993)

126 *Seventeenth-Century British Nondramatic Poets, Second Series,* edited by M. Thomas Hester (1993)

127 *American Newspaper Publishers, 1950–1990,* edited by Perry J. Ashley (1993)

128 *Twentieth-Century Italian Poets, Second Series,* edited by Giovanna Wedel De Stasio, Glauco Cambon, and Antonio Illiano (1993)

129 *Nineteenth-Century German Writers, 1841–1900,* edited by James Hardin and Siegfried Mews (1993)

130 *American Short-Story Writers Since World War II,* edited by Patrick Meanor (1993)

131 *Seventeenth-Century British Nondramatic Poets, Third Series,* edited by M. Thomas Hester (1993)

132 *Sixteenth-Century British Nondramatic Writers, First Series,* edited by David A. Richardson (1993)

133 *Nineteenth-Century German Writers to 1840,* edited by James Hardin and Siegfried Mews (1993)

134 *Twentieth-Century Spanish Poets, Second Series,* edited by Jerry Phillips Winfield (1994)

135 *British Short-Fiction Writers, 1880–1914: The Realist Tradition,* edited by William B. Thesing (1994)

136 *Sixteenth-Century British Nondramatic Writers, Second Series,* edited by David A. Richardson (1994)

137 *American Magazine Journalists, 1900–1960, Second Series,* edited by Sam G. Riley (1994)

138 *German Writers and Works of the High Middle Ages: 1170–1280,* edited by James Hardin and Will Hasty (1994)

139 *British Short-Fiction Writers, 1945–1980,* edited by Dean Baldwin (1994)

140 *American Book-Collectors and Bibliographers, First Series,* edited by Joseph Rosenblum (1994)

141 *British Children's Writers, 1880–1914,* edited by Laura M. Zaidman (1994)

142 *Eighteenth-Century British Literary Biographers,* edited by Steven Serafin (1994)

143 *American Novelists Since World War II, Third Series,* edited by James R. Giles and Wanda H. Giles (1994)

144 *Nineteenth-Century British Literary Biographers,* edited by Steven Serafin (1994)

145 *Modern Latin-American Fiction Writers, Second Series,* edited by William Luis and Ann González (1994)

146 *Old and Middle English Literature,* edited by Jeffrey Helterman and Jerome Mitchell (1994)

147 *South Slavic Writers Before World War II,* edited by Vasa D. Mihailovich (1994)

148 *German Writers and Works of the Early Middle Ages: 800–1170,* edited by Will Hasty and James Hardin (1994)

149 *Late Nineteenth- and Early Twentieth-Century British Literary Biographers,* edited by Steven Serafin (1995)

150 *Early Modern Russian Writers, Late Seventeenth and Eighteenth Centuries,* edited by Marcus C. Levitt (1995)

151 *British Prose Writers of the Early Seventeenth Century,* edited by Clayton D. Lein (1995)

152 *American Novelists Since World War II, Fourth Series,* edited by James R. Giles and Wanda H. Giles (1995)

153 *Late-Victorian and Edwardian British Novelists, First Series,* edited by George M. Johnson (1995)

154 *The British Literary Book Trade, 1700–1820,* edited by James K. Bracken and Joel Silver (1995)

155 *Twentieth-Century British Literary Biographers,* edited by Steven Serafin (1995)

156 *British Short-Fiction Writers, 1880–1914: The Romantic Tradition,* edited by William F. Naufftus (1995)

157 *Twentieth-Century Caribbean and Black African Writers, Third Series,* edited by Bernth Lindfors and Reinhard Sander (1995)

158 *British Reform Writers, 1789–1832,* edited by Gary Kelly and Edd Applegate (1995)

159 *British Short-Fiction Writers, 1800–1880,* edited by John R. Greenfield (1996)

160 *British Children's Writers, 1914–1960,* edited by Donald R. Hettinga and Gary D. Schmidt (1996)

161 *British Children's Writers Since 1960, First Series,* edited by Caroline Hunt (1996)

162 *British Short-Fiction Writers, 1915–1945,* edited by John H. Rogers (1996)

163 *British Children's Writers, 1800–1880,* edited by Meena Khorana (1996)

164 *German Baroque Writers, 1580–1660,* edited by James Hardin (1996)

165 *American Poets Since World War II, Fourth Series,* edited by Joseph Conte (1996)

166 *British Travel Writers, 1837–1875,* edited by Barbara Brothers and Julia Gergits (1996)

167 *Sixteenth-Century British Nondramatic Writers, Third Series,* edited by David A. Richardson (1996)

168 *German Baroque Writers, 1661–1730,* edited by James Hardin (1996)

169 *American Poets Since World War II, Fifth Series,* edited by Joseph Conte (1996)

170 *The British Literary Book Trade, 1475–1700,* edited by James K. Bracken and Joel Silver (1996)

171 *Twentieth-Century American Sportswriters,* edited by Richard Orodenker (1996)

172 *Sixteenth-Century British Nondramatic Writers, Fourth Series,* edited by David A. Richardson (1996)

173 *American Novelists Since World War II, Fifth Series,* edited by James R. Giles and Wanda H. Giles (1996)

174 *British Travel Writers, 1876–1909,* edited by Barbara Brothers and Julia Gergits (1997)

175 *Native American Writers of the United States,* edited by Kenneth M. Roemer (1997)

176 *Ancient Greek Authors,* edited by Ward W. Briggs (1997)

177 *Italian Novelists Since World War II, 1945–1965,* edited by Augustus Pallotta (1997)

178 *British Fantasy and Science-Fiction Writers Before World War I,* edited by Darren Harris-Fain (1997)

179 *German Writers of the Renaissance and Reformation, 1280–1580,* edited by James Hardin and Max Reinhart (1997)

180 *Japanese Fiction Writers, 1868–1945,* edited by Van C. Gessel (1997)

181 *South Slavic Writers Since World War II,* edited by Vasa D. Mihailovich (1997)

182 *Japanese Fiction Writers Since World War II,* edited by Van C. Gessel (1997)

183 *American Travel Writers, 1776–1864,* edited by James J. Schramer and Donald Ross (1997)

184 *Nineteenth-Century British Book-Collectors and Bibliographers,* edited by William Baker and Kenneth Womack (1997)

185 *American Literary Journalists, 1945–1995, First Series,* edited by Arthur J. Kaul (1998)

186 *Nineteenth-Century American Western Writers,* edited by Robert L. Gale (1998)

187 *American Book Collectors and Bibliographers, Second Series,* edited by Joseph Rosenblum (1998)

188 *American Book and Magazine Illustrators to 1920,* edited by Steven E. Smith, Catherine A. Hastedt, and Donald H. Dyal (1998)

189 *American Travel Writers, 1850–1915,* edited by Donald Ross and James J. Schramer (1998)

190 *British Reform Writers, 1832–1914,* edited by Gary Kelly and Edd Applegate (1998)

191 *British Novelists Between the Wars,* edited by George M. Johnson (1998)

192 *French Dramatists, 1789–1914,* edited by Barbara T. Cooper (1998)

193 *American Poets Since World War II, Sixth Series,* edited by Joseph Conte (1998)

194 *British Novelists Since 1960, Second Series,* edited by Merritt Moseley (1998)

195 *British Travel Writers, 1910–1939,* edited by Barbara Brothers and Julia Gergits (1998)

196 *Italian Novelists Since World War II, 1965–1995,* edited by Augustus Pallotta (1999)

197 *Late-Victorian and Edwardian British Novelists, Second Series,* edited by George M. Johnson (1999)

198 *Russian Literature in the Age of Pushkin and Gogol: Prose,* edited by Christine A. Rydel (1999)

199 *Victorian Women Poets,* edited by William B. Thesing (1999)

200 *American Women Prose Writers to 1820,* edited by Carla J. Mulford, with Angela Vietto and Amy E. Winans (1999)

201 *Twentieth-Century British Book Collectors and Bibliographers,* edited by William Baker and Kenneth Womack (1999)

202 *Nineteenth-Century American Fiction Writers,* edited by Kent P. Ljungquist (1999)

203 *Medieval Japanese Writers,* edited by Steven D. Carter (1999)

204 *British Travel Writers, 1940–1997,* edited by Barbara Brothers and Julia M. Gergits (1999)

205 *Russian Literature in the Age of Pushkin and Gogol: Poetry and Drama,* edited by Christine A. Rydel (1999)

206 *Twentieth-Century American Western Writers, First Series,* edited by Richard H. Cracroft (1999)

207 *British Novelists Since 1960, Third Series,* edited by Merritt Moseley (1999)

208 *Literature of the French and Occitan Middle Ages: Eleventh to Fifteenth Centuries,* edited by Deborah Sinnreich-Levi and Ian S. Laurie (1999)

209 *Chicano Writers, Third Series,* edited by Francisco A. Lomelí and Carl R. Shirley (1999)

210 *Ernest Hemingway: A Documentary Volume,* edited by Robert W. Trogdon (1999)

211 *Ancient Roman Writers,* edited by Ward W. Briggs (1999)

212 *Twentieth-Century American Western Writers, Second Series,* edited by Richard H. Cracroft (1999)

213 *Pre-Nineteenth-Century British Book Collectors and Bibliographers,* edited by William Baker and Kenneth Womack (1999)

214 *Twentieth-Century Danish Writers,* edited by Marianne Stecher-Hansen (1999)

215 *Twentieth-Century Eastern European Writers, First Series,* edited by Steven Serafin (1999)

216 *British Poets of the Great War: Brooke, Rosenberg, Thomas. A Documentary Volume,* edited by Patrick Quinn (2000)

217 *Nineteenth-Century French Poets,* edited by Robert Beum (2000)

218 *American Short-Story Writers Since World War II, Second Series,* edited by Patrick Meanor and Gwen Crane (2000)

219 *F. Scott Fitzgerald's* The Great Gatsby: *A Documentary Volume,* edited by Matthew J. Bruccoli (2000)

220 *Twentieth-Century Eastern European Writers, Second Series,* edited by Steven Serafin (2000)

221 *American Women Prose Writers, 1870–1920,* edited by Sharon M. Harris, with the assistance of Heidi L. M. Jacobs and Jennifer Putzi (2000)

222 *H. L. Mencken: A Documentary Volume,* edited by Richard J. Schrader (2000)

223 *The American Renaissance in New England, Second Series,* edited by Wesley T. Mott (2000)

224 *Walt Whitman: A Documentary Volume,* edited by Joel Myerson (2000)

225 *South African Writers,* edited by Paul A. Scanlon (2000)

226 *American Hard-Boiled Crime Writers,* edited by George Parker Anderson and Julie B. Anderson (2000)

227 *American Novelists Since World War II, Sixth Series,* edited by James R. Giles and Wanda H. Giles (2000)

228 *Twentieth-Century American Dramatists, Second Series,* edited by Christopher J. Wheatley (2000)

229 *Thomas Wolfe: A Documentary Volume,* edited by Ted Mitchell (2001)

230 *Australian Literature, 1788–1914,* edited by Selina Samuels (2001)

231 *British Novelists Since 1960, Fourth Series,* edited by Merritt Moseley (2001)

232 *Twentieth-Century Eastern European Writers, Third Series,* edited by Steven Serafin (2001)

233 *British and Irish Dramatists Since World War II, Second Series,* edited by John Bull (2001)

234 *American Short-Story Writers Since World War II, Third Series,* edited by Patrick Meanor and Richard E. Lee (2001)

235 *The American Renaissance in New England, Third Series,* edited by Wesley T. Mott (2001)

236 *British Rhetoricians and Logicians, 1500–1660,* edited by Edward A. Malone (2001)

237 *The Beats: A Documentary Volume,* edited by Matt Theado (2001)

238 *Russian Novelists in the Age of Tolstoy and Dostoevsky,* edited by J. Alexander Ogden and Judith E. Kalb (2001)

239 *American Women Prose Writers: 1820–1870,* edited by Amy E. Hudock and Katharine Rodier (2001)

240 *Late Nineteenth- and Early Twentieth-Century British Women Poets,* edited by William B. Thesing (2001)

241 *American Sportswriters and Writers on Sport,* edited by Richard Orodenker (2001)

242 *Twentieth-Century European Cultural Theorists, First Series,* edited by Paul Hansom (2001)

243 *The American Renaissance in New England, Fourth Series,* edited by Wesley T. Mott (2001)

244 *American Short-Story Writers Since World War II, Fourth Series,* edited by Patrick Meanor and Joseph McNicholas (2001)

245 *British and Irish Dramatists Since World War II, Third Series,* edited by John Bull (2001)

246 *Twentieth-Century American Cultural Theorists,* edited by Paul Hansom (2001)

247 *James Joyce: A Documentary Volume,* edited by A. Nicholas Fargnoli (2001)

248 *Antebellum Writers in the South, Second Series,* edited by Kent Ljungquist (2001)

249 *Twentieth-Century American Dramatists, Third Series,* edited by Christopher Wheatley (2002)

250 *Antebellum Writers in New York, Second Series,* edited by Kent Ljungquist (2002)

251 *Canadian Fantasy and Science-Fiction Writers,* edited by Douglas Ivison (2002)

252 *British Philosophers, 1500–1799,* edited by Philip B. Dematteis and Peter S. Fosl (2002)

253 *Raymond Chandler: A Documentary Volume,* edited by Robert Moss (2002)

254 *The House of Putnam, 1837–1872: A Documentary Volume,* edited by Ezra Greenspan (2002)

255 *British Fantasy and Science-Fiction Writers, 1918–1960,* edited by Darren Harris-Fain (2002)

256 *Twentieth-Century American Western Writers, Third Series,* edited by Richard H. Cracroft (2002)

257 *Twentieth-Century Swedish Writers After World War II,* edited by Ann-Charlotte Gavel Adams (2002)

258 *Modern French Poets,* edited by Jean-François Leroux (2002)

259 *Twentieth-Century Swedish Writers Before World War II,* edited by Ann-Charlotte Gavel Adams (2002)

260 *Australian Writers, 1915–1950,* edited by Selina Samuels (2002)

261 *British Fantasy and Science-Fiction Writers Since 1960,* edited by Darren Harris-Fain (2002)

262 *British Philosophers, 1800–2000,* edited by Peter S. Fosl and Leemon B. McHenry (2002)

263 *William Shakespeare: A Documentary Volume,* edited by Catherine Loomis (2002)

264 *Italian Prose Writers, 1900–1945,* edited by Luca Somigli and Rocco Capozzi (2002)

265 *American Song Lyricists, 1920–1960,* edited by Philip Furia (2002)

266 *Twentieth-Century American Dramatists, Fourth Series,* edited by Christopher J. Wheatley (2002)

267 *Twenty-First-Century British and Irish Novelists,* edited by Michael R. Molino (2002)

268 *Seventeenth-Century French Writers,* edited by Françoise Jaouën (2002)

269 *Nathaniel Hawthorne: A Documentary Volume,* edited by Benjamin Franklin V (2002)

270 *American Philosophers Before 1950,* edited by Philip B. Dematteis and Leemon B. McHenry (2002)

271 *British and Irish Novelists Since 1960,* edited by Merritt Moseley (2002)

272 *Russian Prose Writers Between the World Wars,* edited by Christine Rydel (2003)

273 *F. Scott Fitzgerald's* Tender Is the Night: *A Documentary Volume,* edited by Matthew J. Bruccoli and George Parker Anderson (2003)

274 *John Dos Passos's* U.S.A.: *A Documentary Volume,* edited by Donald Pizer (2003)

275 *Twentieth-Century American Nature Writers: Prose,* edited by Roger Thompson and J. Scott Bryson (2003)

276 *British Mystery and Thriller Writers Since 1960,* edited by Gina Macdonald (2003)

277 *Russian Literature in the Age of Realism,* edited by Alyssa Dinega Gillespie (2003)

278 *American Novelists Since World War II, Seventh Series,* edited by James R. Giles and Wanda H. Giles (2003)

279 *American Philosophers, 1950–2000,* edited by Philip B. Dematteis and Leemon B. McHenry (2003)

280 *Dashiell Hammett's* The Maltese Falcon: *A Documentary Volume,* edited by Richard Layman (2003)

281 *British Rhetoricians and Logicians, 1500–1660, Second Series,* edited by Edward A. Malone (2003)

282 *New Formalist Poets,* edited by Jonathan N. Barron and Bruce Meyer (2003)

283 *Modern Spanish American Poets, First Series,* edited by María A. Salgado (2003)

284 *The House of Holt, 1866–1946: A Documentary Volume,* edited by Ellen D. Gilbert (2003)

285 *Russian Writers Since 1980,* edited by Marina Balina and Mark Lipovetsky (2004)

286 *Castilian Writers, 1400–1500,* edited by Frank A. Domínguez and George D. Greenia (2004)

287 *Portuguese Writers,* edited by Monica Rector and Fred M. Clark (2004)

## *Dictionary of Literary Biography Documentary Series*

1 *Sherwood Anderson, Willa Cather, John Dos Passos, Theodore Dreiser, F. Scott Fitzgerald, Ernest Hemingway, Sinclair Lewis,* edited by Margaret A. Van Antwerp (1982)

2 *James Gould Cozzens, James T. Farrell, William Faulkner, John O'Hara, John Steinbeck, Thomas Wolfe, Richard Wright,* edited by Margaret A. Van Antwerp (1982)

3 *Saul Bellow, Jack Kerouac, Norman Mailer, Vladimir Nabokov, John Updike, Kurt Vonnegut,* edited by Mary Bruccoli (1983)

4 *Tennessee Williams,* edited by Margaret A. Van Antwerp and Sally Johns (1984)

5 *American Transcendentalists,* edited by Joel Myerson (1988)

6 *Hardboiled Mystery Writers: Raymond Chandler, Dashiell Hammett, Ross Macdonald,* edited by Matthew J. Bruccoli and Richard Layman (1989)

7 *Modern American Poets: James Dickey, Robert Frost, Marianne Moore,* edited by Karen L. Rood (1989)

8 *The Black Aesthetic Movement,* edited by Jeffrey Louis Decker (1991)

9 *American Writers of the Vietnam War: W. D. Ehrhart, Larry Heinemann, Tim O'Brien, Walter McDonald, John M. Del Vecchio,* edited by Ronald Baughman (1991)

10 *The Bloomsbury Group,* edited by Edward L. Bishop (1992)

11 *American Proletarian Culture: The Twenties and The Thirties,* edited by Jon Christian Suggs (1993)

12 *Southern Women Writers: Flannery O'Connor, Katherine Anne Porter, Eudora Welty,* edited by Mary Ann Wimsatt and Karen L. Rood (1994)

13 *The House of Scribner, 1846–1904,* edited by John Delaney (1996)

14 *Four Women Writers for Children, 1868–1918,* edited by Caroline C. Hunt (1996)

15 *American Expatriate Writers: Paris in the Twenties,* edited by Matthew J. Bruccoli and Robert W. Trogdon (1997)

16 *The House of Scribner, 1905–1930,* edited by John Delaney (1997)

17 *The House of Scribner, 1931–1984,* edited by John Delaney (1998)

18 *British Poets of The Great War: Sassoon, Graves, Owen,* edited by Patrick Quinn (1999)

19 *James Dickey,* edited by Judith S. Baughman (1999)

**See also DLB 210, 216, 219, 222, 224, 229, 237, 247, 253, 254, 263, 269, 273, 274, 280, 284**

## Dictionary of Literary Biography Yearbooks

1980 edited by Karen L. Rood, Jean W. Ross, and Richard Ziegfeld (1981)

1981 edited by Karen L. Rood, Jean W. Ross, and Richard Ziegfeld (1982)

1982 edited by Richard Ziegfeld; associate editors: Jean W. Ross and Lynne C. Zeigler (1983)

1983 edited by Mary Bruccoli and Jean W. Ross; associate editor Richard Ziegfeld (1984)

1984 edited by Jean W. Ross (1985)

1985 edited by Jean W. Ross (1986)

1986 edited by J. M. Brook (1987)

1987 edited by J. M. Brook (1988)

1988 edited by J. M. Brook (1989)

1989 edited by J. M. Brook (1990)

1990 edited by James W. Hipp (1991)

1991 edited by James W. Hipp (1992)

1992 edited by James W. Hipp (1993)

1993 edited by James W. Hipp, contributing editor George Garrett (1994)

1994 edited by James W. Hipp, contributing editor George Garrett (1995)

1995 edited by James W. Hipp, contributing editor George Garrett (1996)

1996 edited by Samuel W. Bruce and L. Kay Webster, contributing editor George Garrett (1997)

1997 edited by Matthew J. Bruccoli and George Garrett, with the assistance of L. Kay Webster (1998)

1998 edited by Matthew J. Bruccoli, contributing editor George Garrett, with the assistance of D. W. Thomas (1999)

1999 edited by Matthew J. Bruccoli, contributing editor George Garrett, with the assistance of D. W. Thomas (2000)

2000 edited by Matthew J. Bruccoli, contributing editor George Garrett, with the assistance of George Parker Anderson (2001)

2001 edited by Matthew J. Bruccoli, contributing editor George Garrett, with the assistance of George Parker Anderson (2002)

2002 edited by Matthew J. Bruccoli and George Garrett; George Parker Anderson, Assistant Editor (2003)

## Concise Series

**Concise Dictionary of American Literary Biography,** 7 volumes (1988-1999): *The New Consciousness, 1941-1968; Colonization to the American Renaissance, 1640-1865; Realism, Naturalism, and Local Color, 1865-1917; The Twenties, 1917-1929; The Age of Maturity, 1929-1941; Broadening Views, 1968-1988; Supplement: Modern Writers, 1900-1998.*

**Concise Dictionary of British Literary Biography,** 8 volumes (1991-1992): *Writers of the Middle Ages and Renaissance Before 1660; Writers of the Restoration and Eighteenth Century, 1660-1789; Writers of the Romantic Period, 1789-1832; Victorian Writers, 1832-1890; Late-Victorian and Edwardian Writers, 1890-1914; Modern Writers, 1914-1945; Writers After World War II, 1945-1960; Contemporary Writers, 1960 to Present.*

**Concise Dictionary of World Literary Biography,** 4 volumes (1999-2000): *Ancient Greek and Roman Writers; German Writers; African, Caribbean, and Latin American Writers; South Slavic and Eastern European Writers.*

Dictionary of Literary Biography® • Volume Two Hundred Eighty-Seven

# Portuguese Writers

Dictionary of Literary Biography® • Volume Two Hundred Eighty-Seven

# Portuguese Writers

Edited by
Monica Rector
*University of North Carolina at Chapel Hill*
and
Fred M. Clark
*University of North Carolina at Chapel Hill*

A Bruccoli Clark Layman Book

ST. PHILIP'S COLLEGE LIBRARY

Detroit • New York • San Diego • San Francisco • Cleveland • New Haven, Conn. • Waterville, Maine • London • Munich

**Dictionary of Literary Biography**
**Volume 287: Portuguese Writers**

Monica Rector
Fred M. Clark

**Advisory Board**
John Baker
William Cagle
Patrick O'Connor
George Garrett
Trudier Harris
Alvin Kernan
Kenny J. Williams

**Editorial Directors**
Matthew J. Bruccoli and Richard Layman

© 2004 by Gale. Gale is an imprint of The Gale Group, Inc., a division of Thomson Learning, Inc.

Gale and Design™ and Thomson Learning™ are trademarks used herein under license.

*For more information, contact*
The Gale Group, Inc.
27500 Drake Rd.
Farmington Hills, MI 48331-3535
Or you can visit our Internet site at
http://www.gale.com

**ALL RIGHTS RESERVED**
No part of this work covered by the copyright hereon may be reproduced or used in any form or by any means—graphic, electronic, or mechanical, including photocopying, recording, taping, Web distribution, or information storage retrieval systems—without the written permission of the publisher.

For permission to use material from this product, submit your request via Web at http://www.gale-edit.com/permissions, or you may download our Permissions Request form and submit your request by fax or mail to:

*Permissions Department*
The Gale Group, Inc.
27500 Drake Rd.
Farmington Hills, MI 48331-3535
Permissions Hotline:
248-699-8006 or 800-877-4253, ext. 8006
Fax: 248-699-8074 or 800-762-4058

While every effort has been made to ensure the reliability of the information presented in this publication, The Gale Group, Inc. does not guarantee the accuracy of the data contained herein. The Gale Group, Inc. accepts no payment for listing; and inclusion in the publication of any organization, agency, institution, publication, service, or individual does not imply endorsement of the editors or publisher. Errors brought to the attention of the publisher and verified to the satisfaction of the publisher will be corrected in future editions.

---

**LIBRARY OF CONGRESS CATALOGING-IN-PUBLICATION DATA**

Portuguese writers / edited by Monica Rector and Fred M. Clark.
    p. cm. — (Dictionary of literary biography ; v. 287)
"A Bruccoli Clark Layman book."
Includes bibliographical references and index.
    ISBN 0-7876-6824-9 (hardcover)
    1. Portuguese literature—Bio-bibliography—Dictionaries.
    2. Authors, Portuguese—Biography—Dictionaries.
    I. Rector, Monica. II. Clark, Fred M. III. Series.

PQ9027.P67 2003
869.09'0003—dc22
                                      2003016431

---

Printed in the United States of America
10 9 8 7 6 5 4 3 2 1

# Contents

Plan of the Series .......................... xiii
Introduction ............................. xv

Augusto Abelaira (1926– ) ................... 3
*Maria Guterres*

Sophia de Mello Breyner Andresen (1919– ) ..... 11
*Marco G. Silva*

António Lobo Antunes (1942– ) .............. 18
*Luis Riordan Gonçalves*

Agustina Bessa-Luís (1922– ) ................ 26
*Luciana Camargo Namorato*

Manuel Maria Barbosa du Bocage (1765–1805) .... 34
*Elias J. Torres Feijó*

Raul Brandão (1867–1930) ................... 42
*Rui Torres*

Luís de Camões (1524–1580) ................. 49
*Leodegário A. de Azevedo Filho*

Camilo Castelo Branco (1825–1890) ........... 58
*Elias J. Torres Feijó*

Júlio Dinis (Joaquim Guilherme
Gomes Coelho) (1839–1871) ............... 75
*Paulo Motta Oliveira*

Florbela Espanca (1894–1930) ................ 80
*Anna Klobucka*

Vergílio Ferreira (1916–1996) ................ 89
*Fernando Arenas*

Manuel da Fonseca (1911–1993) .............. 97
*José Carlos Barcellos*

Almeida Garrett (João Baptista da Silva Leitão
de Almeida Garrett) (1799–1854) ........... 101
*Sérgio Nazar David*

Teolinda Gersão (1940– ) .................. 112
*José N. Ornelas*

Ana Hatherly (1929– ) .................... 121
*Nadiá Paulo Ferreira*

Herberto Helder (1930– ) .................. 126
*Rui Torres*

Alexandre Herculano (1810–1877) ............ 133
*Paulo Motta Oliveira*

Abílio Manuel Guerra Junqueiro
(1850–1923) ........................... 143
*Elias J. Torres Feijó*

Irene Lisboa (1892–1958) .................. 149
*Alice R. Clemente*

Fernão Lopes (1380/1390?–1460?) ............ 157
*Andréia Cristina Lopes Frazão da Silva*

Helena Marques (1935– ) .................. 165
*Monica Rector*

José Rodrigues Miguéis (1901–1980) .......... 170
*Reinaldo Francisco Silva*

Fernando Namora (1919–1989) ............... 176
*Luís Flávio Sieczkowski*

António Nobre (1867–1900) ................. 183
*Paulo Motta Oliveira*

Carlos de Oliveira (1921–1981) .............. 188
*Reinaldo Francisco Silva*

Camilo Pessanha (1867–1926) ............... 194
*René P. Garay*

Fernando Pessoa (1888–1935) ............... 199
*George Monteiro*

Fernão Mendes Pinto (1509?/1511?–1583) ...... 215
*Leila Rodrigues da Silva*

José Cardoso Pires (1925–1998) .............. 220
*Lênia Márcia Mongelli*

Eça de Queirós (1845–1900) ................. 230
*Maria do Amparo Tavares Maleval*

Antero de Quental (1842–1891) .............. 241
*Ana Maria Almeida Martins*

Alves Redol (1911–1969) ................... 249
*Loida Pereira Peterson*

José Régio (José Maria dos Reis Pereira)
(1901–1969) ........................... 254
*José Carlos Barcellos*

Bernardim Ribeiro (fl. circa 1475–1482–
circa 1526–1544) .........................259
  *Joseph Abraham Levi*

Francisco de Sá de Miranda (1481–1558?) .......268
  *Joseph Abraham Levi*

Mário de Sá-Carneiro (1890–1916) .............275
  *Fernando Arenas*

José Saramago (1922– ) ....................280
  *José N. Ornelas*

Jorge de Sena (1919–1978) ...................298
  *Gilda Santos*

Salette Tavares (1922–1994) ..................307
  *Rui Torres*

Miguel Torga (Adolfo Correia da Rocha)
(1907–1995) .............................312
  *Maria do Amparo Tavares Maleval*

Cesário Verde (1855–1886) ...................322
  *Marina Machado Rodrigues*

Gil Vicente (1465–between 1536 and 1540) .....327
  *Reinhard Krüger*

Appendix 1:
  Medieval Galician-Portuguese Poetry ........337
  *Leodegário A. de Azevedo Filho*

Appendix 2:
  Mariana Alcoforado, the Portuguese Nun .....347
  *Anna Klobucka*

Appendix 3:
  The Three Marias: A Landmark Case in
  Portuguese Literary History ................355
  *Anna Klobucka*

Books for Further Reading ...................365
Contributors ................................371
Cumulative Index ............................375

# Plan of the Series

*... Almost the most prodigious asset of a country, and perhaps its most precious possession, is its native literary product—when that product is fine and noble and enduring.*

Mark Twain*

The advisory board, the editors, and the publisher of the *Dictionary of Literary Biography* are joined in endorsing Mark Twain's declaration. The literature of a nation provides an inexhaustible resource of permanent worth. Our purpose is to make literature and its creators better understood and more accessible to students and the reading public, while satisfying the needs of teachers and researchers.

To meet these requirements, *literary biography* has been construed in terms of the author's achievement. The most important thing about a writer is his writing. Accordingly, the entries in *DLB* are career biographies, tracing the development of the author's canon and the evolution of his reputation.

The purpose of *DLB* is not only to provide reliable information in a usable format but also to place the figures in the larger perspective of literary history and to offer appraisals of their accomplishments by qualified scholars.

The publication plan for *DLB* resulted from two years of preparation. The project was proposed to Bruccoli Clark by Frederick G. Ruffner, president of the Gale Research Company, in November 1975. After specimen entries were prepared and typeset, an advisory board was formed to refine the entry format and develop the series rationale. In meetings held during 1976, the publisher, series editors, and advisory board approved the scheme for a comprehensive biographical dictionary of persons who contributed to literature. Editorial work on the first volume began in January 1977, and it was published in 1978. In order to make *DLB* more than a dictionary and to compile volumes that individually have claim to status as literary history, it was decided to organize volumes by topic, period, or genre. Each of these freestanding volumes provides a biographical-bibliographical guide and overview for a particular area of literature. We are convinced that this organization—as opposed to a single alphabet method—constitutes a valuable innovation in the presentation of reference material. The volume plan necessarily requires many decisions for the placement and treatment of authors. Certain figures will be included in separate volumes, but with different entries emphasizing the aspect of his career appropriate to each volume. Ernest Hemingway, for example, is represented in *American Writers in Paris, 1920-1939* by an entry focusing on his expatriate apprenticeship; he is also in *American Novelists, 1910-1945* with an entry surveying his entire career, as well as in *American Short-Story Writers, 1910-1945, Second Series* with an entry concentrating on his short fiction. Each volume includes a cumulative index of the subject authors and articles.

Since 1981 the series has been further augmented by the *DLB Yearbooks,* which update published entries, add new entries to keep the *DLB* current with contemporary activity, and provide articles on literary history. There have also been nineteen *DLB Documentary Series* volumes, which provide illustrations, facsimiles, and biographical and critical source materials for figures, works, or groups judged to have particular interest for students. In 1999 the *Documentary Series* was incorporated into the *DLB* volume numbering system beginning with *DLB 210: Ernest Hemingway.*

We define literature as the *intellectual commerce of a nation:* not merely as belles lettres but as that ample and complex process by which ideas are generated, shaped, and transmitted. *DLB* entries are not limited to "creative writers" but extend to other figures who in their time and in their way influenced the mind of a people. Thus the series encompasses historians, journalists, publishers, book collectors, and screenwriters. By this means readers of *DLB* may be aided to perceive literature not as cult scripture in the keeping of intellectual high priests but firmly positioned at the center of a nation's life.

*DLB* includes the major writers appropriate to each volume and those standing in the ranks behind them. Scholarly and critical counsel has been sought in

*\*From an unpublished section of Mark Twain's autobiography, copyright by the Mark Twain Company*

# Plan of the Series

deciding which minor figures to include and how full their entries should be. Wherever possible, useful references are made to figures who do not warrant separate entries.

Each *DLB* volume has an expert volume editor responsible for planning the volume, selecting the figures for inclusion, and assigning the entries. Volume editors are also responsible for preparing, where appropriate, appendices surveying the major periodicals and literary and intellectual movements for their volumes, as well as lists of further readings. Work on the series as a whole is coordinated at the Bruccoli Clark Layman editorial center in Columbia, South Carolina, where the editorial staff is responsible for accuracy and utility of the published volumes.

One feature that distinguishes *DLB* is the illustration policy—its concern with the iconography of literature. Just as an author is influenced by his surroundings, so is the reader's understanding of the author enhanced by a knowledge of his environment. Therefore *DLB* volumes include not only drawings, paintings, and photographs of authors, often depicting them at various stages in their careers, but also illustrations of their families and places where they lived. Title pages are regularly reproduced in facsimile along with dust jackets for modern authors. The dust jackets are a special feature of *DLB* because they often document better than anything else the way in which an author's work was perceived in its own time. Specimens of the writers' manuscripts and letters are included when feasible.

Samuel Johnson rightly decreed that "The chief glory of every people arises from its authors." The purpose of the *Dictionary of Literary Biography* is to compile literary history in the surest way available to us—by accurate and comprehensive treatment of the lives and work of those who contributed to it.

The *DLB* Advisory Board

# Introduction

The origins of Portuguese literature are linked to the formation of the nation. At the end of the eleventh century, Alfonso VI, king of León, married his only legitimate daughter, Urraca, to Count Raymond of Burgundy, and his illegitimate daughter Tarasia (or Teresa) to Raymond's cousin, Henry of Burgundy. Alfonso gave the region of Galicia to Raymond, and the area between the Minho River and the Tagus River, which included what was called Portugal at the time, to Henry. When Alfonso died in 1109, several political and military conflicts took place as Portugal attempted to gain its independence. Tarasia's son, Afonso Henriques, was in a constant skirmish over territory with his cousin Alfonso VII (son of Urraca). The two reached a settlement in 1137, but they resumed fighting in 1140 when Afonso Henriques invaded Galicia and Alfonso VII invaded Portugal. The cousins made peace in 1143, and Pope Alexander III finally recognized Afonso Henriques as king (Afonso I) and Portugal as an independent kingdom in 1179.

The Portuguese language derives from Latin, which became more diversified as the Roman Empire expanded. Latin, as it was spoken by the people (vulgar Latin), gave rise to dialectal differences throughout the empire. The Romance languages are a result of this differentiation. The first manifestations of Portuguese literature—*cantigas,* poems that were performed as songs—were written in the Galician-Portuguese dialect. From the twelfth to the fifteenth centuries, Latin was the language of the cultured upper class, but the people spoke Portuguese, which became the official language during the reign of Dinis (1279–1325). The first texts written in Portuguese date from the thirteenth century.

Portuguese oral literature dates from the reign of Sancho I (1185–1211), son of Afonso Henriques. It was transmitted by minstrels and by the troubadours, noblemen who wrote the words (and possibly composed the music) for the poetry that the minstrels sang. While there were women singers called *soldadeiras* because they received *soldo* (money) for their performances, the troubadours were all male. The troubadours' audience was limited to other noblemen, while the minstrels traveled around the country performing for the public. Both King Dinis and Sancho I are credited for some of the songs that belong to the troubadour tradition.

Troubadour literature, composed of *cantigas,* evolved between 1250 and 1350. The *cantigas* may be lyrical or satirical. The lyrical category includes the *cantigas de amigo* (songs of friends) and the *cantigas de amor* (songs of love); the satirical category includes the *cantigas de escárnio* (songs of mockery) and the *cantigas de maldizer* (songs of vilification). The *cantigas de amigo* are verses in which a feminine voice addresses a male lover; in these, the poet portrays his emotions and amorous ambitions as if he were a woman. The *cantigas de amor* express the ideal of courtly love from a male perspective. In the *cantigas de escárnio* the troubadour satirizes a person without mentioning the name; he focuses on personal defects and negative qualities. In the *cantigas de maldizer* the poet specifies the person being criticized by name. Many of the *cantigas* were compiled into collections called *cancioneiros*. Most of the poems surviving from the epoch are in the *Cancioneiro da Ajuda,* which includes 310 *cantigas;* the *Cancioneiro da Biblioteca Nacional,* also referred to as the *Colocci-Brancuti,* which has 1,647; and the *Cancioneiro da Vaticana,* which has 1,205.

Novels of chivalry began to appear in Portugal during Afonso III's reign (1248–1279). These novels were not written by Portuguese authors; they were adaptations or translations, mostly from the French, and appeared toward the end of the thirteenth century. The most notable include the *História de Merlim* (Story of Merlin) and two versions of the Grail stories, *Livro de Josep ab Arimatia* (The Book of Joseph of Arimathea) and *A demanda do Santo Graal* (The Fight for the Holy Grail). In these narratives, the protagonist carries out promises and obligations to his lady. Other types of early prose include *crônicas* (chronicles that deal with historical and legendary topics), *hagiografias* (lives of the saints), and *livros de linhagens,* genealogical tracts that were used to establish family relationships in order to avoid intermarriage of relatives and to solve questions about inheritances.

With the beginning of the period of discovery and expansion, which occurred during the reign of the Master of Avis (who had himself proclaimed King John I in 1385 and ruled until 1433), the interest of medieval man in commerce began to increase. In 1434 King Duarte (1433–1438) commissioned Fernão Lopes to write about the lives of the early kings of Portugal. There are three extant Lopes works considered to be authentic; they narrate the lives of Pedro, Fernando, and John I. Whereas the medieval chroniclers had related facts through a partial and fragmented perspective, Lopes portrays his subjects vividly within the context of palace life and its intrigues.

During this period, Garcia de Resende compiled the *Cancioneiro geral* (General Songbook, 1516), which includes mostly poems written by court poets, dating from the middle of the fifteenth century to the early sixteenth. The greatest author of the time was Gil Vicente, founder of the Portuguese theater. A favorite at the court of Queen Leonor, Vicente focused his theatrical work on criticizing various social classes and customs of the time. His works, which include religious *autos* (plays) as well as farces, focus on the society of his period. Through the use of allegory and symbols, the playwright expresses his concerns about social changes and what he considered to be the loss of traditional values. His preferred verse form in his plays was the *redondilha maior,* lines of seven syllables.

In the sixteenth century, Portugal was caught up in a fervor of change and innovation. The economy, however, retained its medieval structure. In the spirit of expansion and discovery, John III (1521–1557) reformed university education. Throughout the 1530s and 1540s some twenty colleges were founded in Portugal. John III's most important contribution to education was the creation of the Colégio das Artes e Humanidades (School of the Arts and Humanities) in Coimbra in 1547. The director of the school brought in a faculty of French, Portuguese, and Scottish professors to teach a curriculum that ranged from Latin, Greek, and Hebrew to philosophy and mathematics. In spite of the advances in education, there were setbacks to the development of humanistic thought, principally with the introduction into Portugal of the procedures of the Spanish Inquisition in 1536.

The classical epoch of Portuguese literature includes the sixteenth, seventeenth, and eighteenth centuries. This broad temporal and cultural span corresponds to the trends and movements known as the Renaissance, the Baroque, and Arcadianism.

The Renaissance period reintroduced classical Greek and Latin models that shaped and defined literary production during the period. Francisco Sá de Miranda is a key figure of the time; on his return from Italy in 1527, he brought with him various poetic innovations that influenced the *quinhentistas* (poets of the 1500s). These innovations included verse forms and combinations: the heroic decasyllable (a ten-syllable line with stress on the sixth and tenth syllables), the tercet, the *oitava rima* (a stanza of eight lines with the rhyme scheme *abababcc*), and the sonnet (composed of two quatrains and two tercets with various rhyme schemes). Sá de Miranda's new method of writing verse (*medida nova*) broke with the traditional *medida velha* (old measure) that stressed the use of *redondilha maior* (lines of seven syllables) and *redondilha menor* (lines of five syllables). Bernardim Ribeiro, known for his pastoral novel *Menina e moça* (Lass and Maiden, 1554), cultivated the bucolic in his eclogues, the first written in the Portuguese language. Renaissance poets introduced the Petrarchan concept of love through their idealized treatment of women and sensuality in their works.

The most important writer of the Renaissance is Luís de Camões, who retained elements of the Christian tradition of the Middle Ages while composing sensual poems that explore worldly pleasures. His work is a mixture of the Christian and the Neoplatonic concepts of life. Camões's most important work is his epic poem *Os Lusíadas* (The Lusiads, 1572), divided into ten cantos composed in *oitava rima*. While the narrative is focused on Vasco da Gama's expedition to India (1497–1498), the poet extols the accomplishments of the Portuguese people in verses that mingle historical events and legend, Christian religion and pagan mythology, and prosaic and highly lyrical moments.

A figure who stands out in the sixteenth century is Sebastian (1557–1578), son of John (John III's son and heir to the throne) and Juana, Spanish king Philip II's sister. With the intention of expanding the Catholic faith, King Sebastian invaded Morocco but was totally defeated in the battle of Alcácer-Quibir (1578). He and many of his country's noblemen were killed, but Sebastian was transformed into a legend of mythic proportions that has reappeared in Portuguese literature many times. *Sebastianismo* consists of the hope that King Sebastian will return, and with him, the past glory of Portugal.

Sebastian's successor, Cardinal Henry (1578–1580), had no children; when he died, the forces of Philip II entered Portugal, making him Philip I of Portugal. The country was thus under Spanish domination, which lasted until 1640. Economic problems and unpopular political decisions by the Spaniards created a spirit of Portuguese nationalism and the desire for self-identity, which finally led to revolution: John, Duke of Bragança, drove out the Spaniards, restoring Portugal's independence and becoming John IV (1640–1656). In this period there also emerged an antagonism between noblemen and the rising bourgeoisie, who assumed economic power of the country. The ideals of this new social class were also often at odds with the church.

The Baroque, which was a reaction against the classical concepts of the Renaissance, dominates art and literature of the period. The Baroque spirit reflects certain basic antitheses, such as the opposition between faith and reason, derived from the Middle Ages and the Renaissance. The opposition is captured in the literary styles known as *cultismo* or *gongorismo* (cultism or gongorism), influenced by the Spanish poet Luis de Góngora y Argote, and *conceptismo* (conceptism), influenced by the Spanish writer Francisco de Quevedo. *Cultismo* is characterized by elaborate and extravagant language, complicated metaphors, and obscure symbols, while *conceptismo* emphasizes logical reasoning and the expression of a concept or idea in clear and precise language. Father António Vieira, who was born in Portugal but spent most of his life in Brazil as a Jesuit priest, represents well the Baroque spirit. He used sermons to express both his religious faith and his political views, often incurring the disapproval of his superiors in the church. Although he cultivated both conceptism and cultism, his sermons are characterized by precision and clarity. He even used the pulpit at times to preach against the lack of clarity in the sermons of other priests. For Vieira, the mission of the perfect orator was to "ensinar, deleitar e mover" (teach, delight, and move) his audience.

Other works that stand out during the restoration period include the didactic prose in *Carta de guia de casados* (A Guide for Married Couples, 1651), by Francisco Manuel de Melo, and *Lettres portugaises traduites en françois* (Portuguese Letters Translated into French, 1669), for many years attributed to Soror Mariana Alcoforado but now thought to be the work of a Frenchman, Gabriel-Joseph Lavergne de Guilleragues. Nevertheless, Alcoforado and another nun, Soror Violante do Céu, appreciated for her clever conceits and mystic tone, represent the first feminine voices of importance in Portuguese literature. Poetry, which had reached moments of brilliance in the verses of Camões, entered a state of decadence toward the end of the Baroque period. Much of the poetry of the seventeenth century is collected into *Postilhão de Apolo* (Apollo's Messenger, 1761-1762) and *A fênix renascida* (The Phoenix Reborn, 1716-1728). Many of the poems in these volumes are the results of the cultural phenomenon referred to as the *academias* (academies; a society or group of poets and writers) and are characterized by excessive influences of cultism and conceptism.

The Enlightenment, the movement of intellectual renovation that had its origins in England and reached its greatest moments with the French Revolution (1789), arrived late in Portugal. The Portuguese bourgeoisie had increased their numbers and in the eighteenth century began to demand more freedom and economic and political power. Sebastião José de Carvalho e Melo, Marquês de Pombal, whose prestige had been enhanced by the rebuilding of Lisbon after the earthquake of 1755, instituted reforms throughout the country. As prime minister of José I (1750-1777), he reorganized the university system. He also founded several new schools, including the Escola de Comércio (for the sons of the bourgeoisie); established the Academia Real das Ciências (1779); set up a royal printing press; and turned the king's library into the first public library in Portugal. The number of literary academies increased, the most notable ones being the Arcádia Lusitana (1756) and the Nova Arcádia (1790), to which many of the important poets belonged. The Arcadians produced the best poetry of this period, in which French neoclassicism replaced Spanish models of influence.

Arcadianism, an artistic reaction against the excesses of the Baroque, dominated literature of the eighteenth century. This movement represents a critical attitude of the educated bourgeoisie toward the ideals and lifestyles of the nobility and the clergy. The Arcadians, well within the principles of the Enlightenment, were guided by a rational vision that resulted in writing characterized by order and verisimilitude. Writers favored simplicity over the exaggeration of the Baroque spirit; poets cultivated blank verse and experimented freely with the decasyllabic line. One of the most important poets of the period was Manuel Maria Barbosa du Bocage. Known for his bohemian lifestyle, Bocage produced pastoral poems, including sonnets of great lyrical and sensual qualities. He and rival poet José Agostinho de Macedo were the two most noteworthy members of the Nova Arcádia. Like his fellow Arcadians, Bocage adopted a shepherd's name (Elmano Sadino) and wrote poems in which he searches for the "locus amenus" (an idyllic place in nature) to escape the stifling environment of the city.

Although poetry dominated literary output in the eighteenth century, there were some important prose pieces and drama. Luís Antônio Verney wrote *Verdadeiro método de estudar* (True Method for Studying, 1746), in which he criticizes prevalent educational methods of the first half of the century. Attempts at reviving the theater include the works of Antônio José da Silva. Born in Brazil, the dramatist spent most of his life in Portugal, where, influenced by Italian opera, he displayed his comic talents in prose dialogues intermingled with songs and music.

The nineteenth century was a period of political chaos in Portugal. At the end of 1806, Napoleon Bonaparte set up the continental blockade (1806-1814) and closed ports to the English. The French army, allied with the Spanish, invaded Portugal in 1807. The royal family fled to Brazil, where it remained for fourteen years, during which Portugal was ruled by a regency while Brazil served as the seat of the Portuguese empire. John VI (1816–1826) returned to Portugal in 1821, and Brazil declared its independence in 1822. The economic and financial situation of Portugal worsened as discontent with John VI, who had been reluctant to return, increased. Liberals were persecuted, and the country suffered a looting of art treasures and manuscripts.

The first liberal revolution occurred in 1820, and an ongoing struggle between absolutists and liberals ensued. The absolutists defended the traditional monarchy; the liberals advocated a constitutionally based government. At times, absolutist despotism was worse than it had been under Pombal in the eighteenth century. Thousands of people were jailed or executed, and thousands fled the country. In 1851, after much turmoil, the country settled into a period of tranquility with the establishment of the government of "Regeneration," supported by a unified bourgeoisie that had increased in size since the eighteenth century.

Romanticism, which had its most important representatives in poetry and in drama, evolved in Portugal during this period of political chaos. Many writers of the epoch were also journalists who took advantage of a cultural democratization from which emerged a new reading public among the bourgeoisie. Portuguese Romanticism, which is closely associated with the bourgeois reader and the evolution of the press, may be divided into three distinct phases: the emergence of the movement with Almeida Garrett's epic *Camões* in 1825 and the works of Alexandre Herculano and António Feliciano de Castilho; the ultra-Romanticism of the works of Camilo Castelo Branco, António Soares de Passos, and Maria da Felicidade do Couto Browne; and the transition to realism with Júlio Dinis (Joaquim Guilherme Gomes Coelho) and João de Deus Ramos.

Garrett's strong neoclassical background links him to eighteenth-century Arcadianism. His liberal ideas and nationalism, seen in the ballads in *Romanceiro* (1843), however, tie him to the Romantic movement. He cultivated three genres without falling into the excesses of Romanticism seen in other authors of the period. In prose, he denounces the Portuguese oligarchy in *Viagens na minha terra* (Travels in My Country, 1846). His innovative drama *Frei Luís de Souza* (Brother Luís de Sousa, 1843) explores social prejudices. *Folhas caídas* (Fallen Leaves, 1853), inspired by his love affair with Rosa Montufar Barreiros, Viscountess of Luz, includes the best of his lyric poetry.

Alexandre Herculano was an historian and fiction writer. He reconstructs Portuguese history, giving special attention to the intervention of the social classes in past events, in his four-volume *História de Portugal* (History of Portugal, 1846–1853). He also wrote the three-volume *Da origem e estabelecimento da Inquisição em Portugal: Tentativa histórica* (On the Origin and Establishment of the Inquisition in Portugal: A Tentative History, 1854–1859) and edited the document collection *Portugaliae monumenta historica* (begun in 1856). History plays an important role in his fiction as well. His novel *O bobo* (The Fool, 1843) deals with the formation of the nation; *Eurico, o presbítero* (Eurico, the Presbyter, 1844), with its love story and questioning of clerical celibacy, takes place during the late eighth century. The writer combines sociohistorical explanations with moral and religious reflection as he intermingles dramatic, descriptive, and didactic elements.

Castelo Branco used the techniques of serialized journalistic fiction, following in the path of Honoré de Balzac and Eugène Sue. He was the first Portuguese author to be able to live solely on the earnings from his writing. Castelo Branco was a controversial figure; he married twice, had mistresses, and ended up contracting syphilis, which led to his blindness and suicide. With a vast literary output, he was a master of language and of the melodramatic plot. His novel *Amor de perdição* (Doomed Love, 1862) serves as a paradigm of his love stories, which generally involve a triangle with a heroine in love with two men. Ultimately, she is condemned for adultery and punished according to the social code of the patriarchy. Castelo Branco's works had a didactic effect on the behavior of women, who constituted the majority of his reading audience. The author also deals with love relationships in satirical novels in which he ridicules the customs and mores of the age. In *Coração, cabeça e estômago* (Heart, Head, and Stomach, 1862), for example, the protagonist attempts to achieve happiness through three different types of relationships. First, he tries love (heart), but fails; then, he opts for an intelligent companion (head); finally, he chooses a peasant woman who feeds him well every day (stomach).

Dinis, a liberal educated in the English manner, cultivated the rural novel at a time that literature was in a transitional phase moving toward realism. His novels are characterized by psychological conflicts among people living in a rural setting, as in *As pupilas do senhor reitor* (The Rector's Pupils, 1867). Dinis stands out for his treatment of *o amor português* (Portuguese love–a pure, simple love) in his *Campos de flores* (Fields of Flowers, 1869, 1893), in which he combines Romantic traits with optimism and bourgeois feelings.

Realism began to take hold in Portuguese literature around 1865 with the "Questão Coimbrã" (The Coimbra Question). This reaction against Romanticism was led by a group of young liberal writers and intellectuals, later called the Generation of '70, who were involved in the political issues of the period. The "Questão Coimbrã" began over a literary disagreement. Poet António Feliciano de Castilho wrote an afterword for his disciple Pinheiro Chagas's *Poema da mocidade* (Poem of Youth, 1865). In the text Castilho criticized what he considered to be the poor quality of the work of the group of writers associated with the University of Coimbra, including Antero de Quental and Teófilo Braga. Quental, one of the most significant poets of the period, responded in a pamphlet titled *Bomsenso e bom-gosto* (Good Sense and Good Taste, 1865). The polemic was continued by another group of intellectuals referred to as Cenáculo (Cenacle). In Lisbon, this group sponsored a series of lectures, "Conferências Democráticas do Casino Lisbonense" (Democratic Lectures of the Lisbon Casino), with the intention of introducing new ideas and scientific knowledge from other parts of Europe. In one of the lectures Eça de Queirós attacked Romanticism and spoke of the social function of art. In another, Quental linked the decadence of the Iberian Peninsula to the Counter Reformation. The government halted these conferences when the group announced a lecture titled "Os historiadores críticos de Jesus" (Historians Critical of Jesus).

Naturalism is linked to realism in its attempt to portray reality in an almost photographic manner through words. Naturalism focuses more on mechanical and deterministic elements while trying to show a cause and effect relationship among all aspects of reality. In Portugal, the tendency is to refer to *realismo-naturalismo*, with no clear-cut distinction between the two. The movement, a reaction against the excesses of Romanticism, is characterized by socially committed literature that attempts to present the truth. It reveals a strong anticlerical element in its criticism of the church's conservative position as an impediment to social advancement. Reform and democratization of society are important tenets of the naturalist mission.

Queirós is undoubtedly the most important and best-known author, both nationally and internationally, of the second half of the nineteenth century. His work is marked by an ideological tension between his conservative attitudes and his liberal sense of the need for reform. He began to write under the influence of Romanticism, adding a social dimension to that movement. Queirós's pessimistic vision characterizes his realist-naturalist phase, in which he dissects Portuguese society. In his famous novels, he criticizes the clergy (*O crime do Padre Amaro,* 1875; translated as *The Sin of Father Amaro,* 1963), amorous and conjugal relationships (*O primo Basílio,* 1878; translated as *Cousin Bazilio,* 1953), and the decadent aristocratic family (*Os Maias,* 1880; translated as *The Maias,* 1965). His reformist spirit stresses the needs for social conscience and social equality. Queirós avoided the more radical aspects of naturalism, revealing instead a highly refined sense of irony.

Cesário Verde is another important voice during the second half of the nineteenth century. In his only work, which was published posthumously in 1887 under the title *O livro de Cesário Verde* (The Book of Cesário Verde), Verde adapted naturalism to poetry. His poems focus on concrete details of bourgeois existence and question the problems of urban progress and the plight of the workers. He uses the metaphor of woman to describe the city as a sensual being fatigued by capitalist development and also as a cold force that dehumanizes the workers. Verde reveals the city through a technique of verbal flashes that approaches the cinematographic. António Duarte Gomes Leal, Abílio Manuel Guerra Junqueiro, and José Valentin Fialho de Almeida also contributed to the prose and poetry of the realist-naturalist period.

The relative calm of the 1870s and 1880s was terminated by social, political, and economic crises. A dissatisfied population, especially in the agrarian sector (which was being emptied by mass movements to the cities), began to participate more actively in political movements against the bourgeois establishment. More women, contrary to tradition in the profoundly patriarchal society, also became involved in the new political consciousness. The famous mythical figure of Maria da Fonte had emerged during a peasant revolt led by women in 1846 in the region of the Mondego River. For the poor rural workers, the only option for survival was migration to the cities, but industrialization had not created the necessary conditions to absorb more workers. Capitalist development of the country had remained tied to the import rather than export of products. The British government contributed to the political crisis when, in 1890, it issued an ultimatum for Portugal to give up claims to large portions of its empire in southeastern Africa. The English interference created resentment toward the monarchy (because people felt King Carlos I had capitulated too easily to the ultimatum) and provoked riots and a republican uprising in 1891. Social and economic conditions continued to worsen as the country moved into the twentieth century. Illiteracy in the population reached 80 percent around 1900.

In 1908 Carlos I (1889–1908) and his son Prince Luis Felipe were assassinated. King Manuel II inherited the throne but lasted only until 1910, when a military and popular revolt put a definite end to monarchy in Portugal. The Republic was established, and Braga assumed provisional control of the government (1910–1911). Braga promulgated a divorce law, the separation of church and state, and a law that allowed workers to strike. He also created the University of Lisbon and the University of Porto.

Toward the end of the nineteenth century there had been a return to Romanticism, and Charles Baudelaire influenced a new generation of writers. Eugénio de Castro, inspired by the work of Paul Verlaine, introduced the symbolist movement to Portugal with his work *Oaristos* (Intimate Dialogues) in 1890. The symbolist aesthetic focuses on the notion of a pure art divorced from social causes. Symbolist poets removed themselves from daily reality in an elitist art that turned inward. The neo-Romantic trend was composed of two currents: one that followed the traditional writing of Garrett (*neogarrettismo*), and the more progressive *saudosismo* (a literary movement, based on the word *saudade* [nostalgia], that appeared after the establishment of the Republic in 1910 and stressed the need for a new Portugal). Reality was perceived as a process from which impressionistic art, with its colors disconnected from the object, originates. The artist takes refuge in technique, as content becomes secondary. In literature, rational vision gives way to the irrational through the abundant use of ambiguous metaphors and symbols. The formal construction of the poem provides an escape from concrete reality. António Pereira Nobre's poetry in *Só* (Alone, 1892) portrays a mythical paradise and idealizes the past in an extremely subjective tone. Camilo Pessanha, the greatest of the Portuguese symbolists, uses a delicate, musical language in the intellectualized, melancholic poems of his *Clepsidra* (1920). In prose, Raul Brandão, influenced by Fyodor Dostoevsky, denounced the ills of society through the use of tragic and grotesque elements in works such as *Os pescadores* (The Fishermen, 1923) and *Os pobres* (The Poor, 1906).

The first phase of Portuguese modernism corresponds to the politically unstable period of the first Republic (1910–1926). This period, however, had its progressive aspects. Free public education, for example, was made available to all children. Literary currents of this phase of modernism were organized around the vanguard journal *Orpheu* (Orpheus, 1915). Only two numbers of the journal were published, but that was sufficient to give rise to the movement known as *Orfismo*. The writers of this group were opposed to the neo-Romantic and symbolist traditions; its main objective was to scandalize and shock the bourgeoisie. Mário de Sá-Carneiro, who collaborated in the creation of *Orpheu,* was heir to some of the traits of symbolism. He breathed new life into traditional forms in which he strongly criticized the bourgeoisie. During this time several important literary journals appeared, including *Exílio* (Exile), *Centauro* (Centaur), *Portugal Futurista* (Futurist Portugal), *Contemporânea* (Contemporary), and *Athena*.

The European vanguard movements of the early twentieth century had a great impact on Portugal. The various "–isms" were absorbed by Fernando Pessoa, one of the greatest poets in the Portuguese language. In his *Mensagem* (Message, 1934), an esoteric collection with nationalistic and mystic tones, Pessoa takes up the heroic trajectory established by Camões. He wrote his experimental poetry under different names and personalities in addition to his own, including Alberto Caeiro, Ricardo Reis, and Álvaro de Campos. He also wrote poetry in English under the name Alexander Search. Through the use of these various "masks" the poet explores the fine line between sincerity and deception.

José de Almada Negreiros, painter and writer, also collaborated on the journals *Orpheu* and *Portugal Futurista*. In addition to novels, theater, and poetry, he wrote interesting, provocative essays such as the *Manifesto anti-Dantas* (1915), in which he opposes the literary conservatism of older writer Júlio Dantas.

The second phase of Portuguese modernism is referred to as *Presencismo* and had as its official journal *Presença* (Presence, 1927–1940). Writers associated with the movement include João Gaspar Simões, José Régio (José Maria dos Reis Pereira), and Miguel Torga (Adolfo Correio da Rocha). The authors of this phase advocated originality and sincerity in literature. The influence of Henri-Louis Bergson, Marcel Proust, and André Gide can be noted in the emphasis the writers placed on psychological theory. Torga, who withdrew from the group in 1930, expresses a humanism and individualism tied to nature and his rural origins.

During the first Republic there was a constant tension between nationalist and liberal groups, on the one hand, and dissident or extreme-right groups such as the communists or the Catholics, on the other. The discord culminated in the establishment of the Estado Novo (New State), which was a dictatorial government under the control of António de Oliveira Salazar; it lasted from 1932 until 1974. Except for the União Nacional, political parties were forbidden. The government exercised a repressive force throughout the country through the Polícia de Vigilância e Defesa do Estado (PVDE), which, after World War II, was given more power and was renamed Polícia Internacional e de Defesa do Estado (PIDE). The conservative totalitarian government showed little flexibility in its policies, and censorship was practiced in all means of communication, especially in the arts. Literature was particularly affected, since all publications required prior governmental approval. With the death of Salazar in 1968 there was an easing of political and cultural restrictions, but the country was undergoing serious economic difficulties and was intensely involved in military conflicts in its African colonies. On 25 April 1974 the remainder of Salazar's policies were overturned by the Revolução dos Cravos (The Carnation Revolution), which used the carnation as a symbol of liberation. The Estado Novo fell, and the fighting in Africa ended when the government granted independence to the colonies. The new political regime marked a return to democracy and inclusion in the European Union. The improved financial situation began to modify the face of the country.

Postmodernism began with the neorealist movement in the decade of the 1930s. Neorealist writing is characterized by its commitment to social causes and its desire to create an awareness in the people of the socio-economic situation of the country. Neorealism emerged through several literary journals: *O Diabo* (1934–1940), *Sol Nascente* (1937–1940), *Vértice, Árvore* (1945), and *Novo Cancioneiro*. The neorealist vanguard influenced diverse cultural sectors: historiography, with Joel Serrão and Vitor de Sá; literary history, with Oscar Lopes and António José Saraiva; linguistics, with Herculano de Carvalho and Luís Felipe Lindley Cintra; and literary criticism, with Jacinto Prado do Coelho.

In 1939 Alves Redol introduced neorealism to the novel with his *Gaibéus* ("gaibéus" refers to fieldworkers in the Ribatejo region), in which he portrays poor rural workers. Carlos de Oliveira, in his *O aprendiz de feiticeiro* (The Apprentice Sorcerer, 1971), captures the philosophy of neorealism: "o meu ponto de partida, como romancista e poeta, é a realidade que me cerca; tenho que equacioná-la em função do passado, do presente e do futuro; e, noutro plano, em função das características nacionais e locais" (my point of departure, as a novelist and as a poet, is the reality that surrounds me; I have to consider it in terms of the past, the present, and the future; and, on another level, in terms of national and local characteristics). Manuel da Fonseca contributed cinematographic narratives and poems that express man's inability to grasp the causes of the anxiety of alienation. José Cardoso Pires's *O delfim* (The Dauphin, 1968), influenced by the techniques of the French *nouveau roman,* displays neorealist characteristics. Augusto Abelaira and Vergílio Ferreira, using stream-of-consciousness techniques, wrote novels with philosophical and existentialist themes. Fernando Namora's talents as a storyteller made him one of the most popular neorealist writers.

French literary Surrealism had emerged in 1924 with André Breton's *Manifesto*. Poet Mário Cesariny de Vasconcelos embraced the tenets of the movement throughout his career, beginning with *Corpo visível* (Visible Body) in 1950. There was a renewed spirit of experimentation with poetic language in the 1950s with Jorge de Sena, Sophia de Mello Breyner Andresen, and António Ramos Rosa. In the 1960s, a group of university students, including Fiama Hasse Pais Brandão, Gastão Cruz, and Maria Teresa Horta, launched the movement *Poesia 61*. The anthology *Poesia Experimental* (Experimental Poetry) includes verses by Herberto Helder, Ana Hatherly, and E. M. de Melo e Castro, some of whom exhibit close connections to Brazilian *concretismo* (concretism), a poetic movement that explored the visual aspects of verbal art and attempted to make the poem a tangible object.

In 1998 José Saramago became the first Portuguese author to win the Nobel Prize in literature. In his work, characterized by a mixture of concrete reality and poetic imagination, Saramago uses historiographic devices to demystify history, as seen in *Memorial do convento* (1982; translated as *Baltasar and Blimunda,* 1987). Other outstanding representatives of the contemporary Portuguese novel include Almeida Faria and António Lobo Antunes.

After the revolution of 1974, two specific trends flourished and began to receive more critical attention: literature written by women, and literature of the former African colonies written in Portuguese (which will not be included in this volume). Florbela Espanca, known especially for the highly lyrical and personal tone of her sonnets, was the first Portuguese woman writer to break with tradition, both in her personal life and in her writing. Irene Lisboa, with her melancholic treatment of the educated woman dealing with the restrictions and prejudices of provincial society, followed. Agustina Bessa-Luís portrays the force of various generations of women of the rural aristocracy in *A sibila* (The Sibyl, 1954). In 1972 the "Three Marias"–Horta, Maria Isabel Barreno, and Maria Velho da Costa–created a stir with their *Novas cartas portuguesas* (translated as *The Three Marias: New Portuguese Letters,* 1975). The work–which was originally suppressed by the government because it was considered "an outrage to public decency" and "pornographic," and because it includes sensitive political references–is based on the *Lettres portugaises traduites en françois* attributed to Alcoforado. The authors were put on trial (but exonerated after the 1974 revolution), causing the book to become an important symbol for the feminist movements of the period. Other women have written about the problems the female faces in a patriarchal society when she tries to establish her own identity. In the majority of the works by these writers, the woman is seen as caught in an incessant struggle, accompanied by suffering and anxiety. Helena Marques, however, breaks with this tendency in the 1990s with her portrayals of the happy, liberated woman in control of her own life.

Although there is a considerable body of literature written in the Portuguese language in Europe, Africa, and South America, it is still not as well known as the literatures written in other Romance languages. Portuguese is spoken by 250 million people, but these speakers have been isolated in a small country on the Iberian Peninsula and in overseas colonies away from the mainstream of Western culture. The use of language has been limited almost exclusively to native speakers, and the literary works have only recently begun to be translated into other languages. Since the 1990s, more translations (especially into Spanish and into English) have gained a larger reading public for Portuguese literature, as well as for the literatures of Brazil and the former African colonies.

*–Monica Rector and Fred M. Clark*

## Acknowledgments

This book was produced by Bruccoli Clark Layman, Inc. Tracy Simmons Bitonti and Patricia Hswe were the in-house editors.

Production manager is Philip B. Dematteis.

Administrative support was provided by Ann M. Cheschi and Carol A. Cheschi.

Accountant is Ann-Marie Holland.

Copyediting supervisor is Sally R. Evans. The copyediting staff includes Phyllis A. Avant, Caryl Brown, Leah M. Cutsinger, Melissa D. Hinton, Philip I. Jones, Rebecca Mayo, and Nancy E. Smith.

Editorial associates are Jessica Goudeau, Michael S. Martin, Catherine M. Polit, Joshua M. Robinson, and William Mathes Straney.

In-house prevetting is by Nicole A. La Rocque.

Permissions editor and database manager is Amber L. Coker.

Layout and graphics supervisor is Janet E. Hill. The graphics staff includes Zoe R. Cook and Sydney E. Hammock.

Office manager is Kathy Lawler Merlette.

Photography supervisor is Paul Talbot. Photography editor is Scott Nemzek.

Digital photographic copy work was performed by Joseph M. Bruccoli.

Systems manager is Donald Kevin Starling.

Typesetting supervisor is Kathleen M. Flanagan. The typesetting staff includes Patricia Marie Flanagan, Mark J. McEwan, and Pamela D. Norton.

Walter W. Ross did library research. He was assisted by Jo Cottingham and the following librarians at the Thomas Cooper Library of the University of South Carolina: circulation department head Tucker Taylor; reference department head Virginia W. Weathers; reference department staff Laurel Baker, Marilee Birchfield, Kate Boyd, Paul Cammarata, Joshua Garris, Gary Geer, Tom Marcil, Rose Marshall, and Sharon Verba; interlibrary loan department head Marna Hostetler; and interlibrary loan staff Bill Fetty, Nelson Rivera, and Cedric Rose.

Dictionary of Literary Biography® • Volume Two Hundred Eighty-Seven

# Portuguese Writers

# Dictionary of Literary Biography

## Augusto Abelaira
*(18 March 1926 –    )*

Maria Guterres
*Liverpool University*

BOOKS: *A cidade das flores* (Lisbon: Bertrand, 1959);
*Os desertores* (Lisbon: Bertrand, 1960);
*A palavra é de oiro* (Lisbon: Bertrand, 1961);
*O nariz de Cleópatra* (Lisbon: Bertrand, 1961);
*As boas intenções* (Lisbon: Bertrand, 1963);
*Enseada amena* (Lisbon: Bertrand, 1966);
*Bolor* (Lisbon: Bertrand, 1968);
*Quatro paredes nuas* (Lisbon: Bertrand, 1972);
*Sem tecto entre ruínas* (Lisbon: Bertrand, 1978);
*Anfitrião, outra vez* (Lisbon: Bertrand, 1980);
*O triunfo da morte* (Lisbon: Sá da Costa, 1981);
*O bosque harmonioso* (Lisbon: Sá da Costa, 1982);
*O único animal que?* (Lisbon: O Jornal, 1985);
*Deste modo ou daquele* (Lisbon: O Jornal, 1990);
*A meu ver,* by Abelaira and Carlos Pinto Coelho (Lisbon: Pégaso, 1992);
*Outrora agora* (Lisbon: Presença, 1996).

*Augusto Abelaira (from the cover for the 1984 edition of* A cidade das flores, *1959; Thomas Cooper Library, University of South Carolina)*

Augusto Abelaira has assembled a considerable body of work: eleven novels, three plays, and one collection of short stories. He is considered a neorealist writer, and on the whole he has remained faithful to the ideals of neorealism. This movement, which began in the late 1930s, in its first phase was devoted above all to the progress of the working class, and most of its fiction was set in rural Portugal. However, from the late 1950s onward, although neorealist writers still believed in the ultimate ideal of a transformation of man and society and of a collective happiness, they began to be concerned with the middle classes and their problems.

Abelaira's urban novels take place in Lisbon, with the exception of the first, which is set in Italy in order to avoid the censorship of the time. These novels deal mainly with the politically dissatisfied intellectuals of the middle class. As literary critic João Camilo dos Santos points out: "For Abelaira, individual accomplishment never boiled down to the simple resolution of political and economic problems, nevertheless he always accorded these factors the enormous importance that they merited."

Augusto Abelaira was born in Ança (Beira Litoral) on 18 March 1926, but he has lived in Lisbon for most of his life. His mother, Mandelina de Freitas, a farmer's daughter, came from Ança and was a housewife. His father, José Abelaira Gomez, came from Galicia (Spain) and worked for Mobil Corporation, first in the north of Portugal and later in Lisbon, where his son went to school. After graduating from the Classic University of Lisbon in 1953 with a degree in arts (history and philosophy), Abelaira taught in a secondary school but soon became a journalist working for *Seara Nova* (New Harvest), *Vida Mundial* (World Life), *O Século* (The Century), and *O Jornal* (The Newspaper). Later, he also contributed a column every two weeks to *Jornal das Letras e das Artes* (Journal of Letters and Arts), titled "Escrever na água" (To Write in the Water), which reflects the ephemeral nature of writing. In 1955 Abelaira married Susana Vasques, with whom he has a daughter, Sílvia. The marriage ended in divorce, and Abelaira has not remarried.

Abelaira made his literary debut with *A cidade das flores* (The City of Flowers, 1959), which is an attack on dictatorship. By the time this novel appeared, António de Oliveira Salazar had ruled Portugal as prime minister for twenty-seven years. His was a brutal and repressive regime that crushed all opposition and silenced writers or made them practice a kind of self-censorship. The work shows the relationship between power and politics and the methods of repression Salazar practiced during this period to achieve complete control. *A cidade das flores* is set in Florence just before and at the beginning of World War II. It portrays a group of idealistic young people who are unable to live fully in an unfree society. These friends (Fasio, Soldati, Vianello, Villani, Rosabianca, and Renata) are intelligent and well educated, and they are opposed to the regime and still committed to political honesty. They dream about an impossible revolution and speculate whether a world war might not be the only way for Italy to get rid of her dictator. Vianello is the only one active in the resistance movement against Benito Mussolini; he believes that it is necessary to encourage young people to fight so that they can regain what they have lost. Friendship plays an important role in the novel. The friends meet in a café, where they argue about politics, art, literature, current affairs, and the possibility of individual happiness under a fascist dictatorship. Villani, for a short time, betrays his principles and his friends' trust and later is imprisoned for a crime that he did not commit. Fasio, the skeptic, who no longer believes in the possibility of a social revolution, admires Vianello for his commitment to his cause. Fasio is the "deserter" in a long list of characters who choose inaction and try to placate their guilty consciences over not acting against oppression and injustice.

*A cidade das flores* is also the love story of Rosabianca, who is pure, beautiful, and full of life. She is loved by Fasio, Soldati, and Vianello, but she falls in love with Fasio and marries him. Unlike Fasio, she believes in the future and in the possibility of a social utopia after the war. In the first part of the novel, the author depicts Rosabianca and Fasio's courtship in a series of tableaux, conveying their love and happiness. In the second part, he reflects on their marriage and their inability to communicate with each other. For Abelaira's male characters, courtship and seduction are exciting, but marriage dulls or kills their love. Asked if he loves his wife, Fasio answers that he would have loved her forever had he been free and not married to her. This criticism of the institution of marriage is a constant in Abelaira's work. The novel closes with Italy entering World War II and with Fasio's pessimism about its outcome. Mussolini and Adolf Hitler lost the war, but Salazar's regime continued, and in 1959 it seemed as if the dictatorship would go on forever. Abelaira voices this fear.

Abelaira's constant preoccupation with language, especially with the choice and power of words, is explored in this novel. As he says, "As palavras são arquipélagos onde o tempo é o oceano. Arquipélagos ricos, densos de florestas, de enigmas e que brilham na bruma. . . . Neste momento não são escravos. Vão livres e sorriem no meio das palavras" (Words are archipelagos where time is the ocean. Rich archipelagos, thick woods where enigmas shine through the mist. . . . At this time they are not slaves. They are free and smile amidst words).

In the preface to his second novel, *Os desertores* (The Deserters, 1960), Abelaira remarks that "there is only one novel inside me"; and indeed, he has devoted most of his work to the "deserters" of Portuguese society. This novel, like the first, deals with a group of friends. These young intellectuals talk a lot, fall in love, marry, and continue to look for the ideal love. To the question "What have you done for the Portuguese?" the answer is "not much." Although the characters concentrate on love and interpersonal relationships, they never lose their guilty social consciences. They dream of a better society, but they know that they are not contributing to human happiness. The narrator questions what happiness is: perhaps it is only the search for an ideal love. Ramiro and Beatriz are happily married; yet, when he goes to Italy, he starts looking for the love of his life, Berenice (who may be dead), and he does not return to Portugal. He meets

Francesca, and they stay together for a month. Love is ephemeral; yet, for Abelaira, individual salvation can only be achieved through love.

Abelaira is also the author of three satirical comedies that develop the same themes found in the novels. In the first, *A palavra é de oiro* (Words Are Made of Gold, 1961), the author demonstrates how characters can exercise control through the mechanical manipulation of language. By patenting the invention of language, the central character achieves extreme wealth and power. Language becomes a commodity like gas, water, and electricity, and, in the same way, it has to be metered and paid for. The result is that only the rich can speak at length. The poor work even harder, since they do not waste time talking. The status quo is maintained, and the regime has a firmer grip on the people. The author's conclusion is that, without language, civilization cannot progress and human relationships will die.

*O nariz de Cleópatra* (Cleopatra's Nose, 1961) is a satire on the historical process. The author speculates on how history might have changed if certain events had never occurred or had happened differently. Like Jean Giraudoux in *The Trojan War Will Not Take Place* (1935), Abelaira questions whether the world would be different if the outcome of the Trojan War were changed. He concludes, however, that the world really would not be different, for human beings are still the same, and they still defend the use of war to settle disagreements between nations.

The novel *As boas intenções* (Good Intentions, 1963) is set during the period between 1908 and 1912, which includes the end of the monarchy (1910) and the beginning of the Republic in Portugal. In this novel, time is not chronologically linear. Small variations and repetitive descriptions recurring throughout the narrative emphasize the nature of time as cyclical and life as transitory. The action is seen not only from the present and the past of the characters but also from their future. Through this device, the author illuminates the characters' lives and allows the reader to see how history developed. This knowledge of the characters' future gives the action a new perspective. Abelaira stressed, when receiving the Ricardo Malheiros Prize from the Academia das Ciências de Lisboa for this novel, that he had been influenced by the nineteenth-century writer Eça de Queirós. Following Queirós, this novel treats the themes of the corruption of the state and the decadence of the upper classes, which lead to the end of the monarchy.

In *As boas intenções* Abelaira portrays two generations of the same family, while also relating what will happen to their descendants. The first generation, represented by Alexandre and Carlota Soares, observe the corruption of the monarchy but do nothing about it.

*Paperback cover for the 1984 edition of Abelaira's first novel, about six friends in pre–World War II Italy (Thomas Cooper Library, University of South Carolina)*

On the other hand, their daughter Maria Brenda chooses to help Vasco, a republican journalist, in his fight to end it. Both Vasco and Bernardo (a wealthy monarchist) love Maria Brenda; she tosses a coin and marries Bernardo. Even though she criticizes her husband's politics, she feels more comfortable with him than with Vasco. They belong to the same social class and share a love of art and music. Bernardo is interested in love, Vasco in the revolution, which will be successful. Although the Republic brings freedom, it does not bring social equality, and Abelaira attacks the inequality of this society. The irony of the title, *As boas intenções,* is that all individual good intentions, whether moral, political, or aesthetic, are doomed to fail. Perhaps, in the end, salvation can only be achieved through writing, for writing is a form of acting. Without books the world will not progress; Maria Brenda's descendants will still be fighting fear and oppression, for nothing will have changed.

In 1965 Abelaira was imprisoned briefly in Caxias, along with literary critic Alexandre Pinheiro Torres and writer Manuel da Fonseca. Their offense was having served on the committee that awarded the Fiction Prize of the Portuguese Writers' Society to Luandino Vieira for his 1963 short-story collection, *Luuanda*. Vieira was an Angolan who had fought against the Portuguese colonial government of his country; he had been imprisoned since 1961, and *Luuanda* had been banned. After this prize incident Salazar closed down the Writers' Society.

In the novel *Enseada amena* (Pleasant Bay, 1966) Abelaira analyzes the institution of marriage. The *enseada amena* is the city of Lisbon, which has been populated by the Romans, the Moors, and now the Portuguese. For the central character, Osório, Lisbon is a dead city, waiting for a revelation and a change. Disillusioned, he admits that he does not know where his historic vocation lies and tries to justify his apathy. Happily married (or so he says), he soon becomes bored and unfaithful, considering adultery the only adventure left to him. He starts a relationship with Ana Isa, also married, who like him is looking for the ideal love. Osório knows, however, that even ideal love is not eternal and that if he loves women, it is because the feeling enables him to probe the depths of his soul. For Osório, who feels alienated from this authoritarian society, love is at first the ultimate quest—only love can satisfy him, at least while it lasts. Finally, Osório comes to the realization that he cannot recover his youth through love and that love leads to boundless grief. He knows that love cannot be an absolute, for there are no absolutes in this world.

Osório leaves his wife, Maria José, who begins to build her future alone with her son. In the 1960s increasing numbers of middle-class Portuguese women were beginning to go to universities and to work outside their homes; Maria José fulfills herself through a career as a teacher of English in a secondary school. She devotes her time to her students, who reward her by acknowledging that they like and respect her. The novel closes with a victory of a sort for Maria José: she manages to respond positively to her changed circumstances and in the process regains her own identity.

*Bolor* (Mildew, 1968), Abelaira's seventh book, is a complex and ambitious novel that explores the increasing significance of language in the structure of his fiction. The narrator begins to write a diary; he begins on page 115, then goes backward as well as forward. He is conscious of his creative power, for he can move in all directions within time. In his work Abelaira destroys real time and replaces it with fictional time; he realizes that he cannot alter the first, but he can create the second and control the universe he is inventing. Real time, measured by a calendar or a clock, where the characters exist, is depicted in detail, but the characters' reactions to real events are shown ambiguously. This ambiguity reflects the characters' inner life, which is analyzed through the outside world.

Nelly Novais Coelho points out that Abelaira uses the diary as a symbol of human immobility. Indeed, *Bolor* is written in a succession of monologues; it never becomes a dialogue. The narrator communicates with his diary but not with the other characters. What the narrator wants to do is to discover, to know, and to repossess his wife and invent a life for her, as well as overcome the emptiness of his life. The narrator of *Bolor* duplicates himself in a multiplicity of narrators (Humberto, Maria dos Remédios, Aleixo), each with something different to write. There is no confrontation between husband and wife, and communication is only achieved when they reinvent themselves into different characters: Humberto and Aleixo into Daniel and Catarina, and Maria dos Remédios into Julieta. This transformation is part of the narrator's past, and it depicts the beginning of his amorous life. In *Bolor* the word replaces action, and words show the narrator's frustration at the impossibility of "doing." The title of the novel, taken from Carlos de Oliveira's poem "O bolor nas paredes deste quarto deserto" (The mildew on the walls of this empty room), illustrates the impossibility of love, in what is really a love story. In *Bolor* Abelaira reveals both the power of language as a creator of reality and its failure as a means for human communication.

*Bolor* was followed by a collection of seven short stories, *Quatro paredes nuas* (Four Empty Walls, 1972), which the author thought could have been called "Bolor/2." It certainly echoes the novel, but without its complexity. There are recurrent characters: Maria dos Remédios from *Bolor* and Ana Isa from *Enseada amena*. These stories help to clarify Abelaira's novels and demonstrate his approach to writing. The narration revolves around the images that each character has of the others. The images are a source of illusion, and the author engages in a subtle game between the real and the imaginary. In the title story Maria dos Remédios wants to get rid of all her furniture so that she can forget the past. She wants to be free of her memories. In "Teatro" (Theatre), on the other hand, Ana Isa attempts to re-create the past; she wants to reinvent it so that the present can be different. Both characters are anchored to a world they are unable to change. Abelaira uses the past in order to enlighten the present.

Abelaira's next novel, *Sem tecto entre ruínas* (Roofless among Ruins, 1978), published after the 1974 revolution, covers the transition from Salazar to Marcelo Caetano, who replaced the dictator in 1968 but followed his same policies. The authoritarian state

Four founders of the journal Almanaque: *Abelaira, José Cutileiro, José Cardoso Pires, and Alexandre O'Neill, 1960* (from Ines Pedrosa, José Cardoso Pires: Fotobiografia, *1999; University of California, Berkeley, Library*)

remained through 25 April 1974. In this book the author denounces the emptiness of a language that is a means of avoiding silence, not of communication. *Falar* (to speak) is identified with *fazer* (to do). Language plays an important role in the structure of the novel. There are many repetitions, reiterations, flashbacks, and flashforwards, as chronological time is replaced by time seen and experienced subjectively by the characters. The dialogues do not reveal the real feelings of the characters: the reader does not always know whether the characters are talking seriously, ironically, or just for the sake of talking. Like the nation itself, the characters in *Sem tecto entre ruínas* are inert and static. As in the previous novels, the characters are intelligent and cultured, but they are alienated by their inability to act effectively in their society. They wait for a future in which they do not believe. The present is like the past, and the future may be the same.

The protagonist, João Gilberto, constantly questions his identity and his behavior; he is unable to find an answer to what is important in his life. He reaches the conclusion that he is incapable of loving a woman. Although he no longer loves Maria Eugénia, he still clings to her, for she is the only refuge left to him. His friend Bruno, who loves Maria Eugénia and wants to live with her, sees love in a different way. He thinks that love at forty is not a romantic sentiment but rather a desire for stability, understanding, tenderness, and respect for each other.

Since the characters cannot be political and social beings, they are reduced to having amorous adventures and questioning their concept of love. The only future left to them is a new love, or the hope of a new affair, which leads to adultery yet again. The novel is circular; the final scene repeats the first, except that João Gilberto sees himself as he is seen by others. Completely disillusioned, he admits that love is dead and that utopia is nothing but a myth.

Through the conversations of the characters, the reader can see the effects of the end of Salazar's rule on the population. People waited so long for that moment, but when it came, it was an anticlimax. Caetano did not bring the liberalization of the country—Salazarism continued with him. Thus, the novel ends in despair; freedom has not yet been achieved.

Abelaira's third satirical play, *Anfitrião, outra vez* (Amphitryon, Yet Again, 1980), is a twentieth-century re-creation of Plautus's *Amphitryon*. Abelaira is concerned with the nature of truth, and he also questions whether justice can exist in the contemporary world. Both gods and humans behave badly; their only aim is to satisfy their desires. All characters wear electronic *dialogadores* (producers of dialogue) around their necks so that they do not have to make conversation. They only have to choose the right topic, and the machine answers automatically. It is another invention for exploiting and controlling people; as a result, personal relationships suffer. As in the previous plays, the heroine represents positive ethics, and Abelaira's dialogue is invariably polished, elegant, and witty.

*O triunfo da morte* (The Triumph of Death, 1981) takes a satirical view of consumer society. The first-person narrator, at first an observer and a potential revolutionary, ends up as a powerful capitalist. He invents "burujandu," an artificial drink that becomes wildly popular thanks to massive publicity. Although harmful to human beings, burujandu is globally accepted and gives rise to erudite but useless studies. This acceptance demonstrates the lack of criticism of modern society and its consumption of fashionable products. Burujandu becomes a symbol of power and destruction and takes on mythical proportions. When the narrator realizes how harmful burujandu is and wants to stop production, he cannot. The workers threaten to rebel, since they would become unemployed. Besides burujandu, the narrator also creates "pterossauro," an artificial meat that neutralizes aggression and changes people by dehumanizing them, an element intended to show that the consumer society contributes to its own alienation.

The narrator invents not only the consumer goods in the plot but also the story itself. He treats the characters as objects, getting rid of them when they are a threat to his power. Finally, the narrator even kills himself off, and the reader is left to interpret the novel. The narrator's identity is questioned, as is the story he narrates. Nothing is what it seems, and it falls to the reader or critic to unmask the narrator and read between the lines.

In *O bosque harmonioso* (The Harmonious Forest, 1982) Abelaira continues his search for adventure, for love, for God, and for a social utopia. The narrator admits knowing that life does not make sense. Nevertheless, he still looks for meaning; that is his continual quest. Again, the reader has to discover the thread that links different stories and discordant voices in this book. The story "O bosque harmonioso," which gives the book its title, is a modern parody of the medieval text *Bosco deleitoso* (The Pleasant Forest), dating from the fifteenth century. Abelaira subverts its sense; "O bosque harmonioso" is not the wood where the sinner went to purify himself but rather the grove where Simão Montalegre finds complete bliss in the pleasure of a woman. Redemption comes through physical pleasure, through the senses. This woman's sex is *o bosque harmonioso;* it is, in fact, Paradise. However, if the senses are important, so is the spirit; human beings will always dream and use their imaginations to create a new reality. The narrator searches for freedom, for a sociopolitical "Paradise." In *O bosque harmonioso,* as in *O triunfo da morte,* both written after the 1974 revolution, Abelaira attempts to rethink and to understand the new Portugal.

*O único animal que?* (The Only Animal That? 1985) is a satirical novel set in the future. Like *O triunfo da morte,* the work exposes the evils of modern society: scientific experiments on animals, which are detrimental to both animals and humans. The narrator is a monkey who has been taught to speak by an American scientist, Professor Garden, whose aim is to transform the monkey into a man. The professor believes that language determines the nature of human beings. Another scientist also tries to teach a female monkey, Washoe, to become a woman. Both scientists observe the monkeys' behavior in order to develop their own research. The monkeys, however, observe their masters' behavior and make fools of them. The monkeys' conclusion is that, although man is the last link in the long chain of life, men are not born men; they become men. Like monkeys, they are taught to behave in a certain way, which is assumed to be the way human beings should behave. The narrator and Washoe fall in love and at first have an idyllic life together. Men, however, soon intervene. Washoe ends up in Africa and the narrator in Lisbon, where a great sociological experiment is taking place—a study of human beings as pure consumers of anything, be it goods, images, or words. The monkey muses on the reasons for this experiment and believes that, in the midst of a crisis, Portugal is trying to solve its external debt by becoming a vast laboratory. The experiment of the "human-monkey" does not work, because he ends up being neither. The narrator entices his readers with exotic stories (which may not be true as he tells them), aiming to keep his audience's attention to the end of the book. This novel is witty and provocative, for indeed, man is the only animal who can differentiate water from holy water.

For his next novel, *Deste modo ou daquele* (In This or That Way, 1990), Abelaira uses as a starting point the diary of a secondary-school teacher of history and philosophy. The teacher lives in Lisbon and is beginning his retirement. The omniscient narrator, a biologist, reads this diary, and from the beginning he intervenes in the narrative, questioning what he reads and commenting on it. He identifies with the diarist and tries to understand him through his writing. The narrator searches for the truth, interpreting language in order to find the real self of this character. He looks behind the mask, for living is not merely surviving, it is also a form of retelling one's life experiences in this or that way. *Deste modo ou daquele* tells what was, what was not, and what might and might not have been. The narrator refers to a world of limitless variations. Fiction mirrors reality–or perhaps reality mirrors fiction. In this novel Abelaira reflects on being and existing. The narrator and the teacher are two voices constructing the novel, writing about events that could also have been told in a different way. They could even have been written solely by the narrator. The identity of the narrator/teacher remains open, since the two lives seem to intertwine and become one.

*Outrora agora* (Then and Now, 1996) takes its title from a poem by Fernando Pessoa: "Com que ânsia tão raiva / Quero aquele outrora! / E eu era feliz? / Não sei / Fui–o outrora agora" (With what anxious rage / I long for yesteryear! / Was I happy? / I don't know / I was–then and now). As the title suggests, the past and the present intermingle, and a recovery and revival of the past is used to illuminate the present. The novel is set in Lisbon, where the central character, Jerónimo, lives, and in the Algarve, where he goes to finish his translation of Dorothy Richardson's work *Pilgrimage* (1938). *Outrora agora* is Jerónimo's pilgrimage through life from childhood to death. He reflects on his experiences as an individual and as a Portuguese who has spent his life on a quest for personal happiness and political freedom. He wonders what cruel fate made his birthplace in Portugal, where more than forty years of fascism were followed by a right-wing democracy. It is twenty years after the 1974 revolution, and the utopia dreamed of by Abelaira's characters has not been achieved. It seems now that it never will be. In several interior monologues the narrator visits important moments of his past, including his first marriage, which ended in divorce after his son's death in a motorbike accident; his former wife's suicide; and his second marriage, happy but boring. The remembrance of the past brings happiness and despair, and he speculates whether at his age (early sixties) he can still fall in love.

*Paperback cover for the fourth edition (1978) of Abelaira's 1960 novel, about a group of young intellectuals who have "deserted" Portuguese society (Thomas Cooper Library, University of South Carolina)*

On his arrival in the Algarve, he meets Cristina, a married lawyer, whom he had known briefly when they attended the same university and were involved in leftwing politics. This meeting is the starting point for a renewal of his love for her, but he begins an affair with her young cousin Filomena instead. He admits to himself that he loves Cristina, but he desires Filomena. They are the same women at different times. The past and the present are seen as one and the same as Jerónimo remembers all the important events in Portugal that shaped him and his life.

The novel closes with a long interior monologue in which Jerónimo, driving to the Algarve to see Cristina and confess that he loves her, is killed in an accident. It is difficult to imagine an Abelairan character who finally stops looking for the great adventure and the ideal love; so it seems appropriate that Jerónimo dies on the point of finding his "true" love. Jerónimo has come to the end of his quest for an absolute love, having despaired of finding a social utopia before that. Convinced that the author's task is to ask uncomfortable questions, Abelaira does just that in this novel, which is one of his greatest achievements.

Abelaira constantly reminds the reader that his works constitute a whole. There is only one voice, that of the creator; this voice determines the unity of vision of the work. Abelaira's characters are similar, not only from book to book but also within the same book. They belong to the same class (the educated middle class); they use the same language and argue constantly about politics, current affairs, art, literature, music, travel, and love. They are cultured, and they care about what goes on in the world and in their own country. Abelaira reflects on important questions that have affected Portugal and the Portuguese for several decades. Natália Nunes acknowledges this contribution and believes that Abelaira's work "is one of the most courageous and lucid fictional examinations of conscience, of the socio-political and ethical reality of the Portuguese in the last 50 years."

**References:**

Nelly Novais Coelho, *Escritores portugueses* (São Paulo: Quiron, 1973);

Lélia Pereira Duarte, "*O triunfo da morte,* novo caminho para o Neo-Realismo," *Colóquio,* 81 (1984): 34–39;

Ângela Beatriz de Carvalho Faria, "Augusto Abelaira–a busca do fio invisível da harmonia polifônica," in *XIII Encontro de Professores Universitários Brasileiros de Literatura Portuguesa* (Rio de Janeiro, 1992), pp. 408–414;

Maria Lúcia Lepecki, *Meredianos do Texto* (Lisbon: Assírio & Alvim, 1979);

Óscar Lopes, *Os sinais e os sentidos-literatura portuguesa do seculo XX* (Lisbon: Editorial Caminho, 1986);

António Apolinário Lourenço, *Biblos-Enciclopédia Verbo das literaturas de língua portuguesa* (Lisbon: Verbo, 1995);

Natália Nunes, *As batalhas que nós perdemos* (Porto: Livraria Paisagem Editora, 1973);

Vera Lúcia Felício Pereira, "O sentido da (des) construção da narrativa e do sujeito em *Bolor:* A ironia existencial," *Boletim do centro de estudos portugueses,* 11 (1991): 25–33;

Lucília Gonçalves Pires, "A reiteração no romance de Augusto Abelaira," *Cadernos de literatura,* 7 (1980): 38–44;

Manuel Poppe, *Temas de literatura viva–35 escritores contemporâneos* (Vila da Maia: Imprensa Nacional-Casa da Moeda, 1982);

Mário Sacramento, *Ensaios de domingo II* (Porto: Editorial Inova, 1974);

João Camilo dos Santos, "Belles lettres, Revolutionary Promise and Reality," in *The New Portugal: Democracy and Europe,* edited by Richard Herr (Berkeley: International and Area Studies, University of California at Berkeley, 1992);

Maria Alzira Seixo, *Discursos do texto* (Lisbon: Livraria Bertrand, 1977);

Alexandre Pinheiro Torres, *O Neo-realismo literário português* (Lisbon: Moraes, 1976);

Torres, *Romance: o mundo em equação* (Lisbon: Portugália Editora, 1982).

# Sophia de Mello Breyner Andresen

*(6 November 1919 - )*

Marco G. Silva
*University of North Carolina at Chapel Hill*

*Sophia de Mello Breyner Andresen (photograph by U. Andersen/SIPA PRESS)*

BOOKS: *Poesia* (Coimbra: Privately printed, 1944; revised and expanded, Lisbon: Ática, 1975);
*Dia do mar* (Lisbon: Ática, 1947);
*Coral* (Porto: Simões Lopes, 1950);
*No tempo dividido* (Lisbon: Guimarães, 1954);
*O rapaz de bronze* (Lisbon: Minotauro, 1956);
*Mar novo* (Lisbon: Guimarães, 1958);
*A menina do mar* (Porto: Figueirinhas, 1958);
*A fada Oriana* (Lisbon: Ática, 1958);
*A noite de Natal* (Lisbon: Ática, 1959);
*O Cristo cigano, ou, A lenda do Cristo cachorro* (Lisbon: Minotauro, 1961);
*Contos exemplares* (Lisbon: Moraes, 1962);
*Livro sexto* (Lisbon: Moraes, 1962);
*O cavaleiro da Dinamarca* (Porto: Figueirinhas, 1964);
*Os três reis do Oriente* (Lisbon: Estúdio Cor, 1965);
*Geografia* (Lisbon: Ática, 1967);
*Antologia, 1944-1967* (Lisbon: Portugália, 1968);
*A floresta* (Porto: Figueirinhas, 1968);
*Grades: Antologia de poemas de resistência* (Lisbon: Dom Quixote, 1970);
*11 poemas* (Lisbon: Movimento, 1971);
*Dual* (Lisbon: Moraes, 1972);
*O nome das coisas* (Lisbon: Moraes, 1977);
*O nu na antiguidade clássica* (Lisbon: Portugália, 1978);
*Tesouro* (Porto: Figueirinhas, 1978);
*Contos: 1979* (Lisbon: Galeria São Mamede, 1979);
*A casa do mar* (Lisbon: Galeria São Mamede, 1980);
*Poemas escolhidos* (Lisbon: Círculo de Leitores, 1981);
*Navegações* (Lisbon: Imprensa Nacional-Casa da Moeda, 1983);
*Histórias da terra e do mar* (Lisbon: Salamandra, 1984);
*Antologia* (Porto: Figueirinhas, 1985);
*No tempo dividido; e, Mar novo* (Estoril: Salamandra, 1985);
*A árvore: O espelho ou o retrato vivo* (Porto: Figueirinhas, 1985);
*Ilhas* (Lisbon: Texto, 1989); bilingual edition translated by Richard Zenith as *Islands* (Lisbon: Texto, 1995);
*Obra poética,* 3 volumes (Lisbon: Caminho, 1990-1991);
*Primeiro livro de poesia: Poemas em língua portuguesa para a infância e a adolescência* (Lisbon: Caminho, 1991);
*Obra poética,* 2 volumes (Lisbon: Círculo de Leitores, 1992);
*Musa* (Lisbon: Caminho, 1994);
*Signo (escolha de poemas)* (Lisbon: Presença, 1994);
*Poemas de Sophia (1944-1989),* bilingual edition, translated into Chinese by Yao Jing Ming (Macao: Instituto Cultural / Hebei, China: Montanha das Flores, 1995);
*O búzio de Cós e outros poemas* (Lisbon: Caminho, 1997);
*Era uma vez uma praia atlântica* (Lisbon: Expo 98, 1997);
*O Bojador* (Lisbon: Caminho, 2000);
*O colar: Teatro* (Lisbon: Caminho, 2001);
*Mar* (Lisbon: Caminho, 2001);
*Orpheu e Eurydice* (Lisbon: Galeria 111, 2001).

**Editions in English:** *Marine Rose: Selected Poems,* translated by Ruth Fainlight (Redding Ridge, Conn.: Black Swan Books, 1986);

*Log Book: Selected Poems,* translated by Richard Zenith (Manchester: Carcanet Press, 1997).

TRANSLATIONS: Paul Claudel, *A anunciação de Maria* (Paris: Aster, 1962);

Dante, *O purgatório* (Lisbon: Minotauro, 1962);

William Shakespeare, *Hamlet* (Porto: Lello, 1965);

Emile Mireaux, *A vida quotidiana no tempo de Homero* (Lisbon: Livros do Brasil, [1979]).

Sophia de Mello Breyner Andresen has been recognized since the 1940s as one of the most inspired poets of Portuguese literature. She was influenced by the classic authors of ancient Greece and by the magical environment of their Mediterranean landscapes. Her work expresses a poetic knowledge of human existence, and it reaches a sort of substantial transparency that is closely linked with her search for what she calls "the undivided time"–that is, an original, undisrupted time, before the appearance of chaos, when all things were united as part of the same whole. Her work does not consist solely of poetry: she has also published novels, essays, literature for children, and translations. Her translations include Dante's *Purgatory,* Paul Claudel's *The Tidings Brought to Mary,* William Shakespeare's *Hamlet,* and Emile Mireaux's *Vie quotidiane au temps d'Homère* (Everyday Life in Homer's Time).

Andresen was born in Porto on 6 November 1919, the first child of João Henrique Andresen and Maria Mello Breyner. Her mother was a housewife, and her father was a businessman who supported the family with many investments. Andresen spent her childhood at the family's fancy home in the city (the Quinta do Campo Alegre) and their summer place in the coastal town of Espinho with her brothers—João Henrique, Thomaz, and Gustavo—and many cousins. This happy childhood left an undeniable mark on the author's work, which portrays a woman's search for the beauty of life.

Andresen had her first contact with poetry when she was three years old. Her babysitter read for her, and long before learning how to read, Andresen was able to recite the works of sixteenth-century poet Luís Vaz de Camões, to the delight of her proud grandfather Thomaz de Mello Andresen. Her love for the sea as a vibrant and inspiring entity was encouraged by reading Homer at the age of twelve. She developed a passion for classical literature, which left a clear influence on her poetic voice. As a child, she had a naive view of the world that led her to identify poems not as a specific author's work but rather as elements that had life by themselves, suspended in thin air. Childhood memories form the basis for Andresen's notion of the poet as a listener and of poetry as a state of pure concentration. Following the steps of Rainer Maria Rilke, she also cultivates the image of the poet as a "possessed" being, engulfed by the mystic quality of poetry.

Andresen entered the Colégio do Sagrado Coração de Maria in Porto in 1926 and studied there until the age of seventeen. She was considered a dedicated student by most of her teachers, although she was never fond of disciplines such as mathematics and chemistry, preferring the classics and the study of modern languages, especially her mother tongue. She had written her first poems when she was twelve; from the age of sixteen her passion for poetry increased. In 1936 Andresen went to the University of Lisbon to study classical philology, but she did not complete her degree. Three years later she returned to Porto and lived there until she married lawyer Francisco Sousa Tavares on 27 September 1946, a union that lasted until Tavares's death in 1993. Soon after their marriage, the couple moved to Lisbon, where they raised their five children: Maria, Isabel Sophia, Miguel, Sophia, and Francisco Xavier.

Andresen's first book, *Poesia* (Poetry), was published in 1944. Three hundred copies were printed and paid for by her father, with the help of a family friend. *Poesia* was republished in 1975 by Editora Ática, and this revised edition includes additional poems that Andresen had written between the ages of sixteen and twenty-three–a period that, according to the poet, represents the most productive phase of her career. The book, in which the author reveals a strong connection with the reality of things and clarity of images, was the beginning of an impressive career. Andresen's poetic works have maintained this characteristic of dealing with the real rather than the ideal.

Andresen's poetry is distinctive in its presentation of seductive themes and forms of expression and in its visible demand for essentiality. Unlike other Portuguese female poets, she has avoided the use of biographical or picturesque elements and theatricality. Detached from both the physical and mythical worlds, yet aware of them, her poetry examines scientific and literary themes such as an existentialist concept of life, the values of classical antiquity (harmony, balance, and justice), and the didactic function of literature. Other important subjects include individualism, psychological idealism, Christian humanism, the social and ethical aspects of artistic production, and nature. Her work reflects the notion of the poet as the shepherd of the absolute and man as the shepherd of beings.

*Andresen (center) with fellow writer Agustina Bessa-Luís and Eugenio Andrade in Amarante, 1958 (from Alvaro Manuel Machado,* A vida e a obra de Agustina Bessa-Luis, *1979; Alderman Library, University of Virginia)*

With *Dia do mar* (Day of the Sea, 1947), Andresen's second book, the poet started exploring one of her most frequent subjects: the sea. The poems in *Dia do mar* create images that evoke the sensation of waves rolling through the pages. In "Navegação" (Navigation), for instance, Andresen writes:

Distância da distância derivada
Aparição do mundo: a terra escorre
Pelos olhos que a vêem revelada
E atrás um outro longe imenso morre.

(Distance derived from distance
Apparition of the world: the land flows
Through the eyes that see it revealed
And behind this another far off immensity dies.)

These lines give the reader a sharp vision of the clarity of the ocean, its endless nature, and its relationship with the earth. For Andresen, the sea is a living element that communicates to humans, and it has a magical role in the epiphany of the world.

In her next book, *Coral* (Coral, 1950), Andresen continues to explore connections with the ocean, especially in the Mediterranean world. Since her first work, she has been attracted to ancient Greece, particularly to the Greek islands. Every sign of the brightest beauty in the world is closely attached to the sea, seen in her work as the origin of all things. The sea creates a holy and mythical environment where human beings achieve a primordial wisdom inspired by the natural elements: the water, the animals, the wind, and the vegetation. In many of her poems, the narrative voice reaches the purest joy of a body and soul united with the water.

Overall, Andresen's poems are true exercises in thought and reflection. The capacity to listen to all the sounds of the world is a crucial issue for her; in order to listen to the beautiful elements of nature, one only needs to be quiet and attentive. For the poet, poetry is an explanation of the universe. Because she believes a poem should talk about a concrete life rather than an ideal one, prosaic elements are sources of inspiration: common sights, sounds, and images, such as the angle of a window, the resonance of the streets, the shadow of the walls, the appearance of faces, silence, or the distance and brilliance of the stars, become deep objects of expression in her work.

Other characteristics of Andresen's poetic works, besides the ubiquity of the sea, include a creative and sensory imagination, the transformation of the real into the poetic, a use of strong rhythms and auditory images, and the magical language present in the myth of Orpheus. Orphism (the teachings of an ancient Greek philosophical cult that exerted great influence on Greek culture, and later on Western mysticism and occultism) has a definite impact on her work. Following the style of authors such as Rilke and Friedrich Hölderlin, Andresen also celebrates poetry as a form of possession and as a divine expression of being. Nevertheless, Andresen subverts and reinterprets the classical myth of Orpheus, an ultimate symbol of poets. Diverging from the traditional interpretation of the myth, the author turns the hero's act of descending into the underworld to recover his beloved Eurydice into a metaphor for the poetic quest for meaning. The poem "Soneto de Eurydice" (Sonnet for Eurydice, from *No tempo dividido* [In The Divided Time], 1954) is an example of Andresen's reinterpretation of the Greek myth. In this poem she inverts the roles of the two lovers: Eurydice is searching for Orpheus. For Andresen, this search symbolizes the "true face" of poetry: "Eurydice perdida que no cheiro / E nas vozes do mar procura Orpheu" (Dazed Eurydice searches for Orpheus / In the voices and scents of the ocean). Orpheus cannot be found anywhere except within the poet: "E deixei de estar viva e de ser eu / Em procura de um rosto que era o meu / O meu rosto secreto e verdadeiro" (And I ceased to be alive and to be myself / While I searched for a face that was mine / My own secret and true face). Orphism in Andresen's work also stresses the "magical" function of language, which becomes an instrument for the materialization of poetry in the real world.

Nearly all of the academic studies and general criticism of the work of Andresen focus on her poetry. She is, however, also an appreciated writer of fiction, particularly short stories and books for children, beginning with *O rapaz de bronze* (The Bronze Boy, 1956). Her children's stories tend to attract adults as well: mature readers are often captivated by the intrinsic poetic power of her prose and by her symbols and images. Her short stories written for an adult audience develop themes that are related to the human being's relationships with nature and with fellow human beings. Andresen's writing is linear, using traditional narrative structures and a simple vocabulary. Her way of organizing the material is creative yet accessible to the reader, who easily recognizes the basic themes and messages of the text. The simplicity of her writing, however, does not compromise the communicative power of the implied messages, as she explores complex human behavior and thought on both the connotative and symbolic levels. Andresen's writing, which maintains a balance between clarity of text and complexity of meaning, demands an intellectual response from the reader.

Andresen's fiction, besides its literary and aesthetic qualities, has been studied from other contemporary perspectives. Environmental issues, for example, have been in vogue since the last two decades of the twentieth century, and Andresen's stories for children are being used in primary and secondary schools in Portugal to help develop environmental awareness in children. Portugal is a country in which the coast is threatened by intensive building and the growing occupation of the landscape; Andresen's *A menina do mar* (The Sea Girl, 1958) has been used by teachers to address such issues. In this story a boy makes a voyage to find his girlfriend. The descriptions of the girl's sea companions and the terrestrial elements, given in conversations between the two protagonists, are interesting starting points for a deeper understanding of these features, their reasons for being, and their possible material and symbolic extensions. The emphasis placed on the superiority of the Sea Kingdom provides material for studying and analyzing myths that deal with whatever is different or unknown. Above and beyond the environmentalist aspect of the project, Portuguese teachers are also applying Andresen's stories as a tool in the formation of children's humanistic and civil consciousness.

The poet's experience with the social and political problems of Portugal, combined with her analytical view of post–World War II society, resulted in the search for a more direct and simple literary language. She sought a way in which she could present a variety of everyday themes while at the same time expressing her preoccupation with the essence of life. The poem "Exílio" (Exile) from *Livro sexto* (The Sixth Book, 1962) illustrates the author's political concerns: "Quando a pátria que temos não a temos / Perdida por silêncio e por renúncia / Até a voz do mar se torna exílio / E a luz que nos rodeia é como grades" (When we do not have the homeland that we have / Lost through silence and renunciation / Even the voice of the sea becomes an exile / And the light surrounding us is like bars). Andresen's political attitude has always been straightforward, ideologically developed through aesthetic and ethical dimensions. As a citizen sensitive to the cultural implications of politics and the feeling of freedom, Andresen sometimes expresses the pettiness involved when environments are suffocated by social oppression.

The 1970s were a significant decade in Andresen's literary and personal life. Besides publishing two of her most acclaimed books of poetry, *Dual* (Dual, 1972) and *O nome das coisas* (The Name of Things,

1977), Andresen decided during this period to get more involved with her political career. She expresses in many of her essays and interviews the importance of a dual dimension in her life and work as she supports values such as freedom and justice. She has actively participated in the cultural and political life of Portugal for many years. She served as president of the Assembléia Geral da Associação Portuguesa de Escritores (General Assembly of the Association of Portuguese Writers) in 1973, and she was one of the founders of the Comissão Nacional Portuguesa de Ajuda a Prisoneiros Políticos (Portuguese National Commission for the Aid of Political Prisoners) in 1974. She was also a representative of the opposition to the government of the city of Porto in the beginning of the 1970s. Her political career flourished after the Revolution of 1974, in which the officers and men of the Movimento das Forças Armadas (Armed Forces Movement) ousted Prime Minister Marcello Caetano and President Américo Tomás. She was elected deputy for the Assembléia Constitucional Portuguesa (Portuguese Constitutional Assembly) in 1975.

In many of Andresen's later works, such as *Navegações* (Navigations, 1983), *Histórias da terra e do mar* (Stories from the Land and the Sea, 1984), and *Ilhas* (Islands, 1989), the sea is still a frequent theme, though her approach to it takes different shapes. As illustrated in *Navegações,* Andresen's relationship with the sea is sometimes also connected to Portuguese history, especially with the Portuguese explorers during the sixteenth century. Andresen writes about the adventures of these Portuguese navigators as they moved toward the East and along the coasts of Africa and India. In a style close to that of the chronicles by her countryman Fernão Lopes, Andresen seeks to share the epic feelings of the explorers. She tells the reader what these explorers saw, as if she were sailing with them as part of the same crew. Her point of view sometimes shifts to the twentieth century as she tries to describe the navigators in their historical context. *Navegações* illustrates that Andresen's work is also concerned with voyages and the search for identity found and lost by the Portuguese maritime discoveries.

*O búzio de Cós e outros poemas* (The Seashell of Cós and Other Poems), Andresen's 1997 collection, takes its title from one of the poems, "O búzio de Cós," which ambiguously evokes the poet's memories of worlds conquered in the past. These worlds are again objects of Andresen's conquest, though fragmented and lost in time and space. Her means to recover such worlds is to listen attentively to the sounds of a seashell as it holds "Cântico da longa vasta praia / Atlântica e sagrada / Onde para sempre minha alma foi criada" (The chanting of the long beach / Atlantic and sacred / Where my soul was created forever). These lines summarize the

*Front cover for Andresen's 1977 collection of poetry, one of her most acclaimed books (Joint University Libraries, Tulane University)*

main concern of Andresen's poetry: every poem hides in itself a lost world ruled by an irrecoverable order based on simplicity, truth, and beauty. Poetry is therefore the word of a sacred world with no gods and suspended in time. The seashell has the power to connect the poet to this world.

Andresen's work has for many years been the object of literary criticism and study. She has published an extensive number of books, both in poetry and prose, and many of these have been translated into different languages, including Chinese, French, English, Italian, and Dutch. She has won many literary awards in Portugal, including the two major ones: the Fundação Luís Miguel Nava Award in 1998 and the Camões Prize in 1999. The Fundação Luís Miguel Nava, a foundation whose major concern is the international promotion of poetry, is responsible for the editing and publication of the periodical *Relâmpago* (Lightning). The award was unanimously granted to *O búzio de Cós e outros poemas* in May 1998. The Camões Prize was created in 1989 by an agreement between the

*Front cover for the second edition (1998) of Andresen's 1997 volume of poetry, which won the Fundação Luís Miguel Nava Award in 1998 (Lauinger Library, Georgetown University)*

governments of Brazil and Portugal. It is the highest award given for literature in the Portuguese language. The prize is awarded annually to distinguished writers whose work is considered as having contributed to the development of the cultural and literary patrimony of the Portuguese language. Andresen was the second Portuguese female poet and the fifth Portuguese writer in general to be granted this honor.

In March 2001 she won the prestigious Max Jacob Prize in France. Andresen, whose poems were translated by Joaquim Vital into French in a collection titled *Malgré les ruínes et la mort* (Despite the Ruins and Death, 2000), was the first international writer to be honored with this distinguished award. In June 2003, Andresen became the second poet writing in the Portuguese language (the first was Brazilian writer João Cabral de Melo Neto in 1994) to win the Premio Reina Sofia de Poesia Iberoamericana (Queen Sofia's Prize), the most important Spanish literary award. Created in 1992 by the University of Salamanca and the Spanish National Patrimony, the award recognizes the importance of the work of living authors whose poetic and literary achievements are relevant to the common cultural patrimony of Iberian-America and Spain.

Andresen's prose and poetry already stand at the level of other recognized Portuguese authors such as Fernando Pessoa and 1998 Nobel Prize winner José Saramago. However, she still considers her definition of poetry as being something far beyond any poet's understanding. Andresen claims to write without any kind of preconceptions. She says that she thinks of neither the image nor the sentence structures but rather focuses on the literal meaning of the words that flow spontaneously when she begins to write.

**References:**

Fernando Pinto de Amaral, "Sophia e Eugénio de Andrade, discurso e imagens da melancolia na poesia do séc. XX," dissertation, Faculdade de Letras, Universidade de Lisboa, 1997;

Maria de Lourdes Belchior, "Itinerário poético de Sophia," *Colóquio/Letras,* 89 (1986): 36–42;

Maria Graciete Besse, *Sophia de Mello Breyner, contos exemplars* (Lisbon & Mem-Martins: Europa-América, 1990);

Maria João Quirino Borges, "A arte poética de Sophia de Mello Breyner como 'Arte do Ser': Os contos como explicação de uma poética," dissertation, Faculdade de Letras, Universidade de Lisboa, 1987;

Fiama Hasse Pais Brandão, "O triplo nome Sophia," in *A Phala: Um Século de Poesia,* edited by Manuel Hermínio Monteiro (Lisbon: Assírio & Alvim, 1988);

Casimiro de Brito, *Fevereiro: textos de poesia* (Lisbon: Tipografia Ideal, 1972);

Helena Carvalhão Buescu, "Sophia au pays des merveilles," in *Sophia de Mello Breyner Andresen: Prix Camões 1999: Lumière et nudité des mots* (Lisbon: Instituto Camões, 2000), pp. 17–42;

Carlos Ceia, *Iniciação aos mistérios da poesia de Sophia de Mello Breyner Andresen* (Lisbon: Vega, 1996);

Ceia, "Monólogo crítico: nos 50 anos de vida literária de Sophia Breyner Andresen," *Colóquio/Letras,* 132–133 (1994): 182–187;

Ceia, "The Way of Delphi, A Reading of the Poetry of Sophia de Mello Breyner Andresen," dissertation, University of Wales, 1990;

Maria da Conceicão Pires Coelho and Maria Teresa Azinheira, *Sophia de Mello Breyner Andresen: Histórias da terra e do mar* (Lisbon: Europa-América, 1995);

José Antônio Gomes, *Sophia, infância e apelo do mar: Elementos para uma leitura da obra para crianças* (Matosinhos: Contemporâne, 2000);

Anna Klobucka, "O formato mulher: As poéticas do feminino na obra de Florbela Espanca, Sophia de Mello Breyner Andresen, Maria Teresa Horta, Luíza Neto Jorge," dissertation, Harvard University, 1993;

Estela Pinto Ribeiro Lamas, *Sophia de Mello Breyner Andresen, da escrita ao texto* (Lisbon: Caminho, 1998);

Jean R. Longle, ed., *Contemporary Portuguese Poetry* (New York: Harvey House, 1966);

Silvina Rodrigues Lopes, *Poesia de Sophia de Mello Breyner Andresen* (Lisbon: Editorial Comunicação, 1990);

Marta Martins, *Ler Sophia: Os valores, os modelos e as estratégias discursivas nos contos de Sophia de Mello Breyner Andresen* (Porto: Porto Editora, 1995);

Maria Luísa Sarmento de Matos, *Os itinerários do maravilhoso: Uma leitura dos contos para crianças de Sophia de Mello Breyner Andresen* (Lisbon: Texto Editora, 1994);

Inmaculada Báez Montero, "Literatura infantil: Sophia de Mello Breyner Andresen," dissertation, Universidade de Santiago de Compostela, 1986;

José Augusto Mourão, "Semiótica do espaço: 'O anjo' de Sophia de Mello Breyner," *Colóquio/Letras,* 74 (1983): 37–44;

David Mourão-Ferreira, "Mitos, rituais e paixão em Sophia de Mello Breyner," in *Letras, sinais,* edited by Mourão-Ferreira and others (Lisbon: Cosmos, 1999);

Clara Crabbé Rocha, *Os "Contos exemplares" de Sophia de Mello Breyner* (Coimbra: Instituto Nacional de Investigação Científica, 1978);

Rocha, "Sophia de Mello Breyner Andresen: poesia e magia," *Colóquio/Letras,* 132–133 (1994): 165–181;

Mário Sacramento, "Sophia de Mello Breyner Andresen: Contos Exemplares," in his *Ensaios de Domingo II* (Porto: Inova, 1974);

Sérgio Telles, ed., *Encontros* (Lisbon: Centro do Livro Brasileiro, 1970);

Alexandre Pinheiro Torres, *Poesia: programa para o concreto: Ensaios* (Lisbon: Editora Ulisséia, 1966);

Maria Elizabeth de Vasconcelos, "A harmonia da procura: A obra de Sophia de Mello Breyner e seu modelo ciclo," dissertation, Faculdade de Letras da Faculdade Federal do Rio de Janeiro, 1980;

Vasconcelos, "Sophia, a paixão da palavra," *Metamorfoses,* 1 (2000): 47–59;

Maria Adelina Vieira, "Arte poética: dom, descrença e desafio de Horácio, Sá de Miranda e Sophia de M. B. Andresen," dissertation, Universidade Católica Portuguesa, 1996.

# António Lobo Antunes
(1 September 1942 - )

Luis Riordan Gonçalves
*University of North Carolina at Chapel Hill*

BOOKS: *Memória de elefante* (Lisbon: Vega, 1979);

*Os cus de Judas* (Lisbon: Vega, 1979); translated by Elizabeth Lowe as *South of Nowhere* (New York: Random House, 1983; London: Chatto & Windus, 1983);

*Conhecimento do inferno* (Lisbon: Vega, 1980);

*Explicação dos pássaros* (Lisbon: Vega, 1981); translated by Richard Zenith as *An Explanation of the Birds* (New York: Grove, 1991; London: Secker & Warburg, 1992);

*Fado alexandrino* (Lisbon: Dom Quixote, 1983); translated by Gregory Rabassa as *Fado Alexandrino* (New York: Grove Weidenfeld, 1990);

*Auto dos danados* (Lisbon: Dom Quixote, 1985); translated by Zenith as *Act of the Damned* (London: Secker & Warburg, 1993; New York: Grove, 1995);

*As naus* (Lisbon: Dom Quixote, 1988); translated by Rabassa as *The Return of the Caravels: A Novel* (New York: Grove, 2002);

*Tratado das paixões da alma* (Lisbon: Dom Quixote, 1990);

*A ordem natural das coisas* (Lisbon: Dom Quixote, 1992); translated by Zenith as *The Natural Order of Things* (New York: Grove, 2000);

*A morte de Carlos Gardel* (Lisbon: Dom Quixote, 1994);

*Crónicas* (Lisbon: Dom Quixote, 1995);

*O manual dos inquisidores* (Lisbon: Dom Quixote, 1996); translated by Zenith as *The Inquisitors' Manual* (New York: Grove, 2003);

*O esplendor de Portugal* (Lisbon: Dom Quixote, 1997);

*Diálogos,* by Antunes and José Luís Tinoco (Lisbon: Escritor, 1998);

*Livro de crónicas* (Lisbon: Dom Quixote, 1998);

*Exortação aos crocodilos* (Lisbon: Dom Quixote, 1999);

*Não entres tão depressa nessa noite escura* (Lisbon: Dom Quixote, 2000);

*Que farei quando tudo arde?* (Lisbon: Dom Quixote, 2001);

*Algumas crónicas* (Lisbon: Dom Quixote, 2002).

*António Lobo Antunes (photograph by Jerry Bauer; from the dust jacket for* The Natural Order of Things, *2000)*

OTHER: William Faulkner, *O som e a fúria,* translated by Ana Maria Chaves, introduction by Antunes (Lisbon: Dom Quixote, 1994);

Joseph Mitchell, *O segredo de Joe Gould,* translated by José Lima, preface by Antunes (Lisbon: Dom Quixote, 2001).

António Lobo Antunes belongs to the generation of writers that appeared immediately after the Portuguese Revolution of 1974. Through his distinctive personal style he has established himself as one of the most representative voices of contemporary Portuguese literature. The success of his novels can be confirmed by the frequent reprintings that are almost always sold out. Antunes is also one of the most translated and well-known Portuguese writers abroad; his works have appeared in Danish, Dutch, English, Finnish, French, German, Italian, Norwegian, Romanian, Spanish, and Swedish translations. He narrates the history of his country as family stories of power and passion. He draws the reader into a web of unrelated lives whose links become clear only progressively, merging the voices and memories of characters into a tragicomic description of a decayed society. Antunes has been consistently nominated for the Nobel Prize in literature.

Antunes was born in the neighborhood of Benfica, Lisbon, on 1 September 1942, to a family of aristocratic ancestry. Antunes, the oldest of six brothers, was particularly close to his brother João Lobo Antunes, a prominent Portuguese doctor, with whom he shared a room when they were children. His parents were conservative and strict, but they also encouraged their children's intellectual interests and curiosity. Antunes's father, who was a well-educated doctor, was especially concerned with his children's education and exposed them to French literature. Antunes wrote his first poems and short stories when he was seven years old. He acknowledges that North American and Italian cinema, as well as the authors he read when he was a teenager (Louis-Ferdinand Céline, Ernest Hemingway, Jean-Paul Sartre, Albert Camus, André Malraux, Jules Verne, Emilio Salgary, William Faulkner, F. Scott Fitzgerald, and Thomas Wolfe), have influenced his work. He later discovered the works of Georges Simenon, Leo Tolstoy, and Anton Pavlovich Chekhov, figures who he admits have also had an impact on him.

When Antunes was sixteen, his father asked him about his future, and Antunes responded that he would like to be a writer. His father, however, convinced him that a technical course would better prepare him for life; Antunes therefore applied to the school of medicine at the University of Lisbon. He never stopped writing during his university studies. He specialized in psychiatry because he thought it was the branch most similar to literature. When he graduated in 1971 he went to London, because he wanted to be in the same hospital where Somerset Maugham had worked. As soon as he arrived in England, however, he was recalled to Portugal to serve in the army in Angola, where Portugal was involved in a colonial war. He received part of his clinical experience during his military service. Even though he had little practice in surgery, he had to perform amputations and other operations on soldiers wounded in battle. He took his book on surgery from medical school and had a nurse read from it while he proceeded with the operations. No one died as a result of his surgery, but the experience was traumatic for Antunes. He returned to Lisbon in 1973 and only then saw his oldest daughter, who had been born two years earlier. In Lisbon he joined the psychiatric services of the hospital where his father worked.

Antunes published his first novel, *Memória de elefante* (Elephant's Memory), in 1979. This novel was followed by *Os cus de Judas* (translated as *South of Nowhere*, 1983) in the same year and by *Conhecimento do inferno* (Knowledge of Hell) in 1980. These three books form his Romanesque Trilogy. The work of this first phase of his career is characterized by violent language and metaphorical exaggeration with expressionist overtones. The writer reveals a sense of disillusionment with the colonial conflicts and their impact on his country. He observes amorous relationships and sentimental forces in great detail, and he laments the loss of a mythical childhood. The important themes of his first phase include death, the obliteration of the soul, human cruelty, and the impact of the Portuguese dictatorship on national life. Antunes's works reveal a great concern for the tortuous and chaotic reality of his country, which he portrays with a nightmarish quality. He prefers elaborate structures that complicate his novels as the narratives constantly shift from past to present and from reality to delirium. He concentrates mostly on the period that followed the revolution of 1974, capturing the chaos and confusion of the time with a blending of narrative voices.

Antunes wrote *Memória de elefante* after his divorce in 1976. In this novel of separation, the existential crisis of the main character, a psychiatrist, is presented within a twenty-four-hour period. The narrative, which coincides with the last hours of a long-term crisis, is marked by depression and aggression. At the end of the work, however, the reader is left with the feeling that a change is going to come. This book is filled with references to other texts, authors, and historical characters. The language is marked by rich imagery and abundant comparisons and metaphors. Antunes combines poetic syntax and vocabulary with everyday discourse and slang. The success of this novel confirmed Antunes as a prominent new Portuguese novelist of the twentieth century.

In 1979 Antunes published *Os cus de Judas*, which won the Franco-Português Prize in 1987. This violent novel about the Portuguese colonial war in Angola is a clinical description, inspired by the author's experience as a young doctor there. It is also

Paperback cover for the 1986 edition of Antunes's first novel (1979), which covers twenty-four hours in the life of a depressed psychiatrist (Thomas Cooper Library, University of South Carolina)

a satire that explains how the revolution of 1974 actually began in Angola and how the young officers in Lisbon revolted against this absurd conflict. The story is about a man and a woman who meet in a zoo. Their conversation reveals their reasons for staying in Angola during the colonial war, their perplexity when the war started, and ultimately their horror at the situation. Through the narrator's description of his experiences and the way he interprets and deals with them, the reader perceives the enormous absurdity of war.

In *Conhecimento do inferno,* the third novel in his Romanesque Trilogy, Antunes takes the reader inside a psychiatric hospital in Lisbon, where the narrator criticizes the outdated and dehumanizing practice of psychiatry. The narrative provides a delirious vision of the anguish of madness in a psychiatric hospital where insanity is looked upon with cruelty or indifference.

The hardship of living and loving is also found in *Explicação dos pássaros* (1981, translated as *An Explanation of the Birds,* 1991), less complex in structure than the previous novels because the narration is limited to one character. Rui S. is a bourgeois intellectual who is displeased with his life and lacks self-esteem. His first marriage failed and continues to upset him. He lives with an intellectual woman who is a communist from the working class. Their two worlds, however, are not compatible. In the four days in which the novel takes place, the present is always linked to moments of rupture–in the family, social relationships, and the social discourse of the text. These ruptures indicate the disintegration of the protagonist's world and the loss of the social meaning of family, class, and group that leads ultimately to death.

*Fado alexandrino* (1983; translated as *Fado Alexandrino,* 1990), portrays Portuguese history of the previous decade. The author blends time and space and creates a sense of ceaseless movement through which the reader is invited to see the present reality of the country and its people. The characters consist of a group of former military men who meet for dinner with the former commander of their platoon in Mozambique. During the dinner their conversation reconstructs the last ten years, before and after the revolution of 1974. Their memories are a blend of personal, professional, and social incidents that reveal the lack of meaning in their lives. The novel ends with the dissolution of the group.

In 1985 Antunes decided to stop practicing medicine and devote himself exclusively to writing. At the same time, his novels began to be translated into several languages and to gain more recognition at the international level than he had achieved in Portugal. Antunes, unhappy with this inequality, has refused interviews to the Portuguese press and invitations to social functions. In 1985 he also published *Auto dos danados* (translated as *Act of the Damned,* 1995) and won the Grand Prize of the Portuguese Writers' Association. The background of this novel is the postrevolutionary period in the south of Portugal and the expansion of Communism. The narrative focuses on the breakup of a family after the death of the patriarch and the ensuing fight over an illusory inheritance. There are several characters that act as narrators over a period of several generations in which the family members destroy each other through their hatred and greed. The theme of economic decadence is linked to the degradation of family relationships that are characterized by infidelities, distrust, violence, and hatred. The characters fight to

Dust jacket for the 1983 English translation of Antunes's second novel, Os cus de Judas *(1979), based on his experiences as a surgeon during the Portuguese colonial war in Angola (Richland County Public Library)*

survive by using all types of cruelty to satisfy their egocentric needs.

In 1988 Antunes published *As naus* (translated as *The Return of the Caravels: A Novel*, 2002), which combines historical figures and events from the time of the Portuguese expansion with the present. There is a negative evocation of that period that seems to have contaminated all of Portuguese history. Alluding to *Os Lusíadas* (1572), Luís de Camões's epic poem about Portuguese maritime discoveries in the fifteenth century, Antunes shows the heroic navigators on the returning ships as disillusioned men carrying diseases and spitting blood. They are the ruins of the Portuguese colonial empire returning home. In these caravels the reader finds those whom official history has traditionally marginalized. This picture of the past is merged with the present to explain the contemporary decay and resignation. The work presents a grotesque and surreal picture of the Portuguese expansion in a text that also includes modern figures such as Spanish movie director Luís Buñuel and abstract and Surrealist artist Joan Miró.

The second stage of Antunes's work, a period he calls the "Ciclo do Benfica" (Cycle of Benfica–the neighborhood where he spent his youth), begins with *Tratado das paixões da alma* (Treatise on the Passions of the Soul, 1990) and includes *A ordem natural das coisas* (1992, translated as *The Natural Order of Things,* 2000), and *A morte de Carlos Gardel* (The Death of Carlos Gardel, 1994). In these novels the author pays more attention to formal structure as he abandons the biographical elements of his early works. He depicts a disillusioned country that has lost the possibility of any hope for the future. In this trilogy Antunes's art reaches its highest level of expression in the meticulously worked polyphony of the texts, the mixture of individual stories and fundamental moments of contemporary Portuguese history, and characters who impersonate possible key figures of this history. The narratives are permeated by a sadness embedded in

*Dust jacket for the 1991 English translation of Antunes's 1981 novel,* Explicação dos pássaros, *about a bourgeois man's disintegrating relationship with an intellectual working-class woman (Richland County Public Library)*

the tensions of opposing spaces such as city/jail and countryside/desert.

In *Tratado das paixões da alma* the late-twentieth-century history of Portugal is portrayed through two characters who were childhood friends and find themselves face-to-face in Lisbon. The relationship between the men is a blend of love, hatred, competition, and envy. One is a judge, and the other is on trial as a member of a terrorist organization. During the narrative the memories and monologues of the different characters merge to produce both humorous observations and sordid situations, as visions of the past are mixed with the complexity of the present. The novel portrays a Portugal in which the dreams of revolution fade and the manipulation of power produces a new history and hierarchical structures. The work is a ruthless depiction of a degraded social world from which there is no escape.

*A ordem natural das coisas* presents all of the important characteristics of Antunes's work in general: his activity as a psychiatrist, his disenchantment with the revolution of 1974, his skepticism regarding the new Portuguese society, the drama of emotional involvement, and the theme of childhood as a lost paradise. The novel, which is narrated by several voices in the first person, portrays the disintegration of a family between 1950 and 1990. The dialogues and memories of the characters produce a dream-like reality that captures the Portugal of the moment. A middle-aged man, who lost his job doing surveillance and wiretapping after the fall of the dictatorship, falls in love with a diabetic girl young enough to be his granddaughter. She fantasizes about younger men who will take her away from him. Their story blends with those of the other characters: an old man who was once a miner in South Africa and dreams of "flying underground"; an army officer who during the dictatorship was arrested on charges of conspiracy and now lives with the memories of being tortured in prison; and the army officer's sister, who was locked away for being illegitimate. The novel portrays the country in chaos and disintegration, and it attacks the past by showing the historical distortions produced by the secrecy and repression of the dictatorship.

*A morte de Carlos Gardel* won the France-Culture Prize. Like most of Antunes's novels, the work is written in the form of interior monologues with descriptive realism and a skeptical, pessimistic attitude toward life. The story opens in the parking lot of a hospital in Lisbon, where a young man, Nuno, has been admitted as a victim of a drug overdose. As Nuno lies dying, his father and mother (who separated a long time ago) and his aunt take turns visiting his bedside. While they surround him, each becomes absorbed in his or her own memories, which include impudence, bitterness, hatred, sickness, and death. In his coma Nuno observes the agitation around him while memories merge in his hallucination. The story is told by each of the protagonists, who are joined by distant and close members of the family. The different characters' memories focus on the state of the young addict, revealing various perceptions of the same events.

*Livro de crónicas* (Book of Chronicles, 1995) consists of short pieces that Antunes wrote in previous years. The work introduces the reader to different aspects of the author's personal life. Antunes writes with irony of his childhood and teenage years in the severe Lisbon of Prime Minister Antonio Salazar's regime. He talks about his sports heroes, his first love, his writing, and his solitude.

*O manual dos inquisidores* (translated as *The Inquisitors' Manual,* 2003), which came out in 1996, won the

*Antunes (right) and fellow novelist José Cardoso Pires, 1982 (from Ines Pedrosa,* José Cardoso Pires: Fotobiografia, *1999; University of California, Berkeley, Library)*

prize for the Best Foreign Book Published in France in 1997. It also won the Prize Portugal-Frankfurt in Germany for best translation in the same year. In this novel Antunes re-creates the decadent world of the period of Salazar's dictatorship. The protagonist is one of Salazar's ministers, who acts like a feudal master in his rural village. Throughout the narrative all the corruption surrounding this absolute master comes to light. The story shows the actions of corrupt businessmen, the political police, the old military chiefs, and Salazar himself, the true "unseen" protagonist who walks through the novel like a ghost. The minister is a man whom everyone obeys in Lisbon; he is the right arm of the dictator. Through the figure of Salazar's minister, Antunes portrays the breakdown of a society in which the ridiculous and the tragic come together through an ironic narrative that caricatures behaviors as it denounces the inquisitorial ways of those in power. The interior voices, the monologues, and the memories are part of the consciousness of the protagonists that expose the depravation, the secrets, and the private lives of the authoritarian regime in all its indifferent cruelty, hatred, and irrationality.

The title of *O esplendor de Portugal* (The Splendor of Portugal, 1997) comes directly from one of the lines of the Portuguese national anthem. This book is considered Antunes's most anti-Portuguese work, focusing on the horror of the colonial war in Angola. Through the monologues of a mother and her three children, who come from a rich family of Portuguese settlers in Angola, the book describes the degradation of the feudal society of farmers. The woman, who grew up and became a mother in Africa, refuses to leave her deteriorating house and country. The characters reveal traces of insanity; they are trapped between their connection to the Africa of their childhood and the shame of admitting that the Africa of their dreams is in reality a nightmare.

The Portuguese presence in Africa during the dictatorship of Salazar is a recurrent theme in Antunes's work. In the first chapter the author makes it clear that all the ties with Africa have been broken and that the four characters describe a world that no long exists. The characters, however, remain desperately attached to what is left of the splendor of the nation, but the world that Antunes describes is the opposite of splendor. The novel deals with the human being's capacity to explore his or her own misery and pain.

Antunes published *Exortação aos crocodilos* (Exhortation to the Crocodiles) in 1999. This novel won the D. Dinis Prize given by the Casa de Mateus Foundation. Without being a political novel, the narrative depicts a right-wing terrorist group that attempts to reestablish the order destroyed by the revolution of 1974. The story takes place in 1975 as a group of female companions of influential men try to revive a violent movement of the extreme right. During the course of the story they look at various aspects of life, many times connected to their childhood. The novel explores themes of nostalgia, violence, and fear. The monologues (or streams of consciousness) of the four women form the narrative structure. The protagonists move between reality and dream. The novel takes the reader to the tormented world of these women, presenting their anguish, traumas, passions, humiliations, and childhood recollections. The women are different from each other, but they are all obsessed with failure, horror, and death. There is no hope or happiness in this novel.

In 2000 Antunes published *Não entres tão depressa nessa noite escura* (Do Not Go So Fast into That Dark Night). In this narrative various marginal perspectives lead the reader to a hospital and explore such subjects as dementia, old age, and the permanent uneasiness of living to die. The work resembles a collection of clinical reports. The action takes place during seven days that correspond with the seven days of creation in Genesis. As the narration progresses, each day brings everything closer to death.

Antunes's blend of his military experience in the Portuguese colonial war in Angola and his profession as a psychiatrist make him one of the most disconcerting and complex of contemporary Portuguese novelists. His works are characterized by an apparent complacency with abjection and with miserable or cruel situations. Antunes opens each of his novels in medias res; in some cases one has to read several pages before fully understanding what is occurring. Antunes's writing is characterized by multiple voices that offer various perspectives, often on the same thing. His characters are frequently obsessive, looking for something they have lost: the hope of living well or being loved. In his novels there is a compassion for women and men who, although they appear motionless, are fighting to live.

Antunes also writes chronicles for the Portuguese newspaper *O público*. In these pieces he continues his critique of contemporary Portuguese society by portraying a country that is losing its cultural identity. As in his novels, Antunes exposes a cruel picture of the mediocrity of everyday tragedies.

Antunes writes every day. He usually starts at 2:00 P.M. and finishes at 2:00 or 3:00 A.M., and he stops only for dinner. He lives in a small apartment in Lisbon. He says that he writes to correct what he has written before. For him, life is a constant battle against depression, and writing is his way of finding the necessary equilibrium for living.

**References:**

Sarah Adamopoulos, "Leituras com o Lobo," *O Independente*, 14 January 1994;

Clara Ferreira Alves, "*Fado Alexandrino*," *Jornal de Letras, Artes e Ideias*, 72 (November 1983): 3–4;

Pedro Alvim, "*As naus* (regressadas) de António Lobo Antunes–protoplasma e futuro," *Jornal Diário de Lisboa*, 21 April 1988, p. 1;

Alvim, "*Tratado das paixões da alma* de António Lobo Antunes–festa com infância e morte," *Jornal Diário de Lisboa*, 21 November 1990;

Baptista-Bastos, "Lobo Antunes a Baptista-Bastos: Escrever não me dá prazer," *Jornal de Letras, Artes e Ideias*, 176 (November 1985): 3–5;

Margarida Barahona, "*Explicação dos pássaros*–a fragmentação e o modelo perdido," *Jornal de Letras, Artes e Ideias*, 37 (August 1982): 26;

Agustina Bessa-Luis, "O incorrígivel," *Jornal de Letras, Artes e Ideias*, 27 (November 1990);

Patrícia Cabral, "O psicodrama de Lobo Antunes," *Jornal Diário de Notícias*, 21 January 1993, p. 8;

João Camilo, "Alguns aspectos da tecnica narrativa em *Os cus de Judas*, de Antonio Lobo Antunes," *Cahiers-d'Etudes-Romanes*, 10 (1985): 231–249;

António Carvalho, "O exílio de Lobo Antunes," *Revista Visão*, 22 March 1996;

Luís Coelho, "Da ordem natural às pequenas razões," *Jornal Expresso*, 7 November 1992, pp. 99–100;

Tereza Coelho, "Memória de um escritor," *Jornal Público*, 4 April 1994, pp. 26–27;

Liberto Cruz, "António Lobo Antunes–*Auto dos danados*," *Colóquio/Letras*, 97 (May–June 1987): 118–119;

Ana Sousa Dias, "António Lobo Antunes–Um escritor reconciliado com a vida," *Jornal Público*, 18 October 1992, pp. 24–32;

Dias, "*A ordem natural das coisas*, de Lobo Antunes, nas livrarias–Silencioso e tímido," *Jornal Público*, 30 October 1992, p. 32;

Teolinda Gersão, "António Lobo Antunes–*Explicação dos pássaros*," *Colóquio/Letras*, 72 (March 1983): 102–104;

António Guerreiro, "Crónica da vida vulgar," *Jornal Expresso*, 16 April 1994;

Guerreiro, "Matéria de romance," *Jornal Expresso,* 26 October 1996, pp. 25;

Luis Madureira, "The Discreet Seductiveness of the Crumbling Empire: Sex, Violence and Colonialism in the Fiction of Antonio Lobo Antunes," *Luso-Brazilian Review,* 32 (Summer 1995): 17–29;

Luís Almeida Martins, "António Lobo Antunes: não merecemos o Nobel," *Revista Visão,* 26 September 1996, pp. 88–91;

Martins, "Uma bela e alegre declaração de amor a um país," *Jornal de Letras, Artes e Ideias,* 12 April 1988, p. 7;

Marcello Duarte Mathias, "Ferocidade e ternura," *Jornal de Letras, Artes e Ideias,* 642 (May 1995): 22;

João de Melo, "António Lobo Antunes–*Fado alexandrino,*" *Colóquio/Letras,* 82 (November 1984): 104–106;

Fernando Mendonça, "António Lobo Antunes–*Tratado das paixões da alma,*" *Colóquio/Letras,* 125/126 (July-December 1992): 296–297;

Maria do Carmo Monterio, "Elements pour une lecture de *Os Cus de Judas* de Antonio Lobo Antunes," *Recherches et Etudes Comparatistes Ibero-Francophes de la Sorbonne-Nouvelle,* 4 (1982): 110–119;

Alexandre Pastor, "*Fado alexandrino,*" *Jornal de Letras, Artes e Ideias,* 489 (November 1991);

Inês Pedrosa, "Que estão eles a ler?" *Jornal de Letras, Artes e Ideias,* 156 (July 1985);

Phyllis Peres, "Love and Imagination among the Ruins of Empire: Antonio Lobo Antunes's *Os cus de Judas* and *O fado alexandrino,*" in *After the Revolution: Twenty Years of Portuguese Literature, 1974–1994,* edited by Helena Kaufman and Anna Klobucka (Lewisburg, Pa.: Bucknell University Press, 1997);

J. David Pinto-Correira, "António Lobo Antunes–*Memória de elefante,*" *Colóquio/Letras,* 62 (July 1981): 87–89;

Luís Francisco Rebello, "*Fado alexandrino,*" *Jornal de Letras, Artes e Ideias,* 89 (March 1984): 5;

Isabel Risques, "Lobo Antunes: o artista é um ladrão bom," *O Jornal,* 30 October 1992;

Mário Santos, "António Lobo Antunes–cada vez tenho mais medo de escrever," *Jornal Público,* 24 September 1993, p. 8;

João Botelho da Silva, "Escrevo o que gostava de ler," *Jornal Diário de Notícias,* 27 April 1994, pp. 30–31;

Rodrigues Silva, "A constância do esforço criativo," *Jornal de Letras, Artes e Ideias,* 25 September 1996, p. 13;

Francisco José Viegas, "António Lobo Antunes–Nunca li um livro meu," *Revista Ler,* 37 (1997): 30–43;

Viegas, "O regresso das caravelas e da tristeza," *Jornal Mais Semanário,* 31 March 1988, p. 14.

# Agustina Bessa-Luís
*(15 October 1922 - )*

Luciana Camargo Namorato
*University of North Carolina at Chapel Hill*

BOOKS: *Mundo fechado* (Coimbra: Mensagem, 1948);
*Os super-homens* (Porto: Portugália, 1950);
*Contos impopulares,* 5 volumes (Porto: Imprensa Portuguesa, 1951–1953);
*A sibila* (Lisbon: Guimarães, 1954);
*Os incuráveis* (Lisbon: Guimarães, 1956);
*A muralha* (Lisbon: Guimarães, 1957);
*O inseparável ou o amigo por testamento* (Lisbon: Guimarães, 1958);
*O susto* (Lisbon: Guimarães, 1958);
*Ternos guerreiros* (Lisbon: Guimarães, 1960);
*Embaixada a Calígula* (Lisbon: Bertrand, 1961);
*O manto* (Lisbon: Bertrand, 1961);
*O sermão de fogo* (Lisbon: Bertrand, 1962);
*As relações humanas,* 3 volumes (Lisbon: Guimarães, 1964–1966)–comprises volume 1, *Os quatro rios* (1964); volume 2, *A dança das espadas* (1965); and volume 3, *Canção diante de uma porta fechada* (1966);
*A bíblia dos pobres,* 2 volumes (Lisbon: Guimarães, 1967, 1970)–comprises volume 1, *Homens e mulheres* (1967); and volume 2, *As categorias* (1970);
*A Brusca* (Lisbon: Verbo, 1971);
*Santo António* (Lisbon: Guimarães, 1973);
*As pessoas felizes* (Lisbon: Guimarães, 1975);
*Crónica do cruzado Osb* (Lisbon: Guimarães, 1976);
*As fúrias* (Lisbon: Guimarães, 1977);
*Conversações com Dimitri e outras fantasias* (Lisbon: A Regra do Jogo, 1979);
*Fanny Owen* (Lisbon: Guimarães, 1979);
*A vida e a obra de Florbela Espanca* (Lisbon: Arcádia, 1979);
*O mosteiro* (Lisbon: Guimarães, 1980);
*A mãe de um rio,* text by Bessa-Luís, photographs by Jorge Molder (Lisbon: Contexto, 1981);
*Sebastião José* (Lisbon: Imprensa Nacional-Casa da Moeda, 1981);
*Longos dias têm cem anos: Presença de Vieira da Silva* (Lisbon: Imprensa Nacional-Casa da Moeda, 1982);
*Os incuráveis,* 2 volumes (Lisbon: Guimarães, 1982–1983)–comprises volume 1, *Os retratos* (1982); and volume 2, *Os irmãos* (1983);

*Agustina Bessa-Luís (from the cover for* A bela portuguesa, *1986)*

*A memória de giz* (Lisbon: Contexto, 1983);
*Os meninos de ouro* (Lisbon: Guimarães, 1983);
*Adivinhas de Pedro e Inês* (Lisbon: Guimarães, 1983);
*Um bicho da terra* (Lisbon: Guimarães, 1984);
*Os incuráveis: Revelação e criação* (Lisbon: Guimarães, 1984);
*"Menina e moça" e a teoria inacabada* (Lisbon: Univ. Nova. Fac. de Ciências e Tecnologia, 1984);
*A monja de Lisboa* (Lisbon: Guimarães, 1985);
*Apocalipse de Albrecht Dürer* (Lisbon: Guimarães, 1986);
*A bela portuguesa* (Lisbon: Rolim, 1986);

*Martha Telles: O castelo onde irás e não voltarás* (Lisbon: Imprensa Nacional-Casa da Moeda, 1986);
*Contos amarantinos* (Porto: Asa, 1987);
*A corte do norte* (Lisbon: Guimarães, 1987);
*Dentes de rato* (Lisbon: Guimarães, 1987);
*Aforismos* (Lisbon: Guimarães, 1988);
*Prazer e glória* (Lisbon: Guimarães, 1988);
*A torre* (Lisbon: Associação Portuguesa de Escritores, 1989);
*Eugénia e Silvina* (Lisbon: Guimarães, 1989);
*Vento, areia e amoras bravas* (Lisbon: Guimarães, 1990);
*Breviário do Brasil* (Porto: Asa, 1991);
*Vale Abraão* (Lisbon: Guimarães, 1991);
*Estados eróticos imediatos de Sören Kierkegaard* (Lisbon: Guimarães, 1992);
*Ordens menores* (Lisbon: Guimarães, 1992);
*As terras do risco* (Lisbon: Guimarães, 1994);
*Camilo: Génio e figura* (Lisbon: Notícias, 1994);
*O concerto dos flamengos* (Lisbon: Guimarães, 1994);
*Um outro olhar sobre Portugal* (Porto: Asa, 1995);
*Aquário e Sagitário* (Porto: Civilização, 1995);
*Alegria do mundo,* 2 volumes (Lisbon: Guimarães, 1996);
*Memórias laurentinas* (Lisbon: Guimarães, 1996);
*Party: Garden-party dos Açores: Diálogos* (Lisbon: Guimarães, 1996);
*Um cão que sonha* (Lisbon: Guimarães, 1997);
*Garrett: Eremita do chiado: Teatro* (Lisbon: Guimarães, 1998);
*O Porto em vários sentidos,* text by Bessa-Luís, photographs by Nicolas Sapieha (Lisbon: Quetzal, 1998);
*O comum dos mortais* (Lisbon: Guimarães, 1998);
*A quinta-essência* (Lisbon: Guimarães, 1999);
*O Presépio: Escultura de Graça Costa Cabral,* text by Bessa-Luís, photographs by Pedro Vaz (Lisbon: Inapa, 2000);
*As meninas,* text by Bessa-Luís, paintings by Paula Rego (Lisbon: Três Sinais, 2001);
*O princípio da incerteza,* 2 volumes (Lisbon: Guimarães, 2001, 2002)–comprises volume 1, *Jóia de família* (2001); and volume 2, *A alma os ricos* (2002);
*Agustina Bessa-Luís: O livro de Agustina* (Torres Vedras: Três Sinais, 2002).

Agustina Bessa-Luís began writing at a time when many women writers were unsuccessfully fighting for emancipation. Bessa-Luís, however, was able to publish her work regularly, standing out as a prolific writer of Portuguese literature. Her novels are characterized by detailed descriptions and a concern for time and its passage. Her characters are generally presented as being in conflict with the indifference of a technologically oriented society. Bessa-Luís, especially in her novels, attempts to solve the age-old conflict between the regional and the universal as she reflects on Portuguese reality and its relation to the world. Her work, closely connected to Portuguese culture and at the same time extremely universal, has earned her a place not only as an important woman writer but also as a prominent Portuguese author.

As a member of the third phase of Portuguese modernism, Bessa-Luís escapes the rigid classification of being a neorealist writer. Although her work has been characterized by a resistance to the dissolution of individuality in a superficial and mechanical society, it goes beyond social criticism and explores other issues. Bessa-Luís refuses to see language as a mere form of communication. In her works, she assembles and organizes important moments without great concern for linearity. Bessa-Luís, according to the Portuguese critic António José Saraiva, is the "second miracle of the twentieth Portuguese century" (the first one being the writer Fernando Pessoa).

Maria Agustina Ferreira Teixeira Bessa (she adopted the name Bessa-Luís after marriage) was born in Vila Meã in Douro on 15 October 1922. Her mother, Laura Jurado Ferreira, was Spanish, and her father, Artur Teixeira Bessa, was a Portuguese landowner. She had one brother. At the age of six she was reading *The Thousand and One Nights,* and at ten, she read stories from the Bible. She found books by eighteenth-century French, English, and Spanish writers in her grandfather's library. Her mother, who was from Zamora, Spain, is the source of the aspects of the Spanish culture seen in her works.

Bessa-Luís spent her childhood and adolescent years at Amarante, a recurrent setting in her works. Her favorite course in school was history, which she considered to be her pastime. She attended Colégio das Doroteias, at Póvoa do Varzim, and spent most of her vacations at Douro. During a monotonous and rainy winter there when she was sixteen, she wrote her first novel. The work was never published. At that time she also read the important authors of Portuguese literature, including Luís de Camões, João de Barros, and Pessoa. She wrote another novel while she was a teenager, but it also was never published. Bessa-Luís finished her studies in 1936.

In 1945 the author married Alberto de Oliveira Luís, who was studying law. They lived in Coimbra for three years, where their daughter, Laura Monica, was born in 1946. Bessa-Luís published her first book, *Mundo fechado* (Closed World), in 1948. *Mundo fechado* is the story of Pedro, a young man who suffers from an incurable disease. By emphasizing small but significant moments of his daily life, Bessa-Luís stresses the magic that is present in everyone's life. Pairs of oppositions such as life/death, solitude/communion, and isolation/communication resonate in this story, in which each

*Bessa-Luís and her brother with their maternal grandmother, 1924 (from Álvaro Manuel Machado,* A vida e a obra de Agustina Bessa-Luís, *1979; Alderman Library, University of Virginia)*

individual life is presented as an essential part of the whole world. *Mundo fechado* was praised by writers such as Aquilino Ribeiro and Ferreira de Castro, who considered it to be a mature work, without the usual mistakes of beginners. Time, which becomes an important element of her fiction, is already a prominent aspect of this novel.

In 1950 Bessa-Luís moved to Porto and published the novel *Os super-homens* (The Supermen). In this work night is depicted as a symbol of the social-psychological environment and of the situation in which the characters are involved. Between 1951 and 1953, she published the short-story collection *Contos impopulares* (Unpopular Stories) in five volumes. The stories blend real and supernatural elements in imaginative ways and address existential questions. *Contos impopulares* combines the extremely descriptive and the extremely intellectualized, as memory is seen as an essential element of symbolic language. The characters in *Contos impopulares* are significant not for the complexity of their feelings or thoughts, but rather for the complexity of their existence as characters. They live on the edge of a reality that is constantly questioned.

In 1953 Bessa-Luís received the Delfim Guimarães Prize for her then-unpublished novel *A sibila* (The Fortune-Teller, 1954). The prize was granted unanimously by the jury of Álvaro Lins, Branquinho da Fonseca, Tomaz de Figueiredo, and Vitorino Nemésio. In 1954 she also received the Prize Eça de Queirós for the same book.

*A sibila* tells the story of Quina, the youngest daughter of a couple who live in a rural area. Because of financial difficulties, the family is unable to educate Quina properly. Illiterate, she tries to find a way to change her fate. While other neorealist authors saw the novel as a didactic discourse that could be used to transform history and society, *A sibila* goes beyond immediate history, assimilating it through the nontemporal nature of myth and through symbolic language, which had been introduced to Portuguese literature by Raul Brandão in *Húmus* (1917). The flow of Bessa-Luís's prose interrupts the linear sequence of events in the narrative, creating a sense of improvisation in the text.

*A sibila* presents another way of viewing the excess of vitality that torments human nature in *Os super-homens* and the fragmentary complexity seen symbolically in *Contos impopulares*. In *A sibila* there are several limited worlds that open up and mingle with one another. This fragmentary complexity allows the development of a symbolic language. Quina represents the mystery of mankind.

Bessa-Luís believes that a novel should never be written according to the demands of the literary market. For this reason, she thinks the success of *A sibila* changed her view about what she writes. She began to feel a necessity both to defend herself from the fame that she earned with the novel and to observe herself as a writer.

In *Os incuráveis* (Incurable People, 1956) she analyzes symbolically the distinct behaviors of the members of a typical family from Douro. The work is permeated by a sense of the incompleteness of life. In this work there are several stories that are connected to others, creating a series of embedded love stories. Regardless of the detailed analyses of many characters, the reader has the impression that there is something more to the characters, which is more important than the individual and which can establish a connection among them all. *A muralha* (The Wall, 1957) and *O susto* (The Fright, 1958) are characterized by a sense of mystery and a mythical discourse. *A muralha* begins with a scene in which the mystery of the cosmos is revealed through a dream. *O susto* questions the freedom and reason of the literary work in relation to the mystery of time and the cosmos.

Bessa-Luís's play in three acts, *O inseparável ou o amigo por testamento* (The Inseparable or the Friend as Legacy, 1958), is her first dramatic work. The main theme is the game of secret passions that is present in a rich family from a small town. Through the family's habits and relationships, the play analyzes the meaning of the essential mystery of humanity and the search for communication.

In 1959 Bessa-Luís traveled to France to take part in a literary conference at the invitation of the Faculdade de Letras e Ciências Humanas de Aix-en-Provence and the Fundação Laurent-Vibett. There she met writers Camilo José Cela, Julián Marias, and André Chamson. During the 1960s she visited several countries in Europe, and after her experiences abroad she wrote *Embaixada a Calígula* (Caligula's Embassy, 1961), a travel book that was ignored by the critics. As in previous books, in *Embaixada a Calígula* the analysis of the deepest motivations of the characters is connected with the concrete world. In this book Bessa-Luís offers readers almost an essay based on a psychological interpretation of the customs of the Spanish, Italian, and French people.

Many of Bessa-Luís's novels feature a large cast of characters and multiple plots. Her long sentences and difficult phrases, the richness of her vocabulary, and the recurrent interruptions of the narrative and interventions of the narrator have caused some critics to consider Bessa-Luís a difficult and hermetic writer. Through these characteristics the author attempts to show the readers a reality different from their own. She reveals a world in which characters act and react as she observes their souls in their primitive roots. In *Ternos guerreiros* (Gentle Warriors, 1960), for instance, the close analysis of the characters reveals the ignoble actions of Porfírio and his sister Amina. The relationship between these characters is painful and culminates in the establishment of a sadistic atmosphere in the text. The absence of noble qualities and the presence of serious flaws in the characters is recurrent in Bessa-Luís's works. Their behavior often borders on the pathological. In *Ternos guerreiros*, Domingos is a man without self-confidence, a fact that prevents him from being happy. He searches for something that he cannot define. Throughout his life, this constant search makes the character learn and grow, but he can never emerge from his melancholic condition.

In *O manto* (The Mantle, 1961) the title constitutes a metaphor for life. The mantle is seen as an object that touches the ground, leaving its marks wherever it passes. In this work the author uses the two main characters, Lourença and Filipe, to show that even in love man must search for peace. The author shows that individuals are chaotic entities, and they need to make an effort to understand themselves. The characters in the novel are strangers to themselves: they do not know their own values, and for this reason they live a series of frustrating relationships. *O manto* illustrates the author's notion that a novel is never complete. At the end of her work she affirms that the way one finishes a good book is to give the idea that something is missing or untold.

In *O sermão de fogo* (Sermon of Fire, 1962) the writer again deals with the question of the essential mystery of the human being. In *Contos impopulares* and *A sibila* she created a highly symbolic language; in *O sermão de fogo* she presents thematic archetypes that develop into a kind of baroque and conceptualist complexity. The work marks the end of the second phase of Bessa-Luís's work.

From 1961 to 1962 Bessa-Luís was a member of the Conselho Diretivo da "Cummunitá Europea degli Scrittori," whose headquarters are in Rome. In 1966 she received the Prémio Ricardo Malheiros from the Academia de Ciências of Lisbon and in 1967 the Prémio Nacional de Novelística. In 1969 she first tried to become a member of the congress of the Assembléia Nacional, but her name was vetoed several times.

*Embaixada a Calígula* began a new cycle continued in a series of novels collectively titled *As relações humanas* (Human Relationships, 1964–1966). The series begins with the novel *Os quatro rios* (The Four Rivers, 1964). The basic symbols of the novel are portrayed at the beginning: the four rivers represent the concepts of childhood, woman, man, and death. The theme of the soul of a place also appears at the beginning of the novel in the description of the landscape, which acquires a mythic sense as the narrator reflects on human relations. Through one of the main characters, the writer Clemente, Bessa-Luís presents the idea of the couple as the basis of the Christian and Western family.

In the third volume of the series, *Canção diante de uma porta fechada* (Song in Front of a Closed Door, 1966), Bessa-Luís plays with concepts of the baroque and the notion of images. The mirror appears as a principal symbol that captures the essence of the entire cycle of *As relações humanas*: the various ways of seeing the world and humanity.

*Homens e mulheres* (Men and Women, 1967) is the first in a two-volume novel series called *A bíblia dos pobres* (The Bible of the Poor). Both texts include well-defined historical elements, but in the second volume, *As categorias* (The Categories, 1970), Bessa-Luís deals with the uselessness of chronological time and order. Time is shown as something personal and intimate. The essence of the characters is formed by their past, present, and future, and by how they have lived and what they will experience. In Bessa-Luís's subsequent works there is a tendency to give more impor-

*Bessa-Luís in 1946 (from Machado,* A vida e a obra de Agustina Bessa-Luís, *1979; Alderman Library, University of Virginia)*

tance to dialogues and details of daily life. The author also begins to explore cities as settings for her novels.

Her second book of short stories, *A Brusca* (The House of Brusca, 1971), reveals a more concise and less vague development of the stories compared to her first publication in this genre. Some of the stories involve memories, and change is the main theme of the work. In the title story, the author presents the decadence of the old, traditional house called Brusca. The author opposes the rigid habits that lead to the unavoidable disintegration of a family living in a small province.

In 1973 Bessa-Luís participated in the Terceiro Encontro Mundial de Mulheres Jornalistas e Escritoras (Third International Conference of Female Journalists and Writers) in Israel. During the 1970s she became involved in topics related not only to women but also specifically to Portugal, such as the revolution that took place in April 1974 and brought an end to the dictatorial regime of Prime Minister António de Oliveira Salazar and his successor, Marcelo Caetano. This issue is present in many of her novels, such as *As fúrias* (The Furies, 1977), *Os meninos de ouro* (Golden Boys, 1983) and *Vale Abraão* (Abraham Valley, 1991). *As pessoas felizes* (Happy People, 1975) is the main novel related to the historical, social, and political process of the revolution. In this work the author focuses on the city of Porto, the psychology of its inhabitants, and the spirit of the place. The novel ends with a celebration of nature.

In 1975 Bessa-Luís received the Prize Adelaide Ristori from the Centro Cultural Italiano in Rome. Two years later she received the Prémio Ricardo Malheiros from the Academia das Ciências of Lisbon for her novel *As fúrias,* which was later adapted for the theater and produced in Lisbon in 1995.

Bessa-Luís has always known how to combine fictional and real elements, and she sees the writer of fiction as responsible for linking history and real life. Authors, she believes, should give fictional events a sense of experienced reality. Even in the biographies that she wrote, she used fictional elements to fill the lack of information. With *Fanny Owen* (1979), Bessa-Luís inaugurates a series of novels that present characters taken from Portuguese history. The basis of *Fanny Owen* can be found in two texts written by Camilo Castelo Branco in 1849 and 1854. Fanny Owen lived in Portugal in the nineteenth century and carried on a correspondence with Castelo Branco. She went through a turbulent marriage with José Augusto Pinto de Magalhães, who had kidnapped her. Owen died of tuberculosis in 1854, when she was twenty-four years old. Bessa-Luís rewrites history, adding and suppressing parts of it, as she attempts to find and create the deepest and most subjective motivations for the actions of the characters.

In *Adivinhas de Pedro e Inês* (The Guesses of Pedro and Inês, 1983), Bessa-Luís relates the love story between Pedro, son of Afonso IV, and his wife's maid, Inês. In this text, the author shows the inner lives of the characters based not only on what she has read but also on what she has imagined them to be. She goes beyond what is related in the history books. She offers hypotheses and suppositions, trying to show the innermost secrets of the characters. She creates a story that focuses on the individuals and their lives, but she does not follow a chronological sequence of events.

Bessa-Luís has also written the biographies *Santo António* (Saint Anthony, 1973), *A vida e a obra de Florbela Espanca* (Life and Work of Florbela Espanca, 1979), and *Sebastião José* (1981). In her opinion, there are no "simple souls," neither for the artist nor for the psychologist. For that reason, she developed an interest in researching and reconstructing characters from the past. Her description of these figures and the portrayal of their everyday passions are striking: she turns her subjects into characters similar to the great ones of Greek tragedy. She mixes historical and fictional elements, revealing and at the same time distorting the official historical version. For this reason, Bessa-Luís goes beyond the mere influence of Romantic historical narratives. *Santo António,* for example, can be considered a kind of philosophical essay. In this work she points out the importance of the collective memory of a people for the process of writing history. She also questions the concept of history itself. She explores the essence of Saint Anthony's character and discovers a man of great intellectual capacity, which is not totally revealed in his sermons. In the biography of Espanca, a writer from the previous generation, Bessa-Luís tries to reconstruct this complex, unknown, and fleeting character, pointing out the possible forces that led this great name of Portuguese literature to her destiny.

In *Sebastião José* Bessa-Luís presents the figure of the powerful and fearsome minister Sebastião José arvalho e Melo, Marquês de Pombal. She depicts his uncertainties and involvement in the social and political transformations of the eighteenth century, which was marked by the fall of the feudal system. Through the study of the man, the author seeks to comprehend the historical figure that dominated the Portuguese political scene during the phase of transition marked by the Industrial Revolution. She portrays Pombal as a dictator and a tyrant, but at the same time, as a scared and naive man who was both subtle and banal. Bessa-Luís sees biography as useful because she thinks that personal experience, in all its complexity, is at the core of the collective history of all civilizations.

The work *Crónica do cruzado Osb* (Crusader Osb's Chronicle, 1976) also presents a close relationship to history. It depicts the revolution of 1974 and its relation to time and human passions. Through an exploration of the political, social, economic, cultural, and psychological processes of the revolution, the author points out the impossibility of returning to the past, which is filled with hidden and mysterious evils. In this work she once again explores the condition of being Portuguese. Bessa-Luís places many of her characters in small Portuguese villages as she analyzes the parallels and contrasts between the local, petty bourgeoisie and the humble working people. The village of Andriço in *O susto,* the scenery of Beira in *Ternos guerreiros,* and the setting of Douro in *Os incuráveis* are earlier examples of this tendency to focus on the psychological richness of the inhabitants of small towns and villages and on their beliefs and narrow-mindedness.

In 1977 Bessa-Luís published *As fúrias,* a novel written like a fictional chronicle that portrays the characters and facts of the revolution of 1974. The work can be read as a continuation of the *Crónica do cruzado Osb.* In *As fúrias* there are three generations represented succes-

*Bessa-Luís and her husband, Alberto de Oliveira Luís, in the ancient city of Paestum, Italy, 1968 (from Machado,* A vida e a obra de Agustina Bessa-Luís, *1979; Alderman Library, University of Virginia)*

sively by the characters Olga, Ofélia, and Pedro Rodom.

In *Vale Abraão* Bessa-Luís creates a novel similar to the works of Gustave Flaubert. The protagonist of *Vale Abraão* is Ema Paiva, who shares with Emma Bovary a feeling of emptiness. The theme of the emptiness of human beings was a characteristic of the literature written at the end of the nineteenth century. This characteristic is modified by Bessa-Luís, who connects this feeling to the place where the protagonist lived, the region of Douro.

Beginning in the 1970s, Bessa-Luís became involved with journalism. She wrote a series of chronicles for the *Diário de Notícias* (Daily News) from 1972 to 1974 and from 1992 to 1995. She also wrote for the magazine *Factos* (Facts) and the newspaper *Jornal de Letras* (Journal of Literature) in 1988. She worked on the newspaper *O Primeiro de Janeiro* (The First of January) in Porto, becoming its director of publication during the 1980s. In her journalistic work Bessa-Luís has

*Paperback cover for Bessa-Luís's 1979 biography of the first woman to be regarded as a major Portuguese writer (Thomas Cooper Library, University of South Carolina)*

always fought for her political ideas, her cultural beliefs, and the Portuguese language. After she left *O Primeiro de Janeiro,* she was invited to work as a director of the Teatro Nacional D. Maria in Lisbon. She later became director of the Instituto de Artes Cênicas until 1997, when she became involved in a debate with the minister of culture Manuel Carrilho over her criticism of Portuguese society.

Bessa-Luís has also written for television and theater. Her father had owned a movie theater in Porto, and she had attended movies since the age of five. She sees motion pictures as a fascinating art and some of her work has been adapted for the cinema by Manoel de Oliveira. These movie versions include *Francisca* (1981), an adaptation of *Fanny Owen; Vale Abraão* (1993); *As terras do risco* (*O convento*) (1995); and *O princípio da incerteza* (2002). She also wrote dialogue for *Party* (1996).

In *Memórias laurentinas* (Laurentinian Memories, 1996), Bessa-Luís once more explores historical themes and mixes them with personal experiences. This novel is the saga of a family descended from Spanish and Portuguese ancestors. There are many autobiographical elements in this work, particularly memories of Bessa-Luís's grandfather. There are several voices that intermingle in the narrative, and the depiction of the main character, Lourenço, is shown in a nonlinear way. Bessa-Luís says that all her books are exercises of spontaneous confession and that their flaws come from this spontaneity.

In 1997 Bessa-Luís published *Um cão que sonha* (A Dog that Dreams), which deals with the bourgeoisie of Porto and Lisbon during the twentieth century. The characters face constant difficulties in this novel structured around repetitions that give the impression of an eternal starting over. The main character is Léon, an intelligent man with limited ambitions. He is forced to think about his past and his relationships after becoming successful with the publication of a manuscript left by his late wife.

*O comum dos mortais* (Ordinary Mortals, 1998) created controversy with its portrayal of the lives of well-known figures such as Salazar, although the author did not use the real names of people for her characters. Some reviewers criticized the book for being anachronistic and incoherent in some passages. Bessa-Luís defended herself by saying that she was not searching for historical truth but rather was trying to see the past as fiction. Salazar is represented in this work by two characters: the professor of law Marcos da Bodiosa, who is contemplative, solitary, and introspective, like Salazar when he was not in power; and João Barreto, who is outgoing, ambitious, and eager for power.

In the same year, Bessa-Luís wrote the text for *O Porto em vários sentidos* (Porto in Many Senses), a book of photographs by the Mexican Nicolas Sapieha, who was nominated twice for the Pulitzer Prize and who disappeared in 1995. Sapieha had visited Porto to develop a project and was fascinated by its architecture.

Bessa-Luís was honored in 1998 by the Universidade Fernando Pessoa, which was responsible for organizing the first international congress on her work. Representatives from universities all over the world, including the United States, Spain, France, and Great Britain, attended. The congress was also a celebration marking fifty years of her literary production. The event included papers on her work; a documentary about her life and work, produced by the journalist Jorge Campos from the Rádio Televisão Portuguesa (RTP); and a theatrical presentation by the university group Quase Teatro based on Bessa-Luís's unedited text "Três mulheres com máscara de ferro" (Three Women with Iron Masks).

During the 1990s Bessa-Luís visited Macao, which was about to revert to Chinese sovereignty after having been a Portuguese overseas province since 1951; after returning to Portugal, Bessa-Luís decided to write about it. She had visited Macao and China during the 1980s at the invitation of the Fundação Oriente, which requested a written account of the trip. Instead of an account of the journey, she wrote *A quinta-essência* (Quintessence, 1999), a novel in which the protagonist finds intellectual pleasure in trying to solve enigmas. The protagonist, José Carlos, from Porto, goes to Macao seeking revenge: he plans to seduce and abandon the daughter of a captain who had ordered the occupation of his house when he was young. In Macao he is influenced by a different culture and loses his identity to a certain degree. The author sees the East as a suggestive place with hidden secrets for the Portuguese mind. The novel focuses on the eternal human search for perfection and happiness.

In 2001 Bessa-Luís published *As meninas* (The Girls), a novel in which she emphasizes dialogue. The work offers a personal appreciation of a series of twenty paintings by Portuguese artist Paula Rego. In this work Bessa-Luís presents a biography of the painter as well.

When analyzing her own work, Bessa-Luís divides it in three phases. The first is the phase of presentation, an ambitious period in which she emerged as a new figure in literature and during which she wrote *A sibila*. The second phase is the one in which she defined her personality and became accustomed to the act of writing. This phase ended with the beginning of the academic phase, in which her biographies are included. In this phase of wisdom she attempts to eliminate mediocrity without knowledge and also knowledge in excess.

Bessa-Luís usually portrays characters that have a romantic spirit. They have in common a great sense of solitude, and they spend time in meditation, like the mystics or the hermits. Her characters often parallel her own life and are marked by creativity and involvement with history and questions related to human nature. According to the author, the more fully a life is experienced, the less destructive time is upon it. Bessa-Luís found a way to reduce the destructive action of time by incorporating it into her work.

**Interview:**

Artur Portela, *Agustina por Agustina: Entrevista conduzida por Artur Portela* (Lisbon: Dom Quixote, 1986).

**References:**

Laura Bulger, *As máscaras da memória: Estudos em torno da obra de Agustina* (Lisbon: Guimarães, 1998);

Bulger, *A sibila, uma superação inconclusa* (Lisbon: Guimarães, 1990);

Maria do Carmo Castelo Branco, *A fala da sibila: Nótulas para a leitura de "A sibila," de Agustina Bessa Luís* (Porto: Edições ASA, 1993);

Catherine Dumas, *Estética e personagens nos romances de Agustina Bessa-Luís: espelhismos* (Porto: Campo das Letras, 2002);

Georges Guntert, "Literatura como discurso terapêutico: *Eugénia e Silvina* de Agustina Bessa-Luís," *Colóquio/Letras*, 120 (1991): 95–106;

Isabel Vaz Ponce de Leão and Olympio Pinheiro, *Agustina (1948–1998): Bodas escritas de oiro* (Porto: Universidade Fernando Pessoa, 1999);

Álvaro Manuel Machado, *Agustina Bessa Luís: O imaginário total* (Lisbon: Dom Quixote, 1983);

Machado, *Do romantismo aos romantismos em Portugal* (Lisbon: Presença, 1996);

Machado, *A vida e a obra de Agustina Bessa-Luís* (Lisbon: Arcádia, 1979);

Maria de Fátima Marinho, *O romance histórico em Portugal* (Porto: Campo das Letras, 1999);

Fernando Mendonça, *O romance português contemporâneo* (Assis: Faculdade de Filosofia, Ciências e Letras, 1966);

Massaud Moisés, *A literatura portuguesa em perspectiva*, volume 4 (São Paulo: Atlas, 1994);

Hilary Owen, *Gender, Ethnicity, and Class in Modern Portuguese-speaking Culture* (Lewiston, N.Y.: Edwin Mellen Press, 1996);

Maria Helena Padrão, *Os sentidos da paixão* (Porto: Universidade Fernando Pessoa, 1998);

Mônica Rector, *Mulher: Objecto e sujeito da literatura portuguesa* (Porto: Universidade Fernando Pessoa, 1999);

António José Saraiva and Oscar Lopes, *História da literatura portuguesa* (Porto: Porto Editora, 1982).

# Manuel Maria Barbosa du Bocage
*(15 September 1765 – 21 December 1805)*

Elias J. Torres Feijó
*Universidade de Santiago de Compostela*

BOOKS: *Elegia que o mais ingenuo, e verdadeiro sentimento consagra é deploravel morte do illustrissimo e excelentissimo Senhor D. Jozé Thomaz de Menezes* (Lisbon: Na Off. de Lino da Silva Godinho, 1790);

*Queixumes do pastor Elmano contra a falsidade da pastora Urselina: Egloga* (Lisbon: Off. Simão Thaddeo Ferreira, 1791);

*Idyllios maritimos recitados na Academia das Bellas Letras de Lisboa* (Lisbon, 1791);

*Rimas: Tomo I* (Lisbon: Off. Simão Thaddeo Ferreira, 1791; corrected and augmented, 1794);

*Elogio poetico á admiravel intrepidez, com que em domingo 24 de Agosto de 1794 subiu o capitão Lunardi no balão aerostatico* (Lisbon, 1794);

*Rimas . . . dedicadas à amisade: Tomo II* (Lisbon: Off. Simão Thaddeo Ferreira, 1799);

*Aos faustissimos annos do serenissimo príncipe regente, nosso senhor: Elogio para se recitar no theatro da rua dos Condes* (Lisbon: Tip. Caligráfica, Tipoplástica e Literária do Arco do Cego, 1801);

*Epicédio na sentida morte do . . . Senhor D. Pedro José de Noronha, marquez de Angeja* (Lisbon: Régia, 1804);

*Poesias: Dedicadas à Illma. e Exma. Senhora Condessa de Oyenhausen: Tomo III* (Lisbon: Off. Simão Thaddeo Ferreira, 1804);

*Mágoas amorosas de Elmano: Idyllio* (Lisbon: Régia, 1805);

*A saudade materna: Idýllio, na prematura, e chora da morte da Senhora Dona Anna Raimunda Lobo* (Lisbon: Régia, 1805);

*Improvisos de Bocage na sua mui perigosa enfermidade, dedicados a seus bons amigos* (Lisbon: Régia, 1805);

*Collecção dos novos improvisos de Bocage na sua molestia, com as obras, que lhe forão dirigidas por vários poetas nacionaes* (Lisbon: Régia, 1805);

*Armia: Idyllio* (Lisbon: 1806);

*Verdadeiras inéditas, obras poeticas* (Lisbon: Régia, 1813);

*Poesias eroticas, burlescas e satyricas de M. M. de Barboza du Bocage não comprendidas na edição que das obras deste poeta se publicou em Lisboa, no anno passado de MDCCCLIII* (Brussels, 1854).

*Manuel Maria Barbosa du Bocage (frontispiece for* Poesias de Manuel Maria de Barbosa du Bocage, *1853; from the 1985 Dinalivro facsimile edition; Thomas Cooper Library, University of South Carolina)*

**Editions and Collections:** *Poesias de Manuel Maria de Barbosa du Bocage,* 6 volumes, edited by Inocêncio Francisco da Silva (Lisbon: Em casa do editor A. J. F. Lopes, 1853);

*Opera omnia Manuel Maria de Barbosa du Bocage,* 6 volumes, edited by Hernâni Cidade (Lisbon: Bertrand, 1969–1973);

*Apólogos, adivinhações e epigramas* (Mem Martins: Europa-América, 1984).

TRANSLATIONS: François Thomas Marie de Baculard d'Arnaud, *Eufemia, ou O trionfo da religião* (Lisbon: Off. Simão Thaddeo Ferreira, 1793);

*História de Gil Braz de Santilhana,* 4 volumes (Lisbon: Off. Simão Thaddeo Ferreira, 1797–1800);

Jacques Delille, *Os jardins ou a arte de aformosear as paisagens* (Lisbon: Tip. Caligráfica, Tipoplástica e Literária do Arco do Cego, 1800);

José Francisco Cardoso, *Canto heróico sobre as façanhas dos portugueses na expedição de Tripoli* (Lisbon: Off. da Casa Litterária do Arco do Cego, 1800);

La Croix, *O consórcio das flores, epistola de la Croix a seu irmão* (Lisbon: Tip. Caligráfica, Tipoplástica e Literária do Arco do Cego, 1801);

Ricardo de Castel, *As plantas* (Lisbon: Tip. Caligráfica, Tipoplástica e Literária do Arco do Cego, 1801);

*Rogerio e Victor de Sabran ou o trágico efeito do ciume* (Lisbon: Of. António Rodrigues Galhardo, 1802);

Antoine d'Anchet, *Erícia ou a Vestal* (Lisbon: Régia, 1805).

Manuel Maria Barbosa du Bocage is considered to be the most representative Portuguese writer of the eighteenth century, standing out in a period in which Portuguese literature is renowned for its otherwise poor performances. For some, Bocage is the greatest Portuguese poet after Luís de Camões and Fernando Pessoa. Known for his poetry and translations, he was one of the most popular writers of his generation, particularly appreciated for his satiric and erotic poems and, above all, for the anecdotes that circulated about him, the majority of which were false or apocryphal.

Bocage's years spent as a "bohemian" inhabitant of Lisbon also contributed to his rakish image, which evolved over the years to the point of becoming, in the 1970s, a symbol of the defense of freedom. He is considered as the author of, on the one hand, the most consummate expression of the poetics and the practice of enlightened and neoclassical ideals, and on the other hand, the irruption of the irrational or sentimental elements typical of Romanticism. Humanism, individualism, and the defense of freedom in the face of despotism are the values most associated with his life and works. His sonnets, some of which are satirical, and his fables are his best-known pieces.

Bocage, born on 15 September 1765 into a bourgeois family in Setúbal, Portugal, was the second-eldest son of the jurist José Luís Soares Barbosa and Mariana Joaquina Lestoff du Bocage, the daughter of a French admiral who had been posted in Portugal to take charge of the Lusitanian navy. From what is known of Bocage's family background, it seems to have been one in which reading was heartily encouraged. At the age of five he began his primary education and by the age of eight could write with ease. He learned French at home, studied Latin with the help of the Spanish priest Juan de Medina, and later went on to teach himself Italian.

Bocage's mother died when he was ten. As a younger son of a large family, therefore having fewer prospects, he abandoned his studies in the humanities and joined the infantry corps of Setúbal. At the age of eighteen he was admitted to the newly created royal marine academy in Lisbon. Classes were taught in the Colégio dos Nobres and provided the students with a scientific education of sorts, focusing particularly on math and physics applied to nautical activities. He studied various subjects, although his attendance was somewhat sporadic. He finally deserted in June 1784 (though desertion at the time was not a crime).

The young Bocage felt an attraction to freethinking Lisbon with its effervescent ideas and social gatherings in large cafés, debating rooms, and taverns, in particular the Café Nicola and the Botequim das Parras. These places were constantly watched over and repressed by the national police superintendent Diogo Inácio Pina Manique and his officers, or "flies" as they were nicknamed, on the lookout for any manifestation of revolutionary thought or criticism of the Portuguese regime. During this period Bocage forged friendships with some of the most famous people in this milieu, including the poet Maximiano Torres, the eldest son of Assentis Francisco de Pasula Cardoso de Almeida Vasconcelos Amaral e Gaula, translator and freethinker; Pato Moniz, Arcadian poet, dramatist, and politician; Gastão Fausto, poet, dramatist, and translator; and André da Ponte de Quental, poet and liberal politician. Bocage thus entered into a literary circle that thrived on improvised or rehearsed poetic production, composed and/or recited in these social settings, often in exchange for material goods, money, and food. Bocage rapidly earned the reputation of being a good poet.

Despite his popularity, the poet returned to his military career as a means of earning a living, and on 1 April 1786 his posting as a guard in Goa (a state in India that was then controlled by the Portuguese) was announced in the *Gazeta de Lisbon*. On his way to Goa he passed through Rio de Janeiro. Although little is known about his stay there, some accounts suggest that he had a literary and personal impact on the society of Rio de Janeiro, to which he was introduced by the viceroy Luís de Vasconcelos Sousa Veiga Caminha e Faro, who had a great fondness for the arts. In October,

Bocage arrived in India, and judging by some of his more satirical sonnets written at the time, he found the climate, the vanity, and the cultural vacuum there unbearable. While in Goa he continued his military training in the Aula Real da Marinha, which he was later forced to abandon because of serious illness resulting from his use of tobacco and alcohol.

Once recovered, Bocage wrote against the conspiracy engineered by the people of Goa to expel the Europeans from their territory. For his efforts he was promoted to lieutenant in February 1789. Two days after being posted to Damão, however, he deserted alongside the lieutenant Manuel José Dionísio, who, it was said, was deeply in debt because of gambling. In poems such as "Descreve as suas des venturas, longe da Pátria e de Gertrúria" (He Describes His Misfortune, Far from the Homeland and from Gertrúria) Bocage tells of how he traveled through other territories in India, China, and Macao. With the help of the high magistrate Lázaro Ferreira, he returned to Portugal in August 1790, where, according to dubious sources (biographical claims without documentary evidence), he found his sweetheart (the woman known as Gertrúria in his poetry) married to his brother.

At that time, in spite of the presence of Pina Manique's repressive police force, ideas from the French Revolution began to penetrate Lisbon society and were openly discussed in the cafés and bars that were springing up all over the city. Bocage became actively involved in this environment, in which satire was found in abundance in what had become a stagnating Portuguese culture. Bocage's quick rise to fame in this milieu could be attributed to his good memory and his ability to improvise verses. Such verses also provided a significant source of income for the poet, as they were often written to order. During this period he led an irreverent life that ran contrary to prevailing ethics: he smoked and drank excessively and was later accused of heretical conduct.

Bocage published his first known work, *Elegia que o mais ingenuo, e verdadeiro sentimento consagra é deploravel morte do illustrissimo e excelentissimo Senhor D. Józé Thomaz de Menezes* (Elegy on the Death of Don José Tomás de Meneses), about the drowning of the Marquis of Meneses, in 1790. From that moment on, the critique of Portuguese society—including the government, the powerful nouveau riche, mediocrity, social convention, the clergy, the medical profession, avarice, and writers—became his poetic objective. Shortly after his return to Portugal the young Bocage, a known and popular poet, also praised within intellectual circles, was invited to join the Academy of Literature, a mark of the recognition he enjoyed among his peers. This institution, known as the Nova Arcádia—directed by Domingo Caldas Barbosa, sponsored by the Count of Pombeiro, and controlled by Pina Manique—tried to modernize the neoclassical objectives of the older Lusitanian Academy, which, for its part, had looked to the Italian Academy of Arcádia as a model and precedent. The motto of the Nova Arcádia, *Inutilia truncat* (Cut the Useless Things), illustrates its claim to a style of poetry that was spontaneous and simple, harmonious and usable, antibaroque and opposed to counterreformist spirits and practices. Bocage, in the Arcadian tradition, assumed a poetical and pastoral pen name, using the anagram Elmano accompanied by the epithet Sadino (from Sado, the river that flows into the Setúbal).

Bocage's family profile corresponded to that of neoclassical intellectuals, the majority of whom came from middle-class backgrounds and were joined by sectors of the aristocracy and petit bourgeoisie. These intellectuals defended their liberal ideology and wrote with reformist aspirations. In the Academy, Bocage recited a collection of "Idílios marítimos" (Maritime Idylls), a minor genre designed to proclaim the pureness of rustic life. The genre was used as a melancholic expression of life's misfortunes, often those concerning love, which makes it similar to the classical or Renaissance eulogy. Together with other compositions, these idylls were compiled in *Rimas* (The Rhymes), Bocage's first book, which appeared in 1791. The book was subtitled *Tomo I* (Volume 1), and a follow-up was produced in due course.

The *Rimas,* which displayed Bocage's status as member of the Nova Arcádia with the name Elmano Sadino stamped across its front cover and with the inclusion of a quotation by Ovid, presented itself as the product of the author's plight: "súbitas desgraças assombram meus dias" (sudden misfortunes darken my days). Bocage added two introductory sonnets. In the first he effectively shows himself to be a poet persecuted and beset by misfortune; he speaks of his "Incultas produções da mocidade" (Unrefined essays written in youth), indicating that if the readers find some poems of "festival contentamento" (festival contentment) they are the result of "Fingimento" (Pretense) and "Dependência" (Dependency), given that they were written to order. In the second sonnet he reiterates the motif of sadness and adversity, showing himself to be unafraid of satire and slander and depicting himself as a man now with "Um peito, de gemer cansado e rouco" (a tired of whining and hoarse chest). Such comments suggest a setting in which his works were more than likely to be met with criticism and satire in what was a literary field divided into two camps. Apart from employing this presentational style, Bocage avoids the personal abstraction and the pretense that were common poetic practices of the neoclassicists. His poetry reveals instead an author who

*Draft for one of Bocage's sonnets (Biblioteca Municipal de Évora)* wishes to intervene directly in the society that surrounds him.

At the time, his recitations, some of which were improvised in cafés and public debating halls, were received by a public who knew of Bocage's illicit lifestyle and found it impossible to separate the life of the poet from his works. This tendency was compounded by the fact that Bocage's works depict him as an author who is constantly preoccupied with the construction of his image. There are many references in *Rimas* to his personal life, including his illness and his life "longe da Pátria e de Gertrúria." This autobiographical tendency is especially evident in his sonnets, which constitute the main body of the work, and perhaps the compositional pieces that most distinguish themselves from neoclassical schemas.

Bocage's love poems essentially focus on his protests of unrequited love, inconsistency in love, misfortune, and the ingratitude of the lover. A climate of desperation, from which the only escape is often death, is a predominant theme. Few of these poems are written in a neoclassical and balanced vein in which nature suspends its traditional role of the reflection of sorrow to lend itself to something more harmonious. This poetry, which often appears bare and uses a nocturnal and mysterious setting, is indicative of what was already a rupture with the neoclassical repertoire. Some neoclassical traits, however, persist, such as the poetic forms (especially the sonnet) and the occasional reference to patterns of speech. These characteristics can be noted in the sonnet "Convite a Marília" (Invitation to Marília), in which passion and lack of restraint stand out. The speaker, identified with the lyrical self, deems himself mad, blind, miserable, and lost. Specific elements, such as the dream world, delirium or a state of mind and soul no longer subject to reason, and jealousy, begin to emerge in the poems.

There are also religious poems that seek a reconciliation of faith and reason and in which the poet claims to be searching for refuge from his disorderly and depraved life. In addition to the sonnets, other writing forms, neoclassical in nature, appear. For example, there are odes such as the one that he dedicated to Luís de Vasconcelos, a strongly allegorical poem in which the poet thanks the nobleman for his assistance in the face of misfortune. The poem is also an explicit reference to the dependency to which the poet was subjected. There are the epistles he writes to Gertrúria and to his friend and companion in the Nova Arcádia, Josino (José Francisco Cardoso), to the former expressing his sad fate at being separated from his sweetheart, and to the latter communicating his many bad impressions of India and his deep nostalgia for his friends and another lover, Saudade. Bocage also uses the song, neoclassical in content, in which he depicts his bidding farewell to Lisbon, his friend, and his sweetheart before his departure to Goa. He wrote other songs with themes such as jealousy and betrayal. In these songs, despite the use of a highly allegorical repertoire in which reason plays a determinant role, the poet explores sentimental nuances that were relatively unheard of in Portuguese literature at that time. In such songs, as with the sonnets, freedom and passion begin to appear at odds with rationalism, forming the basis of Bocage's future poetic style.

Bocage's lifestyle and beliefs brought many problems upon him. It appears that from its creation, the Nova Arcádia was a place of convention and mutual praise, which led Bocage to overstep the boundaries of critical sense that rigidly defined such academies. He employed harsh satire against some of its members in some of his compositions that circulated around the cafés and meeting rooms. His caustic attitude was aimed at Father António Pereira de Sousa Caldas (poet, lawyer, and president of Nova Arcádia) and others such as Curvo Semedo (Belchior Manuel Curvo Semedo Torres Sequeria, a poet and absolutist militant) and Father José Agostinho de Macedo (an epic poet and absolutist). The poet even turned against those whom he had formerly praised (José Tomás Quintanilha, for example), accusing them of mediocrity in their lives and verses. His adversaries accused him of immoral behavior and reproached him for his atheism. In 1794 he was expelled from the academy, which by this time he had ceased to attend.

That same year Simão Thaddeo Ferreira released the second edition of Bocage's *Rimas,* which attests to his popularity. In this edition the poet no longer alluded to his academic status. The edition omitted some of the poems present in the first, and it included more poems from minor genres. Bocage included Anacreontic poetry in the form of odes and *cançonetas* (poems with graceful content, written in short stanzas). He also included poems concerning jealousy, disappointment in love, and death, as well as a significant ensemble of epigrammatic poems. Along with such compositions, he incorporated a series of moral tales, some original and some translated from the works of Jean La Fontaine. Bocage also added a prologue in which he justified the first edition as being the initial product of youth, affirming that he had not been able to revise the texts and justifying the amendment of others. He thus exposed the new texts to critical judgment, declaring himself to be "nem soberbo nem humilde" (neither arrogant nor humble) and "com o ánimo igualmente disposto para o louvor e para a crítica" (equally open to accept praise as he was to accept criticism). This edition, historically unrecognized and sometimes even dismissed by specialists because it was so difficult to find, is essential to an understanding of Bocage's objectives and poetic styles. At the same time, it provides insight into the author's popularity and the state of the literary scene in the era in which he lived.

At the end of the eighteenth century, in certain circles of Lisbon society, literature assumed a political nature and became the topic of meetings and the vehicle of new ideas. To some, the antibaroque reaction of neoclassicism implied an attack on the cultural and mental backwardness of Portuguese society. The state of economic crisis was evident. The abundant gold mines of Brazil (then a Portuguese colony) did not provide enough for the immense military budget and uncontrollable squandering of the royal court, which had put a halt to the administrative reforms undertaken by Sebastião de Carvalho, Marquês de Pombal, a powerful figure during the reign of King Joseph. The revolutionary events in France were observed with a growing intensity, although the penetration of French terminology into the Portuguese language was resisted in the spirit of nationalism. Books from France found their way into Portugal by way of ports and foreign travelers; thus, ideas derived from the French Revolution soon topped the agenda in the assembly rooms, and subversive texts were put into print. All this ferment took place under a regime in which anyone suspected of deviating from the religious or the political status quo risked incarceration or execution. Bocage's works did not avoid these subjects. Several of his texts, including some that remained unedited until many years after his death, criticized the political climate of the moment and claimed the right to freedom in the face of despotism. A good example of this poetry is "Epístola a Marília" (Epistle to Marília, not published until 1812), also known by its first line, "Pavorosa ilusão da eternidade" (Frightful illusion of eternity). The poem illustrates Bocage's strongly critical sentiment toward religion. "Epístola a Marília" deals with the amorous provocation of passion without respecting dogmas or rules as it asserts the right to freedom. This epistle is the most complete of Bocage's compositions; it reduced the amorous isolation that neoclassical rationalism imposed and that Romanticism opposed.

During a police raid on 7 August 1797, Bocage was detained, and the authorities confiscated various documents that they considered to be mutinous and sympathetic to the cause of the French Revolution. The epistle was among these documents. Bocage was sent to prison for crimes against the monarchy. He was placed under the jurisdiction of the royal justice system managed by Pina Manique and confined to the Lisbon prison of Limoeiro. Benefiting from his popularity, and with the help of friends in high places, such as the minister Jose Seabra da Silva—contacts made during his life as a poet and freethinker—he escaped conviction for these crimes, but on 7 November he was handed over to the Inquisition on the grounds of "disorderly ways" and ungodliness. The Inquisition, however, had had its powers severely reduced by this time.

During February of 1798 Bocage was transferred to the Convent of Saint Bento. On 22 March, accused of blasphemy and immorality, he was sent to the Hospício das Necessidades to be "re-educated." He was released a few months later. Without doubt, Bocage's fame and prestige contributed to the short prison sentence, and even when in 1802 he was denounced to the Inquisition, accused of being a Freemason, the case against him was not pursued. Bocage was suspected of being opposed to both the church and the state. Whether because of genuine conviction or as a result of the repression he was forced to endure, he began to modify his attitude after his release from prison. He was no longer seen drinking in the bars of Lisbon, smoking, entertaining, and impressing all those around him with his irreverent style and satirical, erotic (sometimes pornographic) poems. From the little information available about his life, including some biographical material within his work, it is known that he was a man of modest financial means and was obliged to support a family composed of himself, his sister, and her daughter.

Shortly after he was released from prison, Bocage's second volume of *Rimas* (1799) was published. The work included new minor genres such as a series of satirical epigrams (some heavily veiled in order to avoid the strict precensorship to which they were subjected), songs of lament, and the translation of fragments of the *Metamorphosis*. In the prologue, Bocage suggests that the volume was designed to sidestep criticism, reiterates his aspiration to fame and his pride in his talent, thanks his editor António J. Álvares, and presents these *Rimas* as partly reconstructed from memory after his manuscript was stolen in Santarém. At the time, Bocage was caught up in a tough satirical debate over literary merit with Agostinho de Macedo that he depicted in his work titled "Pena do Talião" (The Sorrow of Torion), first published in *Investigador Portuguez*, 1812.

During his time in prison, Bocage was given access to an excellent classical library. He put his Latin skills to good use, translating, among other works, fragments of Ovid's *Metamorphosis*. The poet earned his meager upkeep in his twilight years doing translations as well as written-to-order poems. He had previously resorted to the translation of pieces by Jean Racine, Voltaire, and Jean-Jacques Rousseau to subsidize publication of the second volume of his *Rimas*. In 1800, however, he began to work translating, proofreading, and

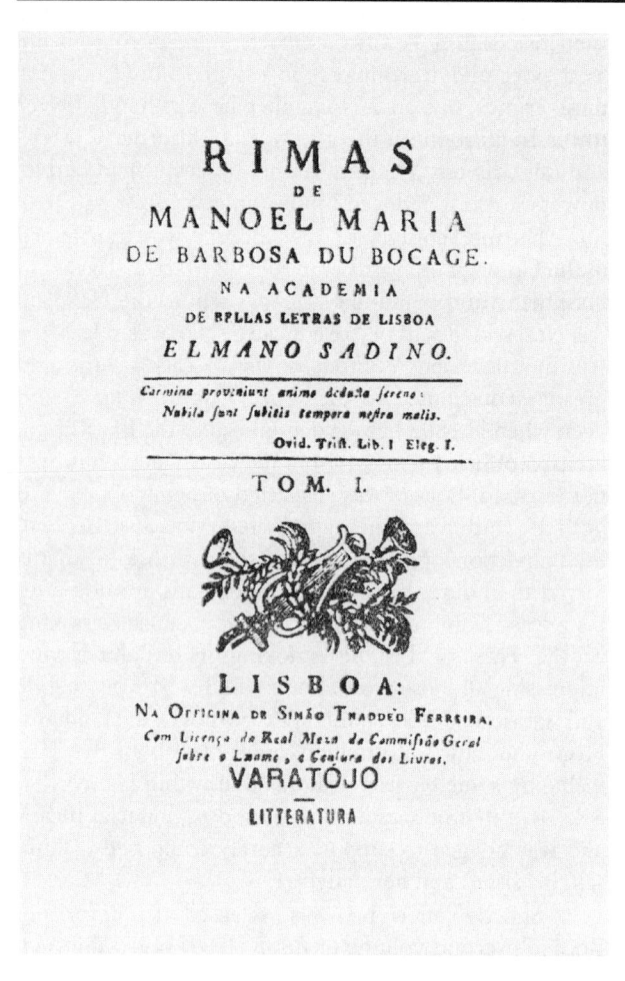

*Title page for the first book-length collection of Bocage's poetry, published in 1791 (Biblioteca Nacional, Lisbon)*

perfecting other authors' works for the publishing firm directed by the scientist José Mariano Veloso. Bocage received a modest salary for endeavors that occupied all of his time, although he considered translation to be an activity that merely imitated and improved on the original.

Bocage preferred to work on didactic poems, which were in vogue at that time. He translated texts such as Jacques Delille's *Os jardins ou a arte de aformosear paisagens* (The Gardens or the Art of Embellishing Landscapes, 1782) in 1800, Ricardo de Castel's *As plantas* (The Plants, 1799) and La Croix's *O consórcio das flores* (The Partnership of Flowers) in 1801, Pierre-Fulcrand de Rosset's *A agricultura* (The Agriculture [1774], which remained unedited until 1831), and sections from *A Colombíada* (Columbus's Feat), written by his famous ancestor Madame du Bocage (Marie Anne Le Page, an important eighteenth-century French intellectual). He also translated lyric poetry and dramas that were popular at the time, including *Canto heróico* (The Heroic Song, 1800) by the Latinist José Francisco Cardoso, Antoine d'Anchet's *Erícia ou a vestal* (Erícia or the Vestal), and Pietro Metastasio's posthumously published *Atílio Régulo* (1740).

Bocage's work reached a turning point with the publication of his short pieces under the titles *Improvisos de Bocage na sua mui perigosa enfermidade, dedicados a seus bons amigos* (Improvisations of Bocage in His Very Dangerous Disease, Dedicated to His Good Friends, 1805) and *Collecção dos novos improvisos de Bocage na sua molestia, com as obras, que lhe forão dirigidas por vários poetas nacionaes* (Collection of the New Improvisations of Bocage in His Disease, with the Works That Had Been Directed to Him by Some National Poets, 1805) and with the third volume of his *Rimas,* titled *Poesias* (1804), which he dedicated to the progressive thinker the Marquise of Alorna. *Poesias* brings together an important collection of eulogies, many of which were aimed at members of royalty or of the court and which were a reflection of the dependency of his poetic vocation. His poetry still depicted the pride he felt for his recognition and his opposition to his critics, as reflected in the poem he dedicated to neoclassical poet Filinto Elísio (Francisco Manuel do Nascimento) upon hearing that the latter held his works in high esteem (a poem that ends with an emphatic "Posteridade . . . es minha!" [Posterity . . . you are mine!]). As his illness progressed, however, his writing began to show increasing signs of regret for his past and indications of reconciliation with old enemies from the era of the Nova Arcádia.

The last poems published during his lifetime, in particular those in the *Improvisos* volumes, were written for friends and as peace offerings to enemies. In these verses he does not abandon his claim to fame and glory. In many of these poems and other compositions, the allusions to nearing death are overwhelming. Bocage was in poor financial circumstances and incurably ill; his only source of income was the charity of his friends, managed on his behalf by his friend and proprietor of the Botequim das Parras. An aneurysm, which seems to have had its roots in his early youth, caused his death at the age of forty. He was buried in the Igreja das Mercês, in the Bairro Alto (High District) of Lisbon.

Bocage's popularity was reflected by the number of poets who lamented his death, the frequent republication of his texts in Portugal and in Brazil, the successive books of anecdotes in which he was made the protagonist of even the most implausible adventures, and even the naming of streets, societies, and newspapers in his honor. His life has been brought to the screen and to the stage and has inspired artistic sequences. Various editions of his work have been posthumously published, notably the six-volume *Poesias de Manuel Maria de Barbosa du Bocage* (1853) edited by Inocêncio Francisco da Silva, who titled all the sonnets.

Thus far, the most outstanding edition of his works is that of Hernâni Cidade, begun in 1969 (also a six-volume set). There is, however, still no version that puts in order the material published under Bocage's supervision and that arranges his works in chronological order.

Considered a poet of excess and contradiction, Bocage produced works that are characterized by the Romanticism that was gathering force in Europe but was still unheard of in Portuguese literature. Bocage is considered to be the master of pre-Romanticism in Portugal: he incorporated aspects of neoclassicism while proclaiming a Romantic vision of life. This vision reveals a vivid expression of cultural reform, which was to be found in the rudimentary schema of the neoclassical model and which in turn integrated new ideas and bourgeois aspirations of freedom and free thinking.

**References**:

Artur Anselmo, "A fortuna editorial de Bocage," in his *Estudos de história do livro* (Lisbon: Guimarães, 1997), pp. 99–116;

Olavo Bilac, *Bocage. Conferências* (Porto: Renascença Portuguesa, 1917);

Teófilo Braga, *Bocage, sua vida e época literária* (Porto: Livraria Chardron, 1902);

Hernâni Cidade, *Bocage, a obra e o homem,* third edition (Lisbon: Arcádia, 1978);

Jacinto do Prado Coelho, "Bocage: A vocação do obscuro," in his *A letra e o leitor,* second edition (Lisbon: Moraes, 1977), pp. 37–55;

Coelho, *Poetas pré-românticos,* second edition (Coimbra: Atlântida, 1970);

António Gedeão, *O sentimento científico de Bocage* (Lisbon: Separata de *Ocidente,* 1965);

Óscar Lopes, "Bocage–fronteiras de um individualismo," in his *Ler e depois* (Porto: Inoa, 1969), pp. 154–162;

Cândido Martins, *Para uma leitura da poesia de Bocage* (Lisbon: Presença, 1999);

João Mendes, *Literatura portuguesa II,* second edition (Lisbon: Verbo, 1982), pp. 241–260;

Carlos Filipe Moisés, "Bocage e o século XVIII," *Colóquio-Letras,* 50 (1979): 35–42;

Maria Antónia C. Mourão and Maria Fernanda P. Nunes, *Bocage. Antologia Poética* (Lisbon: Ulisseia, 1991);

Vitorino Nemésio, João Mendes, and Ester de Lemos, *Bocage* (Lisbon: Verbo, 1972);

Maria Helena da Rocha Pereira, "Bocage e o legado clássico," in her *Temas clássicos da poesia portuguesa* (Lisbon: Verbo, 1972), pp. 131–172;

Maria Aparecida Santilli, "Em torno do soneto de Bocage," *Revista de Letras,* 8–9 (1966): 232–241.

**Papers**:

Major archives of Manuel Maria Barbosa du Bocage's papers are kept at the Casa de Bocage/Galeria Municipal de Artes Visuais and the Centro de Estudos Bocageanos, both in Setúbal, Portugal.

# Raul Brandão
*(12 March 1867 – 5 December 1930)*

Rui Torres
*Universidade Fernando Pessoa, Porto*

BOOKS: *Impressões e paisagens* (Porto: Tipografia de A. J. da Silva Teixeira, 1890);

*História d'um palhaço: A vida e o diário de K. Maurício* (Lisbon: Parceria A. M. Pereira, 1896); republished as *A morte do palhaço e o mistério da àrvore* (Lisbon: Seara Nova, 1926);

*O padre* (Lisbon: Livraria Central de Gomes de Carvalho, 1901);

*A farsa* (Lisbon: Ferreira & Oliveira, 1903);

*Os pobres* (Lisbon: Empresa da História de Portugal, 1906);

*El-rei Junot* (Porto: Renascença Portuguesa, 1912);

*A conspiração de 1817* (Porto: Tipografia da Empresa Literária & Tipográfica, 1914);

*1817: A conspiração de Gomes Freire* (Porto: Renascença Portuguesa, 1917);

*Húmus* (Porto: Renascença Portuguesa, 1917);

*Memórias,* volume 1 (Porto: Renascença Portuguesa, 1919);

*Teatro: O Gebo e a sombra; O rei imaginário; O doido e a morte* (Porto: Renascença Portuguesa, 1923);

*Memórias,* volume 2 (Paris & Lisbon: Aillaud & Bertrand, 1923);

*Os pescadores* (Paris & Lisbon: Aillaud & Bertrand, 1923);

*As ilhas desconhecidas: Notas e paisagens* (Rio de Janeiro: Francisco Alves / Paris: Aillaud / Lisbon: Bertrand, 1926);

*Jesus Cristo em Lisboa,* by Brandão and Teixeira de Pascoaes (Paris & Lisbon: Aillaud & Bertrand, 1927);

*O avejão* (Lisbon: Seara Nova, 1929);

*Portugal pequenino,* by Brandão and Maria Angelina (Lisbon: Privately printed, 1930);

*O pobre de pedir* (Lisbon: Seara Nova, 1931);

*Memórias,* volume 3: *Vale de Josafat* (Lisbon: Seara Nova, 1933);

*A noite de Natal,* by Brandão and Júlio Brandão, edited by José Carlos Seabra Pereira (Lisbon: Imprensa Nacional-Casa da Moeda/Biblioteca Nacional, 1981).

*Raul Brandão, 1925 (from Guilherme de Castilho,*
Vida e obra de Raul Brandão, *1978;*
*Vanderbilt University Library)*

Raul Brandão's literary output was vast and covered many genres, including drama, short stories, novels, diaries, and journalism. Several generations of writers recognize Brandão's importance in the development of the new Portuguese novel. Among them, authors such as Vergílio Ferreira, Agustina Bessa-Luís, and the poet Herberto Helder have talked about his influence on their work. Brandão's work may be divided into two opposing tendencies. On the one hand, there is a negative and pessimistic side, grounded in a metaphysical questioning about the origins of human misery, the incomprehensibility of death, and the problem of defining God. On the other, however, there is the author who writes of hope, affirming the beauty of life and the magnitude of nature. The depiction of the inherent contradictions of life and the frustrated attempts to comprehend it appear in a fragmented and almost repetitive way in Brandão's novels, which are often populated with characters that represent different aspects of his personality. There is a conscious rejection of unity and logic that confers on his works the modern characteristics of other great Portuguese thinkers and writers. More importantly, perhaps, Brandão represents the transition between the literary movements of realism, naturalism, and symbolism in the nineteenth century and premodernism in the twentieth.

Raul Germano Brandão was born in Foz do Douro, Porto, on 12 March 1867, the same year as two other remarkable figures of Portuguese literature: António Nobre and Camilo Pessanha, major figures in the symbolist movement. His parents were José Germano Brandão and Laurentina Ferreira de Almeida. Born into a family of fishermen, Brandão spent his childhood and adolescence in the delta area of the river Douro and at Leça da Palmeira, a small fishing village on the outskirts of Porto. His first contact with the humble and underprivileged people who struggle with the sea in their daily lives later manifested itself as a social concern and as a theme in his work. The type of education he received in the schools and colleges of Porto had a significantly negative impact on his intellectual development. From his time in the Colégio de São Carlos in Porto, for instance, Brandão speaks in his memoirs about the sheer terror and rigidity of the institution. These defining moments projected the young author to an alternative spiritual dimension, which manifested itself at the level of the dream in his novels.

His first work, *Impressões e paisagens* (Impressions and Landscapes), was published in 1890, a politically charged year in Portugal since England had given the country an ultimatum to withdraw its forces from certain areas of Africa. While it is difficult to categorize this book of short stories under a specific literary style, it nonetheless overlaps with the publication of Eugénio de Castros's symbolist work *Oaristos,* published that same year. In the following year, Brandão published *Vidas de santos* (Lives of the Saints) with Júlio Brandão, with whom Raul Brandão shared the first steps of his literary career. During this time Brandão was still searching for a direction of his own, and these works represent practice for something of superior value that was imminent. It is important to mention, however, that Brandão breaks with the literary conventions that define his early works. His first aesthetic

*Title page for Brandão's 1896 novel, which displays some of the antiformalist and grotesque elements that characterize his work (from Castilho,* Vida e obra de Raul Brandão, *1978; Vanderbilt University Library)*

stance results from the contacts with Nobre, Justino de Montalvão, and Júlio Brandão during their gatherings in Porto, as a group called the Nefelibatas. As the name of the group–literally, "those who walk on the clouds"–implies, these writers saw themselves as mavericks on the literary scene. In their work of the same name, *Os nefelibatas,* a short manifesto published in 1892 under the collective pseudonym of Luís de Borja, they publicly expose their passions and hatred of the literature of the moment:

O que os novos querem é a Arte livre . . . Os parnasianos desconsolavam-se coçando adjectivos bonitos: o naturalismo, que em Portugal se sustentara pelo *humour* de Eça de Queirós e pelo seu génio de fantasista–só encontrara seguidores medíocres.

(What the young want is a free Art . . . The Parnassians were afflicted with their scratching up beautiful adjectives: Naturalism, which in Portugal lived on the *humor* of Eça de Queirós and his creative genius—only had mediocre followers).

In 1890 Brandão began writing *História d'um palhaço: A vida e o diário de K. Maurício* (The Story of a Clown: The Life and Diary of K. Mauricio), which was not published until 1896. It is his first significant work, and it indicates a strong sense of his future antiformalist attitude as well as his proximity to the work of the decadent and symbolist poets of the time. Brandão's negation of the efficacy of reason as the only instrument of valid knowledge and his interest in the ineffable and mysterious confirm his adherence to symbolism. The reality that Brandão presents to the reader is fluid and vague, as opposed to the concreteness of positivism and realism dominant at the end of the nineteenth century. The protagonist, K. Maurício—a central character in the works of Brandão—can be understood, like many other characters, as Brandão's alter ego. The work is created around three persons: the author/narrator, K., and the clown. However, the interior conflicts of these characters shift the narrative toward others, such as the Anarchist; Dona Felicidade (Ms. Happiness) in her boardinghouse; and the pessimist Pita, with his disenchanted dream. As in Brandão's later novels, none of these figures seems real; they move between a disenchantment with life and the despair and self-denial that it creates. The escape into their dreams is the only thing that makes life bearable. For most of Brandão's characters, their interior lives determine their interpretations of the external world, which they perceive as a mix of slush and dreams. The grotesque elements that characterize his later works begin to emerge in this novel.

In 1891 Brandão made an important decision: at his mother's insistence, he enrolled in the School of the Army to begin a military career. He despised military life, but it allowed him to spend his time doing what he most enjoyed, writing, even if only bureaucratic documents. In his *Memórias* (Memoirs, 1919, 1923, 1933) there is a sense of the terribly aggressive institution that the Ministry of War represented for him. The positive side to his military career was that it allowed him to travel, which had an impact on his work. In the early years of his profession, he started collaborating on several newspapers, including *O Imparcial* (The Impartial), Pinheiro Chagas's *Correio da Manhã* (Morning Journal), and *O Dia* (The Day). In 1894 he and Júlio Brandão founded the *Revista d'Hoje* (Today's Magazine). The author practiced journalism throughout his career.

In 1896, the year in which he published *História d'um palhaço,* Brandão was promoted to second lieutenant and placed in Infantry Regiment 20 in the town of Guimarães. That same year he met Maria Angelina, whom he married in March 1897 and with whom he shared the rest of his life. In this period Brandão dedicated his time to the construction of a house in Nespereira (near Guimarães), which he named Casa do Alto (House on the Hill). After his marriage, however, he lived for a time in Foz do Douro. In 1901 he was promoted to lieutenant and asked to be transferred to Lisbon, where he became the secretary in the newsroom of *O Dia*. Around this time he also published the pamphlet *O padre* (The Priest).

Brandão published *A farsa* (The Farce) in 1903. Like many of his works, it is a blending of novel and philosophical writing. In this work he creates one of his most striking characters, Candidinha, the embodiment of envy, hatred, falsehood, and stinginess. She is the materialization of the evil that Brandão attempted to identify and define in his works. Candidinha also represents a wish for revenge and death. She lies and pretends because falsehood is what allows her to avoid and flee from the absurdities of her life. The reader sees a transformation in Candidinha, however, after her sister, on her deathbed, gives Candidinha a package of letters and her daughter to raise. In terms of form Brandão distorts chronological time, a characteristic that came to define his narrative technique. Brandão also presents a group of old women, shriveled and paltry, subjugated by absurd conventions and routines. Their features are grotesque, and the author characterizes them as ridiculous and evil. The negative traits that Candidinha presents are the necessary tools for her to confront other types of social masking. *A farsa* condenses several themes that appear throughout Brandão's works, including the masking of reality and simulation and appearance.

In 1903 Brandão published a series of news reports in *O Dia* about hospitals, jails, and mental institutions. This contact with the underworld of misery and crime had an enormous influence on the writing of his important novel *Os pobres* (The Poor, 1906). The work, which is a blend of poetry, philosophical meditation, novella, short story, and chronicle, is a mature attempt at explaining the existence of misery and sorrow. For Brandão, the fact that people endure pain and psychological suffering throughout most of their lives is a sign that something superior must justify it. *Os pobres* reveals the author's evolution, which is best seen through one important character who appears in his future novels as well: Gabiru, the philosopher-poet. Gabiru is the extension of K. from *História d'um palhaço,* believing also that attachment to a dream is

*Brandão and his wife, Maria Angelina Brandão, in 1897 (from Castilho,* Vida e obra de Raul Brandão, *1978; Vanderbilt University Library)*

the only solution for the absurdity of a life of sorrow. The only character that stands up to face his problems is Gabiru. None of the secondary characters is able to rise up and surpass his or her annihilated humanity. The fatalism of the women, for example, is paralyzing, even though they are conscious of the evil that prevents them from going beyond it. Gebo, a male character who reappears in Brandão's play *O Gebo e a sombra* (Gebo and the Shadow, published in *Teatro,* 1923), lives in a hopeless condition, without the possibility of dreaming (literally or figuratively). Brandão uses poverty and the resignation of his characters to present in a disquieting way questions about love, the mystery of death, and the origin and purpose of life.

In 1906 Brandão traveled to Italy with his wife, and from Genoa they went by train to Rome, Naples, Florence, Venice, Milan, and later Switzerland, Paris, and London. In 1910 he was again promoted, this time to captain, and until his retirement in 1911 he divided his time between Guimarães and Lisbon. He lost both of his parents in 1910. In the following years, Brandão wrote *Húmus,* completed during World War I and published for the first time in 1917. Considered by many critics to be Brandão's masterpiece, *Húmus* has provoked many different interpretations. Some scholars have classified it within the Portuguese symbolist movement, and some see in it elements of an emotional grotesque that link it to Portuguese expressionism. *Húmus* is written in the form of a diary. As the title indicates, the novel deals with transformation: humus, composed of vegetable as well as animal detritus, is the fertile part of the soil, where life and death mingle.

The writer develops one main notion throughout his metaphysical wanderings in the text: "Ouço sempre o mesmo ruído de morte, que devagar rói e persiste" (I always hear the same noise of death, which slowly gnaws and persists). The scenery against which the action (or the lack thereof) takes place is presented in a negative language: "Uma vila encardida–ruas desertas–pátios de lajes soerguidas pelo único esforço da erva–o castelo–restos de muralha que não têm serventia: uma escada encravada nos alvéolos das paredes não conduz a nenhures" (A soiled village–deserted streets–courtyards with flagstones lifted only by the effort of the grass–the castle–remains of a useless wall: a staircase stuck in the cavities of the walls leads nowhere). The village constitutes a space of neg-

*Brandão and his wife embarking on a trip to the Azores in 1924 (from João Pedro de Andrade,* Raul Brandão, *1963; Daniel Library, The Citadel)*

ativity, symbolically associated with death. The characters that inhabit this place are beings without a history, caught up in the insignificance of their daily routines. As Brandão states: "a vila é um simulacro. Melhor: a vida é um simulacro" (the village is a simulacrum. Better: life is a simulacrum). These ghost-like humans are provided with a second life that they create and that is formed on the basis of time and tradition. The characters neither contemplate nor understand life. This permanent opposition between an apparent and a true life suggests—in all of Brandão's works, but in a peculiar form in *Húmus*—that human beings are composed of several different layers of subjectivity, "um interior escondido" (a hidden inner world). The characters lack psychological consistency, coming to represent simply the notion of representation itself. This level of self-reflexive narrative presents the reader with a parade of grotesque caricatures with absurd names, which the author playfully constructs in an obvious manner.

The characters, better defined as ghosts, include the Teles, the Sousas, the Fonsecas, and the Albergarias, and also D. Engrácia; D. Biblioteca with her two sons, Elias de Melo and Melias de Melo; D. Restituta, D. Felizarda, and D. Hermengarda; and an old maid, Joana. In the midst of this grotesque landscape, formed by stagnation and immobility, the village faces a sudden possibility of change. The village has the dream of immortality, and this dream lies in the nonconformism of one man–Gabiru. The alter ego of Brandão, Gabiru introduces into this inert space the prospect of revolution. Once again, the dream performs the function of activating the opposition between the farce of everyday life and that which grows from the inside and corresponds to another dimension of life. Uncontrollable forces that agitate both life and death are united within this dream, thus connecting the dead with the living: "Aqui não andam só os vivos–andam também os mortos. A vila é povoada pelos que se agitam numa existência transitória e baça, e pelos outros que se impõem como se estivessem vivos. Tudo está ligado e confundido" (Around here not only the living walk–the dead walk too. The village is inhabited by those who move about in a transitory and dull existence, and by others who pass for being alive. Everything is linked and confused).

Brandão also explores in this book the theme of silence, which is associated with inefficiency and the inability to communicate. As the author repeats several times: "O silêncio . . . O pior de tudo é o silêncio, e o que se cria no silêncio, o que eu sinto que remexe no silêncio" (Silence . . . The worst of all is silence, and what is created within silence, what I feel rummaging in silence). On the other hand, the agent of immobility, as well as of transformation, is time. One of the most interesting features of time is the fact that it points to its own impossibility: "E, como a existência é monótona, o tempo chega para tudo, o tempo dura séculos" (And, because existence is monotonous, time is enough for everything, time lasts for centuries). In this sense, time is not presented as an ordering agent but rather as a symbolic one. With the announcement of a suspension of chronological time, the boundary that divides life and death is eliminated. The author inverts standard values and juxtaposes the realms of reality. In the meantime, the dream takes charge of everything, but this dream represents the fall to hell. *Húmus* ends with a scream of revolt against immobility and tradition as an imposition of values, favoring instead the revolution of creativity and innovation. *Húmus* is Brandão's greatest work, not only because it was the one for which he became most involved with its writing and editing but also because it synthesizes all of the problems that Brandão had presented in his previous works.

After *Húmus,* Brandão dedicated himself to various projects, namely, the completion of the volumes of his *Memórias* and the publication of his collected plays. In 1918 he finished the preface for the first volume of *Memórias,* which was published the following year. *Memórias* epitomizes a game played out on the frontier between history and gossip, as it also vacillates between the literary and the biographical. The volumes of Brandão's diary represent an important effort of the author to explore the problem of what is real and what is fiction. Also in 1919, and following a certain historicist tendency, Brandão published the second edition of *El-rei Junot* (King Junot, 1912). This book appears to be an historical account of the life of Andoche Junot, the general who invaded Portugal by order of Napoleon Bonaparte in 1807, because Brandão includes allusions and references to historical documents. It is, however, a personal vision of the author, who reflects on historical characters from the perspective of his own subjective inner world.

In 1923 Brandão traveled the entire Portuguese coastline and wrote a book about fishermen. The work was meant to be a part of a larger group of works about the lives and customs of the working people. Some of the books that Brandão had in mind included "Os lavradores" (The Agricultural Workers), "Os pastores" (The Shepherds), and "Os operários" (The Factory Workers), but he never finished these. The only one that made its way to the publishers was *Os pescadores* (The Fishermen, 1923), which is a remarkable book for two different reasons. First, the level of intimacy and identification of the author with its theme is high; he was born near the ocean, and his emotional ties to it allowed him to understand these people both physically and psychologically. Second, and most importantly, this book represents an unusually positive and optimistic side of his work.

With the publication in 1923 of his collected plays, Brandão proved that some of his outstanding attributes as a writer were versatility and eclecticism. The collection *Teatro* also reveals the importance of the blurring of the boundaries between the literary genres. Most of his plays are deeply rooted in the same poetic language that permeates his novels. Another interesting characteristic of Brandão's works is the links that are established among them. In *O Gebo e a sombra,* for instance, some notorious secondary characters from *Os pobres*—Gebo, his wife, Dorotéia, and his daughter-in-law Sofia—are transformed into dramatic protagonists. The opposite happens with Candidinha, who assumes a secondary role in the play. Gebo, although he is still a slave to duty and honor, assumes his own personal values. He hides from his wife the fact that their son João is a thief, and he is arrested instead of their son. This type of slavery to honor develops Brandão's belief that cultural constructs, such as honor and duty, sometimes hinder the individual's free will to live.

Brandão and his wife began an ocean voyage in 1924 to the Azores, where he gathered material for his book *As ilhas desconhecidas* (The Unknown Islands), published in 1926. In the same year, he published a new edition of *História d'um palhaço,* under the title of *A morte do palhaço e o mistério da àrvore* (The Death of a Clown and the Mystery of the Tree). Around this time, he and an old friend, the poet Teixeira de Pascoaes, published a tragicomedy that they titled *Jesus Cristo em Lisboa* (Jesus Christ in Lisbon, 1927).

In 1930 Brandão published *Portugal pequenino* (Tiny Portugal), a children's book written with his wife. He also wrote *O pobre de pedir* (The Beggar, 1931), which remained unpublished until after his death. In this fictional work the author sees himself as a tormented spirit searching for a sense of self. He accuses himself of cowardice, falsehood, and simulation, characteristics that during his life as a writer he always ascribed to his characters. This supreme anguish of the last pages of an author who has searched for a self through his writing serves as an indicator of the uselessness of all metaphysical inquiries.

On 17 November 1930 Brandão arrived in Lisbon, and his health began to decline. He died on 5 December 1930 in his house in São Domingos, Lapa.

Raul Brandão occupies an unquestionable place in the history of the modern and contemporary Portuguese novel, particularly with the publication of *Húmus* in 1917. His remarkable production, situated in the transition between Romanticism and modernism, was not adequately acknowledged while Brandão was alive, but his contribution to the renewing of the novel has been recognized by many important writers that followed him. For example, in his article "No limiar de um mundo, Raul Brandão" (On the Threshold of a World, Raul Brandão), included in his *Espaço do invisível II* (Invisible Space, 1991), Vergílio Ferreira accentuates the existentialist strain in Brandão's novels, stating that Brandão is "um dos mais originais e poderosos escritores de toda a literatura portuguesa" (one of the most original and powerful writers in all of Portuguese literature). Brandão's philosophical questioning results in an important account of what is tragic about human experience.

**Letters:**

*Correspondência Raúl Brandão, Teixeira de Pascoaes,* edited by António Mateus Vilhena and Maria Emília Marques Mano (Lisbon: Quetzal, 1994).

**Biography:**

João Pedro de Andrade, *Raul Brandão* (Lisbon: Arcádia, 1963).

**References:**

Guilherme de Castilho, *Vida e obra de Raul Brandão* (Lisbon: Bertrand, 1978);

Jacinto do Prado Coelho, "Da vivência do tempo em Raul Brandão," in his *Ao contrário de Penélope* (Amadora: Bertrand, 1976), pp. 221–226;

Coelho, "O *Húmus* de Raul Brandão: uma obra de hoje," in his *A letra e o leitor* (Lisbon: Portugália, 1969), pp. 320–328;

Vergílio Ferreira, "No limiar de um mundo, Raul Brandão," in his *Espaço do invisível II*, second edition (Lisbon: Bertrand, 1991), pp. 171–225;

Ferreira, "Raul Brandão e a novelística contemporânea," in his *Espaço do invisível*, volume 4 (Lisbon: Portugália, 1987), pp. 253–262;

António Cândido Franco, "O romance lírico de Raul Brandão," in his *Poesia oculta* (Lisbon: Vega, 1996), pp. 47–51;

Oscar Lopes, "Raul Brandão," in his *Entre Fialho e Nemésio: Estudos de literatura portuguesa contemporânea*, volume 1 (Lisbon: Imprensa Nacional-Casa da Moeda, 1987), pp. 343–368;

Álvaro Manuel Machado, *Raul Brandão entre o romantismo e o modernismo* (Lisbon: Bertrand, 1984);

David Mourão-Ferreira, "Releitura do Húmus," in his *Tópicos recuperados* (Lisbon: Caminho, 1992), pp. 181–189;

António Quadros, "O espanto, o absurdo, o sonho, a vida," in his *Estruturas simbólicas do imaginário na literatura portuguesa* (Lisbon: Átrio, 1992), pp. 57–77;

Maria João Reynaud, *Metamorfoses da escrita: Húmus, de Raul Brandão* (Porto: Campo das Letras, 2000);

Reynaud, "No limiar da Modernidade: Raul Brandão," in *Actas do IV Congresso da Associação Internacional de Lusitanistas (Universidade de Hamburgo, 6–11 de Set. de 1993)*, edited by M. Fátima Viegas Brauner-Figueiredo (Lisbon, Porto & Coimbra: LIDEL, 1995), pp. 819–826;

Maria Alzira Seixo, "Raul Brandão," in her *Para um estudo da expressão do tempo no romance português contemporâneo* (Lisbon: Imprensa Nacional-Casa da Moeda, 1987), pp. 45–50;

João Gaspar Simões, "Raul Brandão, mestre de subjectivismo literário," in his *Literatura, literatura, literatura: De Sá de Miranda ao concretismo brasileiro* (Lisbon: Portugália, 1964), pp. 64–68;

Vítor Viçoso, "Apresentação crítica," in *Húmus de Raul Brandão: Textos escolhidos*, edited by Viçoso (Lisbon: Seara Nova, 1978), pp. 9–29.

**Papers:**

Archives of Raul Brandão's papers are located at the Biblioteca Nacional in Lisbon.

# Luís de Camões
## (1524 - 10 June 1580)

### Leodegário A. de Azevedo Filho
*Universidade do Estado do Rio de Janeiro*
*Universidade Federal do Rio de Janeiro*

BOOKS: *Os Lusíadas* (Lisbon: Antonio Gõçaluez, 1572); translated by Sir Richard Fanshawe as *The Lusiad, or, Portugals Historicall Poem* (London: Printed for Humphrey Moseley, 1655);

*Primeira parte dos autos e comédias portuguesas, feitas por Antônio Prestes e por Luís de Camões e por outros autores portugueses, cujos nomes vão nos princípios de suas obras, agora novamente juntas e emendadas nesta primeira impressão,* by Camões and others (Lisbon: Andrés Lobato, 1587)–includes *Anfitriões* and *Filodemo;*

*Rhythmas,* edited by Fernão Rodrigues Lobo Soropita (Lisbon: Manuel de Lyra, 1595); translated by Sir Richard Burton as *Camoens: The Lyricks,* 2 volumes (London: Bernard Quaritch, 1884);

*Rimas . . . Primeira parte, agora novamente emendadas nesta última impressão, e acrescentada hua comédia nunca atègora impressa* (Lisbon: Paulo Craesbeeck, 1645)–includes *El-Rei Seleuco.*

**Editions and Collections:** *Obras de Luis de Camoens,* 3 volumes, edited by Bonardel and Dubeux (Paris: Pedro Gendron, 1759);

*Obras completas,* 7 volumes, edited by Teófilo Braga (Porto: Imprensa Portugueza, 1873–1874);

*Parnaso de Luís de Camões,* 3 volumes, edited by Braga (Porto: Imprensa Internacional, 1880);

*Sonetos acompanhados com um escorço biographico do immortal poeta e com a lista dos sonetos apocriphos que lhe são atribuidos,* edited by Braga (Lisbon: A Educadora, 1913);

*Obras completas,* 5 volumes, edited by Hernâni Cidade (Lisbon: Sá da Costa, 1946–1947);

*Lírica completa,* 3 volumes, edited by Maria de Lurdes Saraiva (Lisbon: Imprensa Nacional-Casa da Moeda, 1980–1981);

*Lírica de Camões. Textos apurados à luz dos manuscritos quinhentistas, em confronto com a tradição impressa,* 8 volumes, edited by Leodegário A. de Azevedo Filho (Lisbon: Imprensa Nacional-Casa da Moeda, 1985–2001).

*Luís de Camões (from* Luís de Camões: Epic & Lyric, *edited by L. C. Taylor, 1990; Thomas Cooper Library, University of South Carolina)*

**Editions in English:** *The Lusiad; or The Discovery of India: An Epic Poem,* translated by William Julius Mickle (Oxford: Jackson & Lister, 1776);

*Luís de Camões: Epic & Lyric,* translated by Keith Bosley, edited by L. C. Taylor (Manchester: Carcanet/ Fundação Calouste Gulbenkian, 1990);

*The Lusíads,* translated and edited by Landeg White (Oxford: Oxford University Press, 1997).

OTHER: "Ao Conde do Redondo, viso Rey da India," in *Colóquios dos simples e drogas he cousas medicinais da India....*, edited by Garcia de Orta (Goa, India: Ioannes de Endem, 1563);

"Ao muito ilustre senhor Don Lionis Pereira sobre o liuro que lhe offerece Pero de Magalhães: tercetos de Luís de Camões," "Começa: 'Depopis que Magalhães teue tecida' e Soneto do mesmo Autor ao senhor Dom Lionis, acerca da victoria que ouue contra el Rey do Achem em Malaca," and "Começa: 'Vos Ninphas da Gangetica espessura,'" in *Historia da prouincia de sācta Cruz a que vulgarme[n]te chamamos Brasil,* edited by Pêro de Magalhães de Gândavo (Lisbon: António Gonçalves, 1576).

Luís de Camões is the major figure of the Portuguese Renaissance and one of the most important writers in the Portuguese language. Although he wrote lyric poetry and dramas, Camões is internationally recognized as the author of the epic poem *Os Lusíadas* (The Lusíads, 1572), which is considered his masterpiece and has been translated into several languages. No other Portuguese author has maintained the prestige that Camões has over the centuries.

Although little is known about the writer's personal life, most scholars agree that Luís Vaz de Camões was born in 1524, possibly in Lisbon, and that his name is of Galician origin. His grandparents, Antão Vaz de Camões and Guiomar Vaz da Gama, lived in Vilar de Nantes, a village in the vicinity of Chaves. Camões's parents, Simão Vaz de Camões and Ana de Sá, were born in the village. There is mention of Camões having studied in Braga. Although there is no record in the school archives, many scholars believe that he studied at the University of Coimbra, where his family moved around 1527. His uncle, Bento de Camões, was the first chancellor of the university, where Latin was the obligatory language at the time. Camões's education would have consisted of a strong background in classical works on natural philosophy, logic, the arts, grammar, and rhetoric. The writer often records his affection for the city of Coimbra in lyric and epic poetry.

Camões probably wrote the play *Anfitriões* (published in 1587) when he was a student at Coimbra. In 1546, performance of classical texts had become obligatory in the university. *Anfitriões,* inspired by Plautus's *Amphitryon,* is filled with comical situations. The text, which reveals a youthful sensuality, is bilingual and presents a constant play between seeming and being. The action focuses on the tricks and cunning of Jupiter and Mercury (the son of Jupiter and Maia), god of eloquence, commerce, and thieves, as they take on the human appearances of Anfitrião and Sósia. The purpose of the trickery is so that Jupiter can court Alcmena, Anfitrião's faithful wife. (Hercules is the son of Jupiter and Alcmena.) Anfitrião resembles a Portuguese naval captain; his servant is humorous but refined and speaks Spanish. Mercury speaks Portuguese, but he begins to speak Spanish when he takes the role of the false Sósia. Jupiter is presented as he appears in classical literature, while Mercury assumes characteristics of the Portuguese. Later Jupiter also becomes more Portuguese when he uses Petrarchan tenderness to communicate with Alcmena.

Camões went to Lisbon before 1550, probably in 1542. He probably participated in the soirees at the court, where he met members of the upper nobility, but he never abandoned his bohemian lifestyle. Although theater was a marginal activity in the totality of Camões's literary work, he had another play, *El Rei-Seleuco* (King Seleucus, published in 1645), staged while he was still in Lisbon. The work was performed in the home of Estácio da Fonseca, an official in the court of João III, and was probably part of a wedding celebration. The play was seen by some as a recrimination against King Manuel, who, in 1518 (three years before his death), had married Leonor of Austria, who was intended for João's son. The play, consisting of only one act, is based on an anecdote from Plutarch and other classical historians. Prince Antiochus, son of King Seleucus of Syria, falls in love with his stepmother. His father is placed in the position of having to chose between losing his son or his wife. He gives his wife to his son with a part of the kingdom. Although *El Rei-Seleuco* is written in the style of Portuguese dramatist Gil Vicente, Camões focuses more on a psychological analysis of the characters and emphasizes Antiochus's conscience while criticizing the sentimental aspects of the story. Camões includes a prologue and an epilogue in prose, with references to the practice of performing *autos* (a type of morality play) in the patios of private homes in Lisbon, with the last-minute problems of uninvited guests.

Camões participated in a military expedition to North Africa from 1549 to 1551, during which he was wounded in the right eye in combat. Back in Lisbon, he was arrested in 1552 and imprisoned for having stabbed an officer named Gonçalves Borges, who was in charge of the king's royal cavalry, in the neck during the procession of Corpus Christi on 16 June. Camões was jailed in Tronco, where he remained until March 1553. The document of pardon for this crime refers to Camões as a *cavaleiro fidalgo,* a person of the lower nobility. This status is confirmed in a letter the author wrote to Francisca de Aragão, first lady to Queen Caterina, widow of João II.

Aragão obtained the pardon for Camões, who, after his release from jail, agreed to five years of military service in India. He set sail on the *São Bento* on 26 March 1553. The ship was under the command of Fernão de Álvares Cabral. There are mentions of Camões having served in various military campaigns in Asia, including one against the king of Chembé. While in the Portuguese-controlled state of Goa in India, the writer enjoyed the friendship and protection of the viceroy, Francisco Redonda, Count of Redondo. This friendship did not, however, allow him any special rights or privileges. In Goa he wrote the play *Filodemo* (published in 1587) as entertainment for the governor of India, Francisco Barreto, when he was inaugurated in 1555. The performance was intended to celebrate this event and to glorify the Portuguese people. The inspiration for the play includes popular sources, the medieval novel, and lyric poetry. The entire play is perhaps a hidden reference to Camões's love for the Infanta Maria, daughter of King Manuel. Such a love would have been difficult since the two people involved were from different social classes. In the text the orphaned twins Filodemo and Florimena are separated. Filodemo falls in love with Dionísia, in whose home he is a servant. Florimena, who had become a shepherdess, falls in love with Venadoro, Dionísia's brother. At the end of the play there is the inevitable recognition of the identity of the twins, which the author uses to underscore the nobility of amorous feelings.

In Goa, Camões was sent to jail again for debts to a man named Miguel Roiz. After his release he went to Macau, where he served as the official charged with handling the affairs of the deceased and orphans. He had to give up this job, however, when he was arrested again (possibly as the result of a dispute with the captain of a trade ship, or possibly because he was in debt again) and returned to Goa. Scholars believe that Camões refers to this fact in *Os Lusíadas* in Canto X, verse 128, when he describes the world as "mundo injusto" (an unjust place). In 1568, with the help of Captain Pero Barreto Rolim, Camões went to Mozambique, where he lived in poverty. Among Camões's friends in Asia was historian Diogo de Couto, who recorded in his *Década VIII da Ásia* a visit with Camões in Mozambique. Couto found the poet desolate over the death of Dinamene, "china muy fermosa" (a very pretty Chinese woman) who traveled with him and had died in a shipwreck at the mouth of the Mekong River on the return from India. According to Couto, the famous sonnet "Alma minha gentil, que te partiste" (Gentle soul of mine, separate yourself) was dedicated to her. With the help of some friends, Camões was able to leave Mozambique and

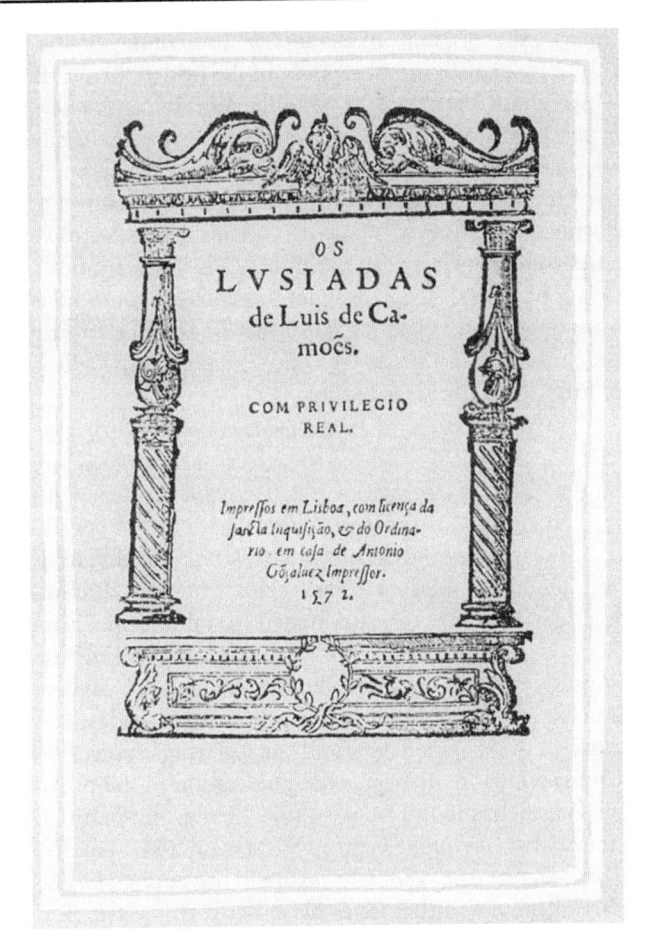

*Title page for Camões's epic poem praising Portugal and its people (from* Luís de Camões: Epic & Lyric, *edited by L. C. Taylor, 1990; Thomas Cooper Library, University of South Carolina)*

departed for Lisbon in November 1569. He arrived in Cascais on the ship *Santa Clara* in April 1570.

In Lisbon, Camões dedicated himself to the publication of his epic, *Os Lusíadas*. In September 1571 he obtained authorization to publish the work, which was printed in October 1571 and July 1572 by António Gonçalves. Two editions of the work appeared in 1572; the one with a cover depicting the head of a pelican with its beak turned to the reader's left is considered the authentic edition. The texts of the two editions present many variants, some of which are major.

*Os Lusíadas,* considered the "poema da raça" (poem of the race), is a vision and glorification of the Portuguese world and people of the fifteenth century. In that century Portugal had reached the height of its historical and cultural development. The word "lusíadas" of the title was taken from a 1531 letter written by antiquities scholar André de Resende and refers to the "lusos," the original inhabitants of present-day Portugal. Camões uses the word only in the title of the work. Throughout the poem he uses the synonyms *lusitanos, portugueses,* and *filhos de Luso,* words that are more easily adapted to the metrical scheme of the verses. The poem narrates the most glorious episodes of the history of Portugal, focusing on Vasco da Gama's trip to establish a maritime contract with the Indies. The hero is not da Gama but rather the Portuguese nation, of whom he is a representative. Camões states that he is going to sing the praises of "as armas e os barões assinalados" (coats of arms and illustrious barons).

The structure of *Os Lusíadas* consists of 10 cantos, 1,102 stanzas, and 8,816 verses. The stanzas are ottava rima, groupings of 8 ten-syllable verses, with the rhyme scheme *abababcc.* The verses are generally *decassílabos heroícos*—that is, the stress falls on the sixth and tenth syllables of each verse. The introduction (the first 18 stanzas) is subdivided into the Proposition (stanzas 1–3), in which the poet proposes to sing the praises of brave deeds of illustrious men; the Invocation (stanzas 4–5), in which he invokes Tágides, the muse of the Tagus River; and the Offering (stanzas 6–18), in which he dedicates the publication of the poem to King Sebastião. The narration runs from Canto I, stanza 19, through Canto X, stanza 144. Finally, Canto X, stanzas 145–146, provide the epilogue. The part of the poem that takes place between the trip and the conclusion is narrated by Jupiter, in the presence of Venus, and by Tethys on the Isle of Love.

The action of the poem is made up of a mixture of historical aspects of da Gama's trip to India and his return (1497–1499) and episodes based on classical mythology, including a battle between Venus, as the protector of the Portuguese people, and Bacchus. There are lyrical episodes that achieve emotional depth, such as those describing the tragic love affair of Inês de Castro and Pedro I, son of King Afonso IV, and the story of the Velho do Restelo, an old man who rants against the politics of expansion. There are also symbolic episodes, such as King Manuel I's dream, which deals with the expansion of the Portuguese nation; the events that involve a giant, Adamastor, who symbolizes the force of nature; the episode of the Twelve Dames of England, an example of medieval Portuguese chivalry; and the Ilha dos Amores (Isle of Love), in which the Portuguese concept of honor stands out. In certain episodes, such as the storms in Canto VI, the poet focuses on nature. As António José Saraiva noted in his 1963 study, the traditional concepts of time, space, history, and death are abolished in the narrative.

*Os Lusíadas* incorporates the spirit of the Renaissance and the classical epics of Homer and Virgil, although the trip to the Indies lacks the mythic and heroic air. Da Gama is simply a spokesperson, a symbol of the Portuguese people. The navigators, as a group, represent the role of the epic hero. There is the coexistence of the marvelous, that is, the intervention of pagan and Christian supernatural beings, in the spirit of Renaissance dualism. There is no coherence until the end of the text, and the epilogue is sad and melancholic, which is contrary to the traditional epic poem. Throughout the verses Camões creates a portrait of a visionary people caught up in the frenzy and glory of overseas expansion. The poet himself is a dramatic presence in the poem, transmitting his feelings and frustrations to the characters. His most inspired moments are in the depiction of de Castro and the prophetic threats of Adamastor.

Three elements combine in this work: the real, the mythical, and the miraculous. The real is made up of true events, including battles and storms, and the psychological states of the characters involved in the actions. These persons include Afonso Henriques and Nuno Álvares Pereira, who are active participants in the action; the prudent and reflective Egas Moniz and Martim de Freitas; and persons such as Maria, the daughter of Afonso IV, who participate only indirectly in the story. There are also characters who are not involved in the action, such as de Castro, but who reflect the poet's elevated sentiments. The mythical beings of the text include those who determine events, such as Jupiter, Neptune, and the members of the Council of Olympus; those who soften the many crude deeds of the Council, including the Nereids; those who praise the Portuguese people and those who act against them but who, once defeated, glorify them, including Bacchus and Adamastor; those who figure intimately in the lives of the heroes, such as Tethys and the nymphs on the Isle of Love; and messengers, such as Mercury. The miraculous is seen in episodes such as the appearance of Saint Elmo's fire and an encounter with a waterspout in Canto V.

The action of the poem, which begins in stanza 19, opens in medias res. While da Gama's ships are in the Indian Ocean, the gods meet on Mount Olympus to determine the sailors' fate. Bacchus opposes the Portuguese, but Jupiter, Venus, and Mars support them and rule in their favor. When the Portuguese arrive in Mozambique, da Gama goes ashore and barely escapes problems instigated with the Muslims by Bacchus. In Canto II the Portuguese arrive in Mombasa, where Bacchus again attempts to destroy them. Venus and the Nereids, however, save them. Jupiter foresees the great discoveries of the Portuguese in the East, and he sends Mercury ahead to ensure that they are well received in Melindi. Canto III, after an invocation to the epic muse, focuses on Portugal, its geography and history. The poet relates the emergence of Portugal as a country under the rule of Henriques, the reconquest of the peninsula from the Arabs, the stories of other kings and their conquests, the tale of de Castro's execution, and an account of how Fernando I jeopardized the country's independence. In Canto IV the poet tells of the death of Fernando, Afonso V's battle with Castile, and his conquests in North Africa, including Ceuta. King Manuel I sends da Gama to search for India after a dream of the River Ganges and the River Indus. Da Gama departs, and in Canto V he reaches Melindi, where the king visits da Gama's ship to hear of the trip up to this point. There are several incidents involving natural phenomena and predictions of disaster by the giant Adamastor. Many crew members fall ill along the way.

Canto VI relates the voyage across the Indian Ocean. Bacchus again attempts to create problems for the Portuguese navigators when he speaks against them at Neptune's underwater court. Aeolus releases violent winds against the fleet, but Venus and her nymphs hear da Gama's prayers and stop the storm. At daybreak the sailors sight India. In Canto VII, Monçaide, a Muslim from Berberia and a friend of the Portuguese who speaks Spanish, comes to da Gama's ships and tells him about the Malabar coast. After da Gama lands, he goes to Samorin to establish a treaty of friendship. Da Gama's fleet flies banners that depict various episodes of Portuguese history, and the poet invokes the help of the nymphs of the Mondego and Tagus Rivers as he describes them. Canto VIII continues with the descriptions of the banners, and the story becomes complicated as Bacchus conspires with the Muslims to destroy the Portuguese. Da Gama is detained, but he secures his freedom for a portion of the merchandise that he was allowed to carry ashore. In Canto IX da Gama takes some Muslims hostage and exchanges them for two of his agents who were held on land. He then begins the journey home. Venus leads the fleet to her Isle of Love, where Tethys and the Nereids fall in love with the sailors. After a banquet at which one of the nymphs prophesies future exploits by the Portuguese in Canto X, the fleet departs for Portugal. The canto is filled with descriptions of Africa and Asia.

Each canto includes the poet's thoughts and musings on different topics, including heroism, materialism, the uncertainty of human existence, the power of love, and the evil of ambition. Narrative is accompanied by reflection as Camões glorifies the people and history of Portugal and creates a national epic for the country.

In addition to *Os Lusíadas,* Camões wrote an impressive body of lyric poetry and *autos* that were cir-

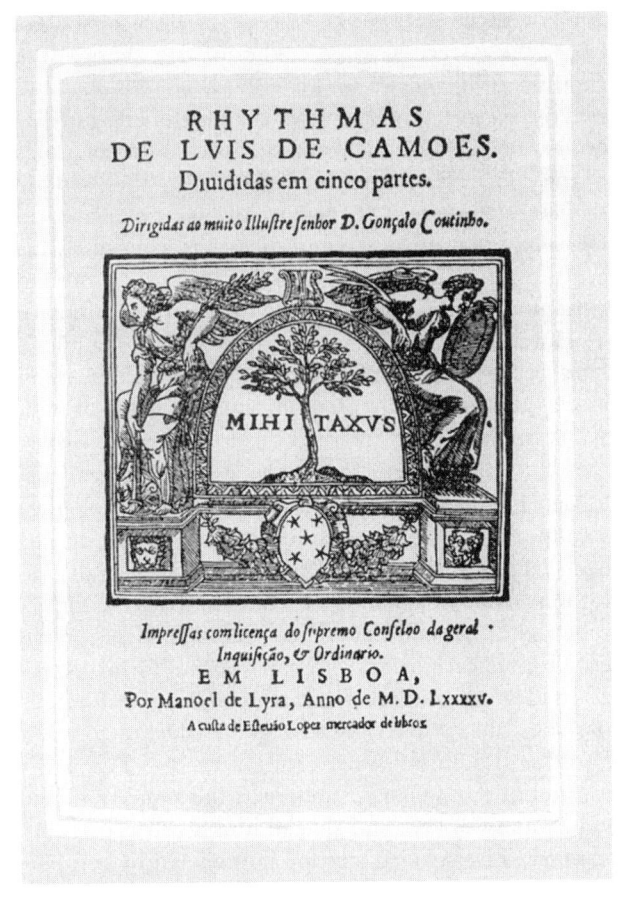

*Title page for Camões's collection of lyric poetry (from* Luís de Camões: Epic & Lyric, *edited by L. C. Taylor, 1990; Thomas Cooper Library, University of South Carolina)*

culated in manuscript form during his lifetime. There has been a long and often harsh debate among specialists about the chronology and authenticity of the poems. Many editions have been released, focusing on different theories to prove their authenticity. The Escola Camoniana Brasileira, a group of Brazilian scholars under the direction of Leodegário A. de Azevedo Filho, has prepared several volumes using philological methods of comparison of texts to prove authorship and establish dates of composition.

Camões worked in several Renaissance lyric forms, including the sonnet, ottava rima, tercet, sextet, eclogue, ode, elegy, and song. He also wrote in the traditional forms of the *redondilha maior, redondilha menor,* and *cantigas.* He wrote both in Portuguese and in Spanish (all the writers of that time were bilingual). Camões's lyric poetry is characterized by a spontaneity that lends it a sense of interior discourse. At times, the poet assumes the artificiality of the *conceptista* poets and reveals an erudite knowledge of classical writers from the Greco-Roman tradition. He varies the rhythms of his verses to accommodate emotions, and his *redondilhas* reveal a sense of the playful and humorous as they capture the contradictions and ambiguities of the epoch. His sonnets are marked by the baroque *cultismo* (exaggerated refinement of literary form) and *conceptismo* (an artful game of ideas and concepts); his eclogues discourse on the contradictions of human existence; and his odes vacillate between the influence of Horace and a highly personal lyricism. Camões's lyric poetry resembles that of Dante and Petrarch in its resistance to a supposed destiny. His sense of individualism battles hostile reactions to nonconformism.

Camões's poetry resembles a philosophical dialogue. The most frequent theme from an ideological standpoint is the contradiction between what he has been taught and what he experiences in terms of philosophy and religion. His Platonic background is reflected in his concept of love, inherited from medieval Provençal poetry. Woman appears in his verses as an idealized, angelic figure who cleanses and purges the soul of her lover. Beatriz guided Dante through Paradise; Laura, after her death, served as Petrarch's inspiration; and Camões inherited this concept of the woman and of love and shaped it in his own personal manner. The beloved appears illuminated by a supernatural light that transforms her human features into divine ones: her hair is always bright and golden; her resplendent look has the power to calm nature; and her presence makes the flowers bloom. Camões's verses, however, also reveal a contrast between carnal desire and idealized longing. The poet seems to pose the question: If love is a "feito da alma" (deed of the soul), how does one explain that the lover desires the beloved in a carnal manner? Corporeal beauty is a reflection of pure beauty, for which carnal desire must be sacrificed. In his reflections on the dichotomy between carnal and pure love, Camões concludes by condemning love that is not divine. Eroticism is intermingled with mysticism, and in this way, spiritual love overcomes carnal desire.

Another frequent theme throughout his verses is the contradiction between individual aspirations to happiness and the impossibility of concretely attaining this happiness. Change brings hope to the human being, but happiness is always something of the past, only to be remembered in the present. Camões also focuses on the contrast between worthiness and individual destiny. He sees evil and mediocre people as content in this life, while the good (and he included himself in that category) are pursued by misfortune. Thus, the world is incomprehensible. This theme is apparent in the poem "Ao desconcerto do mundo" (This Disconcerting World), written before the poet's trip to India. Individual destiny makes the poet contemplate the *desconcerto* of life, and he finds that the key to happiness is in God, whose designs are unknown.

Camões's lyric work consists of a psychological analysis of feelings, at times abstract and subtle, an anguished examination of conscience, and a metaphysical and religious theory of the sentimental experiences of the poet. Several themes stand out in his works, including love, *saudade* (a mixture of yearning and nostalgia), nature, and religion. There is a constant conflict between the divine and the mundane, from which emerges a Petrarchan melancholy. This expression of the inner being is the fusion of the dominant spiritual forces of the epoch: Petrarchism and Platonism, which refine the medieval troubadour concept of love; Christian doctrine that stressed restraint of carnal desire; and vigilance of the state and the church in their moralizing role. Poetry assumes a form that tends toward impassionate thought.

The poet goes from one love to the other, which purifies his soul. Love is always the same ideal exaltation and sublimation, and it is never impaired as the poet changes places and customs. On the contrary, love is strengthened and unified through various experiences. Love becomes something permanent, beyond ephemeral infatuations and desire: "O desejo que não quer o desejado, só porque se quer perpétuo" (Desire that the desired one does not want because it wants that which is eternal). This permanent love goes beyond momentary desire that is translated into acts. This love is sublimated in the beloved to the point of seeing in her a divine beauty.

The beloved, on an intellectual level that is divine, is a demigoddess and is totally united with her lover. Her soul is transformed into the object of love for which the poet searches. He loses his sense of self but retains a lucid consciousness of the reason that explains such a loss. Throughout Camões's works the notion of the ascent from specific to general beauty, and from personal experience to spiritual concept, is implicit. The poet surpasses the physical man, tied to the concrete reality of amorous experiences, and arrives at a state in which he is capable of theorizing metaphysically on his emotional experiences. The poet never forgets that he is a man made of flesh, blood, and feelings, as seen in the poem "Mande-me Amor" (Send Me Love, included in *Rhythmas*, 1595). At times, however, his inner life dominates external reality, and he becomes involved in his thoughts.

Camões associates nature with love in his lyric works. Nature frames and provides a background for love, or it serves as a projection of the "I" of the poet in his moments of emotional outpouring. The poet

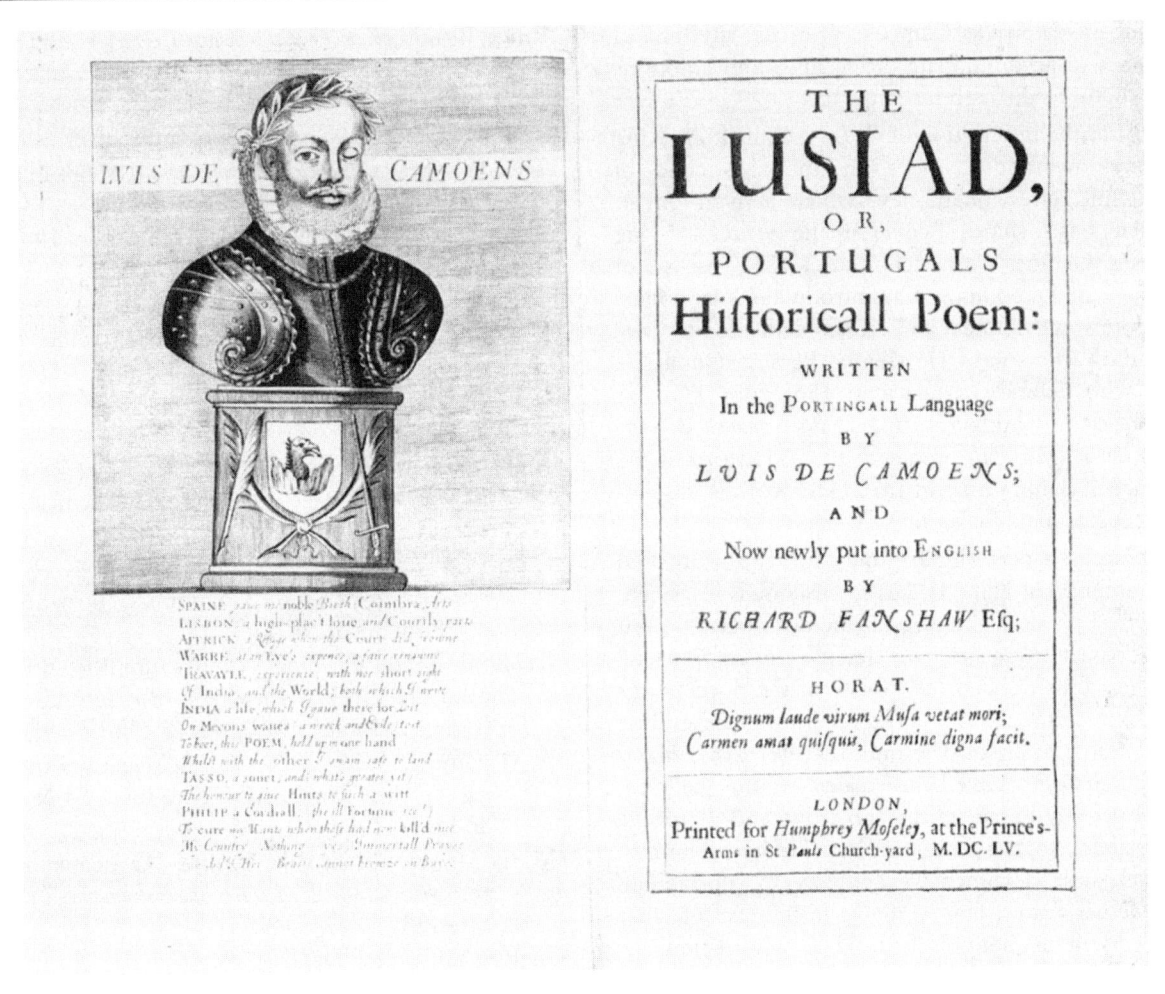

*Frontispiece and title page of the first English edition of* Os Lusíadas *(from* Luís de Camões: Epic & Lyric, *edited by L. C. Taylor, 1990; Thomas Cooper Library, University of South Carolina)*

also contemplates nature in itself, independent of its relationship to his emotional states or to his artistic devices. Nature provokes the poet's senses through its multiple aspects, but, above all, it nurtures the philosophical intuition of its essence and meaning. As in the medieval *cancioneiros,* Camões appeals to the waves of the sea to be messengers, and to the birds, the fields, and the sun to attest to the sincerity of his suffering. Nature itself, however, like love, is filled with paradoxical games that reflect the contradictory state of the tormented soul.

Camões's texts reveal a faithful rendering of Catholic thought and doctrine. His lyric poetry expresses spiritual tones as his Christian faith becomes a special aspect of his verses. His Catholic spirit is fed by convictions imposed by dogmatism and tradition, particularly the intervention of Providence in the lives of individuals and nations. The poet censures vain people who blame their suffering and misfortune on bad luck.

Specific geographical settings in Camões's poems include Coimbra, with its landscape and its intellectual life; Lisbon, with its cosmopolitan population and social refinement; Ceuta, with its military garrison; and the Orient. These places were the bright spots of the empire and figured into the drama of its decline.

Camões's style is marked by certain recurring traits that were a part of the artistic conventions of his times, including the use of mythological characters and situations. From the classics he inherited the use of periphrasis, but above all, a sense of equilibrium and harmony of expression. His language is characterized by the abundant use of metaphor and hyperbole and a rhythm that resembles that of classical music, with short and even intervals. The sense of unity demanded by the classics, however, does not create a sense of monotony as Camões varies the rhythms of his verses to accommodate the feelings and emotions being captured through his language.

After the publication of *Os Lusíadas* in 1572, King Sebastião awarded Camões an annual stipend of 15,000 mil réis. The money, which arrived on an irregular basis, hardly covered the writer's living expenses. Camões's production after 1572 consists of a few poems he composed as introductions to books. He wrote some sonnets and tercets dedicated to Leonis Pereira (the son of D. Manuel Pereira, Conde de Feira, who defended Malaca in 1568), for Pêro de Magalhães de Gândavo's *Historia da prouincia de sãcta Cruz a que vulgarme[n]te chamamos Brasil* (History of the Province of Santa Cruz) in 1576. The work is the first ethnogeographic description of Brazil.

Camões's death on 10 June 1580 is documented in the archives of Filipe II. His gravestone is inscribed: "Aqui jaz Luís de Camões, príncipe dos poetas do seu tempo. Viveu pobre e miseravelmente e assim morreu" (Here lies Luís de Camões, prince of the poets of his time. He lived in poverty and died in it). Since so little factual information on the author's life exists, many myths and stories have been created around the great poet, especially based on the subjective and debatable interpretations of the poems attributed to him. There is, however, little documentary evidence to substantiate them. Other than a few verifiable facts, most of what has been written about his life has been speculation.

Camões is considered the most important poet of the Portuguese language. He captured in his epic poem the heroism and daring of the Portuguese during a period of expansion and discovery of the world. In the twentieth century, poet Fernando Pessoa attempted to create a new Portuguese epic in his work *Mensagem* (Message, 1934), and novelist José Saramago represented the heroic Portuguese past in his historiographical novel *Memorial do convento* (Memoir of the Convent, 1982). Neither of these two works, however, captures the glory of that period of Portuguese history in the same epic spirit as the work of Camões.

**References:**

Eugênio Asênsio, *Estudios portugueses* (Paris: Fundação Calouste Gulbenkian, 1974);

Asênsio and José V. de Pina Martins, *Luís de Camões. El humanismo en su obra poética. Los Lusíadas y las Rimas en la poesía española* (Paris: Fundação Calouste Gulbenkian, 1982);

Leodegário A. de Azevedo Filho, *Camões, o desconcerto do mundo e a estética da utopia* (Rio de Janeiro: Tempo Brasileiro, 1995);

Roger Bismut, *Camões et son oeuvre lyrique. Visages de Luís de Camões* (Paris: Fundação Calouste Gulbenkian, 1972), pp. 33–53;

Bismut, *La lyrique de Camões* (Paris: PUF, 1970);

Theophilo Braga, *Bibliografia camoneana* (Lisbon: Imprensa de Cristóvão. A. Rodrigues, 1880);

Braga, *Camões: Epoca e vida* (Porto: Chardron, 1907);

Braga, *Camões: A obra lyrica e épica* (Porto: Chardron, 1911);

José Gonçalo (Herculano) Chorão de Carvalho, "Sobre o texto da lírica camoniana," *Revista da Faculdade de Letras de Lisboa,* 14 (1948): 224–238; 15 (1948): 53–91;

Aníbal Pinto de Castro, *Camões e a língua portuguesa. Quatro orações camonianas* (Lisbon: Academia Portuguesa de História, 1980);

Castro, *Retórica e teorização literária em Portugal. Do humanismo ao neoclassicismo* (Coimbra: Centro de Estudos Românicos, 1973);

Jacinto do Prado Coelho, "Camões: um lírico do transcendente," in his *A letra e o leitor,* second edition (Lisbon: Moraes, 1977), pp. 15–29;

A. G. Cunha, *Índice analítico do vocabulário de "Os Lusíadas"* (Rio de Janeiro: Presença-Instituto Nacional do Livro, 1980);

Maria Helena Ribeiro da Cunha, "O neoplatonismo amoroso na Ode VI," *Revista Camoniana,* 2 (1965): 116–128;

A. Epiphanio da Silva Dias, *Syntaxe historica portuguesa,* fourth edition (Lisbon: Livraria Clássica, 1959);

Antonio Houaiss, "O texto das 'Rimas' de Camões," in his *Estudos vários sobre palavras, livros, autores* (Rio de Janeiro: Paz e Terra, 1979), pp. 143–160;

Augusto C. Pires de Lima, ed., *Auto de El-Rei Seleuco* (Porto: Domingos Barreira, 1941);

J. V. de Pina Martins, *Camões et la pensée platonicienne de la Renaissance. Visages de Luís de Camões* (Paris: Fundação Calouste Gulbenkian, 1972), pp. 55–94;

Maria Vitalina Leal de Matos, *O canto na poesia épica e lírica de Camões: Estudo de isotopia enunciativa* (Paris: Fundação Calouste Gulbenkian, 1981);

George Monteiro, *The Presence of Camões: Influences on the Literature of England, America, and Southern Africa* (Lexington: University of Kentucky Press, 1996);

Vasco Graça Moura, *Luís de Camões: Alguns desafios* (Lisbon: Vega, 1989);

Joaquim Nabuco, *Camões* (Rio de Janeiro: Biblioteca Nacional, 1980);

Elizabeth Naïque-Dessai, *Die Sonette Luís de Camões* (Münster: Aschendorff, 1969);

Afrânio Peixoto, *Ensaios camonianos* (Rio de Janeiro: W. M. Jackson, 1944);

Emmanuel Pereira Filho, *Estudos de crítica textual* (Rio de Janeiro: Gernasa, 1972);

Pereira Filho, *Uma forma provençalesca na lírica de Camões* (Rio de Janeiro: Gernasa, 1974);

Pereira Filho, *As rimas de Camões* (Rio de Janeiro: Aguilar-Instituto Nacional do Livro, 1974);

Luciana Stegagno Picchio, *Ars combinatoria e algebra delle proposizioni in una lirica de Camões* (Rome: Società Filologica Romana, 1973);

A. J. da Costa Pimpão, ed., *Rimas, autos e cartas* (Barcelos: Ed. do Minho, 1944);

Luís Francisco Rebello, *Variações sobre o teatro de Camões* (Lisbon: Caminho, 1980);

António José Saraiva, *Camões* (Lisbon: Jornal do Foro, 1963);

Jorge de Sena, *A estrutura de Os Lusíadas e outros estudos camonianos e de poesia peninsular no século XVI*, second edition (Lisbon: Edições 70, 1980);

Sena, *Estudos sobre o vocabulário de 'Os Lusíadas'* (Lisbon: Edições 70, 1982);

Sena, *Os sonetos de Camões* (Lisbon: Portugália, 1966);

Sena, *Trinta anos de Camões 1948–1978*, 2 volumes (Lisbon: Edições 70, 1980);

Vítor Manuel de Aguiar e Silva, *Camões: Labirintos e fascínios* (Lisbon: Cotovia, 1994);

Silva, "Notas sobre o cânone da lírica camoniana–II," *Revista de História Literária de Portugal*, 4 (1975): 87–122;

Sousa da Silveira, *Textos quinhentistas* (Rio de Janeiro: Fundação Getúlio Vargas, 1971);

Barbara Spaggiari, "Doces águas e claras do Mondego," *Quaderni portoghesi*, 6 (1979): 17–30;

Spaggiari, "L'Ode IX. Per la conoscenza della lirica camoniana," *Annali della Scuola Normale Superiore di Pisa*, 10 (1980): 1003–1064;

Wilhelm Storch, *Vida e obra de Luís de Camões* (Lisbon: Typographia da Academia Real das Sciências, 1897);

Carolina Michaëlis de Vasconcelos, "O texto das *Rimas* de Camões e os apocryphos," *Revista da Sociedade de Instrução do Porto*, 2 (1882): 105–125.

**Papers:**

Archives of Luís de Camões's papers are held at the Biblioteca Geral in Coimbra, and at the Biblioteca Nacional and the Biblioteca do Arquivo Geral da Torre do Tombo, both in Lisbon.

# Camilo Castelo Branco
*(16 March 1825 - 1 June 1890)*

Elias J. Torres Feijó
*Universidade de Santiago de Compostela*

BOOKS: *Os pundonores desagravados,* anonymous (Porto: Tipografia da Revista, 1845);

*O juízo final e o sonho do inferno* (Porto: Tipografia da Revista, 1845);

*Agostinho de Ceuta* (Porto: Tipografia de Bragança, 1847);

*A murraça,* anonymous (Porto: Privately printed, 1848);

*Maria! não me mates, que sou tua mãe!* anonymous (Porto: Tipografia do Ecco, 1848);

*O Marquês de Torres Novas* (Porto: Tipografia do Nacional, 1849);

*O caleche* (Porto: J. Lourenço de Sousa, 1849);

*O clero e o senhor Alexandre Herculano,* anonymous (Lisbon: Impresso de Francisco Xavier de Sousa, 1850);

*Inspirações* (Porto: J. J. Gonçalves Basto, 1851);

*Anátema* (Porto: Francisco Gomes da Fonseca, 1851);

*Revelações* (Porto: J. J. Gonçalves Basto, 1852);

*Hossana!* (Porto: F. P. d'Azevedo, 1852);

*Folhas cahidas, apanhadas na lama* (Porto: Francisco Gomes da Fonseca, 1854);

*A vespa do Parnaso!* (Porto: J. A. de Freitas Junior, 1854);

*Duas épocas na vida* (Porto: A. da S. Santos, 1854)—comprises *Preceitos do coração* and *Preceitos de consciência;*

*Um livro* (Porto: J. A. de Freitas Júnior, 1854);

*Mistérios de Lisboa,* 3 volumes (Porto: J. J. Gonçalves Basto, 1854);

*A filha do arcediago* [*Cenas Contemporâneas I*] (Porto: Faria Guimarães, 1854);

*Livro negro de Padre Dinis* (Porto: Francisco Gomes da Fonseca, 1855);

*Cenas contemporâneas II* (Porto: Faria Guimarães, 1855);

*A neta do arcediago* [*Cenas Contemporâneas III*] (Porto: António José da Silva Teixeira, 1856);

*Onde está a felicidade?* (Porto: Cruz Coutinho, 1856);

*Um homem de brios* (Porto: Rodrigo José d'Oliveira Guimarães, 1856);

*Justiça* (Porto: Boaventura José Vaz Murta, 1856);

*Duas horas de leitura* (Porto: António Moutinho de Sousa, 1857);

*Camilo Castelo Branco ( from João Bigote Chorão,* Camilo: A obra e o homem, *1979; Brigham Young University Libraries)*

*Solemnia Verba–Cenas da Foz* (Viana: Tipografia da Aurora do Lima, 1857);

*Purgatório e paraíso* (Porto: Cruz Coutinho, 1857);

*Espinhos e flores* (Porto: António Moutinho de Sousa, 1857);

*Lágrimas abençoadas* (Porto: António José da Silva Teixeira, 1857);

*Carlota Ângela* (Viana: Tipografia da Aurora do Lima, 1858);

*O que fazem as mulheres* (Porto: Cruz Coutinho, 1858);

*Vingança* (Porto: Cruz Coutinho, 1858);

*Doze casamentos felizes* (Porto: Tipografia da Revista, 1861);

*O romance dum homem rico* (Porto: Tipografia da Revista, 1861);

*O morgado de Fafe em Lisboa* (Lisbon: António Maria Pereira, 1861);

*Abençoadas lágrimas!* (Lisbon: António Maria Pereira, 1861);

*Coisas espantosas* (Lisbon: António Maria Pereira, 1862);

*Memórias do cárcere*, 2 volumes (Porto: Viúva Moré, 1862);

*Coração, cabeça e estômago* (Lisbon: António Maria Pereira, 1862);

*Amor de perdição* (Porto: Viúva Moré, 1862); translated by Alice R. Clemente as *Doomed Love (A Family Memoir)* (Providence, R.I.: Gávea-Brown, 2000);

*Estrelas funestas* (Porto: Viúva Moré, 1862);

*As três irmãs* (Porto: Viúva Moré, 1862);

*O último acto* (Lisbon: A. M. Pereira, 1862);

*Anos de prosa; A Gratidão; O Arrependimento* (Porto: António José da Silva Teixeira, 1863);

*Aventuras de Basílio Fernandes Enxertado* (Lisbon: António Maria Pereira, 1863);

*Estrelas propícias* (Porto: Viúva Moré, 1863);

*Cenas inocentes da comédia humana* (Lisbon: António Maria Pereira, 1863);

*Noites de Lamego* (Lisbon: António Maria Pereira, 1863);

*O bem e o mal* (Lisbon: Campos Júnior, 1863);

*Agulha em palheiro* (Rio de Janeiro: Tipografia do Correio Mercantil, 1863);

*Memórias de Guilherme de Amaral* (Lisbon: Campos Júnior, 1863);

*No Bom Jesus do Monte* (Porto: Viúva Moré, 1864);

*A filha do doutor Negro* (Porto: Tip. do Comércio, 1864);

*Amor de salvação* (Porto: Viúva Moré, 1864);

*Vinte horas de liteira* (Lisbon: Campos Júnior, 1864);

*O esqueleto* (Lisbon: Campos Júnior, 1865);

*A sereia* (Porto: Viúva Moré, 1865);

*Luta de gigantes* (Lisbon: Campos Júnior, 1865);

*O morgado de Fafe amoroso* (Lisbon: António Maria Pereira, 1865);

*Esboços de apreciações literárias* (Porto: Viúva Moré, 1865);

*Divindade de Jesus e tradição apostolica* (Porto: Viúva Moré, 1865);

*Horas de paz: Escriptos religiosos* (Porto: Francisco Gomes da Fonseca, 1865);

*A queda d'um anjo* (Lisbon: Campos Júnior, 1866);

*O santo da montanha* (Porto: Tipografia do Comércio, 1866);

*O judeu*, 2 volumes (Porto: Viúva Moré, 1866);

*Vaidades irritadas e irritantes* (Porto: Viúva Moré, 1866);

*A enjeitada* (Lisbon: Campos Júnior, 1866);

*O olho de vidro* (Lisbon: Campos Júnior, 1866);

*Cavar em ruínas* (Lisbon: Campos Júnior, 1867);

*O senhor do Paço de Ninães* (Porto: Tipografia do Comércio, 1867);

*A bruxa de Monte-Córdova* (Lisbon: Campos Júnior, 1867);

*Cousas leves e pesadas* (Porto: Luiz José d'Oliveira, 1867);

*A doida do Candal* (Lisbon: Campos Júnior, 1867);

*O sangue* (Lisbon: Campos Júnior, 1868);

*Mosaico e silva de curiosidades históricas, literárias e biográficas* (Porto: Anselmo de Moraes, 1868);

*Mistérios de Fafe* (Lisbon: Campos Júnior, 1868);

*O retrato de Ricardina* (Lisbon: Campos Júnior, 1868);

*As virtudes antigas ou a freira que fazia chagas, e o frade que fazia reis* (Lisbon: Campos Júnior, 1868);

*Os brilhantes do brasileiro* (Lisbon: António Maria Pereira, 1869);

*A mulher fatal* (Lisbon: Campos Júnior, 1870);

*D. António Alves Martins: Bispo de Vizeu: Esboço biografico* (Porto: Viúva Moré, 1870);

*O condenado: Drama . . . seguido do drama . . . Como os anjos se vingam* (Porto: Viúva Moré, 1870);

*A morgadinha de Val-de-Amores* (Porto: Viúva Moré, 1871)–includes *Entre a flauta e a viola;*

*Voltaréis, ó Cristo?* (Porto: Viúva Moré, 1871);

*Livro de consolação* (Porto: Viúva Moré, 1872);

*O carrasco de Vitor Hugo José Alves* (Porto & Braga: Ernesto and Eugénio Chardron [Livraria Internacional], 1872);

*Quatro horas inocentes* (Lisbon: Campos Júnior, 1872);

*O Visconde de Ouguella: Perfil biographico* (Porto: Pereira da Silva, 1873);

*O demónio do ouro*, 2 volumes (Lisbon: Matos Moreira, 1873, 1874);

*O regicida* (Lisbon: Matos Moreira, 1874);

*Noites de insônia: Oferecidas a quem não pode dormir* (Porto: Ernesto Chardron / Braga: Eugenio Chardron, 1874);

*Ao anoitecer da vida: Ultimos versos* (Lisbon & Porto: Imp. Literario-Comercial, 1874);

*A filha do regicida* (Lisbon: Matos Moreira, 1875);

*A caveira da mártir*, 3 volumes (Lisbon: Matos Moreira, 1875–1876);

*Curso de literatura portuguesa*, by Castelo Branco and José Maria de Andrade Ferreira, 2 volumes (Lisbon: Matos Moreira, 1875, 1876);

*Novelas do Minho*, 12 volumes (Lisbon: Matos Moreira, 1875–1877)–comprises volume 1, *Gracejos que matam* (1875); volume 2, *O commendador* (1876); volume 3, *O cego de Landim* (1876); volume 4, *A morgada de Romariz* (1876); volumes 5–6, *O filho natural* (1876); volumes 7–8, *Maria Moisés* (1876–1877); volume 9, *O degredado* (1877); and volumes 10–12, *A viúva do enforcado* (1877);

*História e sentimentalismo–Eusébio Macário* (Porto: Ernesto Chardron / Braga: Eugenio Chardron, 1879);

*Cancioneiro alegre de poetas portugueses e brasileiros* (Porto: Ernesto Chardron, 1879);

*Os criticos do Cancioneiro alegre* (Porto & Braga: Ernesto Chardron, 1879);

*Sentimentalismo e história–A Corja* (Porto: Ernesto Chardron, 1879);

*A senhora Rattazzi* (Porto & Braga: Livraria Internacional de Ernesto Chardron, 1880);

*Luís de Camões: Notas biograficas* (Porto & Braga: Livraria Internacional de Ernesto Chardron, 1880);

*Suicida* (Porto & Braga: Livraria Internacional de Ernesto Chardron, 1880);

*Ecos humorísticos do Minho*, 4 volumes (Porto & Braga: Livraria Internacional de Ernesto Chardron, 1880);

*Perfil do Marquês de Pombal* (Porto: Clavel / Rio de Janeiro: L. Couto, 1882);

*Narcóticos*, 2 volumes (Porto: Clavel, 1882);

*A brasileira de Prazins* (Porto: Ernesto Chardron, 1882);

*Catálogo da preciosa livraria do eminente escritor Camilo Castelo Branco* (Lisbon: Matos Moreira e Cardosos, 1883);

*A cavalaria da sebenta: Resposta a theologo* (Porto: Ernesto Chardron, 1883);

*Notas ao folheto do Doutor Avelino César Calisto* (Porto: Ernesto Chardron, 1883);

*Segunda carga da cavalaria* (Porto: Ernesto Chardron, 1883);

*Carga terceira* (Porto: Ernesto Chardron, 1883);

*D. Luís de Portugal neto do Prior do Crato* (Porto: Livraria Civilização de Eduardo da Costa Santos, 1883);

*O vinho do Porto: Processo de uma bestialidade inglesa: Exposição a Tomas Ribeiro* (Porto: Livraria Civilização de Eduardo da Costa Santos, 1884);

*O general Carlos Ribeiro: Recordações da mocidade* (Porto: Livraria Civilização de Eduardo da Costa Santos, 1884);

*Maria da Fonte: A propósito dos apontamentos para a História da Revolução do Minho em 1846* (Porto: Livraria Civilização de Eduardo da Costa Santos, 1885);

*Serões de S. Miguel de Ceide*, 6 volumes (Porto: Livraria Civilização de Eduardo da Costa Santos, 1885–1886);

*Boémia do espírito* (Porto: Livraria Civilização de Eduardo da Costa Santos, 1886);

*Vulcões de lama* (Porto: Livraria Civilização de Eduardo da Costa Santos, 1886);

*A diffamação dos livreiros successores de Ernesto Chardron* (Porto: Livraria Civilização de Eduardo da Costa Santos, 1886);

*Obolo ás crianças,* by Castelo Branco and Francisco Martins Sarmento (Porto: Joaquim Ferreira Moutinho, 1887);

*Nostalgias: Ultima prosa rimada* (Porto: M. L. de Souza Ferreira, 1888);

*Delictos da mocidade: Primeiros attentados literarios* (Porto: Livraria Civilização de Eduardo da Costa Santos, 1889);

*Nas trevas: Sonetos sentimentaes e humorísticos* (Lisbon: Tavares Cardoso e Irmão, 1890);

*O lobisomem* (Lisbon: Livraria Editora, 1900).

**Edition:** *Obras completas,* 17 volumes to date, edited by Justino Mendes de Almeida (Porto: Lello & Irmão, 1982–1994).

PLAY PRODUCTIONS: *Agostinho de ceuta,* Vila Real, 1846; Porto, Teatro Camões, 1848;

*O Marquês de Torres Novas,* Porto, Teatro Camões, 1855;

*Poesia ou dinheiro?* Porto, Teatro de S. João, 1855;

*Justiça,* Porto, Teatro de S. João, 1856;

*Espinhos e flores,* Porto, Teatro de S. João, 1857; Lisbon, Teatro Nacional de Lisboa D. Maria II, 1857;

*Purgatório e paraíso,* Lisbon, Teatro Nacional de Lisboa D. Maria II, 1857;

*O último acto,* Lisbon, Teatro Nacional de Lisboa D. Maria II, 1858;

*Abençoadas lágrimas!* Lisbon, Teatro Nacional de Lisboa D. Maria II, 1860;

*O morgado de Fafe em Lisboa,* Lisbon, Teatro Nacional de Lisboa D. Maria II, 1860;

*O morgado de Fafe amoroso,* Lisbon, Teatro Nacional de Lisboa D. Maria II, 1863;

*O condenado,* Porto, Teatro Baquet, 1870;

*Como os anjos se vingam,* Porto, Teatro Baquet, 1870;

*O assassino de Macário,* Coimbra, Teatro Académico, 1886.

TRANSLATIONS: François-René de Chateaubriand, *O genio do christianismo,* 2 volumes (Porto: Cruz Coutinho, 1860);

Ernest Feydeau, *Fanny* (N.p., 1861);

Chateaubriand, *Os martyres,* 2 volumes (Lisbon: A. M. Pereira, 1865);

Octave Feuillet, *Romance de um rapaz pobre* (Lisbon: Livraria Universal, 1865);

Augusto Callet, *O inferno* (Porto: Livraria Nacional, 1871).

Camilo Castelo Branco was the most celebrated Portuguese writer of his time and still occupies a central place in the Portuguese literary canon. The prestige in Europe of realist narratives as opposed to the Romantic mode in which Castelo Branco wrote, the increased recognition of work by realists such as Eça de Queirós, and the pronounced biographical tendencies of many scholars (nourished by Castelo Branco's own work) have contributed to relegating Castelo Branco to the margins of the nineteenth-century literary scene. He has, nonetheless, endured by virtue of the continuous reprints of his works (subject to the demands of the market), his inclusion in school curricula, and studies by prestigious scholars. Although his work is recognized mainly within his own country, he is one of the most widely read Portuguese novelists of all time.

Born in Lisbon on 16 March 1825, Camilo Ferreira Botelho Castelo Branco firmly believed that he was born in 1826, a conviction that went unrefuted by the press even in the notice of his death. The discrepancy is perhaps owing to the fact that he was illegitimate; he and his sister, Carolina, were officially registered as children of an unknown mother. Their mother, Rosa Jacinta, died on 6 February 1827. Their father, the unmarried Manuel Joaquim Botelho Castelo Branco, was the son of an important magistrate; he was an adventurer who never had a stable job. He acknowledged Carolina and Camilo as his children in 1829, but he passed away when Camilo was ten and his sister was fourteen. In that same year, the two siblings were sent with a maid from their native Lisbon to Vila Real (a small provincial capital in northern Portugal) to live with their aunt Rita Emília. They traveled by steamship, and a storm forced them to dock in Vigo, Spain—the only time that Castelo Branco set foot outside of Portugal.

At age fourteen he went to live with his sister and her husband, a medical student named Francisco José de Azevedo, in a small village near Vila Real, where his brother-in-law set up a medical practice. Castelo Branco received a traditional Catholic education under the guidance of Father Antonio J. de Azevedo, Franciso José's brother. He then moved to Friúme, another small village, where he worked as an administrative assistant and furthered his education under the tutelage of a local priest. While in Friúme he married Joaquina Pereira de França, and his daughter Rosa was born in 1843.

According to Castelo Branco, he abandoned his family at the age of eighteen because of the persecution he suffered for his criticism of a local nobleman. That same year (1843) he traveled to Lisbon in a frustrated attempt to collect his legal inheritance, disputed by his aunt. He never received the inheritance in its entirety. In October of 1843 he enrolled in the School of Surgical Medicine in Porto, in an attempt to earn a university degree. The events of Castelo Branco's life are somewhat obscure up to this point, and several legends that make his biography even more complex emerge after his arrival in Porto. The primary source of information is Castelo Branco's own accounts, which are not always reliable. According to some biographers, he abandoned his wife and daughter in 1843 and ran away to Lisbon with his lover, Maria do Adro (possibly Margarida Maria Dias, who probably died of tuberculosis). Castelo Branco and a doctor later exhumed her cadaver, an event that can be inferred from his collection *Duas horas de leitura* (Two Hours of Reading, 1857). It is a known fact that he continued his medical studies but failed the second year, prompting his return to Vila Real in 1845.

Castelo Branco's failure at his studies was a direct result of the bohemian lifestyle he led while in Porto. He adopted the role of the young dandy fond of subverting and attacking the system, especially the morals of the commercial middle class. He became a poet, and his first two works were published in 1845: the unsigned *Os pundonores desagravados* (The Niceties of Honor), a ten-page comical-heroic poem, and *O juízo final e o sonho do inferno* (Final Judgement and the Dream of Hell), an antireligious satire, the first work to carry the signature C. F. B. C. Branco. In Porto he formed his first friendships with other writers, many of whom were connected to journalism or literature and were members of the middle-class and aristocratic circles of the city. These friendships facilitated his access to literary and social gatherings and to publishing houses.

For the first time Castelo Branco had access to the world of Romantic literature, both Portuguese and foreign. Foreign literature dominated the Portuguese literary scene, which was steadily growing as a result of the increase in both middle-class and female readers. The works of writers such as Sir Walter Scott, Ann Radcliffe, Johann Wolfgang von Goethe, Wenceslao Ayguals de Izco, and particularly the French novelists Alexandre Dumas *père,* the Vicomte d'Arlincourt, Victor Hugo, Charles Antoine Guillaume Pigault-Lebrun, Eugène Sue, George Sand, Honoré de Balzac, and Alfred de Musset were popular. At that time Portuguese writers Almeida Garrett and Alexandre Herculano attempted a liberal Romanticism that reacted against the exaggeration and conventions that the second generation of Romantic writers, with António Feliciano de Castilho as their mentor, practiced. This literary field was the one in which Castelo Branco actively participated. According to his own declarations to the biographer José Cardoso Vieira de Castro, in 1845 he had already begun "Mistérios de Coimbra" (Mysteries of Coimbra, not published) and an historical novel, which was the literary trend at the time.

In an 1846 letter to Herculano, Castelo Branco claimed to have studied law from 1845 to 1846 while living in Coimbra. However, his foremost biographer, Alexandre Cabral, questions the truth of this claim. In

*Castelo Branco with Ana Plácido and their son Manuel, 1860 (from Nuno Júdice,* Portugal, língua e cultura, *1992; Lauinger Library, Georgetown University)*

the letter Castelo Branco speaks of how financial circumstances frustrated his desire to become somebody important in the humanities, and he requests a meeting with Herculano in Lisbon to ask him for support. Although Castelo Branco contended that the death of a benefactor had forced him to discontinue his studies, the annual sum he received from his inheritance guaranteed him sufficient economic means to continue. He was addressing a self-made man, who was capable of overcoming financial and social obstacles. A mirror image of the intellectual who was not influenced by economic interests (unlike the middle-class merchants he so despised), Herculano was the quintessence of the austere Romantic who was willing to understand the vicissitudes of a talented young man on whom fortune and politics had turned their backs. Whether the content of the letter is really true or was a biographical invention, the persona defined in it is one that Castelo Branco adopted throughout his professional life.

Some biographers who accept Castelo Branco's testimonies place him in 1846 in the guerrilla band led by Reinaldo MacDonnell, the Scottish general who fought for Miguel I during the revolt of Maria da Fonte (a popular revolt in Minho, led by local women, against the government of António Bernardo da Costa Cabral). Cabral, however, situates the author in Porto living as man and wife with Patrícia Emília de Barros, a young woman from Vila Real. In October of that year both ended up in prison in Porto (where he presented himself as single), accused by her uncle of stealing. The year 1846 marked two important phases in Castelo Branco's career as a writer: the first was his contributions to many Porto newspapers with differing ideologies, and the second was his debut as a playwright in Vila Real with *Agostinho de Ceuta* (Agostinho of Ceuta, published in 1847), an historical drama influenced by Herculano. In addition, he is believed to have written the incomplete and anonymous novel *Lágrimas para quatro vítimas do despotismo* (Tears for Four Victims of Despotism). This novel, written in the same vein as French novels of the time, was published in *O Nacional,* a newspaper that opposed the government of Costa Cabral and whose owner, a rich progressive businessman named Gonçalves Basto, received Castelo Branco favorably.

Castelo Branco's wife died in 1846, an event of which he was apparently unaware. With the civil war over, some say he abandoned the guerrilla band and took refuge with his sister in Samardã, where he was appointed clerk for the provincial government of Vila Real. His daughter Rosa died in March. The following June his daughter Amelia, from his relationship with Barros, was born. He also published "A última vitória de um conquistador" (The Last Victory of a Conqueror) in the newspaper *O Eco Popular* (The Popular Echo). The story is filled with love relationships aggravated by third-party meddlers and crimes presented beneath a moralistic veneer.

At the end of 1848 Castelo Branco returned to Porto. The move was apparently motivated by threats made against him for his criticism of the provincial governor of Vila Real. In Porto he began friendships with a priest named António Alves Martins, with the director of *O Nacional,* and with other members of the intellectual elite. He published, in several newspapers, satirical texts that describe urban life, as well as his unsigned *Maria! não me mates, que sou tua mãe!* (Maria! Don't Kill Me, Because I Am Your Mother! 1848). The work, based on a true account of a macabre matricide in Lisbon, was in the vein of the sensationalist stories that appeared in popular newspapers. The work enjoyed such success that imitations began to spring up around Portugal, which provided the impetus for Castelo Branco finally to claim authorship in the fourth edition (in 1852). He later published the incomplete "Um episódio de Alcácer-Quibir" (An Episode from Alcácer-Quibir, 1848) in *O Eco Popular,* though it was never published in book form. The work is a serialized historical novel that reveals the influence of Herculano and Garrett. Castelo Branco continued to contribute to newspapers and magazines, and he also became a theater critic, which automatically increased his contact with the Porto bourgeoisie. That year, 1849, he published *O Marquês de Torres Novas* (The Marquis of Torres Novas), "a drama in five acts and a prologue" with gothic overtones, and *O caleche* (The Calash), a two-part leaflet filled with anti–Costa Cabral propaganda. Despite its ultra-Romantic elements, *O caleche* was more favorably received by the public than his previously published works.

In February of 1850 Castelo Branco took up residence in Lisbon and began to work as a writer for *A Semana* (The Week), a position possibly obtained through his involvement with Herculano. Castelo Branco, however, was also a friend of the founding director of the magazine, João de Lemos, a jurist, Miguelist diplomat, and poet. The author was finally reaping the fruits of the friendships from his bohemian youth in Porto. The first fifteen chapters of *Anátema* (Anathema, 1851) were published in *A Semana*. The serialized version, however, for unknown reasons was never completed. Several chapters were republished in the first issues of the newspaper *O Portugal*, to which Camilo contributed actively in 1850 and 1851. Once again, however, the publication of the work was thwarted, this time for several reasons, including a disagreement between editor and author over the author's delayed delivery of texts and a lack of public interest.

In 1850 Castelo Branco wrote *O lobisomem* (The Werewolf, 1900), a rather unoriginal and naive comedy full of reproductions of rural customs and speech. He did not sign his name to this work or to *O clero e o senhor Alexandre Herculano* (The Clergy and Mr. Alexandre Herculano, 1850), which became a part of the polemic created by Herculano's *Eu e o clero* (I and the Clergy, 1850). Herculano had written his work in response to the criticism he received from the clergy for the first volumes of his *História de Portugal* (History of Portugal, 1846–1853). Castelo Branco had quickly come to the historian's defense in the form of a letter written in 1846; his efforts, however, were received with condescending indifference by Herculano, who either did not receive the letter or simply failed to remember having received it.

Upon his return to Porto in 1850, Castelo Branco enrolled in the seminary in an attempt to put a stop to his unbridled social and love life, which instead were prolonged by his simultaneous affairs with the owner of the guest house in which he lived and a nun named Isabel Cândida Vaz Mourão. This activity unleashed acrimonious polemics in the press, in which insults and personal attacks on the author abounded.

By the age of twenty-five, the author had written in almost all genres, including drama, comedy, novel, poetry, and the short story. He had published extensively in magazines and newspapers, a medium that reached such importance in the following decades that no writer who sought public recognition could escape it. He also had made new friendships while destroying others, especially among the ruling class in Porto, who had often been the object of his attacks. His agitated life, filled with dandyism and immorality, was increasingly becoming publicly known. There are occasional moments in his biography that suggest a sense of disgrace and fatalism (which the author nourished in his work, justifying his life as a product of destiny) that complete the figure of the Romantic intellectual who fought the economic power of the ruling class through his art.

Castelo Branco left the seminary in 1852 without having taken the vows, and he had finally seen the publication of *Anátema* in its entirety as a book the year before. The volume brought him some prestige despite the contemporary tendency to publish translations of foreign works that had already enjoyed success in Paris. *Anátema* relates as factual a tragic love story that ends in the suicide of the female protagonist, who is kidnapped by a priest seeking vengeance for his mother's rape by the protagonist's father. Secondary intrigues include murder, seduction, revenge, and illegitimate children. The work has a touch of medievalism, which was much in fashion among the writers of the time, and critiques of the ruling class, presented in a melodramatic structure with suspense in every installment and direct references to the reader. The novel includes elements found in contemporary melodramatic French novels dealing with the world of terror and fantasy. These elements reflect the prevailing preferences and literary styles such as the historical and so-called topical novel. Certain features of the work reveal Castelo Branco's erudition and classicism, but the vernacular nature of his work was what made him competitive with foreign authors.

To gain the sympathy of a larger readership, Castelo Branco adopted a highly Romantic stance, which proved his awareness of the existing preferences of the public at the time. Often, however, he employed irony, which, with its potential for parody, created a distance between the work and the reader, but this distance was compensated by lyrical, dramatic, and passionate outbursts in which the author bared his soul. Castelo Branco's Romantic irony, which used ambiguity as one of its main devices even in his earliest works, establishes a contradiction between the status of the idealistic and altruistic Romantic writer and his socio-economic and cultural interests. These strategies allowed him to com-pete with national and foreign writers, either by making them the object of his parodies or by alluding to the works of those with whom he believed himself to be on a par, such as Hugo, Sue, and Dumas. He also was able to introduce his own conceptions of the novel. Since many of his works were previously published in serial format, he was already familiar with his readers' reactions and thus could perfect his literary objectives.

With the emergence of a commercial literary market, there arose in Portugal a split between the literary production of those who wrote to satisfy the tastes of the economically and politically dominant classes and those who were seeking to gain the recognition of their fellow writers and the sympathetic public. The latter group scorned the former's production, known as "literatura industrial" (industrial literature), which they considered banal. In a letter to Garrett in 1851 concerning literary property, Herculano declared an ethical and aesthetic condemnation of modern novelists (including Sand and Balzac) whom he considered uneducated and immoral manufacturers of "useless, frivolous, ephemeral writing." Castelo Branco cautiously avoided being identified with industrial literature by presenting himself as a writer who was not influenced by literary trends and whose methods were less pedagogical, self-centered, and fantastic. By not being bound to any literary group, Castelo Branco could utilize any trend that satisfied his objectives at the time. He added to this freedom his ambiguous conviction of the social uselessness of novels, which released him from the "intellectual's sacred obligation" denounced by Herculano in his critique of industrial literature. Castelo Branco, however, failed to incorporate one element that could have made his work reach a larger public: social and political criticism on a global scale.

Castelo Branco understood the literary world well enough to accomplish his goals. He wanted to become popular, sell books, and earn money. At the same time, he wished to achieve the approval of other writers and critics to legitimize his activity in the intellectual arena. What he apparently was not determined to do was to make journalism and literature his career; he continued to seek other jobs, complaining that as a journalist he made too little money and worked too much. Castelo Branco had failed in his attempts to earn an academic degree that would help him make a living, and he had been frustrated that the priesthood had not served this purpose either. He had made a name for himself, although not one that in and of itself stimulated interest in his writing. He published extensively, mainly poetry. In 1852 he cofounded the magazine *O Cristianismo: "Semanario Religioso"* (The Christianity: "Religious Seminary"), which he later abandoned because of ideological differences with the other editors. He contributed poetry, translations, narratives, and polemical debates to other publications.

After attempting various economic ventures, Castelo Branco began to supplement his income by editing *A Cruz* (The Cross, 1853), and publishing his novel *Mistérios de Lisboa* (Mysteries of Lisbon) as a serial in *O Nacional* from March 1853 to January 1855. The novel also came out in three volumes in 1854. Castelo Branco had created this work as a moneymaking opportunity. Several novels of this type, imitating Sue's *Les Mystères de Paris* (1842–1843), had already appeared in Portugal and had enjoyed great success. In this work Castelo Branco repeated nearly the same strategy used in *Anátema,* re-creating the most stereotypical settings found in the novels popular at the time, although his character portrayals sometimes reflected his own vision of the world. Castelo Branco accepted the novel as the genre that would produce income and allow him to sign publishing deals. This realization led to the appearance of the same characters in different novels and, on occasion, to the production of novelistic series.

As Castelo Branco approached the age of thirty, the majority of writers of his generation were already well established. Unlike Castelo Branco, they were not subjected to the instability of sporadic employment. Lacking academic degrees and social position and far from having any political commitments that would guarantee him a post in the government, Castelo Branco had a clearly subordinate professional status. His last recourse was either to continue journalistic or editorial activities or to look for other means of earning a living. Opting for the latter, in 1853 he presented his application for the position of customs officer. He did not obtain the job, however, because there were apparently few influential people in Porto who were willing to support his candidacy. He turned over the education of his daughter Amelia, who was living with her mother in Vila Real, to Sister Vaz Mourão.

Castelo Branco continued to publish extensively, occasionally producing works, such as the collection of poems *Um livro* (A Book, 1854), at his own expense. He told José Barbosa e Silva, who had helped him with the book, that it would be the decisive work to solidify his reputation as a writer. This prediction, however, did not prove true. The author's vast correspondence at the time often includes pleas for financial help, accompanied by a romantic portrayal of himself as the misunderstood and ill-fated writer.

Between poems and antibourgeois satires, *A filha do arcediago* (The Archdeacon's Daughter) came out in 1854. This novel of love affairs and satires of Portuguese traditions and institutions (such as the baronies or the Royal Academy of Science) was the first volume in the series *Cenas contemporâneas* (Contemporary Scenes), published in serial format in *A Concórdia* (The Concord). Influences of Balzac are seen in the author's criticism of the Porto elite and in the emphasis on money and daily life.

In 1855 Castelo Branco became the editor of *O Porto e a Carta* (Porto and the Letter). He published *Cenas contemporâneas II,* a compilation of brief texts including new ones such as the successful play *Poesia ou dinheiro?* (Poetry or Money?). That same year he published *Livro negro do Padre Dinis* (Father Dinis's Black Book), which followed the lines of *Mistérios de Lisboa,* and *A neta do arcediago* (The Archdeacon's Granddaughter) in *A Verdade* (The Truth). This last novel was published the following year in book format carrying the subtitle *Cenas contemporâneas III.* In it certain themes are more prominent than in previous works: amorous passion unrealized because of social conventions or human malice; sexual desire, as the romantic femme fatale is placed in the forefront; and punishment and chastisement. The religion of love was a central theme in Castelo Branco's fiction. The well-known contemporary critic José Maria de Andrade Ferreira considered this religion of love in line with Balzac's and Sue's novels, a point that, whether or not it made Castelo Branco a follower of a particular school of writing, singled him out as modern, especially because of his successful attempts to make certain imported literary models seem authentically Portuguese.

The novel, a rising genre, brought Castelo Branco his greatest success and earnings as well as his important position in Portuguese literature. In 1856 he published the book version of *A neta do arcediago,* as well as the serialized versions of *Onde está a felicidade?* (Where Is Happiness?) and *Lágrimas abençoadas* (Blessed Tears, 1857) in *A Verdade.* In May of that year the play *Justiça* (Justice) came out (performed earlier in the Teatro de S. João in Porto), portraying love affairs and emigrants to Brazil who return to Portugal wealthy. The author began to contribute to *A Aurora do Lima* (The Aurora's Lima), a newspaper in Viana founded by people associated with the Progressive Party, including his well-to-do friend Barbosa e Silva. Castelo Branco, together with the distinguished journalist Evaristo Basto and the two prominent writers Alexandre José da Silva Braga Júnior and António José Coelho Lousada, edited *O Clamor Público* (The Public Outcry). Castelo Branco promised the owner of *O Clamor Público,* Faria Regras, that he would write *Um homem de brios* (A Man of Courage) as a continuation of *Onde está a felicidade?* In 1857, however, Castelo Branco, Basto, and Lousada left the newspaper, and the novel, dated 1856, was published by Oliveira Guimarães, owner of the printing press that published *O Clamor Público.*

*Onde está a felicidade?* represented a turning point in Castelo Branco's work. He toned down his imitation of the French models dealing with the world of the fantastic

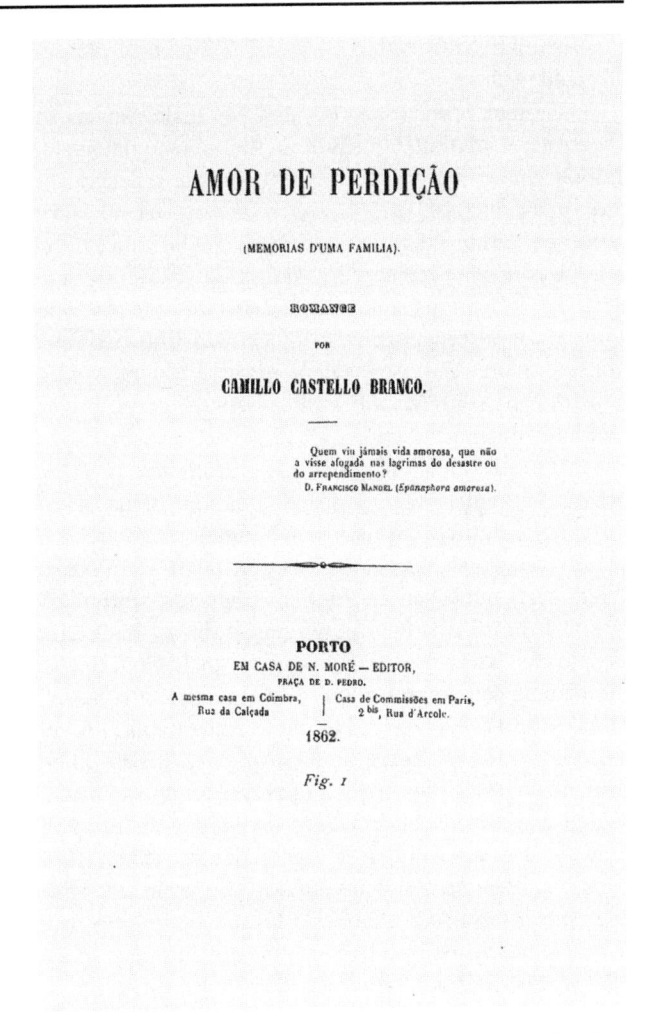

*Title page for Castelo Branco's novel about a doomed love triangle, written while he was in prison on charges of adultery (from Gustavo d'Ávila Perez,* As traduções do "Amor de perdição," *1964; Thomas Cooper Library, University of South Carolina)*

and simplified the plot. The protagonist, Guilherme de Amaral, is a young man negatively influenced by the same type of novel that had once nurtured Castelo Branco's literary production. Criticism of Porto society, with overtones of Balzac's works, reappears without the author foregoing the lucrative intrigue of love affairs. Amaral abandons Augusta, his fiancée, for Leonor. When Leonor betrays him, he regrets having left Augusta. He wants to return to her, but it is too late: distraught, she has married a rich cousin. The work has a more balanced structure, a more fluid language, and greater moderation in the presence and narration of dramatic scenes, in contrast to the melodramatic works of some of his contemporaries. The critics began to appreciate Castelo Branco's literature of manners, in which he explores national themes and speech. The book eventually sold well.

Castelo Branco incorporated the main aspects of *Onde está a felicidade?* (including the main characters, among whom the unnamed journalist is a reflection of the author himself) in *Um homem de brios,* which lacks action even more than its predecessor. This time, however, action is not replaced by analysis but rather by sentimental expansions and digressions. In its story line some readers recognize traces of Castelo Branco's relationship with Ana Augusto Vieira Plácido, a young woman married to Manuel Pinheiro Alves, a much older and influential merchant.

Castelo Branco had attained a prominent position on the Portuguese literary scene, although perhaps not the one he desired. He was not included in *Viagem pela literatura contemporânea* (A Journey through Portuguese Literature), published in 1856 by the critic and playwright Ernesto Biester. The writer attributed his exclusion to the "society of mutual praise" in Lisbon and to his blatant contempt for the Porto milieu. His work, however, was well received by the reading public, and in the prestigious magazine *A Revolução de Setembro* (The September Revolution) critic Lopes de Mendonça underscored its satire of the commercial ruling class. In addition to this recognition, Castelo Branco achieved a certain professional stability by signing contracts with publisher António Rodrigues da Cruz Coutinho to produce various works and by receiving advance payments. This activity did not, however, entirely satisfy his financial needs. He constantly appealed to his friends for help, expressing the desire to leave behind his unstable life and complaining about his health, particularly his eyesight. Castelo Branco was not entirely honest about his income, which, on average, was that of a high-level civil servant. He published often, always paying close attention to the public's and editors' preferences.

In 1857 Castelo Branco moved to Viana, where he briefly edited *A Aurora do Lima.* The reason for his moving perhaps had to do with Plácido, who was caring for her sick sister there. When she returned to Porto, Castelo Branco left the newspaper and followed her. There he worked as literary director of *O Nacional* in the midst of escalating rumors about their love affair. He responded to these rumors in the serialized edition of the feuilleton "O mundo patarata" (The Humbug World, 1857), giving rise to a disagreement with the owner of the newspaper and the eventual abandonment of his position. He sent his daughter back to Vila Real and saw the publication in book form of *Duas horas de leitura,* a compilation of journalistic contributions (some previously published in three different newspapers); *Lágrimas abençoadas;* two dramatic pieces about love and adventure titled *Espinhos e flores* (Thorns and Flowers, 1857), dedicated to Herculano and premiered successfully in Porto; *Purgatório e paraíso* (Purgatory and Paradise), which premiered in the Teatro D. Maria II in Lisbon; and two brief satirical novels of customs, previously printed in serialized form in *A Aurora do Lima* and combined under the collective title *Cenas da Foz* (The Foz Scenes).

In 1858 Castelo Branco published the novels *Carlota Ângela, Vingança* (Vengeance) and *O que fazem as mulheres* (What Women Do). Several of his works were republished, which meant that he had more than ten books in circulation at the same time, more than any other Portuguese writer. In the pages of *O Nacional* he was hailed as a distinguished and successful writer. Herculano proclaimed him a great novelist of the future (an opinion quickly seconded by others), which, apart from earning Castelo Branco the recognition of one of the greatest authorities in the field, pointed the author to the path he followed in the future: the novel of passion. In the prologue of the second edition of *Lendas e narrativas* (Legends and Narratives, 1851) Herculano reserves a founding role for himself in literature and suggests that Castelo Branco will be his successor.

*Carlota Ângela,* a serialized novel printed in *A Aurora do Lima,* is predominantly a novel of passion without much psychological treatment of the characters. The work is set at the time of the French invasion of Portugal and deals with the saving presence of religion while criticizing certain aspects of Porto society. *O que fazem mulheres,* with the subtitle "a philosophical novel," is an equally passionate work that narrates the love affairs of its two heroines. Castelo Branco mocks the writers of Gothic narratives that once served as his models. The work, which reveals the author's gift as a keen observer of the Portuguese world, combines devices such as sudden turns of events and melodrama with social criticism and moral lessons. This formula allowed him to expand his readership, although at times satisfying popular demand did not always coincide with the demands of his literary critics, as was the case with *Vingança,* which was not critically well received.

Castelo Branco's unsatisfactory financial situation continued and was exacerbated by new expenses originating from his love affair with Plácido. His friends tried to find him work as a civil servant, but the ruling class of Porto, perpetual victims of his attacks (and sensitive to the rumors that Plácido's newborn son, Manuel, was indeed Castelo Branco's), raised obstacles that thwarted these efforts. As his literary fame increased, the author's financial situation worsened. At Herculano's request, Castelo Branco was named corresponding member of the Royal Academy of Sciences of Lisbon. He became the editor of the magazine *O Mundo Elegante* (Elegant World, 1858–1860); however, he continued his attacks on the Porto elite, and they continued to boycott him.

He applied for a position in the Porto Public Library and was backed by Herculano who, in *O Jornal do Comércio* (The Commerce Newspaper), described him as "indisputably the best Portuguese novelist," whose exclusion from the post would be scandalous. Castelo Branco, however, did not get the job. Although he did not publish anything in book form in 1859, he continued to write and indulge in polemical issues in the press. He published various texts (some about happy marriages) as contributor to the *Revista Contemporânea de Portugal e o Brasil* (Contemporary Review of Portugal and Brazil), which counted on the collaboration of the most renowned writers in the country, especially those from Lisbon. Castelo Branco, thus, had become part of the literary network that he had openly rejected previously.

The scandal surrounding his love affair had reached outstanding proportions. Under enormous social pressure to leave Castelo Branco or to join a convent, Plácido ran away with her child, maid, and Castelo Branco—who, according to some, even received death threats. The lovers fled to Lisbon, but financial problems caused Plácido to yield to the wishes of Pinheiro Alves and to join the Convento da Conceição in Braga, from which she later fled again with the writer. Once again, Castelo Branco appealed to his friends for help. Among them was Duarte Gustavo Nogueira Soares, an important politician and diplomat, who was asked to speak directly with Minister Fontes Pereira de Melo to offer the writer's services. The requests were of little avail. Thus, finding himself in a precarious economic situation, Castelo Branco was forced to sell part of his personal library to Coutinho.

Apart from some isolated pamphlets, the only publication to carry his name in 1860 was the translation of *Génie du christianisme* (The Genius of Christianity) by François-René de Chateaubriand, commissioned by Coutinho. As a way of humiliating the author for failing to honor his contracts, Coutinho had his name on the translation accompanied by the qualifying phrase "revised by Augusto Soromenho." While Castelo Branco and Plácido were on the run, his comedy *O morgado de Fafe em Lisboa* (The First-Born of Fafe in Lisbon, published in 1861) and *Abençoadas lágrimas!*, a play version of *Lágrimas abençoadas*, premiered in the Teatro D. Maria II. The premieres were a guaranteed success given the morbidity of the public, who opted for a biographical interpretation of the adulterous drama represented on stage. Pinheiro Alves denounced both Castelo Branco and Plácido as adulterers, and Plácido was arrested on 6 June 1860. The writer spent that entire summer fleeing the law in the northern part of the country until he finally decided to turn himself in on 1 October. He was incarcerated in Porto, where Plácido was already being held.

The ensuing social movement for and against the prisoners was tremendous. While in jail they received visits from King Pedro V and intellectuals from Porto and Lisbon. Newspaper articles praising Castelo Branco's work appeared; he had become the most recognized contemporary Portuguese writer of the time and was also proclaimed to be the best peninsular novelist. Under the pseudonym "Felizardo," he even advertised his biography in the magazine *A Revolução de Setembro*. Granted permission to leave his jail cell for health-related reasons, he rode around the main streets of Porto on horseback. His adversaries put pressure on the courts and tried to produce witnesses willing to testify against the lovers. Nonetheless, his friends who were members of the Institute of Coimbra halted these attempts in order to name him a member. On 14 October several sectors of the Porto elite circulated the *Revista do Porto,* which reproduced the author's attacks on them written eleven years earlier.

In 1861 Castelo Branco published his translation of Ernest Feydeau's 1858 novel *Fanny,* revealing his understanding of the realist novel, which had not been reflected previously in his repertoire. In addition to that translation and book versions of *O morgado de Fafe em Lisboa* and *Abençoadas lágrimas!* commissioned by the Lisbon publisher António Maria Pereira, two more narratives appeared from the printing press of *A Revista* (The Review) in Lisbon: *Doze casamentos felizes* (Twelve Happy Marriages), a collection of stories, some of which had previously been published; and *O romance dum homem rico* (The Novel of a Rich Man), a story about a man and his compassion for his unfaithful lover. The subject matter of these two texts inevitably led readers to see the author's personal life in them.

With many people in Portugal following the trial in the press, Plácido and Castelo Branco were absolved of adultery on 16 October 1861. At that stage, the writer's life and work appeared to be in absolute harmony with each other, summed up in a compendium of romantic values associated with love as the supreme good, the femme fatale, scorn of the bourgeois, and adventure. In the eyes of many readers, Castelo Branco and Plácido personified the romantic heroes who appeared in his novels about abductions, persecutions, and imprisonments. The couple moved to Lisbon, where he received the support of prominent writers and intellectuals such as Castilho, Biester, Tomás Ribeiro, and J. C. Machado.

Castelo Branco's economic situation had become complicated. He had worked while in jail, and he had signed contracts with a diverse group of publishers. These contracts were the source of the greatest volume of his professional activity and of his income. Such a diversity of publishing contracts was the result not only of the fact that no publisher was willing to risk signing an exclusive deal for the writer's vast literary production but also of his own strategy to better manage his business relationships. Castelo Branco was always pressed for money and generally contracted the absolute sale of his originals, which gave him greater immediate remuneration but little guarantee for future royalties. Confronted with this situation almost from the beginning of his career, he repeatedly lamented and celebrated his independence, which he claimed to have achieved by writing copiously and living modestly. He was not independent, however, of the market and his publishers. Proof of this dependence was the translation of *Les Martyrs* by Chateaubriand, which was work done to make a living. It was completed in 1862 but came out only in 1865, along with *O morgado de Fafe amoroso* and the second edition of *Duas épocas da vida* (Two Epochs of Life, first published in 1854), the last of his works published by Pereira. Publications prior to these included the humorous works *Coração, cabeça e estômago* (Heart, Head and Stomach), *Coisas espantosas* (Frightening Things), and *O último acto* (The Last Act) in 1862, and *Aventuras de Basílio Fernandes Enxertado* (The Basílio Fernandes Enxertado Adventures), *Cenas inocentes da comédia humana* (Innocent Scenes of the Human Comedy), and *Noites de Lamego* (The Lamego Nights) in 1863.

While he was still in jail, Castelo Branco, with the help of an old friend, secured a publishing deal with the conservative newspaper *Comércio do Porto* (Commerce of Porto) for his translation of Octave Feuillet's 1858 novel and play *Le Roman d'un jeune homme pauvre* (The Romance of a Poor Young Man). In the following years he published *As três irmãs* (The Three Sisters, 1862), *Estrelas funestas* (Sinister Stars, 1862), *Estrelas propícias* (Benevolent Stars, 1863), *O bem e o mal* (Good and Evil, 1863), *A filha do doutor Negro* (Doctor Negro's Daughter, 1864), and *Vinte horas de liteira* (Twenty Hours in the Sedan, 1864). He also produced several historical novels, in which his classicism is mixed with his awareness of the public's interest in the past: *Luta de gigantes* (Battle of the Giants, 1865), *O santo da montanha* (The Saint from the Mountain, 1866), *O senhor do Paço de Ninães* (The Master-House of the Ninães, 1867), and *A enjeitada* (The Foundling Girl, 1866), which was published directly in book form. Because of the moralizing tendency of some of these novels, the author was accused of succumbing to the puritanical mission of the newspaper. Castelo Branco defended himself by averring his belief in the morals found in his works and denying any outside pressure. Around the same time he signed another deal, once again through a friend, with the Porto publisher Viúva Moré, which eventually published many Castelo Branco titles.

In *Amor de perdição* (Ruined Love), published in 1862 and dedicated to Fontes Pereira de Melo (head of the Regenerative Party and a prominent politician), the romantic aura of Castelo Branco's biography interacts with the narrated story, intensified by his declaration that it was written in "fifteen tormented days" in jail, thus contributing to the myth of the inspired and incorrigible writer. The story deals with a hopeless love triangle involving one of Castelo Branco's ancestors, who had served time in the same prison as the author. The critics applauded the writer's talent, imagination, and subtle observation of Portuguese life. In the preface to the second printing (1863), the author, who did not believe the work to be his best and had not expected such a "sad" book to be successful, declares that the only usefulness of the contemporary novel is in the "purity of the telling." Now comfortably successful, Castelo Branco reinforced his standing in the field with a justification of the exclusivity of genuine Portuguese elements in his work and the classicism of the modern novel.

Although he was now a successful writer, Castelo Branco continued to have problems with his health (poor eyesight, migraines, and premature aging) and with his finances. He once again sought work as a public official. Despite moments of separation from Plácido, which were aggravated by health problems and his attacks of jealousy, their situation changed with the death of Pinheiro Alves in the summer of 1863 (days after Plácido's second son, Jorge, was born). Pinheiro Alves's estate went to Manuel, including a house in São Miguel de Ceide (located in the region of the Minho River). Plácido and Castelo Branco made the house their permanent residence, and their son Nuno was born there in 1864.

Castelo Branco's literary success continued with the publication of the novel of passion *O esqueleto* (The Skeleton, 1865), the historical novel *O olho de vidro* (The Glass Eye, first published in the *Jornal de Comércio* of Lisbon, 1866), and the republication and theatrical adaptation of other works. The novel of passion became a key part of his literary production, which won him the approval and support of critics in Lisbon and Porto without his having to abandon the melodramatic character of some narrations, the moralizing weight of others, or his criticism and irony.

The famous polemic "Questão Coimbrã" (The Coimbra Case) was a journalistic controversy that began in 1865. The younger generation of writers criticized what they considered the vacuous conventionalism and the absence of ethical values of the literary production of the older artists. The attacks were centered on Castilho and his supporters. Some of the most prominent writers of the time intervened, including Castelo Branco (but only at Castilho's insistence). The intervention, however, came too late. The feared and ferocious polemicist did not show his customary enthusiasm, but in his pamphlet *Vaidades irritadas e irritantes* (Irritating and Irritated Vanities, 1866) he did censure those critics whom he judged excessively materialistic, analytical, and lacking in sensitivity and lyricism. Everything indicated that Castelo

*Interior of Castelo Branco's home in São Miguel de Ceide, where he lived from 1863 until his death (from João Bigote Chorão,*
Camilo: A obra e o homem, *1979; Brigham Young University Libraries)*

Branco did not make the battle his own and was not worried about his status in the field. He was the consecrated writer, the great observer, and the cultivator of the language, along with Castilho. That year, 1866, Manuel António de Campos Júnior, one of the author's important publishers, printed in his newspaper *O Jornal do Comércio* the serial *A queda d'um anjo* (The Fall of an Angel). The work is a satire without any moralistic overtones, about a provincial deputy and his wife who are corrupted by life in the capital.

The "Questão Coimbrã" signaled the advent of new ideological and cultural currents and new writers in Portugal. The essence of those currents is captured in Júlio Dinis's critically acclaimed *As pupilas do senhor reitor* (The Rector's Pupils), published in 1866 in serialized form in *O Jornal do Porto*. This novel reflects the influence of the first English realists, with their focus on rural themes and natural dialogues. Herculano praised the work as the best Portuguese novel of the century. In a letter to Castelo Branco (2 November 1867), Castilho compared Dinis to Balzac, an attribute already assigned to Castelo Branco, who replied that the new generation was pushing ahead.

In 1867, according to Castelo Branco in his letters, the fundamental threat to his career was the worsening condition of his health. He continued to work hard, however, and in diverse endeavors. He published more works that year, including *A doida do Candal* (The Crazy Woman from Candal), a moralizing novel of passion, and the historiographical work *Cavar em ruínas* (To Dig in the Ruins). The effect of the new ideas and currents is manifest in the prologue of the second edition of *A doida do Candal*, in which Castelo Branco affirms that he wrote to entertain and not to philosophize, because there was no readership for that type of writing in Portugal. He claimed that what he wrote to please the critics did not sell, and that only writers who were secure financially could afford the luxury of writing for the sake of posterity.

Castelo Branco published three works of fiction in 1868: *O retrato de Ricardina* (The Portrait of Ricardina), *O sangue* (Blood), and *Mistérios de Fafe* (The Mysteries of Fafe), subtitled "a social novel." The latter work, however, deals less with social issues and more with how a poor but honorable man's honesty triumphs over that of a person of higher social class. Well received by the critics, the other two novels are about passionate love. The author, at the time, edited the weekly newspaper *Gazeta Literária de Porto* (Porto Literary Gazette). This job ended after the sixteenth issue of the paper because of disagreements with its owner.

In 1869 Castelo Branco published one new novel, *Os brilhantes do brasileiro* (The Brazilian's Diamonds), and he received several awards, including the commendation of Carlos III of Spain. In 1870 he published four titles but only one novel, attesting to an unusual change of pace possibly caused by his failing health. Commissioned by Campos Júnior, the novel *A mulher fatal* (The Fatal Woman) is about adulterous love. Critics underscored the burlesque treatment of romantic excess in the work. The successful premieres and subsequent publication in 1870 of *Como os anjos se vingam* (How the Angels Take Revenge) and *O condenado* (The Convict), dedicated to Vieira de Castro, who was incarcerated for killing his wife, followed. Halfway through that same year, Castilho was granted the title of viscount. While not an infrequent honor, this one was unusual in that it could be passed along to the recipient's firstborn son. Some biographers believe that Castelo Branco, an illegitimate child (one of the most frequent character types in his novels), saw in this title of nobility an opportunity to unite social recognition and economic guarantees for his family. With that in mind, in September he wrote to the Bishop of Viseu and Minister to the King, Alves Martins (whose biography Castelo Branco later wrote), to request the title for himself. The response was harsh; as long as the writer lived in sin, the king (Luís I, of the House of Bragança, the ruling monarchical family from the seventeenth century) would not grant him the title. Despite the fact that in subsequent years Castelo Branco became even more important in the literary world, his objective to join the ranks of the nobility became a priority. His literary activity continued, but he published infrequently. Financial difficulties forced him once again to sell part of his personal library (around one thousand books) and to write prefaces and do translations.

Castelo Branco's main rival in the literary field, Dinis, died in 1871. The importation of literary works, the realist novel, the new French trends in poetry, and the Portuguese elite's favor of the "Ideia Nova" (New Idea) gradually modified the hierarchy of the field. Some of the participants in the "Questão Coimbrã," together with other intellectuals such as Queirós, organized a series of lectures called the Conferências Democráticas (Democratic Conferences) in Lisbon. Queirós spoke on realism in art, beginning a campaign that criticized ultra-Romanticism and was anti–Castelo Branco in nature. This campaign included publications such as *As Farpas* (The Splinters), "a monthly chronicle on the politics of the arts and tradition" written by Queirós and Ramalho Ortigão.

Castelo Branco acknowledged indirectly this incipient threat to his professional status in the preface of his work *Quatro horas inocentes* (Four Innocent Hours), dated 1872 but consisting of texts published in 1871. He responded with a meager production (in which he comments that the new public was looking for the new novel), a search for economic stability (he apparently was even thinking about becoming a businessman), and a new attempt to achieve a title of nobility. He appealed to Castilho and wrote to the influential politician Rodrigues Sampaio, whose response was similar to that of Alves Martins. Castelo Branco's reaction to Sampaio's refusal to help came in the form of an anti-Bragança novel of passion titled *A infanta capelista* (The Little Salesgirl). After the novel was printed, some of Castelo Branco's friends had the edition destroyed, to avoid scandals and in hopes that the monarchy would change its stance. This shift did not occur, and the result was the publication of *O carrasco de Vitor Hugo José Alves* (Vitor Hugo José Alves's Executioner), a recycling of *A infanta capelista* published by Ernesto Chardron, who in 1868 had published two prefaces on historical topics by Castelo Branco. *Livro de consolação* (The Book of Consolation) also came out in 1872. The protagonist of this work is a political idealist who has just killed his wife's lover out of his frustration with the brutality of a false and corrupt social reality. The book is dedicated to the emperor of Brazil, Pedro II, whom the author had met in March. Luís I had granted Castelo Branco the Ordem da Rosa (Order of the Rose), a title added to that of member of the Instituto Vasco da Gama, which was given to him around the same time.

Castelo Branco published only two books in 1873. The first, *O Visconde de Ouguella* (The Viscount of Ouguela), is the biography of a childhood friend, a democratic mason who was incarcerated after being accused of conspiring against the government. The second was the first volume of the novel *O demónio do ouro* (The Golden Devil), the plot of which centers on love and the corruptive power of money.

Motivated by his desire for a title of nobility, Castelo Branco in December 1873 solicited the help of the prominent politician Tomás Ribeiro. The king responded that he would only grant Castelo Branco himself the title of viscount, and that if he wanted to pass it on to his son he would have to legalize his family's situation. The author's response was virulent; Chardron published his *Noites de insônia: Oferecidas a quem não pode dormir* (Sleepless

Nights: Offered to Those Who Cannot Sleep, 1874), a mixture of literary and polemical pieces that were critical of the House of Bragança. His literary production increased with the publication of *Ao anoitecer da vida: Ultimos versos* (The Darkening of Life: Last Verses), a collection of partly autobiographical love poetry written twelve years earlier. The romantic tone of this work contrasted with that of emerging young writers such as Abílio Manuel Guerra Junqueiro and with Castelo Branco's novel *O regicida* (The King's Killer, 1874), a new attack on the Braganças, published by Matos Moreira. Although the novel is subtitled "an historical novel," amorous intrigue and the exploration of injustice are central themes. In 1874 Castelo Branco and some partners established the publishing house Leitura Para Todos, which did not survive long.

In 1875 the author left Porto to be with his younger children, who were studying in Coimbra, and Manuel returned from Luanda, where he had lived for two years. Castelo Branco wrote the anti-Bragança novels *A filha do regicida* (The Daughter of the King's Killer) and the three-volume *A caveira do mártir* (The Skull of the Martyr). In this trilogy Castelo Branco offers a gloomy panorama of the repressive and hypocritical kingdoms of the seventeenth and eighteenth centuries. The work, a mixture of erudition and love affairs, presents honor and religious morality as a just conclusion to the work. In opposition to what he considered an obscene fashion, he maintained that he wrote not to satisfy the demands of the market but rather to look for the truth behind human pain and suffering.

Castelo Branco's humanistic posture later took a more defined shape. Castilho's death in June of 1875 and the publication of Queirós's *O crime do padre Amaro* (The Sin of Father Amaro, 1876) reinforced Castelo Branco's position as a representative of "old-fashioned" literature. The new realist narrative was enthusiastically greeted by the critics for its modernity and pioneering nature. These circumstances, in accordance with the prevailing polemics, converted Castelo Branco into a labeled defender of the dominant repertoire in the literary system and, to some extent, of a society and political system that were synonymous. The author's defense of his romantic viewpoints began to increase, and he began to change his attitude about the House of Bragança because he thought that would facilitate the concession of a noble title. He even attempted to withdraw the volumes of *A caveira do mártir* from circulation.

Castelo Branco was, nonetheless, influenced by some elements of realism, which can be seen in the eight-novel series *Novelas do Minho* (The Minho Novels), which he began to publish in 1875. Equally significant was his dedication of the fourth novel in the series, *A morgada de Romariz* (The First-Born Daughter of Romariz, 1876), to Teixeira de Queirós, a realist writer who with his help began to publish that same year a series of "country comedies." Castelo Branco, perhaps because he still did not see his professional status threatened, greeted the first Portuguese realist productions positively, but not without some critical mentions of *O crime do padre Amaro* or *As Farpas*. Castelo Branco was famous for being an erudite, and his *Curso de literatura portuguesa* (Course on Portuguese Literature, 1875, 1876) had been in circulation since the beginning of the year. It was a continuation of a work by Andrade Ferreira, who had been studying the modern period when he died in 1875.

The *Novelas do Minho* are characterized by the same world of intrigue and surprises found in Castelo Branco's successful novels. That was not, however, the case of *Os mistérios de Lisboa, Amor de perdição,* or *O regicida;* what was the exception in these works had now almost become the rule. The writer had taken advantage of a method that he knew well, one that was filled with violence and tragedy. In order not to abandon the strong religious components out of which he molded plots and denouements, he turned to naturalist explanations of his characters' actions. He called attention to their psychological makeup and their portrayal with ethnographic expressions in their speech and customs. He was thus more attentive to the systematic precision of the realists than to the florid digressions of the Romantics.

Faced with the behaviorally evident schizophrenia of his son Jorge, the author returned to Ceide at the end of 1876. The following summer his son Manuel died of a fever. Castelo Branco did not publish a single novel that year. In 1878 Chardron printed the unheard-of quantity of three thousand copies of Quierós's *O primo Basílio* (Cousin Basílio), which sold quickly. Castelo Branco, who for some had become the old author of Romantic and historical novels, now saw his professional status threatened. His books were not selling as well as those of his young rivals; a new public, for whom the world and characters about which he wrote seemed remote, had emerged. He was faced with a group of emerging writers who practiced a literature perceived as different. This writing offered new techniques, themes, and objectives, and it was more urban and topical. The majority of the new writers claimed to be socialists or republicans, as opposed to Castelo Branco, who was vox populi and yearned for the title of viscount. He was becoming increasingly embittered because of incessant physical and family problems.

Still holding a prominent position in the field nevertheless, the writer in 1879 switched to a direct attack against the already familiar "Ideia Nova," using irony and sarcasm as his most vigorous weapons. Since January he had been the almost exclusive writer for the monthly magazine *Revista de Bibliografia Nacional e Estrangeira*

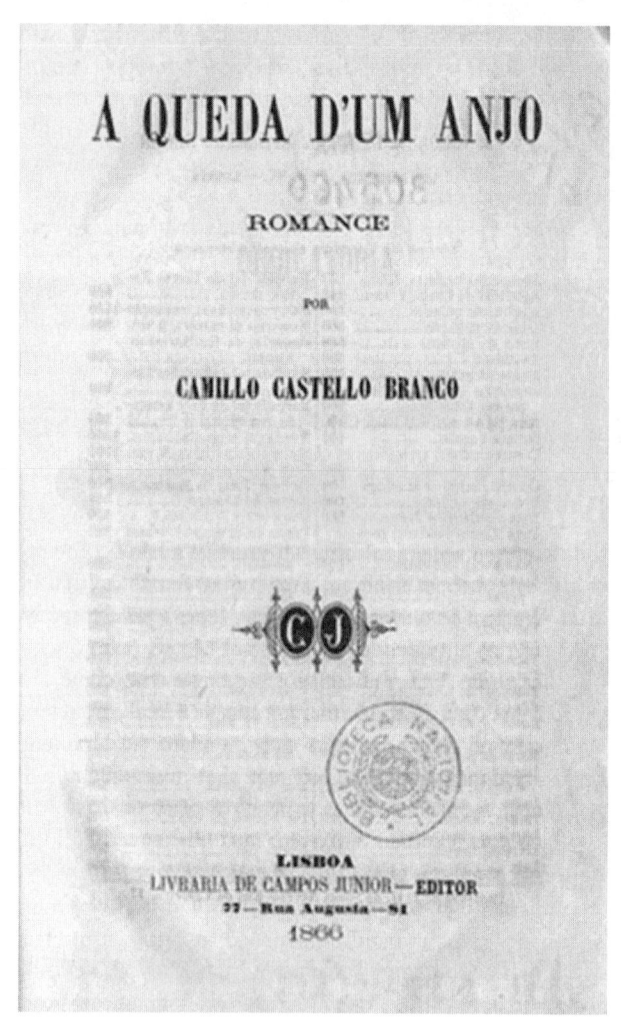

*Title page for Castelo Branco's 1866 satiric novel about a provincial deputy and his wife who become corrupted by city life (Biblioteca Nacional, Lisbon)*

(Journal of National and Foreign Bibliography), published by Chardron. The magazine was a propagandistic platform in which he entrenched himself as a supporter of good Portuguese (as opposed to the idiomatic corruption he attributed to his adversaries), as a scholar of the most varied disciplines, and, especially, as a man experienced in the arts. In the spring Chardron printed the highly publicized *Cancioneiro alegre de poetas portugueses e brasileiros* (Collection of Merry Poems of Portuguese and Brazilian Poets), an extremely partial view of contemporary poets in which Castelo Branco appears just as condescending toward the writers who share his ideas as he is aggressive toward the followers of the "Ideia Nova." A polemic arose, but now the principal figures of the opposing group did not intervene. Because of this confrontation and the support of various critics who praised him as the best contemporary Portuguese writer, Castelo Branco regained attention and prestige. He filled pages of the *Revista de Bibliografia Portuguesa e Estrangeira* and published in book format *Os críticos do Cancioneiro alegre* (The Critics of the Book of Merry Poems).

In the summer of 1879, in the middle of the polemic, Chardron published the equally propagandistic *Eusébio Macário,* announced as an "interminable" series of "humorous novels." In this series (subtitled "The Natural and Social History of a Family in the Times of the Cabrals" to ridicule Emile Zola's twenty-volume series *Les Rougon-Macquart,* 1871–1893), Castelo Branco's aggressiveness intensified. *Eusébio Macário* is a realist work set in the north of the country, but with a humor that distorts the realist objectives. The novel is, thus, an ironic tug-of-war directed at the leaders of the new trend and their public; it exaggerates the so-called portrait of immorality and vice, the use of language, and the narrative techniques of realism. The novel met with enough success to require an immediate second printing. Many critics saw in it a fierce censure of the realists (whom the conservatives applauded and the critics scorned) while others thought that Castelo Branco had switched over to the enemy's side. His allies in the literary field once again applauded him as the best Portuguese writer, and with his constant resources of irony and ambiguity he defended himself in the preface of the new edition. There he stated that *Eusébio Macário* was his most banal work because of the facility with which he wrote it, imitating "the processes of naturalism."

The press had hardly begun to receive *Eusébio Macário* when the magazine *A Arte* began to publish *A brasileira de Prazins* (The Brazilian Woman from Prazins, published in book form in 1882). Although the publication was interrupted after the first few chapters, the reader could sense the signs of a novel of passion, which clearly showed Castelo Branco's versatility and constant adaptation to his surroundings. In addition to some reprints, prefaces, and the collection *Ecos humorísticos do Minho* (Humorous Echoes from Minho), he published in 1880 a biography of key Renaissance literary figure Luís de Camões as well as the novel *A corja* (The Mob), "a continuation of *Eusébio Macário.*" The latter unleashed a virulent polemic occurring simultaneously with another controversy caused by his criticism of a book by Princess Maria Letizia Studolmire Wise Rattazzi, a noblewoman who traveled extensively throughout Europe. The princess had insinuated that Castelo Branco's works were a constant repetition of models (one of the most frequent criticisms of his work). The controversy escalated and almost ended in a duel with the princess's husband. The polemic raised by *A corja* lasted several months, encouraged by articles that appeared in the *Revista de Bibliografia Portuguesa e Estrangeira*. Its chief protagonists were Alexandre da Conceição, who sided with the "Ideia Nova," and António José da Silva Pinto, a friend from Ceide who took Castelo Branco's side.

Castelo Branco did not publish any books in 1881, as his personal problems intensified. In addition to Jorge's violent madness, his other son Nuno's lifestyle was becoming increasingly dissolute. Nuno, perhaps with his father's help, abducted and married a rich Brazilian heiress, seemingly as a way to secure his financial future. In 1882 Castelo Branco published only two works: *Perfil do Marquês do Pombal*, a critical biography of the eighteenth-century political reformer Sebastião José de Carvalho e Melo, Marquês de Pombal; and *Narcóticos* (Narcotics), which included many previously published texts. Although bearing the same date as these works, the book version of *A brasileira de Prazins* really came out in January of 1883. The work is another story of impossible love, narrated by a sensible priest, a frequent figure in the author's work. The story is interlaced with episodes of civil war and the appearance in Minho of a false King Miguel. *A brasileira de Prazins* does not use realist techniques, but it does rely on determinism to explain some of the characters' behavior. The work includes detailed annotations, straightforward drama, irony, humor, and the author's usual means of relating to his public, with the explicit and skeptical conclusion that the work does not aspire to social reform. It is, perhaps, an example of a work that conforms to the public's preferences while resisting any realist ideology.

Chardron also published the polemic called "Questão da Sebenta" (The Filthy One's Question), a series of articles initiated by a professor from Coimbra who accused Castelo Branco of being mercenary. The author's biography of the Portuguese gentleman *D. Luís de Portugal neto do Prior do Crato* (Dom Luís de Portugal, Grandson of the Prior of Crato), commissioned by his new publisher, Eduardo da Costa Santos, came out when he was breaking his ties with Chardron. In a 3 September 1883 letter to Luís Augusto Palmeirim, Castelo Branco attributed this break to the fact that Chardron had asked him to produce "really spicy realist novels."

Castelo Branco's problems continued to abound: his medical ailments and his eyesight continued to worsen, and his precarious financial situation forced him not only to sell another large portion of his personal library in 1883, some two thousand volumes, but also to continue his prior attempts to sell some of his historical studies on the House of Bragança to the government. The only two books to come out in 1884 were *O vinho do Porto: Processo de uma bestialidade inglesa* (The Port Wine: A Process of English Brutality) and *O general Carlos Ribeiro: Recordações da mocidade* (General Carlos Ribeiro: Memories of Youth). The first one, a combination of historical and memorialist narrative, caused new controversies with young naturalist writers. The second, a biography dedicated to Tomás Ribeiro, initiated the polemic surrounding Castelo Branco's pretensions of nobility. Some interpreted his gift to the king of a copy of the work as an act of submission. Despite his scant novelistic production, Castelo Branco was still considered to be the most important writer at the time, followed by Manuel Joaquim Pinheiro Chagas, proof of which is the relatively reliable literary survey taken by the journal *Imparcial de Coimbra* (Coimbra's Impartial).

On 18 June 1885 Castelo Branco was finally named viscount of Correia Botelho. By then he was publishing even less than before. That year he published the study *Maria da Fonte: A propósito dos apontamentos para a História da Revolução do Minho em 1846* (Maria da Fonte: With Regard to the Notes for the History of the Revolution of Minho in 1846). Between then and the following year his next work published was *Serões de S. Miguel de Ceide* (The Soirées of São Miguel de Ceide, 1885–1886), newspaper serials dedicated to criticism and to cultural and social chronicles. The serial was discontinued, however, with the sixth installment. In 1886 *Boémia do espírito* (Bohemianism in Spirit) came out. This work is an extremely broad compilation of texts, some reworked to soften the author's criticism of the monarchy. However, Chardron's successors Lugan and Genelioux were the copyright owners of a great majority of these texts, and they ordered the confiscation of the edition. Finally, his so-called sensationalist novel *Vulcões de lama* (Volcanos of Mud) came out but did not attain the success he had expected. The work is a rural novel of passion set in times of civil war (the historical setting that Castelo Branco preferred). The work is realist in many aspects, and partly pessimistic, but with a romantic and sentimental ending.

Family and health problems hounded the author, and the idea of death, even of suicide (an already old idea), was becoming more present in his mind. In 1887 he did not publish any books and, by now almost blind, visited several doctors in search of a cure. He did publish, however, "Nota àprocissão dos moribundos" (Annotations about the Procession of the Dying) in *Novidades* (New Features), his retort to Queirós's prologue to the Count of Arnoso's *Azulejos* (1886) in which Queirós attacks but never mentions him directly. Queirós, however, avoided the polemic.

Castelo Branco married Plácido in 1888, perhaps fulfilling an obligation made when he obtained the title of viscount. He only published *Nostalgias: Ultima prosa rimada* (Nostalgias: Last Rhymed Prose), which he dedicated to João António de Freitas Fortuna, his chief financial protector during his last few years. Freitas Fortuna may have paid for the publication of the work. In 1889 students and intellectuals paid a tribute to Castelo Branco in Lisbon, organized by the well-known writer João de Deus. He also received a visit from the dethroned Pedro II of Brazil as well as an allowance from the government and the king for Jorge. He published more compilations but nothing new. In 1890 his book of sonnets, *Nas trevas* (In the Darkness), was printed by Tavares Cardoso and Irmão, after having been rejected by several publishers, perhaps because they considered it of inferior quality or feared it would not sell.

By the end of May 1890, Castelo Branco was completely blind. On 1 June the author received the visit of a prestigious doctor in whom he had placed his last hope of finding a cure for his illness. Finding that there was, however, no such remedy, Castelo Branco shot himself. His funeral and burial in Porto in the Freitas Fortuna family mausoleum was treated objectively in the press. Almost all of the Porto elite and the prestigious writers of the time were absent from the ceremony. The Chamber of Deputies passed a resolution of "profound sentiment" on the death of a "glory of our national literature" and closed as a sign of mourning. The author received no other major honors. Camilo Castelo Branco was one of the first professional writers in Portugal: his writing was his source of income. Several aspects of his career are of continuing interest to scholars and readers, especially the adventurous and romantic characters of his works. Although the works of Queirós, Garrett, and Herculano are considered to be of higher literary value, Castelo Branco occupies a privileged place in the Portuguese canon of the nineteenth century.

**Letters:**

*Correspondência epistolar entre José Cardoso Vieira de Castro e Camilo Castelo Branco: Escripta durante os dous ultimos annos da vida do illustre orador,* 2 volumes (Porto & Rio de Janeiro: Livr. Portugueza e Estrangeira, 1874);

*Cartas de Camilo Castelo Branco,* 2 volumes, edited by M. Cardoso Marta (Lisbon: H. Antunes, 1918–1923);

*Correspondência de Camilo Castelo Branco,* edited by Alexandre Cabral, 6 volumes (Lisbon: Livros Horizonte, 1984–1988).

**Biographies:**

José Cardoso Vieira de Castro, *Camilo Castelo Branco: Noticia da sua vida e obras* (Porto: J. da Silva Teixeira, 1863);

Alexandre Cabral, *Camilo Castelo Branco. Roteiro dramático dum profissional das letras* (Vila Nova de Famalicão: Centro de Estudos Camilianos, 1995).

**References:**

Abel Barros Baptista, *Camilo e a revolução camiliana* (Lisbon: Quetzal, 1988);

*Bibliotheca portucalensis: Colectânea de Estudos da Biblioteca Pública Municipal do Porto,* special Castelo Branco issue, no. 5 (1990);

Alexandre Cabral, *Dicionário de Camilo Castelo Branco* (Lisbon: Caminho, 1989);

Aníbal Pinto de Castro, *Tempo e leitor na novela camiliana* (São Miguel de Ceide: Casa de Camilo, 1976);

João Bigote Chorão, *Camilo: A obra e o homem* (Lisbon: Arcádia, 1979);

Jacinto do Prado Coelho, *Introdução ao estudo da novela camiliana* (Lisbon: Imprensa Nacional-Casa da Moeda, 2001);

*Colóquio/Letras,* special Castelo Branco issue, edited by David Mourão Ferreira, 119 (1991);

Comissão Nacional das Comemorações Camilianas, *Congresso Internacional de Estudos Camilianos (24–29 de Junho de 1991). Actas* (Coimbra: Universidade de Coimbra, 1994);

João de Araújo Correia, *Uma sombra picada das bexigas* (Porto: Inova, 1973);

Ángel Marcos de Dios, ed., *Camilo Castelo Branco. Perspectivas. Actas de las Jornadas Internacionales sobre Camilo* (Salamanca: Universidad de Salamanca, 1991);

Maria de Lourdes A. Ferraz, ed., *Dicionário de personagens da novela Camiliana* (Lisbon: Caminho, 2002);

Ferraz, ed., *In Memoriam. Camilo. Centenário da morte* (Porto: Comissão Nacional das Comemorações Camilianas, 1992);

Francisco Martins, *Camilo quando jovem escritor* (Porto: Afrontamento, 1990);

*Prelo,* special Castelo Branco issue, edited by Diogo Pires Aurélio, no. 18 (1990);

Aquilino Ribeiro, *O romance de Camilo,* 3 volumes (Lisbon: Bertrand, 1961);

Ribeiro, ed., *Camiliana & vária: Revista enciclopédica do círculo camiliano* (Lisbon: Impr. Portugal-Brasil, 1951–1954);

João Camilo dos Santos, ed., *Camilo Castelo Branco no centenário da morte. Colloquium of Santa Barbara. Proceedings of the Camilo Castelo Branco International Colloquium* (Santa Barbara: Center for Portuguese Studies, 1995);

Maria de Lourdes Costa Lima dos Santos, *Intelectuais portugueses na primeira metade de oitocentos* (Lisbon: Presença, 1988).

**Papers:**

Archives of Camilo Castelo Branco's papers are held at the Casa-Museu de Camilo and the Centro de Estudos Camilianos in São Miguel de Ceide. The Houghton Library at Harvard University also has a collection of Castelo Branco's correspondence with Joaquim Ferreira Moutinho.

# Júlio Dinis
# (Joaquim Guilherme Gomes Coelho)
*(14 November 1839 – 12 September 1871)*

Paulo Motta Oliveira
*Universidade de São Paulo*

BOOKS: *As pupilas do senhor reitor: Crônica da aldeia* (Porto: Typografia do Jornal do Porto, 1867);

*Uma família inglesa: Cenas da vida do Porto* (Porto: Tipografia do Jornal do Porto, 1868);

*A morgadinha dos canaviais: Crônica da aldeia* (Porto: Tipografia do Jornal do Porto, 1868);

*Serões da província* (Porto: Viúva More, 1870);

*Os fidalgos da Casa Mourisca: Crônica da aldeia*, 2 volumes (Porto: Tipografia do Jornal do Porto, 1871); translated by Roxana L. Dabney as *The Fidalgos of Casa Mourisca* (Boston: Lothrop, 1891);

*Poesias* (Porto: Tipografia do Jornal do Porto, 1874);

*Inéditos e esparsos,* edited by Sousa Viterbo (Lisbon: Tipografia a Editora, 1910);

*Teatro inédito,* 3 volumes, edited by Egas Moniz (Porto: Civilização, 1946–1947);

*Cartas e esboços literários,* edited by Moniz (Porto: Civilização, 1947);

*Serões da província, 2o. Volume,* edited by Moniz (Porto: Civilização, 1947);

*Obras de Júlio Dinis* (Porto: Lello & Irmão, n.d.).

PLAY PRODUCTIONS: *Bolo quente,* 1856;
*O casamento da condessa de Vilar Maior,* 1856;
*O último baile do Dr. José da Cunha,* 1857;
*Os anéis ou inconvenientes de amar às escuras,* 1857;
*As duas cartas,* 1857;
*Um rei popular,* 1857;
*Similia similibus,* 1858;
*Um segredo de família,* 1860;
*A educanda de Odivelas,* 1860.

*Júlio Dinis (Joaquim Guilherme Gomes Coelho), circa 1865 (from João Gaspar Simões,* Júlio Dinis: A obra e o homem, *1963; Daniel Library, The Citadel)*

Júlio Dinis is the most important pseudonym of Joaquim Guilherme Gomes Coelho. He wrote under other pseudonyms (for example, Diana de Avelada) in some newspapers, and for a short period of time he signed his literary works with his own surname, Gomes Coelho. Dinis's works constitute an important bridge between the movements of Romanticism and realism in Portuguese literature: his novels have Romantic characteristics yet, at the same time, show a critical attitude typical of realism. His works portray a society in transition and explain the impact that the liberal revolution of 1820, the civil war, and the political instability that ended in the 1850s had on life in the small villages in the north of Portugal. The plots of his narratives generally end with the marriage of important characters from different social classes and backgrounds, which may be seen as a metaphor of a country in search of an ideal middle ground where tensions between these groups do not exist. Although Dinis's point of view was optimistic for the reality of his day, his novels present a detailed look at a society in crisis and change.

Gomes Coelho was born in Porto on 14 November 1839 to José Joaquim Gomes Coelho, a doctor, and Ana Constança Potter Pereira Lopes. His mother died of tuberculosis when he was six. In 1855 he lost his two older brothers to the same disease.

Gomes Coelho began his undergraduate studies at the Academia Politécnica do Porto (Porto Polytechnic Academy) in 1853. From 1855 to 1861 he attended the Escola Médico-Cirúrgia (College of Surgery) in Porto, from which he graduated after defending his thesis, "A importância dos estudos metereológicos para a medicina" (The Importance of Meteorological Studies for Medicine).

Gomes Coelho began his literary career while he was still a medical student in 1856 with the plays *Bolo quente* (Hot Cake) and *O casamento da condessa de Vilar Maior* (The Wedding of the Countess of Vila Maior). He wrote two other theatrical works the following year: *O último baile do Dr. José da Cunha* (Dr. José Cunha's Last Ball) and *As duas cartas* (Two Letters). Some critics date the play *Os anéis ou inconvenientes de amar às escuras* (The Rings or the Inconveniences of Love in the Dark) as 1857, the year he wrote the two-act comedy *Um rei popular* (A Popular King); others believe that it dates from 1858, the year he wrote his first short story, "Justiça de sua majestade" (His Majesty's Justice). He probably began to write the novel *Uma família inglesa: Cenas da vida do Porto* (An English Family: Scenes from Life in Porto, 1868) during the same year. In 1860 he published his first poems—"A.J.," "Aparências" (Appearances), and "O despertar da virgem" (The Virgin's Awakening)—in the newspaper *A Grinalda* (The Wreath), using for the first time the pseudonym Júlio Dinis; why he decided to use this or any of his pseudonyms is unknown. He wrote two more plays in 1860: *Um segredo de família* (A Family Secret) and *A educanda de Odivelas* (Odivelas's Pupil).

In 1862 the newspaper *Jornal do Porto* published the short stories "Apreensões de uma mãe" (Concerns of a Mother) and "O espólio do Senhor Cipriano" (Estate of Mr. Cipriano). That same year *A Grinalda* published his poems "A Noiva" (The Bride) and "Thereza." Another short story, "Os novelos da tia Filomena" (Aunt Filomena's Skeins), appeared in the *Jornal do Porto* in 1863, and in that year Dinis wrote his first two articles using the pseudonym Diana de Avelada. The articles, both under the title "Coisas verdadeiras. Ao folhetinista do *Jornal do Porto*" (True Things. To the Feuilleton Writer of the *Porto Newspaper*), were a review of a piece written by Ramalho Ortigão. Dinis also used this feminine pseudonym for a letter published in 1863 in the *Jornal do Porto* and for three articles, all titled "Impressões do campo–À Cecilia" (Impressions from the Countryside–To Cecília), published in 1864 and 1865 in the same newspaper. During 1864 the writer signed some works with his surname, Gomes Coelho. These works include the short novel *Uma flor dentre o gelo* (A Flower Amidst the Ice), published in serialized form in *Jornal do Porto* from November to December, and the poems "A intercessão da virgem" (The Virgin Mary's Help), "No altar da pátria" (On the Nation's Altar), and "A despedida da ama" (The Nursemaid's Farewell).

After some unsuccessful attempts, Dinis became a professor at the Escola Médico-Cirúrgia in 1865. He probably never really wanted to pursue a medical or teaching career. In 1867 he became the secretary and librarian of the Escola Médico Cirúrgica, which provided him a higher income than teaching at the medical school had. He published his first novel, *As pupilas do senhor reitor: Crônica da aldeia* (The Rector's Pupils: Village Chronicle), in serialized form in the *Jornal do Porto* from May to June 1866. Two subsequent novels were also serialized there before appearing in book form. *Uma família de ingleses* (A Family of English People; the title was changed to *Uma família inglesa* when the work was published as a book) ran from March to May 1867, and *A morgadinha dos canaviais* (The Young Madam of the Sugarcane Field), the last novel published during the author's lifetime, appeared from April to July 1868. The first of these novels appeared in book format in 1867, the other two in 1868. In 1870 Dinis published *Serões da província* (Gatherings in the Countryside), which included some of the short stories that had already appeared in the *Jornal do Porto*. *Os fidalgos da Casa Mourisca* (1871; translated as *The Fidalgos of Casa Mourisca*, 1891) was the first novel he wrote not to be published first in serialized form. The book appeared only after his death, however, and he died before revising all the proofs.

Dinis's popularity and importance in nineteenth-century Portuguese literature rest mainly on his novels. Three of these take place in small towns or rural settings; the only exception, *Uma família inglesa*, is set in Porto, a city that was not as urbanized as Lisbon. The Portuguese novel with a predominant rural background has its antecedents in Alexandre Herculano's short story "Pároco de Aldeia" (The Prior of the Village, 1843) and in Rodrigo Paganinos's *Os contos de tio Joaquim* (Uncle Joaquim's Stories, 1861). These works, however, do not possess the quality and importance of Dinis's four novels that were published from 1866 to

*Dinis's home in Ovar, where he began writing* As pupilas do senhor reitor *(The Rector's Pupils, 1867), his first novel (from João Gaspar Simões,* Júlio Dinis: A obra e o homem, *1963; Daniel Library, The Citadel)*

1871, a period chronologically situated between the Romantic and the realistic movements in Portugal. Almeida Garrett had died in 1854, more than ten years before Dinis's first novel appeared in print, and Herculano, the other key figure of the first generation of Romantic writers, had already published his novels and short stories in that period. *O monge de Cister* (The Monk of Cister), his last novel, was published in 1848 and *Lendas e narrativas* (Legends and Narratives) in 1851. The most important author writing in the period, Camilo Castelo Branco, had by that time published his most impressive work, the novel *Amor de perdição* (Doomed Love), which was released in 1862. He continued writing until his death in 1890, but the central place in Portuguese literature was quickly occupied by the realist writers of the so-called Generation of the 1870s, a prestigious group of intellectuals that included Antero de Quental, Eça de Queirós, Oliveira Martins, Teófilo Braga, and Guerra Junqueiro. In fact, *Os fidalgos da Casa Mourisca* appeared in the same year as the journal *As Farpas* (The Barbs) and the Conferências Democráticas do Casino Lisbonense (Democratic Conferences of the Lisbon Casino), which were intended to provoke the general population to participate in discussions that would contribute to reforms in Portuguese society. As a product of the period between two major literary movements, Dinis's novels constitute important examples of the changes Portuguese prose was undergoing throughout the 1860s.

All of Dinis's novels are constructed around a love affair. In each work there is at least one pair of characters involved in a difficult sentimental relationship. The difficulty stems from their contrasting social classes; but these conflicts are resolved in a happy ending. The important relationships in the novels include Daniel and Margarida in *As pupilas do senhor reitor;* Carlos and Cecília in *Uma família inglesa;* Henrique and Cristina and Madalena and Augusto in *A morgadinha dos canaviais;* and Jorge and Berta in *Os fidalgos da Casa Mourisca.* These couples represent, in one way or another, a happy solution not only to a sentimental affair but also to a social conflict, as new contracts are established between people of different classes or cultural backgrounds. The marriages symbolize the victory of a new social order in the fight against prejudice and sometimes against a traditional and anachronistic sense of honor. Carlos and Cecília, for instance, represent a possible union of a boss and a worker; Jorge and

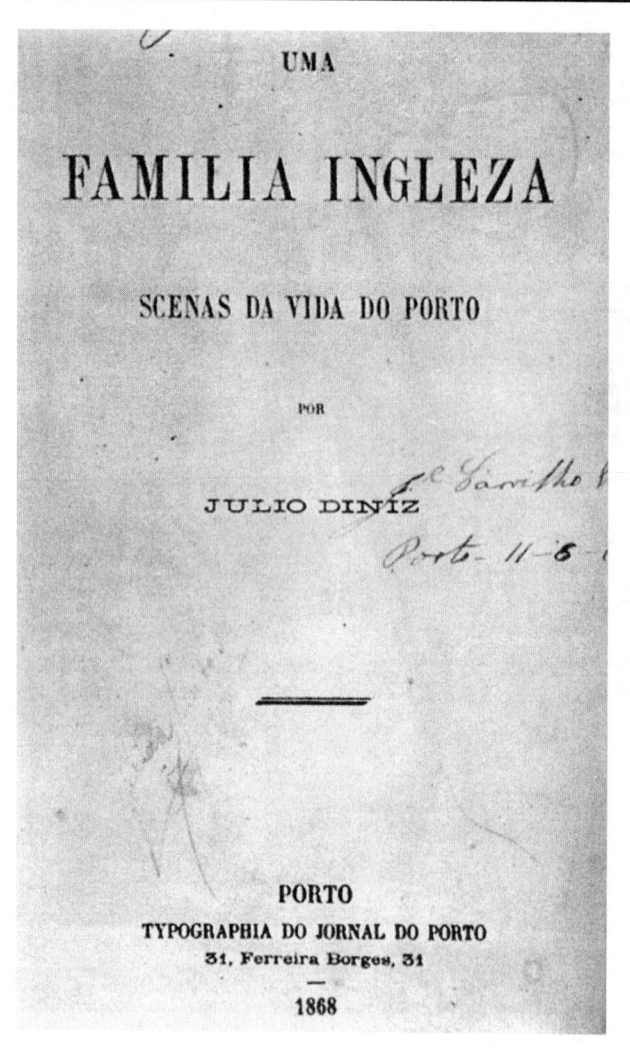

*Title page for Dinis's second novel, set in Porto (from João Gaspar Simões,* Julio Dinis: A obra e o homem, *1963; Daniel Library, The Citadel)*

Berta, the linking of aristocracy and the new bourgeoisie; Madalena and Augusto, the coming together of a rich landowner and a rural intellectual; and Henrique and Cristina, the union of two different cultural and educational backgrounds. This last situation is almost the same as that of Margarida and Daniel; in both cases, the men represent urban values (Lisbon or Coimbra), while the women represent healthy rural principles. The happy endings, the slow rhythms of the plots, the absence of significant events or adventures, and the sense of integrity and rectitude that wins out in the stories create similarities between Dinis's works and those of other nineteenth-century novelists such as Charles Dickens and George Eliot.

Dinis's fictional works create a world in which social reality plays a significant role not limited to the main characters or to their amorous relationships. There is also a link established between love and the social environment in his novels, which is handled with remarkable skill in *A morgadinha dos canaviais*. In this work, the author mixes fictional events with certain ideological issues and historical facts of the period. In terms of ideology, the author portrays the opposition between the urban and the rural; the city is seen as an unhealthy environment while country life is seen as embodying all that is good and healthy in life. The character Henrique, who undergoes a major transformation when he leaves the city for the countryside, is a good example of this opposition. He is a hypochondriac city dweller in the beginning of the story; by the end, however, he has become a man working his own land and has married a gentlewoman from the region. In many aspects, Henrique's development is similar to that of the character Jacinto, who appears in two works by Queirós: the short story "Civilização" (Civilization; first published in a Brazilian newspaper in 1892) and the novel *A cidade e a serra* (The City and the Hills, 1901). There is a striking similarity between the first chapter of Dinis's book and the scenes that involve Jacinto's arrival in Torges in the short story and in Tormes in the novel. This similarity shows that Dinis prefigures some characteristics that emerged at the end of the century.

The character Ermelinda, who constitutes the inverse to Henrique's development in the plot, goes from happiness to disgrace. Her story supports another ideological issue treated in the novel: the pernicious influence of religion on the poor and less educated of the population. Ermelinda, seen first as a happy teenager, discovers her love for her childhood friend Ângelo. The influence of the priest Father Domingos, however, turns her into an ill and unhappy person who dies a slow, torturous death. As a victim of his control, she becomes obsessed with the notions of sin and divine punishment. There are interesting parallels between this vivid story and the most important of the Conferências, "As causas da decadência dos povos peninsulares nos últimos três séculos" (The Causes of the Decadence of Peninsular Peoples of the Last Three Centuries), in which Quental attributes the apathy of nineteenth-century Spain and Portugal to the negative influence of the Church. It is also possible to see Father Domingos as a precursor of Queirós's protagonist in *O crime do Padre Amaro* (The Sin of Father Amaro), which was first published in the magazine *Revista Ocidental* from February to May 1875. Queirós's work portrays the extremely destructive power of the Church in the small Portuguese city of Leiria. The importance of Dinis's novels in the change of the paradigm of the Romantic narrative may be noted in a comparison between Father Domingos, Father Amaro, and the priests of Castelo Branco's works. Dinis's priest is more similar to Father Amaro than to the figure of the sometimes silly, sometimes guilty, gentle priest of Castelo Branco's narratives. Father Amaro, however, is more immoral and cynical than Father Domingos. On the other hand, Dinis's priest in *As pupilas do senhor reitor,* with his kindness and his sense of justice, resembles some of Castelo Branco's religious figures.

Dinis adds a realistic dimension to his novels as he incorporates important historical facts of nineteenth-century Portugal into the fictional world of the text. In *A morgadinha dos canaviais,* for example, the author uses the death of Ermelinda to show the popular reaction against the prohibition of the burial of corpses inside the churches. This issue had provoked the famous 1846 revolt of Maria da Fonte, one of the most important popular riots in Portugal in the nineteenth century. Dinis touches on the imperfections of the electoral system, showing the dishonest practices of politicians in their bid for power and the lack of knowledge of the less educated about their electoral choices. The work also explores the question of the destructive impact of material progress on the rural areas of the nation, symbolized in the book especially by the construction of a new road. The road not only modifies the physical and human geography of those areas but also has a harmful impact on individual characters such as Vicente, who dies after seeing his home destroyed because it was in the way of the new road. Dinis interweaves these actual events into the plots of his novels, establishing strong links between his work and that of the realist writers of the 1870s. *A morgadinha dos canaviais,* however, also clearly establishes his relationship to the Romantic writers.

Some of the most important similarities between Dinis and the Romantic writers, especially Castelo Branco, are the frequent commentaries and digressions of the narrative voice. In *A morgadinha dos canaviais,* as in other Dinis novels, the narrator often interrupts the development of the plot to comment on subjects such as the political and social system, comparisons between a Portuguese and a Spanish nativity scene, and the courage a timid woman has when her true love needs her help. Dinis's narrator, unlike the narrator in realist works, does not pretend to be impartial. This type of narration, and the great importance of love in Dinis's novels, show the relationship between the author and Romantic literature. All of these characteristics reveal the importance that the analysis of Dinis's novels has to a better understanding of the multiple strategies that are represented in nineteenth-century Portuguese literature.

The author's other works are significant, but they did not achieve the same importance as the novels. His short stories, compiled in *Serões da província,* are interesting mainly because of their use of irony to show the discrepancies of the narrative voice. Dinis died of tuberculosis on 12 September 1871. Other posthumous works include *Poesias* (Poems, 1874) and *Inéditos e esparsos* (Unpublished and Other Pieces, 1910), which includes interesting excerpts of Dinis's ideas about literature and the process of literary creation; in these fragments he reveals his own strategies for writing novels, plays, and stories. *Teatro inédito* (Unpublished Theater, 1946–1947) includes seven plays. His four novels, however, are what guarantee Dinis's place in the canon of Portuguese literature.

**References:**

Alexandre Cabral, *Dicionário de Camilo Castelo Branco* (Lisbon: Caminho, 1989);

Fidelino Figueiredo, *História da literatura romântica* (São Paulo: Anchieta, 1946);

José Augusto França, "Júlio Dinis ou cinco anos de felicidade," in his *O romantismo em Portugal: Estudo de factos socioculturais* (Lisbon: Horizontes, 1993), pp. 425–434;

Maria Lívia Diana de Araújo Marchon, *A arte de contar em Júlio Dinis: Alguns aspectos de sua técnica narrativa* (Coimbra: Almedina, 1980);

A. H. de Oliveira Marques, *História de Portugal* (Lisbon: Caminho, 1989);

A. Campos Matos, *Dicionário de Eça de Queiroz* (Lisbon: Caminho, 1988);

Egas Moniz, *Júlio Dinis e a sua obra* (Porto: Civilização, 1946);

António José de Saraiva and Óscar Lopes, *História da literatura portuguesa* (Porto: Porto Editora, 1982);

João Gaspar Simões, *Júlio Dinis: A obra e o homem* (Lisbon: Editora Arcádia, 1963).

**Papers:**

Some of Júlio Dinis's papers are at the Casa-Museu Júlio Dinis (Museum House of Júlio Dinis) in Ovar, Portugal.

# Florbela Espanca

*(8 December 1894 – 8 December 1930)*

Anna Klobucka
*University of Massachusetts Dartmouth*

BOOKS: *Livro de mágoas* (Lisbon: Tip. Maurício, 1919);
*Livro de Soror Saudade* (Lisbon: Privately printed, 1923);
*Charneca em flor* (Coimbra: Livraria Gonçalves, 1931; second edition, expanded, 1931);
*Cartas,* edited by Guido Battelli (Coimbra: Livraria Gonçalves, 1931);
*Juvenília,* edited by Battelli (Coimbra: Livraria Gonçalves, 1931);
*As máscaras do destino* (Porto: Maranus, 1931);
*Cartas,* edited by Azinhal Abelho and José Emídio Amaro (Lisbon, 1952?);
*Diário do último ano* (Amadora: Bertrand, 1981);
*O dominó preto* (Amadora: Bertrand, 1982);
*Obras completas,* 6 volumes, edited by Rui Guedes (Lisbon: Dom Quixote, 1985–1986)—comprises volume 1, *Poesia, 1903–1917;* volume 2, *Poesia, 1918–1930;* volume 3, *Contos;* volume 4, *Contos e diário;* volume 5, *Cartas, 1906–1922;* and volume 6, *Cartas, 1923–1930;*
*Trocando olhares,* edited by Maria Lúcia Dal Farra (Lisbon: Imprensa Nacional–Casa da Moeda, 1994).

**Editions and Collections:** *Sonetos completos* (Coimbra: Livraria Gonçalves, 1934);
*Antologia de poesia,* edited by Fernando Pinto do Amaral (Lisbon: Dom Quixote, 2003).

*Florbela Espanca, 1925 (from Agustina Bessa-Luís,*
Florbela Espanca, *1984; Thomas Cooper Library, University of South Carolina)*

Unlike some western European countries, most notably England and France, Portugal had extremely few prominent women writers prior to the twentieth century. Although in her lifetime Florbela Espanca received relatively little public and critical recognition, she is now recognized as a major author, the first Portuguese woman poet to have achieved this status. She is not only a significant figure in her own right but also an important precursor to the flourishing literary production by women writers in contemporary Portugal.

Florbela d'Alma da Conceição Espanca was born out of wedlock on 8 December 1894 in Vila Viçosa in the province of Alentejo. Her father, João Maria Espanca, was an avid photographer who in 1887 had opened his own shop, the Photo Calypolense, in addition to various business dealings. He later became one of the pioneering distributors of cinematography in Portugal. Her mother, Antónia da Conceição Lobo, was an orphan and a servant. The fifteen-year-old Lobo's pregnancy and the birth of her daughter appear to have occurred with full cognizance of João Espanca's wife, Mariana do Carmo Inglesa Espanca, who was unable to have any children of her own. By mutual arrangement, the newborn Florbela was taken into her father's house, where she was cared for by both her biological mother and Mariana Espanca. Nevertheless, she was baptized on 20 June 1895 as Flor Bela Lobo, a natural daughter of Antónia Lobo and an unknown father. Although in all practical respects João Espanca acted as Florbela's father throughout her life, he never formally adopted her as his legitimate child.

In 1903, at the age of eight, Espanca wrote her first known poem, ambitiously titled "A vida e a morte" (Life and Death). Her second known poem, written the next day, follows the same metrical pattern (seven-syllable *redondilha,* the most common meter of Portuguese popular verse), but it takes on the strophic shape of a sonnet. This lyric form, which Espanca went on to cultivate almost exclusively, eventually brought her the greatest renown. Not until around 1915, however, did she begin to write maturely and prolifically. In the meantime, she completed several more years of formal education, enrolling in 1908 in the Liceu André de Gouveia in Évora as one of the first female students at that traditionally male school. Earlier the same year, Espanca's natural mother died at the age of twenty-nine; in 1897 she had given birth to João Espanca's second child, Florbela's beloved brother, Apeles (also baptized as the son of an unknown father). Antónia Lobo's cause of death was officially recorded as "neurosis"; Espanca later came to regard her mother's condition as a prefiguration of her own multiple ailments and mysterious afflictions.

In 1913, having failed the final exam for the academic year ending in June, Espanca dropped out of school. Six months later, on 8 December (the day she turned nineteen), she married Alberto Moutinho, her longtime friend and schoolmate. The newlyweds moved to Redondo, halfway between Évora and Vila Viçosa, where they started a school. Moutinho became its science teacher, while Espanca taught French, English, geography, and history. Economic difficulties, however, forced them to move back to Évora in September 1915, where they took up residence in the house of Espanca's father and continued to work as teachers.

While living in Redondo and in Évora, probably around May 1915, Espanca began to write poetry in a steady and systematic manner. By early 1916 she had enough material to contemplate composing a book of poems. *Trocando olhares* (Exchanging Glances) was the name she gave to the notebook in which, over a year and a half, she came to assemble copies of 145 poems and 3 short stories. First published in the 1985–1986 edition of Espanca's *Obras completas* (Complete Works) and republished in a thoroughly revised edition by Maria Lúcia Dal Farra in 1994, *Trocando olhares* offers important insights into the writer's artistic growth and maturation, as well as into her creative struggle with exclusionary patterns of the male-identified poetic tradition that she was attempting to make her own. In the sonnet "Errante" (Wandering) the speaker appears as a mother lamenting the departure of a wayward son, who is none other than her own personified heart, longing to be "um santo e um poeta" (a saint and a poet). Striking textual similarities suggest that the poem is a rewriting, from a female perspective, of a well-known sonnet by the nineteenth-century poet Antero de Quental, "O palácio da ventura" (The Palace of Fortune, 1862–1866). In "A Anto" (To Anto) Espanca's lyric "I" addresses António Nobre, arguably the most influential among her acknowledged literary idols, called her "mythical double" by the critic José Carlos Seabra Pereira in his introductory essays for the 1985–1986 *Obras completas*. The poem—on the surface an unqualified tribute to "Anto"—documents a dynamic transformation of a reader (of Nobre's poetry) into a writer (of her own) and performs a subtle reversal of literary genealogies, with Nobre's poetic "daughter" metaphorically assuming the identity of his grieving mother.

In January 1916 Espanca wrote to Mme. Carvalho, the editor of the supplement *Modas e Bordados* (Fashion and Needlework), published in conjunction with the Lisbon daily *O Século*. The supplement, published since 1912, was directed at female readers and offered, in addition to reports on current fashion and customary beauty advice, more unusual and significant fare: literary pieces by aspiring women writers, along with suggestions for improvement of poetic diction for those readers whose submissions failed to reach the editors' standards. On 22 March 1916 *Modas e Bordados* published Espanca's "Crisântemos" (Chrysanthemums), her first composition to appear in print, albeit marred by arbitrarily introduced modifications and typographical errors. In the course of 1916 four more of Espanca's poems were accepted for publication in *Modas e Bordados*. By the summer of that year, however, Espanca gained enough confidence to start sending her poems to other publishing venues, particularly two regional newspapers, *Notícias de Évora* (Évora News) and *A Voz Pública* (The Public Voice), which in the period from July to September 1916 published twenty-five of her compositions (including "A Anto").

The advice and support Espanca received from Carvalho, in the course of her correspondence with *Modas e Bordados,* were important incentives in her artistic development. One of Carvalho's suggestions was that Espanca should not write under a pseudonym, a common practice at the time among the female contributors to the magazine. As the journalist put it in a letter to Espanca (19 April 1916), "Se quer vir a prezar o seu

*Espanca and her brother, Apeles (from Espanca,* Sonetos, *1978; Thomas Cooper Library, University of South Carolina)*

nome literário e se tem consciência da originalidade das suas produções poéticas não deve tomar agora um pseudónimo" (if you wish to be able to come to value your literary name, and if you are conscious of the originality of your poems, you should not adopt a pseudonym now). Another crucial consequence of that (relatively short-lived) relationship was Espanca's epistolary friendship with Júlia Alves, the associate editor of *Modas e Bordados,* who first wrote to the poet in June 1916 in connection with a new magazine Alves was hoping to start. The twenty-six extant letters written by Espanca to Alves between June 1916 and April 1917 (published in a book by Carlos Sombrio in 1948) are a rich source of information regarding the formative period of her literary career. They offer reflections on life and literature, record Espanca's readings and her poetic projects, and comment on the situation of women in early-twentieth-century Portugal.

Toward the end of 1916, clearly a watershed year for Espanca with regard to her development as a writer, she resolved to complete her secondary education, with the ultimate goal of moving to Lisbon and enrolling at the university. In July 1917 she graduated from the Liceu de Évora, and three months later she was able to enroll at the Universidade de Lisboa. There she chose to study law, in spite of her earlier declarations to Alves that her desire was to become a student of literature. In the same year, Espanca's brother graduated from the Naval School with the rank of midshipman. Six months after she and her husband moved to Lisbon, Espanca suffered the first in a series of miscarriages. She temporarily interrupted her studies and left the capital for the southern region of Algarve in order to recover. She continued, however, to write poetry and to explore the opportunities for the publication of a volume of sonnets. She contacted Raul Proença, a well-known writer who was a brother of one of her father's friends and who had earlier (in 1916) offered an encouraging, if somewhat condescending, assessment of the poetry submitted to his attention by "Mr. Espanca's daughter," as he referred to her in a letter to his brother Luís, who had transmitted the poems to Proença. This time Proença proved to be less forthcoming; of the thirty-five sonnets Espanca had sent him, he judged none to be good, although he also described some as "absolutely reasonable." Attempting to secure a more positive response, the poet followed with two more sonnets, "Mais triste" (Sadder) and "Castelã" (Chatelaine), later published in her first volume, *Livro de mágoas* (Book of Sorrows, 1919), which suggests that the poems sent to Proença coincided, in the main, with the thirty-two compositions assembled in that collection.

In September 1918 Espanca returned alone to Lisbon, leaving her husband behind in Algarve. She resumed her study of law at the second-year level, which she was able to do owing to the liberal higher-education reform of 1911. Students were not required to pass any exams in order to advance through the curriculum, and many chose to postpone their examinations until the final year. According to various contemporary reports, Espanca was a less than assiduous student of law but participated with great enthusiasm in informal discussions with her classmates. She appears to have been the only female participant in these gatherings, which is not surprising given the fact that there were only 7 women among the 313 students enrolled at the School of Law of the Universidade de Lisboa in the academic year 1917–1918. Espanca's discussions with her colleagues and her familiarity with their poetry echo from the pages of *Livro de mágoas,* which she was finally able to publish, with Proença's support, in June 1919. At least three of Espanca's male friends (Américo Durão, João Boto de Carvalho, and Vasco Camélier) wrote poems dedicated to her, and Espanca's lyric self-portrait in *Livro de mágoas* is replicated in their idealizing vision of her as a tragic and misunderstood superior being, variously imagined as a remote princess or a cloistered nun. As scholar Cláudia Pazos Alonso commented in a 1995 article, it is difficult to determine whether Espanca's elaborate self-fashioning should be read "as a cause or as a consequence" of the poetic vision that she inspired in her adoring colleagues. In any case, their intellectual and sentimental companionship was clearly an important formative experience for Espanca and one of the leading sources of inspiration for the sonnets of *Livro de mágoas*.

In keeping with its title, *Livro de mágoas* is a collection imbued with pessimism and desolation, which incorporates a varied repertoire of themes and images common to the symbolist and decadent poetry of the late nineteenth century. Suffering, darkness, and loneliness are its key motives. The word *Dor* (suffering, pain), almost always spelled with a capital D, appears in no fewer than eleven out of the thirty-two poems included in the volume. The forlorn atmosphere of the work acquires, however, a particular inflection that distinguishes it from its many counterparts on the contemporary Portuguese literary scene (unaffected, for the most part, by the modernist explosion of 1915). One of the dominant themes in the collection is metapoetic anxiety. Espanca's lyric "I" repeatedly questions her own ability to assume the exalted stature of the poet, who is imagined, in keeping with the Romantic tradition, as an extraordinarily gifted, god-like—and invariably male—creative individual. Espanca's poetic subject recurrently, if often indirectly, compares and contrasts herself with this "impossible" ideal. The final sonnet in *Livro de mágoas*, titled "Impossível" (Impossible), concludes with a statement of discursive impotence, as the speaker declares herself unable to articulate her suffering—in contrast, once again, to Nobre, whose pain "toda a gente ... sabe" (everyone knows) through his poems.

In the fall of 1919 Espanca registered for her third year at the Universidade de Lisboa, where she continued her lively social and intellectual interaction with her poetically inclined classmates. In late December, Durão, her closest and most influential interlocutor within the group, published in the literary page of the newspaper *O Século* a sonnet in which he addressed Espanca, nicknaming her "Soror Saudade" (Sister Nostalgia). Together with Durão's poem, *O Século* printed Espanca's lyric response, titled "O meu nome" (My Name) and dedicated to Durão. "O meu nome" (the title of which the author later changed to "Soror Saudade") expressed Espanca's grateful acceptance of the "nome lindo" (beautiful name) bestowed on her by Durão; indeed, she later adopted it as the title of her second volume of poems, *Livro de Soror Saudade* (1923). This episode illustrates the way in which Espanca's penchant for dramatic self-mythification (in her 1981 introduction to Espanca's *Diário do último ano* [Diary of the Last Year] the poet and critic Natália Correia called her an "actriz do seu ser mítico" [actress of her mythic

*Espanca and her first husband, Alberto Moutinho, on their wedding day in 1913 (from Agustina Bessa-Luís, A vida e a obra de Florbela Espanca, 1979; Thomas Cooper Library, University of South Carolina)*

self]) was stimulated and reinforced, often in a problematic way, by the feats of artistic imagination that her personality inspired in her male literary companions.

In early 1920 Espanca met and fell in love with António Guimarães, a second lieutenant in the Guarda Nacional Republicana, who was stationed in Lisbon. She began sketching out a new book of poems around that time, with the working title of "Claustro das quimeras" (Cloister of Fancy), which later became *Livro de Soror Saudade*. It was dedicated to Guimarães, Espanca's "único amor de verdade, maior que todos os amores de quimera e ilusão que tão cedo passaram" (only true love, greater than all those loves, full of illusion and fancy, that disappeared so quickly). Although still legally married to Moutinho, Espanca joined Guimarães in July 1920 when he was transferred to a post in the Artillery Detachment of Porto, in the north of Portugal. Among other consequences, the move brought a definitive end to her university education, particularly given the fact that in her three years of course work she had not taken a single exam and therefore could not claim any formal credit for the courses she had attended. Since Guimarães's military superiors looked askance at his extramarital cohabitation with Espanca, she accelerated her divorce proceedings. The divorce between Espanca and Moutinho became final on 30 April 1921, and two months later, on 29 June, Espanca and Guimarães were married in Porto.

Espanca's second book of poems took another year to develop. She declared it complete in a letter to her brother on 10 March 1922, announcing also her determination to have it published in the fall. She rejected the original projected title, since another poet, Alfredo Pimenta, had published a similarly titled book, *Livro de quimeras* (Book of Fancy, 1922). Apeles Espanca provided a watercolor portrait of his sister for the cover; however, although the painting was completed, it was not used. It depicts a slender woman reclining on a chaise longue, looking away from the viewer and through an open window at a desert-like landscape with a single palm tree visible on the horizon (the painting belongs to the Biblioteca Pública of Évora and is reproduced on the cover of Alonso's 1997 study of Espanca's poetry). Also in March 1922, Espanca and her husband returned to Lisbon, where Guimarães was offered the post of a senior official in the Ministry of War. In spite of Espanca's eagerness to publish *Livro de Soror Saudade,* the volume did not appear until January 1923. Its publication was fostered by Francisco Laje, author of several plays and an actor in the Teatro Nacional.

While Espanca's first book of poems had not attracted the attention of reviewers, seven generally positive reviews of *Livro de Soror Saudade* were published between 19 January and 1 April 1923. One of the critics (writing in *Ilustração Portuguesa* on 10 February 1923) accused Espanca of imitating Virgínia Vitorino, the most popular Portuguese woman poet of the early 1920s. Vitorino's volume *Namorados* (Lovers), published in 1920, had become an unprecedented bestseller (though her work is now a footnote in Portuguese literary history). The critic Câmara Lima commented in *Correio da Manhã* (20 February 1923) on the contemporary proliferation of women authors in Portugal and criticized, in a parodic vein, the two common traits of their lyric production: they all wrote sonnets and they all wrote about love.

Like her many female contemporaries, Espanca almost exclusively wrote sonnets, and love remained her favorite theme throughout her literary life. Through writing about love, she developed in *Livro de Soror Saudade* what proved to be a winning formula for overcoming the disabling perception of her artistic inferiority that had still haunted *Livro de mágoas*. In Espanca's second volume, the troubling issue of intertextual relationships with (superior) male poets becomes intimately interwoven with amorous discourse. This combination is manifest from the opening pages: the two initial poems are dedicated, respectively, to Durão (the poet) and to A[ntónio] G[uimarães] (the lover). This structural arrangement was partly motivated by the change of the originally projected title to *Livro de Soror Saudade,* which made it desirable for the sonnet that explained the nickname (Espanca's response to Durão) to be placed at the beginning of the volume. It can also be attributed to the fact that the book was a fusion of two distinct manuscript notebooks, the "Claustro das quimeras" and its earlier, alternative version that opened with the sonnet "Livro do nosso amor" (Book of Our Love) dedicated to Guimarães. Whatever the reasons, however, the prefatory juxtaposition of the two sonnets established an implicit parallel between poetic composition and amorous involvement. In fact, the sonnet "O nosso livro" (Our Book) presents *Livro de Soror Saudade* as an organic outgrowth of the love uniting its two protagonists, a flower-like creation that springs directly from the lovers' joined bodies (thus displacing and questioning its intertextual indebtedness made explicit in the sonnet "Soror Saudade").

The often intense and sometimes playful intertwining of metapoetic commentary and amorous confession recurs throughout the volume. In the sonnet "Os versos que te fiz" (The Verses I Made for You) the speaker prides herself on having composed some exquisitely wrought verses for her beloved; she has, however, refrained from spelling them out since "a boca da mulher é sempre linda / Se dentro guarda um verso que não diz" (a woman's mouth is always lovely / When it contains a poem it does not utter). This ironic comment on the complicated relationship between female allure, creativity, and silence testifies to a sense of confidence, and even amused detachment, that Espanca had gradually acquired in her conflicted quest to define herself as a woman poet. This achievement manifests itself in the most explicit way at the end of the volume, where the last sonnet, "Exaltação" (Exaltation), establishes a striking counterpoint with "Impossível," the final poem of *Livro de mágoas*. The exuberantly sensuous lyric "I" of "Exaltação" boasts of the intensity of both her amorous desire and her cre-

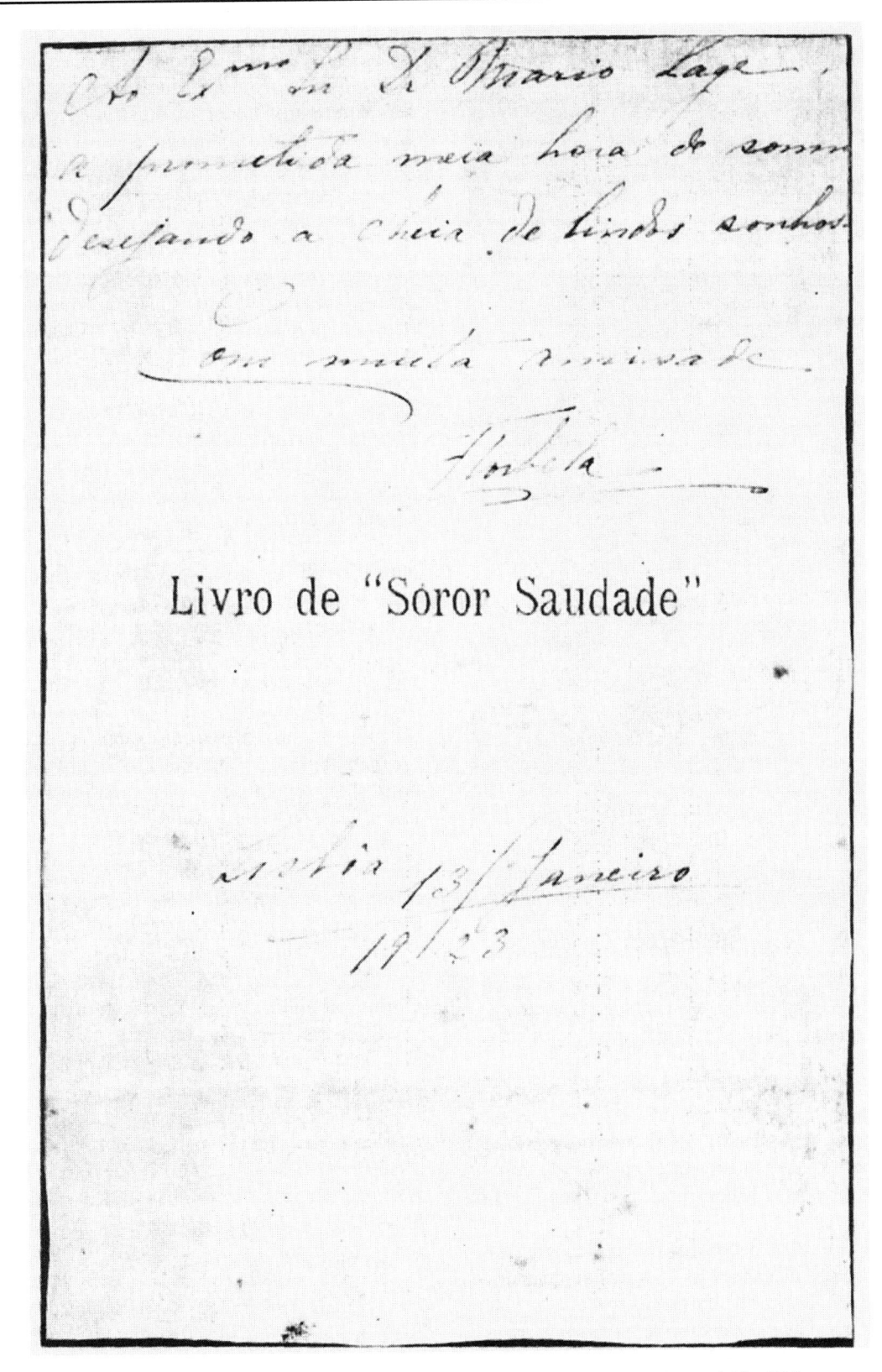

*Inscription in Espanca's second volume of poetry (1923) to Mário Lage, whom she married in 1925 (from Agustina Bessa-Luís, A vida e a obra de Florbela Espanca, 1979; Thomas Cooper Library, University of South Carolina)*

*One of the last photographs of Espanca before her suicide in 1930 (from Espanca,* Sonetos, *1978; Thomas Cooper Library, University of South Carolina)*

ative drive, describing herself, in the concluding verses, as a "Sister" to her male counterparts, "Boémios, vagabundos, e poetas" (bohemians, vagabonds, and poets).

In November 1923 Espanca suffered another miscarriage, officially diagnosed as "abortus syphiliticus," and left Lisbon for the countryside to recover. Her departure marked also the end of her second marriage. In the same month, Guimarães filed for divorce, citing effective separation and unspecified "grave injuries." The divorce became final in June 1925, and in October of the same year Espanca married Mário Lage, the physician who had treated her since 1921 and with whom she had been involved for some time. In June 1926 the couple moved to Matosinhos, Espanca's final residence in her lifetime. Although in a May 1927 letter to José Emídio Amaro (editor of the Vila Viçosa newspaper *Dom Nuno*) Espanca complained of not having written any poetry in a long while, she also indicated that she had in hand a new volume of sonnets, *Charneca em flor* (Flowering Heath, 1931). The title poem of the collection had already appeared in the third (and last) issue of the magazine *Europa,* directed by the freethinking, openly lesbian poet Judite Teixeira (while several others had been published in *Dom Nuno*). "Charneca em flor" is an explicit rejection of Espanca's earlier poetic persona, the melancholy Soror Saudade bestowed on her by Durão. The lyric "I" of the later sonnet slips out of her nun's habit and becomes one with the flowering, uncultivated heath of Espanca's native Alentejo. The entire volume, while continuing to gloss many of Espanca's earlier favorite themes, strikes a chord of intense vitality and sensuality, and the poet's staging of her lyric self is replete with images of unprecedented self-confidence and protomythic excess, as in the sonnet "Mais alto" (Higher Up), in which the speaker effectively performs her own apotheosis as an all-powerful, redemptive female divinity.

In the same 1927 letter to Amaro, Espanca also mentioned working on translations (of French novels for the publishing house Civilização in Porto) and on a book of her own prose. This project was most likely the first of her two collections of short stories, *As máscaras do destino* (Masks of Fate, 1931) and *O dominó preto* (Black Domino, 1982), neither of which she was able to publish in her lifetime. This intense activity was, however, interrupted by an accident: Espanca's brother, who had reached the rank of first lieutenant in the navy and was training to become a pilot, died in a seaplane crash. During the following months, Espanca, devastated by her brother's death, was unable to write. Nevertheless, in a letter to her father written in November 1929, she indicated having completed both *Charneca em flor* and *As máscaras do destino*. Since she was unable to find a commercial publisher and had no financial means to publish them herself, both volumes remained unpublished. Also, her deteriorating health and deepening depression likely had a negative impact on her desire to assert herself as an author.

In June 1930 Espanca began what soon became an abundant and intense correspondence with Guido Battelli, a professor of Italian literature at the Universidade de Coimbra. He admired her poems and had translated several of them into Italian. Battelli took it upon himself to publish *Charneca em flor*. Espanca's letters to Battelli, written in the last months of her life, describe her excitement at the proximity of the publication of this volume and her conviction that it included her best work to date.

The precise causes and nature of Espanca's worsening physical and psychological condition remain unclear. Surrounded by doctors, she was painfully thin and complained of insomnia and of shattered nerves. She attempted suicide twice before making the final attempt on her life (by an overdose of barbiturates) on 8 December 1930, the date of her thirty-sixth birthday. *Charneca em flor* appeared in early January 1931, less than a month after Espanca's death. In addition to the poems, it included an "In Memoriam" section composed of pieces by various authors (including two by Battelli), which projected a melodramatic image of Espanca as a great, misunderstood, and isolated poet who throughout her life had struggled to reach an unobtainable ideal and who ultimately had died for her art. In July 1931 Battelli published several more volumes of Espanca's poetry: a second edition of *Charneca em flor* augmented by a section of twenty-eight additional sonnets, titled *Reliquiae;* a new one-volume edition of *Livro de mágoas* and *Livro de Soror Saudade;* a volume of *Juvenília;* and a collection of Espanca's letters to Alves and to Battelli himself.

Although the poet's dramatic and untimely death, along with the flurry of publications that followed her demise, contributed to bringing her into the public spotlight and gained her a large and enthusiastic readership, critical recognition of the artistic value of her work was much slower in coming. The prominent writer and critic Jorge de Sena was the first, in a lecture given in 1946, to interpret seriously and favorably Espanca's insistence on making her female identity the centerpiece of her poetic world. In later decades, critics relying on feminist methods of interpretation traced the poet's formative trajectory and exposed complex and ingenious strategies of artistic emancipation that may be discerned in her poetry and other writings. While Espanca remains a perennial sentimental favorite of Portuguese (and Brazilian) readers of both sexes, her work has attracted a growing number of new critical readings, particularly since the 1990s, and she has been recognized as an important protagonist on the scene of early-twentieth-century Portuguese literature.

**References:**

José Augusto Alegria, *A poetisa Florbela Espanca: O processo de uma causa* (Évora: Centro de Estudos D. Manuel Mendes da Conceição Santos, 1956);

Maria Alexandrina, *A vida ignorada de Florbela Espanca* (Porto, 1964);

Cláudia Pazos Alonso, *Imagens do eu na poesia de Florbela Espanca* (Lisbon: Imprensa Nacional–Casa da Moeda, 1997);

Alonso, "'Tanto poeta em versos me cantou': The Role of Florbela Espanca's Colleagues in Her Poetic Development," *Portuguese Studies,* 11 (1995): 168–178;

Agustina Bessa-Luís, *A vida e a obra de Florbela Espanca* (Lisbon: Arcádia, 1979); republished as *Florbela Espanca* (Lisbon: Guimarães, 1984);

Aurélia Borges, *Florbela Espanca e a sua obra* (Lisbon: Edições Expansão, 1946);

Thomas J. Braga, "The Limbs of a Passion," *Hispania,* 73 (1990): 978–982;

Lúcia Castello Branco, "As incuráveis feridas da natureza feminina," in *A mulher escrita,* edited by Castello Branco and Ruth Silviano Brandão (Rio de Janeiro: Casa-Maria Editorial, 1989), pp. 87–109;

Narino de Campos, *A poesia, o drama e a glória de Florbela Espanca* (Lisbon, 1955);

Maria Tecla Portela Carreiro, *Florbela Espanca, quimera y saudade* (Madrid: Torremozas, 1991);

Maria Lúcia Dal Farra, "A condição feminina na obra de Florbela Espanca," *Estudos Portugueses e Africanos,* 5 (1985): 111–122;

Dal Farra, "Florbela, os sortilégios de um arquetipo," *Estudos Portugueses e Africanos,* 2 (1983): 53–66;

Dal Farra, "A interlocução de Florbela com a poética de Américo Durão," *Colóquio/Letras,* 132–133 (1994): 99–110;

Dal Farra, "A nascente poética de Florbela Espanca," *Estudos Portugueses e Africanos,* 17 (1991): 97–108;

António Freire, *O destino em Florbela* (Porto: Salesianas, 1977);

Rui Guedes, *Acerca de Florbela* (Lisbon: Dom Quixote, 1986);

Guedes, *Florbela Espanca: Fotobiografia* (Lisbon: Dom Quixote, 1985);

Renata Soares Junqueira, "O arquetipo do herói na poesia de Florbela Espanca," *Estudos Portugueses e Africanos,* 9 (1987): 27–41;

Junqueira, "O embasamento arquetípico da literatura florbeliana. Uma análise da poesia de Florbela Espanca à luz da psicologia analítica jungueana," *Estudos Portugueses e Africanos,* 7 (1986): 159–169;

Junqueira, "Florbela Espanca e . . . 'O Resto é Perfume,'" *Estudos Portugueses e Africanos,* 16 (1990): 27–37;

Anna Klobucka, "*On ne naît pas poétesse:* A aprendizagem literária de Florbela Espanca," *Luso-Brazilian Review,* 29 (1992): 51–61;

António da Costa Leão, *Poetas do sul: Bernardo de Passos e Florbela Espanca* (Lisbon: Portugália, 1947);

Oscar Lopes and others, eds., *A planície e o abismo: Actas do Congresso sobre Florbela Espanca realizado na Univer-*

sidade de Évora, de 7 a 9 de Dezembro de 1994 (Lisbon: Vega, 1997);

Billie Maciunas, "Voice as Thematics in the Poetry of Florbela Espanca," *Hispanófila,* 103 (1991): 61–72;

Joaguim Manuel Magalhães, "Demasiado poucas palavras sobre Florbela," in his *Rima pobre: Poesia portuguesa de agora* (Lisbon: Presença, 1999), pp. 18–30;

Vitorino Nemésio, "Florbela Espanca," in his *Conhecimento da poesia* (Salvador: Universidade da Bahia, 1958), pp. 227–232;

Maria Manuela Moreira Nunes, "Florbela Espanca: Sarça ardente de fogos fátuos," *A cidade de Évora,* 45–46 (1962–1963): 160–224;

Haquira Osakabe, "Florbela e os esteriótipos da feminilidade," *Estudos Portugueses e Africanos,* 2 (1983): 67–77;

José Rodrigues de Paiva, ed., *Estudos sobre Florbela Espanca* (Recife: Assoc. de Estudos Portugueses Jordão Emerenciano, 1995);

Júlia Serpa Pimentel, "Freud e Florbela Espanca: Dois discursos paralelos sobre a depressão e o narcisismo," *Análise psicológica,* 4 (1983): 425–432;

Mário Sacramento, "Florbela num verso," in his *Ensaios de Domingo* (Coimbra: Coimbra Editora, 1959), pp. 155–161;

Victor Santos, *A paisagem alentejana em Florbela Espanca, Mário Beirão e Monsaraz* (Lisbon, 1936);

Jorge de Sena, *Florbela Espanca ou a expressão do feminino na poesia portuguesa* (Porto: Biblioteca Fenianos, 1947);

Zina Bellodi Silva, "Florbela Espanca," *Cadernos de teoria e crítica literária,* 15 (1988): 66–92;

M. J. da Silva Jr., "Através da obra de Florbela Espanca," *Gil Vicente,* 13 (1937): 33–40, 68–77;

Silva, *Florbela Espanca: Discurso do outro e imagem de si* (Araraquara: Universidade Estadual Paulista, 1992);

Carlos Sombrio, *Florbela Espanca* (Figueira da Foz: Homo, 1948);

Diogo Ivens Tavares, "O narcisismo de uma poetisa," *Portucale,* 51–52 (1936): 106–120;

Tavares, "O sentimento de solidão na obra de Florbela Espanca," *Gil Vicente,* 14 (1938): 19–23, 48–55, 71–81;

Amélia Vilar, *O drama de Florbela Espanca* (Porto: Costa Carregal, 1947).

**Papers:**
Collections of Florbela Espanca's papers can be found at the Biblioteca Nacional in Lisbon; the Biblioteca Pública de Évora; and the Grupo de Amigos de Vila Viçosa.

# Vergílio Ferreira
*(28 January 1916 – 1 March 1996)*

Fernando Arenas
*University of Minnesota*

BOOKS: *O caminho fica longe* (Lisbon: Inquérito, 1943);
*Sobre o humorismo de Eça de Queiros* (Coimbra: Faculdade de Letras da Universidade, 1943);
*Onde tudo foi morrendo* (Coimbra: Coimbra, 1944);
*Vagão J* (Coimbra: Coimbra, 1946);
*Mudança* (Lisbon: Portugália, 1949);
*A face sangrenta* (Lisbon: Contraponto, 1953);
*Manhã submersa* (Lisbon: Sociedade de Expansão Cultural, 1954);
*Do mundo original* (Coimbra: Vértice, 1957; expanded, Amadora: Bertrand, 1979);
*Mãe Genoveva: Contos* (Lisbon: Edição de Fomento de Publicações, 1957);
*Carta ao futuro* (Venda Nova: Bertrand, 1958);
*Aparição* (Lisbon: Portugália, 1959);
*Cântico final* (Lisbon: Ulisseia, 1960; revised, Lisbon: Arcádia, 1975);
*Estrela polar* (Lisbon: Portugália, 1962);
*Apelo da noite* (Lisbon: Portugália, 1963);
*André Malraux: Interrogação ao destino* (Lisbon: Presença, 1963);
*Alegria breve* (Lisbon: Portugália, 1965);
*Espaço do invisível I* (Lisbon: Portugália, 1965);
*Invocação ao meu corpo* (Lisbon: Portugália, 1969);
*Nítido nulo* (Lisbon: Portugália, 1971);
*Apenas homens* (Porto: Inova, 1972);
*Rápida, a sombra* (Lisbon: Arcádia, 1975);
*Contos* (Lisbon: Arcádia, 1976);
*Espaço do invisível II* (Lisbon: Arcádia, 1976);
*Espaço do invisível III* (Lisbon: Arcádia, 1977);
*Signo sinal* (Venda Nova: Bertrand, 1979);
*Conta-corrente I* (Venda Nova: Bertrand, 1980);
*Conta-corrente II* (Venda Nova: Bertrand, 1981);
*Conta-corrente III* (Venda Nova: Bertrand, 1983);
*Camões e a identidade nacional* (Vila de Maia: Imprensa Nacional-Casa da Moeda, 1983);
*Para sempre* (Venda Nova: Bertrand, 1983);
*Conta-corrente IV* (Venda Nova: Bertrand, 1986);
*Uma esplanada sobre o mar* (Lisbon: DIFEL, 1986);
*Espaço do invisível IV* (Lisbon: Imprensa Nacional-Casa da Moeda, 1987);

*Vergílio Ferreira (from http://vferreira.no.sapo.pt/main.html)*

*Até ao fim* (Venda Nova: Bertrand, 1987);
*Conta-corrente V* (Venda Nova: Bertrand, 1987);
*A estrela: Um conto de Vergílio Ferreira* (Lisbon: Quetzal, 1987);

*Arte tempo* (Lisbon: Rolim, 1988);

*Em nome da terra* (Venda Nova: Bertrand, 1990);

*Pensar* (Venda Nova: Bertrand, 1992);

*Conta-corrente–nova série I* (Venda Nova: Bertrand, 1993);

*Conta-corrente–nova série II* (Venda Nova: Bertrand, 1993);

*Na tua face* (Venda Nova: Bertrand, 1993);

*Conta-corrente–nova série III* (Venda Nova: Bertrand, 1994);

*Conta-corrente–nova série IV* (Venda Nova: Bertrand, 1994);

*Cartas a Sandra* (Venda Nova: Bertrand, 1996);

*Espaço do invisível V* (Venda Nova: Bertrand, 1998);

*Escrever,* edited by Helder Godinho (Venda Nova: Bertrand, 2001).

TRANSLATION: Jean-Paul Sartre, *O existencialismo é um humanismo,* introduction by Ferreira (Lisbon: Presença, 1970).

OTHER: Michel Foucault, *As palavras e as coisas,* introduction by Ferreira and Eduardo Lourenço (Lisbon: Edições 70, 1988).

Vergílio Ferreira, who actively published from 1939 until his death in 1996, is considered one of the greatest Portuguese writers of the twentieth century. His output includes more than twenty works of fiction (mostly novels but also some collections of short stories), more than a dozen works of nonfiction (essays on philosophy as well as on literary and cultural criticism), and approximately ten volumes of diaries. Several of his novels have been awarded major literary prizes, and late in his life the importance of Ferreira's literary career was recognized through various prestigious international awards such as the Femina Prize in France (1990), the Európalia Prize (1991), and the Camões Prize (1992), the highest literary honor in Portugal.

Ferreira is also regarded as one of the most highly philosophical modern writers in the Portuguese language, alongside Fernando Pessoa, João Guimarães Rosa, Clarice Lispector, and Maria Gabriela Llansol. Some of his main thematic interests include the destiny of humanity, the meaning of death, the phenomenological aspects of human existence, the relationship between language and being, music and the arts as transcendental sites of human experience, aging, the body, and the relationship with the "Other." What distinguishes Ferreira from other philosophically inclined authors is that his interest in existential questions is widely disseminated throughout his fiction as well as his nonfiction. Another significant characteristic is the fact that in Ferreira's work, Portugal as a cultural reality is secondary or altogether absent in favor of more individualized existential concerns—within a national context where questions of national identity have been central to the work of major writers since the fifteenth and sixteenth centuries. Furthermore, Ferreira is one of few major Portuguese authors whose literary and philosophical sources of influence lie largely outside of Portugal; these influences include Lucretius, Marcus Aurelius, St. Augustine, Blaise Pascal, Fyodor Dostoevsky, Ernest Hemingway, André Malraux, Albert Camus, Jean-Paul Sartre, Martin Heidegger, and Karl Theodor Jaspers.

Born in the Serra da Estrela region in the Portuguese interior (Melo) on 28 January 1916, Ferreira spent most of his childhood with his maternal aunts (Eulália and Joaquina de Oliveira) after his parents (António Augusto Ferreira and Josefa de Oliveira) immigrated to the United States. He had three siblings: Judite, César, and Virgínia. At age ten he entered the seminary in Fundão, where he stayed between 1926 and 1932. His negative associations with the seminary experience later inspired him to write the novel *Manhã submersa* (Deep Morning, 1954). Ferreira graduated from high school in Guarda in 1935 and finished his college degree in classics at Coimbra University in 1940. For most of his life he taught in various high schools throughout the country (Coimbra, Faro, Bragança, Évora, and Lisbon, where he taught at the renowned Liceu Camões from 1959 until 1981). Ferreira married Regina Kasprzykowsky in 1946. Together they had a son, Vergílio (or Gilo) Kasprzykowsky.

Ferreira's evolution as a thinker and writer is best appreciated through an understanding of the major themes that interested him and how these are developed in his fictional and nonfictional production. Ferreira was above all a secular humanist who struggled intensely with the question of the existence of God and the meaning of life in a world devoid of an "absolute prescriber." In Ferreira's fiction the human subject is located at an existential and cultural crossroads beyond universal truths, where the sole ontological horizon is himself. In his solitude, hyperaware of the limits of his body and of his language, the Ferreiran subject searches for his own instances of truth in order to fulfill, however briefly, his fragile existence. Ferreira's novels present protagonists who strive to overcome cultural discourses or myths that frustrate their attempts at finding their own truths or constructing their own measure of freedom independently.

Ferreira's earliest period is characterized by a half-hearted adherence to the Marxist-inspired neorealist movement, which dominated the Portuguese literary scene under right-wing dictator António de Oliveira

Salazar. Neorealism emerged from the crisis of capitalism, the upsurge of right-wing regimes throughout Europe in the 1930s, and the experience of World War II. Aside from challenging the prevailing social inequality and politically authoritarian structures of the time period, it also sought to represent social reality as authentically as possible. Ferreira's first three novels—*O caminho fica longe* (The Path Is Far Away, 1943), which was written in 1939; *Onde tudo foi morrendo* (Where Everything Was Dying, 1944); and *Vagão J* (Carriage J, 1946)—constitute his brief passage through neorealism. The novel that signals a transition away from neorealist literary practices and onto more existentialist concerns is *Mudança* (Change, 1949). In this novel, socio-economic concerns are gradually superseded by existential conflicts within the lives of the protagonists. The crisis of the bourgeoisie as a class gives way to the crisis of the bourgeois subject. In *Mudança* the impossible harmony with the Other and consequent solitude that surrounds the protagonist, along with his absolute certainty of death and his disbelief in religious or political narratives of redemption, ultimately displace the class issues that frame the novel initially.

Yet, as Ferreira continued to distance himself from the most dogmatic aspects of neorealism, venturing increasingly into the existential realm, he never ceased to criticize the oppressive power structures that prevailed in Portugal between the 1950s and early 1970s, even in implicit, veiled, or allegorical fashions. Ferreira's distance from the neorealists stemmed from the fact that he opposed their views regarding the status of art and literature in society and the notion that literature and the arts should be subservient to ideological dogma (in this case, Marxism). The novel *Apelo da noite* (Call of the Night, 1963) best illustrates Ferreira's difficult position as he rejected the oppressive Salazar regime at the same time as he rejected its staunchest source of opposition—the Portuguese Communist Party (which was outlawed at the time but to which many neorealists adhered). The protagonist of *Apelo da noite* is caught in the dilemma of being an intellectual who opposes the authoritarian right-wing regime of the time, yet cannot submit himself to Communist Party dogma. In this way, Ferreira anticipates his own struggle with the April 1974 revolution that ended the regime of Salazar and his successor, Marcelo Caetano; in particular, Ferreira wanted to maintain intellectual and political independence at an historical moment in which political dogmas of the Right and Left were dominant. This situation caused great strife between Ferreira and the Portuguese leftist intelligentsia that haunted him for the rest of his life (as he himself expressed in a personal interview in 1992).

Among Ferreira's novels, *Manhã submersa* is probably his most widely read and accessible (it is required reading in Portuguese high schools). It portrays the oppressive experience of a young man at the seminary, and the author has stated that some elements are autobiographical. The authoritarian sociopolitical structure and stifling environment at the seminary in this novel have been read as an allegory of the Salazar regime, with the Catholic Church standing in for the right-wing dictatorship. Still, the author's critical stance ultimately aims at both Salazar and the church, who were staunch allies. The central theme of this novel is the question of freedom and the ability to exercise one's individual freedom in defiance of authoritarian power structures. *Manhã submersa* represents the passage from childhood to a new stage of consciousness for the self who is in search of his own truth and who desires to assume his own individual will. This particular life transition inevitably entails questioning the existence of God, and the skepticism regarding God's existence is one of the most dominant themes throughout all of Ferreira's writings.

The novel *Aparição* (Appearance, 1959) has become Ferreira's existential manifesto, and it revolves around the narrator-protagonist's epiphanic moments of "coming into being," whereby he achieves a heightened awareness of the metaphysical substratum of life. Ferreira defines such a particular phenomenological event as an *aparição*, which is, according to the author, a fleeting moment of being in the world or of perceiving the "I" in relationship to the world. It is the expression of the inner side of being, its furtive and unfathomable depths that only reveal themselves in these "miraculous instances," which may occur through the subject's interaction with art, music, nature, or a lover. Ferreira clearly aligns himself with the existential subjectivity of Heidegger and Jaspers as well as the phenomenological nature of the literary works by Brazilian writer Lispector. In *Aparição* the struggles of Évora schoolteacher Alberto to adjust to a stifling sociopolitical context during the times of Salazar, as well as the complications related to his amorous involvement with a woman named Sofia, become subordinated to the philosophical issues that most interest the author: what lies beneath the surface of everyday human existence. In fact, throughout Ferreira's novels of this period there is a tension between story lines and philosophical problems that is reflected in their disjointed form: in *Apelo da noite*, *Aparição*, and *Cântico final* (Final Song, 1960), readers see two simultaneous texts differentiated by regular font and italics. In some cases, as in *Aparição*, the two texts function to separate the action of the novel from the philosophical reflections. This separation is not always clear-cut, as philosophical reflections permeate the novels in different instances.

*Paperback cover for the 1983 edition of Ferreira's semi-autobiographical 1954 novel, about a young man in a seminary (Thomas Cooper Library, University of South Carolina)*

Beginning with *Alegria breve* (Brief Happiness, 1965), plot and philosophical reflections are no longer differentiated through typography but instead become completely enmeshed in a highly fragmented structure, revealing a world in crisis where new meanings of life must be found and where faith in God is withering. Thus, narrative fragmentation as well as formal and linguistic experimentation become more accentuated in Ferreira's later novels, as meditations on being and truth become inseparable from meditations on the limits of language and the expressive possibilities of literature. This dynamic can be most clearly observed in *Nítido nulo* (Bright Nothingness, 1971) and *Signo sinal* (Sign Signal, 1979), culminating with his most groundbreaking novel, *Para sempre* (Forever, 1983).

The revolution of 1974 plays a key role in the novel *Signo sinal*. The revolution is referred to as an "earthquake" that nearly destroys everything. This cataclysmic event results in an era of not only material reconstruction but also philosophical reckoning. The struggle between the Left and the Right is intense, although the narrator suggests that the dogmatic impulse that governs both ideological camps is much the same. Luís, the protagonist, is a factory owner, and the ideological struggles of the revolution are enacted through him and his difficult socio-economic position during this time of change. *Signo sinal* is a novel that portrays a moment of profound reflection and new historical possibilities. It is the most fragmented work by Ferreira before *Para sempre;* there is a proliferation of incomplete sentences and a deliberate blurring of narrative facts and the temporal sequence of events, suggesting the tenuousness of truths as well as the contingency of life. These traits are coupled with an accentuated parody of Marxist and Christian ideological dogma. For the author, their respective dogmas are indistinguishable from one another: "–Que é que ele disse? Pergunta-me uma velha ainda com a mão em concha no ouvido. –Disse que Cristo estava filiado no partido. –Estava quê?" (–What did he say? An old woman asks me with her hand around her ear. –He said that Christ was a member of the party. –He said what?). Both Marxism and Christianity become primary targets of Ferreira's deconstructive strategies in the novels that belong to his later phase.

*Para sempre* is a novel of beginnings and endings. It is situated on the limits of linear conceptions of time and space. The narrator, Paulo, returns home at the end of his life and is stripped of everything except memory. Home becomes the materialization of memory, the space from which he will establish a bridge with himself and with his past. Paulo is situated in an atemporal dimension. All of his past converges simultaneously into the narrative present. *Para sempre* goes full circle–albeit in nonsequential order–through key episodes of Paulo's life: the loss of his mother (she becomes insane and is sent to an asylum; later, she dies); the loss of his aunts Luísa and Joana, who become the substitute mothers; his first sexual experience, with prostitute Adelaide; the courtship of the woman, Sandra, who later becomes his wife; the birth of his daughter, Xana; the eventual rebellion and estrangement of the adolescent Xana; the illness and eventual death of Sandra; Paulo's increasing age and solitude; and even his own death (which he witnesses).

Paulo opens doors and windows in order to initiate the search for the fundamental word, a word that may contain all of life itself, a word that may signify everything, a word that may encompass a whole human being. But at a time beyond the existence of God, beyond ideologies, beyond the notion of a unified subject, where can truth be found? The affective realm becomes a location where one can search for the truth. The narrator constructs a series of epiphanies that serve as a platform in order to reflect on several interrelated issues such as the limits of language, the neutralization of grand narratives, and the possibility or impossibility of arriving at a transcendental truth, at a word that could say the truth of being. In *Para sempre* Ferreira establishes a dialogue with several philosophers who have also dwelled on these issues to varying degrees and in diverse ways, including Heidegger, Friedrich Nietzsche, Ludwig Wittgenstein, and Jean-François Lyotard.

*Até ao fim* (Until the End, 1987) revolves around a conversation between the narrator-protagonist, Cláudio, and his son, Miguel (who is dead). Like Paulo in *Para sempre,* Cláudio finds himself at a turning point in his life: between life and death, beginnings and endings. As the conversation evolves, events in Cláudio's life interrupt the conversation and, at the same time, illuminate it: his family experience as a child in a village; his early love affairs; the marriage to his wife, Flora; the birth of Miguel and the close relationship with him; the tyranny of his wife and their subsequent divorce; the son's drug addiction and eventual (premature) death. Toward the end, only lifetime maid Tina survives, but she eventually dies, leaving Cláudio completely alone in the world at the end of his life. In contrast to *Para sempre* this novel pays closer attention to the events of everyday life; at the same time, it is much less fragmented and includes fewer philosophical interludes. The authorial thematic interests are much the same as in Ferreira's other works: the meanings of life and death, religion, the destiny of human civilization without gods, family life, the expressive possibilities of music and painting, and the future of literature. He places much greater emphasis, however, on the issue of the relationship with the Other, in particular, within the family. The overarching question that remains is: what is the meaning of life after it has been lived? While the answers offered are manifold, the author suggests that the relationship with the Other plays a key role in the search for a life purpose.

The novel *Em nome da terra* (In the Name of the Earth, 1990) is a long, passionate, and profoundly vivid "letter" addressed by João, the narrator and protagonist, to his deceased wife, Mónica. João, a former judge, is living his last days in a nursing home. From the limits of his life, João evokes the past: flashes from his childhood, the courtship of his wife, his married life, the illness and subsequent death of Mónica, and the lives of his three children. He also reflects upon life in the nursing home, old age, the inexorable decline of the body, the amputation of his leg, the possibility of loving and/ or being sexual in old age, death, God, the family, solitude, and politics. As in *Para sempre,* there is no linear sequence through which actions, feelings, or ideas are evoked. They all occur as they flow within the stream of memory.

In what is probably Ferreira's greatest novel, *Na tua face* (In Your Face, 1993), the categories of beauty and ugliness are stripped of their weight as distinct judgments and hierarchized cultural measures. This particular novel presents itself as a space where what has been traditionally regarded as aesthetically or physically abject, unseemly, incomplete, deformed, or horrendous acquires a new ontological meaning. The ugly and the horrible are posited as human inventions, while nature continues its course, making no judgment one way or another. *Na tua face* desires to push the limits of established aesthetic, philosophical, and religious discourses around beauty by valuing the horrible and by fully incorporating the fragments of the incomplete, deformed, and battered body. The novel rejects exclusive notions of beauty while it valorizes the "ugly" through its images and language, thus challenging Greek and Roman narratives of beauty, which are at the root of Western culture.

In a typically Ferreiran nonlinear and dialogical fashion, the plot of *Na tua face* is interspersed with dramatized and highly poetic philosophical reflections on the questions of beauty, truth, life and death, love, old age, the body, philosophy, and the arts. In *Em nome da terra* the reader witnesses the protagonist coming to terms with the limits and inexorable decline of the physical body, as João seeks through the memory of his beloved Mónica the strength to overcome, although briefly, the physical and temporal limitations of life. In *Na tua face,* however, Ferreira offers a slightly different project. The reader is still confronted with the finitude of life as an ever-present horizon. But finitude, as Ferreira has demonstrated before, is to be lived as a moment of possibilities. In this novel the narrator searches for different ways of seeing the world and being in it as he challenges aesthetic and moral categories that rule everyday life.

In *Na tua face* the protagonist, Daniel, is observed as he struggles to come to terms with a wife and daughter who are portrayed as superbeings—highly creative and successful from an intellectual and artistic point of view. They are also enveloped by a layer of coldness that perplexes Daniel, reflecting a tempered sense of powerlessness on the part of the male protagonist in the face of contemporary women's personal and professional independence, as well as the unattainability of the female object of desire. The latter becomes more evident with Bárbara, a long-lost lover. Bárbara is in fact an unattainable lover, representing archetypal beauty in its most idealized form. Nevertheless, she

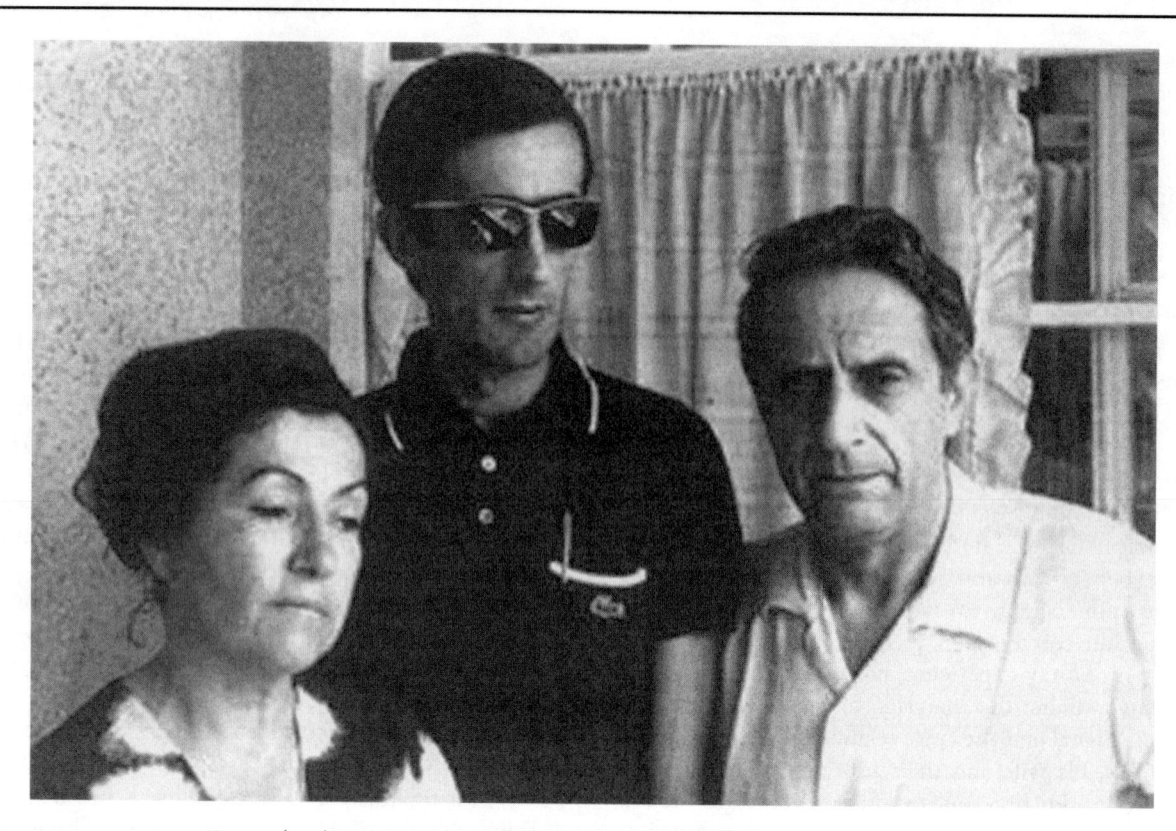

*Ferreira (right) in Lisbon with his wife, Regina Kasprzykowsky, and their son, Vergílio (Gilo) Kasprzykowsky, 1970 (from http://vferreira.no.sapo.pt/main.html)*

eventually appears in the novel as a much older woman whose physical appearance has been ravaged by the passage of time. Thus, archetypal Bárbara only exists as a trace imperfectly evoked by memory. She constitutes an impossible surface of beauty and divine perfection onto which the (heterosexual) male protagonist's desire is projected. Bárbara, together with other female characters in Ferreira's fiction, plays a major role in the (male) protagonists' struggles to accept the limits of life, which in *Na tua face* is played out through the debate around the question of beauty. In *Cartas a Sandra* (Letters to Sandra, Ferreira's last work, which was published around the time he passed away in early 1996), the addressee of the ten letters that make up the fictional work is represented as an idealized female figure of the highest order; she is an illuminated image projected onto a horizon of eternity and perfection. The more absent from physical reality, the more present Sandra is within the boundless hallucinations and imaginings of the narrator.

Ferreira is as much a philosopher as he is a fiction writer. Throughout his work there is an increased mingling of philosophy and fiction, prose and poetry, and fiction and essay. In spite of maintaining genre distinctions (novels, short stories, essay, and diaries), these writings are in constant dialogue with one another. His most important nonfiction works are *Invocação ao meu corpo* (Invocation of My Body, 1969); *Espaço do invisível I, II,* and *III* (The Space of the Invisible, 1965, 1976, and 1977); *Conta-corrente I, II, III, IV,* and *V* (Counter-Current, 1980, 1981, 1983, 1986, and 1987); *Pensar* (Thinking, 1992); *Conta-corrente–nova série I, II, III,* and *IV* (Counter-Current, new series, 1993 and 1994), and *Escrever* (Writing, published posthumously in 2001). *Invocação ao meu corpo* is a philosophical work that explores thematic coordinates such as truth, myth, subjectivity, reason, God, art, and the body. *Espaço do invisível* is made up of essays that focus on art, literature, and philosophy. *Conta-corrente* is a combination of sequentially dated short passages ranging from descriptions of day-to-day life to literary criticism (even of his own novels), philosophical reflections, and his thoughts on art, culture, history, and politics. Stripped of any chronological sequence, *Pensar* is a stream of profoundly lyrical reflections on being, language, time, postmodernism, the end of the Cold War, music, and art. It follows a tradition of aphoristic thinking, reminiscent of Pascal's *Pensées* (Thoughts, 1670) as well as works of Marcus Aurelius, seventeenth- and eighteenth-century French moralists (Jean de La Bruyère, François de La Rochefoucauld, and Luc de Clapiers, Marquis de Vauvenargues), and Nietzsche. *Escrever,* which was left unfinished by the author and has been edited by Helder Godinho, can be described as an aphoristic diary, although less abstract than *Pensar* and closer in tone to *Conta-corrente*. The important themes of this posthumous work are the end of life and the end of the century/millennium.

For Ferreira, humankind represents the ultimate source of truths. However, for as much as Ferreira depicts the absence of the gods and the consequent solitude and contingency that envelop human existence, the gods never completely disappear. They function, rather, as utopian projections of what or where humans are not, but aspire to be. For Ferreira, humankind must confront its own fragility and finiteness, searching for a measure of freedom and happiness, in order to make life more livable and death more endurable.

In 1969, when *Invocação ao meu corpo* was published, Ferreira spoke of humankind as the only permanent value after the emptying or death of all other values (value here refers to myth–the myths of Christianity or Communism, for example). Humankind does not become devalued but rather attempts to recognize itself within the limits of its body. The body and the "I" are indissociable from one another. The absolute of the body becomes the absolute of the "I"–the body is not the site of the person but the actual person *(pessoa efectivada)*. However, by 1990, with *Em nome da terra*, the reader faces (as has been pointed out by Fernanda Irene Fonseca) a subject no longer unified with the body. The irreversibility of death shatters this unity to such an extent that it becomes only a memory. In *Em nome da terra* João calls forth his deceased wife, Mónica:

> Querida. Veio-me hoje uma enorme vontade de te amar. E então pensei: vou-te escrever. Mas não te quero amar no tempo em que te lembro. Quero-te amar antes, muito antes.
>
> (My dear. I've been suddenly overtaken today by a desire to love you. And so I thought: I will write you. But I do not wish to love in the very instant in which I remember you. I wish to love you before, much before).

All events take place in João's memory: Mónica, his absent interlocutor, will be reconstructed, as if in a desire to reconstruct himself through the Other–emotionally, spiritually, ontologically–at the edge of life, now that the corporeal is slowly and irremediably falling apart. João can only exist as long as he expresses the passion he feels for his loved one, as long as the Other's presence is called forth–the force of the novel is then extracted from its very dialogical structure:

> Meu amor–que amor? Não és tu. És, és. Não és. Na realidade não sei. Na realidade há o que existe, o que se diz um facto, o que se avalia ao quilo ou ao quilómetro. E há o que nos existe, aquilo que está por dentro disso–vou amar o teu corpo como nunca te amei.
>
> (My love–what love? It isn't you. Yes it is. No it isn't. I really don't know. In truth, all that exists is what is, that which calls itself a fact, whatever can be measured by the pound or by the mile. And there is also what exists within us and whatever that is–I will love your body as I've never loved you).

In his later works Ferreira emphasized the decline or weakening of utopias or myths that have dominated the Western cultural landscape throughout the twentieth century. There is, however, a detectable nostalgia for "the whole" or lasting myths that may provide an affectional as well as ideological basis for human existence. This nostalgia, which is so palpable throughout Ferreira's fictional and non-fictional production, is the underlying theme of Godinho's *O universo imaginário de Ferreira* (1985), the first major critical work on Ferreira. The nostalgia for the whole is apparent in the constant search for absolute beauty in *Na tua face,* in spite of the narrator's hyperawareness of living in a time beyond absolute beauty. In *Em nome da terra* the desire for absolute communicability between the narrator and his forever-lost lover becomes a metaphor of the longing for a time in which the belief in the correspondence between word and object of representation was held to be true. In *Para sempre* there is an endless desire to achieve a plenitude of being that may be expressed through language. In all three novels, the search or the desire–for absolute beauty, communicability, or a plenitude of being–is invariably framed within the context of the longing for a loved Other. The desire for the Other as a metonymic expression of the search for lasting truths becomes a propelling force for the act of literary creation, as well as for the act of living–which are inseparable in Ferreira.

It was reported that on the day of his death, 1 March 1996, Ferreira was writing in his Lisbon apartment. His body is now buried in his hometown of Melo, in the Serra da Estrela region.

Vergílio Ferreira was one of the most prolific Portuguese writers of the twentieth century, having written approximately fifty works of fiction and essays, as well as diaries. Even as he was strongly rooted in the literary traditions of Portugal, few Portuguese writers have been as intimately engaged with the saga of canonical Western philosophy and literature as was Ferreira. His literary and philosophical legacy will endure as one of the most original to emerge in Portugal during the world's most turbulent century.

**Bibliography:**

"Bibliografia de y sobre Vergílio Ferreira," *Anthropos,* 101 (1989): 17–26.

**References:**

Fernando Arenas, "Beauty at the Surface of Love's Face: Myth and Metanarrative in Vergílio Ferreira's Contemporary Writing," *Santa Barbara Portuguese Studies,* 4 (1999): 157–169;

Arenas, "Being Here with Clarice Lispector and Vergílio Ferreira: At the Limits of Language and Subjectivity," *Portuguese Studies,* 14 (1999): 1–14;

Arenas, "A Breath on the Edge of Earth: The Limits of Language and Subjectivity in Vergílio Ferreira and Clarice Lispector," dissertation, University of California, Berkeley, 1994;

Arenas, *Utopias of Otherness: Nation and Subjectivity in Portugal and Brazil* (Minneapolis: University of Minnesota Press, 2003);

Maria Lúcia Dal Farra, *O narrador ensimesmado* (São Paulo: Ática, 1978);

Fernanda Irene Fonseca, *Vergílio Ferreira: A celebração da palavra* (Coimbra: Almedina, 1992);

Helder Godinho, *O universo imaginário de Ferreira* (Lisbon: Instituto de Investigação Científica, 1985);

Godinho, ed., *Estudos sobre Vergílio Ferreira* (Lisbon: Imprensa Nacional-Casa da Moeda, 1982);

Godinho and Serafim Ferreira, eds., *Vergílio Ferreira: Fotobiografia* (Venda Nova: Bertrand, 1993);

Rosa Maria Goulart, *Romance lírico: O percurso de Vergílio Ferreira* (Lisbon: Bertrand, 1990);

José Luis Gavilanes Laso, *Vergílio Ferreira: espaço simbólico e metafísico* (Lisbon: Dom Quixote, 1989);

Eduardo Lourenço, "Uma aparição sem fim," *Público,* 28 January 1993;

Lourenço, "Literatura e revolução," *Colóquio/Letras,* 78 (1984): 7–16;

Lourenço, "Vergílio Ferreira: Do alarme à jubilação," *Colóquio/Letras,* 90 (1986): 24–34;

Ivo Lucchesi, *Crise e Escritura: Uma leitura de Clarice Lispector e Vergílio Ferreira* (Rio de Janeiro: Forense Universitária, 1987);

Aniceta de Mendonça, *O romance de Vergílio Ferreira: Existencialismo e ficção* (São Paulo: ILHPA-HUCITEC, 1978);

Luís Mourão, "Conta-corrente 6: Ensaio sobre o diário de Vergílio Ferreira," M.A. thesis, Faculdade de Ciências Sociais e Humanas da Universidade Nova de Lisboa, 1990;

Mourão, *Vergílio Ferreira: Excesso, escassez, resto* (Braga: Angelus Novus, 2001);

Maria da Glória Padrão, ed., *Um escritor apresenta-se* (Lisbon: Imprensa Nacional-Casa da Moeda, 1981);

José Rodrigues Paiva, *O espaço-limite no romance de Vergílio Ferreira* (Recife: Encontro-Gabinete Português de Leitura, 1984);

"Vergílio Ferreira (Dossier)," *Letras & Letras,* 33 (1990).

**Papers:**

Vergílio Ferreira's original manuscripts as well as unpublished materials are currently housed at the Biblioteca Nacional in Lisbon. Ferreira's private library and personal objects are housed at the Biblioteca Municipal Vergílio Ferreira in Gouveia, Portugal.

# Manuel da Fonseca
*(15 October 1911 – 11 March 1993)*

José Carlos Barcellos
*Universidade Federal Fluminense*

BOOKS: *Rosa dos ventos* (Lisbon: Imprensa Baroeth, 1940);

*Planície* (Coimbra: Portugália, 1941);

*Aldeia Nova* (Lisbon: Portugália, 1942; revised edition, Lisbon: Caminho, 1984);

*Cerromaior* (Lisbon: Inquérito, 1943; revised edition, Lisbon: Caminho, 1982);

*O fogo e as cinzas* (Lisbon: Gleba, 1951; revised edition, Lisbon: Caminho, 1983);

*Poemas completos* (Lisbon: Iniciativas, 1958); revised as *Obra poética* (Lisbon: Caminho, 1984);

*Seara de vento* (Lisbon: Ulisseia, 1958; revised edition, Lisbon: Caminho, 1984);

*Um anjo no trapézio* (Lisbon: Prelo, 1968; revised edition, Lisbon: Caminho, 1986);

*Tempo de solidão* (Lisbon: Arcádia, 1973; revised edition, Lisbon: Caminho, 1985);

*Crónicas algarvias* (Lisbon: Caminho, 1986);

*À lareira, nos fundos da casa onde o Retorta tem o café,* edited by Artur da Fonseca (Lisbon: Caminho, 2000).

OTHER: Fialho d'Almeida, *Antologia,* compiled by Fonseca (Beja: Câmaras Municipais de Cuba e Vidigueira, 1984).

*Manuel da Fonseca (from the paperback cover for Aldeia Nova, 1984; Thomas Cooper Library, University of South Carolina)*

Manuel da Fonseca is one of the most important Portuguese writers of the period known as neorealism, which dominated Portuguese literature from 1940 to 1974. The neorealists were deeply concerned with social and political issues from a leftist point of view. Writers such as Fonseca, Alves Redol, Soeiro Pereira Gomes, Fernando Namora, and José Cardoso Pires engaged in a literary project opposed to that developed by José Régio and his group, who founded *Presença* magazine (published from 1927 until 1940). Régio's group paid more attention to psychological and metaphysical questions. The neorealists considered literature primarily as a political weapon to be used against the fascist dictatorship in Portugal (1928–1974), led by António de Oliveira Salazar until 1968, then by Marcelo Caetano.

Manuel Lopes da Fonseca was born in Santiago do Cacém, Baixo Alentejo, on 15 October 1911. His parents were Carlos Augusto da Fonseca and Maria Silvina Lopes da Fonseca, who belonged to the provincial middle class. His native Santiago, which appears under the name of Cerromaior in some of his works, constitutes a symbol of Portuguese society as a whole, with its rigid gap between rich and poor, its authoritarian practices, its many prejudices, and the lack of opportunities for working-class people. During his childhood and adolescence in Santiago, Fonseca had many opportunities to meet people from different social backgrounds, to observe their way of life, and to talk with them and hear their stories. This experience was important for his career as a writer.

In his youth, after secondary school Fonseca attended classes in the Fine Arts Academy in Lisbon, but he never graduated. Throughout his life he undertook many different jobs. Nevertheless, his main concern was always literature. When he was twenty-nine years old he published his first book of poems, *Rosa dos ventos* (Compass, 1940), and one year later, *Planície* (Plain, 1941). The poetry in these two works offers a rich and varied presentation of characters taken from Portuguese rural life, specifically from the Alentejo region. Most of these characters reappear later in his short stories and in the novel *Cerromaior* (1943). Through these characters, Fonseca's poetry follows the neorealist literary and political goals of denouncing the bourgeois way of life and speaking on behalf of the victims of social and economic oppression.

In *Planície,* Fonseca published one of his most acclaimed poems, "Para um poema a Florbela" (Toward a Poem for Florbela), in which he pays homage to the Portuguese poet Florbela Espanca, who had committed suicide in 1930. She was from the Alentejo region, and Fonseca, in this poetic tribute, presents her as a symbol of personal freedom. He depicts her deep concern for poor people and her nonconformity to bourgeois prejudices.

Fonseca's first book of fiction is a collection of short stories published under the title of *Aldeia Nova* (New Village, 1942); most of them had already been published in newspapers and magazines. The book was received well by the critics. João Gaspar Simões, the most important literary critic linked to the *Presença* group, wrote in the *Diário de Lisboa* on 12 November 1942: "Sim, *Aldeia Nova* é uma bela estreia" (*Aldeia Nova* is indeed a nice beginning).

The stories of *Aldeia Nova* reveal the most characteristic features of Fonseca's fiction: the rural scenery of Alentejo, a sympathetic view of the impoverished and oppressed workers, an ironic view of the bourgeois elite, and the projects and dreams for a new and better world, to which the title of the book refers. In the title story Zé Cardo, a young employee on a pig farm, endures a miserable life of poverty and solitude. At the same time, however, he feels confident and hopeful of going one day to Aldeia Nova, a village until then still unknown to him, but which his naive imagination pictures as a sort of paradise. Aldeia Nova, therefore, is a symbol of the new and better society that the communists expected would emerge from the revolution—a society in which there was no hunger, poverty, or oppression.

Some of the short stories of *Aldeia Nova,* however, present characters such as António Vargas and Rui do Parral, two rich young men who are neither workers nor poor. Regardless of their social position, they do not feel comfortable within bourgeois society and its strict patterns of power, behavior, and respectability. Fonseca's most influential innovation in neorealist literature, at least in the beginning of the 1940s, is the attention he pays to these kinds of characters. They do not belong to the working class; nevertheless, they recognize the oppressive social, economic, and political structures under which the working class is forced to live, and they try to engage themselves in one way or another in a struggle against those structures.

The plot of *Cerromaior* is directly concerned with this subject. Adriano Serpa is a nineteen-year-old student who is a member of one of the ruling families of Cerromaior. Adriano has lost his parents, and his uncle and cousins succeed in keeping him apart from the administration of the family's properties and businesses. Thus, although belonging to the bourgeoisie, he becomes a friend to many workers. He talks and learns with them, and he is able to understand the complex mechanisms of the social structure. He recognizes, from a leftist point of view, the injustice intrinsic to this structure.

In a society in which, as his cousin Carlos Runa puts it, "há duas categorias . . . os que mandam e os que obedecem" (there are only two sides . . . those who command and those who obey), Adriano finds himself in an unexpected outside position. This position allows him the necessary freedom and leisure to understand and acknowledge the truth about social and economic oppression. *Cerromaior* is, thus, a novel about the emergence of the hero's political and social conscience. Adriano finally decides to undertake a positive and combative role beside the workers and against the class of landowners to which his own family belongs.

The publication of *Cerromaior* created a polemic among the critics. Some Marxist critics did not find the novel to be a faithful embodiment of neorealist aesthetic and political principles. They were displeased with Adriano's middle-class ethics and failed to understand that the novel was precisely about the surpassing of these beliefs in a move toward revolutionary politics. Perhaps because of this criticism, Fonseca rewrote the work in 1981, stressing for the revised edition Adriano's political consciousness much earlier in the plot. In 1980 director Luís Filipe Rocha released a movie based on *Cerromaior*, with the same title.

In 1951 Fonseca published another collection of short stories, *O fogo e as cinzas* (The Fire and the Ashes). This book, as most of Portuguese neorealist fiction of the 1950s, expresses a generally pessimistic view of the possibility of quick changes in Portuguese society under the enduring conservative dictatorship of Salazar in the period immediately after World War II. As a matter of fact, the opponents of the Salazar government, among whom were the neorealist writers, were surprised and disappointed with Salazar's great ability for surviving politically the defeat of Nazi fascism in 1945.

Significantly, many stories in *O fogo e as cinzas* deal with personal defeat. In the title story, for example, three close friends—the narrator, André Juliano, and Mestre Poupa, a fireman—are involved in different ways in the burning of a house, which puts an end to their group. Oppressed and humiliated by his old father, Juliano kills him by setting fire to their house. Poupa dies while trying to put out the fire, and the narrator sees the woman he is in love with being rescued almost naked by another man. Poupa's death, Juliano's imprisonment, and what seems to the narrator a shameful and public humiliation link their lives and friendship in a single and definite process of defeat and failure.

After 1974, when a military rebellion led to the end of the authoritarian government in Portugal and to its replacement by a democratic one, *O fogo e as cinzas* became obligatory reading in Portuguese schools for many years. This requirement explains why, of all Fonseca's books, *O fogo e as cinzas* has sold the most copies.

In 1958 Fonseca published *Poemas completos* (Complete Poems) and *Seara de vento* (Plantation of Wind). The first is an expanded collection of the author's poetry, including the contents of *Rosa dos ventos* and *Planície,* and other poems. In general, the poems included in this collection for the first time do not add any remarkable new feature or perspective to Fonseca's two previous books of poetry. *Seara de vento,* on the other hand, is unanimously considered Fonseca's most important work and one of the best Portuguese neorealist novels.

*Seara de vento,* which was based upon real events, tells the story of a man's resistance to a police siege. Having been unjustly accused of theft, António de Valmurado, alias Palma, cannot find a job and is forced to engage in smuggling to feed his family. The police convince his wife to betray him by telling them about her husband's activities as a smuggler. She kills herself when she realizes what she has done. In revenge, Palma murders Elias Sobral, the rich farm-owner who accused him of the initial theft, and Sobral's son, who confesses to being the real thief. With his mother-in-law, Amanda

*Paperback cover for the 1984 revised edition of Fonseca's 1942 collection of short stories set in the rural Alentejo region (Thomas Cooper Library, University of South Carolina)*

Carrusca, Palma closes himself up in his house and fights against the police until he is shot and killed.

The novel reveals the political message that a single individual's resistance is not enough to overcome the oppression of the entire working class. The workers must organize as a class to end the injustice of their oppressors. Many critics have pointed out how deeply Fonseca's novel is indebted to Greek tragedy. Indeed, as a tragic hero, Palma goes straight to his ruin because he cannot understand his true situation. Everything he does contributes to his own destruction. From a Marxist point of view, working-class people need to develop a critical awareness of their social, political, and economic situation to be able to play an active and positive role in their own liberation.

In 1965 Fonseca was sent to prison for a short time, along with Alexandre Pinheiro Torres, one of the best-known neorealist literary critics, and Augusto Abelaira, an acclaimed novelist. Their "crime" was that as members of a committee appointed by the Portuguese Writers' Society, they had awarded a literary prize to *Luuanda* (1963), a short-story collection by Luandino Vieira. This important Angolan writer was at that time in prison himself for having participated in his country's liberation movement against Portuguese colonialism, and *Luuanda* had been banned.

*Um anjo no trapézio* (An Angel on the Trapeze, 1968) and *Tempo de solidão* (Time of Solitude, 1973) are collections of short stories in which Fonseca leaves the rural scenery of Alentejo for the urban world of Lisbon. Although the stories do not have the same direct concern with social and political problems as Fonseca's previous works, they do present an analogous atmosphere of solitude, despair, and lack of opportunities that affects the lives of common people. In both books Fonseca maintains a rather traditional manner of presenting characters and developing plot that avoids the more audacious innovations of modern fiction. Critics agree that *Um anjo no trapézio* and *Tempo de solidão* do not add any significant contribution to Fonseca's reputation, which is built almost entirely on his poetry, the stories of *Aldeia Nova* and *O fogo e as cinzas,* and his two novels, *Cerromaior* and *Seara de vento.*

In the 1980s Fonseca revised his books for an edition of his complete works, published between 1983 and 1989 by Editorial Caminho in Lisbon. In 1984 he edited an acclaimed anthology of the works of Portuguese naturalist writer Fialho de Almeida. Under the title of *Crónicas algarvias* (Chronicles from Algarve, 1986), Fonseca added to his works a volume including a series of sixteen articles on the Algarve region. These articles had previously been published in *A capital,* a Lisbon newspaper, in August 1968. Fonseca died in Lisbon on 11 March 1993.

In 2000 Fonseca's complete works were enriched by the collection of short stories *À lareira, nos fundos da casa onde Retorta tem o café* (By the Fire, in the Back of the Building Where Retorta's Café is Located). These stories had already been published in the newspaper *Diário Popular* between 1969 and 1971. In this book, editor Artur da Fonseca announced other posthumous volumes of short stories and articles by Fonseca to be published in the future by Editorial Caminho.

Manuel da Fonseca's body of work is not large, but it presents notable literary achievements and a deep ethical and aesthetic coherence. His poetry and fiction are unanimously considered among the best in Portuguese literature of the 1940s and 1950s. According to Mário Sacramento, one of the leading Portuguese literary critics of that period, Fonseca is the greatest of the Portuguese neorealist writers.

**References:**

José Carlos Barcellos, *O herói problemático em Cerromaior: Subsídios para o estudo do neo-realismo português* (Niterói: EDUFF, 1997);

Maria de Lourdes Belchior, Maria Isabel Rocheta, and Maria Alzira Seixo, *Três ensaios sobre a obra de Manuel da Fonseca* (Lisbon: Seara Nova/Comunicação, 1980);

Gregory Rust McNab Jr., "The Neo-Realist Novel in Portugal: Literature as a Political Weapon," dissertation, New York University, 1973;

Carlos Reis, *O discurso ideológico do neo-realismo português* (Coimbra: Almedina, 1983);

Urbano Tavares Rodrigues, *Um novo olhar sobre o neo-realismo* (Lisbon: Moraes, 1981);

Mário Sacramento, *Há uma estética neorealista?* (Lisbon: Vega, 1985);

Maria Aparecida Santilli, *Arte e representação da realidade no romance português contemporâneo* (São Paulo: Quíron, 1979);

Alexandre Pinheiro Torres, *O movimento neo-realista em Portugal na sua primeira fase* (Lisbon: Instituto de Cultura e Língua Portuguesa, 1977).

# Almeida Garrett
## (João Baptista da Silva Leitão de Almeida Garrett)
### (4 February 1799 - 9 December 1854)

Sérgio Nazar David
*Universidade do Estado do Rio de Janeiro*

BOOKS: *O dia vintequatro d'agosto* (Lisbon: Typografia Rollandiana, 1821);

*O retrato de Vénus* (Coimbra: Imprensa da Universidade, 1821);

*Catão* (Lisbon: Imprensa Liberal, 1822; London: S. W. Sustenance, 1830)–includes *O corcunda por amor*, by Garrett and Paulo Midosi;

*Camões* (Paris: Livraria Nacional & Estrangeira, 1825; Lisbon: Typografia de José Baptista Morando, 1839);

*Dona Branca ou a conquista do Algarve* (Paris: J. P. Aillaud, 1826; Lisbon: Chardron de Melo & Irmão, 1848);

*Carta de guia para leitores* (Lisbon: Typ. de Desiderio Marques Leão, 1826);

*Adozinda* (London: Boosey/V. Salva, 1828);

*Lírica de João Mínimo* (London: Sustenance & Stretch, 1829; Lisbon: Casa Viúva Bertrand & Filhos, 1853);

*Da educação* (London: Sustenance & Stretch, 1829);

*Portugal na balança da Europa* (London: Sustenance & Stretch, 1830);

*Elogio fúnebre de Carlos Infante de Lacerda, Barão de Sabrosa* (London: R. Greenlaw, 1830);

*Mérope / Gil Vicente* (Lisbon: Typ. José Baptista Morando, 1841);

*O alfageme de Santarém ou a espada do Condestável* (Lisbon: Imprensa Nacional, 1842);

*Memória histórica do Conselheiro A. M. L. Vieira de Castro* (Lisbon: Typ. José Baptista Morando, 1843);

*Romanceiro e Cancioneiro Geral* (Lisbon: Typ. da Soc. Propagadora dos Conhecimentos Uteis, 1843); expanded as *Romanceiro*, 3 volumes (Lisbon: Imprensa Nacional, 1851);

*Frei Luís de Sousa* (Lisbon: Imprensa Nacional, 1844); translated by Edgar Prestage as *The "Brother Luiz de Sousa" of Viscount de Almeida Garrett* (London: Elkin Mathews, 1909);

*Flores sem fructo* (Lisbon: Imprensa Nacional, 1845);

*Almeida Garrett, circa 1853 (from João Gaspar Simões, ed., Garrett, 1954; Joint University Libraries, Vanderbilt University)*

*O arco de Sant'Ana*, 2 volumes (Lisbon: Imprensa Nacional, 1845, 1850);

*Filipa de Vilhena* (Lisbon: Imprensa Nacional, 1846);

*Viagens na minha terra*, 2 volumes (Lisbon: Typ. Gazeta dos Tribunais, 1846); translated by John M. Parker as *Travels in My Homeland* (London: Peter Owen / Paris: UNESCO, 1987);

*Memória histórica da excellentissima Duqueza de Palmella, D. Eugénia Francisca Xavier Telles da Gama* (Lisbon: Imprensa Nacional, 1848);

*A sobrinha do marquês* (Lisbon: Imprensa Nacional, 1848);

*Memória histórica de José Xavier Mouzinho da Silveira* (Lisbon: Imprensa da Epocha, 1849);

*Folhas caídas,* anonymous (Lisbon: Casa Viúva Bertrand & Filhos, 1853);

*Um noivado no Dafundo ou cada terra com seu uso cada roca com seu fuso* (Lisbon: Viúva Marques & Filha, 1857);

*Discursos parlamentares e Memórias biográficas* (Lisbon: Imprensa Nacional, 1871)–includes *Elogio fúnebre de Carlos Infante de Lacerda, Barão de Sabrosa,* and *Memória histórica de José Xavier Mouzinho da Silveira;*

*Helena: Fragmento de um romance inedito* (Lisbon: Imprensa Nacional, 1871);

*O bastardo do fidalgo* (Porto: Typ. Commércio e Indústria, 1877);

*Obras completas,* 2 volumes (Porto: Lello & Irmão, 1963);

*O roubo das sabinas: Poemas libertinos I,* edited by Augusto da Costa Dias (Lisbon: Portugália, 1968);

*Narrativas e lendas,* edited by Dias (Lisbon: Estampa, 1979);

*Escritos do vintismo,* edited by Dias, Maria Helena da Costa Dias, and Luis Augusto Costa Dias (Lisbon: Editorial Estampa, 1985);

*Doutrinação liberal,* edited by António Reis (Lisbon: Alfa, 1990).

**Editions and Collections:** *Obras completas de Almeida Garrett,* 2 volumes, edited by Teófilo Braga (Lisbon: Empreza da História de Portugal, 1904);

*Frei Luís de Sousa,* edited by Rodrigues Lapa (Lisbon: Seara Nova, 1943);

*Viagens na minha terra,* edited by Augusto da Costa Dias (Lisbon: Portugália, 1963);

*Flores sem fruto / Folhas caídas,* edited by R. A. Lawton (Paris: Presses Universitaires de France, 1975);

*Romanceiro de Almeida Garrett,* edited by Maria Ema Tarracha Ferreira (Lisbon: Ulisseia, 1997).

PLAY PRODUCTIONS: *Xerxes,* Coimbra, Teatro dos Grilos, February 1819;

*Lucrécia,* Coimbra, Teatro dos Grilos, February 1819;

*Catão,* by Garrett, and *O corcunda por amor,* by Garrett and Paulo Midosi, Lisbon, Teatro do Bairro Alto, 29 September 1821;

*Os namorados extravagantes,* Sintra, 26 May 1822;

*Um auto de Gil Vicente,* Lisbon, Teatro da Rua dos Condes, 15 August 1838;

*Filipa de Vilhena,* Lisbon, Teatro do Saltre, 30 May 1840;

*Frei Luís de Sousa,* Sete Rios, Teatro da Quinta do Pinheiro, 4 July 1843;

*O alfageme de Santarém,* Lisbon, Terreiro do Paço, 11 July 1846;

*A sobrinha do marquês,* Lisbon, Teatro Maria II, 4 April 1848.

OTHER: *Parnaso lusitano ou poesias selectas dos autores portugueses antigos e modernos,* 6 volumes, edited by Garrett (Paris: J. P. Aillaud, 1826–1834)–includes Garrett's *Bosquejo da história da poesia e língua portuguesa.*

Scholars agree on the importance of Almeida Garrett's participation in the cultural and literary transformations in Portugal from 1820 to 1854. Garrett worked in various literary genres and produced a highly diversified body of work. In the field of epic poetry, specifically in his *Camões* (1825), he turned the image of sixteenth-century poet Luís de Camões into a Romantic myth of the beggar poet rather than a heroic one. In his novels Garrett not only created love stories but also mingled fiction with philosophical, aesthetic, and historical reflections. In his plays Garrett added a didactic element through his plots and characters in which the literate public of the nineteenth century could recognize their own dilemmas. In his pedagogical and historiographical essays there are two main trends: the defense of Christianity and the duty Garrett imposes on himself and his readers, along with the rest of Europe, of following the path of eighteenth-century philosophical rationalism against tyranny and ignorance. Garrett's popular narrative poems still constitute an important reference for themes from oral literary tradition and folklore. Finally, the conception of love and sexual desire in his lyric poems became the dominant one in Portuguese literature throughout the nineteenth century. His commitment to the truths of Christianity and liberalism appears throughout all his works.

João Leitão da Silva was born on 4 February 1799 in Porto. He was the second son of the five children–four boys and a girl–of António Bernardo da Silva and Ana Augusta de Almeida Leitão. His father worked at the Porto customhouse and was responsible for supervising the application of lead stamps on goods. In 1804 the family moved to Quinta do Castelo, south of the Douro River. Quinta do Sardão, the estate of his maternal grandmother, was a few kilometers away. Da Silva spent his childhood between these two places and refers to them in his works.

In 1807 Napoleon Bonaparte's troops, commanded by Andoche Junot, invaded Portugal, and King João VI and his court moved to Brazil. In 1808 António da Silva took his family to his native town, Angra do Heroísmo on Terceira Island in the Azores. Da Silva's uncle Alexandre José da Silva, then known as Friar Alexandre da Sagrada Família, returned to the Azores in 1811 as bishop of Angra do Heroísmo, and da Silva learned classical literature and modern philosophy from him. He also studied Latin, Greek, French, Italian, arithmetic, and geometry, because his parents wanted him to become a priest.

In 1815 da Silva left for Coimbra, abandoning plans for an ecclesiastical career, and enrolled in law school on 23 November 1816. While in law school, he founded a secret society similar to the Freemasons. Also during this period he began to receive recognition as an orator, founded an academic theater, and combined the maiden names of his grandmothers to become known as Almeida Garrett. He presented the play *Xerxes* (1819) in Coimbra. He did not publish the work, nor did he keep a copy of it. His tragedy *Lucrécia* was performed in 1819 at the Teatro dos Grilos in Coimbra. In the same year he started writing the tragedies "Afonso de Albuquerque" and "Sofonisba," but he never finished them.

In 1820 Garrett became enthusiastic about the liberal revolution that took place in Porto on 24 August and spread to Lisbon on 15 September. The revolution installed a temporary government with members from both Lisbon and Porto. These events affected Coimbra, where rebellious students demanded to participate in the municipal elections.

After finishing his fifth year of law school in May 1821, Garrett visited his family in Angra do Heroísmo. The city was governed by the absolutist Francisco de Borja Stockler, but Garrett participated in the writing of a liberal constitution that forced Stockler to return to the Continent. Garrett left for Lisbon, where he published the essay *O dia vintequatro d'agosto* (The Twenty-Fourth of August) on the first anniversary of the 1820 revolution. This text attacks absolutist government and defends religion and constitutional monarchy. The representative government is presented in the opening of the work as the natural defender of the "nation's majesty," the "crown's rights," the "holiness of religion," and the "law's empire."

Around this time Garrett's friend Luis Francisco Midosi introduced Garrett to his brother, the journalist and writer Paulo Midosi. Garrett met their sister, Luísa Cândida Midosi, on 29 September 1821 at the opening of his tragedy *Catão* (published in 1822) at the Teatro do Bairro Alto in Lisbon. The work was inspired by Joseph Addison's *Cato* (1713), and its main character is the Roman Cato, defender of freedom against Julius Caesar's tyranny. The play *O corcunda por amor* (Hunchback for Love's Sake), written with Paulo Midosi, was presented along with this tragedy. The term "corcundas" (hunchbacks) was used by liberals to refer to the absolutists to suggest the act of bowing to royalty.

Garrett returned to Coimbra in October 1821 to take his final examinations. He received only a conditional pass, possibly the university's way of responding

*Title page for Garrett's 1821 poem, whose description of Venus undressing for portrait painters provoked a scandal (Biblioteca Nacional, Lisbon)*

to his *O dia vintequatro d'agosto*. In early 1821 his poem *O retrato de Vénus* (The Portrait of Venus) was published in Coimbra. Venus hides Adonis on a remote island to protect him from her husband, Vulcano, and from her other lover, Mars, who is outraged that his rival is young, beardless, and effeminate. She wants to leave Adonis a portrait so that he will remember her, and she sends Cupid in search of painters able to reproduce her beauty. All of the painting schools respond to the goddess's request. When she undresses, the painters drop their brushes, and all nature trembles. José Agostinho de Macedo wrote a violent criticism of the work for the Lisbon newspaper *Gazeta Universal* in which he accused Garrett of obscenity. Garrett responded on 13 February and 11 March 1822 in the *Portuguez Constitucional Regenerado* (Regenerated Portuguese Constitutional). In the same year he was charged with abuse of freedom of the press in Coimbra. He defended himself personally in Lisbon, and the judge suspended the confiscation of copies of the work.

In 1822 Garrett composed *Os namorados extravagantes* (The Extravagant Lovers) and had it performed in Sintra. He founded the Sociedade Literária Patriótica (Literary Patriotic Society), in which he and the most important members from the Partido Constitucional (Constitutional Party) participated. Garrett was nominated an official of the Ministry of the Kingdom. He married the fourteen-year-old Luísa Midosi on 11 November. He changed his middle name from Leitão to Baptista in honor of his father-in-law.

On 27 May 1823 some troops rebelled against the constitutional government, and Miguel, the youngest son of João VI, joined the troops in Vila França. In June, João VI suspended the liberal constitution, and most of the radical liberals fled the country. Garrett was exiled to England on 9 June 1823. Luísa remained in Portugal with her father. On 4 July, Garrett arrived in London, where he devised a plan to return to Portugal. The only thing he accomplished, however, was to be granted the right to take his wife into exile with him.

In England, Garrett's financial situation deteriorated. He requested a subvention from the British government, but it was denied. His friend António Joaquim Freire Marreco found him a job at Laffite Bank in Le Havre, France. Garrett and his wife arrived there in March 1824. They lived at Ingouville Hill, on the right bank of the Seine, where Garrett wrote *Camões* and *Dona Branca ou a conquista do Algarve* (Mrs. Branca or the Conquest of Algarve, 1826). In 1825 he was fired from Laffite Bank. He tried unsuccessfully to publish *Camões* in London; with the help of some of his countrymen, he was able to publish the book in Paris in February. He regained his position at Laffite Bank after the book appeared. He requested that João VI lift his banishment from Portugal, but the king refused.

In early 1826 Garrett was fired again from the bank. João VI died in March, and Garrett's hope of returning to Portugal increased. Luísa Garrett returned first and, with the help of her father, obtained an authorization for Garrett's return. He would have to sign a document declaring that he accepted the "legitimately established government" in Portugal; Garrett refused to sign it. When Pedro I abdicated the Portuguese throne on behalf of his daughter, Maria da Glória, he promulgated the Constitution of 1826. Shortly afterward, Garrett and other exiles were allowed to return to Lisbon, where Garrett was reinstated as an official of the Ministry of the Kingdom.

At the time that the ballots for new elections were being prepared, Garrett published his *Carta de guia para leitores* (Guide for Voters, 1826) in which he discouraged the election of *afidalgados* (men who were not born into the nobility but rather were given titles of nobility) to office. He claimed that they were ashamed of the class into which they were born.

In October 1826 Garrett founded the newspaper *O Portuguez* with his friend Paulo Midosi. The following year he founded the newspaper *O Chronista*. The main objective of these newspapers was the defense of the liberal cause. On 19 September, Garrett, Paulo Midosi, Luis Francisco Midosi, and the other editors were arrested. Some friends helped them gain their freedom around Christmas. In 1827 the Garretts had a daughter, who died in infancy.

In February 1828 Prince Miguel returned to Portugal, intending to restore the absolute monarchy. Garrett and his wife moved back to London, where they lived with the help of an organization created to aid the refugees. Garrett published *Adozinda* in 1828. This work, along with "Bernal Francez," became part of the first volume of his *Romanceiro*, published in 1843.

In early 1829 Garrett published *Lírica de João Mínimo* (João Mínimo's Lyric), a selection of poems that he had written from his youth until 1826. This book and *Adozinda* were published with the help of his friend José Gomes Monteiro. In the same year, Garrett and Paulo Midosi founded in London the newspaper *O Chaveco Liberal* (The Liberal Sailing Boat). The aim of the paper was the encouragement of the growth of the liberal cause. Soon afterward, Garrett wrote the treatise *Da educação* (On Education, 1829), inspired by Jean-Jacques Rousseau's *Emile ou de l'éducation* (Emile, or, On Education, 1762). Women, he says, should be good mothers, procreate, and educate their children. The queen's case, however, was extraordinary: she should disobey the "laws of nature" to take over a male function.

In 1830 Garrett collected the articles he had published in *O Popular* as *Portugal na balança da Europa* (Portugal in the European Balance). Garrett analyzes the political relationships among European nations in an attempt to understand Portugal's position in this power game and concludes that Portugal must follow the path of civilized societies: Christianity and liberalism.

On 27 September 1830 Garrett published the *Elogio fúnebre de Carlos Infante de Lacerda, Barão de Sabrosa* (Eulogy for Carlos Infante de Lacerda, the Baron of Sabrosa); Lacerda was a liberal who had died in Paris. Throughout 1831 the liberals won important victories in the Azores and occupied many islands: Pico, São Jorge, Faial, and São Miguel. During this period Garrett met three English sisters in London who inspired some of the adventures in his novel *Viagens na minha terra* (Travels in My Homeland, 1846). Francisco Gomes de Amorim, Garrett's most important biographer, admits in *Garrett. Memórias biográficas* (Garrett: Biographical Memoirs, 1881–1884) that Garrett had a serious affair with one of the sisters. Later in 1831 Garrett founded the newspaper *O Precursor* to encourage the liberal cause.

The liberals were preparing an expedition that was to leave the Azores to put an end to "Miguelismo." Luísa Garrett stayed in London with her aunt while Garrett went to Paris to await the organization of this venture, which would take him back to Portugal. In Paris he met the famous duchess of Abrantes, Junot's widow, whom he also later remembered in *Viagens na minha terra*. In 1832 Garrett went to Terceira Island and collaborated on the writing of new laws with the lawyer José Xavier Mouzinho da Silveira.

On 10 July liberal forces occupied Porto. During his stay in Porto, Garrett was lodged at the Grilos Convent, where he began to write the two-volume novel *O arco de Sant'Ana* (Saint Anne's Arch, 1845, 1850). In August 1832 he participated on the committee responsible for writing the criminal and commercial codes for the liberal government. In November he went with Luís da Silva Mouzinho de Albuquerque on a mission to London. Fearing reprisals, Garrett did not return to Portugal after Mouzinho da Silveira was dismissed from the Department of the Treasury.

Garrett moved from London to Paris. In July 1833 the liberals took Lisbon, and he was finally able to return there with his family. In November he served on a commission to reform public education. In February 1834 he was nominated representative of trade and consul in Brussels. He arrived in the Belgian capital in July, and the following year he was given the badge of honor by the Portuguese government and then by the king of Belgium.

Garrett did not participate in the negotiations concerning the engagement of Maria II and Prince Fernando de Saxe-Coburgo, cousin of Leopold of Belgium, which indicates his lack of prestige with the queen. During this period he fell ill and, while in Paris for a medical examination, he discovered that he had tuberculosis. Garrett returned to Portugal in June 1836, replaced in Brussels by Luís da Camara by order of the queen. He did not recover from his illness, and he and Luísa Garrett separated. In October of 1836 he started a relationship with Adelaide Pastor, a seventeen-year-old girl who moved in with him. On 2 July 1836 the *Portuguez Constitucional* was published for the first time. Garrett was one of the founders and the main editor of the newspaper. On the fourth anniversary of the liberals' landing in Mindelo, Garrett attacked the ministry members in the *Portuguez Constitucional* with the exception of the duke of Terceira, claim-

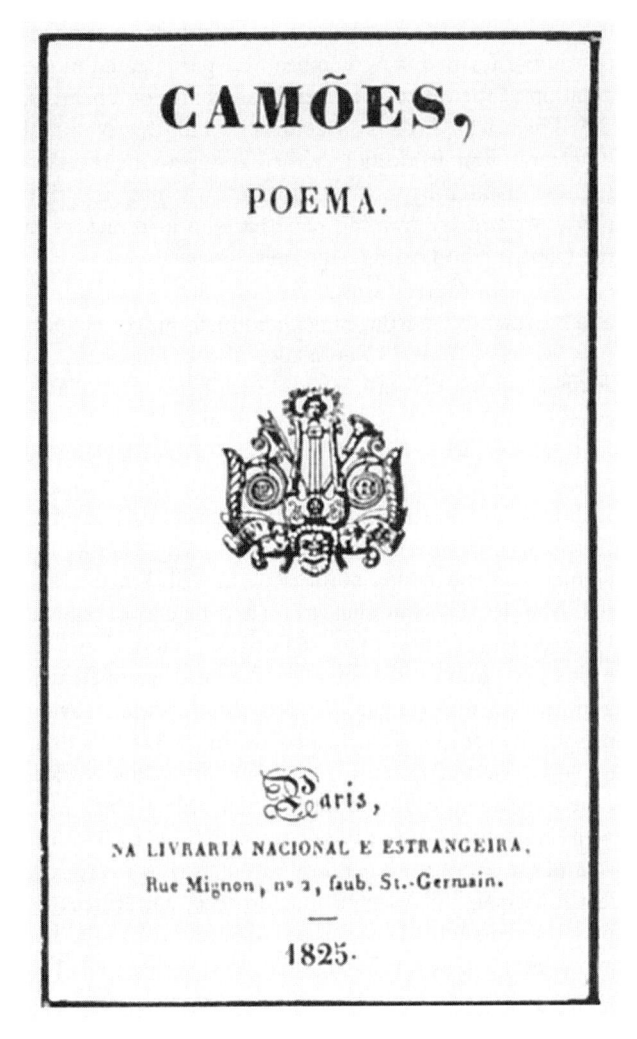

*Title page for Garrett's book-length poem about sixteenth-century writer Luís de Camões (from Simões, ed.,* Garrett, *1954; Joint University Libraries, Vanderbilt University)*

ing that time would confirm that they had not been Pedro IV's loyal friends.

Many *vintistas* (liberals from the 1820 movement), who were opponents of the government, were elected to office in the north of Portugal. After the elections of 15 August 1836, they came to Lisbon and were well received by the people. Manuel da Silva Passos (known as Passos Manuel), Garrett's friend who appears on the trip to Santarém in *Viagens na minha terra,* was among them. The members of parliament and many members of the military praised the Constitution of 1822. On 10 September 1836 the queen commissioned Marquêz Sá da Bandeira (Bernardo de Sá Nogueira) and the earl of Lumiares to form a new government.

Despite the fact that Garrett was considered a *cartista* (defender of the 1826 constitution imposed by Pedro IV after João VI's death), he collaborated with the new *setembrista* government (a reference to the fact that it was formed in September). He participated in the creation of the office of General Inspection of Theaters, the Theatrical Arts Conservatory, and the National Theater. These institutions aimed at improving the Portuguese theater by encouraging a truly national dramatic art and by training new actors and directors in the latest methods and techniques.

In 1837 Garrett was elected member of parliament as a representative from Braga, and he founded the journals *Jornal de Teatros* (Newspaper of the Theatres) and *Entre-Acto* (Intermission). The following year he collaborated on the writing of the Constitution of 1838, and the first staging of his *Um auto de Gil Vicente* (A Play by Gil Vicente) took place at the Teatro da Rua dos Condes in Lisbon on 15 August. Garrett was inspired by Vicente's *As cortes de Júpiter* (The Court of Jupiter, 1521), performed on the occasion of the departure of Princess Beatriz, Manuel III's daughter, to marry the earl of Saboia. He used this historical fact, making Vicente a character in his play, and added the alleged love story of Beatriz and the poet Bernadim Ribeiro. In this text Garrett introduces the notion of a play within a play, and he explores national themes. The originality of the work is especially noted in the scene in which Ribeiro bids farewell to Beatriz. One of the actresses who is to play the role of the Moor at the end of Vicente's play misses the last rehearsal, and Vicente ends up accepting Ribeiro to play the female role. Instead of the text that Vicente has given him, Ribeiro recites a poem he himself wrote. The success of *Um auto de Gil Vicente* may be interpreted as a kind of a revival of the Portuguese theater. In his introduction to the first printing of the work in 1841, Garrett evaluates the development of the national theater and reveals his intentions of restoring it through a revival of Vicente's works.

The year 1839 was an eventful one for Garrett. He was named official chronicler of the country, and at the Carmo Convent he began a series of public lectures on various themes from the history of Portugal. He was reelected member of parliament from the Azores, and he presented one of his most important projects to the government, dealing with the laws concerning artistic and literary property. He legalized his separation from Luísa Garrett. Two of his and Pastor's three sons died that year: Nuno, born on 25 November 1837, died on 9 February; and João, born on 6 November, died on 16 December. Sá de Bandeira's *setembrista* government fell that same year, and the members of the new government, presided over by the earl of Bonfim, included António Bernardo da Costa Cabral and Garrett's friend Rodrigo da Fonseca Magalhães.

After the first staging of *Filipa de Vilhena* in May 1840 in Lisbon, Garrett continued to prepare the first volume of *Romanceiro,* but it was not published until 1843. On 8 February 1840 Garrett delivered his well-known "Porto Pireu" speech in parliament, in which he defended freedom and the new government, together with the throne and Christianity. That same year he was reelected to parliament and was assigned to the Department of Foreign Trade to negotiate a commercial agreement with the United States of America. Anti-British sentiment was strong in Lisbon at the time, and the negotiations would affect British interests. The Americans insisted on including a clause stating that any commercial advantage given to a third country would automatically be extended to the United States. Garrett represented the Portuguese at the negotiations, which were concluded on 26 August 1840. The agreement was approved in March 1841. Shortly afterward, two new treaties were signed with England: one concerning the abolition of slave traffic, and one on trade and navigation. Both were based on the liberal rules of the Luso-American agreement. Also in 1841 Maria Adelaide, Garrett's only child who reached adulthood, was born. Adelaide Pastor died in childbirth. She was only twenty-two years old.

The reorganization of the government, now headed by Joaquim António de Aguiar, on 9 June 1841 brought Garrett great irritation. Although Magalhães still directed the Department of Foreign Trade, he was unable to prevent friction between Garrett and Antonio José de Avila, head of the Department of the Treasury, when the latter proposed budget cuts for the Conservatório Dramático. Garrett's vigorous opposition resulted in his being fired on 10 July from his positions of chronicler, director of the conservatory, and general inspector of theaters.

In the municipal elections of 1841 the *cabralistas* (partisans of Costa Cabral) won all over the nation. There were popular manifestations of support in Porto. Costa Cabral went there as soon as the results were known in Lisbon. The queen was forced to turn the government over to the earl of Terceira, who nominated *cabralistas* as ministers. One of his first official acts was to restore the constitution imposed by Pedro IV in 1826. In spite of being a *cartista,* Garrett wrote to his friend Manuel Rodrigues da Silva on 12 April 1842 expressing his dissatisfaction with the new government. When he was reelected to parliament in 1843, he opposed the arrest of his peers, the general violence in the country, and the military's abuse of the people.

The first staging of Garrett's play *Frei Luís de Sousa* (Friar Luís de Sousa) took place at the Teatro da Quinta do Pinheiro in Sete Rios on 4 July 1843. Garrett himself performed the role of Telmo, a servant. In his lecture "Ao Conservatório Real" (To the Conservatório Real) on 6 May 1843 the author stated that he had read *Memória histórica e crítica acerca de Frei Luís de Sousa* (Historical and Critical Memoir on Frei Luís de Sousa) written by a bishop of Viseu, D. Francisco Alexandre Lobo, in the eighteenth century, and also *Vida de Frei Luis de Sousa* (The Life of Frei Luís de Sousa) written by Friar António da Encarnação in the seventeenth century, as preparation for writing his work. The lecture is included in some editions of *Frei Luís de Sousa*.

The sixteenth-century prose writer known as Friar Luís de Sousa was born Manuel de Sousa Coutinho and was married to Madalena de Vilhena, João de Portugal's widow. When their only daughter, Maria, died, they separated and went to live in different convents. According to the legend, the separation and the choice of a religious life were motivated by the return of de Vilhena's first husband, supposedly killed in the battle at Alcácer-Quibir.

*Frei Luís de Sousa* is considered Garrett's theatrical masterpiece. The work is a moral and historical drama, composed of dialogues in prose. The revelation that de Vilhena was in love with Coutinho before João de Portugal went to war brings in the notion of divine punishment. At the same time, Coutinho led the resistance to the Spanish domination of Portugal (1580–1640), which highlights the struggle for national values. *Frei Luís de Sousa* portrays Garrett's belief in progress and his fight against *Sebastianismo* (the belief in King Sebastian's return). According to the author, progress could only take place if examples of virtue and patriotism from the past were revived. Thus, when literature is based on national topics, it could lead the way to a civilization built on reason and religion.

On 17 July 1843 Garrett began the trip to the Santarém Valley that inspired his most important novel, *Viagens na minha terra*. He had been invited by da Silva Passos, the former head of the *setembristas*. The first six chapters were published from August to December 1843 in the *Revista universal lisbonense* (Universal Journal of Lisbon). In June 1845 the journal published these six chapters again and continued to publish the rest of the work through November 1846. In this same year the work appeared as a book, in two volumes, including a "Prólogo da primeira edição" (Prologue to the First Edition). Although the prologue was not signed and hence was attributed to the editors, Garrett has been identified as the author.

The plot of *Viagens na minha terra* develops in two different time periods. In the first (1843), the character identified as the Author travels to Santarém. On the way, he comments on various episodes from the past as he analyzes and criticizes the society of his own time, specifically Costa Cabral's government. He weaves aesthetic and philosophic reflections into his analysis. The second period (1832) occurs within this trip, when the Author's

*Front page for one of the periodicals Garrett founded to promote liberal ideas (Biblioteca Nacional, Lisbon)*

companion tells him a story about Carlos and Joaninha, "the girl of nightingales." The Author decides to write the tale after convincing himself that it is "um romance todo inteiro, todo feito como dizem os franceses" (a complete novel, fully conceived as the French say).

Many episodes from Garrett's life can be identified in the adventures of the Author as well as in those of Carlos. Carlos is presented as a man whose goodness comes from his nature, according to Rousseau's literary and philosophical heritage. But society pushes him to doubt, uncertainty, vanity, and lies, and he turns into "um tíbio reflexo do homem natural" (a weak reflection of the natural man). At the end of the work the Author transcribes a long letter from Carlos to Joaninha. In the letter Carlos confesses himself powerless in the presence of social forces and thereby justifies his decision to become a baron. He sees himself unworthy of Joaninha's love. Although he believes that she is the right woman for him, he cannot give up other women. Both Carlos and the Author believe in a society without lies, and also in the power of love to unite a man and woman completely. When these ideals fail, Carlos is left with the option of confessing his weakness in the presence of the forces that make him "monstruoso e aleijão" (monstrous and crippled), "o mais absurdo animal, o mais disparatado e incongruente que habita na terra" (the most absurd animal, the most nonsensical and incongruous one that inhabits the Earth). In the letter Carlos presents himself as unable to be reformed by the power of love.

*Viagens na minha terra* is considered by the critics to be a landmark in the history of the Portuguese novel. With this work, Portuguese novelists began to investigate the human being within both his physical and psychological worlds. Garrett introduced formal innovations from eighteenth-century English classics into his novel: narrative digression, the imprecise and fragmentary retrieval of history, a tone of uncertainty, and a sense of humor that breaks narrative sequences strongly marked by sentimentality.

When he traveled to Santarém, Garrett accepted an invitation to visit da Silva Passos. At the height of the dictatorship of Costa Cabral, the visit to this *setembrista* leader was seen as a political act. On 4 February 1844 there was an uprising in Torres Novas against the government. Costa Cabral reacted promptly by firing the officials who were involved, suspending individual freedom, closing down opposition newspapers, and imprisoning suspects. In the same year Garrett's home was searched while he was having dinner at a friend's house.

Garrett published the first volume of *O arco de Sant'Ana* in 1845. He finished the second volume in 1849, and it appeared in print in 1850. He had begun writing this novel in 1832 at Grilos Convent in Porto, after coming from the Azores with Pedro IV's liberal troops. The novel revives an episode from chapter 7 of Fernão Lopes's seventeenth-century *Crónica de D. Pedro* (Chronicle of Pedro I). The action takes place during the reign of Pedro I, who came to be known both as "the maker of justice" and as "the cruel." In the prologue of the first edition, Garrett clearly states that although the novel is set in the Middle Ages, it refers to the fight against the oligarchy that came to replace the aristocracy in his own time.

The protagonist of the novel is Vasco, son of a Jewish woman and of the bishop of Porto. Moved by love of a woman named Gertrudinhas, Vasco leads a popular uprising against the bishop's tyranny when the bishop orders the abduction of Gertrudinhas's friend Aninhas (whom he intends to seduce while her husband is absent). Vasco was raised and educated by the bishop, but he does not know that this man is really his father. Vasco seeks justice from King Pedro for the people of Porto. In the end Pedro I, the guardian of good manners and interpreter of bourgeoisie aspirations, intervenes on behalf of the people. *O arco de Sant'Ana* ends up being a fictional treatment of the balance between elections and the constitutional monarchy.

In 1845 Garrett published in the newspaper *A Revolução de Setembro* the "Memória histórica do Conde de Avilez" (Historical Memoirs of the Earl of Avilez), and in *Revista Universal Lisbonense* the study "Da antiga poesia portuguesa" (Ancient Portuguese Poetry). The fourth edition of *Catão* and the first edition of the poetry collection *Flores sem fructo* (Flowers without Fruit) were also published.

According to Gomes de Amorim, during this period Garrett met Rosa Montufar, the wife of an army official, Joaquim Antonio Velez Barreiros, who had taken part in Pedro IV's liberal expedition with Garrett in 1832. The writer's love for Montufar, Viscountess of Luz, is immortalized in his letters and in his poems from the book *Folhas caídas* (Fallen Leaves, 1853). In the poem "Cascais," about the place where they used to meet secretly, for example, he writes: "Como ela vivia em mim, / Como eu tinha nela tudo, / Minha alma em sua razão, / Meu sangue em seu coração!" (How she lived inside me, / How I had everything in her, / My soul in her reason, / My blood in her heart). Their affair became public knowledge, but, according to scholar José Calvet de Magalhães, Garrett's friendship with Montufar's husband remained unaffected.

At the end of 1845 Garrett was reelected to parliament by the opposition to the government. In March 1846 the revolt led by Maria da Fonte broke out in Minho. Costa Cabral had prohibited burials inside the churches and had imposed new taxes; Maria da Fonte and other women armed themselves with sickles and opposed these decrees. The uprising spread to Porto, and the government was obliged to resign, ending Costa Cabral's first government. The duke of Palmela was made head of the new government, and on 10 August 1846 Garrett was returned to his position as official chronicler of the kingdom. The Teatro Maria II was finally inaugurated in the spring of 1846. Garrett's historical drama *O alfageme de Santarém* (The Armorer of Santarém) was performed at a reception for the returning exiles in the Terreiro do Paço on 11 July 1846. The work deals with the political crisis of 1383–1385, after which the Avis dynasty was established in Portugal. In early 1846 the Grêmio Literário (Literary Association) was created, with the aim of promoting science, literature, and art. Garrett and Alexandre Herculano were among its founders. In August of the same year some politicians who opposed the duke of Palmela formed an alliance around the duke of Saldanha. On 6 October a military coup took place, and civil war spread all over the country. Costa Cabral returned to Portugal after

Saldanha's victory and was elected to parliament in 1848. In 1849 he became the president of the new government.

Among Garrett's important works of this time, the comedy *A sobrinha do marquês* (The Marquis's Niece, 1848) stands out. He had begun writing the play in 1837 but finished it only in 1847. Its first staging was at the Teatro Maria II in April 1848. That year Garrett added three cantos to a new edition of *Dona Branca ou a conquista do Algarve*. Around this time he also wrote a funeral prayer in memory of Mouzinho da Silveira as well as the conclusion of *O arco de Sant'Ana*, which he published in 1850. Garrett and Montufar separated in the spring of 1849. According to Garrett's letters, the reason was jealousy. After the breakup he went to Herculano's house in Ajuda, but in the summer the lovers reconciled.

The duke of Palmela died in 1850. Costa Cabral's new government published in the *Diário do Governo* (Government Newspaper) a law restricting freedom of the press that became known as the "lei das rolhas" (law of corks). The newspaper *A Revolução de Setembro* published a protest written by Garrett and Herculano titled "Protesto contra o projecto sobre a liberdade de imprensa" (Outcry against the Freedom of the Press Project). Fifty-eight literary and political personalities signed the protest, in which the authors accused the new government of destroying freedom of thought.

In 1851 Saldanha's coup d'état ended the Costa Cabral government. The period known as the *regeneração* (regeneration), based on the reconciliation of the *cartistas* and the *setembristas*, began. Garrett received the title of viscount and asked to have the title extended to his daughter. The queen, however, denied this request, probably because Maria Adelaide was illegitimate. Moreover, it was known by then that Garrett was having an affair with a married woman, Montufar.

Garrett did not participate in the government formed by Saldanha, although he was always invited to collaborate on the writing of official documents. When he was reelected, he took office at the Department of Foreign Trade. In 1852 he began work on changes to the Constitution of 1826.

On 17 August 1852 Garrett resigned as minister because of political intrigues in which he was accused of tampering with the budgets. Evidence, however, showed that these denunciations were unfounded. Garrett reassumed his parliamentary activities in 1853. He also published the first edition of *Folhas caídas*, anonymously, but everybody seemed to know that only Garrett would write such verses. This first edition was out of print within one month.

According to Gomes de Amorim, readers wanted to know the identity of the woman referred to in the dedication of the volume as "ignoto deo" (unknown god). The number of times the words "rosa" (rose) and

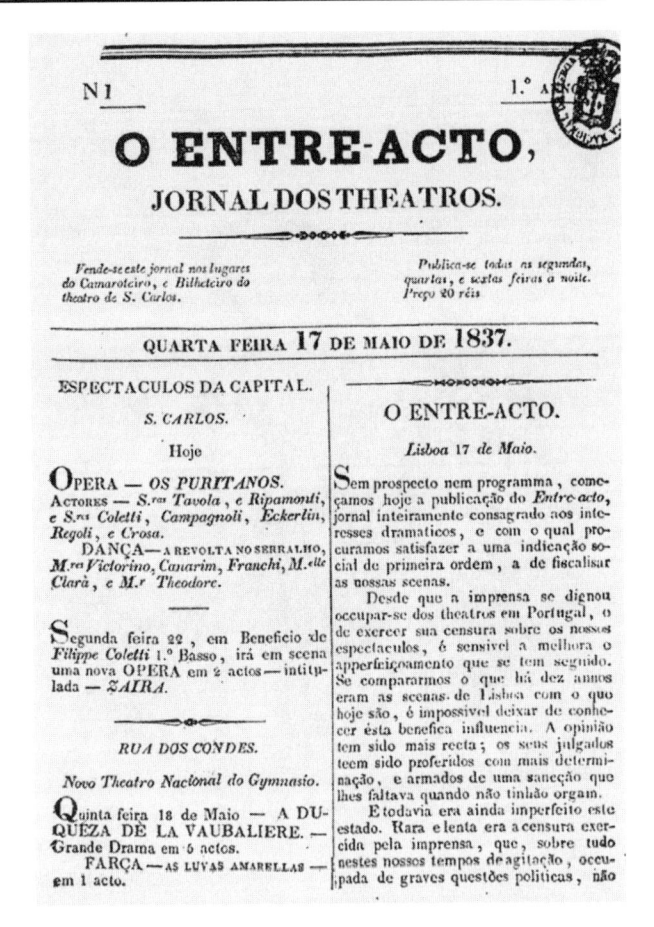

*Front page for one of the periodicals Garrett founded to support the theatrical arts in Portugal (Biblioteca Nacional, Lisbon)*

"luz" (light) appear points to one person: Montufar. Garrett's enemies accused him of immorality because although Montufar was married, some of the poems clearly express the poet's sexual desire.

During this period the friendship between Garrett and his future biographer Gomes de Amorim grew stronger. Gomes de Amorim lived in Brazil; after reading *Camões,* he had written to the author, who suggested that they meet on Gomes de Amorim's next trip to Lisbon to visit his parents. The meeting began a lasting friendship between the two men. Gomes de Amorim declares in *Memórias biográficas* that sometimes he preferred going out to taverns with friends his own age rather than being with Garrett, but that many times the writer insisted on going with them, saying that he needed to study the popular manners.

Garrett could no longer dedicate himself to his parliamentary activities in 1854 because his health had begun to worsen. When he moved into a new house on Santa Isabel Street, his health was so bad that he needed the care of Gomes de Amorim.

Garrett wanted to write a history either of the liberal campaign or of restoration of freedom. The author

*Rosa Montufar Barreiros, Viscountess of Luz, whose affair with Garrett inspired his love poems in* Folhas caídas *(Fallen Leaves), 1853 (from Simões, ed.,* Garrett, *1954; Joint University Libraries, Vanderbilt University)*

relied on Amorim's help with this project, but he never finished it, and the little that he wrote of the book disappeared. Gomes de Amorim refers to this episode in *Memórias biográficas* and suggests that someone, whose identity he does not reveal, destroyed it. Garrett also released the fourth edition of *Camões*, which he had revised, adding some notes.

Garrett lived little more than a month in the new house. The tuberculosis that had been diagnosed twenty years earlier had weakened him. Both Montufar and Herculano visited him, and Amorim says that during this visit Garrett and Montufar talked privately. When she left the house looking depressed, Garrett asked his friend not to allow her to visit again. He spent his last days with his daughter, Maria Adelaide, and Amorim.

Francisco Martins Pupilo, Garrett's friend and a physician, visited him at the end of November 1854 but saw no hope for the writer's recovery. Gomes de Amorim says that Garrett remained in a good mood during his final days. He asked that his poems and those of his friends be read to him. One night he asked Maria Adelaide to bring *Flores sem fructo* and for Gomes de Amorim to read aloud "As minhas asas" (My Wings). He received last rites on 6 December 1854, and on 9 December he died at his home on Santa Isabel Street, with his daughter and Gomes de Amorim at his side.

Almeida Garrett is one of those cases in which the author's life and work are difficult to separate. Author of an impressive body of work in various genres, he stands out in Portuguese literature, especially in the nineteenth century, for his personal style and for the themes that he explored in his works. These themes include his reevaluation of Portuguese history, love and sexual desire, and his treatment of political liberalism. In "Ao Conservatório Real" Garrett had written that readers and spectators of his time wanted works that dealt with substantial subjects: "é povo, quer verdade" (they are people, they want the truth). In Garrett, Portuguese Romanticism found an author whose work raised and explored the questions of national identity and of human existence.

**Letters:**

*Cartas de amor à Viscondessa da Luz,* edited by José Bruno Carreiro (Lisbon: Empresa Nacional de Publicidade, 1955);

*Correspondência inédita do Arquivo do Conservatório 1836–1841,* edited by Duarte Ivo Cruz (Lisbon: Imprensa Nacional-Casa da Moeda, 1995);

*Relações de Garrett com os Bertrand: Cartas inéditas: 1834–1853,* edited by Manuela D. Domingos (Lisbon: Biblioteca Nacional, 1999);

*Cartas a Garrett,* edited by Eduardo Honório Pinto da Costa (Maia: Câmara Municipal, 2000).

**Biographies:**

Francisco Gomes de Amorim, *Garrett: Memórias biográficas,* 3 volumes (Lisbon: Imprensa Nacional, 1881–1884);

Latino Coelho, "O visconde de Almeida Garrett," *Garrett e Castilho: estudos biográficos* (Lisbon: Santos & Vieira, 1917);

José Calvet de Magalhães, *Garrett, a vida ardente de um romântico* (Venda Nova: Bertrand, 1996).

**References:**

Maria Fernanda de Abreu, *Cervantes no romantismo português. Cavaleiros andantes, manuscritos encontrados e gargalhadas moralíssimas* (Lisbon: Estampa, 1997);

Joaquim de Araújo, "Garrett no estrangeiro," *Revista Moderna,* no. 28 (1899): 145–148;

Teófilo Braga, *Garrett e os dramas românticos* (Porto: Chardron, 1905);

Braga, *História de romantismo em Portugal* (Lisbon: Internacional, 1880);

Jacinto do Prado Coelho, "Garrett prosador," "A Dialéctica da História em Garrett," and "Garrett, Rousseau e o Carlos de *Viagens*," in his *A letra e o leitor* (Lisbon: Portugália, 1969), pp. 57–84;

Sérgio Nazar David, "Almeida Garrett: Sua viagem, sua vertigem," in *Paixão e revolução,* edited by David (Rio de Janeiro: EdUERJ, 1996);

David, "Imperativcos da educação e desígnios da natureza em 'Da Educação'" and "Garrett e o medevailismo," in his *O paradoxo do desejo. O masoquismo moral nas literaturas portuguesa e brasileira (1829–1899),* dissertation, Universidade Federal do Rio do Janeiro, 2001, pp. 41–97, 104–149;

Lélia Parreira Duarte, ed., "Almeida Garrett," *Scripta,* 3, no. 5 (Belo Horizonte: PUC, Minas, 1999);

Alberto Ferreira, "Garrett e o poder burguês," in his *Estudos de cultura portuguesa (século XIX)* (Lisbon: Moraes, 1980), pp. 113–123;

Ferreira, "A primeira geração romântica: Esforços de actualização cultural" and "O caminho encruzilhado do romantismo português," in his *Perspectiva do romantismo português* (Lisbon & Porto: Litexa Editora, 1984): 37–88;

Nadiá Paulo Ferreira, "Eu te amo. Tu me amas. Nós sofremos e assim morremos de e por amor," *Boletim do Centro de Estudos Portugueses,* 19, no. 25 (2000): 85–101;

José-Augusto França, "Catão e a primavera," "Camões e a saudade," and "Garrett ou a ilusão desejada," in his *O romantismo em Portugal,* volume 1 (Lisbon: Horizonte, 1974), pp. 67–91, 93–113, 239–283;

Marquês de Fronteira, *Memórias do Marquês de Fronteira e d'Alorna,* 5 volumes, edited by Ernesto de Campos de Andrada (Coimbra: Impr. da Universidade, 1926–1932);

R. A. Lawton, *Almeida Garrett. L'intime Contrainte* (Paris: Didier, 1966);

Henrique de Campos Ferreira Lima, *Estudos Garrettianos* (Porto: Imprenso Portuguesa, 1923);

Lima, *Inventário do Espólio de Almeida Garrett* (Coimbra: Publicação da Biblioteca Geral da Universidade, 1948);

Eduardo Lourenço, "Le Romantisme et Camoëns," in his *Nós e a Europa* (Lisbon: Imprensa Nacional-Casa da Moeda, 1988): 103–109;

Álvaro Manuel Machado, *Do romantismo aos romantismos em Portugal* (Lisbon: Presença, 1996);

Machado, "Garrett, Eça e o romantismo," in *Suplemento ao Dicionário de Eça de Queiroz,* edited by A. Campos Matos (Lisbon: Caminho, 2000), pp. 199–204;

Machado, *Les Romantismes au Portugal. Modèles étrangers et orientations nationales* (Paris: Fondation Calouste Gulbenkian, 1986);

Víctor J. Mendes, *Almeida Garrett. Crise na representação nas "Viagens na minha Terra"* (Lisbon: Cosmos, 1999);

Ofélia Milheiro Caldas Paiva Monteiro, "Ainda sobre a coesão estrutural de 'Viagens na minha terra,'" in *Afecto às letras: homenagem da literatura portuguesa contemporânea a Jacinto do Prado Coelho* (Lisbon: Imprensa Nacional-Casa da Moeda, 1984), pp. 598–600;

Monteiro, *O essencial sobre Almeida Garrett* (Lisbon: Imprensa Nacional-Casa de Moeda, 2001);

Monteiro, *A formação de Almeida Garrett. Experiência e criação,* 2 volumes (Coimbra: Centro de Estudos Românicos, 1971);

Lia Noémia Rodrigues Correia Raitt, *Garrett and the English Muse* (London: Tamesis, 1983);

Carlos Reis, *Introdução ao estudo de "Viagens na minha terra"* (Coimbra: Almedina, 1987);

Andrée Cabrée Rocha, *O Teatro de Garrett* (Coimbra: Coimbra Editora, 1954);

Maria Antonieta Salgado, ed., *A polémica sobre O retrato de Vénus* (Lisbon: Imprensa Nacional-Casa da Moeda, 1983);

António José Saraiva, "A evolução do teatro de Garrett," "A expressão lírica do amor nas *Folhas caídas*" and "Garrett e o romantismo," in his *Para a história da cultura em Portugal,* volume 2 (Lisbon: Europa-América, 1961), pp. 11–45;

Joel Serrão, "Introdução ao estudo do pensamento político português na época contemporânea (1820–1920)," in *Liberalismo, socialismo, republicanismo,* edited by Serrão (Lisbon: Livros Horizonte, 1979), pp. 10–41.

**Papers:**

Manuscripts and papers of Almeida Garrett are in the Biblioteca Geral da Universidada de Coimbra, the Biblioteca Nacional in Lisbon, and the Municipal Library of Ponta Delgada in the Azores.

# Teolinda Gersão
*(30 January 1940 –   )*

José N. Ornelas
*University of Massachusetts Amherst*

BOOKS: *Liliana* (Coimbra, 1954);

*Poemas* (Coimbra: Coimbra Editora, 1960);

*Alfred Döblin: Indivíduo e natureza* (Lisbon: Universidade Nova, 1979);

*O silêncio* (Amadora: Bertrand, 1981);

*Paisagem com mulher e mar ao fundo* (Lisbon: O Jornal, 1982);

*História do homem na gaiola e do passáro encarnado* (Amadora: Bertrand, 1982);

*Os guarda-chuvas cintilantes* (Lisbon: O Jornal, 1984);

*O cavalo de sol* (Lisbon: Dom Quixote, 1989);

*A casa da cabeça de cavalo* (Lisbon: Dom Quixote, 1995);

*A árvore das palavras* (Lisbon: Dom Quixote, 1997);

*Os teclados* (Lisbon: Dom Quixote, 1999);

*Os anjos* (Lisbon: Dom Quixote, 2000);

*Histórias de ver e andar* (Lisbon: Dom Quixote, 2002).

PLAY PRODUCTION: *Os teclados,* Lisbon, Centro Cultural de Belém, February 2001.

OTHER: *Dada: Antologia bilingue de textos teóricos e poemas,* edited and translated by Gersão (Lisbon: Dom Quixote, 1983).

Teolinda Gersão is the author of a significant body of literary work and one of the most innovative female voices of Portugal in the decades following the 25 April 1974 revolution. This military coup put an end to a repressive fascist dictatorship that had endured for almost fifty years and set the stage for a reform process that reshaped the entire country's socio-economic, political, and cultural landscape. As a consequence of the sweeping changes that took place in the aftermath of the coup, many cultural and political theorists embarked on an evaluation of the victories and losses associated with the postrevolutionary period. Similarly, many writers also began attempts to interpret the new Portugal and to redefine and reevaluate the country's past in order to better understand its present conjuncture. The revolution, which led to freedom of expression in the country, gave Portuguese

*Teolinda Gersão ( from the cover for* Os anjos, *2000; Widener Library, Harvard University)*

writers a golden opportunity to reimagine and to engage critically with their country; and Gersão was at the forefront of this movement. Besides her creative work, Gersão has also published extensively on other writers. Her membership in several associations reflects both her interests as a fiction writer and as a literary critic: she is a member of the PEN Club, the Portuguese Association of Writers, the International Association of Literary Critics, and the Portuguese Association of Comparative Literature.

Teolinda Maria Sanches de Castilho Gersão Gomes Moreno was born on 30 January 1940, in Coimbra, a city that is known for being home to the oldest Portuguese university, the University of Coimbra, founded originally in Lisbon in 1290. Her father, Manuel Liberato Faria Gersão, was a medical doctor; her mother, Teolinda Sanches de Castilho Costa Gersão, was a homemaker. Gersão completed elementary and secondary school in Coimbra and graduated from the University of Coimbra with a degree in English and German studies in 1963. To further her academic career, she did postgraduate studies in Germany at the Universities of Tüebingen and Berlin from 1962 to 1965. She finished her master's degree in German philology during this period and also completed several of the courses for her doctorate. During her last year in Germany, she was a lecturer at the Technical University of Berlin. Upon her return to Portugal, she became an assistant professor at the University of Lisbon, a position that she held until 1974, when she became a professor at the New University of Lisbon. She received her doctorate in German philology in 1976 with a dissertation on the work of Alfred Döblin.

In 1976 and 1977 Gersão resided in São Paulo, Brazil, a stay that is reflected in her diary, *Os guarda-chuvas cintilantes* (Shimmering Umbrellas, 1984). She went to Brazil to accompany her husband, Luís Moreno, a jurist and company executive who was in the country on business matters. She and Moreno, who were married in 1966, have two daughters, Maria Luís and Sílvia.

Gersão's literary career was launched in 1981 with her first major book, the highly acclaimed novel *O silêncio* (The Silence). The book was awarded the prestigious PEN Club Fiction Prize. *O silêncio* focuses on the unequal relationships between men and women, the difficult links between the natural and cultural worlds, the refusal to accept linear time and tradition, and the constant subversion of both language and cultural spaces. Another major concern relates to language, writing, and the need for women and the disenfranchised to create a discourse of their own. The author constructs a bipolar fictional world where seemingly there is no contact between the male and female spheres, and women still inhabit the asphyxiating traditional space of silence without apparent bridges to a liberating reality. Nevertheless, as the narrative makes clear, the dichotomy that keeps the sexes separated is a boundary that can be and is transposed through the subversive behavior of certain characters, especially women. Such characters refuse to accept the fixed aspects of old and traditional models and reality, and instead stress the power of imagination, dream, and invention in the construction of the world.

*O silêncio,* which is considered an experimental novel because of its fragmented structure, is divided into three narrative segments that correspond to three different periods in the life of Lídia, the protagonist. The first segment is concerned with the establishment of a dialogue between Lídia and her lover, Afonso, a dialogue that is meant to find some contact points between their different worlds. Lídia's transparent desire is to transform Afonso. She wants someone who is not restricted by an exterior repressive and imposed order and who strives instead to break free from the rigid constraints of traditional society. She needs Afonso to accompany her in her search for a world of uncertainty and without any limits. The second segment deals with a clash between the feminine and masculine characters in the novel. On one hand, there is Lídia's desire to inhabit a limitless and chaotic world where everything can be invented anew. On the other hand, there is Afonso's world, which follows a set of rules and regulations in order to be meaningful. Lídia's attempt to convince Afonso to use language in an imaginative way in order to find liberty and love in linguistic chaos ends in failure. Her lover only understands an objective and limited use of language: language that cannot question the real and only serves to express the order of society.

The constant and explicit tension between order and disorder present throughout the novel does not have a resolution. Lídia cannot convince Afonso of the superiority of her transgressive relationship to the world. Also, unlike her, he cannot be open, unfinished, and in constant movement, and at the same time inhabit a world without boundaries. As a consequence of their inability to construct a world together, Lídia, in the third segment of the novel, decides that she must depart lest she be confined to a world of silence and repetition. As she walks away from Afonso's house in search of a new life and freedom, she affirms that his voice cannot any longer influence or control her because she is out of his reach.

In addition to the focus on the lives of the two main characters and their conflicting worlds, *O silêncio* also touches upon the lives of Lavínia and Alfredo, Lídia's parents, as well as of Alcina, Afonso's wife. Alfredo and Afonso lead parallel lives, and Lavínia's world has many affinities with her daughter's. Although the two men have different professions—Afonso is a medical doctor, and Alfredo is a teacher of

*Paperback cover for the second edition (1981) of Gersao's experimental first novel (1981), about romantic and linguistic conflicts (Howard-Tilton Memorial Library, Tulane University)*

Portuguese—they both want their respective lovers to live within rigid and established structures and accept social norms and rules. As a professor of language, Alfredo feels that Lavínia, who is Russian, must learn Portuguese so that she can function within prescribed rules and regulations, proper usage of language being a way of entering the norm and living within it. However, his wife looks at languages in general as a form of oppression: she feels that she is exiled in a world of words that she cannot really comprehend, words that cannot construct her own world. Unable to express herself and realizing that she is living in a rigid and limiting environment that she cannot question, she decides to take refuge in silence as a form of transgression and resistance. However, even silence does not buy Lavínia freedom from the rigid impositions of society, and she eventually commits suicide to escape her imprisonment in language and social order.

Alcina, in contrast, is compliant to the surrounding circumstances: her docile behavior and her immaculate, orderly home are projections of her unproblematic relationship with social order. She mimics the codes and conventions of traditional society. However, her blind allegiance to the well-ordered program of society and her ability to play the wife's role so perfectly are the factors that create instability and monotony in her marriage to Afonso, who decides to find a lover. But instead of finding variety with Lídia, he finds chaos and resistance to his way of representing the world.

*O silêncio* is a fragmented narrative that does not follow conventional compositional techniques. Time and space are collapsed; there are no references to specific historical events that might help the reader locate the text in a specific context. Chronological development is seldom followed: past, present, and future are fused, a fact that confounds the reader trying to follow the sequence of events. Lavínia's and Lídia's actions overlap each other, so that many times the reader loses the thread regarding the two characters. Finally, there is no single narrative voice but rather multilayered voices that create a polyphonic text.

Gersão's second novel, *Paisagem com mulher e mar ao fundo* (Seascape with Woman, 1982), although similar in some respects to *O silêncio,* also differs substantially from her first novel. As in the previous work, the new novel focuses on the expansion of reality and on social and cultural movement through rupture and transgression. *Paisagem com mulher e mar ao fundo* also stresses that transformation of the social order can occur if all forms of repression and violence against the individual are denounced and if abusive power is undermined. Contrary to *O silêncio,* however, the 1982 novel is placed in a specific sociopolitical context: the fascist dictatorship of António de Oliveira Salazar and his successor, Marcelo Caetano; the colonial wars; and the 1974 Portuguese revolution and its aftermath.

In *Paisagem com mulher e mar ao fundo* the figure of Salazar (known by the initials O.S. in the novel) plays a crucial role in the development of the narrative. Although his omnipotent and omnipresent power is felt throughout the novel, he never appears as a character. He is only a symbolic force that controls all the actions, words, and movements of the Portuguese. He is everywhere, but physically he is nowhere. Gersão structures her narrative against the repressive backdrop of fascism as personalized in the figure of O.S. On the one hand, there is the dominant order claiming that it possesses knowledge and truth and therefore has the moral authority to impose its view of the world on others and force them to accept it without question. On the other hand, there are the adversaries of Salazar, led by Hortense, the protagonist; Horácio, her husband; and others who constantly try to break through the limits imposed on them by fascist rhetoric and create an alternative space.

The tension between the two worldviews is the backbone of the novel. The conflict between the opposing forces is a struggle for representation, that is, a conflict over the words, actions, gestures, and images that will shape reality and the worldview of the Portuguese. As Hortense finds out, the castrating force of fascism—and its capacity to reinvent its repressive mechanisms as changing circumstances dictate—controls all actions and the representation of reality. However, Hortense consistently counters the force of O.S. through personal acts of transgression and resistance. As a child in school, she creates compositions and drawings that let her subversive imagination construct other worlds. As Hortense gets older, she eventually marries Horácio, an individual who becomes an ally in her struggle against O.S. Subsequently, Hortense gives birth to a son who dies in the colonial wars defending the morally corrupt fascist regime. However, before his departure for Angola, he impregnates his wife; Hortense's daughter-in-law and her future grandson also become allies in her fight against the regime. Eventually victorious after the 1974 Portuguese revolution, Hortense is given the opportunity to invent a new world through her own words.

The reactionary figure Áurea, a schoolteacher and a supporter of O.S.'s ideological program, is Hortense's rival in *Paisagem com mulher e mar ao fundo*. Not only does this character blindly accept the ideas that fascist rhetoric espouses, but she, unlike Hortense, also repudiates femininity in all its sexual and erotic manifestations. She is a strong believer that the nation needs and must have a manly outlook and that only strong masculine principles, O.S.'s principles, can preserve the integrity of Portugal. Áurea has two missions in life: the first is to educate the future citizens of the country, and the second is to attack lust, femininity, and pleasure, all threats to the perfection of an ideal state engendered by male figures to preserve their power and privilege. She views pleasure as a form of moral degradation that corrupts and destroys the nation. She also accepts without question the fascist idea that pleasure and culture rise and fall proportionately. Therefore, she keeps herself incorruptible and above the base pleasures of the flesh as an example for others to follow.

Again in *Paisagem com mulher e mar ao fundo* there is great tension between opposing worldviews. Although it is not really a conflict resulting from a repressive patriarchal system, as is the case with *O silêncio,* the conceptualization of fascism encompasses many ideas and elements that are present in patriarchy. Similarly, both novels feature characters whose actions support the repressive sociopolitical structure and those whose actions not only oppose it but also are the basis for the construction of a liberating and alternative space.

Gersão's next work is a fictional diary, *Os guarda-chuvas cintilantes*. The book, written partly in Brazil, where the author lived for almost two years, is not a traditional diary. Its focus is not on the confessional registering of daily events, personal experiences, intimate details, feelings, and emotions. The laying bare of the soul and/or of the interior of the individual, typical of the diary form, plays an insignificant role in the structure of this work. The author has stated that the diary is not autobiographical, even if it pretends to be so. Details and references in the text do indeed, at times, create the impression that the author is writing about her personal experiences and feelings and daily occurrences of her life, but it would be misleading to assume that they are autobiographical.

*Os guarda-chuvas cintilantes* deals with many themes that are of great interest to the author: war, hunger, social inequities, the relationship between life and writing, the struggle with the word, the search for the other through the written word, and the word as a means to construct different worlds—the real, the imaginary, and the symbolic. In fact, the passion for words and writing becomes the predominant theme in this fictional diary. Given the ambiguous nature of the meaning of words and the fact that words are inscribed in a system that she wants to undermine, the author has to constantly struggle against the difficulty and even the impossibility of writing. How can she write her world, feelings, and thoughts in a male-centered language that feels foreign to her? This question is the crux of the diary, and it becomes an issue for which she cannot really find a solution.

Gersão's third novel, *O cavalo de sol* (Sun Horse, 1989), has many similarities to her two previous novels but also differs significantly from them. The narrative centers around Vitória and her problematic relationship with her cousin Jerónimo. Just like the heroines of *O silêncio* and *Paisagem com mulher e mar ao fundo,* Vitória also has to struggle against a repressive system that constantly tries to control and silence her. The novel focuses on the representation of the rural Portuguese bourgeoisie in the 1920s and its hierarchical system of values, which are undermined by the protagonist through her transgressive actions. The story begins a few days prior to the marriage of Vitória to Jerónimo—a marriage that is not consummated because Vitória decides to flee the repressive space in which she finds herself. She had moved into her cousin's home, the "House of the Horse's Head," when she lost her mother at an early age. From the beginning, Jerónimo

*Paperback covers for Gersão's second novel (1982), about the protagonist's struggles against the fascist regime that controlled Portugal until 1974 (Howard-Tilton Memorial Library, Tulane University)*

establishes with Vitória a relationship that is based on domination and submission; his objective is to possess Vitória totally, to control all her movements and actions. As he eventually finds out, however, his idea that he possesses absolute control over her wild and subversive nature is pure delusion.

The tension between the two main characters builds up slowly at first, but then it grows in intensity and eventually ends with the final revolt of Vitória, her abandonment of her cousin's home in search of a new, liberating space. The novel is divided into four sections, or chapters, named after the movements of a horse: walk, trot, gallop, and jump. The heroine is associated with the horse, a symbol of the solar principle, life, and sex. There is a strong symbiotic relationship between Vitória and her horse: both are wild, unpredictable, and extremely difficult to tame. Both cannot be confined or controlled; they will use all four movements in order to escape any predator. In the case of Vitória, her escape is from Jerónimo and the bourgeois society that the "House of the Horse's Head" represents. At the end, Vitória and her horse jump the wall that has contained her in a submissive, obedient, and compliant state. The final leap into the unknown signifies independence and the possibility of freedom.

While Vitória identifies with her horse, Jerónimo feels repulsed by horses because he is aware that they cannot ever be tamed. He prefers the relationship that he establishes with his dog. The dog is compliant, always faithful, and submits totally to the wishes of Jerónimo; the dog is really the shadow of its owner. Jerónimo relishes the relationship of power and total submission that characterizes the association between man and dog, and he expects the same type of relationship with his cousin. However, he cannot exert the same power over Vitória that he exerts over his dog. She remains forever the "other" and eventually causes the destruction of his ordered world. *O cavalo de sol* earned Gersão her second PEN Club Fiction Prize.

In 1995 Gersão decided to retire from the New University of Lisbon to dedicate herself exclusively to her creative-writing interests. Her fourth novel, *A casa da cabeça de cavalo* (The House of the Horse's Head, 1995), was awarded the Grand Prize of the Portuguese Association of Writers as the best novel published that year. As in *O cavalo de sol,* the horse plays an important role in the structure of *A casa da cabeça de cavalo*. Both novels take place in the same house, and some characters even have the same names. However, there are no overlapping characters, since the action for the two novels occurs about one hundred years apart. In this narrative of events that take place during the nineteenth century, the dark bronze horse's head facing east on the wall of the house is an ambivalent and enigmatic symbol of time, and thus of life and death. The animal's presence and impact in the house as well as its constant disappearances and appearances in different parts of the town and surrounding areas are connected with the appearances and disappearances of the characters in the novel. The author constructs a narrative that eschews linear time and instead focuses on memory in order to reconstruct events.

In the "House of the Horse's Head" the souls of its former inhabitants get together to tell stories about their lives in order to keep memory alive, because they understand quite well that total loss of memory signifies death. However, as the characters narrate their stories, they start to realize that many inaccuracies begin to appear in their retellings. Consequently, they feel a need to write them down in order to preserve accuracy. By writing down their stories in notebooks—or one of the characters writes what is told by others, since many of them cannot read or write—they will be able to preserve the reality of the house, from its initial construction, to a gutting fire, to its reformation and its final demise, along with the deaths of all its inhabitants.

The characters deal humorously with their own deaths and recount other episodes of their everyday lives: love affairs, births, marriages, likes and dislikes, family fights and struggles, and experiences of wars and the Napoleonic invasions of Portugal. The novel, through the many conversations of the dead inhabitants, re-creates a fairly accurate view of Portuguese society during the nineteenth century. Although the society that is represented is traditional—women constantly make references to the task of embroidery and taking care of household chores and the family, while men deal mainly with worldly affairs—the reader can still gather from those memories that Portuguese society was not fixed or immobile. Some of the women were raising their voices against the abuse, including physical beatings, to which they were subjected by men. In spite of the fact that the work focuses on three generations of a family, it never attains the status of an historical novel. Rather, it is a disjointed re-creation of the past through memory, where different time frames overlap and a subjective reconstruction of the past is paramount.

Eventually, memory begins to waste away, and the characters of the novel—Januário, Horácia, Benta, Inácio, Carmo, Ercília, and Paulinho—also lose all points of reference and their voices. Since the characters are unable to speak, memory cannot be kept alive either. With the loss of memory comes final death. However, the act of writing will always preserve the memory of those who are no longer able to narrate stories.

In contrast to her previous novels that used Portugal as a background, Gersão's next novel, *A árvore das palavras* (The Tree of Words, 1997), takes place in Mozambique's capital, Lourenço Marques, now Maputo. Two trips to Mozambique—the first in 1960, when the writer spent a whole summer there, and the second for a month in 1995—played a crucial role in the composition of this book. She uses the 1950s and the 1960s, the years prior to and at the beginning of the colonial war, as the sociohistorical background for her novel. As many other Portuguese writers have done since the 1974 revolution, the writer also uses the space of Portuguese-speaking Africa for her novel. Essentially, two opposing feminine points of view are presented: the reality of Mozambique as observed and lived by Amélia, a Portuguese woman who had migrated to the country to marry Laureano Capítulo in response to an advertisement she saw in a Portuguese newspaper, and the reality of the country as seen and felt through the eyes of Gita, Amélia's daughter, who takes over the narration of the novel when her mother abandons Laureano and disappears.

Amélia's point of view is influenced by her personal background as a white woman who migrates to Mozambique from rural Portugal in search of better economic conditions but realizes that her dream cannot be attained because the inequality and the injustice to which human beings are subjected are a result not only of racial differences but also of social differences. She never really adapts to the exuberance and richness of nature in Mozambique; she cannot live in harmony with the sensuality and the chaos of that nature. Her attempts to build a garden around her house lose out against the wilderness of Mozambique. She is disdainful of white people who do not consider material progress and social climbing to be the main objectives of life and instead adopt local customs, living as if they were black natives. To a great extent, she tries to re-create Portuguese reality in her new country but fails miserably. There is danger lurking everywhere in nature, and she feels that blacks are a threat to her ordered way of life because they are a source of all illnesses and they practice magic. She compares the African continent to quicksand: it sucks all strength, and it also sucks in all

*Paperback cover for Gersão's 1989 novel, about a woman who rebels against the dominating cousin she has married (Library Communications Center, University of Massachusetts, Dartmouth)*

people. Her decision to leave is based on her fear of being trapped by a reality she cannot comprehend and on her desire to domesticate her world, something she is unable to do in Africa.

Gita, on the other hand, feels at home in Mozambique. She has a symbiotic relationship with nature; the sensuality and the force of nature flow through her. Gita is initiated into all the rhythms, the myths, the love of nature and the need to live in harmony with it and the cult of the ancestors of her native country. It is conceivable that Amélia's departure is related to the fact that both her husband and daughter have become totally integrated into Mozambican society. She tries hard to force her daughter to conform to Portuguese customs and values, but she fails because of Gita's rebellious nature. The initiation that Gita undergoes is not only sensual and social, it is also political and sexual. Her awakening to the political situation of Mozambique parallels in many ways her acceptance and opening up to the social, natural, and sensual aspects of the country. Consequently, the novel is more than the dichotomous representation of Mozambican reality; it is also a vision of the political and historical turmoil that confronted the country during the 1950s and 1960s and of the problematic colonizer/colonized relationship that existed between Portugal and Mozambique. In fact, there is a constant juxtaposition between the colonizer and the colonized in the novel. In addition, Portuguese society is represented as being immobile, static, and stagnant, while Mozambican society is characterized as dynamic and full of vitality, just like its nature.

*Os teclados* (The Keyboards, 1999) and *Os anjos* (The Angels, 2000) have to be considered novellas rather than novels. *Os anjos* may even be classified as a short story, since the text is fewer than fifty pages. *Os teclados,* which may be characterized as an apprenticeship novel, is a story about an adolescent, Júlia, who attains knowledge and discovers her essence through her conflictive and problematic relationship with music. She is a pianist, and what music signifies in her life and how she relates to sounds are the bases for her newfound knowledge of the self. Through her personal journey she finally recognizes that the world has lost its transcendence and that it is only her work on the keyboard that is transcendent. In spite of her feeling that she inhabits a world of silence and nothingness, she will still sit at the piano and play, because playing is a way for her to be united with the universe. According to her, music is linked to the movement of the planets; music is the beginning of everything; and each celestial body possesses a note and a specific accord. All of them together create the harmony that governs the universe. In a sense, music plays the same role in *Os teclados* that writing has played in some of the other works written by Gersão: music, like writing, prevents the world from falling into chaos, and it also preserves memory.

Music is linked to the destinies of several characters in the novella, including all the members of Júlia's family, especially her crazy uncle Eurico; her friend Lúcia; and her two music teachers, Claudemiro Palrinha and Severiano Mendonça. In the same way, Júlia's destiny is traced through her relationship with the keyboard. However, it is also through words that Júlia–and Gersão–can express the idea that music structures and governs the universe. Thus, music and writing are correlated.

*Os anjos* is a story of secrets and revelations narrated by a prepubescent girl named Ilda. Her family is in a state of crisis: her father is an alcoholic; her mother is mentally disturbed and beats Ilda frequently; her grandmother has passed away; and her grandfather, who has an unnamed, incurable illness, comes to live with the family after his wife's death. Ilda's mother, father, and Serafim, the male predator of the village, are also involved in a love triangle. Given that the story is narrated from Ilda's perspective, there are many silences and gaps, which make the narrative enigmatic and mysterious. Surely, there is conflict between Ilda's mother and father, but she cannot explain the source of the conflict. Neither can she explain her mother's state of mind nor the reasons for her violent outbursts, her suicide attempts, and her constant wandering off day and night.

One day Ilda receives a package from Serafim to give to her mother. He tells her that it is medicine for her grandfather, but it is never made clear whether that package and subsequent ones that Ilda receives really contain medicine. However, from the first time Ilda receives the package from Serafim, the mental state of her mother improves dramatically, and she becomes her old self, beautiful and loving. On the other hand, the father becomes more irritated and depressed, and he begins to drink even more than before. It seems that Ilda's mother has returned to the arms of her old lover, Serafim, with the approval and consent of the grandfather. He believes that for his daughter-in-law to be cured and return to her old self she must be encouraged to have regular clandestine sexual encounters with Serafim. And he tells his grandchild not to worry any longer about her mother wandering off from the house, because she is being guided by angels.

The angels that the grandfather alludes to in the story are not orthodox; they are revelations that touch a human being and allow the individual to ascend to a higher state of being and knowledge. In this particular case, they are the angels of sexual revelation or gratification, appropriately the seraphim of love, but Ilda is still too young to comprehend the allusion. On the day of her first communion, she also expects a revelation from the seraphim, the archangels, and angels, just like her mother has had and the prophet Muhammad had a long time ago, but it does not happen. She is truly disappointed and decides to stop going to church. Eventually, Ilda has her revelation at the end of the story. The angels finally descend upon her body while she is carrying a tray with food and, as a consequence, she drops it. She does so because she is unhappy and tired of being ordered around. Her act of rebellion receives approval from her mother, who used to exhibit the same type of minor defiances prior to the much more significant acts of rebellion, her adulterous encounters with Serafim. Ilda now comprehends what it means to be a female in a male-oriented world. The angel of darkness has illuminated her as it did her mother. She finally understands that it is through acts of subversion and rebellion that the female will attain a state of happiness, the state inhabited by the angels of the title of the book.

Through an illustrious literary career spanning more than twenty years, Teolinda Gersão has produced a remarkable number of books dealing with various aspects of her homeland, including the colonial conditions that prevailed in the former Portuguese colony of Mozambique. Her work has begun to receive international attention, with translations into languages such as English, French, and Romanian. An English translation of her story "A dedicatória" (The Dedication) appeared in *Beacons: A Magazine of Literary Translation* in 2002. The author also maintains a website, <http://www.teolinda-gersao.com/>, in English and Portuguese.

Whether she is addressing the colonial situation, fascism, love, the multitude of historical events of the nineteenth century, the problematic relations between men and women, or the force of institutions, Gersão's novels always draw upon the resourcefulness of her characters to create alternative worlds, to denounce the conditions that repress and imprison human beings, and to carry out actions that undermine the institutions that confine them. Although Gersão does not consider herself a feminist writer and is offended by the application of such labels to her body of work, her writing deals precisely with the challenges that women face in a male-centered society. Gersão's novels are not only texts of transgression against an oppressive system but also transgressive in their use of poetic language and of a narrative structure that eschews linear time and clearly defined spaces.

**References:**

Sandra Regina Goulart Almeida, "Writing from the Place of the Other: The Poetic Discourse of Transgression in the Works of Virginia Woolf, Clarice Lispector and Teolinda Gersão," dissertation, University of North Carolina, 1994;

Helena Barbas, "*Os teclados:* um romance de aprendizagem em que a autora se ultrapassa a si própria," *Jornal de Letras,* 34 (1982);

Eduardo Prado Coelho, "A Seda do Lenço," in his *A mecânica dos fluídos: Literatura, cinema, teoria* (Lisbon: Imp. Nac. Casa da Moeda, 1984), pp. 91–100;

Maria Heloísa Martins Dias, "O pacto primordial entre mulher e escrita na obra ficcional de Teolinda Gersão," dissertation, University of São Paulo, 1992;

Dias, "Teolinda Gersão: Uma voz expressiva da ficção portuguesa contemporânea," *Letras & Letras,* 60 (1991): 241;

Ana Teresa Diogo, "*O cavalo de sol,*" *Colóquio/Letras,* 121–122 (1991): 241;

Maria de Lourdes Ferrari Horta, "*Paisagem com mulher e mar ao fundo* de Teolinda Gersão," M.A. thesis, Universidade Católica do Rio Grande do Sul, 2000;

Nuno Júdice, "Romance: os elementos na *Paisagem,*" *Expresso,* 10 July 1982, p. R28;

Catherine Kong-Dumas, "Teolinda Gersão: *Paisagem com mulher e mar ao fundo,*" *Colóquio/Letras,* 73 (1983): 78–80;

Fábio Lucas, "Teolinda Gersão: Música nas esferas," *Jornal de Letras,* 757 (1999): 21;

Isabel Allegro de Magalhães, "O tempo de *O silêncio*" and "O tempo de *Paisagem com mulher e mar ao fundo,*" in her *O tempo das mulheres* (Lisbon: Imp. Nac. Casa da Moeda, 1987), pp. 389–460;

Maria de Fátima Marinho, "Teolinda Gersão: *A casa da cabeça de cavalo,*" in her *O romance histórico em Portugal* (Porto: Campo das Letras, 1999);

Cristina Cordeiro Oliveira, "Teolinda Gersão: *O silêncio,*" *Colóquio/Letras,* 65 (1982): 81–83;

José N. Ornelas, "*Paisagem com mulher e mar ao fundo:* Positividade e afirmação de diferença," in *O despertar de Eva,* edited by Maria Luiza Ritzel Remédios (Porto Alegre: Coleção Memória das Letras, 2000), pp. 145–164;

Ornelas, "Subversão da topografia cultural do patriarcado em *O cavalo de sol* de Teolinda Gersão," *Discursos: Estudos de Língua e Cultura Portuguesa,* 5 (1993): 115–137;

Carlos Reis, "Inscrição ficcional de África: *A árvore das palavras* de Teolinda Gersão," *Jornal de Letras,* 693 (1997): 22–23;

Darlene J. Sadlier, "The Language of Silence in Teolinda Gersão's *O silêncio,*" in her *The Question of How: Women Writers and New Portuguese Literature* (New York: Greenwood Press, 1989), pp. 93–112;

Maria Alzira Seixo, "*Os guarda-chuvas cintilantes* de Teolinda Gersão," in her *A palavra do romance* (Lisbon: Horizonte, 1986), pp. 237–241;

Inês Alves de Sousa, "Teolinda Gersão: O processo de uma escrita," dissertation, University of Oporto, 1988.

# Ana Hatherly
*(15 June 1929 –   )*

Nadiá Paulo Ferreira
*Universidade do Estado do Rio de Janeiro*

BOOKS: *Um ritmo perdido* (Lisbon: Privately printed, 1958);

*As aparências: Sombra, claro-escuro, luz* (Lisbon: Sociedade de Expansão Cultural, 1959);

*A dama e o cavaleiro* (Lisbon: Guimarães, 1960);

*Nove incursões* (Lisbon: Sociedade de Expansão Cultural, 1962);

*O mestre* (Lisbon: Arcádia, 1963);

*Sigma* (Lisbon: Privately printed, 1965);

*Eros frenético* (Lisbon: Moraes, 1968);

*39 Tisanas* (Porto: Colecção Gémeos 2, 1969);

*Anagramático, 1965–70* (Lisbon: Moraes, 1970);

*Mapas da imaginação e da memória* (Lisbon: Moraes, 1973);

*63 Tisanas* (Lisbon: Moraes, 1973);

*O escritor: 1967–1972* (Lisbon: Moraes, 1975);

*A reinvenção da leitura: Breve ensaio crítico seguido de 19 textos visuais* (Lisbon: Futura, 1975);

*Crónicas, anacrónicas, quase-tisanas e outras neo-prosas* (Lisbon: Iniciativas Editoriais, 1977);

*O espaço crítico: Do simbolismo à vanguarda* (Lisbon: Caminho, 1979);

*Para uma arqueologia da poesia experimental: Anagramas portuguesas do século XVII* (Lisbon: Fundacão Calouste Gulbenkian, 1979);

*Poesia: 1958–1978* (Lisbon: Moraes, 1980);

*Joyciana,* by Hatherly, E. M. Melo e Castro, António Aragão, and Alberto Pimenta (Lisbon: & Etc., 1982);

*A experiência do prodígio: Bases teóricas e antologia de textos-visuais portugueses dos séculos XVII e XVIII* (Lisbon: Imprensa Nacional-Casa da Moeda, 1983);

*Anacrusa: 68 sonhos* (Lisbon: & Etc., 1983);

*O cisne intacto: Outras metáforas: Notas para uma teoria do poema-ensaio* (Porto: Limiar, 1983);

*A cidade das palavras* (Lisbon: Quetzal, 1988);

*Escrita natural* (Lisbon: Galeria Diferença, 1988);

*Poemas em língua de preto dos séculos XVII e XVIII* (Lisbon: Quimera, 1990);

*A preciosa de Sóror Maria do Céu* (Lisbon: Instituto Nacional de Investigação Científica, 1990);

*Volúpsia* (Lisbon: Quimera, 1994);

*Ana Hatherly (photograph by Graça Sarsfield; from <http://www.mulheres-ps20.ipp.pt/Ana_Hatherly.htm>)*

*A casa das musas: Uma releitura crítica da tradição* (Lisbon: Estampa, 1995);

*O ladrão Cristalino: Aspectos do imaginário barroco* (Lisbon: Cosmos, 1997);

*351 Tisanas* (Lisbon: Quimera, 1997);

*A idade da escrita* (Lisbon: Tema, 1998);

*Rilkeana* (Lisbon: Assírio & Alvim, 1999);

*Elles: Um epistolado,* by Hatherly and Alberto Pimenta (Lisbon: Escritor, 1999);

*Um calculador de improbabilidades* (Lisbon: Quimera, 2001);
*Poesia incurável* (Lisbon: Estampa, 2003);
*O pavão negro* (Lisbon: Assírio & Alvim, 2003);
*Itinerários* (N.p.: V. N. Famalicão, 2003).

OTHER: *Operação 1,* edited by Hatherly and E. M. Melo e Castro (Lisbon: Privately printed, 1967);
*Operação 2: Estruturas poéticas,* edited by Hatherly and Melo e Castro (Lisbon: Privately printed, 1967);
*Caminhos da moderna poesia portuguesas,* edited by Hatherly (Lisbon: Dir. Geral do Ensino Primário, 1969);
*PO. EX: Textos teóricos e documentos da poesia experimental portuguesa,* edited by Hatherly and Melo e Castro (Lisbon: Moraes, 1981);
*Defesa e condenação da Manice,* introduction by Hatherly (Lisbon: Quimera, 1989);
Luís Nunes Tinoco, *Elogio da pintura,* edited by Hatherly and Luís de Moura Sobral (Lisbon: Instituto Português do Património Cultural, 1991);
António Barbosa Bacelar, *Desafio venturoso,* edited by Hatherly (Lisbon: Assírio & Alvim, 1991).

TRANSLATIONS: Nikolai Aleksandrovich Berdiaev, *Cinco meditações sobre a existência* (Lisbon: Guimarães, 1961);
Cesare Pavese, *Férias de agosto* (Lisbon: Arcádia, 1965);
Leopold von Sacher Masoch, *A Vénus de Kazabaika* (Lisbon: Fernando Ribeiro de Mello, 1966);
Pierre Klossowski, *Sade, meu próximo* (Lisbon: Moraes, 1968);
J. A. S. Collin de Plancy, *Dicionário infernal* (Lisbon: Galeria Panorama, 1969);
Robert Littell, *O peão agressivo* (Lisbon: O Século, 1974);
Malcolm Lowry, *Ouve-nos Senhor do Céu que é a tua morada: Através do Canal do Panamá* (Lisbon: Iniciativas Editoriais, 1976);
G. R. Elton, *A Europa duranta a reforma: 1517–1559* (Lisbon: Presença, 1982);
Leland Robert Guyer, *Imagística do espaço fechado na poesia de Fernando Pessoa* (Lisbon: Imprensa Nacional-Casa da Moeda/Centro de Estudos Pessoanos, 1982);
Denis Rougemont, *O amor e o ocidente* (Lisbon: Vega, 1989);
Maria do Céu, *Triunfo do rosário repartido em cinco autos* (Lisbon: Quimera, 1992);
Jerónimo Baía, *Lampadário de cristal* (Lisbon: Comunicação, 1992);
Gunnar Ekelöf, *Antologia poética* (Lisbon: Quetzal, 1992);
Ruth Fainlight, *Visitação* (Lisbon: Quetzal, 1995).

Ana Hatherly's extensive production in both literature and the plastic arts is characterized by a strong sense of the poetic and by elements of the baroque. Great attention to form, wordplay, and the doubling of images are aspects of the artistic style in her fiction, which is dominated by themes of the drama and pain of human existence, language and writing as signifying processes, and writing as a questioning of and search for the truth. The author's particular preference for baroque literature is also seen in her many critical studies and editions of Portuguese writers of that period.

Hatherly was born Ana Maria de Lourdes Rocha Alves on 15 June 1929 in Porto to Celeste Rocha Pereira and Jaime C. Alves, but she moved to Lisbon in her youth and has lived there since then. In 1952 she married a British subject, Henry Mário Frank Hatherly, who died in 2000. They had one daughter, Catherine, who died in 1970 at age eighteen.

Hatherly graduated from the University of Lisbon with a degree in Germanic philology in 1977. During the 1970s she also majored in cinema technique at the International London Film School in England. In the 1980s she earned a doctorate in Hispanic literature of the Golden Age from the University of California at Berkeley. She also obtained a doctorate in modern Portuguese studies from the Universidade Nova de Lisboa in 1986.

Her professional experience includes classes at the Art and Visual Communication Center in Lisbon from 1975 to 1978. From 1977 to 1979 she taught at Lisbon Superior Cinema School, and from 1981 to 1982 she was a visiting professor at King's College in London. From 1982 to 1986 she taught Portuguese literature at Berkeley. Beginning in 1984 she also taught at the Universidade Nova de Lisboa, where she founded the Portuguese Studies Institute. Later she became head professor at this university.

Hatherly published her first books of poetry–*Um ritmo perdido* (A Lost Rhythm, 1958), *As aparências: Sombra, claro-escuro, luz* (Appearances: Shadow, Light-Dark, Light, 1959), and *A dama e o cavaleiro* (The Lady and the Knight, 1960)–in an atmosphere of political intolerance and lack of freedom, under the dictatorship of António de Oliveira Salazar and his successor, Marcelo Caetano, who ruled Portugal with an iron fist through repression of any sort of opposition, including censorship of the press. Hatherly says that this atmosphere had an impact on her choice of subjects, but not on her ability to publish.

In *Um ritmo perdido* the image of love as Sphinx corresponds to the experience of something nameless, metaphorically called "a rhythm," that is lost for ever. In *As aparências* Hatherly uses a theme that dominates most of her writing: the idea that language makes it difficult for man to reach the truth. After being introduced to the rules of language (the symbolical order), man becomes a being divided between subjectivity and appearances. Hatherly uses the desert as a metaphor for the mysteries of life and death and departure and return. The image of the arrow captures the notion of time, which is "Entre o que está assustadoramente aquém / E o que misteriosamente além / Se imagina" (Between that which is frighteningly beneath / And that which is mysteriously beyond / One imagines). In *A dama e o cavaleiro* the themes are centered on the pain of existence, since living implies dealing with mysteries: "conviver com cifras ocultas, que ficaram perdidas, que ficaram suspensas" (to live with hidden figures that remain lost and suspended).

In 1960 Hatherly and E. M. Melo e Castro, also a poet, led the Movimento da Poesia Experimental Portuguesa, whose objective, like that of the modernist movement in 1915, was the renewal of Portuguese poetry. In the 1960s poets faced the same issue the modernists had dealt with, namely the preference for national themes that resulted in a sentimental, redundant, and rhetorical discourse. At the end of the 1960s Hatherly took part in many individual and collective art exhibitions, installations, and performances, developing her career as an artist. She worked primarily on painting and visual poetry. In 1969 she also began to work on short experimental movies and videos.

Several important features characterize the experimental poetry with which Hatherly worked in the 1960s: the visualization and spatialization of words; the creation of a new syntax (combinatory syntax), which allowed for semantic invention (nondiscursive); and a new structure through which readers participate in the process of creation. Portuguese experimental poetry earned its place among the international avant-garde movements. In a debate focused on experimental Portuguese poetry, held in São Paulo, Brazil, during the Art Biennial (1977), Hatherly emphasized that the rupture proposed by experimentalism should be understood as a rejection of the present moment but not as a total rejection of the past.

Words, with their qualities of sound, rhythm, and time, have to be regarded as objects, the raw material of the text. The concept of a "verbivocovisual" poetry was proposed by the "Plano Piloto para poesia concreta" (Pilot Plan for Concrete Poetry) by Augusto de Campos, Décio Pignatari, and Haroldo de Campos; this text, first published in the Brazilian journal *Noigandres* in 1958, became the basis of experimental poetry in Portugal and all over the world. The impact of Concrete poetry on Hatherly's poetry of the 1960s is evident.

Hatherly and Melo e Castro launched issues 1 and 2 of *Operação,* an experimental poetry magazine, on

*Cover for Hatherly's first poetry collection (University of California, Santa Barbara)*

13 April 1967, at the Galeria-Livraria Quadrante in Lisbon, where an event titled CONFERÊNCIA-OBJETO was held. Her *Estruturas poéticas* (Poetic Structures) was a part of the second and last issue of the magazine. Other works of hers were also part of the experimental poetry movement: *Sigma* (1965), *Eros frenético* (Frenetic Eros, 1968), *39 Tisanas* (39 Tisanes, 1969), and *Anagramático* (Anagrammatic, 1970).

*O mestre* (The Master, 1963) is Hatherly's only novel. According to the author, she wrote it when she joined with experimentalism and abandoned the style of her former production.

*O mestre* reveals close links to the myth of love and the Romanesque style. The complex structure of the work goes beyond the traditional structure of the novel in terms of time, space, characters, and plot. *O mestre* poses new questions, especially concerning several different literary theories of prose and verse. The novel is based on the articulation of love and knowledge, the latter becoming a requisite of true love. Truth has to be discovered, and love depends on it.

*Cover for Hatherly's only novel (1963), about a Disciple's frustrated love for a Master (Miami Public Library)*

The traditional Romanesque trickery is avoided in the plot. The drama of the heroine, reflected in the story of a nameless character, represents the destiny of all women who believe in the promise of everlasting happiness through love. The proper names of the characters are replaced by nouns that express their participation in the plot: a Disciple who searches persistently for a Master to be loved by and to love. This process of idealization places the loved one beyond the realm of everyday existence, and the conjugation of love and knowledge reinforces the idea of "matching souls."

The Disciple dedicates herself to the Master and tries to seduce him because she desires to be his favorite and to have him exclusively for herself. The Master is presented as one who does not speak much but laughs and makes his pupils laugh. The narrator warns that the insistence on being loved may not end well for the Disciple. The Master himself tells her that she should not try to understand everything and that "há coisas que a gente não deve querer" (there are things that one should not desire).

The Master refuses the idea of being loved, and his attitude frustrates the Disciple. She believes that he is a joker who uses his laughter to attract and betray the disciples. Therefore, her love turns into anger; she enters a dark cave where he is sleeping, surrounded by dead disciples and hunting trophies, and she stabs him in the heart. She searches for an exit, but when she turns to look at the Master one last time, she sees him standing there holding her head, with the dagger still in his chest. Master and Disciple thus symbolize how dangerous and lethal passionate love can become.

The heart as a symbol of love and the head as a symbol of knowledge are the emblematic agents of the double murder. Lover and loved one cannot fulfill each other's needs, because what one needs does not exist in the other. Denying this truth, as the Disciple did, or just simply laughing at it, as the Master did, constitutes a tragedy.

At the end of the 1960s Hatherly became interested in experimenting with the letters of the alphabet as a visual expression. In *Anagramático* she collects ninety-seven drawings and writings. The individual letter as sign and symbol is a means of communication, and writing (especially handwriting) can be regarded as a sort of map, since it describes a route: "um sistema de sinais para indicar um roteiro específico, o que faz com que toda página escrita seja um mapa" (a system of signs to indicate a specific route, which makes each written page a map), as Hatherly writes in *Mapas da imaginação e da memória* (Maps of the Imagination and Memory, 1973). With this research, Hatherly initiates a poetic project in which the letter assumes its real nature as a form of drawing. The books in which she experiments with this type of visual activity, in addition to *Mapas da imaginação e da memória,* include *A reinvenção da leitura* (The Reinvention of Reading, 1975), *O escritor* (The Writer, 1975), and *Escrita natural* (Natural Writing, 1988).

Writing as imagetic representation, however, did not absorb Hatherly completely. Both in verse and in prose she persists in her search for the clue that links words, which becomes an ambiguous search for the truth. After she joined the experimental poetry movement in the 1960s, she began to write the pieces for her books titled *Tisanas*. The 1969 volume *39 Tisanas* includes the first 39, and *63 Tisanas* (1973) has numbers 40 through 102. *A cidade das palavras* (City of Words, 1988) includes *tisanas* 1 to 222, and there are 351 in a 1997 collection.

*Tisanas* are a group of fragments in prose, which according to the author are prose poems. Tisanes are a homeopathic remedy made from barley. *Tisana,* as a metaphor, is a type of writing that captures daily life while focusing on the desires, wishes, and unconscious affections of the human being. Thus, a scene (event) built into another scene (subjectivity) can reveal several things: the pain of an anticipated meeting; an enigma to be solved from thoughts or dreams; a wound that will never be healed; a gesture or a word; or a silence that affects the subject. "Tisana 46," from *63 Tisanas,* is typical: "ontem, eu e a minha irmã resolvemos ir hoje ao cinema quando chegou o momento de nos prepararmos para sair verificamos que o verdadeiro momento já tinha passado" (Yesterday, my sister and I decided to go to the movies today when the moment for getting ready to leave arrived we realized that the real moment had already passed).

Twenty-one years after the start of the experimental poetry movement, Hatherly and Melo e Castro published the collected theoretical guidelines and documents of the movement as *PO. EX* (1981). Hatherly's work as a writer and researcher continues to be recognized through various awards and prizes, including the Oskar Nobling Medal, awarded by the Academia Brasileira de Filologia Românica (1978); the Grande Prémio de Ensaio Literário da Associação Portuguesa de Escritores, for the book *O ladrão Cristalino* (The Crystal Thief, 1997); and the Prémio de Poesia do PEN Club Português, for her book *Rilkeana* (1999). She received the Prix Evelyne Encelot from the Maison des Ecrivains in Paris (awarded in 2003 for poetry) and the Hanibal Lucic Poetry Prize in Hvar, Croatia, also in 2003. In 2000, Hatherly retired from her post as professor at the Universidade Nova de Lisboa. She continues to write, to publish, and to teach, and she participates in congresses in Portugal and abroad.

**References:**

Augusto de Campos, Décio Pignatari, and Harold de Campos, "Plano Piloto para poesia concreta," in *Vanguarda européia e modernismo brasileiro,* edited by Gilberto Mendonça Teles (Petrópolis: Vozes, 1997);

Nadiá Paulo Ferreira, "O lugar do sujeito em *Tisanas,*" in *Estudos universitários de língua e literatura,* edited by Tempo Brasileiro (Rio de Janeiro: Tempo Brasileiro, 1993), pp. 349–361;

Linda Hutcheon, "Modes et formes du narcisisme littéraire," *Poétique,* 29 (February 1977): 104;

Antônio Sérgio Mendonça, *Bovarismo & Paixão* (Porto Alegre: Centro de Estudos Lacaneanos, 1992);

Maria Elisabeth Graça de Vasconcelos, "*O Mestre–Romance de Prometeu e o tema do labirinto,*" *Revista Ocidente,* 80 (1971): 182–196.

**Papers:**

An archive of Ana Hatherly's papers is at the Biblioteca Nacional in Lisbon.

# Herberto Helder
*(23 November 1930 –    )*

Rui Torres
*Universidade Fernando Pessoa, Porto*

BOOKS: *O amor em visita* (Lisbon: Contraponto, 1958);
*A colher na boca* (Lisbon: Ática, 1961);
*Poemacto* (Lisbon: Contraponto, 1961);
*Lugar* (Lisbon: Guimarães, 1962);
*Os passos em volta* (Lisbon: Portugália, 1963);
*Electronicolírica* (Lisbon: Guimarães, 1964);
*Húmus* (Lisbon: Guimarães, 1967);
*Retrato em movimento* (Lisbon: Ulisseia, 1967);
*Ofício cantante* (Lisbon: Portugália, 1967);
*O bebedor nocturno* (Lisbon: Portugália, 1968);
*Apresentação do rosto* (Lisbon: Ulisseia, 1968);
*Vocação animal* (Lisbon: Dom Quixote, 1971);
*Poesia toda* (2 volumes, Lisbon: Plátano, 1973; revised and expanded, 1 volume, Lisbon: Assírio & Alvim, 1981);
*Cobra* (Lisbon: & Etc., 1977);
*O corpo, o luxo, a obra* (Lisbon: & Etc., 1978);
*Photomaton & vox* (Lisbon: Assírio & Alvim, 1979);
*Flash* (Lisbon: Privately printed, 1980);
*A plenos pulmões* (Porto: Oiro do Dia, 1981);
*A cabeça entre as mãos* (Lisbon: Assírio & Alvim, 1982);
*As magias: Versões de Herberto Helder* (Lisbon: Hiena, 1987); revised as *As magias: Alguns exemplos* (Lisbon: Assírio & Alvim, 1988);
*Última ciência* (Lisbon: Assírio & Alvim, 1988);
*Do mundo* (Lisbon: Assírio & Alvim, 1994);
*Doze nós numa corda: Poemas* (Lisbon: Assírio & Alvim, 1997);
*Oulof* (Lisbon: Assírio & Alvim, 1997);
*Poemas ameríndios* (Lisbon: Assírio & Alvim, 1997);
*Fonte* (Lisbon: Assírio & Alvim, 1998);
*Ou o poema contínuo: Súmula* (Lisbon: Assírio & Alvim, 2001).

TRANSLATIONS: Hans Christian Andersen, *Contos*, translated by Helder and Elsa Taveira (Lisbon: Verbo, 1964);
Italo Calvino, *O cavaleiro inexistente*, translated by Helder and Fernanda Ribeiro (Lisbon: Portugália, 1965);
Gine Victor Leclercq, *Veloz como o vento* (Lisbon: Verbo, 1967);
Louis Althusser, *Lenine e a filosofia*, translated by Helder and A. C. Manso Pinheiro (Lisbon: Estampa, 1970).

OTHER: "Aviso indispensável," in *Poemas bestiais*, edited by Carlos Camacho (Funchal: Tipografia Camões, 1954);
Edmundo de Bettencourt, *Poemas de Edmundo de Bettencourt (1930-1962)*, introduction by Helder (Lisbon: Portugália, 1963);
António José Forte, *Uma faca nos dentes*, introduction by Helder (Lisbon: & Etc., 1983);
*Eloi Lelia Doura: Antologia das vozes comunicantes da poesia moderna portuguesa*, edited by Helder (Lisbon: Assírio & Alvim, 1985).

SELECTED PERIODICAL PUBLICATIONS–
UNCOLLECTED: "Declaram que . . . ," *Nova* [s.d.]: 1-5;
"Ofício de poeta," *Êxodo* (1961): 32-34;
"Paisagem de caras," *Diário Popular* (suplemento *Quinta-feira à tarde*), 1 August 1968, pp. 1, 9;
"Carta a Eduardo Prado Coelho," *Abril* (1977): 46.

Herberto Helder's poetry cannot easily be catalogued under any literary genre, because in each of his books Helder reworks previously used poetic motifs. Every poem that he writes is a transformation of a previous text, which can be his own or that of another writer. The fact that the poet is currently dedicated to the translation of poetry–or what he prefers to call "versions"–is a sign of the textual instability that characterizes all of his works. His biography also reveals a sense of constant change and transformation, which is developed in his *Photomaton & vox* (1979). In this work he recognizes that "Nada há de mais apaziguador do que ter falhado em todos os lados da biografia" (There is nothing more appeasing than having failed all parts of my biography), and in a straightforward fashion he says that "[a] nota biográfica é: desempregado por dentro e por fora como um pai ou como um filho" (the biographical entry is: unemployed on the inside and on the outside like a father or like a son).

Helder's poetry persistently reminds the reader that the function of the poetic word is to denaturalize any stable meanings, pointing to semantic contents that are beyond the limits imposed by daily routines. The indecipherable poem can only be fully accessed by the poet; however, he includes in the text the key for its translation, which allows for the reader's own transformation and evolution. The obscure loneliness of the poet holds the possibility of its own deciphering, which places Helder on the level of self-reflexive poetics and the reader in a position of co-authorship. The reading experience resulting from the texts of Helder is, thus, an empowering one in that its translation of the world contains, simultaneously, the will to change and the resistance to the world of rules and rationalization.

Helder shuns public visibility. A view of his life, however, may help the reader to understand his rejection of the literary canon and his refusal to project a public image of himself. Helder was born Luís Bernardes Oliveira on 23 November 1930, in Funchal, in the Madeira Islands. His mother, who had been ill since his birth, died in 1938. In that same year he entered the Colégio Lisbonense, from which he graduated in 1946. Helder says in *Photomaton & vox* that his adolescence was "apenas ira e dor" (only anger and pain). During this period the young poet left Funchal for Lisbon, where he enrolled in the Escola Luís de Camões for two years. In 1948 he completed the first year of law school at the University of Coimbra, but then he decided to change to Romance philology. After three years, however, he also left this program and traveled throughout Portugal. During this time Helder also published his first poems, in the literary journal *Arquipélago* (1952). In the meantime, he moved from one job to another, a habit that has accompanied him throughout his life.

In 1954 Helder published three more poems in the journal *Poemas Bestiais,* and in that same year he returned to Funchal, where he started working as a meteorologist in the Serviço Meteriológico Nacional. There he saw his father for the last time, and in the following year he joined the group of Surrealist poets that came to be known as the group of Café Gelo (Lisbon). The group included poets such as Mário Cesariny de Vasconcelos, Manuel Castro, Luiz Pacheco, Manuel de Lima, and António José Forte. This Surrealist experience, which lasted until 1957, was important for Helder's work. Some of the themes and techniques that characterize Surrealism appear in most of his later poems: eroticism, occultism, the exploration of the unconscious, textual montage, and collage. During this time Helder worked in the publicity section of the Pasteur Institute, and he also collaborated on many newspaper literary supplements and journals, including the weekly *Re-nhau-nhau* (1955), the magazine *Búzio* (1956), and the journals *Folhas de Poesia* (Leaves of Poetry), *Graal,* and *Cadernos do Meio-Dia* (Mid-Day Cahiers)

His first book of poetry, *O amor em visita* (Love on Visit), was written in 1955 but not published until 1958. This work is a long poem that was later fully integrated into his second book, *A colher na boca* (The Spoon in the Mouth, 1961). In *O amor em visita* Helder explores some of the motifs that pervade his later poetry. The first thing that catches the attention of the reader, not only in this poem but in almost all of Helder's poetry, is the absence of rhyme. *O amor em visita* also shows how deeply connected love and death are for the poet. He later develops a love-death relationship in most of his texts. Another important theme in this first book is the self-referential function of language, along with several

*Paperback cover for Herberto Helder's 1964 volume of poetry, in which he develops his experimental methods (Young Research Library, University of California, Los Angeles)*

words frequently used to create unexpected metaphors. These words focus on the feminine and on desire, and the metaphors are derived from the vegetable and animal kingdoms. Later, in response to a growing interest of the poet in alchemic processes, the mineral world replaces the vegetable and animal. The feminine, however, is the central issue of all of Helder's poetry, as captured in the title poem of *O amor em visita*: "começa o tempo onde a mulher começa" (time begins where the woman begins). In 1957 Helder married Maria Ludovina Dourado Pimentel, with whom he has a daughter, Gisela Ester Pimentel de Oliveira, born in 1958.

Silence, one of the most important themes explored by Helder, has a double meaning of death and resurrection, and it is an active component of language. In his poetry Helder understands death as the necessary transitional stage that allows for resurrection: "a morte é como romper uma palavra e passar / através da porta, para uma nova palavra" (death is how to break a word and pass / through the door to a new word). *O amor em visita* shows this primordial image of transformation in a metaphorical symbol of fertilization: the spring. On the other hand, the work of transmutation is a work of love: the love for the text and for reading the world. Helder uses all these symbols in a challenging way for the reader to make connections.

From 1958 to 1960 Helder lived in France, Belgium, Holland, and Denmark. During this time he had a variety of underpaid jobs: helping in bakeries, kitchens, and breweries; loading trucks; and even serving as a tour guide in the zones of prostitution in Amsterdam. He wrote most of the poems for *A colher na boca* and *Os passos em volta* (The Steps Around, 1963) during this time. After a while, however, he was forced to return to Portugal, where he spent some time in Coimbra recovering from avitaminosis. Later in 1960 he started working with the Itinerant Libraries (trucks or vans with books that travel around the country so that people can have access to them) of the Fundação Calouste Gulbenkian, which gave him the opportunity to travel through the areas of Beira-Alta, Ribatejo, and Baixo Alentejo.

He published *A colher na boca* and *Poemacto* (Poem-Act) in 1961. In *A colher na boca* Helder expands his themes to depict the poem as body and earth and adds a preoccupation with the notion of writing itself. The word and the naming of things have had a central place in Helder's poetics since his first poems, but starting with this work there is a clear metalinguistic questioning of language. There emerges throughout the book a parallel between the work of the poet and that of the architect, as the project of the house and the idea of a habitat connect to his reflections on the feminine condition. For the poet the figure of woman or mother is one of loss and need, like the portrait—a presence that is absence at the same time—which shares a central place with death in his works. These initial poems were later modified in the collections *Ofício cantante* (Singing Craft, 1967) and *Poesia toda* (Whole Poetry, 1973), showing that the poem as metamorphosis has a central role in Helder's work.

This search for alteration is illustrated in the use of quotation in the poem "Tranforma-se o amador na coisa amada, com seu" (The Lover is Transformed into the Thing Loved, with His . . .), in which Helder reads a poem of the classical poet Luís de Camões. Helder's erotic treatment of love subverts Camões' notion of idealized love, and the modern poet perceives the past as a system of impositions, thus proposing a redefinition of the present.

*Poemacto,* on the other hand, considers the poem as the undertaking of an actor (the poet) whose voice sings love, madness, and childhood. This act can only acquire consistency within the process of writing, which is seen as both discovery and action: poem-act. In 1962 Helder published *Lugar* (Place), in which he considers the act of reading in a straightforward fashion. In this book he starts using a technique that becomes central to the definition of his literary style: the caesura, or enjambment, which happens with the separation and consequent distribution of parts of certain words throughout the verses. This work also marks the introduction of the mineral element in the thematic conception of the poem. A poetic system develops in which poetry is the naming of the world. It is, however, a world where the eternal return of the same (to use Friedrich Nietzsche's philosophical expression) blurs the limits of what is writing and reading, and of what is love and death.

Around this time Helder began collaborating on the journals *Távola Redonda* (Round Table) and *Jornal de Letras e Artes* (Journal of Letters and Arts). In 1963 he published *Os passos em volta* and wrote the preface for Edmundo de Bettencourt's collected poems. *Os passos em volta* was a significant book in making Helder known to a larger public and is one of the most well-accepted books that he has written. The texts in this book appear under the format of short stories. The level of poeticalness that they contain, however, clearly negates their status as traditional narrative. To further complicate understanding the texts as narratives, only one character in the twenty-three texts, Anemarie, has a name. The book represents an attempt to overcome the dichotomy between prose and poetry. Another aspect that blurs these boundaries is the level of ambiguity that pervades most of the texts. A unity is preserved, however, through a series of themes that recur in Helder's poetry. These include the incommunicability of certain illuminated beings; the house and the inquiring of places; love; innocence; the act of writing; anthropophagy; crime; childhood; and loneliness.

The circularity of the texts is, as indicated in the title, one of the most important characteristics of the volume. All of the texts share the same narrator-character, who oscillates between the self and the other, forming a type of spiral, as Maria de Fátima Marinho has noted. These stories are clearly written from the perspective of an outsider, but they reaffirm a certain nostalgia for the return (to home, to self, and so on) even though this return is embedded with fear and anguish. In the stories "Estilo" (Style) and "Brandy," for example, the narrator is also the main character, and he speaks directly to a mute interlocutor, thus reaffirming the level of isolation to which the poet, as the reader of the world, must necessarily be confined. *Os passos em volta,* which has gone through several editions, represents a type of writing studio for Helder; in this volume the poet rewrites and thus practices the self-metamorphosis that characterizes his poetry. This rewriting of his own texts also contributes to the general characteristic of instability and mutation that his poetry communicates.

Starting in 1963, Helder established a profound relationship with poetic experimentalism, which has determined his attitude toward poetry and its writing. At first influenced by the post-Surrealist approach, Helder soon replaced it with the baroque and started using the wordplay typical of Concrete and visual poetry. *Electronicolírica,* written in 1963 and published in 1964, represents a turning point in the poet's work. In this book he experiments with metaphorical as well as with metonymical transformation, by means of processes that include crossing, substituting, and inverting the elements of a system of words previously created. This work led to Helder's experiences with Concrete poetry, at the same time revealing his usage of the combinatory process that he developed in his later poetry. In the postscript to the first edition of the book Helder mentions one experiment that Italian intellectual Nanni Balestrini accomplished in Milan in 1961 with an electronic calculator. Balestrini processed old as well as modern texts according to certain combinatory rules previously established, resulting in more than three thousand combinations of sentences. Helder explains that the same attitude is behind the conception of his book, except he does not limit himself to any rule. According to the poet, the resulting texts resemble "certos textos mágicos primitivos, a certa poesia popular, a certo lirismo medieval" (certain magical primitive texts, certain popular poetry, certain medieval lyricism). The texts create a peculiar "fórmula ritual mágica, de que o refrão popular é um vestígio e de que é vestígio também o paralelismo medieval, exemplificável com as cantigas dos cancioneiros" (ritual magical formula of which the popular refrain is a vestige, and of which medieval parallelism, exemplified through the songs of the *cancioneiros,* is also a vestige). Helder concludes, with this experiment, that "O princípio combinatório é, na verdade, a base linguística da criação poética" (The combinatory principle is, in truth, the linguistic base of poetic creation).

*Cover for the first volume of the 1973 collection of poems Helder wrote between 1953 and 1971 (Jean and Alexander Heard Library, Vanderbilt University)*

In 1964 Helder and António Aragão organized the first anthology of the Portuguese publication of *Poesia Experimental.* During the same year, Helder and Elsa Taveira translated some fairy tales by Hans Christian Andersen; the following year, Helder worked with Fernanda Ribeiro to translate Italo Calvino's 1959 fantasy *O cavaleiro inexistente* (The Nonexistent Knight). In addition, Helder worked for National Public Radio of Portugal as an international news editor. The poems that Helder wrote for the anthology of experimental poetry represent mere speculations on the form and the visual materiality of the word. They also point to a new poet, more prepared to debate and question the problems inherent to translation, adaptation, and rewriting. The concrete experience opens ways to the discussion of a revision of the literary tradition, and along with Ana Hatherly and E. M. de Melo e Castro, Helder has opened a debate in Portugal and created the necessary vocabulary for future developments. In 1965 he participated with a total of four visual poems in a collective exhibit called Visopoemas and also collaborated on a special issue of the *Jornal do Fundão* dedicated to experimental poetry. In the following year he co-organized, this time with Aragão and Melo e Castro, the second issue of *Poesia Experimental*.

His most famous text—and the one that received the best critical reception—was "A máquina de emaranhar paisagens" (The Landscape Entangling Machine), which first appeared in *Poesia Experimental* and was later included in the collections *Ofício cantante* and *Poesia toda*. In this work Helder freely combines his own poems with fragments of texts from the book of Genesis, the book of Apocalypse, and with the poems of François Villon, Dante, and Camões.

In 1967 Helder published *Húmus* (Humus), *Retrato em movimento* (Portrait in Movement), and *Ofício cantante*. *Húmus* is part of a series of intertextual activities that Helder developed at this time. It is a poem that rewrites another text, Raul Brandão's novel by the same name, which had been published in 1917. As Helder mentions in the epigraph, all the "palavras, frases, fragmentos, imagens, metáforas" (words, phrases, fragments, images, metaphors) of the poem are present in Brandão's text. Helder's work is thus an act of concretization, through writing, of his attentive reading of the novel. This work is one of transformation and metamorphoses of other texts, as well as an expansion of significations. It is a text inscribed in another text.

The structure of *Retrato em movimento* is similar to that of *Os passos em volta*. It rejects even more, however, the conventional structure of the short story and narrative conventions in general. The texts in this book point to an almost absence of narrative structure. Taking as his raw material a series of strange cases gathered from the media, Helder subverts the collective narratives in such a violent way that crime and excess seem to be the only possible way to achieve the combination of woman-love-writing that in other books could be more easily attained. This work also presents as an innovative feature the exploration of colors as a way of understanding the metamorphosis of the world, thus adding to the gallery of metaphors that Helder uses throughout his poems.

In 1968 Helder began to dedicate most of his efforts to the translation of poetry, beginning a series of books in which, as he says, he "changes" poems into the Portuguese. Such is the case of *O bebedor nocturno* (The Nocturnal Drinker), which comes with an important preface that helps the reader to understand his conceptions of anthropophagy and its importance to his poetics. *Apresentação do rosto* (Presentation of the Face), published in 1968, was confiscated by government censors. *Vocação animal* (Animal Vocation) appeared in 1971. In the first edition of this work there is a note that declares the author "deixou de escrever em 1968" (stopped writing in 1968). Helder has published several books of poetry and translations since then; but at the time he made the statement in 1968, he had completely withdrawn from social life. In an article published in the newspaper *Diário Popular* on 1 August 1968, titled "Paisagem de caras" (Landscape of Faces), Helder explains this period of seclusion: "Quanto a mim, apenas desejo alguma distância para apaziguamento das raivas e um pouco de simpatia por essa massa na verdade tão pouco vital e natural e normal, sem um mínimo de qualidade íntima e higiene de projectos. Uma certa distância" (As for me, I only want some distance for pacifying my anger and a little sympathy for the mass of truth, so little vital and natural and normal, without the minimum of intimate quality and hygiene of projects. A certain distance.)

*Apresentação do rosto* once again negates any possible stable relationship between prose and poetry. It is close to an autobiographical novel, but at the same time it presents an unstable alternation of narrators. As the poet warns, "o autobiógrafo é a vítima do seu crime" (the autobiographer is the victim of his own crime), and he also tells the reader that the description of a life is necessarily the description of an invented reality. The themes that pervade this narrated and fictionalized biography are filtered through the image of the mother and given from the perspective of the passage into the adult world. They nonetheless resemble Helder's previous concerns: the discovery of loneliness, the necessity of crime, and the end of innocence.

In 1968 Helder also wrote a book of poems that was only published in the second volume of his anthology *Poesia toda* in 1973. This book is, however, an important work. Titled *Kodak*, it considers writing as a portrait, and therefore as a verbal translation of the world. *Kodak* uses photography as the focusing metaphor, because photography represents, for Helder, a place of possibility as well as of illusion. Therefore, it constitutes a good metaphor for language. Similar to these texts are those of "Cinco canções lacunares" (Five Lacunal Songs), written between 1965 and 1968 and published in volume two of *Poesia toda*. These poems sporadically use rhyme, which is rare in Helder's works. Once again, common concerns include the uselessness of words and their impossibility of translating the illegible.

Helder participated in the publication of *Filosofia na alcova* (Philosophy in the Bedroom), by the Marquis de Sade, in 1968. This activity involved him in an unpleasant judicial process related to censorship, but he received only a suspended sentence. In 1969 he became the literary editor of the publishing firm Estampa, where he began publishing the complete works of the futurist poet José de Almada Negreiros. In the following year he traveled to the south of France, Holland, and London, and in 1971 he left for Angola, where he worked as a reporter for the magazine *Notícia* in Luanda. He wrote under several different pseudonyms. In September of 1972 Helder returned to Lisbon, and in the following year he published the two volumes of his first literary collection, *Poesia toda*. He also traveled to New York and worked as a proofreader for Arcádia Publishing. He worked as a journalist in 1974 for the National Public Radio of Portugal and in 1975 traveled again through Europe. In 1976 he, António Paulouro, and António Sena organized the two numbers of the literary journal *Nova*.

Helder's first marriage ended, and in 1969 he had a son, Daniel João Figueiredo de Oliveira, with Isabel Figueiredo. In 1973 he married Olga da Conceição Ferreira Lima.

Helder published *Cobra* (Snake) in 1977. The work confirms the textual instability that characterizes his perspective on the poetic function. All the copies of this book, which were personally distributed, were different. That is why Helder, in a 1977 letter to Eduardo Prado Coelho published in *Abril*, says of the book: "flutua. É um livro em suspensão" (it fluctuates. It is a book in suspension).

In the following years Helder published *O corpo, o luxo, a obra* (The Body, the Luxury, the Work, 1978) and *Photomaton & vox*, and in 1980 the stories of *Os passos em volta* were rewritten for the fourth edition. In 1981 a new edition of *Poesia toda* was published, this time by Assírio and Alvim. This edition represents a more complete version, updated and edited by the author. He excluded, however, the poems he wrote between 1952 and 1954. The publication of this 650-page volume was carefully supervised by the poet. It represents the most easily obtainable of Helder's works, since most of his books are out of print. The volume also marks one of the last times that Helder rewrote his own poetry.

In 1994 Helder turned down the coveted Pessoa Prize, which carries a substantial monetary award. The rejection, which was expected by the jury that nonetheless wanted to attempt to give it to the author, is consistent with his decision to avoid the public arena. (In 1983 he had also turned down the Prémio de Poesia do

*Cover for Helder's 2001 collection, intended to present the sum of his poetic achievements (University of California, Santa Barbara)*

PEN Club Português for his *A cabeça entre as mãos*.) Rather than being an act of arrogance, Helder's refusal to accept this important recognition constitutes a clear statement of the nonconformist position noted in all his poetry.

Herberto Helder's work has been the object of a growing interest on the part of literary critics. The number of books, scholarly articles, and doctoral dissertations dedicated to his work has increased since the 1990s. Helder has a poetic language of his own and an important place on the Portuguese literary scene. His 2001 book complements the metamorphosis of his texts and his life. It is, like his previous works, a rewriting of some of his poems to create a *sumula poetica*. The open-ended text again finds its continuum, as stated in the title: *Ou o poema contínuo* (Or the Continuous Poem).

**References:**

José Ferreira de Almeida, "Os cantos do corpo: Uma leitura da versão de Herberto Helder do Cântico dos Cânticos," *Brotéria,* no. 140 (May–June 1995): 589–608;

Fernando Pinto do Amaral, "Herberto Helder: O texto sonâmbulo," in *Um século de poesia, 1888–1988,* special issue of *A Phala,* edited by Manuel Hermínio Monteiro (Lisbon: Assírio & Alvim, 1988), pp. 133–137;

Amaral, "Um verso infinito," *Ler,* no. 14 (1991): 5–60;

Ruy Belo, "Poesia e arte poética em Herberto Helder," in his *Na senda da poesia* (Lisbon: União Gráfica, 1969), pp. 237–258;

Eduardo Prado Coelho, "Herberto Helder: A não separabilidade," "Como falar de Herberto Helder?" and "Questão de tacto," in his *O cálculo das sombras* (Lisbon: Asa, 1997), pp. 321–335;

Maria Lúcia Dal Farra, *A alquimia da linguagem: Leitura da cosmogonia poética de Herberto Helder* (Lisbon: Imprensa Nacional-Casa da Moeda, 1986);

Dal Farra, "Herberto Helder leitor de Camões," *Revista Camoniana,* second series, 1 (1978): 67–90;

Dal Farra, "Para o leitor ler de/vagar Herberto Helder," *Revista Letras,* 24 (1975): 219–227;

Dal Farra, "Vôo de teto-teco sobre a poesia de Herberto Helder," *Estudos Portugueses e Africanos,* no. 31 (1998): 17–22;

João Décio, "Introdução ao estudo da poesia de Herberto Helder I," *Alfa,* no. 17 (1971): 37–47;

Décio, "Introdução ao estudo da poesia de Herberto Helder II," *Alfa,* no. 20–21 (1974–1975): 143–146;

A. Lindeza Diogo, *Herberto Helder: Texto, metáfora, metáfora do texto* (Coimbra: Almedina, 1990);

Maria Teresa Dias Furtado, "A dialética do silêncio em Herberto Helder," *Colóquio/Letras,* 35 (1977): 73–76;

Maria Estela Guedes, *Herberto Helder–Poeta obscuro* (Lisbon: Moraes, 1979);

Guedes, "Viagem e utopia em Herberto Helder," *Colóquio/Letras,* 46 (1978): 36–45;

Maria de Fátima Marinho, "A feminilidade na poesia de Herberto Helder," *Colóquio/Letras,* 67 (1982): 72–75;

Marinho, *Herberto Helder: A obra e o homem* (Lisbon: Arcádia, 1982);

Marinho, "Herberto Helder: Para uma estética de modificação," *Jornal de Letras,* 10 (7–20 July 1981): 25;

Manuel Frias Martins, *Herberto Helder, um silêncio de bronze* (Lisbon: Livros Horizonte, 1983);

Juliet Perkins, *The Feminine in the Poetry of Herberto Helder* (London: Tamesis, 1991);

Perkins, "As filhas do tempo: Análise de um poema de Herberto Helder," *Colóquio/Letras,* 65 (1982): 14–22;

António Quadros, "Sentido maravilhoso–despertar para o enigma–*Os passos em volta* de Herberto Helder," in his *Crítica e verdade: Introdução à actual literatura portuguesa* (Lisbon: Livraria Clássica, 1964), pp. 177–181;

*Revista Textos/Pretextos,* special Helder issue, edited by Margarida Gil dos Reis, no. 1 (Winter 2002);

António Ramos Rosa, "Herberto Helder ou a imaginação liberta," in his *Incisões oblíquas: Estudos sobre poesia portuguesa contemporânea* (Lisbon: Caminho, 1987), pp. 75–85;

Rosa, "Herberto Helder–Poeta órfico," in his *Poesia, liberdade livre* (Lisbon: Moraes, 1962), pp. 149–157;

Mário Sacramento, "Herberto Helder–*Retrato em movimento,*" in his *Ensaios de Domingo II* (Porto: Inova, 1974), pp. 303–307.

# Alexandre Herculano

(28 March 1810 – 13 September 1877)

Paulo Motta Oliveira
*Universidade de São Paulo*

BOOKS: *A voz do profeta,* first series (Lisbon: Oficina de Galhardo, 1836);

*A voz do profeta,* second series (Lisbon: Tipografia Patriótica, 1837);

*A harpa do crente* (Lisbon: Tipografia da Sociedade Propagadora dos Conhecimentos Úteis, 1838);

*Da Escola Politécnica e do Colégio dos Nobres* (Lisbon: A. Herculano, 1841);

*O clero portuguez* (Lisbon: Tipografia do Constitucional, 1841);

*Eurico, o presbítero* (Lisbon: Tipografia da Sociedade Propagadora dos Conhecimentos Úteis, 1844);

*Infantes em Ceuta* (Lisbon: Tipografia da Sociedade Propagadora dos Conhecimentos Úteis, 1844);

*História de Portugal,* 4 volumes (Lisbon: Casa da Viúva Bertrand & Filhos, 1846–1853);

*O monge de Cister ou a epocha de D. João,* 2 volumes (Lisbon: Imprensa Nacional, 1848);

*Poesias* (Lisbon: Imprensa Nacional/Viúva Bertrand & Filhos, 1850);

*Eu e o clero* (Lisbon: Imprensa Nacional, 1850);

*Considerações pacíficas sobre o opúsculo "Eu e o clero"* (Lisbon: Imprensa Nacional, 1850);

*Solemnia verba: Cartas ao senhor A. L. Magessi Tavares sobre a questão actual entre a verdade e uma parte do clero* (Lisbon: Imprensa Nacional, 1850);

*Cartas ao muito reverendo em Christo padre Francisco Recreio,* anonymous (Lisbon: Tip. de Castro & Irmão, 1850);

*A batalha de Ourique e a ciência arábico-académica: Carta ao redactor da semana* (Lisbon: Imprensa Nacional, 1851);

*Lendas e narrativas* (Lisbon: Imprensa Nacional/Viúva Bertrand & Filhos, 1851);

*Memoria sobre a origem provavel dos livros de linhagens* (Lisbon: Tip. da Academia, 1854);

*Da origem e do estabelecimento da Inquisição em Portugal: Tentativa histórica,* 3 volumes (Lisbon: Imprensa Nacional, 1854–1859); translated by John C. Branner as *History of the Origin and Establishment of the Inquisition in Portugal* (Stanford, Cal.: Stanford University, 1926);

*Alexandre Herculano (from Cândido Beirante,* Herculano em Vale de Lobos, *1977; Thomas Cooper Library, University of South Carolina)*

*A reacção ultramontana em Portugal ou A concordata de 21 de Fevereiro* (Lisbon: Tipografia José Baptista Morando, 1857);

*Ao partido liberal portuguès, a associação popular promotora da educação do sexo feminino* (Lisbon: Imprensa União Tipográfica, 1858);

*O Fronteiro d'Africa ou três noites asíagas* (Rio de Janeiro: Tip. Económica de J. J. Fontes, 1862);

*Estudos sobre o casamento civil por ocasião do opúsculo do sr. visconde de Seabra sobre este assunto* (Lisbon: Tipografia Universal, 1866);

*Opúsculos,* 10 volumes (Lisbon: Viúva Bertrand, 1873–1908);

*O bobo* (Lisbon: Viúva Bertrand-Sucessores, Carvalho, 1878);

*Composições várias* (Lisbon: Ailland, Alves, Bastos, 1910);
*Cenas de um ano da minha vida e apontamentos de viagem,* edited by Vitorino Nemésio (Lisbon & Rio de Janeiro: Bertrand/Francisco Alves, 1934).

OTHER: *Portugaliae monumenta historica,* 6 volumes, edited by Herculano (Olisipone: Academiae Scientiarum Olisiponensis, 1856–1873).

Alexandre Herculano shares with Almeida Garrett the title of most important writer of the first generation of Romanticism in Portugal. Poet, historian, novelist, polemist, essayist, and editor, Herculano was a key figure in nineteenth-century Portugal, not only because of his multiple and diverse works but also because of his active participation in the political events of the time.

Alexandre Herculano de Carvalho e Araújo was born on 28 March 1810, the year of the third French invasion of Portugal. He was the son of Teodoro Cândido de Araújo, a low-level administrative employee, and Maria do Carmo de São Boaventura. In 1820 Portugal was shocked and changed by the Liberal Revolution (a rebellion against the absolute monarchy that obliged King João VI to return from Brazil and to accept the progressive constitution written by the National Assembly in 1822). Herculano was ten years old at the time. From either 1820 or 1821 to 1825, he studied in the Congregação de S. Felipe Nery, where he did the preparatory studies for attending a university. During this period important events occurred in Portugal: Miguel, the second son of the king, made two unsuccessful attempts (in 1823 and 1824) to force his father to restore the absolute monarchy. The country was divided, and liberalism was weak; as the next few years proved, liberalism could not be easily implanted in Portugal. In 1827 the young Herculano had to give up his plans of becoming a university student; because of his father's blindness he had to find the quickest way to full-time employment. He started his studies at the Aula de Comércio and at the Torre do Tombo, probably with the aim of becoming an administrative employee.

Herculano started writing poems and participating in literary groups during the period of the restoration of the absolute monarchy, a process that began in March and ended in July 1828. During this time Herculano was introduced to the salons of the Marquesa de Alorna, an important Portuguese writer who played in Portugal a role similar to that of Madame de Staël in France. The marquesa introduced the new German literature into Portugal, and Herculano often mentioned her great importance to his literary life.

Herculano's first significant excursion into Portuguese political life occurred in August 1831 when he took part in an unsuccessful uprising against the absolutist King Miguel. To escape being killed, he went into exile, first in England and then in France. He did not have good memories of his stay in England, and he wrote about this period of his life some years later in the narrative "De Jersey a Granville" (From Jersey to Granville). The work first appeared in 1843 in the magazine *O Panorama* as a fragment of the larger text *Cenas de um ano da minha vida* (Scenes of a Year in My Life). The narrative was republished by Herculano in the book *Lendas e narrativas* (Legends and Narratives, 1851); the fragments of *Cenas de um ano da minha vida,* which the author never finished, were published in 1934 by Vitorino Nemésio, an important scholar of Herculano's work.

Herculano's memories of France were not as bad as those he had of England. In France he could do research in the public library of Rennes and the National Library in Paris. This research was important when he began to write his historical papers. The experience in England and France opened what many scholars and critics call the "scar of exile" in Herculano's life and works. The theme of exile, from the time in those two countries to the final self-banishment to his rural property in Vale de Lobos, appears in many of his works, including poems in *A harpa do crente* (Believer's Harp, 1838) and the novel *Eurico, o presbítero* (Eurico, the Priest, 1844).

Herculano returned to Portugal in 1832 from his first exile, as a soldier. In Porto in 1833, even before the final victory of the liberal forces, he became the assistant librarian of the Municipal Library. He stayed there until September 1836, and during this time he did research and wrote the poems that were published in 1838 in *A harpa do crente.* To understand why Herculano gave up this position as librarian, it is necessary to look at the complex relations between certain events in Portuguese history, the character of the writer, and some aspects of his political beliefs. Like all liberal soldiers, Herculano had sworn to obey the Carta Constitucional (Constitutional Letter) created by Pedro IV in 1826 to become the new Portuguese constitution. In 1826, Pedro's father died, and Pedro, who was the emperor of Brazil, had to abdicate to his seven-year-old daughter, who became Queen Maria II in 1834. The document became the constitution of Portugal when liberal forces won the civil war in May 1834. In September 1836 Manuel da Silva Passos (Passos Manuel), one of the most important political figures of the first part of the nineteenth century, in a victorious revolution, succeeded in adopting again the more progressive Constitution of 1822 instead of the Carta Constitucional. This change, which Herculano could not accept, provoked his opposition to the *setembristas* (Septembrists), who were Passos Manuel's allies.

The oath taken by all liberal soldiers, however, was not the only reason for Herculano's disapproval. In

*A voz do profeta* (The Prophet's Voice, 1836), written as an attack on his political enemies, the author stated that the echo of the glorious past of Portugal had been sounding in vain and dying in the middle of the decomposed voice of the common people, and that the *setembristas* had begun a licentious kingdom. Herculano states clearly his political position and beliefs in those and other, similar words. Like other important nineteenth-century thinkers, he was a liberal, but he was not totally democratic in his thought. He believed that a universal suffrage, which in that century meant a suffrage for all men who could read and write, could be dangerous and destroy his country. Herculano's opposition to the Septembrist government obliged him to give up his job at the Municipal Library of Porto. During these events, he and Garrett, who had fought with him against King Miguel's forces, went to different political sides. Garrett was a friend of Passos Manuel and one of the great defenders of the Septembrist ideology.

At that time Herculano edited *O Panorama,* a magazine devoted to current European literature, science, and politics. He published his early historical short stories in this important magazine, which had a circulation of about five thousand readers. He also became, during the short time from January to May 1838, the publisher of the *Diário do Governo*.

*A harpa do crente* includes the main part of Herculano's poetry. He not only began his literary life as a poet but also wrote most of his poems when he was still young. The last poem he wrote was "A cruz mutilada" (The Mutilated Cross, 1849), when he was thirty-eight years old. In 1850 he published *Poesias,* a book in which all of his poetic works are gathered. Although poetry was the first phase of Herculano's literary life, there are few studies and literary analyses dedicated to him as a poet. His poetic works may be analyzed from different and divergent perspectives. Some critics focus on the presence of classical models in his poems, which suggests an obvious relation to neoclassicism. Others, such as Cândido Beirante, consider that it is possible to identify in Herculano's poetry traces of baroque oratory. From an entirely different perspective, critics such as Alberto Ferreira point out the significance of Herculano's poetry for later generations of writers, the ultra-Romantics. These different perspectives reveal his poetry to be a transition between the neoclassical and Romantic worlds. As Vasco Graça Moura has noted in his contribution to *Herculano e sua obra* (Herculano and His Works, 1978), edited by the Instituto Cultural de Porto, in Herculano's poetry it is possible to find subjects and concerns that anticipated many characteristics of Portuguese poetry from the end of the nineteenth through the middle of the twentieth centuries. His work had a definite influence on poets such as João de Deus, Abílio Manuel Guerra Junqueiro, António Nobre, António Duarte Gomes Leal,

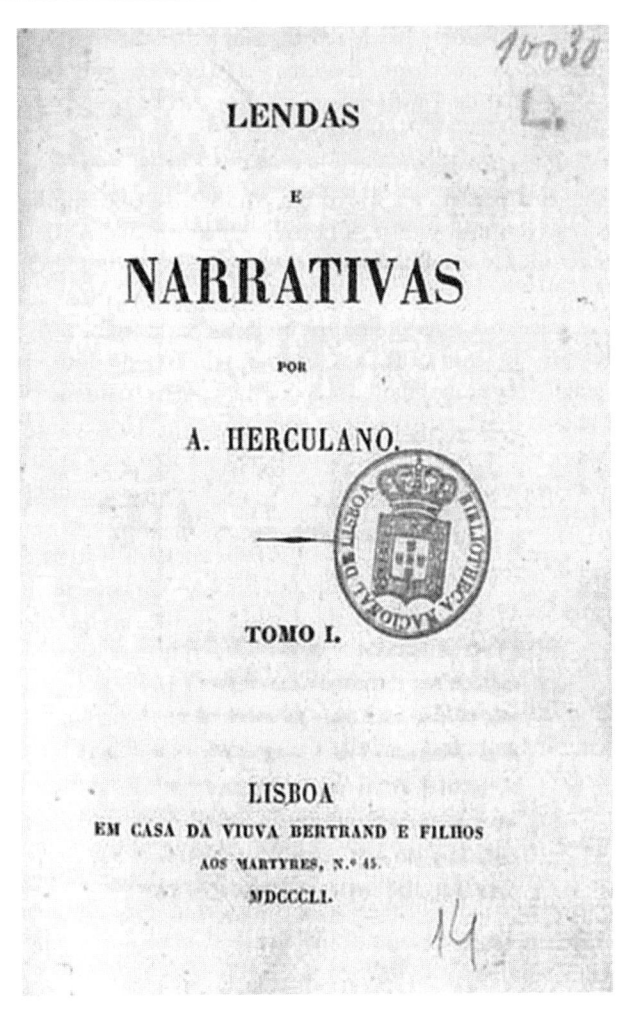

*Title page for a collection of Herculano's stories that had appeared in periodicals (Biblioteca Nacional, Lisbon)*

Teixeira de Pascoaes, Fernando Pessoa, Miguel Torga, Alexandre O'Neill, and Nemésio.

Other aspects of Herculano's work as a poet reveal his importance in Portuguese poetry. As António José Saraiva and Oscar Lopes have indicated in their *História da literatura portuguesa* (History of Portuguese Literature, 1982), Herculano's poems constitute an important poetic document of the period in which liberalism was being established in Portugal. Poems such as "O soldado" (The Soldier), "A vitória e a piedade" (Victory and Piety), "Tristezas do desterro" (Sadness of Exile), "O mosteiro deserto" (The Deserted Monastery), and "A volta do proscrito" (The Return of the Exile) are particularly important because they deal with the civil war and the experience of exile. Oliveira Martins believes that some of these poems capture the universal voice of the sadness and pain of emigration. These poems express the historical moment filtered through Herculano's personal experiences in a way that no other writer, not even Garrett, was able to do at the time they were written. Maria de

Lourdes Belchior has noted the similarities between the poem "Tristezas do desterro" and other important poems that deal with exile, including works by Luís de Camões, Garrett, Nobre, and Pascoaes.

Herculano's poetry has two important axes: one that focuses on nation and liberty and one that emphasizes God and nature. The relationship between these two trends constitutes the theme of some of Herculano's best poems. In "A vitória e a piedade," for instance, the poet defines himself as "Eu cristão, o trovador do exílio" (I, a Christian, the troubadour of exile), revealing the source of his poetic tendencies. These characteristics resemble those of Herculano's most famous creation, Eurico, the title character of his 1844 novel, showing that there are important connections between Herculano's poetry and fiction.

In 1839, one year after the publication of *A harpa do crente*, Queen Maria II's husband, Fernando, made Herculano head of the Royal Library in Ajuda, a position that provided him with the necessary research materials for his *História de Portugal* (History of Portugal, 1846–1853). In 1840 he entered parliament and began campaigning for educational reform on the Committee for Public Education. During this period he wrote important texts on the subject of education, including *Da Escola Politécnica e do Colégio dos Nobres* (On the Polytechnical School and the School for Nobility, 1841) and "Instrução pública" (Public Education, 1841). Herculano was removed from the committee and, probably because of this removal, gave up his position in parliament.

During the authoritarian regime of António Bernardo da Costa Cabral, Herculano was invited to be general inspector of performances, a position that had been occupied by Garrett during the Septembrist government. Although the new government had once more adopted the Carta Constitucional, Herculano could not accept it because of the extremely authoritarian regime. The author refused the position, and he established good relations with the main figures of the opposition. During Costa Cabral's government, which lasted from 1842 to 1846, Herculano published the following important works: "Cartas sobre a história de Portugal" (Letters on the History of Portugal, 1842) in the *Revista universal Lisbonense* (Universal Lisbonese Magazine), and the novels *O bobo* (The Clown, 1843), *Eurico, o presbítero* (1844), and the short novel *O pároco da aldeia* (The Parish Priest, 1842–1843), all in *O Panorama*. In the "Cartas sobre a história de Portugal" Herculano presents some ideas that are central to his way of thinking about the history of his country.

Following the path opened by his contemporaries François Guizot and Augustin Thierry, Herculano developed a concept of history that differs from that of his predecessors in Portugal. These differences stem from the importance Herculano gave to the future of society and from the central role that he assigned to ordinary people, especially to the working class. At the time, historical writing in Portugal consisted mainly of laudatory biographies about eminent persons; Herculano was more concerned with the future and development of society than with a mere retelling of the past.

Herculano's work with history can be divided into four phases: first, the period prior to 1846, in which his main work was five "Cartas sobre a história de Portugal," published from 7 April to 3 November 1842 in the *Revista universal Lisbonense;* second, the years between 1846 and 1853, when he published the four volumes of his *História de Portugal;* third, from 1854 to 1859, when he completed *Da origem e do estabelecimento da Inquisição em Portugal* (The Origin and Establishment of the Inquisition in Portugal); and, fourth, the period from about 1859 to 1873, in which he organized and published the *Portugaliae monumenta historica*. In these works he promoted several new and important ideas in Portuguese history.

Herculano did not think it possible to consider that a history of Portugal existed before the nation began to exist. He considered that Portuguese history began when Portugal split from the kingdom of León, and everything that happened before this date was a part of Spanish history. Before Herculano, historians had considered that the history of Portugal began with the Lusos, a group that lived during the Roman Empire in the territory that later became Portugal. Herculano did not accept this position as historically valid, because there was no relationship between this group and the Portuguese people. The Lusos were only one of many groups that lived in the Iberian Peninsula during the Middle Ages, and Portuguese culture did not inherit anything relevant from them.

Another important idea, which is related not only to Portugal but also to all of Europe, is the way Herculano divided history from the end of the Roman Empire up to his time. He considered the Middle Ages to be a complex period in which the main task was the transformation of the Roman Empire into individual modern nations. The reestablishment of variety is the principle that represents the Middle Ages, and this principle is seen in social institutions and the languages and literatures that emerged. Herculano saw the Renaissance, generally considered by historians as a bright period, as the moment when absolute monarchy destroyed the diversity that Europe had achieved during the Middle Ages. He did not consider the Renaissance to be only a revival of Roman arts and science; to him it was the full restoration of unity as the main and exclusive principle from which only the distinction between nationalities was saved. Herculano saw similarities between his own historical moment and the Middle Ages in that both were periods of struggle between the principles of unity and diversity. He saw the political revolutions of the nineteenth century as a protest against the Renaissance; they were a rejection of the absolute unity and an attempt to restore diversity. This relationship between the Middle Ages and Herculano's time is more than a simple effect of the Romantic tendency to valorize the medieval period. Herculano's perspective is not only related to the way he regarded the Portuguese past but also to the possibilities he saw in his nation at the present moment.

One of the greatest changes Herculano made in the usual way of thinking about his country at that time is how he interpreted the importance of the period of discovery and expansion. His fifth letter produces a radical change of focus on what had been considered Portugal's golden age. Until then, as Herculano notes, the sixteenth century had been considered the apogee of Portuguese power in the world. He opposes, however, this traditional way of viewing the history of Portugal and proposes that the nation's greatest moment had occurred during the Middle Ages when it emerged from the conflicts created by the principles of unity and diversity. The brightness of the sixteenth century was an effect of a generation that had been educated in the previous century. According to Herculano, the most important characteristic of this inheritance was the freedom and independence that people in the Middle Ages had but that could not exist in a period of absolute monarchy. Herculano minimizes the adventurous period of conquests and discoveries that transformed the country into an economic power in Europe. He stresses that the absolute monarchy eventually became corrupted and began to fall apart; thus, the moral forces that motivated expansionism were corrupt, and the period was not as glorious as historians had always considered it to be.

Herculano's point of view made a significant impact on other writers. Some critics consider his perspective to be central to one of the most important texts about Portugal in the nineteenth century: *As causas da decadência dos povos peninsulares nos últimos três séculos* (The Causes of the Decadence of the Nations of the Iberian Peninsula during the Last Three Centuries, 1871), by Antero de Quental. Herculano initiated a questioning of the importance of Portuguese expansion that became central to discussions of Portuguese culture and literature in general. Many important Portuguese writers of the nineteenth and twentieth centuries became involved in this questioning of the national past, including Nobre, Pascoaes, Pessoa, Eça de Queirós, António Sérgio, Jorge de Sena, and José Saramago.

Herculano's letters may be considered central to his historical work. They represent a kind of manifesto, the main ideas of which are developed in later works. His *História de Portugal*, for example, develops some of the theses presented in the letters. In 1846, the year he was accepted as a member of the Academia Real das Ciências

*Mariana Hermínia Meira, whom Herculano married in 1866 (from Beirante,* Herculano em Vale de Lobos, *1977; Thomas Cooper Library, University of South Carolina)*

de Lisboa, Herculano wrote the first volume of the *História de Portugal*. The other three volumes of the work were published in 1847, 1850, and 1853. During these years he also published the novel *O monge de Cister* (The Cisterican Monk, 1848), a companion to *Eurico, o presbítero* under the collective title *O Monasticon* (The Monastic Chronicle).

The *História de Portugal* is distinguished for its use of previously researched manuscripts, to which the writer had access as a librarian. In this work Herculano challenges many of the ideas of previous historians. In the prologue to the first edition he outlines the main aspects to be discussed in his work, and he points out that the reader may find mistakes in his book. He notes, however, that he tried to be as accurate as possible. He affirms that his work, the first to give a critical history of Portugal, was written using the latest scholarly methods, which means that he avoided love stories, patriotic sentiments, and emotional attachment to tradition. There are two radical new ideas in Herculano's perspective on the history of Portugal. First, Herculano claimed that the "Milagre de Ourique" (Miracle of Ourique)–the legend that Christ had appeared to Afonso I, the first king of Portugal, and turned the tides of battle in his favor in 1139–was not authentic, and it could not be authenticated by any document of the period to which it was attributed. The second important concept was that the conquests and the great navigations did not constitute a golden age of the country but, rather, a period of decadence. Herculano challenged the way the Portuguese perceived their past and themselves. He attempted to alter the popular view presented in Camões's epic poem *Os Lusíadas* (1572) that the Portuguese were designated by God to build an empire and spread Christianity.

In the prologue the author was possibly anticipating reactions to the publication. The work was released in a conservative environment, and it created a polemic. The critics attacked Herculano's approach and interpretations: they took issue with the fact that he considered that Portuguese history began with the creation of the Portucalense earldom, and especially with his negation of the Miracle of Ourique. The clergy reacted strongly against the writer's interpretation, and this reaction created a conflict between him and the Church. As a result, he published the booklet *Eu e o clero* (I and the Clergy) in 1850. He followed that with *Considerações pacíficas sobre o opúsculo "Eu e o clero"* (Peaceful Considerations about the Booklet "I and the Clergy") and *Solemnia verba: Cartas ao senhor A. L. Magessi Tavares sobre a questão actual entre a verdade e uma parte do clero* (Solemnia Verba: Letters to Mr. A. L. Magessi Tavares about the Current Debate between the Truth and a Part of the Clergy) the same year.

The ideological struggle between Herculano and the clergy reveals an aspect of his works not often studied: he was a polemist. Critics have considered him to be the greatest Portuguese polemist of the nineteenth century. During his life Herculano took part in several polemics, a usual practice among writers and thinkers at that time. The most important ones include his debate with the Septembrist government in 1836 and 1837, his exchanges with the clergy, the controversy over civil marriage in 1866, and his involvement in the polemic when the conferences of the Casino Lisbonense, organized by Eça de Queirós, Antero de Quental, and other members of the Cenáculo, were forbidden by the government in 1871. Despite the obvious differences among the topics of these debates, Herculano participated with the same emotion, the same sarcasm and irony, and the same logical presentation of thesis. These polemics demonstrate an important side of the writer's intellectual life and his active role in the political life of the country.

Some critics consider the publication of *Da origem e do estabelecimento da Inquisição em Portugal* between 1854 and 1859 to be a consequence of the controversy about the Miracle of Ourique. Significant events had occurred in Herculano's life before he published this new historical work. He had made his opposition to Costa Cabral's government explicit since 1850, when he and other Portuguese intellectuals signed a protest against a law that limited the freedom of the press. In Herculano's house, the following year, the revolution that put an end to Costa Cabral's government was plotted, and the movement of *Regeneração* (Regeneration) began. The revolution, headed by the Duke de Saldanha and supported by important intellectuals such as Garrett, was successful, but it rapidly took directions that did not please Herculano. The main figure of the *Regeneração* period was Fontes Pereira de Melo, an engineer who was the most important Portuguese politician of the second half of the nineteenth century. He was responsible for the material changes, such as the huge increase in railways, that occurred in that period in the country. Herculano did not believe that a nation could be regenerated with these kinds of changes.

Also in 1851 Herculano published *Lendas e narrativas*, a collection of short stories. In the prologue of the work he says that he wanted to preserve these stories, which had appeared mainly in *O Panorama*, from the fate that most stories published in ephemeral newspapers and magazines usually suffered. This book and the two novels *Eurico, o presbítero* and *O monge de Cister* complete the fictional works published in book form by the author during his lifetime.

Herculano used fiction as an effective and pleasing way to teach his reader about different aspects of the history of his country. He showed his readers the multiple and complicated relationships among traditions, legends, history, and truth. His immense knowledge of the history of Portugal, based on extensive research, helped him construct a complex mosaic in which the reader must discover the clue that reveals the exit from the labyrinth where history and fiction merge.

All but two of the pieces in *Lendas e narrativas* are based on historical sources. "De Jersey a Granville" is not a fictional work, and *O pároco da aldeia*, which is fiction, has a contemporary subject. Originally published in *O Panorama* in 1843, this short novel deals with a parish priest who uses his money for the wedding of a poor girl and the son of a greedy mill owner. The work is not typical of Herculano's writing, but it did have an impact on the Portuguese novel with a predominantly rural background, which Júlio Dinis later developed into an important genre.

Herculano's novels and short narratives cover a large historical period, from the tenth century to the end of the fifteenth, focusing on the period of Muslim domination in Portugal, the kingdom of Afonso Henriques, and the period between the last king of the Borgonha dynasty, Fernando, and the first of the Avis dynasty, João I. The plot of "O alcaide de Santarém" (The Mayor of Santarém) takes place between 950 and 971. The story narrates the revenge of Umeyya-ibn-Isahk, the old mayor of the city, against the caliph of Cordoba, who killed his brother. In "A dama pé-de-cabra" (Lady Crowbar) three stories are fused: the marriage of Diogo Lopes to the Lady Crowbar and her disappearance some years later with their daughter; the tale about how a countess in the Visigoth Kingdom

*Herculano's home in Vale de Lobos, Santarém, where he spent the last ten years of his life (from Beirante, Herculano em Vale de Lobos, 1977; Thomas Cooper Library, University of South Carolina)*

had been transformed into Lady Crowbar; and the final story that tells how Diogo's son needed his mother's help to rescue his father from the Muslims.

"O bispo negro" (The Black Bishop) and "A morte do lidador" (The Death of the Fighter) are set in the twelfth century. The first deals with the legend of the imprisonment of Dona Teresa by her son, the first Portuguese king, Afonso Henriques. The story treats the incident as fact. There is a struggle between the king and the Pope, and in spite of the power of Rome, in the story the king is the victor. The second story narrates the death of Gonçalo Mendes de Maia, a ninety-five-year-old warrior, in a battle against the Muslims.

The stories set in the fourteenth century include "Arras por foro d'Espanha" (The Dowry Law of Spain) and "O castelo de Faria" (The Castle of Faria). The first tells the story of the marriage of King Fernando and Leonor Teles, which the people of Lisbon refused to accept. Leonor had been married to another man, but the Pope had annulled the union so that the king could marry her. "O castelo de Faria" also deals with the effects this marriage had on the relations between Portugal and Castile. The Portuguese king had been engaged to the princess of Castile, and when he broke this commitment to marry Leonor, the king of Castile invaded Portugal. The story relates how the Castilians attempted to hold onto the Castle of Faria.

"A abóbada" (The Vault) takes place at the beginning of the fifteenth century. It is the story of the construction of the church of Batalha during the kingdom of João I, the first king of the Avis dynasty. The old blind Portuguese master, Afonso Domingues, had been replaced by the Frenchman Ouget in the mission of constructing the vault of a segment of the church. The vault, however, collapsed, and Domingues was called in to construct a new one.

The novels *Eurico, o presbítero* and *O monge de Cister* are set respectively in the period when the Muslims invaded the Iberian Peninsula in the eighth century and during the kingdom of João I. In the first, there are important similarities between the protagonist, Eurico, and the author. The priest is a Christian and a "troubadour of exile," a position similar to that found in Herculano's poetry. The historical periods of Eurico and Herculano are both times of change in the political and religious life of the country. The novel itself, as the critics have noted, also presents important poetic characteristics. *O monge de Cister* tells of the revenge of Vasco da Silva against Lopo Mendes, who married Vasco's fiancée, Leonor, and against Fernando Afonso, who seduced his sister Beatriz. Vasco kills Lopo, but filled with remorse, he becomes a priest and gives up his hatred. Later, however, at the urging of the Abbot of Alcobaça, Vasco completes his revenge and kills Fernando.

Throughout Herculano's works it is possible to identify three different narrative points of view concerning the relationships among his narrators, characters, and history. One of these can be seen in "A dama pé-de-cabra," in which the narrator not only assumes that he is retelling a legend but also simulates an environment in which oral narratives play a central role. At the beginning of "A dama pé-de-cabra" the narrator warns the reader that his narrative is really a tale. The work, in fact, was created from a medieval tale, in which the devil appears and magical happenings occur. The boundary between history and legend is obliterated as the narrative is set in the Middle Ages, a period in which this distinction does not exist. In this medieval world, speaking, writing, and singing are sources of the truth.

The short story "O bispo negro" exhibits a different narrative point of view, created by the presence of two voices: one narrates the events of the story, and the other is an historical voice that analyzes the materials being narrated and attempts to separate history from legend. While the first voice is responsible for telling the story, the second appears mainly in footnotes to the text and constantly reminds the reader that the first voice is retelling a legend and not historical fact. For example, when the narrator comments that the cathedral of Coimbra was built by either the Visigoths or by the Arabs, there is a footnote that tells the reader that it dates only from the end of the twelfth century. The dual voices of the short story show that fiction can be created from legend, but that legend cannot be accepted as history. At the end of the work there is a long note that reminds the reader that what has been told is not history but rather legend. This note points out that the legend was taken from the Chronicles of Acenheiro, a collection of lies and nonsense stories published by the Academy of Science. A fake historical fact, as the story shows, can constitute a good fictional narrative.

The other stories of *Lendas e narrativas* reveal the same concern with the relationship between narrative and history: all the narrators consider their stories to be history rather than fiction. In "O castelo de Faria," for example, the narrator claims that there is not any difference between this literary story and the historical narratives on which it is based. The story is presented as history. Even the footnotes in this story and others in the book (except "O bispo negro") do not alert the reader to the differences between legend and history. They are used to verify the correct usage of words and to show that a specific piece of information can be verified by historical documents. When the character Diogo Lopes de Pacheco appears in "Arras por foro d'Espanha," there is a footnote that explains that historian Fernão Lopes believed that Pacheco returned to Portugal in 1372 but that certain documents disprove this theory. Footnotes such as this one are used to prove to the reader that the narrative is, at least, constructed close to an historical background and could be more interesting and richer in action than a true historical work.

The narrator of *Eurico, o presbítero* is in a position similar to that of the narrator of "O bispo negro." In the novel there is a narrative voice that pretends to tell a true story. At the beginning of the novel the narrator states that he will deal with the political and moral situation of Spain at the time of the events to be narrated, indicating that the events are taken from history. In the third chapter the narrator reveals that he is working from a lost manuscript, a device often employed by the Romantics. As in the short story, the other narrative voice of the novel appears in the footnotes and shows that the text is fictional. In the first footnote, for example, the narrator, who can be considered a second voice as in "O bispo negro," states that he does not know how this book should be classified since it is neither a poem in prose nor an historical novel; in the last one, he admits that for fictional purposes, some historical dates had to be changed.

In *O monge de Cister* the theme of the "found manuscript" is used throughout the narrative, and the book is full of expressions such as "mui verídica história" (a very truthful story) and "autêntica história" (an authentic story). The last footnote of the work states:

> a precedente narração foi tirada, a bem dizer textualmente, de um manuscrito que estava no mosteiro de *** da comarca de **** da província de *** e que só o autor teve a fortuna de ver. Para que serviriam, pois, citações, notas, emburrilhas? A coisa é de uma autenticidade irrepreensível.
>
> (the previous narration was taken, almost without changes, from a manuscript that was located in the monastery *** of the judicial district of *** of the province of *** that only the author had the good fortune to see. What would be the use, then, of quotations, notes, obsessions? The thing is of an irreproachable authenticity).

As in any ironic process, it is necessary for the reader to realize that the narration was not really extracted from an old manuscript. If the reader does not, he will suppose that he is reading a true history. There is no second voice in this work. There is, however, a game that creates doubt around the theme of the "found manuscript."

Three years after the publication of *Lendas e narrativas*, Herculano began to publish *Da origem e do estabelecimento da Inquisição em Portugal*, probably as an answer to the reaction of the clergy and certain intellectuals against the *História de Portugal*. Although the work is important for the study of the Portuguese Inquisition, it did not have as great an impact on Portuguese culture as *História de Portugal* and "Cartas sobre a história de Portugal." As Saraiva and Lopes have noted, the work on the Inquisition is not a social history like the other two but rather a narration of an intrigue among unscrupulous persons.

From 1851 on Herculano took part in important public matters, such as the controversy over civil marriage. He collected his opinions on the subject into his book *Estudos sobre o casamento civil por ocasião do opúsculo do sr. visconde de Seabra sobre este assunto* (Studies on Civil Marriage on the Occasion of the Publication of a Booklet Written by the Viscount de Seabra about This Matter, 1866). In this book Herculano defends the new marriage legislation. He also edited important collections of Portuguese documents in the *Portugaliae monumenta historica* from 1856 to 1873. This work is a compilation inspired by similar works done in France, Germany, and Italy, especially the *Monumenta Germaniae historica* (1826), edited by Georg Heinrich Pertz. Herculano was able to research, organize, and publish his *Portugaliae monumenta historica* under the auspices of the Academia de Ciências de Lisboa, where he served as vice president. Herculano worked constantly on the study for more than fifteen years. This period can be considered the last segment of Herculano's historical activity.

As scholar José-Augusto França has stated, it is difficult to say at what point in his life Herculano stopped believing in a liberal Portuguese society. He had been disappointed with the Septembrist revolution, then by Costa Cabral's government, and finally, by the politics of the Regeneration, for which he had proposed serious reforms. He had some hope for Pedro V, who became king in 1853. In 1861, however, the king died, and with him, Herculano's last hopes for changes.

In 1859, using the money earned with the copyrights of his books, the writer bought a farm in Vale de Lobos, Santarém. In 1866 he married Mariana Hermínia Meira, and in the following year he moved to his property to live as a farmer. Some critics consider this move to be Herculano's final exile. He transformed the house at Vale de Lobos into a kind of sanctuary and symbol of the failed Portuguese liberalism. From that time on the writer made few public appearances, the most important being the one against the forced interruption of the Conferências Democráticas do Casino Lisbonense in 1871. In spite of the ideological and political divergences between Herculano and the members of Quental and Queirós's generation who had organized the conferences, he could not remain silent when the cabinet of the Duke de Ávila e Bolama forbade them to assemble. Herculano used his afternoons to collect his writings and to write to old and new friends. During this time he began the compilation of his *Opúsculos* (Booklets), in which he organized his most important work published in newspapers and magazines. On 13 September 1877 he died of pneumonia, which he had

*Herculano in Vale de Lobos in 1865 (from a photograph by Henrique Dulac; from Beirante,* Herculano em Vale de Lobos, *1977; Thomas Cooper Library, University of South Carolina)*

contracted on a trip to Lisbon to talk with Brazilian emperor Pedro II.

Some of Herculano's works were published after his death. The novel *O bobo,* which occupies a special place among his writings, was first published in book form in Portugal in 1878 (it had been published in an unauthorized Brazilian edition in 1866). Some critics consider this work, which is a melange of multiple points of view narrating events from different perspectives, to be his masterpiece. The novel presents events that happened in the days before the Battle of São Mamede fought near the Guimarães castle between D. Tereza and her son, Afonso Henriques, who became the first king of Portugal. The novel has four main characters: Dulce and her two lovers, Egas and Garcia, form a love triangle; the clown Dom Bibas is an essential figure in the decisive moments of the plot, including the final victory of Afonso Henriques. At the end of the novel he is the only one of the four who survives. The reader gradually discovers that the official history, like any official story, is always based on only one version, and that truth can perhaps emerge only from fiction. From the shadows in which the clown has changed the life of a nation, to the noble and fake version of the battle between Egas and Garcia, to the gossip about the death and funeral of Dulce, everything in the work suggests that history could be a collection of false fragments that nobody can decipher. This book presents a perspective that could not be accepted by the author of the *História de Portugal,* which is possibly why Herculano never published the novel in book form: perhaps he expected that, like most works published serially, the work would soon be forgotten.

Unpublished works of the author continued to appear until the middle of the twentieth century. The publication of *Opúsculos* was completed only in 1908, and Herculano's many letters to various people were organized and published in different books.

Herculano was active in many different areas of national life. Like Garrett, he worked in any job or position where he was needed as Portugal attempted to establish a new liberal democracy. Some critics have argued that his most important work was as an historian; others consider it to be as a writer of fiction. He introduced both the Romantic novel and a new concept of history into Portugal. Scholars and critics are unanimous in their opinion that all of Herculano's activities, literary and political, make him a complex figure who epitomizes Portuguese culture of the nineteenth century.

**Letters:**

*Cartas inéditas a Joaquim Filipe de Soure,* edited by Luís Silveira (Lisbon: Tipografia Pap. Fernandes, 1946);

*Cartas de Vale de Lobos ao 3º Duque de Palmela e a José Cândido dos Santos,* 3 volumes, edited by Vitorino Nemésio (Lisbon: Bertrand, 1951);

*Cartas,* 2 volumes (Lisbon: Ailland, Alves, Bastos, n.d.).

**References:**

Cândido Beirante, *Alexandre Herculano "as faces do poliedro"* (Lisbon: Veja, 1991);

Beirante, *Herculano em Vale de Lobos* (Santarém: Junta Distrital de Santarém, 1977);

Maria de Lourdes Belchior, "Herculano, trovador do exílio," in her *Os homens e os livros: Séculos XIX e XX,* volume 2 (Lisbon: Verbo, 1980): pp. 199–215;

Teófilo Braga, *Curso de história da literatura portuguesa* (Lisbon: Nova Livraria Internacional, 1885);

Braga, *As modernas idéias na literatura portuguesa* (Porto: Livraria Internacional de Ernesto Chardron, 1892);

Helena Carvalhão Buescu, *"Lendas e narrativas" de Alexandre Herculano* (Lisbon: Editorial Comunicação, 1987);

Joaquim Barradas de Carvalho, *As idéias políticas e sociais de Alexandre Herculano* (Lisbon: Seara Nova, 1971);

Fernando Catroga, "Alexandre Herculano e o historicismo romântico," in *História da história em Portugal,* edited by Luís Reis Torgal, José Amado Mendes, and Catroga (Lisbon: Temas e Debates, 1998), pp. 45–98;

António Borges Coelho, *Alexandre Herculano* (Lisbon: Presença, 1965);

Alberto Ferreira, *Perspectiva do romantismo português* (Lisbon: Edições 70, 1971);

Fidelino Figueiredo, *História da literatura romântica* (São Paulo: Anchieta, 1946);

José-Augusto França, *O romantismo em Portugal,* 6 volumes (Lisbon: Livros Horizonte, 1975–1977);

Instituto Cultural de Porto, ed., *Herculano e sua obra* (Porto: Fundaçao Engenheiro António de Almeida, 1978);

Eduardo Lourenço, *O labirinto da saudade* (Lisbon: Dom Quixote, 1982);

Oliveira Martins, *Portugal contemporâneo* (Lisbon: Guimarães, 1953);

João Medina, *Herculano e a geração de 70* (Lisbon: Terra Livre, 1977);

Vitorino Nemésio, *A mocidade de Herculano* (Lisbon: Bertrand, 1978);

Nemésio, *Ondas médias* (Lisbon: Imprensa Nacional-Casa da Moeda, 2000);

Paulo Motta Oliveira, "Alexandre Herculano: Malhas da história, armadilhas da ficção," in *Romance histórico recorrências e transformações,* edited by Oliveira, Maria Cecília B. Boëchat, and Silvana M. P. De Oliveira (Belo Horizonte: Faculdade de Letras da Universidade Federal de Minas Gerais, 2000), pp. 29–149;

Oliveira, "Alexandre Herculano e Portugal: Da história à ficção," *Intercâmbio,* 1, no. 2 (1997): 28–34;

Oliveira, "Um oceano por achar: Pascoaes, Pessoa e a questão nacional," *Revista da Associação Brasileira de Professores de Literatura Portuguesa (Belo Horizonte),* 1, no. 1 (1999): 329–350;

A. H. de Oliveira Marques, *História de Portugal* (Lisbon: Palas, 1986);

António José Saraiva, *Herculano e o liberalismo em Portugal* (Lisbon: Privately printed, 1949);

Saraiva and Oscar Lopes, *História da literatura portuguesa* (Porto: Porto Editora, 1982);

Joaquim Veríssimo Serrão, *Herculano e a consciência do liberalismo português* (Lisbon: Bertrand, 1977);

João Gaspar Simões, *Perspectiva histórica da ficção portuguesa (das origens ao século XX)* (Lisbon: Dom Quixote, 1987).

**Papers:**

Some of Alexandre Herculano's papers are in the Biblioteca Pública Municipal do Porto.

# Abílio Manuel Guerra Junqueiro
*(15 September 1850 – 7 July 1923)*

Elias J. Torres Feijó
*Universidade de Santiago de Compostela*

BOOKS: *Duas palavras de quatorzes annos: Poesia* (Coimbra: Imp. da Universidade, 1864);

*Mysticae nuptiae: Poemeto* (Coimbra: Imp. da Universidade, 1866);

*Vozes sem eco* (Coimbra: Imp. da Universidade, 1867);

*Baptismo de amor* (Porto: Cruz Coutinho, 1885 [first edition, 1868]);

*Vitória da França: 4 de Setembro de 1870* (Porto: Chardron, 1870);

*A hespanha livre* (Coimbra: Tip. de Manuel Caetano da Silva, 1873);

*A morte de D. João* (Porto: Livraria Moré Editora, 1874);

*Aos veteranos da liberdade: Poesia* (Lisbon: Tip. Universal, 1878);

*A musa em férias: Idílios e sátiras* (Lisbon: Typ. das Horas Romanticas, 1879);

*Viagem à roda da Parvónia: Relatorio em 4 actos e 6 quadros,* by Junqueiro and Guilherme de Azevedo (Lisbon: Of. Tip. da Empreza Litteraria de Lisboa, 1879);

*A velhice do Padre Eterno* (Porto: Chardron / Porto: Alvarim Pimenta & Joaquim Antunes Leitão / Lisbon: Minerva, 1885);

*A lágrima* (Viana do Castelo: João Baptista Domingos, 1892 [first edition, 1888]);

*Marcha do ódio,* book by Junqueiro, music by Miguel Angelo (Porto: Civilisação, ca. 1891);

*Finis patriae* (Porto: Empreza Litteraria e Typographica, 1891);

*Os simples* (Porto: Tip. Occidental, 1892);

*Pátria* (Porto: Lello & Irmão, 1896);

*Oração ao pão* (Porto: Chardron, 1902);

*Oração à luz* (Porto: Chardron, 1904);

*Poesias dispersas* (Porto: Chardron, 1920);

*Prosas dispersas* (Porto: Chardron, 1921);

*Horas de combate* (Porto: Chardron, 1924);

*Horas de luta* (Lisbon: Lello & Irmão, 1924);

*O caminho de céu* (Porto: Chardron, 1925);

*Prometheu libertado: Esboço do poema,* edited by Luís de Magalhães (Porto: Chardron, 1926).

*Abílio Manuel Guerra Junqueiro, circa 1876 (from Manuela de Azevedo,* Guerra Junqueiro: A obra e o homem, *1981; Thomas Cooper Library, University of South Carolina)*

PLAY PRODUCTION: *Viagem à roda de Parvónia,* Lisbon, Teatro Gymnasio, 1878.

Abílio Manuel Guerra Junqueiro was the most popular poet of his time. Nineteenth-century critics praised the visual strength of his work and the elaboration of his rhetoric. His poetry incorporated realist-naturalist, scientific, and socialist projects with the Romantic, Christian influences of his childhood. He was considered the apostle of the masses and prophet in verse of the Republic. From an artistic point of view, his detractors saw his work as an empty and contradictory rhetoric, unskillful, and simply echoing the topics of the times. He was the target of important criticism, initiated by António Sérgio in 1920, who criticized his "histeria romantesca" (romanesque hysteria). His work is today seen as incoherent and a prisoner of its time, and he is considered by some to be a minor poet in the Portuguese literary canon.

Junqueiro was born on 15 September 1850 to a traditional and religious farming family in one of the most backward regions in Portugal, Trás-os-Montes. His parents were José António Junqueiro and Ana Maria Guerra. Five years after having Abílio, his mother died. His father later married Francisca Marcelina, his sister-in-law, and they had five children: Amândio, Ana, Inês, Laura, and Julia. In 1860 his father sent him to study at the Instituto Portuense in Porto, where he met Bernardino Machado, future professor in Coimbra and president of the Republic. In 1862 he moved to Coimbra, where he continued his studies, especially French and Latin. This type of education was common among persons of his social background. During this period Junqueiro began to participate in literary activities in Coimbra and Porto, with writers who were renowned in his country and with young men such as Antero de Quental and Teófilo Braga. A gifted child, he published *Duas palavras de quatorzes annos* (Two Words at Fourteen) in 1864, printed at the University of Coimbra. The work, which the author gave away to his friends, is characterized by verses of an ultra-Romantic flavor.

In 1866 Junqueiro enrolled in theology at the University of Coimbra, following his father's wishes that he pursue an ecclesiastical degree. That same year he wrote *Mysticae nuptiae* (Mystical Marriages), which was included in *Vozes sem eco* (Voices without Echo, 1867). The poet, who was sixteen, produced an intimate and lyrical poetry, which was typical of the Romantic atmosphere that dominated the era. The verses are marked by pain, nostalgia for childhood, and an intimacy similar to that in the work of Alfred de Musset and Camilo Castelo Branco. Although in a secondary manner, his poetry reveals traces of social criticism, following the direction that the young intellectuals of Coimbra had set in the famous polemic of the "Questão Coimbrã" (The Coimbra Case), a controversial literary dispute that lasted almost two years. That same year Junqueiro wrote the poem "À Espanha" (To Spain), an ode to liberty that he dedicated to Victor Hugo, the "bold giant in the battles of progress."

Junqueiro began to receive public praise for his poetry in 1867. There was a review of his work, under a pseudonym, by Ana Plácido, Castelo Branco's partner, in her *Revista literária* (Literary Review) of Porto. Perhaps it was her intervention that encouraged Castelo Branco, the most famous writer of the time, to write a prologue in 1868 for Junqueiro's new poem *Baptismo de amor* (Baptism of Love). This work completed Junqueiro's cycle of ultra-Romantic poetry, in which melancholic, painful, and religious sensitivity mixed with traces of social concerns predominate. That same year, he abandoned his studies in theology and enrolled in the School of Law. He also began to collaborate on a new project, a journal called *A Folha* (The Paper), with João Penha, a poet who introduced the Parnassian movement in Portugal. (This movement, which had appeared in France in the middle of the nineteenth century in opposition to Romanticism, represented in poetry the positivist and scientific spirit of the time.) *A Folha* quickly earned prestige in literary circles. Many important writers such as Castelo Branco published in the magazine, along with a new group of innovative writers including Quental, Braga, and Eça de Queirós. This group's first compositions in the magazine are reminiscent of the work of Alexandre Herculano and Hugo and reflect the socialist ideas of Quental.

Junqueiro was starting to make contact, directly or indirectly, with the works of thinkers such as Hugo, Pierre-Joseph Proudhon, Joseph Ernest Renan, and Jules Michelet who influenced him with ideas of social transformation and scientific principles. A few years later, as a doctrinaire group, these ideas were presented in the Democratic Conferences in Lisbon by his older friends. These conferences were a series of lectures in 1871 in Lisbon; also known as "Conferências do Casino" (Casino Conferences), they were given by members of the cultural group called Cenáculo (Cenacle), led by Quental. Their intention was to end Portugal's stagnation and backward ideas and to promote the moral, economic, and political transformation of the country within a European cosmopolitan social spirit. After five such presentations, the government forbade subsequent lectures because they were an attack on political and religious institutions. This prohibition provoked a great controversy. The influence of people such as Penha and the Parnassian poet Gonçalves Crespo also contributed to Junqueiro's move away from the late, dominant Romanticism.

That influence is evident in two poems he wrote in 1870, "Vitória da França" (France's Victory) and "Saudação à França" (Greeting to France), in which he expresses social and political concerns. A declamatory, even pamphleteering, tone emerged in his work as he began to collaborate with important presses in the country such as the newspaper *O Primeiro de Janeiro* (The First of January). In 1873 he published "A Espanha livre" (To Free Spain), a political poem that praises a republican system rather than the monarchy. That same year Junqueiro visited Herculano at his retreat in Vale de Lobos and met Guilherme de Azevedo, a poet with whom he shared several interests. Having finished his studies in 1873, he visited with old friends in Lisbon. These friends were now members of Cenáculo, the progressive club. In 1874 Junqueiro's *A morte de D. João* (The Death of Don Juan) was published in Porto and dedicated to Herculano. The work is written in *alexandrinos* (lines with twelve syllables, Junqueiro's favorite meter) and blends poetry and science, in accordance with the positivist ideas of the era. In the preface the poet presents his conception of poetry as "truth turned into feeling." He also expresses his purpose to address the ailments of corrupt society and show their solution. For Junqueiro, all that opposed Justice (with the capital letter of an allegory) can be summarized in what Don Juan and Jehovah stand for: "D. Juan summarizes in himself all that is ill in modern society. Jehovah represents tyranny, the divine right." Junqueiro satirizes *donjuanism*—the absolute rupture of all societal norms and preestablished rules, valuing only life lived in absolute freedom from morality or justice—and the poor state of education for bourgeois women, on the one hand, and the clergy and clericalism, on the other. The work had already been planned and was implicitly announced as part of a triptych with the objective of showing the triumph of Justice on earth. The second part would be included as a criticism of the Catholic religion, and the third would be shown as the triumph of Justice personified in the symbiosis of the figures of Christ and Prometheus.

The dramatized poem, inspired by the philosophy of Proudhon, was an important success for Junqueiro. The public and critics were impressed by the imagery in the work, its declamatory and visionary character, the accumulation of comparisons, metaphors, allegories, and parallelisms, and its strong lyricism. There was also praise for its satirical and vehement character, expressing a certain ideology that some progressive sectors tried to spread among the Portuguese people. It was not so much the originality or depth of Junqueiro's ideas but rather the rhetorical construction of the work that impacted the readers. As was expected, the Catholic sectors strongly criticized the work. As Amorim de Carvalho indicated in his 1998 study, *A morte de D. João* is a work with a fighting objective carried out by a lyricist. Carvalho pointed out Junqueiro's constructive errors, such as the weak nexus and lack of balance between the different episodes. However, the demolishing criticism by Sérgio in 1920 was the first to demonstrate the enormous contradictions in the text.

*Junqueiro and his wife, Filomena Augusta da Silva Neves (from Manuela de Azevedo,* Guerra Junqueiro: A obra e o homem, *1981; Thomas Cooper Library, University of South Carolina)*

In 1875, with money he had inherited from his mother, Junqueiro established himself in Lisbon, where he led a bohemian lifestyle. Around this time he collaborated on *A Lanterna Mágica,* a satirical publication on which the caricaturist Rafael Bordalo Pinheiro worked. He was more settled in his political and social activities, and in 1876 he wrote *Aos veteranos da liberdade* (For the Veterans of Freedom) for the festivity commemorating the entrance of the forces of Pedro IV into Porto. The tribute followed the model of civic and lay celebrations imported from France around that time. In September of that same year, Junqueiro was named secretary general of the civil government of Angra do Heroísmo in the Azores. The success of *A morte de D. João* was confirmed with a second edition in 1877. Junqueiro was now a famous writer and collaborator for important newspapers, including *Crónicas da Europa* in Rio de Janeiro, for which he began to write in 1878. At the end of that year he presented the play *Viagem à roda da Parvónia* (Journey around the Land of Foolish Country People) in Lisbon. Written with Azevedo, the work is a social and political satire; its success and scandal were such that the civil government prohibited more performances. The work was published in 1879 with a supporting manifesto signed by many Portuguese intellectuals.

In 1879 Castelo Branco published his *Cancioneiro alegre de poetas portugueses e brasileiros* (Collection of Merry Poems of Portuguese and Brazilian Poets), in which he criticized Junqueiro and other progressive writers. That same year Junqueiro collaborated on a satirical magazine called *António Maria,* in which the work of Bordalo Pinheiro stood out. The aim of the magazine was to criticize the monarchic and conservative Partido Regenerador (Regenerative Party) led by António Maria Fontes de Melo and, generally, the corruption of power. At the same time, Junqueiro's *A musa em férias: Idílios e sátiras* (The Muse on Holiday: Idylls and Satires) was published, combining social criticism with the lyrical influence of his youth.

During those years the poet spent his time alternating between the Azores and Lisbon. Unhappy with Angra do Heroísmo from the beginning and feeling ill, he returned to the Continent, posted to the northern city of Viana do Castelo. Around that time he offered the publisher Ernesto Chardron his "A morte de Jeová" (The Death of Jehovah), the second book of his planned trilogy. Chardron, however, rejected the work on the advice of Father Sena Freitas, an influential newspaper writer who had previously quarreled with Junqueiro. The work eventually became *A velhice do Padre Eterno* (The Old Age of the Eternal Father, 1885).

Junqueiro married Filomena Augusta da Silva Neves on 1 February 1880. They later had two daughters, Maria Isabel and Julia Francisca.

Linked to the Partido Progressista (Progressive Party), Junqueiro was elected deputy of the Portuguese parliament (Courts) and established himself once more in Lisbon. The fall of José Anselmo Brancaamp's prime ministry in 1881 provoked the dissolution of the Courts, and Junqueiro returned to Viana do Castelo, unemployed. He stayed there, aiming to lead a life that was closer to nature (he bought an estate in the region of the Douro) without abandoning his poetic and anticlerical activities. He participated actively in the anniversary celebrations of the Marqués do Pombal, who had decreed the expulsion of the Jesuits in the previous century. In 1884 some of Junqueiro's poems appeared in *Cancioneiro musical* (Musical Collection of Poems) by Gustavo Romanof Salvini, and, finally, in 1885, Chardron published *A velhice do Padre Eterno*. From a projected fifty poems, announced as being "like fifty bullets," came twenty-eight poems linked by their anticlerical and rationalist views. In these poems Junqueiro, inspired by Proudhon, Renan, and Hugo, attacked fanaticism and Catholic morality.

The structure of the work manifests the poet's allegorical objective. *A velhice do Padre Eterno* opens with a poem dedicated to "Aos simples," in which Junqueiro praises the simple and humble religion of his main characters. The positive nature of this first poem is transformed by the end of the work into a satirical vision of a religion turned into pure commercial exercise. Halfway through the book, the poet begins to focus on some of what he considered to be the ills of the Catholic religion, including the fanaticism of the early Church and the current polemics, such as the dichotomy between charity and justice. He makes personal reference to specific figures within the Catholic hierarchy of his time, especially to Leo XIII. Junqueiro glorifies the scientific progress of the era, personifying, for example, the locomotive as a symbol of social progress. Once again, the spirited poetry of the *Geração de 70* (Generation of the 1870s, the name given to the group of young intellectuals led by Quental and José Fontana) could be appreciated in this book, which was an ode to Liberty, Fraternity, and Equality as values of modernity. The work, however, is not antireligious; in it Junqueiro seeks a reconciliation between reason and faith. His vision, which was more between a popular religion and one inspired by the Gospels, was filled with lyricism and nostalgia for his mother. As Sérgio noted, the book is a series of contradictions and, despite the objective, an impossible harmony between opposites. The success and scandal of the work were once again enormous.

In 1886, amid the criticism that his followers directed at the government led by D. Luís, who was king at the time, in which he participated, he presented himself again for deputy. He was prepared to help his friend Joaquim Pedro de Oliveira Martins, who at his urging entered the Partido Progressista to further his political objectives. Elected deputy for Viana do Castelo, Junqueiro visited Paris, taking an interest in humanitarian affairs such as child welfare and the penitentiary system. The publication of the poem *A lágrima* (The Tear) in 1888, aimed at economically helping the victims of a fire at the Teatro Baquet in Porto, renewed his popularity. While he was collaborating with various newspapers in Lisbon and Porto, the poet also participated in the formation of the group Os vencidos da vida (The Losers of Life), a famous dilettante club formed by some intellectuals of his generation, including Queirós and Oliveira Martins.

The political events of 1890 accentuated Junqueiro's ideological views. The year was marked by an ultimatum that Great Britain imposed on Portugal to prevent the creation of a territorial nexus between Angola and Mozambique. The king, D. Carlos I, signed the treaty imposed by the British; his move was seen by some sectors of Portuguese society as an act of treason. Junqueiro participated in antitreaty activities and made a definite step toward the Republican line of thought. He broke off relations with Martins, who, against rec-

*Monument to Junqueiro in the garden of the Casa-Museu Guerra Junqueiro in Porto (from Manuela de Azevedo,*
Guerra Junqueiro: A obra e o homem, *1981; Thomas Cooper Library, University of South Carolina)*

ommendations of the Partido Progressista, had accepted well-paid posts with the monarchy. Junqueiro gave harsh speeches against the monarchy and its government, and he wrote expressive poems, such as *Marcha do ódio* (March of Hatred, 1891), with music by Miguel Ângelo. In October he resigned from his post as deputy and returned to Viana do Castelo. There he wrote *Regresso ao lar* (Return Home), later printed as part of *Os simples* (The Simple Ones, 1892). Toward the end of December, he wrote the poem *Finis patriae* (The End of the Homeland, 1891) with profound pessimism for the political situation of the country; the volume included a text titled *O caçador Simão* (The Hunter Simon). This poem was about the king, who liked to hunt and was called Simão by the people. These poems, together with previous works, made him stand out as a spokesperson for popular aspirations, which increased his success.

Junqueiro helped several of his friends who were directly involved in the failed Republican rising of 31 January 1891 against the monarchy in Porto. The following year, he published *Os simples,* which he dedicated to his wife. *Os simples* is a poem in two parts, the first a dramatized poem and the second a collection of smaller poems. The immediate translations of the work into Italian and Spanish indicate that his fame had crossed borders. Considered a lyrical epic, the new dramatic poem tells the story of a pilgrim who, after having traveled the world in search of fame and fortune, returns home, disappointed, where he finds happiness in nature. *Os simples* reflects a pantheistic, panpsychic, and at the same time, evangelical vision of life, in which nature, children, and the poor achieve a status similar to that of religion. Junqueiro was no longer the civil poet who had left a deep mark on authors such as the pro-Galician and Republican Curros Enríquez. He was, in part, the poet of religious and vague melancholy recollecting his beginnings. *Os simples* was presented as a psychological autobiography, in which the bucolic customs of the north of Portugal are intertwined with his own vision of life.

Junqueiro had not abandoned his interest in social and political issues. In 1894 he published fragments of *Pátria* (Homeland, 1896), a dramatic poem that is considered by many to be his best work. The poem was, like *Finis patriae,* a satirical text in which his visionary and prophetic expression was in accordance with the Republican ideas of the times. Critics, who once again detected Hugo's influence, said that the work had better structure than his previous works. The theme was nationalist and Republican: the king, after anguishing doubts and terror inspired by a Madman (symbol of the homeland), signs, with his ministers' agreement, the 1890 treaty with England. The work is full of the specters of the king's predecessors, all shown as being corrupt and favoring the treaty, except Pedro V, who, having died young, remained in liberal memories as the hope that never took place. The ending of the work is an ode to the spirit of the medieval captain Nuno Alvares. The work has a tinge of Greek tragedy, and its atmosphere is reminiscent of William Shakespeare's tragedies. The pessimistic tone of the work reveals the influence of Oliveira Martins's analyses in *Portugal contemporâneo* (Contemporary Portugal, 1881), but simplified by Junqueiro's grandiloquence.

Around this time, Junqueiro entered into what scholar Leonardo Coimbra calls a "spiritualist reconstruction." He sought a reconciliation between his growing obsession with science (and metaphysical search) and neo-romanticism and Franciscanism, which were common at the turn of the century in Portugal. His image as a prophet was augmented by the fact that he let his beard grow long after a bout with tertian fever.

In 1902 Junqueiro published *Oração ao pão* (Prayer for Bread) and in 1904 *Oração à luz* (Prayer for Light), two works that continued the pantheism of *Os simples* but more accentuated by Romantic symbolism. In 1904 he published in *La Revue des Revues* "Le Radium et la radiation universelle." In 1906, his Republican activity was intense, and he was arrested in 1907 for having insulted the king, D. Carlos I, in a harsh article published during the electoral campaign of 1906. His defense was led by Afonso Costa, the Republican leader, who was unable to get him out of the sentence of fifty days' arrest and a fine of 1,000 *réis* a day. When the king and his successor were killed in 1908, Junqueiro was accused of being the prophet and poet of the crime, for *O caçador Simão*.

In 1910 Junqueiro faced difficult personal controversies, but he joyfully witnessed the proclamation of the First Republic. In 1911 he refused the post of ambassador to Spain and accepted a post in Switzerland instead. He was not well, and he believed that Switzerland would be better for his health. He resigned, however, in 1913, amid accusations of fraud against the state. Once retired from his intense political and social life, and with his anticlerical attitudes softened, Junqueiro published *Poesias dispersas* (Scattered Poetry, 1920) and *Prosas dispersas* (Scattered Prose, 1921), which included a note linked to the article "Sacre Coeur," in which he retracts some of his previous attitudes, especially those expressed in *A velhice do Padre Eterno*. Amid rumors that he was mentally ill and that he had become a Catholic integrationist, in his last days he seemed to have embraced Christianity.

On 7 July 1923, with the second edition of *Viagem à roda da Parvónia* out, Abílio Manuel Guerra Junqueiro died in his daughter Isabel's home. The funeral was an immense manifestation of mourning: the last important figure that had created the First Republic was dead. The honors that he had requested for Castelo Branco were bestowed on him, and he was buried in the pantheon of the Convento dos Jerónimos in Lisbon. Three years later, a draft of his *Prometheu libertado* (Prometheus Freed) was published, completing the trilogy that began in 1874 with *A morte de D. João* and continued with *A velhice do Padre Eterno*. Junqueiro was one of the most important poets of his time, surpassed only by Quental. After having been forgotten for a long time, his works, particularly *A morte de D. João, A velhice do Padre Eterno,* and *Pátria,* are receiving attention from readers and scholars.

**References:**

Manuela de Azevedo, *Guerra Junqueiro: A obra e o homem* (Lisbon: Arcádia, 1981);

Amorim de Carvalho, *Guerra Junqueiro e a sua obra poética: Análise crítica* (Porto: Lello, 1998);

Leonardo Coimbra, *Guerra Junqueiro* (Porto: Renascença Portuguesa, 1923);

António Cândido Franco, *A epopeia pós-camoniana de Guerra Junqueiro* (Rio de Janeiro & Porto, 1920; Lisbon: Gazeta do Mundo de Língua Portuguesa, 1996);

Pierre Hourcade, *Guerra Junqueiro et le probléme des influences françaises dans son oeuvre* (Paris: Les Belles Lettres, 1932);

Lopes de Oliveira, *Guerra Junqueiro, a sua vida e a sua obra* (Lisbon: Excelsior, 1982);

Maria Helena Rocha Pereira, *As imagens e os sons na lírica de Guerra Junqueiro* (Porto: Portugália, 1950);

Manuela Rêgo, *Poesia de Guerra Junqueiro* (Lisbon: Presença, 1997);

Paulo Samuel, ed., *Colóquio Guerra Junqueiro e a Modernidade: Actas* (Porto: Universidade Católica Portuguesa e Centro Regional do Porto / Lello, 1998);

António Sérgio, "O caprichismo romântico do Sr. Guerra Junqueiro," in his *Ensaios, I* (Rio de Janeiro & Porto, 1920; Lisbon: Sá da Costa, 1976), pp. 2–368.

**Papers:**

An archive of Abílio Manuel Guerra Junqueiro's papers is housed at the Casa-Museu Guerra Junqueiro in Porto.

# Irene Lisboa
*(25 December 1892 – 25 November 1958)*

Alice R. Clemente
*Brown University*

BOOKS: *13 Contarelos que Irene escreveu e Ilda ilustrou para a gente nova* (Lisbon: Privately printed, 1926);

*Um dia e outro dia . . . Diário de uma mulher,* as João Falco (Lisbon: Seara Nova, 1936);

*Outono havias de vir latente triste,* as Falco (Lisbon: Seara Nova, 1937);

*Froebel e Montessori: O trabalho manual na escola,* as Manuel Soares (Lisbon: Seara Nova, 1937);

*O primeiro ensino,* as Soares (Lisbon: Seara Nova, 1938);

*Solidão: Notas do punho de uma mulher,* as Falco (Lisbon: Seara Nova, 1939);

*Começa uma vida,* as Falco (Lisbon: Seara Nova, 1940);

*A iniciação do cálculo,* as Soares (Lisbon: Seara Nova, 1940);

*Folhas volantes,* as Falco (Lisbon: Seara Nova, 1940);

*Lisboa e quem cá vive,* as Falco (Lisbon: Seara Nova, 1940);

*Esta cidade!* (Lisbon: Privately printed, 1942);

*Modernas tendências da educação* (Lisbon: Cosmos, 1942);

*A psicologia do desenho infantil* (Lisbon: Associação Feminina Portuguesa para a Paz, 1942);

*Apontamentos* (Lisbon: Privately printed, 1943);

*Educação* (Lisbon: Seara Nova, 1944);

*Inquérito ao livro em Portugal,* 2 volumes (Lisbon: Seara Nova, 1944, 1946);

*Uma mão cheia de nada, outra de coisa nenhuma* (Lisbon: Portugália, 1955);

*O pouco e o muito: Crónica urbana* (Lisbon: Portugália, 1956);

*Voltar atrás para quê?* (Lisbon: Bertrand, 1956);

*Título qualquer serve: Para novelas e noveletas* (Lisbon: Portugália, 1958);

*Queres ouvir? Eu conto* (Lisbon: Portugália, 1958);

*Crónicas da serra* (Lisbon: Bertrand, 1958);

*Solidão II* (Lisbon: Portugália, 1966);

*A vidinha da Lita* (Coimbra: Atlântida, 1971);

*Folhas soltas da Seara Nova: 1929–1955,* edited by Paula Morão (Lisbon: Imprensa Nacional-Casa da Moeda, 1986);

*10 mandamentos para a felicidade feminina,* as Maria Moira (Lisbon: Oficina do Livro, 2002).

*Irene Lisboa, 1946 (from Paula Morão, ed.,* Irene Lisboa 1892–1958, *1992; Davis Library, University of North Carolina at Chapel Hill)*

**Edition:** *Obras de Irene Lisboa,* 10 volumes, edited by Paula Morão (Lisbon: Presença, 1991–1999).

For Irene Lisboa, the effects of an irregular childhood, a traumatic adolescence, and an unintentional clash with political dictatorship lingered to the end of her life. At a time when relatively few Portuguese

*Lisboa in 1915 (from Paula Morão, ed.,* Irene Lisboa
1892–1958, *1992; Davis Library, University
of North Carolina at Chapel Hill)*

women were writing for publication, Lisboa found in literature a vehicle for confronting the cumulative injustices that she faced from early childhood onward. She also found in poetry and prose a means for compassionately reaching out to and validating other victims of life, the normally anonymous masses, to whom she gave names and faces. In addition, she found in literature an intellectually and artistically challenging medium that she shaped to her own ends more often than not in opposition to traditional practices but in keeping with the fundamental tenets of the contemporary literary movement known as the *Presença,* or the second phase of Portuguese modernism.

Irene do Céu Vieira Lisboa was born on 25 December 1892 in Casal da Murzinheira, a village in the outskirts of Lisbon, to an eighteen-year-old peasant girl and an elderly lawyer with a reputation for seducing vulnerable young women. Early on, the mother abandoned the child. Lisboa remained nominally in the custody of her father, Luís Emílio Vieira Lisboa; she was, in fact, in the care of her elderly godmother, another of the father's victims. Lisboa's father refused to acknowledge his paternity legally, though he did give her his name. Irene lived with him and her godmother until she went off to boarding school, but the irregularity of her civil status and the innuendo surrounding it marginalized her both at the convent school that she first attended and in her own mind. Then in early adolescence she found herself forced out of her father's life by his marriage to a young woman with a calculating and opportunistic mother who was intent upon ensuring Lisboa's disinheritance to the benefit of her own daughter. With help from her godmother, Lisboa was able to complete her secondary education and enter normal school. She prepared herself to become an elementary-school teacher and, while still a student, began to distinguish herself as an activist. She founded a short-lived journal, *Educação Feminina* (Feminine Education), in which she published her first critique of the educational system.

Lisboa began her teaching career in the elementary grades in 1915, but in 1920 her pedagogical interest shifted to the preschool years. She soon became one of the country's authorities in that field. In 1929, with a scholarship awarded her by the Department of Education, she left for Geneva to study at the prestigious Institut des Sciences de l'Education with some of the most renowned pedagogical scholars of the day, among them Jean Piaget. In 1931 she received her diploma and moved on to Brussels and Paris to study at her own expense and to observe classes utilizing the newest methodologies. Lisboa returned to Portugal intent on putting into practice what she had learned and advocating an early-learning program based on the latest theories of child development. Her program incorporated such participatory practices as multidisciplinary study units, group projects, and open classrooms, all revolutionary concepts for the time. In 1934 she was appointed to the post of director of education for the preschool field and set about instructing other teachers on how to organize classrooms conducive to stimulating the development of children's creative potential.

Lisboa also engaged in an intensive public-education initiative, lecturing and publishing books as well as articles in *Seara Nova, Revista Escolar,* and *Revista Portuguesa* on such topics as advanced pedagogical theory, the Montessori method, and the place of art and crafts in early education. She published these essays under the pseudonym Manuel Soares, presumably sensing that in the conservative climate that prevailed in Portugal in the 1930s such ideas would be more acceptable coming from a man than from a woman. Her fears appear to have been justified. As the dictatorship of António de Oliveira Salazar became increasingly entrenched and intransigent, Lisboa's innovative theories became anathema. Experimental schools were closed, and Lisboa was removed from her post and given a routine office job in the Ministry of Education. In 1940 she was forced into an early retirement. The abrupt termination of her teaching career was a blow from which she never recovered. Never married, Lisboa moved in with her widowed friend and colleague, Ilda Moreira, and Moreira's children. She eked out a meager living from her writing.

During these years Lisboa also published her first fiction, not surprisingly a collection of children's stories, illustrated by Moreira: *13 Contarelos que Irene escreveu e Ilda ilustrou para a gente nova* (13 Little Stories that Irene Wrote and Ilda Illustrated for Young People, 1926). She wrote other stories for adolescents but published them in book form only years later in the last decade of her life. These include *Uma mão cheia de nada, outra de coisa nenhuma* (A Hand Full of Nothing, Another of Nothing More, 1955) and *Queres ouvir? Eu conto* (Do You Want to Hear Something? I'll Tell You, 1958). In composing these tales, she took full account of what she had learned about children, their needs, and their interests.

Lisboa began to make a name for herself as a serious writer not with children's literature, but rather with poetry. She published two books of poetry during these early years: *Um dia e outro dia . . . Diário de uma mulher* (One Day and Another Day . . . Diary of a Woman, 1936) and *Outono havias de vir latente triste* (Autumn, You Arrived Hazy and Sad, 1937), both under another pseudonym, João Falco. Her readers understood that it was a woman writing, and her colleagues at *Seara Nova* as well as her fellow writers knew who Falco was all along. From 1940 to 1942 she used the byline "Irene Lisboa (João Falco)," and from 1942 on, she used her own name. This masculine identity is surprising, since the first of the two books proclaims in its subtitle that it is the diary of a woman. Several critics have sought to account for the use of this pseudonym. One theory was that it was an accommodation to one of her superiors who detested women writers. Another was that Lisboa resorted to the male mask out of social reticence; it was considered unseemly for women to speak openly of personal problems. Yet another explanation was fear, specifically fear that the dictatorship would look upon the author's openness as subversive. Whatever the explanation, there is no doubt that Lisboa creates a corpus of poetry that in subject matter is highly original for its time. The style is also innovative, breaking with tradition in its use of a poetic idiom without ornament. Her poetic language, in its metric and stanzaic irregularity, approximates the naturalness of spoken language.

*Um dia e outro dia,* the so-called diary of a woman, eschews one of the conventions of diary form, identifying each of the entries (or poems) simply as "One

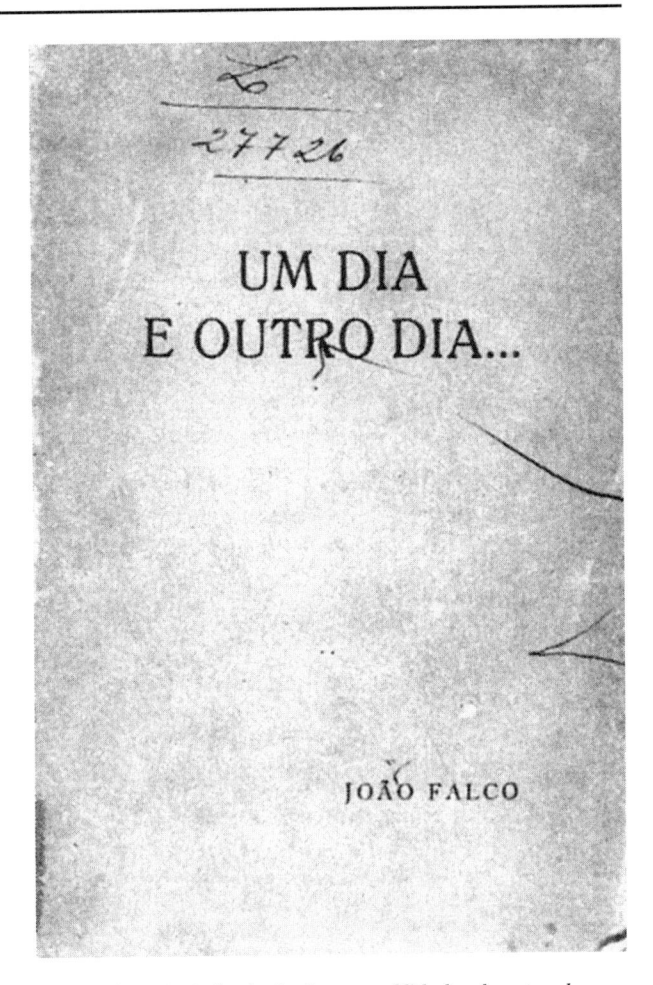

*Cover for Lisboa's first book of poetry, published under a pseudonym in 1936 (from Paula Morão, ed.,* Irene Lisboa 1892–1958, *1992; Davis Library, University of North Carolina at Chapel Hill)*

day," "Another day," or "Another day," with no further indication of date or even, at times, sequentiality. It does share other conventions of the diary; the book is presumably an account of the poet's quotidian experience and an expression of her subjectivity.

On the surface, *Um dia e outro dia* is a record of an unexceptional, monotonous, and banal existence. In reality, however, it plunges the reader into the poet's solitude and her sense of having been forever marginalized by the irregularities of her life. Drawing from memory, Lisboa alludes to deprivation, to specific details of her disturbed childhood and adolescence, and to the sense that it created in her of an almost congenital inadequacy, of being a person *sem casta* (without lineage). Her poetry registers Lisboa's anguished yearning for fulfillment, her need to validate her very existence. Time is an important element as it encompasses not only time remembered but an unending *esperar,* a waiting/hoping for what might yet come to fill the void. Writing is another recurrent

*First page of a letter from Lisboa to fellow writer Vitorino Nemésio (Biblioteca Nacional, Lisbon)* theme; it is important because, after reviewing the conventions of canonical poetry, she asserts her right to go her own way. Writing is also a place to hide and a place to find herself as she reaches both inward and outward toward people, things, and nature. Pain is the creative impulse for her writing.

The first book of verse is unusually long for its day; the second, *Outono havias de vir latente triste,* is short. The poems are free-form, but the lines are longer and more fluid. Enjambment is common. The familiar themes reappear, but they are distanced somewhat by an apparent fatigue and by a greater attentiveness to the external world. The tone is more resigned, meditative, and reflective; the treatment, as a whole, is more lyrical and less prosaic. Suspecting perhaps that she would be criticized for any prose-like passages similar to some in the earlier volume that she herself called *prosa versejada* (versified prose), Lisboa begins *Outono havias de vir latente triste* with a prefatory statement to the reader: "Ao que vos parecer verso chamai verso e ao resto chamai prosa" (What appears to be verse call it verse and the rest, call it prose).

The third major book of this early period was *Solidão: Notas do punho de uma mulher* (Solitude: Notes from the Fist of a Woman, 1939). Perhaps the most widely read of Lisboa's writings, it is a book of prose again akin to a diary or journal. There are passages connected simply by theme and by the presence of a first-person consciousness. Like the other books of poems, it was published under the pseudonym João Falco.

From its beginning, *Solidão* is a lament, tearful in its recognition of frustrated hope, of life never lived. The dominant image of the first segment is one that is common in women's writing, the metaphor of the house. In this case, it is a cold, dark, and inhospitable house. The lament continues in the next segment as the woman questions life in the midst of this perceived aridity, sensing a difference between herself and others in her emotional isolation. She turns to her pen "to free herself from herself"; then, reflecting on the situation, she decides not to vent her pain. She observes others, dramatizing her interactions with them, whether they be visitors or people on the street, and she often stands at her window and looks out over the rooftops of Lisbon toward the Tagus River with its own rhythm of life. She returns once again to her self-absorbed musings, attempting to identify and elucidate the exact nature of her feelings. In the process, she examines the many facets of such complex psychological states as depression and inevitably, repeatedly, the sense of solitude. The latter, however, is not always negative:

*Cover for Lisboa's 1940 autobiographical novella (from Paula Morão, ed.,* Irene Lisboa 1892–1958, *1992; Davis Library, University of North Carolina at Chapel Hill)*

A pesar de tudo, há momentos da minha solidão em que me sinto ultrapassando todos os ordinários interesses, desgarrada deles e dominando-os. E isto sem correr mundo nem ver gente. . . . Será uma forçada sublimação da abstinência?!

(In spite of it all there are moments in my solitude when I feel myself transcending all ordinary interests, cut off from them, dominating them. And this without going out into the world or seeing people. . . . Can it be a forced sublimation of abstinence?!).

Lisboa writes also about her readings, often without identifying the author by anything more than an initial. Some authors, Thomas Mann for example, are identified fully and merit more extensive commentary. Lisboa continues to explore the nature of writing. The novel in particular draws her attention (as it did throughout her career as a writer). Writing novels, she believes, requires a dispassionate and lengthy observation of others that she herself is not capable of sustaining: "A minha análise é repentina e a minha composição muito fraccionária" (My analysis is swift and my composition very fragmentary). Again, this fractured narrative is a characteristic of much women's writing. But women's writing itself is a concept that Lisboa questions:

> Ainda não percebí que bases tem uma tal arte. Nem até o que chega a significar *intelectualidade feminina*, inteligência de mulheres, distinta da dos homens.... Distinguir, como se tem pretendido, arte feminina de arte masculina, parece-me coisa bem temerária e difícil.
>
> (I have not yet come to understand such an art. Nor even the meaning of *feminine intellectuality*, the intelligence of women distinguished from that of men.... To distinguish, as people have tried to do, feminine art from masculine art seems to me to be a rash and difficult thing).

Her own writing, she claims, is a writing of "nothings" of interest only to the author herself. Those nothings include more revelations about her childhood, the early abandonment and abuse (notably by her stepmother and the latter's family) that led her to seek refuge in the intellectual life, and information about her life in Geneva, where she again found refuge from isolation in intellectual excitement. (Details of her sense of estrangement in Geneva can be found in her letters to another budding writer then studying in Brussels, José Rodrigues Miguéis.) Lisboa also addresses her use of pseudonyms. After acknowledging others' comments on them, she states:

> A mim, porém, qualquer coisa mais grave e mais indeterminada me tem levado a adoptar o anonimato, os pseudónimos. Talvez um subtil espírito utilitário de defesa. De inversão da arrogância, da combatividade, também. De timidez, ou de fuga à responsabilidade intelectual, ainda ... Não posso precisar perfeitamente o que seja!
>
> (But something more serious and more indeterminate has led me to adopt anonymity, pseudonyms. Perhaps a subtle utilitarian sense of self-defense, the opposite of arrogance, of combativeness, also. Of timidity or flight from intellectual responsibility ... I can't say exactly what it is!).

In one excursus, Lisboa plays with the notion of another way of writing:

> Deviam ter certa graça *novelas,* que têm menos extensão que *romances,* feitas quase só por figuras. E não por acções, choques, desenlaces. Não será bem, bem desclassificar a *acção,* diminuí-la, reduzí-la à passividade e impotência; era dispensá-la. Ver cada criatura, cada figura de novela em disponibilidade, isto é, na disposição de....
>
> (There would be a certain charm in *novellas,* shorter than *novels,* made up almost exclusively of characters. And not of actions, clashes, denouements. It wouldn't be exactly a declassification of *action,* a diminishing of it, or a reducing of it to passivity and impotence; it would be simply to dispense with it. To see each being, each novella figure as is, that is, in the process of....).

This kind of narrative without action dominates a substantial portion of her writing during the 1940s and 1950s. From 1929 until the end of her life, Lisboa wrote regularly for the literary and intellectual journals of the time, notably for the prestigious journal of the liberal intelligentsia, *Seara Nova,* under both her own name and the pseudonym Maria Moira (used from 1937 to 1939 for "crónicas"). Her contributions include poems, commentary, criticism, short sketches, and longer narratives of the kind she described in *Solidão.* Many of the pieces were later revised for publication in book form; many continued to develop the themes of her earlier work. The books published between 1940 and the end of her life were essentially of two kinds. On the one hand, there are the works that continue the autobiographical strain. On the other, there are collections of narratives focused at first on the people of her city (cleaning women, shopkeepers, street vendors, theatergoers) and later on the mountain folk of the north. She spent increasing amounts of time in that area after the forced termination of her teaching career.

Her first book of the 1940s, *Começa uma vida* (A Life Begins), published earlier in *Seara Nova,* is an autobiographical novella in which the author seeks the "roots and sediments" of her early life. Relying solely on memory and acknowledging its imperfect nature, the author realizes that the effort will be, at best, incomplete. There will be details not remembered and others never really known but suspected by the child she once was. The author aborts her story at the onset of adolescence, defeated in her narrative effort by an overwhelming impotence in dealing with a period as difficult as her adolescent years were. A decade and a half later, in *Voltar atrás para quê?* (Return to the Past, What For? 1956), she finally returns to that adolescence because, as she confesses, at the end of her life she is still trying to reclaim the shattered self whose traumatic beginnings left her forever timid, reserved, oppressed, and now, in old age, invalid and inconsolable. Lisboa shifts from the first-person narrative of the earlier work to the third person in *Voltar atrás para quê?* in an effort, perhaps, to distance her present from her former selves to better understand just what her life has been. Yet, the result is, if anything, even more stark and anguished than the earlier text. Her situation is revisited in *Solidão II* (Solitude II, 1966), a posthumously published continuation of the 1939 *Solidão*.

Lisboa was anything but reclusive; her isolation was a psychological one. Her social reality included the people with whom she lived through much of her adult life (Moreira and her children). They also included the many people who came to visit, old friends and associates, cleaning women past and present, the merchants in the streets and shops of Lisbon, and the many figures who peopled the rural world that she so loved and returned to with greater frequency. Lisboa communicated with these people, listened to their stories, and then reproduced them in the important books of the 1940s and particularly the 1950s: *Esta cidade!* (This City, 1942), which included revisions of material published earlier in *Seara Nova*; *O pouco e o muito: Crónica urbana* (A Lot and a Little: An Urban Chronicle, 1956); *Título qualquer serve: Para novelas e noveletas* (Any Title is Fine: For Novellas and Novelettes, 1958); and finally *Crónicas da serra* (Stories from the Mountains, 1958). These are, for the most part, sketches and vignettes (only toward the end are there authentic short stories) with a purpose that is set forth in a piece published in *Seara Nova* in 1942: "O fim duma literatura destas, que deixa de ser romanesca, é de anotar muitas verdades insignificantes, sem lhes dar, porém, excessivo realce—é de trazer para o campo expressivo, artístico, uma grande naturalidade de observação e de conceitos" (The purpose of this kind of literature, which is not novelistic, is to record many insignificant truths, without overly stressing them—it is to bring into the artistic, expressive field a naturalness of observation and ideas).

An example is the figure of her former cleaning woman Adelina, who appears in several books:

Ela era um *tipo,* uma figura que me parecia bem enquadrada no seu meio, nas suas condições de existência. Ora, este meio, e as reacções que ele provocava na pessoa da Adelina; a sua acomodação umas vezes, os seus assomos de revolta, outras, a sua consciência e a sua personalidade, enfim, interessavam-me.

(She was a *type,* a figure who seemed to me to fit well into her environment, into her lifestyle. This environment and the reactions it provoked in Adelina: her accommodation sometimes, her rebellion other times,

*Cover for the 1956 volume in which Lisboa reexamines her early life (from Paula Morão, ed.,* Irene Lisboa 1892–1958, *1992; Davis Library, University of North Carolina at Chapel Hill)*

her conscience and her personality, in short, interested me).

Adelina's language (like that of all of Lisboa's characters) drew the author's attention. She reproduced it scrupulously with all its faults and strengths. Lisboa's own language and her narrative technique were constantly honed while remaining close to the models that inspired her.

Lisboa died on 25 November 1958 in Lisbon, after a long period of illnesses that included at least two surgical procedures. The final paragraph of *Solidão II,* published after her death, expresses another disappointment that she endured: "Tive meia dúzia de leitores, simpáticos, graciosos. (Letrados, já se sabe.) E continuei esquecida e solitária" (I had a half dozen readers, very nice ones, charming. [People of letters, of course.] And I remained forgotten and solitary). While her work was enthusiastically received by the critics and she was given a high place in the literary firmament of her time, her books had virtually no success among the reading public during her lifetime. This lack of popular interest changed when, several decades after Lisboa's death, her work was rediscovered by another writer, Paula Morão. The result has been not only critical attention (including a major exhibit at the Biblioteca Nacional in Lisbon) but also the reediting of Lisboa's complete works, published by Presença beginning in 1991. Each volume includes an introduction by Morão. The response of the readers has been one that the author could never have imagined. There are now streets and other places named after her, and Maria Velho da Costa (one of the "Three Marias" of *Novas cartas portuguesas* [New Portuguese Letters, 1972]) has published a novel based on Lisboa's life: *Irene ou o contrato social* (Irene or The Social Contract, 2000). Irene Lisboa's books have never become best-sellers, but they are read by anyone interested in women's writing and women's issues.

**References:**

Maria Ondina Braga, "Irene Lisboa," in her *Mulheres escritoras* (Lisbon: Bertrand, 1980), pp. 103–123;

*Colóquio/Letras,* special Lisboa issue, 131 (January–March 1994);

Paula Morão, *O essencial sobre Irene Lisboa* (Lisbon: Imprensa Nacional-Casa da Moeda, 1985);

Morão, *Irene Lisboa: Vida e escrita* (Lisbon: Presença, 1989);

Morão, ed., *Irene Lisboa 1892–1958* (Lisbon: Biblioteca Nacional, 1992);

Raymond L. Sayers, "Irene Lisboa as a Writer of Fiction," *Hispania,* 45 (1962): 224–232;

Maria Alzira Seixo, "Irene Lisboa, *Solidão II*," in her *Discursos do texto* (Lisbon: Bertrand, 1977), pp. 237–243.

**Papers:**

Manuscripts of Irene Lisboa's works are at the Biblioteca Nacional in Lisbon; Lisboa's correspondence with José Rodrigues Miguéis is among his papers at the John Hay Library at Brown University in Providence, Rhode Island.

# Fernão Lopes
*(1380/1390? – 1460?)*

Andréia Cristina Lopes Frazão da Silva
*Universidade Federal do Rio de Janeiro*

**BOOKS:** *Crónica del Rey D. João I de Boa Memória e dos reis de Portugal o décimo,* 2 volumes (Lisbon: Antônio Álvares, 1644);

*Crónica do El Rei Dom Pedro I deste nome, e dos reis de Portugal o oitavo cognominado o Justiceiro na forma em que a escreveu Fernão Lopes,* edited by José Pereira Baião (Lisbon: Na Offic. de Manoel Fernandes Costa, 1735);

*Crónica do Senhor Rei D. Fernando,* edited by Aragão Morato, in *Colecção de livros inéditos da história portuguesa,* volume 4 (Lisbon: Academia Real das Ciências, 1816), pp. 121–525.

**Editions:** *Crónica de El-Rei D. Pedro I,* edited by Luciano Cordeiro (Lisbon: Escriptorio, 1895);

*Crónica de D. Fernando,* 3 volumes, edited by Cordeiro (Lisbon: Escriptorio, 1895–1896);

*Chronica de El-Rei D. Fernando* (Lisbon: Edição Mello D'Azevedo, 1896);

*Crónica de El-Rei D. João I, Primeira parte,* 3 volumes, edited by Cordeiro (Lisbon: Escriptorio, 1897);

*Crónica de El-Rei D. João I, Segunda parte,* 4 volumes, edited by Cordeiro (Lisbon: Escriptorio, 1898);

*Primeira parte da crónica de D. João I,* edited by Anselmo Braamcamp Freire (Lisbon: Arquivo Histórico Português, 1915);

*Fernão Lopes,* 3 volumes, edited by Agostinho de Campos (Lisbon: Bertrand, 1921–1922)—comprises volume 1, *Crónicas de D. Pedro e D. Fernando;* volume 2, *Primeira parte da crônica de D. João I;* and volume 3, *Primeira crônica de D. João I;*

*Crônica de D. Pedro I,* edited by Damião Peres (Barcelos: Portucalense, 1932);

*Crônica de D. Fernando,* 2 volumes (Barcelos: Portucalense, 1933, 1935);

*Crônica de D. Pedro I,* edited by Torquato de Sousa Soares (Lisbon: A. M. Teixeira, 1943);

*Crônica de D. João I,* 2 volumes, volume 1 edited by António Sérgio, volume 2 edited by M. Lopes de Almeida and A. Magalhães Basto (Porto: Civilização, 1945, 1949);

*Fernão Lopes (portrait by Nuno Gonçalves, from the Archbishop's Panel at the monastery of São Vicente de Fora)*

*Crônica de D. Fernando,* edited by Soares (Lisbon: Clássica, 1945);

*Crônica do senhor rei Dom Pedro oitavo rei destes regnos,* edited by Peres (Porto: Civilização, 1965);

*Crônica de D. Pedro,* edited by Giuliano Macchi (Rome: Ateneo, 1966);

*Crônica do senhor rei Dom Fernando nono rei destes regnos,* edited by Salvador Dias Arnaut (Porto: Civilização, 1966);

*Fernão Lopes: Crônicas,* edited by Adolfo Casais Monteiro (Rio de Janeiro: Agir, 1968);

*Crônica del rei D. Joham I, de Boa Memória e dos reis de Portugal o decimo,* edited by William J. Entwistle and Luís F. Lindley Cintra (Lisbon: Imprensa Nacional, 1968);

*Crônica de D. Fernando,* edited by Macchi (Lisbon: Imprensa Nacional-Casa da Moeda, 1975);

*Crônica de D. Pedro,* edited by Antônio Borges Coelho (Lisbon: Horizonte, 1977);

*História de uma revolução: Primeria parte da "Crônica de El-Rei D. João I de Boa Memória,"* edited by José Hermano Saraiva (Lisbon: Europa-América, 1977);

*Crônica de D. João I,* edited by Teresa Amado (Lisbon: Seara Nova Comunicação, 1980);

*Crónicas de Fernão Lopes,* edited by Maria Ema Tarracha Ferreira (Lisbon: Ulisseia, 1984);

*As crónicas de Fernão Lopes,* edited by António José Saraiva, fourth edition (Lisbon: Gradiva, 1997).

**Editions in English:** *The Chronicles of Fernão Lopes and Gomes Eannes de Zurara,* edited and translated by Edgar Prestage (Watford: Voss & Michael, 1928);

*The English in Portugal, 1367–1387: Extracts from the Chronicles of Dom Fernando and Dom João,* edited and translated by Derek W. Lomax and R. J. Oakley (Warminster, U.K.: Aris & Phillips, 1988).

Chronicler Fernão Lopes is an important early figure in the intellectual and literary history of Portugal. His output was not enormous, but the works he produced in the fifteenth century are of a magnitude that earned him the title of "father of Portuguese historiography." Lopes was not only an historian but also a creative writer who produced texts of high literary quality. His chronicles possess a hybrid character: they cannot easily be classified under a specific literary genre because they incorporate elements from several different ones, including the novel of chivalry, epic poetry, ecclesiastical oratory, classical rhetoric, and above all, the Bible.

The only materials available for reconstructing Lopes's biography include some letters, notarial documents, and information in his works and those of other authors. In the preserved documentation regarding Lopes, there is no information about his family or the date or place of his birth. Scholars believe that he was born between 1380 and 1390, but they have conjectured this date based on indirect evidence. It is known that Lopes's son Martinho was the physician of the infante D. Fernando, son of King John I of Portugal, around the year 1437. Since this position would have demanded a certain amount of experience, it is reasonable to assume that Lopes's son was about thirty years old at the time. Therefore, he would have been born around 1407, and it is likely that Lopes was already then between twenty and thirty years old. Lopes lived a large portion of his life in Lisbon, because of the professional activities he performed. In his chronicles he refers frequently to urban life, so it is possible that he was born or educated in a city, perhaps Lisbon.

Several biographical details accepted as fact have led specialists to assume that Lopes (which means son of Lopo) was born into a family of humble origins. He married Mor Lourenço, the daughter of a manual laborer, with whom he had at least one son, Martinho; and he maintained relationships with several people outside the nobility until around 1446. His father was probably a peasant, artisan, or even a small-time merchant. Even so, Lopes ascended socially, receiving the title of vassal of the king and acquiring some wealth. He also attained a certain amount of recognition in Lisbon society of his day. His importance is supported by the fact that several scholars agree that he is the subject of a portrait by well-known painter Nuno Gonçalves. The painting is a part of the Archbishop's Panel in the monastery of São Vicente de Fora.

Lopes was born at a time of internal conflicts within the nobility and deep social differences in Portuguese society. These culminated in a revolt after King Fernando I died in 1383, leaving no masculine heirs. His only daughter, Beatriz, was married to John I of Castile, according to an agreement made by the two countries. This arrangement stipulated that Leonor Teles, the king's widow, would rule as regent until Beatriz produced a son to succeed his grandfather.

The dissatisfaction of several groups inside Portuguese society, the regent's politics that favored Castile, and economic and social problems resulted in the revolt. John, bastard son of King Peter I and half brother of King Fernando I, was chosen in 1385 by the court in Coimbra as the new king, thus establishing the Avis Dynasty. As a reaction to the acclamation of John I as sovereign, the traditional Portuguese nobility, with the support of Castile, was at odds with the small nobility, merchants, artisans, part of the clergy, and the Portuguese people in general.

Lopes was probably still a child when these events occurred. In his writing, however, he reveals an awareness of the revolt, the ascension of John I to the Portuguese throne, and the victory of the Portuguese against Castile at Aljubarrota (1385). The chronicler developed his literary skills and achieved social recognition during the Avis Dynasty. It is difficult to separate his biography and his literary production from the historical events and the lives of Portuguese royalty of this period. Not only was a new dynasty inaugurated but also a new balance of social and political forces was established. The king, with the support of the lesser nobility, merchants, laborers, and common people, assumed a dominant position in the life of the nation. The powerful families, who had been so prominent in politics until then, were pushed into the background.

The first extant document that directly concerns Lopes is a certificate that bears his signature and is dated 29 November 1418. The certificate names him curator of the general archives of the kingdom, kept in the Torre do Tombo. Documents such as certificates, contracts, and wills were maintained there.

As curator of the Torre do Tombo, Lopes managed the archives, issued certificates, and authenticated diplomas by order of the king. He was the first to occupy this position. Before him, such tasks were performed by the Inspector of the State or by the king's accountant. The creation of the position indicates the growing importance of the government's administrative apparatus at the time. Lopes's appointment has led scholars to believe that he already had a certain amount of experience, perhaps having worked as a public notary. Notaries made copies of original documents; they wrote certificates, contracts, and wills; and they were clerks of the courts, keeping police records for their jurisdictions. To be a general notary was a privilege granted only by the king himself; Lopes, at the beginning of the 1430s, achieved this rank. His activities as curator of the archives of the Torre do Tombo and as a notary gave him access to the information that he used in the writing of his chronicles.

There is a certificate dated 12 December 1418 in which he is declared clerk of the books–a type of secretary–of D. Duarte, son of John I. In the following year, he added this function to that of clerk of the king's books. Another document, dated 4 September 1422, states that he became the confidant and private secretary for a son of King Fernando, which implies an intimacy and trust between the chronicler and the infante. In 1437 Lopes wrote, in his own handwriting, Fernando's will, for which he received an inheritance of a certain amount of money. The administrative offices exercised by Lopes demonstrate a recognition by royalty of his professional capacity, as well as his proximity to the court. About 1433, John I granted Lopes the title of King's Vassal.

In a letter dated 19 March 1434, King Duarte entrusted Lopes with the composition of chronicles of the kings of Portugal. He was given an annual income to perform the task. Some scholars, however, believe that Lopes had already begun his work as chronicler in 1419. The income and the responsibility given to Lopes were renewed in 1439 by the regent D. Peter, the other son of John I. And in 1449, Afonso V not only renewed Lopes's assignment as chronicler but also increased his wages. Lopes wrote his works, therefore, as an official chronicler, in the service of royalty. Thus, his perspective on the events narrated in the chronicles are not the result of a personal analysis but rather constitute an expression of the hegemonic thought present in the court of the Avis dynasty.

There is no direct information about Lopes's academic background. Based on references to Livy, Cicero, Ovid, Augustine, Bede, and Eusebio of Caesarea in his chronicles, some scholars believe that he attended a monastic school or a cathedral school. Gomes Eanes de Zurara, Lopes's successor as curator of the Torre de Tombo and official chronicler of the court, wrote in the third part of the *Crónica de D. João I* (probably after 1450) that Lopes was an outstanding person, of great authority, but that he had only a basic culture, similar to that of most of the population. Zurara's testimony, in addition to evidence from several other sources, has led scholars to conclude that Lopes had only an elementary education. This assumption could be correct, since he was of humble origins, and the notarial activity did not require a university education. Generally, notaries came from the families of artisans or small merchants, and they obtained the position after an exam presided over by the king's chancellor. Lopes's works do not reveal great erudition, although his texts are well organized, clear, and coherent.

School, however, is not the only place where it is possible to acquire academic culture. It would have been possible for Lopes to complete his education with knowledge obtained orally, especially in the court, and through reading. In the Portuguese libraries, such as the Monastery of Alcobaça and the Real Library, Lopes had access to several books, such as the *Crónica geral de Espanha* (General Chronicle of Spain, 1270–1289), *Demanda do Santo Graal* (Demand for the Holy Grail, a French work translated for the Portuguese in the thirteenth century), *Regimento de príncipes* (The Regiment of Princes, 1287) of Gil Roman, *De re militari* (By the Military, early fifteenth century) of Vegecio, plus works by Aristotle, Augustine, Cicero, Seneca, Dante, Petrarch, Boccaccio, and Marco Polo.

In the beginning of the fifteenth century, there was in Portugal a secular culture among the new royalty that had ascended to power after 1383. This group needed to affirm its moral superiority, its effectiveness, and its sincerity in governing the kingdom. Thus, many books were translated or written, such as historical books and practical texts, some by members of the royal family: *Livro de montaria* (Book of Riding) by John I; *Livro da ensinança de bem cavalgar toda sela* (Book Teaching How to Ride All Kinds of Saddles) and *Leal conselheiro* (Loyal Counselor) by Duarte; and *Virtuosa benfeitoria* (Virtuous Benefit) by Peter.

Lopes acquired a basic mastery of Latin–which he used to read his sources–and of Latin rhetoric,

*First page of the will of the infante D. Fernando, handwritten by Lopes in 1437 in his capacity as private secretary (Biblioteca Nacional, Lisbon; from a 1915 edition of Lopes's* Crónica del Rey D. Joao I, *Thomas Cooper Library, University of South Carolina)* which he used in the composition of his chronicles. There are three works that, incontestably, were written by him: *Crónica del Rey D. Pedro* (Chronicle of King Peter); *Crónica del Rey D. Fernando* (Chronicle of King Fernando); and *Crónica del Rey D. João I de Boa Memória e dos reis de Portugal o décimo* (Chronicle of King John I of Glorious Memory and the Tenth King of Portugal), referred to as the *Crónica del Rey D. João I*.

The *Crónica del Rey D. Pedro* covers the ten years of this king's rule (1357–1367). The events before his reign are omitted, but the narration includes some information about events after his death. The work is composed of a foreword and forty-four chapters. Lopes probably began to write it in 1434, when Duarte entrusted him with this task.

The *Crónica del Rey D. Fernando* relates the events that followed King Peter I's death in March of 1367. The volume ends shortly after Fernando I's death, and it includes an account of the reaction of the Portuguese people to the regency of Leonor Teles, the king's widow. This work opens with a foreword, followed by 178 chapters. Lopes probably began its composition around 1436.

The *Crónica del Rey D. João I* is considered Lopes's masterpiece. It is the product of a mature historian and writer. In this work he covers a longer time period than in the previous chronicles, and he also talks about the crisis of succession (1383–1385). This chronicle is divided into two parts. The first presents the events that occurred from King Fernando I's death in December 1383 to John's acclamation as king of Portugal in April of 1385. The second part covers the period from April 1385 to 1411; it focuses on the conflicts between Portugal and Castile in the court of Coimbra, which chose Peter I's illegitimate son John to be the new king. A few events posterior to this date are also mentioned.

The work includes 193 chapters in the first part and 204 in the second. Scholars believe that it was written during Peter's regency, which began in 1438. Lopes did not complete the chronicle because John's reign was prolonged to 1433, and the narrative finishes in 1411. Lopes's successor, Zurara, wrote the third part. Some specialists believe that Lopes had already gathered the documents to compose the final part of this work when Zurara took his place as chronicler.

Lopes's individual chronicles possess an internal coherence: they are the result of the same writing project, which the author skillfully planned and executed. The narratives are developed carefully along time coordinates, following closely the chronology of the episodes. This organization is broken at some points when Lopes concentrates on certain characters, because the author is concerned, above all, with causality. The chapters are thus grouped according to themes and are relatively autonomous. The writer provides transitional sentences to guide the reader through the various parts of the narrative. Lopes's text, therefore, ends up building several plans of action and sequences.

There are references in both Lopes's and Zurara's works that allow the reader to assume that Lopes wrote chronicles about some Portuguese kings before Peter I. Damian of Gois, a Portuguese writer of the sixteenth century, insists that Lopes wrote a chronicle about all the kings of the Afonsina Dynasty, but this work would have been adapted by Rui of Pina, curator of the Torre do Tombo in the beginning of the sixteenth century. This information, in addition to the anonymous manuscripts of the fifteenth century discovered in Portuguese institutions in the 1940s, led many scholars to believe that the chronicler was also the author of a *Crónica geral do reino* (General Chronicle of the Kingdom). The first manuscript was found at the Municipal Public Library of Porto; it is known as the *Crónica dos cinco reis* (Chronicle of the Five Kings), because it covers the period from the reign of Afonso Henriques to Afonso III. The second, discovered in the archives of the House of the Dukes of Cadaval, includes a text that was denominated *Crónica de 1419* (Chronicle of 1419), because, according to the chronicle itself, its composition began in that year. This text is also known as *Crónica dos sete reis* (Chronicle of the Seven Kings) because it includes information about Portuguese kings up to the reign of Afonso IV.

The *Crónica dos cinco reis* and *Crónica dos sete reis* are expansions of passages from the *Crónica geral de Espanha de 1344* (General Chronicle of Spain of 1344) that deal with the Portuguese monarchs. This work is incomplete, and many specialists have considered it to be a first draft. Some authors believe that Lopes wrote this material at the request of Duarte in 1419; others, however, disagree with this hypothesis, in spite of the similarities between Lopes's chronicles and these manuscripts.

Another work that has been attributed to Lopes is the *Crónica do Condestabre* (Chronicle of Condestabre, which was probably written by 1431). Most scholars, however, now question his authorship of the text. This chronicle, in a version different from the one that was preserved, was one of the most important sources Lopes used in the composition of his work and of which he made many transcriptions. Only the chronicles of the reigns of Peter I, Fernando I, and John I are accepted without any doubt as Lopes's works.

As a mature man working as official chronicler of the kingdom, Lopes witnessed and probably took part in the dispute for the regency by Peter after Duarte's death from the plague on 9 September 1438. The throne should have passed to Afonso V, but he was only six years old; in this case the regency would have gone to the widowed queen. Peter, however, supported by the same groups that had earlier supported his father, was chosen as regent. These events happened around the time of the composition of part 1 of the *Crónica del Rey D. João I,* and certainly influenced Lopes. Some of the details that the author included about the events of 1383 belong, in fact, to the crisis of 1439. When Afonso V was sixteen years old, the traditional noble families restored him to power. As a result, Peter was discharged and later killed in the battle of Alforrobeira.

As a contemporary of the Avis Dynasty, Lopes wrote his chronicles at the time that Portugal began its Atlantic expansion. Starting in 1415, the Portuguese began to reach more remote areas: the Canary Islands in 1424; Tangier in 1437; White Cable, Furna, and Arguim in 1442; and Gambia and Geba in 1456. Several areas were discovered, conquered, and colonized: Ceuta, the Azores, the archipelago of Cape Verde, and the area of Alcácer-Ceguer.

The Atlantic expansion was an initiative of the nobility, supported by the royalty, and with merchant participation and papal recognition of the territorial rights of the Portuguese. These discoveries enlarged the Portuguese Empire, intensified trade, generated wealth, and eased some of the social and economic tensions of the moment. At the same time, however, there were disputes with Castile, such as the one over human losses and failures that took place during the expedition to Tangier, in which Lopes's son, Martinho, and the infante D. Fernando died.

As an adult living in the court, Lopes witnessed many events from a privileged position: the final years of João I's reign and the beginning of the Atlantic expansion; the entire reign of Duarte; the crisis of succession and Pedro's regency; and the first years of the rule of Afonso V. Since he concluded his chronicles with the year 1411 and the beginning of the Avis Dynasty, Lopes did not write about what he had witnessed. What he saw at the court, however, influenced his perspective as he wrote his works.

Although he exercised important positions in the court and reached the rank of king's vassal, Lopes was not of noble origins. Having come from another social and economic class, his perspective was that of an outsider. His chronicles are not limited to presenting facts; they include analyses and judgments about what is narrated. Everything in his text focuses on the defense of a central thesis. Lopes's narrative is the result of an individual's understanding of the events, made from a social and political stance, and within a specific intellectual context.

Lopes's work as chronicler has its climax in the events of 1383. He narrates these in the first part of the *Crónica del Rey D. João I,* which argues that the Avis dynasty, raised to power after the events between 1383 and 1385, was legitimate. In Lopes's work, John I is presented not as a usurper but rather as a legitimate sovereign on the basis of ethical and juridical reasons as well as through divine choice.

The justification of the revolt was Lopes's main interest, rather than the events prior to it. The change of dynasty created a new political organization, in which new groups were integrated into the power structure, including the lesser nobility, small merchants, and even artisans. Lopes's perspective is that of the triumphant group, and from that point of view he apprehended and interpreted the events, which he saw as a turning point inaugurating a "new age" in the history of mankind.

The purpose of Lopes's work was to establish a new code of behavior and to educate and inform the new group of leaders. His books, at first, had a small circulation, restricted to the court. In fact, the form of composition of the chronicles indicates that they were intended to be read aloud to the members of the court of Avis.

Since Lopes was not an eyewitness of the events he narrates in his work, he used several documents to reconstruct the past. His main sources for the *Crónica del Rey D. Pedro I* were Lopes de Ayala's *Crônica de D. Pedro de Castela* (Chronicle of D. Peter of Castile, written, probably, after 1366 and 1407); the *Crônica geral de Espanha* (General Chronicle of Spain), written between 1270 and 1289; documents from the King's Chancellery, diplomatic letters, papal bulls, coins, oral testimonies, and monuments. For the composition of the *Crónica del Rey D. Fernando,* he consulted Ayala's *Crônicas de D. Henrique e D. João I de Castela* (The Chronicles of D. Henrique and D. John I of Castile), written, probably, after 1366 and before 1407; Martim Afonso Melo's books, such as *Da guerra* (Of the War) and *Cronica de D. Fernando* (Chronicle of D. Fernando), dated at the end of the fourteenth century and now lost; and books of lineage records, ecclesiastical treatises, books from the royal chancellery, diplomatic correspondence, monastic archives, and military documents. And, finally, for the *Crónica del Rey D. João I* he used a Latin chronicle on the reign of John I, written by Christoforus, probably a clergyman; he also consulted sermons, Ayala's *Crônica de D. João I de Castela* (Chronicle of D. John I of Castile), books from the chancellery, the work of Afonso Melo, epitaphs of the monastery of Alcobaça, bulls, diplomatic documents, letters, and notarial texts.

Many of the documents Lopes used, especially the notarial and diplomatic ones, have been preserved only through his works. To gather so many sources that included not only Portuguese but also Castilian, Aragonese, and English documents, the chronicler traveled to several places and consulted many civil, religious, military, and private archives. His investigative and critical works were based on the collection, selection, ordination, and critical appraisal of these sources. His treatment of this material was diverse: he translated and transcribed; he summarized and elaborated; he changed the narrative order of his sources and dramatized events, creating dialogues and fictitious speeches for his characters; he commented on his sources and compared different versions of the same event; and he even omitted some information. For example, when he presents two different versions of the same event, he indicates the one that seems to him to be the most reasonable. The chronicler presents the reader with his personal version of the truth that he built through the selection and combination of materials from various sources.

Lopes is innovative in his treatment of the past, including economic aspects. He dedicates pages and even entire chapters to revealing the public's opinion on some episodes. He mentions social conflicts and considers Portugal as having its own political individuality, different from that of Castile. He constructs an orderly narrative, based on cause and effect, as the Scholastics had done. Lopes, however, believed in the division of history into ages, in loyalty to his sponsors, and in the exaltation of heroes. He also accepted divine providence as the guiding principle of history.

His editorial style is simple and direct, approaching oral speech. The narrator participates in the work, and sometimes it is difficult to distinguish narrator from author. The narrator creates a dialogue with his readers. Lopes's chronicles are replete with dialogues between the characters, emphatic exclamations from the narrator, and descriptions of landscapes and people. His texts possess a dynamic and dramatic character.

The people in Lopes's chronicles are complex creations; he makes these historical figures come alive and reveal themselves through their speech, acts, and behavior. The author concentrates his narrative on concrete, sensory, and visual elements, but at times he also uses allegory and metaphor to vivify the narrative. Lopes's Portuguese is archaic and filled with syntactical irregularities. Overall, however, his language is simple and incorporates several oral expressions. His vocabulary is colloquial, fluid, and familiar, which makes it extremely clear. His narrative at times resembles an informal chat, in which the listener is invited to participate.

With the ascension of Afonso V to the throne and the reestablishment of the old families in power, Zurara replaced Lopes as official chronicler in 1450. In 1454, Lopes was also removed from his position as curator of the Torre do Tombo. The king sent him a letter on 6 June stating that Lopes was too old and weak to perform the job. The last time that Lopes's name officially appears is in a 1459 document in which he disinherits a grandson, the bastard son of Martinho. Lopes was probably about seventy to eighty years old at the time. After

*Title page for the second volume of one of Lopes's chronicles (Biblioteca Nacional, Lisbon)*

this date, he does not appear in any preserved documentation, and it is believed that he died around 1460.

The original manuscripts of Lopes's three chronicles with his signature have not been preserved. What is preserved today was passed down from copies made at the end of the fifteenth and throughout the sixteenth centuries. These manuscripts are either anonymous or attributed to Zurara or to Rui of Pina. More than seventy-five manuscripts with his work were preserved, which shows that there was some interest in maintaining them. There is no evidence, however, that these works were circulated.

The first publication of Lopes's work was in 1644, when Antônio Álvares printed the *Crónica del Rey D. João I*. In 1735, José Pereira Baião published the *Crónica del Rey D. Pedro I*. The *Crónica del Rey D. Fernando*, however, was not printed until 1816. Specialists have offered several explanations for this indifference to Lopes's works, including their archaic language and the fact that the descendants of many figures criticized by the chronicler were displeased. There were also reasons of a political nature; the present king was different from the humanized sovereign presented in Lopes's narrative. In addition to that, men of the Renaissance and the Enlightenment were unsympathetic toward anything that was medieval. Finally, there was the Spanish occupation of the Portuguese throne from 1580 to 1640.

During the twentieth century, several editions of the chronicles, complete or in selections, were published, including some in modern Portuguese. Critical editions, however, only began to appear after the 1960s. Giuliano Macchi is responsible for a 1966 annotated edition of the *Crónica del Rey D. Pedro* and a 1975 edition of the *Crónica del Rey D. Fernando*. There is no critical edition of the *Crónica del Rey D. João I*, nor a critical edition of the complete works of Lopes.

Many scholars have devoted time to study of Lopes's work. They have published articles and books, or they have written forewords and notes for the editions of his chronicles. Most of the studies written about Lopes and his chronicles in the first half of the twentieth century, with few exceptions, were not done in a systematic way; they were based mostly on personal tastes and impressions. After the 1980s, more systematic and conclusive works appeared, following modern theories and methods. These have tended to focus on particular aspects of Lopes's work, such as language, literary style, the organization of the narrative, the description of character, and the study of the sources of the chronicles. Lopes's work has been studied mainly for the historical reconstruction of the reigns of Peter I, Fernando I, and John I. With recent progress and interest in cultural history and linguistics, however, the works have been looked at more as documents for the understanding of the historical and cultural context of the author.

General public access to Lopes's work is limited, especially in countries where Portuguese is not spoken. Many of the modernized Portuguese versions do not present the complete text of the work, but rather only selected passages. Also, the complete chronicles have not yet been translated into other languages, prohibiting access by students and specialists who do not know Portuguese.

Despised by the age of humanists and the men of the Enlightenment, Lopes was deified by the Romantics as a patriot and nationalist and considered the father of Portuguese history. The positivist historians, who valued empirical work, narrative, and political facts, loved his work for the author's attention to detail and his incessant search for the truth. In the last few decades of the twentieth century, the chronicler has been viewed from another perspective: as a man of humble origins who ascended socially during the Avis dynasty and served as its official chronicler. He wrote to justify the events of 1383–1385 and to legitimize the new dynasty.

Fernão Lopes was not truly the father of Portuguese historiography, which had already produced some texts before his chronicles. He, in fact, used some of these works as his sources. Lopes, however, opened a new phase of this historiography. His work represents the passage from an approach to history based on the memory of the events, often mixed with the invented, to a more coherent and systematic text produced after the collection, selection, ordering, and critical appraisal of the records. Lopes's activities as notary and curator of the Torre do Tombo brought him into contact with documents in which he found vestiges of the past. He had the ability to observe in these documents a moment of which he was not a direct witness, and he was able to record and bring that moment to life in his prose.

**References:**

Teresa Amado, *Fernão Lopes: Contador de histórias. Sobre a Crônica de D. João I* (Lisbon: Estampa, 1997);

Artur de Magalhães Basto, *Fernão Lopes suas "Crônicas Perdidas" e a Crônica Geral do Reino: A propôsito duma crônica quatrocentista inedita dos cinco primeros reis de Portugal* (Porto: Progredior, 1943);

António Afonso Borregana, *Poesia trovadoresca. Crónicas de Fernão Lopes: O texto em análise* (Lisbon: Texto, 2001);

Ablin Eduard Beau, "Características da manifestação do sentimento nacional em Fernão Lopes," *Acta Universitatis Conimbrigensis*, 1 (1959): 63–72;

Maria Ângela Beirante, *As estrutras sociais em Fernão Lopes* (Lisbon: Horizonte, 1984);

Aubrey F. G. Bell, *Fernão Lopes* (Coimbra: Universidade de Coimbra, 1931);

Hernâni Cidade, *Fernão Lopes é ou não autor da Crónica do Condestabre?* (Coimbra: Universidade de Coimbra, 1931);

Julio López-Arias, *Peculiaridades estilísticas de Fernäo Lopes* (New York: Peter Lang, 1993);

Adolfo Casais Monteiro, *Fernão Lopes* (Rio de Janeiro: Agir, 1968);

João Gouveia Monteiro, *Fernão Lopes: Texto e contexto* (Coimbra: Minerva, 1988);

Luis de Sousa Rebelo, *A concepção do poder em Fernão Lopes* (Lisbon: Horizonte, 1983);

P. E. Russel, *As fontes de Fernão Lopes* (Coimbra: Coimbra, 1941);

Antônio José Saraiva, *Fernão Lopes* (Lisbon: Europa-América, 1965);

Valentino Viegas, *Fernão Lopes e os arquivos do país* (Lisbon: V. M. Viegas, 1989);

Viegas, *Lisboa, a força da revolução, 1383–1385: Os documentos comprovam Fernão Lopes* (Lisbon: Livros Horizonte, 1985).

# Helena Marques
(17 May 1935 -   )

Monica Rector
University of North Carolina at Chapel Hill

BOOKS: *O último cais* (Lisbon: Circulo de Leitores, 1992);
*A deusa sentada* (Lisbon: Dom Quixote, 1994);
*Terceiras pessoas* (Lisbon: Dom Quixote, 1998);
*Os íbis vermelhos de Guiana* (Lisbon: Dom Quixote, 2002).

OTHER: "O tratado," in *Doze escritores portugueses contemporâneos: Antologia* (Lisbon: Dom Quixote, 1997), pp. 26-31.

SELECTED PERIODICAL PUBLICATION–UNCOLLECTED: "Sou uma jornalista que escreveu um romance," *Jornal de Letras,* 30 March 1993: 16-17.

Helena Marques's work has made her one of the most recognized Portuguese writers of the end of the twentieth century. Her books, which began appearing in the 1990s, are among the first works in Portuguese literature to portray older and independent women who are accomplished both professionally and personally. Her female characters stand out for the choices they make as they take control of their own destinies in a traditional patriarchal society.

Helena Maria Pereira Gonçalves Marques was born in Carcavelos, Portugal, near Lisbon, on 17 May 1935. Her parents are Ernesto Gonçalves Marques, a radiotelegraphist for the Western Telegraphy Company, and Maria Helena Pereira Gonçalves Marques. When Marques was born, the Western Telegraphy Company, a British manufacturer of underwater cables, had stations in Portugal and in the islands of Madeira and the Azores. At the age of three months Marques was taken to Funchal, capital of the Madeira Islands, where she later completed her elementary and secondary studies. She did not attend college because at that time there was no university in Funchal. Marques, who was born during the regime of Portuguese dictator António de Oliveira Salazar, received a strong republican influence from her grandfather, Vasco Gonçalves Marques–doctor, senator of the Portuguese republic, and president of the regional government of Madeira before the advent of the dictatorship–who transmitted to her his values of liberty and equality. She was brought up near the harbor, which, with its constant arrival and departure of ships, plays an important role in her work. She married journalist Rui Camacho in 1958 and has four children, three of whom are also journalists. Marques has worked most of her life in the field of journalism, beginning her career at the *Diário de Notícias* of Funchal in March 1957, where she remained until 1971. She then moved to Lisbon, where she worked for various newspapers: *A Capital, Jornal do Comércio, República, Luta,* and finally for the Lisbon *Diário de Notícias* from 1978 to 1992. She was adjunct director of the paper from 1986 to 1992. In 1986 she received the prize of Jornalista do Ano (Journalist of the Year), awarded by the magazine *Mulher.* She retired from *Diário de Notícias* in 1992.

Marques began to write fiction after she had completed her career as a journalist. At a mature age, and without any professional demands, she has written four novels. Although each is a separate unit and coherent in itself, her first three works form a trilogy. Some critics, however, consider only the first two books as sequential. Over the course of the trilogy times change, and women gain more rights and responsibilities. The author chronicles the growth of women as human beings and the difficulties the male characters face in dealing with this development. Marques's novels may be analyzed from a feminist perspective, and the author has referred to herself as a "rational feminist."

Her first novel, *O último cais* (The Last Harbor, 1992), won the Prémio Revista Ler / Círculo dos Leitores; the Grande Prémio de Romance e Novela of the Associação Portuguesa de Escritores; the Prémio Máxima-Revelação; the Prémio Bordallo de Literatura by Casa da Imprensa; and the Prémio Procópio de Literatura, all in 1992. *O último cais* and *A deusa sentada* (The Seated Goddess, 1994) relate the saga of the Vella or Villa family. The first novel takes place in the nineteenth century and the second in the twentieth. *O último*

*Helena Marques (photograph by João Vilhena; from the cover for* A deusa sentada, *1994; Davis Library, University of North Carolina at Chapel Hill)*

*cais* reflects the feelings of isolation and confinement of the Funchal natives, who are portrayed as always awaiting a ship to bring news from the outside world. The image of a last harbor creates a sensation of finality and ending, which is seen in the lives of those who cannot leave the island.

The trilogy begins on the island in the nineteenth century with the Vella family and focuses on the women. Raquel, the principal character, is a happily married woman with a positive perspective on life. The other characters consist of the immediate and extended family and an array of other islanders who interact with the family. Constança, Raquel's aunt, is a lonely and unhappy person, the product of a frustrating marriage that drained her spirit. Catarina Isabel is a professional woman at a time when women had just been granted the privilege of working. Violante is a good wife who loses interest in sex when she realizes that she cannot have children. Raquel's daughter Benedita is conservative and proper. Charlotte is a foreigner and fights for women's right to vote until she discovers that most of the women are not interested in voting. Clara, Raquel's other daughter (Raquel dies giving birth to her), is a candid woman, peaceful and harmonious. Luciana is a free spirit, symbolic of women of the following century. These women compose an intricate and complicated world of feminine relationships in a traditional patriarchal society isolated from the mainstream of Portuguese life.

*O último cais* opens with a page from a shipboard diary, dated 4 September 1879. The narrative ends around 1904. The story centers on the extremely happy relationship between Raquel and her husband, Marcos Vaz de Lacerda. He is an officer in the navy and is deeply in love with Raquel, to whom he has been married for many years. Unlike most males in this traditional society, he is not afraid to express his feelings. Marcos is not an ambitious male figure; his greatest desire in life is to be Raquel's husband. In portraying a sensitive male totally dedicated to his wife and uninterested in professional success, Marques creates a pattern of behavior that subverts the traditional gender roles of nineteenth-century Portuguese society.

Raquel is an unusual female character. Throughout her life she has manifested a rebellious, nonconformist spirit. She is fascinated by the sea, which offers a sense of freedom in contrast to the claustrophobic life on the island. Raquel is an intelligent woman who appreciates classical music and literature. She suffers, however, an anxiety caused by an incomplete sense of identity. Her great desire in life is to research the family origins on the island of Malta, home of her grandfather André Villa (the family name Villa had been changed to Vella in Funchal). Raquel longs to know about her ancestors from Malta, especially the women from whom she inherited her long legs, wine-colored hair, and rebellious nature. In spite of her adventurous personality, she chooses to marry and remain in Funchal, leaving her dreams of traveling to a future generation. She enjoys a full life as wife and mother. Eventually, Raquel's dream to go abroad is fulfilled when her husband takes her on a trip to the British Guianas. Before she can experience any sense of liberation in her life, however, Raquel dies giving birth in a foreign country.

Marques conveys a strong feeling for life and love in her narrative. She portrays love as a powerful force that allows dreams to come true. This feeling is seen when, some years after the death of Raquel, Marcos falls in love with Luciana. Their union, like Marcos's first marriage, is an extremely happy one. The two are totally devoted to each other. The reader senses that this love is not only a feeling between two people but also the author's caring for humanity and her love for Portugal and those isolated islands that make up part of the country's history.

In general, Portuguese writers have given little consideration in their works to peripheral areas of the empire. In *O último cais,* however, Marques gives special attention to the Madeira Islands, and in *A deusa sentada* she turns this attention to other islands. In *O último cais* periphery is transformed into center as Funchal becomes a microcosm that represents the female in search of identity. Each woman in the narrative possesses specific characteristics that contribute to a representative view of nineteenth-century Portuguese society. The author combines these perspectives of a specific group of women and the metaphor of geographical periphery to universalize woman's attempt to overcome her marginalization in the patriarchy.

In *A deusa sentada* Marques continues the theme of the search for a feminine identity. The main characters are Laura and Matilde, two independent professional women in the twentieth century. Laura is happily married to Lourenço, whom the reader knows only from Laura's perspective throughout the text. She owns a bookshop. Matilde is divorced and makes a living as a translator. Laura and Matilde have a close relationship, in spite of the difference of age (Laura is forty-six, Matilde is thirty-eight). Both are mature and self-made women, yet they still have the dreams and anxieties of their youth. Matilde was married to Artur, a victim of the war to free the Portuguese colonies in Africa (1961–1974), who never readjusted to society. They have separated, but he remains an important part of her life. Matilde fears a new relationship, but when she meets Ian, he brings passion, tenderness, confidence, and faith into her life again.

*A deusa sentada* is linked to the previous novel because Raquel's daughter Clara is Laura's grandmother. The work resembles a detective novel, as the narrator's objective is to find the origin of André Vella or Villa in Malta. Raquel's dream in *O último cais* of rediscovering the family past is thus ultimately fulfilled by her great-granddaughter in *A deusa sentada.* The author uses Malta to evoke a sense of history. Its capital, La Valletta, is of Roman origin, but the island's history extends back to 3600 B.C., when temples and

Cover for Marques's second novel, the title of which refers to
The Seated Goddess, *a statue representative of
Portuguese women (Davis Library, University
of North Carolina at Chapel Hill)*

*Paperback cover for Marques's 1998 novel, in which a modern woman must choose between her personal life and her career (Yale University Library)*

statues of female figures were erected by an ancient people. The island's past constitutes a rich mingling, from that point on, of different peoples and cultures, including the Phoenicians, Greeks, Romans, Vandals, Berbers, and Arabs. Napoleon Bonaparte was there in 1798 and the British in 1814. The island was bombed in World War II. The past is fundamental for Laura, and the history and geography of Malta are relived through a movie on the islands that she sees in a museum there.

In *O último cais* the past is told through female speech; in *A deusa sentada* it is re-created through constant descriptions of and allusions to the statue of the seated goddess of the title. This statue of a female figure from the temple of Hagar Qim, which Laura and Matilde see in a museum, is a seated peasant woman with great inner beauty. She is headless and has tiny feet and hands, strong torso and thighs; her knees are folded laterally and rest on the ground in a position of tranquility and dignity. As Laura says: "Malta é como a pequena *Deusa Sentada*. Malta é a própria *Deusa Sentada*" (Malta is like a small Seated Goddess. Malta is the Seated Goddess). The seated goddess represents the figure of the Portuguese woman, who has assimilated and preserved traditional values from several cultures over the history of the country. André Villa had taken this history to the island and passed it on to future generations. Matilde regains the traditions and values, and through her marriage to Ian, an English journalist living temporarily in Malta, she adds to and continues them.

In *O último cais* and *A deusa sentada* Marques recovers the national past and establishes an identity for the Portuguese woman, using the peripheral areas of the empire as symbols. *Terceiras pessoas* (Third Persons, 1998) is narrated at the end of the twentieth century. In this novel Marques places her characters on the Portuguese mainland. The novel does not continue the sequence of actions of the two previous novels; there is, however, a great similarity in the characters' behavior and attitude toward life. Unlike the two previous novels, which were set in concrete locations, *Terceiras pessoas* takes place in a fictional area of the Ribatejo region. Here João Bernardo wants to build a house, plant vineyards, and start a family. He chooses this location because it evokes pleasant memories of his childhood.

This area of the Ribatejo region reflects contemporary Portuguese society and shows the family relationship at the turn of the millennium. Three generations play a role in it, but Natália, João Bernardo's wife, is the centerpiece. The couple, who were once close as well as great lovers, change with time. At first, he is the professional, and she is the housewife. He always holds a stable and coherent position; she is in a constant search for change. Natália grows out of the relationship, becomes independent, and does not need a man anymore. Because she is an efficient executive, her place is not at home, but rather in the sky. She flies from Manhattan, to Santiago, to Lisbon, in a continuous movement. Her professional agitation contrasts with his tranquility.

The "third persons" of the title are the anonymous heroes of everyday life:

> o mundo não é constituído só por *nós,* os que conhecemos desde sempre, os que nós encontramos todos os dias. O mundo é sobretudo constituído por *elas,* pelas *terceiras pessoas,* aquelas de quem nada sabemos ou de quem pouco sabemos e que, um dia, inesperadamente, saem do desconhecimento ou das sombras e vêm ao nosso encontro.
>
> (the world is not constituted only by *us,* by those that we have always known, those whom we meet every day. The world is mainly made of *them, third person,*

those about whom we know nothing or very little, but that one day unexpectedly come out of the dark into our lives).

Natália could not be an executive without these people. Even João Bernardo was a third person for her, as well as those who took care of her household and children while she was traveling. These "third persons" assure the continuity of the home, the land, and the memories that constitute history.

Natália had everything, but she began to leave it all behind—the land, her husband, and her children. In Santiago she meets another loving and caring man, who offers her a new and secure life. But then she is offered a better professional position in Holland; this new job represents the maximum she can achieve in her career. She is caught in the dilemma of choosing between her professional and her personal life. Natália questions herself: "mas onde está a vitória? Que faço dela?, ou que fez ela de mim?" (but where is victory? What do I do with it, or what did it do to me?). Natália is symbolic of woman, at the turn of the millenium, caught between the options of home and profession. The book has an open ending. The author indicates that the solution remains an individual choice; to reconcile both with responsibility and without guilt is, however, extremely difficult.

Marques, in this third novel, shows that women have found their identity and have arrived where they wanted. Now the individual must make choices to achieve happiness. The author suggests that love should be a part of any decision, in which the "third persons" should never be forgotten because they are the ones who make life happen.

The author's next work, the novel *Os íbis vermelhos da Guiana* (The Red Ibis of Guiana, 2002), portrays the lives of two family members who are separated by time and geography. They share, however, a similar character, ambitions, and memories. The story begins in British Guiana in the nineteenth century, when the colony received several young middle-class emigrants who had left the Madeira Islands in search of their fortune. The narrative extends into twenty-first-century England and Portugal, where the past and present finally meet.

Helena Marques emphasizes the geography and history of the Portuguese empire in all of her novels. She especially focuses on the woman in the patriarchal system and follows the development and the growth of the female into her own being within this system in which liberation has come at slow pace. She stresses individual choice in achieving fulfillment and happiness, which is never complete. Her novels tend to be open-ended and encourage the reader's use of imagination in seeing continuity in the women's lives.

**References:**

Branca Lizardo, "*A deusa sentada,* ou um paradigma da dignidade humana," *Margem* (1995): 11–13;

Monica Rector, *Mulher, objecto e sujeito da literatura portuguesa* (Porto: Edições Fernando Pessoa, 1999).

# José Rodrigues Miguéis
*(9 December 1901 – 28 October 1980)*

Reinaldo Francisco Silva
*University of Aveiro, Portugal*

BOOKS: *Páscoa feliz* (Lisbon: Edições Alfa, 1932); translated by John Byrne as *Happy Easter* (Manchester, U.K.: Carcanet, 1995);

*Onde a noite se acaba* (Rio de Janeiro: Dois Mundos, 1946);

*Saudades para Dona Genciana* (Lisbon: Iniciativas Editoriais, 1956);

*Léah e outras histórias* (Lisbon: Estúdios Cor, 1958);

*Uma aventura inquietante* (Lisbon: Iniciativas Editoriais, 1958);

*Um homem sorri à morte com meia cara* (Lisbon: Estúdios Cor, 1959); translated by George Monteiro as *A Man Smiles at Death with Half a Face* (Hanover, N.H.: Brown University Press, 1990);

*A escola do paraíso* (Lisbon: Estúdios Cor, 1960);

*O passageiro do expresso* (Lisbon: Estúdios Cor, 1960);

*Gente da terceira classe* (Lisbon: Estúdios Cor, 1962); translated by George Monteiro as *Steerage and Ten Other Stories* (Providence, R.I.: Gávea-Brown, 1983);

*É proibido apontar: Reflexões de um burguês I* (Lisbon: Estúdios Cor, 1964);

*Nikalai! Nikalai!* (Lisbon: Estúdios Cor, 1971);

*O espelho poliédrico* (Lisbon: Estúdios Cor, 1973);

*Comércio com o inimigo* (Porto: Inova, 1973);

*As harmonias do canelão: Reflexões de um burguês II* (Lisbon: Estúdios Cor, 1974);

*O milagre segundo Salomé*, 2 volumes (Lisbon: Estúdios Cor, 1974);

*O pão não cai do céu* (Lisbon: Estampa, 1981);

*Paços confusos* (Lisbon: Estampa, 1982);

*Idealista no mundo real* (Lisbon: Estampa, 1986);

*Aforismos & desaforismos de Aparício,* edited by Onésimo Teótonio Almeida (Lisbon: Estampa, 1996).

**Collection:** *Contos de José Rodrigues Miguéis,* edited by Margarida Barahona (Lisbon: Comunicação, 1981).

*José Rodrigues Miguéis, 1928 (from Mário Neves,* José Rodrigues Miguéis: Vida e obra, *1990; Hayward Library, California State University)*

José Rodrigues Miguéis is an important figure in twentieth-century Portuguese literary history mainly because of his contributions to the novel and short-story genres. His work is noted for his use of irony and humor, minute attention to details, interior monologues, and sharp analyses of a character's psychology. While some of his novels and short stories are imbued with an autobiographical impulse, inspired by his experiences abroad in Belgium and the United States, these writings also reflect his enthusiasm with the Republican movement in Portugal and his frustration when it was replaced by dictator António de Oliveira Salazar's Estado Novo (New State) and fascist propaganda in the 1930s. Miguéis's writings have been widely acclaimed because he capitalized on his self-imposed exile and successfully explored the problems and feelings of the immigrant. Miguéis's acute perception in those stories of immigrants torn between their native land and country of adoption–especially in the United States–continues to draw the attention of emerging Portuguese American writers and scholars interested in Portuguese American literature.

Miguéis was born on 9 December 1901 in Lisbon. His father, Manuel Maria Miguéis Pombo, was originally from Galicia, Spain, and worked as a doorman at the Hotel Francfort (Frankfurt) in Lisbon. His mother, Maria Adelaide Rodrigues Miguéis, worked for a rich family as a maid. The couple had two children. Miguéis earned a degree in law from the University of Lisbon in 1924 and followed it with another in education and pedagogy from the University of Brussels in 1933. For a while he was simultaneously an attorney, a public prosecutor, and a high-school teacher.

Although Miguéis had been an outstanding student and orator, he was not enthusiastic about a career in law. As he kept himself abreast of what was being published in Portuguese newspapers, he submitted a few articles to *A República* (The Republic), *Alma Nova* (New Soul), *Revista de Portugal* (Magazine of Portugal), and *Seara Nova* (New Harvest). In *História da literatura portuguesa* (History of Portuguese Literature, 1996) António José Saraiva and Oscar Lopes contend that in 1930 or 1931 Miguéis withdrew from the *Seara Nova* group because of his criticism of the group's lack of commitment to any type of organized mass movement. In addition, while editing and managing the weekly *O Globo* (The Globe) in 1933 with Bento de Jesus Caraça (a mathematician, writer, and instructor at the Universidade Técnica de Lisboa), he took part in various democratic movements. At the time, Salazar's fascist dictatorship (contemporary historians prefer to call it a right-wing dictatorship) was in the process of establishing and asserting itself. Salazar, the prime minister of the Estado Novo, had been sworn in in 1932. He quickly thwarted the ideals of the Republican revolution, which had taken place on 5 October 1910 and had brought about the downfall of the monarchy in Portugal. As Miguéis became more involved in these political movements, he began to see his name censored in the newspapers, and he was finally banned from teaching in the public schools controlled by the regime. With no other option available to him, in 1935 he immigrated to the United States and settled in New York City. He remained there for the rest of his life, sporadically returning to Portugal.

In 1932, Miguéis had married Pecia Cogan Portnoi, a Russian woman of Jewish descent who was a special-education teacher. She was unable to find work in her field or adapt to life in Portugal, so she returned

*Cover, with art by Miguéis, for one of the periodicals to which he contributed in the 1920s (from Mário Neves,* José Rodrigues Miguéis: Vida e obra, *1990; Hayward Library, California State University)*

to Belgium, and the couple divorced. After he moved to the United States, Miguéis married Camila Pitta Campanella, a Portuguese American woman who was a translator and worked in an office in Manhattan. Four years after their marriage in 1940, they adopted a daughter, Patricia. Miguéis became an American citizen in 1942.

Once settled in America, Miguéis was responsible for bringing together various groups of Portuguese immigrants to establish several democratic movements. After 1942 and for a period of about ten years, he held the office of assistant editor of *Reader's Digest*. In addition to being a freelance translator during his spare time, he regularly submitted pieces to various newspapers and magazines in Lisbon.

In her 1994 study, Teresa Martins Marques has outlined the influences from both the *Presença* (Presence) and neorealist movements in Miguéis's work. Although indebted to both trends, he remained relatively inde-

*Miguéis with his second wife, Camila Pitta Campanella, and their daughter, Patricia, in the 1950s (from Mário Neves,* José Rodrigues Miguéis: Vida e obra, *1990; Hayward Library, California State University)*

pendent of the rigid tenets endorsed by these literary movements. Marques posits that Miguéis was incapable of avoiding what she refers to as an area of intersection, where both movements crisscross, often creating original compositions. In addition, scholars have noted that his painstaking reading of the works of Camilo Castelo Branco and Eça de Queirós may account for his mastery of irony and humor in several of his writings. In these works he is given to depicting the contradictions in society while analyzing each character individually. Miguéis draws the reader's attention to a character's heart-wrenching anguish and loss, and he often portrays the character as if on a quest for identity. At times, he or she is portrayed as if torn between the possibility of returning to a given place so as to fulfill his or her hopes and expectations and giving up and running away. In his exploration of these themes, Miguéis has openly admitted his indebtedness to Raul Brandão and Fyodor Dostoevsky.

Scholars contend that Miguéis is at his best in the genres of the novella and the short story. Most regard his shorter pieces as among the best in Portuguese literature. Published in 1932 and awarded the Casa da Imprensa Prize, *Páscoa feliz* (translated as *Happy Easter,* 1995) is an engrossing portrayal of a character's gradual mental breakdown. The story culminates in madness and crime, a theme Miguéis eventually recycles (less successfully) in his play, *O passageiro do expresso* (The Express Passenger, 1960). "A mancha não se apaga" (The Stain Will Not Go Away), a story in *Onde a noite se acaba* (Where Night Ends, 1946), published in Brazil, reflects Miguéis's fondness for the theme of a character's disintegration. In this story, however, the author adds grotesque and gothic nuances.

Scholars agree that "Léah" and "Saudades para a Dona Genciana" (Missing Miss Genciana) are among the most important pieces in *Léah e outras histórias* (Leah and Other Stories, 1958), awarded the Camilo Castelo Branco Prize. The former tale is a mixture of the epistolary and diary genres. The story revolves around a timid and easily frightened narrator, who, as he evokes his beloved, comes to the realization that he has lost her forever. Although these emotions are conveyed through a monologue, in the course of the story the narrator gains more confidence in himself. The complexity and intricacy of "Saudades para Dona Genciana" stems from its double usage of the stylistic device known as synecdoche. Miguéis has applied this rhetorical device to the character of Dona Genciana, who is depicted as representing the people who stroll through the Almirante Reis Avenue in Lisbon; this thoroughfare, in turn, represents the city of Lisbon. The narrator's perception of these is twofold. On the one hand, the narrator's consciousness is clouded by unpleasant images of the capital that hark back to his youth; on the other hand, he is assailed by a certain enthusiasm as he recalls them in the present. At first, the narrator undervalues these recollections; later, however, they are also glorified. These emotions are conveyed through the process of memory. As the narrator longs for these moments, his intense feelings allow him to relive and retrieve his past. As a whole, the stories in *Léah* criticize the hypocrisy of ordinary Portuguese citizens of the time as well as their way of life.

Miguéis wrote six novels. Published in 1958, *Uma aventura inquietante* (A Disturbing Adventure) is written in the tradition of the detective story. The plot demonstrates the arbitrary ways of justice, and the protagonist

Sketch by Miguéis for an illustration to accompany one of his stories in the magazine Ver e Crer
(John Hay Library, Brown University)

*Miguéis and Camila Miguéis (from Mário Neves,* José Rodrigues Miguéis: Vida e obra, *1990; Hayward Library, California State University)*

archy in Portugal and the dawn of the proclamation of the Republic in 1910. While bringing the figure of the mother to the fore, the author takes the reader on a guided tour of Lisbon streets and monuments. The novel stresses the contributions of Lisbon's dynamic lower middle class to the Republican cause. In *O milagre segundo Salomé* (The Miracle According to Salomé, 1975) Miguéis explores Lisbon in greater depth. The city inhabitants and the depressing and stifling environment capture the ambience of the capital as Republican ideals began to wane, eventually culminating in the inauguration of the Estado Novo on 28 May 1926.

Miguéis's experience as an immigrant comes full circle in the stories that compose *Gente da terceira classe* (translated as *Steerage and Ten Other Stories*, 1983), published in 1962. In the 1992 *Dicionário de literatura* (Dictionary of Literature) Jacinto do Prado Coelho states that in this volume, of all the Portuguese writers who have written about the theme of emigration, Miguéis is the one who most fully explores the problems and feelings of the immigrant. The author is especially sensitive and perceptive in those stories of people torn between their native land and country of adoption.

*Nikalai! Nikalai!* (1971) is a picaresque novel that depicts a community of Russians in Brussels, after the Soviet revolution, who aim at restoring Czar Nikolai's throne. Of all of Miguéis's novels, the one with the most ties to the neorealist movement in Portugal is *O pão não cai do céu* (Bread Does Not Fall from the Sky), written in exile between the years of 1943 and 1975 and published posthumously in 1981. The protagonist, a gypsy character, is portrayed as an epic hero and a galvanizing force who successfully brings the farmers of Alentejo together to struggle for freedom and a piece of land.

is an expatriate residing in Belgium. The immigrant experience—which Miguéis refined in other stories and novels—has its origins in *Uma aventura inquietante*. In this story the author emphasizes the protagonist's feelings of nostalgia by stressing how much he misses Portuguese cuisine and his native country.

His autobiographical impulse was channeled into *Um homem sorri à morte com meia cara* (1959; translated as *A Man Smiles at Death with Half a Face*, 1990), in which the protagonist's resilience is tested in a New York City hospital as he is confronted with imminent death. Miguéis had been seriously ill in 1946 and had spent time both in a New York City hospital and convalescing in Portugal. In the book, pain and anxiety are overcome thanks to the narrator's courage and strong desire to live, and the story ends with life and hope prevailing.

*A escola do paraíso* (School of Paradise), published in 1960, has strong affinities with the bildungsroman since it follows up on the protagonist's childhood, more specifically, the period comprising the end of the mon-

Miguéis's essays and sketches have been collected with short stories into three volumes: *É proibido apontar: Reflexões de um burguês I* (Pointing Prohibited: Reflections of a Bourgeois I, 1964), *O espelho poliédrico* (The Polyhedric Mirror, 1973), and *As harmonias do canelão: Reflexões de um burguês II* (The Harmonies of a Bully: Reflections of a Bourgeois II, 1974). *Paços confusos* (Confused Steps, 1982) includes material previously published in *Comércio com o inimigo* (Business with the Enemy, 1973), a collection of short stories as well as a series of scattered pieces published in newspapers. Also published posthumously, *Idealista no mundo real* (An Idealist in the Real World, 1986) is a novel that explores the contradictions of a young public prosecutor, a regular contributor to the *Seara Nova* movement, in search of his own ideological and social identity.

*Aforismos & desaforismos de Aparício* (Aparício's Aphorisms and Disaphorisms, 1996), edited by Onésimo Teótonio Almeida, includes a variety of Miguéis's short pieces formerly published in the newspaper *Diário Popular* (The People's Daily) under the title "Tablóides" (Headlines). They cover issues of politics and culture, such as freedom of expression and art; the role of intellectuals in modern societies; and other pieces often charged with an undercurrent of anguish and anxiety, feelings motivated by Miguéis's status as a solitary writer in exile. This self-imposed exile ended on 28 October 1980 with the writer's death from a heart attack in New York City. His ashes were taken to the Alto de São João Cemetery in Lisbon.

José Rodrigues Miguéis's work has received much scholarly attention both in Portugal and the United States. In addition to his ability to evoke many different emotions through the ambience and humor of a story, Miguéis paid attention to details. Moreover, his acute character analyses have had great appeal to readers. His versatility as a writer enabled him to adjust to several novelistic techniques, both in the Portuguese and foreign traditions. The author's work addresses several themes, including ethical and pedagogical matters reflecting the writer's academic training; the Republican ideals fostered by the writer's father; and the writer's involvement—along with other important writers such as José Gomes Ferreira, Irene Lisboa, Jaime Cortesão, Raul Proença, Câmara Reys, António Sérgio, and other intellectuals from the *Seara Nova* movement—in political causes aimed at toppling the fascist dictatorship. Coelho has noted Miguéis's mastery in describing specific settings and characters, especially those from Lisbon of the first decades of the twentieth century.

**References:**

Onésimo Teótonio Almeida, ed., *José Rodrigues Miguéis: Lisbon in Manhattan* (Providence, R.I.: Gávea-Brown, 1984);

João José Cochofel, "O último romance de Miguéis," in his *Críticas e crónicas* (Lisbon: Imprensa Nacional-Casa da Moeda, 1982), pp. 238–241;

José Martins Garcia, "Um paraíso sempre ameaçado," in *A escola do paraíso* by Miguéis (Lisbon: Círculo de Leitores, 1986), pp. xvii–xxv;

John Austin Kerr Jr., *Miguéis—To the Seventh Decade* (University, Miss.: Romance Monographs, 1977);

Maria Lúcia Lepecki, "Rodrigues Miguéis: O código e a chave," in her *Meridianos do texto* (Lisbon: Assíro e Alvim, 1979), pp. 71–96;

Oscar Lopes, "O pessoal e o social na obra de Miguéis," in his *Cinco personalidades literárias* (Porto: Divulgação, 1961), pp. 53–86;

Eduardo Lourenço, "As marcas do exílio no discurso de Rodrigues Miguéis," in his *O canto do signo: Existência e literatura* (Lisbon: Presença, 1994);

Teresa Martins Marques, *O imaginário de Lisboa na ficção narrativa de José Rodrigues Miguéis* (Lisbon: Editorial Estampa, 1994);

David Mourão-Ferreira, "Avatares do narrador na ficção de Miguéis," in his *Sob o mesmo tecto: Estudos sobre autores de língua portuguesa* (Lisbon: Presença, 1989), pp. 185–196;

Mário Neves, *José Rodrigues Miguéis: Vida e obra* (Lisbon: Caminho, 1990);

Mário Sacramento, "A problemática do Eu em José Rodrigues Miguéis," in his *Ensaios de domingo* (Coimbra: Coimbra Editora, 1959), pp. 279–292.

**Papers:**

The José Rodrigues Miguéis Archives at the John Hay Library, Brown University, include drafts, typescripts, correspondence, drawings, notebooks, diaries, photographs, and portions of the author's personal library. There is an introduction to the collection at <http://www.brown.edu/Facilities/University_Library/libs/hay/collections/migueis/>. Copies of his papers are also stored on microfilm at the Biblioteca Nacional in Lisbon.

# Fernando Namora
(15 April 1919 - 31 January 1989)

Luís Flávio Sieczkowski
*Centro Universitário da Cidade–UniverCidade*

BOOKS: *Cabeças de barro,* by Namora, Carlos de Oliveira, and Artur Varela (Lousa: Moura Marques & Filho, 1937);

*As sete partidas do mundo* (Coimbra: Portugália, 1938);

*Terra* (Coimbra: Atlântida, 1941);

*Fogo na noite escura* (Coimbra: Coimbra Editora, 1943);

*Casa da Malta* (Coimbra: Coimbra Editora, 1945);

*Minas de San Francisco* (Coimbra: Casa Minerva, 1946);

*Retalhos da vida de um médico,* volume 1 (Lisbon: Inquérito, 1949);

*A noite e a madrugada* (Lisbon: Inquérito, 1950);

*Deuses e demónios da medicina* (Lisbon: Livros do Brasil, 1952);

*O trigo e o joio* (Lisbon: Guimarães, 1954); translated by Dorothy Ball as *Fields of Fate* (New York: Crown, 1970);

*O homem disfarçado* (Lisbon: Arcádia, 1957?);

*Cidade solitária* (Lisbon: Arcádia, 1959);

*As frias madrugadas* (Lisbon: Arcádia, 1959);

*Domingo à tarde* (Lisbon: Livros do Brasil, 1961);

*Retalhos da vida de um médico,* volume 2 (Lisbon: Arcádia, 1963);

*Diálogo em Setembro* (Lisbon: Europa-América, 1966);

*Um sino na montanha: Cadernos de um escritor* (Lisbon: Europa-América, 1968);

*Marketing (1959–1960)* (Lisbon: Europa-América, 1969);

*Os adoradores do sol* (Mem Martins: Europa-América, 1971);

*Os clandestinos* (Mem Martins: Europa-América, 1972);

*Estamos no vento* (Amadora: Bertrand, 1974);

*A nave de pedra* (Amadora: Bertrand, 1975);

*Cavalgada cinzenta* (Amadora: Bertrand, 1977);

*Encontros com Fernando Namora* (Porto: Nova Crítica, 1979; enlarged edition, Lisbon: Bertrand, 1981);

*Resposta a Matilde* (Amadora: Bertrand, 1980);

*O rio triste* (Amadora: Bertrand, 1982);

*Nome para uma casa* (Lisbon: Bertrand, 1984);

*Sentados na relva* (Venda Nova: Bertrand, 1986);

*URSS, mal amada, bem amada: Cadernos de um escritor* (Venda Nova: Bertrand, 1986);

*Autobiografia* (Lisbon: O Jornal, 1987);

*Jornal sem data* (Venda Nova: Bertrand, 1988).

Fernando Namora lived during the social dynamism in Portugal that changed the shape of Lusitanian literature. He participated in the new literary movement called neorealism. Some writers tried to take fiction in new directions in defiance of the aesthetic ideals established by authors of the Presença Movement (*Presença* was a literary journal, published between 1927 and 1940, which gave its name to the movement), whose motto was "art for art's sake." If the Generation of 1870, a milestone for realism as exemplified by the works of Eça de Queirós, was able to articulate the thoughts of society at that time, such articulation was possible only through listening to the voice of the middle class. Neorealism initiated a whole new process of questioning and trying to change this conservative socialism, and it is where Namora made his greatest contribution. He distinguished himself as a neorealist novelist and chronicler at a time when other writers wanted to break with what was already an outdated mode of thinking. The ideals of this new current pried open a space in the consciousness of the people, demystifying and reconciling a Portuguese way of life that had been disagreeable to the population at large.

Son of António Mendes Namora and Albertina Augusta Gonçalves Namora, Fernando Gonçalves Namora was born in Condeixa, a village in the county of Coimbra, on 15 April 1919. Although he spent most of his childhood in Condeixa, where his father had opened a business, his ancestors came from Vale Florido village. Just a few miles from Condeixa, Namora's parents owned a small property that had been in the family for generations. Namora took extended walks, encountering shepherds, millers, farmworkers, old women—simple people, dreamers, and loners—all of whom were well acquainted with the details of rural life. These walks in the valleys and the mountains influenced him greatly and determined his future fate as a tireless traveler. Both his uncle, Antero Mendes Namora, a pharmacist who loved seventeenth- and eighteenth-century classical music and good prose, and the social universe of Condeixa had a positive

*Fernando Namora (photograph by Gustavo de Almeida Ribeiro; from the cover for the 1988 edition of* O homem disfarçado, *Thomas Cooper Library, University of South Carolina)*

impact on Namora's budding vocation. Painting, design, and sculpture were the passions of his youth.

When Namora was ten years old, he entered the Colégio Camões in Coimbra and stayed there for two years. He also studied at the Liceu Camões in Lisbon before returning to Coimbra to finish his schooling. After leaving secondary school, he considered studying architecture but then enrolled at an engineering college. He finally entered medical school, fulfilling his mother's wish.

His experience as a boarder at Colégio Camões left its mark in his novel *As sete partidas do mundo* (The Seven Departures from the World), published in 1938. Life at boarding school is no different from any other: "a reputable education was one of discipline comprised of humiliation and punishment." Although subjective dramatization is present in the novel, revealing the lingering influence of the Presença style of writing, *As sete partidas do mundo* represents the starting point from which his future works develop. Literary critics attest that this novel reveals a sense of rebellion and the need to make a bold statement. The romantic plot is ideological, centering on the need to break with some forms of authority. Past experience is quite important in this context; it reflects those earliest discoveries within the family unit, at school, among friends, during puberty–first disillusions, disappointments, and minor triumphs that Namora explores in a more complicated historical context.

Namora made important contributions to two typically neorealist series: his volume *Terra* (Land, 1941) was part of the "Novo cancioneiro" series published by Atlântida, and his novel *Fogo na noite escura* (Fire in the Dark Night, 1943) was part of Coimbra

*Cover for Namora's first novel, published in 1938 (from Mário Sacramento,* Fernando Namora, *1967; Daniel Library, The Citadel)*

Editora's "Novos prosadores" series. The publication of *Terra* aims to put into verse the youthful desires of neorealist supporters. Namora went on to publish other works of poetry, such as *As frias madrugadas* (The Cold Dawns, 1959), *Marketing (1959–1960)* (1969), and *Nome para uma casa* (Name for a House, 1984). He made his name as a writer, however, in the genre of narrative fiction.

In 1940 Namora married Arminda Bragaça de Miranda. She died nine months later, after giving birth to their daughter, Arminda Maria.

In 1942 Namora graduated with a degree in medicine, and the following year he published *Fogo na noite escura*. In this novel he investigates and re-creates the history of an era. Although on the surface the novel seems to be about love, in reality it discusses the alienating social-political-cultural system that pervades Coimbra University. In August 1943 Namora moved to Tinalhas, a village in Beira Baixa. He resumed his passion for travel, acquired during his childhood encounters with simple people of the land. His wanderings led him to make both grueling and spectacular discoveries about peasants, miners, smugglers, and great and minor citizens. He was beginning his "rural" phase, during which he wrote and published *Casa da Malta* (House of the Rabble, 1945), *Minas de San Francisco* (Mines of San Francisco, 1946), volume one of *Retalhos da vida de um médico* (Remnants of the Life of a Doctor, 1949), *A noite e a madrugada* (The Night and the Dawn, 1950), *O trigo e o joio* (1954; translated as *Fields of Fate,* 1970), and volume two of *Retalhos da vida de um médico* (1963).

In 1944 Namora married for a second time. A year later his wife, Isaura de Campos Mendonça Namora, gave birth to his second daughter, Margarida Maria.

Namora established his medical practice opposite an abandoned hut, where vagrants, tramps, gypsies, and peasants formed the wandering circus portrayed in his short novel *Casa da Malta*. Bringing together all kinds of people, the house of the rabble becomes a place in which camaraderie triumphs over all the wrongs of the outside world.

With the outbreak of World War II, the world powers entered a frenetic race for tungsten. In *Minas de San Francisco* he criticizes the historical and social impact of this mania. The character João Simão, one of the landless workers, symbolizes the heroism of former peasants and day laborers in their fight for a decent living. Namora portrays their dreams and illusions as they face the inclemency of nature and excessively authoritarian land stewards, as well as disease, poverty, and hunger. The question of landownership is fundamental because it is inherent to the national reality. The peasant "dialogues" with a backward country, which forces its citizens to drift with no destination. This political criticism camouflages Namora's disillusionment and anguish concerning the destiny of Portugal.

In the first volume of *Retalhos da vida de um médico,* an anthology of narratives, Namora describes in detail his experiences serving as a physician to the rural poor. Involving himself in their lives, he takes on their miseries of body and soul, capturing the simple moments of country life that emerge from both collective and individual dramas. On the bases of these tiny flashes, or moments, Namora rails at the fact that basic necessities are not being provided, and he appeals for social transformation. His attitude conforms to the tenets of neorealism as he echoes the voices of the oppressed and the forgotten who live in a social system that is both cruel and alienating. Namora's 1950 novel, *A noite e a madrugada,* also depicts a devastated world–represented by peasants, smugglers, and vagrants–in desperate need of change. Trained as a doctor, he perceives the anguish of these pariahs of society and looks for some hope that will give them relief.

In 1951 Namora published *Deuses e demónios da medicina* (Gods and Devils of Medicine), which collects romanticized biographies of Hippocrates, Galen, Paracelsus, Ambroise Paré, John Hunter, Claude Bernard, Ivan Petrovich Pavlov, and Sigmund Freud. Perhaps Namora's style is less pronounced this time, but his character and scientific background are evident throughout as he follows the evolutionary progress of the history of medicine, from Hippocrates to the present day.

In his 1954 novel, *O trigo e o joio,* Namora captivates the reader through the character Loas, a soothsayer, whose greatest wish in life is to buy a she-ass. The animal will allow him to make a better life for himself, his wife, Joana, his little daughter, Alice, and his friend Barbaças. The story is divided into three parts: the dreams of cultivating the small piece of arable land and the purchase of the she ass; the acquisition of the animal and how it becomes a part of the family; and finally, the death of the she-ass, or the total destruction of the characters' dreams. Before dying, the she-ass represents hope in a corrupted world. Loas, a man of the moorland, is irredeemably condemned to remaining a stranger in his own country, which refuses to bring him comfort, love, and trust in the relationship between man, land, and homeland.

Before publishing *O trigo e o joio,* Namora moved to Lisbon in order to work at the Lisbon Cancer Institute, an experience that later added a new dimension to his work. The world had been through difficult times, such as the tensions of the Cold War, the creation of the North American Treaty Organization and the Warsaw Pact, the threat of nuclear war, and the construction of–and subsequent incidents of violence at–the Berlin Wall. Some writers expressed their distress through the existentialist literary movement, which arrived in Portugal through the voices of Albert Camus, Jean-Paul Sartre, Anton Chekhov, Martin Heidegger, Søren Kierkegaard, and Karl Jaspers. Namora knew how to listen to them and, soon afterward, articulated the fearfulness and bewilderment of a man caught up in a brutal battle for power.

The second wave of neorealism–also called "urban" or "existential" literature–reflects a change from the use of the first-person plural pronoun, "we," to the first-person singular, "I." This development did not imply that the writer was distancing himself from the

*Namora in 1959 (from Mário Sacramento,* Fernando Namora, *1967; Daniel Library, The Citadel)*

social and economic troubles of his country. During the so-called rural wave, an adverse economic situation was a prerequisite to a man achieving awareness. The presence of "I" in this new phase of neorealism reveals the worries of man in a ruined world. If the use of "we" in the previous phase had revealed and criticized the difficulties and injustices within a country, the "I" of the following phase also suffered, agonizing over the same problems–the only difference existing in terms of the literary focal point.

Within this new context, in *O homem disfarçado* (The Masked Man, 1957?), *Cidade solitária* (Lonely City, 1959), and *Domingo à tarde* (Sunday Afternoon, 1961) Namora replaced his rural character with an urban dweller who experiences modern man's conflict between his inner desires and the horrifying outside world. In *O homem disfarçado* a renowned doctor, João Eduardo, fights to survive in a society that has taught him to pretend and act. The character's difficult dilemma, which the reader senses acutely, is whether to take part in the dirty games of life. With the subtlety of existentialism, Namora expresses his writerly commitment to life, the individual, and society. The book plots a course toward a humane justice that fights ferociously against a backdrop of troubled history. The idea of disguise in the novel is synonymous with alienation: whether they remove or keep their masks on, characters in *O homem disfarçado* are trapped "between four walls," which leave their inner selves marooned. In *Cidade solitária,* an anthology of narratives, Namora portrays a vast universe of lonely people who experience deep silences, distrust, secrets, and failures. The creation of silence enables man to be known—his inner depths are explored and "the masks" are removed.

The novel *Domingo à tarde* includes some of the themes presented in *O homem disfarçado*. The central character, a doctor named Jorge, works in the difficult area of malignant diseases. Through the figure of Clarisse, who suffers from leukemia, Jorge begins to perceive that the society in which he lives is also sick; the escape is the recognition that he is not alone and that he can cure himself of existing secret illnesses by socializing with others. The idea of mortality becomes more acute when Clarisse dies, and, although some critics consider this idea pessimistic, death is seen here as a means to motivate man; it simply marks a point of reference. The existence of death, in fact, serves as a reminder to celebrate life, so that man can experience his presence in the world more intensely. In the face of death, man strips off his selfishness in order to communicate with others.

In 1963 Namora published the second volume of *Retalhos da vida de um médico,* another anthology in largely the same vein as the first but with more psychological depth. In volume two the vision of the doctor-writer goes beyond the mere clinical diagnosis of a disease, the fruit of his patients' imagination, and their possible cure. His mission, rather, is to give them his solidarity—to offer them ways to survive and to soothe their woes.

In 1965 Namora was invited to take part in the International Conference in Geneva, where he gathered many experiences that were incorporated later in a book. His work began to develop in a new direction; it became more of a combination of essay and fiction, as seen in *Diálogo em Setembro* (Conversations in September), a romanticized chronicle published in 1966. After this human and cultural experience, the Portuguese context of the author's work begins to move toward a more universal context. Geneva serves as the stage for observing the atrocities of daily life, for which solutions are found through man's increasing awareness of self. That same year, Namora resigned his position at the Lisbon Cancer Institute.

With the 1968 publication of *Um sino na montanha* (A Mountain Bell), subtitled *Cadernos de um escritor* (A Writer's Notes), Namora reveals a new side—that of "chronicler of daily life." His composition enters the realm of personal confidences, of fiction and testimony about the world in which he has been living. A continuation of the first "writer's notes," *Os adoradores do sol* (The Sun Worshippers, 1971) continues to underline the distinctive characteristic of the traveling man—his insightful observation of all the places through which he passes during his travels.

In his novel *Os clandestinos* (The Secret Ones), published in 1972, Namora does not tire of explaining that the fight should never end. Despite the central character's political past, the oppression—though extremely difficult—did not create a generation of disconsolate souls. On the contrary, even amid great tragedies, the repressed demonstrated extraordinary resolve or firmly held convictions that nothing could destroy. *Estamos no vento* (We Are in the Wind, 1974), a fictional sociological narrative, is a profound and intense testimony to generation gaps. It puts itself at the forefront of a new era, creating a dialogue with reality. Once again, Namora is critical of past efforts in the search for new ways to live and to rethink new concepts; he reminds the reader that he is a traveling man and a follower of the wind; neither type ever stops.

*A nave de pedra* (The Stone Ship), published in 1975, is the third book that Namora wrote as a chronicler of daily life. In some ways this narrative represents a return to the roots of his professional career. Namora converses with himself, comparing the image he used to have of beings and objects with the reality he came to discover twenty years later. *Cavalgada cinzenta* (Grey Cavalcade, 1977), a narrative from 1975, consists of the images he picked up on his travels throughout the United States and Canada. The trip was an extremely gratifying experience for Namora, a European from an old country that was behind the times. In North America he was able to see another way of being in the world, which was in total contrast with his previous personal experiences. In 1979 the book *Encontros com Fernando Namora* (Encounters with Fernando Namora) came out; it comprises interviews with Namora, in which he talks about his literary life and his personal relationship to the history of Portugal. After a general introduction, which outlines Namora's background, the book features several interviews by foreign journalists between 1963 and 1965, as well as interviews by Portuguese journalists and scholars from 1969 to 1978.

The publication of *Resposta a Matilde* (Response to Matilde) in 1980, considered an entertaining work, came as a surprise to Namora's readers and critics. The narrator asks the reader for help to produce a text that

*Page from the manuscript for the second volume of* Retalhos da vida de um médico *(Remnants of the Life of a Doctor, 1963), a collection of narratives drawing on Namora's experiences as a rural physician (from Mário Sacramento,* Fernando Namora, *1967; Daniel Library, The Citadel)* they will write together during the course of the book. During this witty process, which uses humor to the utmost, nonsensical absurdities are perceived in what is ultimately a game, whereby Namora manages to entertain the reader by including him in the narrative process. As with Namora's other fiction, the existential questions constitute an intrinsic part of the work. The 1982 novel *O rio triste* (The Sad River) re-creates the atmosphere of Lisbon during the 1960s and tells about the character Rodrigo, who seems to have had problems with the Salazar police as a result of his political activism. The open narrative of the novel invites the reader's active participation, so that its possible meanings can be fully appreciated.

*Sentados na relva* (Sitting on the Grass), one of two works that Namora published in 1986, is not only a novel but also a kind of "report" on the International Culture Meetings held in Lahti, Finland. The discussions there focused on the long-standing question of whether the intelligentsia are responsible for denouncing the suffering and oppression of their time. Namora talks of totalitarianism, genocide, the left wing, and the right wing as one who has come back from a journey and describes what he has seen. In *URSS, mal amada, bem amada* (U.S.S.R., Unloved, Loved, 1986), another work subtitled *Cadernos de um escritor,* Namora presents his personal analysis of the Soviet Union. He discusses the question of recruiting youth for war and the emergence of unemployment and alcoholism–in sum, the various problems plaguing the citizens of that superpower.

Namora's *Autobiografia* (Autobiography), dated 1987, recalls the keen eye of the traveler, the writer, and the doctor and relates his journeys, criticisms, and compassion. *Jornal sem data* (Undated Diary, 1988) continues the narrative of his travels and his quest for awareness. It shows him as a writer rethinking man's existence, examining and exploring the world, society, and literature.

Fernando Namora died on 31 January 1989 in Lisbon. During his lifetime he incorporated everything that he saw on his travels, both within Portugal and abroad, into his writings. By relating the hard life of downtrodden people in conflict with some form of alienating system, he became aware of his own reality. The era of myth had been extinguished. There were no longer any Portuguese values and ideals. His narratives and chronicles always pose the questions "Who are we?", "Where do we come from?", and "Where are we?" Namora created books that reflected the images of tired and suffering faces and allowed the flame of collective consciousness to glow. This journey began in his youth, throughout which he was able to observe the outside world and confront it with his inner reality, giving him cause to cry out in protest.

**References:**

*Biblos: Enciclopédia verbo das literaturas de língua portuguesa,* volume 3 (Lisbon & São Paulo: Verbo, 1999), pp. 1015-1017;

Elêusis M. Camocardi, *Fernando Namora: Um cronista no território da ficção* (São Paulo: ILHPA-HUCITEC, 1978);

Camocardi, "As relações metafóricas e metonímicas em *O trigo e o joio*," *Revista de Letras,* 22 (1982): 27-36;

Pierrette Chalendar and Gérard Chalendar, "A fabricação do sentido em *O Rio Triste* de Fernando Namora," *Colóquio/Letras,* 86 (July 1985): 24-32;

Chalendar and Chalendar, *Temas e estruturas na obra de Fernando Namora* (Lisbon: Moraes, 1979);

Chalendar and Chalendar, "*URSS mal amada bem amada*," *Colóquio/Letras,* 97 (May-June 1987): 115-116;

Nelly Novaes Coelho, Preface, in Namora's *Fogo na noite escura* (São Paulo: Verbo, 1973);

João Palma Ferreira, "Os clandestinos," *Colóquio/Letras,* 10 (November 1972): 71-73;

Pierre Hourcade, "A Nave de Pedra," *Colóquio/Letras,* 32 (July 1976): 84-85;

André Kedros, Preface, in Namora's *A noite e a madrugada* (Rio de Janeiro: Nórdica, 1986);

Cremilda de Araújo Medina, "Fernando Namora," in her *Viagem à literatura portuguesa contemporânea* (Rio de Janeiro: Nórdica, 1983);

Maria Teresa Arsénio Nunes, "Sentados na Relva," *Colóquio/Letras,* 97 (May-June 1987): 114-115;

António Pedro Pita, "A partida e o fogo: metamorfose na juventude na obra de Fernando Namora (1935-1943)," *O Escritor,* 51 (1995): 22-134;

Mário Sacramento, *Fernando Namora* (Lisbon: Arcádia, 1967);

Álvaro Salema, "Os adoradores do sol," *Colóquio/Letras,* 6 (March 1972): 82-83;

Maria Alzira Seixo, "Uma personalidade, um tempo, uma obra: Fernando Namora fala a Maria Alzira Seixo," *Revista ICALP,* 1 (March 1985): 33-51;

Taborda de Vasconcelos, *Fernando Namora* (Lisbon: Arcádia, 1972).

# António Nobre
*(16 August 1867 – 18 March 1900)*

Paulo Motta Oliveira
*Universidade de São Paulo*

BOOKS: *Só* (Paris: Leon Vanier-Henri Jouve, 1892; revised and enlarged edition, Lisbon: Guillard Aillaud, 1898);

*Despedidas: 1895–1899,* with a preface by José Pereira de Sampaio (Porto, 1902);

*Primeiros versos: 1882–1889* (Porto: A Tribuna, 1921);

*Ave e outras poesias desconhecidas* (Porto: Parnaso-Jardim de Poesia, n.d.);

*Cartas inéditas de António Nobre,* with an introduction by Adolfo Casais Monteiro (Coimbra: Edições Presença, 1934);

*Cartas e bilhetes-postais a Justino de Montalvão,* with a preface by Alberto de Serpa (Porto: Figueirinhas, 1956);

*Correspondência,* with an introduction by Guilherme de Castilho (Lisbon: Portugália, 1967; revised and enlarged edition, Lisbon: Imprensa Nacional-Casa da Moeda, 1982);

*Correspondência com Cândida Ramos,* with a preface by Mário Cláudio (Porto: Biblioteca Pública Municipal do Porto, 1981);

*Primeiros versos e cartas inéditas,* with a preface by Viale Moutinho (Lisbon: Notícias, 1983);

*Alicerces seguido de Livro de Apontamentos* (Lisbon: Imprensa Nacional-Casa da Moeda, 1983);

*Poesia completa* (Lisbon: Círculo dos Leitores, 1988).

Although he published only one book during his lifetime, António Nobre is considered, along with his contemporary Cesário Verde, a founder of twentieth-century Portuguese poetry. Not easily classified in any one specific literary movement, Nobre's verses are characterized by a sentimental tone, a colloquial style and humor, and, at times, a tendency toward the realistic. He was undoubtedly one of the most preeminent Portuguese poets, and his book *Só* (Alone, 1892) is considered by some critics a masterpiece of Portuguese literature.

António Pereira Nobre was born in Porto on 16 August 1867 to José Pereira Nobre, who had lived in Brazil for about twenty years, and Ana de Sousa Nobre.

*António Nobre, circa 1893 (from Guilherme de Castilho,*
António Nobre: A obra e o homem, *1977;*
*Thomas Cooper Library, University*
*of South Carolina)*

When Nobre was a child, he and one of his brothers, Augusto, attended the Colégio Padre Loureiro Dias and the Colégio São Lázaro. Later, Nobre studied at the Colégio Glória. During his childhood he spent the summers in the country at Seixo or at the beach at Leça da Palmeira. These two settings, as well as Coimbra and Paris, are the locations described with the most frequency in his poetry.

Nobre's first poem, "Intermezzo ocidental" (Occidental Intermezzo), was written in May 1882, when he was only fourteen years old, and published in *Primeiros versos: 1882–1889* (First Verses: 1882–1889, 1921). Beginning at that early age, Nobre sought the companionship of people who shared his intellectual and artistic interests, including Eduardo Coimbra, who died in 1884 and with whom Nobre wrote the poem "Tremulante" (Glimmering), first published in a small newspaper with the same title; José de Oliveira Macedo; Augusto de Mesquita; and Júlio Brandão. Brandão's first book, *O Livro de Aglaïs* (Book of Aglaïs), was published in 1892, with a preface by Abílio Manuel Guerra Junqueiro; Nobre's first book also came out that year. He and his group of friends frequented the Palace and Camanho coffe shop, and they created *A Mocidade de Hoje* (The Youth of Today), a newspaper of modest size first published on 4 March 1883. During this period, from 1883 to 1886, Nobre wrote some of the poems subsequently collected in the posthumous volume *Primeiros versos*.

In 1888 Nobre went to the University of Coimbra to study law. He failed his exams twice in the first two years of the program. In spite of his lack of academic success, this period was important for him in other respects. In Coimbra he met other writers, such as Alberto de Oliveira, who became a close friend, and he participated in the establishment of a new literary review, *Boémia Nova* (New Bohemia). Lasting only sixteen issues, the periodical made its initial appearance on 1 February 1889, while the final issue came out on 12 April. *Boémia Nova* represented one of two important groups of the Generation of 1890, the movement that is considered responsible for the emergence of symbolism in Portugal. The main writers associated with *Boémia Nova* included Nobre, de Oliveira, and Osório de Castro. The other important group of this generation, which included Eugénio de Castro, João de Menezes, and Francisco Bastos, wrote for *Os Insubmissos* (The Unsubmissive Ones), a magazine as ephemeral as *Boémia Nova*.

After failing at his studies at Coimbra, Nobre decided to go to Paris, where he stayed from 1890 to October 1892. In his first year in Paris, while studying at the Sorbonne, he wrote most of the poems for the volume *Só*. The work came out in Paris in 1892, the same year that Arthur Rimbaud published his *Une saison en enfer* (A Season in Hell). In Portugal, Junqueiro, who was considered the most important living poet at the time, also published his work *Os simples* (The Simple People) in 1892. As Nobre said in a letter to his friend Silva Gaio, his experiences in Paris had a defining impact on the way he viewed Portugal: "Comecei a amar Portugal depois que o deixei, se é na ausência que se reconhece o amor. Perdida a ilusão do estrangeiro, voltei-me para a nossa terra e é lá que moram as minhas predileções e para lá vão as minhas saudades" (I started to love Portugal after I left it, if it is in absence that we recognize love. When I lost my fascination for that which is foreign, I turned myself toward our land, and it is there that my predilections live, and there is what I long for so much [*Correspondência*, 1967]). Living in Paris also gave him the opportunity to know the works of important contemporary French poets such as Paul Verlaine, Jean Moréas, and Jules Laforge. Since his youth, one of Nobre's main objectives was to publish a book of poetry. Critical reaction to his work, however, was mostly negative. His friend de Oliveira was one of the few who praised his verse, while eminent critics and writers—including Moniz Barreto, Abel Botelho, and Pinheiro Chagas—attacked it. The book was neither representative of the old way of writing poetry nor could it easily be connected with the new tendencies, represented by the symbolists.

Some critics and literary historians speak of Nobre's work together with that of the poet Verde. Guilherme de Castilho, writing in his *António Nobre: A obra e o homem* (António Nobre: The Work and the Man, 1977), considers both writers to be authors of only one work. Helena Carvalhão Buescu and Vergílio Ferreira have indicated the similarities between the two important poets, and António José Saraiva and Oscar Lopes believe that Nobre's innovations in lyric poetry are a product of a popular, almost child-like view of the world, while Verde's poems reflect a bourgeois outlook. Both Nobre and Verde renovated the tone of the lyrical language of Portuguese with their works by introducing colloquial elements into poetry. Nobre's poetic language tends to be rural, however, while Verde's is more urban.

The similarities between the two writers extend beyond the quite different but complementary ways in which they changed the course of Portuguese poetry at the end of the nineteenth century. They were born within twelve years of each other—Verde in 1855 and Nobre in 1867—and both died of tuberculosis. Verde's *Livro de Cesário Verde* (The Book of Cesário Verde, 1887) and Nobre's *Só* appeared within five years of each other. Nobre's and Verde's poetic innovations were overshadowed during their lifetime by their more recognized contemporaries Junqueiro and Antero de Quental. The importance of Nobre and Verde to the development of Portuguese poetry and their acceptance into the canon came only years later, when poets associated with the movement centered on the review *Orpheu* (two issues were published, both in 1915). In particular Fernando Pessoa began to appreciate their poetic innovations.

Nobre and Verde came from similar social and literary backgrounds. Both writers portray a Portugal that was making a traumatic transformation into the industrial world. They saw the traditional way of life and values disappearing rapidly and being replaced by something they perceived as negative. The end of the nineteenth century was a time of despair in Portugal. After almost half a century of invasions, civil wars, and revolutions from 1808 to 1851, Portugal underwent important changes in its infrastructure, but those changes did not represent the hope for a better country. The English issued their ultimatum in 1890 for Portugal to withdraw its troops from certain areas of Africa, which ended the dream of creating on the continent a colony that would extend from the coast of Angola to Mozambique. There was a heightened sense of fear and disillusionment throughout the country, culminating in a failed Republican revolution on 31 January 1891. The British ultimatum symbolized to many the failure of the country in general, and it created a reaction against England's attitude toward the feelings of smaller nations.

Nobre constructed his work *Só* from materials provided by these difficult historical moments. The work, with its explicit autobiographical elements, occupies a special place in Portuguese poetry of the late nineteenth century, a period in which French symbolism had exerted a major influence. *Só* is characterized by a pessimistic tone deriving from both Nobre's personal life and the historical situation of a country in which traditions are being threatened. Two years after the first edition of *Só*, de Oliveira in his *Palavras loucas* (Mad Words, 1894) assessed Nobre as the most important writer of *neogarrettismo*, an artistic movement, named after the well-known Romantic writer Almeida Garrett, which perceived modernization as the destruction of the essence of Portugal. The writers of the group believed that the mission of the writer was the perpetuation of Portuguese traditions and values. Nobre's poetry incorporates many symbols and aspects of Portuguese life, including the emotional and fatalistic way of being; the great importance of *saudade* (a profound longing for that which is missing, resulting in feelings of both pain and pleasure); and the beliefs and language of the simple people. Twentieth-century poet Fernando Pessoa understands Nobre's poetic language as capturing the true essence of the Portuguese people. He sees Nobre as representative of a specific tendency in late-nineteenth-century Portuguese poetry, which regards the past with great sadness, while poets such as Junqueiro look happily to the future.

Urbano Tavares Rodrigues recognizes the importance of Nobre's references to Portuguese culture and his incorporation of colloquial language into his poetry. The critic notes, however, that Nobre was influenced in these aspects of his writing not only by Portuguese writers—such as Garrett and Júlio Dinis—but also by the French poet Laforge. Paula Mourão (1991) has shown that *Só* is a mingling of diverse influences, including

*Title page for Nobre's collection of poetry about Portuguese life and culture (Biblioteca Nacional, Lisbon)*

both Portuguese writers—such as Camões, Garrett, and Bernardim Ribeiro—and classic authors, such as Virgil, William Shakespeare, and Edgar Allan Poe.

The 1892 definitive edition of *Só* is apparently a confessional and prosaic work. In fact, it presents a mélange of Portuguese and European references, and its complex and refined fictional construction reveals, as many critics noticed, Nobre's sophisticated knowledge of literature and culture in general. The work captures the pessimism so characteristic of Portuguese literature written between 1890 and 1910. His pessimism blends personal feelings and emotions with the national sense of failure. A strong relationship exists between Nobre's view of his own life as the ruins of a lost infancy and his view of the nation in a state of decadence after a glorious past. These perceptions can be seen in many poems, including "Memória" (Memory), which opens the second edition of *Só*, published in 1898. The poem declares the book to be "o livro mais triste que há em Portugal" (the saddest book that there is in Portugal). The relationship between Nobre's personal situation

*Nobre in the Madeira Islands, circa 1897 (from Guilherme de Castilho,* António Nobre: A obra e o homem, *1977; Thomas Cooper Library, University of South Carolina)*

and the national destiny stands out in the second sonnet, in which Portugal is minimized as "certo Reino, à esquina do Planeta" (a certain kingdom on the corner of the planet). The poem ends on a highly pessimistic note: "Que desgraça nascer em Portugal" (What a misfortune to be born in Portugal).

In October 1892 Nobre returned from Paris to Portugal, where he stayed until November 1893. That year he experienced the first symptoms of tuberculosis. In spite of his illness, he returned to Paris and remained there until 1895 when he graduated with a degree in political science from the Sorbonne. As his illness grew worse, he took several trips within Portugal and abroad, searching for a cure or at least some relief from his suffering. He went to sanatoriums in Switzerland and France. In 1897 he made a trip to the United States, and later he stayed for some time in the Madeira Islands, considered a healthy place for victims of tuberculosis. Nobre also visited different places in Portugal, and during this period he published the second edition of *Só,* a version differing from the first. He eliminated some poems from the original and added new ones in their stead. He also changed the order of the poems, grouping some under specific titles.

From 1895 to 1899 Nobre wrote the poems that appeared in *Despedidas* (Farewells, 1902), published by his brother, Augusto, with a preface written by Nobre's friend José (Bruno) Pereira de Sampaio. The first part of the book consists of twenty-five sonnets and other poems. Nobre did not revise these poems, and some are unfinished. The second part of *Despedidas* is composed of fragments of a book, to be called "O desejado" (The Wanted Man). This part is especially noteworthy because it concerns the figure of King Sebastião, the Portuguese monarch who disappeared in 1578 in the battle of Alcácer-Quibir and later became legendary in Portuguese culture. *Sebastianismo,* the belief in the return of D. Sebastião, was an important popular movement in Portuguese culture. It began immediately after the disappearance of the king and remained strong at least until the middle of the nineteenth century, as pointed out by some critics. In the nineteenth century this myth began appearing in the highest Portuguese literature, as seen in Garrett's *Frei Luís de Sousa* (1844; translated as *The "Brother Luiz de Sousa" of Viscount de Almeida Garrett,* 1909). Nobre's "O desejado" has a crucial importance in this process. In the book the poetic voice talks directly to the Portuguese people and says, "Para os mortos os séculos são meses, / Ou menos que isso, nem um dia, um ai" (For the deceased the centuries are months, / Or less than this, less than a day, perhaps one second). This statement means that they have to wait ("esperai, ó Portugueses"), because the child-king D. Sebastião will not delay appearing, and when the king returns to his people, Portugal will be ready to be born again. In this magical moment of rebirth the nation will return to the influential position that it enjoyed in the time of the great navigations, and Lisbon will become, once again, a universal seaport. Altering completely the position presented in the second sonnet of *Só,* the poetic voice believes that to live in Portugal is a grace. Like a child, the voice says repeatedly that the king "há-de vir, há-de vir, há-de vir" (will return, will return, will return). This belief appeared in several important Portuguese literary works during the first decades of the twentieth century. Pessoa, for instance, took it up in his masterpiece *Mensagem* (Message, 1934). In spite of its relevance to a main branch of Portuguese literature, "O desejado" and the whole book *Despedidas* needs a more accurate critical study.

António Pereira Nobre never married. He died of tuberculosis on 18 March 1900 in Foz do Douro. Few Portuguese writers have left such an important mark on the literature of their country with only one work published during their lifetime and a few posthumous publications. Besides *Despedidas,* Nobre's posthumous volumes include *Primeiros versos* and *Alicerces seguido de Livro de Apontamentos* (Foundation, followed by Book of

Notes, 1983), which feature his first works and show the influence of poets such as Verde, Junqueiro, Gomes Leal, Gonçalves Crespo, and João de Deus. The early poems, some of which achieve the same high literary level as those collected in *Só,* reveal the relationships that Nobre and his contemporaries shared. His correspondence, which has not been published in its entirety, also provides a rich source regarding his writing life and activities within his literary environment. In his letters, especially those written to his friend de Oliveira, Nobre talks about his favorite authors and comments on the books he was reading at that time. One critic, José Carlos Seabra Pereira, understands the significance of Nobre's letters: they create the conditions necessary for understanding better the play between sincerity, fate, and literary construction—themes that Nobre presented in all of his works.

**References:**

Ida Maria Santos Ferreira Alves, "Deambulações de António Nobre," in *Os Centenários: Eça, Nobre, Freyre,* edited by Marli Fantini Scarpelli and Paulo Motta Oliveira (Belo Horizonte: Faculdade de Letras da UFMG, 2001), pp. 103–115;

José van den Besselaar, *O sebastianismo–história sumária* (Lisbon: Instituto de Cultura e Língua Portuguesa, 1987);

Helena Carvalhão Buescu, "Dois poetas da evocação–Cesário Verde e António Nobre," *Colóquio /Letras,* 75 (September 1983): 28–39;

Guilherme de Castilho, *António Nobre* (Lisbon: Bertrand, 1950);

de Castilho, *António Nobre: A obra e o homem* (Lisbon: Arcádia, 1977);

Augusto da Costa Dias, *A crise da consciência pequeno-burguesa* (Lisbon: Estampa, 1977);

Vergílio Ferreira, "Serás poeta e desgraçado," *Colóquio/ Letras,* 127–128 (January–June 1993): 17–26;

Maria Madalena Gonçalves, "Apresentação crítica," in *António Nobre* (Lisbon: Comunicação, 1987), pp. 9–51;

Eugénio Lisboa, ed., *Dicionário cronológico de autores portugueses,* volume 3 (Mem Martins: Europa-América, 1994), pp. 52–54;

Oscar Lopes, *Entre Fialho e Nemésio* (Lisbon: Imprensa Nacional-Casa da Moeda, 1987);

Lopes and António José Saraiva, *História da literatura portuguesa* (Porto: Porto Editora, 1982);

João Louro, *António Nobre. O sonho de Portugal e a procura do sagrado* (Lisbon: Universitária Editora);

Paula Mourão, *O Só de António Nobre–Uma leitura do nome* (Lisbon: Caminho, 1991);

Alberto de Oliveira, *Palavras loucas* (Coimbra: F. França Amado, 1894);

Paulo Motta Oliveira, "Antônio Nobre: para além do *Só,* um rei menino de fantástica memória," *Voz Lusíada,* 17 (January–June 2002): 151–166;

José Carlos Seabra Pereira, *António Nobre projecto e destino* (Porto: Caixotim, 2000);

Fernando Pessoa, *Obras em prosa* (Rio de Janeiro: Nova Aguilar, 1986);

António Machado Pires, *D. Sebastião e o encoberto* (Lisbon: Fundação Calouste Gulbenkian, 1982);

Urbano Tavares Rodrigues, "NOBRE, António Pereira," in *Dicionário de literatura brasileira, portuguesa e galega,* edited by Jacinto do Prado Coelho, António Soares Amora, and Ernesto Guerra da Cal (Rio de Janeiro: Companhia Brasileira de Publicações, 1969), pp. 731–733.

**Papers:**

Some of António Nobre's papers are at the Biblioteca Pública Municipal in Porto, Portugal.

# Carlos de Oliveira
*(10 August 1921 – 1 July 1981)*

Reinaldo Francisco Silva
*University of Aveiro, Portugal*

BOOKS: *Cabeças de barro,* by Oliveira, Fernando Namora, and Artur Varela (Coimbra: Moura Marques & Filho, 1937);

*Turismo* (Coimbra: Novo Cancioneiro, 1942);

*Casa na duna* (Coimbra: Coimbra Editora, 1943);

*Alcateia* (Coimbra: Coimbra Editora, 1944);

*Mãe pobre* (Coimbra: Coimbra Editora, 1945);

*Colheita perdida* (Coimbra: Tipografia Casa Minerva, 1948);

*Pequenos burgueses* (Coimbra: Coimbra Editora, 1948);

*Descida aos infernos* (Porto: Tipografia Emp. Ind. Gráfica, 1949);

*Terra de harmonia* (Lisbon: Centro Bibliográfico, 1950);

*Uma abelha na chuva* (Coimbra: Coimbra Editora, 1953);

*Cantata* (Lisbon: Iniciativas, 1960);

*Poesias 1945–1960* (Lisbon: Portugália, 1962);

*Sobre o lado esquerdo* (Lisbon: Iniciativas, 1968);

*Micropaisagem* (Lisbon: Dom Quixote, 1968);

*Entre duas memórias* (Lisbon: Dom Quixote, 1971);

*O aprendiz de feiticeiro* (Lisbon: Dom Quixote, 1971);

*Trabalho poético,* 2 volumes (Lisbon: Sá da Costa, 1976);

*Finisterra: Paisagem e povoamento* (Lisbon: Sá da Costa, 1978).

Carlos de Oliveira is a central figure in twentieth-century Portuguese literary history mainly because of his novel *Uma abelha na chuva* (A Bee in the Rain, 1953). But he is also important because in most of his work he has captured the ambience of stagnation, frustration, oppression, and quiet despair in Portuguese society during the dictatorship of António de Oliveira Salazar. Oliveira endorses some of the ideological tenets of the neorealism movement; in *Uma abelha na chuva* he does so through a sharp analysis of the power relations between the lower-middle-class yeomanry in the Gândara region and the defenseless peasants. Oliveira is acknowledged as a writer with a strong sense of place at a regional level, and his novels mirror Portuguese society during the middle of the twentieth century. His work produced during the later phase of his career has generated a widespread interest because of its postmodern appeal.

*Carlos de Oliveira (photograph © Arquivo Diário de Notícias)*

Born on 10 August 1921, in Belém do Pará, Brazil, Carlos Alberto Serra de Oliveira returned to Portugal with his family in 1923 because his mother, Aurora Serra de Oliveira, a native of Lousã, had been ill and bedridden during their years overseas. His father, Américo de Oliveira, was a doctor. Oliveira had an older brother, Fernando Serra de Oliveira, born in 1918 in Portugal; he eventually became a professor of medicine (surgery) in the School of Medicine at the University of Coimbra. Upon arriving from Brazil, the family settled in the Gândara region—at first in the village of Camarneira, and afterward in Febres, both part of the municipality of Cantanhede, where Américo de Oliveira had been born. He practiced medicine in both villages, traveling on horseback from one place to another to assist the sick and dying. At times he refused to charge the needy for his services.

Gândara is located in the area made up of Cantanhede (district of Coimbra) on the east, the dunes of Tocha on the west, and Montemor-o-Velho on the south. The region left a profound imprint on Oliveira, who lived there for about thirty years. In his works he has immortalized its farmers, sandy fields, and pine forests, as well as the insalubrious swamps and lagoons. He enrolled at the University of Coimbra in 1941, where he met Ângela de Jesus, a native of the island of Madeira. They married in 1949, two years after his graduation. Both earned degrees in history and philosophy. They had no children.

Although in 1937 Oliveira published *Cabeças de barro* (Heads of Clay), a book he wrote with Fernando Namora and Artur Varela, the first work he acknowledges as his own is *Turismo* (Tourism), published in 1942. *Turismo* is, in essence, a collection of poetry dating as far back as 1941, fulfilling the social and ideological tenets set forth by the *Novo Cancioneiro* (New Songbook). The *Novo Cancioneiro* was a cultural movement initiated by several young poets with literary interests similar to those who belonged to the neorealism movement. Jacinto do Prado Coelho has noted in the 1992 edition of his *Dicionário de literatura* (Dictionary of Literature) that the neorealism movement appeared in Portugal around the beginning of World War II. The poets' common ground was their perception of poetry as a means to focus on social issues. While scholars regard *Turismo* as imbued with the spirit of *Novo Cancioneiro*, they also consider its poems a signal of the arrival of the poet as the most representative voice of neorealism. Osvaldo Manuel Silvestre claims that the poems in the first version of *Turismo*, which oscillate between the Amazon and the Gândara region, are an attempt to re-create the story in Genesis of man's downfall. In the process the poet has shaped his materials so as to reflect his own political views: his denunciation and criticism of social and economic exploitation, the struggles between the social classes, and capitalism.

During the most intense phase of the neorealism movement—the first half of the 1940s, while World War II was being fought—Oliveira published the novels *Casa na duna* (House on the Dune, 1943) and *Alcateia* (Pack of Wolves, 1944), in addition to *Mãe pobre* (Poor

*Paperback cover for the collection of poetry that marks the beginning of Oliveira's mature work (Widener Library, Harvard University)*

Mother, 1945), a collection of poems. While *Casa na duna* stresses stagnation and the decadence of a middle-class family from the Gândara region, the other two works reflect the writer's commitment to broadcasting his political beliefs. The writings from this phase constitute repositories of proletarian experience and beliefs. Speculations as to why the author later downplayed and even rejected *Alcateia* range from his growing distaste for its tragic Gothic scenario to his enthusiasm for leftist politics. Friends and relatives, however, are of the opinion that he feared Salazar's fascist political police, the Polícia Internacional e de Defesa do Estado (International Police and Defense of the State), or PIDE. The author of *Alcateia* was well aware of the regime's policy of censorship, deportation, terror, and torture, and he feared for himself and for his family because of the Marxist overtones of the work; it deals with the exploitation of poor farmers and journeymen by rich and powerful landowners in the Gândara region. The collection of poems *Colheita perdida* (Lost Harvest, 1948),

*Manuscript for one of the poems that appeared in Oliveira's 1960 collection,* Cantata *(from Oliveira's* Poesias 1945–1960, *1962; Vanderbilt, Joint University Libraries)* the novel *Pequenos burgueses* (The Petite Bourgeoisie, 1948), the first version of the long poem *Descida aos infernos* (Descent into Hell, 1949), and the volume of poems titled *Terra de harmonia* (Land of Harmony, 1950) close this first cycle of Oliveira's literary output, which had lasted for about a decade. As a whole, the works from this period are imbued with the spirit of neorealism; for example, *Pequenos burgueses* capitalizes on the tensions between the local bourgeoisie and various marginal characters. Oliveira is universally acknowledged as having contributed to the neorealist movement with a style and vision that are distinctively his own. *Terra de harmonia* is often considered a pivotal work because it marks the beginning of a new decade and it demonstrates a considerable maturity over earlier works. Through time the author's vocabulary becomes increasingly selective; often, he reduces it to a nucleus of words such as *insomnia, desert, silence, lime, ice, ruins, dawn* or *twilight, dune, sand, whiteness,* and *blindness*. Such a selection, scholars contend, reinforces the atmosphere of anxiety that permeates his works.

Published in 1953, the novel *Uma abelha na chuva* has been critically acclaimed as Oliveira's greatest work. It is often considered the culmination of what Alexandre Pinheiro Torres has defined as the "Tetralogy of the *Gândara*," consisting of the author's first four novels. (In actuality, it had been reduced to a trilogy since Oliveira had disavowed *Alcateia*.) *Uma abelha na chuva*, which inspired Fernando Lopes's motion picture of that title in 1972, is populated by several characters who belong to a shabby, lower-middle-class yeomanry. In his exploration of their spiritual barrenness, Oliveira highlights these characters' stifled aspirations and discontent. The novel includes a subtle criticism of the status quo during Salazar's fascist political regime (contemporary historians prefer to call it a right-wing dictatorship), generally characterized by poverty, oppression, and silence. The metaphor of the defenseless bee in the rain, as suggested by the title, is quite meaningful in this sense. The major themes of his earlier novels have been condensed into this book: social and conjugal sterility; alienation; unfulfilled sexuality; the oppression of laws and the violent behavior they elicited from the society of the time; and the fate of an individual or of a given family. Finally, it has been argued that in this novel, Oliveira updates the narrative technique of the nineteeth-century writer Camilo Castelo Branco.

In *Cantata*, published in 1960, a mature poetic voice emerges in poems that are predominantly short and structured around a single image. In this collection Oliveira eschews the rhetoric centered on ideological intervention and heroism so often encountered in his earlier poetry.

During most of the 1960s Oliveira strove to fulfill two important personal goals. The first was the collection of his poems in *Poesias 1945-1960* (Poetry 1945-1960, 1962); the poems in *Turismo* are not included. The second objective is related to his constant desire to rewrite his poems; his novels about the Gândara region are subject to the same impulse. While some of these have been slightly revised, others have been revised to the point of becoming completely different poems. In 1968 Oliveira published two important volumes of poetry: *Sobre o lado esquerdo* (On the Left Side) and *Micropaisagem* (Microlandscape). Afterward, his steady release of new titles slowed. Instead, Oliveira preferred to reread his earlier writings, thus returning to the themes he explored at the beginning of his career. Scholars have called attention to the importance and achievement of his prose poems in *Sobre o lado esquerdo,* which have secured him a prominent position in contemporary Portuguese poetry. In *Micropaisagem,* Oliveira experiments with the techniques of the avant-garde poetic movements of the 1960s. Oliveira further explores this style in *Entre duas memórias* (Between Two Memories, 1971), a volume of poems that are heavily fragmented, especially at the level of syntax. As the poems become more descriptive, the poetic voice focuses on minute details, as in a famous sequence in Pablo Picasso's 1937 Spanish Civil War painting, *Guernica*. Silvestre has argued that the poetic voice in this sequence wants to warn the reader of the impossibility of contemplating the totality of a given object or work of art.

*O aprendiz de feiticeiro* (The Apprentice Sorcerer), published in 1971, is a breakthrough for the author both at a personal and literary level. Oliveira had never written anything similar to it, and there was no record of an analogous work in Portuguese literature. Basically, it is a composite of texts with various styles. Old and new texts, all by Oliveira, are set side by side. The book is metaphorically compared to a writer's workshop where the readers are invited to appreciate and assess the various directions and styles that have coexisted in Oliveira's works, including the pastiche, theoretical and autobiographical entries, and comments and personal impressions.

In 1976 Oliveira published *Trabalho poético* (Poetic Work), an anthology in which he again assembled his volumes of poetry, including a substantially reformulated *Turismo*. At the end he added a sequence of ten poems titled *Pastoral*. The author's innovative experimentation with grammar and stylistics in *Pastoral* has attracted much scholarly attention. The work highlights the current crisis of representation through its elegiac mode and personification. It also focuses on how a particular scenario, way of writing, and memory gradually fade away or became blurred.

*Paperback cover for the 1984 edition of Oliveira's last novel (1978), about a rural bourgeois family (Thomas Cooper Library, University of South Carolina)*

*Finisterra: Paisagem e povoamento* (Finisterra: Landscape and Population), published in 1978, is Oliveira's last piece of writing and represents the culmination of his career as a novelist and poet. This last novel also recycles the major themes in Oliveira's works. Through a kaleidoscope of images, the writer recaptures, for example, his childhood drawings, the peculiar sight obtained from a given window, old pictures, and a sketch of a few sand dunes. These are placed in a story that focuses on a family from the lower ranks of the rural bourgeoisie. The work explores this family's feelings of guilt, which are motivated by the exploitation of journeymen. While the family members are depicted as excelling at this type of behavior, they are also brought down by it. Scholars have been attracted to—and puzzled by—the atmosphere of shadows and how the voices do not match with the speakers. Most importantly, the speakers are incapable of recognizing familiar places within their memories. Whereas the Gândara region is no longer a physical place but rather a symbol in Oliveira's work, *Finisterra* is emblematic of a fleeting world. *Finisterra* is marked by a sense of timelessness, or rather, it is a place where different times often clash with one another: cosmic and geological time; the cycles of life or generations; and the time for settling down to found a particular community.

Contemporary readers, as well as the scholars who have written extensively on Oliveira's work, are drawn mostly to the works written during the last phase of his career. These pieces often address topics that are paramount in current theoretical and critical debates, specifically the issues of literary representation; time and crisis; discourse and metadiscourse; and modernism and postmodernism. As Oliveira's position within the canon of twentieth-century Portuguese literature strengthens even further, contemporary scholars have shifted their focus and interest in his work. Whereas in the past scholars directed their attention to his novels with a strong neorealist imprint and scope, current critics prefer his later writings and the themes that they address.

Scholars also distinguish between Oliveira's roles as a writer of fiction and a poet. The consensus is that the two roles are equally balanced. As a novelist, Oliveira adopted a style and tone of voice marked by seriousness and tragedy so as to unmask the characters from the rural middle class who unscrupulously oppress and exploit the underprivileged. Other critics have been drawn to his Marxist and socialist ideology, which often comes to the surface in specific situations or passages. Finally, others have noticed how a few of Oliveira's novels fall into the tradition of specific novels written by Castelo Branco. As for his poetry, scholars have noticed two major phases. The first is characterized by poems with an emphasis on strong emotions and socialist discourse (*Mãe pobre* and *Descida aos infernos* being his most representative pieces during this phase); the second is marked by a more personal and intimate tone, especially after *Sobre o lado esquerdo*.

In the 1996 edition of *História da literatura portuguesa* (History of Portuguese Literature) António José Saraiva has noted the feelings of personal attachment to land and place that permeate Oliveira's works. Such an interest further attests to a Portuguese cultural trait that has been explored by many other writers. With the Gândara region as the backdrop in most of his poems, Oliveira remains faithful to what Saraiva refers to as a strong "sense of place," hence giving shape to a literary theme found, for example, in the work of writers such as Teixeira de Pascoaes, Miguel Torga, and Afonso Duarte.

On 1 July 1981 Oliveira died in Lisbon. He is buried in the Cemitério dos Prazeres. The people of

Febres have perpetuated his memory by naming the local middle school and a street after him, in recognition not only of his importance in the neorealist movement in Portugal but also of his immortalization of the Gândara region and its way of life in his writings during the first half of the century.

## References:

João Camilo, *Carlos de Oliveira et le Roman* (Paris: Fondation Calouste Gulbenkian, Centre Culturel Portugais, 1987);

Eduardo Prado Coelho, "Itinerário poético de Carlos de Oliveira," in his *A letra litoral* (Lisbon: Moraes, 1979), pp. 155–179;

Gastão Cruz, "Carlos de Oliveira: Uma poética da brevidade no contexto do neo-Realismo," in *Um século de poesia (1888–1988)*, edited by Manuel Hermínio Monteiro (Lisbon: Assírio & Alvim, 1988), pp. 83–86;

Américo Lindeza Diogo, *Aventuras da mimese na poesia de Carlos de Oliveira e na poesia de António Franco Alexandre* (Pontevedra & Braga: Irmandades da Fala da Galiza e de Portugal, 1995);

Rosa Maria Goulart, "Carlos de Oliveira: Arte poética," in her *Artes poéticas* (Braga & Coimbra: Angelus Novus, 1997);

Manuel Gusmão, *A poesia de Carlos de Oliveira* (Lisbon: Seara Nova/Comunicação, 1981);

Nuno Júdice, "Guia (Sumário) para ler *Finisterra*," in his *O processo poético* (Lisbon: Imprensa Nacional-Casa da Moeda, 1992);

Silvina Rodrigues Lopes, *Carlos de Oliveira: O testemunho inadiável* (Sintra: Câmara Municipal, 1996);

Eduardo Lourenço, "Carlos de Oliveira e o trágico neo-realista," in his *Sentido e forma da poesia neo-realista* (Lisbon: Ulisseia, 1968), pp. 173–249;

Rosa Maria Martelo, "Reescrita e efeito de invariância em trabalho poético de Carlos de Oliveira," *Colóquio/Letras*, 135–136 (1995);

Carlos Reis, *O discurso ideológico de neo-realismo português* (Coimbra: Livraria Almedina, 1983);

Maria Alzira Seixo, "Paisagem e narração em *Finisterra* de Carlos de Oliveira," in her *A palavra do romance: Ensaios de gemologia e análise* (Lisbon: Horizonte, 1986);

Osvaldo Manuel Silvestre, *Slow Motion: Carlos de Oliveira e a pós-modernidade* (Braga & Coimbra: Angelus Novus, 1993);

Alexandre Pinheiro Torres, "Carlos de Oliveira ou algumas das necessidades não equacionadas pelo neo-realismo," in his *Ensaios escolhidos I* (Lisbon: Caminho, 1989);

*Vértice: Revista de cultura e arte,* special Oliveira issue, 450–451 (1982).

## Papers:

As of 2003, Carlos de Oliveira's manuscripts were in the possession of his wife in Lisbon; but planning was under way for a museum, archive, and cultural center to be established in the house in Febres where he grew up.

# Camilo Pessanha

*(7 September 1867 – 1 March 1926)*

René P. Garay
*City College–Graduate School, City University of New York*

BOOKS: *Clepsidra* (Lisbon: Lusitânia, 1920);
*China. Estudos e traduções* (Lisbon: Agência Geral das Colónias, 1944).

**Editions and Collections:** *Clépsidra* (Lisbon: Ática, 1945);
*Clepsidra e outros poemas de Camilo Pessanha* (Lisbon: Ática, 1969);
*Obras de Camilo Pessanha*, 2 volumes, edited by António Quadros (Lisbon: Europa-América, 1988)–comprises volume 1, *Clepsidra e poemas dispersos;* and volume 2, *Contos, crónicas, cartas escolhidas e textos de temática chinesa;*
*Clepsidra e outros poemas*, edited by Barbara Spaggiari (Porto: Lello, 1997).

Although Camilo Pessanha published only one collection, *Clepsidra* (1920), he is considered a leading figure in the world of Portuguese poetry. The well-known modernist poet Fernando Pessoa considered Pessanha a master of modern thought. His artistic originality contributed to the development of Portuguese literature not only within the premodern period of renovation (that is, Parnassian, decadent, and symbolist movements of the late nineteenth century) but also in the phase of Portuguese modernism that began in the early twentieth century. This important period of transition–from a state of decay to the introduction of modern aesthetics–fostered artistic innovation that defined the modern style in Portuguese letters.

Pessanha was heir to the name of an illustrious family: the founder of the eminent Genovese family by that name had taken a prominent position as admiral in the court of the Portuguese king D. Dinis in 1317. Camilo d'Almeida Pessanha's own life, however, was marred with the taint of illegitimacy. He was born on 7 September 1867 to Francisco António Pessanha, a law student at the University of Coimbra, and Maria do Espírito Santo Duarte Nunes Pereira, the family housekeeper from the Beira Alta region. His father's refusal to marry his mother because of her humble origins was a lasting source of disillusionment for Pessanha.

*Camilo Pessanha, 1916 (from Daniel Pires, ed.,* Homenagem a Camilo Pessanha, *2000; University of Southern California Library)*

The sonnet "Madalena" (Magdelene), written in 1890, reveals some of the symbols of impurity and the torturous existence that the poet associates with his own illegitimacy, disclosing only marginally the possible recovery of his mother's good name as represented by the woman who, although a sinner, was forgiven by Jesus: "Ó Madalena, ó cabelos de rastos, / Lírio poluído, branca flor inútil" (Oh Magdalene, your trailing tresses / polluted lily, fruitless flower, colorless). Pessanha's sister was named Madalena; after her death at age five, another sister received the telling appellative of Madalena da Purificação.

After Pessanha's primary education, which began in Lamego, he entered preparatory school in Coimbra. In 1891, following his father's career, Pessanha received his law degree from the University of Coimbra. Graduation was followed by positions in Miranda (1892) as assistant to the royal solicitor and then as a lawyer in Óbidos. While still at the university he wrote a short story, "Segundo Amante" (Second Lover), that echoes the feeling of endless guilt for his mother's inadvertent social infraction. In this early work Pessanha returns to the theme of frustrated love and a disillusionment with family life. The story recounts the sad circumstances of Sofia, an unwed mother abandoned by Teles, a university student: "Com o Teles vivera apenas onze meses e dessa doidice nada lhe ficara . . . senão o pequerrucho" (she had lived with Teles for only eleven months and from that folly nothing remained . . . except the little one). After Teles's death, Sofia takes on another lover, Luis Vila Nova, who abandons her after their first encounter: "Ao retirar-se, o Luís deixou três moedas . . . sobre o toucador . . . Náo voltou" (When he left her, Luis put three coins . . . on the dressing table . . . He never returned). For its time, the story appears unusually sympathetic to Sofia as a woman, and more specifically to her predicament as an unwed mother. More than just solidarity with a feminist sensibility, however, Pessanha is confessing his own longing for a conventional family life. The first-person narrator often betrays the author's own anxiety by interrupting the narrative to add comments such as the observation that children of unwed mothers are the "frutos condenados dum amor promíscuo" (condemned fruit of promiscuous love). In both "Madalena" and "Segundo Amante" the writer uses similar metaphors of decadence that convey the sterility and hopelessness of his state, a wretched existence that conditioned his unending and illusive search for individual love that would lead to the stability of a family life.

The same fin-de-siècle feeling of decadence prevailed in all of Europe, now spiritually and morally exhausted after a dizzying century of technological discoveries that, in turn, facilitated colonial exploitation. In Portugal, after years of exploration, the political and social scene had been eroded by these frustrated colonial ventures. Pessanha saw the need for the modern cultural renovations that the new economic and political scenario demanded. In the poem "Eu vi a luz" (I Saw the Light), which serves as an epigraph to *Clepsidra*, one may observe this declining sense of empire:

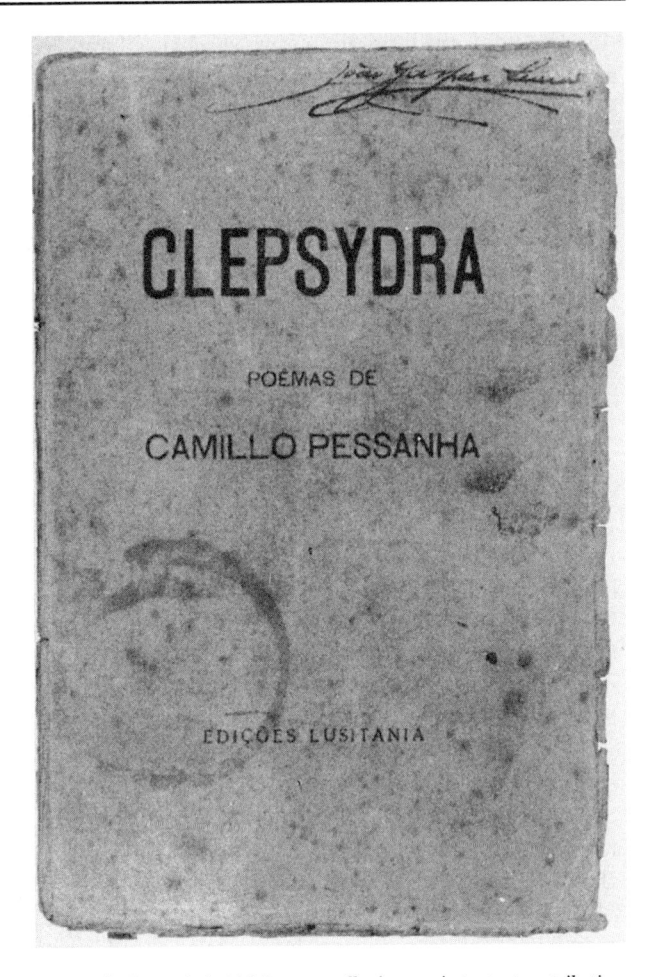

*Cover for Pessanha's 1920 poetry collection, an important contribution to Portuguese modernism (from João Gaspar Simões,* Camilo Pessanha, *1967; Daniel Library, The Citadel)*

Eu vi a luz em um pais perdido
A minha alma é lânguida e inerme.
Oh! Quem pudesse deslizar sem ruído
No chão sumir-se, como faz um verme . . .

(I saw the light of a defeated nation
My soul is languid and listless.
Oh! Would that one could slither away quietly
Like a worm, on the ground, dissipating . . .)

As António Quadros pointed out in his notes to a 1988 edition of Pessanha's works, "Eu vi a luz" is a desperately solemn poem that echoes the creed of Pessanha's avowed master, Paul Verlaine: "Je suis l'Empire à la fin de la décadence" (I am the empire at the end of its decadence). In its starkness, brevity, and simplified use of words to create an image of social abandonment, this grave poem also expresses the author's rejection of the decadent aesthetic creeds of a failed poetics. In this sense he is again remembering the voice of Verlaine, who, in his "golden rule" of defiance, suggests "wringing rhetoric's neck!" The poem titled "Inscrição"

(Inscription) is the inspiration for *Clepsidra* itself and carries the germ of Pessanha's poetic precept, in which personal longing *(saudade)* is associated with a decadent, national reality.

In 1893 Pessanha was appointed professor of philosophy in a secondary school in Macao, where he began teaching the following year. In Macao he met Venceslau de Morais, a writer known not only for his translation of oriental motifs into the language of Portuguese *saudosismo* (nostalgic yearning), but also for his realistic depiction of the ills introduced by the West into the Eastern world after centuries of colonial expansion. In this environment Pessanha also took up smoking opium, a habit that, along with his chronic ill health and the abuse of absinthe and alcohol, sealed his fate. In 1900 Pessanha was named Conservador do Registro Predial (Administrator of the Real Estate Office), and he also served as a justice of the peace in 1904. After leaving his job as conservador in 1905, he returned to his former teaching position. During this period he returned to Lisbon several times in search of better health.

Much has been written about Pessanha's orientalism, and Esther de Lemos has reviewed some of these opinions in the context of his stay in Macao. Lemos has noted in the author a tendency toward a disarticulated rhetoric that often seems to escape the logical sequence of the intended discourse. She adds that this fracturing may have been learned from his knowledge of Chinese literature: "as far as techniques are concerned, it is possible that Chinese literature helped shape the tendency towards a disarticulation of logic," but she insists that Pessanha's orientalism is not authentic but rather a stereotypical, Western rendition of the East.

Pessanha is by far the most representative poet of the symbolist-decadent period in Portuguese literature, as evident not only in his careful insistence on the musical cadence of his verse but also in the vague and suggestive quality of his poetic language. He was an innate dreamer who was able to translate his vision of total frustration within the symbolist precepts outlined by Verlaine and later Stéphane Mallarmé: verse is above all the harmonious suggestions projected from the poet's soul. It is the condensation of the world of dream and illusion.

Pessanha's use of opium and absinthe, common drugs in this age of decadence, was no doubt responsible not only for his euphoric flights of fantasy but also for the pessimism that almost always ensued, informing his solemn poetic vision: a world paralyzed by physical exhaustion and inertia. These changes in mood inevitably turned to absolute depression and the frustration resulting from unrequited love. This dissipation of his energy could be further related to Pessanha's experience in the East, for it had a profound effect on his writing. An untitled poem, for example, reflects an Eastern passivity closely allied to the Buddhist quiescent tradition:

Porque o melhor emfim,
É não ouvir nem ver'
Passarem sobre mim
E nada me doer!
—Sorrindo interiormente
Co'as pálpebras cerradas,
Às águas da torrente
Já tão longe passadas.—
. . . . . . . . . . . . . . . . . .
E eu sob a terra firme
Compacta, recalcada,
Muito quietinho. A rir-me
De não me doer nada.

(For it is ultimately better
Not to hear nor see
Stampede over one's body
And not feel a thing!
—Laughing all the while, inside,
With closed eyelids,
At those torrential waters
So long ago receded.—
. . . . . . . . . . . . . . . . . .
And underneath this firm soil,
Compact and footed,
So very quiet. I laugh
At my painless existence.)

This poetic imagery follows closely the dispirited temper of a life in pursuit of love, from the earliest poems of a heady adolescent sensuality, such as "Lúbrica" (Lubricious), and its later, more naturalistic renunciation of the feminine in "Vénus I e II," to the ultimate, nirvana-like indifference that underscores the poet's unstable vision of life: "Imagens que passais pela retina / Dos meus olhos, porque não vos fixais?" (Images that pass the retinas / Of my eyes, why do you not abide?). In the poem "Olvido" (Oblivion) a final stage of Pessanha's writing invokes images of agony and death as the only solution to a defeated life: "Dorme emfim sem desejo e sem saudade / Das coisas não logradas ou perdidas" (Sleep, then, without desire or longing / For that which has been thwarted or lost).

These ideas of decadence molded by the pangs of forsaken love are summarized in an 1893 letter to Ana de Castro Osório, one of at least three women who rejected Pessanha's marriage proposals. In the letter, the poet claims that "nada verdadeiramente e para mim tem realidade no mundo—por onde tenho passado como um sonâmbulo" (nothing, in truth, has any reality for me in this world—a world that I have traversed like a sleepwalker). Pessanha was never legally married. He had a son, João Manuel, in 1897 with a Chinese housekeeper whose name is not known. Later he entered into a relationship with her daughter, N'gan-Yeng, and still later with another Chinese woman, Same-Khun.

Pessanha's use of language–and his rejection of the Romantic tendency toward wordiness–is one of the essential elements of his modern poetics. Following the precepts of earlier models Verlaine and Rubén Darío, Pessanha emphasized the musical cadence of the written word, created a new syntax to express psychological states, and developed a surprising ability for bold imagery, all of which announce a truly modernist aesthetics. The almost surrealistic mixture of different states of consciousness–blending past, present, and future–reveals a deliberate play with presence and absence that announces Pessoa's poetics of *interseccionismo* (intersectionism).

The sonnet "Na Cadeia" (In Prison), for example, exhibits this technique of *interseccionismo*. Pessanha achieves the intersectionist ideal of harmonizing two distinct and, apparently, irreconcilable planes of reality by blending the melancholic state of consciousness of the first-person poetic voice with the desolate plight of the confined convicts:

> Coração, quietinho . . . quietinho . . .
> Porque te insurges e blasfemas?
> Pschiu . . . Não batas . . . Devagarinho . . .
> Olha os soldados, as algemas!
>
> (Heart of mine, slow down, be still,
> Why rebel, why curse thy fate?
> Hush now . . . Arrest your palpitations . . . Slow down . . .
> Mind those soldiers, those handcuffs!)

His startling associations of sound, sight, and smell all come together to render a postsymbolist poetics of great expressive quality and singular beauty. In this respect, Jorge de Sena saw Pessanha as one of the most extraordinary artists who have written in the Portuguese language, a statement that echoes the modernist poets of the early twentieth century. Among these, Pessoa, António Ferro, Luis de Montalvo, and Mário de Sá-Carneiro saw in Pessanha a precursor of the new sensibility that ultimately opened the way for the modernist movement in Portugal. Tereza Coelho Lopes, in her 1979 study, observes that Pessanha became a genuine precursor of many elements of modernism: from his poetics of *interseccionismo*, similar to the blending of different levels of reality in Pessoa's poetic sequence "Chuva oblíqua" (Oblique Rain, written in 1914), to the emblematic fragmentation of the poetic subject, inspiring such strategies as Pessoa's literary use of heteronyms (multiple voices and personalities).

*Pessanha's grave, Macao (from João Gaspar Simões,* Camilo Pessanha, *1967; Daniel Library, The Citadel)*

Pessoa asked Pessanha, in a letter dated 1915, to collaborate on the never-published third volume of the modernist review *Orpheu,* adding that Pessanha's work was to him a "Fonte continua de exaltação estética" (Never-ending fountain of aesthetic exaltation). For Pessoa, Pessanha was a literary mentor, an avowed master of the modern temper who taught him how to feel in hidden ways and took him through untrodden paths ("ensinou[-me] a sentir veladamente") and whom Pessoa considered the epitome of an aesthetic ideal: "O mais que é tudo, é Camilo Pessanha" (the more that is all, that is Camilo Pessanha).

**Letters:**

*Cartas a Alberto Osório de Castro, João Baptista de Castro e Ana de Castro Osório,* edited by Maria José de Lancastre (Lisbon: Imprensa Nacional-Casa da Moeda, 1984).

**References:**

Eugénio de Andrade, "Camilo Pessanha, o mestre," *Persona,* 10 (July 1984);

Rui de Avintes, "A sensibilidade misteriosa de Camilo Pessanha," *Mosaico* (Macao), nos. 68–70 (April–June 1956);

Reis Brasil, "Camilo Pessanha, mestre do Simbolismo esotérico," *O Primeiro de Janeiro,* 26 April 1967;

João Camilo, "Sobre a 'abulia' de Camilo Pessanha," *Persona,* 11/12 (December 1985);

Jacinto do Prado Coelho, "De Verlaine a Camilo Pessanha," *Colóquio/Letras,* 26 (1975);

Paulo Franchetti, *Nostalgia, exílio e melancolia: Leituras de Camilo Pessanha* (São Paulo: Eduspe, 2001);

Franchetti, "Pessanha e a China," *Estudos Portugueses e Africanos,* no. 11 (1989);

Anna Klobucka, "A (de)composição de Vénus: Reflexões sobre dois sonetos de Camilo Pessanha," *Colóquio/Letras,* nos. 104–105 (July–October 1988);

Esther de Lemos, *A Clépsidra de Camilo Pessanha* (Porto: Tavares Martins, 1956);

Tereza Coelho Lopes, *Clepsidra de Camilo Pessanha (Textos Escolhidos)* (Lisbon: Seara Nova, 1979);

Maria Ofélia Paiva Monteiro, "O universo poético de Camilo Pessanha," *Arquivo Coimbrão,* 24 (1969);

João Augusto Máttar Neto, *O processo simbólico na Clepsidra de Camilo Pessanha* (São Paulo: Centro de Estudos Portugueses da Universidade de São Paulo, 1996);

Edgard Pereira, "O conflicto existencial em 'Clepsidra,'" *Letras & Letras,* 4 (21 August 1991);

Fernando Pessoa, "Obras em prosa de Fernando Pessoa," in his *Páginas de estética e de teoria e crítica literárias,* edited by Georg Rudolf Lind and Jacinto do Prado Coelho (Lisbon: Ática, 1966);

Urbano Tavares Rodrigues, "Reflexão sobre três sonetos de Camilo Pessanha. A Estátua, A Vénus viva e a Vénus morta," in his *Ensaios de Após–Abril* (Lisbon: Moraes, 1977);

Ana Teresa de Castro Santos, "Pessanha e Pessoa: Uma leitura do mar português," *Estudos Portugueses e Africanos,* no. 13 (1989);

Maria Alzira Seixo, "O pensamento da morte na poesia de Camilo Pessanha," *Análise,* no. 13 (1990);

Barbara Spaggiari, *O simbolismo na obra de Camilo Pessanha,* translated by Carlos Moura (Lisbon: Instituto de Cultura e Língua Portuguesa, 1982).

**Papers:**

A collection of Camilo Pessanha's papers is at the Biblioteca Nacional in Lisbon.

# Fernando Pessoa
*(13 June 1888 – 30 November 1935)*

George Monteiro
*Brown University*

BOOKS: *Antinous* (Lisbon: Monteiro, 1918);

*35 Sonnets* (Lisbon: Monteiro, 1918);

*English Poems I-II* (Lisbon: Olisipo, 1921)–comprises *Antinous* and *Inscriptions;*

*English Poems III* (Lisbon: Olisipo, 1921)–comprises *Epithalamium;*

*Mensagem* (Lisbon: A. M. Pereira, 1934);

*Poesias,* 2 volumes, edited by Adolfo Casais Monteiro (Lisbon: Confluência, 1942);

*Obras completas de Fernando Pessoa,* 11 volumes (Lisbon: Ática, 1942-1974)–comprises volume 1, *Poesia de Fernando Pessoa,* by João Gaspar Simões and Luís de Montalvor (1942); volume 2, *Poesias de Álvaro de Campos,* edited by Simões and Montalvor (1944); volume 3, *Poemas de Alberto Caeiro,* edited by Simões and Montalvor (1946); volume 4, *Odes de Ricardo Reis,* edited by Simões and Montalvor (1946); volume 5, *Mensagem* (1945); volume 6, *Poemas dramáticos de Fernando Pessoa,* edited by Eduardo Freitas da Costa (1952); volume 7, *Poesias inéditas: 1930-1935,* edited by Jorge Nemésio (1955); volume 8, *Poesias inéditas: 1919-1930,* edited by Nemésio (1956); volume 9, *Quadras ao gosto popular,* edited by Georg Rudolf Lind and Jacinto do Prado Coelho (1965); volume 10, *Novas poesias inéditas,* edited by Maria do Rosário Marques Sabino and Adelaide Maria Monteiro Sereno (1973); and volume 11, *Poemas inglesas: Antinous, Inscriptions, Epithalamium, 35 Sonnets e Dispersos,* bilingual edition, translated by Jorge de Sena, Monteiro, and José Blanc de Portugal (1974);

*Páginas íntimas e de auto-interpretação,* edited by Lind and Coelho (Lisbon: Ática, 1966);

*Páginas de estética e de teoria e crítica literárias,* edited by Lind and Coelho (Lisbon: Ática, 1966);

*Textos filosóficos,* 2 volumes, edited by António de Pina Coelho (Lisbon: Ática, 1968);

*Livro do desassossego por Bernardo Soares,* 2 volumes, edited by Jacinto do Prado Coelho, Maria Aliete Galhoz, and Teresa Sobral Cunha (Lisbon: Ática, 1982);

*Fernando Pessoa (photograph by Vitoriano Braga; from João Gaspar Simões,* Vida e obra de Fernando Pessoa, *1987; Thomas Cooper Library, University of South Carolina)*

*Canções de beber na obra de Fernando Pessoa,* edited by Galhoz (Lisbon: Tiragem Limitada, 1997);

*Alexander Search: Poesia,* edited by Luísa Freire (Lisbon: Assírio & Alvim, 2000).

**Editions and Collections:** *O manuscrito de O guardador de rebanhos,* edited by Ivo Castro (Lisbon: Dom Quixote, 1986);

*Edição crítica de Fernando Pessoa,* 6 volumes published (Lisbon: Imprensa Nacional-Casa da Moeda, 1990- );

*Mensagem: Poemas esotéricos,* edited by José Augusto Seabra (Madrid: Consejo Superior de Investiga-

ciones Científicas / Porto: Fundação A. Almeida, 1993);
*Poemas completos de Alberto Caeiro,* edited by Teresa Sobral Cunha (Lisbon: Presença, 1994);
*Livro de desassossego composto por Bernardo Soares, ajudante de guarda-livros na cidade de Lisboa,* edited by Richard Zenith (São Paulo: Companhia Das Letras, 1999);
*Poesia inglesa,* 2 volumes, edited by Luísa Freire (Lisbon: Assírio & Alvim, 2000);
*Crítica: Ensaios, artigos e entrevistas,* edited by Fernando Cabral Martins (Lisbon: Assírio & Alvim, 2000).

**Editions in English:** *Selected Poems,* translated by Peter Rickard (Edinburgh: Edinburgh University Press, 1971; Austin: University of Texas Press, 1972);
*Sixty Portuguese Poems,* translated by F. E. G. Quintanilha (Cardiff: University of Wales Press, 1971);
*Selected Poems,* second edition, translated by Jonathan Griffin (Harmondsworth, U.K. & New York: Penguin, 1982);
*The Keeper of Sheep,* translated by Edwin Honig and Susan M. Brown (Riverdale-on-Hudson, N.Y.: Sheep Meadow Press, 1986);
*Always Astonished: Selected Prose,* translated by Honig (San Francisco: City Lights Books, 1988);
*Self-Analysis and Thirty Other Poems,* translated by George Monteiro (Lisbon: Calouste Gulbenkian Foundation, 1988);
*Message/Mensagem,* bilingual edition, translated by Griffin (London: Menard/King's College, 1992);
*Fernando Pessoa & Co.: Selected Poems,* translated by Richard Zenith (New York: Grove, 1998);
*Poems of Fernando Pessoa,* translated by Honig and Brown (San Francisco: City Lights Books, 1998);
*The Selected Prose of Fernando Pessoa,* translated by Zenith (New York: Grove, 2001);
*The Book of Disquiet,* translated by Zenith (London: Penguin, 2002; New York: Penguin, 2003).

OTHER: *Antologia de poemas portuguêzes modernos,* edited by Pessoa and António Botto (Lisbon: Solução, 1929).

The achievement of Fernando Pessoa has no parallel in modern literature. Yet, while widely recognized as one of the greatest twentieth-century writers in the Portuguese language, he nevertheless remains the most obscure of the acknowledged masters of Western literary modernism. Recognition of the magnitude of his work beyond the confines of Portugal and other Portuguese-speaking lands has come slowly if steadily as his work has found readers and translators across linguistic boundaries. Especially captivating to Pessoa's readers has been the striking aspect of his creativity that enabled him to bring into being the poetry and prose of several other imaginary writers.

Pessoa started out as an English-language poet, writing poems in a still undefined poetic style. He began creating various voices, different from his own; he called them heteronyms and gave them individual biographies to go along with their names and the body of work assigned to them. In 1928 in the journal *Presença,* Pessoa defined his use of the term heteronym by distinguishing it from the term pseudonym:

> A obra pseudónyma é do autor em sua pessoa, salvo no nome que assina; a heterónyma é do auctor fóra da sua pessoa, é de uma individualidade completa fabricada por êle, como o seriam os dizeres de qualquer personagem de qualquer drama seu.
>
> (A pseudonymous work is, except for the name with which it is signed, the work of an author writing as himself; a heteronymic work is by an author writing outside his own personality: it is the work of a complete individuality made up by him, just as the utterances of some character in any of his plays would be).

His first important heteronyms, Charles Robert Anon and his brother Alexander Search, were eventually succeeded by others, including Alberto Caeiro, Álvaro de Campos, Ricardo Reis, and Bernardo Soares, but not before Pessoa had attributed enough work to Alexander Search to make up a sizable volume, though no such volume was published during Pessoa's lifetime.

Pessoa published the best of the poems and essays he assigned to his major heteronyms–Caeiro, Campos, and Reis–in journals and newspapers during his lifetime, just as he did the best of his so-called orthonymic poetry, which he presented under his own name. Although he left various outlines and schemes for collecting and publishing the work of his heteronyms as different books, none appeared during his lifetime. Only one book of related poems, *Mensagem* (Message, 1934), a work Pessoa assigned to *êle-mesmo* (himself), appeared a year before his death. The critic Jorge de Sena has called Pessoa "the man who never was," meaning that the poet had lived no outward life to speak of, that his work was the whole of his existence. What was said of one of his fictitious poets might have been said about him: "A vida de Caeiro não pode narrar-se pois que não há nela de que narrar. Seus poemas são o que houve nele de vida." (It's impossible to narrate Caeiro's life because there is nothing to narrate. His poems are what there was of him in life.)

Fernando António Nogueira Pessoa was born in Lisbon on 13 June 1888. His father, Joaquim de Seabra Pessoa, who died when his son was five, was a public employee who also wrote music reviews for a Lisbon newspaper. Pessoa never took on his father's role of music critic, but over his lifetime he practiced the art of a man of letters, writing poetry, fiction, drama, reviews, translations, and essays—literary, historical, sociological, philosophical—much of which was published only after his death in 1935.

Pessoa had a younger brother, Jorge, who died in 1894. His mother, Maria Madalena Nogueira Pessoa, married her second husband, Commander João Miguel Rosa, the Portuguese consul in Durban, South Africa, when Fernando was six. Pessoa had five half siblings from this marriage. He lived in Durban until he was seventeen, returning alone to Portugal in 1905. So except for a few weeks at the University of Lisbon in 1906, Pessoa received his formal education in English. He considered himself bilingual and bicultural. Unpublished in England (except for one minor lyric in the *Athenaeum* in 1920), Pessoa nevertheless always thought of himself as a poet in the English tradition, even as he was earning a place in Portuguese literary history.

Pessoa's serious attempts to launch a career in Portugal began with two essays on the nature and properties of modern Portuguese poetry. He published these in 1912 in successive issues of *A Águia* (The Eagle), the voice of the Nova Renascença, a term applied to a group of authors seeking to renew Portuguese writing. In these essays Pessoa predicts the appearance of a poet destined to lead a modern movement in Portuguese poetry. This poet, who would be even more important than sixteenth-century poet Luís de Camões, would write the new poetry of matter conceived as spirit. Although he was not at that time identified with this supra-Camões of the future, Pessoa has come to be so considered by some of his later, more enthusiastic adherents. Pessoa's association with *A Águia* was short-lived, coming to an end in 1914 over an unexplained delay in publishing *O marinheiro* (The Sailor), Pessoa's "drama estático em um quadro" (static play in one scene). Pessoa withdrew his play and later published it in *Orpheu,* a journal he cofounded. Two pieces in *A Águia* in 1913—a mildly satiric critique of caricatures by the young artist José de Almada Negreiros, who helped to create Portuguese modernism, and "Na floresta do alheamento" (In the Forest of Estrangement), which was the first fragment from *Livro do desassossego por Bernardo Soares* (The Book of Disquiet, 1982) to be published—were his last contributions to that periodical. *Livro do desassossego,* attributed at first to the now obscure heteronym Vicente Guedes but later definitively assigned to Soares, engaged Pessoa intermittently for the rest of his life, and he left at his death a large collection of segments and fragments but no definitive plan for their sequence or any stated principle of organization.

*Pessoa in 1898 (from João Gaspar Simões,* Vida e obra de Fernando Pessoa, *1987; Thomas Cooper Library, University of South Carolina)*

Of Soares, an assistant bookkeeper employed in the Rua dos Douradores in the commercial center of Lisbon, whose notes, observations, and meditations constitute the fragments put together by scholars to make up *Livro do desassossego,* Pessoa wrote: "apparece sempre que estou cansado ou somnolento, de sorte que tenha um pouco suspensas as qualidades de raciocinio e de inhibição" (He appears always when I am tired or sleepy, when my qualities of rationality and of inhibition are somewhat in suspension). He decided that Soares was not a heteronym but rather a "semi-heteronym": "não sendo a personalidade a minha, é, não diferente da minha, mas uma simples multilação della. Sou eu menos o raciocinio e a affectividade" (His personality is not my personality. It does not differ from mine but is a mutilation of it. He's me minus the rationality and the feeling). At an early stage in his literary career Pessoa admitted that when depressed he could write nothing but the entries destined for *Livro do desassossego.* Thus, everything that Soares wrote, except for a few lyric poems, was in prose intended for this twentieth-century anatomy of melancholy. Soares's themes, including anonymity, solitude, boredom, and the dream-like nature of existence, are the same as Pessoa's themes in the poetry he attributed to himself. In Soares's prose, however, they are expressed more bitterly and with greater contempt. The enthusiastic reception accorded *Livro do desassossego* in the languages into which it has been translated since its publication in 1982 has brought its semi-heteronymic author the widespread recognition previously enjoyed only by Pessoa's three major heteronyms or by the poet himself.

With "Na floresta do alheamento" in 1913 Pessoa effectively broke away from both *A Àguia* and the founders and leaders of the Nova Renascença. He never entirely rejected, however, their ideals of Portuguese character or their sanguine prophecies for a new and revived Portugal.

In February 1914 Pessoa published "Impressões do crespúsculo" (Impressions of Twilight) in the first and only issue of the journal *A Renascença*. The title covers two loosely related poems. That spring, on the commission of a London publisher, he compiled and translated into English a collection of Portuguese proverbs. The outbreak of World War I that summer compelled the publisher to put off publication, and the work never appeared in print.

In 1912 Pessoa had conceived the idea of Ricardo Reis as a "pagan" poet, though not until June 1914 did Pessoa write the first poems that gave Reis his identity as one of Pessoa's major Portuguese-language heteronyms. These poems followed the creation in March of both Alberto Caeiro, the second such heteronym who resulted from the impulse to play a friendly joke on the writer Mário de Sá-Carneiro, and, later on the same day, Álvaro de Campos, the third heteronymic poet that makes up what Pessoa calls his "coterie inexistent." Pessoa later explained, in answer to a question posed to him in 1935 by the young poet-critic and editor Adolfo Casais Monteiro, how this triumvirate of poets had emerged in his consciousness. Pessoa's reply has become, perhaps, the most widely quoted document in modern Portuguese literary history. Recalling and undoubtedly reimagining the past, he related how the voices of his heteronyms came to him, revealed their identity, and wrote their poetry through him. In this way he set down the whole of Caeiro's *O guardador de rebanhos* (The Keeper of Sheep) at once, followed by major odes by Campos. Even his own personality asserted itself, as if in resistance to his having been taken over by his heteronyms, and he wrote the autobiographical sequence "Chuva oblíqua" (Oblique Rain) in his own voice. It was the greatest day of his life, he said.

Of seventy or so heteronyms, semiheteronyms, and pseudonyms ultimately imagined by Pessoa, the three comprising his "coterie inexistent" stand out, each in his own right as well as in relationship to one another. Each one became the author of a substantial body of work sufficiently elaborated and original enough to ensure the poet an honored place in Portuguese literary history. Along with the Pessoa who also laid claim to a singular body of work, they made up the major and best-known portion of what Pessoa called his "drama-en-gente" (drama-in-people). This phrase, which he might have taken from the English poet Robert Browning, was meaningful in two major senses: Pessoa was interested in the drama that came from within individuals, and he was interested in the imaginary dramatic world created through the interactions among the members of his group of imagined poets.

Alberto Caeiro was the recognized and gratefully acknowledged "master" of Reis, Campos, and Pessoa himself. Caeiro was "born" on 16 April 1889 in Lisbon, but spent most of his life in rural Portugal. His parents died when he was young, and he himself died in his mid twenties, of tuberculosis, in 1915. He followed no profession, having had little formal education beyond the primary level. He lived at home with an aged aunt. He was blond, blue-eyed, and of medium height. His major work was *O guardador de rebanhos,* which Pessoa claimed came to him fully formed on that remarkable day in March 1914. Surviving manuscripts, however, show that he worked the poems over in considerable detail after their original composition. Reis considered Caeiro's supreme line to be: "A Natureza é partes sem um todo" (Nature is parts without a whole).

While Pessoa often composed poetry and prose in English and considered himself more often than not to be a poet in the English tradition, the English-speaking Álvaro de Campos wrote only in Portuguese. Occasionally, however, he displayed his knowledge of English by assigning English titles to poems, such as "Lisbon Revisited (1923)" and "Clearly non-Campos" (pun intended), and by signing essays and letters from British locations such as Newcastle upon Tyne or Glasgow. A five-sonnet sequence, unpublished in Pessoa's lifetime, bears the title "Barrow-in-Furness." As the English shipbuilding center along the western coast, Barrow-in-Furness is in keeping with the fictional biography imagined for Campos. A naval engineer trained in Glasgow, he finds himself at the end of a job at the Barrow-in-Furness ship works, anticipating his return to Lisbon. Credited with some of the most strikingly original lyrics in modern Portuguese poetry, Campos is also a master of the sustained open-form poem. Especially

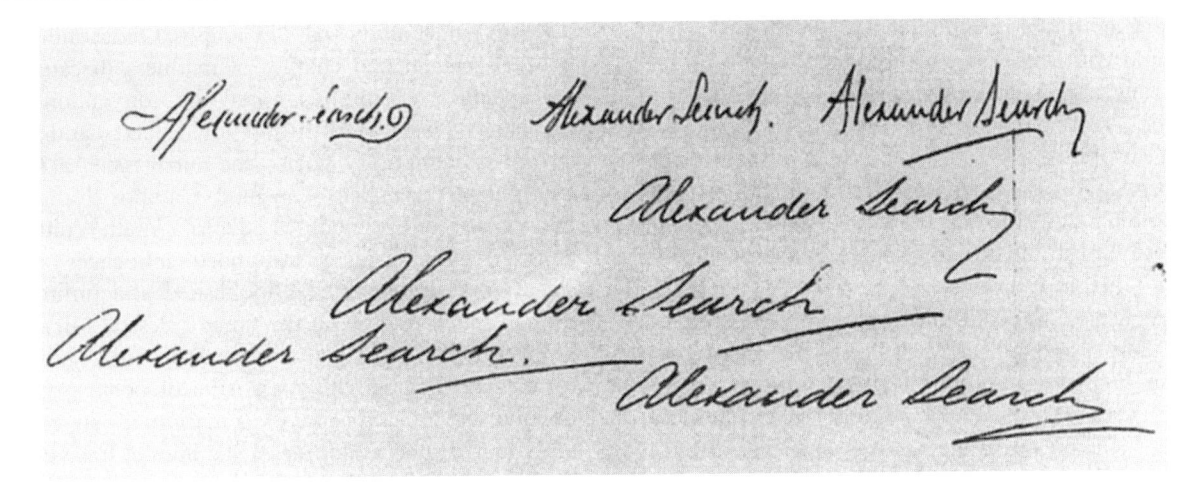

*Pessoa's experiments with a signature for one of his "heteronyms," or alter egos (Pessoa Archive, Biblioteca Nacional, Lisbon)*

remarkable among these poems are "Tabacaria" (Tobacco Shop, 1933), one of the great poetic meditations of the twentieth century; the sometimes savage "Ode marítima" (Maritime Ode, 1915); and the raucous "Saudação a Walt Whitman" (Salutation to Walt Whitman, 1915), which greets the American poet as "Grande pederasta roçando-te contra a diversidade das cousas" (Great pederast brushing up against the diversity of things).

Of Pessoa's many fictional companions, Campos was the closest to his creator, even participating, at times, in the actual public and private events of the poet's daily life. Pessoa assigns to him a date and hour of birth, 15 October 1890, at 1:30 P.M., in Tavira. Pessoa describes the adult Campos as tall, thin, with a tendency to stoop, and in complexion somewhere between white and swarthy. He was, as Pessoa states, "typo vagamente de judeu portuguez, cabello porém liso e normalmente apartado ao lado, monoculo" (vaguely of the Portuguese Jewish type, with straight hair, therefore, normally parted to the side, a monocle). The artist Almada Negreiros took his cue from this description for the portrait of Campos he cut into the façade of the Faculdade de Letras building at the University of Lisbon.

Nowhere does Pessoa indicate that he had ever met either Reis or Caeiro. He did, however, become something of an intimate with Campos. This extroverted but moody heteronym was entrusted with important tasks. As Pessoa's alter ego, he sometimes intervened in public debates with letters and polemical articles in the Lisbon newspapers. Sometimes he took on tasks that Pessoa found potentially unpleasant or tricky. After meeting with the poet in a Lisbon café, two of the young editors of the journal *Presença*, who were trumpeting Pessoa as Portugal's greatest modern poet, were convinced that they had met not with Fernando Pessoa but with the unpleasant Álvaro de Campos. The befuddled Monteiro and João Gaspar Simões were not the only ones to suffer the slights and sarcasm so characteristic of the unpredictable Campos. Even Pessoa was not exempt from Campos's often splenetic behavior. His most familiar heteronym went so far as to criticize publicly his creator's only published play.

Pessoa wrote the words he attributed to Campos, as he said, when he had an impulse to write some unknown thing: "quando sinto um subito impulso para escrever e não sei o quê" (when I feel a sudden impulse to write though I do not know what). As Campos said, in Pessoa's first contribution to *Presença:* "Fingir é conhecer-se" (To fake is to know oneself). At the end of Pessoa's life only Campos, of all his imagined companions, had not left him.

According to a January 1935 letter from Pessoa to Monteiro, Ricardo Reis was born in 1887 in Porto. Although Pessoa could not then recall the day or month, he claimed to have the information somewhere. Reis was a physician, having first been educated by the Jesuits. Pessoa calls him a "Latinist" by education and, by self-education, a "semi-Hellenist." The philosophy behind Reis's poetry, explains his brother Frederico (a semiheteronym), is "um epicurismo triste" (a sad Epicureanism). A monarchist in politics, Reis emigrated from Portugal to Brazil in 1919–the year, not entirely incidentally, following the assassination of the president of the Republic, Sidónio Paes. In 1935, at the time of Pessoa's letter to Monteiro, Reis was presumably still living somewhere in Brazil. Most, if not all, of Reis's conservatively formalist poetry is written in the form of what Pessoa called the ode. Those poems came, according to Pessoa, after abstract deliberation. Like Campos and Pessoa himself, Reis considered himself to be a "disciple" of Caeiro, about whom he wrote after Caeiro's death and with whom he corresponded during his lifetime. Reis also exchanged views on aesthetics with Campos. Audaciously, in *O ano da morte de Ricardo Reis* (The Year of the Death of Ricardo Reis, 1984), the novelist José Saramago brings Reis back to Lisbon in 1937 to encounter both the self left behind when he immigrated to Brazil and the ghost of his master, Pessoa, who had died in 1935.

As central as Caeiro, Campos, and Reis became to the temper and substance of Pessoa's growing posthumous literary reputation, it would be a mistake to think that they dominated his life as he was living it. Having brought into being, on the same day in 1914, those three important Portuguese poetic voices, Pessoa then returned promptly to his day-by-day literary tasks. Three weeks after that day of remarkable creativity, in early April, he took the time to answer a survey by the editors of the newspaper *República* asking the question: "Qual é o mais belo livro dos últimos trinta anos?" (What is the most beautiful book of the past thirty years?) His choice was *Pátria* (Homeland, 1894), Abílio Manuel Guerra Junqueiro's elegiac poem on patriotism, which he called not only the greatest work of the previous thirty years but also the greatest work ever produced in Portugal. He relegated Camões' *Os Lusíadas* (1572), surprisingly, to second place. In late spring he sent off his play *O marinheiro* to *A Águia*. In mid June Pessoa returned to Reis, composing the first of his odes. In early September, however, he complained in a letter to his friend and fellow poet Armando Côrtes-Rodrigues that with the outbreak of war all writing by Reis and Campos had come to a halt and that even Caeiro had managed to write no more than a few lines. He had made headway only with *Livro do desassossego*, the only writing that suited the darkness of his current temper.

By January 1915 Pessoa had recovered sufficiently from his sense of depression to set down his long poem *Antinous* (1918). In late February, in the Coimbra journal *A Galera* (The Gallery) he paid tribute to Antonio Nobre, the perfectionist poet of *Só* (Alone, 1892). Shortly thereafter, Pessoa turned to planning, financing, and founding a new journal, an idea that seems to have first surfaced when Caeiro and his other major heteronyms made their appearance. The new journal, *Orpheu,* aimed at selecting new talent and providing it with meaningful direction.

The group that brought out the first issue of *Orpheu* in April 1915 included (besides Pessoa) Sá-Carneiro, Negreiros, Ronald de Carvalho, Luís de Montalvor, Côrtes-Rodrigues, and António Ferro. Pessoa contributed *O marinheiro* under his own name, and "Ode triunfal" (Triumphal Ode) and "Opiário" (Opium Eater) under that of Campos. Occasioning outcries of scandal and charges of madness (because the work defied or simply ignored the conventions and familiar concerns of both traditional poetry and mainstream contemporary poets), the initial issue of *Orpheu* sold out in three weeks. In June, Campos drafted the first version of his poem "Saudação a Walt Whitman," celebrating one of the greatest poetic influences on Pessoa's work. It remained unpublished and unfinished, though much revised, at the time of Pessoa's death. In the second issue of *Orpheu,* which appeared in July, editor Pessoa included his own suite of poems "Chuva oblíqua" and Campos's "Ode marítíma," an exuberantly futurist poem running to 904 lines of free verse. A third issue of *Orpheu* reached the page-proof stage but went no further when the money to cover the costs of printing ran out. Those pages included, besides a clutch of Sá-Carneiro's poems and Almada Negreiros's long poem "A scena do odio" (The Scene of Hatred), Pessoa's own poems "Gladio" (Sword) and "Além-Deus" (Beyond-God), along with "Para além doutro oceano" (Beyond Another Sea), the only poem ever published by the heteronym C. Pacheco.

In the meantime, to support himself, Pessoa agreed to do several translations from English. The Livraria Clássica Editora of Lisbon published the first of these, *Compendio de theosophia* (Compendium of Philosophy) and *Os ideaes da theosophia* (Theosophical Ideas), Pessoa's translations of work by C. W. Leadbeater and Annie Besant, respectively. On 6 December 1915 Pessoa revealed in a letter to Sá-Carneiro that in doing these translations he had learned the doctrines of theosophy, bringing him to an intellectual crisis. He continued to translate similar books over the course of the next year or so. In 1916 the Livraria Clássica Editora brought out *A clarividência* (Clairvoyance) and *Auxiliares invisíveis* (Invisible Auxiliaries), Pessoa's translations of two other works by Leadbeater. Pessoa's translations of *A voz do silencio* (The Voice of Silence) and *Luz sobre o caminho e O karma* (Light over the Way and Karma), both of unidentified authorship, appeared in the same series. He even considered becoming an astrologer but abandoned the idea. He later incorporated the ideas of theosophy, alchemy, and Masonic lore and ritual into several poems. The verses collected as "No túmulo de Christian Rosencreutz" (In the Tomb of Christian Rosencreutz) and published posthumously by Monteiro in *Poesias* in 1942 are typical of Pessoa's poetry in this vein.

Earlier in 1916, Sá-Carneiro, Pessoa's best friend and fellow poet, had written him from Paris saying that he intended to commit suicide. After putting off the date several times, Sá-Carneiro died of strychnine poisoning in his room at the Hotel de Nice on 26 April.

Pessoa became his literary executor, taking on the tasks of publishing his poems in journals and planning for a collected works. In April, Pessoa published in *Exílio* a book review and his own poem, "Hora absurda" (Absurd Hour). In September the third issue of *Orpheu* was announced but was never published. Also in September he published in *Terra Nossa* (Our Land) a major orthonymic poem, "A ceifeira" (The Reaper), a critical poem "answering" William Wordsworth's "Solitary Reaper" (1807). On 4 September he announced to a friend that he had made "a great change" in his life. He had dropped the circumflex over the "o" in his surname. Intending to publish in English, he thought it wise to "dis-adapt" himself to the circumflex, because it might be injurious to the cosmopolitan image he hoped to encourage. In the first issue of the journal *Centauro* (Centaur), dated October–December 1916, the orthonymic Pessoa published "Passos da cruz" (Steps of the Cross), the first poem of what turned out to be a sequence of fourteen sonnets.

On 1 July 1917, Pessoa published under his own name the poem "A casa branca nau preta" (The Black Ship White House) as part of the series of futurist poems the Faro newspaper *O Heraldo* (The Herald) was then publishing. Filippo Tommasso Marinetti's Italian futurist movement and its gospel of action in the arts, launched at the end of the first decade of the twentieth century, had quickly spread to Paris and several other centers of Europe. Its more-or-less official arrival in Lisbon came only with the publication of the first issue of *Portugal Futurista* in November 1917. Pessoa contributed generously to the issue, both under his own name and under that of Campos. Under his own name Pessoa contributed two poetic series, "A Múmia" (The Mummy) and "Ficções do interludio" (Fictions of the Interlude), and under Campos's name, a manifesto in prose excoriating all recent literary movements and virtually all European and English writers. In its title, "Ultimatum," Campos evokes the memory of one of his country's darkest hours: when the British, in 1890, compelled the Portuguese to withdraw from African territory that they had claimed for themselves. The issue also included a transcription of Almada Negreiros's notorious lecture, "Ultimatum futurista às gerações portuguesas do século XX" (Futurist Ultimatum to the Portuguese Generations of the Twentieth Century), originally delivered in Lisbon at the Teatro República on 14 April 1917 and angrily received. As expected, the police confiscated the first and only issue of *Portugal Futurista*.

In 1917 Pessoa offered the London publisher Constable "The Mad Fiddler," a collection of English-language poems to be published under his own name. He was turned down. Pessoa then published in

*Ofélia Queiroz, with whom Pessoa began a romance in 1920 (from Martin Claret, ed.,* O pensamento vivo de Fernando Pessoa, *1986; Thomas Cooper Library, University of South Carolina)*

Lisbon two chapbooks of English-language poetry under his own name and at his own expense. *Antinous* (1918), a late-Edwardian poem narrated in explicitly sensual terms, tells the story of the Emperor Hadrian's grief at the death of his lover, a young man he later attempts to elevate into a deity. *35 Sonnets* (1918), on the other hand, is a sequence of poems written in a strikingly original neo-Elizabethan style. In these, he intellectualizes and objectifies the emotions of an unnamed, unidentified, and never described poet-speaker. Sent to newspapers and libraries in England and Scotland, the poems received only a few perfunctory notices and brief reviews.

Also during this period, asserted Pessoa, Caeiro wrote his "Poemas inconjunctos" (Unassembled Poems)–despite the contradictory "fact," established elsewhere, that Caeiro had died in 1915. To a potential future contributor Pessoa detailed plans for a new journal, which would be the work of Portuguese writers but would be published, alternately, in English and French. The journal would present the true selves of the Portuguese (not the "servile" Portuguese all too familiar to foreigners) and would contribute to the creation of an authentic Portuguese culture. This journal did not materialize. Pessoa's translation of Elizabeth Barrett Browning's poem "Catarina to Camoens," first published in 1911 in the multivolume *A biblioteca internacional de obras célebres* (International Library of Famous Works), was reprinted in Mário de Almeida's "Os sonetos From the Portuguese e Elisabeth Barrett Brow[n]ing," a thesis published in Coimbra. In London, in January 1920, the *Athenaeum,* whose contributors included Aldous Huxley, E. M. Forster, Bertrand Russell, T. S. Eliot, Conrad Aiken, and Virginia Woolf, published Pessoa's "Meantime," a dreamy poem of love and loss culled from his unpublished collection "The Mad Fiddler." It was the only poem he managed to place in Great Britain.

At the end of February 1920 Pessoa contributed the poem "À memoria do presidente Sidónio Paes" (To the Memory of President Sidónio Paes) to *Acção* (Action), a politically and socially conservative newspaper. In this somewhat belated tribute, Pessoa elegizes the Cromwellian figure of the powerful and autocratic president assassinated in Lisbon at the Rossio train station on 14 December 1918. It is of more than passing interest to those interested in Pessoa's often far from liberal politics that in 1940, five years after his death, "À memoria do presidente Sidónio Paes"–retitled "À memória do presidente-rei Sidónio Paes" (To the Memory of the President-King Sidónio Paes)–was republished as a pamphlet, presumably by Pessoa's friend and business associate Augusto Ferreira Gomes, an act not out of keeping with the norms and policies of Prime Minister António de Oliveira Salazar's autocratic state.

On 1 March 1920, at the age of thirty-one, Pessoa sent off his first love letter. It was directed to Ofélia Queiroz, a nineteen-year-old office worker employed by one of the firms for which Pessoa handled French and English correspondence. On 25 March he moved to Rua Coelho da Rocha, 26, to live with his now widowed mother and his siblings, who arrived in Lisbon five days later. He lived there for the rest of his life. At a crucial moment in his affair with Queiroz, his only known love interest, Pessoa deputized Campos to inform her that his mental illness was such that he could not meet with her as planned. Queiroz was so upset at being visited by Pessoa's messenger that, maintaining Pessoa's fiction, she insisted he never again send that "mauzinho" (bad boy) to visit her. In mid October 1920 Pessoa revealed to Queiroz that he was seriously considering having himself committed to a psychiatric hospital. At the end of November he sent a letter breaking off the courtship.

Also in 1920 Pessoa wrote a series titled *Inscriptions,* short English poems patterned after elegies in the *Greek Anthology*. In 1921 he spent a modest inheritance to set up "Olisipo," a combined printing shop and publishing firm, a commercial venture that, like all of Pessoa's business ventures, was doomed to a short existence. But under this imprint, before going out of business, he did manage to publish his *English Poems I–II* (a republication of *Antinous,* revised, with *Inscriptions*) and *English Poems III* (*Epithalamium,* a rather frank marriage poem written in 1913).

By the early 1920s Pessoa had abandoned his overtures to the English press and publishers. Those early, largely unsuccessful efforts at self-promotion in the newspapers and journals of Great Britain gave way, after a decade of trying to establish himself as both an English poet and a Portuguese writer, to a more concentrated focus on building a career in Portugal as a critic-poet-editor. He continued to compose both prose and poetry in English, however, until the end of his life.

*Contemporanea* was an important journal that ran to nine issues (May 1922–March 1923) with a tenth somewhat later. Its first issue included Pessoa's first published piece of fiction, *O banqueiro anarquista* (The Anarchist Banker). In this satiric novella of social and economic ideas Pessoa presents an extended monologue on the realities of anarchism, espoused somewhat paradoxically by a highly successful banker. The first issue of *Contemporanea* presented "Poemas de Paris" (Poems of Paris), a selection of quatrains by Sá-Carneiro submitted to the journal by Pessoa in his capacity as his friend's literary executor. Pessoa's printing house, Olisipo, also managed to publish a second edition of *Canções* (Songs, 1920), poems by António Botto, a contemporary whose work Pessoa persistently defended and championed over the years. In June *Contemporanea* published Sá-Carneiro's poem "O Lord." In July it published Pessoa's essay on Botto and the course of aesthetic idealism in Portugal, and in October, two poems by Pessoa appeared (under the collective title "Mar portuguez" [Portuguese Sea]). The issue also included a letter from Campos that he signed from Newcastle upon Tyne, keeping up the fiction of his English adventures. In the same issue appeared Álvaro Maia's "Literatura de Sodoma" (Literature of Sodom), an essay attacking Pessoa's advocacy of sensual and literary aestheticism as evidenced in his essay on Botto. In December *Contemporanea* published both Pessoa's poem "Natal" (Christmas) and Campos's "Soneto já antigo" (An Old Sonnet), a poem replete with references to the heteronym's putative English experiences.

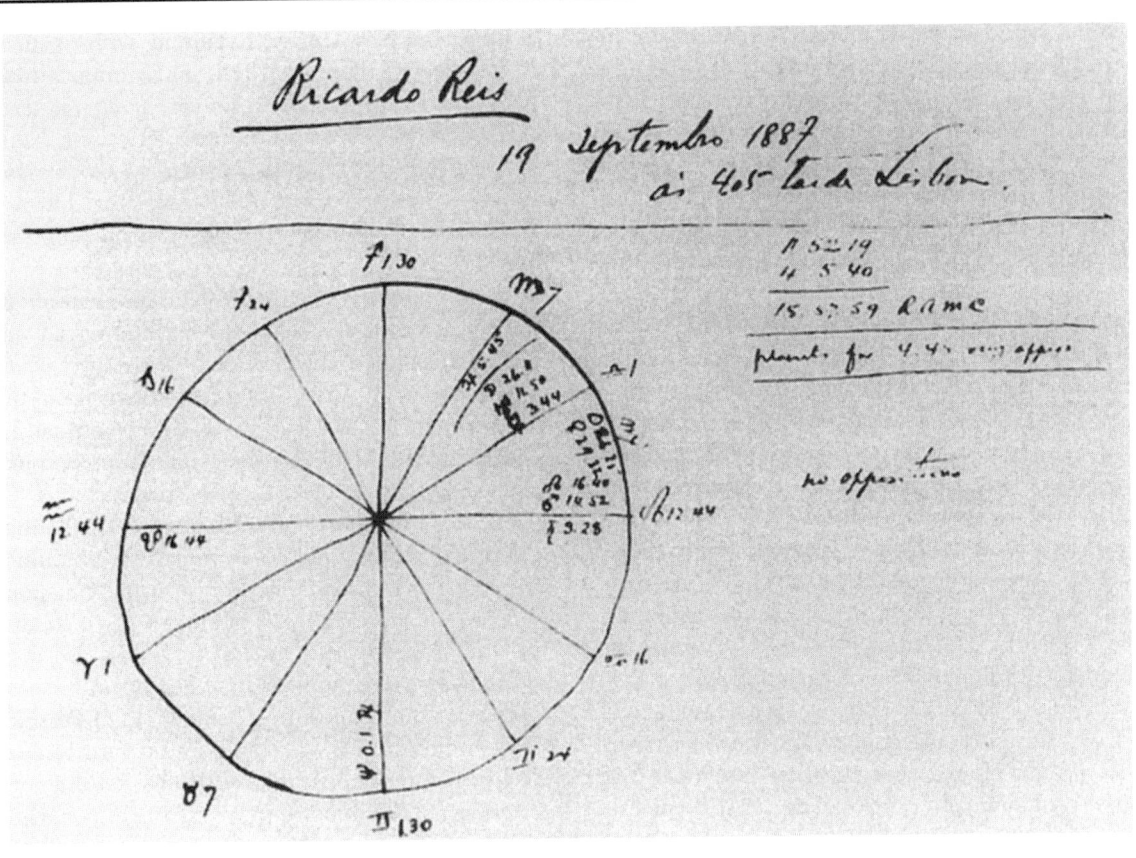

*The horoscope Pessoa charted for another of the personalities he created (Pessoa Archive, Biblioteca Nacional, Lisbon)*

In January 1923 *Contemporanea* published a three-poem sequence in French that Pessoa later dismissed as whimsical. In February, Olisipo published Raul Leal's *Sodoma divinizada* (Sodomy Praised), a defense of Pessoa's position as expressed in the May 1922 issue of *Contemporanea*. In February 1923 *Contemporanea* published Campos's poem "Lisbon Revisited (1923)," the title of which not only shows off the poet's English training but also suggests Campos's sense of himself as something of an exile now visiting his nation's capital city. It also included Pessoa's review of the morally controversial "novella-film" *Sáchá* (a text by Francisco Manuel Cabral Metello), presented as an open letter to its author. As was Pessoa's custom, he used the occasion to put forth theories of poetry and aesthetics. In March *Contemporanea* published "Spell," an English-language poem by Pessoa from "The Mad Fiddler." On 6 March of that year, the Liga de Acção dos Estudantes de Lisboa, a conservative, Catholic-oriented organization, distributed a manifesto attacking the "literature of sodomy" as exemplified and promoted in recent publications–the second edition of Botto's *Canções* and Leal's *Sodoma divinizada*. Pessoa reacted personally to this attack by having Campos reply to the student attack with a manifesto titled "Aviso por causa da moral" (Warning in the Cause of Morality), a broadside. In April, Pessoa found it necessary to distribute his own manifesto both defending Leal and answering the specifics of the student manifesto. At the same time, Leal published a second manifesto, this one aimed more directly at the Catholic Church as the force behind the protesting students. The cause was lost when the authorities cracked down on the publication of the so-called literature of sodomy.

In February 1924, the four-hundredth anniversary of Camões's birth, Pessoa joined in commemorating Camões in the pages of the *Diário de Notícias*, concluding cryptically: "A epopeia que Camões escreveu pede que aguardemos a epopeia que ele não pode escrever. A maior coisa nele é o não ser grande bastante para os semi-deuses que celebrou" (The epic that Camões wrote asks us to await the epic that he was unable to write. The greatest thing about him is his not being great enough for the half-gods he celebrated). That same year Pessoa joined the artist Ruy Vaz in the editing of a new and ambitious journal called *Athena*. This journal, which lasted five issues, ending in February 1925, became for a time the major outlet for Pessoa's work in various genres. Its first issue came out in October and included eight sonnets by the recently deceased Henrique Rosa, the brother of Pessoa's stepfather; twenty odes by Reis (his first appearance in print, more than a decade after he had first emerged from Pessoa's imagination); and Pessoa's translation of Edgar Allan Poe's "The Raven" (1845). The second issue, in November, included Pessoa's appreciative biographical essay on Sá-Carneiro, along with six of his friend's "final" poems; Pessoa's translation of an excerpt from Walter Pater's seminal collection *Studies in the Renaissance;* Pessoa's own poems based on themes from the *Greek Anthology;* and the first part of an important essay attributed to Campos presenting his ideas on the subject of a non-Aristotelian metaphysics. In November 1924 Pessoa granted an interview to the *Diário de Lisboa* on the subject of *Athena*. In the December issue of *Athena* Pessoa published sixteen of his own poems (some of them for a second time), including "Sacadura Cabral," "Gladio" (Sword), "Ó sino da minha aldeia" (O Bell of My Village), and "Ela canta, pobre ceifeira" (She Sings, Poor Reaper); his translations of two stories by the popular American writer of short stories O. Henry; and the first installment of Campos's programmatic essay calling for a theory of aesthetics that would not be based on Aristotelian principles. Pessoa also continued his publication of the work of Rosa, with three additional sonnets. Also in 1924, the journal *Folhas de Arte* reproduced, in facsimile, in its inaugural issue, the holograph manuscript for Pessoa's poem titled "Canção" (Song), beginning "Silfos ou gnomos tocam?" (Do sylphs or gnomes play music?).

Caeiro, whose poems were first set down by Pessoa in 1914, finally made an initial appearance in print in the January 1925 issue of *Athena* with a healthy selection of poems from the poetic sequence *O guardador de rebanhos.* The great theme of the poet who called himself a "místico materialista" (materialist mystic) is stated in his "Poem IX," in which he declares:

Sou um guardador de rebanhos.
O rebanho é os meus pensamentos
E os meus pensamentos são todos sensações.

(I am a keeper of sheep.
The herd is my thoughts
And my thoughts are all sensations).

The same issue also included the second half of Campos's essay calling for a non-Aristotelian aesthetics, along with Pessoa's translation of two of Poe's most famous poems, "Annabel Lee" (1849) and "Ulalume" (1847). In the last issue of *Athena,* in February 1925, besides sixteen poems selected from Caeiro's "Poemas inconjunctos," Pessoa published his translation of another story by Henry. Beginning with its inaugural issue, dated 1 January 1926, and running until mid February 1927, the Lisbon journal *Illustração* serialized *A letra encarnada,* Pessoa's translation of Nathaniel Hawthorne's 1850 novel, *The Scarlet Letter.* Pessoa was not, however, identified as the translator. This translation was not published in book form during Pessoa's lifetime.

In January 1926 the entrepreneurial Pessoa joined his brother-in-law in a new commercial venture, the publication of the *Revista de Comercio e Contabilidade* (Magazine of Business and Accounting). From the outset Pessoa contributed regularly to this journal. Late in May he took the time to answer an inquiry, conducted nationally, by *O Jornal do Comercio e das Colonias* (Journal of Business and the Colonies) on the theme of "Portugal, vasto imperio" (Portugal, a Vast Empire). In May *Contemporanea* published his orthonymic poem "O menino da sua mãe" (His Mother's Boy), following it in the July–October issue with his poem titled "Rubaiyat." The publication of this poem was the only outward indication during his lifetime of Pessoa's sustained interest in the British poet Edward FitzGerald's putative translations published as *Rubáiyát of Omar Khayyám* (1859), attested to by dozens of poems written and translations made by Pessoa through the years. Pessoa's own poems employing the form of the *rubai* were not collected until 1997, when they were published in an expensive illustrated edition under the title of *Canções de beber na obra de Fernando Pessoa,* which casually grouped them all under the debatable rubric of "drinking songs."

Through 1926 Pessoa's name or that of Campos was signed to a variety of publications, the most important of which was "Lisbon Revisited (1926)" in June in *Contemporanea,* a poem in which Campos complains he is "estrangeiro aqui como em tôda a parte" (a stranger here as I am everywhere else). Newspapers reprinted Pessoa's articles on commerce, business, and organization from the *Revista de Comercio e Contabilidade*. In October the first installment of his translation of an Anna Katharine Green detective story came out in *Sol: Diário independente*. A projected later number of *Contemporanea* survives only in a handful of proofs, but those pages include "D. Sebastião," Pessoa's two-stanza lyric expressed in the posthumous voice of Portugal's doomed young king, as well as "Quasi" (Nearly), a poem by Campos.

The year 1927 was an important one for Pessoa and his literary reputation as a poet. On 8 April 1927, in its third number, the Coimbra-based journal *Presença*– which was the force behind and became the voice of what has been called the second modernist movement in Portugal–published the young editor José Régio's essay "Da geração modernista" (On the Modernist Generation). In this work Régio sought to define Portugal's place in the international modernist movement by invoking the names of Sá-Carneiro, Almada Negreiros, and Pessoa. After having established contact with Pessoa, the *Presença* editors were able to publish, in the 4 June issue, poems by Pessoa ("Marinha" [Seascape]), Campos ("Ambiente" [Ambient]), and Sá-Carneiro ("Ápice" [Summit]). They followed up in the July issue with three odes by Reis. Pessoa's only other publication in 1927 came in *O Imparcial*, which, in June, published his appreciation of *Poemas* (1927) by Montalvor, one of the original editors of *Orpheu*.

In mid March 1928 *Presença* published two additional odes by Reis, a short poem by Campos ("Escripto num livro abandonado em viagem" [Written in a Book Abandoned in Transit]), a poem by Pessoa ("Qualquer música" [Some Music or Other]), and another poem by Sá-Carneiro. In November, *Presença* published Pessoa's poem "Depois da feira" (After the Fair) and his unsigned checklist of Sá-Carneiro's published work; in December it published a primary bibliography for Pessoa's own work, which appeared under Monteiro's signature but was actually prepared by Pessoa himself.

Also in 1927 came Pessoa's first appearances in *O Notícias Ilustrado*, beginning with Campos's "Apostilha" (Marginalia), a poem that sounds that heteronym's customary note of melancholy and depression, followed by Pessoa's essay on Portuguese provincialism, a short biographical piece on Poe, a poetic tribute to the poet Gomes Leal, and, on the ninth anniversary of the World War I armistice, a reprinting of his poem "O menino da sua mãe."

In late 1928 Pessoa published a pamphlet titled *O interregno: Defeza e justificação da dictadura militar em Portugal* (Interregnum: Defense of and Justification for a Military Dictatorship in Portugal), a bold apologia for what was considered to be a temporary dictatorship. According to Pessoa scholars, this intervention in current politics in a time of crisis had been written months earlier, and by the time it was published, it no longer reflected the poet's views on a military dictatorship as the necessary solution to the real problems of Portugal's political chaos. Pessoa omitted this publication from the bibliography he prepared for *Presença*.

In 1929 Pessoa and Botto edited and published the first installment of *Antologia de poemas portuguêzes modernos* (Anthology of Modern Portuguese Poems). Pessoa wrote the unsigned preface. He also continued his association with *O Notícias Ilustrado*. "Prece" (Prayer), identified as lines taken from the poem "Mar portuguez," and reprinted from the October 1922 issue of *Contemporenea*, appeared in the January issue. In April he answered a

*Dust jacket for the only collection of poetry in Portuguese that Pessoa published during his lifetime (James S. Jaffe Rare Books/Lame Duck Books, lot 93, n.d.)*

survey on Portuguese music, taking the opportunity to comment on "sebastianism," the symbolic meaning of the Portuguese longing for the return of King Sebastian. A poem taken from his own "Passos da cruz" series appeared in the April issue, and for the July issue Pessoa provided "Tomamos a villa depois de um intenso bombardeamento" (We Took the Village after Heavy Bombing), an antiwar poem written a decade or so earlier.

Throughout 1929 Pessoa also wrote regularly for *Presença*. To its January issue, Campos contributed "Gazetilha" (News in Brief), a rather pedestrian poem naming those contemporary heroes for whom the future holds only obscurity, and to the April–May issue he contributed "Apontamento" (Note), a poem entertaining the fond thought that perhaps a surviving shard from his shattered soul will someday be seen by the gods. In the first issue of *A Revista da Solução Editora* (The Review of Solution Publications) Campos continued the publication of his poetic record of his melancholia, acedia, and procrastination with "Addiamento" (Postponement). In the succeeding issue Pessoa published "Trecho" (Excerpt), a prose fragment from *Livro do desassossego,* the work-in-progress attributed to Bernardo Soares. And in the fourth issue he published "Outro trecho" (Another Excerpt), an additional fragment from, as Pessoa put it, Soares's "composition." To the same issue he contributed Campos's poem "A Fernando Pessoa depois de ler o seu drama statico 'O marinheiro' em *Orpheu 1*" (To Fernando Pessoa after Reading his Static Drama 'The Sailor' in *Orpheu 1*). This complaint about Pessoa's own play was published fourteen years after the play had appeared in the first issue of *Orpheu*. It exemplifies one aspect of the interplay among his major heteronyms and himself.

In early September 1929 an anxious Pessoa expressed the desire to leave Lisbon and move up the coast to Cascais so that he could bring his otherwise unspecified "work" to completion. Yet, just two days later, on 11 September, Pessoa began once again to correspond with Ofélia Queiroz, after a silence of nearly a decade. Whatever passion Pessoa had felt the first time could not be rekindled, and this reconciliation of sorts was short-lived. Four months later, in January 1930, Pessoa again broke off with Queiroz, this time permanently. He explained that he had obligations to the life of the mind: "quero organizar essa vida de pensamento e de trabalho *meu*" (I want to organize that life of thought and of work that is *mine*). Except for a couple of additional letters, there appears to have been no further contact between them. Queiroz, who did not marry until after Pessoa's death, lived well into her nineties.

Also in 1930 Pessoa initiated his correspondence with Aleister Crowley, offering a correction to the English poet-magician-necromancer's reading of his own horoscope. Impressed, Crowley visited with Pessoa in Lisbon. He arrived on 2 September. In late September, newspapers reported that Crowley had disappeared mysteriously off the seacoast beyond Cascais, at the Boca do Inferno. In October Pessoa wrote about the inexplicable circumstances surrounding Crowley's disappearance for *O Notícias Ilustrado,* and in December he granted *Girassol* (Sunflower) an interview on the subject. Crowley's disappearance was later found to be a hoax when he turned up alive in Germany. To what extent Pessoa was in on Crowley's escapade has never been satisfactorily established.

To the June–July issue of *Presença,* Campos contributed "Anniversario" (Birthday), a poem about childhood birthdays that is the source of "This Was a Wonderful Night" (1987), a poem by the contemporary American poet Gerald Stern. The same issue included another excerpt from *Livro do desassossego*. In December *Presença* published "O último sortilegio" (The Last Sortilege), a poem Pessoa assigned to himself.

For its January–February 1931 issue Pessoa sent *Presença* the "eighth poem" of Caeiro's *O guardador de rebanhos,* which fantasizes longingly on play in the domestic life of the infant Jesus (a poem that, after Pessoa's death, evoked much critical commentary and conflicting interpretations), along with a complementary essay by Campos about "his Master, Caeiro." The March–June issue of the same year was dominated by Pessoa's work, including Campos's poem "Trapo" (Rag), Pessoa's poem "O andaime" (The Scaffold), two odes by Reis, "O penúltimo poema" (The Penultimate Poem) by Caeiro, and a poem by Sá-Carneiro. In its July–October issue appeared Pessoa's translation of Crowley's poem "Hymn to Pan" (1929), a sign to the editors of *Presença* that Pessoa, unlike them, was also interested in the occult.

Pessoa chose to contribute the next five fragments from *Livro do desassossego* not to *Presença,* however, but to the autumn issue of *Descobrimento* (Discovery), followed up, in the winter 1931–1932 issue, by the orthonymic poem "Guia me a só razão" (Guided by Reason Alone) and Campos's poem beginning "Quero acabar entre rosas, porque as amei na infância" (I want to end up among roses because I loved them in childhood). Later in the year, to the summer–autumn issue, he contributed a book review of *Poemas* (1932) by Paulino de Oliveira. To *Presença,* for its November 1931–February 1932 issue, he sent Campos's poem "Ah, um soneto" (Ah, a Sonnet), along with a fragment from *Livro do desassossego,* followed by an ode by Reis in its February issue. The March–May issue of *Presença* carried a poem by Pessoa, "Iniciação" (Initiation), along with Monteiro's piece chastising Pessoa for having written a laudatory preface to a now forgotten book of poems by Luiz Pedro, an acquaintance. After characterizing the poems as juvenile, derivative, and artificial, Monteiro, who had started out his essay by calling Pessoa "o maior poeta Português de hoje" (the greatest Portuguese poet of the day), attacks Pessoa the critic. Although there seems to have been no correspondence exchanged between Pessoa and his young critic over the matter of Pedro's modest poems, Pessoa did not remain entirely silent about Monteiro's criticism. Instead of answering him directly, he countered with a poem. He sent *Presença* verses that could be taken as his own statement on the poet's endemic insincerity, both in intention and in the art of poetry itself. That the poet and the critic must be sincere was a given in Monteiro's piece. It was a tenet dear as well to Régio and Simões, his co-editors at *Presença*. In November, with no sign whatsoever that Pessoa's poem "Autopscicografia" (Autopsychography) might be construed as a reply to Monteiro's criticism, *Presença* published the poem that to this day remains Pessoa's best known and most widely translated poem, which opens:

> O poeta é um fingidor.
> Finge tão completamente
> Que chega a fingir que é dor
> A dor que deveras sente.
>
> (The poet is a forger.
> He forges so completely
> That he forges as pain
> The pain that is truly his).

In early June 1931 the daily newspaper *Revolução* published another fragment from *Livro do desassossego*. In November, in the monthly *Fama* (Fame), Pessoa published an essay on the "estado mental dos nossos homens de talento" (the mental state of our men of talent). Continuing to follow his custom of contributing to the first issues of new journals, he published in *A Revista* what appears to have been the last fragment of *Livro do desassossego* to achieve print in his lifetime. For Botto's *Cartas que me foram devolvidas* (Letters that were Returned to Me, 1932), he updated his sympathetic essay "António Botto e o ideal estético creador" (Antonio Botto and the Ideal Aesthetic Creator). Pessoa, who thought himself to be part Jewish (like Campos), wrote a preface for *Alma errante* (Errant Soul, 1932), a book of poems by Eliezer Kamenezky, a Ukrainian Jew living in Lisbon.

During 1933 *Presença* continued its determined effort to promote Pessoa as Portugal's greatest living poet. In February it published a somewhat didactic poem by Reis, which advises:

> Para ser grande, sê inteiro: nada
>     Teu exagera ou exclui.
>
> (To be great, to be whole: nothing
>     Your own exaggerate or exclude).

In April the orthonymic poem "Isto" (This) appeared. The verses return to Pessoa's theme of poetic insincerity, reinforcing the message of "Autopsicografia," along with "Crise lamentável" (Lamentable Crisis), a poem by Sá-Carneiro. To the July number Pessoa contributed "Tabacaria," Campos's modernist masterpiece. Assigning the poem a place and a date–"Lisboa, 15 de Janeiro de 1928"–Pessoa locates it in troubling times, exactly three months before the military dictator General António Oscar de Fragoso Carmona was proclaimed the president of Portugal and Salazar became minister of finance. Exemplary of Campos's melding of concrete experience with meditative sadness, "Tabacaria" is an expression of the paradoxical fusing of its putative author's angst and ennui. Contrasted with Campos's

*Pessoa in 1935, the year he died (from Simões,* Vida e obra de Fernando Pessoa, *1987; Thomas Cooper Library, University of South Carolina)*

optimistic "Ultimatum," which appeared in the midst of World War I, "Tabacaria" becomes not only a revelation of its author's depressed spirit but also an implied criticism of the national situation. The image of a child's unselfconscious act of eating chocolates, which haunts the poem, furnishes Campos with an ironic analogy for what he considers to be his own wasted life.

As much as he had committed himself to *Presença* from the beginning, Pessoa did not forgo the opportunity to publish in other journals as well. In June, for example, he returned to *Revolução* with a reprinting of "Mar portuguez," a suite of twelve poems on historical themes. Pessoa also continued to work on behalf of his friends; he wrote an afterword for Botto's *António* (1933), and he prepared for publication a collection of Sá-Carneiro's poetry, which did not appear.

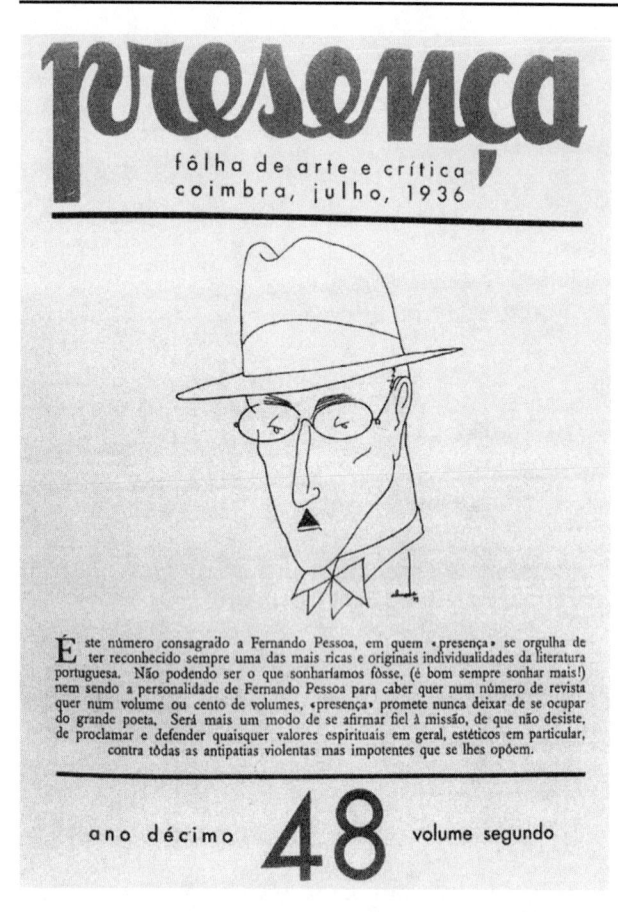

*Cover for the Pessoa commemorative issue of the influential journal to which he had contributed frequently (from Darlene J. Sadlier, An Introduction to Fernando Pessoa: Modernism and the Paradoxes of Authorship, 1998; Thomas Cooper Library, University of South Carolina)*

In February 1934 Pessoa published one of his most richly suggestive pieces in the newspaper *Fradique*. Its subject was the English poet Samuel Taylor Coleridge's anecdote about the "Man from Porlock" that fatefully and conclusively interrupted his composition of "Kubla Khan" (1816). In March, Pessoa published the uplifting poem "Fresta" (Opening) in the journal *Momento*. In May *Presença* published Pessoa's poem "Eros e Psique" (Eros and Psyche). In its double issue for July–August, the journal *O Mundo Português* (Portuguese World), which carried the explanatory subtitle of "Revista de Cultura e Propaganda, Arte e Literaturas Coloniais" (A Review of Culture and Propaganda, Colonial Art and Literature), published as a "Tríptico" (Triptych) three of Pessoa's historical poems: "O Infante D. Henrique," "D. João o Segundo," and "Afonso de Albuquerque." Pessoa also contributed a preface in the same historical vein to *Quinto império* (Fifth Empire), a book of patriotic poems by his friend Augusto Ferreira Gomes.

In December 1934 Pessoa published *Mensagem*, the one book of his poetry in Portuguese that he saw into print. Based on a plan possibly dating back two decades, *Mensagem* is modernist in form but traditional in subject matter. It comprises fifty-four discrete poems, largely elegiac, orphic, and prophetic, on Portuguese history and culture.

"Ulysses," the third poem of the work, sets the stage and ventures a tone for the reader's response to the principles, prophecies, glories, and disasters dramatized in the poems that, collectively, compose the major master narrative of Portuguese history. Imbedded in its accumulation of lyrics is the "message" of the poem. A wry meditation on the idea that myth ("the nothing that is everything") shapes reality and empowers life, "Ulysses" poses larger questions concerning the course and predictive nature of Portuguese history. Interpretations of the meaning of *Mensagem* and of its author's intentions and overall tone are varied and contradictory–ranging from the unquestionably patriotic, which sees in the poem the prophecy of a "Fifth Empire" of the spirit for contemporary Portugal, to a deeply ironic vision of the sources for Portugal's history of decadence and diminishment.

Entered in the Antero de Quental poetry competition sponsored by the Secretariado de Propaganda Nacional under the direction of Ferro–a member of the original *Orpheu* group–*Mensagem* was awarded what amounted to a second first prize. The other first prize in this first-time competition went to *A romaria* (The Pilgrimage, 1934) by Vasco Reis, a Franciscan cleric. In mid December the newspaper *Diário de Notícias* published an interview with Pessoa and reprinted three poems from *Mensagem*: "O Infante" (The Infant), "O mostrengo" (The Monstrous One), and "Prece." In late December the same newspaper reprinted Pessoa's seasonal poem "Natal."

On 4 January 1935 the *Diário de Notícias* published Pessoa's seemingly favorable but ambiguous commentary on *A romaria,* and two days later *O Notícias Ilustrado* reprinted two poems from *Mensagem*. In mid January, in reply to Monteiro's questioning, Pessoa offered his detailed account of the genesis of Caeiro, Reis, and Campos. In the *Diário de Lisboa,* in early February, Pessoa published a defense of "secret societies," which were under governmental and legislative fire. The piece was altered in wording and by cuts for clandestine publication as a pamphlet titled *A maçonaria vista por Fernando Pessoa* (Freemasonry as Seen by Fernando Pessoa). In March, in the newspaper *Diário de Lisboa,* Pessoa championed Botto's *Ciume* (Jealousy, 1934), his last effort on behalf of his friend's poetry. In the same month he composed his first poem on the subject of Salazar and his Estado Novo (New State, as the regime was called), following it up in

July with other bits of satirical doggerel. Pessoa did not publish these poems. In *Momento,* in April, he published the poem "Intervalo" (Interval). In November, complying with a request from Almada Negreiros for contributions to his new journal *Sudoeste* (Southwest), Pessoa sent him notes, one by Campos and another by himself, along with an orthonymic poem, "Conselho" (Advice), and a poem by Sá-Carneiro.

On 29 November 1935 the suddenly ill Pessoa was admitted to the Hospital de S. Luís. He died the next day, possibly of cirrhosis of the liver. His last written words, set down in pencil on the eve of his death, were, significantly for this bilingual, bicultural poet, in English: "I know not what to-morrow will bring."

Obituaries appeared throughout Portugal and its overseas possessions, including the Azores and Madeira. In December it was announced that the next issue of *Presença* would be dedicated to Pessoa in memoriam. Published in July, it featured an elegy by Gil Vaz and tributes or critical pieces by Leal, Montalvor, Carlos Queiroz (nephew of Ofélia Queiroz), Pierre Hourcade, Guilherme de Castilho, and Simões. Of Pessoa's work, the memorial issue included fragments quoted from Pessoa's love letters to Ofélia Queiroz (supplied by her nephew), though their recipient was not identified, along with a scrap of Campos's prose. That there was so little original work by Pessoa in the memorial issue indicates that the editors had nothing on hand when the poet died suddenly. Indeed, nothing by Pessoa had appeared in *Presença* after May 1934.

If Fernando Pessoa did not contribute to *Presença* for the final eighteen months before his death, it was not because he had nothing to offer to the editors. In fact, he had left a trunk full of work, including many unpublished poems, essays, manifestos, stories, and notes of all sorts. Monteiro, Simões, and Montalvor began the task of preparing Pessoa's work for publication. The first volume to appear was *Poesia,* a general anthology of the poetry that Pessoa had published during his lifetime but had never been collected in book form. It was published by Confluência in 1942. Almost immediately, however, Ática announced that it would publish the *Obras completas de Fernando Pessoa* (Complete Works of Fernando Pessoa). Under the direction of Montalvor, this publisher began the project (after an introductory and critical volume published in 1942) with *Poesias de Álvaro de Campos* in 1944, a new edition of *Mensagem* in 1945, and *Poemas de Alberto Caeiro* and *Odes de Ricardo Reis* in 1946. These first volumes had an immediate and powerful impact on Portuguese writing. They also initiated the still increasing flow of editions, studies, and translations of Pessoa that have given his work an international readership, beyond the borders of the Portuguese-speaking world.

**Letters:**

Mário de Sá-Carneiro, *Cartas a Fernando Pessoa,* second edition, 2 volumes (Lisbon: Ática, 1992);

*Cartas de amor de Ofélia a Fernando Pessoa,* edited by Manuela Nogueira and Maria da Conceição Azevedo (Lisbon: Assírio & Alvim, 1996);

*Correspondência [de Fernando Pessoa] 1905–1935,* 2 volumes, edited by Manuela Parreira da Silva (Lisbon: Assírio & Alvim, 1999).

**Bibliographies:**

José Blanco, *Fernando Pessoa: Esboço de uma bibliografia* (Lisbon: Imprensa Nacional-Casa da Moeda/Centro de Estudos Pessoanos, 1983);

João Rui de Sousa, *Fotobibliografia de Fernando Pessoa* (Lisbon: Imprensa Nacional-Casa da Moeda/Biblioteca Nacional, 1988).

**Biographies:**

João Gaspar Simões, *Vida e obra de Fernando Pessoa: História duma geração,* 2 volumes (Lisbon: Bertrand, 1954; revised edition, Lisbon: Publicaçoes Dom Quixote, 1987);

Maria José de Lancastre, *Fernando Pessoa: Uma fotobiografia,* third edition (Lisbon: Imprensa Nacional-Casa da Moeda/Centro de Estudos Pessoanos, 1984);

Ángel Crespo, *La vida plural de Fernando Pessoa* (Barcelona: Seix Barral, 1988);

Robert Bréchon, *Étrange étranger: Une biographie de Fernando Pessoa* (Paris: Christian Bourgois, 1996).

**References:**

*Actas do 1º congresso internacional de estudos pessoanos* (Porto: Brasília/Centro de Estudos Pessoanos, 1979);

*Actas do 2º congresso internacional de estudos pessoanos* (Porto: Centro de Estudos Pessoanos, 1985);

[*Actas do 3º congresso internacional de estudos pessoanos*] *Um século de Pessoa: encontro International do centenário de Fernando Pessoa* (Lisbon: Secretaria de Estado da Cultura/Fundação Calouste Gulbenkian, 1990);

*Actas IV congresso internacional de estudos pessoanos (secção brasileira),* 2 volumes (Porto: Fundação Eng. António de Almeida, 1990);

*Actas IV congresso internacional de estudos pessoanos (secção norte-americana)* (Porto: Fundação Eng. António de Almeida, 2000);

Onésimo Teotónio Almeida, *Mensagem: Uma tentative de reinterpretação* (Angra do Heroísmo: Secretaria Regional da Educação e Cultura, 1987);

António Cirurgião, *O "Olhar esfíngico" da Mensagem de Pessoa* (Lisbon: Instituto de Cultura e Língua Portuguesa/Ministério da Educação, 1990);

Jacinto do Prado Coelho, *Diversidade e unidade em Fernando Pessoa,* eighth edition (Lisbon: Verbo, 1985);

Zbigniew Kotowicz, *Fernando Pessoa: Voices of a Nomadic Soul* (London: Menard, 1996);

Gilberto de Mello Kujawski, *Fernando Pessoa, o outro,* third edition (Petrópolis: Vozes, 1979);

George Rudolf Lind, *Estudos sobre Fernando Pessoa* (Lisbon: Imprensa Nacional-Casa da Moeda, 1981);

Teresa Rita Lopes, *Fernando Pessoa et le drame Symboliste: Heritage et creation,* second edition (Paris: Fondation Calouste Gulbenkian/Centre Culturel Portugais, 1985);

Lopes, *Pessoa por conhecer,* 2 volumes (Lisbon: Estampa, 1990);

Eduardo Lourenço, *Fernando, rei da nossa Baviera* (Lisbon: Imprensa Nacional-Casa da Moeda, 1986);

Lourenço, *Pessoa revisitado: Leitura estruturante do drama em gente,* third edition (Lisbon: Gradiva, 2000);

Adolfo Casais Monteiro, *A poesia de Fernando Pessoa,* second edition, edited by José Blanco (Lisbon: Imprensa Nacional-Casa da Moeda, 1985);

George Monteiro, *Fernando Pessoa and Nineteenth-Century Anglo-American Literature* (Lexington: University Press of Kentucky, 2000);

Monteiro, *The Presence of Pessoa: English, American, and Southern African Literary Responses* (Lexington: University Press of Kentucky, 1998);

Monteiro, ed., *The Man Who Never Was: Essays on Fernando Pessoa* (Providence, R.I.: Gávea-Brown, 1982);

David Mourão-Ferreira, *Nos passos de Pessoa: Ensaios* (Lisbon: Editorial Presença, 1988);

Octavio Paz, "El desconocido de sí mismo," in Fernando Pessoa, *Antología,* selected and translated by Paz (Mexico: Universidad Nacional Autónoma de México, 1962), pp. 9–40;

António Quadros, *Fernando Pessoa: Vida, personalidade e génio,* second edition (Lisbon: Dom Quixote, 1984);

Darlene J. Sadlier, *An Introduction to Fernando Pessoa: Modernism and the Paradoxes of Authorship* (Gainesville: University Press of Florida, 1998);

Irene Ramalho Santos, *Atlantic Poets: Fernando Pessoa's Turn in Anglo-American Modernism* (Hanover & London: University Press of New England, 2003);

José Augusto Seabra, *O heterotexto pessoano* (Lisbon: Dinalivro, 1985);

Jorge de Sena, *Fernando Pessoa & cª heterónima,* 2 volumes (Lisbon: Edições 70, 1982);

Alexandrino E. Severino, *Fernando Pessoa na África do Sul* (Lisbon: Dom Quixote, 1983);

João Gaspar Simões, *Heteropsicografia de Fernando Pessoa* (Porto: Inova, 1973);

Ronald W. Sousa, "Pessoa: The Messenger," in his *The Rediscoverers: Major Writers in the Portuguese Literature of National Regeneration* (University Park: Pennsylvania State University Press, 1981), pp. 131–160;

Yara Frateschi Vieira, *Sob o ramo da bétula: Fernando Pessoa e o erotismo vitoriano* (Campinas: Editora da UNICAMP, 1989).

**Papers:**

The Fernando Pessoa Papers in the Biblioteca Nacional, Lisbon, Portugal, are inventoried in *Bibliotecas e Arquivos de Portugal,* 3–5 (1973–1979). The books in Pessoa's personal library are kept at the Casa Fernando Pessoa, Lisbon.

# Fernão Mendes Pinto
*(1509?/1511? – 8 July 1583)*

Leila Rodrigues da Silva
*Universidade Federal do Rio de Janeiro*

BOOK: *Peregrinaçam de Fernam Mendez Pinto em que da conta de muytas e muyto estranhas cousas que vio & ouuio no reyno da China, no da Tartaria, no do Sarnau . . . e tambem da conta de muytos casos particulares que acontecerão assi a elle como a outras pessoas* (Lisbon: Pedro Crasbeeck, 1614); translated by H. C. Gent as *The Voyages and Adventures, of Fernand Mendez Pinto, a Portugal: During his Travels for the Space of One and Twenty Years in the Kingdoms of Ethiopia, China, Tartaria . . . Japan and a Great Part of the East-Indies* (London: Printed by J. Macock for Henry Cripps & Lodowick Lloyd, 1653).

Editions: *Peregrinação de Fernão Mendes Pinto, e por elle escrita . . . e no fim della trata brevemente de alguas noticias, e da morte do Santo Padre Mestre Francisco Xavier . . . accrecentada com o itenerario de Antonio Tenreiro . . . e a conquista do Reyno de Pegu* (Lisbon: Na Offic. de Joam de Aquino Bulhoens, 1762);

*Peregrinação*, 4 volumes (Lisbon: Rollandiana, 1829);

*Excerptos seguidos de uma noticia sobre sua vida e obras e estudos de lingua por José Feliciano de Castilho,* 2 volumes, Livraria classica, excerptos dos principaes autores de boa nota, nos. 4–5 (Rio de Janeiro: Garnier, 1865);

*Peregrinação*, 4 volumes, Livros de oiro da literatura portuguêsa, no. 1 (Lisbon: Livraria Ferreira, 1908–1910);

*Peregrinação,* 7 volumes (Ajuda: Cosmopolis Editora, 1930);

*Peregrinação* (Vila Nova de Gaia: Ajuda, 1931);

*Peregrinação,* 7 volumes (Porto: Portucalense, 1944);

*Peregrinação* (Lisbon: Lisbonense, 1946);

*Peregrinação* [Excertos], edited, with a preface, by Rodrigues Lapa (Lisbon: Seara Nova, 1946);

*Peregrinação* (Porto: Portucalense, 1962);

*Peregrinação e outras obras,* 4 volumes (Lisbon: Sá da Costa, 1963–1974);

*Peregrinação e outras obras,* with a preface by António José Saraiva (Lisbon: Sá da Costa, 1981);

*Peregrinação* (Lisbon: Imprensa Nacional-Casa da Moeda, 1983);

*Peregrinação* (Porto: Lello & Irmãos, 1984);

*Peregrinação e outras cartas,* 2 volumes, with critical commentaries by Fernando António Almeida, Eduardo Lourenço, and José Augusto Seabra (Lisbon: Afrodite, 1989);

*Peregrinação,* 2 volumes, with an introduction by Aguás Neves (Lisbon: Europa América, 1995).

Editions in English: *The Voyages and Adventures of Ferdinand Mendez Pinto, the Portuguese,* translated by Henry Cogan, with an introduction by Arminius Vambéry (London: Unwin, 1891);

*The Great Peregrination* (London: Faber & Faber, 1949);

*The Travels of Mendes Pinto,* edited and translated by Rebecca D. Catz (Chicago: University of Chicago Press, 1989);

*The Peregrination of Fernão Mendes Pinto* (London: Carcanet in association with the Calouste Gulbenkian Foundation and the Discoveries Commission, 1992).

Fernão Mendes Pinto is an important figure in the literary history of Portugal. He wrote only one text, but it is considered a literary masterpiece. Pinto's work describes his twenty-one years of adventures around the East in the mid sixteenth century. The great popularity of Pinto's manuscript during the seventeenth and eighteenth centuries is indisputable, and the work became an important source for people who wanted to know more about the East.

Pinto was born between 1509 and 1511, in Montemor-o-Velho, close to Coimbra. Even though he is the author of *Peregrinaçam de Fernam Mendez Pinto em que da conta de muytas e muyto estranhas cousas que vio & ouuio no reyno da China, no da Tartaria, no do Sarnau . . . e tambem da conta de muytos casos particulares que acontecerão assi a elle como a outras pessoas* (1614; translated as *The Voyages and Adventures, of Fernand Mendez Pinto, a Portugal: During his Travels for the Space of One and Twenty Years in the Kingdoms of Ethiopia, China, Tartaria . . . Japan and a Great Part of the East-Indies,* 1653), one of the best-known works in Portuguese literature, extremely little is known about

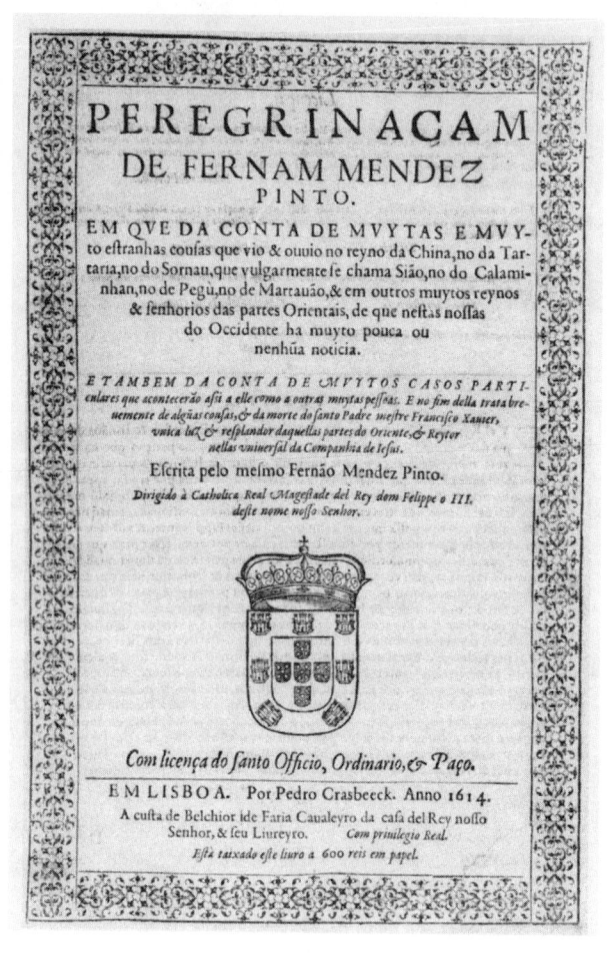

*Title page for Fernão Mendes Pinto's account of his extensive travels through the Far East (James Ford Bell Library, University of Minnesota)*

Pinto's life. No primary sources addressing his biography are extant; most of what is known about his family relationships, religion, and ideology has been reconstructed from his work. The autobiographical nature of the *Peregrinação*, as the work is popularly known, is revealed in its opening lines. Pinto gives his readers a basic indication of what they will find in the narrative, which is made up of reports about his twenty-one years of travels throughout the Far East.

The life and the work of Pinto are deeply marked by the historical moment. The period comprising the fourteenth and fifteenth centuries consists of a series of crises, including starvation, plagues, and wars. This era preceded the great transformations of sixteenth-century Europe, where in the cultural sphere, for example, there was a break with the medieval period: artists and writers returned to Greco-Latin culture in their attempt to reproduce the art and spirit of the classical age. In addition, the invention of the printing press made possible a more dynamic diffusion of knowledge through the circulation of books. The ideals of medieval chivalry slowly gave way to more pragmatic bourgeois values. New geographical areas were incorporated into the European political system, and the exotic flora, fauna, and population of the new areas stimulated European interest and imagination.

Mankind became the center of his universe, and the doubts that arose in relation to theological discourse culminated in the Protestant Reformation and the Counter Reformation. Religious intolerance, one of the facets of this period, often legitimized political actions that were not always in keeping with religious doctrine. The Portuguese Inquisition, created in 1536 during the reign of João III, was thus often used to suppress political adversaries and critics.

In the area of economics the crisis that characterized the previous period provoked the exploration and incorporation of large territories outside of Europe. These new lands were a source of considerable raw materials and general wealth and led to inflationary pressure in Europe. The consolidation of bourgeois groups, already present in the previous century, was accelerated, and the great trading companies, with their complex organization, competed fiercely for the control of imports. In politics the absolutist monarchies consolidated with their military and diplomatic actions of expansionism. The Tudors in England, the Valois in France, and the Hapsburgs in Spain were the most important representatives of this process. Also a participant in the politics of the time, the papacy used its religious authority to legitimize its own expansionist interests, as well as those of select groups and individuals.

The involvement of Portugal in this entire process is reflected in Pinto's work. He lived through two important political periods of Portuguese history. The first was one of triumph and glory, with the conquest of territories spread over three continents. Regions distant from each other were completely or partially brought under Portuguese control. These areas included the coasts of Brazil, West and East Africa, Persia, the Malabar Coast in India, Ceylon, and the archipelagos of Malala and of the Moluccas. The largest territorial expansion of the Portuguese Empire occurred during this time. The second period was characterized by a loss of political autonomy that resulted from the expansionist actions of the absolutist monarchies. In 1580 Portugal was incorporated into Felipe II's Spanish Empire and suffered the loss of juridical authority over its vast territories.

Some scholars recognize a resemblance between Pinto and the main character of the *Peregrinação*. These specialists tend to emphasize the autobiographical tone of the first and last chapters of the *Peregrinação*. The confirmation of the knowledge embodied in the work, however, has been possible in only a few specific instances. The scarcity of other sources is a fact recognized by all the scholars dedicated to an analysis of Pinto's life and work. Besides the *Peregrinação*, direct testimonies of contact with Pinto are evidenced by only three letters and some references made to him by members of the Society of Jesus.

Pinto was associated with the Society of Jesus during the last years of his stay in the East, between 1554 and 1557. As a result of his association with the order, as its archives support, there are some mentions made of him by the Jesuits. The first of his letters was written in Malaca, on 5 December 1554, and the second one in Macau on 20 November of the following year. The third was written in Almada on 15 March 1571. This last letter discusses aspects of Pinto's religious mission to Japan and replies to a request from an Italian for information about the East. At this time Pinto had already gone back to Portugal and was dedicating himself to being, among other things, a consultant on the regions that he had visited. The most interesting piece of information included in the Jesuit writings concerning Pinto is provided by Father Francisco Xavier, with whom the author maintained a friendship after meeting him in 1553. In a letter to King João III, dated 31 January 1552, the Jesuit mentions two siblings of Pinto: Álvaro, who would have been in the siege of Malaca in 1547, and Antonio.

The pieces that compose the few sources for the study of the life and work of Pinto add little to what is found in the *Peregrinação* itself. This lack of sources, however, has led some specialists to show considerable caution in using information drawn exclusively from the work. The pertinent aspects of Pinto's life are placed in doubt, as are the meticulous and extremely detailed elements that he presents in the reports of his adventures in the East. The reliability of the facts narrated by Pinto has been a point of concern for most scholars. Since the first edition of the *Peregrinação*, many of its readers have assumed the same position as these scholars and have doubted the veracity of the work. Although since the twentieth century there has been considerable debate surrounding the question of what is fact and what is fiction in the *Peregrinação*, the number of studies dedicated to an understanding and analysis of the work within its historical context is still limited. There is, however, a consensus among most scholars that the historical and literary value of the *Peregrinação* does not rest on an exact measurement of the truth of Pinto's narrative.

Among the information presented in the first chapter of the *Peregrinação*, most specialists accept the following items as facts: Pinto was brought from the village where he was born to Lisbon by an uncle on 13 December 1521, when he was between ten and twelve years old. He probably was born to a family of modest means, since he mentions explicitly the misery and the poverty that prevailed in his parents' home. In Lisbon, Pinto was placed by his uncle in the service of a rich family, where he stayed for a year and a half until, for reasons not revealed in his writings, he ran away. The consequences of his escape constitute the central argument of the entire *Peregrinação*.

Pinto left for the East on 11 March 1537, and thus began the adventures that later became the source of his work. The *Peregrinação* was divided into 226 chapters for publication by the king's chronicler Francisco de Andrade, and all but two of them are devoted to the period of Pinto's Eastern travels. According to the text of Pinto's work, he embarked for Setúbal on a caravel that, before reaching its destination, was sacked by French pirates. He was taken prisoner, tortured, and abandoned in Melides. He spent some time there recovering from his wounds and then continued to Setúbal, where he remained in the service of a nobleman, Francisco de Faria—possibly until 1537, when he left to seek his fortune in India. Throughout his travels in Asia, Pinto was enslaved thirteen times and sold seventeen times; he suffered shipwrecks and survived many life-threatening situations. He was a nobleman's servant, a soldier, occasionally a doctor, missionary, ambassador, and pirate, among other things. Around 1539 he settled down in Malaca, where he was at the service of the captain of the local fortress and where he met Antonio de Farias, with whom he undertook several adventures. He also lived in Pegú, Burma (now Myanmar), and Siam (now Thailand). As a merchant he worked mostly in China and Japan. After meeting Xavier, to whom he had lent money for the construction of the first Christian temple in Japan, he entered the Society of Jesus. As a member of this religious order, Pinto shed most of the wealth he had accumulated and went on to spend his time between evangelical and ambassadorial activities in Japan. He served the vice king of Goa, India, establishing diplomatic relationships between Japan and Portuguese India. Shortly before returning to Portugal, for reasons that he does not explain clearly, Pinto left the Society of Jesus.

Using the structure of the chronicle for the *Peregrinação*, Pinto addresses several themes, including botany, zoology, anthropology, geography, history, religion, and military strategy. His descriptions are detailed and interspersed with his personal opinions and impressions of the system of power established by

*Sculpture of Pinto by A. Duarte, Almada, 1983 (from Rebecca D. Catz, ed.,* The Travels of Mendes Pinto, *1989; Thomas Cooper Library, University of South Carolina)*

the Eastern colonies of the Portuguese Empire, the organization of other European nations involved in maritime expeditions, and the different people and cultures that he encounters in his travels.

Pinto reveals a fascination for the unknown, as well as the differences between the Portuguese and the inhabitants of the lands that he visits. This interest leads him to fill his narrative with many details and comparisons. It also leads him to be concerned with the quantification of everything that he comes across—from the length of a river to the number of steps relative to the leap of a certain animal. The value placed on quantification was much appreciated during the Renaissance.

Pinto's focus on the superiority of the Christian faith adds another interesting aspect to the *Peregrinação*. There are few chapters in which Pinto does not mention God or Jesus Christ. He is highly critical of Islam and the indigenous religious practices with which he becomes acquainted. He is also critical, but in a subtle manner, of those Christians of whose behavior and moral conduct he does not approve. When such criticisms appear in the narrative, they are voiced by secondary characters rather than by the protagonist. The unconditional nature of Pinto's faith—a position fundamental to the maintenance of orthodoxy in times of the Inquisition—is obvious throughout his work.

In the *Peregrinação,* Pinto also criticizes those who eagerly accumulate wealth, particularly when he talks about expeditions bound for the East simply for financial gain and, right before his return to Portugal, when his scorn for material goods begins to manifest itself. The episodes about his association with the Society of Jesus and the donation of his wealth to the order reveal a change in his own personal attitudes, leading to such criticisms.

When Pinto arrived in Portugal on 22 September 1558, as recorded in the last chapter of the *Peregrinação,* he requested a pension from the regent D. Catarina as payment for the services that he had rendered to the Portuguese Crown in the East. The pension, however, was not granted until January 1583 by Felipe I. Registering his indignation about the delay in the last pages of his work (written after 1569), Pinto alleges that four and a half years have elapsed since he first made his request. Although the pension recognized his devotion to the Crown, as well as the services rendered, its value was extremely low and contributed little to the improvement of Pinto's life. Pinto died six months after the stipend was granted.

While waiting for a response to his request during that period, Pinto settled down on a farm in Pragal, without any real source of income. He married Maria Correia de Brito, with whom he had two daughters. He devoted the next years to writing the *Peregrinação* and to consulting activities concerning Eastern subjects. Among the people who sought his expertise was João de Barros, one of the great Portuguese writers during the Renaissance. At the time Barros was writing his *Décadas* (Decades, first published in Lisbon, 1552–1553), a type of historical and geographical encyclopedia of the world discovered by the Portuguese.

Written between the years 1569 and 1578, the *Peregrinação* was only published in 1614, thirty-one years after Pinto's death on 8 July 1583. In spite of its late publication, the work had already been mentioned in 1569 in a letter written by the Jesuit Cipriano Soares. The delay was in part because of Pinto's request to his daughters, to whom he had dedicated the work. In accordance with his will, his daughters gave the manuscript to the Casa Pia das Penitentes de Lisbon, a charitable institution dedicated to helping destitute women.

Much conjecture about Pinto's decision not to publish the *Peregrinação* followed as soon as he had completed the work. Scholars have speculated that he was worried about the Inquisition. Possibly, he was conscious of the repercussions that criticism of the work could draw during that time of religious intolerance. The Holy Office, however, granted a license to publish Pinto's manuscript without difficulties on 25 May 1603. The publication of the *Peregrinação,* however, had to wait for a special license from the Casa Pia das Penitentes de Lisbon, which was obtained only on 6 November 1613.

The great popularity of Fernão Mendes Pinto's *Peregrinação* during the seventeenth century is undeniable. It was published at least nineteen times and in six different languages before the end of that century. Today there are more than 165 complete or partial editions of the *Peregrinação*. The popularity of the work stems from its attractive content, which emphasizes the exotic and a sense of adventure. The *Peregrinação* also became an important source for people who wanted to know more about the East, especially in the seventeenth and eighteenth centuries. It was considered a reliable source for the official history of the discoveries and for the Jesuits dedicated to reconstructing Xavier's work.

**References:**

Cristovão Aires, *Fernão Mendes Pinto, subsídios para a sua biografia e para o estudo da sua obra* (Lisbon: Academia Real de Lisboa, 1904);

Luís Filipe Barreto, "Introdução à *Peregrinação* de Fernão Mendes Pinto," in *A abertura do mundo: Estudos de história dos descobrimentos europeus em homenagem a Luís de Albuquerque,* volume 1, edited by Barreto and Francisco Contente Domingues and Barreto, volume 1 (Lisbon: Presença, 1986), pp. 101–118;

Rebecca D. Catz, *A sátira social em Fernão Mendes Pinto* (Lisbon: Prelo, 1978);

António Álvaro Dória, *Um aventureiro português do século XVI: Fernão Mendes Pinto* (Guimarães: Separata da Revista Gil Vicente, 1951);

Gilberto Freyre, "Em tôrno da 'Peregrinaçam' de Fernão Mendes Pinto," in his *Vida forma e cor* (Rio de Janeiro: Olímpio, 1962), pp. 373–390;

Georges Le Gentil, *Les portugais en extreme-orient: Fernão Mendes Pinto, un précurser de l'exotisme au XVI$^{eme}$ siècle* (Paris: Hermann, 1947);

Francisco Ferreira Lima, *O outro livro das Maravilhas. A Peregrinação de Fernão Mendes Pinto* (Rio de Janeiro: Relume Dumará, 1998);

Alfredo Margarido, "Fernão Mendes Pinto: Um herói do cotidiano," *Colóquio/Letras,* 74 (1983): 23–28;

Aquilino Gomes Ribeiro, "Quem era Fernão Mendes Pinto?" in *Peregrinação de Fernão Mendes Pinto—Aventuras extraordinárias de um português no Oriente* (Lisbon: Sá da Costa, 1976), pp. 199–212.

# José Cardoso Pires
*(2 October 1925 – 26 October 1998)*

Lênia Márcia Mongelli
*Universidade de São Paulo, Brazil*

(Translated by Lillian DePaula)

BOOKS: *Os caminheiros e outros contos* (Lisbon: Centro Bibliográfico, 1949);
*Histórias de amor* (Lisbon: Gleba, 1952);
*O anjo ancorado* (Lisbon: Ulisséia, 1958);
*O render dos heróis* (Lisbon: Gleba, 1960);
*Cartilha do Marialva ou das negações libertinas* (Lisbon: Ulisséia, 1960);
*Jogos de azar* (Lisbon: Arcádia, 1963);
*O hóspede de Job* (Lisbon: Arcádia, 1963);
*O delfim* (Lisbon: Moraes, 1968);
*Dinossauro excelentíssimo* (Lisbon: Arcádia, 1972);
*E agora, José?* (Lisbon: Moraes, 1977);
*O burro-em-pé* (Lisbon: Moraes, 1979);
*Corpo-delito na sala de espelhos* (Lisbon: Moraes, 1980);
*Balada da praia dos cães* (Lisbon: O Jornal, 1982); translated by Mary Fitton as *Ballad of Dogs' Beach: Dossier of a Crime* (London: Dent, 1986);
*Alexandra Alpha* (Lisbon: Dom Quixote, 1987);
*A república dos corvos* (Lisbon: Dom Quixote, 1988);
*A cavalo no diabo* (Lisbon: Dom Quixote, 1994);
*De profundis, valsa lenta* (Lisbon: Dom Quixote, 1997);
*Lisboa, livro de bordo: Vozes, olhares, memorações* (Lisbon: Dom Quixote, 1997).

PLAY PRODUCTIONS: *O render dos heróis,* Lisbon, Teatro Moderno, 1965;
*Corpo-delito na sala de espelhos,* Lisbon, Teatro Aberto, 1979.

TRANSLATIONS: Horace McCoy, *O pão de mentira* (N.p., 1952);
Arthur Miller, *Morte dum caixeiro viajante,* translated by Pires and Victor Palla (Lisbon: Imp. Libanio da Silva, 1954).

*José Cardoso Pires (from the cover for the 1983 edition of* O hóspede de Job; *Thomas Cooper Library, University of South Carolina)*

Since José Cardoso Pires's debut as a fiction writer in 1949, political engagement and the declared objectives of critical and analytical independence were distinctive characteristics of his work. He was an extreme-left activist, and three historical developments aid in understanding the choice for this political position: the dictatorial regime of António de Oliveira Salazar and his successor, Marcelo Caetano, in Portugal (1926–1974); the outbreak of World War II (1939–

1945); and the appearance of neorealism (1940), inspired by American (John Steinbeck, Sinclair Lewis, Ernest Hemingway) and Brazilian (Jorge Amado, José Lins do Rego, Graciliano Ramos) models. The development of Portuguese and European surrealism also had an impact on Pires's works. The author presents a thematically uniform body of writing that assumes a distinctive and personal style after the 1974 Revolução dos Cravos (Carnation Revolution), when the Portuguese dictatorial regime ended, allowing the novelist more freedom of expression.

José Augusto Neves Cardoso Pires was born in the village of São João do Peso, Castelo Branco District, on 2 October 1925. Son of naval officer José Antonio Neves and Maria Sofia Cardoso Pires, he was the descendant, on the maternal side, of rural middle bourgeoisie, and on the paternal side, of immigrants who settled in the United States. In a 1991 interview with Artur Portela, Pires spoke of these "uncles from America," who had to emigrate after having served as child laborers in the fields of the Alentejo region. Pires's family moved to Lisbon when he was only a few months old. He maintained, however, some ties with his origins in Beira, a large meridional region in Portugal, where his mother returned to give birth. Questioned on the insignificant presence of the rural area in his fiction, Pires answered that he only remembered the countryside as a place of melancholy and conservatism. In Lisbon the family lived in the Arroios neighborhood, at 7 Carlos José Barreiros Street, which Pires called "the atlas of his childhood."

In 1932 Pires began primary school at Largo do Leão, and in 1936 he enrolled at the Liceu Camões for his secondary studies. Those childhood and adolescent days were, on the one hand, filled with the common experiences of innocence and mischief, despite the family's paltry income. On the other, they were filled with memories of the threat of war and an oppressive church and government. These memories define the anticlericalism and the sense of rebellion and refusal to be a part of a fixed, rigid structure that surface throughout Pires's writings, in which he denounces the "apostolic massification" he saw in the activities of the church in Portugal. Pires had his first contact with this "massification" at the Liceu Camões, where he met fellow students in the paramilitary group Mocidade Portuguesa (Portuguese Youth). These students wore uniforms and greeted their professors with a fascist salute.

Influenced by the mathematicians Câmara Reyes, Antônio Gedeão, and Luis de Matos during his last years at the Liceu, Pires entered the Faculdade de Ciências de Lisbon. During this time there emerged the Estado Novo (New State), a name (coined in 1930) by which the political regime installed in Portugal around 1926 came to be known. Salazar, who became synonymous with the Estado Novo, took power in Portugal definitively when he became prime minister in 1932. In 1940 the famous Exposition of the Portuguese World, organized at the request of the secretary of national propaganda, brought together the best architects, artists, and designers from around Portugal, with the objective of proposing a new interpretation of the past. This new perspective on Portuguese history was to be firmly based on traditional concepts of family, religion, and state. The exposition coincided with the appearance of neorealism in the arts, a movement strongly committed to class struggles and to the defense of the poor. (Alves Redol's *Gaibéus* [1966], a saga that focuses on the collective drama of farm workers who are treated as serfs, became a profession of faith in the movement.)

Within this intense moment of national history, Pires drafted his first literary works. In 1943, at the age of eighteen, he published a short essay, "Loti, o sonhador" (Loti, the Dreamer), in *Cidade dos Rapazes* (City of Youth), a journal of restricted circulation. Since he had always wanted to be a writer and realized that he would never be more than an average student at the Liceu, he began to contribute to the literary section of the newspaper *O Globo* (The Globe) and to write book reviews for the magazine *Afinidades* (Affinities). In a documentary made by Rosa Filmes for Rádio e Televisão Portuguesa in 1998, Pires stated that he abandoned the study of mathematics because "my life was at the Cervejaria Portugália, playing pool, because I didn't have a great affinity with the students." At the end of World War II he signed up with the merchant marine as an apprentice pilot and embarked on a trip to Africa on a cargo ship transporting troops to Timor. But in Lourenço Marques he deserted because of his dissatisfaction with colonial morality and was then arrested and returned to Lisbon. In 1947 he did military service in Vendas Novas and in Figueira de Foz. During those last two years Pires's literary activities began to gain momentum; he published his first short story, "Salão de vintém" (Penny Saloon, 1944), in the anthology *Bloco* (Block), edited by a group of university students. Together with Mario Cesariny, Luis Pacheco, Alexandre O'Neill, and Pedro Oom, surrealists of the first order, he reacted against the neorealists' populist concept that subjects art to political intentions. He always, however, maintained a sense of independence from any specific group.

After military service Pires attempted several professions to support himself. He worked as a sales agent, an English correspondent, an interpreter for an airline company, and a translator. He translated Arthur Miller's *Death of a Salesman* (1949) in 1954 and Horace McCoy's *No Pockets in a Shroud* (1937) in 1952. He also tried his hand at journalism, which, with its roots in

*Cover for Pires's first book, published when he was twenty-four (from Ines Pedrosa, José Cardoso Pires: Fotobiografia, 1999; University of California, Berkeley, Library)*

everyday life and language, exercised a significant influence on his fiction. According to Pires, the journalistic method of "writing under pressure" and using colloquial language provided excellent lessons in style. All of this experience is evident in his first book, *Os caminheiros e outros contos* (The Travelers and Other Stories, 1949), published at the author's own expense. He was twenty-four years old at the time and was editor of the magazine *Eva*. Fellow writer Mário Dionísio first believed in and encouraged the talent of the young author. Pires was also a member of the recently founded Movimento de Unidade Democratica (MUD, Movement of Democratic Unity), which served as a first step toward his later entrance into the Portuguese Communist Party (PCP).

Until the appearance of his second book, *Histórias de amor* (Love Stories, 1952), Pires published in various magazines and journals. Many of these works were collected in *Histórias de amor*, which was confiscated by Salazar's police force. Reorganized in the 1930s and formally called the Police Vigilance and State Defense (PVDE), it maintained, as the name suggests, strict control over the people of Portugal, particularly the intellectuals and writers. Pires was jailed for a short time when his book was confiscated because, in spite of the title, one of the short stories describes a student who was made a prisoner for being antifascist. The repression, however, did not end there; the censors (who worked hand in hand with the political police) later ordered him to make substantial changes to the text, taking out all the references against fascism. Pires kept the copy marked by the censors' famous blue pencil, "as a precious reference of my life as a writer, because it is the evidence of prepotency and the superstitious analysis of what Salazar would call the politics of the spirit," as he says in his interview with Portela. As a response to the arbitrary political actions of the PVDE, the first Editorial Cooperative for Writers was founded in 1952.

In 1963 many of the short stories from *Os caminheiros e outros contos* and *Histórias de amor* were published in the volume *Jogos de azar* (Games of Chance), which also included stories previously unpublished in book form. Those stories are clear witnesses to the period. "Ritual dos pequenos vampiros" (Ritual of the Little Vampires), for example, portrays the marginal lives of the students in Lisbon and their outings to the bars on the outskirts of the city, long nights of gambling, and sexual exploits in the houses of prostitution. In "Os caminheiros" (The Travelers) the characters' dialogues reveal the difficulties and the plundering that the marginalized segments of the population suffered. There are also autobiographical elements in "Amanhã, se Deus quiser" (Tomorrow, God Willing), which deals with an absent father, a weak mother, and a poor, sick young seamstress and her unemployed brother. Pires always struggled against subservience to reality, as seen in the short story "A charrua entre os corvos" (The Plow Among Crows), and against the popularity of certain literary trends. His two inaugural books, however, were tied to formulas dictated by the styles current in the 1940s and 1950s.

Pires was quite familiar with Portuguese literary tradition. He was conscious of its qualities and shortcomings, and of the necessity of innovation by bringing in foreign and national contributions. In authors such as Anton Pavlovich Chekhov and Edgar Allan Poe, and later Hemingway and Stephen Crane, Pires found his inspiration for conciseness and precision in his dialogue. He felt that through style and careful attention to form, the writer could effect change in literature. Beginning with his first novel, *O anjo ancorado* (The Anchored Angel, 1958), in which he contrasts the world of the village with the modernity of technology, Pires remained committed to this objective. The author's mature view of his country in search of an identity, particularly throughout the years of totalitarian oppression, caused critics to view this novel as a work of transition.

*Pires in Sines, a southwestern port, circa 1950s (from Ines Pedrosa, José Cardoso Pires: Fotobiografia, 1999; University of California, Berkeley, Library)*

During the 1950s, when literary criticism speaks of a "second moment" in neorealism, Pires's life took definite direction. At the atelier of the painter Júlio Pomar and the sculptor Vasco de Conceição he met a twenty-two-year-old nurse, Edite Pereira, whom he nicknamed "Esquilo" (Squirrel); she became his lifelong companion (they married in 1954), and they had two daughters, Ana and Rita. In 1953 he lost his brother in a military plane accident. As a member of the Portuguese Writers' Society, founded by Aquilino Ribeiro, Pires took part in the World Congress for Peace in Stockholm (1958). The following year he worked as a trainee for the magazine *Epoca* (Epoch) in Milan, with plans to publish a weekly periodical that had been banned by censorship. In 1959 he founded the magazine *Almanaque* (Almanac) with O'Neill, Luis Sttau Monteiro, Vasco Pulido Valente, Augusto Abelaira, and José Cutileiro. Pires was head editor. There he began his productive journalistic experience. As he says in his interview with Portela, the main objective of the periodical was "to ridicule cosmopolitanism as a synonym for provincialism, shake up hypocrisy and demonstrate that austerity is a coat of fear and lack of imagination." At that time Alvaro Cunhal and other communist companions escaped from the Peniche prison, and Ribeiro was prosecuted for an antifascist article he published in *Quando os lobos uivam* (When the Wolves Howl). Because of the persecution of intellectuals, Pires went into exile–first to London, then to Paris, and finally to Brazil. He returned to Portugal a year later, in 1961.

In the early 1960s Pires made his incursion into theater with the publication of *O render dos heróis* (The Vanquishing of the Heroes, 1960), subtitled "a dramatic narrative in three parts and a grotesque apotheosis." The work takes place in the backwoods of Alto Minho and deals with the Maria da Fonte revolt in 1846 against increased taxation. The play was presented with great success in 1965 at the Teatro Moderno de Lisbon. Pires did not achieve the same success with his second and last play, *Corpo-delito na sala de espelhos* (Corpus Delecti in the Hall of Mirrors, performed in 1979 and published in 1980), which deals with the PVDE and its ghosts. Pires demonstrated more enthusiasm for the essay genre than he did for the theater, which he considered a subjective activity dependent on the freedom of the actor and the director. His essays, beginning with *Cartilha do Marialva* (Marialva's Primer, 1960), which targets the eighteenth-century government reforms of Sebastião José de Carvalho e Melo, Marquês de Pombal, reveal a satirical verve and irreverent sharpness. Through "marialvismo" Pires criticized social injustices and privileges.

On returning to Portugal in 1961, Pires resumed the editorship of *Almanaque* and also participated in the Portuguese Writers' Society for three years. In 1962 he traveled as a delegate to the International Writers' Congress in Florence and was elected vice president of the Portuguese Delegation of Writers of the Comunitá Europea degli Scrittori (European Community of Writers). Along with others, he restructured the *Gazeta musical e de todas as artes* (Journal of Music and of All Arts). He also took part in the meeting of the Peninsular Writers in Barcelona, which was held secretly, as many of these writers were persecuted in Portugal. These activities paralleled the agitated Portuguese political movements of the moment: the beginning of the war in Angola in 1961; the election of Cunhal as general secretary of the Communist Party; and the severe educational and economic crisis in the universities in Lisbon, Coimbra, and Porto. At the time, Portuguese intellectuals counted on the support of the French intelligentsia (including Louis Aragon, Simone de Beauvoir, François Mauriac, and Jean-Paul Sartre) in their protests against the excesses of Salazar.

In 1963, the same year *Jogos de azar* was withdrawn from circulation for being antifascist, Pires published his novel *O hóspede de Job* (Job's Guest). This novel earned him the Camilo Castelo Branco Award in 1964 and an award granted by the Regional Press Congress. Pires stated in 1988 that the novel was "naive" but "political." In this story about Gallagher, an arrogant representative of a great military power who moves to the house of the humble Job, the author explores the themes of the imbalance between power and weakness, wealth and poverty, and class struggles.

After an assault on the Portuguese Writers' Society in 1965, Salazar had the association officially dissolved and government awards for literature reactivated. Many writers refused to accept the honors. At the same time, Pires and a few others joined the Portuguese branch of the Association Internationale pour la liberté de la culture–a movement of resistance against repression in the Iberian Peninsula. In 1967 he published a series of weekly columns titled "Os lugares comuns" (Common Places) in the *Diário Popular* and founded the "Magazine das Letras, das Artes e dos Espetáculos" in the *Jornal do Fundão*. The experience led him to the "Suplemento Literário" of the *Diário de Lisboa* and, months later, to the supplement "A Mosca" in the same paper.

Pires published *O delfim* (The Dauphin) in 1968. Written between 1963 and 1967, this novel is considered by some critics to be the author's masterpiece. It deals with the tragic adventures of the infante (or "delfim") Tomás Manuel da Palma Bravo, the Engineer, the last descendent of the fictional Palma Bravo lineage, which dates back to the seventeenth century. This family, established in Gafeira, was involved in poaching. The fame of this novel does not derive from the theme of the decadence of powerful families but rather from the techniques employed in the narration. The plot is constructed in a nonlinear, dispersed manner; it is made up of stories casually collected by the main narrator, who places himself by a window overlooking a lake. The author uses imprecision, haziness, mystery, doubts, and police-like curiosity as he shows that historical facts should not take the place of that which belongs to the imagination. In a postscript to *O anjo ancorado* Pires defines what history is to the writer of fiction: "uma generalização de caráter romanesco que, como tudo quanto há no romanesco, é pessoal, *intemporal* e seletiva" (a generalization in a Romanesque way which, as everything found in the Romanesque, is personal, *atemporal* and selective). In the interview with Portela, Pires spoke of the influence of cinema, television, and photography on "the structure of narrative discourse, that is, the assembling, the rhythm and the sequence of the narrative." This influence can be seen in "the visual focus his manner of telling presents" in *O delfim*.

Pires's interest in painting is also obvious in the novel. From painting he learned the art of going beyond the rules to escape the commonplace and to observe more carefully in order to achieve verisimilitude in his writing. The author's involvement with this art form is perhaps responsible for his sense of the coherence between life and work, and between aesthetic notions and political convictions. It also shows his affinity with the surrealist presuppositions at this moment in neorealism.

The University of London invited Pires to teach Portuguese and Brazilian literature at King's College in 1969. Pires worked intensely in London until 1971, teaching and sending columns to the *Diário de Lisbon* on a regular basis. In 1970 the great innovator of Portuguese letters, José de Almada Negreiros, died. According to Pires, Almada Negreiros was his "stylistic mentor" in a field of invention that the author of *O delfim* considers the foundation of literature. Questioned on the "stylistic" theme, he answered categorically:

*Pires with his wife, Edite Pereira, and their daughters, Ana and Rita, 1967 (photograph by Eduardo Gageiro)*

Recusa da evidência, fundamentalmente . . . Para mim o estilo nao é uma caligrafia, o estilo que se "vê" não se sente e por isso é que eu admiro a escrita *ao gume da lâmina,* digamos assim. Desgastar, afiar, ir até o osso, como faz por exemplo o João Cabral de Melo Neto . . . O projeto é esse. E, como tal, prefiro pecar por defeito a pecar por excesso.

(Refusal of the evidence, fundamentally . . . For me style is not calligraphy, the style that one "sees" one does not feel, and that is why I admire the writing *done with a razor's edge,* let's say. To wear down, to sharpen, to go to the very marrow, as, for example João Cabral de Melo Neto does . . . That is the project. And, as such, I prefer to sin for the lack rather than to sin for the excess).

In 1971, preserving the spirit of the extinct Portuguese Writers' Society, the Portuguese Writers' Association was founded. Motivated by the increasingly favorable climate for Portuguese intellectuals, Pires published *Dinossauro excelentíssimo* (Most Excellent Dinosaur, 1972), a fable dedicated to his daughters, Ana and Rita. The story is about a young dinosaur that becomes emperor. The emperor is all-powerful but also schizophrenic. Pires classified his work as entertainment, but its grotesque portrait of Salazar provoked a scandal that reached the National Assembly. During one session Professor Miller Guerra claimed that there was no freedom in Portugal. The ultrafascist congressman Cazal Ribeiro denied this charge, using the recent publication of *Dinossauro excelentíssimo* as evidence to the contrary. Since a supporter of Salazar had thus acknowledged the book, the censors could not remove it from circulation. In his interview with Portela, Pires later called the dispute, from which he benefited, a "repulsive carnival."

Salazar became incapacitated in 1968 and was replaced by Caetano. After Salazar's death in 1970 general dissatisfaction in Portugal intensified. Mário Soares, who had been deported to São Tomé in 1968, returned and published *Portugal amordaçado* (Portugal Gagged). In London and Paris in 1972 Pires published his study "Técnica do golpe da censura" (Techniques of Censorship; included in *E agora, José?* [What Now, José?], 1977). The text, perhaps the most incisive analysis of the Portuguese dictatorship, is indispensable for understanding what goes on behind the scenes in an authoritarian regime. The work had this interesting dedication: "I dedicate these reflections to a citizen without letters, Simplício Barreto Magro, veterinarian

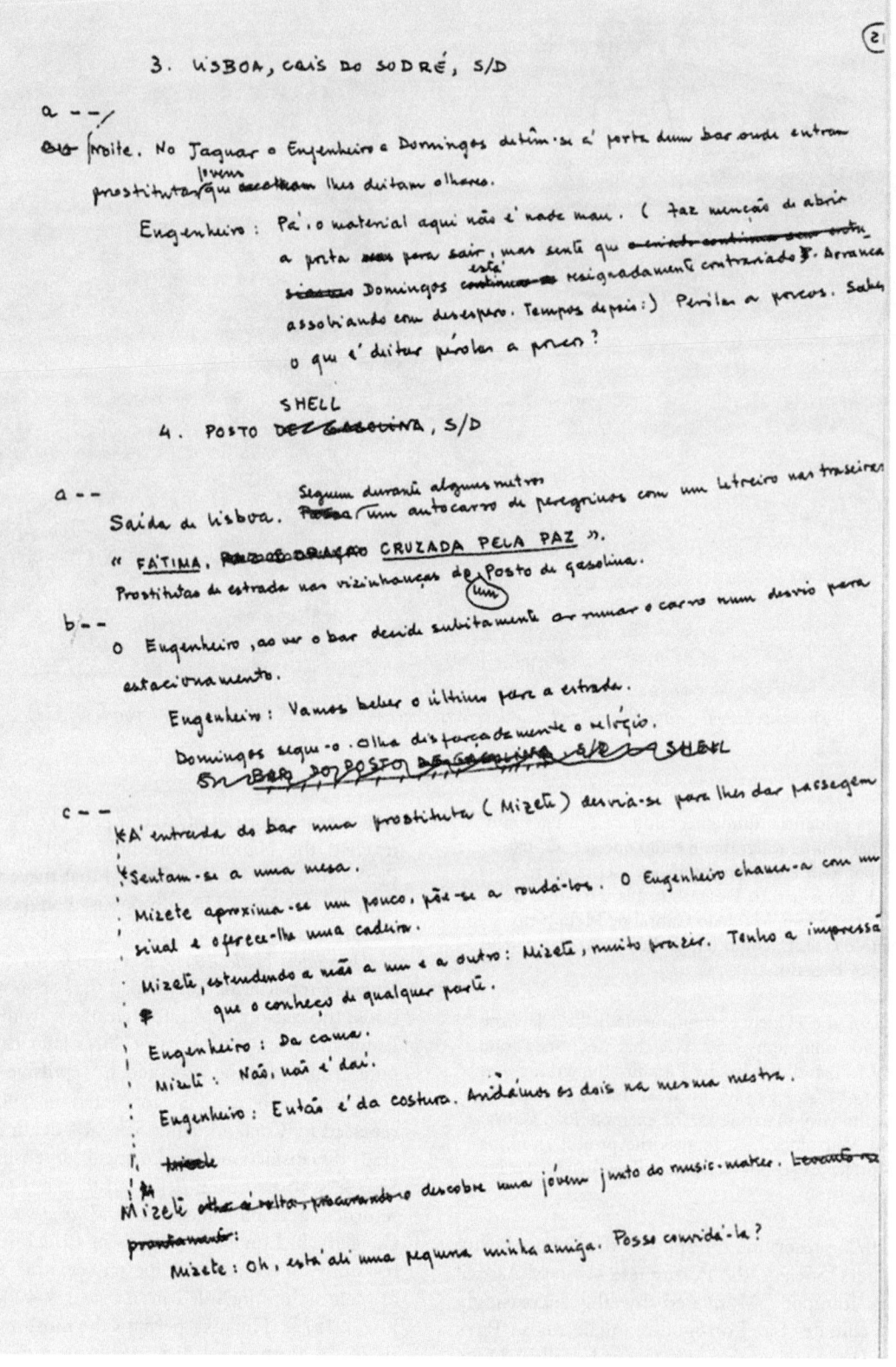

*Page from the manuscript for the unpublished screenplay (circa 1972) that Pires based on his novel* O delfim *(The Dauphin), which appeared in 1968 (from Ines Pedrosa,* José Cardoso Pires: Fotobiografia, *1999; University of California, Berkeley, Library)*

and fascist governor, who, prohibiting me, forced me to speak of freedom in a territory dominated by him." Pires showed similar fearlessness in 1973 when he appeared in defense of João Abel Manta, accused of using the national flag offensively in a cartoon in the *Diário de Lisbon*. In 1974 Pires came to the defense of the authors of the *Novas cartas portuguesas* (New Portuguese Letters, 1972; translated as *The Three Marias: New Portuguese Letters,* 1975), who had been charged with pornography. As he stated, "The witness considers that pornography is in the eyes of those who fear the reality of their own bodies and not in the eyes of the writer of this book."

The Revolução dos Cravos took place on 25 April 1974. The dictatorship ended, and Antônio Sebastião Ribeiro de Spinola took over the presidency of the National Salvation Council and, later, of the Republic. Censorship and the PVDE were abolished. In May the statue of Salazar at the door of the Palácio da Cultura was taken down, and many writers began to return from exile, welcomed by the Portuguese Writers' Association. Pires, a euphoric and indefatigable militant, was nominated town councillor for Lisbon and president of the Cultural Commission of the county. In 1975 he took part in the National Conference for the Independence of Puerto Rico, in Havana, and he attended the twenty-fifth Berlin City Festival. The following year, he attended the Copenhagen PEN Club meeting against the cultural repression in Spain and Latin America, and he also served as an official delegate for Portuguese writers at the Book Biennial in São Paulo, Brazil.

Most of the texts that Pires wrote during these international travels were published in *E agora, José?* in 1977, his first book since the revolution. The work, with its metaphorical title taken from a poem by the Brazilian Carlos Drummond de Andrade, reflects the doubts most Portuguese had about how to handle their new freedom after almost half a century of repression. It was a time in which writers were examining the relationship between writing and power. The essays in the section "Auto-retrato" (Self-Portrait), especially "Atento, venerador e obrigado" (Attentive, Praising and Thankful), are characterized by a sharp sense of irony.

At the time of the publication of *O burro-em-pé* (The Jackass on Foot, 1979), a series of the author's most liked short stories, Pires was in London as a university writer-in-residence. In 1980 he wrote a report on Vietnam ("Apocalipse 2") for the magazines *Triunfo* (Triumph) in Madrid and *Hoy* (Today) in Mexico. The article was also excerpted in the *Diário de Lisbon*. He bought a house in Costa da Caparica, which became his favorite place for writing, and dedicated himself, as he stated in the Portela interview, to uncovering "the sub-world of the political police and the psychological tissue of his identification with terror."

The novel *Balada da praia dos cães* (1982; translated as *Ballad of Dogs' Beach: Dossier of a Crime,* 1986) resulted from these efforts and went through thirteen editions in five years. In 1983 the work was awarded the Grande Prêmio de Romance e Novela da Associação Portuguesa de Escritores (Portuguese Writers' Association Grand Prize for the Novel and Short Story), and in 1986 it was on the list of "the best foreign novels of the year" in *The Sunday Times* of London. The novel also inspired the 1986 motion picture of the same title, directed by José Fonseca e Costa. The book, in police-story style, deals with an assassination committed in April 1960, when the PVDE was in full force. Pires was cautious, however, to avoid creating an historical novel. He wanted to use a real-life event to escape literary conventions and to explore his own creativity. In the novel he exploits events that surround an episode of this type: the gathering of testimonies and documents about the victim's lifestyle, the relationships among the policemen responsible for the investigation, the questioning of suspects, laboratory analyses, and reports with dates and schedules. Hidden aspects of dictatorship emerge as the narrator delves into the hallucinatory and fantastic atmosphere created by the protagonist, Major Dantas C.

In 1983 Pires's short story "Week-end" was adapted for the movies, with the title *Casino Oceano;* in 1985 he was decorated by the president of the republic, Ramalho Eanes, with the Ordem da Liberdade (Order of Freedom). "Les pas perdus" (The Lost Steps) was published in *Le monde diplomatique* in 1986, and a series of five chronicles titled "Poker aberto" (Open Poker) appeared in the weekly periodical *O Jornal*.

Pires published the novel *Alexandra Alpha* in 1987 and was awarded the Prêmio da Associaçao de Críticos (Award of the Association of Critics) in São Paulo, Brazil. In the Portela interview Pires offers precious clues for understanding *Alexandra Alpha,* which treats with bitter irony the periods before and after the 1974 revolution:

A consciência da desidentificação é quase sempre desagradável, para não dizer dolorosa. É como sentir-se emigrante na sua própria terra: a pessoa tem dois rostos que se contrariam um ao outro. Sim, é isso. . . . *Alexandra Alpha* está povoada de figuras a dois rostos, como se pode verificar.

(The awareness of lacking an identity is almost always unpleasant, if not painful. It is like feeling like an immigrant in your own country: the person has two faces that contradict one another. Yes, that is it. . . . *Alexandra*

*Cover for Pires's 1982 novel about the police investigation of a 1960 assassination (from Ines Pedrosa,* José Cardoso Pires: Fotobiografia, *1999; University of California, Berkeley, Library) and dust jacket for its 1986 English translation (Richland County Public Library)*

*Alpha* is populated by figures with two faces, which can be verified).

In this novel the author vigorously resumes the cinematographic style of *O anjo ancorado* and *O hóspede de Job*, as well as the nonsense-filled detective plot of *Balada da praia dos cães*. The work relates the story of Alexandra Alpha, marketing and publicity director of the multinational Alpha Linn, and her "double," Maria (the "two faces," according to Pires, who live on the edge of social and moral prejudice and who supposedly die, hand in hand, in a plane accident). The reader is constantly involved in the mysteries of the narrative and is never completely certain of anything. The political and human portrait of Portugal, which is seen as facing a mirror in discouraging "before" and "after" images, is characterized by the author: "o nosso inconsciente político está carregado de obscurantismos que foram regras entre nós durante séculos. Complexos de inferioridade, fatalis-mos, álibis providencialistas" (our political unconsciousness is full of obscurantisms that were rules among us for centuries. Inferiority complexes, fatalism, providential alibis).

Between 1988 and 1994 Pires published two more books. *A república dos corvos* (The Republic of Crows, 1988), which he defined in the Portela interview as "dramatic zoology"—that is, "Kafkan insects, birds with voices, police-dogs"—is a collection of short stories (including *Dinossauro excelentíssimo*). *A cavalo no diabo* (The Devil's Horse, 1994) consists of short pieces written for the periodical *Público;* these describe his travels to New York, London, and Paris. He also talks about his days in the cafés and pubs, restaurants, bookstores, and streets and squares from his childhood and adolescence. Lisbon, a combination of the new and the old, serves as a symbol of a Portugal on the verge of losing its rural features. These two books brought Pires more awards: in Rome, the Prêmio Internacional da

União Latina (1991) for the totality of his works; and in Pisa, the Golden Astrolabe for the Prêmio Internazzionale Ultimo Novecentos (1992).

Following this international acknowledgment, in 1995 Pires was struck with a vascular brain disease that affected his speech and writing centers. He fell into a coma but recovered in fifteen days. Two years afterward, Pires related this experience in a new book, *De profundis, valsa lenta* (De Profundis, Slow Waltz), at the request of his neurologist. He called the event "white death," or a temporary loss of consciousness, and he gave various interviews describing his sensation of having been "on the other side." More than the circumstantial misfortune of the illness, Pires explores the peculiar state of the human being who loses all of his points of reference.

During 1995 Pires received other important awards: the Fernando Pessoa Award; the Prêmio D. Dinis da Fundação da Casa de Mateus; and the Prêmio de Crítica da Associação International de Críticos Literários. At the same time, his last literary work, *Lisboa, livro de bordo: Vozes, olhares, memorações* (Lisbon, a Ship's Log: Voices, Looks, Memories, 1997), was released at the Frankfurt Fair. The author told Rodrigues da Silva:

> Neste livro quis fazer outro coisa: uma espécie de levantamento que desse, com toda a sinceridade, o modo como sinto Lisboa. E é aí que o livro me parece muito diferente da Lisboa convencional do Tejo que é bonito, etc. . . . Falta ainda a sintaxe lisboeta. Está abordada, mas não aprofundada. E os cheiros. . . . E o humor, que é um dos mais característicos e criativos aspectos da personalidade de Lisboa.
>
> (In this book I wanted to do something else: a sort of investigation that would state, with total sincerity, how I feel about Lisbon. And it is at this point that the book seems very different from the conventional descriptions of Lisbon with the beautiful Tejo River, etc. . . . The syntax of the speech from Lisbon is still missing. It is approached but not entirely grasped. And the smells. . . . and the humor, one of the most characteristic and creative aspects of the personality of Lisbon).

The work constitutes a farewell to the city and the country he loved so much.

In April of 1998 Pires suffered another vascular attack. In the following month, still at home, he personally received the Associação Internacional de Críticos de Arte (International Association of Art Critics [AICA]) award. Immediately afterward, he was taken to the hospital with respiratory failure. He was in a coma until his death on 26 October. His death occurred ten days after José Saramago won for Portugal the first Nobel Prize in literature in its history. In September, Pires's wife had accepted, on his behalf, the Prêmio de Vida Literária awarded by the Portuguese Writers' Association. This prize recognized Pires's achievements as an important Portuguese writer who made a revolution in neorealism through his innovations in literary narrative and his depictions of social problems.

**Interview:**

*Cardoso Pires por Cardoso Pires: Entrevista de Artur Portela* (Lisbon: Dom Quixote, 1991).

**References:**

Jacinto Baptista, *Caminhos para uma revolução* (Lisbon: Bertrand, 1975);

Pierrette Chalendar and Gérard Chalendar, "Da balada da praia dos cães de José Cardoso Pires," *Letras & Letras*, 45 (1991): 15;

Liberto Cruz, *José Cardoso Pires. Análise crítica e seleção de textos* (Lisbon: Arcádia, 1972);

João Décio, "Uma nova faceta da ficção de José Cardoso Pires," *Letras & Letras*, 45 (1991): 14;

Álvaro Cardoso Gomes, *A voz itinerante* (São Paulo: Editora da Universidade de São Paulo, 1993);

L. W. Keats, *Thesis and the Craft of Prose Fiction in the Work of José Cardoso Pires* (Leeds: University of Leeds, 1966);

Maria Lúcia Lepecki, *José Cardoso Pires* (Lisbon: Moraes, 1977);

Rodrigues da Silva, "Lisboa em livros(s). Cidade, minha cúmplice," *Letras & Letras* (19 November 1997);

Alexandre Pinheiro Torres, *O neo-realismo literário português* (Lisbon: Moraes, 1976).

# Eça de Queirós
*(25 November 1845 – 16 August 1900)*

## Maria do Amparo Tavares Maleval
*Universidade do Estado do Rio de Janeiro*

BOOKS: *O mistério da estrada de Sintra,* by Queirós and José Duarte Ramalho Ortigão (Lisbon: A. M. Pereira, 1870; revised, 1885);

*Singularidades de uma rapariga loira* (Lisbon: Tip. Universal de T. Q. Antunes, 1874);

*O crime do padre Amaro* (Lisbon: Tipografia Castro Irmão, 1876; revised edition, Porto: Chardron, 1880); translated by Nan Flanagan as *The Sin of Father Amaro* (New York: St. Martin's Press, 1963; London: Transworld, 1964);

*O primo Basílio* (Porto: Chardron, 1878; revised, 1878); translated by Roy Campbell as *Cousin Bazilio* (London: Max Reinhardt, 1953; New York: Noonday Press, 1953);

*O mandarim* (Porto: Chardron, 1880); translated by Richard Franko Goldman as *The Mandarin and Other Stories* (Athens: Ohio University Press, 1965; London: Bodley Head, 1966);

*A relíquia* (Porto: Tipografia de A. J. da Silva Teixeira, 1887); translated by Aubrey F. G. Bell as *The Relic* (New York: Knopf, 1930; London: Max Reinhardt, 1954);

*Os Maias,* 2 volumes (Porto: Chardron, 1888); translated by Patricia McGowan Pinheiro and Ann Stevens as *The Maias* (London: Bodley Head, 1965; New York: St. Martin's Press, 1965);

*Uma campanha alegre,* 2 volumes (Lisbon: Companhia Nacional, 1890, 1891);

*Dicionário de milagres* (Lisbon: A. M. Pereira, 1900);

*A ilustre casa de Ramires* (Porto: Chardron, 1900); translated by Stevens as *The Illustrious House of Ramires* (London: Bodley Head, 1968; Athens: Ohio University Press, 1968);

*A correspondência de Fradique Mendes* (Porto: Lello & Irmão, 1900);

*A cidade e as serras* (Porto: Chardron, 1901); translated by Campbell as *The City and the Mountains* (London: Max Reinhardt, 1955; Athens: Ohio University Press, 1967);

*Contos* (Porto: Chardron de Lello & Irmão, 1902);

*Prosas bárbaras* (Porto: Chardron, 1903);

*Eça de Queirós (from Fidelino de Figueiredo,* Historia de la literatura portuguesa, *1927; Thomas Cooper Library, University of South Carolina)*

*Cartas de Inglaterra* (Porto: Chardron, 1905); translated by Stevens as *Letters from England* (London: Bodley Head, 1970; Athens: Ohio University Press, 1970);

*Ecos de Paris* (Porto: Chardron, 1905);

*Cartas familiares e bilhetes de Paris* (Porto: Chardron, 1907);

*Notas contemporâneas* (Porto: Chardron, 1909);

*Últimas páginas* (Porto: Lello & Irmão, 1912);

*Alves & C* (Porto: Chardron, 1925); translated by John Vetch as *The Yellow Sofa*, in *The Yellow Sofa & Three Portraits*, translated by Vetch, Goldman, and Luís Marques (Manchester, U.K.: Carcanet, 1993; New York: New Directions, 1996);

*O Conde de Abranhos e A catástrofe* (Porto: Lello & Irmão, 1925);

*A capital* (Porto: Chardron, 1925); translated by Vetch as *To the Capital* (Manchester, U.K.: Carcanet, 1995);

*O Egipto* (Porto: Chardron / Lisbon & Paris: Aillaud & Bertrand, 1926);

*Cartas inéditas de Fradique Mendes e mais páginas esquecidas* (Porto: Chardron, 1929);

*Crónicas de Londres* (Lisbon: Aviz, 1944);

*Polêmicas de Eça de Queirós*, edited by João Luso (Rio de Janeiro & Lisbon: Edições Dois Mundos, 1945);

*Folhas soltas* (Porto: Lello & Irmão, 1966);

*Lendas de santos*, edited by Helena Cidade Moura (Lisbon: Livros de Brasil, 1970);

*A tragédia da Rua das Flores*, edited by João Medina and A. Campos Matos (Lisbon: Moraes, 1980); translated by Margaret Jull Costa as *The Tragedy of the Street of Flowers* (Sawtry: Dedalus, 2000).

**Editions and Collections:** *Obras de Eça de Queirós*, 15 volumes (Porto: Lello & Irmão, 1946–1948);

*Prosas esquecidas*, 5 volumes, edited by Albert Machado da Rosa (Lisbon: Presença, 1965–1966)—comprises volume 1, *Ficção, 1866–1872;* volume 2, *Crítica, 1867;* volume 3, *Política, 1867;* volume 4, *Polémica, 1867;* and volume 5, *Farpas, 1871.*

**Editions in English:** *The Sweet Miracle*, translated by Edgar Prestage (Portland, Me.: Printed for T. B. Mosher, 1906);

*Perfection*, translated by Charles Marriott (London: Selwyn & Blount, 1923).

TRANSLATION: H. Rider Haggard, *As Minas de Salomão* (Porto: Chardron, 1891).

Eça de Queirós is the most representative writer of Portuguese realism. In his novels and short stories he portrays diverse aspects of Portuguese society, showing its shortcomings and defects. His detailed and profound treatment of issues associated with religion and the church, the family structure, education, and the political and economic life of nineteenth-century Portugal have earned him respect as a gifted prose writer both in Portugal and abroad.

José Maria Eça de Queirós was born on 25 November 1845 in Póvoa de Varzim. He was registered as the natural son of the magistrate José de Almeida Teixeira de Queirós. His mother's name, Carolina Augusta Pereira de Eça, does not appear on the birth certificate, probably because she and Queirós's father did not marry until four years after his birth. Queirós spent those years with his godmother, Ana Joaquina Leal de Barros. After his parents' marriage he was moved to his paternal grandparents' house in Verdemilho, where he lived until 1855. The local priest, António Gonçalves Bartolomeu, taught him to read and write.

When his paternal grandmother, Teodora Joaquina, died in 1855, Queirós was sent to the boarding school Colégio de Nossa Senhora da Lapa in Porto. This school, considered one of the best at that time, was directed by Joaquim da Costa Ramalho, father of writer José Duarte Ramalho Ortigão, who was a French teacher at the school. Even though Ramalho Ortigão was nine years older than Queirós, the two developed a lasting friendship. During his years at the school, Queirós demonstrated a gift for writing, which pleased his father.

Between 1858 and 1861 Queiros's father served as the judge in two scandalous trials. The first involved the powerful count of Bolhão, who was accused of making counterfeit money. The strict magistrate found him guilty, but the count's political allies had the ruling overturned. The second case involved his friend, the writer Camilo Castelo Branco, who was accused of committing adultery with Ana Plácido. The judge was forced to rule against his friend, who was eventually absolved of the crime. Before being released, however, the couple was held for several months in prison. Upset with these two cases, the judge moved from Porto to Vila França de Xira. These events occurred about the time Queirós began law school at the University of Coimbra. The future writer became disillusioned with the immorality of society and the fragility of the juridical system, subjects his father addressed in a letter to the king.

In 1861 Queirós began his studies at the University of Coimbra, where he met Teófilo Braga and Antero de Quental. The academic atmosphere at the time was agitated, since the students were unhappy with the strict policies of the dean, Basílio Alberto de Souza Pinto. The students created a secret society to combat his despotism; they called themselves the Sociedade do Raio (The Ray Society), and their most eloquent representative was Quental. Two years later, in 1863, the dean submitted his resignation.

Queirós did not belong to the Sociedade do Raio, but he signed their protests. A shy individual, he accomplished his academic work without enthusiasm. He read many works, including novels and French poetry. His preferred authors were Victor Hugo, Alfred de Musset,

Théophile Gautier, Charles Baudelaire, and Heinrich Heine. He liked to recite passages from those authors' works for his friends, interpreting them with gestures as if he were on stage. His dramatic abilities, inherited from his father's family (his uncle Fernando José Queirós was a famous actor), led him in October 1863 to the university theater. At the Teatro Acadêmico he was able to overcome some of his shyness.

The theatrical sessions were filled with discussions on art and literature and were often accompanied by dinners of fried fish and wine. Queirós had a voracious appetite and over the years developed intestinal problems. Some of his biographers consider these problems to be the first manifestations of his intestinal tuberculosis. He also participated in the bohemian life in Coimbra. In 1863 he moved from José Doria's house on the Rua do Loureiro to a room at 16 Rua do Salvador, where he lived until he finished his studies. There he received his friends for serious debates on philosophy and art. Around this time Queirós met Carlos de Lima Mayer, a rich man who became his friend for life. Mayer later moved to Paris during Queirós's assignment as consul in that city.

Like many of his classmates, Queirós had a profound appreciation for Quental, whom he called "Saint Antero." He got to know him in 1864 during a student movement against the government. The group was called Rolinada, taken from the surname Rolim of the duke of Loulé, the head of the government. Quental's work *Bom senso e bom gosto* (Good Sense and Good Taste, 1865) was the catalyst for the "Questão Coimbrã" (Coimbra Affair), in which he defended a new approach to art: realism. The Questão Coimbrã began in 1865 when the author, translator, journalist, and professor of literature Pinheiro Chagas published *Poema da Juventude* (Poem of Youth). A postscript to the poem by António Feliciano de Castilho, one of the first Romantics in Portugal, referred derogatorily to the writers Antero de Quental, Teófilo Braga, and Antonio Manuel Lopez Vieira de Castro. Quental responded in a pamphlet, and the quarrel that became the Questão Coimbrã began. Proponents of an arcadian aesthetic and Romantic literature, led by Castilho, fought against the scientific and realistic spirit. This new generation was solidified six years later with the Conferências Democráticas do Casino (Casino Democratic Conferences). Queirós was a silent and loyal observer, and later in his essay on Quental he stated that the artist's protest was more against society than against art.

Quental and Mayer had left Coimbra by 1866, Queirós's last year as a university student. Around this time he became friends with poet João Penha, who was six years older and a popular figure at the university. Penha was a fun-loving bohemian and was involved in several pranks with Queirós and his friends during his last year at school. One such incident occurred on a night at the cathedral in Coimbra. Queirós, at the portal of the church, invoked in his theatrical voice the memory of Sancho I. A few minutes later they heard the sound of running footsteps on the wooden floor. Penha jokingly said that it must have been the sound of a dead lady running from the devil. The group fled, but Queirós insisted on returning to "face the danger." Later, he joined fiction to history and fantasized that it could have been Mécia Fufes de Anaia, who had been buried in the dungeons of the cathedral after her death in 1371 in Santa Clara monastery. Her father, Arnulfo Eanes Zurara, was the murderer of Iñigo Ansur, her boyfriend. Some days after the incident in the cathedral, in March 1866, Queirós published his first poem in the *Gazeta de Portugal,* a prestigious magazine directed by António Augusto Teixeira de Vasconelos, a friend of Queirós's father. The morbid character of the poem, possibly inspired by the incident, was the first of his romantic compositions published in the *Gazeta de Portugal* from October 1866 to December 1867. Ten were included in the volume *Prosas bárbaras* (Barbarous Prose, 1903).

In June 1866 Queirós graduated with a degree in law. That same year he sent his translation of Joseph Bouchardy's play *Philodor* (1863) to the Teatro D. Maria I. The play, however, was never performed. After he graduated, Queirós moved to Lisbon and settled into his parents' house on the fourth floor of 26 Rossio. His father had been transferred from Porto to Vila França de Xira in 1861, and in 1862 to Almada. After a short period in Évora, he returned to Lisbon on 21 October 1862. Queirós, possibly at his father's insistence, applied for the position of lawyer in the Supreme Tribunal of Justice on 10 October 1866. The dedication to literary activities and bohemian habits, however, contributed to his short juridical career. At the end of 1866 Queirós left for Évora to run the opposition political newspaper *Distrito de Évora*. The paper was launched on 6 January 1867 and was published twice a week. Queirós also worked as a lawyer. Life in the provinces, without his friends with whom he could talk about art and literature, proved too boring after a while, so in July 1867 Queirós left the newspaper and the city and returned to Lisbon. He took up his work at the *Gazeta de Portugal,* and on 6 October he published "O Milharfe" (The Glede), a narrative that tells of a bird's metaphysical reflections on the image of Christ on a rat-gnawed cross.

At the end of 1867 Queirós joined a group of young intellectuals at the home of Jaime Batalha Reis, whose father was a friend of the poet Almeida Garrett, to discuss topics including art, philosophy, politics. The author had met Reis earlier while serving on the editorial board of the *Gazeta de Portugal*. The enthusiastic gatherings were known as the Cenáculo (Cenacle), and Queirós was one of the first members. Reis, Mayer, Ramalho Ortigão, Salomão Sáraga, Augusto Fuschini, Oliveira Martins, Abílio Manuel Guerra Junqueiro, and others soon joined the group. The group eventually merged with one led by Quental, who had just arrived from his birthplace, São Miguel, where he had lived since 1868 after leaving Coimbra. Quental introduced the group to Pierre-Joseph Proudhon's socialism, and they often read his books far into the night.

The first verses of Carlos Fradique Mendes, "the satanic poet," appeared in 1869. Reis, Quental, and Queirós invented this pen name for verses they wrote. According to *A correspondência de Fradique Mendes* (The Correspondence of Fradique Mendes, 1900), Queirós alone wrote the verses under this name from 1888 to 1900. In October 1869 the author reestablished contact with Luís and Manuel Resende, who had been his classmates at the Colégio da Lapa in Porto. The Resende family was descended from a long line of noblemen, including Álvaro Pires de Castro, brother of Inês de Castro, Pedro I's lover. That same year, in November, Queirós and Luís de Castro Pamplona, fifth Earl of Resende, visited Egypt for the inauguration of the Suez Canal. Pamplona was a notable man, with a great sense of justice and dignity. He was also, however, a great spendthrift. Although his fortune was not as great as when he had received his inheritance, he financed Queirós's trip in luxurious style. They stayed at the exclusive Shepherd's Hotel in Cairo. When they returned to Lisbon on 3 January 1870, Queirós was dressed in fine clothes and wore a monocle on his right eye. He published the reports of the trip under the title "De Port-Said a Suez" (From Port Said to the Suez) in the newspaper *Diário de Notícias*.

On 21 July 1870 Queirós was named Administrator of the Council of Leiria, probably because of his father's influence. A short time before leaving for Leiria, he and Ramalho Ortigão drafted the fantastic and melodramatic story *O mistério da estrada de Sintra* (The Mystery on the Highway to Sintra) in the form of anonymous letters. They published these in the *Diário de Notícias* from July to September 1870. The work, which is the first example of the police novel in Portuguese literature, is a blend of mystery and romance. The story deals with an accidental crime of passion, focusing on adultery as a product of the tedium of leisure. There are certain thematic similarities between the work and Queirós's later novel *O primo Basílio* (1878; translated as *Cousin Bazilio,* 1953), and the adulterous female character in both works has the name Luísa. The authors play with the concept of verisimilitude,

*Queirós's parents, Carolina Augusta Pereira de Eça and José de Almeida Teixeira de Queirós (Biblioteca Nacional, Lisbon)*

using the last letter to explain finally to the reader that all the letters were fictitious.

Queirós probably sketched out the first chapters of his first great novel, *O crime do padre Amaro* (1876; translated as *The Sin of Father Amaro,* 1963) during his days in Leiria. At the time, Europe was devastated by the Franco-Prussian War, which had begun on 19 July 1870. Queirós followed the military actions in the newspapers with great interest. Later, in a letter to Reis and Quental, he expressed his joy at Napoleon III's defeat.

In September 1870 Queirós competed for a diplomatic position and came in first; the person who came in second, however, got the job. Disillusioned, the writer left Lisbon for Leiria and threw himself into the life of the local high society. He began a love affair with the baroness of Salgueiro, but it ended when they were caught in her bedroom during a party at the Salgueiro home.

In 1871 Queirós and Ramalho Ortigão began to publish a regular series of supplements titled *As Farpas* (The Barbs) in which they criticized various aspects of Portuguese society. At the same time, the meetings of the Cenáculo led them to the project of the "democratic conferences," whose program of May 1871 was planned and organized by Quental and signed by Quental, Queirós, Martins, Fuschini, Braga, Reis, Sáraga, Adolfo Coelho, Augusto Soromenho, Germane Vieira de Meireles, Guilherme de Azevedo, and Manuel de Arriaga. The conferences aimed at the modernization of Portugal, using more-advanced nations as a model, and at a transformation in Portuguese politics, economy, and religion. The conferences took place in the Casino Lisbonense on Praça da Abegoaria, at 9:00 P.M. on Mondays. The public had to pay an admission fee to help cover general costs. At the first conference, which took place on 22 May, Quental explained the purpose of the project. On Saturday, 27 May, he discussed "the reasons for the decadence in the peninsula during the last three centuries."

Soromenho gave the third conference, on Portuguese literature, on 5 June. An elegantly dressed Queirós gave the fourth one on 12 June; his topic was the "New Literature," which, as he explained in *As Farpas,* was a statement on realism as the new expression of art. This manifesto, based mainly on Proudhon's *Du principe de l'art et de sa destination sociale* (The Prince of Art and His Social Destination, 1865), proposes an art "perfectly connected with its time," based on daily life and with science as the basis of experience, temper, and character.

Adolfo Coelho, brother of Eduardo Coelho (director of the *Diário de Notícias*), held the fifth conference, titled "The Question of Teaching," on 19 June. Coelho violently attacked the educational system of the country, which so displeased the authorities that they prohibited the next conference, scheduled for 26 June. The Jewish scholar Sáraga was scheduled to speak on critical histories of Jesus. The government accused the speakers of presenting and defending ideas that attacked religion and the state. Writers Alexandre Herculano and Quental responded, and Pinheiro Chagas, in turn, declared that all the speakers were subversives.

On 6 June, before the conference, Queirós had resigned his post on the Council of Leiria. On the same day he had asked to have his name removed from the membership of the Internacional Socialista. This action shows his lack of esteem for political militancy. In a letter to Ramalho Ortigão in 1871 Queirós expressed concerns about his health. He decided to take the sea baths prescribed by his physician for nerves, anemia, and eyesight. At the time, Queirós was slim and prone to colds and frequent intestinal problems inherited from his father's family. He avoided extreme temperatures of heat and cold, but his bohemian lifestyle and insatiable appetite undermined his health.

In September 1871 the government fell, and Queirós denounced in *As Farpas* the injustice he had suffered in his bid for consul. On 16 March 1872 he was named first class consul to the Spanish Antilles. Later, however, when he was gathering his writings from *As Farpas* into the volumes titled *Uma campanha alegre* (A Happy Campaign, 1890, 1891), he did not include the article in which he had made his complaint.

At the end of 1872 Queirós assumed the office in Havana for a period of two years. During that time he concerned himself with combating the exploitation of Chinese workers from Macao. Because of his delicate health, he got permission to leave Cuba to escape the heat and fevers of the summer. On 30 May 1873 he left for a long trip of five and a half months to Canada, the United States, and Central America. In an undated letter to Raul Brandão, Queirós's son revealed that his father had gone to the United States to pursue Mollie Bidwell, a beautiful American woman who was the daughter of a wealthy industrialist from Pittsburgh. He had been seriously involved with her, but she refused to marry him. In Havana he had a platonic relationship with another American, Anna Conover, who was already married and a religious person.

In the memoirs of his trip described by José Calvet Magalhães, Queirós says that he adored Chicago but both loved and hated New York City. He disliked the brutality of the metropolis but admired its great avenues and parks, the Gothic churches, the countless theaters, the incomparable schools, and the beautiful women. Before returning to Cuba he stayed three months in New York City and then visited Montreal. After arriving in Havana on 15 November 1873, he became bored, finding the city ugly and dirty, with rude and ill-mannered people. He continued to work on *O crime do padre Amaro,* which he had begun in Leiria, and he wrote *Singularidades de uma rapariga loira* (Singularities of a Blonde Girl, 1874), published as a "gift to subscribers of the *Diário de Notícias* of 1873." The work focuses on the kleptomania of a man's fiancée, who steals a diamond ring. Once she is exposed for her crime, she loses her future husband, who is the narrator of the story.

With the help of influential friends in Lisbon, Queirós left Havana again in May 1874 to await a new assignment as attaché in the administration of the consular division. He finished the first version of *O crime do padre Amaro*. In spite of the imperfections he saw in the work, he published it in serialized form in the *Revista Oriental* from 15 February to 15 May 1875. The *Revista Oriental* was a respectable journal founded by Martins and directed by Reis and Quental. The publication, however, done without his revisions taken into account, upset Queirós; he accused Quental of suppressing the passages he considered too realistic.

In 1874 Queirós was designated consul in Newcastle-upon-Tyne. His literary production there was prolific, despite the various official reports he had to write on the conflicts between the coal miners of the area and their employers. While there he wrote *O primo Basílio*, fifteen articles for the Porto newspaper *A Actualidade,* and a revision of *O crime do padre Amaro*. He also launched a project of a series of short novels called *Cenas da vida real* (Scenes of Real Life) or *Cenas portuguesas* (Portuguese Scenes); the works *A tragédia da Rua das Flores* (1980; translated as *The Tragedy of the Street of Flowers,* 2000), *A capital* (1925; translated as *To the Capital,* 1995), *O Conde de Abranhos* (1925), and *Alves & C* (1925; translated as *The Yellow Sofa,* 1993) were part of the project. This intense literary activity was a way to compensate for the lack of intellectual companionship and a way to escape the gloomy atmosphere of the city.

In July of 1876 Queirós published the first book edition of *O crime do padre Amaro* in Porto. His father helped to subsidize the costs of publication. Although totally rewritten, the novel was not a great success and did not receive favorable reviews from the critics. Antonio José da Silva Pinto, a well-known critic and admirer of novelists Camilo Castelo Branco and Honoré de Balzac, considered Queirós's book to be ideologically linked to Balzac's psychological realism in its focus on the inner man, and to the works of Gustave Flaubert. Queirós, who considered Balzac one of his masters and Flaubert to be an important contemporary writer, was pleased with this evaluation. Quental welcomed the new version of the work, considering Queirós to be above all schools and masters.

The novel focuses on a man driven to the priesthood by external pressures. He seduces a young girl who becomes pregnant, has the baby, and then commits suicide. The baby boy is delivered to a "fazedora de anjos," a woman who specializes in killing unwanted babies. Hypocrisy is an important theme of this work and others by Queirós. In a piece on Queirós's *O primo Basílio* in the *Jornal do Comércio* (13 August 1878), the great Brazilian novelist Joaquim Maria Machado de Assis accused him of imitating the French novelists. In the foreword to the second edition of *O crime do padre Amaro,* totally recast and published in 1880, Queirós responds to accusations that he copied Emile Zola in the work. Several changes were made between the first and second editions of the book: the first edition analyzes feelings and represents the tragedy of prohibited love; the second criticizes ecclesiastical tradition and focuses on Amaro's callousness. Although there are some similarities between Queirós's novel and Zola's *La faute de l'Abbé Mouret* (The Transgression of Abbé Mouret, 1875), there are basic differences: Zola's priest possesses a true gift for the priesthood. He gives up the profession, however, when he becomes seriously ill and loses his memory.

In 1877 Queirós published *Cartas inglesas* (English Letters) in *A Actualidade,* on which he collaborated until 1878. He also established contact with Chardron, the publisher to whom he presented the twelve-volume project of *Cenas da vida portuguesa,* and he finished *O primo Basílio,* which he had started in 1876. Critic Ramalho Ortigão attacked the novel, but the reading public appreciated it. The first edition of three thousand copies, released in February 1878, sold out within three months. The author revised and republished the novel that same year. Most of the critics were positive in their reviews. Machado de Assis, however, criticized the work for slavishly following the tenets of realism. He found the characters to be superficial and too strictly governed by the laws of determinism. Luísa, the protagonist, is easily seduced by an old boyfriend while her husband is away. She contrasts strongly with her maid and blackmailer Juliana, whom Machado de Assis considered "the most true and complete character in the work."

Queirós stated that his novel was an attack on the bourgeois families of Lisbon, through their more representative symbols: the poorly educated wife, who is idle, lustful, nervous, and negatively influenced by her reading and her libertine friends; the unscrupulous lover; the envious maid; and the faithful friend. The work is an expression of realist art that explores the weakness of a society on the brink of ruin.

In 1878 Queirós was transferred to the consulate in Bristol, where he lived for the next eight years. He continued his intense literary activity, and he traveled extensively through England, France, and Portugal. He rewrote *O primo Basílio* and worked on the manuscripts of *A catástrofe* (The Catastrophe, 1925) and *A tragédia da Rua das Flores.*

*A tragédia da Rua das Flores* is the sketch of a novel that was conceived from 1877 to 1878 in Newcastle. The work was left among Queirós's manuscripts for almost a century and finally published in 1980. A. Campos Matos, in his 1987 study, posited that the Queirós family was not interested in publishing the novel because the author never really finished it, and possibly also because of some rather crude passages and the theme of involuntary incest between mother and son. Queirós had stated that he wanted the work to be a part of a series of novels titled "As crónicas da vida" (Chronicles of Life). He did not think, however, that it should be the initial piece for the series, deciding instead on the more generic *A capital*.

In 1879, as a part of the project *Cenas da vida real,* Queirós wrote the novel *O Conde de Abranhos,* a short political satire that was not published until twenty-five years

Title page for Queirós's novel about a confidence man trying to win an inheritance from his pious aunt (Biblioteca Nacional, Lisbon)

after his death. His son José Maria made extensive modifications in the manuscript before allowing it to appear in print. Also in 1879 Queirós began his collaboration with the *Gazeta de Notícias,* a newspaper in Rio de Janeiro, Brazil. He wrote for the paper until 1897, publishing many of his stories in its pages.

The second edition of *O crime do padre Amaro* appeared in 1880. Queirós also published in *O Atlantico* the short stories "Um poeta lírico" (A Lyric Poet) and "No moinho" (In the Mill). In the first, he deals with the question of literary aesthetics disguised in the story of an impossible love affair. In "No moinho" he presents a plot similar to that of *O primo Basílio* as he focuses on the process of the degradation of the female character, caused by the books she reads. The protagonist goes from being a woman totally dedicated to her family to being an adulteress.

Queirós also published *O mandarim* (The Mandarin, 1880) in serial form in the *Diário de Portugal*. He wrote this work during his vacations in Angers as a substitute for *Os Maias* (1888; translated as *The Maias,* 1965), which he had promised to the paper but had not completed yet. Teodoro, the narrator, works for the Ministério do Reino and inherits a huge fortune–which does not bring him happiness. Tedium and excessive leisure dominate his life. António Coimbra Martins, in his 1967 volume, sees Teodoro as a metaphor for the dominant West, and the character Ti-Chin-Fu as a metaphor for the exploited East. The antithesis captured in the theme of the confrontation of East and West also appears in some of Queirós's other works.

In 1883 Queirós was elected corresponding member of the Royal Academy of Sciences, and he rewrote *O mistério da estrada de Sintra*. Published in 1885, the revision includes a prologue by Queirós and notes by the editors based on a study of José Sampaio Bruno in which he identifies contributions from Queirós and Ramalho Ortigão. He probably wrote *Alves & C* around this time. The work, however, was not published until 1925. The work narrates another story of adultery. In this case, however, the husband, Godofred, a bourgeois merchant who catches his wife, Lulu, in the act in their home, forgives her. Rather than being tragic, the narrative includes much humor, and the concern with honor is replaced by the pragmatic interests of comfort and profit in the bourgeois world.

The second edition of *O mistério da estrada de Sintra* appeared in late 1884 (dated 1885), and several important events occurred in the writer's love life that year. He traveled to the north of Portugal and visited Costa Nova in the company of the countess of Resende and her daughters Emília and Benedita. He wanted to court Emília, but she had turned him down because she was engaged to someone else. After that relationship ended, Emília's brother Manuel interceded on Queirós's behalf, and she accepted his offer of marriage in 1885.

On his return to Bristol from Portugal in 1885, Queirós stopped in Paris with the founder and director of the magazine *A Ilustração* (The Illustration), Mariano Pina, to visit Zola. That same year he published "Outro amável milagre" (Another Pleasant Miracle) in the volume *Um feixe de penas* (A Handful of Feathers), organized for charity purposes by Maria Amália Vaz of Carvalho. He returned to Lisbon on 2 November 1885 to finish the preparations for the wedding. To avoid Queirós's embarrassment over having been born illegitimate, the writer's parents signed a document on 23 December declaring him legitimate.

On 10 February 1886 Queirós married Emília de Castro Pamplona Resende in the private chapel of Quinta de Santo Ovídio in Porto. They left by train the same day for Madrid and went on to Paris, where they spent their honeymoon. They arrived in Bristol in the middle of March and started their married life in Stoke Bishop, on the outskirts of the city. There, they hosted many friends and their families. In 1886 Queirós wrote the prefaces for *Azulejos* (Wall Tiles), by Conde de Arnoso, and *O brasileiro Soares* (The Brazilian Soares), by Luiz de Magalhães.

On 16 January 1887 Queirós's daughter Maria was born. He finished *A relíquia* (1887; translated as *The Relic*, 1930) and entered it in the contest for the D. Luís Prize offered by the Royal Academy of Sciences. Henrique Lopes of Mendonça, however, won the prize with his book *O Duque de Viseu* (The Duke of Viseu). Queirós published *A relíquia* initially in serial form in the *Gazeta de Notícias* in Rio de Janeiro from 24 April to 10 June 1887. It also appeared as a book that year in Porto.

*A relíquia* is narrated in the first person by the protagonist, Teodorico Raposo, nicknamed "Raposão" (Big Fox). The word "raposo" means fox and refers to the cunning character of the picaresque hero. Teodorico's mother died when he was born, and his father died when he was seven. His maternal aunt raised him and saw to his education. She is the "Titi," Maria do Patrocínio, a fanatic bigot who has an exaggerated fear of sexuality. When Raposão goes to the University of Coimbra to study law, he leads a bohemian lifestyle. He deceives his aunt, however, making her think that he is a fervently religious person, because he wants to inherit her fortune. After graduation he leaves on a trip to Palestine in the company of the scholar Topsius. In Alexandria he has a love affair with a woman named Mary, who gives him her nightgown as a present. In Jerusalem he has a dream of Jesus Christ's last days on earth, which takes up a large portion of the work. He acquires a false crown of thorns of Christ as a gift for his aunt, hoping to curry her favor. When he returns to Lisbon, the package with the crown of thorns and the one containing Mary's nightgown get switched, and he gives the nightgown to his aunt. She immediately understands that her nephew is not the religious person he has claimed to be, and she orders him out of the house. Raposão lives for some time from the sale of false relics from the Holy Land. After a while, however, he becomes convinced of the uselessness of his hypocrisy and asks an old schoolmate to arrange a job for him. He ends up marrying the sister of this friend, living without financial problems and perfectly integrated into family and social life. He seems to be a totally different person until he learns that a priest, who was an old friend of his aunt, had inherited her property. The reader sees that he has not changed as he laments not having told his aunt that the nightgown had belonged to Mary Magdalene.

Around the end of 1887 Queirós joined a newly formed group in Lisbon called the Vencidos na Vida (Defeated in Life). Whenever he was in Lisbon he participated in this association of friends, which had as its members some of the outstanding writers and politicians of the day, including Ramalho Ortigão, Martins, Mayer, Guerra Junqueiro, António Cândido, Luís Soveral, Carlos Ávila Wolf, and Conde de Ficalho. The objective of the group was the conviviality of similar mentalities at dinners and banquets. The air of snobbery that surrounded the group provoked the antipathy of other intellectuals such as Chagas, Fialho de Almeida, and Abel Botelho. The "dining group," as Queirós defined it, lasted until 1894. Its dissolution was possibly caused by the political division provoked by King Luís's death. In his 1969 study, Ernesto Guerra da Cal points out that the meetings were not just aristocratic dinners; on the contrary, they captured the ideals of the Generation of 1870, which opposed constitutionalism and "demagogic plebeism."

On 26 February 1888 the Queiróses' son, José Maria, was born. On 28 August, Queirós was named consul to Paris, taking the place of the Viscount Augusto de Faria, who had had a disagreement with his superior and was dismissed. Queirós obtained the position with the help of Martins, who was a close friend of the minister of foreign affairs, Barros Gomes. In October, Queirós moved his family to Paris.

Queirós had an argument with Chagas, who had ignored the publication of *A relíquia*, concerning the awarding of the D. Luís Prize. He published in the *Reporter*, a paper run by Martins, some of his "Cartas de Fradique Mendes," which also appeared in the *Gazeta de Notícias* in Rio de Janeiro and, the following year, in *Revista de Portugal*. The character, originally created by Reis, Quental, and Queirós, became from this point on the work of Queirós. Fradique Mendes is a "satanic poet" and resident of Paris, where he had met Baudelaire, Charles-Marie-René Leconte de Lisle, Théodore de Banville, and all of the poets of the new French generation. He was destined to modernize the outdated ideas that were still in force in Portugal. His letters, published from 1888 to 1900, were presented as posthumous. They are directed to different readers and deal with several subjects. Queirós, in a letter to Martins (10 October 1885), characterizes Mendes as a "man, poet, traveler, and philosopher in the spare time." He appears as a rich aristocrat, a participant in heroic campaigns, a polyglot, a Cartesian, and a dandy. Some critics pointed out Mendes's superficiality and the lack of verisimilitude. Through this character, however, Queirós was able to make interesting social and cultural observations on his time and capture the general skepticism of his generation.

In 1888 Queirós published his masterpiece, *Os Maias*, on which he had worked since 1881. He had completed two volumes in 1882 but took the next six years to finish and polish the work. There were various interruptions during these years, including the time he took to write *A relíquia*.

The novel is the tragic story of the Maia family. Afonso da Maia, a nobleman, opposes his son Pedro's marriage to Maria Monforte, the daughter of a slave merchant. Pedro is a weak man, the product of a doting mother. His father's opposition to the marriage is based not only on the woman's origins but also on his premonitions of the bad fortune she could bring his son. Maria betrays Pedro and leaves him for a Neapolitan, taking their daughter, Maria Eduarda, but leaving behind their son, Carlos Eduardo. Pedro da Maia commits suicide, and Afonso raises his grandson, Carlos. Afonso believes that Maria Eduarda has died. Years later, however, brother and sister meet in Lisbon, where Maria Eduarda has come with her Brazilian husband, the rich Castro Gomes. They fall in love, not knowing that they are brother and sister. Afonso opposes their union, once again based on his premonitions. When Carlos learns the truth through documents given to him by an old friend of Maria Monforte, he has one last sexual encounter with his sister, who is still ignorant of their relationship. When the truth comes out, Afonso dies, and Maria Eduarda leaves for France, after having her family rights recognized.

Queirós criticizes the idle and futile lifestyle of Lisbon high society of his time through some of its most representative types among the supporting characters: the ridiculous romantic poet (Alencar); the mediocre politician (the conde de Gouvarinho); the slanderer, who is a product of a devout and provincial education (Eusebiozinho); the corrupt journalist (Palma Cavalão); and the misunderstood conductor (Cruges). In spite of the English-style education his grandfather gave him to make his character strong, Carlos is a physician who lives like a parasite. His friend João da Ega, who mercilessly comments on the mediocrity of Portuguese society, is also a useless idler. In *Os Maias* Queirós combines psychological elements and social criticism in his portrayal of the saga of a traditional Portuguese family.

In 1889 Queirós wrote the preface for João Dinis's *Aquarelas* (Water Colors). He also launched the first number of the *Revista de Portugal,* and his son António was born on 28 December. On 11 January 1890 the English government sent an ultimatum to the Portuguese government to withdraw its troops from the area between Angola and Mozambique in Africa. The occupation of this zone was part of a project dating back to the fourteenth century, when Portugal began to acquire a vast colonial empire. Recently crowned King Carlos had to accept England's demands to avoid a threatened naval attack. The Republican Party took advantage of the protests of indignity that occurred throughout Portugal, which dealt a mortal blow to the monarchy.

Queirós followed this crisis with great concern, and he wrote about it in one of Fradique Mendes's letters. He considered it "the most severe, maybe the most decisive" event of his time. In a letter to Martins, however, he referred with skepticism and irony to the purposeless excess of patriotism in Portugal. That same year he published the first volume of *Uma campanha alegre,* made up of several texts from *As Farpas*. He also finished the publication of Fradique Mendes's letters in the *Revista de Portugal*.

In 1891 Queirós translated H. Rider Haggard's novel *King Solomon's Mines* (1885), and his fourth child, Alberto, was born. Quental committed suicide on 11 September 1891, in São Miguel; his friend's death had a great impact on Queirós and other intellectuals of his generation.

Queirós published the tale "Civilização" (Civilization) in the *Gazeta de Notícias* in Rio de Janeiro in 1891. This story and "Um dia de chuva" (A Rainy Day), which was left unpublished and undated by the author, became the embryo of the naturalist novel *A cidade e as serras* (1901; translated as *The City and the Mountains,* 1955). The novel, however, goes beyond the tenets of realist-naturalist art with the ambiguity that comes from the narrative focus, given through the perspective of narrator and character Zé Fernandes.

*Gazeta de Notícias* in Rio de Janeiro published the story "A aia" (The Nursemaid, 1893), set in a medieval atmosphere. The work explores the theme of everlasting loyalty, represented by a humble maid. In 1894 Queirós's good friend Martins died. That same year he published in the *Gazeta de Notícias* the short story "O tesouro" (The Treasure), which takes place in the medieval kingdom of Asturias, Spain. The work is based on the proverb that "Greed is the origin of all evils." The story "Frei Genebro" appeared in the same issue and focuses on one of the followers of St. Francis and the exercise of compassion.

In 1895 Queirós, José Sarmiento, and Henrique Marques organized the 1896 version of the *Almanaque Enciclopédico*. In 1896 the same collaborators organized the 1897 version, in which Queirós included the story "Adão e Eva no paraíso" (Adam and Eve in Paradise). Also in 1896 he contributed the text "Um génio que era um santo" (A Genius Who Was a Saint) to *Antero de Quental, In Memoriam,* organized in memory of Quental. *Gazeta de Notícias* also ran his "O Defunto" (The Corpse), a story set in the Middle Ages and based on the themes of jealousy and the intervention of the supernatural in defense of innocent worshipers of the Virgin. Queirós also finished the novel *A ilustre casa de Ramires* (1900; translated as *The Illustrious House of Ramires,* 1968) in 1896.

Queirós started the publication of the *Revista Moderna* in Paris in 1897. In the first two numbers he published the stories "A perfeição" (Perfection) and "José Matias." The November issue was dedicated to Queirós and

*Queirós at the time he was writing his novel* A ilustre casa de Ramires *(1900; translated as* The Illustrious House of Ramires, *1968), which he completed in 1896 (from Ronald W. Sousa,* The Rediscoverers, *1981; Thomas Cooper Library)*

carried the first installment of the serialization of *A ilustre casa de Ramires*. Part of this novel appeared in twenty numbers of *Revista Moderna*, from 20 November 1897 to 29 March 1899. The complete work came out in one volume in Porto in 1900, the year of Queirós's death.

*A ilustre casa de Ramires* presents two parallel narratives. One focuses on Portugal at the end of the nineteenth century, with an impoverished nobleman, Gonçalo Mendes Ramires, as the protagonist. Ramires is a graduate in law from the University of Coimbra and has political aspirations. The other narrative focuses on Ramires's writing of a history based on the life of one of his ancestors, Tructesindo Mendes Ramires, a faithful vassal of Sancho I and the Infantas Teresa and Sancha. Queirós's work, which took seven years to complete, is based on extensive research of the medieval world. Queirós's research on the Middle Ages is also documented in his writings published by his daughter in *Folhas soltas* (Various Papers, 1966). Ramires's ancestor is characterized not only by his honesty and courage but also by cruelty, pride, foolishness, and lack of compassion. These characteristics contrast with those of Ramires, who is dominated by cowardice, inertia, and a lack of scruples. By the end of the narrative, however, he is redeemed by his generosity. He is seen as a metaphor of Portugal, as he leaves his country to explore Africa, where he becomes rich.

In 1898 Queirós published in the *Revista Moderna* the story "O suave milagre," in which he talks about Jesus' preference for the simple and the humble and his objection to the rich and powerful. This story was a revision of "Outro amável milagre," which had first been revised in 1897 and published in *Revista Cor de Rosa* under the title "O milagre." The story not only had various published versions but also had an adaptation by Arnoso for the theater, published in 1902. Arnoso adapted the work with the title *O suave milagre;* it was billed as a mystery in four acts and six scenes. Alberto de Oliveira wrote the lyrics, and Óscar Silva composed the music. The first performance of the play took place on 28 December 1901 in the Teatro D. Maria in Lisbon. The royal family attended the opening to raise funds to subsidize a monument for Eça by Teixeira Lopes.

Queirós died on 16 August 1900 in Paris after a long illness, identified by some biographers as intestinal tuberculosis. In September his body was sent to Portugal for the funeral, which took place in the Alto de São João cemetery in Lisbon. Some of his books were published after his death, including *A correspondência de Fradique Mendes* and *A ilustre casa de Ramires*. Among his posthumous publications, *Últimas páginas* (Last Pages, 1912) stands out; it focuses on legends of the saints but includes some letters and the article "O Francesismo" (Francesism). In this work he deals with the saints to whom he was devoted in the final years of his life. He had started writing the life of St. Frei Gil in 1891, but he never completed it. He also wrote the life of St. Onofre and that of St. Christopher, in which he condemns asceticism in favor of religious practices that were more effective. The legend of St. Christopher is placed in fourteenth-century France, during the farmers' revolution. The gigantic saint takes the side of the oppressed farmers, but without embracing violence in the conflict. After the group is defeated, he begins to transport people from one side of the river to the other, as in the original story. This work advocates charity, humility, and work, and it marks the end of Queirós's works in which he combats idle leisure, boredom, opulence, arrogance, and hypocrisy.

Eça de Queirós's works, according to most critics, have guaranteed him the position of one of Portugal's greatest writers. He has reached a vast public in Portugal with his many novels and stories and the adaptations of these to theater, cinema, and television. He has also reached a larger international audience through the many translations of his works into other languages.

**Letters:**

*Eça de Queirós e Jaime Batalha Reis: Cartas e recordações do seu convívio,* edited by Beatriz Cinatti Batalha Reis (Porto: Lello & Irmão, 1966);

*Eça de Queirós: Cartas inéditas,* edited by Beatriz Berrini (Lisbon: Jornal, 1987);

*Eça de Queirós–Emília de Castro: Correspondência epistolar,* edited by A. Campos Matos (Porto: Lello & Irmão, 1995).

**Biographies:**

João Gaspar Simões, *Vida e obra de Eça de Queirós* (Lisbon: Bertrand, 1980);

José Calvet Magalhães, *Eça de Queirós: A vida privada* (Lisbon: Bizâncio, 2000).

**References:**

Jacinto do Prado Coelho, "Para a compreensão d' *Os Maias* como um todo orgânico," in his *Ao contrário de Penélope* (Lisbon: Bertrand, 1976), pp. 167–188;

Sérgio Nazar David, "O paradoxo do desejo: O masoquismo moral nas literaturas portuguesa e brasileira (1829–1899)," dissertation, Universidade Federal de Rio de Janeiro, 2001;

Ernesto Guerra da Cal, *Língua e estilo de Eça de Queirós,* translated by Estella Glatt (São Paulo: EDUSP / Rio de Janeiro: Tempo Brasileiro, 1969);

Valery Larbaud, "Jaune bleu blanc," in his *Oeuvres* (Paris: Gallimard, 1970), pp. 1272–1274;

Joaquim Maria Machado de Assis, "Literatura realista. *O primo Basílio,* romance de Eça de Queirós," *Jornal do Comércio,* 13 August 1878;

Maria do Amparo Tavares Maleval, "Eça, leitor de *exempla* medievos," *Boletim do Centro de Estudos Portugueses da Faculdade de Letras da UFMG,* 14, no. 18 (1994): 91–98;

Maleval, "A Idade Média na obra de Eça de Queirós," in *Atas da IV Semana de Estudos Medievais* (Rio de Janeiro: IFCS/UFRJ, 2001), pp. 22–33;

António Coimbra Martins, *Ensaios queirosianos* (Lisbon: Europa-América, 1967);

A. Campos Matos, *Imagens do Portugal queirosiano,* second edition, revised and augmented (Lisbon: Imprensa Nacional-Casa da Moeda, 1987);

Matos, ed., *Dicionário de Eça de Queirós* (Lisbon: Caminho, 1993);

Matos, ed., *Suplemento ao dicionário de Eça de Queirós* (Lisbon: Caminho, 2000);

João Medina, *E.Q. e o seu tempo* (Lisbon: Livros Horizonte, 1972);

Maria Filomena Mónica, *Vida e obra de José Maria Eça de Queirós* (Rio de Janeiro: Record, 2001);

Isabel Pires de Lima, *As máscaras do desengano: Para uma abordagem sociológica de Os Maias* (Lisbon: Caminho, 1987);

Carlos Reis, ed., *Eça de Queirós: A escrita do mundo* (Lisbon: Biblioteca Nacional/Edições Inapa, 2000);

Alberto Machado da Rosa, "Nova interpretação d' *Os Maias,*" in his *Eça, discípulo de Machado?* (Lisbon: Presença, 1964);

António José Saraiva, *As idéias de Eça de Queirós* (Lisbon: Gradiva, 2000);

António Sérgio, "Notas sobre a imaginação, a fantasia e o problema psicológico-moral da novelística de Queirós," in Eça de Queirós, *Obra completa,* vol. 1 (Rio de Janeiro: Aguilar, 1970), pp. 47–87;

Frank F. Sousa, *O segredo de Eça: Ideologia e ambigüidade em A cidade e as serras* (Lisbon: Cosmos, 1996);

Miguel Torga, *Diário I* (Coimbra: Privately printed, 1941).

**Papers:**

Eça de Queirós's papers are in the Fundação Eça de Queirós, Casa de Tormes, in Baião; the Biblioteca Nacional and the Biblioteca do Museu João de Deus in Lisbon; the Fundação da Casa de Bragança in Vila Viçosa; the Fundação Joaquim Nabuco in Recife; the Biblioteca Nacional, the Biblioteca da Academia Brasileira de Letras, the Biblioteca e Arquivo do Itamarati, and the Real Gabinete Portugês de Leitura in Rio de Janeiro; and the Instituto Histórico e Geográfico in São Paulo.

# Antero de Quental
*(18 April 1842 – 11 September 1891)*

## Ana Maria Almeida Martins

BOOKS: *Sonetos de Anthero de Quental* (Coimbra: Imprensa Literária, 1861);

*Beatrice* (Coimbra: Imprensa da Universidade, 1863);

*Fiat lux!* (Coimbra: Imprensa da Universidade, 1863);

*Bom-senso e bom-gosto: Carta ao [excellentissimo] senhor Antonio Feliciano de Castilho* (Coimbra: Imprensa da Universidade, 1865);

*Defesa da carta encyclica de Sua Santidade Pio IX contra a chamada opinião liberal* (Coimbra: Imprensa Literária, 1865);

*A dignidade das lettras e as litteraturas officiaes* (Lisbon: Universal, 1865);

*Odes modernas* (Coimbra: Imprensa da Universidade, 1865; enlarged edition, Porto: Chardron, 1875);

*Portugal perante a revolução de Hespanha* (Lisbon: Tip. Portugueza, 1868);

*Carta ao Exmo Sr. António José D'Ávila, Marquês de Ávila, Presidente do Conselho de Ministros* (N.p., 1871);

*Causas da decadencia dos povos peninsulares nos ultimos tres seculos* (Porto: Tip. Commercial, 1871);

*Primaveras românticas, versos dos vinte anos* (Porto: Imprensa Portuguesa, 1872);

*Considerações sobre a philosophia da história litterária portugueza (a proposito d'alguns livros recentes)* (Porto Braga: Livraria Internacional, 1872);

*Thesouro poético da infância* (Porto: Ernesto Chardron, 1883);

*Os sonetos completos de Anthero de Quental,* edited by J. P. Oliveira Martins (Porto: Livraria Portuense de Lopes, 1886);

*Raios de extinta luz poesias inéditas (1859–1863) com outras pela primeira vez colligidas Anthero de Quental* (Porto: Ernesto Chardron, 1892);

*Algumas poesias suas pouco conhecidas Anthero de Quental* (Barcelos: Rodrigo Veloso, 1894);

*Oliveira Martins* (Lisbon: Tip. Companhia Nacional Editora, 1894);

*O Infante Dom Henrique,* with a preface by Rodrigo Veloso (Lisbon: M. Gomes, 1894);

*Zara* (Lisbon: Imprensa Nacional, 1894);

*Lopes de Mendonça* (Barcelos: Aurora do Cavado, 1894);

*Antero de Quental (photograph by Roger-Viollet)*

*A bíblia da humanidade* (Barcelos: Aurora de Carvalho, 1895);

*Da reorganisação social aos trabalhadores e proprietarios,* by de Quental and João Bonança (Barcelos: Aurora do Cavado, 1896);

*Manifesto dos estudantes da Univesidade de Coimbra a opinião illustrada do pais: 1862–1863* (Barcelos: Aurora do Cavado, 1896);

*Liga patriotica do norte* (Barcelos: Aurora do Cavado, 1896);

*Prosas opusculos publicados nos annos de 1893–1897,* 2 volumes (Barcelos: Editor - R.V., 1897);

*Prosas,* 3 volumes (Coimbra: Imprensa da Universidade, 1923–1931);

*Obras completas,* 4 volumes (Lisbon: Editorial Comunicação, 1989–1994);

*Poesia completa [1842–1891],* edited, with a preface, by Fernando Pinto do Amaral (Lisbon: Dom Quixote, 2001).

**Editions in English:** *Sonnets and Poems of Anthero de Quental,* translated by Griswold Morley (Berkeley: University of California Press, 1922);

*Sixty-Four Sonnets,* translated by Edgar Prestage (London: David Nutt, 1984).

OTHER: *Cantos na solidão versos Manuel Ferreira da Portela,* introduction by Quental (Coimbra: Imprensa Literária, 1865).

The poet, essayist, and politician Antero de Quental was an active member of the Generation of 1870, which was responsible for the establishment of the literary movement known in Portugal as realism. He was a leader in the writers' group Questão Coimbrã, named for a polemic that took place throughout 1865 and 1866 in the form of newspaper and journal articles. At times militant in his politics, he is linked to the introduction of socialist thought in Portugal.

A descendant of one of the oldest families of the provincial captaincies on the island of São Miguel, Antero Tarquínio Quental was born in Ponta Delgada, Azores, on 18 April 1842. After he completed his primary education on his native island, he enrolled in law school at the University of Coimbra and quickly became a leader among his fellow students; he assumed the role of spokesman for those who opposed the intellectual and political conservatism of the time. In the early 1860s Quental wrote several protests against the rector of the university, including the important "Manifesto dos estudantes da Universidade de Coimbra à opinião illustrada do país" (Manifesto of the Students of the University of Coimbra Concerning the Enlightened Opinion of the Country), published in 1896 as *Manifesto dos estudantes da Univesidade de Coimbra a opinião illustrada do pais: 1862–1863.* Among the more than three hundred students who signed the protest were the writers Eça de Queirós and Teófilo Braga. The students opposed university legislation, which, according to Quental, was antiquated and unjust. The manifesto expressed the need for urgent academic reform, which the university took into serious consideration when it fired the rector after his repeated confrontations with the students.

During his student years Quental regularly contributed poems and essays to Coimbra literary journals such as *Fósforo, Académico,* and *Prelúdios Literários.* His articles on feminine emancipation merit special distinction and include titles such as "A educação das mulheres" (The Education of Women, 1859), "A influência da mulher na civilização" (The Influence of Women on Civilization, 1860), "O sentimento da imortalidade" (The Feeling of Immortality, 1862), "A ilustração e o operário" (Erudition and the Worker, 1860), "A indiferença em política" (Political Indifference, 1862), and "*A bíblia da humanidade* de Michelet" (Michelet's *Humanity's Bible,* 1865).

In 1861 Quental published his first book, *Sonetos de Anthero de Quental* (Sonnets of Antero de Quental), a collection of twenty-one sonnets. That same year he was selected to welcome the brother-in-law of King Luís, Prince Humberto de Sabóia, who was passing through Coimbra. In his welcoming address Quental greeted the guest not as a representative of the royal house but rather as the son of Victor Manuel, then king of a unified Italy. More importantly, however, he greeted him as the friend of the revolutionary Giuseppe Garibaldi, who had been the hero of Italian unification.

In the summer of 1865 Quental published *Odes modernas* (Modern Odes), which immediately found itself at the center of a major controversy that had just begun in Portuguese literature: "A Questão Coimbrã ou do Bom Senso e Bom Gosto" (The Coimbra Question or Concerning Good Sense and Good Taste). *Odes modernas,* soon perceived as the "Voz da Revolução" (Voice of the Revolution), was greatly influenced by Jules Michelet, Pierre-Joseph Proudhon, (Joseph-)Ernst Renan, and Georg Wilhelm Friedrich Hegel. Quental even characterized it as the union of Hegelian naturalism and radical French humanism. Its importance in the panorama of Portuguese literature during the second half of the nineteenth century is enormous. Camilo Castelo Branco considered *Odes modernas* "o crépusculo de moderna poesia portuguesa" (the dawning of modern Portuguese poetry). In 1902 the French writer Valery Larbaud, corresponding with a friend, announced that he had chosen Quental's book to begin teaching the Portuguese language and liberally praised the poems in it. Nevertheless, António Feliciano de Castilho, one of the most powerful figures in Portuguese literature at that time, as well as a symbol of traditionalism and ultra-Romanticism, initiated a campaign that sought to ridicule new authors who had begun publishing without first gaining his consent. An important artist in his own right, Castilho was an admirable stylist and an excellent translator of the classics, but he was not innovative or original in his ideas. When he exaggerated his praise of a book by a favorite author, yet disparaged new works that had been written by the up-and-coming generation—among which were *Odes modernas* and Braga's *Tempestades Sonoras* (Sonorous Storms, 1864)—Castilho found himself attacked by Quental, then only twenty-three, in the form of a bellicose pamphlet. *Bom-senso e bom-gosto: Carta ao [excellentissimo] senhor Antonio Feliciano de Castilho* (Good Sense and Good Taste: A Letter to his [Excellency] Mr. António Feliciano de Castilho, 1865) soon became a landmark of Portuguese literature and culture. In the pamphlet Quental accuses Castilho of attacking the Escola de Coimbra (Coimbra School) with no logical grounds and, furthermore, of attempting to silence the voice of the youngest and most up-to-date authors. These accusations were repeated in 1865 in Quental's second pamphlet, *A dignidade das lettras e as litteraturas officiaes* (The Dignity of the Official Letters and Literature). In this text, although he further develops the ideas expressed in *Bom-senso e bom-gosto*, Quental refrained from writing in a personal, irritated manner in order to give his argument a more moral and social tone.

In the Questão Coimbrã there were around forty-four pamphlets and books, and, for more than six months, the old and new authors argued ferociously. In February 1866, on the outskirts of Porto, the polemic culminated in a sword fight between Quental and Ramalho Ortigão, a highly esteemed swordsman who was defending Castilho's views. In the end Castilho's ideas were defeated by his younger adversary, and the Coimbra School emerged victorious. As a result, with the exception of Oliveira Martins, the most important names of Portuguese literature in the second half of the nineteenth century came from, or were influenced by, the Coimbra School.

Quental had already received an advanced law degree in 1864, and given that he had not been enthusiastic in his pursuit of a legal career, he abandoned his law studies, yet without deciding upon a definite course for his life. He considered enlisting in Garibaldi's army but instead felt a greater attraction to the socialist ideas of Michelet and Proudhon. As a result he began to learn typography, after which he moved to Paris in October 1866 to work in his new profession. He wanted to "live" the problems faced by the proletariat in general but specifically in France. At that time Portugal was a predominantly agricultural country and thus unprepared to face the future problems created by industrialization.

During his time in France, Quental attended the Collège de France, and he visited his idol and teacher, Michelet, to whom he presented himself as Bittencourt, borrowing a Quental family name. According to Quental's inventive "back story," which he needed for an introduction to Michelet, this Bittencourt had been charged by the writer Quental with the responsibility of offering Michelet a copy of *Odes modernas*. As Bittencourt, Quental translated the book for Michelet so that the latter could appreciate *Odes modernas* without feeling compelled to give it praise merely because of the circumstances. Michelet, however, took a liking to Quental's imagined friend and in a letter, dated 2 August 1867, thanked Quental for his book. In his letter Michelet mentioned the sympathy that he had felt for his visitor. The encounter with Michelet was the only highlight of Quental's short stay in Paris. He felt that his experience with the French proletariat was an enormous failure.

Disillusioned and sick, Quental returned to Lisbon in 1868. After the triumph of the republican revolution in Spain, he was invited by the party of Castellar and Pi y Margell to contribute a Portuguese perspective to an Iberian democratic newspaper. He entertained the idea of moving to Madrid. Near the end of 1868 Quental published the pamphlet titled *Portugal perante a revolução de Hespanha* (Portugal and the Spanish Revolution). In it he defends the idea of a democratic federation of the five Iberian states: Catalonia, Galicia, Portugal, Andalusia, and Castile. In 1869 he traveled to the United States and Canada, spending nearly four months visiting cities such as New York and Halifax. While abroad he studied important social questions and key capitalist organizations.

Upon returning to Lisbon, Quental was reunited with some of his colleagues from his Coimbra days—Queirós, Manuel de Arriaga, and João de Deus—and he met Martins for the first time. This encounter proved to be of great importance in the lives of both men. A group was formed in 1868, known as the Cenáculo (Cenacle) by those who participated in it. Under Quental's direction the group began studying Proudhon, Renan, and Hegel, as well as Charles Baudelaire; Edgar Allan Poe; George Gordon, Lord Byron; Victor Hugo; and Heinrich Heine.

For Quental the year 1870 marked the beginning of a period of great political and social activity in the socialist movement. He contributed to the founding of worker associations, to the publication of propaganda pamphlets—such as *O que é a Internacional* (What Is the International Workers Association, 1871)—and even established a Portuguese chapter of this association, which entertained Karl Marx's son-in-law Paul Lafargue as its guest. Quental also cofounded the Association of Worker Fraternity. Later, however, he distanced himself from the organization because of its rejection of Proudhon's doctrines, which he had defended against Marxist theories.

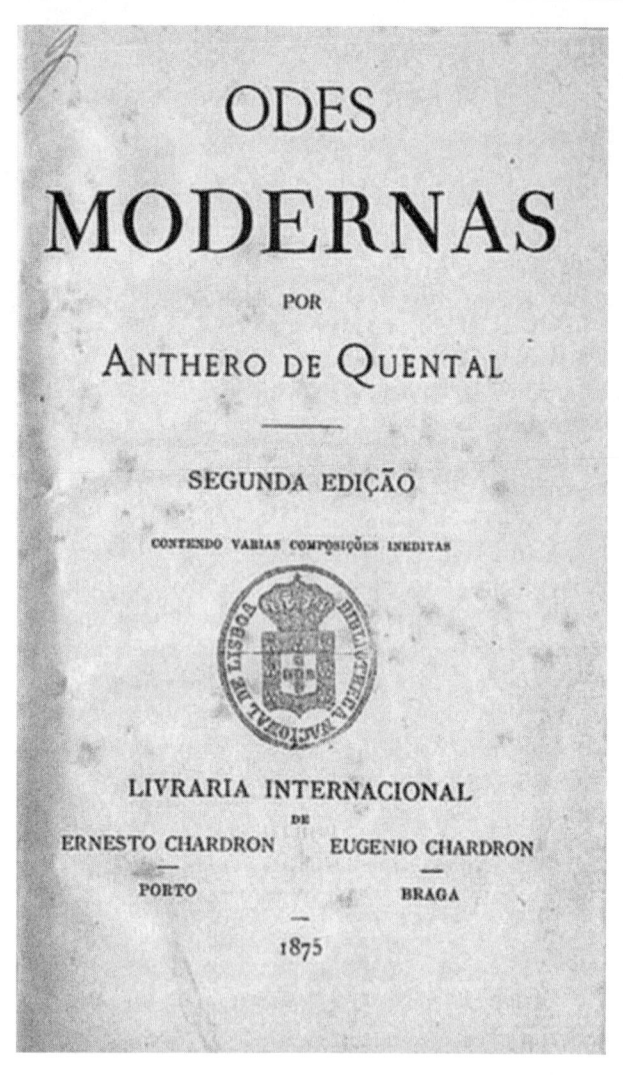

*Title page for the expanded second edition of Quental's 1865 collection, one of the first works of Portuguese modernist poetry (Biblioteca Nacional, Lisbon)*

Quental returned to active journalism and directed the *República–Jornal da Democracia Portuguesa* (Republic–Democratic Newspaper of Portugal). He wrote, but did not sign, an article presenting the editorial agenda of the paper on questions concerning Iberianism and international politics. In partnership with Martins, he also directed the journal *Pensamento Social* (Social Thought). The most agitated period of his public life, however, culminated in the organization of the famous Conferências Democráticas (Democratic Conferences), also known as the Conferências do Casino (Conferences of Casino) because of their venue, the Lisbon Casino, in May 1871.

Quental questioned the political, cultural, economic, and religious conditioning of a Portuguese society that was well behind the rest of Europe. For this reason the objective of these conferences was to stimulate Portugal on an extremely fundamental level and to participate in the movement of renovation common among the foremost European societies. The conference organizers asked for the participation of all parties and opinions, even when they themselves did not share them.

Quental gave the first lecture at the conferences. His presentation, titled "O espírito das conferências" (The Spirit of the Conferences), provided an overview. He also gave the second presentation, which took place on 27 May 1871. It was published as *Causas das decadencia dos povos peninsulares nos ultimos tres seculos* (The Causes of the Decline of the Iberian Peoples During the Last Three Centuries, 1871) and became his best-known work in prose.

In Quental's view the decline of Spain and Portugal, which in the fifteenth and sixteenth centuries were among the most culturally and economically prosperous countries in Europe, was principally the result of religious, political, and economic factors. He believed that these factors stemmed from three basic causes: the effect on Catholicism by the Council of Trent; absolutism; and overseas conquests. After the council Catholicism manifested itself in Portugal through the Inquisition, which was based on the expulsion of Jews and gave rise to serious economic problems in commerce, industry, and agriculture. Quental also attributed the general decadence found in the arts and literature to the Jesuits. Absolutism, the second cause for the state of decadence in Iberia, was to political and social life what Catholicism was to moral life. And overseas conquests provoked economic decay because of the abandonment of lands by a population that sought new places to settle—places where people could attain wealth quickly. At the same time, however, overseas expansion engendered a heroic spirit among the citizens of Iberia, producing a sense of patriotism that they would remember and celebrate for years.

According to Quental, after the Council of Trent the Catholic religion ceased to possess a truly living meaning and became an unintelligible, formal, and mechanical practice. Moreover, the Inquisition weighed heavily on the Portuguese conscience. Hypocrisy had become a national vice, and, consequently, the denouncement of one's friends and neighbors turned into a religious virtue. With the Jesuit movement Christian sensibilities gave way to the most deplorable sophisms—the lowest point to which religion had ever descended, in Quental's opinion. The Catholicism of Trent opposed moral liberty and considered free thought and human reason to be a crime against God. For three centuries the Iberian Peninsula had not produced a single man who excelled in the scientific domains. A more progressive Europe was enlightened through the study of the sciences. Because of a lack of such scientific erudition, the peninsular peoples became decadent. In particular, extreme intolerance of the Portuguese for hundreds of years brought about widespread indifference during the nineteenth century.

Never before had such a controversial and publicly prolonged denunciation of the consequences of the Church's secular power taken place in Portugal. The Portuguese were more accustomed to private criticism and disguised satire–thus Quental's second lecture, given at the Lisbon Casino, had a disturbing effect on his audience. Three more conferences followed in 1871, at which Queirós delivered "A literatura como nova expressão de Arte" (Literature as a New Expression of Art) and Adolfo Coelho gave a lecture titled "O ensino" (Education). In his address Coelho vehemently criticized the interference of religion in society and called for a complete separation of church and state. The revolutionary spirit communicated by these conferences, however, soon became the target of violent campaigns in conservative newspapers. Public powers were equally attentive, and the fate of the remaining conferences was set. On 4 July 1871, the day that Salomão Sáragga's conference "Os historiadores críticos de Jesus" (Historians Critical of Jesus) was announced, the Lisbon Casino was closed, by the prime minister's decree, under the pretext that the conferences were attacking state religion and institutions. Conference organizers were taken by surprise, and the most violent protest to the arbitrary shutdown of the Lisbon Casino was written by Quental. In *Carta ao Exmo Sr. António José D'Ávila, Marquês de Ávila, Presidente do Conselho de Ministros* (A Letter to His Excellency António José D'Ávila, Marquis of Ávila, President of the Council of Ministers, 1871) Quental responds to the attacks on the freedom of thought and opinion and the freedom to assemble. He considers the act inquisitorial–it goes against the tolerant spirit of the time. Politics, he says to Prime Minister D'Ávila, "is an instrument of social justice, almost a religious act."

Thus the conferences at the Lisbon Casino ended. They had been, in the opinion of their principal leader Quental, "a dawn which was not followed by a day, or if it was, only a cloudy one." Quental's conclusion was embittered and pessimistic, and only time could disprove it. The conferences became a fundamental landmark of nineteenth-century Portuguese society, and the group of intellectuals associated with them–known today as the Generation of the 1870s–gathered some of the most brilliant people in Portugal, including not only Quental but also Queirós, Martins, and others in the domains of literature, science, painting, and music.

Although he participated in social and political actions, Quental never abandoned his poetic and literary activities. In 1872 he published *Primaveras românticas, versos dos vinte anos* (Romantic Springs, Verses From My Twentieth Year), which collected poems written in his youth. He translated excerpts from Johann Wolfgang von Goethe's *Faust: Eine Tragedie* (Faust: A Tragedy, 1808) and in that same year published what he considered, until 1887, his best writing: *Considerações sobre a philosophia da história litterária portugueza* (Philosophical Considerations of Portuguese Literary History).

In 1873 Quental returned to his native island, where he suffered a bout of depression that lasted until 1880. Although his illness kept him from participating in most activities, he founded–together with his friend Jaime Batalha Rei–a journal called *Revista Occidental* (Occidental Magazine). He had had the idea for a journal about peninsular themes at the time of the conferences at the Lisbon Casino. *Revista Occidental* helped initiate conversations with Spanish Federalists such as Francisco Maria Tubino, who recruited the services of Canovas del Castillo, Rafael Labra, Pi y Margall, Tomás Rodriguez Pinilla, and others to contribute to the magazine. The Spaniard who participated most in this project was Fernandes de los Rios, who at the time was the Spanish ambassador in Lisbon. One of the main objectives of the *Revista Occidental* was to bring together Portuguese and Spanish intellectuals to form a new literary school. This objective was shared by Martins and Queirós (whose book *O crime do Padre Amaro* [Father Amaro's Crime] first came out in the journal in 1875), as well as many other important figures in the cultural life of Portugal at that time. The short life of *Revista Occidental* (it lasted from February to July of 1875) was filled with mishaps, animosity, and suspicion. Nicknamed *Ibérica,* which startled those Portuguese who still feared the dissolution of their country into an Iberian whole, the magazine was ahead of its time and created positive ties between Spanish and Portuguese intellectuals.

After 1876 Quental embarked on a kind of pilgrimage among physicians in Portugal and abroad because of mental illness. Among these physicians was the neurologist Jean-Martin Charcot, whom he had consulted in Paris and who prescribed hydrotherapeutic treatments in a thermal facility in Bellevue, a suburb of the capital city. Thus, in 1877 and again in 1878 Quental lived in Paris from May until October, but the treatments did not improve his health much. During one of his treatments at the facility, however, he met the baroness of Saillière, with whom he engaged in a relationship for more than three years.

When he returned to Portugal between treatments, Quental devoted himself to political activities,

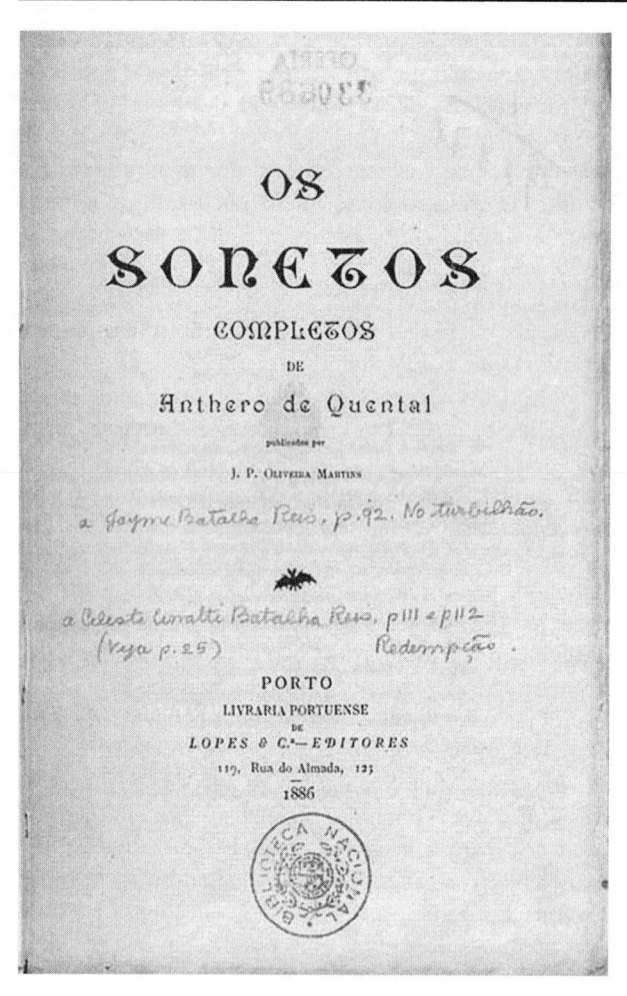

*Title page for the collection of sonnets that Quental considered his poetic autobiography (Biblioteca Nacional, Lisbon)*

and although he never had any hope of being elected, he ran for congress on the Socialist Party ticket in the 1879 and 1880 general elections. In 1881, disillusioned with partisan politics and tired of life in Lisbon, he decided to establish residency in the small picturesque village of Vila do Conde, on the outskirts of Porto. Previous to this decision, he had adopted the children of Germano Meireles, his colleague from Coimbra who had passed away in 1878 and left the care and upbringing of his daughters, four-year-old Albertina and two-year-old Beatriz, to Quental.

The time that he spent at Vila do Conde was the calmest and, in a literary sense, the most productive period of Quental's life. Martins remained close to him while living in Porto. Thinking of his two adopted girls, and because there had not been anything published in Portugal for their age group, Quental organized and wrote the preface for an anthology of poems dedicated to children. *Tesouro poético da infância* (Poetic Treasures of Childhood) appeared in 1883 and includes poems from various Portuguese novels and books of poetry–for example, poets such as Deus from the nineteenth century. Quental also selected works by his favorite Brazilian poets Castro Alves, Casimiro de Abreu, and Junqueira Freire. Quental himself wrote an enchanting poem of twenty-three sextets titled "The Fates" for the anthology.

In Vila do Conde, Quental wrote his last sonnets, in which he reflects on the spiritual nature of his life and how it helped him overcome his pessimism. When he wrote poetry, it consisted mainly of sonnets, for which–according to Quental himself–he had an unexplainable affinity. The influence of the Portuguese poets of the sixteenth century, however, especially of Luis de Camões, was paramount. Quental had also read the sonnets of Byron, William Shakespeare, and, most important, Gérard de Nerval. These authors completed what he considered to be his poetic formation.

Around 1886 Quental was pressured by his closest friends to publish a collection of his complete sonnets. He had written close to a hundred by that time, many of which remained unpublished. He finally assented, and his dear friend Martins wrote the preface for his *Os sonetos completos de Anthero de Quental* (The Complete Sonnets of Antero de Quental, 1886). Quental structured the collection as a poetic autobiography, or a moral and psychological memoir. As he stated in a letter to his friends, the book "contains a portrait of my true intellectual and sentimental evolution. If anything of mine remains to be read in Portuguese literature, it will be this little book." *Os sonetos completos de Anthero de Quental* is one of the most translated works of Portuguese literature.

Quental sent a copy of the sonnets to the German philologist Wilhelm Storck, who had translated the complete works of Camões. Storck, in return, sent Quental German translations of some of the sonnets. In response to a request made by Storck, Quental wrote a short autobiographical letter, dated 14 May 1887, which became the most cited piece of correspondence that he ever wrote. The letter even inspired the Russian writer Leo Tolstoy, who had read Storck's translations, to write in his *Diary* on 15 March 1889 that he completely agreed with Quental's idea of liberty as the secret aspiration of all things and the ultimate end of the universe. *Os sonetos completos de Anthero de Quental* was Quental's final work of poetry. With it came his promise that the philosophical ideas expressed in the sonnets would someday be developed and treated at more length in prose. Consequently, in March of 1886 in Porto he published a series of articles in the newspaper *A Província* (The Province). Titled "A filosofia da natureza dos naturalistas" (The Philosophy of Nature and the Naturalists), the series gave him the opportunity to analyze the Brazilian philosopher Viana de Lima's book *Exposição sumária das teorias transformistas* (Exposition of Transformist Theories). Quental wrote a biting criticism of Lima's work. To the writer, science was merely one sphere of knowledge and never the whole of it. He believed that evolution was the fundamental reason for all human thought in philosophy and science, as well as in history and politics.

Quental expounded in a methodical and definitive manner upon his own philosophical outlook in "Tendências gerais da filosofia na segunda metade do século XIX" (General Tendencies in Philosophy of the Second Half of the 19th Century), which appeared in the *Revista de Portugal* (Journal of Portugal) in 1890. In the work he interprets his own intellectual evolution in the form of a dialogue with the most representative figures of contemporary thought. Quental clearly and incisively criticizes positivism; he points to the limits that must be placed upon mechanistic thought and calls for a restoration of metaphysics.

In 1890 Quental began a series of political pieces titled "Ultimatum inglês de 11 de Janeiro" (The English Ultimatum of January 11). He protested the humiliation imposed on Portugal by its old ally England, when it had placed itself firmly in the way of Portuguese colonial expansion that was intended to link Mozambique with Angola. Such a move on the part of Portugal was contrary to the expansionist plans of the British Empire. Upon this undermining of government authority in Portugal, there emerged a climate of internal strife, almost revolutionary in scope. Any manifestation against the British became a mere pretext that was taken advantage of by the ever-growing Republican Party. A group in Porto conceived the idea of the Northern Patriotic League, which used the patriotic fervor of the time to lead the country out of the collective chaos in which it was living. The supporters of the league felt that it needed as a leader a man whose national prestige could inspire public confidence—one who could impartially oppose the political currents of the day and reorganize the impoverished Portuguese. Quental's name was unanimously chosen, and he finally accepted the task after being asked insistently. The situation with the English influenced his decision because he realized that he could take advantage of it to incite a true restoration of civic sentiment. Almost from the beginning, however, political intrigues plagued the movement, as various political leaders saw that it might develop into a force opposed to their own interests. Enthusiasm soon changed to indifference and finally to hostility. Quental did not wish to disparage the thought that guided the constitution of the Northern Patriotic League. Yet, disillusioned with what turned out to be his last great vision and resisting those who desired to transform the Northern Patriotic League into a political party and an instrument of personal ambition, he presented it with his resignation in April. He decided to return with his adoptive daughters to his native island and make it his permanent home.

Antero de Quental departed for Ponta Delgada on 5 July 1891. The first news that he sent his friends from there seemed quite optimistic. By mid August, however, his health had deteriorated, partly as a result of erratic weather on the island but principally because of a disagreement in the Quental family concerning the presence of his adoptive daughters. Faced with the necessity of returning once again to Lisbon, Quental informed his friend Martins in a letter of 29 August of his plans to leave on 18 September. At seven o'clock in the evening of 11 September 1891, however, he sat down on a bench in the park Campo de São Francisco in Ponta Delgada and committed suicide with a revolver. He was buried the following day in the cemetery of São Joaquim. In his autobiographical letter to Martins he had expressed hope for a much different end to his life. According to the spiritual evolution that he had expressed in *Os sonetos completos de Anthero de Quental,* as well as in "Tendências gerais da filosofia na segunda metade do século XIX," "I shall die after a morally agitated and dolorous life, in the placidness of thoughts close to the most intimate of human aspirations, and, as the ancients say, in the peace of the Lord—Thus I hope."

**Letters:**

*Cartas* (Coimbra: Imprensa da Universidade, 1915);

*Cartas inéditas de Antero de Quental a Oliveira Martins* (Coimbra: Imprensa da Universidade, 1931);

*Cartas inéditas de Antero de Quental a Wilhelm Storck* (Coimbra: Tip. da Coimbra Editora, 1935);

*Cartas a António de Azevedo Castelo Branco* (Lisbon: Signo, 1942);

*Correspondência entre Antero de Quental e Jaime Batalha Reis* (Lisbon: Assírio & Alvim, 1982);

*Novas cartas inéditas de Antero de Quental,* with an introduction by Lúcio Craveiro da Silva (Braga: Faculdade de Filosofia de Braga, 1996).

**Bibliographies:**

José Bruno Carreiro, *Antero de Quental: Subsídios para a sua bibliografia* (Ponta Delgada: Instituto Cultural, 1981);

Maria do Rosário Azenha, "Antero Quental, elementos para uma bibliografia," in *Antero Quental* (Coimbra: Revista da História da Idéias da Faculdade de Letras, 1991);

*Actas do congresso anteriano internacional* (Ponta Delgada: Universidade dos Açores, 1993);

*Catalogo da livraria de Anthero de Quental: Legada á bibliotheca publica de Ponta-Delgada* (Lisbon: Ulmeiro, 1993).

**References:**

Joaquim de Carvalho, "Estudos para a cultura portuguesa do século XIX (Anteriana)," in de Quental's *Obra completa,* volume 4 (Lisbon: Fundação Gulbenkian, 1983);

Joaquim-Francisco Coelho, *Microleituras de Antero* (Lisbon: Difel, 1993);

William B. Edgerton, "Tolstoi and Magalhães Lima," *Comparative Literature,* 27 (1976);

Alberto Ferreira and Maria José Marinho, *Bom senso e bom gosto–a Questão Coimbrã,* 4 volumes (Lisbon: Imprensa Nacional-Casa da Moeda, 1985–1989);

Eduardo Lourenço, *A noite intacta–(I) irrecuperável Antero* (Vila do Conde: Centro de Estudos Anterianos, 2000;

Ana Maria Martins, *Antero de Quental–fotobiografia* (Lisbon: Imprensa Nacional-Casa da Moeda, 1986);

Martins, *O essencial sobre Antero de Quental* (Lisbon: Imprensa Nacional-Casa da Moeda, 2001);

António José Saraiva, *A tertúlia ocidental: Estudos sobre Antero de Quental, Eça de Queirós e outros* (Lisbon: Cradiva, 1990);

Jorge de Sena, "Antero revisitado," in his *Estudos de literatura portuguesa* (Lisbon: Edições 70, 1982);

António Sérgio, "Os dois Anteros," in *Ensaios IV,* by Castel Branco Chaves and others (Lisbon: Clássicos Sá da Costa, 1972).

# Alves Redol

(29 December 1911 - 29 November 1969)

Loida Pereira Peterson

BOOKS: *Glória: Uma aldeia do Ribatejo* (Barcelos: Companhia Editora do Minho, 1938);
*Gaibéus* (Barcelos: Companhia Editora do Minho, 1939);
*Nasci com passaporte de turista* (Lisbon: Portugália, 1940);
*Marés* (Lisbon: Grafica Portuguesa, 1941);
*Avieiros* (Lisbon: Portugália, 1942);
*Fanga* (Lisbon: Portugália, 1943);
*Espólio* (Lisbon: Municipalista, 1943);
*Anúncio* (Lisbon: Inquérito, 1945);
*Porto manso* (Lisbon: Inquérito, 1946);
*A França—da resistência à renascença* (Lisbon: Inquérito, 1948);
*Forja* (Lisbon, 1948);
*Ciclo port-wine: Horizonte cerrado* (Lisbon: Graf. Lisbonense, 1949);
*Os homens e as sombras* (Lisbon: Europa-América, 1951);
*Vindima de sangue* (Lisbon: Europa-América, 1953);
*Olhos de água* (Lisbon: Centro Bibliográfico, 1954);
*A barca dos sete lemes* (Lisbon: Europa-América, 1958); translated by Linton Lomas Barrett as *The Man with Seven Names* (New York: Knopf, 1964);
*Uma fenda na muralha* (Lisbon: Portugália, 1959);
*Noite Esquecida* (Lisbon: Estúdios Cor, 1959);
*O cavalo espantado* (Lisbon: Portugália, 1960);
*Barranco de cegos* (Lisbon: Portugália, 1961);
*Constantino guardador de vacas e de sonhos* (Lisbon: Portugália, 1962);
*Histórias afluentes* (Lisbon: Portugália, 1963);
*O muro branco* (Lisbon: Europa-América, 1966);
*Teatro I: Forja; Maria Emília* (Lisbon: Europa-América, 1966);
*Teatro II: O destino morreu de repente* (Lisbon: Europa-América, 1967);
*A flor vai ver o mar* (Lisbon: Europa-América, 1968);
*A flor vai pescar num bote* (Lisbon: Europa-América, 1968);
*Maria flor abre o livro das surpresas* (Lisbon: Mem Martins, 1970);

*Alves Redol (from Alvaro Salema,* Alves Redol, a obra e o homem, *1980; Thomas Cooper Library, University of South Carolina)*

*Os reinegros* (Lisbon: Europa-América, 1972);
*Teatro III: Fronteira fechada* (Lisbon: Europa-América, 1972);
*Nasci com passaporte e outros contos,* with a preface by José Manuel Mendes (Lisbon: Caminho, 1991);
*A vida mágica da sementinha* (Lisbon: Caminho, 1995);

*Alves Redol, testemunhos dos seus contemporâneos,* edited by Maria José Marinho and António Mota Redol (Lisbon: Caminho, 2001).

OTHER: *Cancioneiro do Ribatejo,* notes and preface by Redol (Vila Franca de Xira: Centro Bibliográfico, 1964);

*Romanceiro geral do povo português,* notes and preface by Redol (Lisbon: Iniciativas Editoriais, 1964).

Alves Redol is best known for the works of prose he wrote during the neorealist literary period of Portuguese literature. He also published short stories, children's literature, theatrical pieces, and several studies on the social injustices of everyday life in the Ribatejo and Alentejo regions of Portugal. Works of both Italian and Brazilian literature inspired Redol in his writing. He especially admired Jorge Amado, Graciliano Ramos, Rachel de Queirós, and José Lins do Rego, novelists of northeastern Brazil who were known for their objective observation of reality and a deep concern for the social problems of their country. Documenting in prose such problems in his own country, Redol depicts the enslaving labor that connects the common man to the land on which he works. He narrates in detail how physical work exhausts the laborer's energy and well-being yet does not enable him to better his financial position in life. His writings explore the lives and conditions of various groups of lower-class workers throughout Portugal, including the *avieiros* (fishermen), the *fangueiros* (street vendors), and the *vinhateiros* (vineyard workers). He describes the relationships formed between these groups of the working class and those of the bourgeois. Redol concludes that the different groups of the lower class share a similar way of life, which is best characterized by a sense of unrealized potential and unfulfilled destinies. Ranked with Carlos de Oliveira, Manuel da Fonseca, Mário Dionísio, and Fernando Namora, Redol is viewed as one of the most influential writers of neorealist literature in Portugal. He was the first literary writer of his time to be considered a popular author by Portuguese society.

António Alves Redol was born on 29 December 1911 in Vila Franca de Xira, Portugal, to António Redol da Cruz and Inocência Alves Redol. He came from a family of humble origins. From 1921 to 1923, while still a boy, he worked at his father's hardware shop. In 1923 he began attending school at the Colégio Arriaga in Junqueira. Redol was unable to finish his studies during this time not because of any lack of desire but because of financial hardship. He took on many jobs, including part-time work in publicity; he also labored as a cabinetmaker, tire salesman, typographer, and office assistant. In 1927, when Redol turned sixteen, he moved to Luanda, Angola, in search of better living conditions. While residing in Africa, he worked as an office assistant and migrant laborer by day and taught several courses in shorthand and grammar by night. His temporary residence in Angola was not a happy one, although it brought certain positive experiences to his life, as well as insight into a new vision of the world—insight that later played an important role in the development of his literary career.

Redol returned to Vila Franca de Xira in 1931 because of failing health. His interest in pursuing a career as a writer began during this time, as he worked for the local newspaper while completing his last courses in high school. He graduated from high school with honors in the study of economics. At the age of twenty-five Redol joined his first political party, Movimento de Unidade Democrática—MUD—which opposed the Estado Novo, the political regime established and headed by António Salazar, who was dictator of Portugal from 1928 to 1970. Redol's participation as a speaker at these revolutionary activities involved several political movements, and his activism against the Estado Novo made life as a writer difficult. The movements were fronted by the Communist Party, which led him to become a militant follower of its beliefs. These beliefs are reflected both ideologically and emotionally in Redol's writings.

Beginning in 1926 Portuguese society fell under strict control and censorship by a fascist military government, resulting in political events that prompted the start of the neorealist period in Portuguese literature. The neorealist style of writing was strongly influenced by American authors such as John Steinbeck, Upton Sinclair, and Ernest Hemingway, as well as by novelists of northeastern Brazil in the 1930s—in particular, Amado and Ramos. During the early 1930s a group of neorealist writers and intellectuals reacted against the literary movement called "Presencismo." The members of Presencismo, which existed from 1927 to 1939, emphasized the sensations and emotions evoked by beauty and attempted to produce literature that was spontaneous in character.

Redol began his literary career in 1936 as a contributor to the literary journal *O Diabo,* in which he published a series of short stories about the common people of the Ribatejo region. That same year he married Maria dos Santos Mota. Their only son, António Mota Redol, was born in 1943.

In 1939, with the publication of his first novel, *Gaibéus,* Redol became well established as an author. The overwhelming success of *Gaibéus*—along with that of Soeiro Pereira Gomes's *Esteiros* (Tributaries, 1941)—effectively solidified neorealism, which was also referred to as the socialist realist literary movement in Portugal. Redol expresses his main purpose in writing works of literature in the prologue to *Gaibéus*: "*Gaibéus* não pretende ficar na literatura como obra de arte. Quer ser, antes de tudo, um documentário humano fixado no Ribatejo. Depois disso será o que os outros entenderem" (*Gaibéus* does not intend to become a work of art in literature. Above all, it attempts to be a human documentary focused on everyday life in the Ribatejo region. After this purpose is achieved, it will be what others understand it to be). Furthermore, he states, he does not want his prose to be interpreted merely as a work of "art for art's sake," but rather as a novel that exposes the social problems of the time. Redol advocates the use of fiction as an instrument for demonstrating social action and change; he believes that revolution is possible through the written word. As a writer he is therefore committed to describing reality, but, at the same time, he writes fiction as a way of denouncing one's reality. For this reason specifically, he describes the protagonist of *Gaibéus* as a "human type," a character who represents all those who labor physically on rice plantations. Redol's main objective is to regain dignity for workers oppressed and alienated by the subordination of the upper social class. In *Gaibéus* he concludes that the misery of the poor and oppressed is caused by the cruelty and greed of those controlling the political and economic power in Portugal.

The ideological beliefs present in *Gaibéus* reveal Redol's personal search to find the significance that the role of "art for art's sake" plays in neorealism. When he first wrote *Gaibéus*, he did not directly intend to use prose as a political tool in highlighting current social problems in Portugal. He did, however, intentionally create in the dialogue of his first novel a passionate voice that served as a testimonial to the common man and to his everyday experiences. By not giving his protagonists detailed personal characteristics, Redol better illustrated their alienation from the rest of society.

In most cases Redol's literary characters lack the cohesion and desire to revolt against the established social order of the Salazar regime. His writings are motivated by the conflicts that arise from members of the working class interacting with the upper social class. Conveying in a realist manner the many clashes that occur in relationships between people of different social groups, Redol especially emphasizes the connections formed between the wealthy landowner and the poor laborer—the two figures who present the contrasting points of view in his narrations. His prose delves into the ideological synchronicities extant in certain patterns that have evolved from this socialist-realist type of environment.

Many of Redol's works illustrate his important contributions to neorealist literature, including *Anúncio* (Announcement, 1945), *A barca dos sete lemes* (1958; translated as *The Man with Seven Names*, 1964), *Uma fenda na muralha* (A Crack in the Wall, 1959), and *Barranco de cegos* (Trenches of the Blind, 1961). With *Gaibéus*, Redol introduced certain characteristics that established the preliminary stages of neorealism, including both its positive and negative aspects. Through his writings he subtly demonstrates how, during the early twentieth century, the social order in Portugal suppressed individual human freedom, a notion not depicted in works of Portuguese literature until the late 1930s.

*Redol in 1929 (from Alvaro Salema,* Alves Redol, a obra e o homem, *1980; Thomas Cooper Library, University of South Carolina)*

The same year that Redol turned thirty, *Marés* (1941) was published. *Marés* is a story that depicts the joys and hardships of man's survival. The plot of this novel focuses on a group of field laborers—men who gave up the freedom of their youth to fight the misery of harsh physical labor and the hardships brought on by exploration of the land. As the narrative ends, Redol leaves the reader with a sense of hope for a better future and states that hope is present as long as man does not give up his struggle for survival: "Aquele grito ia para o futuro. E era ele que guiava os homens que tomavam toda a estrada" (That cry went toward the future. And it was the one that guided the men who took the path).

The hardships of a poor fisherman in the Ribatejo region are described in *Avieiros* (1942). In this particular work the protagonist is a young woman, Olinda, whose parents work diligently to give her every opportunity for

*Redol autographing copies of his 1958 novel,* A barca dos sete lemes, *which was translated in 1964 as* The Man with Seven Names *(from Alvaro Salema,* Alves Redol, a obra e o homem, *1980; Thomas Cooper Library, University of South Carolina)*

a better future. Against their wishes, however, she chooses to marry a poor fisherman, Tóino da Vala, and the union seals her fate of work and life by the sea. Redol relates an intimate portrait of a young couple who, like Olinda's parents before her, weather temporal and physical difficulties in hopes of improving their situation for the sake of their children's futures.

In 1945 *Anúncio,* a novel depicting urban life in Portugal, was published. Demonstrating neorealist tendencies in a dramatic, caustic tone, it explores the trying interactions that can occur between a worker and an owner. Set in a large office building in Lisbon, the narrative focuses mainly on the arbitrary orders of a proprietor toward his employees and his exploitation of them. In *Anúncio,* as in many of his other works, Redol provides an almost obsessive account of how the common man must constantly struggle to achieve what he believes is his rightful place in life. The protagonist, an ordinary office employee, holds onto his job, despite the miserable conditions, in order to secure an income that ensures his family's survival. *Anúncio*

paints an intimate and painful portrait of how the bourgeois take advantage of members of the working class—forgetting that without workers it could not survive as a class.

In *Uma fenda na muralha,* published in 1959, Redol purues a different approach to his writing style. This new direction is best exemplified by his detailed descriptions of the riches found in the provincial fishing town of Nazaré, where the main action of the story takes place. Instead of focusing the narrative mainly on the physical beauty of the sea, Redol concentrates on describing the social segregation of the poor, individual fisherman. He describes the physical environment not only in terms of its greatness and power but also as a symbol of certain basic human attributes and instincts. The storyline of *Uma fenda na muralha* emphasizes the reality of how extensively man depends upon the sea for his survival. Redol conveys this notion through his constant use of colloquialisms and vocabulary specific to the region where the novel is set.

*A barca dos sete lemes* and *Barranco de cegos* also model neorealist characteristics. In each work the protagonist is a man, born into a lower social class, who will spend his entire life struggling to change his destiny. Redol suggests that in both cases, however, the poor individual cannot change his plight regardless of how hard he works toward improving his station in life. These narratives depict how the financial and political power remains in the hands of the conservative patriarchy. Both *A barca dos sete lemes* and *Barranco de cegos* reveal an emotional vision of a world in which the common man attempts, but is unable, to fulfill his aspirations in life. Redol believes that this vision includes the willingness to love, live, and communicate better with other human beings.

In *Barranco de cegos* the story line also addresses the family unit and its feudal origins. For the first time in his fiction Redol tells the story from the point of view of several characters belonging to the upper social class. The main character, Diogo Relvas, fights to keep the traditional structures of the patriarchal system intact while he struggles with the advances of industrialization. The character of Diogo not only symbolizes the conservative ideology of the decadent upper class but also represents the revolutionary beliefs of the younger generation. By narrating the story from Diogo's perspective, Redol wants the reader to comprehend how human relationships can be built on opposing social forces. The dialogue is spoken in a way that avoids the simplistic division into oppressor and oppressed.

After the publication of *A barca dos sete lemes,* Redol's prose began to change thematically. Around the late 1950s and early 1960s, his novels present a more complex and psychological analysis of Portuguese life and its social contradictions. During the later part of his literary career, abandoning the collective portrait of society to concentrate on the individual, Redol depicts a portrait of alienation. Alcides, the protagonist of *A barca dos sete lemes,* for example, loses his humanity; he symbolizes a historical moment whereby the weakening of human relationships is documented. The reader sees that the individual is alienated from everyone around him and, therefore, does not reflect on his presence in the world alongside others.

On 29 November 1969 António Alves Redol died at the Santa Maria Hospital in Lisbon; he was buried in the oldest cemetery in Vila Franca de Xira. During his career he wrote what were effectively documentary narratives, the main purpose of which was to show human beings in social conflict. By intimately characterizing members of the Portuguese working class, Redol emphasized some of the most intense yet universal aspects of human reality. He employed rich poetic language to depict the voice of the common man who is imprisoned in life by an unchangeable fate, or destiny. Redol's writing style is best described as simple yet at times artificial and repetitive. It does not, however, detract from the expressive, image-filled mannerisms and exalted lyrical passages that are also found in his narrative fiction. In the evolution of his particular writing style, beginning with *Gaibéus* and ending with *Os reinegros* (The Black Kings), published posthumously in 1972, a certain pattern emerges. It consists of a rhythmic and poetic prose that Redol adapted depending on both the social issues that he was treating and the time frame in which they were current.

In his writings Redol held true to certain social and political beliefs formed early in his youth. He believed that literature should not be written simply to accomplish a work of "art for art's sake." Instead, he used the literary text to re-create crucial moments in the everyday lives of different groups of people in Portuguese society. His works highlighted the limitations and alienation that society imposes on the individual, especially the poor laborer, who is seen as a victim. The laborer is a marginalized being who survives by working for others and is never totally integrated into society. As a result Redol is perceived in Portuguese literature as one of the most important voices of the worker.

**References:**

Maria Graciete Besse, *Alves Redol—o espaço e o discurso* (Lisbon: Ulmeiro, 1997);

Besse, "O mundo rural no romance português: Realidade, mitos e representações," *Quadrant,* 7 (1990): 119–146;

Ana Paula Ferreira, *Alves Redol e o neo-realismo português* (Lisbon: Caminho, 1992);

Ferreira, "As histórias do desejo e o desejo da história 'Os reinegros' de Redol," *Colóquio/Letras,* 120 (1991): 87–94;

Maria Fernandes Mendes, *Apontamentos Europa-América explicam Alves Redol* (Lisbon: Europa-América, 1992);

Massaud Moisés, *Presença da literatura portuguesa: Modernismo* (São Paulo: Difusão, 1983);

Carlos Reis, "Da literariedade em *Gaibeus,*" *Colóquio/Letras,* 52 (1979): 33–38;

Reis, *O discurso ideológico do neo-realismo português* (Coimbra: Almedina, 1989);

Alvaro Salema, *Alves Redol, a obra e o homem* (Lisbon: Arcádia, 1980);

Maria Aparecida Santilli, *Arte e representação da realidade no romance português contemporâneo* (São Paulo: Quíron, 1979);

Garcez da Silva, *Alves Redol e o grupo neo-realista de Vila Franca* (Lisbon: Caminho, 1992);

Silva, *A experiência africana de Alves Redol* (Lisbon: Caminho, 1993);

Alexandre Pinheiro Torres, *Os romances de Alves Redol: Ensaio e interpretação* (Lisbon: Moraes, 1979);

António Manuel Couto Viana, *Breve dicionário de autores portugueses* (Lisbon: Verbo, 1985).

# José Régio
# (José Maria dos Reis Pereira)
### (17 September 1901 – 22 December 1969)

### José Carlos Barcellos
*Universidade Federal Fluminense*

BOOKS: *As correntes e as individualidades na moderna poesia portuguesa,* as Pereira (Vila do Conde: Privately printed, 1925); revised as *Pequena história da moderna poesia portuguesa* (Lisbon: Inquérito, 1941);

*Poemas de Deus e do Diabo* (Coimbra: Privately printed, 1925);

*Biografia* (Coimbra: Privately printed, 1929);

*Jogo da cabra cega* (Coimbra: Atlântida, 1934);

*As encruzilhadas de Deus* (Coimbra: Atlântida, 1935);

*Críticos e criticados: Carta a um amigo* (Lisbon: Inquérito, 1936);

*António Botto e o amor* (Porto: Editora Livraria Progredir, 1937); republished as *Estudos: António Botto e o amor* (Porto: Civilização, 1938; enlarged edition, Porto: Brasília Editora, 1978);

*Em torno da expressão artística* (Lisbon: Inquérito, 1940);

*Primeiro volume de teatro* (Porto: Editora Livraria Progredir, 1940)—comprises *Jacob e o anjo, Três máscaras,* and *Post-facio;*

*Davam grandes passeios aos domingos . . .* (Lisbon: Inquérito, 1941)—includes "Davam grandes passeios aos domingos . . .";

*Fado* (Coimbra: Arménio Armado, 1941);

*O príncipe com orelhas de burro* (Lisbon: Inquérito, 1942);

*Mas Deus é grande* (Lisbon: Inquérito, 1945);

*Uma gota de sangue,* volume 1 of *A velha casa* (Lisbon: Inquérito, 1945);

*Histórias de mulheres* (Porto: Portugália, 1946)—includes "A menina Olímpia e sua criada Belarmina" and "O vestido cor de fogo"; enlarged as *Histórias de mulheres: Conto e novela* (Lisbon: Portugália, 1968);

*As raízes do futuro,* volume 2 of *A velha casa* (Porto: Educação Nacional, 1947);

*Benilde ou a virgem-mãe* (Porto: Portugália, 1947);

*El-Rei Sebastião* (Coimbra: Atlântida, 1949);

*Os avisos do destino,* volume 3 of *A velha casa* (Vila do Conde: Edições Ser, 1953);

*A chaga do lado* (Lisbon: Portugália, 1954);

*A salvação do mundo* (Lisbon: Inquérito, 1954);

*José Régio (José Maria dos Reis Pereira), circa 1929 (from Régio,* Escritos de Portalegre, *1984; Thomas Cooper Library, University of South Carolina)*

*Três peças em um acto* (Lisbon: Inquérito, 1957)—includes *O meu caso* and *Mário ou eu próprio—o outro;*

*As monstruosidades vulgares,* volume 4 of *A velha casa* (Lisbon: Portugália, 1960);

*Filho do homem* (Lisbon: Portugália, 1961);

*Há mais mundos* (Lisbon: Portugália, 1962);

*Ensaios de interpretação crítica Camões, Camilo, Florbela, Sá-Carneiro* (Lisbon: Portugália, 1964);

*Vidas são vidas,* volume 5 of *A velha casa* (Lisbon: Portugália, 1966);

*Três ensaios sobre arte* (Lisbon: Portugália, 1967)—comprises "Em torno da expressão artística," "A expressão e o expresso," and "Vistas sobre o teatro";

*Cântico suspenso* (Lisbon: Portugália, 1968);

*Música ligeira* (Lisbon: Portugália, 1970);

*Colheita da tarde,* edited by Alberto de Serpa (Porto: Brasília, 1971);

*16 poemas dos não incluídos em colheita da tarde* (Póvoa de Varzim: Tip. Camões, 1971);

*Confissão de um homem religioso* (Porto: Brasília, 1971);

*Páginas de doutrina e crítica da "Presença,"* with preface and notes by João Gaspar Simões (Porto: Brasília, 1977);

*Escritos de Portalegre,* with an introduction by António Ventura (Portalegre: A Cidade, 1984).

**Editions and Collections:** *Jacob e o anjo* (Vila do Conde: Edições Ser, 1953);

*Jogo da cabra cega* (Lisbon: Portugália, 1963);

*Histórias de mulheres* (Lisbon: Portugália, 1968);

*Contos* (Mem Martins: Europa-América, 1984);

*Poesia de todos os tempos* (Rio de Janeiro: Record, 1985);

*Obra completa,* with an introduction by José Augusto Seabra, revised by Luís Amaro (Lisbon: Imprensa Nacional-Casa da Moeda, 2001).

**Edition in English:** *The Flame-Coloured Dress and Other Stories,* translated by Margaret Jull Costa (Manchester, U.K.: Carcanet, 1999)—comprises "They Used to Go for Walks on Sundays . . . ," "A Sad Smile," "Miss Olimpia and Her Maid Belarmina," "The Story of Rosa Brava," "María do Ahú," "The Flame-Coloured Dress," and "A Brief Comedy."

OTHER: "António Botto: Ensaio crítico," in Botto's *Cartas que me foram devolvidas* (Lisboa: Anuário Comercial, 1932);

Joaquim Pacheco Neves, *Contos sombrios,* preface by Régio (Porto: A. Portuense, 1942);

*As mais belas líricas portuguesas,* compiled, with an introduction, by Régio (Lisbon: Portugália, 1944); revised and enlarged as *Líricas portuguesas* (Lisbon: Portugália, n.d.);

Luís de Camões, *Luís de Camões,* selected, with notes, by Régio (Lisbon: Rodrigues, 1944);

Florbela Espanca, *Sonetos completos,* preface by Régio (Famalicão: Minerva, 1946);

*Alma minha gentil: Antologia da poesia de amor portuguesa,* compiled by Régio and Alberto de Serpa (Lisbon: Portugália, 1957);

*Na mão de Deus: Antologia da poesia religiosa portuguesa,* compiled by Régio and de Serpa (Lisbon: Portugália, 1958);

Pedro Hommem de Melo, *Povo que lavas no rio,* preface by Régio (Porto: Gráficos Reunidos, 1978).

A prolific novelist, dramatist, poet, and literary critic, José Régio is the leading figure of the *Presença* movement, which dominated the Portuguese literary scene from 1927 until 1940–that is, between the *Orpheu* generation and neorealism. The *Presença* writers had a deep concern with psychological and metaphysical questions and adopted an aesthetic posture based on the well-known axiom "art for art's sake." They did not accept any form of compromise with religious, political, or ethical principles, because they believed that such an attitude would affect artistic freedom and authenticity. For them, literature had to be completely personal and sincere in order to be genuine.

Régio was born José Maria dos Reis Pereira in Vila do Conde, in the north of Portugal, on 17 September 1901 to José Maria Pereira Sobrinho and Maria da Conceição Reis Pereira. Pereira spent his childhood in the provincial environment of his native town. His family was religious and inclined toward the arts. Owing to this influence, both the Roman Catholic faith and his sense of aesthetics were enduring concerns in Régio's life and affected his works with great intensity. In addition to literature and literary criticism, he was also interested in drawing, music, and theater. Some editions of Régio's poetry are illustrated with his own drawings.

When Pereira was sixteen, he and his brother, Júlio, were sent to Porto to finish their studies. Pereira lived for two years in a boarding school before attending the University of Coimbra, one of the oldest in Europe. *Uma gota de sangue* (A Drop of Blood, 1945) and *Os avisos do destino* (Notices from Destiny, 1953)—the first and third volumes, respectively, of Regio's autobiographical novel *A velha casa* (The Old House, published in five volumes, 1945–1966)—are based on his high-school and university experiences. At the University of Coimbra, Pereira studied Romance languages and literatures and founded the journal *Presença* with students he had befriended—among them, Adolfo Rocha (alias Miguel Torga), João Gaspar Simões, and António José Branquinho da Fonseca.

In 1925, after writing his thesis, *As correntes e as individualidades na moderna poesia portuguesa* (Currents and Individualities in Modern Portuguese Poetry), published privately that same year, Pereira graduated from the university. He later revised his thesis and, as Régio, published it in 1941 as *Pequena história da moderna poesia portuguesa* (Short History of Modern Portuguese Poetry). In it he criticized and praised the works of the most distinguished *Orpheu* poets: Fernando Pessoa, Mário de Sá-Carneiro, José de Almada Negreiros, and António Botto.

The first work that Pereira published as José Régio was *Poemas de Deus e do Diabo* (Poems of God and the Devil, 1925), in which the most characteristic features of his poetry are easily recognized: religious and sexual anxiety together with a deep cry for freedom, expressed in a rather traditional style, in that his poems do not reveal the influence of the major formal achievements of modernism. "Cântigo negro" (Black Song), his best-known poem, summarizes Régio's attitude toward life and literature in his categorical refusal to accept any previously established truth or identity. For Régio, one should create one's own way in life as well as in art. The two books that he published in 1925–his thesis and *Poemas de Deus e do Diabo*–exemplify the basic contradiction of his work. As many critics have pointed out, he was an open-minded enthusiast of modern art and literature. Yet, as far as his own works were concerned, he held conservative aesthetic attitudes.

The first issue of *Presença* magazine, subtitled "Folha de Arte e Crítica" (Paper for Art and Criticism), appeared in Coimbra on 10 March 1927. The directors included Régio, the novelist and literary critic Simões, and Branquinho da Fonseca, the author of "O barão," (The Baron, 1942), one of the most acclaimed short stories in Portuguese literature. This first issue includes one of Regio's best-known and most praised texts. Titled "Literatura viva" (Living Literature), it is considered the ultimate expression of Régio's and his fellow editors' opinions regarding literature and aesthetics. The essay "Literatura viva" became the literary manifesto of the *Presença* generation. Although Régio and his friends stopped publishing their magazine in 1940, the year that neorealism essentially began in Portugal, the aesthetic principles expressed in it were highly influential over the years–both in Régio's own work and in that of his former colleagues.

In "Literatura viva" Régio criticizes contemporary Portuguese literature for its inadequate emphasis on rhetoric and style. He argues that in literature the author must have a strong and original personality in order to create a genuine artistic style. By virtue of his sensibility, intelligence, and imagination, an artist must be a sort of superior man; his personality is the unquestionable basis for his literary achievements. According to this theory, literature is the expression of a highly personal and individual view of the world. The writer must put his own life in his work, if he wants to produce what Régio calls "literatura viva"; otherwise, the text is simply "literatura livresca" (bookish literature). This distinction is significant, according to Régio, especially in the domain of modernism, in which it is quite easy to mistake "literatura viva" for "literatura livresca," owing to the general search for originality.

In 1927 Régio left Coimbra and began a career as a high-school teacher, first in Porto and then, after 1929, in Portalegre, Alentejo. Never marrying, he lived in Portalegre until 1962, the year of his retirement, and moved back to his native Vila do Conde. Régio's second book of poetry, *Biografia* (Biography), appeared in 1929, the year he left Porto for Portalegre.

In 1934 he published what many critics consider his masterpiece, *Jogo da cabra cega* (The Giddy Goat Game). This novel, one of the most accomplished examples of the *Presença* literary ideal, focuses on a group of young men who meet regularly in a café in a provincial town to discuss matters such as art, literature, and philosophy. Two of them–the narrator, Pedro Serra, and his friend Jaime Franco–develop an intense and ambiguous relationship fraught with sexual tension. In this particular domain, as in others, the novel suggests, rather than states, the truth of the situation.

*Jogo da cabra cega* addresses the complex psychology of human beings. It depicts ambiguities in feelings, relationships, and situations, and the variety in reality perception that can occur, especially in abnormal states of mind. Through such themes, the work draws a distinction between the prosaic life of ordinary people–who are full of prejudices and ruled by common sense–and the superior yet unknown, or even despised, life of an original and artistic personality. Why the novel was forbidden by the censors under the fascist dictatorship of Salazar is not quite clear; perhaps the regime found the novel obscure and pointless. The second edition appeared only in 1963, almost thirty years later. Today, *Jogo da cabra cega* is widely considered one of the highlights in the development of the novel in twentieth-century Portuguese literature.

In the ensuing years Régio published his third book of poems, *As encruzilhadas de Deus* (God's Crossroads, 1935), and three works on literary criticism–*Críticos e criticados: Carta a um amigo* (Critics and the Criticized: A Letter to a Friend, 1936), *António Botto e o amor* (António Botto and Love, 1937), and *Em torno da expressão artística* (On Artistic Expression, 1940)–in which he develops and stresses his ideas about literature and art. *António Botto e o amor* is a clever and open-minded study of Botto's polemical gay poetry. Defying Portuguese conservative religious and literary establishments, Régio argues that in literature what really matters is the writer's commitment to authenticity, regardless of the morality of the human experiences upon which he bases his work.

During this period Régio also began publishing plays. As a dramatist he developed an aesthetic universe quite similar to that of his poetry. In one of his best-known plays, *Jacob e o anjo* (Jacob and the Angel), published in *Primeiro volume de teatro* (First Volume of Theater, 1940), sexual desire and religious doubts are the axis upon which the characters revolve as they search for meaning in their lives. As in all his plays, Régio shows a clear opposition between someone with a marked individuality and society as a whole. In his view the inner life of superior men is the only realm of truth and beauty in which salvation is possible to find.

"Davam grandes passeios aos domingos . . ." (1941; translated as "They Used to Go for Long Walks on Sundays," 1999) is a highly acclaimed short story. Rosa Maria is a poor orphan girl, twenty-four or twenty-five years old, who comes to Portalegre to live with her rich Aunt Alice and cousin Fernando, with whom Rosa Maria falls in love. The story portrays Rosa Maria's sadness and pain as she comes to realize that she will never be more than a pleasant pastime for her cousin. *O príncipe com orelhas de burro* (The Prince with Donkey Ears, 1942) is a novel that, under the guise of a children's storybook, presents the same features of *Jacob e o anjo* and an analogous view of human life. In this novel, as well as in *Jacob e o anjo,* Régio tries to create a fairy-tale atmosphere.

In 1945 Régio published *Uma gota de sangue*—the first volume of his autobiographical opus, *A velha casa,* a project that he left unfinished. The fifth and final volume, *Vidas são vidas* (Lives are Lives), came out in 1966. *A velha casa* is, for the most part, a fictional transposition of Régio's life. The hero, Manuel Trigueiros (alias Lèlito), has many things in common with Régio himself—among which are a delicate sensibility, a rather introspective personality, and a deep interest in literature. Lèlito's experiences in boarding school in Porto and at the University of Coimbra resemble those lived by Régio, and both author and protagonist have similar family lives.

In 1946 Régio published *Histórias de mulheres* (Women Stories), a collection of short stories about female characters. Some of these, such as "A menina Olímpia e sua criada Belarmina" (translated as "Miss Olimpia and Her Maid Belarmina," 1999) and "O vestido cor de fogo" (translated as "The Flame-Coloured Dress," 1999), are generally counted among his best works. The first one tells about an impoverished and half-mad aristocratic lady who, notwithstanding her actual miserable situation, lives in an imaginary world of grandeur and distinction. "O vestido cor de fogo" concerns a man's difficulty in coping with his wife's sexual desires. In both stories, as is typical of Régio's works, the inner lives of the characters are seen as stronger and more real than reality itself. Since the third edition, published in 1968, *Histórias de mulheres* has included "Davam grandes passeios aos domingos. . . ."

*Portrait of Régio by Arlindo Vicente (Casa-Museu José Régio, Portalegre)*

In the play *Benilde ou a virgem-mãe* (Benilde or the Virgin Mother, 1947) Régio returns to the same themes of *Jacob e o anjo*—sexual anxiety connected to religious questions in a somewhat metaphysical perspective. In another play, *El-Rei Sebastião* (King Sebastian, 1949), he pays homage to the young king who disappeared in 1578 in Morocco during a battle against the Moors; over the centuries King Sebastian's life became one of the most important national myths of Portugal. *A salvação do mundo* (The Salvation of the World, 1954) concerns the Christian theme of world redemption. The orthodoxy of Régio's religious conceptions, however, is a matter subject to many disputes. In *Mário ou eu próprio—o outro* (Mário or Myself—the Other), published in *Três peças em um acto* (Three One-Act Plays, 1957), Régio turns his attention to Sá-Carneiro, one of the most important poets of the *Orpheu* generation, about whom he had already written in his critical works.

During the 1950s and 1960s, while writing *A velha casa,* Régio published volumes of poetry, such as *A chaga do lado* (The Wound in the Side, 1954), *Filho do homem* (Son of Man, 1961), and *Cântico suspenso* (Delayed Song, 1968); the short-story collection *Há mais mundos*

(There are Other Worlds, 1962); and works of literary criticism, including *Ensaios de interpretação crítica Camões, Camilo, Florbela, Sá-Carneiro* (Essays of Critical Interpretation: On Camões, Camilo, Florbela, Sá-Carneiro, 1964) and *Três ensaios sobre arte* (Three Essays on Art, 1967). Two more poetry collections—*Música ligeira* (Light Music, 1970) and *Colheita da tarde* (Afternoon Harvest, 1971)—and his autobiography, *Confissão de um homem religioso* (Confession of a Religious Man, 1971) appeared posthumously.

José Régio died in Vila do Conde on 22 December 1969. The house where he lived for more than thirty years in Portalegre is now a museum dedicated to his work and to the works of art that he collected throughout his life. His contribution to Portuguese modern literature is widely considered as one of prime importance, chiefly in the areas of fiction and literary criticism. His acute, early, and open-minded recognition of the importance of such authors as Pessoa and Sá-Carneiro is highly appreciated as a sign of cleverness and sophisticated literary taste. Some of his short stories, as well as the novel *Jogo da cabra cega,* are also regarded as key achievements. On the other hand, his work in poetry and drama does not enjoy the same favorable judgment of many critics. In this domain Régio's rather traditional aesthetic principles are perceived as dated or old-fashioned. Nevertheless, he remains one of the most important and influential Portuguese writers of his time.

**Letters:**

*Correspondência Jorge de Sena, José Régio,* edited by Mécia de Sena (Lisbon: Imprensa Nacional-Casa da Moeda, 1984).

**References:**

Luis Amaro, ed., *Ensaios críticos sobre José Régio* (Porto: Asa, 1994);

Nádia Battela Gotlib, *A poesia de José Régio: O símbolo nos poemas de Deus e do Diabo* (São Paulo: Universidade de São Paulo / Faculdade de Filosofia, Letras e Ciências Humanas, 1981);

Eugénio Lisboa, *O essencial sobre José Régio* (Lisbon: Imprensa Nacional-Casa da Moeda, 2001);

Lisboa, *José Régio: A obra e o homem* (Lisbon: Arcádia, 1976);

José Gaspar Simões, *José Régio e a história do movimento da "Presença"* (Lisbon: Brasília, 1977);

Yara Frateschi Vieira, *Níveis de significação no romance: Um estudo do Jogo da Cabra Cega* (São Paulo: Ática, 1974).

# Bernardim Ribeiro

*(fl. circa 1475–1482 – circa 1526–1544)*

Joseph Abraham Levi
*Rhode Island College*

BOOKS: *Trovas de Dous pastores. f. Silvestre & Amador. Feytas por Bernaldim Ribeyro. Nouamente empremidas. Com outros dois romãces com suas grosas: que dizem: O' Belerma e Justa fue mi perdicion. E passando el mar Leandro* (Lisbon: Germão Galharde, 1536);

*Hystoria de menina e moça per Bernaldim Ribeyro agora de novo estampada e com summa deligencia emendada e assi alguãs eglogas suas com homais que na pagina seguinte se vera* (Ferrara: Samuel & Abraão Usque, 1554).

**Editions and Collections:** *Primeira e segunda parte do liuro chamado as Saudades de Bernardim Ribeiro com todas suas obras; treladado de seu proprio original* (Évora: André de Burgos, 1557);

*História de menina e moça* (Cologne: Arnold Birckmann / Lisbon: Francisco Graseo, 1559);

*Primeira e segunda parte das Saudades. Hora novamente impressas,* edited by Manuel da Silva Mascarenhas (Lisbon: Paulo Craesbeeck, 1645);

*Menina e moça ou Saudades,* edited by António Luiz Guadalupe (Lisbon: Domingos Gonsalves, 1785);

*Obras de Bernardim Ribeiro,* edited by José da Silva Mendes Leal and F. I. Pinheiro (Porto: Bibliotheca Portugueza, 1852);

*Obras. Bernardim Ribeiro e Cristóvão Falcão. Nova edição conforme à edição de Ferrara,* 2 volumes, edited by Anselmo Braamcamp Freire (Coimbra: Imprensa da Universidade, 1923, 1932);

*Obras poéticas,* edited by Delfim de Brito Guimarães (Lisbon: Guimarães, 1930);

*Obras completas,* 2 volumes, edited by Aquilino Ribeiro and Manuel Marques Braga (Lisbon: Sá da Costa, 1949–1950);

*Menina e moça, ou, Saudades,* edited by Hélder Macedo (Lisbon: Dom Quixote, 1990);

*Menina e moça,* edited by Maria de Lourdes Saraiva, fourth edition (Mem Martins: Europa-América, 1996).

**Edition in English:** "The Young Girl's Story; or, The Book of Longing: A Translation of the Prologue of *Menina e moça ou Saudades* by Bernardim Ribeiro," translated by Suzette Macedo, *Portuguese Studies,* 1 (1985): 58–67.

Bernardim Ribeiro–in medieval Portuguese also spelled Bernaldim Ribeyro–lived during the last two decades of the fifteenth century and the first half of the sixteenth century. He achieved fame during the reign of King Manuel I (1495–1521), who also appointed him *moço fidalgo* (gentleman of the royal chambers). Unlike many of his contemporaries, Ribeiro wrote exclusively in Portuguese. He was primarily a poet and a lyric writer and is credited with having introduced bucolic poetry to Portugal. His prose is characterized by an innovative and well-balanced combination of three novelistic trends: the sentimental, derived from the Renaissance tradition started by Giovanni Boccaccio's *Elegia di Madonna Fiammetta* (Elegy to Lady Fiammetta, 1343–1344); the pastoral, inaugurated by Jacopo Sannazzaro's *Arcadia* (1501); and the chivalrous, a prose version of the *chansons de geste* (Old French epic poems) that flourished in Portugal between the thirteenth and the sixteenth centuries. An overall sense of delicateness, at times equated to a feminine sensibility, and a yearning for something that is not there yet–*saudade* (longing), that is, an ever-present and ever-changing "nostalgia"–are perhaps what make Ribeiro's compositions distinctive among Portuguese letters.

Mystery, reality, and myth are intertwined in Ribeiro's life to such a degree that it is impossible to separate truth from fiction. As a consequence, little is known about his private or public life. His writings are, thus, the only source for reconstructing his biography. Since almost all the biographical information on Ribeiro comes directly from his writings, most scholars consider it unreliable or fabricated by other scholars to fit their theories. The scholars who reject the biographical material derived from the text include Hernâni Cidade, Hélder Macedo, Marcelino Menéndez y Pelayo, and José Augusto Ramalho Teixeira Rego. Teófilo Braga's *Bernardim Ribeiro e o bucolismo* (1897), an earlier version of which was first published in 1872, was used by many scholars as the basis for their approach to and textual exegesis of Ribeiro's work. Braga's biography became an uncontrollable syncretism of different sources, legends, and forgeries. Among the scholars who followed in Braga's footsteps are the Visconde de Augusto Romano Sanches de Baêna, Manuel da Silva Gaio, Delfim de Brito Guimarães, and Carolina Michaëlis de Vasconcelos. The latter author, however, was aware of the faults and unfounded grounds of some of the proposed theories.

From his *Éclogas* (Eclogues, 1554), Ribeiro's first literary compositions, scholars have inferred that he was born at Torrão, a hamlet between the Tagus and the Guadiana Rivers, in the Alentejo region, in or around 1475. Most likely Ribeiro's parents were Damião Ribeiro and Joana Dias Zagalo. If that is true, then Ribeiro spent most of his early childhood between Torrão and Sintra, where his parents had relatives. According to some sources, on 23 August 1484, Ribeiro's father left Portugal for Castile, where he was assassinated for having been involved in a conspiracy against King João II (1481–1495).

Internal evidence from the second eclogue, "Écloga II (Jano e Franco)"–in which the protagonist flees the land because of famine and the plague–could be used as an indication that in 1496 Ribeiro went to the capital to escape these natural disasters and possibly to complete his education. The famine occurred in 1494, preceded and followed by various waves of the plague (1480–1496). In 1496 the Portuguese nobility moved from Évora, capital of the Alentejo region, to Lisbon. In "Écloga II (Jano e Franco)" the shepherd Jano abandons his native Torrão at the age of twenty-one. If Jano is the poet himself, then Ribeiro was born in 1475. However, given that the plague occurred over a span of sixteen years, some scholars push the date of birth ahead by seven years; in other words, young Ribeiro would have been fourteen years old and not twenty-one when he finally went to Lisbon. Thus, 1482 has been chosen by many as the year of his birth. Ribeiro's assumed arrival in Lisbon in 1496 coincides with the disastrous end of the reign of King João II–probably poisoned by some members of the nobility–and the beginning of King Manuel's reign.

According to Braga–who based his statements on a passage in the 1645 edition of the 1554 work known by its common title, *Menina e moça* (Maiden and Lass)– one of Ribeiro's ancestors was João de Freitas Mascarenhas of Évora, whose first wife was Maria Ribeiro Meigas. She was the daughter of the famous scholar Pedro Meigas, also mentioned in "Écloga II (Jano e Franco)." The Mascarenhas were known protégés of King João II. Ribeiro's lineage was, thus, the key to his success at the Portuguese court, where he was surrounded by members of the aristocracy as well as men and women of letters, such as the poets Leonor de Mascarenhas, maid of Queen Maria, and Francisco Sá de Miranda, who became his best friend. Both writers, as well as Garcia de Resende and Gil Vicente, belonged to the circle of Portuguese court poets of the time.

In the sixteenth century alone, however, there were at least six or seven personages by the name Bernardim Ribeiro. Though plausible, it is still not certain that Ribeiro is the same *Doutor* (Doctor) Bernardim Ribeiro who attended and subsequently received a degree in law from the University of Lisbon and who in 1524 was also appointed *escrivão da câmara* (secretary) to King João III (1521–1557) for his "bondade, saber, discrição, e prática e ensino que tem" (goodness, knowledge, discretion, and practice and teaching that he possesses). There is no substantial evidence that the author attended the University of Lisbon. Had Ribeiro received his law degree, most likely he would have used his title of *Doutor* and, most of all, his title would have been used after his name in the few documents that are extant today. It would also have appeared on the covers of the first editions of all his published works.

Ribeiro's proximity to the court might have led to a few rumored amorous liaisons with noblewomen, including Lucrécia Gonçalves; his cousin Joana Tavares Zagalo; and Princess Beatriz, twenty-two years his junior. There are some serious doubts, however, about the veracity of these affairs, especially the latter two. Ribeiro's alleged affair with King Manuel's daughter Beatriz later inspired the Romantic writer Almeida Garrett to write *Um auto de Gil Vicente* (A Play by Gil Vicente, 1838). In order to forget a woman who did not return his love, according to Braga, Ribeiro decided to leave Portugal for Italy. Braga's theories, almost all unfounded, have been refuted by nearly all scholars.

Whether these events really happened or not, it is likely Ribeiro was in Italy from 1520 to 1524, where he had contacts with Garcilaso de la Vega and Sá de Miranda. It is not known if Ribeiro accompanied Sá de Miranda to Venice, Milan, Florence, Naples, and Palermo. Most likely he met Sá de Miranda in Rome. Ribeiro's stay in Italy proved to be instrumental for his literary development. There, he had the chance of being directly exposed to Italian and classical literature, among the latter Virgil's *Eclogues,* as well as the science of the Cabala.

Ribeiro's literary development can be divided into two sections: one of formation, in which he conforms, though in his own way, to the established literary canons of Iberia, and one in which he finally breaks from tradition, introducing new forms and ideas. These innovations derive mainly from the Italian literary tradition. Ribeiro, however, reworked these to fit his personality as well to embody the Portuguese character and spirit. His works represent the *saudade* and the eternal suffering found in the Portuguese *coita de amor* (pain of love), or rather, the sadness of the lover whose love is not returned, also sung by the medieval troubadours.

Ribeiro's bucolic literary production includes dramas, eclogues, idylls, novellas, and poems wherein his characters are usually shepherds and herdsmen who move within a rural background dominated by mountains, rivers, solitude, sadness, and a sense of distance, both in time and space. He is the author of several entries in Garcia de Resende's *Cancioneiro geral* (General Songbook, 1516)–a collection of courtly poetry from the middle of the fifteenth century to the actual year of publication–as well as the *Trovas de Dous pastores. f. Silvestre & Amador* (The Ballads of Two Shepherds. f. Sylvester & Amador, 1536) and five *Éclogas*, which are usually known by the names of the shepherds who appear in them, namely: "Écloga I (Pérsio e Fauno)," "Écloga II (Jano e Franco)," "Écloga III (Silvestre e Amador)," "Écloga IV (Jano)," and "Écloga V (Agrestes e Ribeiro)." The author also wrote a few minor verse compositions, which are characterized by the sense of melancholy present in almost all of his literary production.

Ribeiro's first poetic phase started with "Cantiga à senhora Maria Coresma" (Song to Ms. Maria Quaresma [Coresma being the medieval form]) and "Memento," a composition in stanzas of ten verses in which couplets "a uma mulher que servia" (to a woman whom I used to serve) are also dedicated to Quaresma. Maria Gonçalves Quaresma was the daughter of Gonçalo Martins Quaresma of Lisbon, who eventually gave her in marriage to Álvaro Mendes Casco, a widower from the Alentejo region. If read correctly, "Écloga IV (Jano)" could allude to the fact that Ribeiro had a love affair with Quaresma for a year (1495). In 1496 he went to Lisbon, while Quaresma proceeded to Viseu.

"Memento," four *cantigas* (songs), three *esparsas* (poems with six-syllable verses), and four *vilancetes* (pastoral poems) constitute Ribeiro's contributions to Resende's *Cancioneiro geral*. Until the beginning of the nineteenth century another work in *Cancioneiro geral*, "Écloga Crisfal" (Eclogue Crisfal, circa 1543–1547), was attributed to Cristóvão de Sousa Falcão, also known as Crisfal. Based mainly on internal evidence, however, as well as contrastive analyses between Ribeiro's works and the "Écloga Crisfal," scholars no longer doubt that it was in fact composed by Ribeiro. There are striking similarities in genre, style, and meter that link the "Écloga Crisfal" to Ribeiro's five *Éclogas*, especially "Écloga III (Silvestre e Amador)" and his *Trovas de Dous pastores*. These works use the *redondilha* (lines of five or seven syllables), a technique that was common among the poets at the courts of King Manuel and King João III. Furthermore, in the "Écloga Crisfal" there are thirty-three passages that are similar to other passages used by Ribeiro.

Though presented in oneiric voyages, the "Écloga Crisfal" is decisively a romantic eclogue in which the protagonist flies like a bird from the Alentejo region to Lorvão (district of Coimbra). Ribeiro describes nature, the Tagus River, the woods, and the mountains of southern, south-central, and central Portugal. The imaginary, however, overshadows the pastoral scenery as well as the romantic dialogues. In linguistic terms, the "Écloga Crisfal" represents an earlier stage of the writer's work when compared to "Écloga I (Pérsio e Fauno)," "Écloga II (Jano e Franco)," and "Écloga IV (Jano)."

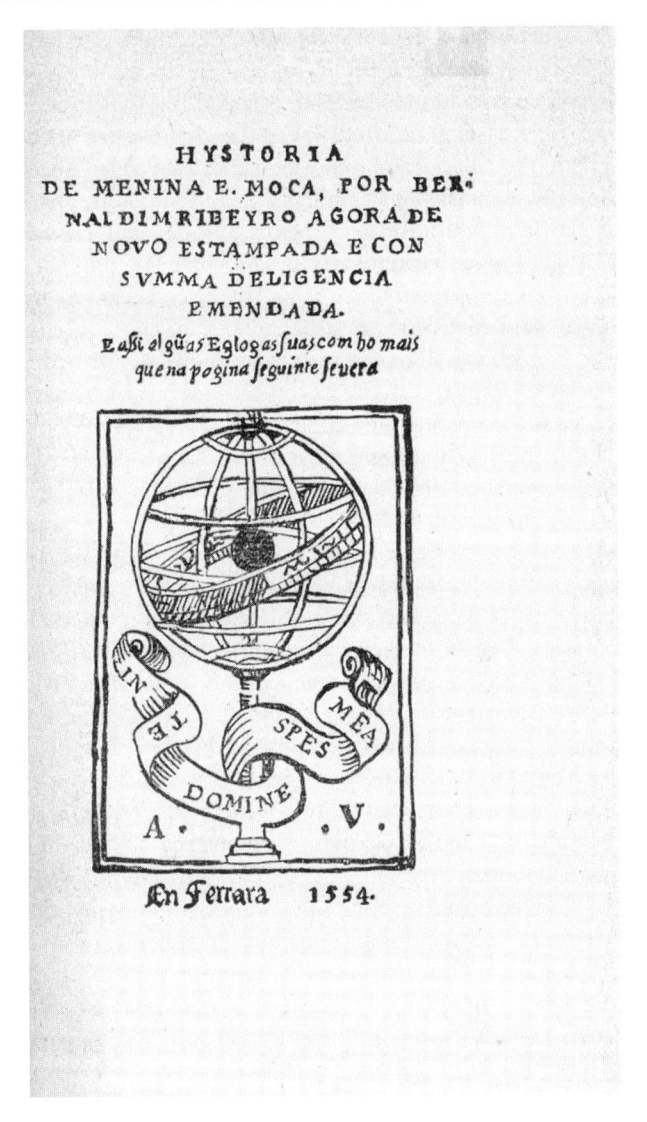

*Title page of Bernardim Ribeiro's work commonly known as* Menina e moça *(Maiden and Lass), first published in Italy (from Ribeiro,* Obras, *volume 2, 1932; Louis R. Wilson Library, University of North Carolina at Chapel Hill)*

Ribeiro's *Éclogas* are among the earliest eclogues ever composed in either Portuguese or Spanish. They are all composed in *redondilhas,* grouped together in *décimas* (stanzas of nine or ten verses each). Despite their length, the *Éclogas* can be considered as full-fledged anecdotes written as song-like poems. Images of nature, particularly with the Alentejo region, Lisbon, and central Portugal as a background, predominate as the poet describes the vicissitudes of his characters. The rivers Tagus and Mondego, the Atlantic Ocean, cities, towns, and hamlets are all represented in ways that stimulate the reader's imagination. The pastoral scenes in which shepherds such as Fauno, Franco, Jano, Pérsio, Silvestre, Costança, and Joana appear and move about perhaps recall the noble circles of the courtly life with which Ribeiro was familiar. All of Ribeiro's *Éclogas* have a common denominator, namely, a disconsolate lover in the *coita de amor* and the ever-present feeling of *saudade* that reflects the overall theme and genre of Portuguese sentimentality, sung by the medieval Portuguese troubadours. For example, in "Écloga I (Pérsio e Fauno)" the action is between two shepherds, Pérsio and Fauno, the former representing Love, the latter Reason. Pérsio is betrayed by Maria, who left him for a shepherd with more cattle. As he wanders aimlessly through the fields, Fauno sees him and tries to console him by putting reason ahead of any emotion.

From a courtly point of view, eclogues usually idealize rural life in a nostalgic manner. In Ribeiro's *Éclogas* the bucolic atmosphere is best represented in the form of dialogues or monologues. "Écloga IV (Jano)" is a soliloquy in which the main character is surrounded by pure nature: rivers, mountains, hills, and forests. The pain, longing, and suffering of the shepherds are lived, experienced, and expressed to the fullest. These techniques make Ribeiro more a precursor of the Renaissance than a son of the late-medieval period. Besides the examples of classical authors, such as Ovid and Virgil, the *Éclogas* show clear echoes of Petrarch's *Canzoniere,* Sannazzaro's *Arcadia,* Boccaccio's *Elegia di Madonna Fiammetta,* and Dante's *Inferno.*

The *estância* (stanza) and the *redondilhas* of the *Éclogas* are a direct development and logical continuation of his *cantigas* found in Resende's *Cancioneiro geral.* The *estâncias* become *motes* (poetic mottoes) in which love scenes are placed in a pastoral setting. There are many hidden but still recognizable allusions to real-life events, people, and places from the Alentejo region and the courtly life of his time.

Ribeiro's *cantigas* can be seen as a good example of Iberian literary production during the fifteenth century. The main idea at the beginning of the *cantigas* is paraphrased in the form of a *volta* (gloss), with a free number of lines. This form of song is modeled upon medieval Iberian ecclesiastical hymns. The *cantiga* "Para mim nasceo cuidado, desaventura, para mim nasceo tristura" (For Me Worry and Misfortune Were Born, for Me Sadness Was Born), which was included in the 1559 Cologne edition of *Menina e moça,* most likely was written by Ribeiro. It is a *mote* with a *glosa* (rondel) written in the *leixa-prem* style (Provençal for "leave and take"), that is, a device in which each stanza begins with the phrase or sentence that ended the previous one. Most likely this *cantiga* was composed after 1532, since the *leixa-prem* technique was introduced by Sá de Miranda in 1524 or, at the latest, in 1526, when he returned from Italy. Ribeiro's poems, instead, normally use the *sextina* (sestina), heavily inspired by their Italian counterparts, but in trochaic verses; that is, stressed syllables are followed by unstressed syllables or long syllables are followed by short syllables, a device that better fits the phonetic inventory of the Portuguese language.

The heptasyllabic sestina "Hontem pos-se o sol, e a noute cobriu de sombra esta terra" (Yesterday the Sun Set, and the Night Covered with a Shadow this Land) appears in the 1554 Ferrara edition of *Menina e moça* and in the 1559 Cologne edition of that work, following "Écloga V (Agrestes e Ribeiro)." This sestina follows the poetic style of the Provençal troubadour Arnaut Daniel de Ribérac (who died in 1189), one of the most admired poets of medieval literature, who also inspired Dante, Petrarch, and Boccaccio. Ribérac's skillful and difficult art of *trobar clus* (to make closed rhymes) was that of taking the noun of the first *sextilha* (six-line stanza) and repeating it in the first verse of the second *sextilha,* and so forth. Menéndez y Pelayo and Vasconcelos refer to "Hontem pos-se o sol, e a noute cobriu de sombra esta terra" as Ribeiro's Italian sestina, since he must have composed it after 1524, when both he and Sá de Miranda, back from Italy, were frequenting the Portuguese court and experimenting with the new trends acquired on their sojourn.

The *Cancioneiro de Évora* (Songbook of Évora), an anonymous collection of poems written in Portuguese and Spanish, composed in the sixteenth century and now kept at the Biblioteca de Évora, includes a contribution that might be by Ribeiro, namely, the "Mote do Capitão Bernaldim Ribeiro, feito ao proposito do mesmo, e pede ajuda aos senhores da sua companhia" (Motto of Captain Bernardim Ribeiro, Done for this Purpose by Himself, and He Asks the Messrs. of His Captaincy for Help). The fact that the poet is called *capitão* (captain, or rather, administrator) might allude to his having been granted a captaincy (overseas territory under Portuguese administration but governed by a Portuguese aristocrat), most likely the captaincy of São Jorge da Mina, in the Gulf of Guinea, along the coast of present-day Ghana. Further evidence, however, is needed before accepting this conclusion as fact. The consensus among scholars is that in all likelihood this Capitão Bernaldim was one of the author's many homonyms.

Ribeiro was already an acclaimed writer when, in 1536, his *Trovas de Dous pastores* was printed in Lisbon by Germão Galharde, together with works by other authors. In 1548 in Antwerp the idyllic novel *Ao longo de uma ribeira* (Along a Riverside) appeared in the Spanish *Cancionero de romance* (Romance Songbook), found between folios 160 and 162, a work that also portrays the anguish and pain of Ribeiro's characters in the midst of a gloomy natural environment.

Ribeiro's contributions to Portuguese letters are best seen in his prose. Though at times archaic, it combines both an elegant and courtly style with the oral language, especially the one employed by shepherds and women of rural Portugal. Ribeiro is chiefly acclaimed for his book of *Saudades* (Longings, circa 1530 or 1532–1544), which is better known as *Menina e moça,* that is, the first three words with which the story begins. The 1554 edition of *Hystoria de menina e moça per Bernaldim Ribeyro agora de novo estampada e com summa deligencia emendada e assi alguãs eglogas suas com homais que na pagina seguinte se vera* (Story of the Maiden and Lass by Bernaldim Ribeyro Now Again Printed and with Great Diligence Emended and Therefore Some of His Eclogues with More Which in the Following Page Will Be Seen) also includes the *Éclogas.*

Ribeiro's masterpiece was published in Ferrara by Samuel and Abraão Usque. The title adverb *de novo* (again), in its modern Portuguese meaning, led some late-nineteenth- and early-twentieth-century scholars to assume the existence of at least one or two previous editions of Ribeiro's work. In medieval and early-modern Portuguese, however, *de novo* also meant "for the first time" or "newly." The appendix of this first 1554 edition includes works by Ribeiro as well as poems written by other Portuguese authors. Among Ribeiro's compositions are his five *Éclogas,* the "Écloga Crisfal," the novel *Ao longo de uma ribeira,* and other works previously included in Resende's *Cancioneiro geral*. The order of the *Éclogas* as they appear in the 1554 Ferrara edition does not correspond to the dates of their composition. "Écloga III (Silvestre e Amador)" and "Écloga V (Agrestes e Ribeiro)" most likely are the oldest eclogues, whereas "Écloga IV (Jano)" and "Écloga II (Jano e Franco)" are the latest.

Another edition of *Menina e moça* was printed at Évora in 1557 and edited by the Spaniard André de Burgos under the title *Primeira e segunda parte do liuro chamado as Saudades de Bernardim Ribeiro com todas suas obras; treladado de seu proprio original* (First and Second Part of the Book of Longings of Bernardim Ribeiro with All His Works:

Taken from the Original). This edition differs from the Ferrara manuscript not only textually but also in its content: forty-one new chapters were added to the unfinished original story, thus bringing the total to eighty-nine chapters. Burgos, in his "Aviso" (Foreword) to the 1557 edition, mentions that he wanted to reproduce both parts in their entirety so that the readers could discern the differences between the two. Burgos's words suggest that most likely he knew who wrote this second part, but for some reason he chose not to disclose the author's name. The general consensus among scholars is that this forty-one-chapter addendum is apocryphal, most likely written by someone else. The original composition probably remained in manuscript form at least a decade, and it must have suffered significant changes through time.

On 20 March 1559 Arnold Birckmann in Cologne and Francisco Graseo in Lisbon published and sold the third edition of *História de menina e moça*. The Ferrara, Évora, and Cologne editions of *Menina e moça* all suggest the existence of a previous edition from which they are derived. They are, thus, amended and altered versions of the original archetype, having had many "translators," that is, editors who made modifications in spelling, lexicon, and content from one version to the other.

There are two additional manuscripts of *Menina e moça,* both transcribed circa 1560. One is kept at the Real Academia de Madrid; it consists of forty-eight chapters. The other, a manuscript bought by the Spanish scholar Eugenio Asensio, includes the original forty-eight chapters of the 1554 Ferrara edition.

As for the reason why *Menina e moça* was printed by Samuel and Abraão Usque in Italy rather than in Portugal, the most plausible explanation (though still not popular among scholars) is that Ribeiro was Jewish, most likely a *converso,* that is, an Iberian Jew forced to convert to Catholicism. During this period, Livorno, Venice, Ancona, and Ferrara became the recipients of a large contingent of Sephardim (Portuguese and Spanish Jews) forced to leave the Iberian Peninsula because of their faith. The first Jewish books of the Modern Era were, in fact, printed in Ferrara by Portuguese Jews of the Diaspora. According to Rego, the most prominent proponent of the opinion that the author was Jewish, Ribeiro's work is characterized by an almost complete lack of references to Christianity. Rego notes that, contrary to what seems to be the norm in Portuguese letters of the time, in Ribeiro's work there is no mention of or allusion to Jesus, Mary, or the myriad of saints that usually are seen in medieval and Renaissance Portuguese works. Similarly, when the situation calls for the inclusion of Christian rites, as in the case of weddings and funerals, once again, there are no references to a Christian, that is, Catholic, function. Most scholars, however, have pointed out that other editions of *Menina e moça* do

*Frontispiece for a retitled edition of* Menina e moça, *augmented with forty-one chapters probably written by someone other than Ribeiro (Biblioteca Nacional, Lisbon)*

include references to Christianity—as in the invocation "Santa Maria, val-me!" (Holy Mary, help me!), instead of the more generic expression "Valha-me Deus!" (God help me!) of the 1554 Ferrara edition. Furthermore, Ribeiro always kept close contacts with the aristocracy and the nobility, including the devout Catholics Quaresma and Mascarenhas, and the Portuguese court, all staunch defenders of Christianity. In addition, as António José Saraiva has suggested, Ribeiro's "heretical ideas" that often appear in his writings are a form of heresy that also goes against Judaism.

The second part of *Menina e moça,* that is, the section that was added posthumously, includes direct mentions of the cross, candles, confession, and communion. This fact, coupled with the overall change in style and content, is further proof that this addendum to the *Menina e moça* is apocryphal. Had Samuel and Abraão Usque been the editors of the second part, most certainly they would have also replaced these words with more neutral and universal symbols of religiosity.

These pieces of evidence suggest that Ribeiro might have been a Portuguese Jew or, most likely, a *marrano*—*conversos* were also known as *marranos* (pigs) or *cristãos-novos* (new-Christians)—and that he was either an exiled Jew or that he was only visiting his coreligionists of the Diaspora in Ferrara. According to Rego, a certain symbolism in *Menina e moça* also may suggest Ribeiro's Jewish origins. As Samuel Usque does in his *Consolaçam às tribulaçoens de Israel* (Consolation to the Tribulations of Israel, 1553; translated as *A Consolation for the Tribulations of Israel. Third Dialogue,* 1964), Ribeiro perhaps uses his narration to vent his anguish and frustration over how the Jews of the Diaspora, particularly the Sephardim, had suffered. The symbolism of the beast—mainly the wolf, that is, Christianity—and the sheep or any other meek animal, representing, in its turn, the Jews, may be seen as indirect allusions to the persecutions of the Jews, including the atrocities of the Iberian High Tribunals of the Holy Inquisition of Spain and Portugal. The wolf/sheep dichotomy is a common metaphor used by European Jews of the Diaspora, since all the European countries at one time or another persecuted, banned, or imposed some restrictions against the Jews living in their midst. Samuel Usque openly referred to Spain as a "cruel and hypocritical wolf." Hence, this "Jewish theme" was appropriated by Ribeiro, a *converso* writer of the time. Maria de Lourdes Saraiva, in her introduction to *Menina e moça,* is also of the opinion that in this work Ribeiro is possibly alluding, though in a camouflaged way, to the Inquisition.

Rego and António Baião (in his *Itinerários da Índia a Portugal por terra,* 1923) refer to an episode that occurred in 1562 along the coast of present-day Guiné-Bissau, where some Portuguese *conversos* were apparently caught mocking the Nativity using Ribeiro's "Écloga II (Jano e Franco)." The Portuguese Inquisition was immediately notified, and the culprits were sent to Lisbon to face the consequences. Between 1581 and 1624 *Menina e moça* was among the many censored and banned books in Portugal. Among the most plausible reasons why Ribeiro's work was banned by the Portuguese Inquisition is the fact that it was published in a known haven for many Sephardic Jews; more important, it was printed by the Usques, who, upon their arrival in Ferrara, had openly declared their ties with Judaism. Finally, several scholars have alleged that *Menina e moça* is full of hidden references to Judaism, the wandering of the Jews, and Jewish mysticism, that is, the Cabala. Prominent modern scholars such as Saraiva and Macedo have considered the possibility of Ribeiro being a *converso,* especially in light of his use of cabalistic images in the *Menina e moça.* They have focused particularly on the mystical and theosophical approach to nature as well as the interaction between the latter and the human soul.

If Ribeiro were a *converso* then there would be the question of his Jewish name since, besides a secular name that follows the customs of the country or region in which they reside, all Jews must also have a Hebrew name. Many theories have been postulated as to which name might have been used by Ribeiro. As most Jews of the Diaspora, Iberian Jews first tried to translate their Hebrew names into the local vernacular(s). If that was not possible, then they tried to use a name that closely fit the original Hebrew name or etymon. Another solution, though, was that of creating from the Hebrew letters of their name a new name by means of an anagram. If this produced an acceptable Christian name, then it was used as the secular name. In an anagram each letter could be used at least once or more than once, with no additional letters being added to the set. The nasals *m* and *n*, the front vowel *i* and the palatal *j*, the back vowels *o* and *u*, and the uvulars *q* and *g* are for this purpose interchangeable. Samuel Usque's anagram was Manuel Gomes. In the same manner, Rego argues, Ribeiro's Hebrew name would have been Juda Abarbanel, Abarbinel, or Abravanel, also known as Leão Hebreu.

*Menina e moça* is the best example of the sixteenth-century Portuguese sentimental novel, following in the footsteps of Boccaccio's *Elegia di Madonna Fiammetta* and, most of all, the *Decameron* (particularly the fourth day). Spanish antecedents of this genre include Juan Rodríguez de la Cámara, also known as Juan Rodríguez del Padrón, with his allegoric and sentimental novel *Siervo libre de amor* (Free Servant of Love, 1440), and Diego Fernández de San Pedro, whose sentimental *Tratado de amores de Arnalte y Lucenda* (Treatise of the Love of Arnalte and Lucenda, 1491) had a decisive impact on the first part of *Menina e moça*.

The prologue to the story of *Menina e moça* is narrated in the first person by an unnamed female character who, because of circumstances beyond her control, has withdrawn from society and is confined in a rural and solitary spot along the Portuguese coast. This character says that when she was still a young and innocent girl ("menina e moça"), she was taken from her father's house and brought to foreign lands, feeling predestined to lead a life of suffering and complete isolation. She bemoans her many sorrows, surrounded only by an inhospitable nature, where the cliffs, the mountains, and the rough sea are her sole companions and witnesses to her endless pain.

The initial monologue of *Menina e moça*, written in rhythmic prose, recalls the medieval troubadour lyrics of the *cantigas de amigo* (songs of friend) genre, in which the object was usually a story of unrequited love or a tale of separation, written by a male from a female or feminine perspective. The fantastic, imaginary, and unreal are intertwined with reflections on sadness and longing. For this reason the protagonist expounds that "o livro há-de ser o que vai escrito nele" (the book has to be about what will be written in it). The girl, thus, wrote the work for herself, not for posterity. That is the reason why she has no intention of finishing it, since, as she also says, "tristeza e lamentações nunca chegam ao fim" (sadness and lamentations never come to an end).

From chapter 2 to the end of chapter 4 the monologue eventually leads to a dialogue between the young girl and an older woman (*dona do tempo antigo,* a woman of bygone days), though the latter also suffers from the *coitas de amor*. This section exemplifies what most critics have called Ribeiro's "feminist" approach to literature. In his view, men, by their very nature that takes them outside of the hearth, ignore the meaning of love, its ramifications and complications, since these are reached only after being confined alone at home. Hence, women are the only repositories of truly noble feelings. Given the times in which Ribeiro lived, perhaps his approach to the issue could be better labeled as "proto-feminist." Although he recognizes the unfairness of the predicament in which women find themselves in society, there is still no analysis of the reasons why men behave the way they do. In other words, there is no blame put on the patriarchal system that for centuries has forged a binary way of conduct for men and women within a given society.

From chapter 5 through chapter 9, Ribeiro makes a chivalrous parenthesis in which the deaths of the *cavaleiro da ponte* (the knight of the bridge) and his lover Bilesa are sadly narrated. From chapter 10 to the end of chapter 31, the author unfolds the story of the love between the knight Narbindel and Aónia, betrothed to Fileno. In order to win Aónia, Narbindel changes his name to Binmarder and becomes a shepherd. The story ends with Aónia marrying Fileno and being carried away to a distant place, while Binmarder disappears. At this point, Ribeiro tells the readers, who supposedly are waiting to know more of the story, that "mudança possui tudo. Deixemo-la agora porém ficar assim" (change is everywhere. Let's leave it at that for now).

The first eleven chapters of the second part describe the tragic love between Arima, Bilesa's daughter, and Avalor. The setting is entirely courtly, filled with adventure and imaginary chivalric episodes. António Salgado Júnior is of the opinion that Ribeiro wanted to recreate a "sentimental *Decameron*," that is, he wished to write a series of novels linked to each other by a central connection, namely, the encounter of the protagonist with the *dona do tempo antigo*.

The ultimate theme of *Menina e moça*–considered by some to be a half pastoral and half chivalrous autobiographical novel–is love, especially the degrees of one's commitment to it. Ribeiro introduces fantastic and fatalistic events, forewarning dreams, good and bad omens, and supernatural voices, perhaps as an indication of the frailty and impotence of humanity and nature versus destiny. The medieval concept of nature as a monolithic, powerful, and transcendent block, dominating all creatures, is completely rejected by the author, who seems to anticipate the Romantic depiction of nature. The autobiographical vein in *Menina e moça* stems from Ribeiro's familiarity with the Portuguese court as well as with the Portuguese spirit; that is, the desire to express *saudade*, the longing for a happiness that is gone forever, with nostalgic sadness.

Nature in *Menina e moça* is represented as a multifaceted entity. It is a mirror in which humans can see each other and, more important, they can contemplate their own shortcomings. As a mirror, nature can also tell love stories, with a happy or sad ending, or no ending at all, since, as Ribeiro often says, "mudança possui tudo" (everything changes). The author represents nature as a driving force that gives strength to humans, animals, and supernatural beings. All living creatures are, thus, part of nature; furthermore, the often described remoteness of faraway places echoes the overall feeling of alienation and despair of the person in pain. For this reason, Ribeiro has been called the precursor of Romanticism, not only in Portuguese letters but also in all of Western literature, in which the emphasis is on the longing for a distant, uncertain, and misty place, that is, a re-creation of an idealized past that can never repeat itself.

Ribeiro's male characters in *Menina e moça*, such as Avalor and Binmarder, are perhaps among the first Romantic characters to appear on European soil, thus making his work one of the earliest modern psychological novels. His female characters in *Menina e moça*, especially Arima, show compassion and, above all, a kind of anxiety that is revealed only after she expresses her feelings of *saudade*, this longing for the indefinite, the unreachable, something that once was and could be again, and yet, it is still too far away and almost impossible to regain.

Like many of the details of his life, the story that Ribeiro died senile and demented in the Hospital de Todos os Santos of Lisbon in 1552 is most likely a legend. Internal evidence from two of Sá de Miranda's eclogues, one written soon after 1526 and the other around 1532 (according to some scholars, before 1544), suggests that Ribeiro's death occurred between 1526 and 1544. There are no references to the writer being interned in an asylum. There is, however, a royal pension dated 9 October 1549, which was used to defray the costs of keeping a certain Bernardim Ribeiro in the Hospital de Todos os Santos of Lisbon. This person was initially hospitalized for mental depression. Scholars are still divided as to whether this individual is the author or just one of his many homonyms.

Ribeiro's verses reveal two main features of his education. One, he belonged to the *eschola hespanhola* (Spanish School), which, among other things, made a parody of the religious hymns such as the *memento*, the *cantigas*, the *voltas*, the *glosas* of the romances, the *esparsas*, and the *vilancetes*. Two, he deeply admired Italian poetry, particularly Dante's allegorical works and Boccaccio's literary innovations. In fact, in the *Cancioneiro geral* Ribeiro explicitly imitates Dante's tercet in *Inferno* V: 121–123. As for *Menina e moça*, it is the only work of sixteenth-century Portugal in which Boccaccio's mixture of the erotic–in this case sensual–and sentimental appear in a novel. These characteristics are fundamental because they indicate when Ribeiro linked the Iberian poetic tradition, mainly of Spanish provenance, with the Italian lyric legacy, though adapting it to the Portuguese language and frame of mind. He was instrumental in introducing Portugal to the Hispano-Italic school and its trends, thus opening the door to experiments and innovations in Portuguese letters in the sixteenth century.

Bernardim Ribeiro embodied trends that were latent in the courtly poets who contributed to Resende's *Cancioneiro geral*. In his prose and lyrics, he displays a strong desire to explore the subconscious of his characters, thus providing his readers with clear portraits of the characters' states of mind, particularly of their self-analyses. Saraiva has noted a common denominator in Ribeiro's literary production: a relentless, pervasive drive that brings his characters to look for strength in things, nature, and ultimately in themselves. Ribeiro's specific longing for the distant and unreachable in life, as well as for the pleasure in feeling pain or suffering for a particular loss, influenced many Portuguese writers and philosophers, including Frei Heitor Pinto, Jorge Ferreira de Vasconcelos, Almeida Garrett, Luís de Camões, the nineteenth-century *saudosista* movement (the doctrine of longing for the good old days in poetry and philosophy), as well as many twentieth-century Portuguese writers. In addition, he transformed the Portuguese landscape, mainly that of the Alentejo region, into a reflection of the souls of his characters and their suffering and longing for a better tomorrow.

**References:**

Visconde de Sanches de Baêna, *Bernardim Ribeiro* (Lisbon: A. M. Pereira, 1895);

António Baião, ed., *Itinerários da Índia a Portugal por terra* (Coimbra: Imprensa da Universidade, 1923);

Teófilo Braga, *Bernardim Ribeiro e o bucolismo,* volume 6 of his *Historia da litteratura portugueza,* 32 volumes (Porto: Chardron, 1897);

Braga, *Obras de Christóvam Falcão: Trovas de Chrisfal, Cartas, Cantigas e Esparsas* (Porto: Renascença Portuguesa, 1915);

João Malaca Casteleiro, "A influência da *Fiammetta* de Boccaccio na *Menina e moça* de Bernardim Ribeiro," *Ocidente*, 74 (1968): 145–168;

Hernâni Cidade, *Lições de cultura e literatura portuguesas*, seventh edition, 2 volumes (Coimbra: Coimbra Editora, 1984);

Manuel da Silva Gaio, *Bucolismo*, 2 volumes (Coimbra: Imprensa da Universidade, 1932, 1933)—comprises volume 1, *Bernardim Ribeiro*; and volume 2, *Cristóvão Falcão*;

Lindolfo Gomez, *O problema Crisfal, subsídios histórico-literários* (Juiz de Fora, Brazil, 1912);

Delfim de Brito Guimarães, *Teófilo Braga e a lenda de Crisfal* (Lisbon: Guimarães, 1909);

Hélder Macedo, *Do significado oculto da "Menina e moça"* (Lisbon: Guimarães, 1999);

Narciso Bernardino de Sá Magalhães, *Bernardim Ribeiro* (Lisbon: Typographia de Castro Irmão, 1893);

Izabel Margato, *As saudades da "Menina e moça"* (Lisbon: Imprensa Nacional-Casa da Moeda, 1988);

José Vitorino de Pina Martins, *Humanisme et Renaissance de l'Italie au Portugal: Les deux regards de Janus* (Lisbon: Fondation Calouste Gulbenkian, 1989);

Marcelino Menéndez y Pelayo, *Orígenes de la novela*, fourth edition, 4 volumes (Buenos Aires: Emece, 1945);

Achille Pellizzari, "Bernardim Ribeiro e la poesia italianeggiante in Portogallo agli inizi del secolo XVI," in his *Portogallo e Italia nel secolo XVI. Studi e ricerche* (Naples: Francesco Perrella, 1914), pp. 19–40;

Pellizzari, *Portogallo e Italia nel secolo XVI. Studi e ricerche storiche e letterarie* (Naples: Società Editrice Francesco Perrella, 1914);

José Augusto Ramalho Teixeira Rego, "Bernardim Ribeiro" and "Notas sobre Bernardim Ribeiro," in his *Estudos e controvérsias, 2.ª série*, 2 volumes (Porto: Faculdade de Letras, 1931), I: 57–79;

Rego, "Um problema da história literária. (Da aparição do estilo pitoresco na literatura portuguesa)," *Revista de Estudos Históricos*, 1 (1925): 47–67;

Michael Ricciardelli, "Relazione tra *Menina e moça* di B. Ribeiro e l'Arcadia di J. Sannazzaro," *Italica*, 42 (1965): 370–377;

Giuseppe Carlo Rossi, "Il Boccaccio nelle letterature in portoghese," in *Il Boccaccio nelle culture e letterature nazionali*, edited by Francesco Mazzoni (Florence: Leo S. Olschki, 1978), pp. 209–242;

António Salgado Júnior, *A "Menina e moça" e o romance sentimental no Renascimento* (Aveiro: Gráfica Aveirense, 1940);

Guilherme G. de Oliveira Santos, ed., *Trovas de Crisfal* (Lisbon: Portugal, 1965);

António José Saraiva, "Ensaio sôbre a poesia de Bernardim Ribeiro," *Revista da Faculdade de Letras*, 7, no. 1-2 (1940–1941): 13–120;

Saraiva and Oscar Lopes, "Bernardim Ribeiro," in their *História da literatura portuguesa*, eleventh edition (Porto: Porto Editora, 1979), pp. 237–252;

Jorge de Sena, "A sextina e a sextina de Bernardim Ribeiro," *Revista de Letras da Faculdade de Filosofia e Ciências e Letras de Assis*, 4 (1963): 137–176;

Raul Soares, *O poeta Crisfal. Subsídios para o estudo de um problema histórico-literário* (Campinas, Brazil: Typographia Livro Azul, 1909);

Carolina Michaëlis de Vasconcelos, *Nótulas relativas à "Menina e moça" na edição de Colónia (1559)* (Coimbra: Imprensa da Universidade, 1924);

Vasconcelos, "Novos estudos sôbre Sá de Miranda," *Boletim da Segunda Classe da Academia das Sciências de Lisboa*, 5 (1911 [1912]): 9–230;

Vasconcelos, "Uma passagem escura do *Crisfal*," *Revista Lusitana*, 3 (1895): 347–362;

Vasconcelos, *Poesias de Francisco de Sá de Miranda* (Halle, Germany: Max Niemeyer, 1885).

**Papers:**

Most of Bernardim Ribeiro's archives are held at the Biblioteca Nacional in Lisbon as well as the Biblioteca de Évora.

# Francisco de Sá de Miranda

*(28 August 1481 – 17 May 1558?)*

Joseph Abraham Levi
*Rhode Island College*

BOOKS: *Comedia dos estrangeiros* (Coimbra: Joam de Barreyra, 1559); republished as *Comedia, intitulada, Os estrangeiros* (Coimbra: António de Maris, 1561);

*Comedia dos vilhalpandos* (Coimbra: António de Maris, 1560);

*As obras do celebrado Lusitano o doutor Francisco de Sá de Miranda* (Lisbon: Manoel de Lyra, 1595);

*As obras do Doctor Francisco de Saa de Miranda,* edited by Gonçalo Coutinho (Lisbon: Vicente Alvares, 1614);

*Satyras de Francisco de Saa de Miranda* (Porto: João Rodriguez, 1626);

*Obras do Doutor Francisco de Sá de Miranda* (Lisbon: Paulo Craesbeek, 1651);

*Poesias de Francisco de Sâ de Miranda. Edição feita sobre cinco manuscriptos ineditos e todas as edições impressas. Acompanhada de um estudo sobre o poeta, variantes, notas, glossario e um retrato,* edited by Carolina Michaëlis de Vasconcelos (Halle, Germany: Max Niemeyer, 1885);

*Obras completas,* 2 volumes, edited by Manuel Rodrigues Lapa (Lisbon: Sá da Costa, 1937);

*Poesias escolhidas,* edited by José V. de Pina Martins (Lisbon: Verbo, 1969).

Francisco de Sá de Miranda (in medieval Portuguese Sá was also spelled Saa or Sâ) is credited with having introduced into Portuguese literature the comedy in prose and a new lyric meter, the decasyllable. Literary historians praise his contributions to the development of new creations or adaptations to already-existing Iberian forms, such as the tercet, the sestina, the octave, and the sonnet. He gave new meaning to the lyric subgenres of the *canção* (song), the *elegia* (elegy), the *écloga* (eclogue), and the *carta* (letter in verse), almost always satiric in nature, thus paving the way for later writers such as Diogo Bernardes and Luís de Camões.

Sá de Miranda introduced these new elements from Italy, where he resided between 1521 and 1526. His merit, however, rests on his originality in acclimatiz-

*Francisco de Sá de Miranda (Biblioteca Nacional, Lisbon)*

ing these imported Italian and classical trends to the Iberian literary tradition and style–the *medida velha* (old meter)–thus forging a new genre, usually referred to as *medida nova* (new meter). Like most Portuguese writers of the time, the poet also felt comfortable composing in Latin and in Spanish. More than half of his work is written in Spanish, although critics unanimously agree that his best literary compositions were in Portuguese.

Sá de Miranda is best known for his poetic epistles, collected in 1938 by Teixeira Leite as *Cartas de Sá de Miranda* (Sá de Miranda's Letters); his *Éclogas,* particularly the "Écloga Basto" (Eclogue Basto, 1626); and his *Sátiras* (Satires), published posthumously as *Satyras de Francisco de Saa de Miranda* (Francisco de Saa de Miranda's Satires, 1626). These works are characterized by an overall satirical and didactic vein. Unlike many of his contemporaries, the writer disapproved of the Portuguese expansion overseas and its colonial policy. He also condemned the love of material wealth and glory, advocating instead rectitude, moral values, and a simple life, preferably within a rural environment. Sá de Miranda's work is usually divided into two parts: one in which his emotions predominate, and one characterized by deep reflections and thought, as in his *Cartas* and *Éclogas.*

Sá de Miranda was born on 28 August 1481 in Coimbra. He was one of the twelve illegitimate sons of Gonçalo Mendes de Sá, archdeacon of Coimbra, and Inês de Melo, a single woman of aristocratic lineage. Later his father legitimized eight of the sons, including the author and his brother Mem de Sá, who served as governor general of Brazil from 1558 to 1572. Francisco spent his childhood in Coimbra, where he completed his secondary education. He then moved to the capital to pursue his studies at the University of Lisbon. Like most of his contemporaries, Sá de Miranda studied law, though with little enthusiasm. On receiving his degree, he obtained a position as *lente substituto* (substitute fellow) in jurisprudence at the University of Lisbon, where he taught with great success until 1520. During this time he began frequenting the royal palace, particularly the court of King Manuel I. His friend the writer Bernardim Ribeiro was also a regular guest there. He also began trying his hand at what became his true vocation–writing.

Sá de Miranda's masterpieces, the *Cartas,* all but one written in Portuguese, and the *Éclogas,* by far his most original works, were composed in the *medida velha.* Sá de Miranda used the *medida velha* as a vehicle to express his strong moral and pedagogical convictions on the trend of getting easy wealth from India and other exotic places where gold was readily available. As a remedy, the writer advocated a return to nature and traditional human and moral values that had been lost in this rush to riches. These ideas, couched in an elliptic and yet concrete language, at times satiric, are among Sá de Miranda's best qualities as a writer.

At first Sá de Miranda wrote compositions in the old style using the *cantiga* (song), the *vilancete* (pastoral poem), the *esparsa* (six-syllable poem), the *redondilha* (five- or seven-syllable verses), and the *trova* (minstrel's ballad). His first poems appeared in Hernán del Castillo's *Cancionero general* (General Songbook, 1511) in Spain. Thirteen were included in Garcia de Resende's *Cancioneiro geral* (General Songbook, 1516). These works were written in both Portuguese and Spanish in the *medida velha;* as an experiment, however, some were also composed in the *medida nova.*

Most of the literary contributions to Resende's *Cancioneiro geral* are *redondilhas, vilancetes,* or *cantigas,* some of the most prominent forms found in fifteenth-century Portugal and Spain. Their common denominators were the *mote* (poetic motto) and the *glosa* (rondel), the characteristics of *medida velha.* The new Italian verse and style, known as *dolce stil nuovo* (sweet new style), which began to appear in the Italian peninsula and in Sicily during the early part of the thirteenth century, was composed of the decasyllable, a ten-syllable verse that bore the stress on either the fourth and eighth syllable (sapphic verse) or on the sixth (heroic verse). According to the Italian phonetic system, if the last word was grave (open and stressed), then the post-tonic syllable (which follows a stressed vowel) had to be counted. As a consequence, the decasyllable became a hendecasyllable, that is, an eleven-syllable verse. Given its length, this new method allowed for a greater flexibility of stress and pauses, which eventually was used by poets to fit the needs of the poem. When compared to the Iberian *redondilha,* the hendecasyllable showed more adaptability and a greater variety of results. With this verse, poets were free to give a more personal tone and, most of all, to express a wider range of topics in their poetry.

According to the biography in *As obras do Doctor Francisco de Saa de Miranda* (The Works of Doctor Francisco de Sá de Miranda, 1614), edited by Gonçalo Coutinho, the writer's father died around 1520. This loss, coupled with an ever-growing dissatisfaction with the system, led Sá de Miranda to abandon the teaching of jurisprudence and take up the private study of moral and Stoic philosophy, clearly visible in the content of most of his sonnets.

In 1521, after a brief sojourn in Spain, Sá de Miranda left for Italy, where he visited and at times resided in Rome, Venice, Naples, Milan, Florence, Palermo, and a few other cities in Sicily. Thomas Foster Earle suggests in his *Theme and Image in the Poetry of Sá de Miranda* (1980) that the author might have reached Italy as early as 1519, since there are good reasons to believe that he was present at the tenth-anniversary presentation of Ludovico Ariosto's *I suppositi* (The Supposed, 1509; translated as *Supposes,* 1566) in Rome.

*Title page for the first collection of Sá de Miranda's works (from Sá de Miranda,* Obras, *1994; Main Library, Indiana University)*

Most scholars are of the opinion that the poet Vittoria Colonna, famous for her *Rime* (Rhymes, 1536–1546) and related to the Miranda family, introduced the young writer to the major Italian authors of the time, including Ariosto, Pietro Bembo, Jacopo Sannazzaro, Giovanni Ruccellai, Luigi Alamanni, Francesco Guicciardini, and Lattanzio Tolomei, all of whom had a decisive influence on Sá de Miranda's career. Besides his best friend Ribeiro, who was there from 1520 to 1524, other Portuguese poets who had been to Italy to benefit from the teachings of the classical scholar and poet Angelo Poliziano included Luís Teixeira Lobo, Henrique Caiado, João Roiz de Sá e Meneses, Diogo Pacheco, and Aires Barbosa. Critics believe that Sá de Miranda's journey to Italy was mainly motivated by his desire to experience firsthand the Italian literary innovations, as well as the Italian renderings of classical Greek and Latin authors.

The sonnets, songs, sestinas, and tercets used by Provençal poets and minstrels were adapted by Petrarch, Dante, and Giovanni Boccaccio, as well as poets from the Sicilian School. Besides these models, the Italians made extensive use of Greek and Latin forms, such as the eclogue (mainly following the examples of the Greek poets Theocritus and Virgil); the elegy (after the Roman poets Albus Tibullus and Sextus Propercius); the ode (particularly the Greek and Roman poets Pindar, Sappho, Alcaeus, Anacreon, Catullus, and Horace); the epistle, or letter in verse (inspired by the Roman satirist Horace); the epigram (as established by the Romans Juvenal and Martial); and the epithalamium, or bridal song. The Italian creation introduced a new way of making poetry that, contrary to the courtly love of the Portuguese troubadour lyric poets, called for a more direct participation of the poet in the subject matter that was being sung.

Italian influence on Iberian letters started during the first half of the fifteenth century, where clear forms of Petrarchism and its new idea of love are found in the Castilian *cancioneros* as well as in some of the poets included in Resende's *Cancioneiro geral*. Only in the sixteenth century, however, did the new Italian trend finally take root in Iberia.

Aside from his use of the *medida nova,* Sá de Miranda is known for having written the first two comedies in a classical style. The Portuguese word *comédia* (comedy), adapted from the Italian *commedia,* was introduced by Sá de Miranda in 1523 or 1524 when he wrote *Os estrangeiros* (The Foreigners), the first comedy in prose in Portuguese. Besides betraying a strong influence from Plautus and Terence, *Os estrangeiros* also has features common to works by Ariosto, Bernardo Dovizi da Bibbiena, and Niccolò Machiavelli.

*Os estrangeiros* is a five-act play set in Palermo during the Spanish domination of the island. The work respects the Aristotelian unities of time, place, and action. Unlike any other Portuguese play of the period, the action takes place in a section of a street, a metaphorical crossroad where all conflicts eventually converge. Surprisingly, it has no Portuguese characters. In his dedication to Cardinal Henrique, Sá de Miranda acknowledges Terence, Plautus, and Ariosto as his sources and inspirations. Unlike Terence, however, Sá de Miranda does not emphasize the age difference of his characters; instead, he focuses on the fact that they are all living in a foreign place and behaving in a foreign manner. In the prologue he personifies the voice of the play itself; the comedy thus addresses the Portuguese audience and takes them, as foreigners, to Palermo to witness life in a different country. Besides the local Sicilian population, there are Aragonese and Italians from the peninsula, among the latter Pisans and Florentine men and women. Sá de Miranda's foreigners speak Portuguese well. They are neither caricatures nor stereotypes of the preconceived idea of foreigners that a sixteenth-century Portuguese audience might have had. They are to be taken seriously. *Os estrangeiros* portrays everyday life in an ordinary Italian town, a place (and an island) caught between political events and personal struggles. The prologue to the work must have surprised audiences of the time when they realized that the play is not a medieval Portuguese *auto* (morality play), performed in verse and rhyme, but rather a sixteenth-century "foreign" comedy that they could understand and follow, though perplexed by its novelty.

After the unification of the Crowns of Aragon and Castile, Sicily passed from Aragonese rule to Spanish sovereignty. During this time Palermo was also a preferred place of refuge for many Pisans who wanted to flee Florentine dominion and prosper economically, away from the political turmoil of the peninsula. The Spanish presence in Sicily—be it Aragonese or Castilian—was seen as a negative contribution to overall stability. Sá de Miranda seems to confirm the feelings of these Italians when he portrays many, if not all, Spaniards in a bad light. A complex love affair unfolds surrounded by intrigue, subterfuge, boastful Spanish soldiers, parasites, and the inevitable matchmakers. In the end, all the schemes lead to the expected, but never certain, happy ending: the marriage of the couple.

*Os estrangeiros,* as Earle states in *The Comedy of the Foreigners* (1997), should be placed within the more general frame of Portuguese literature on faraway places during the age of expansions, as the opening of new sea routes increased Portuguese interest in foreign countries and peoples. In this case, however, the exotic place was Europe itself, specifically Italy, a place still unknown to most Portuguese. *Os estrangeiros* is also a portrayal of an era filled with turmoil, intrigues, and scandals, including the schism within the Church and the subsequent formation of Anglicanism and Protestantism; the problems with the Ottoman presence in the Balkans and the rest of the Mediterranean Sea basin; war between Florence and Pisa; and the political maneuvers to divide the Italian peninsula, Sicily, and Sardinia among Spain, France, and the Papal States.

Sá de Miranda returned to Portugal in 1526 completely transformed and determined not to transplant but rather to adapt what he had learned to the Iberian literary tradition. After his return to Portugal, he visited Spain, where he met the poets Garcilaso de la Vega and Juan Boscán y Almogéver. As his Iberian counterparts had done before him, the author was determined to introduce his country to the *dolce stil nuovo* and, more specifically, to Petrarchism, which he believed could express an even wider range of literary genres and styles than the traditional Iberian forms.

When he returned from Spain, in late 1526 or early 1527, Sá de Miranda frequented the court of King João III, distinguishing himself by his literary talents.

During his voluntary and lifelong exile from court and city life, Sá de Miranda engaged in activities such as studying, writing, playing the violin and viola, enjoying the company of friends and fellow poets, fishing, and hunting, particularly wolf hunting. The countryside gave him the opportunity to observe and enjoy nature and to have contacts with peasants and ordinary people, struggling more than ever to make ends meet in a rapidly changing society. Life in the country provided a backdrop against which he launched his invectives against social oppression and injustice of the poor and the peasants by noble, aristocratic, and absentee landlords. He regarded city life as evil and a source of corruption, as the accumulation of wealth brought the death of the human soul. Around 1527 he began working on the new verse imported from Italy, the hendecasyllable, which largely supplanted the Iberian *redondilha*. He also restructured the Iberian tercet, the sonnet, the ode, the *canção,* the *oitava rima* (strophe with eight hendecasyllabic verses), and the eclogue. The poet's debut in the new Italian style included "Fábula do Mondego" (Fable of the Mondego River, 1528–1529); an eclogue written in Petrarchan stanzas, the "Écloga Alejo" (Eclogue Alejo, circa 1527–1530); and the "Sonetos" (Sonnets). During the same time, he also wrote the "Canção a Nossa Senhora" (Song to Our Lady, circa 1527–1528).

In the "Écloga Alejo" the old and new styles coexist. In the "Écloga a António Ferreira" (Eclogue to António Ferreira, 1626) Sá de Miranda reiterates the value of the old Iberian forms such as the *mote,* the *vilancete,* the *glosas,* and the *esparsas.* The "Carta a António de Meneses" (Letter to António de Meneses) also includes praises to the older, and by then already gone, *momos* (satirical farces) and *serões* (literary compositions accompanied by music), a form he himself had tried during his first attempts at writing poetry. His *Cartas* blend bucolic poetry and classical tradition, mainly of Horatian provenance. The content is moralistic and at times pedantic and prolix. Perhaps for that reason Sá de Miranda chose the term *cartas* instead of the more appropriate *epístolas* (epistles): it appears that he wished to emphasize the individual nature of his missives. He never forgot, however, that he was sending an educational message as well as displaying his scholarly knowledge. His *Cartas* are addressed to the king, family members, friends, and simple acquaintances. The topics range from life in the countryside and all the amenities that derive from it (applicable to both body and soul), to life in the city and all the negative effects that such a lifestyle has, especially on Portuguese society of the time. Sá de Miranda had serious reservations regarding the moral and social effects that the Portuguese colonial

*Title page for an edition of Sá de Miranda's works based on a 1564 manuscript that he probably sent to Prince João (Biblioteca Nacional, Lisbon)*

policy had on Portugal and the Portuguese people in general.

The "Écloga Basto" and all of the *Cartas* are written in *redondilha menor*. In the "Écloga Basto" Sá de Miranda speaks from his voluntary confinement in northern Portugal and launches invectives against the moral decadence of his time. City life is contrasted with the simple, safer, and more stable rustic environment found in the Portuguese countryside. Horace is the model for his invectives at the artificial life at court; the author, however, also includes social commentaries in his writings. Being away from the court, he felt free of all intrigues and political subterfuges of the royal palace. His attacks, however, are directed not at the Portuguese Crown but rather at the maritime expansion in Africa, Asia, and the rest of the world. He has harsh words against gold and greed, which cause war. By 1532 the Atlantic slave trade was being carried on by various European nations, including Portugal; Sá de Miranda considered slavery a violation of "heavenly souls." He saw the latest inventions in the field of weaponry as further examples of the evil that can befall humankind when it abandons nature. Aristocracy taking over the communal land of the peasants, the idea of private property, and the accumulation of money and gold are presented as the roots of all evil and moral decadence.

Sá de Miranda idealizes the rural scene depicted by Horace, as opposed to the unjust system of the proletariat and aristocracy of sixteenth-century Portugal. In this respect, Sá de Miranda's views could be seen as idealistic, comparable to those of a late-nineteenth-century socialist or perhaps even a utopian. A few scholars have compared him to his contemporary Sir Thomas More in this regard. Sá de Miranda's attacks on the Portuguese court as the center of corruption are tempered by a firm belief in a just and well-balanced monarchy at the service of the people. It is not surprising, then, that in his *Cartas* Sá de Miranda also chooses old Portuguese words and forms, as if he wished to emphasize the old and just values of Portuguese society. In 1533 the king awarded Sá de Miranda the Comenda de Santa Maria das Duas Igrejas (Estate of Saint Mary of the Two Churches), which had belonged to the Cavaleiros do Convento de Tomar (Knights of the Convent of Tomar). It was a small property on the left bank of the Neiva, in the Minho region in northern Portugal. The writer retired to his newly acquired estate, where he spent the rest of his life with his wife, Briolanja de Azevedo, with whom he had two sons.

Sá de Miranda's second comedy, *Os vilhalpandos* (The Vilhalpandos), composed circa 1538, is set in Rome. Most likely, *vilhalpando* was the name used by Spanish soldiers of the time to connote the idea of a brave and fearless fighter. Sá de Miranda uses the term in a negative, anti-Spanish sense, as a synonym for bullies. In the work there is an echo of Plautus's exchange of characters and all the clichés used in his plays, including swindlers, servants, parasites, and matrons. The comedy is anticlerical, denouncing the corruption of the Church, especially the selling of indulgences and the practice of simony.

In the introduction to *Os vilhalpandos,* dedicated to Cardinal Henrique, Sá de Miranda mentions the works of Plautus, Terence, and Ariosto as models for the play. The main characters include two arrogant and pretentious soldiers, a courtesan, a mother who is a matchmaker, and a hypocritical notary. The inevitable intrigue involves the ill-fated courtesan, a son lost in perdition, his heartbroken parents, and in-laws fearing for the safety of their daughter. There is the usual confusion caused by people sharing the same name, and there is a happy ending.

*Os vilhalpandos* and *Os estrangeiros* are not only written in an Italian style but also placed within Italian settings. Both comedies are different from the traditional plays with which the Portuguese audience was familiar. Unlike their allegorical antecedents, Sá de Miranda's plays are realistic; the action occurs between real people, and the emphasis is on the consequences of their interactions and not on their souls or their moral qualities. The playwright thus gives a human dimension to comedy. Almost all the scenes are set in the open air, in the middle of the street. Both plays, therefore, represent an urban theater in which merchants, soldiers, doctors, lawyers, and everyday people dominate the entire plot. From the traditional classical repertoire the author took characters such as maids, old men, arrogant soldiers (represented here as Spaniards), young couples in love, tutors, parasites, and matchmakers. Also unlike their models, Sá de Miranda's comedies lack a proper plot; in other words, as Frederick Bouterwek stated in his *Portuguese Literature* (1823), his "scenes are strung together, rather than drawn out of each other." There is, however, an overall bourgeois feeling, a sense of equality among the different characters in the urban environment. In *Os estrangeiros* and *Os vilhalpandos* the writer launches a satire against the Church and the corruption of the clergy. Both works foreshadow the characteristics of Renaissance Europe: the ridicule of military bravery and a critique of monasticism, the corruption of the Church, simony, and the antiquated scholasticism. Sá de Miranda proposes classical models coupled with ideals of peace and simplicity, which he advocated in almost all of his writings.

Cardinal Henrique was so impressed with these two comedies that he made arrangements for them to be performed at the royal palace, and, after Sá de Miranda's death, he also ordered that they be published. *Os estrangeiros* was first printed in 1559, followed by another edition in 1561; *Os vilhalpandos* was published in 1560.

Sá de Miranda had begun his poetic career in the *medida nova* imitating Petrarch's love poems while filtering them through a sense of melancholy, perhaps foreshadowing the theme of his future compositions. These poems were also the first expressions of his inner self, a persona who preferred an elliptic, condensed, and concise style. His imitation of Petrarch, as in the "Canção a Nossa Senhora," although tinged with sadness, is a reflection on the destiny of humankind and the inexorable passing of time.

In later poems in which the *medida nova* is predominant, the writer tried his hand at different literary genres. His *Éclogas* show a predilection for mythological and historical accounts, particularly those belonging to the classical tradition. Like his *Éclogas*, Sá de Miranda's elegies, sonnets, and songs are a mirror of Renaissance Europe, where refinement of the spirit was preferred at all costs over the chivalry and the arms of the past. Although the model was foreign, the topic for the heroic poems covers the national arena. Sá de Miranda's sonnets explore the emotions stirred by love, while highlighting the simplicity of country life and a general disillusionment with life and the uselessness of everything outside of love and nature. He considered both love and nature essential for living in harmony in the world.

Given the nature of the pastoral poems, particularly the sections written in dialogue, Sá de Miranda's first *Éclogas* can be seen as indirect attacks against the moral debauchery of Portuguese society of the time. The writer's disenchantment with the court and the social injustices are even more noticeable in the "Écloga Alejo," in which many scholars see allusions to the ill treatment by some members of the court of his best friend and fellow poet Ribeiro. The work also includes indirect invectives against the count of Castanheira, a favorite of King João III.

The poem "Vida de Santa Maria Egipciaca" (Life of Saint Mary of Egypt, 1544–1554) narrates the life of the famous courtesan from Alexandria who became canonized. Some scholars have questioned the authorship of this poem, considering it too well composed when compared to the monotone character of most of the author's work of this kind. Most likely, however, it was composed by Sá de Miranda. Its difference in style and character from his other works perhaps rest on the fact that he used the "Vida de Santa Maria Egipciaca," written in *quintilhas* (five-verse metrical compositions), as an educational tool for his sons Gonçalo and Jerónimo.

In his compositions inspired by the new Italian style, Sá de Miranda preferred Castilian Spanish rather than Portuguese. Of his 189 lyrics, 74 are composed in Castilian. According to Giuseppe Carlo Rossi, Spanish was more suitable to the new Italian meters than Portuguese, which Sá de Miranda did not consider suitable for the new Italian genre. Form and context, the latter imbued with classical tradition, appealed to the writer, although he deplored the moral decadence that he observed in Italy, especially within the Church.

Sá de Miranda's stylistic innovations encountered great resistance in both Spain and Portugal. Over time, however, more poets tried their hand at the *medida nova,* and in little more than a century this new style became part of the Portuguese and Spanish literary repertoire. His disciples who adapted the *medida nova* to their own writings include the poets Bernardes, António Ferreira, Pêro de Andrade Caminha, Francisco de Sá de Meneses, and Manuel de Portugal. Bernardes is perhaps one of Sá de Miranda's most faithful and talented followers, whose lyric poetry has been surpassed only by Camões.

Sá de Miranda's wife died in 1554; the following year, Sá de Miranda wrote *Aquele espirito ja tam bem pagado* (That Spirit Already So Well Paid) in her memory. The previous year his eldest son, Gonçalo Mendes de Sá, had been killed in the seizure of Ceuta. Sá de Miranda died around 17 May 1558; his son Jerónimo and Jerónimo's fiancée, Maria de Melo e Lima da Silva e Menezes, were at his bedside. He was buried in the church of the nearby hamlet São Martinho de Carrazedo.

Sá de Miranda is one of the main poets of the sixteenth century who found himself in the midst of the polemic between Iberian and foreign forms–namely, the Italian tradition–which dominated the aesthetic and artistic arena of Portugal. The rest of the sixteenth century, as well as the first decade of the seventeenth, was characterized by a predominance of the new trend introduced by Sá de Miranda. Despite these innovations, which eventually brought Portugal into the modern era and the Renaissance, Sá de Miranda remained deeply rooted in traditional and conservative values. High morals, patriotism, respect for nature, religion, and the establishment–hopefully ruled by an impartial and ethically sound Portuguese crown–were the inspiration for his literary production.

**Letters:**

*Cartas de Sá de Miranda,* edited by Teixeira Leite (Lisbon: Empresa Nacional de Publicidade, 1938).

**References:**

Eugenio Asensio, "Texto integral y comentarios del poema de Sá de Miranda *Al son de los vientos que van murmurando,*" *Revista da Faculdade de Letras,* 13 (1971): 1–19;

Aubrey Fitz Gerald Bell, "Lyric and Bucolic Poetry," in his *Portuguese Literature* (Oxford: Clarendon Press, 1970), pp. 139–145;

Bell, *Studies in Portuguese Literature* (New York: Gordon Press, 1975);

Frederick Bouterwek, "Saa de Miranda," in *Portuguese Literature,* volume 2 of his *History of Spanish and Portuguese Literature,* translated by Thomasina Ross (London: Boosey & Sons, 1823), pp. 61–85;

Teófilo Braga, *Sá de Miranda e a eschola italiana,* volume 9 of his *Historia da Litteratura Portugueza,* 32 volumes (Porto: Chardron, 1896);

JoAnne McCaffrey Busnardo-Neto, "The Eclogue in Sixteenth-Century Portugal," dissertation, University of Michigan, 1974;

Carlota Almeida de Carvalho, *Glossário das poesias de Sá de Miranda* (Lisbon: Centro de Estudos Filológicos, 1953);

Duarte Ivo Cruz, *Introdução à história do teatro português* (Lisbon: Guimarães, 1983);

Agostinho Domingues, ed., *Homenagem a Sá de Miranda* (Braga: Câmara Municipal de Amares, 1987);

Thomas Foster Earle, *The Comedy of the Foreigners: Renaissance Sicily through Portuguese Eyes, An Inaugural Lecture Delivered before the University of Oxford on 6 May 1997* (Oxford: Clarendon Press, 1997);

Earle, *Theme and Image in the Poetry of Sá de Miranda* (Oxford: Oxford University Press, 1980);

Achille Pellizzari, "Sá de Miranda e la poesia italianeggiante in Portogallo nel secolo XVI," in his *Portogallo e Italia nel secolo XVI. Studi e ricerche* (Naples: Società Editrice Francesco Perrella, 1914), pp. 43–86;

Adrien Roig, *O teatro clássico em Portugal no século XVI* (Lisbon: Instituto de Cultura e Língua Portuguesa, 1983);

Giuseppe Carlo Rossi, "Il Boccaccio nelle letterature in portoghese," *Studi sul Boccaccio,* 8 (1974): 273–309;

Rossi, *La civiltà portoghese. Profilo storico e storico-letterario* (Milan: Mursia, 1975);

Rossi, "Sá de Miranda introduttore dell'italianismo," in his *La letteratura italiana e le letterature di lingua portoghese* (Turin: Società Editrice Internazionale, 1967), pp. 29–32;

António José Saraiva and Óscar Lopes, "Sá de Miranda entre as tradições medievais e as inovações italianas," in their *História da literatura portuguesa,* eleventh edition (Porto: Porto Editora, 1979), pp. 253–264;

Jorge de Sena, *Os sonetos de Camões e o soneto quinhentista peninsular* (Lisbon: Edições 70, 1980).

**Papers:**

Archives of Francisco de Sá de Miranda are mainly located at the Biblioteca Nacional de Lisboa. MS. CXIV/2-2, also known as M.S.E., is instead located at the Biblioteca Pública e Arquivo Distrital de Évora; whereas MS. 8.924 is found at the Bibliothèque Nationale de Paris, number 60 of the Fonds Portugais.

# Mário de Sá-Carneiro
*(19 May 1890 – 26 April 1916)*

Fernando Arenas
*University of Minnesota*

BOOKS: *Princípio: Novelas originais* (Lisbon: Ferreira–Ferreira, 1912);

*Amizade: Peça original em 3 actos,* by Sá-Carneiro and Tomás Cabreira Júnior (Lisbon: Arnaldo Bordalo, 1912);

*A confissão de Lúcio* (Lisbon: Tip. do Comércio, 1914 [i.e., 1913]); translated by Costa as *Lúcio's Confession* (Sawtry, U.K.: Dedalus, 1993);

*Dispersão* (Lisbon: Tip. do Comércio, 1914);

*Céu em fogo* (Lisbon: Brazileira Monteiro, 1915); translated by Margaret Jull Costa as *The Great Shadow and Other Stories* (Sawtry, U.K.: Dedalus, 1996);

*Indícios de oiro* (Porto: Presença, 1937);

*Poesias: com un estudio crítico de João Gaspar Simões* (Lisbon: Ática, 1946);

*A grande sombra* (Porto: Arte e Cultura, 1960);

*Além: Sonhos* (Porto: Arte e Cultura, 1961);

*O incesto* (Lisbon: Rolim, 1984);

*Loucura* (Lisbon: Rolim, 1984);

*Un conte inédit de Mário de Sá-Carneiro: Biographie ou autoportrait?* edited by François Castex (Coimbra: Coimbra Editora, 1984);

*Mário de Sá-Carneiro em "Azulejos": Contos breves* (Lisbon: Contexto, 1986);

*Poemas juvenis (1903–1908): Inéditos,* edited by Castex (Porto: Centro de Estudos Pessoanos, 1986);

*Alma: Original em 1 acto,* by Sá-Carneiro and Ponce de Leão (Lisbon: Rolim, 1987);

*A estranha morte do Professor Antena* (Lisbon: Rolim, 1987);

*Gentil amor: Un inédit de Mário de Sá-Carneiro,* edited by Castex (Lisbon: Biblioteca Nacional, 1993);

*Juvenília dramática,* edited by Maria Aliete Galhoz (Lisbon: Imprensa Nacional-Casa da Moeda, 1995);

*No lado esquerdo da alma* (Coimbra: Alma Azul, 2000).

*Mário de Sá-Carneiro (from Sá-Carneiro,* Poemas completos, *1996; Thomas Cooper Library, University of South Carolina)*

Mário de Sá-Carneiro is considered one of the great literary figures of early-twentieth-century Portugal and one who had a profound impact on the emergence of the modernist movement. Critics and literary historians alike widely agree that Fernando Pessoa—the key figure of Portuguese modernism and one of Europe's greatest modern poets—is largely indebted to the friendship, existential complexity, and artistic genius of Sá-Carneiro.

Sá-Carneiro was born on 19 May 1890 into a wealthy family. His mother died when Sá-Carneiro was only two years old, so his father left him with his grandparents and a governess. Meanwhile, his father dedicated himself to a life of business travels. As Sá-Carneiro grew up, he traveled with his father to

Paris, Switzerland, and Italy. Sá-Carneiro's writing experience started early in school and included poetry, journalism, short stories, and a play. In 1911 he became a law student at Coimbra, but he lasted there less than a year. At that time he befriended Pessoa and left for Paris with the goal of studying law at the Sorbonne. Sá-Carneiro spent most of his remaining years in Paris, though he traveled frequently to Lisbon.

While in Paris, he dedicated most of his time to writing, and he frequented literary, artistic, and bohemian circles at various cafés and music halls. Living in Paris afforded Sá-Carneiro the opportunity to experience firsthand the effervescence of what was then the cultural capital of the world, where an aesthetic rupture with the past, artistic experimentation, and the rejection of bourgeois conventionality were the norm. Thus, the Portuguese writer was able to share with his fellow poets and artists back in Lisbon, most particularly with Pessoa, the latest literary and artistic developments as they were unfolding.

Sá-Carneiro's own poetry is heavily influenced by avant-garde trends, and the letters exchanged with Pessoa during 1913 became a veritable poetry workshop that gave rise to the Portuguese modernist movement. In fact, their letters are key documents in providing a greater understanding of both poets as well as what was at stake in the Portuguese avant-garde. An important part of the aesthetic vision and poetic production of both Sá-Carneiro and Pessoa was developed through these letters—for instance, the various Portuguese avant-garde poetic styles such as *paulismo, interseccionismo,* and *sensacionismo.*

When visiting Lisbon in 1915, Sá-Carneiro, together with Pessoa, as well as José Pacheco, Luís de Montalvor, Armando Cortes-Rodrigues, Alfredo Guisado, Raul Leal, José de Almada Negreiros, and others, founded the journal *Orpheu,* which became the official publication of Portuguese modernism. *Orpheu,* and especially the writings of Pessoa and Sá-Carneiro, took the Portuguese cultural establishment by storm while creating enormous controversy. Only two numbers were published that year as Sá-Carneiro's father, then living in colonial Mozambique, decided to stop subsidizing the journal. In spite of its short-lived existence, *Orpheu* represents one of the highest moments in the history of Portuguese literature. Sá-Carneiro was most creative during this particular period (1914–1916), producing some of his best poetry and prose, while leaving a profound imprint on Portuguese letters. Several emotional and financial crises, however, led Sá-Carneiro to commit suicide on 26 April 1916, at the height of his literary career.

Several critics have noted that both the prose and poetry of Sá-Carneiro reflect, to varying degrees, recurrent themes that are related in part to autobiographical circumstances. Some of the most representative poems include "Dispersão" (Dispersion, 1914), "Quase" (Almost), "Como eu não possuo" (Since I Do Not Possess), and "Sete canções de declínio" (Seven Songs of Decline). The existential anguish that permeates most of Sá-Carneiro's literary production derives from a complex array of feelings: profound solitude; an incommensurable gap between what one desires and the means that life provides in order to fulfill such desires; the paradoxical chasm between what is felt and what one would want to feel; the reality of an unfulfilled sexuality; the incapacity to love or to allow oneself to be loved; a frequently misunderstood sensibility; and a sense of self-alienation caused by feelings of physical inadequacy. Sá-Carneiro shared with Pessoa the profound disenchantment stemming from the infinite desire for a total sensorial experience and its impossibility in the mediocre routine of everyday life. Sá-Carneiro's vision of art and the place of the artist within society was, like Pessoa's, essentially elitist. Sá-Carneiro shunned bourgeois society in favor of an aristocratic sensibility that is more closely connected to an antihumanist decadence. In synchronicity with avant-garde movements, he favored the idea of shocking bourgeois society and subverting its established notions of good taste.

The novel *A confissão de Lúcio* was published in 1913 (although the cover gives the date as 1914; it was published in English as *Lúcio's Confession,* 1993). This work of fiction has been historically described as exemplary of literary "decadence," and it has always been rumored to have some connection to homoerotic desire. The narrative is centered on a triangle involving two men and a woman; but the woman, who is supposedly the object of desire of both men and eventually the object of transaction between them as well, is in fact nonexistent. The novel oscillates between an explosion of sensuality and polymorphous desire and a near total containment of the possibility of homoerotic impulses. In *A confissão de Lúcio* there is profound anxiety and anguish vis-à-vis the possibility of a homosexual love affair between the two male characters. The concretization of this love affair is eventually forestalled, but at the same time purportedly stable sexual and gender identities are put into question.

As its title implies, *A confissão de Lúcio* is framed around a confessional narrative written by the central character, Lúcio, who is completing a sentence of ten years in prison for a crime he apparently did not commit. The crime involves the mysterious deaths of the other two characters, Ricardo and Marta. The action of the novel alternates between Paris and Lisbon at the turn of the century, and it centers on the relationship between playwright Lúcio and poet Ricardo. As the friendship deepens and evolves between the men, Ricardo marries Marta. Eventually, as Lúcio is brought closer to the intimacy of the couple, Marta and Lúcio develop a love affair, with the tacit approval of Ricardo. As the affair progresses, Marta's material and ontological status and the borders between Lúcio and the dual being Marta/Ricardo become increasingly tenuous. This ambiguity unleashes a profound identity crisis between the two male characters that eventually leads to a bizarre, tragic finale.

In *A confissão de Lúcio* what is ultimately at stake is the status of truth. Truth is profoundly problematic at the fictional and ontological levels. The narrative moves between verisimilitude and its opposite, and between the real and the fantastic. As a consequence, subjectivity, gender, and sexuality are constantly in flux. The lack of an emotional and physical fulfillment with the other contributes decisively to a sense of disjuncture within the subject. In *A confissão de Lúcio* such disjuncture can be largely attributed to the impossibility of a homosexual relationship in a traditional, homophobic society. Since erotic realization is closely linked to the possibility of an existential self-realization of the subject, the consequences of this impasse are a profound sense of malaise, incompleteness, and dissatisfaction. Ultimately, homoerotic desire not only appears negatively charged in the writings of avant-garde poets such as Pessoa and Sá-Carneiro but also becomes a signifying device whereby both poets articulate their critique of modernity. It also functions as a compensatory mechanism for a desire that cannot take place in everyday reality. It can only be named and lived—albeit in the most impossible of circumstances—in the realm of avant-garde literature.

The poems "Manucure" and "Apoteose" (both published in 1915) are Sá-Carneiro's most avant-garde. In fact, they are considered seminal for the emergence of two of Pessoa's most astonishing poems (written as Álvaro de Campos), "Maritime Ode" and "Triumphant Ode" (also published in 1915). These poems aim not only to represent the modern moment but also to be the embodiment of modernity. Sá-Carneiro attempts to enlarge the scope of expressive possibilities within poetry, which is reflected in both the content and form of these particular texts. Although there appears to be on the surface an outright celebration of the modern moment, there is a painful sense of loss of the possibility of ever attaining pure beauty. There is also a realization that the awe-inspiring advances in technology, telecommunications, and transportation are ultimately ephemeral and superficial in relationship to the inexorable reality of death. Sá-Carneiro shared with Pessoa the desire of

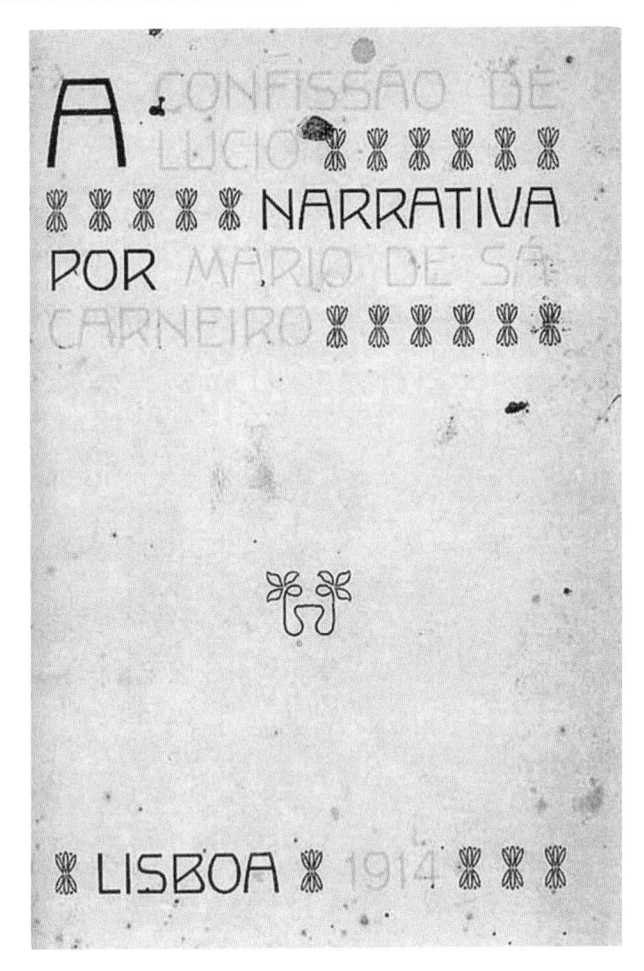

*Cover for Sá-Carneiro's novel about a love triangle involving two men and a woman (Biblioteca Nacional, Lisbon)*

being one with the modern moment by absorbing the sounds, numbers, forms, images, and movement of the city, of technology, and of industrialization.

Sá-Carneiro wrote prose and poetry in tandem; therefore, common themes, images, and even fragments of phrases appear both in his prose writings and poetry. The narratives in *Céu em fogo* (The Sky on Fire, 1915) display a symbiotic relationship with the author's poetry. The gap between the expressive possibilities of modernist literature and the limitations of real life is one of the primary sources of the acute existential malaise that is present throughout the writings of this period, and it is a constant theme in Sá-Carneiro's poetry and prose. *Céu em fogo* was considered at the time a bizarre work of literature; like most of Sá-Carneiro's literary production, it was misunderstood by the public. The author was deeply dissatisfied with the common uses of language or realistic approaches to literary representation, which were prevalent at the time. Thus, in these

*Cover for Sá-Carneiro's 1915 collection of short fiction, in which he emphasizes atmosphere over plot (Biblioteca Nacional, Lisbon)*

short narratives he places greater attention on the creation of atmosphere rather than on the construction of plot. There is a tendency to capture vaguely an array of sensations, images, and memories, while the narratives are often permeated by fantastic and surprising elements, usually ending unexpectedly.

The novella "Ressurreição" (Resurrection) from *Céu em fogo,* like *A confissão de Lúcio,* centers on the issue of homoerotic desire and presents a love triangle between two men and a woman: Inácio (a Portuguese writer living in Paris), Paulette (a performer at a music hall), and Étienne (an actor). Both men desire the same woman–but far from causing any jealousy, this desire brings the men closer together. Soon after Paulette's death, the love affair between the men is consummated, and the narrative suddenly ends. The "resurrection" suggested by the title is the consummated homoerotic affair as a result of the young actress's death. The affair between Inácio and Étienne emerges out of a "mútuo desdobramento psíquico da Saudade comum" (mutual psychic unraveling of a common nostalgia) for the woman that both men once desired.

One of the most recurrent themes in the works of Sá-Carneiro is that of the divided self, which is expressed through the fragmentation of the "I" in much of his poetry or through the doubling of the self in some of his narratives. The subject of suicide is also prominent in some of his poetry and in the letters sent to Pessoa. Suicide is posited as a courageous act on the part of the individual, and in several of his texts–for example, "Dispersão," "A um suicida" (To a Suicidal Man), "Caranguejola" (Crab Man), and "Fim" (End)– the poet forecasts his own death. As its title indicates, the earlier poem "Dispersão" is about the fragmentation and dispersal of the self. The poetic subject loses himself in his obsessions, insecurities, and anxieties, without actually living life. The poet inhabits the margins of society by virtue of being an artist, and while this particular circumstance affords him greater lucidity and a heightened consciousness vis-à-vis the world, it also leads to a greater existential malaise. The poet appears self-alienated because of his sense of physical inadequacy, solitude, misunderstood sensibilities, and unfulfilled desires. There is an acute feeling that life is all about a profound and unavoidable loss, where nothing is what it should be and where only death awaits the individual.

Sá-Carneiro's later poems, featured in the collection *Indícios de oiro* (Traces of Gold, 1937), portray the ontological decline of the poet, leading ultimately to the morbidly humorous expression in "Fim" of his final wish for the kind of funeral he desires. The predominant feelings in the collection are profound disillusionment, existential pain, gloominess, and self-ridicule. The euphoria of his earlier years expressed in "Manucure" or "Apoteose" had dissipated. "Sete poemas de declínio" traces the various emotional/existential stages lived by the poetic subject, ending in a note of defeat that is dramatically exemplified in the final stanza: "Meu alvoroço de oiro e lua / Tinha por fim que transbordar . . . / Caiu-me a Alma ao meio da rua, / E não a posso ir apanhar!" (My commotion of gold and moon / One day was bound to overflow . . . / I dropped my soul in the middle of the street / And now I can no longer recover it whole).

Although brief, Mário de Sá-Carneiro's writing career is considered one of the most spectacular, as far as literary creativity and experimentation are concerned, in the history of Portuguese letters. Portuguese modernism would not have come into being without his presence. Any discussion of the Portuguese literary avant-garde–one of Europe's most astonishing–cannot afford to ignore the role of Sá-Carneiro.

**Letters:**

*Cartas a Fernando Pessoa,* 2 volumes (Lisbon: Ática, 1958, 1959);

*Cartas de Mário de Sá-Carneiro a Luís de Montalvor, Cândida Ramos, Alfredo Guisado, José Pacheco,* edited by Arnaldo Saraiva (Porto: Limiar, 1977);

*Correspondência inédita de Mário de Sá-Carneiro a Fernando Pessoa,* edited by Saraiva (Porto: Centro de Estudos Pessoanos, 1980);

*Cartas a Maria e outra correspondência inédita,* edited by François Castex and Marina Tavares Dias (Lisbon: Quimera, 1992);

*Cartas de Mário de Sá-Carneiro a Fernando Pessoa,* edited by Manuela Parreira da Silva (Lisbon: Assírio & Alvim, 2001).

**References:**

François Castex, *Mário de Sá-Carneiro: Lisbonne 1890 – Paris 1916* (Paris: Centre Culturel Calouste Gulbenkian, 1999);

Marina Tavares Dias, *Mário de Sá-Carneiro: Fotobiografia* (Lisbon: Quimera, 1988);

Maria José de Lencastre, *O eu e o outro: Para uma análise psicanalítica da obra de Mário de Sá-Carneiro* (Lisbon: Quetzal, 1992);

Fernando J. B. Martinho, *Mário de Sá-Carneiro e o(s) outro(s)* (Lisbon: Hiena, 1990);

Fernando Cabral Martins, *O modernismo em Mário de Sá-Carneiro* (Lisbon: Estampa, 1997);

Ana Nascimento Piedade, *A questão estética em Mário de Sá-Carneiro* (Lisbon: Universidade Aberta, 1994);

Clara Crabbé Rocha, *O essencial sobre Mário de Sá-Carneiro* (Lisbon: Imprensa Nacional-Casa da Moeda, 1985);

António Vieira, *Metamorfose e jogo em Mário de Sá-Carneiro* (Lisbon: & etc, 1997);

Dieter Woll, *Realidade e idealidade na lírica de Mário de Sá-Carneiro* (Lisbon: Delfos, 1968).

# José Saramago
*(16 November 1922 -   )*

## José N. Ornelas
*University of Massachusetts Amherst*

See also the Saramago entry in *DLB Yearbook: 1998*.

BOOKS: *Terra do pecado* (Lisbon: Minerva, 1947; corrected edition, Lisbon: Caminho, 1997);

*Os poemas possíveis* (Lisbon: Portugália, 1966; revised edition, Lisbon: Caminho, 1982);

*Provavelmente alegria* (Lisbon: Livros Horizonte, 1970; revised and augmented edition, Lisbon: Caminho, 1985);

*Deste mundo e do outro* (Lisbon: Arcádia, 1971);

*A bagagem do viajante* (Lisbon: Futura, 1973);

*O embargo* (Lisbon: Estúdios Cor, 1973);

*As opiniões que o Diário de Lisboa teve* (Lisbon: Seara Nova/Futura, 1974);

*O ano de 1993* (Lisbon: Futura, 1975);

*Os apontamentos* (Lisbon: Seara Nova, 1976);

*Manual de pintura e caligrafia* (Lisbon: Moraes Editores, 1976); translated by Giovanni Pontiero as *Manual of Painting and Calligraphy* (Manchester, U.K.: Carcanet, 1994);

*Objecto quase* (Lisbon: Moraes Editores, 1978);

*A noite* (Lisbon: Caminho, 1979);

*Levantado do chão* (Lisbon: Caminho, 1980);

*Que farei com este livro?* (Lisbon: Caminho, 1980);

*Viagem a Portugal* (Lisbon: Círculo de Leitores, 1981); translated by Amanda Hopkinson and Nick Caistor as *Journey to Portugal: In Pursuit of Portugal's History and Culture* (New York: Harcourt, 2000);

*Memorial do convento* (Lisbon: Caminho, 1982); translated by Pontiero as *Baltasar and Blimunda* (San Diego: Harcourt Brace Jovanovich, 1987; London: Cape, 1988);

*O ano da morte de Ricardo Reis* (Lisbon: Caminho, 1984); translated by Pontiero as *The Year of the Death of Ricardo Reis* (San Diego: Harcourt Brace Jovanovich, 1991; London: Harvill, 1992);

*A jangada de pedra* (Lisbon: Caminho, 1986); translated by Pontiero as *The Stone Raft* (London: Harvill, 1994; New York: Harcourt Brace, 1995);

*A segunda vida de Francisco de Assis* (Lisbon: Caminho, 1987);

*José Saramago ( photograph by U. Andersen/SIPA PRESS)*

*História do cerco de Lisboa* (Lisbon: Caminho, 1989); translated by Pontiero as *The History of the Siege of Lisbon* (London: Harvill, 1996; New York: Harcourt Brace, 1996);

*O Evangelho segundo Jesus Cristo* (Lisbon: Caminho, 1991); translated by Pontiero as *The Gospel According to Jesus Christ* (London: Harvill, 1993; New York: Harcourt Brace, 1994);

*In nomine Dei* (Lisbon: Caminho, 1993);

*Cadernos de Lanzarote,* 5 volumes (Lisbon: Caminho, 1994–1998);

*Ensaio sobre a cegueira* (Lisbon: Caminho, 1995); translated by Pontiero as *Blindness* (London: Harvill, 1997; New York: Harcourt Brace, 1998);

*Moby Dick em Lisboa* (Lisbon: Expo '98, 1996);

*Todos os nomes* (Lisbon: Caminho, 1997); translated by Margaret Jull Costa as *All the Names* (London: Harvill, 1999; New York: Harcourt Brace, 1999);

*O conto da ilha desconhecida* (Lisbon: Expo '98/Assírio & Alvim, 1997); translated by Christine Robinson as *The Tale of the Unknown Island* (Lisbon: Expo '98/Assírio & Alvim, 1997); translated by Costa (London: Harvill, 1999; New York: Harcourt Brace, 1999);

*Uma voz contra o silêncio* (Lisbon: Caminho, 1998);

*Discursos de Estocolmo* (Lisbon: Caminho, 1999);

*Folhas políticas, 1976–1998* (Lisbon: Caminho, 1999);

*A caverna* (Lisbon: Caminho, 2000); translated by Costa as *The Cave* (London: Harvill, 2002; New York: Harcourt, 2002);

*A maior flor do mundo* (Lisbon: Caminho, 2001);

*O homem duplicado* (Lisbon: Caminho, 2002).

OTHER: "Ouvido," in *Poética dos cinco sentidos,* edited by Figueiredo Magalhães (Lisbon: Bertrand, 1979), pp. 19–26.

In October 1998 José Saramago became the first writer of the Portuguese-speaking world to receive the Nobel Prize in literature. The Swedish Academy's citation for Saramago called his novels "parables sustained by imagination, compassion, and irony," an apt characterization of the universal significance of the writer's work. In 1997 the writer Edmund White had already declared that no candidate for the Nobel Prize had a better claim to lasting recognition as a novelist than Saramago. Although Saramago's first novel, *Terra do pecado* (Land of Sin), appeared in print in 1947, he did not begin to receive national and international acclaim for his work until he was almost sixty years old. His rise to the top of the literary establishment was meteoric. Indeed, during the 1980s and 1990s no other Portuguese writer attained greater national and international recognition, a fact substantiated by the many prestigious awards that Saramago has received both in Portugal and abroad, the translation of many of his works into more than thirty different languages, and the multiple editions of his books in Portugal and in foreign countries.

Even though he is better known for his writings subsequent to the revolution of 25 April 1974, especially his novels, Saramago was already a published author prior to the 1974 events that ended the fascist dictatorship of António de Oliveira Salazar and his successor, Marcelo Caetano. Like many other writers of the postrevolutionary generation, Saramago was affected by the repression and the censorship associated with the Portuguese fascist state and by the long-lasting African colonial wars in which Portugal was involved during the 1960s and early 1970s. These wars affected the national psyche so profoundly and disrupted the lives of so many of its citizens that ultimately they created the conditions for the 1974 military coup, an event responsible for the creation of democratic rule in Portugal and for the independence of the Portuguese African colonies.

In this new political setting, which was initially defined by extreme revolutionary fervor and zeal eventually moderated by Portugal's acceptance of Western European parliamentary democratic ideals, Saramago wrote most of his books. The author, like other writers of the postrevolutionary period, turned to Portuguese history as a source of inspiration for many of his writings. The turn to history occurred for two reasons. First, a more open political climate after the 1974 revolution allowed Saramago to deal with a subject, Portuguese history, that was off-limits during the fascist period. Second, the changing political and social circumstances of the country created a need to reinvent Portugal through a revisionist recoding and reevaluation of Portuguese history as the country emerged from almost fifty years of a nationalistic fascist discourse that had completely distorted Portuguese history for political and ideological motives. Saramago felt that through an engagement with Portuguese history he would achieve a greater understanding of his own country, and he would also be able to contribute to a new imagery and identity for the nation.

Saramago was born in the small village of Azinhaga, in the province of Ribatejo, about a hundred kilometers northeast of Lisbon, on 16 November 1922, into a family of rural workers. His parents were José de Sousa and Maria da Piedade, but the registrar, on his own, decided to write the family's nickname "Saramago" on the identity card. Thus, the boy was officially registered as José de Sousa Saramago, which was later shortened to José Saramago when he began grammar school. Before he turned two, his parents decided to move to Lisbon. Although he grew up in Lisbon and went to school there, he still spent long periods of his childhood and youth in the countryside with his grandparents, who greatly influenced his view of the world. In his Nobel lecture the writer addressed the simple but meaningful peasant life of his grandparents, and he acknowledged that he was so impressed by his illiterate grandfather Jerónimo that he imagined that Jerónimo was the master of all the knowledge in the world. Life in Lisbon was difficult for the Sousa family. A few months after the family settled in the city, Saramago's only sibling, an older brother named Francisco, died.

Saramago was an excellent student in elementary school, but the financial situation of the family did not allow him to continue his studies in an academic high

*Dust jacket for the 1987 American edition of Saramago's 1982 novel,* Memorial do convento, *about the construction of the Mafra Convent in the eighteenth century (Bruccoli Clark Layman Archives)*

school. Consequently, he enrolled in a technical school to learn a trade. After finishing his studies in 1939, he worked for two years as a mechanic in a car repair shop. During this time he became more involved with literature, a subject in which he had developed a keen interest while he was in technical school. Lacking the financial means to buy books, he began to go to a public library during the evening hours to read. In 1944, when he was working with the Social Welfare Services as a civil servant, he married Ilda Reis, who bore his only child, Violante, in 1947. Coincidentally, that same year, his first novel, *Terra do pecado,* was published.

*Terra do pecado,* with its anachronistic indebtedness to nineteenth-century naturalism, has mostly a referential interest for scholars of the author's fiction. Most critics and the author himself consider it an experiment in fiction writing, an aesthetic practice destined to have a short life and written by an individual who was not yet ready to be a novelist. Saramago was conscious of the shortcomings of his initial incursion into the novel genre, and it took him another thirty years before he published another novel, *Manual de pintura e caligrafia* (1976; translated as *Manual of Painting and Calligraphy,* 1994). However, he did not remain totally silent during this period since he published several collections of poetry, chronicles, and essays before he returned to the novel, the genre that eventually brought him international acclaim.

*Terra do pecado* does not fit into the aesthetic parameters of either modernism or neorealism, which were then in vogue in Portugal. Saramago was seemingly unaware of the existence of Jorge Amado, José Lins do Rego, and Graciliano Ramos, writers from the northeast region of Brazil whose influence paved the way for the development and the establishment of neorealism in Portugal. This literary movement was intent on producing socially and politically engaged works of art that focused on ending repression, classism, alienation, oppression, exploitation, and censorship. Neorealism, in which the representation of reality followed a strict and dogmatic Marxist perspective, had as its main ideological goal the undermining and subversion of Salazar's regime. However, *Terra do pecado,* in its political intent and aesthetic conception, cannot be regarded as an ideological weapon in the war against state fascism. It is, rather, a work that has much in common with the nineteenth-century novel and its theories of evolution, which played an important role in the design of naturalist narrative. The novel undeniably has great affinities, in terms of plot and themes (especially those associated with sexual taboos), with the novels of Eça de Queirós and Camilo Castelo Branco, nineteenth-century Portuguese novelists who frequently focused on sordid sexual affairs and the moral degeneration of a decadent rural and urban bourgeoisie. *Terra do pecado,* through its focus on the sexual dissatisfaction of the main character, Leonor, and her blind obedience to sexual impulses, reveals that it follows closely the aesthetics of naturalism, in which a character's behavior is subordinated to physiology and determined by the social and cultural space that he or she inhabits.

Saramago, after his debut with *Terra do pecado,* waited another nineteen years before he published another book. His only excuse for not writing during such a long period of time was that he had nothing worthwhile to say. Between the publication of his novel and his collection of poetry *Os poemas possíveis* (Possible Poems, 1966) he worked in different jobs; initially, he was employed with a metal company, and toward the end of the 1950s he got a job as a production manager with a publishing company. He also began to translate books from French into Portuguese in order to supplement his family income. His activities as a translator only stopped in 1981, when his increasing stature as an author allowed him to dedicate himself totally to his creative writing.

Between 1966 and 1975, Saramago produced three volumes of poetry: *Os poemas possíveis, Provavelmente alegria* (Probably Joy, 1970), and *O ano de 1993* (The Year 1993, 1975). The author has said that whenever he reflects upon his poetry he has a sense of uneasiness because he feels he is expressing himself and creating an identity through the wrong genre. In a preface to the second edition of *Os poemas possíveis* (1982), an edition significantly revised by the author, Saramago observes that the book owes its merits to the themes and the obsessions present in his poetry that link it to his later novels. Several critics have commented on the connections between his poetry and the novels, especially *O ano de 1993*, a work viewed as a fundamental step toward his fiction, but they also point to an intrinsic organic coherence and a thematic unity in his poetry. In addition, his poems have a certain degree of originality, even if they conform to the tradition of the Portuguese modern lyric—the roots of his poetry can be found in Portuguese modernism, especially in the work of Fernando Pessoa, the most distinguished poetic voice of the first wave of modernism in Portugal in the early twentieth century.

*Os poemas possíveis* is divided into five sections: the first and the last have, respectively, forty-eight and sixty-seven poems, while the other three have altogether only thirty-two poems. These poems are, as a rule, short; the majority are one-stanza decasyllabic poems. Among the important themes present in *Os poemas possíveis* are the constant confrontation and struggle with poetic creation, the inability to find the proper word to convey meaning in a world of chaos, and simulation as the reality of poetry. In the three central sections, the writer focuses on oppression and solidarity and on love as a way to overcome death and time. He strikes out against censorship and the denial of freedom, and he constructs a world where the creative act has been returned to humans since they have been abandoned by the gods. Although Saramago's world vision may seem utterly pessimistic and dark throughout the book, the last section does restore a semblance of balance to his vision. A pessimistic tone, disillusionment, and an insistence on the insufficiency of the power of the word to stop the irreversible flow of time and/or construct the unity of the subject may still prevail in the last section, but these themes are counterbalanced by a more optimistic vision of the world that singles out physical and sensual love and eroticism as human attributes that can, through their redeeming qualities, stop the flow of time and foster rebirth. Poetry, love, and time are the structural bases for Saramago's book. The author also seems to indicate that any meaningful knowledge of the world can be achieved only through a constant questioning of the multiple possibilities of language.

*Provavelmente alegria* extends and adds to the thematic lines established in the writer's first book of poetry. Unlike *Os poemas possíveis,* this new volume is not divided into sections, and each poem is not constituted as part of a whole. The composition is much more fragmented, and some of his poetic compositions, especially the prose poems, anticipate the later fiction through their lyrical qualities and suggestive imagery. Through the very act of reading, encountering images that generate new surprises, discoveries, and illuminations, the reader makes sense of the text. These poems, through their visual imagery and the role played by the reader in uncovering their significance, reveal in their aesthetic beauty many similarities with Saramago's mature texts.

It is difficult to classify the genre of *O ano de 1993*. There are indications that Saramago prefers the label of poetry, which is justifiable since the text is divided into thirty different parts that structurally resemble poems. However, some critics disagree with the author's classification. Since *O ano de 1993* resembles a narrative with a plot that develops until it reaches its climax, and it has a sententious and moralizing tone, they feel the book is closer to being a novel or a chronicle.

The title of this experimental text suggests strong affinities with George Orwell's *Nineteen Eighty-Four* (1949). Like Orwell's novel, Saramago's work is a depiction of an imaginary and primitive futurist-dystopian world where repression and abuse of power run rampant. Unlike *Nineteen Eighty-Four,* however, *O ano de 1993* does not resort to language to repress its citizens and to create a nightmarish world characterized by violence, terror, and anarchy. The book begins with an invasion of a city by nameless despotic forces. The inhabitants of the city are already sick with the plague; even light has been infected. Subsequently, an elevator malfunctions, and a man who leaves his home after curfew is subjected to an interrogation for many days. He is asked a question every sixty minutes for which he must give fifty-nine different answers. Without any explanation, the inhabitants of the city find themselves outside of the city walls, with wolves now occupying their former homes—inverting, as the author claims, the natural order of things. The despots occupying the city begin building mechanized elephants and eagles to hunt people down, and a witch doctor reduces the city to the size of a human body, so that when the commander of the occupying forces whips the body, all of its inhabitants get welts. Finally, crystal prisons are built with cells shaped like beehives so that all prisoners can be observed in their most intimate acts.

Slowly, the tribe that occupies the plateau outside the city begins to organize in a fraternal and human way with the objective of putting an end to the apocalyptic atmosphere in the city and to beat back the invading forces. As the tribe struggles against the despots, it receives support from the natural elements, which come to its defense. Trees begin attacking the invaders, and a bird destroys a mechanized eagle, which cannot defend itself since it has been programmed to attack only humans. Language, which had been lost, slowly emerges as a man and a woman look at each other during the sexual act, an act enveloped in silence but which eventually allows the painful birth of a new world. Sex, indeed, is a key element in making society whole again. Sexual acts, along with rites of fertility, occur prior to the insurrection of the terrorized tribe and its subsequent expulsion of the invaders from the occupied city.

In reality, *O ano de 1993* is the narration of the cycle of life and death or of destruction and procreation through an imaginary construction of a futurist dystopia located in an urban space, which is eventually destroyed by sexual love, reproduction, and humanity. In a more political and ideological sense, the book illustrates the vision of an author who strongly believes that revolutionary acts can redeem humanity. Saramago's construction of a dark and apocalyptic city space underscores his pessimistic view of the situation in Portugal one year after the 1974 revolution. Nevertheless, the conclusion of the book reveals that not all is hopeless, since change is always possible.

During the 1960s and 1970s, as he began to publish on a regular basis, Saramago kept busy with other professional activities. He was a literary critic for the review *Seara Nova*. In 1972 and 1973 he worked for the newspaper *Diário de Lisboa* (Lisbon Daily), where he wrote political essays and commentaries. For part of this period he was also in charge of the cultural supplement of the newspaper. In 1975, for a short period of time, he was the associate editor of the *Diário de Notícias* (Daily News), a post he filled until 25 November, when the Portuguese government took a more rightward turn on the heels of a counterrevolution that blocked the ascendancy and the gains of the left in the country. Saramago, a staunch defender of communism and its ideals (and still a card-carrying Communist), was fired by the newspaper. Nevertheless, his dismissal from *Diário de Notícias* paved the way for his career as a professional writer. He decided then to abandon his career as a journalist and to dedicate himself exclusively to creative writing.

While Saramago was writing and publishing his poetry during these decades, he was also trying his hand at writing chronicles. These works, which first appeared in newspapers, were later compiled by the author and published as volumes. *Deste mundo e do outro* (From This World and From the Other, 1971) is a collection of texts that appeared in print between 1968 and 1969 in the daily *A Capital* (The Capital), and *A bagagem do viajante* (The Traveler's Baggage, 1973) assembles texts published between 1971 and 1972 in the same newspaper as well as in the weekly *O Jornal do Fundão* (The Fundão Daily). In addition to these volumes, the author published another two: *As opiniões que o Diário de Lisboa teve* (The Opinions That the Diário de Lisboa Had, 1974), texts that appeared first in print between 1972 and 1973 in the daily *Diário de Lisboa,* and *Os apontamentos* (Notes, 1976), a collection of texts written between April and September of 1975 and published in the daily *Diário de Notícias*.

In the chronicles of the last two volumes, which are a compilation of Saramago's political writings a few years prior to the 1974 revolution and during the revolutionary process itself, the author assumes an explicit and involved posture vis-à-vis the political situation and the events occurring in his country. In *As opiniões que o Diário de Lisboa teve* the writer questions and attacks the repressive Portuguese political system and vents his indignation against the lack of freedom at a time when Caetano had already replaced Salazar as the leader of the country. In some chronicles there is a sense of expectation and hope that the political situation may change. In *Os apontamentos* the reader notices the writer's deep involvement with the revolutionary events. He never fails to attack and criticize sharply what he considers are the failings of both the revolution and the democratic process.

Both books have greater historical and social value than literary value. Even though there is a strong ideological link between these chronicles and Saramago's later novels, it is hard to make the case that they contribute significantly to the evolution of Saramago as a novelist. However, they help the reader understand the political intrigue, the maneuvers, the wishes and hopes, and the emotional state of mind of Portuguese citizens during the prerevolutionary period and also immediately after the 1974 revolution. The convulsion, the chaos, the struggle for the definition of democracy and freedom, and the constant ideological and interparty wars are also some of the postrevolutionary issues that Saramago addresses.

Unlike the two volumes that deal chiefly with political events and issues, *Deste mundo e do outro* and *A bagagem do viajante* anticipate in different ways the mature novelist. The writer himself has asserted that there is a strong correlation between these two books and his novels. Saramago's comment in his 1998 interview with Carlos Reis that "everything is there" in the chronicles is well known. The creative impulse is already present in the chronicles, and the reader can discern in them the first rough sketches of the fictional characters that undergo greater development in his novels. The chronicles also focus on issues and themes to which he returns in the novels of the 1980s and 1990s: current events; the urban and rural landscapes; human types and personalities; the recuperation of the past through memory; the voyage through the cultural and historical landscapes; the act of writing; the interrelationship between history and fiction, history as fiction, and the reinvention of history; the use of the fantastic and the magic in the construction of reality; and the intersection of past, present, and future. Although Saramago is writing chronicles, he takes great pleasure in narrating stories with a variety of characters and personalities that reappear in his mature work: phantoms, apparitions, kings, animals, and all kinds of lovers. Moreover, the inquisitive, critical, ironic, and tender narrating voice that questions and makes comments about everything and everyone, which makes his novels so original, is already present in these chronicles.

*Deste mundo e do outro* and *A bagagem do viajante,* through their thematic and structural connection with Saramago's mature work, play an important role in the transition between the author's formative and mature literary phases; they open up narrative paths that the author reuses in his mature novels. In one of his chronicles, "Viagens na minha terra" (Travels in My Land), Saramago observes that chronicles are bridges that are hurled into the emptiness in search of firm ground.

Thirty years after the publication of his first novel, Saramago returned to the genre with *Manual de pintura e caligrafia,* a work that was attuned to the contemporary literary environment of Portugal and Europe but that only received critical notice and praise after Saramago had become a highly regarded novelist in the 1980s. Thematic concerns that resurface in later novels, as well as the many digressions that are fundamental to the structure of the writer's mature fiction, play a crucial role in the construction of the fictional world of *Manual de pintura e caligrafia.* These themes include the relationship between the self and the "Other," the tensions between life and art and reality and imagination, the rejection of classical realism as a valid aesthetic form for the representation of reality, the unceasing questioning of truth or the plural truths of the text, the impossibility of ever reaching a singular truth because of its duplicitous nature, the discovery of narrative as revelation of the world, the constant subversion of canonized images and historical events, the writer as an artisan, the relationships between voyage and self-knowledge and narrative, and the novel as artifice. Finally, there is the author's preoccupation with

*Dust jacket for the 1991 American edition of Saramago's 1984 novel,* O ano da morte de Ricardo Reis, *which continues the adventures of a literary persona created by modernist poet Fernando Pessoa in 1912 (Richland County Public Library)*

the crisis of representation and the (re)construction of reality through his focus on two essential facets of the act of creation: one that stresses the visual (painting), and one that emphasizes the evocative and signifying power of the word (calligraphy).

*Manual de pintura e caligrafia,* which Saramago considers his most autobiographical novel, is a first-person narrative about a mediocre painter, a portraitist, designated only by an initial, H. The story coincides chronologically with the last few months of the Portuguese Estado Novo (New State), the fascist dictatorship, and the beginning of the revolutionary period in 1974. In fact, the novel ends with the euphoria brought about by the unfolding events in the dawn of 25 April 1974. H., who is well aware of his limitations and ineptitude as a painter and who senses that he is trapped in a predictable and banal social network of friendships, makes a conscious decision to start writing a diary, which he hopes will lead him to self-knowledge, a goal that so far has eluded him as a portrait artist. He begins to write because he recognizes that through his previously chosen form of artistic expression he is condemned to be and do what others want him to be and do. As a painter he is conditioned by a whole system of patronage instituted by those who pay him sizable commissions for his portraits, which place him at their mercy and force him to paint within strictly defined aesthetic codes that are culturally institutionalized. Before H. has his existential crisis, which forces him to reflect on the function of art, he seems content doing the same repetitive things: he engages in loveless love affairs; he separates from lovers without suffering; and he experiences time after time the same predictable adventures. In essence, he lives a life without history, a life of mediocrity and inertia, a life without any big or dramatic risks. His approach to painting mirrors these characteristics. In fact, there is a strong correlation between his personal and artistic lives.

When H. begins his diary, he finds himself restricted by the codes and conventions that bind language and the act of narration. It seems as if writing and painting are following the same beaten and traditional paths. However, a journey to Italy, where he comes into contact with a variety of artistic manifestations, makes H. realize that only through imagination and magic is the artist free to shape the creative process. His diary reflects clearly this transformation. As the novel comes to a close, his love affair with M.—the female protagonist of the novel—reinforces his transformation, since it becomes a catalyst for H.'s further development as an artist. At this point H. decides not to paint a portrait commissioned by the "Senhores da Lapa" in a conventional manner. Instead, he opts to paint it using a risky and imaginative pictorial language that breaks all canonical rules, an act that indicates his rupture with a dying political system, a death that occurs with the 1974 revolution. The event also allows Portuguese society to undergo a transformation. With his decision to use imagination in the painting of a portrait, H. finally shows that he is capable of clinging to his ideals in a world that is still obsessed with material bourgeois values.

In 1978 *Objecto quase* (Almost an Object) became the first and only collection of short stories published by Saramago. The volume, which comprises six short stories mixing the fantastic and science fiction, focuses on themes that are valuable to the writer, such as the struggle against consumer society and totalitarian systems that have stripped individuals of their humanity and/or subjectivity and are the direct cause of their alienation. The stories of the collection are "Cadeira" (The Chair), "Embargo" (Embargo), "Refluxo" (Reflux), "Coisas" (Things), "Centauro" (Centaur), and "Desforra" (Revenge). The main objective of these stories is the restoration of the humanity that has been taken from the individual by alienating and repressive measures. Some of these stories are political and/or social allegories, such as "Cadeira," "Embargo," and "Refluxo," while others, such as "Coisas," portray a Kafkaesque vision of the world.

"Ouvido" (Hearing), another short story, appeared in 1979 in a collective volume titled *Poética dos cinco sentidos* (Poetics of the Five Senses). Besides Saramago, five other major Portuguese writers collaborated in the effort. The stories are all inspired by a famous tapestry belonging to the series *La Dame à la Licorne,* exhibited in the Cluny Museum in Paris. Saramago's contribution on hearing is thematically related to *Manual de pintura e caligrafia,* since both works focus on the connection between writing and the plastic arts.

In the same year that "Ouvido" appeared, Saramago published his first play, *A noite* (The Night), which was followed in 1980 by another play, *Que farei com este livro?* (What Will I Do With This Book?). The first play deals with events taking place on the night of 24 April 1974 in the editorial room of a newspaper, as the first signs of the Portuguese revolution are clearly felt. The second focuses on the poet Luís de Camões, the greatest literary figure of the Portuguese Renaissance, as his poetry and life become intertwined symbolically with the new revolutionary Portugal. Camões had been used in the official fascist discourse for different reasons: to prop up patriotism, belligerent nationalism, and glorification of the Portuguese past. Coincidentally, the play appeared in the same year that the fourth centenary of the poet's death was being commemorated in Portugal.

On several occasions Saramago has claimed that he never had much of a vocation for the theater and that he has never been a great reader of plays. The four plays that he has written in his lifetime have, in his own words, always been written because of an invitation or a suggestion that he has received. Probably for these reasons, *A noite* and *Que farei com este livro?* as well as the other two plays, *A segunda vida de Francisco de Assis* (The Second Life of Francis of Assis, 1987) and *In nomine Dei* (In the Name of God, 1993), do not display the linguistic innovations or the formal inventions that characterize his mature prose. Nevertheless, like his novels, his dramaturgy aims at transformation of society, and it is highly interventional. The focal point of Saramago's theater is never the play as spectacle. It is, rather, theater as a genre that allows the author to question writing and the multiple meanings of words, and to refocus the reader's attention on problems relevant to contemporary Portugal through a dramatization of historical events.

The year 1980 represents a watershed in Saramago's literary career; he emerged as a writer of great talent and significance with the publication of his novel *Levantado do chão* (Raised from the Ground). The innovative use of narrative language in this novel and the ability to reflect upon Portuguese history in order to question its supposed objectivity and its role in the representation of events brought its author immediate critical acclaim. Saramago's groundbreaking use of a novelistic language dispenses with orthodox punctuation, diacritical marks, periods at the ends of sentences, and quotation marks for dialogue, and only uses commas to indicate stops in the narrative. Saramago's language also distinguishes itself by a variety of linguistic registers from every social class, which makes it closer to oral tradition. His prose, with its sudden shifts in tenses and voices, ironic interjections by the narrator, constant digressions, and fusion of the narrator's perspective with that of the characters, has many affinities with the baroque style of Father António Vieira, a seventeenth-century Brazilian/Portuguese author known for his sententious sermons written in an ornate manner. The re-creation of language and the oral tone of the prose in *Levantado do chão* become permanent features in most of Saramago's subsequent novels. No less original in this novel is the author's ability to mix and intersect the real and the historical with the fantastic and the imaginary, which not only allows Saramago to give the reader a more exact picture of reality but also links his writings to those of Gabriel García Márquez and other Latin American writers associated with magic realism.

The idea that all truths are plural and that all knowledge about history is filtered though the subjectivity that re-creates it—a lesson that H. in *Manual de pintura e caligrafia* learned well—also plays a fundamental role in the development of the plot of *Levantado do chão*, a work dealing with three generations of rural workers from the Alentejo region: Domingos Mau-Tempo, his son João, and his grandchildren. At the beginning of 1976, Saramago had embarked on a journey to Alentejo to familiarize himself with the lives, the desires, and the economic and social problems of rural workers, with the purpose of writing a novel that would mark the presence of those who barely register in the social hierarchy. *Levantado do chão* deals with his personal observations in rural Alentejo.

The novel begins a few years prior to the overthrow of the monarchy and the foundation of the Portuguese Republic in 1910 and ends just after the 1974 revolution. In between these major events others abound: World War I, Salazar's Estado Novo, the Spanish Civil War, World War II, and the Portuguese colonial wars in Africa. All these events are seen through the eyes of different generations of the Mau-Tempo family, peasants working the land and struggling against the oppressive conditions imposed by the absent latifundium owners. The saga of the Mau-Tempo family, presented as an epic struggle for better living conditions, emancipation, and the attainment of human dignity, is the axis around which history becomes fiction and fiction becomes history, a dominant theme in all Saramago's novels. It is extremely difficult for the peasant workers to effect change, because the laws of the powerful have turned them into voiceless creatures. However, the heroic struggle of the landless Alentejo farmhands against tyranny never dies. Their redemption finally takes place when the peasants take over the land and evict the latifundium owners from their lands or, better yet, evict their lackeys, those men who have enslaved and oppressed the rural workers in the name of absent landowners. The revolutionary action includes as one of its leaders the daughter of João Mau-Tempo, Maria Adelaide Espada, a woman who rises from the ground along with many male supporters to launch a new chapter in Portuguese history. Maria Adelaide inaugurates the presence of strong female characters in Saramago's works.

When Saramago lived among the rural Alentejo workers in 1976, listening to their personal stories, he had informed them that someday he would publish their narratives. He kept his promise by making sure that *Levantado do chão* was the recorded oral testimony of those who were silenced by official history, those who construct the country but whose deeds are absent from official documents. The author's objective in writing the book, as the title of the novel explicitly suggests, is to "raise from the ground" of Alentejo (and, by extension, of Portugal) those who are unable to raise themselves because they never had a voice in the writing of history.

With *Levantado do chão,* Saramago's career as an influential novelist was launched. Nonetheless, the fact that he had already toiled for years on his writing craft prior to the critical acclaim conferred on *Levantado do chão* should not be overlooked, since it was that earlier work that prepared the writer for his seemingly overnight literary success, which for him arrived at the advanced age of fifty-eight. Although he is best known for the novels that he has published beginning with *Levantado do chão,* a fact that reinforces the idea of the existence of two Saramagos—a more original writer after 1980 and a much lesser one before 1980—it would be wrong to assume this dichotomy in Saramago's literary trajectory as some critics have done. Most critics have focused more on the innovative qualities of his prose in the 1980s and 1990s and have a tendency to

*Dust jacket for the 1994 American edition of Saramago's controversial 1991 novel,* O Evangelho segundo Jesus Cristo, *in which Jesus is the pawn of a mean-spirited God (Bruccoli Clark Layman Archives)*

overlook his earlier work, but his production prior to 1980 is still of high quality. As José Horácio Costa and Maria Alzira Seixo have shown through their analyses of the writer's pre-1980 period, there are many formal and thematic connections between the pre-1980 and the post-1980 periods, which indicate that the programmatic roots and routes for the writer's later development were already present in embryonic form in many of the chronicles, poetry, short stories, and novels of the first phase of his literary career.

In 1981 Saramago published *Viagem a Portugal* (1981; translated as *Journey to Portugal: In Pursuit of Portugal's History and Culture,* 2000), a travel narrative that mingles characteristics of fiction, chronicles, and tourist guides. The book is a voyage through Portuguese culture, as a traveler, referred to in the third person, journeys throughout the country inciting the reader to other voyages. Although the narrative gives information and comments on the places visited by the traveler, the information has a subjective quality, since it distances itself from the stereotypical language found in a tourist guide. As Saramago claims in the introduction to the book, *Viagem a Portugal* is a history about a traveler and a voyage searching for a fusion between the one who sees and what is seen, an encounter between subjectivity and objectivity. By calling attention to the subjective nature of the book, Saramago underscores that the narrative act plays an important role in the traveler's journey. He discusses constantly the different ways of narrating and describing. Instead of just describing what he sees, the traveler focuses on the act of seeing and on his feelings and reflections regarding what is seen. There is a strong correlation between the voyage to the interior of the self and the voyage through Portugal. In the interior voyage, the traveler finds out about himself; he constructs an autobiography. In the exterior voyage, he recaptures Portuguese culture and history through a personal focus on the manifestations and the voices of the people, as well as on small villages and other enchanting places and monuments, which are significantly related to Portuguese history and culture.

*Memorial do convento* (Memoir of the Convent, 1982; translated as *Baltasar and Blimunda,* 1987) was Saramago's first novel to win critical acclaim abroad. This novel, which mixes fantasy with reality, centers on the early-eighteenth-century construction of the Mafra Convent, a monument built to satisfy the megalomaniac desires and vanity of the Portuguese clergy, nobility, and king. It also describes the construction of an airborne vehicle by Father Bartolomeu Gusmão, with the help of Baltasar and Blimunda, the two protagonists, who are romantically involved. The Mafra Convent came to be built because of a pledge made by King John V, in return for the queen giving him an heir. Notwithstanding the pledge, the construction of the convent, as Saramago highlights in his narrative, represents a victory for the forces of religious fanaticism, waste, and corruption, since thousands of peasants were involved for many years in the building of this monument, depriving Portugal of essential manual labor for farming and building the country up in other areas.

*Memorial do convento* is a satirical account of the pomp and ceremony that characterizes an era, the baroque period, known for its festivities, autos-de-fé, bullfights, convents as bordellos, and processions chiefly for the delight and the enjoyment of the upper classes. The work is a story about love (Baltasar and Blimunda), hope and idealism (the airborne machine), and lunacy and abuse (the construction of the Mafra Convent). In the context of the eighteenth century, the airborne machine, associated with the human will and dreams, is the antithesis of the Mafra Convent, a symbol of corruption and repression to satisfy the king's dreams of vanity and grandiosity. The novel focuses on the monument and the machine for different reasons. The machine symbolizes the valuing of humanity and people's ability to effect change and to realize dreams. The focus on the monument challenges the truth of official history, which has always credited the king for the convent construction. The novel narrates a different history of the convent, one with epic dimensions. The epic, in this instance, is not grandiose and heroic for those who write official history, since they never participate in its making. It is heroic for those, the lower classes, who sacrifice, suffer, and even die to carry out the lunatic dreams of a monarch. As the novel indicates, for the new heroes the task is painful and absurd. At the end, the construction is a hollow victory, because the workers are denied their role in the construction of the Mafra Convent in official documents–an omission that is rectified by *Memorial do convento,* the story of those who have not been written into history but who are, in reality, the true makers of history.

Saramago's next novel, *O ano da morte de Ricardo Reis* (1984; translated as *The Year of the Death of Ricardo Reis,* 1991), is set in the early years of Salazar's dictatorship and the beginning of the Spanish Civil War. The tale follows the romantic, social, political, psychological, and artistic adventures of Ricardo Reis through the labyrinthine streets of Lisbon and the village of Fátima. Reis, a poet-physician, was one of the many literary personas created by Fernando Pessoa, the most eminent Portuguese modernist poet; Saramago makes Reis a separate character. The novel is thus a continuation of Pessoa's work. Reis has been in exile in Brazil since 1919 because of his monarchist sympathies; Saramago brings him back from exile to become reacquainted with Lisbon and its changing reality after he learns of Pessoa's death. The narrative begins in late 1935 with the arrival of Reis from Brazil on the *Highland Brigade,* a British ship, just a few days after Pessoa's death on 30 November. Pessoa himself is also brought back as a ghost who acts as an observer and critic of the events occurring in Portugal and the world in 1936 and as an advisor to his poetic creation, Reis. The two have heated discussions on politics, aesthetics, life, religion, history, and philosophy.

A negative image of political and social turbulence greets Reis upon his arrival in Lisbon in late 1935. To the newcomer, Lisbon looks like a silent and somber city enclosed within walls and facades, which on this particular day are being battered by a deluge. The severe weather and the violent storms that continue for days during the winter of 1935–1936 set the tone for a political landscape characterized by a climate of vigilance, fear, and repression affecting all Portuguese citizens. The gloominess of the city and its inhabitants is precipitated by the somber and suffocating images of a fascist state supported by the secret police, the military, paramilitary groups, censorship, newspapers, radio, and even the church. As Reis begins to take daily walks through the Lisbon streets, the same negative images prevail. The cemetery where Pessoa is buried, which Reis visits, is a continuation of the city and completes it metaphorically. The cemetery, with all its streets, pathways, roads, avenues, and numbers, is a portrait of Lisbon and, by extension, Portugal. The inhabitants of the cemetery, just like those of the city, can only watch impassively as the political situation deteriorates and as events occurring in Portugal and in other countries limit personal freedom even further and threaten to create a more oppressive climate.

Reis, a classicist who is a strong believer in a philosophy of contemplation, indifference, and impassibility, is not truly interested in engaging actively with the city. Mostly, he walks aimlessly through the streets, attracted by the cultural and literary aspects of his surroundings, such as monuments, statues, and buildings, an attraction that gives rise to reflections and divagations. As Reis contemplates with indifference the spectacle of the real city, he imaginatively re-creates another that is an embodiment of different cultural and literary textures, patterns, tonalities, and allusions as well as stylistic harmonies, ambiguities, and discordances, which underscores his perception of the world as text. The fact that he only relates to the world through the texts with which he is familiar prevents him from understanding the political situation. Fascism does not really fit into his mental makeup or values. He reads about what is happening in the rest of Portugal, sees a movie being filmed for propagandistic reasons, participates in a political rally, hears about Adolf Hitler and his youth brigades, reads the many lies being published in newspapers, and is even harassed by the secret police; but he observes and feels everything through the prism of his classical detachment. He is simply content with the contemplation of reality.

*A jangada de pedra* (1986; translated as *The Stone Raft,* 1994) narrates the imaginary and futuristic separation of the Iberian Peninsula from the rest of Europe. In the Pyrenees Mountains, in the frontier dividing France from Spain, a deep crack occurs, which leads not only to the separation of the peninsula but also to its ensuing aimless voyage through the Atlantic as a gigantic stone raft. After changing direction several times, the peninsula ends up anchored in the South Atlantic, in a location that is exactly equidistant from Africa and South America. The inexplicable separation of the peninsula from Europe coincides with several strange and supernatural events that occur in both Portugal and Spain.

The novel was written at a time that an inflamed polemic on identity and nationalism was taking place in Portugal between individuals who supported the union of Portugal with the European Community (EC) and those who staunchly opposed it. Most government officials supported the integration, while many intellectuals opposed it. *A jangada de pedra* is written against the absorptive capacity of official history. A few years prior to the writing of the novel, the Portuguese geopolitical space had been reduced with the loss of the African empire. The country was still trying to figure out its new position in the European landscape, as well as its changing identity, when the political machinery decided to join the EC. Many intellectuals, including Saramago, felt that those in power, the creators of history, were in fact not allowing Portugal to have a new rebirth after the loss of the empire. They were strongly opposed to integration. Thus, *A jangada de pedra* must be interpreted as a counterintegration narrative. On the one hand, it seeks to dismantle the ideologies of the EC integration; on the other, it tries to suggest alternatives to integration and to rethink other political options before the two Iberian countries become full EC members. The writer himself has said that he did not write this novel because of a fear of loss of cultural identity. He wrote it because he believed that the peninsula needed to redirect itself toward something from which it had been cut: the countries of the Iberian-American and the Iberian-African spheres. Within this political context the peninsula/raft functions not as a sign of a debilitating isolationism but rather as a metaphor for the construction of a new Iberian history and culture that takes into account its linguistic, cultural, and social affinities with its American and African "Others."

Saramago's utmost desire in *A jangada de pedra* is to reject the integrative discourse through an imaginary search for a new national identity or a common Iberian identity, which conforms to his views on integration. The peninsula/raft voyage stresses the communal characteristics of the peninsula: it unites the Spaniards and the Portuguese; it forces the governments of the two countries to work in unison in order to solve the crisis and to prevent chaotic conditions; and it reveals the connections between the cultural productions of the two countries. The common pilgrimage of the Iberian Peninsula is a conscious authorial strategy of resistance against more powerful European cultural productions, which the writer feels will impose themselves on Portugal and Spain if integration runs its full course. In fact, *A jangada de pedra* represents the revolt of the people against a peninsula ruled by foreign cultural and economic powers.

The play *A segunda vida de Francisco de Assis* (1987), like many of Saramago's novels, also resorts to history to craft its artistic world. In the play, Saramago, as he had done before with Pessoa in *O ano da morte de Ricardo Reis*, brings back to life an historical figure–St. Francis of Assisi–and places him in a modern city where he has to confront a capitalist, mercantilist, and computerized society. *A segunda vida de Francisco de Assis,* which is a political allegory, focuses on Francis's return to a world of commercialism that is antithetical to his romanticized ideal of poverty. The Franciscan Company that he encounters, as opposed to the Company that he founded centuries before, is a capitalist enterprise regulated strictly by market forces. As he realizes that he is not going to be able to force the Company to return to the Franciscan ideal of poverty, he comes also to the conclusion that a life of poverty does not mean, as he believed before, sainthood and salvation. The new Francis accepts that only in the struggle against poverty will he find his humanity, his salvation. In essence, the play is about the transformation of Francis from saint to man, from Francis to João (John), which was Francis's original name.

*História do cerco de Lisboa* (1989; translated as *The History of the Siege of Lisbon,* 1996) is Saramago's novel that most explicitly focuses on the relationship between history and fiction. The interplay between the two occurs because the plot of the book contradicts the official version of the siege of Lisbon in the Middle Ages. In the twelfth century, the Portuguese had taken over Lisbon from the Moors with the help of the crusaders. However, in Saramago's novel, the protagonist, Raimundo Silva, who is a proofreader correcting the galley proofs of a history book about the siege of Lisbon, decides to change the official history of Portugal through a creative act. He inserts a "not" in the galleys in the passage referring to the aid that the crusaders rendered the Portuguese in their conquest of Lisbon. By inserting a "not," the proofreader subverts and inverts one of the great foundational myths of Portugal: the altered text now falsely claims that the crusaders did not come to the aid of the Portuguese. The falsified version of the siege should not be interpreted as a lesser truth; it is just a different truth, another version of a registered historical event that leads to the transformation of past reality. As the protagonist finds out, changing the past also changes the present.

Raimundo's creative act, which makes him realize that he has the power to produce meaning, must be viewed as a necessary correction of Portuguese history. The new history takes into account the blending of Christian and Muslim cultures occurring during the Middle Ages in Portugal. The proofreader's subversive act restores Muslim culture to its rightful place in the construction of Portuguese national identity, since the focus of the altered historical document is on the acceptance of Muslim culture rather than its rejection.

Although Raimundo's text may be considered a novel within a novel, it ultimately becomes *História do cerco de Lisboa,* a text that simultaneously deconstructs the official and inherited history of Portugal and also questions the very nature and essence of historical truth and how it relates to fiction. Raimundo's quest leads him to the realization that there are no certainties and that truth is just as absent from history as it is from fiction. The conclusion is that truth is always constructed in a specific context by human beings. The novel may have started with an alteration of factual reality, but it subsequently evolves into a questioning of the capacity of history to represent a single and objective truth. Even the epigraph of the book, which is taken from an imaginary *Book of Exhortations,* addresses the issue of the importance of correction in seeking truth.

Through a defiant act, the insertion of one small word in an historical narrative, Raimundo is redeemed by liberating himself from the conventions that control his existence. Through the free rein of his imagination, he finally allows himself to love someone for the first time: Maria Sara, one of the editors in the publishing house where Raimundo works, becomes his lover and confidante. He is a confirmed bachelor in his fifties who, as far as anyone can tell, has never had a love affair before in his life. With his newly acquired freedom, he is able to narrate another story that acts as a counterpoint to his affair with Maria Sara: the affair between Mogueime and Oruana, two lovers from the time of the real siege of Lisbon. This parallel affair, which sheds light on Raimundo's affair, informs the reader that the past explains the present and interprets it critically, and vice versa.

Saramago's novel *O Evangelho segundo Jesus Cristo* (1991; translated as *The Gospel According to Jesus Christ,* 1993) created an uproar in Portugal because of its controversial subject. In this bitter satire of an apocryphal biography of Jesus, a mean-spirited God uses the innocently human Jesus to found a repressive religion, Catholicism, which has spawned violence and intolerance through time. Like Nikos Kazantzakis's *The Last Temptation of Christ* (1951), the story of a self-doubting Savior, *O Evangelho segundo Jesus Cristo* is also a rewriting of Christ's life, an account of Jesus' journey on earth from Bethlehem to Gethsemane that departs from traditional interpretations. The Portuguese church attacked the novel as heresy, and a member of the conservative Portuguese government took the book out of competition for the 1992 European Literary Prize for which it had been nominated, on the grounds that it was an attack on the Christian values and the religious faith on which Portugal was founded. The decision, which Saramago called a case of censorship, prompted the author to leave Portugal and to take up residence in Lanzarote,

*Saramago receiving the Nobel Prize in literature from King Carl XVI Gustaf, Stockholm, 1998 (photograph © AFP/CORBIS)*

in the Canary Islands, where he lives with his wife, the Spanish journalist Pilar del Río (María del Pilar del Río Sanchez), whom he married in 1988 (Saramago had been divorced from his first wife since 1970).

The book, which begins and ends with Jesus' crucifixion, is narrated by an unnamed evangelist whose authority comes from his wide range of knowledge about different historical periods. There is some ambiguity about who fathers Jesus, since at his nonvirginal conception God mixes his seed with Joseph's. As in most of Saramago's novels, supernatural and fantastic occurrences also play an important role in the plot of *O Evangelho segundo Jesus Cristo.* Jesus' youth follows the normal pathways found in the Bible, although the composition of his family is decidedly different, including several brothers and sisters. Joseph fails to warn the other parents when he finds out about Herod's planned massacre of all boys under three; he simply runs away with his family to escape it. Joseph's guilt about this failure results in his crucifixion at the hands of the Romans for a crime he does not commit.

In *O Evangelho segundo Jesus Cristo* Jesus is not really God disguised as a man; he is someone who is victimized by God in a cynical and selfish ploy in order for God to extend his influence over the whole world, not just in Judea. The powers given to Jesus are meant only to convince the rest of the world that he is God's son. Jesus does not wish to be the son of God or to make miracles to help God's cause. Neither is he willing to sacrifice himself, as determined by God, to create the illusion of a loving and caring God who gives his life for others.

God in this novel is sly, bloodthirsty, vengeful, and interested in power for power's sake. God's ambition allows him to finally achieve his ultimate goal: the establishment of a church, a symbol of his power, which will be dug in flesh, its walls made of agony, anguish, and death. After God's reference to the establishment of his church, he begins a litany of sorrows, tears, tortures, and deaths that human beings suffer for his sake. The litany goes on for four pages—in alphabetical order, so as not to hurt any feelings about precedence and importance.

For a time, the pressure of God over Jesus is so strong that the son reluctantly accepts his destiny. Nevertheless, as the novel is about to conclude, Jesus begins to question the role that he has been coerced into playing and denies his divinity. He becomes a leader of a revolutionary group fighting against Roman power. He is imprisoned and condemned to die on the cross as an enemy of Rome. He is certain he will die as a son of man and not as the son of God. However, as he is about to die, God appears in the heavens and proclaims him his beloved son. Jesus responds by inverting the famous words that he said on the cross: men forgive him, for he knows not what he has done.

The irony of the final words focuses on God's inhumanity and Jesus' humanity. God is the authoritarian figure who only understands the languages of power and self-interest, and Jesus is the symbol of generosity and human life when he becomes one with all men. In *O Evangelho segundo Jesus Cristo* Jesus learns from several sources: his biological parents, his pastor, and God. However, he learns the most from Mary Magdalene. Jesus, through his relationship with Mary, awakens to sexual life and learns the true meaning of freedom, something that God does not allow any individual in the novel to enjoy, particularly the one person he chooses to be his son. Thus, the novel may be construed as an exaltation of human love combined contrapuntally with the nonhuman dogmatism of transcendental power.

Saramago's fourth and last play, *In nomine Dei*, was published in 1993. As in previous plays and most of the author's novels of the 1980s, history continues to be an object of scrutiny. Religion, the theme of both *O Evangelho segundo Jesus Cristo* and *A segunda vida de Francisco de Assis*, is also the author's main concern in this play. A blind and fanatic religious dogmatism plays a crucial role in the dramatic events. *In nomine Dei* focuses on the fights between Catholics and Protestants in Münster, Germany, from 1532 to 1535, which led to the destruction of the city and the perpetration of horrendous crimes against humanity, all in the name of God.

*In nomine Dei* is divided into three acts, which are preceded by a prologue focusing on religious intolerance and irrationality and followed by a chronology of events taking place in Münster. The play clearly aims to tackle issues of abuse of power, intolerance, and incendiary fanaticism, all by-products of different and opposing religious points of view. *In nomine Dei* depicts the consequences that befall humanity when certain individuals are totally guided by fanaticism, intolerance, and violence in their attempt to achieve their religious objectives. The play is also a condemnation of those who surrender to blind faith and irrationality, metaphors of a dehumanized world.

Every year from 1994 to 1998, Saramago published a diary. These five volumes are titled collectively *Cadernos de Lanzarote* (Notebooks from Lanzarote). Saramago's diaries focus on a variety of themes ranging from the documentary to the literary, the political, and the philosophical. On the documentary level, the diaries record many of the author's private moments and experiences, address domestic problems, and recount his many travels to attend congresses, to receive prizes, or to be interviewed. On other levels, he registers his reactions to specific events, such as Portugal's integration into the EC, the polemic unleashed by the publication of *O Evangelho segundo Jesus Cristo,* and the success of *In nomine Dei*. He also comments on such prevailing and relevant issues as religious intolerance, atrocities committed against humanity, the multiplicity of mechanisms used by power to repress world citizens, and censorship, especially as it relates to the publication of *O Evangelho segundo Jesus Cristo* and his self-exile to Lanzarote because of the ensuing controversy. Furthermore, Saramago uses his diaries to engage in dialogue or polemic with other writers, to discuss the act of writing, and to comment about books he has published or is writing.

*Ensaio sobre a cegueira* (Essay on Blindness, 1995; translated as *Blindness*, 1997) initiates a new cycle in Saramago's literary career. *Ensaio sobre a cegueira* and the novels *Todos os nomes* (1997; translated as *All the Names*, 1999) and *A caverna* (2000; translated as *The Cave*, 2002) constitute a trilogy that addresses concerns and themes that are more universal in character than those in previous novels, since these earlier works were deeply rooted in Portuguese history. The three novels, which do not make specific references to time and space, fall within the mode of allegorical fiction.

In *Ensaio sobre a cegueira* the characters, beginning with a man who is stopped at a traffic light, are struck with a white blindness. Within a few days, everyone in the city seems to have gone blind, with the exception of the wife of the doctor who had examined the first blind man. She remains unaffected by the malady throughout the whole novel. The devastating epidemic that strikes the city and country (which, like the characters, are unnamed) creates havoc everywhere and brings a reign of terror with nightmarish conditions: a state of moral and social degradation and abjection characterized by gang rapes, murders, filth, lack of hygiene, humiliation, a total breakdown of technical support, and even exploitation at the hands of other blind men. As the blindness epidemic spreads, those who have fallen victim to it are quarantined in a mental asylum, where they are subjected to cruel and inhuman conditions. Abandoned by an outside world that is fearful of the contagious disease and full of bigots, a group led by the optometrist's wife (who has feigned her blindness) begins to organize itself in response to the abusive behavior of the other inmates. These inmates have also organized themselves to preserve their selfish interests, privilege, and power, which translates into better living accommodations, greater quantities of food, and even sexual favors in exchange for food. The group led by the optometrist's wife is founded on principles of the humane aspects of all relationships: generosity, solidarity, respect for others, and self-sacrifice. However, as the optometrist's wife finds out, there comes a moment when killing someone is a moral obligation, if humanity is to survive. Her killing of a violent leader of a rival gang must be viewed within this context, since it averts a complete meltdown of civilization.

The people who are quarantined finally regain their freedom because all the outside forces that have kept them imprisoned have become blind as well. As the group led by the optometrist's wife journeys through the city, they discover that the same apocalyptic conditions of the asylum now prevail in the city: thirst, hunger, cold, filth, and chaos. In such a world there can only be "a government of the blind trying to rule the blind, that is to say, or nothingness trying to organize nothingness." The group eventually ends up at the home of the optometrist's wife; and just as mysteriously as they had lost their sight, they regain it, one by one. The recuperation of sight occurs when the characters realize that life is organization and death is disorganization, and that individuals must act and have faith in each other in order to regain their reason, their lucidity. The blindness in the novel is not a physical ailment but rather a political and philosophical illness. The novel is an allegory of irrationality, of a contemporary society that has lost its will to be rational and human, that is, to see. However, the recovery of sight at the end suggests that humanity is still alive and that utopia is still a possibility.

Unlike in *Ensaio sobre a cegueira,* in *Todos os nomes* there is not a breakdown of order. On the contrary, this novel-parable offers a nightmarish vision of order taken to its extreme. An inflexible bureaucratic hierarchy that reduces every employee to a function within the organization runs the Registry where protagonist José works. He is the only character with a name in the novel, and he has just a first name, an indication of the insignificance of the person. The room where the clerks work is arranged according to hierarchy in a harmonious way, which reveals a connection between aesthetics and authority.

The Kafkaesque world of *Todos os nomes,* as the description of the Registry indicates, has reduced human life to some dates and statistics and a few other inconsequential and meaningless details recorded in a file. In the apparently tranquil and secure space of the Registry, the human spirit is really entrapped. One evening José sneaks without authorization into the Registry to pick five card indexes of important figures, to further his hobby of collecting information on famous people, but in his haste to retrieve the indexes he picks up six instead of five, which he brings home. In the sixth index, the name (which is never divulged to the reader) and birth, marriage, and divorce dates of an ordinary female citizen are recorded. Two days later, José decides to begin a quest to find out more about this woman.

José's search for the real person who lies behind the few biographical details on an index card is also a search for self-knowledge. His quest, which he considers absurd, is something that he needs to undertake anyway in order to find his own identity. Through an act of insubordination, he has taken the first step to free himself from the quasi-mythical space of the Registry with its suffocating and deadening atmosphere. His quest, which acquires mythical overtones, leads him to seek information about the woman from several individuals, including her parents, and to break into a school where she had been a student to find out more about her. When he finally locates her, he discovers that she had committed suicide only a few days earlier. Thus, he never gets a chance to meet the woman who has become the source of his obsession and with whom he has fallen in love. He can only go to the cemetery where she is buried.

*Dust jacket for the 2002 American edition of Saramago's 2000 novel,* A caverna, *the last in a trilogy about urban dystopias (Richland County Public Library)*

At the end of the novel, as he returns home one evening, José finds the Registrar in his house. The Registrar is not there to reprimand José or to fire him, however; he is there to tell him that he admires what José has done, because through his actions José has revealed to the Registrar the real meaning of life. The Registrar decides that it is totally absurd to separate the dead from the living, and he even suggests that José place the woman's file among those of the living. The Registrar's subversive notion of no longer viewing the past as death and the present as life will change the whole organizational structure of the Registry. The dead will also partake of the present, because the files of the dead will no longer be separated from the living. The dead will live in the memory of the living and their love.

In 1999, Saramago published *Discursos de Estocolmo* (Stockholm Speeches) and *Folhas políticas, 1976–1998* (Political Papers, 1976–1998). *Discursos de Estocolmo* is a compilation of Saramago's speeches related to his being awarded the Nobel Prize in literature for 1998. The speeches shed light on the public and the private Saramago, since they deal with the author's personal background, his family, and his reflections on some controversial issues. *Folhas políticas* is a compilation of political articles written by the author between 1976 and 1998 and published in newspapers and magazines, both in Portugal and abroad. About half of the essays were published prior to 1980; the others appeared in print after that date.

Although the essays that were written in the 1980s and 1990s are not as concerned with political transformation as those written earlier, they are still political in nature, as the author deals with such controversial topics as the 1994 uprising of the Zapatista National Liberation Army in Chiapas, Mexico; the ETA (a terrorist organization seeking an independent Basque state in Spain); and the fall of the Berlin Wall. In the later essays, the writer also examines and reflects on issues of globalization; immigration; transnational relations, especially those between Portugal and Brazil; the relationship between the political and the cultural; the effects on writers and the reading public as a result of certain political trends; and the role of the writer in society, national identity, and local culture. In a few of the essays there is a nostalgic look at the past, specifically at the Portuguese revolution with its promise of liberty, which leads the writer to question whether that moment in 1974 was a dream or a perfect moment in his life.

*A caverna*, Saramago's first novel after receiving the Nobel Prize, closes the trilogy about urban dystopias that began with *Ensaio sobre a cegueira* and was followed by *Todos os nomes.* Teresa Cristina Cerdeira da Silva has called these novels "a triptych reflecting humanity's quest for meaning in the midst of its end-of-millennium crisis." *A caverna,* which is not a re-creation of Plato's allegory of the cave but has many affinities with it, is an allegorical satire of the shopping center as a symbol of consumer society, the new cave where humanity is currently entrapped. As the author claims, the shopping center is the new cathedral or university of commercialism and free-market capitalism, which have transformed reality into virtual reality. The people living in the Center, a residential and commercial compound in a nameless metropolis, inhabit a world where they assume that the shadows they see going by on the walls are reality. The writer satirizes this gigantic space of global consumer capitalism multiplying rapidly like a mirror game creating deceitful illusions that pass for reality. The Center, which threatens to swallow everything in its periphery, including a city, is a microworld that determines and programs everything and controls the movement of its inhabitants, as well as their leisure activities, through the creation of virtual recreational spaces. The dwellers have become virtual prisoners of the Center; all their needs are satisfied within its walls.

*A caverna* is not only about a nightmarish urban dystopia, as exemplified by a Center that controls the destiny of its dwellers; it is also the story of Cipriano Algor, a sixty-four-year-old potter living in a nearby village, who sells his earthenware vessels to the Center. He lives with his daughter, Marta, who is married to Marçal Gacho, a security guard at the Center. Marçal anxiously awaits a promotion to resident guard so that he can actually move into the Center with his family. In his current position, he has to work ten-day shifts before he has a few days off, which leads to long separations from his wife. When the promotion arrives, the young couple and Cipriano relocate to the Center. Cipriano is reluctant to move, because the Center has unscrupulously canceled the sales contract it has with him, claiming that Center consumers prefer objects made from a plastic that imitates clay. With the termination of the contract, Cipriano decides to produce 1,200 decorative figurines, which the Center also rejects because a survey of its dwellers indicates that consumers are not interested in buying them. Cipriano, realizing that he is no longer necessary to the functioning of the world, moves to the Center with his family, all along disguising his sadness for having abandoned his rural home, a home that is harmoniously integrated with his trade. In fact, the home is an extension of himself.

Dissatisfied with the Center, Cipriano rebels subtly against its organization and rules. Eventually, he trespasses into a cave within the Center where archaeological excavations are being undertaken. He and his son-in-law enter the off-limits area—Plato's cave, as a billboard posted in the Center soon advertises—and discover inside six petrified figures, the stone bodies of six individuals who had failed to understand the meaning of defiance. As a consequence of their failure, they were condemned to live in a world of shadows without any possibility of escape. In a sense, they were the ones who rejected light and liberty by their lack of action. By choosing illusion and simulacrum instead of reality, and ignorance instead of knowledge, they became petrified. Cipriano realizes that the petrified figures in the cave are really bodies of individuals, like him, who have failed to defy the encroachment of commercialism. The discovery of this dystopian vision of the world changes Marçal's dependent and submissive relationship with the Center, and he and his wife decide to leave, just like Cipriano.

As the novel comes to a close, the three characters—accompanied by Isaura, Cipriano's new love interest—are seen leaving in search of a new life, but not before Marta states that they are finished with the Center, that the pottery has come to an end, and that from one day to another they have become strangers in this world. Notwithstanding her words, the journey to the unknown holds the promise of life: Marta is pregnant. There is no final triumph of the spirit over the inhuman and evil forces of the Center, only a hint that not all is lost yet. Although the novel does not offer any concrete solutions to limit the growth and the devouring power of the Center, Saramago shows that unless human beings are willing to fight and reject the apocalyptic images of the Centers of the world, as the four characters have done, then humankind is condemned to live in a world of virtual reality characterized by deceit, shadows, and mirror games.

José Saramago has achieved literary mastery in a wide range of genres. Even though Saramago is better known for the novels that he has written in the 1980s and 1990s, the reader can find the major thematic concerns of the more mature work in the writer's earlier works, those published in the 1960s and 1970s. In addition, those earlier works already display the fantastic and supernatural elements that Saramago incorporates in most of his novels, including those in which the subject matter is more deeply rooted in Portuguese history, such as *Memorial do convento, O ano da morte de Ricardo Reis,* and *A jangada de pedra.* As Saramago's fiction takes a more allegorical turn, especially in his dystopian trilogy, the reader encounters a writer who has a gloomier view of the world and no longer seems to believe that individuals have the capacity to stop the continuous destruction of human dignity and values or to confront the evil power of a mercantilist and commercialized society. Despite Saramago's increasing pessimism regarding humanity's capacity to effect change, to use reason to curb abusive power, and to stop the dehumanizing tendencies of all institutions, he continues to call attention to the destructiveness and irrationality that afflict the world. Saramago may not really believe that a work of art has the potential to change human nature; but he, through his focus on the role played by human beings in confronting political tyranny and the forces that blind humanity, seems to be suggesting that not all is lost yet.

**Interviews:**

Juan Arias, *José Saramago: El amor posible* (Barcelona: Planeta, 1998);

Carlos Reis, *Diálogos com José Saramago* (Lisbon: Caminho, 1998);

Jorge Halperín, *Conversaciones con Saramago: Reflexiones desde Lanzarote* (Barcelona: Icaria, 2002).

**Bibliography:**

Orlando Grossegesse, *Saramago lessen: Werk, Leben, Bibliographie* (Berlin: Tranvía/Walter Frey: 1999).

**References:**

Ana Paula Arnaut, *Memorial do convento: História, ficção e ideologia* (Coimbra: Fora do Texto, 1996);

Armando Baptista-Bastos, *José Saramago: A aproximação a um retrato* (Lisbon: Dom Quixote, 1996);

Beatriz Berrini, *Ler Saramago: O romance* (Lisbon: Caminho, 1998);

Berrini, ed., *José Saramago: Uma homenagem* (São Paulo: EDUC, 1999);

Harold Bloom, "The One With the Beard Is God, the Other Is the Devil," *Portuguese Literary & Cultural Studies*, 6 (2001): 155-166;

Eduardo Calbucci, *Saramago: Um roteiro para os romances* (Cotia, São Paulo: Ateliê, 1999);

Maria de Lourdes Cidraes, "Da possibilidade da poesia: *Os poemas possíveis* de José Saramago," *Colóquio/Letras*, 151-152 (1999): 37-51;

Maria da Conceição Coelho and Teresa Azinheira, *Memorial do convento de José Saramago* (Mem Martins: Europa-América, 1997);

José Horácio Costa, *Saramago. O período formativo* (Lisbon: Caminho, 1998);

Costa, "Saramago's Construction of Fictional Characters: From *Terra do pecado* to *Baltasar and Blimunda*," *Portuguese Literary & Cultural Studies*, 6 (2001): 33-48;

Mary Lou Daniel, "Ebb and Flow: Place as Pretext in the Novels of José Saramago," *Luso-Brazilian Review*, 27, no. 2 (1990): 25-39;

Daniel, "Symbolism and Synchronicity: José Saramago's Jangada de Pedra," *Hispania*, 74, no. 3 (1991): 536-541;

Ana Paula Ferreira, "Cruising Gender in the Eighties: From *Levantado do chão* to the *History of the Siege of Lisbon*," *Portuguese Literary & Cultural Studies*, 6 (2001): 221-238;

Attore Finazzi-Agrò, "Da capo: o texto como palimpsesto na *História do cerco de Lisboa*," *Colóquio/Letras*, 151-152 (1999): 341-351;

Douwe Fokkema, "The Art of Rewriting the Gospel," *Colóquio/Letras*, 151-152 (1999): 395-402;

David Frier, "Ascent and Consent: Hierarchy and Popular Emancipation in the Novels of José Saramago," *Bulletin of Hispanic Studies*, 71, no. 1 (1994): 125-138;

Frier, "In the Beginning Was the Word: Text and Meaning in Two Dramas by José Saramago," *Portuguese Studies*, 14 (1998): 215-226;

Frier, "José Saramago's Stone Boat: Celtic Analogues and Popular Culture," *Portuguese Studies*, 15 (1999): 194-206;

Frier, "Writing Wrongs, Re-Writing Meaning and Reclaiming the City in Saramago's *Blindness* and *All the Names*," *Portuguese Literary & Cultural Studies*, 6 (2001): 97-122;

Orlando Grossegesse, "Journey to the Iberian God: Antonio Machado Revisited by José Saramago," *Portuguese Literary & Cultural Studies*, 6 (2001): 167-184;

Adrián Huici, "Perdidos en el laberinto: El camino del héroe en '*Todos os nomes*'," *Colóquio/Letras*, 151-152 (1999): 453-462;

Maria Joaquina Nobre Júlio, *Memorial do convento de José Saramago: Subsídios para uma leitura* (Lisbon: Replicação, 1999);

Helena Kaufman, "A metaficção historiográfica de José Saramago," *Colóquio/Letras*, 120 (1991): 124-136;

Kenneth Krabbenhoft, "Saramago, Cognitive Estrangement, and Original Sin?" *Portuguese Literary & Cultural Studies*, 6 (2001): 123-136;

Giulia Lanciani, ed., *José Saramago. Il bagaglio dello scritore* (Rome: Bulzoni, 1996);

Isabel Pires de Lima, "Dos 'anjos da História' em dois romances de José Saramago: *Ensaio sobre a cegueira* e *Todos os nomes*," *Colóquio/Letras*, 151-152 (1999): 415-426;

Lilian Lopondo, ed., *Saramago: Segundo terceiros* (São Paulo: Humanitas, 1998);

Conceição Madruga, *A paixão segundo José Saramago* (Porto: Campo das Letras, 1998);

Fernando J. B. Martinho, "Para um enquadramento periodológico da poesia de José Saramago," *Colóquio/Letras*, 151-152 (1999): 21-33;

Adriana Alves de Paula Martins, "A crónica de José Saramago ou uma viagem pela oficina do romance," *Colóquio/Letras,* 151–152 (1999): 95–105;

Martins, *História e ficção–um diálogo* (Lisbon: Fim de Século, 1994);

Martins, "José Saramago's Historical Fiction," *Portuguese Literary & Cultural Studies,* 6 (2001): 49–72;

Vibha Maurya, "Construction of Crowd in Saramago's Texts," *Colóquio/Letras,* 151–152 (1999): 267–278;

António Moniz, *Para uma leitura de Memorial do convento de José Saramago: Uma proposta de leitura crítico-didáctica* (Lisbon: Presença, 1995);

Margarida Braga Neves, "Nexos, temas e obsessões na ficção breve de José Saramago," *Colóquio/Letras,* 151–152 (1999): 117–139;

Odílio José de Oliveira Filho, *Carnaval no convento: Intertextulaidade e paródia em José Saramago* (São Paulo: UNESP, 1993);

José N. Ornelas, "Resistência, Espaço e Utopia em *Memorial do Convento* de José Saramago," *Discursos: Estudos de Língua e Cultura Portuguesa,* 13 (1996): 115–133;

Giovanni Pontiero, "José Saramago and *O ano da morte de Ricardo Reis,*" *Bulletin of Hispanic Studies,* 71, no. 1 (1994): 139–148;

Richard Preto Rodas, "A View of Eighteenth-Century Portugal: José Saramago's *Memorial do convento,*" *World Literature Today,* 73, no. 1 (1987): 27–31;

Miguel Real, *Narração, maravilhoso, trágico e sagrado em Memorial do convento de José Saramago* (Lisbon: Caminho, 1996);

Luiz Francisco Rebello, "Teatro, tempo e história," *Colóquio/Letras,* 151–152 (1999): 143–150;

Mark J. L. Sabine, "Once But No Longer the Prow of Europe: National Identity and Portuguese Destiny in José Saramago's *The Stone Raft,*" *Portuguese Literary & Cultural Studies,* 6 (2001): 185–203;

Maria Alzira Seixo, *O essencial sobre José Saramago* (Lisbon: Imprensa Nacional-Casa da Moeda, 1987);

Seixo, *Lugares da ficção em José Saramago: O essencial e outros ensaios* (Lisbon: Imprensa Nacional-Casa da Moeda, 1999);

Teresa Cristina Cerdeira da Silva, *José Saramago. Entre a história e a ficção: Uma saga de portugueses* (Lisbon: Dom Quixote, 1989);

Silva, "On the Labyrinth of Text, or, Writing, as the Site of Memory," *Portuguese Literary & Cultural Studies,* 6 (2001): 73–96;

Maria Almira Soares, *Memorial do Convento de José Saramago: Um modo de narrar* (Lisbon: Presença, 1999);

Luciana Stegagno Picchio, *José Saramago: Instantanee per un ritratto* (Firenze: Passigli, 2000);

Carmen Chaves Tesser, ed., "A Tribute to José Saramago," *Hispania,* 82, no. 1 (1999): 1–28;

Francisco José Viegas, *José Saramago: Uma voz contra o silêncio* (Lisbon: Caminho, 1998).

**Papers:**

An archive of some of José Saramago's papers is housed at the Biblioteca Nacional in Lisbon.

# Jorge de Sena
(2 November 1919 - 4 June 1978)

Gilda Santos
*Universidade Federal do Rio de Janeiro*

BOOKS: *Perseguição* (Lisbon: Cadernos de Poesia, 1942);

*Coroa da terra* (Porto: Lello, 1946);

*Florbela Espanca: Ou a Expressão do feminino na poesia portuguesa* (Porto: Clube Fenianos Portuenses, 1947);

*Pedra filosofal* (Lisbon: Confluência, 1950);

*O indesejado António, Rei* (Porto: Portucale, 1951);

*A poesia de Camões* (Lisbon: Libânio da Silva, 1951);

*As evidências* (Lisbon: Centro Bibliográfico, 1955); translated by Phyllis Sterling Smith as *The Evidences: Poems,* with a preface by George Monteiro (Santa Barbara: Center for Portuguese Studies, University of California, Santa Barbara, 1994);

*Fidelidade* (Lisbon: Moraes, 1958);

*Da poesia portuguesa* (Lisbon: Ática, 1959);

*Andanças do demônio* (Lisbon: Estúdios Cor, 1960)—includes "Razão de o Pai Natal ter barbas brancas" and "A Comemoração";

*Poesia* (Lisbon: Moraes, 1961);

*"O poeta é um fingidor"* (Lisbon: Ática, 1961);

*O reino da estupidez* (Lisbon: Moraes, 1961; enlarged, 1978);

*Metamorfoses; Quatro sonetos a Afrodite Anadiómena,* with an afterword and notes by Sena (Lisbon: Moraes, 1963)—includes "Carta a meus filhos sobre os fuzilamentos de Goya," "Camões dirige-se a seus contemporâneos," and "A morte, o espaço, a eternidade"; *Metamorfoses* translated by Francisco Cota Fagundes and James Houlihan as *Metamorphoses* (Providence, R.I.: Copper Beach Press, 1991);

*A literatura inglesa* (São Paulo: Cultrix, 1963);

*Uma canção de Camões* (Lisbon: Portugália, 1966);

*Novas andanças do demônio* (Lisbon: Portugália, 1966);

*Estudos de história e de cultura* (Lisbon: Ocidente, 1967);

*Arte de música* (Lisbon: Moraes, 1968); translated by Fagundes and Houlihan as *The Art of Music* (Huntington, W.Va.: University Editions, 1988);

*Peregrinatio ad loca infecta* (Lisbon: Portugália, 1969);

*Jorge de Sena (photograph by Eduardo Gageiro)*

*Os sonetos de Camões e o soneto quinhentista peninsular* (Lisbon: Portugália, 1969);

*A estrutura de Os Lusíadas e outros estudos camonianos e de poesia peninsular do século XVI* (Lisbon: Portugália, 1970);

*Exorcismos* (Lisbon: Moraes, 1972);

*Trinta anos de poesia* (Porto: Inova, 1972);

*Camões dirige-se a seus contemporâneos e outros textos* (Porto: Inova, 1973);

*Dialécticas da literatura* (Lisbon: Edições 70, 1973); enlarged as *Dialécticas teóricas da literatura* (Lisbon: Edições 70, 1977);

*Conheço o Sal . . . e outros poemas* (Lisbon: Moraes, 1974);

*Maquiavel e outros estudos* (Porto: Paisagem, 1974);

*Os Grão-Capitães* (Lisbon: Edições 70, 1976);

*O físico prodigioso* (Lisbon: Edições 70, 1977); translated by Mary Fitton as *The Wondrous Physician* (London: Dent, 1986);

*Sobre esta praia . . . Oito meditações à beira do Pacífico* (Porto: Inova, 1977); translated by Jonathan Griffin as *Over This Shore . . . Eight Meditations on the Coast of the Pacific* (Santa Barbara: Mudborn Press, 1979);

*Régio, Casais, a presença e outros afins* (Porto: Brasília, 1977);

*Antigas e novas andanças do demônio* (Lisbon: Edições 70, 1978);

*Dialécticas aplicadas da literatura* (Lisbon: Edições 70, 1978);

*40 anos de servidão* (Lisbon: Moraes, 1979);

*Sinais de fogo,* edited by Arnaldo Saraiva (Lisbon: Edições 70, 1979);

*Trinta anos de Camões,* 2 volumes (Lisbon: Edições 70, 1980);

*Sequências* (Lisbon: Moraes, 1980);

*Fernando Pessoa & Ca. Heterónima* (Lisbon: Edições 70, 1982);

*Visão perpétua,* with a preface by Mécia de Sena (Lisbon: Imprensa Nacional-Casa da Moeda, 1982);

*Estudos sobre o vocabulário de Os Lusíadas* (Lisbon: Edições 70, 1982);

*Estudos de literatura portuguesa,* 3 volumes (Lisbon: Edições 70, 1982–1988);

*Génesis* (Lisbon: Edições 70, 1983);

*Post-Scriptum II,* 2 volumes, transcribed, with notes, by Mécia de Sena (Lisbon: Imprensa Nacional-Casa da Moeda, 1985);

*Inglaterra revisitada* (Lisbon: Edições 70, 1986); translated by Christopher Damien Auretta as *England Revisited* (Lisbon: Calouste Gulbenkian Foundation, 1986);

*Sobre o romance ingleses: Norte-americanos e outros,* with an introductory note by Mécia de Sena (Lisbon: Edições 70, 1986);

*Estudos de cultura e literatura brasileira* (Lisbon: Edições 70, 1988);

*Sobre cinema,* edited by Mécia de Sena and M. S. Fonseca, with an introduction by Mécia de Sena (Lisbon: Cinemateca Portuguesa, 1988);

*Do teatro em Portugal* (Lisbon: Edições 70, 1989);

*Mater imperialis: Amparo de mãe e mais 5 peças em 1 acto seguido de um apêndice* (Lisbon: Edições 70, 1990);

*Amor e outros verbetes* (Lisbon: Edições 70, 1992);

*Monte cativo e outros projectos de ficção* (Porto: ASA, 1994);

*O dogma da trindade poética (Rimbaud) e outros ensaios,* with an introduction by Mécia de Sena (Porto: ASA, 1994);

*Dedicácias* (Lisbon: Três Sinais, 1999).

**Collections:** *Poesia II* (Lisbon: Moraes, 1978);

*Poesia III* (Lisbon: Moraes, 1978).

**Editions in English:** *The Poetry of Jorge de Sena* [bilingual edition], edited, with a introduction, by Frederick G. Williams, with a foreword by Mécia de Sena, translated by Helen Barreto and others (Santa Barbara: Mudborn Press, 1980);

*In Crete, with the Minotaur, and Other Poems* [bilingual edition], translated, with a preface, by George Monteiro (Providence, R.I.: Gávea-Brown, 1980);

*By the Rivers of Babylon and Other Stories,* translated and edited, with a preface, by Daphne Patai (New Brunswick, N.J. & London: Rutgers University Press/Polygon, 1989);

*Signs of Fire,* translated by John Byrne (Manchester, U.K.: Carcanet, 1999).

OTHER: Fernando Pessoa, *Páginas da doutrina estética,* edited, with a preface, by Sena (Lisbon: Inquérito, 1947);

*Líricas portuguesas* [third series], edited, with a preface, by Sena (Lisbon: Portugália, 1958);

A. C. Ward, *História da literatura inglesa,* translated by Rogério Fernandes, revised and annotated, with a preface, by Sena, História ilustrada das grandes literaturas, no. 6 (Lisbon: Estúdios Cor, 1960);

Luis de Camões, *Lusíadas,* 2 volumes, with an introduction by Sena (Lisbon: Imprensa Nacional-Casa da Moeda, 1972).

TRANSLATIONS: Constantine Cavafy, *90 e mais quatro poemas,* translated, with a preface, by Sena (Porto: Inova, 1975?);

Eugene O'Neill, *Jornada para a noite,* translated by Sena (Lisbon: Cotovia, 1992);

DuBose Heyward, *Porgy e Bess,* translated by Sena (Lisbon: Livros do Brasil, 19?).

A prolific and multitalented author, Jorge de Sena wrote poetry, drama, short stories, critical essays, a novel, and a novella. He had an erudite interest in culture, and his fascination in several aspects of the cultural world are reflected in the richness and diversity of his writings. Scholars of Sena generally emphasize in his work the importance of biography, the concept of metamorphosis, and the experience of "double exile." Sena spent much of his life in Brazil and the United States, but, as he stated more than once: "I have always been in exile, even before I left Portugal." The statement lays bare the feelings of an intellectual, born only seven years before the longest-running dictatorship of twentieth-century Europe began in Portugal and surrounded in his childhood and youth by abuses of power and censorship.

Family circumstances did little to attenuate the feeling of displacement that haunted Sena for most of his life. Born in Lisbon on 2 November 1919, he was the only child of a merchant marine commander, Augusto Raposo de Sena, who was away from home for long periods of time, and of a gifted, submissive woman of fine education, Maria da Luz Teles Grilo. With his mother's encouragement, Sena learned to read at the age of three, and by the age of ten he could read French fluently. He found refuge from loneliness in books. Judging from the short story "Homenagem ao papagaio verde" (Homage to the Green Parrot), which Sena always characterized as autobiographical, his domestic environment was hardly harmonious. The situation became even worse in 1933, the year his father suffered an accident at sea and had to have one of his legs amputated. The family was forced to live on a small monthly allowance that the Companhia Nacional de Navegação gave Augusto, who had served them for forty years. The family was almost always in debt; financial difficulties beset Sena throughout his life, and this period was only the beginning. In his unhappy childhood, only his maternal grandmother, Isabel, stands out. Sena was her favorite grandson. Isabel and Maria gave the boy, who had shown an early artistic sensitivity, great intellectual incentives. At ten he began piano lessons and developed a lifelong affinity for music.

Sena studied in the best schools in Lisbon. He finished high school in 1936 and that same year took the preparatory course for the Escola Naval. Receiving the highest grades in the course, he enrolled in the school with his family's support. He earned first cadet in the "Curso do Condestável." In February 1937 he set out on his first journey, on the teaching ship *Sagres*, and visited Cape Verde, São Tomé, Brazil, Angola, Senegal, and the Canary Islands–places that impressed him and were later depicted in his work. Yet, for reasons still not exactly known, Sena was discharged from the navy in March 1938. Because a naval career had been the prevailing dream of his life, the discharge caused him enormous personal trauma, noted later in his work through the recurring theme of exclusion. Feeling sad, wronged, and humiliated, he shut himself up at home until the beginning of the new academic year in October. When he finished his courses in 1940, he moved to Porto and enrolled in the school of engineering at the university there.

The period between 1936 and 1940 was a formative one in Sena's life. He started his career as a writer in 1936, the same year that the Spanish Civil War began, a fact that he remarks upon in his novel *Sinais de fogo* (Signs of Fire, 1979) and the short stories "Os salteadores" (The Assailants) and "A Grã-Canária" (Grand Canary). At age sixteen, influenced by Claude Debussy's prelude "La Cathédrale Engloutie" (The Engulfed Cathedral, written in 1909–1910), he began to write poetry, as reflected in the prologue-poem of *Arte de música* (1968; translated as *The Art of Music*, 1988). Between 1936 and 1940 he wrote the short stories "Paraíso perdido" (Paradise Lost) and "Caim" (Cain). Both stories include autobiographical elements, and, although written by a seventeen-year-old, they reveal immense narrative strength. The year 1938 was particularly productive for Sena. Not only did he write 256 poems but he also started a novel; wrote a one-act comedy; and composed a *Lied*, or song, inspired by the poem "Pobre velha música" (Poor Old Music) by Fernando Pessoa. Sena has been one of the few poets in Portugal who, in his own innovative diction, has managed to respond to the challenges created by the polyphonic poetics of Pessoa. He is also one of the most recognized scholars of Pessoa's work. Sena's poetry writing provided a catharsis during the anguished months of his isolation after his discharge from the navy. The following year, in 1939, he wrote 168 poems and published his first work, the poem "Nevoeiro" (Mist), in a university review, under the name Teles de Abreu, which Sena used until 1942. In the next issue of the same review, he published the essay "Em prol da poesia chamada moderna" (In Favor of the So-Called Modern Poetry). In 1940 he published a letter on Pessoa's poem "Apostila" (Apostil) in the last issue of *Presença* (Presence), and he began to collaborate on the journal *Cadernos de Poesia* (Poetry Notebooks), for which he later served as a codirector. During these early years Sena was a voracious reader and focused his attention on the established names in literature and philosophy.

Associated with the *Cadernos de Poesia* since his early days as a writer, Sena–along with Eugénio de Andrade and Sophia de Mello Breyner Andresen–attempted to reconcile competing tendencies in the Portuguese literary scene of the 1940s and 1950s. Backed by his theory of *testemunho* (witnessing), which he openly opposed to that of Pessoa's *fingimento* (pretending), Sena proposed the creation in verse of what he called a "poetic diary." He explains this concept as

> um desejo de independência partidária da poesia social; um desejo de comprometimento humano da poesia pura; um desejo de expressão lapidar, clássica, da libertação surrealista; um desejo de destruir pelo tumulto insólito das imagens, qualquer disciplina ultrapassada (e assim: a lógica hegeliana deve sobrepor-se à aristotélica; uma moral sociologicamente esclarecida à moral das proibições legalistas); e sobretudo um desejo de exprimir o que entende ser a dignidade humana–uma fidelidade integral à responsabilidade de estarmos no mundo.

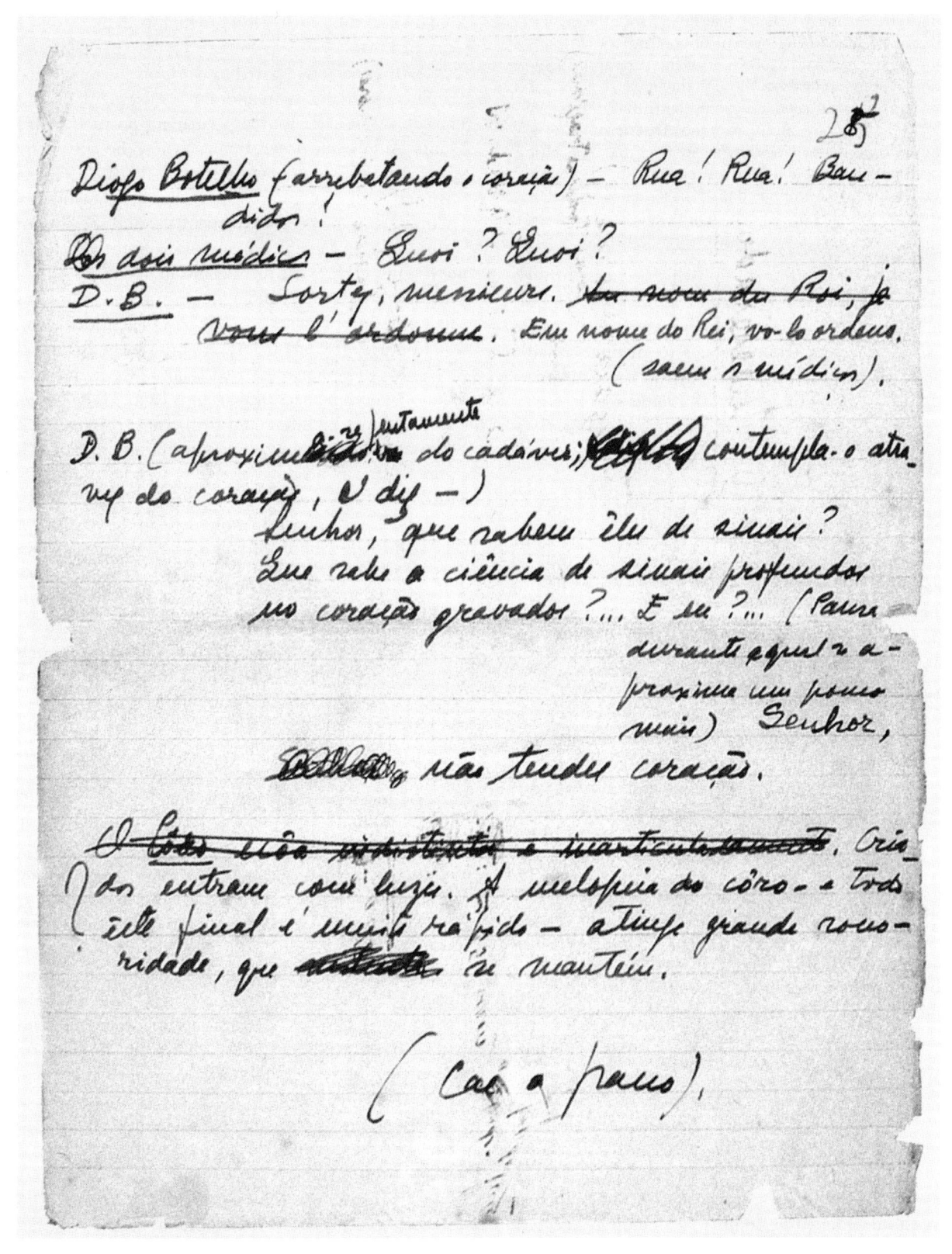

*Page from a 1945 manuscript of Sena's verse tragedy,* O indesejado António, Rei *(The Unwanted Antonio, King), published in 1951 (from Eugénia Vasques,* Jorge de Sena: Uma ideia de teatro [1938–1971]), *1998; University Research Library, University of California, Los Angeles)*

(a desire for independence that favors social poetry; a desire for human engagement of pure poetry; a desire for lapidary, classic expression of the surrealist liberation; a desire to destroy, through the unusual rioting of images, any outdated discipline [and, thus: Hegelian logic must impose itself over the Aristotelian one; a moral which is sociologically aware over that of legalist prohibitions]; and above all a desire to express what it understands to be human dignity—a complete loyalty to the responsibility of us being in the world).

One can see Sena's humanism, which echoes throughout much of his poetry, especially in the book *Metamorfoses* (Metamorphosis), published with *Quatro sonetos a Afrodite Anadiómena* (Four Sonnets to Afrodite Anadiómena) in 1963, and in poems such as the emblematic "Carta a meus filhos sobre os fuzilamentos de Goya" (Letter to My Children on the Executions of Goya).

From October 1940 to November 1944 Sena lived in Porto while attending the university. He would leave the city only for vacation, for health reasons, and for military duty—to which he was called in the summers of 1942 and 1943. These new military experiences, which lasted until 1945, are described in rather unflattering terms in the short stories of *Os Grão-Capitães* (The Grand Captains, 1976). Sena's years at the University of Porto were extremely active ones. In 1941 he gave his first public lecture, "Rimbaud, ou o dogma da trindade poética" (Rimbaud, or the Dogma of the Poetic Trinity), commencing what developed into a long career as a well-received public speaker. The following year, he published his lecture in a Lisbon magazine, and *Perseguição* (Persecution), his first book of poetry, appeared under the aegis of *Cadernos de Poesia*. In 1943 he started contributing to the Lisbon paper *Diário Popular* (Popular Journal) as a literary critic (his area of concentration later expanded to include motion pictures, music, and the theater), thus beginning a dual career in essay writing and journalism that he pursued throughout his life. The year 1944 was his last in the engineering program, which he would not have been able to complete without the financial help of his friends.

Sena finished his verse tragedy *O indesejado António, Rei* (The Unwanted Antonio, King, 1951), which he had read frequently at gatherings of friends and other artists, in 1943. That same year, despite his status in the military, he signed one of the public lists that circulated in the country demanding free elections. He escaped prison by direct intervention of his Brazilian friend Ribeiro Couto, who was then in Portugal working at the Brazilian Embassy. The following year Couto convinced a Porto editor, Lello, to publish Sena's second volume of poetry, *Coroa da terra* (Crown of the Earth, 1946), which is dedicated to the city of Porto.

In 1946 Sena started to work professionally as an engineer—initially as an apprentice in some public organizations. He later took a permanent position with the Junta Autónoma das Estradas, where he stayed from 1948 to 1959, the year he moved to Brazil. The job assured him a regular, though modest, income and allowed him to travel extensively around the country—trips that later benefited many of his historical and literary studies. He went to England in 1952 and 1957 for further professional training in engineering. During the first visit, he read a series of six chronicles titled "Cartas de Londres" (Letters from London) for the BBC.

In 1949 Sena married Maria Mécia de Freitas Lopes, whom he had known since 1940. Over the years they had nine children, and she became his greatest collaborator in life and work. With Mécia's emotional support Sena was productive in the decade that followed their marriage, and his position in Portuguese literary and intellectual life grew more defined. In 1950 he published his third book of poetry, *Pedra filosofal* (Philosopher's Stone), which was followed by the verse collections *As evidências* (The Evidences, 1955) and *Fidelidade* (Fidelity, 1958).

Among the most significant themes in Sena's verse is love, which—along with the themes of homeland and poetry—structures much of Sena's work: "De amor e de poesia de ter pátria / aqui se trata" (Love and poetry and having a country / are dealt with in here). In his poetry Sena often writes about love in erotic and sexual metaphors and images that some readers find pornographic in manner. While the language used to convey the poet's feelings and ideas is often direct and daring, Sena's approach to love is less to shock the reader than to celebrate a consecration of the body; in his love poems the body is a primordial, constructive, and cosmogonic force. After its publication, the poetry collection *As evidências* was seized from distribution, because the regime of then president António Salazar considered it "subversive and pornographic"; the intervention of the authorities confirmed the impact of Sena's politico-erotic discourse on a Portuguese nation that was intensely sexually repressed. Later poems, including ones featured in *Exorcismos* (Exorcisms, 1972), continue the theme of "o sexo em tudo visto" (sex seen in everything) in Sena's poetic universe.

In 1951 both *O indesejado António, Rei* and *A poesia de Camões* (The Poetry of Camões) appeared. The latter, a reproduction of a lecture given in Porto on 10 June 1948, is the starting point of his many critical studies on the sixteenth-century poet Luís de Camões. Sena edited, and wrote the preface for, the poetry anthology *Líricas portuguesas* (Portuguese Lyric Poetry, 1958), as well as published the book of essays *Da poesia portuguesa* (On Portuguese Poetry, 1959). He started working as a literary consultant for the publishing house Livros do Brasil, and as a translator he published the following: *90 e mais quatro poemas* (1975?), a translation of Constantine Cavafy's poems; *Porgy e Bess* (19?), a translation of DuBose Heyward's *Porgy and Bess* (1935); and *Jornada para a noite,* a rendering of Eugene O'Neill's *Long Day's Journey into Night* (1956) that came out posthumously in 1992. Sena's work with literature in English was a novelty in the Portuguese cultural scene of the time, which was still heavily influenced by French literature and culture. A diversity of tasks and interests became a permanent aspect of his life, as evidenced by the volume and variety of his publications.

One subject about which Sena rarely spoke, perhaps owing to excessive caution, was that of political activism. He was always associated with individuals who opposed the Salazar regime. After 1953, when he moved to the house in Restelo (which belongs to his family to this day), he was always willing to facilitate contacts or meetings of different groups. Special mention should be made of the failed attempt to overthrow the regime, known as the "Golpe da Sé" (Strike from the Holy See), which was to take place on 12 March 1959. Sena had been deeply involved in this plan, and after witnessing the imprisonment and disappearance of companions who were as politically engaged as he was, he left for exile in Brazil.

Sena arrived in Brazil on 7 August 1959, and his family arrived a few months later. He had been invited to participate in the fourth Colóquio Internacional de Estudos Luso-Brasileiros (International Colloquy of Luso-Brazilian Studies), organized by the University of Bahia, where his friends Adolfo Casais Monteiro and Eduardo Lourenço were lecturers. They had a decisive role in planning the event, which took place in Salvador from 10 to 21 August. This international conference in literary and cultural studies was the first of many in which Sena participated in his lifetime. Facing an audience of various specialists in Salvador, he chose Pessoa as the theme of his lecture.

The most important consequence of Sena's Brazilian exile was the advancement of his academic career. Soon after his arrival he was invited by Antônio Soares Amora to teach in the new Faculdade de Filosofia, Ciências e Letras (College of Philosophy, Science, and Literature) of Assis. He stayed in Assis until July 1961 and then moved to Araraquara, where he taught Portuguese literature and literary theory until moving to the United States in 1965. In 1962 he taught a course on English literature, on which he published a book the following year. At that time Assis and Araraquara had prestigious teaching staffs that contrib-

*Maria Mécia de Freitas Lopes in 1945, four years before her marriage to Sena (from Vasques,* Jorge de Sena: Uma ideia de teatro [1938–1971]), *1998; University Research Library, University of California, Los Angeles)*

uted to the high quality of the intellectual atmosphere of both institutions.

Sena also had a keen interest in research. In Brazil he had managed to secure institutional support to develop his scholarship on Camões. His work led to volumes that today are fundamental references, such as *Uma canção de Camões* (A Song of Camões, 1966), *A estrutura de Os Lusíadas e outros estudos camonianos e de poesia peninsular do século XVI* (The Structure of *Os Lusíadas* and Other Studies of Camões and Sixteenth-Century Peninsular Poetry, 1970) and the two-volume *Trinta anos de Camões* (Thirty Years of Camões, 1980). Sena's critical writings in these books are based on a thorough study of the photocopies of all editions and manuscripts of Camões's lyrical works. Sena evaluates the state of Camonian studies and questions the work of established authorities, while proposing new ideas and notions on Camões's dialectics and mannerism movement.

In Brazil, Sena undertook many responsibilities and tasks. He lectured and did research; he gave seminars and conferences; he collaborated on literary and nonliterary journals, did translations and editorial work, and traveled extensively. At the same time, for years he wrote the section "Letras Portuguesas" (Portuguese Literature) for the well-known newspaper *O Estado de São Paulo* (The State of São Paulo).

Sena's literary production is truly astonishing. He took advantage of the freedom of the intellectual climate in Brazil, but he always insisted on being considered a Portuguese writer. He published almost all his works in Portugal. He wrote around 120 poems, mostly found in the books *Arte de música, Metamorfoses,* and *Peregrinatio ad loca infecta* (Pilgrimage to the Unfinished Place, 1969). At this stage Sena wrote his first text in which Camões appears as the protagonist—"Camões dirige-se a seus contemporâneos" (Camões Addresses His Contemporaries) from *Metamorfoses*—and inaugurated one of the most fertile veins in his poetry: that in which the sixteenth-century poet is transformed into a persona, or alter ego, of the poetic "I."

Like Camões, Sena was torn between an acute sensitivity and the vicissitudes of his world. Sena's work is characterized by an enormous capacity for indignation and ethical questions, which he transforms into theological and metaphysical queries, as in a poem from *Metamorfoses:* "A morte, o espaço, a eternidade" (Death, Space, Eternity). Sena composed many metalinguistic texts, in which he explores the notion of writing poetry, as well as establishes harmonious dialogues between poetry and the arts—especially the visual arts (as seen in *Metamorfoses*) and music (as exemplified in *Arte de música*).

In Brazil between late 1964 and June 1965 Sena wrote the first and most substantial segment of his only novel, *Sinais de fogo,* which remained unfinished. Although he returned to the text later, in the United States, he never managed to complete it. The novel was intended to portray life in Portugal from 1936 to 1959, but Sena was able to finish writing only the part that takes place during some months in 1936, when the protagonist, Jorge, discovers love, poetry, and war. Though incomplete, the work is frequently included in the list of the best Portuguese novels of the century.

Sena's only novella, *O físico prodigioso* (1977; translated as *The Wondrous Physician,* 1986), was written in Araraquara in May 1964. Praised by critics, it represents an important moment, if not just an important work. The allegorical atmosphere, with medieval and fantastic elements, accentuates a political reading of the text. The reader can detect easily that Sena is writing about, in part, the Brazilian military dictatorship that had just come to power.

Of the eight short stories that constitute the book *Andanças do demônio* (The Devil's Doings, 1960), only two—"Razão de o Pai Natal ter barbas brancas" (The Reason Why Santa Claus Has a White Beard) and "A Comemoração" (Commemoration)—were kept unaltered. The others were either written or revised in Brazil. The seventeen short stories that make up *Novas andanças do demônio* (New Devil's Doings, 1966) and *Os Grão-Capitães* were written in either Assis or Araraquara. Some of the stories included in these collections, such as "Super Flumina Babylonis," "A Grã-Canária," and "Os amantes" (The Lovers), are true masterpieces of short fiction. Sena was fully aware of the difficulties of publishing *Os Grão-Capitães*. Extremely critical of military life, it could not be distributed in Portugal before the revolution.

While in Brazil, Sena wrote two one-act plays in March 1964: *A morte do Papa* (The Death of the Pope) and *O império do oriente* (The Empire of the Orient). He pointed out the relation between the texts and the military assumption of power in Brazil that year, attesting to how much the political situation had affected him. Rather than dedicating a lot of time to writing plays, Sena became involved with the people working in Brazilian theater.

During the 1960s he also maintained close contacts with Brazilian intelligentsia, some of whom he had known through reading or correspondence. His exchanges with poet Manuel Bandeira deserve special attention, as does his encounter with the concretist poets Augusto de Campos, Haroldo de Campos, and Décio Pignatari. Sena published his "asemic" (emphasizing images, or the unreadable) poems that evoke Afrodite Anadiômena, of the final part of *Metamorfoses,* in their journal *Invenção* (Invention).

In Brazil, Sena was involved in his most intense political activity. He could never have been so engaged openly in Portugal without running risks, which he could not afford to do while providing for his large family. Soon after his arrival in São Paulo, he joined the board of editors at the opposition newspaper *Portugal Democrático* (Democratic Portugal) where he published thirty-seven articles between November 1959 and October 1962. Most of these were signed, but some were anonymous or written under a pseudonym. Sena's collaboration on *Portugal Democrático,* published by a group of intellectuals who shared anti-Salazarist ideas, lent prestige and respectability to the paper. Fighting against Salazar from a distance, quixotic as it may seem to some, was still a form of connection with his native land. The Portuguese political police, Polícia Internacional de Defesa do Estado (PIDE, International and State Defense Police), maintained a dossier on Sena, with copies of his articles, and in January 1962 issued an order of arrest against him. In July of the same year, he was banned from entering Portuguese national territory. This ban was only lifted in 1968. In addition to this intense participation in *Portugal Democrático*, Sena was also involved in other similar political activities, such as the Portuguese Republican Center in São Paulo, where he often lectured.

The notion of homeland, closely linked to the concepts of pilgrimage, roots, and exclusion, constitutes an important aspect of Sena's poeticization of his personal experiences. Sena's relationship to his country was a complex, dichotomous one of love and hate; Portugal is often perceived in his works as the mother that forced him out of his home into a life of wandering and into many exiles. The title of one of his books of poetry, *Peregrinatio ad loca infecta,* captures well the result of the feeling. Sena was a citizen of the world, and images of his many travels appear in all of his works, which serve as witnesses to the chaotic historical moment of transformation in which he lived.

In spite of the physical distance between Sena and Portugal, his attention and activities remained focused on that country. Nonetheless, he also took an interest in the politics of his country of exile, of which he became a citizen in 1963. He followed Brazilian politics quite closely, but he did not take any conspicuous political stand. Many of his texts, however, reveal his close connection with the events that he witnessed in Brazil. He had arrived in the country when it was governed by Juscelino Kubitschek; Sena followed the rise and resignation of Jânio Quadros, as well as the rise of João Goulart; and he witnessed the military coup of 1964. This last event, for many reasons, including the threat to his own survival, disquieted him. The evolution of the dictatorial process only enhanced the anguish and sadness that he knew so well and that was further increased by the imprisonment and expulsion of several intellectuals and artists. As a consequence of this insecurity, Sena decided to leave Brazil. He accepted an invitation to be a visiting professor at the University of Wisconsin, Madison, in the United States. He moved there in October 1965 with Mécia and their children, two of whom had been born in Brazil.

The following year Sena was promoted to the rank of professor of Portuguese and Brazilian Literature and granted tenure. He plunged with characteristic intensity into the life of professor, scholar, and lecturer. He attended many conferences and meetings of professional societies and organizations. He also became a member of well-known American associations, such as the Hispanic Society and the Modern Languages Association. In 1968 he returned to Portugal for the first time since his departure for Brazil in 1959. From the late 1960s onward, he traveled regularly to Portugal

*Sena in 1947 (from Vasques,* Jorge de Sena: Uma ideia de teatro [1938–1971]), *1998; University Research Library, University of California, Los Angeles)*

and visited other European countries to attend conferences and give lectures. The trips that he took abroad while based in the United States brought him international renown as a writer and scholar.

Sena moved to the University of California at Santa Barbara in 1970 where he served as the chairman of the Departments of Portuguese and Brazilian Literature and of Comparative Literature. Two years later, he had the opportunity to travel to Angola, South Africa, and Mozambique. His wife affirmed that the visit to the Isle of Mozambique, where Camões had lived in misery, was "one of the most touching moments in his whole life." In 1974 Sena was named head of the Spanish and Portuguese department and of the Interdepartmental Program in Comparative Literature, posts that he held until his death. For his efforts in the diffusion of Portuguese culture, he was awarded the Order of Infante D. Henrique in Portugal in 1977. That same year he received the Italian Etna-Taormina Poetry

International Prize, and, invited by the president of Portugal, Ramalho Eanes, Sena delivered the renowned "Discurso da Guarda" (Speech on Vigilance) on 10 June, known as Camões's Day.

A year later Sena was dying of lung cancer. In a phone conversation with President Eanes three days before Sena passed away, the poet learned that he would receive the Order of Santiago de Espada. Sena died on 4 June 1978.

During his four decades of writing poetry, Sena participated in many aesthetic trends. His early books reveal an influence of Surrealism; he wrote asemic creations in *Quatro sonetos a Afrodite Anadiómena*; *Sequências* (Sequences, 1980) embodies his private experimentalism; and he wrote excellent classical poems of formal rigor and semantic depth. He was able, nonetheless, to establish his own style and build a solid body of works that has been, and continues to be, influential to various generations. In fact, critics such as Eduardo Prado Coelho describe him as a "figura titular" (a guarding figure), as Coelho writes in *A noite do mundo* (The Night of the World, 1988). Sena is someone, Coelho continues, who "condiciona, em níveis diversos, quase tudo o que a poesia portuguesa contemporânea considera e partilha" (conditions, in various levels, almost everything that contemporary Portuguese poetry considers and shares).

Several critics agree that the single unifying link among Jorge de Sena's multifaceted body of works is the figure of Camões. In his dialogue with the sixteenth-century poet, Sena's writings gain a dimension that is simultaneously one of deprivation and plenitude, which are sought by all who use words as instruments of expression. Like the image of Camões that he created, Sena "era um grande poeta, transformava em poesia tudo o que tocava mesmo a miséria, mesmo a amargura, mesmo o abandono de poesia" (was a great poet, transformed everything he touched into poetry, even misery, even bitterness, even the abandonment of poetry). These words communicate Sena's concept of metamorphosis, which in turn articulates the essence of this great poet.

**Letters:**

*Correspondência Jorge de Sena e José Régio,* edited by Mécia de Sena (Lisbon: Imprensa Nacional-Casa da Moeda, 1984).

**Bibliography:**

Jorge Fazenda Lourenço, "Bibliografia sobre Jorge de Sena (1942–1997)," *Boletim do Centro de Estudos Portugueses Jorge de Sena,* 13 (1998).

**References:**

Luis Fernando Adriano Carlos, *Fenomenologia do discurso poético* (Porto: Campo das Letras, 1999);

Eduardo Prado Coelho, "A poesia portuguesa contemporânea," in his *A noite do mundo* (Lisbon: Imprensa Nacional-Casa da Moeda, 1988), pp. 113–132;

Francisco Cota Fagundes, *In the Beginning There Was Jorge de Sena's Genesis: The Birth of a Writer* (Santa Barbara, Cal.: Bandanna Books, 1991);

Fagundes, *Metamorfoses do amor: Estudos sobre a ficção breve de Jorge de Sena* (Lisbon: Salamandra, 1999);

Fagundes, *A Poet's Way with Music: Humanism in Jorge de Sena's Poetry* (Providence, R.I.: Gávea-Brown, 1988);

Fagundes and Paula Gândara, eds., *Para emergir nascemos . . . estudos em rememoração de Jorge de Sena* (Lisbon: Salamandra, 2000);

Fagundes and José Ornelas, eds., *Jorge de Sena: O homem que sempre foi* (Lisbon: ICALP, 1992);

Eugénio Lisboa, ed., *Estudos sobre Jorge de Sena* (Lisbon: INCM, 1984);

Jorge Fazenda Lourenço, *O essencial sobre Jorge de Sena* (Lisbon: INCM, 1987);

Lourenço, *A poesia de Jorge de Sena: Testemunho, metamorfose, peregrinação* (Paris: Centre Culturel Calouste Gulbenkian, 1998);

Lourenço, ed., *Jorge de Sena–Antologia poética* (Porto: ASA, 1999);

Lourenço and Frederick G. Williams, eds., *Uma bibliografia cronológica de Jorge de Sena* (Lisbon: INCM, 1994);

Luciana Stegagno Picchio, ed., *Quaderni Portoghesi,* 13–14 (Pisa: Giardini, 1983);

Gilda Santos, ed., "Evocação de Jorge de Sena," *Boletim do SEPESP,* 6 (1995): 8–236;

Santos, ed., *Jorge de Sena em rotas entrecruzadas* (Lisbon: Cosmos, 1999);

José Augusto Seabra, ed., "Homenagem a Jorge de Sena," *Nova Renascença,* 32-33 (1988–1989);

Maria Alzira Seixo, ed., *O corpo e os signos: Ensaios sobre O físico prodigioso, de Jorge de Sena* (Lisbon: Comunicação, 1990);

Mécia de Sena, *Índices da poesia de Jorge de Sena* (Lisbon: Cotovia, 1990);

*O Tempo e o Modo,* special Sena issue, 59 (1968);

Eugénia Vasques, *Jorge de Sena: Uma ideia de teatro (1938–1971)* (Lisbon: Cosmos, 1998);

Frederick G. Williams and Harvey L. Sharrer, eds., *Studies on Jorge de Sena* (Santa Barbara, Cal.: Bandanna Books, 1981).

# Salette Tavares
*(31 March 1922 – 30 May 1994)*

Rui Torres
*University Fernando Pessoa, Porto*

BOOKS: *Aproximação do pensamento concreto de Gabriel Marcel* (Lisbon: Gráfica Boa Nova, 1948);
*Espelho cego* (Lisbon: Ática, 1957);
*Concerto em mi maior para clarinete e bateria* (Lisbon, 1961);
*14563 letras de Pedro Sete* (Lisbon: Fomento de Cultura, 1965);
*Quadrada* (Lisbon: Moraes, 1967);
*Lex icon* (Lisbon: Moraes, 1971);
*Menez* (Lisbon: Imprensa Nacional-Casa da Moeda, 1983);
*Obra poética (1957–1971)*, introduction by Luciana Stegagno Picchio (Lisbon: Imprensa Nacional-Casa da Moeda, 1992).

OTHER: "O lugar da estética na filosofia," in *Actas do I Congresso Nacional de Filosofia* (Lisbon: Revista de Filosofia, 1955);
"Três poemas espanhóis," in *Hidra*, edited by E. M. de Melo e Castro (Porto: ECMA, 1966), pp. 55–56;
"Os efes," in *Antologia da poesia concreta em Portugal*, edited by Melo e Castro and José Alberto Marques, Documenta Poética, no. 2 (Lisbon: Assírio & Alvim, 1973), pp. 122–124;
"Dois jardins Românticos de Sintra," in *Actas do Colóquio Estética do Romantismo em Portugal* (Lisbon: Grémio Literário, 1974);
"Comunicação de Salette Tavares," in *1º Congresso dos Escritores Portugueses 10/11 de Maio 1975* (Lisbon: APE, 1975), pp. 1–2;
"Brincar," in *Catálogo da Exposição Brincar* (Lisbon: Galeria Quadrum, 1984);
"Brincando brincando" and "Curriculum vitae," in *Poemografias: Perspectivas da poesia visual portuguesa*, edited by Fernando Aguiar and Silvestre Pestana, with photographs by Jorge Lopes (Lisbon: Ulmeiro, 1985), pp. 57–61, 262–268;
*José de Guimarães*, by Tavares and Gillo Dorfles (São Lourenço: Centro Cultural, 1985), pp. 11–15.

SELECTED PERIODICAL PUBLICATIONS–UNCOLLECTED: "Forma poética e tempo," *Brotéria*, 81 (1965): 40–63;
"Teoria da informação e Abraham Moles," *Brotéria*, 84 (1967): 152–173;
"Arquitectura, semiologia e mass média," *Brotéria*, 88 (1969): 196–220;
"A semântica do abstrato em Vieira da Silva," *Colóquio Artes*, 58 (1970): 30–37;
"Brincar, A propósito de Amélia Toledo," *Colóquio Artes*, 7 (1972): 31–34;
"Fragmento dum poema de Pedro Sete," *Colóquio/Letras*, 9 (1972): 54;
"Cesário, in disciplinada mente," *Colóquio/Letras*, 93 (1986): 95–96;
"Os olhos," *Colóquio/Letras*, 103 (1988): 61–64;
"Algumas questões de crítica de arte e de estética na sua relação," *Colóquio Artes*, 82 (1989): 42–49.

The work of poet Salette Tavares is extremely varied. Her theoretical articles employ tenets from schools of art and literature as diverse as information theory (to which her friend Abraham Moles introduced her), the new aesthetics of Wilhelm Worringer, and structuralism (particularly its impact upon architecture, painting, and sculpture). While Tavares, as a poet, was concerned with invention and innovation, she also developed in her verse a sense of vigilance and attention that situated her in the tradition of mid-twentieth-century self-reflexive poetics. Her works also illustrate a dislike for Romantic confessionalism. Her preference for wordplay, often achieved through irony and self-irony, suggests the influence of baroque poetics and aesthetics, which she admired and studied throughout her life. Other important influences on Tavares's works derive from French surrealism and twentieth-century Spanish poetry–mainly that of Federico García Lorca. Some central themes of her poetry include the importance of understanding relationships between people and objects, the musical nature of language, and the key role that music plays in language. These themes are made manifest by the special treatment of sound in her poems and her use of silence, which, as in contemporary music, is understood as a significant component determining rhythm. Noise, on the other hand, is expressed in Tavares's verse through the use of onomatopoeia.

Tavares was born Maria de La Salette Arraiano Tavares on 31 March 1922 in Mozambique–the birthplace of many Portuguese writers–when the African country was still a colony of Portugal. She was the daughter of Francisco Tavares Duarte and Guilhermina Amélia Arraiano Tavares. She refers to this period as the "maior privilégio da vida" (greatest privilege of my life). Yet, at the age of eleven she left the country with her parents and moved to Portugal, where the family chose Sintra as the place for their new home. The Romantic Gardens of Sintra exercised an important influence on Tavares throughout her life.

Tavares often associates her childhood and its "natural and permanent" activity of *brincar* (playing, or amusing oneself) to the discovery of language and identity. In "Brincar" (1984) she describes a child's interest in playing in terms of discovery and invention: "com poucos brinquedos, tudo era brinquedo, folhas, frutos, gafanhotos, terra, lata e até nada. E este nada é importantíssimo" (with few toys, everything became a toy, leaves, fruits, grasshoppers, soil, a tin and even nothing). This "nothing" is important because it allows the poet to find verse later on: "Bastava a palavra que se coisificava. Era tão fácil jogar com ela como jogar à bola" (The word becoming a thing was enough. Playing with it was as easy as playing with a ball).

Tavares's literary personality was marked early in her life by the literature courses that she audited from 1940 to 1941 with Vitorino Nemésio. Around this time, she also began her adventurous discovery of languages in some of Nemésio's lectures, as well as in the company of other intellectual figures, such as Carlos Queiróz. She enrolled at the University of Lisbon in 1943 to study history and philosophy. By the age of twenty-two she was participating in radical, vanguardist activities such as performance art. These experiences anticipated not only Tavares's own experimental and visual poetry but also, in both a Portuguese and worldwide context, the experimental generation that started in the late 1950s. Her interest in learning new ideas and methods led her to study Spanish under the philologist Manuel Albar and Spanish painting under Lafuente Ferrari and Camon Aznar. Tavares later incorporated aspects of these studies into the complex "fabric" of texts that make up most of her poetry.

In 1947 Tavares traveled to Switzerland, where she studied at the Basel Museum. She graduated the following year from the University of Lisbon and published her monograph, *Aproximação do pensamento concreto de Gabriel Marcel* (Approaches to the Concrete Thought of Gabriel Marcel, 1948), which may be considered the first book of Portuguese existentialist philosophy.

Tavares traveled to Paris in 1949. There she established contact with Marcel and Maurice Merleau-Ponty and took courses with important figures of the rising new aesthetic thought–Jeanne Delhomme, Jean Valle, and René Huyghe. These individuals encouraged her studies and developing interest in aesthetics and the theory of art. At the end of the year Tavares was both learning how to work with clay and writing her famous spatial poems–actually sculptures made of several different materials, including written poems, clay, wood, gold, and crystal.

On 2 August 1951 Tavares's daughter Miniña was born; on 27 October 1952 she had her second daughter, Saletinha. In 1953 she started experimenting with pottery. In 1955 she participated in the Philosophy Congress of Braga, where she delivered a paper on aesthetics and created a small scandal: philosophers at the time did not accept the integration of aesthetics into the study of philosophy, which was the subject of Tavares's presentation. On 31 December 1956 a son, Francisco de Assis, was born. The next year Tavares began work on her first book of poems, *Espelho cego* (Blind Mirror), published in 1957. This book represents Tavares's search for the themes that she expanded later in her work and presents a poet who is quite refined in the art of parody. It starts with a dedication to "ao mar onde colhi o sal do meu tormento" (the sea where I harvested the salt of my torment) and reveals some of the experimental techniques that subsequently characterized her work. Her ironic challenge of the literary canon–one of the most important features of Tavares's poetry–is particularly noticeable in the division of the book into three parts, which are prefaced by a "Soneto pateta" (literally, a silly sonnet) that reflects the importance of playfulness in her work. Showing links to concrete poetry, *Espelho cego* reveals Tavares's (and the concrete poets') belief that the work of the writer is no longer related to systems of traditional communication but has initiated a focus specifically on language and its materiality. She pursues this focus by experimenting with spatial organization, techniques that were developed later by visual and concrete poets. *Espelho cego,* in some of its more serious moments, engages the reader to notice the tension between words and things in space and time, as the Brazilian poet Augusto de Campos later did in his "Plano-pilôto para poesia concreta" (Pilot-Plan for Concrete Poetry, published in the journal *Noigrandes,* 1958) and as James Joyce had done earlier through his invented words in works such as *Finnegans Wake* (1939). These poets attempted the writing of verse that appealed to the senses in terms of a synthesis of the verbal, the vocal, and the visual.

In 1958, as proof of her intellectual eclecticism, Tavares translated Blaise Pascal's *Pensées de M. Pascal sur la religion et sur quelques autres sujets, qui ont esté trouvées après sa mort parmy ses papiers* (1669; translated as *Monsieur Pascall's Thoughts, Meditations, and Prayers Touching Matters Moral and Divine*, 1688) and Georges Sadoul's *Les merveilles du cinema* (The Marvels of Cinema, 1957). In 1959 she received an important scholarship from the Calouste Gulbenkian Foundation and used it to fund graduate studies in aesthetics in France with Mikel Dufrenne and in Italy with Gillo Dorfles. During this period she wrote *Concerto em mi maior para clarinete e bateria* (Concert in E minor for Clarinet and Drums, 1961), the title of which acknowledges the importance of music in her poetry. It also indicates the way in which her poems resist boundaries imposed by genre. *Concerto em mi maior para clarinete e bateria* is divided into different *andamentos*, or movements—specifically, *Andamento alegro ma non troppo, Andamento tempo giusto*, and *Andamento allegro con fuoco*.

In 1961 Tavares wrote *Quadrada* (the feminine form of the Portuguese word for "square"); it was published six years later. By that time she had contracted a serious illness. Nevertheless, she was writing at her fastest pace during this period. Between 1961 and 1963 she completed *Quadrada* and *14563 Letras de Pedro Sete* (14,563 of Pedro Sete's Letters, 1965).

Tavares's ability to rewrite tradition associates her with the generation of experimental poets that was prevalent at the time in world literature and in Portuguese letters, in particular. She was an active member of the movement Po. Ex (short for Poesia Experimental), which allowed her to share her ideas with others who were addressing the poetics of word disintegration in verse forms. She participated in many of the happenings and publications that took place in Portugal in the early 1960s, including a series of exhibitions that reached Spain, Italy, France, and the United States. Tavares's graphic and spatial poetry was rendered not only by typographers but also by potters, weavers, and goldsmiths.

Tavares postulates a noninstrumental conception of language and poetry. For her, form and content are intimately connected. If content changes with the reader's altering interpretation of the world, so, too, does form. For this reason some of her spatial poems have different configurations on repeated publication. One example is her well-known "Aranha" (Spider), a poem laid out in the form of a spider. Tavares later developed this poem into a group of more-complex spiders, and titled it "Borboleta de aranhas" (Butterfly of Spiders) and then into "Aranhão" (Big Spider). A matrix that evolves and is transformed, the text communicates the idea that change is inevitable and universal.

*Paperback cover for Salette Tavares's 1971 collection of experimental poetry (Young Research Library, University of California, Los Angeles)*

In 1964 Tavares traveled to New York City, where she visited most of the museums with Frank O'Hara as her guide. She also used this trip to study modern architecture with Philip Johnson and to visit many private collections. She moved on to Philadelphia, where she viewed some of the paintings of Marcel Duchamp. This encounter was an important moment for Tavares's maturity; she recognized Duchamp as the main influence in all of her work—the visual and spatial poems, as well as the traditional verses. She then went to Chicago to study the architectural landmarks of that city.

Tavares taught aesthetics at the National Society for the Study of Arts in Lisbon in 1965. She intended to publish her lectures as a book titled "A dialética das formas" (The Dialectics of Forms), but in 1972 the publisher Livros Horizonte rejected the work. Excerpts from the lectures were published in the journal *Brotéria* as "Forma poética e tempo" (1965), "Teoria da informação e Abraham Moles" (1967), and "Arquitectura, semiologia e mass média" (1969). During the late 1960s

Tavares, still struggling with illness, underwent a critical surgical procedure and afterward suffered from depression. She nonetheless managed to take part with her friends in the student demonstrations of May 1968 in Paris.

In 1969–1970 Tavares devoted most of her time to writing *Lex icon* (1971). She also finished two more book-length works, "O livro do soporífero" (The Book of the Soporiferous) and "O fazer da mão" (The Making of the Hand); they appeared in her *Obra poética (1957–1971)* (Poetic Works, 1992). *Lex icon* is the result of her study of the arts, structuralism, and information theory. In this work Tavares puts into practice her 1965 lectures on aesthetics. The book opens with a dedication that expresses her notion on the informational value of silence: "Discretamente dedico a X alguém / da minha adolescência, / que aXei, / numa antiga casa / secretamente feXada na gaveta" (Carefully dedicated to X someone / from my adolescence, / that I have found / in an old house / secretly locked in the drawer). Here, as in the other poems of the book, Tavares undertakes the task of providing words–and specific characters of words–with a value that otherwise would go unidentified. She explains the important role of sounds themselves as opposed to the transcription of them. In the rest of the lyrics in *Lex icon* she uses the names of everyday objects as titles: "O sapato" (The Shoe), "O pó" (The Dust), "O talher" (Cutlery), "O bule" (The Teapot), "O lixo" (The Garbage), "A toalha" (The Towel), "O copo" (The Glass), "Guardanapos" (Napkins), and "O pires" (Saucer). By questioning the linguistic value of the words for these objects, Tavares examines their ontological status. Furthermore, she tries to expose in these names a magical primary formula that, she apparently believes, may have been lost over time with usage.

These poems also cast into question the polarized dichotomy of form and content by approximating the sound of the word to the concept associated with it. Tavares understood art as a daily construct, a human creation through which to escape daily routines, and an act of re-creation (as well as recreation), rather than a mimetic representation of the world. Furthermore, for her an object is never simply an object; it always carries with it the experience of the reader. She argues that one should take into account that everything associated with a cupboard (as in the poem "O louceiro" [The Cupboard]), although it does not have a sound of its own, is related to noise.

*Lex icon* condenses Tavares's inquiry into the difference between triviality and originality, as well as into the relationship between form and content. The work is divided into three parts. The first two are made up of single poems; "Lex" is composed of "As lições" (The Lessons) and "Icon" is made up of "Os objectos" (The Objects). The third part, "Lex icon," includes twenty-six poems.

"Lex" points to the fact that human reality is inevitably created through language and, therefore, through a constructed law–that is, through culture. Tavares, however, inverts the traditional values of linguistics that, after the work of Swiss linguist Ferdinand de Saussure, stress the arbitrariness of language. Initially, the inversions that she offered were the result of the artist's role in the world. She had written in *Espelho cego* that the silence of the poet is a "Silêncio mudo, cerrado, feroz, / silêncio nascimento que se fez originalmente / Contra" (Mute, gloomy, fierce silence, / silence beginning that was originally made / Against), and in "As lições" revolt is one vital inversion of taught values: "Ensinaram-me a falar / aprendi a escrever. / Ensinaram-me a escrever / aprendi a falar" (They taught me to talk / I learned to write. / They taught me to write / I learned to talk). Of all the inversions proposed by Tavares, one of them presents an important indication for the understanding of the universe in which she writes: "Ensinaram-me a ler / aprendi a ver" (They taught me to read / I learned to see). Here the reader understands that, for Tavares, the verbal icon is essentially visual, and therefore the image is central to the understanding of any object. From here, to move to the realm of the image–the *icon* of the title–is to move to the fabrication of reality. Poetry is the spiritual space of creation, inscribed in an apparently profane world that finally becomes sacred–which is why the poem "Os objectos" insists, "Fabricar é o mais religioso serviço do homem. / A fábrica é uma igreja de pé. / Os produtos são salmos para uso diário / dos ofícios permanentes da fé" (To create is the most religious duty of human beings. / The factory is like a standing church. / The products are psalms for our daily use / in the permanent crafts of faith).

Regaining the sacred significance of human work implies an inversion of the values on which consumer society is founded, given that religious space turns into multiple manifestations of the same alienation. In *Lex icon*, as in many of Tavares's poems, the house is the phenomenological space in which the lessons occur, and she guides the reader through an initiation ceremony in which the secret and the often complex relations between objects and their names are fully revealed. For Tavares, this faith is a true one but only in that it denotes a faith in poetry–in the correspondence between words and things. The verse inaugurates a poetics of everyday life, while her playful attention to the relationship between the object and the word obscures the arbitrary bond between signifier and signified. As she states in "Algumas questões de crítica de arte e de estética na sua relação" (Some Questions of Art Criticism, Aesthetics, and Their Relation, 1989), under the conditions of a technological society liberation implies the "activa penetração poética em todos os planos da vida humana ao nível do quotidiano" (active poetic penetration in every realm of human life at the level of our daily life). The objects of daily routines become in this sense poetic objects. Poems such as "O sapato" are liturgical, and they include reading instructions for the participation of one officer and several devotees. In the poem "O pires" the poet expresses her beliefs in the following manner: "Dêem-me palavras que eu descobrirei as coisas / dêem-me coisas que eu descobrirei as palavras. / Entre a palavra e a coisa o intervalo é nenhum / palavra ou coisa a eloquência pertence-lhes: / à palavra porque diz a coisa / à coisa porque diz a palavra" (Give me words and I will discover the things / give me things and I will find out the words. / Between the word and the thing there is no interval / word or thing the fluency belongs to them: / to the word because it says the thing / to the thing because it says the word).

In London in 1972 physicians discovered that Tavares was being treated with the wrong medicine. She lost her ability to read for the next six years. She responded to this situation by saying that her memory assisted her: she knew many poems by heart. These circumstances did not impede her from traveling to Germany to study the baroque and rococo styles of the region. In 1974 she achieved international recognition when she was appointed president of the International Association of Art Critics. She began an important campaign for the protection of the cultural heritage of the nation, successfully requesting that the Portuguese government create an institute for the preservation of national art treasures. The institute, however, did not receive funding until many years later.

Tavares returned to London in 1976 and discovered that the Portuguese doctors had, for the second time, given her the wrong medication. For the next three years she was not able to leave her bed. In 1978 she began writing and reading again. By this time she was working on a book to be titled "Irrar" (an intentional misspelling of *errar*, to make a mistake), which remains unpublished. She also participated as a poet in the Bienale of Venice and in the exhibit "Scriptura 78," and in 1979 she had a retrospective of her works in the Galeria Quadrum, titled "Brincar." In 1981 she wrote the poems "Do corpo" (From the Body) and "Histórias minúsculas" (Minuscule Stories), which remain unpublished. In 1983 Tavares published *Menez,* the pseudonym of the painter Maria Ines Ribeiro da Fonseca; the next year she wrote a book about the Romantic Gardens of Sintra, which has not been published. She also traveled to Germany, Italy, and Spain. In Barcelona she discovered Antonio Gaudi's architecture.

Salette Tavares taught and lectured on art until her death on 30 May 1994. She spent most of her life as a writer and as a thinker in a clear quest for originality and creativity. Most of her works were not published, but the poems that did appear in print reveal a highly creative and innovative artist. They focus on presenting the old and the ordinary in new ways, since she contrasts what things seem to be with what they seem to lose. Her wordplay, often ironic, created a new set of possibilities, which most people were not prepared to accept. As she says of closets and cabinets, "Os armários estão sempre / longamente calados / mas grávidos de som. / São verdadeiras armárias" (Cupboards are always / calmly silent / but pregnant with sound).

Her poems represent cupboards—lines in which everything is pregnant with possibilities, which conformity does not allow the reader to see. The practical side of language obscures its mysticism and the magical realm of words. Tavares nevertheless carries on, through her works, in a peculiar place recognized as language. As she declared in her epigraph to *Quadrada*: "Toma o ouro que o poeta dá" (Accept the gold that the poet presents).

**References:**

Irina Bajini, "Salette Tavares e a poesia portuguesa de vanguarda," *Colóquio/Letras,* 132–133 (1994): 112–122;

António Ramos Rosa, "Lex Icon," *Colóquio/Letras,* 9 (1972): 79–80.

# Miguel Torga
## (Adolfo Correia da Rocha)
*(12 August 1907 - 17 January 1995)*

Maria do Amparo Tavares Maleval
*Universidade do Estado do Rio de Janeiro*

BOOKS: *Ansiedade,* as Adolfo Rocha (Coimbra: Imprensa Academica, 1928);

*Rampa,* as Rocha (Coimbra: Presença, 1930);

*Pão ázimo,* as Rocha (Coimbra: Atlântida, 1931);

*Tributo,* as Rocha (Coimbra: Atlântida, 1931);

*Abismo,* as Rocha (Coimbra: Atlântida, 1932);

*A terceira voz* (Coimbra: Atlântida, 1934);

*O outro livro de Job* (Coimbra: Atlântida, 1936);

*A criação do mundo,* 5 volumes (Coimbra: Atlântida, 1937–1981)–comprises volume 1, *Os dois primeiros dias* (1937), translated by Ivana Rangel-Carlsen as *The Creation of the World: The First and Second Day* (Manchester, U.K.: Carcanet, 1996); volume 2, *O terceiro dia* (1938); volume 3, *O quarto dia* (1939); volume 4, *O quinto dia* (1974); and volume 5, *O sexto dia* (1981);

*Bichos* (Coimbra: Atlântida, 1940; enlarged, 1941; revised, 1943; revised, Coimbra: Edição do Autor, 1970); translated by Denis Brass as *Farrusco the Blackbird and Other Stories from the Portuguese* (London: Allen & Unwin, 1950; New York: Art, 1951);

*Diário* (16 volumes, Coimbra: Edição do Autor, 1941–1977; enlarged, 4 volumes, 1983–1993);

*Teatro: Terra firme: Mar* (Coimbra: Atlântida, 1941);

*Montanha* (Coimbra: Coimbra Editora, 1941); republished as *Contos da montanha* (Rio de Janeiro: Pongetti, 1955; revised and enlarged, Coimbra, 1969); translated by Rangel-Carlsen as *Tales from the Mountain* (Fort Bragg, Cal.: Q. E. D., 1991);

*Um reino maravilhoso–Trás-os-Montes: Paulo Quintela um poeta de Trás-os-Montes. Conferências* (Coimbra: Atlântida, 1941);

*Rua* (Coimbra: Atlântida, 1942);

*Lamentação* (Coimbra: Atlântida, 1943);

*O Senhor Ventura* (Coimbra: Atlântida, 1943);

*O Porto* (Coimbra: Atlântida, 1944);

*Libertação* (Coimbra: Coimbra Editora, 1944);

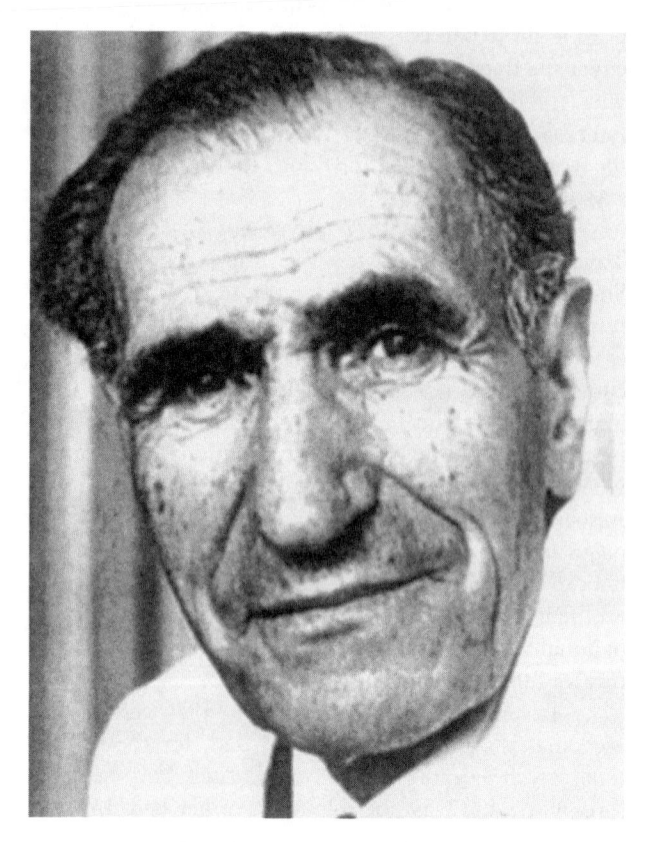

*Miguel Torga (Adolfo Correia da Rocha) (from Nuno Júdice,* Portugal, língua e cultura, *1992; Lauinger Library, Georgetown University)*

*Novos contos da montanha* (Coimbra: Coimbra Editora, 1944);

*Vindima* (Coimbra: Coimbra Editora, 1945);

*Odes* (Coimbra: Coimbra Editora, 1946; revised and enlarged, 1951);

*Sinfonia* (Coimbra: Coimbra Editora, 1947);

*Nihil Sibi* (Coimbra: Coimbra Editora, 1948);

*O paraíso* (Coimbra: Edição do Autor, 1949);

*Cânticos do homem* (Coimbra: Edição do Autor, 1950);

*Portugal* (Coimbra: Coimbra Editora, 1950);

*Pedras lavradas* (Coimbra: Coimbra Editora, 1951);

*Alguns poemas ibéricos* (Coimbra: Coimbra Editora, 1952); revised as *Poemas ibéricos* (Coimbra: Coimbra Editora, 1965);

*Penas do purgatório* (Coimbra: Coimbra Editora, 1954; enlarged, 1954);

*Traço de união* (Coimbra: Edição do Autor, 1955);

*Orfeu rebelde* (Coimbra: Coimbra Editora, 1958; revised, 1970);

*Câmara ardente* (Coimbra: Coimbra Editora, 1962);

*Pena de morte: Centenário da abolição da pena de morte em Portugal* (Coimbra: Coimbra Editora, 1967);

*Fogo preso* (Coimbra: Coimbra Editora, 1976);

*Antologia poética* (Coimbra: Coimbra Editora, 1982);

*Camões* (Coimbra: Coimbra Editora, 1987);

*Poesia completa* (Lisbon: Publicações Dom Quixote, 2000).

**Editions:** *A criação do mundo* (Coimbra: M. Torga, 1991);

*Diário I–VIII* (Coimbra: Graf. de Coimbra, 1995);

*Diário IX–XVI* (Coimbra: Graf. de Coimbra, 1995);

*Teatro* (Lisbon: Dom Quixote, 2001).

**Editions in English:** *Tales and More Tales from the Mountain,* translated by Ivana Rangel-Carlsen (Manchester, U.K.: Carcanet, 1995);

*The Creation of the World,* translated by Rangel-Carlsen and Patricia Odber de Baubeta (Manchester, U.K.: Carcanet, 2000).

Miguel Torga's vast literary production is characterized by a humanist portrayal of the land and the people of Portugal. Although he was not directly involved in politics, he denounced all types of human oppression. He focused specifically on the tyrannical dictatorship of António de Oliveira Salazar, who violated human rights in Portugal for more than forty years, from 1926 to 1974. A contemporary of two major European upheavals–the Spanish Civil War and World War II–Torga was a staunch defender of human rights. His deep concern with these violent conflicts appears in some of his works, especially the multivolume *Diário* (Diary, 1941–1993). Although not officially linked to neorealism, which emerged in Portuguese literature in the 1940s, his work reveals certain characteristics of that trend, such as the denouncement of social injustices. He nonetheless maintained a distance from other literary vanguard movements of the epoch, including Surrealism. Torga produced a body of work marked by a sense of authenticity, a treatment of universal issues through an extremely personal style, and a constant desire to improve (as evidenced by the many rewritings and editions of his short stories and poetry). The subject matter of his work, conveyed in his typically intimate style, remains uniform even after the Revolução dos Cravos (The Carnation Revolution) of 1974, when the Salazar dictatorship fell and writers could create with more freedom of expression.

Torga was born Adolfo Correia da Rocha on 12 August 1907 in São Martinho de Anta, in the region of Trás-os-Montes, in northeastern Portugal, to Francisco Correia Rocha and Maria da Conceição de Barros Rocha. The small villages in the rocky terrain of this region inspired the settings of several of his works. Torga did not limit himself simply to a regionalist portrayal, however, but used the region rather as a real location with which to describe in a symbolic way the universal human condition.

As a boy, Rocha did his elementary studies in the local school of São Martinho de Anta. Yet, the financial situation of the family obliged his mother to remove him from school after the fourth grade so that he could work as a servant in Porto. In 1919, in an attempt to help his son out of poverty, his father insisted that Rocha enter Lamego Seminary for a year to study for the priesthood. While studying at the seminary he performed community service. His experiences are reflected in his writings but with a personal interpretation that rejects the rigid law of the Old Testament and the notion of a vengeful God. The sense of social justice and attacks on oppression that characterize his works derived from these years.

In 1920, after failing to live up to his father's expectations of becoming a priest, Rocha was sent to Brazil, where he worked on his uncle José's farm in the state of Minas Gerais. He toiled at various jobs in Brazil: he cleaned the city square, delivered mail by horseback, worked on a coffee plantation, and trapped poisonous snakes to milk for their venom, which he sold to the Butantan Institute in São Paulo.

In 1924 Rocha attended the Gymnasium Leopoldinense in the city of Leopoldina, in Minas Gerais. In 1925, as a reward for five years of work on the farm, his uncle gave him the choice of working in a store in Rio de Janeiro or continuing his studies. Rocha decided to return to Portugal to study. With financial backing from his uncle, Rocha finished high school in three years and then enrolled in medical school at the University of Coimbra.

Rocha published his first poetry volume, *Ansiedade* (Anxiety), in 1928 but later withdrew the book from the market because he did not like it. Between 1929 and 1930 he collaborated on *Presença* (Presence), a journal created in 1927 by José Régio, Branquinho da Fonseca, and João Gaspar Simões as a vehicle for the aesthetic and ideological ideals of the movement known as *Presencismo.* In various issues of *Presença* Torga published the poems "Altitudes" (Altitudes), "Baloiço" (Sway), "Inercia" (Inertia), "Remendo" (Patch), "Balada da Morger" (Ballad of

*Torga in 1918 (from Jesús Herrero,* Miguel Torga, poetica ibérico, *1979; Thomas Cooper Library, University of South Carolina)*

Morger), and "Compenetração" (Persuasion), as well as the prose piece "O caminho do meio" (The Middle Road).

The writers of the *Presença* group rejected academicism and advocated a new critical attitude toward art. They favored the individual over the collective, the psychological over the social, and emotion over reason. Although the group had a decisive impact on Rocha's literary formation, he–along with Fonseca and Edmundo de Bittencourt–left the movement in 1930. In a letter that the three wrote to Régio and Somões, they criticized the group's dogmatic character and its repression of the individual artist's original idea.

Still, in 1930 Rocha and Fonseca edited the only issue of the magazine *Sinal* (Signal), which consisted of poems and short stories by Rocha, as well as some texts by Fonseca that were co-signed with António Madeira. Before leaving the *Presença* project, Rocha had published another book of poems, *Rampa* (Ramp, 1930), a copy of which he sent to the poet Fernando Pessoa. Although Pessoa apparently liked *Rampa,* he suggested that Rocha undertake a larger work in which to develop a rationalization of his sensibilities. Rocha published his next three books in editions that he personally subsidized–the prose work *Pão ázimo* (Unleavened Bread, 1931) and two books of poetry, *Tributo* (Tribute, 1931) and *Abismo* (Abyss, 1932). In 1933 he graduated from medical school, returned to São Martinho de Anta, in Trás-os-Montes, and began working in a clinic in Vila Nova de Miranda do Corvo.

With the publication of *A terceira voz* (The Third Voice) in 1934 Rocha first used the pen name Miguel Torga–a pseudonym that carries special significance, as it reflects certain themes of his writing, such as the homeland and Iberian unity. A word capturing the telluric character of his works, *torga* is a type of heather that grows wild in the rocky soil of Trás-os-Montes. The root of the plant, which has white or purple flowers, is used to make charcoal. In addition, Torga chose the name Miguel as a tribute to two important figures, the Spanish writers Miguel de Cervantes and Miguel de Unamuno. It also refers to the archangel Michael, to whom Catholic liturgy attributes the triple role of warrior, intercessor, and guide of the church. One can also link the name Miguel to Torga's almost constant use of biblical stories and themes in his works.

Torga published *O outro livro de Job* (The Other Book of Job) in 1936. The liturgical tone and the titles of the poems, such as "O vos omnes" (O You People), "Tantum ergo" (a reference to a famous stanza of the hymn, *Pange Lingua* [Sing My Tongue]), "De profundis" (Out of the Depths), "Livro de horas" (The Book of Hours), and "O Lázaro" (Lazarus), reveal the influence of the Bible. In 1936 Torga and Albano Nogueira founded the journal *Manifesto* (Manifest), on which many important writers collaborated: Afonso Duarte, Álvaro Salema, Madeira, Bento de Jesus Caraça, Carlos Sinde (pseudonym of Martins de Carvalho), Fernando Lopes Graça, Joquim Namorado, Paulo Quintela Sílvio Lima, and Vitório Nemésio. The editor's objective was the creation of a literary humanism that would react against the aestheticism and individualism of *Presença*. *Manifesto* ceased publication after five issues because of problems of censorship by the Salazar government. The fifth issue consisted of only Torga's work, including poems that later appeared in his *Alguns poemas ibéricos* (Some Iberian Poems, 1952).

By the mid to late 1930s Salazar had consolidated the power of the Estado Novo (New State), a name created in 1930 to designate the new political regime. Salazar ran the country with a firm hand through his police force (PIDE, or Polícia Internacional e de Defesa do Estado [International and State Defense Police]). Artists and writers were particularly affected by the laws that imposed censorship and restricted freedom of expression. In addition, the Spanish Civil War broke out in 1936, and as a defender of human rights Torga was disturbed by the events of this struggle. He regretted not only the violence of the conflict and the destruction of democracy in Spain but also its divisive effect on the people of the Iberian Peninsula. His strong impressions of the war emerge in some of the books of *A criação do mundo* (published in five volumes, 1937–1981; translated as *The Creation of the World*, 2000), in many pages of his *Diário*, and in the story "O regresso" (The Return), which appeared in *Novos contos da montanha* (New Stories of the Mountains, 1944). He dedicated one of the poems in *Alguns poemas ibéricos* to the Spanish poet Federico García Lorca, who was killed in August 1936 by General Francisco Franco's police. In another poem he universalizes Dolores Ibarrun's heroic actions during the siege of Madrid.

In 1937 Torga published the first volume of his autobiographical novel *A criação do mundo*, titled *Os dois primeiros dias* (translated as *The Creation of the World: The First and Second Day*, 1996). The work describes his childhood in a small village in Trás-os-Montes and his adolescence in Brazil. That same year he finished his specialization in otolaryngology, and in December he began a trip to Spain, France, Belgium, and Italy. He returned home in January 1938 and published *O terceiro dia* (The Third Day, 1938) of *A criação do mundo*, in which he talks about his return to Portugal from Brazil, his studies in medical school, and his introduction to literature.

Torga met his future wife, Andrée Crabbé, in 1939 at the home of Nemésio. Although he was practicing medicine in Leiria at the time, he spent his weekends in Coimbra with intellectuals such as Nemésio, Paulo Quintela, Martins de Carvalho, and António de Souza. Nemésio had founded the *Revista de Portugal* (Magazine of Portugal) on which Torga collaborated, in 1937. Crabbé had studied with Nemésio in Brussels and was in Portugal for a summer course at the University of Coimbra.

In 1939 Torga also published *O quarto dia* (The Fourth Day), the third volume of his *A criação do mundo*, which was, at the time, one of the few instances of a Portuguese writer addressing the devastation of the Spanish Civil War. Because of Torga's criticism of the Franco dictatorship in *O quarto dia*, the Salazar government seized copies of the book, and Torga was put under arrest. His friends provided tremendous moral support to him during his three-month stay at the Aljube prison in Lisbon. While in jail Torga wrote the sonnet "Pietá" on Christmas Day 1939 and the poem "Ariane" on New Year's Day 1940. On 1 February he composed the poem "Claridade" (Clarity). All three poems, published in volume one of *Diário* in 1941, vividly depict his sense of imprisonment and desire for freedom.

On 27 July Torga and Crabbé were married. They lived in Coimbra in a small house visited by many artists, intellectuals, and politicians–including Brazilian poet Ribeiro Couto and Portuguese poet Eugênio de Andrade. Torga opened an office at the Largo da Portagem, where he practiced medicine for more than fifty years. Devoting his spare time to writing, he published *Bichos* (Animals, 1940), which established him as one of the best storytellers in the Portuguese language. In some of the stories of *Bichos*, which Torga calls a "pequena Arca de Noé" (small Noah's Ark), the characters are animals endowed with the human quality of thought. Some of the pieces present human characters that have no ability to think reflectively. They are victims of the social and political context of the time. This degradation of the human being is seen in the story "Madalena," in which an unmarried woman goes to such extremes as to hide the fact that she is pregnant, and her baby dies. The story "Jesus," however, reveals a warmth and humanity not present in the other stories. Jesus is seen as foreign to the social and political atmosphere; he is an innocent who is moved by love. Torga often uses the figure of Jesus, rather than the image of a vengeful God, in his works. *Bichos* ends with "Vicente," a story of autobiographical elements that reveals Torga's indignation and rebellion against oppression. Vicente is the raven who, "inconformado com o procedimento de Deus" (unhappy with God's procedure), leaves the ark of the cowardly Noah in search of land, freedom, and dignity. The final scene of the story is dramatic in that Vicente, perched on the top of a mountain–the last dry spot on Earth–stubbornly fights against divine power. Years after the publication of *Bichos*, Torga spoke about Vicente in volume six of his *Diário* (1953) and suggested that the poet must act like the raven and fight against tyranny.

The Portuguese government organized the famous Exposition of the Portuguese World in 1940. This event brought together the best architects, artists, and decorators of Portugal for the purpose of proposing a new interpretation of the past, mainly in an effort to provide some orientation toward the present and future of the country. The program, which focused on family, religion, and the state, coincided with the artistic movement known as neorealism. Neorealist writers denounced social injustices and advocated for class rights for the poor. The movement also opposed the psychological subjectivity of the *Presença* writers. Although Torga remained quite independent of literary schools and trends, his own fundamental notion of art as a means of denouncing social ills shares, nonetheless, similarities with certain tenets of neorealism. For example, in *Bichos*, his most revised work, and in other publi-

*Torga in 1981 (from Fernão de Magalhães Gonçalves,* Ser e ler Miguel Torga, *1986; Thomas Cooper Library, University of South Carolina)*

cations he attacks the rigidity of any social system that imposes false, or artificial, codes of conduct.

Torga released the first volume of his *Diário* in 1941 and published fifteen more volumes until 1993, two years before his death. *Diário* is a monumental autobiographical series that registers not only occurrences in Torga's daily life but also his most intimate feelings, thoughts, speeches, and poems. Also in 1941 he published a volume comprising two plays, *Teatro: Terra firme: Mar,* in which he uses the parable of the prodigal son who is awaited, for many tortuous years, by his parents and fiancée. In one of the plays, however, he who abandons the land for the sea never returns. In *Mar* (Sea) the character who is dominant–because of his imagination and stories–dies in the end, while fishing in the ocean, after saying he had finally seen a mermaid. His friends interpret his death as an abduction by the mermaid.

In 1941 Torga also published a book of stories, *Montanha* (Mountain), which the Salazar regime censored. It was later released in Rio de Janeiro in 1955 as *Contos da montanha* (translated as *Tales from the Mountain,* 1991). The work was circulated illegally in Portugal and officially published in Coimbra only in 1969. *Montanha* is a portrait of the mountain people and their communities, myths, and beliefs. The narrator presents the values and primitive existence of the characters through their regional speech, as he identifies with their suffering and fatalistic view of life. An existential sense of the tragic emerges in stories such as "Maria Lionça."

From 1942 to 1945, during World War II, Torga continued his literary production, writing various types of works. Some of his writings of that time reveal an inner conflict, the result of not participating in the war on the side of the democratic forces. In 1942 he published *Rua* (Street), a volume of stories about people in urban settings, which are sometimes identified specifically as Coimbra, Leiria, Lisbon, and Porto. The common themes of Torga's work–the conflict between the oppressed and the oppressors and the struggle between the individual and the authority to which he is subservient–are expressed in these stories through the characters' relationships toward their work.

Torga published the book of poems *Lamentação* (Lament), the second volume of his *Diário,* and the novel *O Senhor Ventura* (Mr. Ventura) in 1943. In the novel he depicts the adventures of a strong and courageous character from the Alentejo region who travels around the world. The next year, Torga published another volume of poetry, *Libertação* (Liberation), and the short-story collection *Novos contos da montanha,* one of his most popular books in Portugal. In these stories he places human beings in the same sphere as animals, plants, and the land and contrasts social law and natural law in the process. Through the characters and situations of the individual narratives he revalidates a mythical way of thinking and affirms that the passive balance between man and the land is permanence and truth.

In February 1944 Torga read the text of his "O porto" (published in *O Porto* in 1944) at a meeting of the Clube dos Fenianos Portuguenses, and in November he gave a lecture on the writer Eça de Queirós at the Ateneu Comercial of Porto. The lecture, "Eça de Queiroz–um problema de consciência" (Eça de Queirós: A Problem of Conscience), was eventually published in the volume *Portugal* (1950). Torga's next novel, *Vindima* (Vintage), appeared in 1945. A work of neorealist characteristics, it denounces the exploitation, poverty, hunger, and illiteracy of the Portuguese. When the owner of a vineyard attempts to pay his workers less than market price for their vines, they rebel, and the owner has to give in to their demands for a fair price. Yet, even with this victory, they return to their home, Penaguião, in the mountains, where life is much worse. The small victory of the workers was important, but, as Torga suggests, it did not create the transformation of a revolution.

In 1946 Torga published *Odes* and the third volume of his *Diário*. He sent a copy of *Diário* to the Brazilian poet Manuel Bandeira, who praised its critical and lyrical tone. In 1947 Torga's wife—by then known as Andrée Rocha and working as a professor at the Faculdade de Letras at the University of Lisbon—was fired, on Salazar's orders, from her position. That same year Torga's dramatic poem "Sinfonia" (Symphony) was published in a book by the same title.

Torga's mother died in 1948. He captured their strong and tender ties in the dramatic poem "Mãe" (Mother), written on 1 July 1948 (it appeared in the fourth volume of *Diário* in 1949). The poem expresses a son's pain as he views his mother's corpse and renders his reflections on death a universal experience. Also in 1948 Torga attempted to publish the magazine *Rebate* (Attack), but government censorship prohibited the progress of the project. The prose drama *O paraíso* (Paradise), as well as another installment of *Diário*, appeared the following year.

*Cânticos do homem* (Man's Chant) came out in 1950. Together with *Orfeu rebelde* (Rebel Orpheus, 1958), the book characterizes another phase of Torga's work, seen mainly in the poems "Ar Livre" (Open Air), "Dies Irae" (Day of Wrath, also published in a booklet of poems, *Notícias do bloqueio*, that had been written against the Salazar regime), and "Hossana" (first published in *Cântico do Homem*). During this period he wrote some biographical notes in which he describes himself as being of medium height and quite thin. He wanted to be a painter, and he even painted a self-portrait, which he threw into the sea. He went to the movies often, and he enjoyed watching cartoons. His favorite painters were Pablo Picasso, David Alfaro Siqueiros, José Clemente Orozco, and Cândido Portinari. He also admired the Brazilian writers Euclides da Cunha and Joaquim Maria Machado de Assis, and he was fond of music—particularly that of Johann Sebastian Bach. Among the authors he most admired were Fyodor Dostoevsky, Marcel Proust, Herman Melville, Cervantes, and Unamuno. He enjoyed solitude, walks in nature, and hunting, which became a theme in his works.

In spite of his passion for Trás-os-Montes, where he spent vacations and holidays, Torga traveled much throughout Portugal. He conveys his impressions of the country in the book *Portugal*. In 1950 he traveled around Italy, visiting Pisa, Venice, Florence, Rome, Naples, Capri, Pompeii, and Sicily. That same year the English translation of *Bichos*, titled *Farrusco the Blackbird and Other Stories from the Portuguese*, was published, and his play *Mar* was staged in London.

In 1951 Torga published the fifth volume of his *Diário* and another book of short stories, *Pedras lavradas* (Carved Stones). In response to an inquiry from the *Journal des Poètes* (Poets' Journal) on 11 March 1951, he describes the mission of the poet as one of insubordination and as a fight against oppression and injustice—qualities that appear throughout his own works.

In 1952 Torga published *Alguns poemas ibéricos*, consisting of verse dedicated to topics such as Iberia and its people; overseas conquests and the most representative historical figures that were involved in them; the greatest poet of the Portuguese language, Camões; Santa Theresa and St. John of the Cross; and martyrs of the Spanish Civil War, including Unamuno, Lorca, and Ibarruri. The next year Torga moved to No. 3 Fernando Pessoa Street in Coimbra. He also published the sixth volume of the *Diário*, and he visited Greece and Turkey with his friend Fernando Vale. Also a physician, Vale opposed the Salazar dictatorship and later founded the Socialist Party.

In 1954 *Penas do purgatório* (Pains of Purgatory) appeared. In the poem "Depoimento" (Testimony) Torga takes responsibility for his actions in relation to the divine. He returned that same year to Brazil to participate in a writers' congress in São Paulo. He gave a lecture titled "Trás-os-Montes," which was later published in the collection *Traço de união* (Trace of the Union, 1955). While in Brazil, he and his wife visited his Uncle José, the places where he had lived during his adolescence, and the farm at Santa Cruz. Also in 1954 Torga was awarded a literary prize by the Ateneu Comercial do Porto during the centennial of Almeida Garrett's death. He donated the money to support the publication of works by young and upcoming writers.

In 1955 Torga published *Traço de união*, a book of essays on Portuguese and Brazilian subjects, and his only daughter, Clara, was born. In the eighth volume of *Diário* (1966) he describes the touching moment when Clara was presented to her grandfather shortly before he died. Torga's father, Francisco, for whom he felt a deep admiration, died in 1956. Beginning in the mid 1950s Torga began exploring his native land and

*Torga and his wife, Andrée Crabbé Rocha, in São Martinho de Anta, 1985 (from Gonçalves,* Ser e ler Miguel Torga; *Thomas Cooper Library, University of South Carolina)*

his rural origins increasingly in his poetry. A clear dislike of the bourgeoisie emerges also at this time.

*Orfeu rebelde,* one of his most aggressive books of poetry, appeared in 1958. The title verse captures the poet's cry of revolt, while another poem, "Mudez" (Silence), reveals his sense of "humanitarian desperation," according to Eduardo Lourenço in *O desespero humanista de Miguel Torga e das novas gerações* (The humanist despair of Miguel Torga and the younger generation, 1955). Other poems, such as "Ameaça de morte" (Threat of Death), display the poet's suffering under the Salazar regime, and "Flor da Liberdade" (Flower of Freedom) expresses a desperate anxiety about freedom. "Profissão" (Profession) articulates the anxious emotions that result from the pain of voicing his torment, which forces him to rewrite his poems constantly in search of a better form. In addition, his play *Mar* was staged in 1958 by Antonio Pedro at the experimental theater in Porto. That same year Torga took part in a three-day celebration of the twenty-fifth anniversary of the School of Medicine at the University of Coimbra. The festivities ended with his friends' decision to pay him a special tribute on 7 December 1958. They placed a memorial stone at the house where he had lived as a student.

In 1958 he also participated in Humberto Delgado's campaign for the presidency of Portugal. No political or ideological faction escaped his criticism in the eighth volume of his *Diário* (1959), and the book was quickly confiscated by police. In this *Diário* Torga declared his feelings about Russian communism, English liberalism, American democracy, and French socialism. During the 1960s Portuguese politics became more agitated, especially after the beginning of the war in Angola; the election of Álvaro Cunhal as a general secretary of the Communist Party; and the crises at the universities of Lisbon, Coimbra, and Porto. At this time intellectuals counted on the support of French writers such as Louis Aragon, Simone de Beauvoir, François Mauriac, and Jean-Paul Sartre, all of whom protested Salazar's excesses.

Torga was nominated for the Nobel Prize in literature in 1960 by Jean Baptista Aquarone, a professor at the University of Montpellier in France. He received the support of both Portuguese and international intellectuals, especially that of Brazilians. In 1962 he published *Câmara ardente* (Ardent Chamber), and in 1964 the ninth volume of *Diário* came out. *Poemas ibéricos* (Iberian Poems), a revision of *Alguns poemas ibéricos,* appeared in 1965. Focusing on the Iberian Peninsula in *Poemas ibéricos,* Torga emphasizes the unity of the peninsula through its myths, heroes, and dialogues with poets and intellectuals such as Camões, Pessoa, Lorca, Unamuno, and Oliveira Martins. In "Ambição" (Ambition, published in the tenth volume of *Diário* in 1968), a 1965 poem of telluric features, he reiterates his desire to attain the universal through the individual. In addition, in 1966 Carlos Avilez staged the play *Mar* at the Cascais Experimental Theater, and Jose de Almada Negreiros, one of the notable writers of the *Orpheu* Generation, was the scenographer for the production.

In 1967 Torga spoke about the death penalty at an international conference commemorating the centenary of the abolition of capital punishment in Portugal. In the text of his speech, which appeared in the tenth volume of *Diário* the following year, he also addresses the Soviet invasion of Prague and the student movements of May 1968 and reaffirms that he could never belong to any political party.

In 1969 Torga refused the national prize for literature in Portugal because of Salazar's dictatorship. He participated in the manifesto "From the Writers to the Country" and fought for the end of coercion and prison. He also took part in the Second Aveiro Republican Congress, where he refused to be interviewed by a journalist; he said that he was there "como povo, e o povo, em Portugal, não diz nada" (as an ordinary person, and ordinary people, in Portugal, usually say nothing). This episode is mentioned in volume eleven of *Diário* (1973), in which he also discusses how man's first walk on the moon expanded his sense of solitude. Furthermore, in an entry dated 30 May 1968 he comments on the French students' movement of the previous year. For him, it marked a manifestation of a bourgeois civilization in crisis:

> . . . a juventude não pretende melhorar, acrescentar ou superar o que está; quer destruílo, simplesmente, e começar de novo. Total demolição e total disponibilidade. O que só dá esperança. Tudo o que seja vincular o futuro a está ambigüidade burguesa, é viciálo. Uma sociedade que comete, ajuda ou permite monstruosidades como as do Vietnã, que burocratizou todos os sentimentos, que, como nenhuma da história, oprime tão universal e sistematicamente o espírito, não merece prosseguir, nem sequer deixar rasto. Por isso, outra ordem, outra economia, outra cultura, outro ensino, outra moral. E outro rosto humano, até, se puder ser, para que amanhã ninguém se possa lembrar com vergonha de que já houve gente com este.

> (. . . young people do not intend to improve, to add or to overcome what there is; they want to destroy it, and to begin all over again. Total demolition and total availability; that really raises hopes. Everything that links the future to that middle-class ambiguity, is to addict it. A society that helps or permits merciless wars like the one in Vietnam, that ignores feelings, oppresses so universally and systematically the spirit, does not deserve to survive, nor even leave any signs. Therefore, we need another order, another economy, another type of teaching, another morality. And, as a consequence, another human face; until this becomes real tomorrow no one can remember with shame what happened to this kind of people).

In 1970 Salazar, who had suffered a blood clot from a blow to the head at the beginning of September 1968, died. Marcelo Caetano assumed presidential powers, ending forty years of nearly absolute government. With Salazar's death, however, discontent in the country intensified. The Socialist politician Mário Soares, who had been deported to São Tomé in 1968, returned to Portugal and published "Portugal amordaçado" (Portugal Gagged), which had a far-reaching effect. Soares's essay was published in September 1972 simultaneously in the first issue of the London magazine *Index*, in the Paris journal *Esprit* (Spirit), and in a condensed form in the German newspaper *Die Zeit* (Time). In 1971, with the new freedom for expression after Salazar's death, the Portuguese Association of Writers was founded.

In 1973 Torga traveled to Angola and Mozambique with Father Valentim Marques, director of a Coimbra publishing house. In *Miguel Torga: Fotobiografia* (Miguel Torga: Photobiography, 2000), a biography of her father, Clara Rocha writes that the notes made by Torga on the occasion of these travels "deixem transparecer um mal-estar de quem sente 'um abismo intransponível com quinhentos anos de largura'" (show the discomfort of one who feels an insuperable abyss five hundred years wide). On 25 April 1974 the Revolução dos Cravos ended the dictatorship of Salazar. Torga, at first, did not trust the revolution since it was staged by the military. Although he attended many meetings of the Socialist Party, he remained an independent.

In 1974 Torga resumed the series *A criação do mundo*. The fourth volume, *O quinto dia* (The Fifth Day), which tells about his experiences in prison, was published that year. In 1975 his short story "O leproso" (The Leper, first published in book form in *Novos contos da montanha*) was made into a movie by Sinde Filipe. In 1976 he published *Fogo preso* (Prison Fire), a collection of interviews, lectures, and speeches. Volume twelve of *Diário* came out in 1977, and Torga was the subject of, and appeared in, the documentary *Eu, Miguel Torga* (I, Miguel Torga), produced by João Roque and filmed by Arca Filmes.

Torga was again nominated for the Nobel Prize in 1978. Among his supporters was Vicente Alexandre, the winner of the prize in 1977. On 26 December he was honored by the Calouste Gulbekian Foundation for his fifty-year contribution to Portuguese literature and culture as a writer. A document on the session was published by the Department of Culture. Also in 1978 the short story "O milagre" (The Miracle), from *Novos contos da montanha*, was adapted for motion pictures by Filipe.

In 1979 Torga was honored by the University of Coimbra. The tribute consisted of a bibliographical exhibition and a session chaired by the chancellor of the University of Coimbra, A. A. Ferrer Correia. The lecture that Professor Carlos Reis gave, titled "Miguel Torga ou o paradigma perdido" (Miguel Torga or the Lost Paradigm), was included in the 1979 publication "Homenagem a Miguel Torga" (Homage to Miguel Torga), a supplement to the journal *Biblos* (Books) that includes the first significant inventory of Torga's works and the critical studies done on them.

In 1980, together with Brazilian poet Carlos Drummond de Andrade, Torga won the Morgado de Mateus Prize. As a part of the continuing celebration of his fifty years as a writer, the Rotary Club de Leiria welcomed him with a speech by his friend Frederico de Moura. The short story "Natal" (Christmas), also from *Novos contos da montanha,* was adapted for television and featured João Àvilon as the lead actor. In 1981 *O sexto dia* (The Sixth Day), the last volume of the *A criação do mundo* series, was published. On 10 March 1981 Torga won the Montaigne Prize from the Fundação F. V. S. de Hamburgo in Germany. The following year Aubier Montaine published an anthology of selections, translated into French, from various volumes of Torga's *Diário,* titled *En franchise intéieure–Pages de journal (1933–1977).*

The thirteenth volume of the *Diário* was published in 1983. That same year he met the president of Mozambique, Samora Machel, at the palace São Marcos, on the outskirts of Coimbra. A great admirer of the African leader, Torga gave Machel a tour of the Douro region. In volume fourteen of *Diário* (1987) he registers his regret at Machel's death on 19 October 1986.

On 12 August 1986 Torga's friends honored him with a birthday celebration, which they organized annually. The participants included Soares, António de Almeida Santos, and Manuel Alegre–all of them important figures in Portuguese politics. According to Santos's testimony in *Miguel Torga: Fotobiografia,* Soares always admired Torga greatly, as both a man and an artist. Torga, however, avoided friendship with Soares for a long time, even when Soares was the prime minister of Portugal. He told Soares that, although he knew he was a good politician, he did not consider him a statesman. Soares confirmed in *Miguel Torga: Fotobiografia* that the two had finally formed a sincere and deep friendship.

To commemorate his eightieth birthday in 1987, Torga recorded "Oitenta poemas" (Eighty Poems), produced by Valentim de Carvalho. Torga was invited to Macau, where he lectured on the poet Camões at the Leal Senado. He took the opportunity to visit Canton, Hong Kong, and Goa. He ironically refers to the comfort of his first-class accommodations, at the expense of his hosts, through the figure of an old and suffering porter in the poem "Errância" (Roaming), written that same summer. The poem appeared in volume fifteen of *Diário* (1990). In 1988 the short story "O vinho," first collected in *Contos da montanha,* was adapted for television by C. J. Michaélis de Vasconcelos, with the actor Raul Solnado in the lead.

Torga received the important Prêmio Camões (Camões Prize) in 1989 in a ceremony chaired by Soares during festivities in June of that year (10 June is the anniversary of Camões's death and the Day of the Portuguese Mother-Country) in Ponta Delgada, Azores. The well-known Brazilian writer Jorge Amado, who was present at the ceremony, suggested that the Nobel Prize be awarded to Torga.

At the time volume fifteen of *Diário* came out, Torga was quite ill. He never stopped writing, however, even during his hospital stays. In 1990 the Goethe-Institut Inter Nationes Lissabon of Coimbra paid him tribute, and his work *Bichos* was adapted for the theater and staged by the group O Bando. The play was later performed in several cities in Portugal and abroad. In 1992 Torga received three more prizes: the Premio Vida Literária from the Associação Portuguesa dos Escritores (Association of Portuguese Writers); the Prêmio Figura do Ano from the Associação dos Correspondentes da Imprensa Estrangeira (Foreign Press Correspondents' Association); and the Prêmio Écureuil de Literatura Estrangeira from the Salão do livro de Bordéus. In October of that year there was a congress dedicated to Torga at the University of Massachusetts at Amherst in which many Portuguese and North American scholars participated. The proceedings of the meeting were published in 1977 as *Sou um homem de granito: Miguel Torga e seu compromiso* (I Am a Man Made of Granite: Miguel Torga and His Commitment).

In 1993 Torga published the sixteenth volume of *Diário,* in which he describes several political and historical events from various countries, including Nelson Mandela's release from prison in South Africa, the reunification of Germany, the Gulf War, the Timor massacre, the presidential elections in Portugal, and Lech Walesa's election in Poland. In this volume, considered the principal one by many critics and readers, Torga begins to discuss old age and death. With the poem "Requiem por mim" (Requiem for Me), which also appears in the sixteenth *Diário,* he ended his literary life.

Fernando Pessoa University in Porto organized the first international congress on Miguel Torga and his works in 1994, and the Spanish writer Gonzalo Torrente Ballester, among others, took part in it. The proceedings of this congress were later published as *Aqui, neste lugar e nesta hora* (Here, in This Place and at This Hour) that same year. In 1994 Torga received many tributes: a prize from the Center for the International Association of Literary Critics; a tribute from the Brazilian embassy in Lisbon in commemoration of Brazilian Independence Day (7 September); and a tribute from the District Council of Lawyers of Coimbra, during which Cunha Rodrigues, then the attorney general, gave the presentation titled "Representations of Justice in Miguel Torga." Rodrigues's address was published as a book in 1995.

Miguel Torga's last text, according to his daughter and biographer, was a message read by his wife at the first meeting of the International Parliament of

Writers in Lisbon. The association was created in July 1994 and chaired by Salman Rushdie. Torga died on 17 January 1995. He was buried in São Martinho de Anta Cemetery. In a testimony in *Miguel Torga: Fotobiografia* his friend António Arnault notes that the name Miguel Torga, rather than the name Adolfo Correia da Rocha, is engraved on the writer's tombstone. He emphasizes that Torga was more than just a pseudonym; it was the true name of an author known for the authenticity, nationalism, and humanism of his many books. Torga left an impressive body of work, including fiction, poetry, drama, essays, and diaries. A passion for Portugal and for justice characterizes his writings, which rank him among the important authors of twentieth-century Portuguese literature.

**References:**

Vilmas Sant'Anna Arêas and Análise Jorge da Silveira, "De *Novos contos da montanha*," *Cadernos da PUC,* 9 (1972): 51–61;

*ATAS do 1º Congresso Internacional sobre Miguel Torga. Aqui, neste lugar e nesta hora* (Porto, 1994);

Eduardo Prado Coelho, *A palavra sobre a palavra* (Porto: Portucalense, 1972);

David Mourão-Ferreira, "Presença," in *Dicionário de literatura brasileira, portuguesa, galega e estilística literária,* volume 2, edited by Jacinto do Prado Coelho (Porto: Figueirinhas, 1973), pp. 868–870;

"Homenagem a Miguel Torga," *Biblos,* special Torga issue, 10 (1979);

Teresa Rita Lopes, *Coimbra vista por Miguel Torga* (Lisbon: INATEL, 1991);

Eduardo Lourenço, *O desespero humanista de Miguel Torga e das novas gerações* (Coimbra: Coimbra Editore, 1955);

Fernando Pessoa, *Correspondência (1923–1935)* (Lisbon: Assírio & Alvim, 1999), pp. 207–210;

Clara Rocha, *O espaço autobiográfico em Miguel Torga* (Coimbra: Almedina, 1977);

Rocha, *Miguel Torga: Fotobiografia* (Lisbon: Dom Quixote, 2000);

José Augusto Seabra, *Um poeta da Ibéria: Miguel Torga. Poligrafias poéticas* (Porto: Lello & Irmão, 1994);

Mônica Rector Toledo Silva, "Miguel Torga: *Novos contos da montanha*," *Cadernos da PUC,* 9 (1972): 95–118;

Maria do Amparo Tavares, "Do paradigma bíblico em Miguel Torga: Bichos," *Boletim Informativo do Centro de Estudos Portugueses,* 7 (1979): 3–11.

# Cesário Verde
*(25 February 1855 – 19 July 1886)*

Marina Machado Rodrigues
*Universidade do Estado do Rio de Janeiro*

BOOKS: *Num bairro moderno* (Lisbon: Universal, 1877);
*O livro de Cesário Verde,* preface by Antonio da Silva Pinto (Lisbon: Elzeviriana, 1887);
*Obra completa,* edited by Joel Serrão (Lisbon: Portugália, 1964);
*Poesia completa e cartas escolhidas,* edited by Carlos Felipe Moisés (São Paulo: Cultrix-Universidade de São Paulo, 1982);
*Obra poética e epistolografia,* edited by Ângela Marques (Porto: Lello, 1999).

Cesário Verde is considered one of the most original and innovative poets of nineteenth-century Portuguese literature. Characterized by a highly personal style, Verde's poetry betrays his intense awareness of reality. He found inspiration in ordinary, everyday circumstances and events: "A mim o que me rodeia é o que me preocupa" (What surrounds me is what concerns me). Strolls down the streets of late-nineteenth-century Lisbon moved Verde to capture through poetry an extensive view of the industrialized landscape of the metropolis. His attention was drawn to palatial residences, modern constructions, wooden buildings, and shop windows as well as to street noise and crowds of people caught up in their daily struggle for survival. Verde's poems also include human portraits, in which he describes the conflicts inherent to the social stratification of the urban environment. His verse offers a rich sociological panorama of the times, ranging in subject matter from aristocrats and the bourgeoisie to the working class and to marginalized persons such as petty criminals. His perspicacious writing not only depicts the city landscape but also delves into what he considered the healthy and practical environment of the countryside and its people. Yet, not everything is perfect in the country, as he warns in his last poem: "nem tudo são descantes" (not everything is melodious).

Verde's poetry is marked by an "antilyric objectivity," which does not prevent him, however, from expressing his ideas and feelings as a man involved in social issues. His respect for positivist philosophy and

*Cesário Verde (from Cesário Verde, 1855–1886, 1986; Thomas Cooper Library, University of South Carolina)*

his tremendous compassion for victims of social injustice is apparent in most of his verses. His sincere feelings for the poor are demonstrated in "Cristalizações" (Crystallizations), in which he sees the worker as symbolic of the energy of the people. The verses assume an almost epic nuance: "Povo! No pano cru rasgado das camisas / Uma bandeira penso que transluz! / Com ela sofres, bebes, agonizas: / Listrões de vinho lançam-lhe divisas, / E os suspensórios traçam-lhe uma cruz!" (People! On the rough torn cloth of your shirts / I think I see a flag shine! / With it you suffer, drink, and agonize: / Broad stripes of wine turn into ribbons / And your suspenders outline a cross on you!).

José Joaquim Cesário Verde was born into a well-to-do family in Lisbon on 25 February 1855. His father owned a rural estate in Linda-a-Pastora and a hardware store in the capital. Around 1865, when Verde was still a child, he started to work in the family business, helping his father at the hardware shop. For the rest of his life he participated in the two economic sectors in which his family had made its living for many years—the agricultural and the commercial. These two areas constitute the main subjects of Verde's work, often in the form of a conflict or contrast between rural and urban life and values. As a young man he attended school for a while in Lisbon to study languages, and he dedicated much of his time to reading literature.

Verde made his lyric debut in 1873 when his first verses were published in two Lisbon newspapers. "A Força" (The Force), "Num tripúdio de corte rigoroso," and "Ó Áridas Messalinas" appeared in the *Diário de Notícias*, while "Eu e ela" (I and She) and "Lúbrica" (Sensual) were published in the *Diário da Tarde*. In 1874 he published seven poems in the *Diário da Tarde*, three in the *Diário de Notícias*, two in the *Tribune*, and one in the *Harpa*. He published only two compositions in 1875, in the *Tribune* and in the magazine *Mosaico*. In 1876 "A débil" (The Weak Woman) appeared in the journal *Evolução* in Coimbra.

Verde's output between 1873 and 1876, as classified by Joel Serrão, was a poetry of youth. These early compositions depict love as the subject and woman as the object. Serrão says that "The poet loves in different ways depending on where he is: in the country or in the city." Verde sees love in rural areas as authentic and true, since women there have not been negatively affected by urban bourgeois behavior. The aristocrats of the city, on the other hand, who are artificial, snobbish, and untrustworthy, make honest love an impossibility.

Early poems such as "Setentrional" (Septentrional) portray an Arcadian vision of the countryside. In "Setentrional" Verde's use of the sea and the countryside as metaphors expresses a sense of the erotic. He sets the pure and the good of rural life in opposition to the city; the urban landscape is an oppressive space that perverts love, while the countryside is where true love occurs: "Mas vinde-me aquecer, que eu tenho muito frio / E quero asfixiar-me em ondas de prazer" (But cuddle me because I am cold / I want to drown in waves of pleasure). The urban atmosphere inspires only that unachievable love granted by the "arid Messalines" or by the superiority of the *miladies*. In "Esplêndida," in which Verde writes, "que atrai como a voragem" (that attracts attracts like a vortex), love acquires its most cruel form, conveyed in the perverse eroticism of humiliation. The poems "Deslumbramentos" (Fascination), "Frígida," (The Cold Woman), and "A débil" show the poet attempting to reconcile himself with the city through the metaphor of an ambiguous relationship with a woman. The sensations of attraction and rejection inspire lines such as "O seu olhar possui um jogo ardente, / Um arcanjo e um demônio a iluminá-lo" (Your gaze is an ardent game, / Brightened by an archangel and a devil). The themes of country versus city, pure love versus impure love, and lyricism versus irony constitute the core of Verde's poetic concerns of this period. As Serrão asserts, although Verde has discovered by now the poetic reality of the urban experience, his fondness for the country is not diminished.

In 1877 Verde wrote and published *Num bairro moderno* (In a Modern Neighborhood); "Em petiz" (Like a Child) was written in 1878 and came out in 1879. In the view of the contemporary poet Hélder Macedo, writing in *Nós—uma leitura de Cesário Verde* (1975), "O sentimento dum ocidental" (The Sentiment of an Easterner, 1880) is Verde's masterpiece. In this verse, capturing the urban life of the poet, Verde makes the city of Lisbon his lyrical subject: "temo que me avives / Uma paixão defunta!" (I fear that you revive in me / an extinguished passion). By the early 1880s, working on a regular basis at his father's shop, he slowly began to take over its management. He published nothing between 1880 and 1884, dedicating himself completely to the family business.

In several poems Verde reveals his sensitivity to the minimal critical attention that his verse has received over the years. He ponders both the lack of reviews for some verses and the moments of unfavorable reception for others. In "Contrariedades" (Oppositions) he indicates his rejection by the critics: "Mais duma redação, das que elogiam tudo / Me tem fechado a porta" (More than one editor's office, of those who praise everything / Have shut the door in my face). The reasons for such a negative response could be Verde's philosophical orientation; for example, the critics did not understand French philosopher Hippolyte Taine's ideas, which left their mark on Verde's writing: "A crítica segundo o método de Taine / ignoram-na" (Criticism according to Taine's method / They are ignorant of it). Macedo believes that reviewers were not familiar with Taine's theories—despite their decisive impact on the intellectual environment in Portugal at that time—and thus did not analyze Verde's poetry in light of them. In addition, perhaps Verde's critics did not like his independent spirit—Verde did not write poetry of circumstance to please the powerful: "Eu nunca dediquei poemas às fortunas" (I never dedicated poems to the powerful). Verde also faults the general reader, whom he considers naive, for preferring the poetry of consumerism (a reference to the work of nineteenth- century French poet Pierre Zaccone). Macedo attributes the critics' lack of interest in Verde's poetry to the nature of his vision toward contemporary Portuguese society.

Verde's worldview was defined by ideas known and accepted at that time—ideas that, besides Taine's philosophical approach, included Pierre-Joseph Proudhon's socialism, Auguste Comte's positivism, Herbert Spencer's sociobiological organicism, and Georg Wilhelm Friedrich Hegel's dialectical idealism. Some scholars believe that Verde did not enjoy much renown during his lifetime because many of his poetic motifs were not considered worthy of poetry. Mário de Sá-Carneiro and Fernando Pessoa see in Verde's poetry aspects of Portuguese modernism. Gaspar Simões acknowledges the originality of the plasticity of Verde's poetic language that, he believes, derives from a natural perception of the world and a sense of the visionary. This element is particularly present in poems in which reality is affected by the poet's fantasy.

Verde incorporates scenes of the quotidian into his poetry, describing them in a prosaic language, as in "De tarde" (In the Evening). He uses words to construct scenes in which the dominant visual effect is underscored by a sensation of movement. Some of these scenes resemble an impressionistic painting. Verde also uses irony and parody, as in "Lágrimas" (Tears), in a more condensed way. In "Sardenta" (The Freckled Woman), for example, he corrodes—beginning with the adjective of the title—the image of ideal feminine beauty. His assignment of a negative value to the metaphor of the woman marks a rejection of the traditional romantic idealization of the feminine. In the first two verses of the poem he establishes the romantic cliché of the woman as flower; in the last two verses, however, he carictures this image when "láctea virgem dourada" (the golden, milky virgin) is seen as a "camélia melada" (a sweet camellia). The sublime is transformed into the grotesque through his critical portrait of the real. The inversion of typical romantic metaphors in "Sardenta" constitutes Verde's reaction to the exaggerated sentimentalism of Romanticism.

In poems that take place in, or mention, the urban environment, Verde's symbolic representation of the feminine usually assumes an ideological aspect. The woman's image consists of archetypes whose role is to point out the inequities existing among the social classes. The woman from the city—the "flor do luxo" (flower of luxury)—is either the oppressive and cruel bourgeois female or the working woman whose poverty and struggle for survival have destroyed her vitality and beauty. The urban environment represents a bourgeois artificiality that exploits the worker. Characters such as the woman in "Contraridedades" who irons clothes reveal their miserable condition: "Uma infeliz sem peito, os dois pulmões doentes / . . . Mal ganha para sopas" (A poor woman without breasts, her two lungs sick / . . . hardly earns enough for soup). These images contrast with those of the palace-like houses on the "ruas macadamizadas" (macadamized streets). Both the middle class and the poor in the city share one characteristic—alienation. This trait emerges in "Um bairro moderno" through a servant's attitude of superiority, as well as through a woman who irons clothes and "cantarola uma canção plangente / duma opereta nova" (warbles a sad song / from a new operetta) but does not know that the "combustão das brasas a asfixia" (the combustion of the flames suffocates her). In the same way, in "Deslumbramentos" the alienation of Milady, who does not know the hardships and difficulties experienced by the poor, motivates the lyric subject's remark that they "para a vingança aguçam os punhais" (sharpen the daggers for their revenge) and that "hão de acabar os bárbaros reais" (the royal barbarians shall disappear). The poet warns the aristocrats that the situation may change in favor of the oppressed.

As Jacinto do Prado Coelho has noted, in some of Verde's poems the stimuli of surrounding reality either generate the evocation of things absent (the calkers remind Verde of stories about the sea and the great ships that he will never see), or imaginatively transform things that he has seen (the lighted shops at night are turned into "rows of chapels," as in a huge cathedral). Such illusions are soon refuted by the lucid poet who returns to the sensorial sphere and is guided by a critical conscience, another trace of modernity revealed in his work.

The poem "Nós" (We), written in 1881 and 1882 and published in 1884, evokes the deaths of the poet's sister (in 1872) and brother (in 1882). It tells about the Verdes departing for the estate of Linda-a-Pastora for two consecutive summers in order to escape the fever and cholera that were plaguing the city at the time. It also dwells on the importance of agricultural activity, which had become the family's main source of income during that period. "Nós" occasions the beginning of an ideological shift in Verde's work. In earlier poems he considered the rural environment an Edenic place. His use of *nós,* a first-person plural pronoun encompassing both the poet and the ones he cared for in this privileged space, reflects an attempt to resolve his own personal and social contradictions. The practical experience makes him search for a more coherent identification with the countryside, which is no longer an idyllic place but rather a concrete reality: "é um mundo útil e sensato" (it is a useful and sensible world). Verde is no longer the estate owner who takes advantage of the land; he has, instead, become the owner involved in production, which according to the theories of Proudhon, provides a sense of moral refinement to land ownership. The country assumes a practical and useful value: "Ah! O campo não é um passatempo / com bucolismos, rouxinóis, luar . . ." (Oh! The country is not amusement / with innocence, nightingales, moonlight . . .). As a metaphor of work, the country provides not only profits but also a real integration of poet and man with the people and their life there. Verde prefers agriculture and the exporting of fruit to the powerful industrial civilization of the big cities. He would rather have "o ritmo do vivo e do real" (the rhythm of that which is alive and real) than "essa perfeição do fabricado" (the perfection of the manufactured).

In the poem "Nós" Verde expands on the opposition of country and city to represent the contrast between agricultural southern Portugal and industrialized northern England–a contrast associated with triumphant urban order and the implicit relationship of English domination over Portugal. The submission of the country to the city thus signifies an alienating and illegitimate foreign imposition, since the poet verifies that the "geração exangue de ricos" (feeble generation of the rich) is doomed to disappear. The ones who survive will be those who have "riqueza química no sangue" (chemical richness in their blood). This perception, which appears in Verde's work following the death of his sister, inverts Spencer's point of view that the progress of the northern countries resulted from their superior capacity for survival. Spencer based this theory on the argument that progress results from the struggle for survival–a fight in which the weak are necessarily eliminated. In Verde's opinion, however, the weak were his own generation ("a geração exangue de ricos"). His sister, a victim of tuberculosis, was extremely beautiful and as kind as a gentle herbivore ("bondades de herbívora mansinha"); Verde wishes, however, that she had been vigorous and plebeian ("vigorosa e plebéia"), with the manners of a ferocious carnivore ("uns modos de carnívora feroz"). The poem pivots on period philosophies of historical, racial, and economic determinism, which supported the notion of the survival of the fittest. The emerging bourgeoisie of the nineteenth century found a moral explanation for its power in these theories.

When Verde rejected the industrial model of the urban bourgeois class to which he belonged, his poetry seemed to consecrate the arcadian metaphor that had

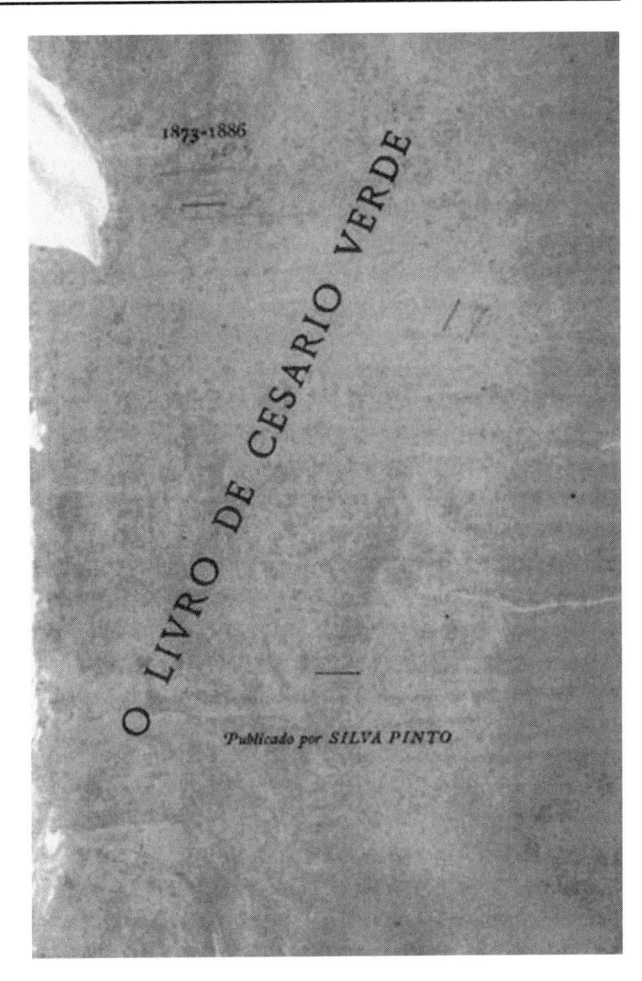

*Cover for Verde's posthumously published 1887 collection (Biblioteca Nacional, Lisbon)*

glorified the image of the countryside in various epochs. Real experience, however, had made him reevaluate the relationship between men and work in both the city and the rural areas. And it had forced him to see that social injustice is inherent to both locations. The origin of the problem lay in the dichotomy between the oppressor and the oppressed, which, in Verde's view, demanded a criticism of the economic model that was valid at the time. This conclusion implies that the opposition of country versus city was surpassed and that a new attitude toward Portuguese social reality was achieved.

Verde's last poem, "Provincianas" (Provincial Women, 1886), which remained unfinished, portrays the evolution of poet and man. The description of the country in springtime vigor is complemented by that of the difficulties faced by peasants working the land, destroying the myth of paradise inscribed in the poem: "Mas nem tudo são descantes / . . . há solos bravios, maninhos, que expulsam seus habitantes" (Not everything is melodious / there is uncultivated and infertile soil that expels everything). The euphoria of Verde's nature description clashes starkly with his questioning of the people's poverty. He now perceives the country as the place where the struggle for life occurs:

> Ei-las que vêm as manadas [as moças]
> com caras de sofrimento,
> Nas grandes marchas forçadas!
> Vêm ao trabalho, ao sustento
> com fouces, sachos, enxadas
>
> (Here comes the cattle [the young girls]
> with their suffering faces,
> On the great forced marches!
> They come to work, for sustenance,
> with scythes, weeding hoes, and spades).

In the second part of the poem an urban scene relates the disparity between the privileged situation of an aristocratic woman and the poor, subhuman condition in which the daughters of her governess live: "Ao meio-dia na cama / branca fidalga . . . / vivem minados de pulgas [as pequenas de sua ama] / negras do tempo e lama" (The white aristocratic woman / at noon in bed / . . . full of fleas [the girls of her governess] / black from mud and time). Verde understands that the difficulties of the peasants and of the urban working class come from the same evil.

In 1886 Verde began to suffer from tuberculosis, and his family took him to Lumiar. He died there on 19 July 1886, without ever having collected his poems into a book. A friend, Silva Pinto, gathered and published Verde's poems in *O livro de Cesário Verde* (The Book of Cesário Verde) in 1887. According to Pinto, the poet had made the selection before his death. Typographia Elzeviriana, the publisher of *O livro de Cesário Verde,* disclosed that Verde had left among his manuscripts an outline of the book, which was supposed to include all variations and rewrites ("fielmente executado, nas variantes e nas supressões, em tudo"). More probable, however, is that Pinto organized the *O livro de Cesário Verde* in terms of his own critical perspective. Scholars such as Serrão do not believe that Verde gave his friend a prepared manuscript. On the contrary, they assert, the book was put together from material collected from newspapers and autographs given to friends. The inclusion of compositions in–and the exclusion of them from–*O livro de Cesário Verde* were probably based on Pinto's decision, as was the division of the work into two sections, which do not follow a chronological order of composition: "Crise romanesca" (Romanesque Crisis) and "Naturais" (Natural).

Commenting in *As mais belas líricas portuguesas* on the various trends that make up *O livro de Cesário Verde,* the poet José Régio points specifically to the preference for concrete details that gave José Joaquim Cesário Verde's sensitive verses the visual force of a realist painting deformed by touches of fantasy. Verde reveals, as Régio notes, "um pendor para o frio cálculo de esteta requintado; o amor do natural e do saudável, com uma íntima inclinação pelo extravagante, o raro, o grotesco artístico . . ." (a propensity for the cold calculation of the refined aesthete, the love for the natural and the healthy, with an intimate inclination for the extravagant, the unusual, the artistic grotesque). By transforming the quotidian into poetry and lending literary dignity to the prosaic, Verde created a new aesthetic in Portuguese literature. This new approach to verse embodied in part the germ of modern Portuguese poetry.

**References:**

*Cesário Verde, 1855–1886* (Lisbon: Biblioteca Nacional, 1986);

Jacinto do Prado Coelho, "Cesário Verde," in *Dicionário de literatura: Literatura portuguesa, literatura brasileira, literatura galega, estilística literária,* 5 volumes, edited by Prado Coelho (Porto: Figueirinhas, 1987);

Hélder Macedo, *Nós–uma leitura de Cesário Verde* (Lisbon: Plátano, 1975);

David Mourão-Ferreira, "Notas sobre Cesário Verde," in his *Hospital das letras* (Lisbon: Guimarães, 1966);

Martinho Nobre de Melo, *Cesário Verde: Poesia* (Rio de Janeiro: Agir, 1975);

José Régio, *As mais belas líricas portuguesas* (Lisbon: Portugália, 1967);

Joel Serrão, *Cesário Verde: Interpretação, poesias dispersas e cartas coligidas e anotadas* (Lisbon: Delfos, 1961);

João Gaspar Simões, "Introdução a Cesário Verde," in his *O mistério da poesia* (Coimbra: Imprensa da Universidade, 1931).

# Gil Vicente
*(1465 – between 1536 and 1540)*

Reinhard Krüger
*University of Stuttgart*

BOOKS: *Copilaçam de todalas obras de Gil Vicente, a qual se reparte em cinco liuros. O primeyro he de todas suas cousas de deuaçam. O segundo as comedias. O terceyro as tragicomedias. No quarto as farsas. No quinto as obras meudas* (Lisbon: Joam Aluarez, 1562; revised, Lisbon: Andres Lobato, 1586); republished as *Obras completas* (Lisbon: Biblioteca Nacional, 1928); republished as *Copilaçam de todalas obras de Gil Vicente*, 2 volumes, edited, with an introduction, by Maria Leonor Carvalhão Buescu (Lisbon: Imprensa Nacional-Casa da Moeda, 1983)—includes *Monológo del vaqueiro; Milagre de São Martinho; Sermão de Abrantes; Auto da Índia; Auto pastoril castelhano; Ecloga dos Reis Magos; Auto da fé ; Farsa do velho da horta; Moralidade dos quatro tempos; Moralidade da Sibila Cassandra; Auto da exortação da guerra; Quem tem farelos?; Os mistérios da Virgem; Auto da barca do inferno; Auto da barca do purgatório; Auto da barca da glória; Auto da fama; Cortes de Júpiter; Comédia de Rubena; Auto das ciganas; Comédia de Dom Duardos; Auto pastoril português; Comédia de Amadis de Gaula; Comédia do viúvo; Os físicos; Frágua do amor; O juiz da Beira; O templo de Apolo; Moralidade da feira; Nao d'amores; Pastoril da Serra da Estrela; A divisa da cidade de Coimbra; Farsa dos Almocreves; Auto das fadas; O clérigo da Beira; Triunfo do inverno (Tragicomédia do inverno e verão); Auto da Lusitânia; O romagem de agravados; Auto da Mofina Mendes; Auto da Cananéia;* and *A floresta de enganos;*

*Poesías,* edited by Dámaso Alonso (Madrid: Cruz & Raya, 1934);

*Auto da moralidade,* edited by I. S. Révah (Lisbon: O Mundo do Livro, 1959).

**Editions and Collections:** *Auto de la sibila Casandra,* with a prologue and notes by Álvaro Giráldez (Madrid: V. Suarez, 1921);

*Farsa de Inês Pereira,* edited, with a preface, by Francisco Torrinha and Augusto C. Pires de Lima (N.p.: F. Torrinha, A. Lima, 1932);

*Exortação da guerra,* with a preface by Pires de Lima (Porto: Ediçao do anotador, 1932);

*Gil Vicente (from Alvaro Cardoso Gomes,* Gil Vicente, *1982; Jean and Alexander Heard Library, Vanderbilt University)*

*Auto chamado da feyra,* edited by Marques Braga (Lisbon: Junta de Educação Nacional, 1936);

*Breve sumário da história de Deus,* edited by João de Almeida Lucas (Lisbon: A. M. Teixeira, 1943);

*Comedia del viudo,* edited by Alonso Zamora Vicente (Lisbon: Instituto de Alta Cultura, 1962);

*Obras dramáticas castellanas,* edited by Thomas R. Hart, Clássicos castellanos, volume 156 (Madrid: Espasa-Calpe, 1962);

*A Critical Edition with Introduction and Notes of Gil Vicente's* Floresta de enganos, edited by Constantine Christopher Stathatos (Chapel Hill: University of North Carolina Press, 1972);

*Auto chamado da Mofina Mendes, mistério,* edited by Mário Fiúza (Porto: Porto Editora, 1978);

*Obras completas,* edited by Alvaro Júlio da Costa Pimpão (Porto: Livraria Civilizacação Editora, 1979);

*Farsa de Inês Pereira,* edited by Albano Monteiro Soares (Porto: Porto Edição, 1979);

*Exortação da guerra,* edited by Soares (Porto: Porto Edição, 1980);

*Comédia sobre a divisa da cidade de Coimbra,* edited by Daniel Rangel-Guerrero (University, Miss.: Romance Monographs, 1980);

*Auto da alma,* edited by Maria Idalina Resina Rodrigues (Lisbon: Seara Nova-Editorial Comunicação, 1980);

*Auto da Feira,* edited by Artur Ribeiro Gonçalves (Lisbon: Comunicação, 1984);

*Auto da Índia* (Lisbon: Comunicação, 1991);

*Lírica,* edited by Armando López Castro (Madrid: Cátedra, 1993);

*Auto da barca da glória; Nao d'amores,* edited by Maria Idalina Resina Rodrigues (Madrid: Castalia, 1995);

*Teatro castellano,* edited by Manuel Calderón, preliminary study by Stephen Reckert (Barcelona: Crítica, 1996);

*Tragicomédia de Don Duardos,* edited by Armando López Castro (Salamanca: Ediciones Colegio de España, 1996);

*A Critical Edition of Gil Vicente's Auto da Índia,* edited by Stathatos (Barcelona: Puvill, 1997);

*Lamento de María la Parda* (Mexico City: Editorial Aldus, 2000);

*Obras Integrais de Gil Vicente,* CD-ROM (Lisbon: Projecto Vercial, 2002).

**Editions in English:** *Four Plays of Gil Vicente,* edited and translated by Aubrey F. G. Bell (Cambridge: Cambridge University Press, 1920)—comprises *The Soul's Journey; Exhortation to War; The Carriers;* and *Tragicomédia pastoril da Serra da Estrella;*

*The Ship of Hell,* translated by A. F. Gerald (Watford, U.K.: Voss & Michael, 1929);

*Three Discovery Plays,* edited and translated by Anthony Lappin (Warminster, U.K.: Aris & Phillips, 1997);

*The Sibyl Cassandra: A Christmas Play with the Insanity and Sanctity of Five Centuries Past,* translated by Cheryl Folkins McGinniss (Lanham, Md.: University Press of America, 2000).

PLAY PRODUCTIONS: *Monológo del vaqueiro,* Lisbon, at court, 7 June 1502;

*Milagre de São Martinho,* Lisbon, Church Igreja das Caldas, 1504;

*Sermão de Abrantes,* Lisbon, unknown theater, 1506;

*Auto da Índia,* Almada, at court, 1509;

*Auto pastoril castelhano,* Lisbon, at court, 25 December 1509;

*Ecloga dos Reis Magos,* Lisbon, at court, 6 January 1510;

*Auto da fé,* Almeirim, at court, 25 December 1510;

*Farsa do velho da horta,* Lisbon, at court, 1512;

*Moralidade dos quatro tempos,* Lisbon, Paços de Alcáçova, Christmas 1513;

*Moralidade da Sibila Cassandra,* Lisbon, Monastery of Xobregas, Christmas morning 1513;

*Auto dos quatro tempos,* 1514?;

*Auto da exortação da guerra,* Lisbon, at court, 1514;

*Quem tem farelos?* Lisbon, Paços da Ribeira, 1515;

*Os mistérios da Virgem,* Lisbon, at court, 25 December 1515; restaged as *Auto da Mofina Mendes,* Lisbon, at court, 25 December 1534;

*Auto da barca do inferno,* Lisbon, at court, 1517;

*Auto da barca do purgatório,* Lisbon, Hospital Todos los Santos, 25 December 1518;

*Auto da alma,* Lisbon, Paços da Ribeira, 1518;

*Auto da barca da glória,* Almeirim, at court, 1519;

*Auto da fama,* Santos-o-Velho (Lisbon), at court, 1520;

*Cortes de Júpiter,* Lisbon, Paços de Ribeira, 1521;

*Comédia de Rubena,* Lisbon, 1521;

*Auto das ciganas,* Évora, at court, 1521;

*Comédia de Dom Duardos,* Lisbon, Court of Almeirim, 1522;

*Farsa de Inês Pereira,* Tomar, Convent of Christ, 1523;

*Auto pastoril português,* Évora, at court, 25 December 1523;

*Comédia do viúvo,* Lisbon, 1524;

*Os físicos,* Lisbon (?), 1524;

*Frágua do amor,* Évora, at court, 1525;

*Auto da festa,* Évora, private residence, 1525;

*O juiz da Beira,* Almeirim, at court, 1525;

*O templo de Apolo,* Lisbon, at court, 1526;

*Farsa dos Almocreves,* Coimbra, at court, circa 1526–1527;

*Moralidade da feira,* Lisbon, at court, 25 December 1527;

*Breve sumário da história de Deus* and *Diálogo sobre a resurreição de Cristo,* Almeirim, at court, 1527;

*Nao d'amores,* Lisbon, at court, 1527;

*Pastoril da Serra da Estrela,* Coimbra, at court, 1527;

*A divisa da cidade de Coimbra,* Coimbra, at court, 1527;

*Auto das fadas,* Lisbon, at court (?), 1527;

*O clérigo da Beira,* Almeirim, at court, 1529;

*Triunfo do inverno* or *Tragicomédia do inverno e verão,* Lisbon, at court, 1529;

*Auto da Lusitânia,* Lisbon, at court, 1532;

*O romagem de agravados,* Évora, at court, 1533;

*Comédia de Amadís de Gaula,* Évora, at court, 1533 (?);

*Auto da Cananéia,* Odivelas, Convent of Odivelas, 1534;

*A floresta de enganos,* Évora, at court, 1536.

A dramatist of immense importance during early modern times in the Iberian Peninsula, Gil Vicente has been called the "inventor of modern Iberian theater": he was the first to write dramas in the main Iberian languages of the postmedieval period. Although there were other dramatic poets before Vicente, their work was part of an oral tradition and disappeared with the advent and popularity of the printing press in the fifteenth and sixteenth centuries. Nonetheless, Vicente thought of his plays as works to be performed. Composed for a purpose, they generally were not staged more than once. Most premiered as part of official celebrations or holidays before royalty or members of the Portuguese political elite; the plays were performed at court or in the palatial residences of upper-class citizens.

Only in his final years, during the mid 1530s, did Vicente make the transition from traditional drama (writing for performance) to published author. (Because of the Inquisition, publication was difficult earlier in his career.) Vicente reveals an awareness of his special situation–the transformation from an oral to a literary poet–in the foreword that he wrote for *Copilaçam de todalas obras de Gil Vicente, a qual se reparte em cinco liuros. O primeyro he de todas suas cousas de deuaçam. O segundo as comedias. O terceyro as tragicomedias. No quarto as farsas. No quinto as obras meudas* (1562), the posthumously published collection of his writings. In the "Prólogo" (Prologue) he relays his concerns about the situation in Portugal when the Inquisition was established. Although he felt that previous writers had attained excellence in all different aspects of poetry, leaving him with little else to say, he also knew that the publication of his writings would rank him with the ancient and modern playwrights whose works were still revered. At the same time, he was aware that the moment was not favorable for him.

Vicente's works have been classified as *moralidades* (spiritual plays), *farsas* (farces), *comédias* (comedies), and *tragicomédias* (tragicomedies). While he himself provided the first information about the essential differences among his works, dividing them into *comédias, farsas,* and *moralidades* in his prologue to *Comédia de Dom Duardos* (Comedy of Don Duarte, performed 1522; published 1562), the notion of *tragicomédias* appears to be a later invention, one that did not originate with him. In addition, Vicente's works reflect an influence of early Renaissance theater theory. Garcia de Resende qualifies Vicente's plays as "muy nova invenções" (very new inventions) and states that his works were written "com mais graça e mais dotrina" (with more humor and more doctrine). Finally, while in the rest of Europe the medieval tradition was flourishing, in Portugal, Vicente began to revive classical themes in his plays, such as the story of Cassandra. Late medieval motifs and settings, including the tradition of farce and the allegory of the garden, which had effectively started with the French *Roman de la Rose* (commenced in 1230 and completed 1270–1275), were still present in his works. They coexisted, however, with typical Renaissance topics such at the boat of souls, Fortuna, and carnivalesque actions.

Vicente was born in 1465, probably in Guimarães, and quite likely was self-educated. Little is known about his personal life, but in some papers of the royal administration there are references to a goldsmith named Gil Vicente. This person was promoted in 1513 to the position of royal goldsmith, and he made a considerable quantity of gold artifacts for the king and the royal household. Vicente is designated in this document as a *trovador mestre da balança* (troubador master of the balance)–in other words, a poet and an officer of the royal mint. He is the poet (*o trovador*) who both satisfies the duties of a goldsmith and oversees the measures in the royal mint (*o mestre da balança*). The designation of a goldsmith as a *mestre de balança* was not unusual–in fact, several European kingdoms recognized such a practice. Royalty of that time was interested in collaborating with intellectuals, such as Vicente, who spoke favorably of monarchical politics. Other evidence that writer and goldsmith were the same individual includes the many references to gold jewelry and its symbolism in Vicente's writings. At the age of approximately thirty-seven he began engaging in a career as a playwright.

The listing of Vicente's works in chronological order is an almost impossible task. Only a few of them were published (in a brochure-like format) during his lifetime, such as *Farsa de Inês Pereira* (Farce of Ines Pereira, performed 1523), *Breve sumário da história de Deus* (Short Summary of the History of God, performed 1527), *Diálogo sobre a resurreição de Cristo* (Dialogue on the Resurrection, performed 1527), and *Pranto de Maria Parda,* none of which has an exact publishing date (each appeared in print sometime between 1536 and 1562). Immediately after Vicente's death censorship by the Inquisition was established in Portugal, and many of his works became targets of criticism by the inquisitors. Vicente's works were published in book form roughly two-and-a-half decades after he died, during a period of political liberalization. His son, Luís Vicente, who undertook the project of securing the publication of his father's writings for the 1562 volume, made some alterations and additions to Vicente's works. As a result, whether a text is completely original or not is sometimes difficult to ascertain. In addition, Luís Vicente did not publish the plays in chronological order. Their chronology has been reconstructed by, rather, A. Braamcamp Freire and Oscar de Pratt. Yet, many questions and doubts regarding the accuracy of the chronology still remain.

*Frontispiece for the earliest collection of Vicente's plays (Biblioteca Nacional, Lisbon)*

There persists, moreover, some doubt about the authenticity of a few works that cannot be clearly attributed to Vicente, mainly because he wrote in more than one language. Twelve of his plays are in Spanish; twenty are in Portuguese; and sixteen were written in both languages. Some of his plays use other Romance languages and dialects, such as Picard and Andalusian, and Latin. This diverse engagement of languages places Vicente within the tradition of early humanism, for he focused on, and observed, the possible kinds and varieties of expressions that people employ for communicative purposes. For instance, many interjections, exclamations, word games, and onomatopoetic expressions can be found in his texts: they belong, even if they are marginal, to the means of human expression.

During the early years of the Renaissance the theater flourished in Portugal, mainly because the Portuguese court was then the most important and richest in Europe. In the early decades of the sixteenth century, when techniques of royal and courtly self-representation and propaganda were being developed, Portuguese royalty recognized that theatrical presentations could be an important medium in which to enhance its image and deliver certain positions of sociopolitical discourse to the public. In the decades that ensued, these performances became an important aspect of Renaissance courtly life, and the practice was imported to the court of France under the influence of the models that Catherine de Médici brought from Florence. In France, however, the type of performance was courtly ballet or royal entrances, which were illuminated through dramatic scenes. Only in late-sixteenth-century England, under the reign of Elizabeth I, and in early-seventeenth-century France, under the government of Armand-Emmanuel du Plessis, Duke of Richelieu, did theater acquire a position similar to what it had achieved in Portugal in the early sixteenth century. Furthermore, Vicente was one of the first European playwrights to provide precise information on the performance of his plays—how the actors should behave and act on the stage. In the text of *O templo de Apolo* (The Temple of Apollo, performed 1526; published 1562), for example, he instructs: "Bebe e depois de beber, diz . . ." (He drinks and after drinking he says . . .) and "Chega um Vilão Português, em trajo de Romeiro, e diz" (A Portuguese peasant arrives, dressed as a pilgrim, and says . . .). Vicente also put himself as a character into some of his dramas.

The coexistence of medieval and Renaissance themes and forms is characteristic of literature during the Portuguese Renaissance. In its incorporation of classical topics and forms, Vicente's plays became a part of Renaissance culture, even though they continued some medieval literary traditions. For example, he employed techniques of theatrical improvisation that were developed in medieval plays, which he knew possibly from oral traditions and presentations. Aristocratic forms, such as the *momo* (a short farce), however, also belong to the dramatic traditions he inherited and put to use in his theatrical works. He was familiar with the Spanish writers Juan del Encina and Lucas Fernández and their eclogues, from which he learned the poetic virtues of medieval Christian symbolism. Beginning in 1514 Vicente was also aware of the more advanced dramatic writings (in terms of technical perfection) of the Spanish author Torres Naharro.

Vicente responded to the literary taste of his time by maintaining the late-medieval, early-humanist idea of an allegorical text open to various interpretations. This approach probably attracted Vicente because of the many obstacles barring the free expression of social and political ideas in Portuguese society. The situation at the end of the fifteenth and the beginning of the sixteenth centuries was complex: the new needs of a transcontinental colonial expansion; the attraction of a transatlantic adventure; the expulsion of the Arabs from Castile; the conversion of Arabs and Jews to

Christianity; and the challenge of a nascent Reformation in Europe, as well as of Christian and pagan humanism. These factors deeply influenced the sociopolitical life of Portugal. Hence, a textual structure that allowed for more than one reading, or understanding–lending a multidimensional sense to a work–was a strategy that filled the needs of the historical complexity that Vicente witnessed and then expressed in his plays.

At the start of his playwriting career, Vicente concentrated mostly on topics inspired by religious themes. On 7 June 1502 he presented his first play, the *Monólogo del vaqueiro* (Cowboy's Monologue), or *Auto de uma visitação* (Drama of a Visit)–written in Castilian–at the court of Dom Manuel and Dona Beatriz. The performance took place on the second night after the birth of their son, the future King João III. The *vaqueiro* arrives to see the newborn child, and the queen greets him with a panegyric on the royal family. Other shepherds arrive to offer gifts. After the premiere Dona Beatriz ordered that *Monólogo del vaqueiro* be performed every Christmas morning. Vicente later added more details concerning the birth of Christ.

In 1504 Vicente wrote *Milagre de São Martinho* (Miracle of San Martinho) and in 1506 he completed *Sermão de Abrantes* (Sermon of Abrantes); each play was performed in the same year that it was written. In 1506, drawing upon his expertise as a goldsmith, he designed and made what has come to be known as a masterpiece of Portuguese jewelry: the "Custódia de Belém," made from the first gold that Vasco da Gama brought with him in tribute to King Quíloa of East Africa.

In *Auto da Índia* (Drama of India, performed 1509) Vicente reconsiders the old epic leitmotiv of marital tension, when a husband leaves his wife to pursue new experiences and adventures in the expanding Portuguese empire. His next play, *Auto pastoril castelhano* (Castilian Shepherds' Drama, performed 1509; published 1562), written in Castilian, is about five shepherds. The first, named Gil, begins a discourse on the *vita contemplativa* (contemplative life), which leads him to isolation. The others criticize Gil's attitude and his increasing withdrawal from them. The critique of the *vita contemplativa* may be considered a critique of *otium* (leisure) under the historical circumstances: at the time Portugal needed a model for a *vita activa* (active life) in the context of its expansion to India and the Americas. By the order of the queen, Vicente finally wrote his third play, dedicated to the story of the magi. *Ecloga dos Reis Magos* (1562) was presented on 6 January 1510. On Christmas of the same year Vicente presented his *Auto da fé* (Drama of Faith).

From 1513 (when he was named *mestre da balança* at the Lisbon mint) until his death, Vicente appeared regularly as the poet who wrote pieces for the most important events in the lives and the households of Portuguese kings and queens. He composed plays to recognize holidays such as Christmas and Easter, as well as to celebrate the birth of royal children. In this sense Vicente was the "master of ceremonies" for the Portuguese kings Manuel and João III.

In *Moralidade da Sibila Cassandra* (Morality of the Sibyl Cassandra, performed 1513; published 1562) Vicente mingles biblical motifs with classical topics. The Hebrew prophets and the Latin sibyls appear as shepherds at the birth of Christ. The anachronisms in this play refer to extraordinary, related facts. The future *autos sacramentales* (holy plays) adopt the same technique of using anachronisms. The *Auto dos quatro tempos* (Drama of the Four Seasons, 1514?) reveals the important impact of Neoplatonist theories and the natural philosophy of Vicente's time. The allegory of the four seasons appears in the presence of Jupiter who, as the highest god, has the right to judge the seasons. King David and Jupiter represent, respectively, Mosaic Law and the law of nature. Both David and Jupiter confess that they have been surpassed by the birth of Christ. Yet, obviously, each belongs to a different culture–and time–and cannot witness the birth of Christ. That Vicente brings David and Jupiter together in the same text, however–rendering them, in an anachronistic way, witnesses of Christ's birth (because they know of its occurrence)–reveals the same spirit of artifice achieved through the anachronisms engendered previously in *Moralidade da Sibila Cassandra*.

*Auto da exortação da guerra* (Drama of an Exhortation to War) appeared in 1514. In this play Vicente criticizes the Portuguese clergy for its refusal to contribute to a new crusade against the Arabs. His criticism makes clear that he clings to the medieval tradition of analyzing the geopolitical constellation in terms of the secular clash between Christian and Islamic cultures. From a Portuguese point of view the crusades held particular meaning: new crusades presented Portugal with a chance to increase its strategic outposts in Africa. Therefore, the *Auto da exortação da guerra* should be seen within the context of the possibility of the *vita activa* under the historical circumstances of colonial expansion–a theme that Vicente had already developed in *Auto da Índia*.

In 1515 Vicente released his *Quem tem farelos?* (1562), a play with close ties to the tradition of farce. On Christmas of that year he also premiered his *Os mistérios da Virgem* (The Mysteries of the Virgin), generally known as *Auto da Mofina Mendes* (Drama of Mofina Mendes). With this work Vicente reinforced the criticism that he had articulated previously against the clergy and the Pope.

In 1518 he presented his *Auto da alma* (Drama of the Soul), which is linked thematically to three other works of that period. Between 1517 and 1519 he wrote his most important plays: the so-called *Trilogía das barcas* (Trilogy of the Boats), which consists of the *Auto da barca do inferno* (Drama of the Boat to Hell, performed 1517; published 1562), the *Auto da barca do purgatório* (Drama of the Boat to Purgatory, performed 1518; published 1562), and the *Auto da barca da glória* (Drama of the Boat to Glory, performed 1519; published 1562). He incorporates the mythological notion of the boat that brings souls to the empire of the dead. On the one hand, the *Auto da barca do inferno* is based on the writings of Lucian of Samosata. For the first time—not only in Portugal but also in all of Europe—a pagan Greek text was used as the basis for a text in a modern European language. On the other hand, the *Trilogía das barcas* resembles the medieval *dança da morte,* the dance of the dead.

The plays of the trilogy share a similar structure. After death the souls leave the bodies to which they belonged and arrive at a river, where they encounter two boats. One boat, guided by an angel, is bound for paradise, while the other one, led by the devil, is headed for purgatory and hell. The souls undergo a trial: if they are found guilty, they will be sent to hell; if they are deemed innocent, they will go to paradise. The souls are those of persons from different social classes, and Vicente uses these people and their souls to create a social critique throughout his texts. *Auto da barca da glória* includes the harshest criticism in the trilogy. The characters include o Conde, o Duque, o Rei, o Imperador, o Bispo, o Arcebispo, o Cardeal, and o Papa. All are found guilty and condemned to hell. After praying to the crucifix, however, they are suddenly freed—by Christ's direct intervention—and allowed to enter paradise.

A shift from religious to worldly topics clearly marks Vicente's work. Of the nineteen plays he wrote before 1520, only five concern profane subjects. After 1520 he wrote twenty-nine plays, four of which are religious in nature. A main reason for this change is the ascension of João III to the throne in 1521, after which Vicente was named master of ceremonies and began orienting his work toward worldly topics, presumably to please his king. As a result, the presence of classical themes and motifs become more apparent in Vicente's plays. Political, social, intellectual, and religious abuse become targets of a severe critique in his *moralidades, farsas, autos,* and *comedias*. This critique, expressed in a poetic manner, attests the mood of crisis in Portuguese society in the first decades of the sixteenth century, and Vicente observed this society from a courtly viewpoint—from the position represented by the king of Portugal.

In 1521 Vicente's *Comédia de Rubena* (Comedy of Rubena, 1562) was performed. This play was his first to be divided into three acts, a result, perhaps, of the increasing influence of Aristotelian theory on drama. In his *Poetics* (after 335 B.C.) Aristotle declares that a drama must have a beginning, a middle, and an end—a tripartite sense of dramatic action. Only in the mid sixteenth century were plays divided into three or five acts as a rule.

In his plays of the *Comédia de Dom Duardos* Vicente incorporates the topic of *amor* (love) and *fortuna* (fortune). The neoplatonic and natural philosophers understood *amor* as the universal power binding all beings and leading them to form new entities. *Amor* defeats everybody and everything because all are subdued by its power. It works in an unforeseeable way; thus, people cannot prepare themselves against its attacks. In this sense *amor* operates as an agent of chance, which had been represented since the Middle Ages by the classical goddess Fortuna. Vicente was aware of this tradition, which had existed since the thirteenth century; it was especially common in the works of Petrarch, for example, who lived and wrote in the fourteenth century. Vicente concludes *Comédia de Don Duardos* with the proverbial sentence: "Al Amor y la Fortuna / no hay defension ninguna" (Against love and fortune / There is no remedy).

In *Farsa de Inês Pereira* Vicente plays with the notion that there exists a difference between public and private morals and ethics. In 1523 he also staged his *Auto pastoril português* (Portuguese Shepherds' Drama, 1562). In the character of the pastoral genre, the language in this piece is colloquial. Interjections ("Ai"), word games ("E um Gil . . . um Gil . . . um Gil . . ."), and songs with senseless syllables ("Cha cha cha, raivarão elas . . .") reveal the linguistic code of shepherds. That same year Vicente wrote his *Comédia de Amadís de Gaula* (Comedy of Amadis of Gaula, performed 1533 [?]; published 1562), presenting for the first time in dramatic form the deeds of a medieval knight. The work reveals the influence of Aristotle's *Poetics* and the early Latin and Italian commentaries on the *Poetics*. Aristotle stressed that the deeds of an aristocrat may fit the needs of dramatic action well, especially the needs of tragedy. The *Comédia de Amadís de Gaula,* however, proves that the difference between dramatic and epic material had not yet been observed in Portugal: the deeds of a hero also fit well the needs of a comedy. This idea was later rejected by Renaissance writers who wanted to eliminate knightly behavior from dramatic action and restrict its use in poetry to the epic. Vicente's comedy provides information about the status of medieval topics in Portuguese Renaissance theater, which presents almost no break with the themes of the Middle Ages.

Some scholars believe that *Comédia do viúvo* (performed 1524; published 1562) is a result of the death of Vicente's wife. According to a chronology that dates the work from 1521, *Comédia do viúvo* could be a sketch for *Tragicomédia de Don Carlos*. In the *Frágua do amor* (1562), performed in 1524 on the occasion of King João III's marriage to Dona Catarina, Vicente presents a long dialogue between the *peregino* (pilgrim) and the goddess Venus. The pilgrim is a symbol of man's journey through life, while Venus represents love. In *Os físicos* (performed 1524; published 1562) Vicente discusses several scientific issues of his time. In keeping with contemporary epistemology, he allows the characters to discuss their problems from the point of view of the unifying force of love.

*O juiz da Beira* (The Judge of Beira, 1525) repeats the main themes of the *Farsa de Inês Pereira*. His 1526 play *O templo de Apolo* (The Temple of Apollo) is a dramatic feast that honors classical knowledge and paganism and reveals the same spirit of Renaissance natural philosophy as the *Cortes de Júpiter*. His next play, *Moralidade da feira* (Morality of the Fair, 1562), was performed on Christmas Day 1527. In it Vicente unmasks the venality of civil and ecclesiastical power. The work incorporates his knowledge of medieval and Renaissance astronomy, displaying long passages that present the structure of the universe. Roma, a character who stands for Rome the city, declares that she might be murdered by the Christians. Her story line appears in the play as a clear reflection of the event known as Sacco di Roma (Sack of Rome), which took place in 1527; the Emperor Charles V, in retaliation for what he saw as King Francis I's betrayal, took the city of Rome. In the comedy *Nao d'amores* (performed 1527; published 1562), as well as in *Moralidade da feira*, Vicente harshly criticizes Pope Clement VII and the Sacco di Roma. At the same time King João III tried to find a new diplomatic balance between the different European forces in the aftermath of the event.

In *Farsa dos Almocreves* (performed circa 1526–1527; published 1562) Vicente deals with the problem of knights who, even if they are impoverished, maintain a huge household that requires more than what they earn. The nobleman in this play never pays his bills. In the comedy *A divisa da cidade de Coimbra* (The Boundary of the City of Coimbra, performed 1527; published 1562) Vicente shares with other humanists an interest in emblems, hieroglyphics, graphic signs, symbols, and idiomatic language. In the same way that Erasmus tried to reconstruct the ancient history of proverbs in his *Chiliades Adagiorum,* or *Adages* (1502), Vicente invents the history of the emblem of Coimbra.

If honor is acquired through antiquity, then the antiquity of the emblem of Coimbra proves the "infinita honra [que] tem esta Cidade" (the infinite honor that this city has). In this play Vicente presents to the public a probable history of the founding of Coimbra.

The allegory of the Coimbra highlands, represented by a female, appears in the comedy *Pastoril da Serra da Estrela* (Shepherds' Play of the Serra da Estrela, performed 1527; published 1562). She meets the shepherd Gonçalvo, who is coming from the court. Social lines are not strictly drawn in Vicente's plays; kings, shepherds, and allegories appear together. He uses the genre of comedy as a poetic form, by which he measures the whole of social reality among the Portuguese people.

*Breve sumário da história de Deus* and *Diálogo sobre a resurreição de Cristo* present a condensed history of the world, from the creation of man to his redemption. The *Auto das fadas* (performed 1527; published 1562) and the *Auto da festa* (performed 1525) were written around the same time. Vicente engages in self-plagiarism in the latter play: he reuses an entire scene from the *O templo de Apolo*. In fact, a frequent recycling of material from previous texts marks his work. He takes his earlier plays and incorporates new dramatic situations and social and political contexts. His work may be defined as imitation and creation, or repetition and invention.

The *Triunfo do inverno* (Triumph of Winter, performed 1529; published 1562) also known as *Tragicomédia do inverno e verão* (Tragicomedy of Winter and Spring), is linked to the medieval and humanistic topic of the beginning of spring, which fights winter and reanimates nature and society. Vicente recasts this theme in a way that is closely linked, however, to Portuguese reality. The battle between winter and spring is essentially a question of navigation and commerce. For this reason a pilot, a seafarer, and the seafarer's whistle appear in *Triunfo do inverno,* which concerns mainly "la marina fortuna" (the maritime fortune), the principal occupation of Portugal at this time.

The farce *O clérigo da Beira* (The Clergyman from Beira, performed 1529; published 1562) plays with the possibility of representing the whole scope of Portuguese society in one play and likely marks one of the first time that the character of a black African appears on the European stage. Vicente allowed the character to speak in "barbarian" Portuguese, which may be of his own invention or modeled after the Portuguese spoken by Africans who came from the Portuguese colonies.

The *Auto da Lusitânia* (Drama of Lusitania, performed 1532; published 1562) is a dramatic allegory in honor of Portugal. The play was performed repeatedly over the ensuing years—a rare occurrence for any of Vicente's works. The comedy *O romagem de agrava-*

*dos* (performed 1533; published 1562), like the *Auto de Cananéia* (Drama of Cananéia, 1534), reveals a strong influence of Erasmus's theories. Vicente's final comedy, *A floresta de enganos* (The Garden of Enchantment, 1536), focuses on a corrupt system of judges and jurisprudence.

In addition to his dramas Vicente wrote poems and other short pieces. Some of these were selected by his son, Luis, for publication as "obras meudas" (smaller works). Vicente is considered one of the most important Portuguese poets, ranking with King Dinis in the fourteenth century and Luís de Camões some decades after Vicente's death. Because of his poems in Spanish, some scholars consider him to be the most outstanding Spanish poet to precede Garcilasso de la Vega. Vicente's other writings consist of hagiographic and encomiastic poems, as well as some letters, one of which is addressed to King João III and addresses the earthquake in Lisbon on 6 January 1531.

Vicente died sometime between 1536 and 1540 in Lisbon. On 29 January 1537 King João III awarded Vicente's son, Belchior, the position of "ao escrivão segundo da feitoria da Mina" (second writer of the factory of Mina). This recognition was probably a royal gesture of gratitude toward the family for the playwright's works.

Before he died Vicente had intended to prepare an edition of his works. In 1536, however, the censorship of the Inquisition was established in Portugal, and he had to abandon his plans for the book—one of the first projects to fall victim to the regime of intolerance. A period of liberalization finally made the collection of Vicente's works a reality, perhaps because of the influence of Queen Catarina, who evidently had some affection for Vicente's work and family. His daughter, Paula Vicente, was a "moça da câmara" (chambermaid) of the queen. Thus, in 1562 the first edition of the *Copilaçam de todalas obras de Gil Vicente, a qual se reparte em cinco liuros. O primeyro he de todas suas cousas de deuaçam. O segundo as comedias. O terceyro as tragicomedias. No quarto as farsas. No quinto as obras meudas* was published by Joam Aluarez. A second edition, published by Andres Lobato, appeared in 1586. Several plays were omitted from the 1562 edition, however, and the 1586 edition was an even more deficient text because of pressure from the Inquisition.

The first Iberian author of the postmedieval period to write plays in both Spanish and Portuguese, Gil Vicente captured the spirit of both the Middle Ages and the Renaissance. He established himself as the creator of modern Portuguese theater, and his importance in that discipline has been repeatedly affirmed over the centuries with the many publications and performances of his plays.

**Bibliographies:**

Constantine C. Stathatos, *A Gil Vicente Bibliography (1940–1975),* with a preface by Thomas R. Hart (London: Grant & Cutler, 1980);

Stathatos, "A Gil Vicente Bibliography (1940–1975)," *Segismundo,* 16, no. 35–36 (1982): 2–25;

Stathatos, *A Gil Vicente Bibliography (1995–2000)* (Kassel: Reichenberger, 2001).

**References:**

Albin Eduard Beau, *Duas conferências inéditas sobre teatro a estrutura dos autos de Gil Vicente; Teatro espectáculo, teatro lírico, teatro ideológico* (Coimbra: Faculdade de Letras, 1977);

D. Becker, *De la musique dans le théâtre religieux de Gil Vicente, ArCCP,* 23 (1987): 461–486;

A. Bell, *Estudos vicentinos* (Lisbon: Nacional, 1940);

C. Berardinelli, *De literatura portuguesa* (Lisbon: Nacional, 1985), pp. 27–76;

A. Braamcamp Freire, *Vida e obras de Gil Vicente "Trovador, mestre da balança"* (Lisbon: Ocidente, 1944);

Teófilo Braga, *Gil Vicente e as origens do theatro nacional* (Porto: Livraria Chardron, 1898);

Reis Brasil, *Gil Vicente e a cidade de Lisboa* (Lisbon: Livraria Portugal, 1968);

Brasil, *Gil Vicente e a evolução do teatro* (Lisbon: Minerva, 1965);

Brasil, *Gil Vicente e o teatro moderno: tentativa de esquematização da obra vicentina* (Lisbon: Minerva, 1965);

José Augusto Cardoso Bernardes, *Sátira e lirismo, modelos de síntese no teatro de Gil Vicente* (Coimbra: Universidade de Coimbra, 1997);

Janet E. Carter, *The Concept of Allegory and Gil Vicente's Auto da Alma* (Johannesburg: Ernest Oppenheimer Institute for Portuguese Studies, University of the Witwatersrand, 1982);

Luisa Maria de Castro e Azevedo, ed., *Bibliografia vicentina* (Lisbon: Pereira Rosa, 1942);

Solange Corbin, *Les textes musicaux de l'Auto da Alma (Identification d'une pièce citée par Gil Vicente)* (Paris: Klincksieck, 1951);

Luís da Cunha Gonçalves, *Gil Vicente e os Homens do Foro* (Lisbon: Ática, 1953);

Ana Paula Dias, *Para uma leitura de "Auto da alma" de Gil Vicente* (Lisbon: Presença, 1999);

José Maria Diez Borque, *Aspectos de la oposición "caballero-pastor" en el primer teatro castellano (Lucas Fernández, Juan del Enzina, Gil Vicente)* (Talence-Pessac: Institut d'études ibériques et ibéro-américaines de l'Université de Bordeaux, 1970);

René Pedro Garay, *Gil Vicente and the Development of the Comedia* (Chapel Hill: University of North Carolina Press, 1988);

Maria Leonor Garcia da Cruz, *Gil Vicente–a sociedade portuguesa de quinhentos leitura crítica num mondo "de Cara Atrás"* (Lisbon: Gradiva, 1990);

Almeida Garrett, *Um auto de Gil Vicente*, edited by Manuel dos Santos Rodrigues (Lisbon: Replicação, 1996);

Garrett, "Gil Vicente," in *Theatro II* (Lisbon: José Baptista Morando, 1841), pp. 131–153;

Hope Hamilton-Faria, *The Farces of Gil Vicente: A Study in the Stylistics of Satire* (Madrid: Playor, 1976);

Thomas R. Hart, *Gil Vicente, Casandra and Don Duardos* (London: Grant & Cutler in association with Tamesis Books, 1981);

Hart, *Gil Vicente Farces and Festival Plays* (Eugene: University of Oregon Press, 1972);

R. Hess, "Die Naturauffassung Gil Vicentes," *APK*, 5 (1965): 1–64;

B. L. Keates, *The Court Theatre of Gil Vicente* (Lisbon: Teorema, 1962);

R. Köhler, "Der Einfluß Gil Vicentes auf das spanische Theater des Goldenen Zeitalters," dissertation, University of Göttingen, 1968;

C. Láfer, *O judeu em Gil Vicente* (São Paulo: Conselho estadual de cultura, 1963);

Cheryl Folkins McGinnis, "La danza literaria como simbolo de metamorfosis: Empleo y sentido en el teatro de Juan del Encina y Gil Vicente," dissertation, 1977;

Carolina Michaëlis de Vasconcelos, *Notas vicentinas* (Lisbon: Ocidente, 1949);

Neil Miller, *O elemento pastoril no teatro de Gil Vicente* (Porto: Inova, 1970);

B. G. M. Moser, *An Index to the Characters in the Dramatic Works of Gil Vicente*, in *Theatre Documentation*, volume 2 (New York: Theatre Library Association, 1970), pp. 19–47;

Maria Amélia Ortiz da Fonseca, *Gil Vicente, Auto da feira* (Mem Martins: Europa-América, 1991);

J. H. Parker, *Gil Vicente* (New York: Twayne, 1967);

Eduardo González Pedroso, *Autos sacramentales desde su origen hasta fines del siglo XVII* (Madrid: M. Rivadeneyra, 1865);

Sebastião Pestana, *O "Auto pastoril castelhano" de Gil Vicente* (Lisbon: S. Pestana, 1978);

Pestana, *Gil Vicente "Auto dos Reis Magos"* (Lisbon: S. Pestana, 1979);

Luciana Stegagno Picchio, *La méthode philologique: Écrits sur la littérature portugaise*, volume 2 (Paris: Calouste Gubelkian Foundation, 1982), pp. 103–116, 137–175;

Alberto Pires de Lima, *A linguagem anatómica de Gil Vicente* (Coimbra: Coimbra Editora, 1938);

H. Post, "As obras de Gil Vicente como elo de transição entre o drama medieval o teatro do renascimento," *ArCCP*, 9 (1975): 101–121;

Oscar de Pratt, *Gil Vicente: Notas e commentários* (Lisbon: Livraria clássica, 1970);

*Quaderni Portoghesi*, special Gil Vicente issue, 9–10 (1981);

S. Reckert, *Gil Vicente: Espíritu y letra. I: Estudio* (Madrid: Gredos, 1977);

I. S. Révah, "Gil Vicente a-t-il été le fondateur du théâtre portugais?" *Bulletin d'histoire du théâtre portugaise*, 1, no. 2 (1950): 153–185;

Maria Idalina Resina Rodrigues, *De Gil Vicente a Lope de Vega, vozes cruzadas no teatro ibérico* (Lisbon: Teorema, 1999);

António José Saraiva, *Gil Vicente e o fim do teatro medieval* (Lisbon: Livraria Bertrand, 1981);

Saraiva, *Teatro de Gil Vicente* (N.p.: Dinalivro, 1988);

Saraiva, *Testemunho social e condenação de Gil Vicente* (Lisbon: Fundao, 1976);

Ugo Serani, *L'immagine allo specchio, il teatro di corte di Gil Vicente* (Rome: Bagatto Libri, 2000);

L. Sletsjøe, *O elemento cénico em Gil Vicente* (Lisbon: Casa Portuguesa, 1965);

Paulo Caratão Soromenho, *Caminhadas lisboetas de Gil Vicente* (Lisbon: Ramos, Afonso & Moita, 1966);

Dulce Pereira Teixeira and Lurdes Aguiar Trilho, *Auto da Índia de Gil Vicente, questões de compreensão global; O autor e a obra; Dissertações; Métodos e técnicas de estudo; Funcionamento da língua; Fichas; Soluções* (Lisbon: Texto Edição, 1997);

Francisco Elías de Tejada Spínola, *As Idéias Políticas de Gil Vicente*, translated by Manoel de Bettencourt e Galvão (Lisbon: Pro Domo, 1945);

Maria J. Teles, Maria Leonor Cruz, and Susana Marta Pinheiro, *O discurso carnavalesco em Gil Vicente* (Lisbon: GEC, 1984);

Paul Teyssier, *Gil Vicente, o autor e a obra* (Lisbon: Instituto de Cultura e Lingua Portuguesa, 1982);

Teyssier, *La langue de Gil Vicente* (Paris: Klincksieck, 1959);

S. Zimic, "Estudios sobre el teatro de Gil Vicente: Obras de crítica social y religiosa," *Acta Neophilologica*, 8 (1985): 11–47;

Zimic, "Estudios sobre el teatro de Gil Vicente (obras de tema amoroso)," *Boletín de la Biblioteca de Menéndez Pelayo*, 57 (1981): 45–103; 58 (1982): 5–66; 59 (1983): 11–78.

# Appendix 1:
# Medieval Galician-Portuguese Poetry

# Appendix 1: Medieval Galician-Portuguese Poetry

Leodegário A. de Azevedo Filho
*Universidade do Estado do Rio de Janeiro*
*Universidade Federal do Rio de Janeiro*

Galician-Portuguese poetry, the first important literary manifestation in Portugal, was cultivated from the twelfth century to the middle of the fourteenth century, when Portugal was still the Condado Portucalense and not a nation in itself. The Galician-Portuguese lyric was not, however, limited only to the area of Portugal and Galicia but also spread to other parts of the Iberian Peninsula, including Castile, León, and Aragon. The earliest known Galician-Portuguese poets, categorized under the general term *trovador* (troubadour), include Sancho I (1154–1211) and João Soares de Paiva (1140?– ?). The poems written in this tradition were recited in different locations; thus, the copies remaining today are probably variations on a long-lost original from the end of the thirteenth, or the beginning of the fourteenth, century.

This early lyric poetry, preserved in manuscript copies called *cancioneiros*, consists of *cantigas* (songs or poems) generally classified into four types, according to subject matter: the *cantigas de amor* (songs of love), the *cantigas de amigo* (songs of friend), the *cantigas de escárnio* (songs of mockery), and the *cantigas de maldizer* (songs of vilification).

The origin of the term *trovador* is the Latin verb *tropare*, which in the Middle Ages referred to the modification of a liturgical text or song through the addition or substitution of parts. An archaic form, *trobar*, is found in the *Cancioneiro da Vaticana* (663): "qual cometeste em vosso trobar." The word ultimately derives from the Greek word *tropos*, used as a rhetorical figure to signify a deviation of meaning. In contemporary Portuguese, the verb *trovar* means to compose poems.

The evolution of the Portuguese language can be divided into three general periods. The first is the protohistoric phase before the twelfth century, with texts written in vulgar Latin. The second—known as the archaic period—extends from the twelfth to the sixteenth centuries and includes two distinct periods: the twelfth to the fourteenth centuries, with texts written in Galician-Portuguese, and the fourteenth to the sixteenth centuries, in which this hybrid language becomes two distinct languages. The Galician-Portuguese language has its origins in the *romanço* (romance), and chronologically it coincides with a period of war, when the Portuguese were trying to reconquer the peninsula from the Arabs. In the middle of the fourteenth century there was a large influence from the south—the region of Lisbon—and the differences between Galician and Portuguese become noticeable. The third period, beginning in the sixteenth century and referred to as modern Portuguese, is when the language acquired the characteristics of contemporary Portuguese. The first grammar books and dictionaries were written in this third phase.

Scholar Carolina Michaëlis de Vasconcelos believes that the medieval period of Portuguese literature begins with the first extant written text, *Canção da Ribeirinha*, also known as *Canção de guarvaia* (Song of the Royal Robe) (1189?) and initially attributed to Father Soares de Taveirós (later he was found to have lived in the thirteenth century). This poem was inspired by Maria Pais Ribeiro, who was also called Ribeirinha. She became the lover of King Sancho, the second king of Portugal. The medieval period is generally subdivided into two phases. The first began in 1189 (or 1198) and lasted through 1434, the date when Fernão Lopes was appointed main chronicler of the Torre do Tombo. The Torre do Tombo is characterized by what scholars call *trovadorismo*, a term used to describe the *cantigas* that were cultivated in Galician-Portuguese poetry. The second phase is known as *humanismo* (humanism) and extends from 1434 to 1527, a period of transition from medieval to classical culture. In 1527 the poet Francisco Sá de Miranda returned from Italy and introduced characteristics of the Renaissance into Portuguese literature.

The *cantigas* were accompanied by music and normally sung in a chorus. A hierarchy among the poets of the period was in place at this time; they were either *trovadores, jograis,* or *soldadeiras*. The *trovador* was of noble birth and wrote and recited his poems for pleasure. The *jogral* was of humble birth, traveled often, and recited his works—and the works of others—for pay. The *soldadeira* or *jogralesa* was a young woman who danced and played an instrument, such as the tambourine.

# Appendix 1: Medieval Galician-Portuguese Poetry

Various scholars have studied the origins of Galician-Portuguese poetry, but no single thesis satisfactorily accounts for the various genres of the tradition. The most popular of these theories include those that trace the lyrics back to Arabic, classical, folkloric, and liturgical sources. Some believe that the troubadour concept of love had its origins in Arabic poetry because of its similarities with Portuguese poetry—including an erotic exaltation of love and an almost masochistic pride expressed in the suffering caused by love. This thesis was formulated in the sixteenth century and popularized by the Romantics of the nineteenth century. The Arabic lyrics, however, were generally addressed to a slave woman and did not involve a lady and her sense of loyalty, a central leitmotiv of the troubadour's poems. The Arabic poets did not address their verses to married women, as was the custom of the troubadours from Provence.

Scholars have not completely accepted the classical thesis of the origin of Galician-Portuguese poetry. Although certain *cantigas* reveal a latent sensuality reminiscent of the pagan aspects of the classical tradition, the chivalric concept of love is basically medieval and Christian. In addition to this, love was, often for the troubadours, merely a pretext for poetic creation and of a mystic and platonic character, thoroughly detached from reality.

The folkloric thesis that traces the Galician-Portuguese tradition back to popular poetry is also flawed. Alfred Jeanroy and Gaston Paris contend that the courtier's love lyrics have their origins in the folk dance of May, the *chanson de la mal mariée* (song of the badly married). The theme of this type of poem is always that of the young married woman who every spring—in the month of May—forgoes her marriage vows and gives herself to a passionate young man. Undoubtedly, popular tradition influenced the Iberian poets, but whether it was the origin of their poetry is difficult to prove.

Some scholars have proposed that Galician-Portuguese verse of the Middle Ages had a liturgical origin in the Latin poetry of the clergy. This approach seems to be a simple case of parallelism between the two traditions, however, since no unequivocal cause-and-effect relationship can be established. Possibly, the troubadours were influenced by certain poetic techniques, such as the form and rhythm of religious verse, but the transformation in the *cantigas* of the Virgin Mary's adoration into the sensual love of a woman is doubtful. Galician-Portuguese lyric poetry is, in essence, secular rather than sacred.

Scholars do not agree on any one specific theory to explain the origins of the rich poetic tradition that developed in the Iberian Peninsula during the Middle Ages. Each thesis, however, contributes interesting and valid points in support of a more ample theory, which views the medieval epoch as a time when multiple and diverse influences were prevalent in Iberian culture. This notion of a plurality of sources would explain the blend of sensual and Platonic love into a certain spirituality that characterizes the tone of the *cantigas*.

Scholars tend to agree that the troubadours from Provence in the south of France found their way to Galicia and had an impact on the poetry developing in the peninsula. King Dinis (1261–1325) was the most famous Portuguese troubadour. Known as the "troubadour king," he was responsible for the first important cultural development of the country. Interested in learning and education, he created the first university in Lisbon in 1290. There are 138 extant *cantigas* by King Dinis. In one of them he suggests Provence as the place of origin for the genre: "Quer' eu en maneira de proençal / fazer agora un cantar d' amor" (I would like to produce now a love song in the fashion of Provence). The considerable movement between the Iberian Peninsula and France during the Middle Ages explains the impact of Provençal poetry on the Galician-Portuguese lyric. Many rural French people went to Portugal to work, and many made the pilgrimages to Santiago de Compostela in Galicia. French knights fought against the Moors, and several marriages between noble Portuguese men and ladies from Provence were celebrated during this period. There was also was an intense commercial trade between Portugal and France.

When the troubadours began making their way from Provence, a primitive, autochthonous verse was already thriving in the peninsula. This popular poetry, which later developed into the *cantiga de amigo*, extended from the north to the south and fused with poetic techniques found in Arabic verse. The *cantigas* were associated with music and dance. The relationship between a male and a female, with the latter as a particular focus, was almost always the subject of the poems. The Galician poets maintained their own language while adapting certain formal aspects of the Provençal lyric, especially for their *cantigas de amor*.

Galician-Portuguese poetry, especially the *cantigas de amor*, expressed a code of courtly love, as well as strong erotic links between the poet and his *senhora* (lady). A young man who revealed a talent for poetry was often given special treatment. When he turned fourteen, his education became the responsibility of the lady of the court, in whose service he remained for seven years. He stayed in her home and traveled with her while he was instructed in courtly behavior. The young man's enthusiasm was focused on this lady, his ideal of love in the verses that he composed.

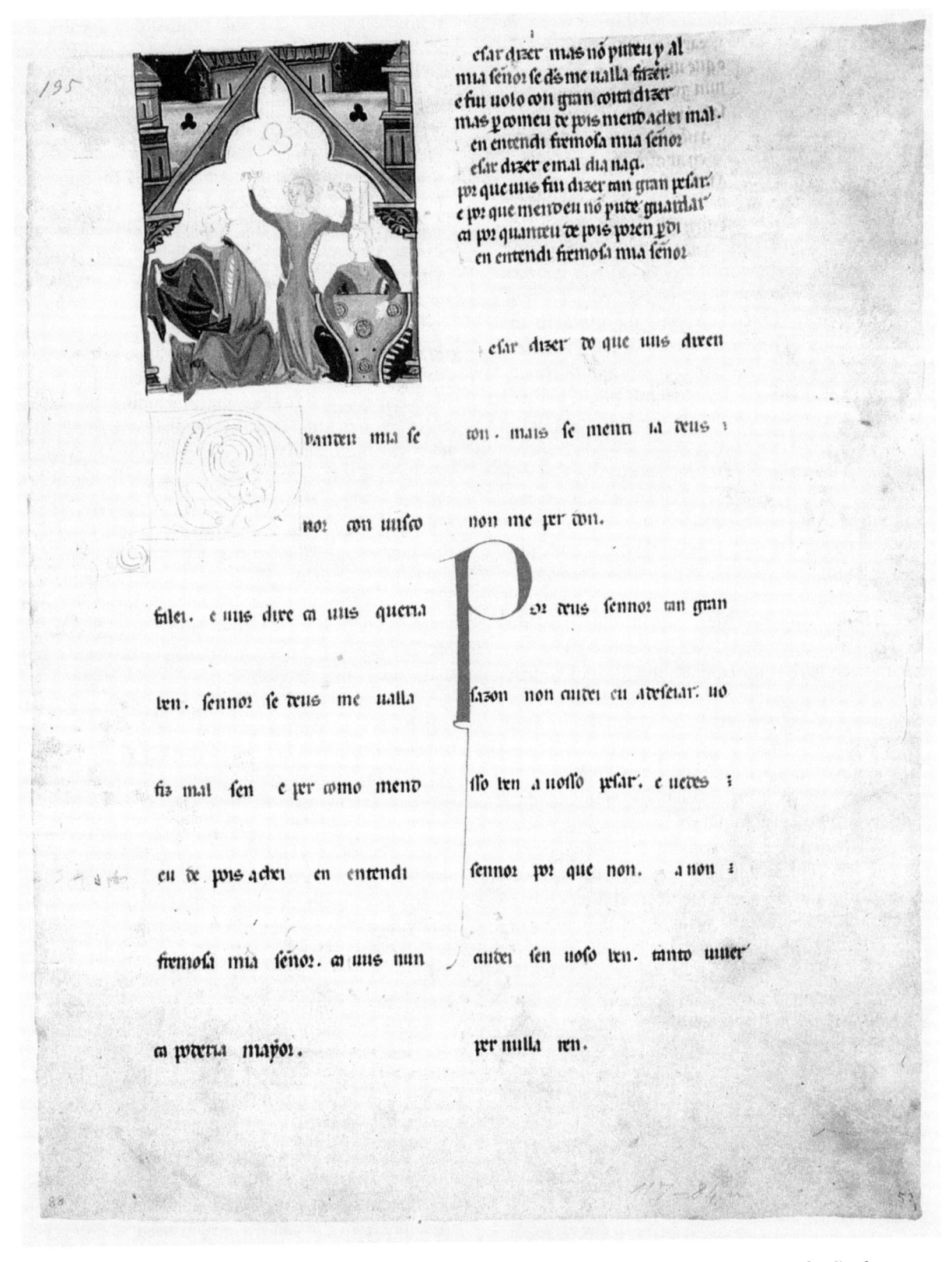

*Page from the manuscript for the* Cancioneiro da Ajuda *(Songbook of Ajuda), one of the major collections of medieval Galician-Portuguese poetry. The manuscript was copied at the end of the thirteenth century and is in the Biblioteca da Ajuda in Lisbon (from Nuno Júdice,* Portugal, língua e cultura, *1992; Lauinger Library, Georgetown University)*

The development of the relationship between the male and the female occurs in four stages. First, the male is a *fenhedor,* an archaic term denoting one who sighs for his lady's love; then he becomes a *precador,* or one who begs for her love; later he is transformed into an *entendedor,* her suitor; in the last stage of the relationship he is her *drudo* (druid)—her lover. The lady is his supreme wealth, and this love is sometimes only a *Minne* (spiritual one). He must possess certain virtues, including patience, fidelity, hope, honor, and—above all—discretion. The behavior of a perfect lover is based on the principle of *mesura* (courteousness), which is reminiscent of chivalry. Discretion was important in the erotic relationship. The woman was usually married, and her husband was jealous. Servants and friends could make her life difficult by gossiping about her and the poet. Therefore, the female had a pseudonym in the verse that was about her.

Although influenced by Provençal poetry, the Galician-Portuguese lyric has its own peculiar characteristics. Unlike in the poetry of Provence, in the *cantigas de amor* the male and female are only suitors and not lovers. This phase is seen only in the *cantigas de escárnio* and *maldizer.*

In the *cantigas de amor,* Portuguese courtly verse of Provençal origin, the poet describes for his lady the anguish and suffering that love has caused him. In poems in which love is unrequited, the ideal of courtly love predominates. Unattainable, the beloved thus symbolizes purity and perfection. Love exists on an ideal level, in which the woman fits a specific type: she is delicate and has light hair, a subtle smile, and refined manners. The poet lives in a servile relationship to this ideal feminine creation. He is faithful to a code of honor and behavior that demands discretion and self-control. Resembling a medieval knight, he demonstrates courage, generosity, and loyalty. Obedient, chaste, courteous, and humble, he maintains a sense of dignity as he serves his lady. The poet, like the knight, has no rights—only duties.

*Coita,* the male's passion and suffering in the service of the maiden, was the main theme of the *cantigas de amor.* Suffering was so intense that for the troubadour death was the only release from his pain. The poet Joan Garcia de Guilhade expresses the *coita* as follows:

> A gran coyta que d'amor ey,
> ca me vejo sandeu andar,
> e com sandece o direy:
> os olhos verdes que eu vi
> me fazem ora andar assí.
>
> (I have a great suffering of love
> because I see myself going crazy,
> the green eyes I saw
> have made me become like this.)

In this *cantiga de amor* the troubadour speaks on his behalf, and he introduces an important motif related to female beauty: green eyes. Before Guilhade's poem "green eyes" symbolized betrayal; after him the eyes were treated as an artistic device.

By contrast, in the *cantigas de amigo* the poet assumes a feminine voice and addresses the verses to the speaker's lover. These poems, which have their origins in the popular poetry of Portugal and Galicia, employ several devices, such as parallelism and refrain, to achieve a highly lyrical quality, as well as suggest a choral aspect; the *cantigas* have been associated with music and dance. The archaic terms that appear in these *cantigas* indicate a long tradition of this type of poetry in the peninsula. The *cantigas de amigo* are generally variations on certain themes and settings, including the separation of lovers, particularly when the male is a *fossado*—that is, he goes on a military expedition for the king, while the female awaits his return, expressing her feelings through sad, teary verse; the pilgrimage to holy places, where the young lady goes in search of her lover; the *barcarolas* (boating songs), which introduce a marine leitmotiv; the songs of a woman who weaves in a domestic setting; and the verses that take place at a fountain where a young lady washes her hair and meets her lover. In playing out the feminine drama as perceived by the male poet, the phenomenon of the *cantigas de amigo* reflects a patriarchal society. In these *cantigas* the woman suffers because she is separated from her *amigo* (lover or boyfriend), and her suffering results from her not knowing whether he will return or simply seek out another woman. The woman in these *cantigas* is always a peasant; thus, the setting is rural—contrary to the *cantigas de amor,* which take place in palaces. The *cantigas de amigo* also introduce other characters in whom the young lady can confide, including her mother, a friend, or even a personified element of nature.

Several poetic symbols recur in the *cantigas de amigo,* including those of the fountain, the deer, the dance, and locks of hair. The fountain is where amorous encounters take place; the water of the fountain represents fertility: "Vay lavar cabelos, na fria fontana" (She washes her hair in the cold fountain, meaning that she is ready for love), from a *cantiga* by Pero Meogo. The deer is a symbol of male virility, and in this type of verse it is associated with the feminine symbolism of the fountain: "o cervo do monte volvia a áugua" (the deer of the mountain returned to the water). The festive atmosphere of the *baile* (dance) is used as an excuse by the young woman to leave her home. Her long curls of hair, or *garcetas,* generally symbolize her virginity.

Galician-Portuguese poetry obeyed specific rules of meter and had certain stylistic devices. The most noticeable device is a regular parallel structure, found

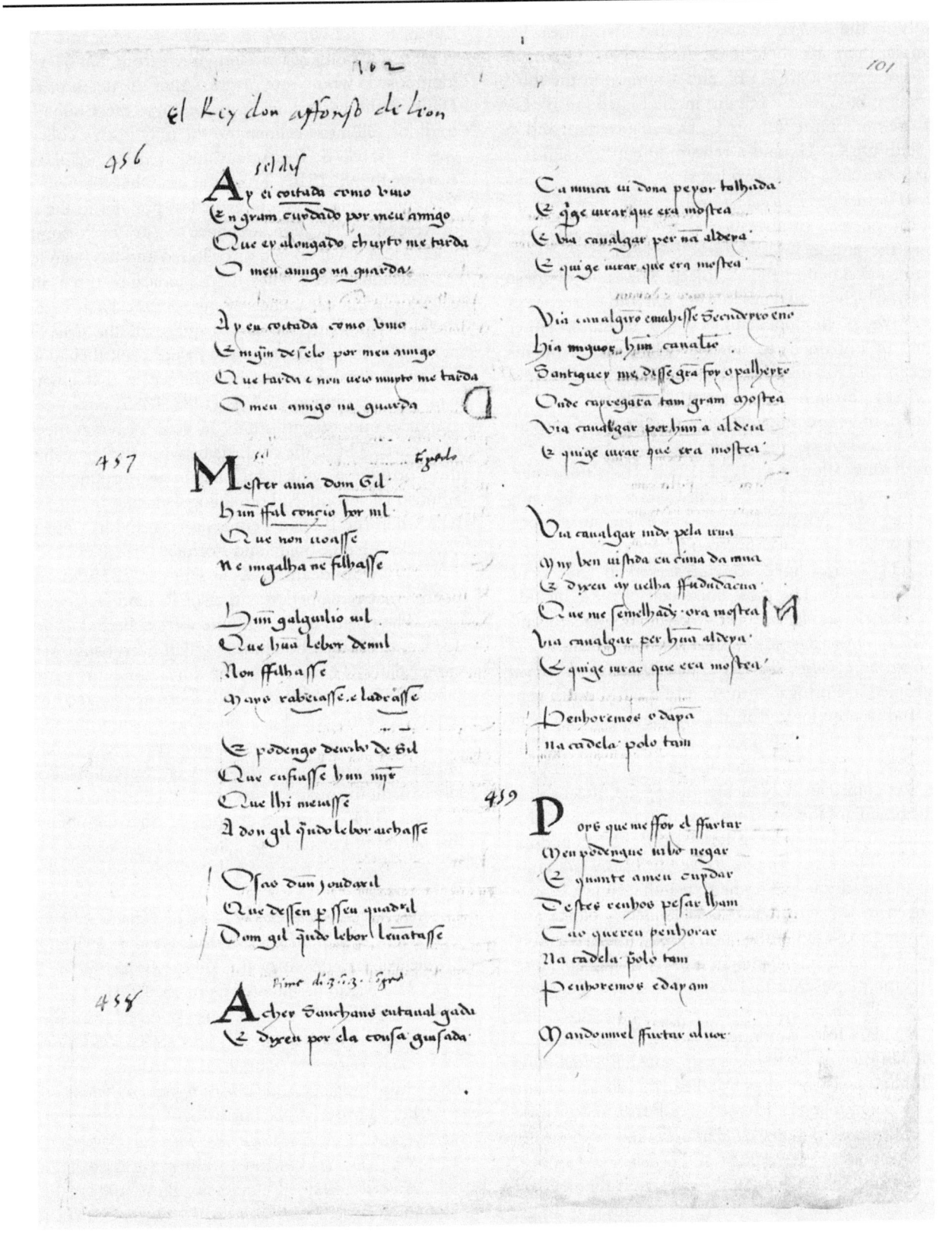

*The* Canção de guarvaia *(Song of the Royal Robe), one of the earliest extant medieval Portuguese texts, included in the* Cancioneiro da Ajuda *manuscript (from Nuno Júdice,* Portugal, língua e cultura, *1992; Lauinger Library, Georgetown University)*

mianly in the *cantigas de amigo*. In the first stanza, for example, there are three lines: A, B, and a refrain. In the second stanza are A', B', and a refrain; in the third stanza are B, C, and a refrain; in the fourth are B', C', and a refrain; in the fifth are C, D, and a refrain; and in the sixth are C', D', and a refrain. Often between two stanzas there is a distic (two lines).

The *cantigas de maldizer* and *cantigas de escárnio* are satirical poems. In the *cantigas de maldizer* the poet names the person under attack; the *cantigas de escárnio* do not individualize their subject. The tone of these poems, which sometimes border on the obscene, is aggressive as the poet subjects his enemies, either named or unnamed, to ridicule. The satirical poems often portray the decadent customs of the nobility and the clergy through the theme of female adultery. In addition, there are religious *cantigas* written in Galician-Portuguese, such as the *Cantigas de Santa Maria* by the Spanish king Alfonso X (1221-1284). His 430 masterfully written poems, dedicated to the miracles surrounding the Virgin Mary, reveal an able poet, influenced by Provençal poetry.

The *cantigas* have been preserved in collections called *cancioneiros*. The most important of these include the *Cancioneiro da Ajuda*, the *Cancioneiro da Vaticana*, and the *Cancioneiro da Biblioteca Nacional*, previously known as the *Cancioneiro Colocci-Brancuti*. The *Cancioneiro da Ajuda* was copied in Portugal at the end of the thirteenth century and is now located in the Biblioteca da Ajuda in Lisbon. Most of its 310 poems are *cantigas de amor*. The *Cancioneiro da Vaticana*, located in the library of the Vatican, was copied in Italy at the end of the fifteenth, or the beginning of the sixteenth, century. Its 1,205 poems are made up of all types of lyrics from the troubadour tradition. The *Cancioneiro da Biblioteca Nacional* is a copy made in Italy at the end of the sixteenth century. It once belonged to the Italian humanist Angelo Colocci and was then discovered in the library of Count Brancuti of Cagli in Ancona. The National Library of Portugal purchased the manuscript in 1924. Of its 1,664 *cantigas* of all types, all except 442 appear in the *Cancioneiro da Vaticana*. Scholars have continued to uncover other *cantigas* in the libraries of Portugal, Spain, and Italy–including the Biblioteca Nacional of Madrid, the library of the Escorial, the Biblioteca Municipal of Porto, and others.

The most famous troubadours and *jograis* were Taveirós, possibly the author of the *Canção de guarvaia*; Martin Codax, who lived in the thirteenth century and wrote *cantigas de amigo* and other lyric poems and songs; Alfonso Mendes de Besteiros, a nobleman from the Portuguese aristocracy who wrote fourteen *cantigas*; Fernando Esquio, a *jogral* from the beginning of the fourteenth century; Joan Garcia de Guilhade, one of the most prolific poets, who wrote fifty-two *cantigas*; João Zorro, a *jogral* who wrote *cantigas de amigo*; and Aires Nunes de Santiago, a clergyman from Santiago de Compostela who wrote *cantigas*. After the death of King Dinis in the early fourteenth century, the troubadour tradition fell into decline, and the only poetry collected was by Garcia de Resende in his *Cancioneiro geral* (General Songbook, 1516). From the time that the Galician-Portuguese lyric began to grow less popular to the year of Resende's collection, an entire century of Portuguese poetry was never copied or collected and has been lost.

Manuel Rodrigues Lapa indicates three main causes for the decadence of *trovadorismo*. First, in 1386 Pedro I eliminated royal patronage of the arts. The poets who had frequented the palace took their poetry to the taverns. Second, the bourgeosie that emerged with the Revolution of Avis (1383-1385) put a strong emphasis on mercantilism in the country but at the cost of the arts. Third, the conflicts between the Spanish and the Portuguese, which had begun in the kingdom of Alfonso IV, produced both a linguistic and literary rupture when the Iberian Peninsula was divided into two countries–that is, Spain and Portugal.

With the death of King Dinis in 1325, the only poetry that remained was that of Resende's *Cancioneiro geral*. The poems in this volume were collected between 1511 and 1516, although many had been composed at earlier dates. There is a gap of almost an entire century (about 1350 to 1450) in which there are no records of poetry collections in Portugal. The books of poems by King Dinis and by King Afonso that existed in the library of King Duarte disappeared. Specialists generally consult the Spanish *cancioneros*, such as the *Cancionero de Baena* (1445), to have an idea of what the poetry of this period in Portugal was like.

**References:**

Eugenio Asensio, *Poética y realidad en el cancionero peninsular de la Edad Media* (Madrid: Gredos, 1957);

Leodegário A. de Azevedo Filho, *As cantigas de Pero Meogo* (Rio de Janeiro: Gernasa, 1974);

Azevedo Filho, "O poema musical de Martin Codax como narrativa," in his *Uma visão brasileira da literatura portuguesa* (Coimbra: Almedina, 1973);

Theophilo Braga, *Cancioneiro portuguez da Vaticana* (Lisbon: Imprensa Nacional, 1876);

Henry H. Carter, *Cancioneiro da Ajuda. A Diplomatic Edition* (New York: Modern Language Association of America, Oxford University Press, 1941);

Hernâni Cidade, *Poesia medieval: I. Cantigas de amigo* (Lisbon: Seara Nova, 1972);

L. F. Lindley Cintra and José Gomes Branco, *Cancioneiro português da Biblioteca da Vaticana* (Cód. 4803) (Lisbon: Centro de Estudos Filológicos, Instituto de Alta Cultura, 1973);

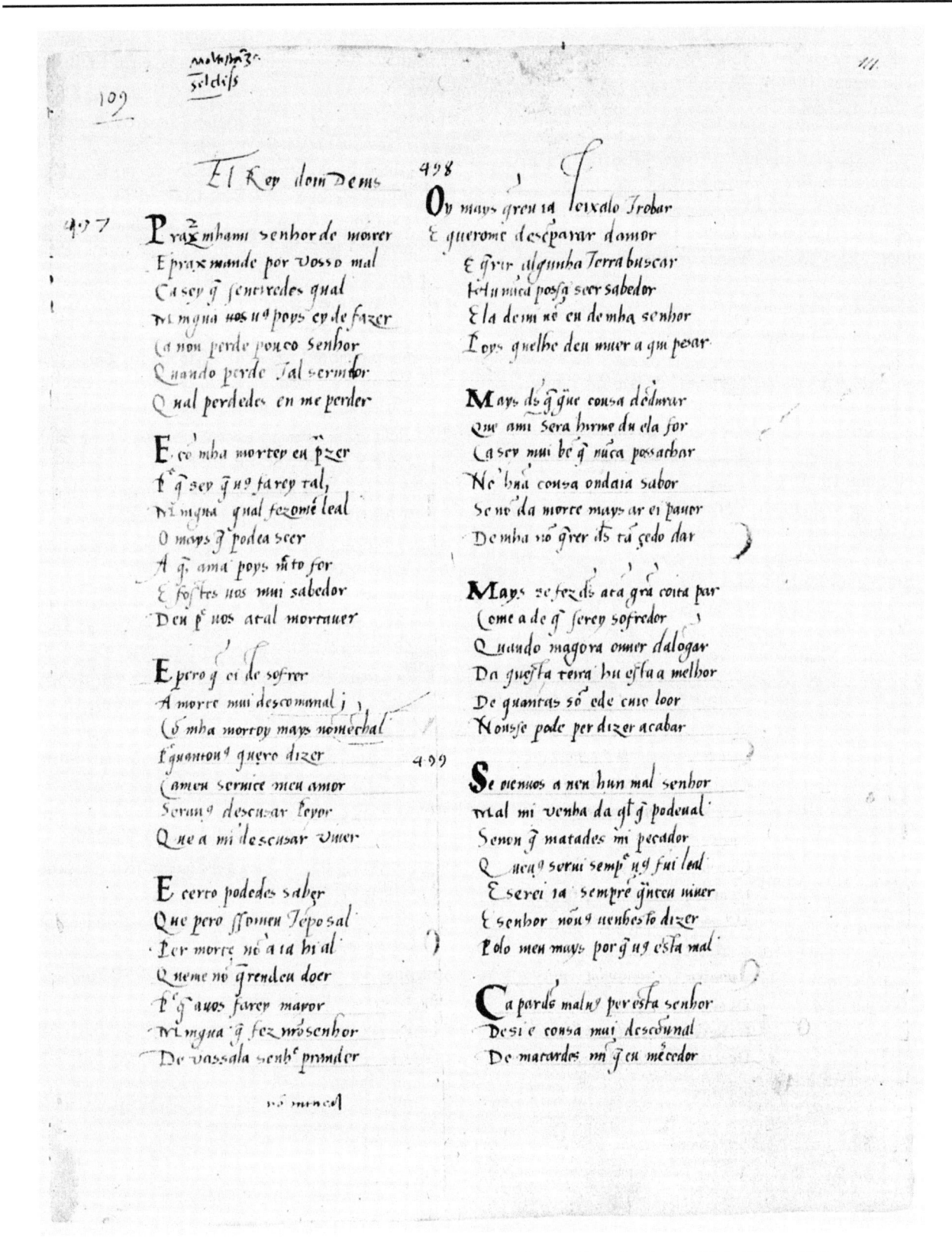

*Page from the manuscript for one of the* cantigas de amigo *(songs of friends) written by Dinis (1261–1325), the "troubadour king," under whose rule cultural development flourished in Portugal (from Nuno Júdice,* Portugal, língua e cultura, *1992; Lauinger Library, Georgetown University)*

Maria Adelaide Valle Cintra, *Bibliografia de textos medievais portugueses* (Lisbon: Centro de Estudos Filológicos, 1960);

Celso Cunha, *O cancioneiro de Joan Zorro* (Rio de Janeiro, 1949);

Cunha, *O cancioneiro de Martin Codax* (Rio de Janeiro: Departamento de Imprensa Nacional, 1956);

Cunha, *Estudos de poética trovadoresca* (Rio de Janeiro: Instituto Nacional do Livro, 1961);

Sílvio Elia, *Sobre as origens do verso românico* (Rio de Janeiro, 1961);

Giulia Lanciani and Giuseppe Tavani, *Dicionário da literatura medieval galega e portuguesa* (Lisbon: Caminho, 1993);

Lanciani, ed., *Il canzoniere di Fernan Velho* (Rome: Japadre, 1977);

Manuel Rodrigues Lapa, *Cantigas d'escarnho e de maldizer dos cancioneiros medievais galego-portugueses* (Coimbra: Galaxia, 1965);

Lapa, *Das origens da poesia lírica em Portugal na Idade Média* (Lisbon: Seara Nova, 1929);

Lapa, *Lições de literatura portuguesa: Epoca medieval* (Coimbra: Coimbra Editora, 1981);

Lapa, "O texto das cantigas d'amigo," in his *Miscelânea de língua e literatura portuguesa medieval* (Rio de Janeiro: Instituto Nacional do Livro, 1965), pp. 9–50;

Pierre Le Gentil, *La poésie lyrique espagnole et portugaise à la fin du Moyen Âge,* 2 volumes (Rennes: Plihon, 1949, 1953);

Mário Martins, *Alegorias, símbolos e exemplos morais da literatura medieval portuguesa* (Lisbon: Brotéria, 1975);

X. L. Mendez-Ferrín, *O cancioneiro de Pero Meogo* (Vigo: Galaxia, 1966);

Enrico Molteni, *Il canzoniere portoghese Colocci-Brancuti* (Halle: Max Niemeyer, 1880);

Ernesto Monaci, *Il canzoniere portoghese della Biblioteca Vaticana* (Halle: Max Niemeyer, 1875);

Vitorino Nemésio, *A poesia dos trovadores, antologia* (Lisbon: Bertrand, 1961);

Oskar Nobiling, *As cantigas de D. Joan Garcia de Guilhade, trovador do século XIII* (Erlangen: Junge & Sohn, 1907);

José Joaquim Nunes, *Cantigas d'amigo dos trovadores galego-portugueses,* 3 volumes (Lisbon: Centro do Livro Brasileiro, 1973);

Nunes, *Cantigas d'amor dos trovadores galego-portugueses* (Lisbon: Centro do Livro Brasileiro, 1972);

Nunes, *Crestomatia arcaica* (Lisbon: Clássica, 1943);

Nunes, "Poesia galego-portuguesa ou trovadoresca," in *História da literatura portuguesa ilustrada,* 3 volumes, edited by Albino Forjaz de Sampaio (Paris & Lisbon: Aillaud & Bertrand, 1929–1932), I: 78–108;

Corrêa de Oliveira and Saavedra Machado, *Textos portugueses medievais* (Coimbra: Coimbra Editora, 1967);

Saveiro Pannunzio, *Pero da Ponte, poesie* (Bari: Adriatica, 1967);

Elza Paxexo and José Pedro Machado, *Cancioneiro da Biblioteca Nacional,* 8 volumes (Lisbon: Revista de Portugal, 1949–1964);

Sílvio Pellegrini, *Auswahl altportugiesischer Lieder* (Halle & Saale: Max Niemeyer, 1928);

Pellegrini, *Repertorio bibliografico della prima lirica portoghese* (Modena: Società Tipografica Modenense, 1939);

Luciana Stegagno Picchio, *Martin Moya, Poesie* (Rome: Ateneo, 1968);

Joseph Piel, "Sobre a origem das cantigas d'amigo: Uma nova hipótese," *Revista Brasileira de Língua e Literatura* (1982): 3–4;

A. J. da Costa Pimpão, *História da literatura portuguesa: Idade Média* (Coimbra: Atlântida, 1959);

Serafim da Silva Neto, *Textos medievais portugueses e seus problemas* (Rio de Janeiro: Casa de Rui Barbosa, 1956);

Barbara Spaggiari, *Il canzoniere di Martin Codax*. Estratto dagli *Studi Medievali,* 3rd series 21.1, 1980;

Segismundo Spina, *A lírica trovadoresca* (Rio de Janeiro: Grifo, 1972);

Spina, *Manual de versificação românica medieval* (Rio de Janeiro: Gernasa, 1971);

Giuseppe Tavani, *Repertorio metrico della lirica galego-portoghese* (Rome: Ateneo, 1967);

Fernanda Toriello, *Fernand' Esquyo, le Poesie* (Bari: Adriatica, 1976);

Carolina Michaëlis de Vasconcelos, *Cancioneiro da Ajuda,* 2 volumes (Halle: Max Niemeyer, 1904; Torino: Bodega d'Erasmo, 1966).

# Appendix 2:
# Mariana Alcoforado, the Portuguese Nun

# Appendix 2: Mariana Alcoforado, the Portuguese Nun

## Anna Klobucka
*University of Massachusetts Dartmouth*

**BOOK:** *Lettres portugaises traduites en françois,* anonymous (Paris: Claude Barbin, 1669); translated by Roger L'Estrange as *Five Love Letters From A Nun To A Cavalier Done Out Of The French Into English* (London: Henry Brome, 1678); translated into Portuguese as *Cartas de uma religiosa portuguesa* by Francisco Manuel de Nascimento (Filinto Elísio), in his *Obras completas* (Paris: A. Bobbe, 1819), and by José Maria de Sousa Botelho (Morgado de Mateus), in *Lettres portugaises. Nouvelle édition* (Paris: Firmin Didot, 1824).

**Editions:** Gabriel-Joseph Lavergne de Guilleragues, *Lettres portugaises, Valentins, et autres oeuvres,* edited by Frédéric Deloffre and Jacques Rougeot (Paris: Garnier, 1962);

Guilleragues, *Lettres portugaises, Chansons et bons mots, Valentins,* revised and edited by Deloffre and Rougeot (Geneva: Librairie Droz, 1972).

Mariana Alcoforado was for a long time considered the most distinguished Portuguese woman writer prior to the twentieth century, and the only one to have acquired widespread international renown. However, the true author of the anonymously published *Lettres portugaises traduites en françois* (Portuguese Letters Translated into French, 1669) was in all probability neither Portuguese nor a woman. Most scholars now accept that the text, presented by its first publisher as an equally anonymous translation from the Portuguese, was in fact composed in French by Gabriel-Joseph Lavergne de Guilleragues, a courtier, diplomat, and onetime French ambassador to Constantinople.

Those original *Lettres portugaises,* as they are known, consisted of five love letters that the publisher claimed were written by a Portuguese nun named Marianne who was cloistered in a provincial convent in the southeastern part of Portugal. Their addressee was a French officer in Louis XIV's army, which took part in the wars of the Restoration following Portugal's loss of independence to Spain (1580–1640). "Marianne" and the chevalier–whose name is never mentioned in the letters–met while the French troops were stationed in her town, and for a time the nun's convent became the stage of their secret, passionate liaison. After the affair ended with the troops' departure, the undiminished intensity of the abandoned nun's feelings for her absent lover was translated into five epistolary laments. From their famous first words, beginning the amorous argument in medias res ("Considère, mon amour, jusqu'à quel excès tu as manqué de prévoyance" [Consider, my love, how extremely lacking you have been in foresight]), to the declaration of independence implicit in their no less famous closure ("je ne vous écrirai plus; suis-je obligée de vous rendre un compte exact de tous mes divers mouvements?" [I will write no more. Am I obliged to give you an accurate account of all my feelings?]), the letters traverse a complex, often contradictory psychological and rhetorical trajectory.

*Lettres portugaises* became a best-seller in France immediately upon its publication in 1669, and its fame spread quickly across European national borders. Also in 1669, several new editions were produced in France and abroad, including three pirated versions; one of the latter, published in Cologne, purported to identify the names of both the nun's lover ("Chevalier de Chamilly") and the translator of her letters ("Cuilleraque"). The original publisher, Claude Barbin, did not limit his activity to new printings of his best-selling volume: spurred by its runaway popularity, he released a 1669 sequel including seven new letters, also titled *Lettres portugaises* but, in this version, said to be written by a Portuguese "femme du monde" (woman of the world). At the same time, others saw an opportunity to capitalize on the success of the original by producing editions of the French officer's alleged epistolary responses to his desolate lover's letters: two such books appeared in 1669, in Paris and Grenoble, and a few more followed, along with a growing number of translations (the first English version was published in 1678). Firmly established in the Western European literary canon, the original *Lettres portugaises,* along with a vast number of paraphrases and sequels, kept alive the story of the provincial Portuguese nun seduced and abandoned by her aristocratic French lover. The female subject's lucidly

# Appendix 2: Mariana Alcoforado, the Portuguese Nun

*The Portuguese Nun, etching by an anonymous artist (from José Cerqueira de Vasconcelos's* As cartas de religiosa portuguesa *[Letters of the Portuguese Nun], 1935; reproduced in Anna Klobucka,* The Portuguese Nun, *2000; Thomas Cooper Library, University of South Carolina)*

voiced emotional anguish and the psychological and rhetorical complexity of her discourse were an inspiration to many prominent writers during the next three centuries. In Stendhal's taxonomy of amorous feeling, *De l'Amour* (1822), the Portuguese Nun figures as one of the paragons of "amour-passion" (passionate love). Elizabeth Barrett Browning's well-known *Sonnets from the Portuguese* (1850) are said to have been inspired by the seventeenth-century text, as are the *Duino Elegies* (1923) by Rainer Maria Rilke, who translated the *Lettres portugaises* into German in 1913.

The notoriety of the Portuguese Nun's letters was not, however, attributable to their literary merit alone; it was also influenced by the tantalizing uncertainty with regard to their origin and the identity of their author. As late as the last decade of the eighteenth century, Mercier de Saint-Léger, the author of the first scholarly study of the letters (*Notice historique et bibliographique sur les Lettres portugaises,* included in the 1796 edition by Delance), had little to say on the subject of their authorship. Another French scholar, Jean-François Boissonade, breathed new life into the debate in 1810: on the basis of an anonymous handwritten note that he claimed he had discovered in his copy of the *Lettres portugaises,* he identified the nun as one "Mariana Alcaforada" and the town where her convent was located as Beja, the capital of the Portuguese province of Lower Alentejo. Following Boissonade's revelations in his weekly column for *Journal de l'Empire* on 5 January 1810, the first translations of the *Lettres portugaises* into what was assumed to be their original language finally appeared, a full century and a half after their publication in French. Both translators were Portuguese expatriates living in France: Francisco Manuel de Nascimento (better known by his Arcadian pseudonym, Filinto Elísio) and José Maria de Sousa Botelho (also referred to by his aristocratic title of Morgado de Mateus). While their translations were published in Paris, in subsequent years they were gradually disseminated in Portugal. Their transmission inaugurated an independent process of reception and interpretation, which eventually led to the formation of one of the most enduring Portuguese cultural myths.

Throughout the second half of the nineteenth century and the first decades of the twentieth, the growing interest of Portuguese historians and writers in Mariana Alcoforado and her epistolary masterpiece led to many inquiries into presumable historical circumstances of its production. Undoubtedly the most significant was the mention by Camilo Castelo Branco, in his *Curso de literatura portuguesa* (Course on Portuguese Literature, 1876), that a nun by the name of Maria Ana (Mariana) Alcoforado had in fact lived in the Convento da Conceição in Beja and was in her mid to late twenties at the time when the French forces, led by the count of Schomberg, adopted Beja as the center of their military operations against Spain between 1666 and 1668. Noel Bouton de Chamilly, a true historical figure who later became the marshall of France, did serve in Portugal as a soldier under Schomberg's command; but it cannot be determined whether he ever met Mariana Alcoforado in her Beja convent, much less whether any secret liaison, followed or not by correspondence, took place between them. While no tangible documentary evidence pointing to Alcoforado's authorship of the love letters came to light, and no Portuguese manuscript that could be presented as the original of their French "translation" was ever found, absent any substantive arguments to the contrary, the *alcoforadista* faction appeared to have carried the day.

While few modern scholars would defend the once dominant claim that the published text was a relatively faithful translation from a lost Portuguese original, it is entirely possible that the author of the *Lettres portugaises* relied on some measure of factual reference, be it as immaterial as mere overheard gossip about sexual exploits of French soldiers in Portugal or as substantial as an authentic exchange of letters between a Portuguese woman and a Frenchman. Although it is unlikely that the mysterious aura surrounding the prehistory of the *Lettres portugaises* will ever be completely dispelled, it is possible to describe the even more extraordinary afterlife of the seventeenth-century love affair the text glosses: that is, the cultural process of invention of Mariana Alcoforado as the author of the *Lettres portugaises* and a figure of mythic prominence in the literary-historical canon of Portuguese national identity.

Following the translation of the *Lettres portugaises* into Portuguese, the awareness of the potential significance of the text for Portugal's national culture grew slowly but surely. However, as late as 1847, José Silvestre Ribeiro, the author of *Beja no anno de 1845* (Beja in the Year 1845), did not mention Mariana Alcoforado among "Naturaes de Beja Grandes em Letras" (Beja Natives Prominent in Literature), and his omission—which stood out conspicuously several decades later—was seemingly caused by ignorance rather than by a censorious exclusion of a morally polluted figure from the roster of the town's prominent sons and daughters, a hypothetical attitude some writers later evoked as an explanation for Beja's protracted lack of recognition of its most famous inhabitant. Inocêncio Francisco da Silva included a reference to the *Lettres portugaises* in the 1862 installment of his multivolume *Dicionário bibliográfico português* (Dictionary of Portuguese Bibliography), although he chose not to pronounce himself on the matter of their national authenticity. A few years later, Castelo Branco voiced his adamant opposition to the inclusion of the letters in the Portuguese literary canon, which he outlined in his *Curso de literatura portuguesa*. He also quoted approvingly Jean-Jacques Rousseau's notorious claim in his *La Lettre à d'Alembert sur les spectacles* (1758) that this masterpiece of amorous discourse could not possibly have been written by a woman. Yet, in spite of his skepticism with regard to the authenticity of the letters, Castelo Branco felt compelled to accord them at least some recognition in his general overview of seventeenth-century Portuguese literature, thus affirming their growing importance in the continuing formation of the national canon.

In 1888 Luciano Cordeiro published a study that was immediately acclaimed as a definitive statement in the authorship controversy and remains the undisputed classic of Portuguese *alcoforadista* literature. Cordeiro's *Soror Mariana, a freira portuguesa* (Sister Mariana, the Portuguese Nun) relied on extensive research conducted by the author in the archives of Beja and presented a great deal of previously unpublished information. The author proved conclusively that Mariana Alcoforado had been a real historical figure, a nun in the Convento da Conceição who was about twenty-five years old at the time of Chamilly's sojourn in Portugal. She had entered the convent as a child and became a nun most likely at the age of sixteen. Cordeiro located records of her baptism on 22 April 1640 in the church of Santa Maria da Feira, as well as her death certificate dating from 1723, along with other documents substantiating Alcoforado's identity. She was the daughter of the nobleman Francisco da Costa Alcoforado, who had moved to Beja from his native Trás-os-Montes, and Leonor Mendes, a daughter of local merchants. Francisco and Leonor Alcoforado had eight children. Their oldest son, Baltasar Vaz Alcoforado, was a soldier who later became a priest; in 1666 he took part in a military foray into Andalusia, which resulted in the seizing of the castle Alcaria de la Puebla. Chamilly's unit had participated in the same expedition, making it plausible that Alcoforado's oldest brother and her hypothetical lover were acquainted. The fact that Baltasar Alcoforado became a priest in 1669, the year of the publication of the *Lettres portugaises,* led Cordeiro to speculate that Alcoforado's brother was motivated by feelings of shame over his sister's now-public disgrace and possibly also over his role in introducing her to Chamilly. Cordeiro also pointed out that, in all her years at the convent, Mariana Alcoforado never exercised any elevated function in its hierarchy, in spite of her noble birth. This fact, according to the researcher, was an indication that she was considered unworthy of such distinction because of her immoral behavior. (In 1709, however, Alcoforado was a candidate and a close runner-up for the post of the mother abbess, obtaining 48 votes of the 109 cast in the election.)

The evidence presented by Cordeiro, although buttressed adroitly with comprehensive background information derived from historical studies of life in seventeenth-century Portuguese convents, was described in a 1935 article by critic A. Gonçalves Rodrigues as Cordeiro's "trabalho de imaginação exuberante . . . castelo de cartas com a arrogância de um arranha-céus" (work of exuberant imagination . . . a house of cards with the arrogance of a skyscraper). In effect, Cordeiro's contribution of new, relatively abundant information on Alcoforado and the environment in which she had lived her long life had purely circumstantial value: it offered no proof of direct contact between the nun and the chevalier, nor did it establish Alcoforado's authorship of the love letters.

*Title page for the volume of letters supposedly written by a nun to the lover who had abandoned her. For years the work was attributed to Mariana Alcoforado (from http://www.pierre-marteau.com/library/f-1669-0001.html).*

At the same time, Cordeiro's work (along with some other early contributions, such as the historian Teófilo Braga's passionate endorsement of the national authenticity of the letters in such works as *Estudos da Edade Média* [Studies of the Middle Ages, 1870]) provided an inspiring basis for a mythographic enterprise of considerable proportions. Both Portuguese enthusiasts of Alcoforado and a significant minority of writers opposed to her inclusion in the national canon have contributed to the mass of writing that in one way or another centers on the Portuguese Nun. Several book-length biographies of Alcoforado coexist with novels, poems, and plays glossing her brief love affair and her long, penitent life. Versions of her story have been featured as case studies in works as diverse as a modernist manifesto (*Manifesto Anti-Dantas* [1915] by José de Almada Negreiros) and a scientific study of masochism by a pioneering practitioner of sexual medicine (Asdrúbal de Aguiar) titled *Masoquismo psíquico de Soror Mariana Alcoforado* (Psychological Masochism of Sister Mariana Alcoforado, 1922). However, the most common leitmotiv of *alcoforadista* writing until at least the mid twentieth century was the question of national authenticity: to reclaim for Portugal the authorship of an internationally renowned literary masterpiece was tantamount to a patriotic duty for many intellectuals engaged in cultural negotiation of national identity that accompanied, particularly since the last decades of the nineteenth century, the gradually unfolding drama of Portuguese marginality in Europe and the world.

The widespread belief in the Portuguese Nun's authorship of the letters was shaken dramatically in 1926 with the publication of a *Modern Language Review* article titled "Who Was the Author of the *Lettres portugaises*?" by F. C. Green, a scholar of French literature. Green brought into play new, previously unexamined evidence: he had located the original official license (*Privilège du Roi*) granted to Claude Barbin in 1668 for the publication of the famous text and verified that the document mentioned "lettres portugaises" among the contents of a collected volume of writings by Guilleragues. Green's identification of the "Cuilleraque" said to be the translator of the letters in their first pirated edition as their legitimate author was supported and amplified by subsequent studies, especially by Frédéric Deloffre and Jacques Rougeot's introductory essay in their 1962 edition of *Lettres portugaises, Valentins, et autres oeuvres* of Guilleragues. This groundbreaking volume was followed ten years later by a revised and expanded edition of Guilleragues's writings, in which the editors' lengthy argument in favor of his authorship of the *Lettres portugaises* was eliminated as no longer necessary: it had become a matter of prevailing consensus that the Portuguese Nun's five extraordinary love letters had been in fact an ingenious literary artifice, their reliance on an exotic Iberian setting having foreshadowed the use of the device of *dépaysement* (exotic displacement) in such later masterpieces of French literature as Montesquieu's *Lettres persanes* (Persian Letters, 1721) or Mme de Grafigny's *Lettres d'une Péruvienne* (Letters of a Peruvian Woman, 1747).

Since the 1960s, Portuguese critics and historians have been virtually unanimous in accepting the *Lettres portugaises* as a literary fiction originating in France. At the same time, however, many contemporary reprises of Sister Mariana's love story (including popular editions of the letters, exhibits, performances, and works of fiction) have taken for granted the prominent place claimed by the letters in the cultural memory of their purported homeland, dismissing as irrelevant the issue of historically verifiable authorial authentication. The most important among those works remains the text that pioneered the postmodern redirecting of the *alcoforadista* discourse away from validation and toward signification, with writers and critics alike choosing to explore the meaning of a particular text or event rather than to establish its truthfulness. This work is the feminist manifesto *Novas cartas portuguesas* (New Portuguese Letters, 1972), collectively authored by Maria Isabel Barreno, Maria Teresa Horta, and Maria Velho da Costa, whose revisionist interpretation of the myth of Sister Mariana took it in new and exciting directions. The "Three Marias" found in the story of Mariana Alcoforado an inspiring source of historical and symbolic substance and a narrative blueprint for the articulation of their political project: an emancipatory chronicle of social and historical realities lived by Portuguese women and a subversive exploration of traditional patterns of thought defining and regulating Portuguese womanhood. Their work may also be credited with revitalizing the potential of the nun's story to inspire present and future generations of Portuguese writers, thus demonstrating that even a fictional author can become an authentically important protagonist in the perpetually unfolding narrative of national literary history.

**References:**

Graça Abreu, "'Le balcon d'où l'on voit Mertola': Le Mirage des points de repère dans les *Lettres portugaises*," *Ariane*, 6 (1988): 81–91;

Luís Cardim, "Les *Lettres portugaises*. A propos de quelques documents récemment publiés," *Bulletin des Etudes Portugaises*, 1 (1931): 161–173;

Luciano Cordeiro, *Soror Mariana, a freira portuguesa* (Lisbon: Livraria Ferin, 1888);

António Belard de Fonseca, *Mariana Alcoforado. A Freira de Beja e as Lettres portugaises* (Lisbon, 1966);

Claude-Henri Frèches, "Une vision française de la féminité portugaise: les *Lettres portugaises* avec les *Responces* traduites en français," in *Les Rapports culturels et littéraires entre le Portugal et la France* (Paris: Fondation Calouste Gulbenkian, 1983), pp. 219–238;

Claire Goldstein, "Love Letters: Discourses of Gender and Writing in the Criticism of the *Lettres portugaises*," *Romanic Review*, 88, no. 4 (1997): 571–590;

F. C. Green, "Who Was the Author of the *Lettres portugaises*?" *Modern Language Review*, 21 (1926): 159–167;

Linda S. Kauffman, *Discourses of Desire: Gender, Genre, and Epistolary Fictions* (Ithaca, N.Y.: Cornell University Press, 1986);

Anna Klobucka, *The Portuguese Nun: Formation of a National Myth* (Lewisburg, Pa.: Bucknell University Press, 2000);

Alice de Oliveira, *Vida amorosa de Soror Mariana* (Lisbon: Parceria A. M. Pereira, 1944);

Leonardo Pereira, *As cartas de Sóror Mariana* (Lisbon: Portugália, 1941);

Manuel Ribeiro, *Vida e morte de Madre Mariana Alcoforado* (Lisbon: Sá da Costa, 1940);

A. Gonçalves Rodrigues, "Mariana Alcoforado. História e crítica de uma fraude literária," *Biblos*, 11 (1935): 85–136;

António Sardinha, "As 'Cartas' da freira," in his *Da hera nas colunas* (Coimbra: Atlântida, 1929), pp. 69–114;

Leo Spitzer, "The *Lettres Portugaises*," in his *Essays on Seventeenth-Century French Literature*, translated and edited by David Bellos (Cambridge: Cambridge University Press, 1988), pp. 355–383;

Katherine Vaz, *Mariana* (London: Flamingo, 1997);

Afonso Lopes Vieira, "Soror Mariana," in his *Em demanda do Graal* (Lisbon: Portugal-Brasil, 1922), pp. 253–259.

# Appendix 3:
# The Three Marias:
# A Landmark Case in Portuguese Literary History

# Appendix 3: The Three Marias: A Landmark Case in Portuguese Literary History

Anna Klobucka
*University of Massachusetts Dartmouth*

BOOK: *Novas cartas portuguesas* (Lisbon: Estúdios Cor, 1972; revised edition, with a preface by Maria de Lurdes Pintasilgo, Lisbon: Moraes, 1980); translated by Helen R. Lane as *The Three Marias: New Portuguese Letters* (New York: Doubleday, 1975).

When in the spring of 1971 Maria Isabel Barreno, Maria Teresa Horta, and Maria Velho da Costa embarked on a collective writing project designed to explore the material as well as symbolic conditions of Portuguese women's lives and works, past and present, they could hardly have foreseen the enormous impact that the final product of their collaboration was to exercise on both a national and an international scale. *Novas cartas portuguesas* (New Portuguese Letters, 1972; translated as *The Three Marias: New Portuguese Letters,* 1975) has been recognized worldwide as one of the great works of modern women's literature and as a rallying cry for the international feminist movement. Based on the seventeenth-century collection of love letters supposedly written by a Portuguese nun named Mariana Alcoforado to her faithless French lover and published anonymously in Paris in 1669 as *Lettres portugaises* (Portuguese Letters), the "new Portuguese letters" of Barreno, Horta, and Velho da Costa engage in a complex renegotiation of their country's historical legacies and contemporary realities shaping gender relations in the family and in the society at large. While the fame of *Novas cartas portuguesas,* not unlike that of its seventeenth-century antecedent, quickly transcended national borders, the revolutionary charge of the book owed as much to its universal appeal as to its wide-reaching and complex engagement with the particular reality of its Portuguese cultural and political context.

The significance of the events that led up to and followed the publication of *Novas cartas portuguesas* is best illuminated within the context of the economic and sociopolitical situation in Portugal in the years immediately preceding the revolution in 1974 that put an end to the longest surviving dictatorship and colonial empire in Europe. The Portuguese Estado Novo (New State) was formally established by the Constitution of 1933 and led by António Oliveira Salazar until his incapacitation in 1968; in subsequent years, Salazar's successor, Marcelo Caetano, effectively continued Estado Novo policies, albeit modified by some superficial measures of liberalization that earned the period its nickname of "Primavera Marcelista" (Marcelo's Spring). The Portuguese dictatorship was partly modeled on the fascist regimes of Adolf Hitler and Benito Mussolini, and although Salazar's regime proved to be somewhat more moderate and haphazard in its application of antiliberal policies, political opposition was nevertheless systematically and violently suppressed. The Colonial Act, passed in 1930 while Salazar was minister of the colonies, had reinforced Portugal's commitment to maintaining possession of its African territories, and from the late 1940s onward there was a rise in primarily working-class migration to Angola and Mozambique. At the same time, the post–World War II international movement toward political emancipation of former European colonies fostered anticolonial opposition in Portugal itself and, most crucially, in its *províncias ultramarinas* (overseas provinces), as they came to be referred to in official parlance. In 1961, after the Indian invasion and subsequent annexation of the Portuguese enclaves of Goa, Daman, and Diu, anticolonial guerrilla war erupted in Angola, soon followed by conflicts in Portugal's other African colonies. The war in Africa profoundly affected Portuguese society, as young men were massively conscripted into the army and shipped overseas to fight against the rebels, while others chose to emigrate in order to avoid the draft.

Social policies adopted by the dictatorship of the Estado Novo fostered a highly conservative, patriarchal model of the family, based on the presupposition of the "natural" subjection of women, who were consequently excluded from equal legal citizenship. Artificial contraception was prohibited, and abortion was punishable by imprisonment of up to eight years. The only indepen-

# Appendix 3: The Three Marias

*Maria Isabel Barreno (photograph by Graça Sarsfield)*

Superiors, 1970), as well as several sociological essays; Horta had produced several volumes of poetry, beginning with *Espelho inicial* (Initial Mirror, 1960), and the novel *Ambas as mãos sobre o corpo* (Both Hands over the Body, 1970); and Velho da Costa had published a collection of short stories, *Lugar comum* (Commonplace, 1966), and a novel, *Maina Mendes* (1969). Barreno and Velho da Costa had been friends since adolescence and worked together as researchers in the Ministry of Economics; Horta was the literary editor of a Lisbon newspaper. All three were in their early thirties, had been educated in convent schools, and were married and mothers of sons.

The idea for the collaboration came from Barreno, as a consequence of the negative public and official response to Horta's book of poems *Minha senhora de mim* (Milady of Me), published in 1971. Horta's highly explicit verbal images of female and male bodies and her intensely solipsistic focus on her own physicality and sexuality provoked an official reaction from the Portuguese censors. Within weeks of its publication, all copies of the volume in the bookstores were confiscated, and the book was banned as "erotic." At that point, as Darlene J. Sadlier wrote in *The Question of How: Women Writers and New Portuguese Literature* (1989), "Barreno decided that, if a book written by a woman 'who wrote freely as a man' could provoke such a reaction, it was time three or four women together wrote about the problems women faced in Portugal."

Barreno, Horta, and Velho da Costa agreed that each of them would compose whatever she chose during the week and distribute a copy of her output to the others. They would meet twice a week: once for lunch in a restaurant, at which time they would share and discuss their childhood memories of growing up and their present-day attitudes and experiences as working women, wives, and mothers; and once in the evening in private, in order to discuss the written material they had produced that week. A portion of the writing was to be in the form of letters addressed to one another; the epistolary model took over, however, as the structural backbone of the emergent book once the writers decided, as English translator Helen R. Lane explained, that the *Lettres portugaises* were to function "as the seed around which their individual contributions would crystallize as a work of literature."

Barreno, Horta, and Velho da Costa found in the story of the Portuguese Nun an extraordinarily fertile vein of inspiration for their guiding objective, a comprehensive exploration of patterns both symbolic and factual, contemporary as well as historical, that have shaped Portuguese women's lives over the centuries. They saw in Mariana Alcoforado's five anguished yet lucid love letters an emblematic representation of the

dent women's organization, the Conselho Nacional das Mulheres Portuguesas (National Portuguese Women's Council), was forcibly disbanded in 1948 and its leader, Maria Lamas, was subsequently persecuted and driven into exile. In 1966 the new Civil Code softened some of the restraints on married women, who were now allowed to manage their own money and no longer needed their husbands' permission to pursue a profession. A year later, however, further legislation reaffirmed the indisputable prerogative of the husband and father as the head of the family who was to decide on and direct all matters concerning marital life and the education of children.

In this political and social climate Barreno, Horta, and Velho da Costa, or "the Three Marias," as they soon came to be nicknamed, undertook their collaborative writing project. All three women were published writers: Barreno was the author of two novels, *De noite as árvores são negras* (At Night the Trees Are Black, 1968) and *Os outros legítimos superiores* (The Other Legitimate plight of all women who are oppressed and confined, whether by societal and familial restraints or by a reactionary political system. Mariana's convent became the symbol of all the obstacles and enclosures that continued to restrict women's lives in contemporary Portugal and in the world at large. At the same time, the relationship between the nun and her French cavalier came to reflect the deep ambivalence underlying interaction and communication between men and women in all times and places.

In keeping with its original design and process of composition, *Novas cartas portuguesas* is a textual collage, a book composed of autonomous yet interconnected fragments written in both prose and verse. Its main overt indicator of chronological progression is the continuum of numbered but otherwise untitled letters that chronicle and question the process of the composition of the volume, reflect on discussions and disagreements among the members of the writing collective, and comment on their social environment and the political meaning of their project. Although structurally modeled on the five (similarly numbered and untitled) letters of the Portuguese Nun, these texts multiply far beyond that number and gradually cease to conform to a neatly ordered sequence. Thus, after the initially disciplined succession in which "First Letter I" is followed by "Second Letter I," then by "Third Letter I" and so on, a note of playful anarchy is introduced by the "Silly Letter VI" and reinforced by the "First Final Letter and Probably a Very Long and Disjointed One" and its sequel, "First Final Letter and Certainly Very Long and Disjointed (te deum)." The narrative voice of all these dispatches alternates between the first-person plural and the first-person singular; the individual writer, however, never names herself, her identity remaining inextricably enmeshed in the exercise of collective expression.

There are texts of a different nature dispersed among the letters whose writing subjects are identifiable with the authors of *Novas cartas portuguesas*. The most distinctive category among those is likewise epistolary, consisting of apocryphal letters attributed to Mariana Alcoforado and to her lover Chamilly, as well as letters written by invented female (and some male) characters, whose names connect them to the Portuguese Nun herself: Maria Ana, Mariana, Maria, Joana, José Maria. One such letter is signed by a peasant woman named Maria Ana and addressed to her husband, António, who emigrated from their village of Carvalhal to Canada twelve years earlier. She gives him news of their three children (one of whom, Júlio, has just been conscripted to go to war in Africa and contemplates fleeing to France instead), reaffirms her love for António, and bemoans her ambiguous semi-widowhood. More than

*Maria Teresa Horta (photograph by Graça Sarsfield)*

a hundred pages later, the husband writes back, enclosing the usual money order but little expression of affection and few signs of hope for an imminent return. On the following page the reader of *Novas cartas portuguesas* finds a letter from another António from the same village, addressed to a young woman named Maria, also from Carvalhal, who is working as a house servant in Lisbon. This António is fighting in the African war against the pro-independence guerilla forces; in the opening paragraph of his letter he mentions Júlio, the son of "auntie" Maria Ana (the emigrant's wife), who has lost a leg in battle and is despairing over his future "pois para o amanho da terra uma perna faz falta e ele não sabe fazer outra coisa e não tem ofício de nada" (because you need two legs to till land and that's the only thing he knows how to do because he's never been trained to do anything else). Open-ended micronarratives such as this one provide another level of cohesion to the volume as a whole, and the repetitive migration of shared proper names and toponyms from one narrative thread to another reinforces the impression of consistency in what is by any standard a radically disjointed textual structure.

The epistolary mode is the dominant formal framework in *Novas cartas portuguesas*. The plot, however, is rooted in the seventeenth-century love affair of Mariana Alcoforado and her French officer. The authors never actually address the much-contested issue of the Portuguese Nun's authorship of "her" letters. As their work clearly demonstrates, Soror Mariana's questionable authenticity does not diminish the potential of her case to serve as a context for an intricate and politically effective analysis of the historical and contemporary predicaments of real Portuguese women; at the same time, it frees the Three Marias from any obligation to follow the more or less established version of the story. Clear textual parallels between *Novas cartas portuguesas* and its seventeenth-century pretext are, however, detectable in the book. Perhaps the most significant of these echoes is the initial apostrophe of the "Third Letter I"–"Considerai, irmãs minhas. . . ." (Consider, my sisters. . . .)–a literal paraphrase of the much-discussed opening invocation of the *Lettres portugaises,* "Considère, mon amour. . . ." (Consider, my love. . . .). This specific instance of intertextual reference points to a radical reorganization of the circuit of literary communication that takes place in *Novas cartas portuguesas.* The solitary woman writer who unilaterally addresses an absent male reader in the *Lettres portugaises* (or who, in an alternative reading of the invocation, narcissistically converses with her own passion), is replaced by the female threesome engaged in a communicative collaboration in which the roles of speakers and addressees are constantly exchanged in an ongoing, open-ended process.

While the authors of *Novas cartas portuguesas* appropriate the original Portuguese Nun's five-letter sequence for the purposes of their own communication (among themselves as well as with their readers), they also accord their heroine ample narrative space of her own. This space opens with a poem titled "Mensagem de invenção de Mariana Alcoforado," which in Lane's English translation becomes "Message Invented by Mariana Alcoforado," but which could also be rendered as "Message/Notice of the Invention of Mariana Alcoforado." The double meaning embedded in this title is aptly symptomatic of the ambivalence surrounding the issue of authorship of the *Lettres portugaises,* leaving open the question of whether Alcoforado had in fact written these famous love letters. In any case, in this poem the invented or inventing Mariana for the first time speaks to the reader directly rather than through the quotations from the *Lettres portugaises* that are embedded in some earlier fragments of *Novas cartas portuguesas.* Her next intervention is in the form of another poem, a "cantiga" addressed to Mariana's mother that recalls the *cantiga de amigo* genre of medieval Galician-Portuguese poetry, in which the female speaker often directly invokes her mother as well as her female companions. Mariana's address is, however, a bitter one, as she expresses her resentment at being sent away from her family: "Que filha posta em convento / não se quer em sua casa" (The daughter placed in the convent / is not wanted at home). Shortly afterward, the reader learns that Mariana was confined in the convent in order to provide a dowry for her sister; further on, it turns out that she is hated by her mother because the latter has also had a passionate adulterous relationship, of which Mariana is an offspring. As Linda S. Kauffman comments in *Discourses of Desire: Gender, Genre, and Epistolary Fictions* (1986), throughout *Novas cartas portuguesas* the "legacy passed down from mothers to daughters is self-loathing and suicide, a blood curse that is the result of a mother's disappointment at having brought forth a child like herself."

What offers an escape route from this fatally flawed mother-daughter relationship, subordinated to the male-centered logic of the patriarchal family, is the authors' creation of the historical lineage of Mariana Alcoforado's female descendants. Mariana herself does not become a biological mother; in this version of her story, a pregnancy by Chamilly ends in a dramatic miscarriage. The Portuguese Nun's descendancy is instead composed of a succession of nieces, beginning with another Mariana, the daughter of one of the nun's siblings and a protofeminist thinker, whose apocryphal letter to her aunt's lover is a devastating deconstruction of their affair. Several generations later, the reader encounters this second Mariana's direct descendant, a D. Maria Ana, born around 1800, who calls herself a "rebento extemporâneo e filosófico desta linhagem feminina" (spontaneous, philosophically minded offshoot of this female line) whose continuity she chronicles in her diary. Unable to tolerate the hypocrisy of the only kind of conjugal contract available in the society in which she lives, she refuses to marry and have children, at the same time as she decides to leave her diary to her own niece. The last link in this chain of displaced heredity is a twentieth-century Ana Maria, a contemporary of the authors of *Novas cartas portuguesas,* who reaffirms, from an historically informed perspective, women's collective need for material and symbolic identities of their own. As she expresses it, addressing her female ancestor:

Bem sei . . . de que te queixavas, do que eras incapaz: de inventares sozinha a mãe, a heroína, a ideologia, o mito, a matriz, que te pusesse espessura e significado perante os outros, que até aos outros abrisse caminho, se não de comunicação, pelo menos de inquietação.

(I am very much aware . . . of what you were complaining of, of what you were incapable of: of inventing, all by yourself, the mother, the heroine, the ideology, the myth, the matrix that would give you substance and meaning in the eyes of others, that would open up a path leading to others, if not a path of communication, at least one of shared concerns and anxieties).

*Novas cartas portuguesas* sought to fulfill this deeply felt imperative, while at the same time charting the authors' own sometimes hesitant and often ambivalent progress toward personal and political emancipation. As a result, according to translator Lane, the book represented

> perhaps the most penetrating record to date of the process of consciousness raising itself—an experience shared over many months by three women determined to tear down the walls of *their* convent, to break the unconscious male-female covenant leading to mutual repression and exploitation by way of the carnal embrace, to use as a kind of revolutionary explosive the power of new sexual freedom they were painfully winning, inch by inch, in their personal lives.

Although the importance of *Novas cartas portuguesas* as a crucial reference point for contemporary women's writing in Portugal is undeniable, it is also safe to assume that at least the initial notoriety of the book, particularly on the international scale, was for the most part a result of the difficulties encountered by the Three Marias, who were taken to court by the Caetano regime on charges of, among other things, "outrage to public decency." After having been rejected by several publishers (who were aware of the risk it represented), *Novas cartas portuguesas* had gained the support of Natália Correia, a poet and novelist and then editor in chief of the publishing firm Estúdios Cor. Some years earlier, Correia herself had experienced Portuguese censorship as the author of *Antologia de poesia portuguesa satírica e erótica* (Anthology of Satyrical and Erotic Portuguese Poetry, 1966); an active oppositionist, she was prepared once more to defy the regime. This time, however, the official reaction was about to exceed all expectations.

Full documentation of the court proceedings was gathered and published (in 1974) by Duarte Vidal, the lawyer for the defense retained by Barreno. In March 1972 Estúdios Cor placed a printing order for 2,000 copies of the book with the Lisbon firm António Coelho Dias. As the owner-manager of the firm later stated in an official deposition to the police, he had not himself seen the typescript in question, but one of his typesetters in charge of the composition of the volume had brought his attention to it, describing it as "pornographic." Dias ordered that the half-completed setting should be stopped and contacted the publisher, who, after a delay of a few days, authorized its continuation. The printing was concluded in late April, and approximately 2,000 copies were delivered to Estúdios Cor; the printer retained in his possession 16 copies destined for

*Maria Velho da Costa (photograph by Graça Sarsfield)*

the National Library and, as required by law, submitted one copy to the Censorship Services. In early May, the publishing house forwarded 1,380 copies to the distributor (Expresso); of those, at least 1,215 were sold in different outlets in Portugal. Most of the remaining copies were sent to Brazil (120), sold at the Lisbon Book Fair (101), offered to the authors (60), distributed among different individuals (199), and sold directly by the publisher (11).

The official case against *Novas cartas portuguesas* took some time to assemble. Although the authors and various individuals involved in the publication were interrogated by the police in June and July of 1972, the formal act of accusation was not composed until 12 December 1972. It encompassed, in addition to the Three Marias, the managing editor of Estúdios Cor (Romeu de Melo) and invoked article 420 of the Penal Code in bringing charges of pornography and offending public morals. Nevertheless, as Hilary Owen stressed in *Portuguese Women's Writing 1972 to 1986: Reincarnations of a Revolution* (2000), it "is now generally accepted in Portugal that the sexual indecency charge against *Novas cartas* was a pretext for suppressing the nationally sensitive issues it refers to, most notably the veiled Colonial War references."

Many Portuguese intellectuals made public statements of support on behalf of the authors of *Novas cartas portuguesas,* including José Gomes Ferreira, then president of the Associação Portuguesa de Escritores (Portuguese Writers' Association); writers Augusto Abelaira and Urbano Tavares Rodrigues; and Correia. They were soon joined by a growing international contingent of supporters. Following Barreno's appeal to Christiane Rochefort in Paris, feminist movements in Western Europe and the United States took up the cause of the Three Marias. The resulting uncommonly close focus on Portugal by the foreign media was mentioned often throughout the court proceedings. Several witnesses referred to the international impact of *Novas cartas portuguesas* and to the attention that the foreign press was paying to the controversy. In her official deposition Barreno herself commented on the "grande interesse" (great interest) that the book had provoked in the "meios intelectuais do mundo civilizado" (intellectual circles of the civilized world), thus becoming a work "que honra as letras portuguesas e já transpôs . . . as fronteiras nacionais" (that honors Portuguese letters and has already crossed . . . national borders). Correia expressed her belief that the book was going to be translated into many more languages, "o que constuirá a maior projecção da literatura portuguesa desde há muitos anos" (which will promote the most widespread propagation that Portuguese literature has seen in many years). Tavares Rodrigues mentioned French, Brazilian, and Spanish writers he had personally asked for an opinion on the matter, and whose responses convinced him that "*Novas cartas portuguesas* contribuiram para uma projecção muito honrosa da literatura portuguesa no mundo civilizado" (contributed toward a most honorable projection of Portuguese literature throughout the civilized world). Further testimonies followed a similar line of argument, stressing the disparity between the widespread success of the book abroad and its condemnation by the Portuguese authorities.

Although the sentencing of the Three Marias was supposed to take place in mid April 1974, the judge chose to delay it for another three weeks; the trial therefore was interrupted by the Marxist coup against the Caetano regime staged by the Movimento das Forças Armadas (Armed Forces Movement) on 25 April 1974, which finally brought the Estado Novo to an end. Shortly thereafter, on 7 May 1974, the same judge who had presided over the proceedings issued a verdict declaring that *Novas cartas portuguesas* was neither pornographic nor immoral and that it was a work of art of high literary quality. The authors and the publisher were completely exonerated of all charges, the conclusion of their trial becoming one of the emblematic events of the 1974 revolution.

In the following weeks and months, however, the memory of the Three Marias' legendary courtroom solidarity was overshadowed by a public quarrel in the press between Velho da Costa, who distanced herself from the international feminist appropriation of *Novas cartas portuguesas* and sought her primary alliances within the Communist-led Portuguese revolutionary movement, and Barreno and Horta, who identified themselves explicitly as feminists. As Owen noted in *Portuguese Women's Writing 1972 to 1986,* the "exchange of published correspondence between Barreno and Velho da Costa provided an acrimonious postscript to the Three Marias' case, not least because both writers ironically prefaced their letters with the type of descriptive titles and modes of address which had characterized the playful, collaborative venture of *Novas cartas.*"

In the years since their memorable collaboration on *Novas cartas portuguesas,* the three writers have followed their own individual paths of intellectual and literary development, as well as (particularly in the case of Horta) political activism. In her writing, Barreno has alternated between works of fiction (novels and short stories) and feminist sociological analyses such as *A imagem da mulher na imprensa* (Images of Women in the Press, 1976) and a study of gender discrimination in the Portuguese educational system titled *O falso neutro* (The False Neuter, 1985). *A morte da mãe* (The Death of the Mother), published in 1979, situates itself between fiction and essay; it provides an extended sequel to many of the themes touched upon (and some that remained untouched) in *Novas cartas portuguesas.* Barreno's collection of short stories *Os sensos incomuns* (Uncommon Senses) won the Grand Prize of the Associação Portuguesa de Escritores and the Portuguese PEN Club prize in 1994. She has also been active as an artist and has exhibited her drawings and tapestries on several occasions. From 1990 to 1993 she directed the Portuguese edition of the women's magazine *Marie Claire.*

Along with Barreno, Horta became one of the founding members of the Portuguese women's liberation movement, the Movimento de Libertação das Mulheres, in 1974. The organization was, however, criticized, denounced, and eventually suppressed by the far larger Portuguese Communist Party women's movement, the Movimento Democrático de Mulheres (MDM). In 1977 Horta became the editor in chief of the *Mulheres* magazine funded by the MDM, which she went on to direct for more than a decade; she was also a frequent contributor to this periodical, which provided a forum for reviewing works by foreign feminist authors and theorists as well as Portuguese women writers. She has continued to write both poetry and narrative fiction; her later collections of poems include *Destino* (Destiny, 1997) and *Só de Amor* (Only of Love, 1999). She has also published a novel, *A paixão segundo Constança H.* (Passion According to Constança H., 1994), which offers a continuation, albeit in a darker, more problematic mode, of Horta's commitment to chronicling what she perceives as a millenary tradition of women's culture and cultural production. Not unlike *Novas cartas portuguesas*, it incorporates a vast gallery of references to literary works by and about women, to real and fictional women's lives that are linked together to form a specifically feminine genealogy. The protagonist reads the works of Marguerite Duras, Sylvia Plath, Clarice Lispector, Florbela Espanca, Zelda Fitzgerald, and Virginia Woolf; in reading, she "reconhece-se em cada parágrafo" (recognizes herself in each paragraph): "na mudez de Maina ou na insanidade apaixonada de Lola Valérie Stein, na imponderabilidade de Mariana Alcoforado" (in Maina's silence, in Lola Valérie Stein's passionate insanity, in Mariana Alcoforado's inscrutability).

Velho da Costa has flourished primarily as a novelist and has emerged as the most highly regarded author among the members of the Three Marias collective. Already with *Maina Mendes* she had been recognized as a profoundly innovative and complex writer whose works combine a high degree of verbal virtuosity and narrative experimentation with a strong commitment to explorations of the Portuguese literary and cultural tradition from the Middle Ages to the present. Among her most consistently republished and most frequently studied novels are (in addition to *Maina Mendes*) *Casas pardas* (Drab Houses, 1977), *Lucialima* (1983), and *Missa in albis* (Mass in White, 1988). In 2001 her novel *Irene ou o contrato social* (Irene, or the Social Contract) was awarded the Grand Prize for the Novel bestowed by the Associação Portuguesa de Escritores, a distinction that, as several commentators pointed out on the occasion, had been long overdue. Velho da Costa has also written for the theater; her play *Madame* (2000) stages an imaginary encounter between two of the most remarkable and notorious female characters of nineteenth-century Portuguese and Brazilian fiction: Maria Eduarda, the heroine of Eça de Queirós's *Os Maias* (The Maias, 1888), and Capitu, the elusive protagonist of Joaquim Maria Machado de Assis's *Dom Casmurro* (1899). In 2002 she was awarded the highest literary honor in the Portuguese-speaking world: the Camões Prize, attributed annually by an international jury to a writer from Portugal, Brazil, or Lusophone Africa. This surprising but widely acclaimed recognition has confirmed Velho da Costa's position as one of the most important authors writing in Portuguese today.

*Cover for the 1979 edition of the 1972 work in which "the Three Marias" explore the cultural and political climates for Portuguese women (Thomas Cooper Library, University of South Carolina)*

Thirty years after its publication, *Novas cartas portuguesas* stands out as a landmark case in modern Portuguese literature and culture. In 1998 a new edition, published on the twenty-fifth anniversary of its first printing, was widely reported in the Portuguese press, with many writers, journalists, and public figures commenting on the importance of the work and especially on the lasting effect the book had on the new generations of Portuguese women writers. At the same time, its place in the canon of Portuguese literary history is not easily defined. To some, *Novas cartas portuguesas* is a dated text, and its undeniable political and cultural impact remains circumscribed by the historical context of its original publication. Others–such as the critic Maria Alzira Seixo in her "Quatro razões para reler *Novas cartas portuguesas*" (Four Reasons to Reread *New Portuguese Letters*)–claim that it should be recognized as a major work of national literature for reasons both aesthetic and political. Seixo sees in *Novas cartas portuguesas* a text of great literary sophistication with feminist insights that are as inspiring and relevant in a democratic and prosperous Portugal in the twenty-first century as they were under the country's authoritarian regime of the early 1970s.

**Interview:**

Antónia de Sousa, "*Novas cartas portuguesas* 25 anos depois. Três Marias abalaram ditadura," *Diário de Notícias,* 7 November 1998, pp. 4–7.

**References:**

Nelly Novaes Coelho, "*Novas cartas portuguesas* e o processo de conscientização da mulher: Século XX," *Letras,* 23 (1975): 165–171;

E. T. Dubois, "A mulher e a paixão: Das *Lettres portugaises* (1669) às *Novas cartas portuguesas* (1972)," *Colóquio/Letras,* 102 (1988): 35–43;

Maria João Guimarães, "Novas cartas de ontem, velhas estórias de hoje," *Público,* 25 November 1998, pp. 4–5;

Maria Teresa Horta, "Novas Cartas . . . tantos anos depois," *Mulheres,* November 1986, p. 33;

Horta, "Três Marias . . . dez anos depois," *Mulheres,* October 1982, pp. 4–6;

Linda S. Kauffman, *Discourses of Desire: Gender, Genre, and Epistolary Fictions* (Ithaca, N.Y.: Cornell University Press, 1986);

Robin Morgan, "International Feminism. A Call for Support of the Three Marias," in her *Going Too Far: The Personal Chronicle of a Feminist* (New York: Vintage, 1978), pp. 201–208;

Hilary Owen, "New Cartographies of the Body in *Novas cartas portuguesas*. The (Counter-) Narrative of the Nation and the Sign of the Voyage Back," *Ellipsis,* 1 (1999): 45–61;

Owen, *Portuguese Women's Writing 1972 to 1986: Reincarnations of a Revolution* (Lewiston, N.Y.: Edwin Mellen Press, 2000);

Owen, "The Three Marias: The Case Re-opened," *ACIS Journal,* 2, no. 1 (1989): 25–32;

Darlene J. Sadlier, "Form in *Novas cartas portuguesas*," *Novel: A Forum on Fiction,* 19, no. 3 (1986): 246–263;

Sadlier, *The Question of How: Women Writers and New Portuguese Literature* (Westport, Conn.: Greenwood Press, 1989);

Maria Alzira Seixo, "*Novas cartas portuguesas:* O jogo das damas," *Jornal de Letras* (27 January – 9 February 1999): 20–21;

Seixo, "Quatro razões para reler *Novas cartas portuguesas*," *Ciberkiosk,* no. 4 (December 1998) <http://www.ciberkiosk.pt/arquivo/ciberkiosk4/livros/seixo.htm>;

Loretta Porto Slover, "The Three Marias: Literary Portrayals of the Situation of Women in Portugal," dissertation, Harvard University, 1977;

Duarte Vidal, *O processo das Três Marias* (Lisbon: Futura, 1974).

# Books for Further Reading

Abdala, Benjamim, Jr., and Maria Aparecida Paschoalin. *História social da literatura portuguesa,* second edition. São Paulo: Ática, 1985.

Amora, Antonio Soares, Massaud Moisés, and Segismundo Spina. *Presença da literatura portuguesa,* 2 volumes. São Paulo: Difusão Européia do Livro, 1961.

Azevedo Filho, Leodegário A. de. *História da literatura portuguesa.* Rio de Janeiro: Tempo Brasileiro / Maceió: EDUFAL, 1983.

Azevedo Filho. *Lírica de Camões,* 2 volumes. Lisbon: Imprensa Nacional-Casa da Moeda, 1984, 1987.

Azevedo Filho. *Literatura portuguesa: história e emergência do novo.* Rio de Janeiro: Tempo Brasileiro / Niterói: Universidade Federal Fluminense EDUFF/PROED, 1987.

Bell, Aubrey. *Portuguese Literature.* Oxford: Clarendon Press, 1970.

Berardinelli, Cleonice. *Estudos camonianos.* Rio de Janeiro: MEC/DAC, 1973.

Berardinelli. *Estudos de literatura portuguesa.* Lisbon: Imprensa Nacional-Casa da Moeda, 1985.

Bourdon, Albert-Alain. *História de Portugal.* Coimbra: Almedina, 1973.

Braga, Maria Ondina. *Mulheres escritoras.* Amadora: Bertrand, 1980.

Braga, Teófilo. *Garrett e o romantismo.* Lisbon: Lello, 1903.

Braga. *História da literatura portuguesa.* Mem Martins: Publ. Europa-América, 1986.

Buescu, Maria Leonor Carvalhão. *Iniciação à literatura portuguesa.* Lisbon: Plátano, 1973.

Buescu. *Literatura portuguesa medieval.* Lisbon: Universidade Aberta, 1990.

Castro, Ernesto Manuel de Melo. *As vanguardas na poesia portuguesa do século XX.* Lisbon: Instituto de Cultura e Língua Portuguesa, 1980.

Castro, ed. *Antologia do conto fantástico português,* second edition. Lisbon: F. Ribeiro de Mello-Ed. Afrodite, 1974.

Chaves, Castelo Branco. *O romance histórico no romantismo português.* Lisbon: Instituto de Cultura Portuguesa, 1979.

Cidade, Hernâni. *Lições de cultura e literatura portuguesas,* seventh edition, corrected, updated, and enlarged. Coimbra: Coimbra Ed., 1984.

Clemente, Alice, ed. *Sweet Marmalade, Sour Oranges: Contemporary Portuguese Women's Fiction.* Providence, R.I.: Gávea-Brown, 1994.

# Books for Further Reading

Coelho, Jacinto do Prado. *Ao contrário de Penélope*. Lisbon: Bertrand, 1976.

Coelho. *Dicionário de literatura: Literatura portuguesa, literatura brasileira, literatura galega, estilística literária,* fourth edition. Porto: Livraria Figueirinhas, 1994.

Coelho. *Introdução ao estudo da novela camiliana*. Coimbra: Coleção Atlântida, 1946.

Coelho. *A originalidade da literatura portuguesa*. Amadora: Instituto de Cultura Portuguesa, 1977.

Coelho, ed. *Antologia da ficção portuguesa contemporânea*. Lisbon: Instituto de Cultura Portuguesa, 1979.

Cunha, Celso. *Estudos de poética trovadoresca: Versificação e ecdótica*. Rio de Janeiro: Ministério da Educação e Cultura, Instituto Nacional do Livro, 1961.

Eminescu, Roxana. *Novas coordenadas no romance português*. Lisbon: Instituto de Cultura e Língua Portuguesa, 1983.

Extremera Tapia, Nicolás and Manuel Correia Fernandez. *Homenaje a Camoens: Estudios y ensayos hispano-portugueses*. Granada: Universidad de Granada, 1980.

Ferreira, Alberto. *Perspectiva do romantismo português*. Lisbon: Edições 70, 1971.

Ferreira, Ana Paula. *Alves Redol e o Neo-Realismo Português*. Lisbon: Caminho, 1992.

Ferreira, João Palma. *Novelistas e contistas portugueses dos séculos XVII e XVIII*. Lisbon: Imprensa Nacional-Casa da Moeda, 1981.

Figueiredo, Fidelino de. *Características da literatura portuguesa,* third edition. Lisbon: Livraria Clássica Ed., 1923.

Figueiredo. *História da literatura de Portugal*. Buenos Aires: Austral, 1948.

Figueiredo. *História da literatura romântica (1825–1870),* third edition, revised. São Paulo: Anchieta, 1946.

Figueiredo. *Literatura portuguesa,* third edition. Rio de Janeiro: Acadêmica, 1955.

Gomes, Álvaro Cardoso. *A estética simbolista,* second edition. São Paulo: Atlas, 1994.

Guimarães, Fernando. *A poesia da Presença e o aparecimento do neo-realismo*. Porto: Brasília, 1969.

Guimarães. *Poética do saudosismo*. Lisbon: Presença, 1988.

Guimarães. *Simbolismo, modernismo e vanguardas*. Lisbon: Imprensa Nacional-Casa da Moeda, 1982.

Hatherly, Ana. *O espaço crítico, do simbolismo à vanguarda*. Lisbon: Caminho, 1979.

Hower, Alfred and Richard A. Preto-Rodas. *Empire in Transition: The Portuguese World in the Time of Camões*. Gainesville: University Press of Florida, 1985.

Kaufman, Helena and Anna Klobucka, eds. *After the Revolution: Twenty Years of Portuguese Literature, 1974–1994*. Lewisburg, Pa.: Bucknell University Press, 1997.

Lapa, Manuel Rodrigues. *Lições de literatura portuguesa: Época medieval,* ninth edition revised. Coimbra: Coimbra, 1977.

Lapa, ed. *Cantigas d'escárnio e maldizer dos cancioneiros galego-portuguese,* third edition. Lisbon: João Sá da Costa, 1995.

Lepecki, Maria Lúcia. *Para uma história das idéias literárias em Portugal*. Lisbon: Instituto Nacional de Investigação Científica, 1980.

Lisboa, Eugênio. *Poesia portuguesa do Orpheu ao neo-realismo*. Lisbon: Biblioteca Breve, 1980.

Lopes, Oscar. *A busca do sentido: Questões de literatura portuguesa*. Lisbon: Caminho, 1994.

Lopes. *Entre Fialho e Nemésio: Estudos de literatura portuguesa contemporânea*, 2 volumes. Lisbon: Imprensa Nacional-Casa da Moeda, 1987.

Lopes. *Os sinais e os sentidos: Literatura portuguesa do século XX*. Lisbon: Caminho, 1986.

Lopes and Antonio José Saraiva. *História da literatura portuguesa*, seventeenth edition, updated. Porto: Porto Editora, 1996.

Lourenço, Eduardo. *O canto do signo: Existência e literatura (1957–1993)*. Lisbon: Presença, 1994.

Lourenço. *O labirinto da saudade: Psicanálise mítica do destino português*. Lisbon: Dom Quixote, 1978.

Lourenço. *Nós e a Europa ou as duas razões,* third edition. Lisbon: Imprensa Nacional-Casa da Moeda, 1990.

Lourenço. *Tempo e poesia*. Porto: Inova, 1974.

Machado, Álvaro Manuel. *Dicionário de Literatura Portuguesa*. Lisbon: Presença, 1996.

Machado. *A novelística portuguesa contemporânea*. Amadora: Instituto de Cultura e Língua Portuguesa, 1984.

Machado. *Quem é quem na literatura portuguesa*. Lisbon: Dom Quixote, 1979.

Magalhães, Isabel Allegro de. *O sexo dos textos e outras leituras*. Lisbon: Caminho, 1995.

Magalhães. *O tempo das mulheres: A dimensão temporal na escrita feminina contemporânea*. Lisbon: Imprensa Nacional-Casa da Moeda, 1987.

Marinho, Maria de Fátima. *O romance histórico em Portugal*. Porto: Campo das Letras, 1999.

Marinho. *O surrealismo em Portugal*. Lisbon: Imprensa Nacional-Casa da Moeda, 1987.

Marques, A. H. de Oliveira. *História de Portugal,* 2 volumes, eighth edition. Lisbon: Palas, 1978.

Martinho, Fernando. *Pessoa e a moderna poesia portuguesa de Orpheu a 1960*. Lisbon: Biblioteca Breve, 1983.

Martins, Oliveira. *História de Portugal,* sixteenth edition. Lisboa: Guimarães, 1972.

Medina, Cremilda de Araújo. *Viagem à literatura portuguesa contemporânea*. Rio de Janeiro: Nórdica, 1983.

Mendonça, Fernando. *A literatura portuguesa no século XX*. São Paulo: HUCITEC / Assis: Faculdade de Filosofia, Ciências e Letras, 1973.

Mendonça. *Para o estudo do teatro em Portugal, 1946–1966*. Assis: Faculdade de Filosofia, Ciências e Letras, 1971.

Mendonça. *O romance português contemporâneo*. Assis: Faculdade de Filolsofia, Ciências e Letras, 1966.

Moisés, Massaud. *Análise literária,* eighth edition. São Paulo: Cultrix, 1987.

Moisés. *A literatura portuguesa,* twenty-fourth edition. São Paulo: Cultrix, 1988.

Moisés. *A literatura portuguesa através de textos.* São Paulo: Cultrix, 1968.

Moisés. *Pequeno dicionário de literatura portuguesa.* São Paulo: Cultrix, 1981.

Moisés. *Presença da literatura portuguesa: Modernismo,* fifth edition. São Paulo: DIFEL, 1983.

Moisés. *Presença da literatura portuguesa: Romantismo, Realismo.* São Paulo: DIFEL, 1978.

Moisés, ed. *A literatura portuguesa em perspectiva,* 4 volumes. São Paulo: Atlas, 1992–1994.

Monteiro, Adolfo Casais. *A poesia portuguesa contemporânea.* Lisbon: Sá da Costa, 1977.

Monteiro, George. *The Presence of Camões: Influences on the Literature of England, America and South Africa.* Lexington: University Press of Kentucky, 1996.

Morão, Paula. *Viagens na terra das palavras: Ensaios sobre literatura portuguesa.* Lisbon: Cosmos, 1993.

Mourão-Ferreira, David. *Conversas com letras: Entrevistas com escritores.* Lisbon: Escritor, 1996.

Nunes, José Joaquim. *Crestomatia arcaica,* eighth edition. Lisbon: Livraria Clássica, 1981.

Osório, João de Castro. *Introdução à história da literatura portuguesa.* Lisbon: Edições Ultramar, 1945.

Pazos Alonso, Cláudia and Glória Fernandes. *Women, Literature and Culture in the Portuguese-Speaking World.* Lewiston, N.Y.: Edwin Mellen Press, 1996.

Picchio, Luciana Stegagno. *História do teatro português.* Lisbon: Portugália, 1969.

Pinheiro, Célio. *Introdução à literatura portuguesa.* São Paulo: Pioneira, 1991.

Poppe, Manuel. *Temas de literatura viva: 35 escritores contemporâneos.* Lisbon: Imprensa Nacional-Casa da Moeda, 1982.

Quadros, Antonio. *A idéia de Portugal na literatura portuguesa dos últimos cem anos.* Lisbon: Fundação Lusíada, 1989.

Quesado, José Clécio Basílio. *Garrett, Camilo e Eça entre Quixote e Sancho.* Rio de Janeiro: PROED/URFJ, 1988.

Rebelo, Luís Francisco. *História do teatro português.* Lisbon: Europa-América, 1968.

Régio, José. *História da literatura portuguesa.* Lisbon: Publicações Alfa, 2001.

Régio. *Página de doutrina e crítica da Presença.* Porto: Brasília, 1978.

Régio. *Pequena história da poesia portuguesa.* Porto: Brasília, 1976.

Reis, Carlos. *O discurso ideológico do neo-realismo português.* Coimbra: Almedina, 1983.

Reis. *História crítica da literatura portuguesa.* Lisbon: Editorial Verbo, 1993.

Reis. *História portuguesa moderna e contemporânea.* Lisbon: Universidade Aberta, 1990.

Remédios, Joaquim Mendes dos. *História da literatura portuguesa desde as origens até a actualidade,* sixth edition. Coimbra: Atlântida, 1930.

Reys, Câmara. *Aspectos da literatura portuguesa.* Lisbon: Seara Nova, 1929.

Rocha, Clara. *Revistas literárias do século XX em Portugal.* Lisbon: Imprensa Nacional-Casa da Moeda, 1985.

Rocha, Ilídio. *Roteiro de literatura portuguesa.* Frankfurt am Main: Verlag Teo Ferrer de Mesquita, 1995.

Rosa, Antonio Ramos. *Incisões oblíquas: Estudos sobre poesia portuguesa contemporânea.* Lisbon: Caminho, 1987.

Rosa. *A poesia moderna e a interrogação do real,* 2 volumes. Lisbon: Arcádia, 1979, 1980.

Sadlier, Darlene J. "Portugal," in *The Bloomsbury Guide to Women's Literature,* edited by Claire Buck. New York: Prentice-Hall, 1992, pp. 89–92.

Sadlier. *The Question of How: Women Writers and New Portuguese Literature.* New York: Greenwood Press, 1989.

Sampaio, Albino Forjaz de. *História da literatura portuguesa ilustrada.* Volumes 1–3, Lisbon: Bertrand, 1929; volume 4, Porto: Fernando Machado, 1942.

Santilli, Maria Aparecida. *Arte e representação da realidade no romance português contemporâneo.* São Paulo: Quirón, 1979.

Saraiva, Antonio José. *O crepúsculo da Idade Média em Portugal.* Lisbon: Gradiva, 1990.

Saraiva. *A épica medieval portuguesa.* Lisbon: Instituto de Cultura Portuguesa, 1979.

Saraiva. *Iniciação na literatura portuguesa.* Mem Martins: Europa-América, 1984.

Saraiva. *Para a história da cultura em Portugal.* Lisbon: Centro Bibliográfico, 1946.

Saraiva and Oscar Lopes. *História da literatura portuguesa: Das origens a 1970.* Amadora: Bertrand, 1979.

Saraiva, José Hermano. *História concisa de Portugal,* sixth edition. Lisbon: Europa-América, 1980.

Seixo, Maria Alzira. *Discursos do texto.* Amadora: Bertrand, 1977.

Seixo. *Para um estudo da expressão do tempo no romance português contemporâneo,* second edition. Lisbon: Imprensa Nacional-Casa da Moeda, 1987.

Sena, Jorge de. *Estudos de literatura portuguesa,* 2 volumes. Lisbon: Edições 70, 1982, 1988.

Sena. *Os sonetos de Camões e o soneto quinhentista peninsular,* second edition. Lisbon: Edições 70, 1980.

Sérgio, Antonio. *Breve interpretação da história de Portugal.* Lisbon: Sá da Costa, 1972.

Serrão, Joel. *Dicionário de história de Portugal,* 4 volumes. Porto: Iniciativas Editoriais, 1979.

Silveira, Jorge Fernandes da. *Portugal maio de/poesia 61.* Lisbon: Imprensa Nacional-Casa da Moeda, 1985.

Simões, João Gaspar. *História da poesia portuguesa,* 3 volumes. Lisbon: Empresa Nacional de Publicidade, 1955–1959.

Simões. *José Régio e a história do movimento da Presença.* Porto: Brasília, 1977.

Simões. *Perspectiva da literatura portuguesa do século XIX,* 2 volumes. Lisbon: Edições Ática, 1947.

Simões. *Perspectiva histórica da ficção portuguesa: Das origens ao século XX.* Lisbon: Dom Quixote, 1987.

Spina, Segismundo. *Introdução à poética clássica,* second edition. São Paulo: Martin Fontes, 1995.

Torres, Alexandre Pinheiro. *O neo-realismo literário português*. Lisbon: Moraes, 1976.

Tufano, Douglas. *Estudos de literatura portuguesa*. São Paulo: Moderna, 1981.

Vieira, Nelson. *Roads to Today's Portugal: Essays on Contemporary Portuguese Literature, Art and Culture*. Providence, R.I.: Gávea-Brown, 1983.

# Contributors

Fernando Arenas . . . . . . . . . . . . . . . . . . . . . . . . . . . . . . . . . . . . *University of Minnesota*
Leodegário A. de Azevedo Filho . . . . . . . . . . . . . . . . *Universidade do Estado do Rio de Janeiro*
José Carlos Barcellos . . . . . . . . . . . . . . . . . . . . . . . . . . . . . *Universidade Federal Fluminense*
Alice R. Clemente . . . . . . . . . . . . . . . . . . . . . . . . . . . . . . . . . . . . *Brown University*
Sérgio Nazar David . . . . . . . . . . . . . . . . . . . . . . *Universidade do Estado do Rio de Janeiro*
Elias J. Torres Feijó . . . . . . . . . . . . . . . . . . . . . . . . . . *Universidade de Santiago de Compostela*
Nadiá Paulo Ferreira . . . . . . . . . . . . . . . . . . . . . . . *Universidade do Estado do Rio de Janeiro*
René P. Garay . . . . . . . . . . . . . . . . . *City College–Graduate School, City University of New York*
Luis Riordan Gonçalves . . . . . . . . . . . . . . . . . . . . *University of North Carolina at Chapel Hill*
Maria Guterres . . . . . . . . . . . . . . . . . . . . . . . . . . . . . . . . . . . . . *Liverpool University*
Anna Klobucka . . . . . . . . . . . . . . . . . . . . . . . . . . . *University of Massachusetts Dartmouth*
Reinhard Krüger . . . . . . . . . . . . . . . . . . . . . . . . . . . . . . . . . . . . *University of Stuttgart*
Joseph Abraham Levi . . . . . . . . . . . . . . . . . . . . . . . . . . . . . . . . *Rhode Island College*
Maria do Amparo Tavares Maleval . . . . . . . . . . . . *Universidade do Estado do Rio de Janeiro*
Ana Maria Almeida Martins . . . . . . . . . . . . . . . . . . . . . . . . . . . . . . . *Lisbon, Portugal*
Lênia Márcia Mongelli . . . . . . . . . . . . . . . . . . . . . . . . . . . . . *Universidade de São Paulo, Brazil*
George Monteiro . . . . . . . . . . . . . . . . . . . . . . . . . . . . . . . . . . . . . . *Brown University*
Luciana Camargo Namorato . . . . . . . . . . . . . . . . . . *University of North Carolina at Chapel Hill*
Paulo Motta Oliveira . . . . . . . . . . . . . . . . . . . . . . . . . . . . . . . *Universidade de São Paulo*
José N. Ornelas . . . . . . . . . . . . . . . . . . . . . . . . . . . . . . *University of Massachusetts Amherst*
Loida Pereira Peterson . . . . . . . . . . . . . . . . . . . . . . . . . . . . . . . . *Lees Summit, Missouri*
Monica Rector . . . . . . . . . . . . . . . . . . . . . . . . . . . *University of North Carolina at Chapel Hill*
Marina Machado Rodrigues . . . . . . . . . . . . . . . . . . *Universidade do Estado do Rio de Janeiro*
Gilda Santos . . . . . . . . . . . . . . . . . . . . . . . . . . . . . . . *Universidade Federal do Rio de Janeiro*
Luís Flávio Sieczkowski . . . . . . . . . . . . . . . . . . . . *Centro Universitário da Cidade–UniverCidade*
Andréia Cristina Lopes Frazão da Silva . . . . . . . . . . . *Universidade Federal do Rio de Janeiro*
Leila Rodrigues da Silva . . . . . . . . . . . . . . . . . . . . . . *Universidade Federal do Rio de Janeiro*
Marco G. Silva . . . . . . . . . . . . . . . . . . . . . . . . . . . *University of North Carolina at Chapel Hill*
Reinaldo Francisco Silva . . . . . . . . . . . . . . . . . . . . . . . . . . . . . *University of Aveiro, Portugal*
Rui Torres . . . . . . . . . . . . . . . . . . . . . . . . . . . . . . . . . . *Universidade Fernando Pessoa, Porto*

# Cumulative Index

*Dictionary of Literary Biography,* Volumes 1-287
*Dictionary of Literary Biography Yearbook,* 1980-2002
*Dictionary of Literary Biography Documentary Series,* Volumes 1-19
*Concise Dictionary of American Literary Biography,* Volumes 1-7
*Concise Dictionary of British Literary Biography,* Volumes 1-8
*Concise Dictionary of World Literary Biography,* Volumes 1-4

# Cumulative Index

**DLB** before number: *Dictionary of Literary Biography,* Volumes 1-287
**Y** before number: *Dictionary of Literary Biography Yearbook,* 1980-2002
**DS** before number: *Dictionary of Literary Biography Documentary Series,* Volumes 1-19
**CDALB** before number: *Concise Dictionary of American Literary Biography,* Volumes 1-7
**CDBLB** before number: *Concise Dictionary of British Literary Biography,* Volumes 1-8
**CDWLB** before number: *Concise Dictionary of World Literary Biography,* Volumes 1-4

## A

Aakjær, Jeppe 1866-1930 ............. DLB-214
Abbey, Edward 1927-1989 ........ DLB-256, 275
Abbey, Edwin Austin 1852-1911 ........ DLB-188
Abbey, Maj. J. R. 1894-1969 .......... DLB-201
Abbey Press ..................... DLB-49
The Abbey Theatre and Irish Drama, 1900-1945 ..................... DLB-10
Abbot, Willis J. 1863-1934 ............. DLB-29
Abbott, Edwin A. 1838-1926 .......... DLB-178
Abbott, Jacob 1803-1879 ........ DLB-1, 42, 243
Abbott, Lee K. 1947- ............. DLB-130
Abbott, Lyman 1835-1922 ............. DLB-79
Abbott, Robert S. 1868-1940 ........ DLB-29, 91
Abe Kōbō 1924-1993 ............... DLB-182
Abelaira, Augusto 1926- ............. DLB-287
Abelard, Peter circa 1079-1142? .... DLB-115, 208
Abelard-Schuman ................ DLB-46
Abell, Arunah S. 1806-1888 ........... DLB-43
Abell, Kjeld 1901-1961 .............. DLB-214
Abercrombie, Lascelles 1881-1938 ....... DLB-19
   The Friends of the Dymock Poets ..................... Y-00
Aberdeen University Press Limited ...... DLB-106
Abish, Walter 1931- .......... DLB-130, 227
Ablesimov, Aleksandr Onisimovich 1742-1783 ..................... DLB-150
Abraham à Sancta Clara 1644-1709 ...... DLB-168
Abrahams, Peter 1919- .......... DLB-117, 225; CDWLB-3
Abrams, M. H. 1912- ............. DLB-67
Abramson, Jesse 1904-1979 .......... DLB-241
*Abrogans* circa 790-800 ............. DLB-148
Abschatz, Hans Aßmann von 1646-1699 .. DLB-168
Abse, Dannie 1923- .......... DLB-27, 245
Abutsu-ni 1221-1283 ............... DLB-203
Academy Chicago Publishers .......... DLB-46
Accius circa 170 B.C.-circa 80 B.C. ...... DLB-211
Accrocca, Elio Filippo 1923-1996 ....... DLB-128
Ace Books ..................... DLB-46
Achebe, Chinua 1930- .... DLB-117; CDWLB-3

Achtenberg, Herbert 1938- ........... DLB-124
Ackerman, Diane 1948- ............. DLB-120
Ackroyd, Peter 1949- .......... DLB-155, 231
Acorn, Milton 1923-1986 ............. DLB-53
Acosta, Oscar Zeta 1935?-1974? ........ DLB-82
Acosta Torres, José 1925- ............ DLB-209
Actors Theatre of Louisville ............ DLB-7
Adair, Gilbert 1944- ............. DLB-194
Adair, James 1709?-1783? ............ DLB-30
Adam, Graeme Mercer 1839-1912 ....... DLB-99
Adam, Robert Borthwick, II 1863-1940 ..................... DLB-187
Adame, Leonard 1947- ............. DLB-82
Adameşteanu, Gabriel 1942- ......... DLB-232
Adamic, Louis 1898-1951 ............. DLB-9
Adams, Abigail 1744-1818 ........ DLB-183, 200
Adams, Alice 1926-1999 ........ DLB-234; Y-86
Adams, Bertha Leith (Mrs. Leith Adams, Mrs. R. S. de Courcy Laffan) 1837?-1912 ..................... DLB-240
Adams, Brooks 1848-1927 ............. DLB-47
Adams, Charles Francis, Jr. 1835-1915 .... DLB-47
Adams, Douglas 1952-2001 ....... DLB-261; Y-83
Adams, Franklin P. 1881-1960 .......... DLB-29
Adams, Hannah 1755-1832 .......... DLB-200
Adams, Henry 1838-1918 ....... DLB-12, 47, 189
Adams, Herbert Baxter 1850-1901 ....... DLB-47
Adams, James Truslow 1878-1949 ................. DLB-17; DS-17
Adams, John 1735-1826 ............ DLB-31, 183
Adams, John Quincy 1767-1848 .......... DLB-37
Adams, Léonie 1899-1988 ............. DLB-48
Adams, Levi 1802-1832 .............. DLB-99
Adams, Richard 1920- ............. DLB-261
Adams, Samuel 1722-1803 .......... DLB-31, 43
Adams, Sarah Fuller Flower 1805-1848 ..................... DLB-199
Adams, Thomas 1582/1583-1652 ....... DLB-151
Adams, William Taylor 1822-1897 ....... DLB-42
J. S. and C. Adams [publishing house] ..... DLB-49
Adamson, Harold 1906-1980 .......... DLB-265
Adamson, Sir John 1867-1950 .......... DLB-98

Adcock, Arthur St. John 1864-1930 ...... DLB-135
Adcock, Betty 1938- ............. DLB-105
   "Certain Gifts" ................ DLB-105
   Tribute to James Dickey ............. Y-97
Adcock, Fleur 1934- ............. DLB-40
Addison, Joseph 1672-1719 ... DLB-101; CDBLB-2
Ade, George 1866-1944 .......... DLB-11, 25
Adeler, Max (see Clark, Charles Heber)
Adlard, Mark 1932- ............. DLB-261
Adler, Richard 1921- ............. DLB-265
Adonias Filho 1915-1990 ............. DLB-145
Adorno, Theodor W. 1903-1969 ........ DLB-242
Adoum, Jorge Enrique 1926- ......... DLB-283
Advance Publishing Company .......... DLB-49
Ady, Endre 1877-1919 ...... DLB-215; CDWLB-4
AE 1867-1935 .............. DLB-19; CDBLB-5
Ælfric circa 955-circa 1010 ............. DLB-146
Aeschines circa 390 B.C.-circa 320 B.C. ..... DLB-176
Aeschylus 525-524 B.C.-456-455 B.C.
   ................. DLB-176; CDWLB-1
*Aesthetic Papers* ..................... DLB-1
Aesthetics
   Eighteenth-Century Aesthetic Theories ..................... DLB-31
African Literature
   Letter from Khartoum ............ Y-90
African American
   Afro-American Literary Critics: An Introduction .............. DLB-33
   The Black Aesthetic: Background ....... DS-8
   The Black Arts Movement, by Larry Neal ................. DLB-38
   Black Theaters and Theater Organizations in America, 1961-1982: A Research List ............... DLB-38
   Black Theatre: A Forum [excerpts] .... DLB-38
   *Callaloo* [journal] ..................... Y-87
   Community and Commentators: Black Theatre and Its Critics ..... DLB-38
   The Emergence of Black Women Writers ............. DS-8
   The Hatch-Billops Collection ........ DLB-76
   A Look at the Contemporary Black Theatre Movement ............ DLB-38

375

The Moorland-Spingarn Research
    Center . . . . . . . . . . . . . . . . . . . . . . DLB-76
"The Negro as a Writer," by
    G. M. McClellan . . . . . . . . . . . . . DLB-50
"Negro Poets and Their Poetry," by
    Wallace Thurman . . . . . . . . . . . . DLB-50
Olaudah Equiano and Unfinished Journeys:
    The Slave-Narrative Tradition and
    Twentieth-Century Continuities, by
    Paul Edwards and Pauline T.
    Wangman . . . . . . . . . . . . . . . . . DLB-117
PHYLON (Fourth Quarter, 1950),
    The Negro in Literature:
    The Current Scene . . . . . . . . . . . DLB-76
The Schomburg Center for Research
    in Black Culture . . . . . . . . . . . . . DLB-76
Three Documents [poets], by John
    Edward Bruce . . . . . . . . . . . . . . . DLB-50
After Dinner Opera Company . . . . . . . . . . . . Y-92
Agassiz, Elizabeth Cary 1822-1907 . . . . . . DLB-189
Agassiz, Louis 1807-1873 . . . . . . . . . . DLB-1, 235
Agee, James
    1909-1955 . . . . . . . DLB-2, 26, 152; CDALB-1
The Agee Legacy: A Conference at
    the University of Tennessee
    at Knoxville . . . . . . . . . . . . . . . . . . . Y-89
Aguilera Malta, Demetrio 1909-1981 . . . . DLB-145
Ahlin, Lars 1915-1997 . . . . . . . . . . . . . . . . DLB-257
Ai 1947- . . . . . . . . . . . . . . . . . . . . . . . . . . DLB-120
Aichinger, Ilse 1921- . . . . . . . . . . . . . . . . . DLB-85
Aickman, Robert 1914-1981 . . . . . . . . . . . DLB-261
Aidoo, Ama Ata 1942- . . . . DLB-117; CDWLB-3
Aiken, Conrad
    1889-1973 . . . . . . . . DLB-9, 45, 102; CDALB-5
Aiken, Joan 1924- . . . . . . . . . . . . . . . . . . . DLB-161
Aikin, Lucy 1781-1864 . . . . . . . . . . . . DLB-144, 163
Ainsworth, William Harrison
    1805-1882 . . . . . . . . . . . . . . . . . . . . . DLB-21
Aistis, Jonas 1904-1973 . . . . . DLB-220; CDWLB-4
Aitken, George A. 1860-1917 . . . . . . . . . . DLB-149
Robert Aitken [publishing house] . . . . . . . . DLB-49
Akenside, Mark 1721-1770 . . . . . . . . . . . . DLB-109
Akins, Zoë 1886-1958 . . . . . . . . . . . . . . . . . DLB-26
Aksakov, Ivan Sergeevich 1823-1826 . . . . . DLB-277
Aksakov, Sergei Timofeevich
    1791-1859 . . . . . . . . . . . . . . . . . . . . . DLB-198
Akunin, Boris (Grigorii Shalvovich
    Chkhartishvili) 1956- . . . . . . . . . . DLB-285
Akutagawa Ryūnosuke 1892-1927 . . . . . . DLB-180
Alabaster, William 1568-1640 . . . . . . . . . . DLB-132
Alain de Lille circa 1116-1202/1203 . . . . . DLB-208
Alain-Fournier 1886-1914 . . . . . . . . . . . . . DLB-65
Alanus de Insulis (see Alain de Lille)
Alarcón, Francisco X. 1954- . . . . . . . . . . DLB-122
Alarcón, Justo S. 1930- . . . . . . . . . . . . . . DLB-209
Alba, Nanina 1915-1968 . . . . . . . . . . . . . . . DLB-41
Albee, Edward 1928- . . . . DLB-7, 266; CDALB-1
Albert, Octavia 1853-ca. 1889 . . . . . . . . . . DLB-221
Albert the Great circa 1200-1280 . . . . . . . . DLB-115
Alberti, Rafael 1902-1999 . . . . . . . . . . . . . DLB-108

Albertinus, Aegidius circa 1560-1620 . . . . DLB-164
Alcaeus born circa 620 B.C. . . . . . . . . . . . . DLB-176
Alcoforado, Mariana, the Portuguese Nun
    1640-1723 . . . . . . . . . . . . . . . . . . . . . DLB-287
Alcott, Amos Bronson
    1799-1888 . . . . . . . . . . . . . . DLB-1, 223; DS-5
Alcott, Louisa May 1832-1888
    . . . DLB-1, 42, 79, 223, 239; DS-14; CDALB-3
Alcott, William Andrus 1798-1859 . . . . DLB-1, 243
Alcuin circa 732-804 . . . . . . . . . . . . . . . . . . DLB-148
Alden, Henry Mills 1836-1919 . . . . . . . . . . DLB-79
Alden, Isabella 1841-1930 . . . . . . . . . . . . . . DLB-42
John B. Alden [publishing house] . . . . . . . . DLB-49
Alden, Beardsley, and Company . . . . . . . . DLB-49
Aldington, Richard
    1892-1962 . . . . . . . . . . . DLB-20, 36, 100, 149
Aldis, Dorothy 1896-1966 . . . . . . . . . . . . . DLB-22
Aldis, H. G. 1863-1919 . . . . . . . . . . . . . . . DLB-184
Aldiss, Brian W. 1925- . . . . . . DLB-14, 261, 271
Aldrich, Thomas Bailey
    1836-1907 . . . . . . . . . . . . DLB-42, 71, 74, 79
Alegría, Ciro 1909-1967 . . . . . . . . . . . . . . DLB-113
Alegría, Claribel 1924- . . . . . . . . DLB-145, 283
Aleixandre, Vicente 1898-1984 . . . . . . . . . DLB-108
Aleksandravičius, Jonas (see Aistis, Jonas)
Aleksandrov, Aleksandr Andreevich
    (see Durova, Nadezhda Andreevna)
Alekseeva, Marina Anatol'evna
    (see Marinina, Aleksandra)
Aleramo, Sibilla (Rena Pierangeli Faccio)
    1876-1960 . . . . . . . . . . . . . . . . . DLB-114, 264
Aleshkovsky, Petr Markovich 1957- . . . DLB-285
Alexander, Cecil Frances 1818-1895 . . . . . DLB-199
Alexander, Charles 1868-1923 . . . . . . . . . . DLB-91
Charles Wesley Alexander
    [publishing house] . . . . . . . . . . . . . . DLB-49
Alexander, James 1691-1756 . . . . . . . . . . . DLB-24
Alexander, Lloyd 1924- . . . . . . . . . . . . . . DLB-52
Alexander, Sir William, Earl of Stirling
    1577?-1640 . . . . . . . . . . . . . . . . . . . . . DLB-121
Alexie, Sherman 1966- . . . . . . DLB-175, 206, 278
Alexis, Willibald 1798-1871 . . . . . . . . . . . . DLB-133
Alfred, King 849-899 . . . . . . . . . . . . . . . . . DLB-146
Alger, Horatio, Jr. 1832-1899 . . . . . . . . . . . DLB-42
Algonquin Books of Chapel Hill . . . . . . . . DLB-46
Algren, Nelson
    1909-1981 . . . . . . DLB-9; Y-81, 82; CDALB-1
    Nelson Algren: An International
        Symposium . . . . . . . . . . . . . . . . . . . Y-00
Aljamiado Literature . . . . . . . . . . . . . . . . . DLB-286
Allan, Andrew 1907-1974 . . . . . . . . . . . . . DLB-88
Allan, Ted 1916-1995 . . . . . . . . . . . . . . . . . DLB-68
Allbeury, Ted 1917- . . . . . . . . . . . . . . . . . DLB-87
Alldritt, Keith 1935- . . . . . . . . . . . . . . . . . DLB-14
Allen, Dick 1939- . . . . . . . . . . . . . . . . . . . DLB-282
Allen, Ethan 1738-1789 . . . . . . . . . . . . . . . DLB-31
Allen, Frederick Lewis 1890-1954 . . . . . . . DLB-137
Allen, Gay Wilson 1903-1995 . . . . . DLB-103; Y-95

Allen, George 1808-1876 . . . . . . . . . . . . . . DLB-59
Allen, Grant 1848-1899 . . . . . . . . DLB-70, 92, 178
Allen, Henry W. 1912-1991 . . . . . . . . . . . . . . Y-85
Allen, Hervey 1889-1949 . . . . . . . . . . . . DLB-9, 45
Allen, James 1739-1808 . . . . . . . . . . . . . . . . DLB-31
Allen, James Lane 1849-1925 . . . . . . . . . . . DLB-71
Allen, Jay Presson 1922- . . . . . . . . . . . . . . DLB-26
John Allen and Company . . . . . . . . . . . . . . DLB-49
Allen, Paula Gunn 1939- . . . . . . . . . . . . DLB-175
Allen, Samuel W. 1917- . . . . . . . . . . . . . . DLB-41
Allen, Woody 1935- . . . . . . . . . . . . . . . . . DLB-44
George Allen [publishing house] . . . . . . . . DLB-106
George Allen and Unwin Limited . . . . . . DLB-112
Allende, Isabel 1942- . . . . . . DLB-145; CDWLB-3
Alline, Henry 1748-1784 . . . . . . . . . . . . . . . DLB-99
Allingham, Margery 1904-1966 . . . . . . . . . DLB-77
    The Margery Allingham Society . . . . . . . . Y-98
Allingham, William 1824-1889 . . . . . . . . . . DLB-35
W. L. Allison [publishing house] . . . . . . . . DLB-49
The *Alliterative Morte Arthure and the Stanzaic
    Morte Arthur* circa 1350-1400 . . . . . . . DLB-146
Allott, Kenneth 1912-1973 . . . . . . . . . . . . . DLB-20
Allston, Washington 1779-1843 . . . . . . DLB-1, 235
John Almon [publishing house] . . . . . . . . DLB-154
Alonzo, Dámaso 1898-1990 . . . . . . . . . . . . DLB-108
Alsop, George 1636-post 1673 . . . . . . . . . . DLB-24
Alsop, Richard 1761-1815 . . . . . . . . . . . . . DLB-37
Henry Altemus and Company . . . . . . . . . . DLB-49
Altenberg, Peter 1885-1919 . . . . . . . . . . . . DLB-81
Althusser, Louis 1918-1990 . . . . . . . . . . . . DLB-242
Altolaguirre, Manuel 1905-1959 . . . . . . . . DLB-108
Aluko, T. M. 1918- . . . . . . . . . . . . . . . . . DLB-117
Alurista 1947- . . . . . . . . . . . . . . . . . . . . . . DLB-82
Alvarez, A. 1929- . . . . . . . . . . . . . . . . . DLB-14, 40
Alvarez, Julia 1950- . . . . . . . . . . . . . . . . . DLB-282
Alvaro, Corrado 1895-1956 . . . . . . . . . . . . DLB-264
Alver, Betti 1906-1989 . . . . . DLB-220; CDWLB-4
Amadi, Elechi 1934- . . . . . . . . . . . . . . . . DLB-117
Amado, Jorge 1912-2001 . . . . . . . . . . . . . . DLB-113
Ambler, Eric 1909-1998 . . . . . . . . . . . . . . . DLB-77
The Library of America . . . . . . . . . . . . . . . DLB-46
The Library of America: An Assessment
    After Two Decades . . . . . . . . . . . . . . . Y-02
America: or, A Poem on the Settlement
    of the British Colonies, by Timothy
    Dwight . . . . . . . . . . . . . . . . . . . . . . . DLB-37
American Bible Society
    Department of Library, Archives, and
        Institutional Research . . . . . . . . . . . Y-97
American Conservatory Theatre . . . . . . . . DLB-7
American Culture
    American Proletarian Culture:
        The Twenties and Thirties . . . . . . . DS-11
Studies in American Jewish Literature . . . . . Y-02
The American Library in Paris . . . . . . . . . . . Y-93
American Literature

The Literary Scene and Situation and . . .
   (Who Besides Oprah) Really Runs
   American Literature? . . . . . . . . . . . . Y-99
Who Owns American Literature, by
   Henry Taylor . . . . . . . . . . . . . . . . . . Y-94
Who Runs American Literature? . . . . . . . Y-94
American News Company . . . . . . . . . . . . . DLB-49
A Century of Poetry, a Lifetime of Collecting:
   J. M. Edelstein's Collection of Twentieth-
   Century American Poetry . . . . . . . . . . . . . Y-02
The American Poets' Corner: The First
   Three Years (1983-1986) . . . . . . . . . . . . . Y-86
American Publishing Company . . . . . . . . . DLB-49
*American Spectator*
   [Editorial] Rationale From the Initial
   Issue of the American Spectator
   (November 1932) . . . . . . . . . . . . . . . DLB-137
American Stationers' Company . . . . . . . . . DLB-49
The American Studies Association
   of Norway . . . . . . . . . . . . . . . . . . . . . . . . Y-00
American Sunday-School Union . . . . . . . . DLB-49
American Temperance Union . . . . . . . . . . DLB-49
American Tract Society . . . . . . . . . . . . . . . DLB-49
The American Trust for the British Library . . Y-96
American Writers Congress
   The American Writers Congress
   (9-12 October 1981) . . . . . . . . . . . . . . Y-81
   The American Writers Congress: A Report
   on Continuing Business . . . . . . . . . . . . Y-81
Ames, Fisher 1758-1808 . . . . . . . . . . . . . . . DLB-37
Ames, Mary Clemmer 1831-1884 . . . . . . . DLB-23
Ames, William 1576-1633 . . . . . . . . . . . . . DLB-281
Amiel, Henri-Frédéric 1821-1881 . . . . . . . DLB-217
Amini, Johari M. 1935- . . . . . . . . . . . . . . . DLB-41
Amis, Kingsley 1922-1995
   . . . . . . . . DLB-15, 27, 100, 139, Y-96; CDBLB-7
Amis, Martin 1949- . . . . . . . . . . . DLB-14, 194
Ammianus Marcellinus
   circa A.D. 330-A.D. 395 . . . . . . . . . . . DLB-211
Ammons, A. R. 1926-2001 . . . . . . . . . DLB-5, 165
Amory, Thomas 1691?-1788 . . . . . . . . . . . DLB-39
Anania, Michael 1939- . . . . . . . . . . . . . . . DLB-193
Anaya, Rudolfo A. 1937- . . . . . DLB-82, 206, 278
*Ancrene Riwle* circa 1200-1225 . . . . . . . . . DLB-146
Andersch, Alfred 1914-1980 . . . . . . . . . . . DLB-69
Andersen, Benny 1929- . . . . . . . . . . . . . . DLB-214
Anderson, Alexander 1775-1870 . . . . . . . . DLB-188
Anderson, David 1929- . . . . . . . . . . . . . . DLB-241
Anderson, Frederick Irving 1877-1947 . . . DLB-202
Anderson, Margaret 1886-1973 . . . . . . . DLB-4, 91
Anderson, Maxwell 1888-1959 . . . . . . DLB-7, 228
Anderson, Patrick 1915-1979 . . . . . . . . . . DLB-68
Anderson, Paul Y. 1893-1938 . . . . . . . . . . DLB-29
Anderson, Poul 1926-2001 . . . . . . . . . . . . DLB-8
   Tribute to Isaac Asimov . . . . . . . . . . . . . Y-92
Anderson, Robert 1750-1830 . . . . . . . . . . DLB-142
Anderson, Robert 1917- . . . . . . . . . . . . . . DLB-7
Anderson, Sherwood
   1876-1941 . . . . . DLB-4, 9, 86; DS-1; CDALB-4

Andreae, Johann Valentin 1586-1654 . . . . DLB-164
Andreas Capellanus
   flourished circa 1185 . . . . . . . . . . . . . . DLB-208
Andreas-Salomé, Lou 1861-1937 . . . . . . . . DLB-66
Andres, Stefan 1906-1970 . . . . . . . . . . . . . DLB-69
Andresen, Sophia de Mello Breyner
   1919- . . . . . . . . . . . . . . . . . . . . . . . . . DLB-287
Andreu, Blanca 1959- . . . . . . . . . . . . . . . DLB-134
Andrewes, Lancelot 1555-1626 . . . . . DLB-151, 172
Andrews, Charles M. 1863-1943 . . . . . . . . DLB-17
Andrews, Miles Peter ?-1814 . . . . . . . . . . . DLB-89
Andrews, Stephen Pearl 1812-1886 . . . . . . DLB-250
Andrian, Leopold von 1875-1951 . . . . . . . DLB-81
Andrić, Ivo 1892-1975 . . . . . . DLB-147; CDWLB-4
Andrieux, Louis (see Aragon, Louis)
Andrus, Silas, and Son . . . . . . . . . . . . . . . DLB-49
Andrzejewski, Jerzy 1909-1983 . . . . . . . . . DLB-215
Angell, James Burrill 1829-1916 . . . . . . . . DLB-64
Angell, Roger 1920- . . . . . . . . . . . DLB-171, 185
Angelou, Maya 1928- . . . . . . . DLB-38; CDALB-7
   Tribute to Julian Mayfield . . . . . . . . . . . . Y-84
Anger, Jane flourished 1589 . . . . . . . . . . . DLB-136
Angers, Félicité (see Conan, Laure)
*The Anglo-Saxon Chronicle* circa 890-1154 . . . DLB-146
Angus and Robertson (UK) Limited . . . . . DLB-112
Anhalt, Edward 1914-2000 . . . . . . . . . . . . DLB-26
Annenkov, Pavel Vasil'evich
   1813?-1887 . . . . . . . . . . . . . . . . . . . . DLB-277
Henry F. Anners [publishing house] . . . . . DLB-49
*Annolied* between 1077 and 1081 . . . . . . . . DLB-148
Anscombe, G. E. M. 1919-2001 . . . . . . . . . DLB-262
Anselm of Canterbury 1033-1109 . . . . . . . DLB-115
Anstey, F. 1856-1934 . . . . . . . . . . . DLB-141, 178
Anthologizing New Formalism . . . . . . . . DLB-282
Anthony, Michael 1932- . . . . . . . . . . . . . DLB-125
Anthony, Piers 1934- . . . . . . . . . . . . . . . . DLB-8
Anthony, Susanna 1726-1791 . . . . . . . . . . DLB-200
Antin, David 1932- . . . . . . . . . . . . . . . . . DLB-169
Antin, Mary 1881-1949 . . . . . . . . DLB-221; Y-84
Anton Ulrich, Duke of Brunswick-Lüneburg
   1633-1714 . . . . . . . . . . . . . . . . . . . . . DLB-168
Antschel, Paul (see Celan, Paul)
Antunes, António Lobo 1942- . . . . . . . . DLB-287
Anyidoho, Kofi 1947- . . . . . . . . . . . . . . . DLB-157
Anzaldúa, Gloria 1942- . . . . . . . . . . . . . . DLB-122
Anzengruber, Ludwig 1839-1889 . . . . . . . DLB-129
Apess, William 1798-1839 . . . . . . . . DLB-175, 243
Apodaca, Rudy S. 1939- . . . . . . . . . . . . . DLB-82
Apollinaire, Guillaume 1880-1918 . . . . . . DLB-258
Apollonius Rhodius third century B.C. . . . DLB-176
Apple, Max 1941- . . . . . . . . . . . . . . . . . . DLB-130
D. Appleton and Company . . . . . . . . . . . . DLB-49
Appleton-Century-Crofts . . . . . . . . . . . . . . DLB-46
Applewhite, James 1935- . . . . . . . . . . . . . DLB-105
   Tribute to James Dickey . . . . . . . . . . . . . Y-97

Apple-wood Books . . . . . . . . . . . . . . . . . . DLB-46
April, Jean-Pierre 1948- . . . . . . . . . . . . . DLB-251
Apukhtin, Aleksei Nikolaevich
   1840-1893 . . . . . . . . . . . . . . . . . . . . . DLB-277
Apuleius circa A.D. 125-post A.D. 164
   . . . . . . . . . . . . . . . . . . DLB-211; CDWLB-1
Aquin, Hubert 1929-1977 . . . . . . . . . . . . . DLB-53
Aquinas, Thomas 1224/1225-1274 . . . . . . DLB-115
Aragon, Louis 1897-1982 . . . . . . . . DLB-72, 258
Aragon, Vernacular Translations in the
   Crowns of Castile and 1352-1515 . . . . DLB-286
Aralica, Ivan 1930- . . . . . . . . . . . . . . . . . DLB-181
Aratus of Soli
   circa 315 B.C.-circa 239 B.C. . . . . . . . DLB-176
Arbasino, Alberto 1930- . . . . . . . . . . . . . DLB-196
Arbor House Publishing Company . . . . . . DLB-46
Arbuthnot, John 1667-1735 . . . . . . . . . . . DLB-101
Arcadia House . . . . . . . . . . . . . . . . . . . . . DLB-46
Arce, Julio G. (see Ulica, Jorge)
Archer, William 1856-1924 . . . . . . . . . . . DLB-10
Archilochhus
   mid seventh century B.C.E. . . . . . . . . DLB-176
The Archpoet circa 1130?-? . . . . . . . . . . . DLB-148
Archpriest Avvakum (Petrovich)
   1620?-1682 . . . . . . . . . . . . . . . . . . . . DLB-150
Arden, John 1930- . . . . . . . . . . . DLB-13, 245
*Arden of Faversham* . . . . . . . . . . . . . . . . . . DLB-62
Ardis Publishers . . . . . . . . . . . . . . . . . . . . . Y-89
Ardizzone, Edward 1900-1979 . . . . . . . . . DLB-160
Arellano, Juan Estevan 1947- . . . . . . . . . DLB-122
The Arena Publishing Company . . . . . . . . DLB-49
Arena Stage . . . . . . . . . . . . . . . . . . . . . . . DLB-7
Arenas, Reinaldo 1943-1990 . . . . . . . . . . DLB-145
Arendt, Hannah 1906-1975 . . . . . . . . . . . DLB-242
Arensberg, Ann 1937- . . . . . . . . . . . . . . . . Y-82
Arghezi, Tudor 1880-1967 . . . DLB-220; CDWLB-4
Arguedas, José María 1911-1969 . . . . . . . DLB-113
Argueta, Manlio 1936- . . . . . . . . . . . . . . DLB-145
Arias, Ron 1941- . . . . . . . . . . . . . . . . . . . DLB-82
Arishima Takeo 1878-1923 . . . . . . . . . . . . DLB-180
Aristophanes circa 446 B.C.-circa 386 B.C.
   . . . . . . . . . . . . . . . . . . DLB-176; CDWLB-1
Aristotle 384 B.C.-322 B.C.
   . . . . . . . . . . . . . . . . . . DLB-176; CDWLB-1
Ariyoshi Sawako 1931-1984 . . . . . . . . . . . DLB-182
Arland, Marcel 1899-1986 . . . . . . . . . . . . DLB-72
Arlen, Michael 1895-1956 . . . . . . . DLB-36, 77, 162
Armah, Ayi Kwei 1939- . . . DLB-117; CDWLB-3
Armantrout, Rae 1947- . . . . . . . . . . . . . . DLB-193
*Der arme Hartmann* ?-after 1150 . . . . . . . DLB-148
Armed Services Editions . . . . . . . . . . . . . . DLB-46
Armitage, G. E. (Robert Edric) 1956- . . DLB-267
Armstrong, Martin Donisthorpe
   1882-1974 . . . . . . . . . . . . . . . . . . . . . DLB-197
Armstrong, Richard 1903- . . . . . . . . . . . DLB-160
Armstrong, Terence Ian Fytton (see Gawsworth, John)
Arnauld, Antoine 1612-1694 . . . . . . . . . . DLB-268

Arndt, Ernst Moritz 1769-1860 . . . . . . . . . DLB-90
Arnim, Achim von 1781-1831. . . . . . . . . . DLB-90
Arnim, Bettina von 1785-1859 . . . . . . . . . DLB-90
Arnim, Elizabeth von (Countess Mary Annette
   Beauchamp Russell) 1866-1941 . . . . DLB-197
Arno Press . . . . . . . . . . . . . . . . . . . . . . . DLB-46
Arnold, Edwin 1832-1904 . . . . . . . . . . . . . DLB-35
Arnold, Edwin L. 1857-1935. . . . . . . . . . . .DLB-178
Arnold, Matthew
   1822-1888 . . . . . . . . . DLB-32, 57; CDBLB-4
   Preface to *Poems* (1853). . . . . . . . . . . . DLB-32
Arnold, Thomas 1795-1842 . . . . . . . . . . . . DLB-55
Edward Arnold [publishing house]. . . . . . DLB-112
Arnott, Peter 1962- . . . . . . . . . . . . . . . . DLB-233
Arnow, Harriette Simpson 1908-1986 . . . . . DLB-6
Arp, Bill (see Smith, Charles Henry)
Arpino, Giovanni 1927-1987. . . . . . . . . . .DLB-177
Arreola, Juan José 1918-2001 . . . . . . . . . DLB-113
Arrian circa 89-circa 155. . . . . . . . . . . . . .DLB-176
J. W. Arrowsmith [publishing house] . . . . DLB-106
Art
   John Dos Passos: Artist . . . . . . . . . . . . . . . Y-99
   The First Post-Impressionist
      Exhibition. . . . . . . . . . . . . . . . . . . . .DS-5
   The Omega Workshops . . . . . . . . . . . . .DS-10
   The Second Post-Impressionist
      Exhibition . . . . . . . . . . . . . . . . . . . . DS-5
Artaud, Antonin 1896-1948 . . . . . . . . . . . DLB-258
Artel, Jorge 1909-1994 . . . . . . . . . . . . . . DLB-283
Arthur, Timothy Shay
   1809-1885 . . . . . . . .DLB-3, 42, 79, 250; DS-13
Artmann, H. C. 1921-2000. . . . . . . . . . . . . DLB-85
Arvin, Newton 1900-1963 . . . . . . . . . . . . DLB-103
Asch, Nathan 1902-1964 . . . . . . . . . DLB-4, 28
   Nathan Asch Remembers Ford Madox
      Ford, Sam Roth, and Hart Crane . . . . Y-02
Ascham, Roger 1515/1516-1568. . . . . . . . DLB-236
Ash, John 1948- . . . . . . . . . . . . . . . . . . . DLB-40
Ashbery, John 1927- . . . . . . . .DLB-5, 165; Y-81
Ashbridge, Elizabeth 1713-1755 . . . . . . . DLB-200
Ashburnham, Bertram Lord
   1797-1878 . . . . . . . . . . . . . . . . . . . . DLB-184
Ashendene Press. . . . . . . . . . . . . . . . . . . DLB-112
Asher, Sandy 1942- . . . . . . . . . . . . . . . . . . Y-83
Ashton, Winifred (see Dane, Clemence)
Asimov, Isaac 1920-1992 . . . . . . . . . DLB-8; Y-92
   Tribute to John Ciardi . . . . . . . . . . . . . . . Y-86
Askew, Anne circa 1521-1546 . . . . . . . . . DLB-136
Aspazija 1865-1943 . . . . . . . . DLB-220; CDWLB-4
Asselin, Olivar 1874-1937 . . . . . . . . . . . . . DLB-92
The Association of American Publishers . . . . . Y-99
The Association for Documentary Editing. . . . Y-00
The Association for the Study of
   Literature and Environment (ASLE) . . . . Y-99
Astell, Mary 1666-1731. . . . . . . . . . . . . . DLB-252
Astley, William (see Warung, Price)

Asturias, Miguel Angel
   1899-1974. . . . . . . . . . . . DLB-113; CDWLB-3
Atava, S. (see Terpigorev, Sergei Nikolaevich)
Atheneum Publishers . . . . . . . . . . . . . . . . DLB-46
Atherton, Gertrude 1857-1948 . . . . .DLB-9, 78, 186
Athlone Press . . . . . . . . . . . . . . . . . . . . . DLB-112
Atkins, Josiah circa 1755-1781. . . . . . . . . . DLB-31
Atkins, Russell 1926- . . . . . . . . . . . . . . . . DLB-41
Atkinson, Kate 1951- . . . . . . . . . . . . . . . DLB-267
Atkinson, Louisa 1834-1872 . . . . . . . . . . DLB-230
The Atlantic Monthly Press . . . . . . . . . . . . DLB-46
Attaway, William 1911-1986 . . . . . . . . . . . DLB-76
Atwood, Margaret 1939- . . . . . . . . DLB-53, 251
Aubert, Alvin 1930- . . . . . . . . . . . . . . . . . DLB-41
Aubert de Gaspé, Phillipe-Ignace-François
   1814-1841 . . . . . . . . . . . . . . . . . . . . . DLB-99
Aubert de Gaspé, Phillipe-Joseph
   1786-1871 . . . . . . . . . . . . . . . . . . . . . DLB-99
Aubin, Napoléon 1812-1890. . . . . . . . . . . . DLB-99
Aubin, Penelope
   1685-circa 1731 . . . . . . . . . . . . . . . . . DLB-39
   Preface to *The Life of Charlotta
      du Pont* (1723) . . . . . . . . . . . . . . . . DLB-39
Aubrey-Fletcher, Henry Lancelot (see Wade, Henry)
Auchincloss, Louis 1917- . . . . . .DLB-2, 244; Y-80
Auden, W. H. 1907-1973 . . DLB-10, 20; CDBLB-6
Audio Art in America: A Personal Memoir . . . Y-85
Audubon, John James 1785-1851 . . . . . . DLB-248
Audubon, John Woodhouse
   1812-1862 . . . . . . . . . . . . . . . . . . . . DLB-183
Auerbach, Berthold 1812-1882. . . . . . . . . DLB-133
Auernheimer, Raoul 1876-1948 . . . . . . . . . DLB-81
Augier, Emile 1820-1889 . . . . . . . . . . . . . DLB-192
Augustine 354-430 . . . . . . . . . . . . . . . . . DLB-115
Aulnoy, Marie-Catherine Le Jumel
   de Barneville, comtesse d'
   1650/1651-1705 . . . . . . . . . . . . . . . . DLB-268
Aulus Gellius
   circa A.D. 125-circa A.D. 180?. . . . . . DLB-211
Austen, Jane 1775-1817 . . . . . DLB-116; CDBLB-3
Auster, Paul 1947- . . . . . . . . . . . . . . . . . DLB-227
Austin, Alfred 1835-1913 . . . . . . . . . . . . . DLB-35
Austin, J. L. 1911-1960. . . . . . . . . . . . . . DLB-262
Austin, Jane Goodwin 1831-1894 . . . . . . . DLB-202
Austin, John 1790-1859 . . . . . . . . . . . . . DLB-262
Austin, Mary Hunter
   1868-1934 . . . . . . . . DLB-9, 78, 206, 221, 275
Austin, William 1778-1841 . . . . . . . . . . . . DLB-74
Australie (Emily Manning)
   1845-1890 . . . . . . . . . . . . . . . . . . . . DLB-230
Authors and Newspapers Association . . . . . DLB-46
Authors' Publishing Company . . . . . . . . . . DLB-49
Avallone, Michael 1924-1999 . . . . . . . . . . . . Y-99
   Tribute to John D. MacDonald . . . . . . . . Y-86
   Tribute to Kenneth Millar . . . . . . . . . . . . Y-83
   Tribute to Raymond Chandler . . . . . . . . Y-88
Avalon Books . . . . . . . . . . . . . . . . . . . . . DLB-46
Avancini, Nicolaus 1611-1686 . . . . . . . . . DLB-164

Avendaño, Fausto 1941- . . . . . . . . . . . . DLB-82
Averroës 1126-1198 . . . . . . . . . . . . . . . . DLB-115
Avery, Gillian 1926- . . . . . . . . . . . . . . . DLB-161
Avicenna 980-1037 . . . . . . . . . . . . . . . . . DLB-115
Ávila Jiménez, Antonio 1898-1965. . . . . . . DLB-283
Avison, Margaret 1918-1987. . . . . . . . . . . DLB-53
Avon Books . . . . . . . . . . . . . . . . . . . . . . DLB-46
Avyžius, Jonas 1922-1999. . . . . . . . . . . . DLB-220
Awdry, Wilbert Vere 1911-1997 . . . . . . . . DLB-160
Awoonor, Kofi 1935- . . . . . . . . . . . . . . .DLB-117
Ayckbourn, Alan 1939- . . . . . . . . DLB-13, 245
Ayer, A. J. 1910-1989 . . . . . . . . . . . . . . . DLB-262
Aymé, Marcel 1902-1967 . . . . . . . . . . . . . DLB-72
Aytoun, Sir Robert 1570-1638 . . . . . . . . DLB-121
Aytoun, William Edmondstoune
   1813-1865 . . . . . . . . . . . . . . . . DLB-32, 159

# B

B.V. (see Thomson, James)
Babbitt, Irving 1865-1933. . . . . . . . . . . . . DLB-63
Babbitt, Natalie 1932- . . . . . . . . . . . . . . . DLB-52
John Babcock [publishing house] . . . . . . . . DLB-49
Babel, Isaak Emmanuilovich 1894-1940. . .DLB-272
Babits, Mihály 1883-1941. . . . .DLB-215; CDWLB-4
Babrius circa 150-200 . . . . . . . . . . . . . . .DLB-176
Babson, Marian 1929- . . . . . . . . . . . . . .DLB-276
Baca, Jimmy Santiago 1952- . . . . . . . . DLB-122
Bacchelli, Riccardo 1891-1985 . . . . . . . . . DLB-264
Bache, Benjamin Franklin 1769-1798 . . . . . DLB-43
Bacheller, Irving 1859-1950 . . . . . . . . . . . DLB-202
Bachmann, Ingeborg 1926-1973 . . . . . . . . . DLB-85
Bačinskaitė-Bučienė, Salomėja (see Nėris, Salomėja)
Bacon, Delia 1811-1859 . . . . . . . . . . . DLB-1, 243
Bacon, Francis
   1561-1626 . . . . DLB-151, 236, 252; CDBLB-1
Bacon, Sir Nicholas circa 1510-1579 . . . . . DLB-132
Bacon, Roger circa 1214/1220-1292 . . . . . DLB-115
Bacon, Thomas circa 1700-1768 . . . . . . . . DLB-31
Bacovia, George
   1881-1957 . . . . . . . . . . . . DLB-220; CDWLB-4
Richard G. Badger and Company . . . . . . . DLB-49
Bagaduce Music Lending Library . . . . . . . . Y-00
Bage, Robert 1728-1801 . . . . . . . . . . . . . . DLB-39
Bagehot, Walter 1826-1877 . . . . . . . . . . . . DLB-55
Bagley, Desmond 1923-1983 . . . . . . . . . . . DLB-87
Bagley, Sarah G. 1806-1848? . . . . . . . . . . DLB-239
Bagnold, Enid 1889-1981 . . .DLB-13, 160, 191, 245
Bagryana, Elisaveta
   1893-1991 . . . . . . . . . . . . DLB-147; CDWLB-4
Bahr, Hermann 1863-1934. . . . . . . . . DLB-81, 118
Bailey, Abigail Abbot 1746-1815. . . . . . . . DLB-200
Bailey, Alfred Goldsworthy 1905- . . . . . DLB-68
Bailey, H. C. 1878-1961 . . . . . . . . . . . . . . DLB-77
Bailey, Jacob 1731-1808 . . . . . . . . . . . . . . DLB-99
Bailey, Paul 1937- . . . . . . . . . . . . .DLB-14, 271

Bailey, Philip James 1816-1902 . . . . . . . . . DLB-32
Francis Bailey [publishing house] . . . . . . . . DLB-49
Baillargeon, Pierre 1916-1967 . . . . . . . . . . DLB-88
Baillie, Hugh 1890-1966 . . . . . . . . . . . . . . DLB-29
Baillie, Joanna 1762-1851 . . . . . . . . . . . . . DLB-93
Bailyn, Bernard 1922- . . . . . . . . . . . . . DLB-17
Bain, Alexander
    *English Composition and Rhetoric* (1866)
    [excerpt] . . . . . . . . . . . . . . . . . . . . . DLB-57
Bainbridge, Beryl 1933- . . . . . . . . DLB-14, 231
Baird, Irene 1901-1981 . . . . . . . . . . . . . . DLB-68
Baker, Augustine 1575-1641 . . . . . . . . . . DLB-151
Baker, Carlos 1909-1987 . . . . . . . . . . . . DLB-103
Baker, David 1954- . . . . . . . . . . . . . . . DLB-120
Baker, George Pierce 1866-1935 . . . . . . . DLB-266
Baker, Herschel C. 1914-1990 . . . . . . . . . DLB-111
Baker, Houston A., Jr. 1943- . . . . . . . . . DLB-67
Baker, Howard
    Tribute to Caroline Gordon . . . . . . . . . . Y-81
    Tribute to Katherine Anne Porter . . . . . . . Y-80
Baker, Nicholson 1957- . . . . . . . DLB-227; Y-00
    Review of Nicholson Baker's *Double Fold:*
    *Libraries and the Assault on Paper* . . . . . . Y-00
Baker, Samuel White 1821-1893 . . . . . . . . DLB-166
Baker, Thomas 1656-1740 . . . . . . . . . . . . DLB-213
Walter H. Baker Company
    ("Baker's Plays") . . . . . . . . . . . . . . . . DLB-49
The Baker and Taylor Company . . . . . . . . DLB-49
Bakhtin, Mikhail Mikhailovich
    1895-1975 . . . . . . . . . . . . . . . . . . . . DLB-242
Bakunin, Mikhail Aleksandrovich
    1814-1876 . . . . . . . . . . . . . . . . . . . . DLB-277
Balaban, John 1943- . . . . . . . . . . . . . . DLB-120
Bald, Wambly 1902- . . . . . . . . . . . . . . . DLB-4
Balde, Jacob 1604-1668 . . . . . . . . . . . . . DLB-164
Balderston, John 1889-1954 . . . . . . . . . . DLB-26
Baldwin, James 1924-1987
    . . . . . . DLB-2, 7, 33, 249, 278; Y-87; CDALB-1
Baldwin, Joseph Glover
    1815-1864 . . . . . . . . . . . . . . . DLB-3, 11, 248
Baldwin, Louisa (Mrs. Alfred Baldwin)
    1845-1925 . . . . . . . . . . . . . . . . . . . . DLB-240
Baldwin, William circa 1515-1563 . . . . . . . DLB-132
Richard and Anne Baldwin
    [publishing house] . . . . . . . . . . . . . . DLB-170
Bale, John 1495-1563 . . . . . . . . . . . . . . DLB-132
Balestrini, Nanni 1935- . . . . . . . . DLB-128, 196
Balfour, Sir Andrew 1630-1694 . . . . . . . . DLB-213
Balfour, Arthur James 1848-1930 . . . . . . . DLB-190
Balfour, Sir James 1600-1657 . . . . . . . . . DLB-213
Ballantine Books . . . . . . . . . . . . . . . . . DLB-46
Ballantyne, R. M. 1825-1894 . . . . . . . . . . DLB-163
Ballard, J. G. 1930- . . . . . . . . DLB-14, 207, 261
Ballard, Martha Moore 1735-1812 . . . . . . DLB-200
Ballerini, Luigi 1940- . . . . . . . . . . . . . DLB-128
Ballou, Maturin Murray (Lieutenant Murray)
    1820-1895 . . . . . . . . . . . . . . . . . DLB-79, 189
Robert O. Ballou [publishing house] . . . . . . DLB-46

Balzac, Guez de 1597?-1654 . . . . . . . . . . DLB-268
Balzac, Honoré de 1799-1855 . . . . . . . . . DLB-119
Bambara, Toni Cade
    1939-1995 . . . . . . . . DLB-38, 218; CDALB-7
Bamford, Samuel 1788-1872 . . . . . . . . . . DLB-190
A. L. Bancroft and Company . . . . . . . . . . DLB-49
Bancroft, George 1800-1891 . . . DLB-1, 30, 59, 243
Bancroft, Hubert Howe 1832-1918 . . . DLB-47, 140
Bandelier, Adolph F. 1840-1914 . . . . . . . . DLB-186
Bangs, John Kendrick 1862-1922 . . . . . DLB-11, 79
Banim, John 1798-1842 . . . . . . . DLB-116, 158, 159
Banim, Michael 1796-1874 . . . . . . . . DLB-158, 159
Banks, Iain (M.) 1954- . . . . . . . . . DLB-194, 261
Banks, John circa 1653-1706 . . . . . . . . . . DLB-80
Banks, Russell 1940- . . . . . . . . . . DLB-130, 278
Bannerman, Helen 1862-1946 . . . . . . . . . DLB-141
Bantam Books . . . . . . . . . . . . . . . . . . DLB-46
Banti, Anna 1895-1985 . . . . . . . . . . . . . DLB-177
Banville, John 1945- . . . . . . . . . . DLB-14, 271
Banville, Théodore de 1823-1891 . . . . . . . DLB-217
Baraka, Amiri
    1934- . . . . DLB-5, 7, 16, 38; DS-8; CDALB-1
Barańczak, Stanisław 1946- . . . . . . . . . . DLB-232
Baratynsky, Evgenii Abramovich
    1800-1844 . . . . . . . . . . . . . . . . . . . DLB-205
Barba-Jacob, Porfirio 1883-1942 . . . . . . . DLB-283
Barbauld, Anna Laetitia
    1743-1825 . . . . . . . . DLB-107, 109, 142, 158
Barbeau, Marius 1883-1969 . . . . . . . . . . DLB-92
Barber, John Warner 1798-1885 . . . . . . . . DLB-30
Bàrberi Squarotti, Giorgio 1929- . . . . . . DLB-128
Barbey d'Aurevilly, Jules-Amédée
    1808-1889 . . . . . . . . . . . . . . . . . . . DLB-119
Barbier, Auguste 1805-1882 . . . . . . . . . . DLB-217
Barbilian, Dan (see Barbu, Ion)
Barbour, John circa 1316-1395 . . . . . . . . DLB-146
Barbour, Ralph Henry 1870-1944 . . . . . . . DLB-22
Barbu, Ion 1895-1961 . . . . . . . DLB-220; CDWLB-4
Barbusse, Henri 1873-1935 . . . . . . . . . . . DLB-65
Barclay, Alexander circa 1475-1552 . . . . . . DLB-132
E. E. Barclay and Company . . . . . . . . . . DLB-49
C. W. Bardeen [publishing house] . . . . . . . DLB-49
Barham, Richard Harris 1788-1845 . . . . . . DLB-159
Barich, Bill 1943- . . . . . . . . . . . . . . . DLB-185
Baring, Maurice 1874-1945 . . . . . . . . . . DLB-34
Baring-Gould, Sabine 1834-1924 . . . . DLB-156, 190
Barker, A. L. 1918- . . . . . . . . . . DLB-14, 139
Barker, Clive 1952- . . . . . . . . . . . . . . DLB-261
Barker, Dudley (see Black, Lionel)
Barker, George 1913-1991 . . . . . . . . . . . DLB-20
Barker, Harley Granville 1877-1946 . . . . . . DLB-10
Barker, Howard 1946- . . . . . . . . . . DLB-13, 233
Barker, James Nelson 1784-1858 . . . . . . . . DLB-37
Barker, Jane 1652-1727 . . . . . . . . . . DLB-39, 131
Barker, Lady Mary Anne 1831-1911 . . . . DLB-166
Barker, Pat 1943- . . . . . . . . . . . . . . . DLB-271

Barker, William circa 1520-after 1576 . . . . DLB-132
Arthur Barker Limited . . . . . . . . . . . . . DLB-112
Barkov, Ivan Semenovich 1732-1768 . . . . . DLB-150
Barks, Coleman 1937- . . . . . . . . . . . . . DLB-5
Barlach, Ernst 1870-1938 . . . . . . . . . DLB-56, 118
Barlow, Joel 1754-1812 . . . . . . . . . . . . . DLB-37
    *The Prospect of Peace* (1778) . . . . . . . . . DLB-37
Barnard, John 1681-1770 . . . . . . . . . . . . DLB-24
Barnard, Marjorie (M. Barnard Eldershaw)
    1897-1987 . . . . . . . . . . . . . . . . . . . DLB-260
Barnard, Robert 1936- . . . . . . . . . . . . DLB-276
Barne, Kitty (Mary Catherine Barne)
    1883-1957 . . . . . . . . . . . . . . . . . . . DLB-160
Barnes, Barnabe 1571-1609 . . . . . . . . . . DLB-132
Barnes, Djuna 1892-1982 . . . . DLB-4, 9, 45; DS-15
Barnes, Jim 1933- . . . . . . . . . . . . . . DLB-175
Barnes, Julian 1946- . . . . . . . . . DLB-194; Y-93
    Notes for a Checklist of Publications . . . . Y-01
Barnes, Margaret Ayer 1886-1967 . . . . . . . DLB-9
Barnes, Peter 1931- . . . . . . . . . . DLB-13, 233
Barnes, William 1801-1886 . . . . . . . . . . DLB-32
A. S. Barnes and Company . . . . . . . . . . DLB-49
Barnes and Noble Books . . . . . . . . . . . . DLB-46
Barnet, Miguel 1940- . . . . . . . . . . . . DLB-145
Barney, Natalie 1876-1972 . . . . . . . . DLB-4; DS-15
Barnfield, Richard 1574-1627 . . . . . . . . . DLB-172
Richard W. Baron [publishing house] . . . . . DLB-46
Barr, Amelia Edith Huddleston
    1831-1919 . . . . . . . . . . . . . . . . DLB-202, 221
Barr, Robert 1850-1912 . . . . . . . . . . . DLB-70, 92
Barral, Carlos 1928-1989 . . . . . . . . . . . . DLB-134
Barrax, Gerald William 1933- . . . . . DLB-41, 120
Barrès, Maurice 1862-1923 . . . . . . . . . . DLB-123
Barreno, Maria Isabel (see The Three Marias:
    A Landmark Case in Portuguese
    Literary History)
Barrett, Eaton Stannard 1786-1820 . . . . . . DLB-116
Barrie, J. M.
    1860-1937 . . . . . . DLB-10, 141, 156; CDBLB-5
Barrie and Jenkins . . . . . . . . . . . . . . . DLB-112
Barrio, Raymond 1921- . . . . . . . . . . . . DLB-82
Barrios, Gregg 1945- . . . . . . . . . . . . . DLB-122
Barry, Philip 1896-1949 . . . . . . . . . . . DLB-7, 228
Barry, Robertine (see Françoise)
Barry, Sebastian 1955- . . . . . . . . . . . . DLB-245
Barse and Hopkins . . . . . . . . . . . . . . . DLB-46
Barstow, Stan 1928- . . . . . . . . DLB-14, 139, 207
    Tribute to John Braine . . . . . . . . . . . . . Y-86
Barth, John 1930- . . . . . . . . . . . . DLB-2, 227
Barthelme, Donald
    1931-1989 . . . . . . . . . . DLB-2, 234; Y-80, 89
Barthelme, Frederick 1943- . . . . . . DLB-244; Y-85
Bartholomew, Frank 1898-1985 . . . . . . . . DLB-127
Bartlett, John 1820-1905 . . . . . . . . . . DLB-1, 235
Bartol, Cyrus Augustus 1813-1900 . . . . DLB-1, 235
Barton, Bernard 1784-1849 . . . . . . . . . . DLB-96

# Cumulative Index

Barton, John ca. 1610-1675............ DLB-236
Barton, Thomas Pennant 1803-1869.... DLB-140
Bartram, John 1699-1777............... DLB-31
Bartram, William 1739-1823............ DLB-37
Barykova, Anna Pavlovna 1839-1893 ....DLB-277
Basic Books........................... DLB-46
Basille, Theodore (see Becon, Thomas)
Bass, Rick 1958-................ DLB-212, 275
Bass, T. J. 1932-..................... Y-81
Bassani, Giorgio 1916-2000........ DLB-128, 177
Basse, William circa 1583-1653........ DLB-121
Bassett, John Spencer 1867-1928....... DLB-17
Bassler, Thomas Joseph (see Bass, T. J.)
Bate, Walter Jackson 1918-1999..... DLB-67, 103
Bateman, Stephen circa 1510-1584...... DLB-136
Christopher Bateman [publishing house] ..DLB-170
Bates, H. E. 1905-1974........... DLB-162, 191
Bates, Katharine Lee 1859-1929........ DLB-71
Batiushkov, Konstantin Nikolaevich
   1787-1855.......................... DLB-205
B. T. Batsford [publishing house]..... DLB-106
Battiscombe, Georgina 1905-........... DLB-155
*The Battle of Maldon* circa 1000......... DLB-146
Baudelaire, Charles 1821-1867......... DLB-217
Bauer, Bruno 1809-1882................ DLB-133
Bauer, Wolfgang 1941-................. DLB-124
Baum, L. Frank 1856-1919.............. DLB-22
Baum, Vicki 1888-1960................. DLB-85
Baumbach, Jonathan 1933-.............. Y-80
Bausch, Richard 1945-................. DLB-130
   Tribute to James Dickey............ Y-97
   Tribute to Peter Taylor............ Y-94
Bausch, Robert 1945-.................. DLB-218
Bawden, Nina 1925-............... DLB-14, 161, 207
Bax, Clifford 1886-1962............ DLB-10, 100
Baxter, Charles 1947-................. DLB-130
Bayer, Eleanor (see Perry, Eleanor)
Bayer, Konrad 1932-1964............... DLB-85
Bayle, Pierre 1647-1706............... DLB-268
Bayley, Barrington J. 1937-........... DLB-261
Baynes, Pauline 1922-................. DLB-160
Baynton, Barbara 1857-1929............ DLB-230
Bazin, Hervé (Jean Pierre Marie Hervé-Bazin)
   1911-1996.......................... DLB-83
The BBC Four Samuel Johnson Prize
   for Non-fiction.................... Y-02
Beach, Sylvia 1887-1962......... DLB-4; DS-15
Beacon Press.......................... DLB-49
Beadle and Adams...................... DLB-49
Beagle, Peter S. 1939-................ Y-80
Beal, M. F. 1937-..................... Y-81
Beale, Howard K. 1899-1959............ DLB-17
Beard, Charles A. 1874-1948........... DLB-17
Beat Generation (Beats)
   As I See It, by Carolyn Cassady.... DLB-16

A Beat Chronology: The First Twenty-five
   Years, 1944-1969................... DLB-16
The Commercialization of the Image
   of Revolt, by Kenneth Rexroth... DLB-16
Four Essays on the Beat Generation .. DLB-16
   in New York City................... DLB-237
   in the West........................ DLB-237
   Outlaw Days........................ DLB-16
   Periodicals of..................... DLB-16
Beattie, Ann 1947-............ DLB-218, 278; Y-82
Beattie, James 1735-1803.............. DLB-109
Beatty, Chester 1875-1968............. DLB-201
Beauchemin, Nérée 1850-1931........... DLB-92
Beauchemin, Yves 1941-................ DLB-60
Beaugrand, Honoré 1848-1906........... DLB-99
Beaulieu, Victor-Lévy 1945-........... DLB-53
Beaumont, Francis circa 1584-1616
   and Fletcher, John
   1579-1625.............. DLB-58; CDBLB-1
Beaumont, Sir John 1583?-1627......... DLB-121
Beaumont, Joseph 1616-1699............ DLB-126
Beauvoir, Simone de 1908-1986..... DLB-72; Y-86
   Personal Tribute to Simone de Beauvoir ... Y-86
Becher, Ulrich 1910-1990.............. DLB-69
Becker, Carl 1873-1945................ DLB-17
Becker, Jurek 1937-1997............... DLB-75
Becker, Jurgen 1932-.................. DLB-75
Beckett, Samuel 1906-1989
   ......... DLB-13, 15, 233; Y-90; CDBLB-7
Beckford, William 1760-1844....... DLB-39, 213
Beckham, Barry 1944-.................. DLB-33
Bećković, Matija 1939-................ DLB-181
Becon, Thomas circa 1512-1567......... DLB-136
Becque, Henry 1837-1899............... DLB-192
Beddoes, Thomas 1760-1808............. DLB-158
Beddoes, Thomas Lovell 1803-1849...... DLB-96
Bede circa 673-735.................... DLB-146
Bedford-Jones, H. 1887-1949........... DLB-251
Bedregal, Yolanda 1913-1999........... DLB-283
Beebe, William 1877-1962.............. DLB-275
Beecher, Catharine Esther
   1800-1878....................... DLB-1, 243
Beecher, Henry Ward
   1813-1887................... DLB-3, 43, 250
Beer, George L. 1872-1920............. DLB-47
Beer, Johann 1655-1700................ DLB-168
Beer, Patricia 1919-1999.............. DLB-40
Beerbohm, Max 1872-1956........... DLB-34, 100
Beer-Hofmann, Richard 1866-1945....... DLB-81
Beers, Henry A. 1847-1926............. DLB-71
S. O. Beeton [publishing house]....... DLB-106
Bégon, Elisabeth 1696-1755............ DLB-99
Behan, Brendan
   1923-1964.............. DLB-13, 233; CDBLB-7
Behn, Aphra 1640?-1689......... DLB-39, 80, 131
Behn, Harry 1898-1973................. DLB-61
Behrman, S. N. 1893-1973............ DLB-7, 44

Beklemishev, Iurii Solomonvich
   (see Krymov, Iurii Solomonovich)
Belaney, Archibald Stansfeld (see Grey Owl)
Belasco, David 1853-1931.............. DLB-7
Clarke Belford and Company............ DLB-49
Belgian Luxembourg American Studies
   Association........................ Y-01
Belinsky, Vissarion Grigor'evich
   1811-1848.......................... DLB-198
Belitt, Ben 1911-..................... DLB-5
Belknap, Jeremy 1744-1798.......... DLB-30, 37
Bell, Adrian 1901-1980................ DLB-191
Bell, Clive 1881-1964................. DS-10
Bell, Daniel 1919-.................... DLB-246
Bell, Gertrude Margaret Lowthian
   1868-1926.......................... DLB-174
Bell, James Madison 1826-1902......... DLB-50
Bell, Madison Smartt 1957-........ DLB-218, 278
   Tribute to Andrew Nelson Lytle..... Y-95
   Tribute to Peter Taylor............ Y-94
Bell, Marvin 1937-.................... DLB-5
Bell, Millicent 1919-................. DLB-111
Bell, Quentin 1910-1996............... DLB-155
Bell, Vanessa 1879-1961............... DS-10
George Bell and Sons.................. DLB-106
Robert Bell [publishing house]........ DLB-49
Bellamy, Edward 1850-1898............. DLB-12
Bellamy, Joseph 1719-1790............. DLB-31
John Bellamy [publishing house]....... DLB-170
*La Belle Assemblée* 1806-1837........... DLB-110
Bellezza, Dario 1944-1996............. DLB-128
Belloc, Hilaire 1870-1953....DLB-19, 100, 141, 174
Belloc, Madame (see Parkes, Bessie Rayner)
Bellonci, Maria 1902-1986............. DLB-196
Bellow, Saul
   1915-...... DLB-2, 28; Y-82; DS-3; CDALB-1
   Tribute to Isaac Bashevis Singer... Y-91
Belmont Productions................... DLB-46
Bels, Alberts 1938-................... DLB-232
Belševica, Vizma 1931-..... DLB-232; CDWLB-4
Bemelmans, Ludwig 1898-1962........... DLB-22
Bemis, Samuel Flagg 1891-1973......... DLB-17
William Bemrose [publishing house].... DLB-106
Ben no Naishi 1228?-1271?............. DLB-203
Benchley, Robert 1889-1945............ DLB-11
Bencúr, Matej (see Kukučin, Martin)
Benedetti, Mario 1920-................ DLB-113
Benedict, Pinckney 1964-.............. DLB-244
Benedict, Ruth 1887-1948.............. DLB-246
Benedictus, David 1938-............... DLB-14
Benedikt, Michael 1935-............... DLB-5
Benediktov, Vladimir Grigor'evich
   1807-1873.......................... DLB-205
Benét, Stephen Vincent
   1898-1943................. DLB-4, 48, 102, 249
   Stephen Vincent Benét Centenary.... Y-97

380

Benét, William Rose 1886-1950..........DLB-45

Benford, Gregory 1941- ................ Y-82

Benjamin, Park 1809-1864.....DLB-3, 59, 73, 250

Benjamin, Peter (see Cunningham, Peter)

Benjamin, S. G. W. 1837-1914.........DLB-189

Benjamin, Walter 1892-1940...........DLB-242

Benlowes, Edward 1602-1676..........DLB-126

Benn, Gottfried 1886-1956............DLB-56

Benn Brothers Limited................DLB-106

Bennett, Arnold
  1867-1931....DLB-10, 34, 98, 135; CDBLB-5

  The Arnold Bennett Society...........Y-98

Bennett, Charles 1899-1995.............DLB-44

Bennett, Emerson 1822-1905..........DLB-202

Bennett, Gwendolyn 1902-1981.........DLB-51

Bennett, Hal 1930- ..................DLB-33

Bennett, James Gordon 1795-1872........DLB-43

Bennett, James Gordon, Jr. 1841-1918.....DLB-23

Bennett, John 1865-1956..............DLB-42

Bennett, Louise 1919- .....DLB-117; CDWLB-3

Benni, Stefano 1947- ................DLB-196

Benoit, Jacques 1941- ................DLB-60

Benson, A. C. 1862-1925..............DLB-98

Benson, E. F. 1867-1940...........DLB-135, 153

  The E. F. Benson Society..............Y-98

  The Tilling Society ..................Y-98

Benson, Jackson J. 1930- .............DLB-111

Benson, Robert Hugh 1871-1914........DLB-153

Benson, Stella 1892-1933...........DLB-36, 162

Bent, James Theodore 1852-1897........DLB-174

Bent, Mabel Virginia Anna ?-?........DLB-174

Bentham, Jeremy 1748-1832 ...DLB-107, 158, 252

Bentley, E. C. 1875-1956..............DLB-70

Bentley, Phyllis 1894-1977............DLB-191

Bentley, Richard 1662-1742............DLB-252

Richard Bentley [publishing house]......DLB-106

Benton, Robert 1932- and
  Newman, David 1937- ..............DLB-44

Benziger Brothers....................DLB-49

*Beowulf* circa 900-1000 or 790-825
  ............... DLB-146; CDBLB-1

Berent, Wacław 1873-1940 ............DLB-215

Beresford, Anne 1929- ................DLB-40

Beresford, John Davys
  1873-1947 ........... DLB-162, 178, 197

  "Experiment in the Novel" (1929)
  [excerpt] .....................DLB-36

Beresford-Howe, Constance 1922- ......DLB-88

R. G. Berford Company ...............DLB-49

Berg, Stephen 1934- ..................DLB-5

Bergengruen, Werner 1892-1964........DLB-56

Berger, John 1926- ............DLB-14, 207

Berger, Meyer 1898-1959 .............DLB-29

Berger, Thomas 1924- ...........DLB-2; Y-80

  A Statement by Thomas Berger ........ Y-80

Bergman, Hjalmar 1883-1931 ..........DLB-259

Bergman, Ingmar 1918- ..............DLB-257

Berkeley, Anthony 1893-1971 ..........DLB-77

Berkeley, George 1685-1753 ....DLB-31, 101, 252

The Berkley Publishing Corporation......DLB-46

Berlin, Irving 1888-1989 .............DLB-265

Berlin, Lucia 1936- .................DLB-130

Berman, Marshall 1940- ..............DLB-246

Bernal, Vicente J. 1888-1915 ..........DLB-82

Bernanos, Georges 1888-1948..........DLB-72

Bernard, Catherine 1663?-1712..........DLB-268

Bernard, Harry 1898-1979..............DLB-92

Bernard, John 1756-1828...............DLB-37

Bernard of Chartres circa 1060-1124?....DLB-115

Bernard of Clairvaux 1090-1153.........DLB-208

Bernard, Richard 1568-1641/1642.......DLB-281

Bernard Silvestris
  flourished circa 1130-1160 ..........DLB-208

Bernari, Carlo 1909-1992 .............DLB-177

Bernhard, Thomas
  1931-1989 .........DLB-85, 124; CDWLB-2

Berniéres, Louis de 1954- ............DLB-271

Bernstein, Charles 1950- .............DLB-169

Berriault, Gina 1926-1999 ............DLB-130

Berrigan, Daniel 1921- ................DLB-5

Berrigan, Ted 1934-1983..............DLB-5, 169

Berry, Wendell 1934- ......DLB-5, 6, 234, 275

Berryman, John 1914-1972 ....DLB-48; CDALB-1

Bersianik, Louky 1930- ................DLB-60

Thomas Berthelet [publishing house].....DLB-170

Berto, Giuseppe 1914-1978 ............DLB-177

Bertocci, Peter Anthony 1910-1989......DLB-279

Bertolucci, Attilio 1911-2000 ..........DLB-128

Berton, Pierre 1920- .................DLB-68

Bertrand, Louis "Aloysius" 1807-1841....DLB-217

Besant, Sir Walter 1836-1901 ......DLB-135, 190

Bessa-Luís, Agustina 1922- ...........DLB-287

Bessette, Gerard 1920- ...............DLB-53

Bessie, Alvah 1904-1985 ..............DLB-26

Bester, Alfred 1913-1987 ..............DLB-8

Besterman, Theodore 1904-1976........DLB-201

Beston, Henry (Henry Beston Sheahan)
  1888-1968....................DLB-275

Best-Seller Lists
  An Assessment ..................... Y-84

  What's Really Wrong With
  Bestseller Lists ................. Y-84

Bestuzhev, Aleksandr Aleksandrovich
  (Marlinsky) 1797-1837.............DLB-198

Bestuzhev, Nikolai Aleksandrovich
  1791-1855 ....................DLB-198

Betham-Edwards, Matilda Barbara
  (see Edwards, Matilda Barbara Betham-)

Betjeman, John
  1906-1984.........DLB-20; Y-84; CDBLB-7

Betocchi, Carlo 1899-1986............DLB-128

Bettarini, Mariella 1942- ............DLB-128

Betts, Doris 1932- ............DLB-218; Y-82

Beveridge, Albert J. 1862-1927 .........DLB-17

Beverley, Robert circa 1673-1722......DLB-24, 30

Bevilacqua, Alberto 1934- ............DLB-196

Bevington, Louisa Sarah 1845-1895.....DLB-199

Beyle, Marie-Henri (see Stendhal)

Białoszewski, Miron 1922-1983.........DLB-232

Bianco, Margery Williams 1881-1944....DLB-160

Bibaud, Adèle 1854-1941...............DLB-92

Bibaud, Michel 1782-1857..............DLB-99

Bibliography
  Bibliographical and Textual Scholarship
  Since World War II ............... Y-89

  Center for Bibliographical Studies and
  Research at the University of
  California, Riverside.............. Y-91

  The Great Bibliographers Series ........ Y-93

  Primary Bibliography: A Retrospective .. Y-95

Bichsel, Peter 1935- .................DLB-75

Bickerstaff, Isaac John 1733-circa 1808 ....DLB-89

Drexel Biddle [publishing house].........DLB-49

Bidermann, Jacob
  1577 or 1578-1639 ...............DLB-164

Bidwell, Walter Hilliard 1798-1881 .......DLB-79

Bienek, Horst 1930-1990 ..............DLB-75

Bierbaum, Otto Julius 1865-1910........DLB-66

Bierce, Ambrose 1842-1914?
  ...... DLB-11, 12, 23, 71, 74, 186; CDALB-3

Bigelow, William F. 1879-1966 ..........DLB-91

Biggle, Lloyd, Jr. 1923- ...............DLB-8

Bigiaretti, Libero 1905-1993 ..........DLB-177

Bigland, Eileen 1898-1970 ............DLB-195

Biglow, Hosea (see Lowell, James Russell)

Bigongiari, Piero 1914-1997............DLB-128

Bilenchi, Romano 1909-1989...........DLB-264

Billinger, Richard 1890-1965...........DLB-124

Billings, Hammatt 1818-1874...........DLB-188

Billings, John Shaw 1898-1975...........DLB-137

Billings, Josh (see Shaw, Henry Wheeler)

Binding, Rudolf G. 1867-1938..........DLB-66

Bingay, Malcolm 1884-1953 ...........DLB-241

Bingham, Caleb 1757-1817..............DLB-42

Bingham, George Barry 1906-1988......DLB-127

Bingham, Sallie 1937- ................DLB-234

William Bingley [publishing house]......DLB-154

Binyon, Laurence 1869-1943............DLB-19

*Biographia Brittanica*..................DLB-142

Biography
  Biographical Documents ............ Y-84, 85

  A Celebration of Literary Biography .... Y-98

  Conference on Modern Biography ...... Y-85

  The Cult of Biography
  Excerpts from the Second Folio Debate:
  "Biographies are generally a disease of
  English Literature" ................ Y-86

  New Approaches to Biography: Challenges
  from Critical Theory, USC Conference
  on Literary Studies, 1990 .......... Y-90

"The New Biography," by Virginia Woolf, *New York Herald Tribune*, 30 October 1927 ............. DLB-149

"The Practice of Biography," in *The English Sense of Humour and Other Essays*, by Harold Nicolson ............. DLB-149

"Principles of Biography," in *Elizabethan and Other Essays*, by Sidney Lee .. DLB-149

Remarks at the Opening of "The Biographical Part of Literature" Exhibition, by William R. Cagle ................ Y-98

Survey of Literary Biographies ......... Y-00

A Transit of Poets and Others: American Biography in 1982 ................ Y-82

The Year in Literary Biography ................... Y-83–01

Biography, The Practice of:
An Interview with B. L. Reid ........... Y-83
An Interview with David Herbert Donald .. Y-87
An Interview with Humphrey Carpenter .. Y-84
An Interview with Joan Mellen ......... Y-94
An Interview with John Caldwell Guilds .. Y-92
An Interview with William Manchester ... Y-85

John Bioren [publishing house] .......... DLB-49

Bioy Casares, Adolfo 1914-1999 ....... DLB-113

Bird, Isabella Lucy 1831-1904 ......... DLB-166

Bird, Robert Montgomery 1806-1854 ... DLB-202

Bird, William 1888-1963 ........ DLB-4; DS-15

The Cost of the *Cantos*: William Bird to Ezra Pound ................... Y-01

Birken, Sigmund von 1626-1681 ....... DLB-164

Birney, Earle 1904-1995 ............. DLB-88

Birrell, Augustine 1850-1933 ......... DLB-98

Bisher, Furman 1918- ............... DLB-171

Bishop, Elizabeth 1911-1979 .......... DLB-5, 169; CDALB-6

The Elizabeth Bishop Society ........... Y-01

Bishop, John Peale 1892-1944 ...... DLB-4, 9, 45

Bismarck, Otto von 1815-1898 ......... DLB-129

Bisset, Robert 1759-1805 ............. DLB-142

Bissett, Bill 1939- ................... DLB-53

Bitzius, Albert (see Gotthelf, Jeremias)

Bjørnvig, Thorkild 1918- ............ DLB-214

Black, David (D. M.) 1941- .......... DLB-40

Black, Gavin (Oswald Morris Wynd) 1913-1998 ................... DLB-276

Black, Lionel (Dudley Barker) 1910-1980 ................... DLB-276

Black, Winifred 1863-1936 ............ DLB-25

Walter J. Black [publishing house] ...... DLB-46

Blackamore, Arthur 1679-? ........ DLB-24, 39

Blackburn, Alexander L. 1929- ........... Y-85

Blackburn, John 1923-1993 ........... DLB-261

Blackburn, Paul 1926-1971 ........ DLB-16; Y-81

Blackburn, Thomas 1916-1977 ......... DLB-27

Blacker, Terence 1948- ............. DLB-271

Blackmore, R. D. 1825-1900 ........... DLB-18

Blackmore, Sir Richard 1654-1729 ..... DLB-131

Blackmur, R. P. 1904-1965 ............ DLB-63

Basil Blackwell, Publisher ............. DLB-106

Blackwood, Algernon Henry 1869-1951 ............. DLB-153, 156, 178

Blackwood, Caroline 1931-1996 ..... DLB-14, 207

William Blackwood and Sons, Ltd. ..... DLB-154

*Blackwood's Edinburgh Magazine* 1817-1980 ................... DLB-110

Blades, William 1824-1890 ........... DLB-184

Blaga, Lucian 1895-1961 ............. DLB-220

Blagden, Isabella 1817?-1873 .......... DLB-199

Blair, Eric Arthur (see Orwell, George)

Blair, Francis Preston 1791-1876 ........ DLB-43

Blair, Hugh
*Lectures on Rhetoric and Belles Lettres* (1783), [excerpts] .................... DLB-31

Blair, James circa 1655-1743 .......... DLB-24

Blair, John Durburrow 1759-1823 ....... DLB-37

Blais, Marie-Claire 1939- ............. DLB-53

Blaise, Clark 1940- ................. DLB-53

Blake, George 1893-1961 ............. DLB-191

Blake, Lillie Devereux 1833-1913 ... DLB-202, 221

Blake, Nicholas (C. Day Lewis) 1904-1972 ................... DLB-77

Blake, William 1757-1827 ...... DLB-93, 154, 163; CDBLB-3

The Blakiston Company ............. DLB-49

Blanchard, Stephen 1950- .......... DLB-267

Blanchot, Maurice 1907-2003 .......... DLB-72

Blanckenburg, Christian Friedrich von 1744-1796 ................... DLB-94

Blandiana, Ana 1942- ..... DLB-232; CDWLB-4

Blanshard, Brand 1892-1987 .......... DLB-279

Blaser, Robin 1925- ............... DLB-165

Blaumanis, Rudolfs 1863-1908 ........ DLB-220

Bleasdale, Alan 1946- ............. DLB-245

Bledsoe, Albert Taylor 1809-1877 ................ DLB-3, 79, 248

Bleecker, Ann Eliza 1752-1783 ......... DLB-200

Blelock and Company ............... DLB-49

Blennerhassett, Margaret Agnew 1773-1842 ................... DLB-99

Geoffrey Bles [publishing house] ....... DLB-112

Blessington, Marguerite, Countess of 1789-1849 ................... DLB-166

Blew, Mary Clearman 1939- .......... DLB-256

The Blickling Homilies circa 971 ....... DLB-146

Blind, Mathilde 1841-1896 ............ DLB-199

Blish, James 1921-1975 .............. DLB-8

E. Bliss and E. White [publishing house] ................ DLB-49

Bliven, Bruce 1889-1977 ............. DLB-137

Blixen, Karen 1885-1962 ............. DLB-214

Bloch, Robert 1917-1994 ............. DLB-44

Tribute to John D. MacDonald ......... Y-86

Block, Lawrence 1938- .............. DLB-226

Block, Rudolph (see Lessing, Bruno)

Blondal, Patricia 1926-1959 ............ DLB-88

Bloom, Harold 1930- ............... DLB-67

Bloomer, Amelia 1818-1894 ............ DLB-79

Bloomfield, Robert 1766-1823 .......... DLB-93

Bloomsbury Group ................... DS-10

The *Dreadnought* Hoax ................ DS-10

Blotner, Joseph 1923- ............. DLB-111

Blount, Thomas 1618?-1679 .......... DLB-236

Bloy, Léon 1846-1917 ................ DLB-123

Blume, Judy 1938- ................. DLB-52

Tribute to Theodor Seuss Geisel ........ Y-91

Blunck, Hans Friedrich 1888-1961 ....... DLB-66

Blunden, Edmund 1896-1974 ....DLB-20, 100, 155

Blundeville, Thomas 1522?-1606 ....... DLB-236

Blunt, Lady Anne Isabella Noel 1837-1917 ................... DLB-174

Blunt, Wilfrid Scawen 1840-1922 ..... DLB-19, 174

Bly, Nellie (see Cochrane, Elizabeth)

Bly, Robert 1926- ................... DLB-5

Blyton, Enid 1897-1968 .............. DLB-160

Boaden, James 1762-1839 ............. DLB-89

Boas, Frederick S. 1862-1957 .......... DLB-149

The Bobbs-Merrill Company ........... DLB-46

The Bobbs-Merrill Archive at the Lilly Library, Indiana University .... Y-90

Boborykin, Petr Dmitrievich 1836-1921 .. DLB-238

Bobrov, Semen Sergeevich 1763?-1810 ... DLB-150

Bobrowski, Johannes 1917-1965 ......... DLB-75

Bocage, Manuel Maria Barbosa du 1765-1805 ................... DLB-287

Bodenheim, Maxwell 1892-1954 ...... DLB-9, 45

Bodenstedt, Friedrich von 1819-1892 .... DLB-129

Bodini, Vittorio 1914-1970 ........... DLB-128

Bodkin, M. McDonnell 1850-1933 ....... DLB-70

Bodley, Sir Thomas 1545-1613 ......... DLB-213

Bodley Head ...................... DLB-112

Bodmer, Johann Jakob 1698-1783 ....... DLB-97

Bodmershof, Imma von 1895-1982 ...... DLB-85

Bodsworth, Fred 1918- ............. DLB-68

Boehm, Sydney 1908- .............. DLB-44

Boer, Charles 1939- ................. DLB-5

Boethius circa 480-circa 524 ........... DLB-115

Boethius of Dacia circa 1240-? ......... DLB-115

Bogan, Louise 1897-1970 .......... DLB-45, 169

Bogarde, Dirk 1921-1999 ............. DLB-14

Bogdanovich, Ippolit Fedorovich circa 1743-1803 ................ DLB-150

David Bogue [publishing house] ........ DLB-106

Böhme, Jakob 1575-1624 ............. DLB-164

H. G. Bohn [publishing house] ......... DLB-106

Bohse, August 1661-1742 ............. DLB-168

Boie, Heinrich Christian 1744-1806 ...... DLB-94

Boileau-Despréaux, Nicolas 1636-1711 ....DLB-268

Bok, Edward W. 1863-1930 ...... DLB-91; DS-16

Boland, Eavan 1944- ............... DLB-40

Boldrewood, Rolf (Thomas Alexander Browne) 1826?-1915 ................... DLB-230

Bolingbroke, Henry St. John, Viscount
 1678-1751 ..................... DLB-101
Böll, Heinrich
 1917-1985 ........ DLB-69; Y-85; CDWLB-2
Bolling, Robert 1738-1775 .............. DLB-31
Bolotov, Andrei Timofeevich
 1738-1833 ..................... DLB-150
Bolt, Carol 1941- .................... DLB-60
Bolt, Robert 1924-1995 ........... DLB-13, 233
Bolton, Herbert E. 1870-1953 ......... DLB-17
Bonaventura ...................... DLB-90
Bonaventure circa 1217-1274 ......... DLB-115
Bonaviri, Giuseppe 1924- ........... DLB-177
Bond, Edward 1934- ................. DLB-13
Bond, Michael 1926- ............... DLB-161
Albert and Charles Boni
 [publishing house] ................ DLB-46
Boni and Liveright ................... DLB-46
Bonnefoy, Yves 1923- .............. DLB-258
Bonner, Marita 1899-1971 .......... DLB-228
Bonner, Paul Hyde 1893-1968 .......... DS-17
Bonner, Sherwood (see McDowell, Katharine
 Sherwood Bonner)
Robert Bonner's Sons ................ DLB-49
Bonnin, Gertrude Simmons (see Zitkala-Ša)
Bonsanti, Alessandro 1904-1984 ....... DLB-177
Bontempelli, Massimo 1878-1960 ...... DLB-264
Bontemps, Arna 1902-1973 ......... DLB-48, 51
*The Book Buyer* (1867-1880, 1884-1918,
 1935-1938 .................... DS-13
The Book League of America .......... DLB-46
Book Reviewing
 The American Book Review: A Sketch... Y-92
 Book Reviewing and the
  Literary Scene ................ Y-96, 97
 Book Reviewing in America ......... Y-87–94
 Book Reviewing in America and the
  Literary Scene ................. Y-95
 Book Reviewing in Texas ............ Y-94
 Book Reviews in Glossy Magazines ..... Y-95
 Do They or Don't They?
  Writers Reading Book Reviews ..... Y-01
 The Most Powerful Book Review
  in America [*New York Times
  Book Review*] ................. Y-82
 Some Surprises and Universal Truths.... Y-92
 The Year in Book Reviewing and the
  Literary Situation ............... Y-98
Book Supply Company ............... DLB-49
The Book Trade History Group ........ Y-93
The Booker Prize .................. Y-96–98
 Address by Anthony Thwaite,
  Chairman of the Booker Prize Judges
  Comments from Former Booker
  Prize Winners .................. Y-86
Boorde, Andrew circa 1490-1549 ...... DLB-136
Boorstin, Daniel J. 1914- ............ DLB-17
 Tribute to Archibald MacLeish ......... Y-82
 Tribute to Charles Scribner Jr. ......... Y-95

Booth, Franklin 1874-1948 ............ DLB-188
Booth, Mary L. 1831-1889 ............ DLB-79
Booth, Philip 1925- ................... Y-82
Booth, Wayne C. 1921- .............. DLB-67
Booth, William 1829-1912 ............ DLB-190
Borchardt, Rudolf 1877-1945 .......... DLB-66
Borchert, Wolfgang 1921-1947 ...... DLB-69, 124
Borel, Pétrus 1809-1859 .............. DLB-119
Borges, Jorge Luis
 1899-1986 ... DLB-113, 283; Y-86; CDWLB-3
 The Poetry of Jorge Luis Borges ........ Y-86
 A Personal Tribute .................. Y-86
Borgese, Giuseppe Antonio 1882-1952 ... DLB-264
Börne, Ludwig 1786-1837 ............ DLB-90
Bornstein, Miriam 1950- ............ DLB-209
Borowski, Tadeusz
 1922-1951 ............ DLB-215; CDWLB-4
Borrow, George 1803-1881 ...... DLB-21, 55, 166
Bosanquet, Bernard 1848-1923 ........ DLB-262
Bosch, Juan 1909-2001 .............. DLB-145
Bosco, Henri 1888-1976 .............. DLB-72
Bosco, Monique 1927- ............... DLB-53
Bosman, Herman Charles 1905-1951 .... DLB-225
Bossuet, Jacques-Bénigne 1627-1704 .... DLB-268
Bostic, Joe 1908-1988 ................ DLB-241
Boston, Lucy M. 1892-1990 .......... DLB-161
*Boston Quarterly Review* .............. DLB-1
Boston University
 Editorial Institute at Boston University ... Y-00
 Special Collections at Boston University .. Y-99
Boswell, James
 1740-1795 ......... DLB-104, 142; CDBLB-2
Boswell, Robert 1953- .............. DLB-234
Bosworth, David ..................... Y-82
 Excerpt from "Excerpts from a Report
  of the Commission," in *The Death
  of Descartes* ................... Y-82
Bote, Hermann circa 1460-circa 1520 .... DLB-179
Botev, Khristo 1847-1876 ............ DLB-147
Botkin, Vasilii Petrovich 1811-1869 ..... DLB-277
Botta, Anne C. Lynch 1815-1891 ..... DLB-3, 250
Botto, Ján (see Krasko, Ivan)
Bottome, Phyllis 1882-1963 .......... DLB-197
Bottomley, Gordon 1874-1948 .......... DLB-10
Bottoms, David 1949- ........ DLB-120; Y-83
 Tribute to James Dickey ............. Y-97
Bottrall, Ronald 1906- ............... DLB-20
Bouchardy, Joseph 1810-1870 ......... DLB-192
Boucher, Anthony 1911-1968 .......... DLB-8
Boucher, Jonathan 1738-1804 .......... DLB-31
Boucher de Boucherville, Georges
 1814-1894 ..................... DLB-99
Boudreau, Daniel (see Coste, Donat)
Bouhours, Dominique 1628-1702 ....... DLB-268
Bourassa, Napoléon 1827-1916 ........ DLB-99
Bourget, Paul 1852-1935 ............. DLB-123

Bourinot, John George 1837-1902 ....... DLB-99
Bourjaily, Vance 1922- ............ DLB-2, 143
Bourne, Edward Gaylord 1860-1908 ..... DLB-47
Bourne, Randolph 1886-1918 .......... DLB-63
Bousoño, Carlos 1923- .............. DLB-108
Bousquet, Joë 1897-1950 ............. DLB-72
Bova, Ben 1932- ..................... Y-81
Bovard, Oliver K. 1872-1945 .......... DLB-25
Bove, Emmanuel 1898-1945 ........... DLB-72
Bowen, Elizabeth
 1899-1973 .......... DLB-15, 162; CDBLB-7
Bowen, Francis 1811-1890 ....... DLB-1, 59, 235
Bowen, John 1924- .................. DLB-13
Bowen, Marjorie 1886-1952 .......... DLB-153
Bowen-Merrill Company ............... DLB-49
Bowering, George 1935- ............. DLB-53
Bowers, Bathsheba 1671-1718 ......... DLB-200
Bowers, Claude G. 1878-1958 .......... DLB-17
Bowers, Edgar 1924-2000 ............. DLB-5
Bowers, Fredson Thayer
 1905-1991 ................ DLB-140; Y-91
 The Editorial Style of Fredson Bowers ... Y-91
 Fredson Bowers and
  Studies in Bibliography ........... Y-91
 Fredson Bowers and the Cambridge
  Beaumont and Fletcher ........... Y-91
 Fredson Bowers as Critic of Renaissance
  Dramatic Literature .............. Y-91
 Fredson Bowers as Music Critic ........ Y-91
 Fredson Bowers, Master Teacher ....... Y-91
 An Interview [on Nabokov] ........... Y-80
 Working with Fredson Bowers ......... Y-91
Bowles, Paul 1910-1999 ...... DLB-5, 6, 218; Y-99
Bowles, Samuel, III 1826-1878 .......... DLB-43
Bowles, William Lisle 1762-1850 ........ DLB-93
Bowman, Louise Morey 1882-1944 ...... DLB-68
Bowne, Borden Parker 1847-1919 ...... DLB-270
Boyd, James 1888-1944 ......... DLB-9; DS-16
Boyd, John 1919- .................... DLB-8
Boyd, Martin 1893-1972 ............. DLB-260
Boyd, Thomas 1898-1935 ........ DLB-9; DS-16
Boyd, William 1952- ................ DLB-231
Boye, Karin 1900-1941 .............. DLB-259
Boyesen, Hjalmar Hjorth
 1848-1895 .............. DLB-12, 71; DS-13
Boylan, Clare 1948- ................ DLB-267
Boyle, Kay 1902-1992 DLB-4, 9, 48, 86; DS-15;
 ............................... Y-93
Boyle, Roger, Earl of Orrery 1621-1679 ... DLB-80
Boyle, T. Coraghessan
 1948- ............... DLB-218, 278; Y-86
Božić, Mirko 1919- ................. DLB-181
Brackenbury, Alison 1953- ............ DLB-40
Brackenridge, Hugh Henry
 1748-1816 ................... DLB-11, 37
 The Rising Glory of America ......... DLB-37
Brackett, Charles 1892-1969 ........... DLB-26

# Cumulative Index

Brackett, Leigh 1915-1978 . . . . . . . . . . DLB-8, 26
John Bradburn [publishing house] . . . . . . . DLB-49
Bradbury, Malcolm 1932-2000. . . . . . DLB-14, 207
Bradbury, Ray 1920- . . . . . DLB-2, 8; CDALB-6
Bradbury and Evans. . . . . . . . . . . . . . . . . DLB-106
Braddon, Mary Elizabeth
  1835-1915. . . . . . . . . . . . . . .DLB-18, 70, 156
Bradford, Andrew 1686-1742 . . . . . . . . DLB-43, 73
Bradford, Gamaliel 1863-1932 . . . . . . . . . DLB-17
Bradford, John 1749-1830. . . . . . . . . . . . . DLB-43
Bradford, Roark 1896-1948 . . . . . . . . . . . DLB-86
Bradford, William 1590-1657 . . . . . . . DLB-24, 30
Bradford, William, III 1719-1791 . . . . . DLB-43, 73
Bradlaugh, Charles 1833-1891 . . . . . . . . . DLB-57
Bradley, David 1950- . . . . . . . . . . . . . . . DLB-33
Bradley, F. H. 1846-1924 . . . . . . . . . . . . DLB-262
Bradley, Katherine Harris (see Field, Michael)
Bradley, Marion Zimmer 1930-1999 . . . . . . DLB-8
Bradley, William Aspenwall 1878-1939 . . . . DLB-4
Ira Bradley and Company . . . . . . . . . . . . . DLB-49
J. W. Bradley and Company . . . . . . . . . . . DLB-49
Bradshaw, Henry 1831-1886 . . . . . . . . . . DLB-184
Bradstreet, Anne
  1612 or 1613-1672 . . . . . . . DLB-24; CDALB-2
Bradūnas, Kazys 1917- . . . . . . . . . . . . . DLB-220
Bradwardine, Thomas circa 1295-1349 . . DLB-115
Brady, Frank 1924-1986. . . . . . . . . . . . . . DLB-111
Frederic A. Brady [publishing house] . . . . . DLB-49
Bragg, Melvyn 1939- . . . . . . . . . . .DLB-14, 271
Charles H. Brainard [publishing house] . . . DLB-49
Braine, John 1922-1986 . DLB-15; Y-86; CDBLB-7
Braithwait, Richard 1588-1673 . . . . . . . . DLB-151
Braithwaite, William Stanley
  1878-1962. . . . . . . . . . . . . . . . . . . DLB-50, 54
Bräker, Ulrich 1735-1798 . . . . . . . . . . . . . DLB-94
Bramah, Ernest 1868-1942. . . . . . . . . . . . DLB-70
Branagan, Thomas 1774-1843 . . . . . . . . . DLB-37
Brancati, Vitaliano 1907-1954 . . . . . . . . . DLB-264
Branch, William Blackwell 1927- . . . . . . DLB-76
Brand, Christianna 1907-1988 . . . . . . . . .DLB-276
Brand, Max (see Faust, Frederick Schiller)
Brandão, Raul 1867-1930 . . . . . . . . . . . . DLB-287
Branden Press. . . . . . . . . . . . . . . . . . . . . DLB-46
Branner, H.C. 1903-1966 . . . . . . . . . . . . DLB-214
Brant, Sebastian 1457-1521 . . . . . . . . . . .DLB-179
Brassey, Lady Annie (Allnutt)
  1839-1887. . . . . . . . . . . . . . . . . . . . DLB-166
Brathwaite, Edward Kamau
  1930- . . . . . . . . . . . DLB-125; CDWLB-3
Brault, Jacques 1933- . . . . . . . . . . . . . . DLB-53
Braun, Matt 1932- . . . . . . . . . . . . . . . . DLB-212
Braun, Volker 1939- . . . . . . . . . . . DLB-75, 124
Brautigan, Richard
  1935-1984 . . . . . . . . .DLB-2, 5, 206; Y-80, 84
Braxton, Joanne M. 1950- . . . . . . . . . . . DLB-41
Bray, Anne Eliza 1790-1883 . . . . . . . . . . DLB-116

Bray, Thomas 1656-1730 . . . . . . . . . . . . . DLB-24
Brazdžionis, Bernardas 1907- . . . . . . . DLB-220
George Braziller [publishing house] . . . . . . DLB-46
The Bread Loaf Writers' Conference 1983 . . . Y-84
Breasted, James Henry 1865-1935 . . . . . . . DLB-47
Brecht, Bertolt
  1898-1956 . . . . . . . .DLB-56, 124; CDWLB-2
Bredel, Willi 1901-1964 . . . . . . . . . . . . . . DLB-56
Bregendahl, Marie 1867-1940. . . . . . . . . DLB-214
Breitinger, Johann Jakob 1701-1776 . . . . . DLB-97
Bremser, Bonnie 1939- . . . . . . . . . . . . . DLB-16
Bremser, Ray 1934-1998 . . . . . . . . . . . . . DLB-16
Brennan, Christopher 1870-1932 . . . . . . . DLB-230
Brentano, Bernard von 1901-1964 . . . . . . . DLB-56
Brentano, Clemens 1778-1842 . . . . . . . . . DLB-90
Brentano's. . . . . . . . . . . . . . . . . . . . . . . . DLB-49
Brenton, Howard 1942- . . . . . . . . . . . . . DLB-13
Breslin, Jimmy 1929-1996. . . . . . . . . . . . DLB-185
Breton, André 1896-1966. . . . . . . . . DLB-65, 258
Breton, Nicholas circa 1555-circa 1626. . . DLB-136
The Breton Lays
  1300-early fifteenth century . . . . . . . . DLB-146
Brett, Simon 1945- . . . . . . . . . . . . . . . .DLB-276
Brewer, Luther A. 1858-1933. . . . . . . . . . DLB-187
Brewer, Warren and Putnam . . . . . . . . . . DLB-46
Brewster, Elizabeth 1922- . . . . . . . . . . . DLB-60
Breytenbach, Breyten 1939- . . . . . . . . . DLB-225
Bridge, Ann (Lady Mary Dolling Sanders
  O'Malley) 1889-1974 . . . . . . . . . . . . DLB-191
Bridge, Horatio 1806-1893 . . . . . . . . . . . DLB-183
Bridgers, Sue Ellen 1942- . . . . . . . . . . . DLB-52
Bridges, Robert
  1844-1930 . . . . . . . . . . DLB-19, 98; CDBLB-5
The Bridgewater Library . . . . . . . . . . . . DLB-213
Bridie, James 1888-1951 . . . . . . . . . . . . . DLB-10
Brieux, Eugene 1858-1932 . . . . . . . . . . . DLB-192
Brigadere, Anna
  1861-1933 . . . . . . . . . . . DLB-220; CDWLB-4
Briggs, Charles Frederick 1804-1877 . . DLB-3, 250
Brighouse, Harold 1882-1958. . . . . . . . . . DLB-10
Bright, Mary Chavelita Dunne (see Egerton, George)
Brightman, Edgar Sheffield 1884-1953 . . . .DLB-270
B. J. Brimmer Company. . . . . . . . . . . . . . DLB-46
Brines, Francisco 1932- . . . . . . . . . . . . DLB-134
Brink, André 1935- . . . . . . . . . . . . . . . DLB-225
Brinley, George, Jr. 1817-1875 . . . . . . . . . DLB-140
Brinnin, John Malcolm 1916-1998 . . . . . . DLB-48
Brisbane, Albert 1809-1890 . . . . . . . . DLB-3, 250
Brisbane, Arthur 1864-1936 . . . . . . . . . . DLB-25
British Academy . . . . . . . . . . . . . . . . . . DLB-112
The British Critic 1793-1843 . . . . . . . . . . . DLB-110
British Library
  The American Trust for the
    British Library. . . . . . . . . . . . . . . . . . Y-96
  The British Library and the Regular
    Readers' Group. . . . . . . . . . . . . . . . . Y-91

Building the New British Library
  at St Pancras . . . . . . . . . . . . . . . . . . . . Y-94
British Literary Prizes. . . . . . . . . . .DLB-207; Y-98
British Literature
  The "Angry Young Men" . . . . . . . . . DLB-15
  Author-Printers, 1476-1599 . . . . . . . . DLB-167
  The Comic Tradition Continued. . . . . DLB-15
  Documents on Sixteenth-Century
    Literature. . . . . . . . . . . . . . . DLB-167, 172
  Eikon Basilike 1649 . . . . . . . . . . . . . . DLB-151
  Letter from London. . . . . . . . . . . . . . . Y-96
  A Mirror for Magistrates . . . . . . . . . . . DLB-167
  "Modern English Prose" (1876),
    by George Saintsbury . . . . . . . . . . DLB-57
  Sex, Class, Politics, and Religion [in the
    British Novel, 1930-1959] . . . . . . . DLB-15
  Victorians on Rhetoric and Prose
    Style. . . . . . . . . . . . . . . . . . . . . . . DLB-57
  The Year in British Fiction. . . . . . . . . Y-99-01
  "You've Never Had It So Good," Gusted
    by "Winds of Change": British
    Fiction in the 1950s, 1960s,
    and After . . . . . . . . . . . . . . . . . . . DLB-14
British Literature, Old and Middle English
  Anglo-Norman Literature in the
    Development of Middle English
    Literature. . . . . . . . . . . . . . . . . . . DLB-146
  The Alliterative Morte Arthure and the
    Stanzaic Morte Arthur
    circa 1350-1400. . . . . . . . . . . . . . DLB-146
  Ancrene Riwle circa 1200-1225. . . . . . . DLB-146
  The Anglo-Saxon Chronicle circa
    890-1154 . . . . . . . . . . . . . . . . . . . DLB-146
  The Battle of Maldon circa 1000 . . . . . DLB-146
  Beowulf circa 900-1000 or
    790-825 . . . . . . . . . DLB-146; CDBLB-1
  The Blickling Homilies circa 971 . . . . DLB-146
  The Breton Lays
    1300-early fifteenth century. . . . . DLB-146
  The Castle of Perseverance
    circa 1400-1425 . . . . . . . . . . . . . . DLB-146
  The Celtic Background to Medieval
    English Literature . . . . . . . . . . . . DLB-146
  The Chester Plays circa 1505-1532;
    revisions until 1575 . . . . . . . . . . . DLB-146
  Cursor Mundi circa 1300 . . . . . . . . . DLB-146
  The English Language: 410
    to 1500 . . . . . . . . . . . . . . . . . . . DLB-146
  The Germanic Epic and Old English
    Heroic Poetry: Widsith, Waldere,
    and The Fight at Finnsburg. . . . . . . DLB-146
  Judith circa 930 . . . . . . . . . . . . . . . DLB-146
  The Matter of England 1240-1400. . . DLB-146
  The Matter of Rome early twelfth to
    late fifteenth centuries . . . . . . . . . DLB-146
  Middle English Literature:
    An Introduction. . . . . . . . . . . . . . DLB-146
  The Middle English Lyric . . . . . . . . DLB-146
  Morality Plays: Mankind circa 1450-1500
    and Everyman circa 1500 . . . . . . . . DLB-146
  N-Town Plays circa 1468 to early
    sixteenth century . . . . . . . . . . . DLB-146

Old English Literature:
An Introduction ............ DLB-146

Old English Riddles
eighth to tenth centuries ....... DLB-146

*The Owl and the Nightingale*
circa 1189-1199 .......... DLB-146

*The Paston Letters* 1422-1509 ........ DLB-146

*The Seafarer* circa 970 .............. DLB-146

The *South English Legendary* circa
thirteenth to fifteenth centuries .... DLB-146

*The British Review and London Critical
Journal* 1811-1825 ................ DLB-110

Brito, Aristeo 1942- ............... DLB-122

Brittain, Vera 1893-1970 ............. DLB-191

Brizeux, Auguste 1803-1858 .......... DLB-217

Broadway Publishing Company ........ DLB-46

Broch, Hermann
1886-1951 ........ DLB-85, 124; CDWLB-2

Brochu, André 1942- ............... DLB-53

Brock, Edwin 1927-1997 ............. DLB-40

Brockes, Barthold Heinrich 1680-1747 .... DLB-168

Brod, Max 1884-1968 ................ DLB-81

Brodber, Erna 1940- ................ DLB-157

Brodhead, John R. 1814-1873 .......... DLB-30

Brodkey, Harold 1930-1996 .......... DLB-130

Brodsky, Joseph (Iosif Aleksandrovich
Brodsky) 1940-1996 ........ DLB-285; Y-87

Nobel Lecture 1987................. Y-87

Brodsky, Michael 1948- ............. DLB-244

Broeg, Bob 1918- .................. DLB-171

Brøgger, Suzanne 1944- ............. DLB-214

Brome, Richard circa 1590-1652 ........ DLB-58

Brome, Vincent 1910- ............... DLB-155

Bromfield, Louis 1896-1956......... DLB-4, 9, 86

Bromige, David 1933- .............. DLB-193

Broner, E. M. 1930- ................ DLB-28

Tribute to Bernard Malamud .......... Y-86

Bronk, William 1918-1999............. DLB-165

Bronnen, Arnolt 1895-1959 ........... DLB-124

Brontë, Anne 1820-1849 ........... DLB-21, 199

Brontë, Charlotte
1816-1855 ..... DLB-21, 159, 199; CDBLB-4

Brontë, Emily
1818-1848 ...... DLB-21, 32, 199; CDBLB-4

The Brontë Society .................... Y-98

Brook, Stephen 1947- ............... DLB-204

Brook Farm 1841-1847 ....... DLB-1; 223; DS-5

Brooke, Frances 1724-1789.......... DLB-39, 99

Brooke, Henry 1703?-1783............. DLB-39

Brooke, L. Leslie 1862-1940 .......... DLB-141

Brooke, Margaret, Ranee of Sarawak
1849-1936 .................... DLB-174

Brooke, Rupert
1887-1915 ........ DLB-19, 216; CDBLB-6

The Friends of the Dymock Poets....... Y-00

Brooker, Bertram 1888-1955........... DLB-88

Brooke-Rose, Christine 1923-  ..... DLB-14, 231

Brookner, Anita 1928- ........ DLB-194; Y-87

Brooks, Charles Timothy 1813-1883...DLB-1, 243

Brooks, Cleanth 1906-1994........ DLB-63; Y-94

Tribute to Katherine Anne Porter....... Y-80

Tribute to Walker Percy............. Y-90

Brooks, Gwendolyn
1917-2000 ........DLB-5, 76, 165; CDALB-1

Tribute to Julian Mayfield............ Y-84

Brooks, Jeremy 1926- ................ DLB-14

Brooks, Mel 1926- .................. DLB-26

Brooks, Noah 1830-1903......... DLB-42; DS-13

Brooks, Richard 1912-1992 ........... DLB-44

Brooks, Van Wyck 1886-1963 ... DLB-45, 63, 103

Brophy, Brigid 1929-1995 ....... DLB-14, 70, 271

Brophy, John 1899-1965 .............. DLB-191

Brossard, Chandler 1922-1993 .......... DLB-16

Brossard, Nicole 1943- ................ DLB-53

Broster, Dorothy Kathleen 1877-1950 .... DLB-160

Brother Antoninus (see Everson, William)

Brotherton, Lord 1856-1930 .......... DLB-184

Brougham, John 1810-1880.............. DLB-11

Brougham and Vaux, Henry Peter
Brougham, Baron 1778-1868.... DLB-110, 158

Broughton, James 1913-1999............. DLB-5

Broughton, Rhoda 1840-1920 ........... DLB-18

Broun, Heywood 1888-1939 ....... DLB-29, 171

Brown, Alice 1856-1948................ DLB-78

Brown, Bob 1886-1959 ........ DLB-4, 45; DS-15

Brown, Cecil 1943- .................. DLB-33

Brown, Charles Brockden
1771-1810 ....... DLB-37, 59, 73; CDALB-2

Brown, Christy 1932-1981 ............. DLB-14

Brown, Dee 1908-2002 ................ Y-80

Brown, Frank London 1927-1962 ........ DLB-76

Brown, Fredric 1906-1972 .............. DLB-8

Brown, George Mackay
1921-1996 ............DLB-14, 27, 139, 271

Brown, Harry 1917-1986 .............. DLB-26

Brown, Larry 1951- ................. DLB-234

Brown, Lew 1893-1958 ................ DLB-265

Brown, Marcia 1918- ................. DLB-61

Brown, Margaret Wise 1910-1952........ DLB-22

Brown, Morna Doris (see Ferrars, Elizabeth)

Brown, Oliver Madox 1855-1874 ........ DLB-21

Brown, Sterling 1901-1989 ....... DLB-48, 51, 63

Brown, T. E. 1830-1897 ............... DLB-35

Brown, Thomas Alexander (see Boldrewood, Rolf)

Brown, Warren 1894-1978 ............. DLB-241

Brown, William Hill 1765-1793 .......... DLB-37

Brown, William Wells
1815-1884 ............. DLB-3, 50, 183, 248

Brown University
The Festival of Vanguard Narrative .... Y-93

Browne, Charles Farrar 1834-1867 ....... DLB-11

Browne, Frances 1816-1879 ........... DLB-199

Browne, Francis Fisher 1843-1913........ DLB-79

Browne, Howard 1908-1999 .......... DLB-226

Browne, J. Ross 1821-1875 ............ DLB-202

Browne, Michael Dennis 1940- ........ DLB-40

Browne, Sir Thomas 1605-1682 ........ DLB-151

Browne, William, of Tavistock
1590-1645 ..................... DLB-121

Browne, Wynyard 1911-1964 ....... DLB-13, 233

Browne and Nolan................... DLB-106

Brownell, W. C. 1851-1928............. DLB-71

Browning, Elizabeth Barrett
1806-1861 .......... DLB-32, 199; CDBLB-4

Browning, Robert
1812-1889 .......... DLB-32, 163; CDBLB-4

Essay on Chatterton ............... DLB-32

Introductory Essay: *Letters of Percy
Bysshe Shelley* (1852)............. DLB-32

"The Novel in [Robert Browning's]
'The Ring and the Book'" (1912),
by Henry James ............... DLB-32

Brownjohn, Allan 1931- .............. DLB-40

Tribute to John Betjeman ............. Y-84

Brownson, Orestes Augustus
1803-1876 ......... DLB-1, 59, 73, 243; DS-5

Bruccoli, Matthew J. 1931- ........... DLB-103

Joseph [Heller] and George [V. Higgins].. Y-99

Response [to Busch on Fitzgerald]....... Y-96

Tribute to Albert Erskine ............. Y-93

Tribute to Charles E. Feinberg ......... Y-88

Working with Fredson Bowers......... Y-91

Bruce, Charles 1906-1971 .............. DLB-68

Bruce, John Edward 1856-1924

Three Documents [African American
poets] ................... DLB-50

Bruce, Leo 1903-1979 ................ DLB-77

Bruce, Mary Grant 1878-1958.......... DLB-230

Bruce, Philip Alexander 1856-1933 ....... DLB-47

Bruce-Novoa, Juan 1944- ............. DLB-82

Bruckman, Clyde 1894-1955............ DLB-26

Bruckner, Ferdinand 1891-1958 ........ DLB-118

Brundage, John Herbert (see Herbert, John)

Brunner, John 1934-1995 ............. DLB-261

Tribute to Theodore Sturgeon ......... Y-85

Brutus, Dennis
1924- .......... DLB-117, 225; CDWLB-3

Bryan, C. D. B. 1936- ............... DLB-185

Bryant, Arthur 1899-1985 ............. DLB-149

Bryant, William Cullen 1794-1878
........ DLB-3, 43, 59, 189, 250; CDALB-2

Bryce, James 1838-1922.......... DLB-166, 190

Bryce Echenique, Alfredo
1939- .............. DLB-145; CDWLB-3

Bryden, Bill 1942- .................. DLB-233

Brydges, Sir Samuel Egerton
1762-1837 ................ DLB-107, 142

Bryskett, Lodowick 1546?-1612 ........ DLB-167

Buchan, John 1875-1940 ....... DLB-34, 70, 156

Buchanan, George 1506-1582 .......... DLB-132

Buchanan, Robert 1841-1901 ....... DLB-18, 35

"The Fleshly School of Poetry and
Other Phenomena of the Day"
(1872)...................... DLB-35

"The Fleshly School of Poetry:
Mr. D. G. Rossetti" (1871),
by Thomas Maitland.......... DLB-35

Buchler, Justus 1914-1991 ............. DLB-279

Buchman, Sidney 1902-1975............. DLB-26

Buchner, Augustus 1591-1661 ......... DLB-164

Büchner, Georg 1813-1837 .. DLB-133; CDWLB-2

Bucholtz, Andreas Heinrich 1607-1671 ... DLB-168

Buck, Pearl S. 1892-1973 .. DLB-9, 102; CDALB-7

Bucke, Charles 1781-1846 ............. DLB-110

Bucke, Richard Maurice 1837-1902 ...... DLB-99

Buckingham, Edwin 1810-1833 ......... DLB-73

Buckingham, Joseph Tinker 1779-1861 ... DLB-73

Buckler, Ernest 1908-1984 ............. DLB-68

Buckley, William F., Jr. 1925- .... DLB-137; Y-80

Publisher's Statement From the
Initial Issue of *National Review*
(19 November 1955) ......... DLB-137

Buckminster, Joseph Stevens
1784-1812..................... DLB-37

Buckner, Robert 1906- .............. DLB-26

Budd, Thomas ?-1698 ............. DLB-24

Budrys, A. J. 1931- ............... DLB-8

Buechner, Frederick 1926- ............. Y-80

Buell, John 1927- ................ DLB-53

Bufalino, Gesualdo 1920-1996 ......... DLB-196

Job Buffum [publishing house]......... DLB-49

Bugnet, Georges 1879-1981 ............ DLB-92

Buies, Arthur 1840-1901............... DLB-99

Bukowski, Charles 1920-1994 ... DLB-5, 130, 169

Bulatović, Miodrag
1930-1991 .......... DLB-181; CDWLB-4

Bulgakov, Mikhail Afanas'evich
1891-1940 ................... DLB-272

Bulgarin, Faddei Venediktovich
1789-1859..................... DLB-198

Bulger, Bozeman 1877-1932 ............DLB-171

Bullein, William
between 1520 and 1530-1576....... DLB-167

Bullins, Ed 1935- ............DLB-7, 38, 249

Bulwer, John 1606-1656................ DLB-236

Bulwer-Lytton, Edward (also Edward
Bulwer) 1803-1873................. DLB-21

"On Art in Fiction "(1838)...... DLB-21

Bumpus, Jerry 1937- ................. Y-81

Bunce and Brother ................. DLB-49

Bunner, H. C. 1855-1896.............DLB-78, 79

Bunting, Basil 1900-1985 ............. DLB-20

Buntline, Ned (Edward Zane Carroll
Judson) 1821-1886................. DLB-186

Bunyan, John 1628-1688 ..... DLB-39; CDBLB-2

The Author's Apology for
His Book.................... DLB-39

Burch, Robert 1925- ............. DLB-52

Burciaga, José Antonio 1940- ........ DLB-82

Burdekin, Katharine (Murray Constantine)
1896-1963 ................... DLB-255

Bürger, Gottfried August 1747-1794 ...... DLB-94

Burgess, Anthony (John Anthony Burgess Wilson)
1917-1993...... DLB-14, 194, 261; CDBLB-8

The Anthony Burgess Archive at
the Harry Ransom Humanities
Research Center ................ Y-98

Anthony Burgess's *99 Novels:*
An Opinion Poll ................ Y-84

Burgess, Gelett 1866-1951 ............. DLB-11

Burgess, John W. 1844-1931 ........... DLB-47

Burgess, Thornton W. 1874-1965 ....... DLB-22

Burgess, Stringer and Company......... DLB-49

Burick, Si 1909-1986..................DLB-171

Burk, John Daly circa 1772-1808 ....... DLB-37

Burk, Ronnie 1955- ............... DLB-209

Burke, Edmund 1729?-1797 ....... DLB-104, 252

Burke, James Lee 1936- ............ DLB-226

Burke, Johnny 1908-1964 ............. DLB-265

Burke, Kenneth 1897-1993 ....... DLB-45, 63

Burke, Thomas 1886-1945 ............ DLB-197

Burley, Dan 1907-1962................ DLB-241

Burley, W. J. 1914- ................DLB-276

Burlingame, Edward Livermore
1848-1922 ..................... DLB-79

Burman, Carina 1960- ............ DLB-257

Burnet, Gilbert 1643-1715............. DLB-101

Burnett, Frances Hodgson
1849-1924 .........DLB-42, 141; DS-13, 14

Burnett, W. R. 1899-1982 ......... DLB-9, 226

Burnett, Whit 1899-1973 ............ DLB-137

Burney, Fanny 1752-1840............. DLB-39

Dedication, *The Wanderer* (1814) ..... DLB-39

Preface to *Evelina* (1778)........... DLB-39

Burns, Alan 1929- ............... DLB-14, 194

Burns, John Horne 1916-1953 ............. Y-85

Burns, Robert 1759-1796 ..... DLB-109; CDBLB-3

Burns and Oates.................... DLB-106

Burnshaw, Stanley 1906- ........DLB-48; Y-97

James Dickey and Stanley Burnshaw
Correspondence ................Y-02

Review of Stanley Burnshaw: The
Collected Poems and Selected
Prose ....................... Y-02

Tribute to Robert Penn Warren ........ Y-89

Burr, C. Chauncey 1815?-1883 ......... DLB-79

Burr, Esther Edwards 1732-1758 ....... DLB-200

Burroughs, Edgar Rice 1875-1950 ........ DLB-8

The Burroughs Bibliophiles........... Y-98

Burroughs, John 1837-1921 .........DLB-64, 275

Burroughs, Margaret T. G. 1917- ..... DLB-41

Burroughs, William S., Jr. 1947-1981 ..... DLB-16

Burroughs, William Seward 1914-1997
......... DLB-2, 8, 16, 152, 237; Y-81, 97

Burroway, Janet 1936- ............... DLB-6

Burt, Maxwell Struthers
1882-1954 ............... DLB-86; DS-16

A. L. Burt and Company ............. DLB-49

Burton, Hester 1913- ............. DLB-161

Burton, Isabel Arundell 1831-1896...... DLB-166

Burton, Miles (see Rhode, John)

Burton, Richard Francis
1821-1890 ............DLB-55, 166, 184

Burton, Robert 1577-1640............. DLB-151

Burton, Virginia Lee 1909-1968......... DLB-22

Burton, William Evans 1804-1860 ....... DLB-73

Burwell, Adam Hood 1790-1849 ........ DLB-99

Bury, Lady Charlotte 1775-1861 ....... DLB-116

Busch, Frederick 1941- ........... DLB-6, 218

Excerpts from Frederick Busch's USC
Remarks [on F. Scott Fitzgerald] ..... Y-96

Tribute to James Laughlin............. Y-97

Tribute to Raymond Carver ........... Y-88

Busch, Niven 1903-1991............... DLB-44

Bushnell, Horace 1802-1876 ...........DS-13

Business & Literature
The Claims of Business and Literature:
An Undergraduate Essay by
Maxwell Perkins ................ Y-01

Bussières, Arthur de 1877-1913.......... DLB-92

Butler, Charles circa 1560-1647 ....... DLB-236

Butler, Guy 1918- ................ DLB-225

Butler, Joseph 1692-1752 ............. DLB-252

Butler, Josephine Elizabeth
1828-1906 ................... DLB-190

Butler, Juan 1942-1981................ DLB-53

Butler, Judith 1956- ............. DLB-246

Butler, Octavia E. 1947- ............ DLB-33

Butler, Pierce 1884-1953................DLB-187

Butler, Robert Olen 1945- ...........DLB-173

Butler, Samuel 1613-1680..........DLB-101, 126

Butler, Samuel
1835-1902 .......DLB-18, 57, 174; CDBLB-5

Butler, William Francis 1838-1910...... DLB-166

E. H. Butler and Company ............. DLB-49

Butor, Michel 1926- ............... DLB-83

Nathaniel Butter [publishing house] .....DLB-170

Butterworth, Hezekiah 1839-1905 ....... DLB-42

Buttitta, Ignazio 1899-1997............ DLB-114

Butts, Mary 1890-1937................ DLB-240

Buzzati, Dino 1906-1972................DLB-177

Byars, Betsy 1928- ................ DLB-52

Byatt, A. S. 1936- ............. DLB-14, 194

Byles, Mather 1707-1788 ............. DLB-24

Henry Bynneman [publishing house].....DLB-170

Bynner, Witter 1881-1968 ............. DLB-54

Byrd, William circa 1543-1623...........DLB-172

Byrd, William, II 1674-1744 ........ DLB-24, 140

Byrne, John Keyes (see Leonard, Hugh)

Byron, George Gordon, Lord
1788-1824.......... DLB-96, 110; CDBLB-3

The Byron Society of America.......... Y-00

Byron, Robert 1905-1941............. DLB-195

# C

Caballero Bonald, José Manuel 1926- .................DLB-108

Cabañero, Eladio 1930- ...........DLB-134

Cabell, James Branch 1879-1958 .......DLB-9, 78

Cabeza de Baca, Manuel 1853-1915 .....DLB-122

Cabeza de Baca Gilbert, Fabiola 1898- .....................DLB-122

Cable, George Washington 1844-1925 ............DLB-12, 74; DS-13

Cable, Mildred 1878-1952 .............DLB-195

Cabral, Manuel del 1907-1999..........DLB-283

Cabrera, Lydia 1900-1991..............DLB-145

Cabrera Infante, Guillermo 1929- ..............DLB-113; CDWLB-3

Cadell [publishing house]..............DLB-154

Cady, Edwin H. 1917- ...............DLB-103

Caedmon flourished 658-680...........DLB-146

Caedmon School circa 660-899 .........DLB-146

Caesar, Irving 1895-1996...............DLB-265

Cafés, Brasseries, and Bistros...........DS-15

Cage, John 1912-1992 ................DLB-193

Cahan, Abraham 1860-1951 .......DLB-9, 25, 28

Cahn, Sammy 1913-1993..............DLB-265

Cain, George 1943- ..................DLB-33

Cain, James M. 1892-1977..............DLB-226

Caird, Edward 1835-1908 ..............DLB-262

Caird, Mona 1854-1932.................DLB-197

Čaks, Aleksandrs 1901-1950 .............DLB-220; CDWLB-4

Caldecott, Randolph 1846-1886 ........DLB-163

John Calder Limited [Publishing house]................DLB-112

Calderón de la Barca, Fanny 1804-1882 ...................DLB-183

Caldwell, Ben 1937- ..................DLB-38

Caldwell, Erskine 1903-1987 .........DLB-9, 86

H. M. Caldwell Company .............DLB-49

Caldwell, Taylor 1900-1985 ............. DS-17

Calhoun, John C. 1782-1850 ..........DLB-3, 248

Călinescu, George 1899-1965 ..........DLB-220

Calisher, Hortense 1911- ...........DLB-2, 218

Calkins, Mary Whiton 1863-1930.......DLB-270

Callaghan, Mary Rose 1944- .........DLB-207

Callaghan, Morley 1903-1990 .....DLB-68; DS-15

Callahan, S. Alice 1868-1894........DLB-175, 221

*Callaloo* [journal]......................Y-87

Callimachus circa 305 B.C.-240 B.C.......DLB-176

Calmer, Edgar 1907- ...................DLB-4

Calverley, C. S. 1831-1884 ...............DLB-35

Calvert, George Henry 1803-1889 .................DLB-1, 64, 248

Calvino, Italo 1923-1985 ...............DLB-196

Cambridge, Ada 1844-1926............DLB-230

Cambridge Press ....................DLB-49

*Cambridge Songs (Carmina Cantabrigensia)* circa 1050 .....................DLB-148

Cambridge University Cambridge and the Apostles...........DS-5

Cambridge University Press ...........DLB-170

Camden, William 1551-1623...........DLB-172

Camden House: An Interview with James Hardin ....................Y-92

Cameron, Eleanor 1912-2000 ..........DLB-52

Cameron, George Frederick 1854-1885 .....................DLB-99

Cameron, Lucy Lyttelton 1781-1858.....DLB-163

Cameron, Peter 1959- .................DLB-234

Cameron, William Bleasdell 1862-1951 ...DLB-99

Camm, John 1718-1778 ................DLB-31

Camões, Luís de 1524-1580.............DLB-287

Camon, Ferdinando 1935- ............DLB-196

Camp, Walter 1859-1925 ..............DLB-241

Campana, Dino 1885-1932 ............DLB-114

Campbell, Bebe Moore 1950- ..........DLB-227

Campbell, David 1915-1979.............DLB-260

Campbell, Gabrielle Margaret Vere (see Shearing, Joseph, and Bowen, Marjorie)

Campbell, James Dykes 1838-1895 ......DLB-144

Campbell, James Edwin 1867-1896 .......DLB-50

Campbell, John 1653-1728..............DLB-43

Campbell, John W., Jr. 1910-1971 ........DLB-8

Campbell, Ramsey 1946- ..............DLB-261

Campbell, Roy 1901-1957 ..........DLB-20, 225

Campbell, Thomas 1777-1844 .......DLB-93, 144

Campbell, William Edward (see March, William)

Campbell, William Wilfred 1858-1918 ....DLB-92

Campion, Edmund 1539-1581 ..........DLB-167

Campion, Thomas 1567-1620 ..........DLB-58, 172; CDBLB-1

Campo, Rafael 1964- ................DLB-282

Campton, David 1924- ...............DLB-245

Camus, Albert 1913-1960 ...............DLB-72

Camus, Jean-Pierre 1584-1652...........DLB-268

The Canadian Publishers' Records Database . Y-96

Canby, Henry Seidel 1878-1961 .........DLB-91

Cancioneros........................DLB-286

Candelaria, Cordelia 1943- ...........DLB-82

Candelaria, Nash 1928- ...............DLB-82

Canetti, Elias 1905-1994 ..........DLB-85, 124; CDWLB-2

Canham, Erwin Dain 1904-1982........DLB-127

Canitz, Friedrich Rudolph Ludwig von 1654-1699 ...................DLB-168

Cankar, Ivan 1876-1918.....DLB-147; CDWLB-4

Cannan, Gilbert 1884-1955 ..........DLB-10, 197

Cannan, Joanna 1896-1961 ............DLB-191

Cannell, Kathleen 1891-1974............DLB-4

Cannell, Skipwith 1887-1957 ...........DLB-45

Canning, George 1770-1827...........DLB-158

Cannon, Jimmy 1910-1973 ............DLB-171

Cano, Daniel 1947- ..................DLB-209

Old Dogs / New Tricks? New Technologies, the Canon, and the Structure of the Profession .........Y-02

Cantú, Norma Elia 1947- ............DLB-209

Cantwell, Robert 1908-1978 ............DLB-9

Jonathan Cape and Harrison Smith [publishing house]................DLB-46

Jonathan Cape Limited .............DLB-112

Čapek, Karel 1890-1938 ....DLB-215; CDWLB-4

Capen, Joseph 1658-1725...............DLB-24

Capes, Bernard 1854-1918 ............DLB-156

Capote, Truman 1924-1984 .......DLB-2, 185, 227; Y-80, 84; CDALB-1

Capps, Benjamin 1922- ..............DLB-256

Caproni, Giorgio 1912-1990 ...........DLB-128

Caragiale, Mateiu Ioan 1885-1936.......DLB-220

Cardarelli, Vincenzo 1887-1959.........DLB-114

Cárdenas, Reyes 1948- ...............DLB-122

Cardinal, Marie 1929-2001 .............DLB-83

Carew, Jan 1920- ...................DLB-157

Carew, Thomas 1594 or 1595-1640.....DLB-126

Carey, Henry circa 1687-1689-1743.......DLB-84

Carey, Mathew 1760-1839............DLB-37, 73

M. Carey and Company ...............DLB-49

Carey and Hart .....................DLB-49

Carlell, Lodowick 1602-1675............DLB-58

Carleton, William 1794-1869............DLB-159

G. W. Carleton [publishing house] .......DLB-49

Carlile, Richard 1790-1843 ........DLB-110, 158

Carlson, Ron 1947- .................DLB-244

Carlyle, Jane Welsh 1801-1866 ..........DLB-55

Carlyle, Thomas 1795-1881 .........DLB-55, 144; CDBLB-3

"The Hero as Man of Letters: Johnson, Rousseau, Burns" (1841) [excerpt].................DLB-57

The Hero as Poet. Dante; Shakspeare (1841) .....................DLB-32

Carman, Bliss 1861-1929 ..............DLB-92

*Carmina Burana* circa 1230 .............DLB-138

Carnap, Rudolf 1891-1970.............DLB-270

Carnero, Guillermo 1947- ............DLB-108

Carossa, Hans 1878-1956 .............DLB-66

Carpenter, Humphrey 1946- ...............DLB-155; Y-84, 99

Carpenter, Stephen Cullen ?-1820?.......DLB-73

Carpentier, Alejo 1904-1980 ............DLB-113; CDWLB-3

Carr, Emily (1871-1945) ...............DLB-68

Carr, Marina 1964- ..................DLB-245

Carr, Virginia Spencer 1929- ......DLB-111; Y-00

Carrera Andrade, Jorge 1903-1978 .......DLB-283

Carrier, Roch 1937- ..................DLB-53

Carrillo, Adolfo 1855-1926 ............DLB-122

Carroll, Gladys Hasty 1904- ............DLB-9

Carroll, John 1735-1815 ................DLB-37

Carroll, John 1809-1884 ................DLB-99

Carroll, Lewis
1832-1898 ..... DLB-18, 163, 178; CDBLB-4
   The Lewis Carroll Centenary .......... Y-98
   The Lewis Carroll Society
     of North America ................ Y-00
Carroll, Paul 1927- ................. DLB-16
Carroll, Paul Vincent 1900-1968 ........ DLB-10
Carroll and Graf Publishers ............ DLB-46
Carruth, Hayden 1921- .......... DLB-5, 165
   Tribute to James Dickey .............. Y-97
   Tribute to Raymond Carver .......... Y-88
Carryl, Charles E. 1841-1920........... DLB-42
Carson, Anne 1950- ................ DLB-193
Carson, Rachel 1907-1964 ............. DLB-275
Carswell, Catherine 1879-1946......... DLB-36
Cartagena, Alfonso de ca. 1384-1456.... DLB-286
Cartagena, Teresa de 1425?-?........ DLB-286
Cărtărescu, Mirea 1956- ............. DLB-232
Carter, Angela 1940-1992....... DLB-14, 207, 261
Carter, Elizabeth 1717-1806 ....... DLB-109
Carter, Henry (see Leslie, Frank)
Carter, Hodding, Jr. 1907-1972........ DLB-127
Carter, Jared 1939- ................ DLB-282
Carter, John 1905-1975............. DLB-201
Carter, Landon 1710-1778.............. DLB-31
Carter, Lin 1930-1988 .................. Y-81
Carter, Martin 1927-1997 .... DLB-117; CDWLB-3
Carter, Robert, and Brothers .......... DLB-49
Carter and Hendee................. DLB-49
Cartwright, Jim 1958- ............. DLB-245
Cartwright, John 1740-1824 ......... DLB-158
Cartwright, William circa 1611-1643 .... DLB-126
Caruthers, William Alexander
1802-1846 ................ DLB-3, 248
Carver, Jonathan 1710-1780 ........... DLB-31
Carver, Raymond 1938-1988... DLB-130; Y-83,88
   First Strauss "Livings" Awarded to Cynthia
     Ozick and Raymond Carver
     An Interview with Raymond Carver.. Y-83
Carvic, Heron 1917?-1980 .............DLB-276
Cary, Alice 1820-1871................ DLB-202
Cary, Joyce 1888-1957 ... DLB-15, 100; CDBLB-6
Cary, Patrick 1623?-1657 ............. DLB-131
Casal, Julián del 1863-1893 ........... DLB-283
Case, John 1540-1600................. DLB-281
Casey, Gavin 1907-1964............... DLB-260
Casey, Juanita 1925- ................ DLB-14
Casey, Michael 1947- ............... DLB-5
Cassady, Carolyn 1923- ............. DLB-16
   "As I See It" ..................... DLB-16
Cassady, Neal 1926-1968 ......... DLB-16, 237
Cassell and Company................ DLB-106
Cassell Publishing Company .......... DLB-49
Cassill, R. V. 1919- ............DLB-6, 218; Y-02
   Tribute to James Dickey .............. Y-97

Cassity, Turner 1929- ..........DLB-105; Y-02
Cassius Dio circa 155/164-post 229 ......DLB-176
Cassola, Carlo 1917-1987 ............DLB-177
Castellano, Olivia 1944- ........... DLB-122
Castellanos, Rosario
1925-1974............DLB-113; CDWLB-3
Castelo Branco, Camilo 1825-1890 ..... DLB-287
Castile, Protest Poetry in ............. DLB-286
Castile and Aragon, Vernacular Translations
   in Crowns of 1352-1515............ DLB-286
Castillo, Ana 1953- .............DLB-122, 227
Castillo, Rafael C. 1950- ............. DLB-209
The Castle of Perseverance circa 1400-1425 . DLB-146
Castlemon, Harry (see Fosdick, Charles Austin)
Čašule, Kole 1921- ................ DLB-181
Caswall, Edward 1814-1878............ DLB-32
Catacalos, Rosemary 1944- ......... DLB-122
Cather, Willa 1873-1947
   ........ DLB-9, 54, 78, 256; DS-1; CDALB-3
   The Willa Cather Pioneer Memorial
     and Education Foundation ......... Y-00
Catherine II (Ekaterina Alekseevna), "The Great,"
   Empress of Russia 1729-1796....... DLB-150
Catherwood, Mary Hartwell 1847-1902... DLB-78
Catledge, Turner 1901-1983 .......... DLB-127
Catlin, George 1796-1872 ......... DLB-186, 189
Cato the Elder 234 B.C.-149 B.C. ...... DLB-211
Cattafi, Bartolo 1922-1979 ........... DLB-128
Catton, Bruce 1899-1978 .............. DLB-17
Catullus circa 84 B.C.-54 B.C.
   .................... DLB-211; CDWLB-1
Causley, Charles 1917- ............. DLB-27
Caute, David 1936- ........... DLB-14, 231
Cavendish, Duchess of Newcastle,
   Margaret Lucas
   1623?-1673............. DLB-131, 252, 281
Cawein, Madison 1865-1914 ........... DLB-54
William Caxton [publishing house] ......DLB-170
The Caxton Printers, Limited .......... DLB-46
Caylor, O. P. 1849-1897.............DLB-241
Cayrol, Jean 1911- ................. DLB-83
Cecil, Lord David 1902-1986......... DLB-155
Cela, Camilo José 1916-2002 .............. Y-89
   Nobel Lecture 1989 ................... Y-89
Celan, Paul 1920-1970 ...... DLB-69; CDWLB-2
Celati, Gianni 1937- ............... DLB-196
Celaya, Gabriel 1911-1991 ........... DLB-108
Céline, Louis-Ferdinand 1894-1961 ..... DLB-72
Celtis, Conrad 1459-1508.............DLB-179
Cendrars, Blaise 1887-1961 ........... DLB-258
The Steinbeck Centennial................. Y-02
Censorship
   The Island Trees Case: A Symposium on
     School Library Censorship ......... Y-82
Center for Bibliographical Studies and
   Research at the University of
   California, Riverside ................ Y-91
Center for Book Research .............. Y-84

The Center for the Book in the Library
   of Congress ........................ Y-93
   A New Voice: The Center for the
     Book's First Five Years ............ Y-83
Centlivre, Susanna 1669?-1723.......... DLB-84
The Centre for Writing, Publishing and
   Printing History at the University
   of Reading ....................... Y-00
The Century Company ................ DLB-49
A Century of Poetry, a Lifetime of Collecting:
   J. M. Edelstein's Collection of
   Twentieth-Century American Poetry .... Y-02
Cernuda, Luis 1902-1963............. DLB-134
Cerruto, Oscar 1912-1981 ............ DLB-283
Cervantes, Lorna Dee 1954- ......... DLB-82
de Céspedes, Alba 1911-1997.......... DLB-264
Ch., T. (see Marchenko, Anastasiia Iakovlevna)
Chaadaev, Petr Iakovlevich
   1794-1856....................... DLB-198
Chabon, Michael 1963- ............DLB-278
Chacel, Rosa 1898-1994............. DLB-134
Chacón, Eusebio 1869-1948............ DLB-82
Chacón, Felipe Maximiliano 1873-? ...... DLB-82
Chadwick, Henry 1824-1908 ......... DLB-241
Chadwyck-Healey's Full-Text Literary Databases:
   Editing Commercial Databases of
   Primary Literary Texts ............. Y-95
Challans, Eileen Mary (see Renault, Mary)
Chalmers, George 1742-1825 ........... DLB-30
Chaloner, Sir Thomas 1520-1565 ...... DLB-167
Chamberlain, Samuel S. 1851-1916 ...... DLB-25
Chamberland, Paul 1939- ........... DLB-60
Chamberlin, William Henry 1897-1969 ... DLB-29
Chambers, Charles Haddon 1860-1921 ... DLB-10
Chambers, María Cristina (see Mena, María Cristina)
Chambers, Robert W. 1865-1933 ...... DLB-202
W. and R. Chambers
   [publishing house] ............... DLB-106
Chamisso, Adelbert von 1781-1838 ...... DLB-90
Champfleury 1821-1889............... DLB-119
Chandler, Harry 1864-1944............ DLB-29
Chandler, Norman 1899-1973 .........DLB-127
Chandler, Otis 1927- .............DLB-127
Chandler, Raymond
   1888-1959 ... DLB-226, 253; DS-6; CDALB-5
   Raymond Chandler Centenary ......... Y-88
Channing, Edward 1856-1931 ..........DLB-17
Channing, Edward Tyrrell
   1790-1856.................. DLB-1, 59, 235
Channing, William Ellery
   1780-1842 .................. DLB-1, 59, 235
Channing, William Ellery, II
   1817-1901 ................... DLB-1, 223
Channing, William Henry
   1810-1884 .................. DLB-1, 59, 243
Chapelain, Jean 1595-1674.............DLB-268
Chaplin, Charlie 1889-1977 ........... DLB-44
Chapman, George
   1559 or 1560-1634............. DLB-62, 121

Chapman, Olive Murray 1892-1977 . . . . . DLB-195
Chapman, R. W. 1881-1960 . . . . . . . . . . DLB-201
Chapman, William 1850-1917 . . . . . . . . . . DLB-99
John Chapman [publishing house] . . . . . . . DLB-106
Chapman and Hall [publishing house] . . . . DLB-106
Chappell, Fred 1936-  . . . . . . . . . . . . DLB-6, 105
 "A Detail in a Poem" . . . . . . . . . . . . . DLB-105
 Tribute to Peter Taylor . . . . . . . . . . . . . Y-94
Chappell, William 1582-1649 . . . . . . . . . DLB-236
Char, René 1907-1988 . . . . . . . . . . . . . . DLB-258
Charbonneau, Jean 1875-1960 . . . . . . . . . DLB-92
Charbonneau, Robert 1911-1967 . . . . . . . . DLB-68
Charles, Gerda 1914-  . . . . . . . . . . . . . DLB-14
William Charles [publishing house] . . . . . . DLB-49
Charles d'Orléans 1394-1465 . . . . . . . . . DLB-208
Charley (see Mann, Charles)
Charteris, Leslie 1907-1993 . . . . . . . . . . . DLB-77
Chartier, Alain circa 1385-1430 . . . . . . . . DLB-208
Charyn, Jerome 1937-  . . . . . . . . . . . . . . Y-83
Chase, Borden 1900-1971 . . . . . . . . . . . . DLB-26
Chase, Edna Woolman 1877-1957 . . . . . . . DLB-91
Chase, James Hadley (René Raymond)
 1906-1985 . . . . . . . . . . . . . . . . . . . . DLB-276
Chase, Mary Coyle 1907-1981 . . . . . . . . . DLB-228
Chase-Riboud, Barbara 1936-   . . . . . . . . . DLB-33
Chateaubriand, François-René de
 1768-1848 . . . . . . . . . . . . . . . . . . . DLB-119
Chatterton, Thomas 1752-1770 . . . . . . . . DLB-109
 Essay on Chatterton (1842), by
  Robert Browning . . . . . . . . . . . . . . DLB-32
Chatto and Windus . . . . . . . . . . . . . . . DLB-106
Chatwin, Bruce 1940-1989 . . . . . . . DLB-194, 204
Chaucer, Geoffrey
 1340?-1400 . . . . . . . . . DLB-146; CDBLB-1
 New Chaucer Society . . . . . . . . . . . . . . . Y-00
Chaudhuri, Amit 1962-   . . . . . . . . . . . . DLB-267
Chauncy, Charles 1705-1787 . . . . . . . . . . DLB-24
Chauveau, Pierre-Joseph-Olivier
 1820-1890 . . . . . . . . . . . . . . . . . . . . DLB-99
Chávez, Denise 1948-  . . . . . . . . . . . . . DLB-122
Chávez, Fray Angélico 1910-1996 . . . . . . . DLB-82
Chayefsky, Paddy 1923-1981 . . . . DLB-7, 44; Y-81
Cheesman, Evelyn 1881-1969 . . . . . . . . . DLB-195
Cheever, Ezekiel 1615-1708 . . . . . . . . . . . DLB-24
Cheever, George Barrell 1807-1890 . . . . . . DLB-59
Cheever, John 1912-1982
 . . . . . . DLB-2, 102, 227; Y-80, 82; CDALB-1
Cheever, Susan 1943-  . . . . . . . . . . . . . . . Y-82
Cheke, Sir John 1514-1557 . . . . . . . . . . . DLB-132
Chekhov, Anton Pavlovich 1860-1904 . . . DLB-277
Chelsea House . . . . . . . . . . . . . . . . . . . DLB-46
Chênedollé, Charles de 1769-1833 . . . . . . DLB-217
Cheney, Brainard
 Tribute to Caroline Gordon . . . . . . . . . . Y-81
Cheney, Ednah Dow 1824-1904 . . . . . . DLB-1, 223
Cheney, Harriet Vaughan 1796-1889 . . . . . DLB-99

Chénier, Marie-Joseph 1764-1811 . . . . . . . DLB-192
Chernyshevsky, Nikolai Gavrilovich
 1828-1889 . . . . . . . . . . . . . . . . . . . DLB-238
Cherry, Kelly 1940  . . . . . . . . . . . . . . . . . Y-83
Cherryh, C. J. 1942-   . . . . . . . . . . . . . . . Y-80
Chesebro', Caroline 1825-1873 . . . . . . . . DLB-202
Chesney, Sir George Tomkyns
 1830-1895 . . . . . . . . . . . . . . . . . . . DLB-190
Chesnut, Mary Boykin 1823-1886 . . . . . . DLB-239
Chesnutt, Charles Waddell
 1858-1932 . . . . . . . . . . . . . DLB-12, 50, 78
Chesson, Mrs. Nora (see Hopper, Nora)
Chester, Alfred 1928-1971 . . . . . . . . . . . DLB-130
Chester, George Randolph 1869-1924 . . . . DLB-78
The Chester Plays circa 1505-1532;
 revisions until 1575 . . . . . . . . . . . . . DLB-146
Chesterfield, Philip Dormer Stanhope,
 Fourth Earl of 1694-1773 . . . . . . . . . DLB-104
Chesterton, G. K. 1874-1936
 . . DLB-10, 19, 34, 70, 98, 149, 178; CDBLB-6
 "The Ethics of Elfland" (1908) . . . . . . DLB-178
Chettle, Henry circa 1560-circa 1607 . . . . . DLB-136
Cheuse, Alan 1940-   . . . . . . . . . . . . . . . DLB-244
Chew, Ada Nield 1870-1945 . . . . . . . . . . DLB-135
Cheyney, Edward P. 1861-1947 . . . . . . . . . DLB-47
Chiara, Piero 1913-1986 . . . . . . . . . . . . DLB-177
Chicanos
 Chicano History . . . . . . . . . . . . . . . . DLB-82
 Chicano Language . . . . . . . . . . . . . . . DLB-82
 Chincano Literature: A Bibliography . DLB-209
 A Contemporary Flourescence of Chicano
  Literature . . . . . . . . . . . . . . . . . . . . Y-84
 Literatura Chicanesca: The View From
  Without . . . . . . . . . . . . . . . . . . . DLB-82
Child, Francis James 1825-1896 . . . . DLB-1, 64, 235
Child, Lydia Maria 1802-1880 . . . . DLB-1, 74, 243
Child, Philip 1898-1978 . . . . . . . . . . . . . DLB-68
Childers, Erskine 1870-1922 . . . . . . . . . . DLB-70
Children's Literature
 Afterword: Propaganda, Namby-Pamby,
  and Some Books of Distinction . . . DLB-52
 Children's Book Awards and Prizes . . . DLB-61
 Children's Book Illustration in the
  Twentieth Century . . . . . . . . . . . . DLB-61
 Children's Illustrators, 1800-1880 . . . . DLB-163
 The Harry Potter Phenomenon . . . . . . . Y-99
 Pony Stories, Omnibus
  Essay on . . . . . . . . . . . . . . . . . . . DLB-160
 The Reality of One Woman's Dream:
  The de Grummond Children's
  Literature Collection . . . . . . . . . . . . Y-99
 School Stories, 1914-1960 . . . . . . . . . DLB-160
 The Year in Children's
  Books . . . . . . . . . . . . . . . . Y-92–96, 98–01
 The Year in Children's Literature . . . . . . Y-97
Childress, Alice 1916-1994 . . . . . . DLB-7, 38, 249
Childs, George W. 1829-1894 . . . . . . . . . . DLB-23
Chilton Book Company . . . . . . . . . . . . . . DLB-46
Chin, Frank 1940-   . . . . . . . . . . . . . . . DLB-206

Chinweizu 1943-  . . . . . . . . . . . . . . . . . DLB-157
Chitham, Edward 1932-   . . . . . . . . . . . . DLB-155
Chittenden, Hiram Martin 1858-1917 . . . . DLB-47
Chivers, Thomas Holley 1809-1858 . . . DLB-3, 248
Chkhartishvili, Grigorii Shalvovich
 (see Akunin, Boris)
Cholmondeley, Mary 1859-1925 . . . . . . . DLB-197
Chomsky, Noam 1928-  . . . . . . . . . . . . . DLB-246
Chopin, Kate 1850-1904 . . . DLB-12, 78; CDALB-3
Chopin, René 1885-1953 . . . . . . . . . . . . . DLB-92
Choquette, Adrienne 1915-1973 . . . . . . . . DLB-68
Choquette, Robert 1905-1991 . . . . . . . . . . DLB-68
Choyce, Lesley 1951-  . . . . . . . . . . . . . . DLB-251
Chrétien de Troyes
 circa 1140-circa 1190 . . . . . . . . . . . . DLB-208
Christensen, Inger 1935-   . . . . . . . . . . . DLB-214
*The Christian Examiner* . . . . . . . . . . . . . . DLB-1
The Christian Publishing Company . . . . . . DLB-49
Christie, Agatha
 1890-1976 . . . . . . . DLB-13, 77, 245; CDBLB-6
Christine de Pizan circa 1365-circa 1431 . . DLB-208
Christopher, John (Sam Youd) 1922-  . . . DLB-255
*Christus und die Samariterin* circa 950 . . . . . DLB-148
Christy, Howard Chandler 1873-1952 . . . DLB-188
Chulkov, Mikhail Dmitrievich
 1743?-1792 . . . . . . . . . . . . . . . . . . . DLB-150
Church, Benjamin 1734-1778 . . . . . . . . . . DLB-31
Church, Francis Pharcellus 1839-1906 . . . . DLB-79
Church, Peggy Pond 1903-1986 . . . . . . . . DLB-212
Church, Richard 1893-1972 . . . . . . . . . . DLB-191
Church, William Conant 1836-1917 . . . . . . DLB-79
Churchill, Caryl 1938-  . . . . . . . . . . . . . . DLB-13
Churchill, Charles 1731-1764 . . . . . . . . . DLB-109
Churchill, Winston 1871-1947 . . . . . . . . . DLB-202
Churchill, Sir Winston
 1874-1965 . . . . . . DLB-100; DS-16; CDBLB-5
Churchyard, Thomas 1520?-1604 . . . . . . . DLB-132
E. Churton and Company . . . . . . . . . . . DLB-106
Chute, Marchette 1909-1994 . . . . . . . . . . DLB-103
Ciardi, John 1916-1986 . . . . . . . . . DLB-5; Y-86
Cibber, Colley 1671-1757 . . . . . . . . . . . . DLB-84
Cicero 106 B.C.-43 B.C. . . . . DLB-211, CDWLB-1
Cima, Annalisa 1941-  . . . . . . . . . . . . . DLB-128
Čingo, Živko 1935-1987 . . . . . . . . . . . . DLB-181
Cioran, E. M. 1911-1995 . . . . . . . . . . . . DLB-220
Čipkus, Alfonsas (see Nyka-Niliūnas, Alfonsas)
Cirese, Eugenio 1884-1955 . . . . . . . . . . . DLB-114
Cīrulis, Jānis (see Bels, Alberts)
Cisneros, Sandra 1954-   . . . . . . . . DLB-122, 152
City Lights Books . . . . . . . . . . . . . . . . . DLB-46
Civil War (1861–1865)
 Battles and Leaders of the Civil War . . DLB-47
 Official Records of the Rebellion . . . . . DLB-47
 Recording the Civil War . . . . . . . . . . . DLB-47
Cixous, Hélène 1937-  . . . . . . . . . . . DLB-83, 242
Clampitt, Amy 1920-1994 . . . . . . . . . . . DLB-105

Tribute to Alfred A. Knopf ............ Y-84

Clancy, Tom 1947- ................ DLB-227

Clapper, Raymond 1892-1944 .......... DLB-29

Clare, John 1793-1864 ............. DLB-55, 96

Clarendon, Edward Hyde, Earl of
1609-1674..................... DLB-101

Clark, Alfred Alexander Gordon
(see Hare, Cyril)

Clark, Ann Nolan 1896- ............. DLB-52

Clark, C. E. Frazer, Jr. 1925-2001 ..DLB-187; Y-01

    C. E. Frazer Clark Jr. and
    Hawthorne Bibliography........ DLB-269

    The Publications of C. E. Frazer
    Clark Jr..................... DLB-269

Clark, Catherine Anthony 1892-1977..... DLB-68

Clark, Charles Heber 1841-1915 ........ DLB-11

Clark, Davis Wasgatt 1812-1871 ........ DLB-79

Clark, Douglas 1919-1993 ............. DLB-276

Clark, Eleanor 1913- ................ DLB-6

Clark, J. P. 1935- ........ DLB-117; CDWLB-3

Clark, Lewis Gaylord
1808-1873............. DLB-3, 64, 73, 250

Clark, Walter Van Tilburg
1909-1971................... DLB-9, 206

Clark, William 1770-1838......... DLB-183, 186

Clark, William Andrews, Jr. 1877-1934 .. DLB-187

C. M. Clark Publishing Company ....... DLB-46

Clarke, Sir Arthur C. 1917- ......... DLB-261

    Tribute to Theodore Sturgeon.......... Y-85

Clarke, Austin 1896-1974 .......... DLB-10, 20

Clarke, Austin C. 1934- ........ DLB-53, 125

Clarke, Gillian 1937- ................ DLB-40

Clarke, James Freeman
1810-1888............. DLB-1, 59, 235; DS-5

Clarke, John circa 1596-1658 ......... DLB-281

Clarke, Lindsay 1939- ............... DLB-231

Clarke, Marcus 1846-1881 ............ DLB-230

Clarke, Pauline 1921- ............... DLB-161

Clarke, Rebecca Sophia 1833-1906 ...... DLB-42

Clarke, Samuel 1675-1729............ DLB-252

Robert Clarke and Company........... DLB-49

Clarkson, Thomas 1760-1846.......... DLB-158

Claudel, Paul 1868-1955........... DLB-192, 258

Claudius, Matthias 1740-1815 .......... DLB-97

Clausen, Andy 1943- ................ DLB-16

Clawson, John L. 1865-1933 .......... DLB-187

Claxton, Remsen and Haffelfinger....... DLB-49

Clay, Cassius Marcellus 1810-1903 ...... DLB-43

Clayton, Richard (seed Haggard, William)

Cleage, Pearl 1948- ................ DLB-228

Cleary, Beverly 1916- ............... DLB-52

Cleary, Kate McPhelim 1863-1905...... DLB-221

Cleaver, Vera 1919-1992 and
Cleaver, Bill 1920-1981............ DLB-52

Cleeve, Brian 1921- ................DLB-276

Cleland, John 1710-1789 ............ DLB-39

Clemens, Samuel Langhorne (Mark Twain)
1835-1910 ......... DLB-11, 12, 23, 64, 74,
186, 189; CDALB-3

    Comments From Authors and Scholars on
    their First Reading of *Huck Finn* ..... Y-85

    Huck at 100: How Old Is
    Huckleberry Finn?................ Y-85

    Mark Twain on Perpetual Copyright .... Y-92

    A New Edition of *Huck Finn*........... Y-85

Clement, Hal 1922- .................. DLB-8

Clemo, Jack 1916- .................. DLB-27

Clephane, Elizabeth Cecilia 1830-1869 .. DLB-199

Cleveland, John 1613-1658............ DLB-126

Cliff, Michelle 1946- ......DLB-157; CDWLB-3

Clifford, Lady Anne 1590-1676 ........ DLB-151

Clifford, James L. 1901-1978 .......... DLB-103

Clifford, Lucy 1853?-1929 .....DLB-135, 141, 197

Clift, Charmian 1923-1969............ DLB-260

Clifton, Lucille 1936- ............... DLB-5, 41

Clines, Francis X. 1938- ............ DLB-185

Clive, Caroline (V) 1801-1873 ......... DLB-199

Edward J. Clode [publishing house] ...... DLB-46

Clough, Arthur Hugh 1819-1861 ........ DLB-32

Cloutier, Cécile 1930- ............... DLB-60

Clouts, Sidney 1926-1982............. DLB-225

Clutton-Brock, Arthur 1868-1924 ...... DLB-98

Coates, Robert M.
1897-1973.............DLB-4, 9, 102; DS-15

Coatsworth, Elizabeth 1893-1986........ DLB-22

Cobb, Charles E., Jr. 1943- ............ DLB-41

Cobb, Frank I. 1869-1923 ............. DLB-25

Cobb, Irvin S. 1876-1944 ........ DLB-11, 25, 86

Cobbe, Frances Power 1822-1904 ...... DLB-190

Cobbett, William 1763-1835..... DLB-43, 107, 158

Cobbledick, Gordon 1898-1969 ........DLB-171

Cochran, Thomas C. 1902- ........... DLB-17

Cochrane, Elizabeth 1867-1922 ..... DLB-25, 189

Cockerell, Sir Sydney 1867-1962 ....... DLB-201

Cockerill, John A. 1845-1896........... DLB-23

Cocteau, Jean 1889-1963 ......... DLB-65, 258

Coderre, Emile (see Jean Narrache)

Cody, Liza 1944- ....................DLB-276

Coe, Jonathan 1961- ............... DLB-231

Coetzee, J. M. 1940- ................ DLB-225

Coffee, Lenore J. 1900?-1984 ........... DLB-44

Coffin, Robert P. Tristram 1892-1955 .... DLB-45

Coghill, Mrs. Harry (see Walker, Anna Louisa)

Cogswell, Fred 1917- ................ DLB-60

Cogswell, Mason Fitch 1761-1830 ....... DLB-37

Cohan, George M. 1878-1942 ......... DLB-249

Cohen, Arthur A. 1928-1986 ........... DLB-28

Cohen, Leonard 1934- ............... DLB-53

Cohen, Matt 1942- .................. DLB-53

Cohen, Morris Raphael 1880-1947.......DLB-270

Colbeck, Norman 1903-1987 ......... DLB-201

Colden, Cadwallader 1688-1776...DLB-24, 30, 270

Colden, Jane 1724-1766 .............. DLB-200

Cole, Barry 1936- .................. DLB-14

Cole, George Watson 1850-1939....... DLB-140

Colegate, Isabel 1931- ........... DLB-14, 231

Coleman, Emily Holmes 1899-1974....... DLB-4

Coleman, Wanda 1946- ............. DLB-130

Coleridge, Hartley 1796-1849.......... DLB-96

Coleridge, Mary 1861-1907 ......... DLB-19, 98

Coleridge, Samuel Taylor
1772-1834.......... DLB-93, 107; CDBLB-3

Coleridge, Sara 1802-1852 ............ DLB-199

Colet, John 1467-1519 ............... DLB-132

Colette 1873-1954.................. DLB-65

Colette, Sidonie Gabrielle (see Colette)

Colinas, Antonio 1946- .............. DLB-134

Coll, Joseph Clement 1881-1921 ....... DLB-188

A Century of Poetry, a Lifetime of Collecting:
J. M. Edelstein's Collection of
Twentieth-Century American Poetry .... Y-02

Collier, John 1901-1980 ............DLB-77, 255

Collier, John Payne 1789-1883 ......... DLB-184

Collier, Mary 1690-1762.............. DLB-95

Collier, Robert J. 1876-1918............ DLB-91

P. F. Collier [publishing house]......... DLB-49

Collin and Small.................... DLB-49

Collingwood, R. G. 1889-1943 ........ DLB-262

Collingwood, W. G. 1854-1932 ........ DLB-149

Collins, An floruit circa 1653 .......... DLB-131

Collins, Anthony 1676-1729........... DLB-252

Collins, Merle 1950- .................DLB-157

Collins, Michael 1964- .............. DLB-267

    Tribute to John D. MacDonald ......... Y-86

    Tribute to Kenneth Millar ............. Y-83

    Why I Write Mysteries: Night and Day .. Y-85

Collins, Mortimer 1827-1876 ........ DLB-21, 35

Collins, Tom (see Furphy, Joseph)

Collins, Wilkie
1824-1889 ....... DLB-18, 70, 159; CDBLB-4

    "The Unknown Public" (1858)
    [excerpt]..................... DLB-57

    The Wilkie Collins Society ............ Y-98

Collins, William 1721-1759............ DLB-109

Isaac Collins [publishing house] ......... DLB-49

William Collins, Sons and Company.... DLB-154

Collis, Maurice 1889-1973 ............ DLB-195

Collyer, Mary 1716?-1763?.............. DLB-39

Colman, Benjamin 1673-1747.......... DLB-24

Colman, George, the Elder 1732-1794 .... DLB-89

Colman, George, the Younger
1762-1836..................... DLB-89

S. Colman [publishing house].......... DLB-49

Colombo, John Robert 1936- ......... DLB-53

Colquhoun, Patrick 1745-1820 ........ DLB-158

Colter, Cyrus 1910-2002 .............. DLB-33

Colum, Padraic 1881-1972............ DLB-19

*The Columbia History of the American Novel*
    A Symposium on.....................Y-92

Columella fl. first century A.D..........DLB-211

Colvin, Sir Sidney 1845-1927..........DLB-149

Colwin, Laurie 1944-1992........DLB-218; Y-80

Comden, Betty 1915- and
    Green, Adolph 1918- .........DLB-44, 265

Comi, Girolamo 1890-1968............DLB-114

Comisso, Giovanni 1895-1969..........DLB-264

Commager, Henry Steele 1902-1998......DLB-17

Commynes, Philippe de
    circa 1447-1511 ..................DLB-208

Compton, D. G. 1930- ...............DLB-261

Compton-Burnett, Ivy 1884?-1969 .......DLB-36

Conan, Laure (Félicité Angers)
    1845-1924.......................DLB-99

Concord, Massachusetts
    Concord History and Life..........DLB-223

    Concord: Literary History
        of a Town...................DLB-223

    The Old Manse, by Hawthorne.....DLB-223

    The Thoreauvian Pilgrimage: The
        Structure of an American Cult...DLB-223

Conde, Carmen 1901-1996............DLB-108

Congreve, William
    1670-1729 .......... DLB-39, 84; CDBLB-2

    Preface to *Incognita* (1692) ...........DLB-39

W. B. Conkey Company..............DLB-49

Conn, Stewart 1936- ...............DLB-233

Connell, Evan S., Jr. 1924- ........DLB-2; Y-81

Connelly, Marc 1890-1980 .........DLB-7; Y-80

Connolly, Cyril 1903-1974..............DLB-98

Connolly, James B. 1868-1957..........DLB-78

Connor, Ralph (Charles William Gordon)
    1860-1937.......................DLB-92

Connor, Tony 1930- ................DLB-40

Conquest, Robert 1917- ..............DLB-27

Conrad, Joseph
    1857-1924 ....DLB-10, 34, 98, 156; CDBLB-5

John Conrad and Company ............DLB-49

Conroy, Jack 1899-1990 ................Y-81

    A Tribute [to Nelson Algren] ........Y-81

Conroy, Pat 1945- .................DLB-6

Considine, Bob 1906-1975..............DLB-241

Consolo, Vincenzo 1933- ............DLB-196

Constable, Henry 1562-1613...........DLB-136

Archibald Constable and Company .....DLB-154

Constable and Company Limited .......DLB-112

Constant, Benjamin 1767-1830...........DLB-119

Constant de Rebecque, Henri-Benjamin de
    (see Constant, Benjamin)

Constantine, David 1944- ............DLB-40

Constantine, Murray (see Burdekin, Katharine)

Constantin-Weyer, Maurice 1881-1964....DLB-92

*Contempo* (magazine)
    Contempo Caravan:
        Kites in a Windstorm............Y-85

The Continental Publishing Company ....DLB-49

A Conversation between William Riggan
    and Janette Turner Hospital..........Y-02

Conversations with Editors...............Y-95

Conway, Anne 1631-1679..............DLB-252

Conway, Moncure Daniel
    1832-1907....................DLB-1, 223

Cook, Ebenezer circa 1667-circa 1732.....DLB-24

Cook, Edward Tyas 1857-1919.........DLB-149

Cook, Eliza 1818-1889................DLB-199

Cook, George Cram 1873-1924.........DLB-266

Cook, Michael 1933-1994..............DLB-53

David C. Cook Publishing Company .....DLB-49

Cooke, George Willis 1848-1923.........DLB-71

Cooke, John Esten 1830-1886........DLB-3, 248

Cooke, Philip Pendleton
    1816-1850 .................DLB-3, 59, 248

Cooke, Rose Terry 1827-1892........DLB-12, 74

Increase Cooke and Company ..........DLB-49

Cook-Lynn, Elizabeth 1930-  .........DLB-175

Coolbrith, Ina 1841-1928...........DLB-54, 186

Cooley, Peter 1940- ................DLB-105

    "Into the Mirror" ................DLB-105

Coolidge, Clark 1939- ..............DLB-193

Coolidge, Susan (see Woolsey, Sarah Chauncy)

George Coolidge [publishing house] ......DLB-49

Cooper, Anna Julia 1858-1964 .........DLB-221

Cooper, Edith Emma 1862-1913........DLB-240

Cooper, Giles 1918-1966................DLB-13

Cooper, J. California 19??- ............DLB-212

Cooper, James Fenimore
    1789-1851 .......DLB-3, 183, 250; CDALB-2

    The Bicentennial of James Fenimore Cooper:
        An International Celebration .......Y-89

    The James Fenimore Cooper Society ....Y-01

Cooper, Kent 1880-1965...............DLB-29

Cooper, Susan 1935- ...........DLB-161, 261

Cooper, Susan Fenimore 1813-1894 .....DLB-239

William Cooper [publishing house].......DLB-170

J. Coote [publishing house] ...........DLB-154

Coover, Robert 1932- ....... DLB-2, 227; Y-81

    Tribute to Donald Barthelme..........Y-89

    Tribute to Theodor Seuss Geisel .......Y-91

Copeland and Day....................DLB-49

Ćopić, Branko 1915-1984 ..............DLB-181

Copland, Robert 1470?-1548..........DLB-136

Coppard, A. E. 1878-1957 ............DLB-162

Coppée, François 1842-1908 ..........DLB-217

Coppel, Alfred 1921- ...................Y-83

    Tribute to Jessamyn West............Y-84

Coppola, Francis Ford 1939- .........DLB-44

Copway, George (Kah-ge-ga-gah-bowh)
    1818-1869 ..................DLB-175, 183

Copyright
    The Development of the Author's
        Copyright in Britain..........DLB-154

The Digital Millennium Copyright Act:
    Expanding Copyright Protection in
    Cyberspace and Beyond..........Y-98

Editorial: The Extension of Copyright...Y-02

Mark Twain on Perpetual Copyright....Y-92

Public Domain and the Violation
    of Texts ........................Y-97

The Question of American Copyright
    in the Nineteenth Century
    Preface, by George Haven Putnam
    The Evolution of Copyright, by
        Brander Matthews
    Summary of Copyright Legislation in
        the United States, by R. R. Bowker
    Analysis of the Provisions of the
        Copyright Law of 1891, by
        George Haven Putnam
    The Contest for International Copyright,
        by George Haven Putnam
    Cheap Books and Good Books,
        by Brander Matthews.........DLB-49

Writers and Their Copyright Holders:
    the WATCH Project .............Y-94

Corazzini, Sergio 1886-1907 ...........DLB-114

Corbett, Richard 1582-1635 ...........DLB-121

Corbière, Tristan 1845-1875 ...........DLB-217

Corcoran, Barbara 1911- ..............DLB-52

Cordelli, Franco 1943- ...............DLB-196

Corelli, Marie 1855-1924............DLB-34, 156

Corle, Edwin 1906-1956 .................Y-85

Corman, Cid 1924- ...............DLB-5, 193

Cormier, Robert 1925-2000....DLB-52; CDALB-6

    Tribute to Theodor Seuss Geisel .......Y-91

Corn, Alfred 1943- ........DLB-120, 282; Y-80

Corneille, Pierre 1606-1684 .............DLB-268

Cornford, Frances 1886-1960 ..........DLB-240

Cornish, Sam 1935- .................DLB-41

Cornish, William circa 1465-circa 1524...DLB-132

Cornwall, Barry (see Procter, Bryan Waller)

Cornwallis, Sir William, the Younger
    circa 1579-1614 ..................DLB-151

Cornwell, David John Moore (see le Carré, John)

Corpi, Lucha 1945- .................DLB-82

Corrington, John William 1932-1988 ..DLB-6, 244

Corriveau, Monique 1927-1976.........DLB-251

Corrothers, James D. 1869-1917 ........DLB-50

Corso, Gregory 1930-2001 ....... DLB-5, 16, 237

Cortázar, Julio 1914-1984 ...DLB-113; CDWLB-3

Cortéz, Carlos 1923- ................DLB-209

Cortez, Jayne 1936- ................DLB-41

Corvinus, Gottlieb Siegmund
    1677-1746.......................DLB-168

Corvo, Baron (see Rolfe, Frederick William)

Cory, Annie Sophie (see Cross, Victoria)

Cory, Desmond (Shaun Lloyd McCarthy)
    1928- ........................DLB-276

Cory, William Johnson 1823-1892 .......DLB-35

Coryate, Thomas 1577?-1617 ......DLB-151, 172

Ćosić, Dobrica 1921- .....DLB-181; CDWLB-4

Cosin, John 1595-1672............DLB-151, 213

Cosmopolitan Book Corporation ........DLB-46

Costa, Maria Velho da (see The Three Marias: A Landmark Case in Portuguese Literary History)
Costain, Thomas B. 1885-1965 .......... DLB-9
Coste, Donat (Daniel Boudreau) 1912-1957 ..................... DLB-88
Costello, Louisa Stuart 1799-1870 ....... DLB-166
Cota-Cárdenas, Margarita 1941- ..... DLB-122
Côté, Denis 1954- ............... DLB-251
Cotten, Bruce 1873-1954 ............. DLB-187
Cotter, Joseph Seamon, Jr. 1895-1919 .... DLB-50
Cotter, Joseph Seamon, Sr. 1861-1949 .... DLB-50
Joseph Cottle [publishing house]......... DLB-154
Cotton, Charles 1630-1687............. DLB-131
Cotton, John 1584-1652 ............... DLB-24
Cotton, Sir Robert Bruce 1571-1631..... DLB-213
Coulter, John 1888-1980 .............. DLB-68
Cournos, John 1881-1966............... DLB-54
Courteline, Georges 1858-1929 ........ DLB-192
Cousins, Margaret 1905-1996 .......... DLB-137
Cousins, Norman 1915-1990 .......... DLB-137
Couvreur, Jessie (see Tasma)
Coventry, Francis 1725-1754 ........... DLB-39
Dedication, *The History of Pompey the Little* (1751) ................ DLB-39
Coverdale, Miles 1487 or 1488-1569 .... DLB-167
N. Coverly [publishing house] .......... DLB-49
Covici-Friede ...................... DLB-46
Cowan, Peter 1914-2002 ............. DLB-260
Coward, Noel 1899-1973.......... DLB-10, 245; CDBLB-6
Coward, McCann and Geoghegan....... DLB-46
Cowles, Gardner 1861-1946............ DLB-29
Cowles, Gardner "Mike", Jr. 1903-1985 ................DLB-127, 137
Cowley, Abraham 1618-1667....... DLB-131, 151
Cowley, Hannah 1743-1809 ............ DLB-89
Cowley, Malcolm 1898-1989 .......DLB-4, 48; DS-15; Y-81, 89
Cowper, Richard (John Middleton Murry Jr.) 1926-2002 .................. DLB-261
Cowper, William 1731-1800....... DLB-104, 109
Cox, A. B. (see Berkeley, Anthony)
Cox, James McMahon 1903-1974....... DLB-127
Cox, James Middleton 1870-1957....... DLB-127
Cox, Leonard circa 1495-circa 1550..... DLB-281
Cox, Palmer 1840-1924 ................ DLB-42
Coxe, Louis 1918-1993................. DLB-5
Coxe, Tench 1755-1824 ............... DLB-37
Cozzens, Frederick S. 1818-1869 ....... DLB-202
Cozzens, James Gould 1903-1978..... DLB-9; Y-84; DS-2; CDALB-1
Cozzens's *Michael Scarlett* .............. Y-97
Ernest Hemingway's Reaction to James Gould Cozzens ............ Y-98
James Gould Cozzens–A View from Afar..................... Y-97

James Gould Cozzens: How to Read Him ..................... Y-97
James Gould Cozzens Symposium and Exhibition at the University of South Carolina, Columbia........ Y-00
*Mens Rea* (or Something) ............. Y-97
Novels for Grown-Ups................ Y-97
Crabbe, George 1754-1832............. DLB-93
Crace, Jim 1946- ................. DLB-231
Crackanthorpe, Hubert 1870-1896...... DLB-135
Craddock, Charles Egbert (see Murfree, Mary N.)
Cradock, Thomas 1718-1770 ........... DLB-31
Craig, Daniel H. 1811-1895 ............ DLB-43
Craik, Dinah Maria 1826-1887...... DLB-35, 163
Cramer, Richard Ben 1950- ........ DLB-185
Cranch, Christopher Pearse 1813-1892 .......... DLB-1, 42, 243; DS-5
Crane, Hart 1899-1932..... DLB-4, 48; CDALB-4
Nathan Asch Remembers Ford Madox Ford, Sam Roth, and Hart Crane .... Y-02
Crane, R. S. 1886-1967................ DLB-63
Crane, Stephen 1871-1900........ DLB-12, 54, 78; CDALB-3
Stephen Crane: A Revaluation, Virginia Tech Conference, 1989............ Y-89
The Stephen Crane Society ......... Y-98, 01
Crane, Walter 1845-1915.............. DLB-163
Cranmer, Thomas 1489-1556 ..... DLB-132, 213
Crapsey, Adelaide 1878-1914 .......... DLB-54
Crashaw, Richard 1612/1613-1649 ..... DLB-126
Craven, Avery 1885-1980............... DLB-17
Crawford, Charles 1752-circa 1815 ..... DLB-31
Crawford, F. Marion 1854-1909......... DLB-71
Crawford, Isabel Valancy 1850-1887 ..... DLB-92
Crawley, Alan 1887-1975 .............. DLB-68
Crayon, Geoffrey (see Irving, Washington)
Crayon, Porte (see Strother, David Hunter)
Creamer, Robert W. 1922- ...........DLB-171
Creasey, John 1908-1973 ............. DLB-77
Creative Age Press .................. DLB-46
Creative Nonfiction ..................... Y-02
William Creech [publishing house]...... DLB-154
Thomas Creede [publishing house] .....DLB-170
Creel, George 1876-1953 .............. DLB-25
Creeley, Robert 1926- .....DLB-5, 16, 169; DS-17
Creelman, James 1859-1915............ DLB-23
Cregan, David 1931- ............... DLB-13
Creighton, Donald 1902-1979 .......... DLB-88
Crémazie, Octave 1827-1879............ DLB-99
Crémer, Victoriano 1909?- ......... DLB-108
Crescas, Hasdai circa 1340-1412?....... DLB-115
Crespo, Angel 1926-1995 ............ DLB-134
Cresset Press..................... DLB-112
Cresswell, Helen 1934- ............ DLB-161
Crèvecoeur, Michel Guillaume Jean de 1735-1813...................... DLB-37
Crewe, Candida 1964- ............ DLB-207

Crews, Harry 1935- .........DLB-6, 143, 185
Crichton, Michael 1942- ............... Y-81
Crispin, Edmund (Robert Bruce Montgomery) 1921-1978 ............. DLB-87
Cristofer, Michael 1946- .............. DLB-7
Criticism
Afro-American Literary Critics: An Introduction................. DLB-33
The Consolidation of Opinion: Critical Responses to the Modernists..... DLB-36
"Criticism in Relation to Novels" (1863), by G. H. Lewes.......... DLB-21
The Limits of Pluralism............ DLB-67
Modern Critical Terms, Schools, and Movements .................. DLB-67
"Panic Among the Philistines": A Postscript, An Interview with Bryan Griffin................ Y-81
The Recovery of Literature: Criticism in the 1990s: A Symposium ........ Y-91
The Stealthy School of Criticism (1871), by Dante Gabriel Rossetti ....... DLB-35
Crnjanski, Miloš 1893-1977.............DLB-147; CDWLB-4
Crocker, Hannah Mather 1752-1829 .... DLB-200
Crockett, David (Davy) 1786-1836.............DLB-3, 11, 183, 248
Croft-Cooke, Rupert (see Bruce, Leo)
Crofts, Freeman Wills 1879-1957........ DLB-77
Croker, John Wilson 1780-1857........ DLB-110
Croly, George 1780-1860 ............. DLB-159
Croly, Herbert 1869-1930 ............. DLB-91
Croly, Jane Cunningham 1829-1901 ..... DLB-23
Crompton, Richmal 1890-1969 ........ DLB-160
Cronin, A. J. 1896-1981 .............. DLB-191
Cros, Charles 1842-1888 .............DLB-217
Crosby, Caresse 1892-1970 and Crosby, Harry 1898-1929 and . DLB-4; DS-15
Crosby, Harry 1898-1929 ............. DLB-48
Crosland, Camilla Toulmin (Mrs. Newton Crosland) 1812-1895 .......... DLB-240
Cross, Gillian 1945- ............... DLB-161
Cross, Victoria 1868-1952 ........DLB-135, 197
Crossley-Holland, Kevin 1941- .... DLB-40, 161
Crothers, Rachel 1870-1958..........DLB-7, 266
Thomas Y. Crowell Company.......... DLB-49
Crowley, John 1942- ................. Y-82
Crowley, Mart 1935- ...........DLB-7, 266
Crown Publishers.................. DLB-46
Crowne, John 1641-1712 .............. DLB-80
Crowninshield, Edward Augustus 1817-1859..................... DLB-140
Crowninshield, Frank 1872-1947 ........ DLB-91
Croy, Homer 1883-1965 ............... DLB-4
Crumley, James 1939- .........DLB-226; Y-84
Cruse, Mary Anne 1825?-1910 ........ DLB-239
Cruz, Migdalia 1958- ............ DLB-249
Cruz, Victor Hernández 1949- ........ DLB-41
Csokor, Franz Theodor 1885-1969 ...... DLB-81

Csoóri, Sándor 1930- ......DLB-232; CDWLB-4
Cuala Press ........................DLB-112
Cudworth, Ralph 1617-1688 ...........DLB-252
Cugoano, Quobna Ottabah 1797-? ......... Y-02
Cullen, Countee
 1903-1946 ........DLB-4, 48, 51; CDALB-4
Culler, Jonathan D. 1944- ....... DLB-67, 246
Cullinan, Elizabeth 1933- ...........DLB-234
Culverwel, Nathaniel 1619?-1651? .....DLB-252
Cumberland, Richard 1732-1811........DLB-89
Cummings, Constance Gordon
 1837-1924 ....................DLB-174
Cummings, E. E.
 1894-1962 ...........DLB-4, 48; CDALB-5
 The E. E. Cummings Society .......... Y-01
Cummings, Ray 1887-1957 .............DLB-8
Cummings and Hilliard................DLB-49
Cummins, Maria Susanna 1827-1866 .....DLB-42
Cumpián, Carlos 1953- ..............DLB-209
Cunard, Nancy 1896-1965 .............DLB-240
Joseph Cundall [publishing house].......DLB-106
Cuney, Waring 1906-1976..............DLB-51
Cuney-Hare, Maude 1874-1936..........DLB-52
Cunningham, Allan 1784-1842 .....DLB-116, 144
Cunningham, J. V. 1911-1985...........DLB-5
Cunningham, Peter (Peter Lauder, Peter
 Benjamin) 1947- .................DLB-267
Peter F. Cunningham
 [publishing house]..................DLB-49
Cunqueiro, Alvaro 1911-1981..........DLB-134
Cuomo, George 1929- ................. Y-80
Cupples, Upham and Company ........DLB-49
Cupples and Leon ....................DLB-46
Cuppy, Will 1884-1949................DLB-11
Curiel, Barbara Brinson 1956- ........DLB-209
Edmund Curll [publishing house] .......DLB-154
Currie, James 1756-1805 ..............DLB-142
Currie, Mary Montgomerie Lamb Singleton,
 Lady Currie (see Fane, Violet)
Cursor Mundi circa 1300 ...............DLB-146
Curti, Merle E. 1897-1996 ............DLB-17
Curtis, Anthony 1926- ...............DLB-155
Curtis, Cyrus H. K. 1850-1933 .........DLB-91
Curtis, George William
 1824-1892 ...............DLB-1, 43, 223
Curzon, Robert 1810-1873 ...........DLB-166
Curzon, Sarah Anne 1833-1898.........DLB-99
Cusack, Dymphna 1902-1981 ...........DLB-260
Cushing, Eliza Lanesford 1794-1886 ......DLB-99
Cushing, Harvey 1869-1939 ...........DLB-187
Custance, Olive (Lady Alfred Douglas)
 1874-1944 .....................DLB-240
Cynewulf circa 770-840 ...............DLB-146
Cyrano de Bergerac, Savinien de
 1619-1655 .....................DLB-268
Czepko, Daniel 1605-1660..............DLB-164
Czerniawski, Adam 1934- .............DLB-232

# D

Dabit, Eugène 1898-1936...............DLB-65
Daborne, Robert circa 1580-1628 .......DLB-58
Dąbrowska, Maria
 1889-1965 ............DLB-215; CDWLB-4
Dacey, Philip 1939- ................DLB-105
 "Eyes Across Centuries:
 Contemporary Poetry and 'That
 Vision Thing,'" ................DLB-105
Dach, Simon 1605-1659................DLB-164
Dagerman, Stig 1923-1954..............DLB-259
Daggett, Rollin M. 1831-1901 ..........DLB-79
D'Aguiar, Fred 1960- ................DLB-157
Dahl, Roald 1916-1990 ...........DLB-139, 255
 Tribute to Alfred A. Knopf............ Y-84
Dahlberg, Edward 1900-1977 ..........DLB-48
Dahn, Felix 1834-1912.................DLB-129
Dal', Vladimir Ivanovich (Kazak Vladimir
 Lugansky) 1801-1872 ..............DLB-198
Dale, Peter 1938- ....................DLB-40
Daley, Arthur 1904-1974 .............DLB-171
Dall, Caroline Healey 1822-1912......DLB-1, 235
Dallas, E. S. 1828-1879 ...............DLB-55
 *The Gay Science* [excerpt](1866)........DLB-21
The Dallas Theater Center .............DLB-7
D'Alton, Louis 1900-1951 ..............DLB-10
Dalton, Roque 1935-1975 ..............DLB-283
Daly, Carroll John 1889-1958 ..........DLB-226
Daly, T. A. 1871-1948 .................DLB-11
Damon, S. Foster 1893-1971 ............DLB-45
William S. Damrell [publishing house] ....DLB-49
Dana, Charles A. 1819-1897 .....DLB-3, 23, 250
Dana, Richard Henry, Jr.
 1815-1882 ...............DLB-1, 183, 235
Dandridge, Ray Garfield ...............DLB-51
Dane, Clemence 1887-1965 .........DLB-10, 197
Danforth, John 1660-1730 ..............DLB-24
Danforth, Samuel, I 1626-1674 ..........DLB-24
Danforth, Samuel, II 1666-1727 .........DLB-24
Daniel, John M. 1825-1865 .............DLB-43
Daniel, Samuel 1562 or 1563-1619 .......DLB-62
Daniel Press........................DLB-106
Daniells, Roy 1902-1979 ...............DLB-68
Daniels, Jim 1956- ..................DLB-120
Daniels, Jonathan 1902-1981 ..........DLB-127
Daniels, Josephus 1862-1948............DLB-29
Daniels, Sarah 1957- .................DLB-245
Danilevsky, Grigorii Petrovich
 1829-1890.....................DLB-238
Dannay, Frederic 1905-1982 ...........DLB-137
Danner, Margaret Esse 1915- ..........DLB-41
John Danter [publishing house] .........DLB-170
Dantin, Louis (Eugene Seers) 1865-1945...DLB-92
Danto, Arthur C. 1924- ..............DLB-279
Danzig, Allison 1898-1987 .............DLB-171

D'Arcy, Ella circa 1857-1937 ..........DLB-135
Dark, Eleanor 1901-1985...............DLB-260
Darke, Nick 1948- ...................DLB-233
Darley, Felix Octavius Carr 1822-1888..DLB-188
Darley, George 1795-1846..............DLB-96
Darmesteter, Madame James
 (see Robinson, A. Mary F.)
Darwin, Charles 1809-1882......... DLB-57, 166
Darwin, Erasmus 1731-1802 ...........DLB-93
Daryush, Elizabeth 1887-1977 ..........DLB-20
Dashkova, Ekaterina Romanovna
 (née Vorontsova) 1743-1810 ........DLB-150
Dashwood, Edmée Elizabeth Monica de la Pasture
 (see Delafield, E. M.)
Daudet, Alphonse 1840-1897...........DLB-123
d'Aulaire, Edgar Parin 1898- and
 d'Aulaire, Ingri 1904- ............DLB-22
Davenant, Sir William 1606-1668 ....DLB-58, 126
Davenport, Guy 1927- ...............DLB-130
 Tribute to John Gardner.............. Y-82
Davenport, Marcia 1903-1996............ DS-17
Davenport, Robert ?-? .................DLB-58
Daves, Delmer 1904-1977 ..............DLB-26
Davey, Frank 1940- ..................DLB-53
Davidson, Avram 1923-1993 ............DLB-8
Davidson, Donald 1893-1968 ...........DLB-45
Davidson, Donald 1917- ..............DLB-279
Davidson, John 1857-1909..............DLB-19
Davidson, Lionel 1922- ..........DLB-14, 276
Davidson, Robyn 1950- ...............DLB-204
Davidson, Sara 1943- ................DLB-185
Davie, Donald 1922- ..................DLB-27
Davie, Elspeth 1919-1995 .............DLB-139
Davies, Sir John 1569-1626 ...........DLB-172
Davies, John, of Hereford 1565?-1618....DLB-121
Davies, Rhys 1901-1978 ..........DLB-139, 191
Davies, Robertson 1913-1995 ..........DLB-68
Davies, Samuel 1723-1761 .............DLB-31
Davies, Thomas 1712?-1785 .......DLB-142, 154
Davies, W. H. 1871-1940..........DLB-19, 174
Peter Davies Limited .................DLB-112
Davin, Nicholas Flood 1840?-1901 .......DLB-99
Daviot, Gordon 1896?-1952 ............DLB-10
 (see also Tey, Josephine)
Davis, Arthur Hoey (see Rudd, Steele)
Davis, Charles A. (Major J. Downing)
 1795-1867 .....................DLB-11
Davis, Clyde Brion 1894-1962 ..........DLB-9
Davis, Dick 1945- ................DLB-40, 282
Davis, Frank Marshall 1905-1987 .......DLB-51
Davis, H. L. 1894-1960............DLB-9, 206
Davis, John 1774-1854 ................DLB-37
Davis, Lydia 1947- ..................DLB-130
Davis, Margaret Thomson 1926- .......DLB-14
Davis, Ossie 1917- .............. DLB-7, 38, 249
Davis, Owen 1874-1956................DLB-249

Davis, Paxton 1925-1994 .................. Y-89

Davis, Rebecca Harding 1831-1910 .. DLB-74, 239

Davis, Richard Harding 1864-1916
............DLB-12, 23, 78, 79, 189; DS-13

Davis, Samuel Cole 1764-1809 .......... DLB-37

Davis, Samuel Post 1850-1918 ......... DLB-202

Davison, Frank Dalby 1893-1970 ...... DLB-260

Davison, Peter 1928- ................. DLB-5

Davydov, Denis Vasil'evich 1784-1839 .. DLB-205

Davys, Mary 1674-1732 ............... DLB-39

   Preface to *The Works of Mrs. Davys*
   (1725).................... DLB-39

DAW Books ....................... DLB-46

Dawson, Ernest 1882-1947 ........ DLB-140; Y-02

Dawson, Fielding 1930- ............. DLB-130

Dawson, Sarah Morgan 1842-1909 ..... DLB-239

Dawson, William 1704-1752 ........... DLB-31

Day, Angel flourished 1583-1599 ....DLB-167, 236

Day, Benjamin Henry 1810-1889 ........ DLB-43

Day, Clarence 1874-1935 ............. DLB-11

Day, Dorothy 1897-1980 .............. DLB-29

Day, Frank Parker 1881-1950 .......... DLB-92

Day, John circa 1574-circa 1640 ......... DLB-62

Day, Thomas 1748-1789 ............... DLB-39

John Day [publishing house]........... .DLB-170

The John Day Company ............. DLB-46

Mahlon Day [publishing house] ........ DLB-49

Day Lewis, C. (see Blake, Nicholas)

Dazai Osamu 1909-1948 ............. DLB-182

Deacon, William Arthur 1890-1977 ...... DLB-68

Deal, Borden 1922-1985 ................ DLB-6

de Angeli, Marguerite 1889-1987 ........ DLB-22

De Angelis, Milo 1951- ............. DLB-128

De Bow, J. D. B. 1820-1867 ...... DLB-3, 79, 248

de Bruyn, Günter 1926- ............. DLB-75

de Camp, L. Sprague 1907-2000 ......... DLB-8

De Carlo, Andrea 1952- ............. DLB-196

De Casas, Celso A. 1944- .......... DLB-209

Dechert, Robert 1895-1975 ........... DLB-187

Dedications, Inscriptions, and
   Annotations .................. Y-01–02

Dee, John 1527-1608 or 1609 ...... DLB-136, 213

Deeping, George Warwick 1877-1950 ... DLB-153

Defoe, Daniel
   1660-1731....... DLB-39, 95, 101; CDBLB-2

   Preface to *Colonel Jack* (1722) ........ DLB-39

   Preface to *The Farther Adventures of*
   *Robinson Crusoe* (1719) ......... DLB-39

   Preface to *Moll Flanders* (1722) ....... DLB-39

   Preface to *Robinson Crusoe* (1719) ...... DLB-39

   Preface to *Roxana* (1724) ........... DLB-39

de Fontaine, Felix Gregory 1834-1896 .... DLB-43

De Forest, John William 1826-1906 .. DLB-12, 189

DeFrees, Madeline 1919- ............. DLB-105

"The Poet's Kaleidoscope: The
   Element of Surprise in the
   Making of the Poem" ......... DLB-105

DeGolyer, Everette Lee 1886-1956 ..... DLB-187

de Graff, Robert 1895-1981 ............. Y-81

de Graft, Joe 1924-1978 ...............DLB-117

*De Heinrico* circa 980? ............... DLB-148

Deighton, Len 1929- ...... DLB-87; CDBLB-8

DeJong, Meindert 1906-1991 .......... DLB-52

Dekker, Thomas
   circa 1572-1632 ..... DLB-62, 172; CDBLB-1

Delacorte, George T., Jr. 1894-1991...... DLB-91

Delafield, E. M. 1890-1943 ............ DLB-34

Delahaye, Guy (Guillaume Lahaise)
   1888-1969 ................... DLB-92

de la Mare, Walter 1873-1956
   ......... DLB-19, 153, 162, 255; CDBLB-6

Deland, Margaret 1857-1945 .......... DLB-78

Delaney, Shelagh 1939- ..... DLB-13; CDBLB-8

Delano, Amasa 1763-1823 ............ DLB-183

Delany, Martin Robinson 1812-1885 ..... DLB-50

Delany, Samuel R. 1942- .......... DLB-8, 33

de la Roche, Mazo 1879-1961.......... DLB-68

Delavigne, Jean François Casimir
   1793-1843.................... DLB-192

Delbanco, Nicholas 1942- ........ DLB-6, 234

Delblanc, Sven 1931-1992 ........... DLB-257

Del Castillo, Ramón 1949- ........... DLB-209

Deledda, Grazia 1871-1936 .......... DLB-264

De León, Nephtal 1945- ............. DLB-82

Delfini, Antonio 1907-1963 .......... DLB-264

Delgado, Abelardo Barrientos 1931- .... DLB-82

Del Giudice, Daniele 1949- .......... DLB-196

Di Libero, Libero 1906-1981 .......... DLB-114

DeLillo, Don 1936- .................DLB-6, 173

de Lint, Charles 1951- ................ DLB-251

de Lisser H. G. 1878-1944 .............DLB-117

Dell, Floyd 1887-1969.................. DLB-9

Dell Publishing Company ............. DLB-46

delle Grazie, Marie Eugene 1864-1931.... DLB-81

Deloney, Thomas died 1600 .......... DLB-167

Deloria, Ella C. 1889-1971 ............DLB-175

Deloria, Vine, Jr. 1933- ...............DLB-175

del Rey, Lester 1915-1993 ............. DLB-8

Del Vecchio, John M. 1947- ............DS-9

Del'vig, Anton Antonovich 1798-1831 ... DLB-205

de Man, Paul 1919-1983............... DLB-67

DeMarinis, Rick 1934- .............. DLB-218

Demby, William 1922- .............. DLB-33

De Mille, James 1833-1880......... DLB-99, 251

de Mille, William 1878-1955........... DLB-266

Deming, Philander 1829-1915 .......... DLB-74

Deml, Jakub 1878-1961............... DLB-215

Demorest, William Jennings 1822-1895 ... DLB-79

De Morgan, William 1839-1917 ........ DLB-153

Demosthenes 384 B.C.-322 B.C. ........DLB-176

Henry Denham [publishing house].......DLB-170

Denham, Sir John 1615-1669 ....... DLB-58, 126

Denison, Merrill 1893-1975 ........... DLB-92

T. S. Denison and Company .......... DLB-49

Dennery, Adolphe Philippe 1811-1899... DLB-192

Dennie, Joseph 1768-1812..... DLB-37, 43, 59, 73

Dennis, C. J. 1876-1938 ............. DLB-260

Dennis, John 1658-1734 ............. DLB-101

Dennis, Nigel 1912-1989 .........DLB-13, 15, 233

Denslow, W. W. 1856-1915........... DLB-188

Dent, J. M., and Sons ................ DLB-112

Dent, Tom 1932-1998 ................ DLB-38

Denton, Daniel circa 1626-1703 ......... DLB-24

DePaola, Tomie 1934- ............. DLB-61

De Quille, Dan 1829-1898 ............ DLB-186

De Quincey, Thomas
   1785-1859.......... DLB-110, 144; CDBLB-3

   "Rhetoric" (1828; revised, 1859)
   [excerpt] .................... DLB-57

   "Style" (1840; revised, 1859)
   [excerpt] .................... DLB-57

Derby, George Horatio 1823-1861....... DLB-11

J. C. Derby and Company ............. DLB-49

Derby and Miller .................... DLB-49

De Ricci, Seymour 1881-1942 ......... DLB-201

Derleth, August 1909-1971 ........DLB-9; DS-17

Derrida, Jacques 1930- ............. DLB-242

The Derrydale Press.................. DLB-46

Derzhavin, Gavriil Romanovich
   1743-1816................... DLB-150

Desai, Anita 1937- .................DLB-271

Desaulniers, Gonzalve 1863-1934 ....... DLB-92

Desbordes-Valmore, Marceline
   1786-1859....................DLB-217

Descartes, René 1596-1650 .............DLB-268

Deschamps, Emile 1791-1871 ...........DLB-217

Deschamps, Eustache 1340?-1404 ...... DLB-208

Desbiens, Jean-Paul 1927- ............ DLB-53

des Forêts, Louis-Rene 1918-2001 ....... DLB-83

Desiato, Luca 1941- .............. DLB-196

Desjardins, Marie-Catherine
   (see Villedieu, Madame de)

Desnica, Vladan 1905-1967 ........... DLB-181

Desnos, Robert 1900-1945............. DLB-258

DesRochers, Alfred 1901-1978 ......... DLB-68

Desrosiers, Léo-Paul 1896-1967 ........ DLB-68

Dessaulles, Louis-Antoine 1819-1895..... DLB-99

Dessì, Giuseppe 1909-1977.............DLB-177

Destouches, Louis-Ferdinand
   (see Céline, Louis-Ferdinand)

DeSylva, Buddy 1895-1950 ........... DLB-265

De Tabley, Lord 1835-1895............ DLB-35

Deutsch, Babette 1895-1982 ........... DLB-45

Deutsch, Niklaus Manuel (see Manuel, Niklaus)

André Deutsch Limited ............. DLB-112

Devanny, Jean 1894-1962............. DLB-260

Deveaux, Alexis 1948- .................DLB-38
De Vere, Aubrey 1814-1902 ...........DLB-35
Devereux, second Earl of Essex, Robert
    1565-1601 ........................DLB-136
The Devin-Adair Company............DLB-46
De Vinne, Theodore Low
    1828-1914 ........................DLB-187
Devlin, Anne 1951- .................DLB-245
DeVoto, Bernard 1897-1955 .........DLB-9, 256
De Vries, Peter 1910-1993..........DLB-6; Y-82
    Tribute to Albert Erskine ............. Y-93
Dewart, Edward Hartley 1828-1903 ......DLB-99
Dewdney, Christopher 1951- ..........DLB-60
Dewdney, Selwyn 1909-1979...........DLB-68
Dewey, John 1859-1952..........DLB-246, 270
Dewey, Orville 1794-1882............DLB-243
Dewey, Thomas B. 1915-1981..........DLB-226
DeWitt, Robert M., Publisher ..........DLB-49
DeWolfe, Fiske and Company ..........DLB-49
Dexter, Colin 1930- .................DLB-87
de Young, M. H. 1849-1925 ...........DLB-25
Dhlomo, H. I. E. 1903-1956 ....... DLB-157, 225
Dhuoda circa 803-after 843 ..........DLB-148
The Dial 1840-1844 .................DLB-223
The Dial Press ........................DLB-46
Diamond, I. A. L. 1920-1988..........DLB-26
Dibble, L. Grace 1902-1998...........DLB-204
Dibdin, Thomas Frognall
    1776-1847........................DLB-184
Di Cicco, Pier Giorgio 1949- ..........DLB-60
Dick, Philip K. 1928-1982 ..............DLB-8
Dick and Fitzgerald ....................DLB-49
Dickens, Charles 1812-1870... DLB-21, 55, 70, 159,
                                   166; DS-5; CDBLB-4
Dickey, James 1923-1997 ........... DLB-5, 193;
                        Y-82, 93, 96, 97; DS-7, 19; CDALB-6
    James Dickey and Stanley Burnshaw
        Correspondence ................ Y-02
    James Dickey at Seventy–A Tribute ..... Y-93
    James Dickey, American Poet .......... Y-96
    The James Dickey Society............. Y-99
    The Life of James Dickey: A Lecture to
        the Friends of the Emory Libraries,
        by Henry Hart .................. Y-98
    Tribute to Archibald MacLeish........ Y-82
    Tribute to Malcolm Cowley ........... Y-89
    Tribute to Truman Capote ............ Y-84
    Tributes [to Dickey] ................ Y-97
Dickey, William 1928-1994 .............DLB-5
Dickinson, Emily
    1830-1886 ..........DLB-1, 243; CDALB-3
Dickinson, John 1732-1808 ............DLB-31
Dickinson, Jonathan 1688-1747 ........DLB-24
Dickinson, Patric 1914- ..............DLB-27
Dickinson, Peter 1927- ...... DLB-87, 161, 276
John Dicks [publishing house]..........DLB-106
Dickson, Gordon R. 1923-2001..........DLB-8

*Dictionary of Literary Biography
    Annual Awards for Dictionary of
    Literary Biography Editors and
    Contributors*................... Y-98–02
*Dictionary of Literary Biography
    Yearbook* Awards .........Y-92–93, 97–02
*The Dictionary of National Biography*........DLB-144
Didion, Joan 1934-
    ....... DLB-2, 173, 185; Y-81, 86; CDALB-6
Di Donato, Pietro 1911- ................DLB-9
Die Fürstliche Bibliothek Corvey .......... Y-96
Diego, Gerardo 1896-1987.............DLB-134
Dietz, Howard 1896-1983 .............DLB-265
Digby, Everard 1550?-1605 ............DLB-281
Digges, Thomas circa 1546-1595........DLB-136
The Digital Millennium Copyright Act:
    Expanding Copyright Protection in
    Cyberspace and Beyond .............. Y-98
Diktonius, Elmer 1896-1961 ...........DLB-259
Dillard, Annie 1945- ...... DLB-275, 278; Y-80
Dillard, R. H. W. 1937- ............DLB-5, 244
Charles T. Dillingham Company ........DLB-49
G. W. Dillingham Company ...........DLB-49
Edward and Charles Dilly
    [publishing house]................DLB-154
Dilthey, Wilhelm 1833-1911 ...........DLB-129
Dimitrova, Blaga 1922- ...DLB-181; CDWLB-4
Dimov, Dimitr 1909-1966 .............DLB-181
Dimsdale, Thomas J. 1831?-1866 .......DLB-186
Dinescu, Mircea 1950- ...............DLB-232
Dinesen, Isak (see Blixen, Karen)
Dingelstedt, Franz von 1814-1881 .......DLB-133
Dinis, Júlio (Joaquim Guilherme
    Gomes Coelho) 1839-1871 ........DLB-287
Dintenfass, Mark 1941- ................ Y-84
Diogenes, Jr. (see Brougham, John)
Diogenes Laertius circa 200............ DLB-176
DiPrima, Diane 1934- ..............DLB-5, 16
Disch, Thomas M. 1940- ...........DLB-8, 282
Diski, Jenny 1947- ..................DLB-271
Disney, Walt 1901-1966 ...............DLB-22
Disraeli, Benjamin 1804-1881 ........DLB-21, 55
D'Israeli, Isaac 1766-1848 ............DLB-107
*DLB* Award for Distinguished
    Literary Criticism .................. Y-02
Ditlevsen, Tove 1917-1976.............DLB-214
Ditzen, Rudolf (see Fallada, Hans)
Dix, Dorothea Lynde 1802-1887......DLB-1, 235
Dix, Dorothy (see Gilmer, Elizabeth Meriwether)
Dix, Edwards and Company............DLB-49
Dix, Gertrude circa 1874-?.............DLB-197
Dixie, Florence Douglas 1857-1905 ..... DLB-174
Dixon, Ella Hepworth
    1855 or 1857?-1932................DLB-197
Dixon, Paige (see Corcoran, Barbara)
Dixon, Richard Watson 1833-1900.......DLB-19
Dixon, Stephen 1936- ................DLB-130

*DLB* Award for Distinguished
    Literary Criticism ................... Y-02
Dmitriev, Andrei Viktorovich 1956- ...DLB-285
Dmitriev, Ivan Ivanovich 1760-1837 .....DLB-150
Dobell, Bertram 1842-1914 ............DLB-184
Dobell, Sydney 1824-1874..............DLB-32
Dobie, J. Frank 1888-1964............DLB-212
Dobles Yzaguirre, Julieta 1943- .......DLB-283
Döblin, Alfred 1878-1957.....DLB-66; CDWLB-2
Dobroliubov, Nikolai Aleksandrovich
    1836-1861........................DLB-277
Dobson, Austin 1840-1921 .........DLB-35, 144
Dobson, Rosemary 1920- ............DLB-260
Doctorow, E. L.
    1931- ..... DLB-2, 28, 173; Y-80; CDALB-6
Dodd, Susan M. 1946- ...............DLB-244
Dodd, William E. 1869-1940............DLB-17
Anne Dodd [publishing house] .........DLB-154
Dodd, Mead and Company.............DLB-49
Doderer, Heimito von 1896-1966 ........DLB-85
B. W. Dodge and Company ............DLB-46
Dodge, Mary Abigail 1833-1896 .......DLB-221
Dodge, Mary Mapes
    1831?-1905 .............DLB-42, 79; DS-13
Dodge Publishing Company ............DLB-49
Dodgson, Charles Lutwidge (see Carroll, Lewis)
Dodsley, Robert 1703-1764 ............DLB-95
R. Dodsley [publishing house]..........DLB-154
Dodson, Owen 1914-1983..............DLB-76
Dodwell, Christina 1951- .............DLB-204
Doesticks, Q. K. Philander, P. B.
    (see Thomson, Mortimer)
Doheny, Carrie Estelle 1875-1958.......DLB-140
Doherty, John 1798?-1854 .............DLB-190
Doig, Ivan 1939- ....................DLB-206
Doinaş, Ştefan Augustin 1922- ........DLB-232
Domínguez, Sylvia Maida 1935- .......DLB-122
Donaghy, Michael 1954- .............DLB-282
Patrick Donahoe [publishing house] .....DLB-49
Donald, David H. 1920- .........DLB-17; Y-87
Donaldson, Scott 1928- ..............DLB-111
Doni, Rodolfo 1919- ................DLB-177
Donleavy, J. P. 1926- .............DLB-6, 173
Donnadieu, Marguerite (see Duras, Marguerite)
Donne, John
    1572-1631 ........DLB-121, 151; CDBLB-1
Donnelly, Ignatius 1831-1901 ..........DLB-12
R. R. Donnelley and Sons Company......DLB-49
Donoghue, Emma 1969- .............DLB-267
Donohue and Henneberry..............DLB-49
Donoso, José 1924-1996 ....DLB-113; CDWLB-3
M. Doolady [publishing house].........DLB-49
Dooley, Ebon (see Ebon)
Doolittle, Hilda 1886-1961 ......DLB-4, 45; DS-15
Doplicher, Fabio 1938- ..............DLB-128
Dor, Milo 1923- .....................DLB-85

George H. Doran Company............ DLB-46
Dorgelès, Roland 1886-1973............ DLB-65
Dorn, Edward 1929-1999............... DLB-5
Dorr, Rheta Childe 1866-1948......... DLB-25
Dorris, Michael 1945-1997..............DLB-175
Dorset and Middlesex, Charles Sackville,
  Lord Buckhurst, Earl of 1643-1706....DLB-131
Dorsey, Candas Jane 1952-   ......... DLB-251
Dorst, Tankred 1925-   ........... DLB-75, 124
Dos Passos, John 1896-1970
  ............. DLB-4, 9; DS-1, 15; CDALB-5
    John Dos Passos: A Centennial
      Commemoration.................Y-96
    John Dos Passos: Artist ...............Y-99
    John Dos Passos Newsletter............Y-00
    *U.S.A.* (Documentary) .............DLB-274
Dostoevsky, Fyodor 1821-1881 ........ DLB-238
Doubleday and Company ............. DLB-49
Dougall, Lily 1858-1923............... DLB-92
Doughty, Charles M.
  1843-1926 ................ DLB-19, 57, 174
Douglas, Lady Alfred (see Custance, Olive)
Douglas, Gavin 1476-1522 ............ DLB-132
Douglas, Keith 1920-1944 ............. DLB-27
Douglas, Norman 1868-1952 ..... DLB-34, 195
Douglass, Frederick 1817-1895
  .......... DLB-1, 43, 50, 79, 243; CDALB-2
    Frederick Douglass Creative Arts Center Y-01
Douglass, William circa 1691-1752....... DLB-24
Dourado, Autran 1926-   ............. DLB-145
Dove, Arthur G. 1880-1946 ........... DLB-188
Dove, Rita 1952-   ........ DLB-120; CDALB-7
Dover Publications................... DLB-46
Doves Press ....................... DLB-112
Dovlatov, Sergei Donatovich 1941-1990 . DLB-285
Dowden, Edward 1843-1913 ....... DLB-35, 149
Dowell, Coleman 1925-1985 .......... DLB-130
Dowland, John 1563-1626 ............DLB-172
Downes, Gwladys 1915-   ............. DLB-88
Downing, J., Major (see Davis, Charles A.)
Downing, Major Jack (see Smith, Seba)
Dowriche, Anne before 1560-after 1613...DLB-172
Dowson, Ernest 1867-1900 ........ DLB-19, 135
William Doxey [publishing house] ....... DLB-49
Doyle, Sir Arthur Conan
  1859-1930 ...DLB-18, 70, 156, 178; CDBLB-5
    The Priory Scholars of New York ....... Y-99
Doyle, Kirby 1932-   .................. DLB-16
Doyle, Roddy 1958-   ................ DLB-194
Drabble, Margaret
  1939-   ....... DLB-14, 155, 231; CDBLB-8
    Tribute to Graham Greene ........... Y-91
Drach, Albert 1902-1995 ............. DLB-85
Dragojević, Danijel 1934-   ............ DLB-181
Drake, Samuel Gardner 1798-1875...... DLB-187
Drama (*See* Theater)

The Dramatic Publishing Company...... DLB-49
Dramatists Play Service ............. DLB-46
Drant, Thomas early 1540s?-1578 ...... DLB-167
Draper, John W. 1811-1882?........... DLB-30
Draper, Lyman C. 1815-1891 .......... DLB-30
Drayton, Michael 1563-1631 .......... DLB-121
Dreiser, Theodore 1871-1945
  ........DLB-9, 12, 102, 137; DS-1; CDALB-3
    The International Theodore Dreiser
      Society.......................Y-01
    Notes from the Underground
      of *Sister Carrie*..................Y-01
Dresser, Davis 1904-1977 ............ DLB-226
Drew, Elizabeth A.
  "A Note on Technique" [excerpt]
  (1926) ....................... DLB-36
Drewitz, Ingeborg 1923-1986........... DLB-75
Drieu La Rochelle, Pierre 1893-1945 ..... DLB-72
Drinker, Elizabeth 1735-1807 .......... DLB-200
Drinkwater, John 1882-1937......DLB-10, 19, 149
    The Friends of the Dymock Poets ....... Y-00
Droste-Hülshoff, Annette von
  1797-1848 ............ DLB-133; CDWLB-2
The Drue Heinz Literature Prize
  Excerpt from "Excerpts from a Report
  of the Commission," in David
  Bosworth's *The Death of Descartes*
  An Interview with David Bosworth...... Y-82
Drummond, William, of Hawthornden
  1585-1649 ................. DLB-121, 213
Drummond, William Henry 1854-1907... DLB-92
Druzhinin, Aleksandr Vasil'evich
  1824-1864 .................... DLB-238
Dryden, Charles 1860?-1931 ...........DLB-171
Dryden, John
  1631-1700...... DLB-80, 101, 131; CDBLB-2
Držić, Marin
  circa 1508-1567 ........DLB-147; CDWLB-4
Duane, William 1760-1835............. DLB-43
Dubé, Marcel 1930-   ................. DLB-53
Dubé, Rodolphe (see Hertel, François)
Dubie, Norman 1945-   ............. DLB-120
Dubin, Al 1891-1945 ............... DLB-265
Dubois, Silvia 1788 or 1789?-1889 ..... DLB-239
Du Bois, W. E. B.
  1868-1963 ....DLB-47, 50, 91, 246; CDALB-3
Du Bois, William Pène 1916-1993 ....... DLB-61
Dubrovina, Ekaterina Oskarovna
  1846-1913 ................... DLB-238
Dubus, Andre 1936-1999............. DLB-130
    Tribute to Michael M. Rea ........... Y-97
Ducange, Victor 1783-1833 ........... DLB-192
Du Chaillu, Paul Belloni 1831?-1903 .... DLB-189
Ducharme, Réjean 1941-   .............. DLB-60
Dučić, Jovan 1871-1943 .....DLB-147; CDWLB-4
Duck, Stephen 1705?-1756 ............ DLB-95
Gerald Duckworth and Company
  Limited. .................... DLB-112
Duclaux, Madame Mary (see Robinson, A. Mary F.)
Dudek, Louis 1918-2001 .............. DLB-88

Dudley-Smith, Trevor (see Hall, Adam)
Duell, Sloan and Pearce .............. DLB-46
Duerer, Albrecht 1471-1528............DLB-179
Duff Gordon, Lucie 1821-1869 ........ DLB-166
Dufferin, Helen Lady, Countess of Gifford
  1807-1867..................... DLB-199
Duffield and Green................... DLB-46
Duffy, Maureen 1933-   .............. DLB-14
Dufief, Nicholas Gouin 1776-1834.......DLB-187
Dugan, Alan 1923-   .................. DLB-5
Dugard, William 1606-1662.......DLB-170, 281
William Dugard [publishing house] ......DLB-170
Dugas, Marcel 1883-1947............... DLB-92
William Dugdale [publishing house] .... DLB-106
Duhamel, Georges 1884-1966 .......... DLB-65
Dujardin, Edouard 1861-1949 ......... DLB-123
Dukes, Ashley 1885-1959 .............. DLB-10
Dumas, Alexandre *fils* 1824-1895....... DLB-192
Dumas, Alexandre *père* 1802-1870 .....DLB-119, 192
Dumas, Henry 1934-1968 ............. DLB-41
du Maurier, Daphne 1907-1989 ........ DLB-191
Du Maurier, George 1834-1896.....DLB-153, 178
Dummett, Michael 1925-   ........... DLB-262
Dunbar, Paul Laurence
  1872-1906......... DLB-50, 54, 78; CDALB-3
    Introduction to *Lyrics of Lowly Life* (1896),
    by William Dean Howells........ DLB-50
Dunbar, William
  circa 1460-circa 1522 ......... DLB-132, 146
Duncan, Dave 1933-   ............... DLB-251
Duncan, David James 1952-   .......... DLB-256
Duncan, Norman 1871-1916 ........... DLB-92
Duncan, Quince 1940-   .............. DLB-145
Duncan, Robert 1919-1988 .......DLB-5, 16, 193
Duncan, Ronald 1914-1982 ............ DLB-13
Duncan, Sara Jeannette 1861-1922........ DLB-92
Dunigan, Edward, and Brother ......... DLB-49
Dunlap, John 1747-1812 ............... DLB-43
Dunlap, William 1766-1839 .......DLB-30, 37, 59
Dunlop, William "Tiger" 1792-1848 ..... DLB-99
Dunmore, Helen 1952-   ............. DLB-267
Dunn, Douglas 1942-   ................ DLB-40
Dunn, Harvey Thomas 1884-1952 ...... DLB-188
Dunn, Stephen 1939-   ............... DLB-105
    "The Good, The Not So Good" .... DLB-105
Dunne, Finley Peter 1867-1936......... DLB-11, 23
Dunne, John Gregory 1932-   .............Y-80
Dunne, Philip 1908-1992 .............. DLB-26
Dunning, Ralph Cheever 1878-1930 ...... DLB-4
Dunning, William A. 1857-1922.........DLB-17
Duns Scotus, John circa 1266-1308 ..... DLB-115
Dunsany, Lord (Edward John Moreton
  Drax Plunkett, Baron Dunsany)
  1878-1957......... DLB-10, 77, 153, 156, 255
Dunton, W. Herbert 1878-1936 ........ DLB-188
John Dunton [publishing house]..........DLB-170

Dupin, Amantine-Aurore-Lucile (see Sand, George)
Dupuy, Eliza Ann 1814-1880..........DLB-248
Durack, Mary 1913-1994..............DLB-260
Durand, Lucile (see Bersianik, Louky)
Duranti, Francesca 1935-  ...........DLB-196
Duranty, Walter 1884-1957...........DLB-29
Duras, Marguerite (Marguerite Donnadieu)
  1914-1996....................DLB-83
Durfey, Thomas 1653-1723...........DLB-80
Durova, Nadezhda Andreevna
  (Aleksandr Andreevich Aleksandrov)
  1783-1866....................DLB-198
Durrell, Lawrence 1912-1990
  .........DLB-15, 27, 204; Y-90; CDBLB-7
William Durrell [publishing house].......DLB-49
Dürrenmatt, Friedrich
  1921-1990.........DLB-69, 124; CDWLB-2
Duston, Hannah 1657-1737...........DLB-200
Dutt, Toru 1856-1877................DLB-240
E. P. Dutton and Company............DLB-49
Duvoisin, Roger 1904-1980............DLB-61
Duyckinck, Evert Augustus
  1816-1878.................DLB-3, 64, 250
Duyckinck, George L.
  1823-1863................DLB-3, 250
Duyckinck and Company............DLB-49
Dwight, John Sullivan 1813-1893.....DLB-1, 235
Dwight, Timothy 1752-1817...........DLB-37
  America: or, A Poem on the Settlement
  of the British Colonies, by
  Timothy Dwight..............DLB-37
Dybek, Stuart 1942-  ................DLB-130
  Tribute to Michael M. Rea...........Y-97
Dyer, Charles 1928-  ................DLB-13
Dyer, Sir Edward 1543-1607..........DLB-136
Dyer, George 1755-1841.............DLB-93
Dyer, John 1699-1757...............DLB-95
Dyk, Viktor 1877-1931...............DLB-215
Dylan, Bob 1941-  ..................DLB-16

# E

Eager, Edward 1911-1964.............DLB-22
Eagleton, Terry 1943-  ..............DLB-242
Eames, Wilberforce 1855-1937........DLB-140
Earle, Alice Morse 1853-1911.........DLB-221
Earle, John 1600 or 1601-1665........DLB-151
James H. Earle and Company...........DLB-49
East Europe
  Independence and Destruction,
  1918-1941....................DLB-220
  Social Theory and Ethnography:
  Language and Ethnicity in
  Western versus Eastern Man....DLB-220
Eastlake, William 1917-1997.........DLB-6, 206
Eastman, Carol ?-  ..................DLB-44
Eastman, Charles A. (Ohiyesa)
  1858-1939....................DLB-175
Eastman, Max 1883-1969.............DLB-91
Eaton, Daniel Isaac 1753-1814.........DLB-158

Eaton, Edith Maude 1865-1914........DLB-221
Eaton, Winnifred 1875-1954..........DLB-221
Eberhart, Richard 1904-  .....DLB-48; CDALB-1
  Tribute to Robert Penn Warren........Y-89
Ebner, Jeannie 1918-  ...............DLB-85
Ebner-Eschenbach, Marie von
  1830-1916....................DLB-81
Ebon 1942-  .......................DLB-41
E-Books' Second Act in Libraries..........Y-02
Ecbasis Captivi circa 1045..............DLB-148
Ecco Press......................DLB-46
Eckhart, Meister circa 1260-circa 1328...DLB-115
The Eclectic Review 1805-1868...........DLB-110
Eco, Umberto 1932-  ............DLB-196, 242
Eddison, E. R. 1882-1945............DLB-255
Edel, Leon 1907-1997................DLB-103
Edelfeldt, Inger 1956-  ...............DLB-257
A Century of Poetry, a Lifetime of Collecting:
  J. M. Edelstein's Collection of Twentieth-
  Century American Poetry...........Y-02
Edes, Benjamin 1732-1803............DLB-43
Edgar, David 1948-  .............DLB-13, 233
  Viewpoint: Politics and
  Performance.................DLB-13
Edgerton, Clyde 1944-  ..............DLB-278
Edgeworth, Maria
  1768-1849..............DLB-116, 159, 163
The Edinburgh Review 1802-1929.........DLB-110
Edinburgh University Press...........DLB-112
Editing
  Conversations with Editors...........Y-95
  Editorial Statements...............DLB-137
  The Editorial Style of Fredson Bowers ... Y-91
  Editorial: The Extension of Copyright ... Y-02
  We See the Editor at Work...........Y-97
  Whose Ulysses? The Function of Editing.. Y-97
The Editor Publishing Company.........DLB-49
Editorial Institute at Boston University......Y-00
Edmonds, Helen Woods Ferguson
  (see Kavan, Anna)
Edmonds, Randolph 1900-1983.........DLB-51
Edmonds, Walter D. 1903-1998..........DLB-9
Edric, Robert (see Armitage, G. E.)
Edschmid, Kasimir 1890-1966..........DLB-56
Edson, Margaret 1961-  ..............DLB-266
Edson, Russell 1935-  ...............DLB-244
Edwards, Amelia Anne Blandford
  1831-1892....................DLB-174
Edwards, Dic 1953-  ................DLB-245
Edwards, Edward 1812-1886..........DLB-184
Edwards, Jonathan 1703-1758......DLB-24, 270
Edwards, Jonathan, Jr. 1745-1801........DLB-37
Edwards, Junius 1929-  ..............DLB-33
Edwards, Matilda Barbara Betham
  1836-1919....................DLB-174
Edwards, Richard 1524-1566..........DLB-62
Edwards, Sarah Pierpont 1710-1758......DLB-200

James Edwards [publishing house].......DLB-154
Effinger, George Alec 1947-  ............DLB-8
Egerton, George 1859-1945...........DLB-135
Eggleston, Edward 1837-1902..........DLB-12
Eggleston, Wilfred 1901-1986..........DLB-92
Eglītis, Anšlavs 1906-1993............DLB-220
Ehrenreich, Barbara 1941-  ............DLB-246
Ehrenstein, Albert 1886-1950.........DLB-81
Ehrhart, W. D. 1948-  ................DS-9
Ehrlich, Gretel 1946-  ............DLB-212, 275
Eich, Günter 1907-1972............DLB-69, 124
Eichendorff, Joseph Freiherr von
  1788-1857....................DLB-90
Eifukumon'in 1271-1342.............DLB-203
Eigner, Larry 1926-1996.............DLB-5, 193
Eikon Basilike 1649...................DLB-151
Eilhart von Oberge
  circa 1140-circa 1195.............DLB-148
Einhard circa 770-840................DLB-148
Eiseley, Loren 1907-1977........DLB-275, DS-17
Eisenberg, Deborah 1945-  ............DLB-244
Eisenreich, Herbert 1925-1986.........DLB-85
Eisner, Kurt 1867-1919...............DLB-66
Ekelöf, Gunnar 1907-1968............DLB-259
Eklund, Gordon 1945-  ................Y-83
Ekman, Kerstin 1933-  ...............DLB-257
Ekwensi, Cyprian 1921-  .....DLB-117; CDWLB-3
Elaw, Zilpha circa 1790-?............DLB-239
George Eld [publishing house].........DLB-170
Elder, Lonne, III 1931-  .........DLB-7, 38, 44
Paul Elder and Company..............DLB-49
Eldershaw, Flora (M. Barnard Eldershaw)
  1897-1956....................DLB-260
Eldershaw, M. Barnard (see Barnard, Marjorie and
  Eldershaw, Flora)
The Electronic Text Center and the Electronic
  Archive of Early American Fiction at the
  University of Virginia Library.........Y-98
Eliade, Mircea 1907-1986....DLB-220; CDWLB-4
Elie, Robert 1915-1973................DLB-88
Elin Pelin 1877-1949........DLB-147; CDWLB-4
Eliot, George
  1819-1880........DLB-21, 35, 55; CDBLB-4
  The George Eliot Fellowship...........Y-99
Eliot, John 1604-1690................DLB-24
Eliot, T. S. 1888-1965
  .........DLB-7, 10, 45, 63, 245; CDALB-5
  T. S. Eliot Centennial: The Return
  of the Old Possum...............Y-88
  The T. S. Eliot Society: Celebration and
  Scholarship, 1980-1999............Y-99
Eliot's Court Press..................DLB-170
Elizabeth I 1533-1603................DLB-136
Elizabeth von Nassau-Saarbrücken
  after 1393-1456..................DLB-179
Elizondo, Salvador 1932-  ............DLB-145
Elizondo, Sergio 1930-  ..............DLB-82

# Cumulative Index

Elkin, Stanley
  1930-1995 ........ DLB-2, 28, 218, 278; Y-80

Elles, Dora Amy (see Wentworth, Patricia)

Ellet, Elizabeth F. 1818?-1877 .......... DLB-30

Elliot, Ebenezer 1781-1849 ....... DLB-96, 190

Elliot, Frances Minto (Dickinson)
  1820-1898 ................... DLB-166

Elliott, Charlotte 1789-1871 .......... DLB-199

Elliott, George 1923- ................ DLB-68

Elliott, George P. 1918-1980 .......... DLB-244

Elliott, Janice 1931-1995 .............. DLB-14

Elliott, Sarah Barnwell 1848-1928 ...... DLB-221

Elliott, Thomes and Talbot ............. DLB-49

Elliott, William, III 1788-1863 ....... DLB-3, 248

Ellis, Alice Thomas (Anna Margaret Haycraft)
  1932- ................... DLB-194

Ellis, Edward S. 1840-1916 ............. DLB-42

Ellis, George E.
  "The New Controversy Concerning
    Miracles ....................... DS-5

Ellis, Havelock 1859-1939 ............. DLB-190

Frederick Staridge Ellis
  [publishing house] ................ DLB-106

The George H. Ellis Company ........ DLB-49

Ellison, Harlan 1934- ................ DLB-8

  Tribute to Isaac Asimov ............... Y-92

Ellison, Ralph
  1914-1994 .... DLB-2, 76, 227; Y-94; CDALB-1

Ellmann, Richard 1918-1987 ...... DLB-103; Y-87

Ellroy, James 1948- ........... DLB-226; Y-91

  Tribute to John D. MacDonald .......... Y-86

  Tribute to Raymond Chandler .......... Y-88

Eluard, Paul 1895-1952 ............. DLB-258

Elyot, Thomas 1490?-1546 ............. DLB-136

Emanuel, James Andrew 1921- ....... DLB-41

Emecheta, Buchi 1944- .... DLB-117; CDWLB-3

Emerson, Ralph Waldo
  1803-1882 ..... DLB-1, 59, 73, 183, 223, 270;
                                DS-5; CDALB-2

  Ralph Waldo Emerson in 1982 ......... Y-82

  The Ralph Waldo Emerson Society ...... Y-99

Emerson, William 1769-1811 .......... DLB-37

Emerson, William R. 1923-1997 ........... Y-97

Emin, Fedor Aleksandrovich
  circa 1735-1770 .................. DLB-150

Emmanuel, Pierre 1916-1984 .......... DLB-258

Empedocles fifth century B.C. .......... DLB-176

Empson, William 1906-1984 ........... DLB-20

Enchi Fumiko 1905-1986 .............. DLB-182

Ende, Michael 1929-1995 .............. DLB-75

Endō Shūsaku 1923-1996 .............. DLB-182

Engel, Marian 1933-1985 .............. DLB-53

Engel'gardt, Sof'ia Vladimirovna
  1828-1894 ....................... DLB-277

Engels, Friedrich 1820-1895 .......... DLB-129

Engle, Paul 1908- ................... DLB-48

  Tribute to Robert Penn Warren ........ Y-89

English, Thomas Dunn 1819-1902 ...... DLB-202

Ennius 239 B.C.-169 B.C. ............ DLB-211

Enquist, Per Olov 1934- ............. DLB-257

Enright, Anne 1962- ................. DLB-267

Enright, D. J. 1920- ................ DLB-27

Enright, Elizabeth 1909-1968 .......... DLB-22

Epictetus circa 55-circa 125-130 ...... DLB-176

Epicurus 342/341 B.C.-271/270 B.C. .... DLB-176

Epps, Bernard 1936- ................. DLB-53

Epshtein, Mikhail Naumovich 1950- .... DLB-285

Epstein, Julius 1909-2000 and
  Epstein, Philip 1909-1952 .......... DLB-26

Editors, Conversations with ............. Y-95

Equiano, Olaudah
  circa 1745-1797 ....... DLB-37, 50; CDWLB-3

  Olaudah Equiano and Unfinished
    Journeys: The Slave-Narrative
    Tradition and Twentieth-Century
    Continuities ................... DLB-117

Eragny Press ........................ DLB-112

Erasmus, Desiderius 1467-1536 ........ DLB-136

Erba, Luciano 1922- ................ DLB-128

Erdman, Nikolai Robertovich
  1900-1970 ....................... DLB-272

Erdrich, Louise
  1954- ...... DLB-152, 175, 206; CDALB-7

Erichsen-Brown, Gwethalyn Graham
  (see Graham, Gwethalyn)

Eriugena, John Scottus circa 810-877 .... DLB-115

Ernst, Paul 1866-1933 ........... DLB-66, 118

Erofeev, Venedikt Vasil'evich
  1938-1990 ....................... DLB-285

Erofeev, Viktor Vladimirovich 1947- .. DLB-285

Ershov, Petr Pavlovich 1815-1869 ...... DLB-205

Erskine, Albert 1911-1993 ............. Y-93

  At Home with Albert Erskine ......... Y-00

Erskine, John 1879-1951 .......... DLB-9, 102

Erskine, Mrs. Steuart ?-1948 ......... DLB-195

Ertel', Aleksandr Ivanovich 1855-1908 .. DLB-238

Ervine, St. John Greer 1883-1971 ...... DLB-10

Eschenburg, Johann Joachim 1743-1820 .. DLB-97

Escoto, Julio 1944- ................. DLB-145

Esdaile, Arundell 1880-1956 .......... DLB-201

Eshleman, Clayton 1935- ............. DLB-5

Espaillat, Rhina P. 1932- ........... DLB-282

Espanca, Florbela 1894-1930 .......... DLB-287

Espriu, Salvador 1913-1985 ........... DLB-134

Ess Ess Publishing Company ......... DLB-49

Essex House Press ................... DLB-112

Esson, Louis 1878-1943 .............. DLB-260

Essop, Ahmed 1931- ................ DLB-225

Esterházy, Péter 1950- .... DLB-232; CDWLB-4

Estes, Eleanor 1906-1988 ............. DLB-22

Estes and Lauriat .................... DLB-49

Estleman, Loren D. 1952- .......... DLB-226

Eszterhas, Joe 1944- ................ DLB-185

Etherege, George 1636-circa 1692 ...... DLB-80

Ethridge, Mark, Sr. 1896-1981 ........ DLB-127

Ets, Marie Hall 1893-1984 ............ DLB-22

Etter, David 1928- .................. DLB-105

Ettner, Johann Christoph 1654-1724 .... DLB-168

Eudora Welty Remembered in
  Two Exhibits ....................... Y-02

Eugene Gant's Projected Works .......... Y-01

Eupolemius flourished circa 1095 ...... DLB-148

Euripides circa 484 B.C.-407/406 B.C.
  ..................... DLB-176; CDWLB-1

Evans, Augusta Jane 1835-1909 ........ DLB-239

Evans, Caradoc 1878-1945 ............ DLB-162

Evans, Charles 1850-1935 ............. DLB-187

Evans, Donald 1884-1921 .............. DLB-54

Evans, George Henry 1805-1856 ........ DLB-43

Evans, Hubert 1892-1986 .............. DLB-92

Evans, Mari 1923- ................... DLB-41

Evans, Mary Ann (see Eliot, George)

Evans, Nathaniel 1742-1767 ........... DLB-31

Evans, Sebastian 1830-1909 ........... DLB-35

Evans, Ray 1915- ................... DLB-265

M. Evans and Company ............... DLB-46

Evaristi, Marcella 1953- ............ DLB-233

Everett, Alexander Hill 1790-1847 ..... DLB-59

Everett, Edward 1794-1865 ...... DLB-1, 59, 235

Everson, R. G. 1903- ................ DLB-88

Everson, William 1912-1994 ...... DLB-5, 16, 212

Ewart, Gavin 1916-1995 .............. DLB-40

Ewing, Juliana Horatia 1841-1885 .... DLB-21, 163

The Examiner 1808-1881 .............. DLB-110

Exley, Frederick 1929-1992 ...... DLB-143; Y-81

Editorial: The Extension of Copyright ... Y-02

von Eyb, Albrecht 1420-1475 .......... DLB-179

Eyre and Spottiswoode ............... DLB-106

Ezera, Regīna 1930- ................ DLB-232

Ezzo ?-after 1065 ................... DLB-148

# F

Faber, Frederick William 1814-1863 .... DLB-32

Faber and Faber Limited .............. DLB-112

Faccio, Rena (see Aleramo, Sibilla)

Facsimiles
  The Uses of Facsimile: A Symposium .... Y-90

Fadeev, Aleksandr Aleksandrovich
  1901-1956 ....................... DLB-272

Fagundo, Ana María 1938- .......... DLB-134

Fainzil'berg, Il'ia Arnol'dovich
  (see Il'f, Il'ia and Petrov, Evgenii)

Fair, Ronald L. 1932- ............... DLB-33

Fairfax, Beatrice (see Manning, Marie)

Fairlie, Gerard 1899-1983 ............ DLB-77

Fallada, Hans 1893-1947 .............. DLB-56

Fancher, Betsy 1928- ................. Y-83

Fane, Violet 1843-1905 ............... DLB-35

Fanfrolico Press .................... DLB-112

Fanning, Katherine 1927- ............ DLB-127

Fanshawe, Sir Richard 1608-1666 . . . . . . .DLB-126

Fantasy Press Publishers . . . . . . . . . . . . . .DLB-46

Fante, John 1909-1983. . . . . . . . . .DLB-130; Y-83

Al-Farabi circa 870-950. . . . . . . . . . . . . . .DLB-115

Farabough, Laura 1949-  . . . . . . . . . . .DLB-228

Farah, Nuruddin 1945-  . . .DLB-125; CDWLB-3

Farber, Norma 1909-1984 . . . . . . . . . . . . . .DLB-61

Fargue, Léon-Paul 1876-1947. . . . . . . . . .DLB-258

Farigoule, Louis (see Romains, Jules)

Farjeon, Eleanor 1881-1965. . . . . . . . . . . .DLB-160

Farley, Harriet 1812-1907 . . . . . . . . . . . . .DLB-239

Farley, Walter 1920-1989 . . . . . . . . . . . . . .DLB-22

Farmborough, Florence 1887-1978. . . . . . .DLB-204

Farmer, Penelope 1939-  . . . . . . . . . . . . .DLB-161

Farmer, Philip José 1918-  . . . . . . . . . . . . . .DLB-8

Farnaby, Thomas 1575?-1647 . . . . . . . . . .DLB-236

Farningham, Marianne (see Hearn, Mary Anne)

Farquhar, George circa 1677-1707 . . . . . . .DLB-84

Farquharson, Martha (see Finley, Martha)

Farrar, Frederic William 1831-1903. . . . . .DLB-163

Farrar, Straus and Giroux . . . . . . . . . . . . .DLB-46

Farrar and Rinehart . . . . . . . . . . . . . . . . .DLB-46

Farrell, J. G. 1935-1979 . . . . . . . . . . .DLB-14, 271

Farrell, James T. 1904-1979 . . . .DLB-4, 9, 86; DS-2

Fast, Howard 1914-  . . . . . . . . . . . . . . . . .DLB-9

Faulkner, William 1897-1962
. . .DLB-9, 11, 44, 102; DS-2; Y-86; CDALB-5

    Faulkner and Yoknapatawpha
        Conference, Oxford, Mississippi . . . . Y-97

    Faulkner Centennial Addresses . . . . . . . . Y-97

    "Faulkner 100–Celebrating the Work,"
        University of South Carolina,
        Columbia . . . . . . . . . . . . . . . . . . Y-97

    Impressions of William Faulkner . . . . . . Y-97

    William Faulkner and the People-to-People
        Program . . . . . . . . . . . . . . . . . . . Y-86

    William Faulkner Centenary
        Celebrations . . . . . . . . . . . . . . . . Y-97

    The William Faulkner Society. . . . . . . . . Y-99

George Faulkner [publishing house] . . . . .DLB-154

Faulks, Sebastian 1953-  . . . . . . . . . . . .DLB-207

Fauset, Jessie Redmon 1882-1961 . . . . . . . .DLB-51

Faust, Frederick Schiller (Max Brand)
1892-1944. . . . . . . . . . . . . . . . . . . . .DLB-256

Faust, Irvin
1924-  . . . . . . DLB-2, 28, 218, 278; Y-80, 00

    I Wake Up Screaming [Response to
        Ken Auletta] . . . . . . . . . . . . . . . . Y-97

    Tribute to Bernard Malamud . . . . . . . . . Y-86

    Tribute to Isaac Bashevis Singer . . . . . . . Y-91

    Tribute to Meyer Levin . . . . . . . . . . . . Y-81

Fawcett, Edgar 1847-1904 . . . . . . . . . . . .DLB-202

Fawcett, Millicent Garrett 1847-1929 . . . . .DLB-190

Fawcett Books . . . . . . . . . . . . . . . . . . . . .DLB-46

Fay, Theodore Sedgwick 1807-1898 . . . . .DLB-202

Fearing, Kenneth 1902-1961 . . . . . . . . . . . .DLB-9

Federal Writers' Project. . . . . . . . . . . . . . .DLB-46

Federman, Raymond 1928-  . . . . . . . . . . . Y-80

Fedin, Konstantin Aleksandrovich
1892-1977 . . . . . . . . . . . . . . . . . . . .DLB-272

Fedorov, Innokentii Vasil'evich
(see Omulevsky, Innokentii Vasil'evich)

Feiffer, Jules 1929-  . . . . . . . . . . . . . .DLB-7, 44

Feinberg, Charles E. 1899-1988. . . .DLB-187; Y-88

Feind, Barthold 1678-1721 . . . . . . . . . . . .DLB-168

Feinstein, Elaine 1930-  . . . . . . . . . .DLB-14, 40

Feirstein, Frederick 1940-  . . . . . . . . . . .DLB-282

Feiss, Paul Louis 1875-1952 . . . . . . . . . . .DLB-187

Feldman, Irving 1928-  . . . . . . . . . . . . .DLB-169

Felipe, Léon 1884-1968 . . . . . . . . . . . . . .DLB-108

Fell, Frederick, Publishers . . . . . . . . . . . . .DLB-46

Fellowship of Southern Writers . . . . . . . . . . Y-98

Felltham, Owen 1602?-1668 . . . . . . .DLB-126, 151

Felman, Shoshana 1942-  . . . . . . . . . . . .DLB-246

Fels, Ludwig 1946-  . . . . . . . . . . . . . . . .DLB-75

Felton, Cornelius Conway
1807-1862 . . . . . . . . . . . . . . . . . . .DLB-1, 235

Mothe-Fénelon, François de Salignac de la
1651-1715 . . . . . . . . . . . . . . . . . . . .DLB-268

Fenn, Harry 1837-1911 . . . . . . . . . . . . . .DLB-188

Fennario, David 1947-  . . . . . . . . . . . . . .DLB-60

Fenner, Dudley 1558?-1587? . . . . . . . . . .DLB-236

Fenno, Jenny 1765?-1803 . . . . . . . . . . . . .DLB-200

Fenno, John 1751-1798. . . . . . . . . . . . . . .DLB-43

R. F. Fenno and Company. . . . . . . . . . . . .DLB-49

Fenoglio, Beppe 1922-1963 . . . . . . . . . . . .DLB-177

Fenton, Geoffrey 1539?-1608. . . . . . . . . . .DLB-136

Fenton, James 1949-  . . . . . . . . . . . . . . .DLB-40

    The Hemingway/Fenton
        Correspondence . . . . . . . . . . . . . . Y-02

Ferber, Edna 1885-1968. . . . . . .DLB-9, 28, 86, 266

Ferdinand, Vallery, III (see Salaam, Kalamu ya)

Ferguson, Sir Samuel 1810-1886 . . . . . . . .DLB-32

Ferguson, William Scott 1875-1954 . . . . . . .DLB-47

Fergusson, Robert 1750-1774 . . . . . . . . . .DLB-109

Ferland, Albert 1872-1943 . . . . . . . . . . . . .DLB-92

Ferlinghetti, Lawrence
1919-  . . . . . . . . . . . .DLB-5, 16; CDALB-1

    Tribute to Kenneth Rexroth . . . . . . . . . . Y-82

Fermor, Patrick Leigh 1915-  . . . . . . . .DLB-204

Fern, Fanny (see Parton, Sara Payson Willis)

Ferrars, Elizabeth (Morna Doris Brown)
1907-1995 . . . . . . . . . . . . . . . . . . . . .DLB-87

Ferré, Rosario 1942-  . . . . . . . . . . . . . .DLB-145

Ferreira, Vergílio 1916-1996 . . . . . . . . . . .DLB-287

E. Ferret and Company . . . . . . . . . . . . . .DLB-49

Ferrier, Susan 1782-1854 . . . . . . . . . . . . .DLB-116

Ferril, Thomas Hornsby 1896-1988 . . . . .DLB-206

Ferrini, Vincent 1913-  . . . . . . . . . . . . . .DLB-48

Ferron, Jacques 1921-1985 . . . . . . . . . . . . .DLB-60

Ferron, Madeleine 1922-  . . . . . . . . . . . .DLB-53

Ferrucci, Franco 1936-  . . . . . . . . . . . . .DLB-196

Fet, Afanasii Afanas'evich
1820?-1892 . . . . . . . . . . . . . . . . . . . .DLB-277

Fetridge and Company . . . . . . . . . . . . . . .DLB-49

Feuchtersleben, Ernst Freiherr von
1806-1849 . . . . . . . . . . . . . . . . . . . .DLB-133

Feuchtwanger, Lion 1884-1958 . . . . . . . . .DLB-66

Feuerbach, Ludwig 1804-1872. . . . . . . . .DLB-133

Feuillet, Octave 1821-1890 . . . . . . . . . . .DLB-192

Feydeau, Georges 1862-1921. . . . . . . . . .DLB-192

Fichte, Johann Gottlieb 1762-1814. . . . . . .DLB-90

Ficke, Arthur Davison 1883-1945 . . . . . . . .DLB-54

Fiction

    American Fiction and the 1930s . . . . . .DLB-9

    Fiction Best-Sellers, 1910-1945 . . . . . . .DLB-9

    The Year in Fiction. . . . . . . .Y-84, 86, 89, 94–99

    The Year in Fiction: A Biased View . . . . . Y-83

    The Year in U.S. Fiction . . . . . . . . . . Y-00, 01

    The Year's Work in Fiction: A Survey. . . Y-82

Fiedler, Leslie A. 1917-  . . . . . . . . . .DLB-28, 67

    Tribute to Bernard Malamud . . . . . . . . . Y-86

    Tribute to James Dickey . . . . . . . . . . . . .Y-97

Field, Barron 1789-1846. . . . . . . . . . . . . .DLB-230

Field, Edward 1924-  . . . . . . . . . . . . . .DLB-105

Field, Eugene 1850-1895 . .DLB-23, 42, 140; DS-13

Field, John 1545?-1588 . . . . . . . . . . . . . . .DLB-167

Field, Joseph M. 1810-1856 . . . . . . . . . . .DLB-248

Field, Marshall, III 1893-1956. . . . . . . . . .DLB-127

Field, Marshall, IV 1916-1965 . . . . . . . . .DLB-127

Field, Marshall, V 1941-  . . . . . . . . . . .DLB-127

Field, Michael (Katherine Harris Bradley)
1846-1914 . . . . . . . . . . . . . . . . . . . .DLB-240

    "The Poetry File" . . . . . . . . . . . . . . .DLB-105

Field, Nathan 1587-1619 or 1620 . . . . . . . .DLB-58

Field, Rachel 1894-1942. . . . . . . . . . . . .DLB-9, 22

Fielding, Helen 1958-  . . . . . . . . . . . . .DLB-231

Fielding, Henry
1707-1754 . . . . . . . .DLB-39, 84, 101; CDBLB-2

    "Defense of *Amelia*" (1752). . . . . . . . . .DLB-39

    *The History of the Adventures of Joseph Andrews*
        [excerpt] (1742) . . . . . . . . . . . . . . .DLB-39

    Letter to [Samuel] Richardson on *Clarissa*
        (1748) . . . . . . . . . . . . . . . . . . . .DLB-39

    Preface to *Joseph Andrews* (1742) . . . . . .DLB-39

    Preface to Sarah Fielding's *Familiar
        Letters* (1747) [excerpt]. . . . . . . . . .DLB-39

    Preface to Sarah Fielding's *The
        Adventures of David Simple* (1744) . . .DLB-39

    Review of *Clarissa* (1748) . . . . . . . . . . .DLB-39

    *Tom Jones* (1749) [excerpt] . . . . . . . . . .DLB-39

Fielding, Sarah 1710-1768. . . . . . . . . . . . .DLB-39

    Preface to *The Cry* (1754) . . . . . . . . . . .DLB-39

Fields, Annie Adams 1834-1915 . . . . . . . .DLB-221

Fields, Dorothy 1905-1974. . . . . . . . . . . .DLB-265

Fields, James T. 1817-1881. . . . . . . . .DLB-1, 235

Fields, Julia 1938-  . . . . . . . . . . . . . . . .DLB-41

Fields, Osgood and Company . . . . . . . . . .DLB-49

Fields, W. C. 1880-1946 . . . . . . . . . . . . . .DLB-44

Fierstein, Harvey 1954-  . . . . . . . . . . . .DLB-266

Figes, Eva 1932-  . . . . . . . . . . . . . .DLB-14, 271

# Cumulative Index

Figuera, Angela 1902-1984 . . . . . . . . . . . DLB-108
Filmer, Sir Robert 1586-1653 . . . . . . . . . DLB-151
Filson, John circa 1753-1788 . . . . . . . . . . . DLB-37
Finch, Anne, Countess of Winchilsea
　1661-1720 . . . . . . . . . . . . . . . . . . . . . DLB-95
Finch, Annie 1956- . . . . . . . . . . . . . . . DLB-282
Finch, Robert 1900- . . . . . . . . . . . . . . . DLB-88
Findley, Timothy 1930-2002 . . . . . . . . . . DLB-53
Finlay, Ian Hamilton 1925- . . . . . . . . . . . DLB-40
Finley, Martha 1828-1909 . . . . . . . . . . . . DLB-42
Finn, Elizabeth Anne (McCaul)
　1825-1921 . . . . . . . . . . . . . . . . . . . . DLB-166
Finnegan, Seamus 1949- . . . . . . . . . . . DLB-245
Finney, Jack 1911-1995 . . . . . . . . . . . . . . DLB-8
Finney, Walter Braden (see Finney, Jack)
Firbank, Ronald 1886-1926 . . . . . . . . . . . DLB-36
Firmin, Giles 1615-1697 . . . . . . . . . . . . . DLB-24
First Edition Library/Collectors'
　Reprints, Inc. . . . . . . . . . . . . . . . . . . . . . Y-91
Fischart, Johann
　1546 or 1547-1590 or 1591 . . . . . . . . DLB-179
Fischer, Karoline Auguste Fernandine
　1764-1842 . . . . . . . . . . . . . . . . . . . . . DLB-94
Fischer, Tibor 1959- . . . . . . . . . . . . . . DLB-231
Fish, Stanley 1938- . . . . . . . . . . . . . . . . DLB-67
Fishacre, Richard 1205-1248 . . . . . . . . . DLB-115
Fisher, Clay (see Allen, Henry W.)
Fisher, Dorothy Canfield 1879-1958 . . . DLB-9, 102
Fisher, Leonard Everett 1924- . . . . . . . . DLB-61
Fisher, Roy 1930- . . . . . . . . . . . . . . . . . DLB-40
Fisher, Rudolph 1897-1934 . . . . . . . . DLB-51, 102
Fisher, Steve 1913-1980 . . . . . . . . . . . . DLB-226
Fisher, Sydney George 1856-1927 . . . . . . DLB-47
Fisher, Vardis 1895-1968 . . . . . . . . . DLB-9, 206
Fiske, John 1608-1677 . . . . . . . . . . . . . . DLB-24
Fiske, John 1842-1901 . . . . . . . . . . . . . DLB-47, 64
Fitch, Thomas circa 1700-1774 . . . . . . . . DLB-31
Fitch, William Clyde 1865-1909 . . . . . . . . DLB-7
FitzGerald, Edward 1809-1883 . . . . . . . . DLB-32
Fitzgerald, F. Scott 1896-1940
　. . . . . . . . . . . . . . . . DLB-4, 9, 86; Y-81, 92;
　DS-1, 15, 16; CDALB-4
　F. Scott Fitzgerald: A Descriptive
　　Bibliography, Supplement (2001) . . . . Y-01
　F. Scott Fitzgerald Centenary
　　Celebrations . . . . . . . . . . . . . . . . . . . Y-96
　F. Scott Fitzgerald Inducted into the
　　American Poets' Corner at St. John
　　the Divine; Ezra Pound Banned . . . . Y-99
　"F. Scott Fitzgerald: St. Paul's Native Son
　　and Distinguished American Writer":
　　University of Minnesota Conference,
　　29-31 October 1982 . . . . . . . . . . . . . Y-82
　First International F. Scott Fitzgerald
　　Conference . . . . . . . . . . . . . . . . . . . Y-92
　*The Great Gatsby* (Documentary) . . . . DLB-219
　*Tender Is the Night* (Documentary) . . . DLB-273
Fitzgerald, Penelope 1916- . . . . . . . . DLB-14, 194
Fitzgerald, Robert 1910-1985 . . . . . . . . . . . Y-80

FitzGerald, Robert D. 1902-1987 . . . . . . DLB-260
Fitzgerald, Thomas 1819-1891 . . . . . . . . DLB-23
Fitzgerald, Zelda Sayre 1900-1948 . . . . . . . Y-84
Fitzhugh, Louise 1928-1974 . . . . . . . . . . DLB-52
Fitzhugh, William circa 1651-1701 . . . . . . DLB-24
Flagg, James Montgomery 1877-1960 . . . . DLB-188
Flanagan, Thomas 1923-2002 . . . . . . . . . . . Y-80
Flanner, Hildegarde 1899-1987 . . . . . . . . DLB-48
Flanner, Janet 1892-1978 . . . . . . . . DLB-4; DS-15
Flannery, Peter 1951- . . . . . . . . . . . . . DLB-233
Flaubert, Gustave 1821-1880 . . . . . . . . . DLB-119
Flavin, Martin 1883-1967 . . . . . . . . . . . . . DLB-9
Fleck, Konrad (flourished circa 1220) . . . DLB-138
Flecker, James Elroy 1884-1915 . . . . . . DLB-10, 19
Fleeson, Doris 1901-1970 . . . . . . . . . . . . DLB-29
Fleißer, Marieluise 1901-1974 . . . . . . DLB-56, 124
Fleischer, Nat 1887-1972 . . . . . . . . . . . DLB-241
Fleming, Abraham 1552?-1607 . . . . . . . . DLB-236
Fleming, Ian 1908-1964 . . . DLB-87, 201; CDBLB-7
Fleming, Joan 1908-1980 . . . . . . . . . . . DLB-276
Fleming, May Agnes 1840-1880 . . . . . . . . DLB-99
Fleming, Paul 1609-1640 . . . . . . . . . . . DLB-164
Fleming, Peter 1907-1971 . . . . . . . . . . . DLB-195
Fletcher, Giles, the Elder 1546-1611 . . . . . DLB-136
Fletcher, Giles, the Younger
　1585 or 1586-1623 . . . . . . . . . . . . . . DLB-121
Fletcher, J. S. 1863-1935 . . . . . . . . . . . . DLB-70
Fletcher, John 1579-1625 . . . . . . . . . . . . DLB-58
Fletcher, John Gould 1886-1950 . . . . . . DLB-4, 45
Fletcher, Phineas 1582-1650 . . . . . . . . . DLB-121
Flieg, Helmut (see Heym, Stefan)
Flint, F. S. 1885-1960 . . . . . . . . . . . . . . DLB-19
Flint, Timothy 1780-1840 . . . . . . . . . DLB-73, 186
Flores, Juan de fl. 1470-1500 . . . . . . . . . DLB-286
Flores-Williams, Jason 1969- . . . . . . . . . DLB-209
Florio, John 1553?-1625 . . . . . . . . . . . . DLB-172
Fludd, Robert 1574-1637 . . . . . . . . . . . DLB-281
Fo, Dario 1926- . . . . . . . . . . . . . . . . . . . . Y-97
　Nobel Lecture 1997: Contra Jogulatores
　　Obloquentes . . . . . . . . . . . . . . . . . . Y-97
Foden, Giles 1967- . . . . . . . . . . . . . . . DLB-267
Fofanov, Konstantin Mikhailovich
　1862-1911 . . . . . . . . . . . . . . . . . . . . DLB-277
Foix, J. V. 1893-1987 . . . . . . . . . . . . . . DLB-134
Foley, Martha 1897-1977 . . . . . . . . . . . DLB-137
Folger, Henry Clay 1857-1930 . . . . . . . . DLB-140
Folio Society . . . . . . . . . . . . . . . . . . . . DLB-112
Follain, Jean 1903-1971 . . . . . . . . . . . . DLB-258
Follen, Charles 1796-1840 . . . . . . . . . . . DLB-235
Follen, Eliza Lee (Cabot) 1787-1860 . . . DLB-1, 235
Follett, Ken 1949- . . . . . . . . . . . . . DLB-87; Y-81
Follett Publishing Company . . . . . . . . . . DLB-46
John West Folsom [publishing house] . . . . DLB-49
Folz, Hans
　between 1435 and 1440-1513 . . . . . . . DLB-179

Fonseca, Manuel da 1911-1993 . . . . . . . DLB-287
Fontane, Theodor
　1819-1898 . . . . . . . . . . . . . . DLB-129; CDWLB-2
Fontenelle, Bernard Le Bovier de
　1657-1757 . . . . . . . . . . . . . . . . . . . . DLB-268
Fontes, Montserrat 1940- . . . . . . . . . . . DLB-209
Fonvisin, Denis Ivanovich
　1744 or 1745-1792 . . . . . . . . . . . . . . DLB-150
Foote, Horton 1916- . . . . . . . . . . . DLB-26, 266
Foote, Mary Hallock
　1847-1938 . . . . . . . . . . DLB-186, 188, 202, 221
Foote, Samuel 1721-1777 . . . . . . . . . . . . DLB-89
Foote, Shelby 1916- . . . . . . . . . . . . . . DLB-2, 17
Forbes, Calvin 1945- . . . . . . . . . . . . . . DLB-41
Forbes, Ester 1891-1967 . . . . . . . . . . . . DLB-22
Forbes, Rosita 1893?-1967 . . . . . . . . . . DLB-195
Forbes and Company . . . . . . . . . . . . . . DLB-49
Force, Peter 1790-1868 . . . . . . . . . . . . . DLB-30
Forché, Carolyn 1950- . . . . . . . . . . . . DLB-5, 193
Ford, Charles Henri 1913-2002 . . . . . . DLB-4, 48
Ford, Corey 1902-1969 . . . . . . . . . . . . . DLB-11
Ford, Ford Madox
　1873-1939 . . . . . . . DLB-34, 98, 162; CDBLB-6
　Nathan Asch Remembers Ford Madox
　　Ford, Sam Roth, and Hart Crane . . . . Y-02
J. B. Ford and Company . . . . . . . . . . . . DLB-49
Ford, Jesse Hill 1928-1996 . . . . . . . . . . . DLB-6
Ford, John 1586-? . . . . . . . . . . DLB-58; CDBLB-1
Ford, R. A. D. 1915- . . . . . . . . . . . . . . DLB-88
Ford, Richard 1944- . . . . . . . . . . . . . . DLB-227
Ford, Worthington C. 1858-1941 . . . . . . . DLB-47
Fords, Howard, and Hulbert . . . . . . . . . DLB-49
Foreman, Carl 1914-1984 . . . . . . . . . . . DLB-26
Forester, C. S. 1899-1966 . . . . . . . . . . . DLB-191
　The C. S. Forester Society . . . . . . . . . . . Y-00
Forester, Frank (see Herbert, Henry William)
Anthologizing New Formalism . . . . . . . . DLB-282
The Little Magazines of the
　New Formalism . . . . . . . . . . . . . . . . DLB-282
The New Narrative Poetry . . . . . . . . . . . DLB-282
Presses of the New Formalism and
　the New Narrative . . . . . . . . . . . . . . DLB-282
The Prosody of the New Formalism . . . . DLB-282
Younger Women Poets of the
　New Formalism . . . . . . . . . . . . . . . . DLB-282
Forman, Harry Buxton 1842-1917 . . . . . . DLB-184
Fornés, María Irene 1930- . . . . . . . . . . . DLB-7
Forrest, Leon 1937-1997 . . . . . . . . . . . . DLB-33
Forsh, Ol'ga Dmitrievna 1873-1961 . . . . . DLB-272
Forster, E. M.
　1879-1970 . . . . . . . DLB-34, 98, 162, 178, 195;
　DS-10; CDBLB-6
　"Fantasy," from *Aspects of the Novel*
　　(1927) . . . . . . . . . . . . . . . . . . . . . DLB-178
Forster, Georg 1754-1794 . . . . . . . . . . . DLB-94
Forster, John 1812-1876 . . . . . . . . . . . . DLB-144
Forster, Margaret 1938- . . . . . . . . . DLB-155, 271
Forsyth, Frederick 1938- . . . . . . . . . . . . DLB-87

Forsyth, William
"Literary Style" (1857) [excerpt] ......DLB-57

Forten, Charlotte L. 1837-1914 ......DLB-50, 239

   Pages from Her Diary..............DLB-50

Fortini, Franco 1917-1994..............DLB-128

Fortune, Mary ca. 1833-ca. 1910........DLB-230

Fortune, T. Thomas 1856-1928..........DLB-23

Fosdick, Charles Austin 1842-1915.......DLB-42

Foster, Genevieve 1893-1979............DLB-61

Foster, Hannah Webster 1758-1840...DLB-37, 200

Foster, John 1648-1681..................DLB-24

Foster, Michael 1904-1956................DLB-9

Foster, Myles Birket 1825-1899..........DLB-184

Foucault, Michel 1926-1984.............DLB-242

Robert and Andrew Foulis
   [publishing house]..................DLB-154

Fouqué, Caroline de la Motte 1774-1831...DLB-90

Fouqué, Friedrich de la Motte
   1777-1843.........................DLB-90

Four Seas Company....................DLB-46

Four Winds Press......................DLB-46

Fournier, Henri Alban (see Alain-Fournier)

Fowler, Christopher 1953- ............DLB-267

Fowler and Wells Company ............DLB-49

Fowles, John
   1926- ........DLB-14, 139, 207; CDBLB-8

Fox, John 1939- .....................DLB-245

Fox, John, Jr. 1862 or 1863-1919....DLB-9; DS-13

Fox, Paula 1923- ....................DLB-52

Fox, Richard Kyle 1846-1922 ..........DLB-79

Fox, William Price 1926- ........DLB-2; Y-81

   Remembering Joe Heller..............Y-99

Richard K. Fox [publishing house].......DLB-49

Foxe, John 1517-1587..................DLB-132

Fraenkel, Michael 1896-1957.............DLB-4

France, Anatole 1844-1924 ............DLB-123

France, Richard 1938- ................DLB-7

Francis, Convers 1795-1863..........DLB-1, 235

Francis, Dick 1920- .......DLB-87; CDBLB-8

Francis, Sir Frank 1901-1988..........DLB-201

Francis, Jeffrey, Lord 1773-1850 ........DLB-107

C. S. Francis [publishing house].........DLB-49

Franck, Sebastian 1499-1542 ...........DLB-179

Francke, Kuno 1855-1930 ..............DLB-71

Françoise (Robertine Barry) 1863-1910....DLB-92

François, Louise von 1817-1893.........DLB-129

Frank, Bruno 1887-1945................DLB-118

Frank, Leonhard 1882-1961 ........DLB-56, 118

Frank, Melvin 1913-1988..............DLB-26

Frank, Waldo 1889-1967...............DLB-9, 63

Franken, Rose 1895?-1988 .....DLB-228, Y-84

Franklin, Benjamin
   1706-1790.....DLB-24, 43, 73, 183; CDALB-2

Franklin, James 1697-1735.............DLB-43

Franklin, John 1786-1847..............DLB-99

Franklin, Miles 1879-1954.............DLB-230

Franklin Library.....................DLB-46

Frantz, Ralph Jules 1902-1979 ............DLB-4

Franzos, Karl Emil 1848-1904 ..........DLB-129

Fraser, Antonia 1932- ................DLB-276

Fraser, G. S. 1915-1980 ................DLB-27

Fraser, Kathleen 1935- ...............DLB-169

Frattini, Alberto 1922- ...............DLB-128

Frau Ava ?-1127.....................DLB-148

Fraunce, Abraham 1558?-1592 or 1593...DLB-236

Frayn, Michael 1933- .....DLB-13, 14, 194, 245

Fréchette, Louis-Honoré 1839-1908.......DLB-99

Frederic, Harold 1856-1898....DLB-12, 23; DS-13

Freed, Arthur 1894-1973 ..............DLB-265

Freeling, Nicolas 1927- ...............DLB-87

   Tribute to Georges Simenon...........Y-89

Freeman, Douglas Southall
   1886-1953 .................DLB-17; DS-17

Freeman, Judith 1946- ...............DLB-256

Freeman, Legh Richmond 1842-1915.....DLB-23

Freeman, Mary E. Wilkins
   1852-1930 ................DLB-12, 78, 221

Freeman, R. Austin 1862-1943 ..........DLB-70

Freidank circa 1170-circa 1233..........DLB-138

Freiligrath, Ferdinand 1810-1876 ........DLB-133

Fremlin, Celia 1914- ................DLB-276

Frémont, Jessie Benton 1834-1902........DLB-183

Frémont, John Charles 1813-1890...DLB-183, 186

French, Alice 1850-1934 .........DLB-74; DS-13

French, David 1939- .................DLB-53

French, Evangeline 1869-1960..........DLB-195

French, Francesca 1871-1960...........DLB-195

James French [publishing house] ........DLB-49

Samuel French [publishing house]........DLB-49

Samuel French, Limited...............DLB-106

French Literature
   Epic and Beast Epic...............DLB-208
   French Arthurian Literature ........DLB-208
   Lyric Poetry .....................DLB-268
   Other Poets.....................DLB-217
   Poetry in Nineteenth-Century France:
     Cultural Background and Critical
     Commentary ................DLB-217
   *Roman de la Rose:* Guillaume de Lorris
     1200 to 1205-circa 1230, Jean de
     Meun 1235/1240-circa 1305.....DLB-208
   Saints' Lives .....................DLB-208
   Troubadours, *Trobairitz,* and
     Trouvères...................DLB-208

French Theater
   Medieval French Drama ..........DLB-208
   Parisian Theater, Fall 1984: Toward
     a New Baroque................Y-85

Freneau, Philip 1752-1832 .........DLB-37, 43

   The Rising Glory of America ........DLB-37

Freni, Melo 1934- ..................DLB-128

Freshfield, Douglas W. 1845-1934.......DLB-174

Freytag, Gustav 1816-1895 ............DLB-129

Fridegård, Jan 1897-1968 .............DLB-259

Fried, Erich 1921-1988 ................DLB-85

Friedan, Betty 1921- .................DLB-246

Friedman, Bruce Jay 1930- ......DLB-2, 28, 244

Friedrich von Hausen circa 1171-1190....DLB-138

Friel, Brian 1929- ...................DLB-13

Friend, Krebs 1895?-1967? ..............DLB-4

Fries, Fritz Rudolf 1935- ..............DLB-75

Frisch, Max
   1911-1991 .........DLB-69, 124; CDWLB-2

Frischlin, Nicodemus 1547-1590 ........DLB-179

Frischmuth, Barbara 1941- ............DLB-85

Fritz, Jean 1915- ...................DLB-52

Froissart, Jean circa 1337-circa 1404......DLB-208

Fromentin, Eugene 1820-1876..........DLB-123

Frontinus circa A.D. 35-A.D. 103/104....DLB-211

Frost, A. B. 1851-1928..........DLB-188; DS-13

Frost, Robert
   1874-1963 .........DLB-54; DS-7; CDALB-4

   The Friends of the Dymock Poets ......Y-00

Frostenson, Katarina 1953- ...........DLB-257

Frothingham, Octavius Brooks
   1822-1895 .....................DLB-1, 243

Froude, James Anthony
   1818-1894 .............DLB-18, 57, 144

Fruitlands 1843-1844..........DLB-1, 223; DS-5

Fry, Christopher 1907- ................DLB-13

   Tribute to John Betjeman .............Y-84

Fry, Roger 1866-1934 ................DS-10

Fry, Stephen 1957- ..................DLB-207

Frye, Northrop 1912-1991......DLB-67, 68, 246

Fuchs, Daniel 1909-1993 .....DLB-9, 26, 28; Y-93

   Tribute to Isaac Bashevis Singer........Y-91

Fuentes, Carlos 1928- .....DLB-113; CDWLB-3

Fuertes, Gloria 1918-1998 .............DLB-108

Fugard, Athol 1932- ................DLB-225

The Fugitives and the Agrarians:
   The First Exhibition ................Y-85

Fujiwara no Shunzei 1114-1204.........DLB-203

Fujiwara no Tameaki 1230s?-1290s?.....DLB-203

Fujiwara no Tameie 1198-1275 .........DLB-203

Fujiwara no Teika 1162-1241 ..........DLB-203

Fulbecke, William 1560-1603?..........DLB-172

Fuller, Charles 1939- ............DLB-38, 266

Fuller, Henry Blake 1857-1929 ..........DLB-12

Fuller, John 1937- ..................DLB-40

Fuller, Margaret (see Fuller, Sarah)

Fuller, Roy 1912-1991 .............DLB-15, 20

   Tribute to Christopher Isherwood ......Y-86

Fuller, Samuel 1912-1997...............DLB-26

Fuller, Sarah 1810-1850..........DLB-1, 59, 73,
      183, 223, 239; DS-5; CDALB-2

Fuller, Thomas 1608-1661..............DLB-151

Fullerton, Hugh 1873-1945 ............DLB-171

Fullwood, William flourished 1568......DLB-236

Fulton, Alice 1952- .................DLB-193

# Cumulative Index

Fulton, Len 1934- .................... Y-86
Fulton, Robin 1937- ............... DLB-40
Furbank, P. N. 1920- ............. DLB-155
Furetière, Antoine 1619-1688 .......... DLB-268
Furman, Laura 1945- ............... Y-86
Furmanov, Dmitrii Andreevich
  1891-1926 .................. DLB-272
Furness, Horace Howard 1833-1912 ..... DLB-64
Furness, William Henry 1802-1896 ... DLB-1, 235
Furnivall, Frederick James 1825-1910.... DLB-184
Furphy, Joseph (Tom Collins)
  1843-1912 .................. DLB-230
Furthman, Jules 1888-1966 ......... DLB-26
  Shakespeare and Montaigne: A
    Symposium by Jules Furthman ..... Y-02
Furui Yoshikichi 1937- ............ DLB-182
Fushimi, Emperor 1265-1317 ........ DLB-203
Futabatei Shimei (Hasegawa Tatsunosuke)
  1864-1909 .................. DLB-180
Fyleman, Rose 1877-1957 ............ DLB-160

## G

Gadallah, Leslie 1939- .............. DLB-251
Gadda, Carlo Emilio 1893-1973 ....... DLB-177
Gaddis, William 1922-1998 ......... DLB-2, 278
  William Gaddis: A Tribute ............ Y-99
Gág, Wanda 1893-1946 ............. DLB-22
Gagarin, Ivan Sergeevich 1814-1882 .... DLB-198
Gagnon, Madeleine 1938- ........... DLB-60
Gaiman, Neil 1960- ............... DLB-261
Gaine, Hugh 1726-1807 ............. DLB-43
Hugh Gaine [publishing house] ........ DLB-49
Gaines, Ernest J.
  1933- .... DLB-2, 33, 152; Y-80; CDALB-6
Gaiser, Gerd 1908-1976 ............ DLB-69
Gaitskill, Mary 1954- .............. DLB-244
Galarza, Ernesto 1905-1984 ......... DLB-122
Galaxy Science Fiction Novels ........ DLB-46
Galbraith, Robert (or Caubraith)
  circa 1483-1544 ............... DLB-281
Gale, Zona 1874-1938 .......... DLB-9, 228, 78
Galen of Pergamon 129-after 210 .....DLB-176
Gales, Winifred Marshall 1761-1839 .... DLB-200
Medieval Galician-Portuguese Poetry.... DLB-287
Gall, Louise von 1815-1855 ......... DLB-133
Gallagher, Tess 1943- ...... DLB-120, 212, 244
Gallagher, Wes 1911- .............. DLB-127
Gallagher, William Davis 1808-1894 ..... DLB-73
Gallant, Mavis 1922- .............. DLB-53
Gallegos, María Magdalena 1935- .... DLB-209
Gallico, Paul 1897-1976 ........... DLB-9, 171
Gallop, Jane 1952- ................ DLB-246
Galloway, Grace Growden 1727-1782.... DLB-200
Gallup, Donald 1913-2000 .......... DLB-187
Galsworthy, John 1867-1933
  ...... DLB-10, 34, 98, 162; DS-16; CDBLB-5

Galt, John 1779-1839 ..........DLB-99, 116, 159
Galton, Sir Francis 1822-1911 ......... DLB-166
Galvin, Brendan 1938- ............... DLB-5
Gambit ........................ DLB-46
Gamboa, Reymundo 1948- .......... DLB-122
*Gammer Gurton's Needle*............... DLB-62
Gan, Elena Andreevna (Zeneida R-va)
  1814-1842 .................. DLB-198
Gandlevsky, Sergei Markovich 1952- .. DLB-285
Gannett, Frank E. 1876-1957 ......... DLB-29
Gao Xingjian 1940- ................... Y-00
  Nobel Lecture 2000: "The Case for
    Literature" ....................... Y-00
Gaos, Vicente 1919-1980 ............. DLB-134
García, Andrew 1854?-1943 .......... DLB-209
García, Lionel G. 1935- ............. DLB-82
García, Richard 1941- .............. DLB-209
García Márquez, Gabriel
  1928- ........DLB-113; Y-82; CDWLB-3
  The Magical World of Macondo....... Y-82
  Nobel Lecture 1982: The Solitude of
    Latin America .................. Y-82
  A Tribute to Gabriel García Márquez .... Y-82
García Marruz, Fina 1923- ......... DLB-283
García-Camarillo, Cecilio 1943- ....... DLB-209
Gardam, Jane 1928- ........ DLB-14, 161, 231
Gardell, Jonas 1963- ............... DLB-257
Garden, Alexander circa 1685-1756 ...... DLB-31
Gardiner, John Rolfe 1936- .......... DLB-244
Gardiner, Margaret Power Farmer
  (see Blessington, Marguerite, Countess of)
Gardner, John
  1933-1982 ........ DLB-2; Y-82; CDALB-7
Garfield, Leon 1921-1996............ DLB-161
Garis, Howard R. 1873-1962 ......... DLB-22
Garland, Hamlin 1860-1940...DLB-12, 71, 78, 186
  The Hamlin Garland Society.......... Y-01
Garneau, François-Xavier 1809-1866..... DLB-99
Garneau, Hector de Saint-Denys
  1912-1943 .................. DLB-88
Garneau, Michel 1939- ............. DLB-53
Garner, Alan 1934- ......... DLB-161, 261
Garner, Hugh 1913-1979 ............ DLB-68
Garnett, David 1892-1981 ........... DLB-34
Garnett, Eve 1900-1991 ............ DLB-160
Garnett, Richard 1835-1906........... DLB-184
Garrard, Lewis H. 1829-1887.......... DLB-186
Garraty, John A. 1920- ............. DLB-17
Garrett, Almeida (João Baptista da Silva
  Leitão de Almeida Garrett)
  1799-1854..................... DLB-287
Garrett, George
  1929- ........DLB-2, 5, 130, 152; Y-83
  Literary Prizes .................... Y-00
  My Summer Reading Orgy: Reading
    for Fun and Games: One Reader's
    Report on the Summer of 2001 ...... Y-01
  A Summing Up at Century's End ....... Y-99

Tribute to James Dickey ............. Y-97
Tribute to Michael M. Rea ........... Y-97
Tribute to Paxton Davis ............. Y-94
Tribute to Peter Taylor ............. Y-94
Tribute to William Goyen ........... Y-83
A Writer Talking: A Collage........... Y-00
Garrett, John Work 1872-1942.........DLB-187
Garrick, David 1717-1779 .......... DLB-84, 213
Garrison, William Lloyd
  1805-1879........ DLB-1, 43, 235; CDALB-2
Garro, Elena 1920-1998 .............. DLB-145
Garshin, Vsevolod Mikhailovich
  1855-1888 ....................DLB-277
Garth, Samuel 1661-1719 ............. DLB-95
Garve, Andrew 1908-2001 ........... DLB-87
Gary, Romain 1914-1980 ............. DLB-83
Gascoigne, George 1539?-1577......... DLB-136
Gascoyne, David 1916-2001........... DLB-20
Gash, Jonathan (John Grant) 1933- ....DLB-276
Gaskell, Elizabeth Cleghorn
  1810-1865 ..... DLB-21, 144, 159; CDBLB-4
  The Gaskell Society ................ Y-98
Gaskell, Jane 1941- ............... DLB-261
Gaspey, Thomas 1788-1871 .......... DLB-116
Gass, William H. 1924- ......... DLB-2, 227
Gates, Doris 1901-1987 ............. DLB-22
Gates, Henry Louis, Jr. 1950- ....... DLB-67
Gates, Lewis E. 1860-1924 ........... DLB-71
Gatto, Alfonso 1909-1976............. DLB-114
Gault, William Campbell 1910-1995 .... DLB-226
  Tribute to Kenneth Millar ............ Y-83
Gaunt, Mary 1861-1942..........DLB-174, 230
Gautier, Théophile 1811-1872 ........ DLB-119
Gauvreau, Claude 1925-1971 ......... DLB-88
The *Gawain*-Poet
  flourished circa 1350-1400......... DLB-146
Gawsworth, John (Terence Ian Fytton
  Armstrong) 1912-1970 ........... DLB-255
Gay, Ebenezer 1696-1787 ............ DLB-24
Gay, John 1685-1732 ............ DLB-84, 95
Gayarré, Charles E. A. 1805-1895 ....... DLB-30
Charles Gaylord [publishing house]...... DLB-49
Gaylord, Edward King 1873-1974 .......DLB-127
Gaylord, Edward Lewis 1919- ........DLB-127
Gébler, Carlo 1954- ...............DLB-271
Geda, Sigitas 1943- ............... DLB-232
Geddes, Gary 1940- ............... DLB-60
Geddes, Virgil 1897- ............... DLB-4
Gedeon (Georgii Andreevich Krinovsky)
  circa 1730-1763................. DLB-150
Gee, Maggie 1948- ............... DLB-207
Gee, Shirley 1932- ............... DLB-245
Geibel, Emanuel 1815-1884 .......... DLB-129
Geiogamah, Hanay 1945- ...........DLB-175
Geis, Bernard, Associates ............. DLB-46
Geisel, Theodor Seuss 1904-1991 ...DLB-61; Y-91

402

Gelb, Arthur 1924- .................DLB-103
Gelb, Barbara 1926- ..............DLB-103
Gelber, Jack 1932- ............DLB-7, 228
Gélinas, Gratien 1909-1999 ............DLB-88
Gellert, Christian Füerchtegott
    1715-1769......................DLB-97
Gellhorn, Martha 1908-1998........... Y-82, 98
Gems, Pam 1925- .................DLB-13
Genet, Jean 1910-1986...........DLB-72; Y-86
Genette, Gérard 1930- ...............DLB-242
Genevoix, Maurice 1890-1980............DLB-65
Genis, Aleksandr Aleksandrovich
    1953- .......................DLB-285
Genovese, Eugene D. 1930- ............DLB-17
Gent, Peter 1942- ..................... Y-82
Geoffrey of Monmouth
    circa 1100-1155.................DLB-146
George, Henry 1839-1897..............DLB-23
George, Jean Craighead 1919- ........DLB-52
George, W. L. 1882-1926 .............DLB-197
George III, King of Great Britain
    and Ireland 1738-1820 ............DLB-213
Georgslied 896?......................DLB-148
Gerber, Merrill Joan 1938- ...........DLB-218
Gerhardie, William 1895-1977...........DLB-36
Gerhardt, Paul 1607-1676............DLB-164
Gérin, Winifred 1901-1981 ............DLB-155
Gérin-Lajoie, Antoine 1824-1882..........DLB-99
German Literature
    A Call to Letters and an Invitation
        to the Electric Chair ............DLB-75
    The Conversion of an Unpolitical
        Man ........................DLB-66
    The German Radio Play..........DLB-124
    The German Transformation from the
        Baroque to the Enlightenment ....DLB-97
    Germanophilism .................DLB-66
    A Letter from a New Germany......... Y-90
    The Making of a People ...........DLB-66
    The Novel of Impressionism........DLB-66
    Pattern and Paradigm: History as
        Design......................DLB-75
    Premisses......................DLB-66
    The 'Twenties and Berlin ...........DLB-66
    Wolfram von Eschenbach's Parzival:
        Prologue and Book 3 ..........DLB-138
    Writers and Politics: 1871-1918.......DLB-66
German Literature, Middle Ages
    Abrogans circa 790-800.............DLB-148
    Annolied between 1077 and 1081 .....DLB-148
    The Arthurian Tradition and
        Its European Context ..........DLB-138
    Cambridge Songs (Carmina Cantabrigensia)
        circa 1050...................DLB-148
    Christus und die Samariterin circa 950 ...DLB-148
    De Heinrico circa 980?.............DLB-148
    Ecbasis Captivi circa 1045 ..........DLB-148
    Georgslied 896?..................DLB-148

    German Literature and Culture from
        Charlemagne to the Early Courtly
        Period ...........DLB-148; CDWLB-2
    The Germanic Epic and Old English
        Heroic Poetry: Widsith, Waldere,
        and The Fight at Finnsburg .......DLB-146
    Graf Rudolf between circa
        1170 and circa 1185 ..........DLB-148
    Heliand circa 850 .................DLB-148
    Das Hildesbrandslied
        circa 820..........DLB-148; CDWLB-2
    Kaiserchronik circa 1147.............DLB-148
    The Legends of the Saints and a
        Medieval Christian
        Worldview .................DLB-148
    Ludus de Antichristo circa 1160........DLB-148
    Ludwigslied 881 or 882.............DLB-148
    Muspilli circa 790-circa 850 ........DLB-148
    Old German Genesis and Old German
        Exodus circa 1050-circa 1130.....DLB-148
    Old High German Charms
        and Blessings ......DLB-148; CDWLB-2
    The Old High German Isidor
        circa 790-800.................DLB-148
    Petruslied circa 854?................DLB-148
    Physiologus circa 1070-circa 1150......DLB-148
    Ruodlieb circa 1050-1075............DLB-148
    "Spielmannsepen" (circa 1152
        circa 1500) ..................DLB-148
    The Strasbourg Oaths 842 .........DLB-148
    Tatian circa 830 .................DLB-148
    Waltharius circa 825 ..............DLB-148
    Wessobrunner Gebet circa 787-815......DLB-148
German Theater
    German Drama 800-1280..........DLB-138
    German Drama from Naturalism
        to Fascism: 1889-1933 .........DLB-118
Gernsback, Hugo 1884-1967.........DLB-8, 137
Gerould, Katharine Fullerton
    1879-1944 ....................DLB-78
Samuel Gerrish [publishing house] .......DLB-49
Gerrold, David 1944- .................DLB-8
Gersão, Teolinda 1940- ............DLB-287
Gershwin, Ira 1896-1983.............DLB-265
    The Ira Gershwin Centenary .......... Y-96
Gerson, Jean 1363-1429.............DLB-208
Gersonides 1288-1344................DLB-115
Gerstäcker, Friedrich 1816-1872 .......DLB-129
Gertsen, Aleksandr Ivanovich
    (see Herzen, Alexander)
Gerstenberg, Heinrich Wilhelm von
    1737-1823......................DLB-97
Gervinus, Georg Gottfried
    1805-1871 ....................DLB-133
Gery, John 1953- ..................DLB-282
Geßner, Solomon 1730-1788 ...........DLB-97
Geston, Mark S. 1946- ................DLB-8
Al-Ghazali 1058-1111................DLB-115
Gibbings, Robert 1889-1958 ..........DLB-195
Gibbon, Edward 1737-1794 ..........DLB-104

Gibbon, John Murray 1875-1952........DLB-92
Gibbon, Lewis Grassic (see Mitchell, James Leslie)
Gibbons, Floyd 1887-1939.............DLB-25
Gibbons, Reginald 1947- ...........DLB-120
Gibbons, William ?-?.................DLB-73
Gibson, Charles Dana
    1867-1944 ............DLB-188; DS-13
Gibson, Graeme 1934- ..............DLB-53
Gibson, Margaret 1944- .............DLB-120
Gibson, Margaret Dunlop 1843-1920 ....DLB-174
Gibson, Wilfrid 1878-1962 ............DLB-19
    The Friends of the Dymock Poets ....... Y-00
Gibson, William 1914- ................DLB-7
Gibson, William 1948- ...............DLB-251
Gide, André 1869-1951................DLB-65
Giguère, Diane 1937- ................DLB-53
Giguère, Roland 1929- ...............DLB-60
Gil de Biedma, Jaime  1929-1990 .......DLB-108
Gil-Albert, Juan 1906-1994 ..........DLB-134
Gilbert, Anthony 1899-1973 ............DLB-77
Gilbert, Sir Humphrey 1537-1583 .......DLB-136
Gilbert, Michael 1912- ..............DLB-87
Gilbert, Sandra M. 1936- .......DLB-120, 246
Gilchrist, Alexander 1828-1861.........DLB-144
Gilchrist, Ellen 1935- ................DLB-130
Gilder, Jeannette L. 1849-1916 .........DLB-79
Gilder, Richard Watson 1844-1909....DLB-64, 79
Gildersleeve, Basil 1831-1924 ..........DLB-71
Giles, Henry 1809-1882...............DLB-64
Giles of Rome circa 1243-1316 ........DLB-115
Gilfillan, George 1813-1878 ..........DLB-144
Gill, Eric 1882-1940..................DLB-98
Gill, Sarah Prince 1728-1771 ..........DLB-200
William F. Gill Company .............DLB-49
Gillespie, A. Lincoln, Jr. 1895-1950........DLB-4
Gillespie, Haven 1883-1975 ..........DLB-265
Gilliam, Florence ?-? ..................DLB-4
Gilliatt, Penelope 1932-1993 ............DLB-14
Gillott, Jacky 1939-1980 ..............DLB-14
Gilman, Caroline H. 1794-1888.....DLB-3, 73
Gilman, Charlotte Perkins 1860-1935....DLB-221
    The Charlotte Perkins Gilman Society ... Y-99
W. and J. Gilman [publishing house]......DLB-49
Gilmer, Elizabeth Meriwether
    1861-1951.....................DLB-29
Gilmer, Francis Walker 1790-1826 .......DLB-37
Gilmore, Mary 1865-1962............DLB-260
Gilroy, Frank D. 1925- .................DLB-7
Gimferrer, Pere (Pedro) 1945- ........DLB-134
Gingrich, Arnold 1903-1976 ..........DLB-137
    Prospectus From the Initial Issue of
        Esquire (Autumn 1933) .........DLB-137
    "With the Editorial Ken," Prospectus
        From the Initial Issue of Ken
        (7 April 1938) ...............DLB-137

# Cumulative Index

Ginsberg, Allen
  1926-1997 .... DLB-5, 16, 169, 237; CDALB-1
Ginzburg, Natalia 1916-1991 .......... DLB-177
Ginzkey, Franz Karl 1871-1963 ......... DLB-81
Gioia, Dana 1950- ............ DLB-120, 282
Giono, Jean 1895-1970 ................ DLB-72
Giotti, Virgilio 1885-1957 ............ DLB-114
Giovanni, Nikki 1943- ... DLB-5, 41; CDALB-7
Gipson, Lawrence Henry 1880-1971 ..... DLB-17
Girard, Rodolphe 1879-1956 ........... DLB-92
Giraudoux, Jean 1882-1944 ............ DLB-65
Girondo, Oliverio 1891-1967 .......... DLB-283
Gissing, George 1857-1903 ..... DLB-18, 135, 184
  The Place of Realism in Fiction (1895) DLB-18
Giudici, Giovanni 1924- ............. DLB-128
Giuliani, Alfredo 1924- ............. DLB-128
Glackens, William J. 1870-1938 ....... DLB-188
Gladkov, Fedor Vasil'evich 1883-1958 ... DLB-272
Gladstone, William Ewart
  1809-1898 .................. DLB-57, 184
Glaeser, Ernst 1902-1963 ............. DLB-69
Glancy, Diane 1941- ................ DLB-175
Glanvill, Joseph 1636-1680 ........... DLB-252
Glanville, Brian 1931- ........... DLB-15, 139
Glapthorne, Henry 1610-1643? ......... DLB-58
Glasgow, Ellen 1873-1945 ........... DLB-9, 12
  The Ellen Glasgow Society ............ Y-01
Glasier, Katharine Bruce 1867-1950 .... DLB-190
Glaspell, Susan 1876-1948 ...... DLB-7, 9, 78, 228
Glass, Montague 1877-1934 ........... DLB-11
Glassco, John 1909-1981 .............. DLB-68
Glauser, Friedrich 1896-1938 ......... DLB-56
F. Gleason's Publishing Hall .......... DLB-49
Gleim, Johann Wilhelm Ludwig
  1719-1803 ........................ DLB-97
Glendinning, Victoria 1937- ......... DLB-155
Glidden, Frederick Dilley (Luke Short)
  1908-1975 ....................... DLB-256
Glinka, Fedor Nikolaevich 1786-1880 .... DLB-205
Glover, Keith 1966- ................ DLB-249
Glover, Richard 1712-1785 ............ DLB-95
Glück, Louise 1943- ................. DLB-5
Glyn, Elinor 1864-1943 .............. DLB-153
Gnedich, Nikolai Ivanovich 1784-1833 ... DLB-205
Gobineau, Joseph-Arthur de 1816-1882 .. DLB-123
Godber, John 1956- ................. DLB-233
Godbout, Jacques 1933- .............. DLB-53
Goddard, Morrill 1865-1937 ........... DLB-25
Goddard, William 1740-1817 ........... DLB-43
Godden, Rumer 1907-1998 ............. DLB-161
Godey, Louis A. 1804-1878 ............ DLB-73
Godey and McMichael ................. DLB-49
Godfrey, Dave 1938- ................. DLB-60
Godfrey, Thomas 1736-1763 ........... DLB-31
Godine, David R., Publisher........... DLB-46

Godkin, E. L. 1831-1902 ............. DLB-79
Godolphin, Sidney 1610-1643 ........ DLB-126
Godwin, Gail 1937- ............... DLB-6, 234
M. J. Godwin and Company .......... DLB-154
Godwin, Mary Jane Clairmont
  1766-1841 ........................ DLB-163
Godwin, Parke 1816-1904 ....... DLB-3, 64, 250
Godwin, William 1756-1836 ...... DLB-39, 104,
              142, 158, 163, 262; CDBLB-3
  Preface to St. Leon (1799) .......... DLB-39
Goering, Reinhard 1887-1936 ......... DLB-118
Goes, Albrecht 1908- ................ DLB-69
Goethe, Johann Wolfgang von
  1749-1832 ............. DLB-94; CDWLB-2
Goetz, Curt 1888-1960 ............... DLB-124
Goffe, Thomas circa 1592-1629 ........ DLB-58
Goffstein, M. B. 1940- ............... DLB-61
Gogarty, Oliver St. John 1878-1957 ... DLB-15, 19
Gogol, Nikolai Vasil'evich 1809-1852 ... DLB-198
Goines, Donald 1937-1974 ............ DLB-33
Gold, Herbert 1924- .............. DLB-2; Y-81
  Tribute to William Saroyan............ Y-81
Gold, Michael 1893-1967 ............ DLB-9, 28
Goldbarth, Albert 1948- ............. DLB-120
Goldberg, Dick 1947- ................. DLB-7
Golden Cockerel Press ................ DLB-112
Golding, Arthur 1536-1606 ........... DLB-136
Golding, Louis 1895-1958 ............ DLB-195
Golding, William 1911-1993
  .......... DLB-15, 100, 255; Y-83; CDBLB-7
  Nobel Lecture 1993 .................. Y-83
  The Stature of William Golding ....... Y-83
Goldman, Emma 1869-1940 ........... DLB-221
Goldman, William 1931- ............. DLB-44
Goldring, Douglas 1887-1960 ......... DLB-197
Goldsmith, Oliver 1730?-1774
  .... DLB-39, 89, 99. 104, 109, 142; CDBLB-2
Goldsmith, Oliver 1794-1861 .......... DLB-99
Goldsmith Publishing Company ....... DLB-46
Goldstein, Richard 1944- ............ DLB-185
Gollancz, Sir Israel 1864-1930 ....... DLB-201
Victor Gollancz Limited ............. DLB-112
Gomberville, Marin Le Roy, sieur de
  1600?-1674 ..................... DLB-268
Gombrowicz, Witold
  1904-1969 ............. DLB-215; CDWLB-4
Gómez-Quiñones, Juan 1942- ........ DLB-122
Laurence James Gomme
  [publishing house] ................ DLB-46
Goncharov, Ivan Aleksandrovich
  1812-1891 ........................ DLB-238
Goncourt, Edmond de 1822-1896 ...... DLB-123
Goncourt, Jules de 1830-1870 ......... DLB-123
Gonzales, Rodolfo "Corky" 1928- .... DLB-122
Gonzales-Berry, Erlinda 1942- ....... DLB-209
  "Chicano Language" .............. DLB-82
González, Angel 1925- ............... DLB-108

Gonzalez, Genaro 1949- ............ DLB-122
Gonzalez, Ray 1952- ................ DLB-122
González de Mireles, Jovita
  1899-1983 ........................ DLB-122
González-T., César A. 1931- ......... DLB-82
Goodis, David 1917-1967 ............. DLB-226
Goodison, Lorna 1947- .............. DLB-157
Goodman, Allegra 1967- ............ DLB-244
Goodman, Nelson 1906-1998........... DLB-279
Goodman, Paul 1911-1972 ....... DLB-130, 246
The Goodman Theatre ................ DLB-7
Goodrich, Frances 1891-1984 and
  Hackett, Albert 1900-1995 ......... DLB-26
Goodrich, Samuel Griswold
  1793-1860 ............... DLB-1, 42, 73, 243
S. G. Goodrich [publishing house] ...... DLB-49
C. E. Goodspeed and Company ........ DLB-49
Goodwin, Stephen 1943- ............. Y-82
Googe, Barnabe 1540-1594 ........... DLB-132
Gookin, Daniel 1612-1687 ............ DLB-24
Goran, Lester 1928- ................ DLB-244
Gordimer, Nadine 1923- ........ DLB-225; Y-91
  Nobel Lecture 1991 ................. Y-91
Gordon, Adam Lindsay 1833-1870 ..... DLB-230
Gordon, Caroline
  1895-1981 ....... DLB-4, 9, 102; DS-17; Y-81
Gordon, Charles F. (see OyamO)
Gordon, Charles William (see Connor, Ralph)
Gordon, Giles 1940- .......... DLB-14, 139, 207
Gordon, Helen Cameron, Lady Russell
  1867-1949 ....................... DLB-195
Gordon, Lyndall 1941- .............. DLB-155
Gordon, Mack 1904-1959 ............ DLB-265
Gordon, Mary 1949- ............. DLB-6; Y-81
Gordone, Charles 1925-1995 ........... DLB-7
Gore, Catherine 1800-1861 ........... DLB-116
Gore-Booth, Eva 1870-1926 .......... DLB-240
Gores, Joe 1931- ................. DLB-226; Y-02
  Tribute to Kenneth Millar ............ Y-83
  Tribute to Raymond Chandler ........ Y-88
Gorey, Edward 1925-2000 ............. DLB-61
Gorgias of Leontini
  circa 485 B.C.-376 B.C. ........... DLB-176
Görres, Joseph 1776-1848 ............. DLB-90
Gosse, Edmund 1849-1928 ..... DLB-57, 144, 184
Gosson, Stephen 1554-1624 ........... DLB-172
  The Schoole of Abuse (1579) .......... DLB-172
Gotanda, Philip Kan 1951- ........... DLB-266
Gotlieb, Phyllis 1926- ............ DLB-88, 251
Go-Toba 1180-1239 .................. DLB-203
Gottfried von Straßburg
  died before 1230 ....... DLB-138; CDWLB-2
Gotthelf, Jeremias 1797-1854........... DLB-133
Gottschalk circa 804/808-869 .......... DLB-148
Gottsched, Johann Christoph
  1700-1766 ........................ DLB-97
Götz, Johann Nikolaus 1721-1781........ DLB-97

Goudge, Elizabeth 1900-1984 .......... DLB-191
Gough, John B. 1817-1886 ............. DLB-243
Gould, Wallace 1882-1940 ............. DLB-54
Govoni, Corrado 1884-1965 ........... DLB-114
Gower, John circa 1330-1408 ......... DLB-146
Goyen, William 1915-1983 ..... DLB-2, 218; Y-83
Goytisolo, José Augustín 1928- ........ DLB-134
Gozzano, Guido 1883-1916 ........... DLB-114
Grabbe, Christian Dietrich 1801-1836 .... DLB-133
Gracq, Julien (Louis Poirier) 1910- ...... DLB-83
Grady, Henry W. 1850-1889 ........... DLB-23
Graf, Oskar Maria 1894-1967 .......... DLB-56
*Graf Rudolf* between circa 1170 and
  circa 1185 ..................... DLB-148
Graff, Gerald 1937- ................. DLB-246
Richard Grafton [publishing house] ...... DLB-170
Grafton, Sue 1940- .................. DLB-226
Graham, Frank 1893-1965 ............. DLB-241
Graham, George Rex 1813-1894 ......... DLB-73
Graham, Gwethalyn (Gwethalyn Graham
  Erichsen-Brown) 1913-1965 ......... DLB-88
Graham, Jorie 1951- ................. DLB-120
Graham, Katharine 1917-2001 .......... DLB-127
Graham, Lorenz 1902-1989 ............. DLB-76
Graham, Philip 1915-1963 ............. DLB-127
Graham, R. B. Cunninghame
  1852-1936 ............... DLB-98, 135, 174
Graham, Shirley 1896-1977 ............. DLB-76
Graham, Stephen 1884-1975 ........... DLB-195
Graham, W. S. 1918-1986 ............. DLB-20
William H. Graham [publishing house] .... DLB-49
Graham, Winston 1910- ............... DLB-77
Grahame, Kenneth 1859-1932 ... DLB-34, 141, 178
Grainger, Martin Allerdale 1874-1941 ..... DLB-92
Gramatky, Hardie 1907-1979 ........... DLB-22
Grand, Sarah 1854-1943 .......... DLB-135, 197
Grandbois, Alain 1900-1975 ........... DLB-92
Grandson, Oton de circa 1345-1397 ..... DLB-208
Grange, John circa 1556-? ............. DLB-136
Granger, Thomas 1578-1627 ........... DLB-281
Granich, Irwin (see Gold, Michael)
Granovsky, Timofei Nikolaevich
  1813-1855 ..................... DLB-198
Grant, Anne MacVicar 1755-1838 ....... DLB-200
Grant, Duncan 1885-1978 ............... DS-10
Grant, George 1918-1988 ............. DLB-88
Grant, George Monro 1835-1902 ........ DLB-99
Grant, Harry J. 1881-1963 ............. DLB-29
Grant, James Edward 1905-1966 ........ DLB-26
Grant, John (see Gash, Jonathan)
War of the Words (and Pictures): The Creation
  of a Graphic Novel .................. Y-02
Grass, Günter 1927- ... DLB-75, 124; CDWLB-2
  Nobel Lecture 1999:
    "To Be Continued..." ........... Y-99
  Tribute to Helen Wolff ............... Y-94

Grasty, Charles H. 1863-1924 .......... DLB-25
Grau, Shirley Ann 1929- ........... DLB-2, 218
Graves, John 1920- ..................... Y-83
Graves, Richard 1715-1804 ............. DLB-39
Graves, Robert 1895-1985
  ... DLB-20, 100, 191; DS-18; Y-85; CDBLB-6
  The St. John's College
    Robert Graves Trust ............... Y-96
Gray, Alasdair 1934- .......... DLB-194, 261
Gray, Asa 1810-1888 ............... DLB-1, 235
Gray, David 1838-1861 ................ DLB-32
Gray, Simon 1936- .................... DLB-13
Gray, Thomas 1716-1771 ..... DLB-109; CDBLB-2
Grayson, Richard 1951- ............... DLB-234
Grayson, William J. 1788-1863 .... DLB-3, 64, 248
The Great Bibliographers Series .......... Y-93
*The Great Gatsby* (Documentary) ......... DLB-219
"The Greatness of Southern Literature":
  League of the South Institute for the
  Study of Southern Culture and History
  .................................. Y-02
Grech, Nikolai Ivanovich 1787-1867 ..... DLB-198
Greeley, Horace 1811-1872 ... DLB-3, 43, 189, 250
Green, Adolph 1915-2002 .......... DLB-44, 265
Green, Anna Katharine
  1846-1935 ................... DLB-202, 221
Green, Duff 1791-1875 ................ DLB-43
Green, Elizabeth Shippen 1871-1954 ..... DLB-188
Green, Gerald 1922- .................. DLB-28
Green, Henry 1905-1973 ............... DLB-15
Green, Jonas 1712-1767 ............... DLB-31
Green, Joseph 1706-1780 .............. DLB-31
Green, Julien 1900-1998 ............ DLB-4, 72
Green, Paul 1894-1981 ....... DLB-7, 9, 249; Y-81
Green, T. H. 1836-1882 ........... DLB-190, 262
Green, Terence M. 1947- .............. DLB-251
T. and S. Green [publishing house] ....... DLB-49
Green Tiger Press ..................... DLB-46
Timothy Green [publishing house] ....... DLB-49
Greenaway, Kate 1846-1901 ........... DLB-141
Greenberg: Publisher .................. DLB-46
Greene, Asa 1789-1838 ................ DLB-11
Greene, Belle da Costa 1883-1950 ....... DLB-187
Greene, Graham 1904-1991
  ........... DLB-13, 15, 77, 100, 162, 201, 204;
                                Y-85, 91; CDBLB-7
  Tribute to Christopher Isherwood ...... Y-86
Greene, Robert 1558-1592 .......... DLB-62, 167
Greene, Robert Bernard (Bob), Jr.
  1947- ......................... DLB-185
Benjamin H Greene [publishing house] .... DLB-49
Greenfield, George 1917-2000 ......... Y-91, 00
  Derek Robinson's Review of George
    Greenfield's *Rich Dust* ............ Y-02
Greenhow, Robert 1800-1854 ........... DLB-30
Greenlee, William B. 1872-1953 ........ DLB-187
Greenough, Horatio 1805-1852 ....... DLB-1, 235

Greenwell, Dora 1821-1882 .......... DLB-35, 199
Greenwillow Books ................... DLB-46
Greenwood, Grace (see Lippincott, Sara Jane Clarke)
Greenwood, Walter 1903-1974 ...... DLB-10, 191
Greer, Ben 1948- ..................... DLB-6
Greflinger, Georg 1620?-1677 ......... DLB-164
Greg, W. R. 1809-1881 ............... DLB-55
Greg, W. W. 1875-1959 ............... DLB-201
Gregg, Josiah 1806-1850 ......... DLB-183, 186
Gregg Press .......................... DLB-46
Gregory, Horace 1898-1982 ............ DLB-48
Gregory, Isabella Augusta Persse, Lady
  1852-1932 ..................... DLB-10
Gregory of Rimini circa 1300-1358 ...... DLB-115
Gregynog Press ...................... DLB-112
Greiff, León de 1895-1976 ............ DLB-283
Greiffenberg, Catharina Regina von
  1633-1694 ..................... DLB-168
Greig, Noël 1944- ................... DLB-245
Grenfell, Wilfred Thomason
  1865-1940 ..................... DLB-92
Gress, Elsa 1919-1988 ................ DLB-214
Greve, Felix Paul (see Grove, Frederick Philip)
Greville, Fulke, First Lord Brooke
  1554-1628 ................... DLB-62, 172
Grey, Sir George, K.C.B. 1812-1898 ..... DLB-184
Grey, Lady Jane 1537-1554 ............ DLB-132
Grey, Zane 1872-1939 .............. DLB-9, 212
  Zane Grey's West Society ............. Y-00
Grey Owl (Archibald Stansfeld Belaney)
  1888-1938 ................. DLB-92; DS-17
Grey Walls Press .................... DLB-112
Griboedov, Aleksandr Sergeevich
  1795?-1829 ..................... DLB-205
Grice, Paul 1913-1988 ................ DLB-279
Grier, Eldon 1917- .................. DLB-88
Grieve, C. M. (see MacDiarmid, Hugh)
Griffin, Bartholomew flourished 1596 .... DLB-172
Griffin, Bryan
  "Panic Among the Philistines":
    A Postscript, An Interview
    with Bryan Griffin ............... Y-81
Griffin, Gerald 1803-1840 ............. DLB-159
The Griffin Poetry Prize ................ Y-00
Griffith, Elizabeth 1727?-1793 ........ DLB-39, 89
  Preface to *The Delicate Distress* (1769) ... DLB-39
Griffith, George 1857-1906 ........... DLB-178
Ralph Griffiths [publishing house] ....... DLB-154
Griffiths, Trevor 1935- ........... DLB-13, 245
S. C. Griggs and Company ............. DLB-49
Griggs, Sutton Elbert 1872-1930 ........ DLB-50
Grignon, Claude-Henri 1894-1976 ...... DLB-68
Grigor'ev, Apollon Aleksandrovich
  1822-1864 ..................... DLB-277
Grigorovich, Dmitrii Vasil'evich
  1822-1899 ..................... DLB-238
Grigson, Geoffrey 1905-1985 ........... DLB-27

405

Grillparzer, Franz 1791-1872 .......... DLB-133; CDWLB-2
Grimald, Nicholas circa 1519-circa 1562 ............. DLB-136
Grimké, Angelina Weld 1880-1958 .. DLB-50, 54
Grimké, Sarah Moore 1792-1873 ....... DLB-239
Grimm, Hans 1875-1959 .............. DLB-66
Grimm, Jacob 1785-1863 .............. DLB-90
Grimm, Wilhelm 1786-1859 ............ DLB-90; CDWLB-2
Grimmelshausen, Johann Jacob Christoffel von 1621 or 1622-1676 ..... DLB-168; CDWLB-2
Grimshaw, Beatrice Ethel 1871-1953 ..... DLB-174
Grin, Aleksandr Stepanovich 1880-1932 .................... DLB-272
Grindal, Edmund 1519 or 1520-1583.... DLB-132
Gripe, Maria (Kristina) 1923- ........ DLB-257
Griswold, Rufus Wilmot 1815-1857................. DLB-3, 59, 250
Grosart, Alexander Balloch 1827-1899 ... DLB-184
Grosholz, Emily 1950- ............. DLB-282
Gross, Milt 1895-1953 ................ DLB-11
Grosset and Dunlap .................. DLB-49
Grosseteste, Robert circa 1160-1253..... DLB-115
Grossman, Allen 1932- ............. DLB-193
Grossman, Vasilii Semenovich 1905-1964 .................... DLB-272
Grossman Publishers ................. DLB-46
Grosvenor, Gilbert H. 1875-1966....... DLB-91
Groth, Klaus 1819-1899 .............. DLB-129
Groulx, Lionel 1878-1967............. DLB-68
Grove, Frederick Philip (Felix Paul Greve) 1879-1948 .................... DLB-92
Grove Press ....................... DLB-46
Groys, Boris Efimovich 1947- ........ DLB-285
Grubb, Davis 1919-1980 ............. DLB-6
Gruelle, Johnny 1880-1938............. DLB-22
von Grumbach, Argula 1492-after 1563?................... DLB-179
Grymeston, Elizabeth before 1563-before 1604........... DLB-136
Gryphius, Andreas 1616-1664............ DLB-164; CDWLB-2
Gryphius, Christian 1649-1706......... DLB-168
Guare, John 1938- ................ DLB-7, 249
Guberman, Igor Mironovich 1936- .... DLB-285
Guerra, Tonino 1920- .............. DLB-128
Guest, Barbara 1920- .............. DLB-5, 193
Guèvremont, Germaine 1893-1968 ...... DLB-68
Guglielminetti, Amalia 1881-1941 ...... DLB-264
Guidacci, Margherita 1921-1992 ....... DLB-128
Guillén, Jorge 1893-1984 ............. DLB-108
Guillén, Nicolás 1902-1989............. DLB-283
Guilloux, Louis 1899-1980 ............ DLB-72
Guilpin, Everard circa 1572-after 1608? .. DLB-136
Guiney, Louise Imogen 1861-1920....... DLB-54
Guiterman, Arthur 1871-1943 ......... DLB-11

Günderrode, Caroline von 1780-1806..................... DLB-90
Gundulić, Ivan 1589-1638 ...DLB-147; CDWLB-4
Gunesekera, Romesh 1954- ........ DLB-267
Gunn, Bill 1934-1989 ................ DLB-38
Gunn, James E. 1923- .............. DLB-8
Gunn, Neil M. 1891-1973............. DLB-15
Gunn, Thom 1929- ........ DLB-27; CDBLB-8
Gunnars, Kristjana 1948- ............ DLB-60
Günther, Johann Christian 1695-1723 ... DLB-168
Gurik, Robert 1932- ................ DLB-60
Gurney, A. R. 1930- ............... DLB-266
Gurney, Ivor 1890-1937................. Y-02
The Ivor Gurney Society ............ Y-98
Gustafson, Ralph 1909-1995 .......... DLB-88
Gustafsson, Lars 1936- ............. DLB-257
Gütersloh, Albert Paris 1887-1973 ....... DLB-81
Guthrie, A. B., Jr. 1901-1991 ...... DLB-6, 212
Guthrie, Ramon 1896-1973 ............ DLB-4
Guthrie, Thomas Anstey (see Anstey, FC)
The Guthrie Theater .................. DLB-7
Gutzkow, Karl 1811-1878.............. DLB-133
Guy, Ray 1939- .................. DLB-60
Guy, Rosa 1925- ................. DLB-33
Guyot, Arnold 1807-1884............... DS-13
Gwynn, R. S. 1948- ............... DLB-282
Gwynne, Erskine 1898-1948 ......... DLB-4
Gyles, John 1680-1755 ............. DLB-99
Gyllensten, Lars 1921- ............ DLB-257
Gysin, Brion 1916-1986 ............ DLB-16

# H

H.D. (see Doolittle, Hilda)
Habermas, Jürgen 1929- ............ DLB-242
Habington, William 1605-1654 ........ DLB-126
Hacker, Marilyn 1942- ........ DLB-120, 282
Hackett, Albert 1900-1995 ............ DLB-26
Hacks, Peter 1928- ................ DLB-124
Hadas, Rachel 1948- ........... DLB-120, 282
Hadden, Briton 1898-1929............. DLB-91
Hagedorn, Friedrich von 1708-1754 ..... DLB-168
Hagelstange, Rudolf 1912-1984 ........ DLB-69
Haggard, H. Rider 1856-1925 .......... DLB-70, 156, 174, 178
Haggard, William (Richard Clayton) 1907-1993................DLB-276; Y-93
Hagy, Alyson 1960- ............... DLB-244
Hahn-Hahn, Ida Gräfin von 1805-1880 .. DLB-133
Haig-Brown, Roderick 1908-1976....... DLB-88
Haight, Gordon S. 1901-1985.......... DLB-103
Hailey, Arthur 1920- .............DLB-88; Y-82
Haines, John 1924- ............. DLB-5, 212
Hake, Edward flourished 1566-1604 .... DLB-136
Hake, Thomas Gordon 1809-1895 ..... DLB-32
Hakluyt, Richard 1552?-1616........... DLB-136

Halas, František 1901-1949 .......... DLB-215
Halbe, Max 1865-1944................ DLB-118
Halberstam, David 1934- ........... DLB-241
Haldane, Charlotte 1894-1969......... DLB-191
Haldane, J. B. S. 1892-1964 .......... DLB-160
Haldeman, Joe 1943- .............. DLB-8
Haldeman-Julius Company ........... DLB-46
Hale, E. J., and Son ................ DLB-49
Hale, Edward Everett 1822-1909 ..........DLB-1, 42, 74, 235
Hale, Janet Campbell 1946- .........DLB-175
Hale, Kathleen 1898-2000 ............ DLB-160
Hale, Leo Thomas (see Ebon)
Hale, Lucretia Peabody 1820-1900....... DLB-42
Hale, Nancy 1908-1988 .........DLB-86; DS-17; Y-80, 88
Hale, Sarah Josepha (Buell) 1788-1879...............DLB-1, 42, 73, 243
Hale, Susan 1833-1910 ............... DLB-221
Hales, John 1584-1656 ............... DLB-151
Halévy, Ludovic 1834-1908 ........... DLB-192
Haley, Alex 1921-1992........ DLB-38; CDALB-7
Haliburton, Thomas Chandler 1796-1865....................DLB-11, 99
Hall, Adam (Trevor Dudley-Smith) 1920-1995 ....................DLB-276
Hall, Anna Maria 1800-1881 .......... DLB-159
Hall, Donald 1928- ................ DLB-5
Hall, Edward 1497-1547 ............. DLB-132
Hall, Halsey 1898-1977............... DLB-241
Hall, James 1793-1868 .............DLB-73, 74
Hall, Joseph 1574-1656 ......... DLB-121, 151
Hall, Radclyffe 1880-1943 ........... DLB-191
Hall, Sarah Ewing 1761-1830 .......... DLB-200
Hall, Stuart 1932- ................ DLB-242
Samuel Hall [publishing house] ........ DLB-49
Hallam, Arthur Henry 1811-1833 ....... DLB-32
On Some of the Characteristics of Modern Poetry and On the Lyrical Poems of Alfred Tennyson (1831).............. DLB-32
Halleck, Fitz-Greene 1790-1867 ...... DLB-3, 250
Haller, Albrecht von 1708-1777 ...... DLB-168
Halliday, Brett (see Dresser, Davis)
Halliwell-Phillipps, James Orchard 1820-1889 .................... DLB-184
Hallmann, Johann Christian 1640-1704 or 1716? .............. DLB-168
Hallmark Editions .................. DLB-46
Halper, Albert 1904-1984.............. DLB-9
Halperin, John William 1941- ........ DLB-111
Halstead, Murat 1829-1908 ........... DLB-23
Hamann, Johann Georg 1730-1788....... DLB-97
Hamburger, Michael 1924- .......... DLB-27
Hamilton, Alexander 1712-1756 ........ DLB-31
Hamilton, Alexander 1755?-1804........ DLB-37
Hamilton, Cicely 1872-1952.........DLB-10, 197

Hamilton, Edmond 1904-1977............DLB-8
Hamilton, Elizabeth 1758-1816.....DLB-116, 158
Hamilton, Gail (see Corcoran, Barbara)
Hamilton, Gail (see Dodge, Mary Abigail)
Hamish Hamilton Limited.............DLB-112
Hamilton, Hugo 1953- ...............DLB-267
Hamilton, Ian 1938-2001............DLB-40, 155
Hamilton, Janet 1795-1873............DLB-199
Hamilton, Mary Agnes 1884-1962......DLB-197
Hamilton, Patrick 1904-1962.........DLB-10, 191
Hamilton, Virginia 1936-2002...DLB-33, 52; Y-01
Hamilton, Sir William 1788-1856.......DLB-262
Hamilton-Paterson, James 1941- ......DLB-267
Hammerstein, Oscar, 2nd 1895-1960 ... DLB-265
Hammett, Dashiell
  1894-1961....DLB-226, 280; DS-6; CDALB-5
  An Appeal in *TAC*..................Y-91
  *The Glass Key* and Other Dashiell
    Hammett Mysteries ..............Y-96
  Knopf to Hammett: The Editoral
    Correspondence .................Y-00
Hammon, Jupiter 1711-died between
  1790 and 1806..................DLB-31, 50
Hammond, John ?-1663................DLB-24
Hamner, Earl 1923- ..................DLB-6
Hampson, John 1901-1955.............DLB-191
Hampton, Christopher 1946- .........DLB-13
Handel-Mazzetti, Enrica von 1871-1955 ...DLB-81
Handke, Peter 1942- .............DLB-85, 124
Handlin, Oscar 1915- ................DLB-17
Hankin, St. John 1869-1909...........DLB-10
Hanley, Clifford 1922- ..............DLB-14
Hanley, James 1901-1985.............DLB-191
Hannah, Barry 1942- ..............DLB-6, 234
Hannay, James 1827-1873.............DLB-21
Hano, Arnold 1922- .................DLB-241
Hansberry, Lorraine
  1930-1965............DLB-7, 38; CDALB-1
Hansen, Martin A. 1909-1955.........DLB-214
Hansen, Thorkild 1927-1989..........DLB-214
Hanson, Elizabeth 1684-1737.........DLB-200
Hapgood, Norman 1868-1937...........DLB-91
Happel, Eberhard Werner 1647-1690 ....DLB-168
Harbach, Otto 1873-1963.............DLB-265
*The Harbinger* 1845-1849...........DLB-1, 223
Harburg, E. Y. "Yip" 1896-1981......DLB-265
Harcourt Brace Jovanovich ............DLB-46
Hardenberg, Friedrich von (see Novalis)
Harding, Walter 1917- ...............DLB-111
Hardwick, Elizabeth 1916- ...........DLB-6
Hardy, Alexandre 1572?-1632..........DLB-268
Hardy, Frank 1917-1994..............DLB-260
Hardy, Thomas
  1840-1928......DLB-18, 19, 135; CDBLB-5
  "Candour in English Fiction" (1890)...DLB-18
Hare, Cyril 1900-1958................DLB-77

Hare, David 1947- ..................DLB-13
Hare, R. M. 1919-2002...............DLB-262
Hargrove, Marion 1919- .............DLB-11
Häring, Georg Wilhelm Heinrich
  (see Alexis, Willibald)
Harington, Donald 1935- ............DLB-152
Harington, Sir John 1560-1612 .......DLB-136
Harjo, Joy 1951- ................DLB-120, 175
Harkness, Margaret (John Law)
  1854-1923......................DLB-197
Harley, Edward, second Earl of Oxford
  1689-1741......................DLB-213
Harley, Robert, first Earl of Oxford
  1661-1724......................DLB-213
Harlow, Robert 1923- ................DLB-60
Harman, Thomas flourished 1566-1573 ..DLB-136
Harness, Charles L. 1915- ............DLB-8
Harnett, Cynthia 1893-1981 ..........DLB-161
Harnick, Sheldon 1924- .............DLB-265
  Tribute to Ira Gershwin .............Y-96
  Tribute to Lorenz Hart ..............Y-95
Harper, Edith Alice Mary (see Wickham, Anna)
Harper, Fletcher 1806-1877 ...........DLB-79
Harper, Frances Ellen Watkins
  1825-1911....................DLB-50, 221
Harper, Michael S. 1938- .............DLB-41
Harper and Brothers ..................DLB-49
Harpur, Charles 1813-1868............DLB-230
Harraden, Beatrice 1864-1943.........DLB-153
George G. Harrap and Company
  Limited ........................DLB-112
Harriot, Thomas 1560-1621 ...........DLB-136
Harris, Alexander 1805-1874..........DLB-230
Harris, Benjamin ?-circa 1720 .......DLB-42, 43
Harris, Christie 1907-2002...........DLB-88
Harris, Errol E. 1908- ..............DLB-279
Harris, Frank 1856-1931 .........DLB-156, 197
Harris, George Washington
  1814-1869...................DLB-3, 11, 248
Harris, Joanne 1964- ................DLB-271
Harris, Joel Chandler
  1848-1908...........DLB-11, 23, 42, 78, 91
  The Joel Chandler Harris Association ...Y-99
Harris, Mark 1922- ...............DLB-2; Y-80
  Tribute to Frederick A. Pottle..........Y-87
Harris, William Torrey 1835-1909 ......DLB-270
Harris, Wilson 1921- ......DLB-117; CDWLB-3
Harrison, Mrs. Burton
  (see Harrison, Constance Cary)
Harrison, Charles Yale 1898-1954........DLB-68
Harrison, Constance Cary 1843-1920....DLB-221
Harrison, Frederic 1831-1923 .......DLB-57, 190
  "On Style in English Prose" (1898)....DLB-57
Harrison, Harry 1925- ...............DLB-8
James P. Harrison Company............DLB-49
Harrison, Jim 1937- ..................Y-82
Harrison, M. John 1945- ............DLB-261

Harrison, Mary St. Leger Kingsley
  (see Malet, Lucas)
Harrison, Paul Carter 1936- .........DLB-38
Harrison, Susan Frances 1859-1935 ......DLB-99
Harrison, Tony 1937- .............DLB-40, 245
Harrison, William 1535-1593 .........DLB-136
Harrison, William 1933- .............DLB-234
Harrisse, Henry 1829-1910 ............DLB-47
The Harry Ransom Humanities Research Center
  at the University of Texas at Austin ....Y-00
Harryman, Carla 1952- ..............DLB-193
Harsdörffer, Georg Philipp 1607-1658....DLB-164
Harsent, David 1942- ................DLB-40
Hart, Albert Bushnell 1854-1943.........DLB-17
Hart, Anne 1768-1834 ................DLB-200
Hart, Elizabeth 1771-1833 ............DLB-200
Hart, Julia Catherine 1796-1867..........DLB-99
Hart, Lorenz 1895-1943 ..............DLB-265
  Larry Hart: Still an Influence ..........Y-95
  Lorenz Hart: An American Lyricist .....Y-95
  The Lorenz Hart Centenary ..........Y-95
Hart, Moss 1904-1961...............DLB-7, 266
Hart, Oliver 1723-1795 ...............DLB-31
Rupert Hart-Davis Limited ............DLB-112
Harte, Bret 1836-1902
  .........DLB-12, 64, 74, 79, 186; CDALB-3
Harte, Edward Holmead 1922- .......DLB-127
Harte, Houston Harriman 1927- ......DLB-127
Hartlaub, Felix 1913-1945 ............DLB-56
Hartleben, Otto Erich 1864-1905 .......DLB-118
Hartley, David 1705-1757 ............DLB-252
Hartley, L. P. 1895-1972 ..........DLB-15, 139
Hartley, Marsden 1877-1943 ..........DLB-54
Hartling, Peter 1933- ................DLB-75
Hartman, Geoffrey H. 1929- .........DLB-67
Hartmann, Sadakichi 1867-1944 ........DLB-54
Hartmann von Aue
  circa 1160-circa 1205....DLB-138; CDWLB-2
Hartshorne, Charles 1897-2000.........DLB-270
Harvey, Gabriel 1550?-1631 ... DLB-167, 213, 281
Harvey, Jack (see Rankin, Ian)
Harvey, Jean-Charles 1891-1967........DLB-88
Harvill Press Limited.................DLB-112
Harwood, Lee 1939- .................DLB-40
Harwood, Ronald 1934- ..............DLB-13
Hašek, Jaroslav 1883-1923 .. DLB-215; CDWLB-4
Haskins, Charles Homer 1870-1937......DLB-47
Haslam, Gerald 1937- ...............DLB-212
Hass, Robert 1941- ..............DLB-105, 206
Hasselstrom, Linda M. 1943- .........DLB-256
Hastings, Michael 1938- .............DLB-233
Hatar, Győző 1914- .................DLB-215
The Hatch-Billops Collection ..........DLB-76
Hathaway, William 1944- ............DLB-120
Hatherly, Ana 1929- .................DLB-287

Hauff, Wilhelm 1802-1827 . . . . . . . . . . . . . DLB-90

Haugwitz, August Adolph von
1647-1706 . . . . . . . . . . . . . . . . . . . . . DLB-168

Hauptmann, Carl 1858-1921 . . . . . . . DLB-66, 118

Hauptmann, Gerhart
1862-1946 . . . . . . . . . DLB-66, 118; CDWLB-2

Hauser, Marianne 1910- . . . . . . . . . . . . . . . . Y-83

Havel, Václav 1936- . . . . . . DLB-232; CDWLB-4

Haven, Alice B. Neal 1827-1863 . . . . . . . . DLB-250

Havergal, Frances Ridley 1836-1879 . . . . DLB-199

Hawes, Stephen 1475?-before 1529 . . . . . DLB-132

Hawker, Robert Stephen 1803-1875 . . . . . . DLB-32

Hawkes, John
1925-1998 . . . . . . . . DLB-2, 7, 227; Y-80, Y-98

    John Hawkes: A Tribute . . . . . . . . . . . . . Y-98

    Tribute to Donald Barthelme . . . . . . . . . . Y-89

Hawkesworth, John 1720-1773 . . . . . . . . . DLB-142

Hawkins, Sir Anthony Hope (see Hope, Anthony)

Hawkins, Sir John 1719-1789 . . . . . . DLB-104, 142

Hawkins, Walter Everette 1883-? . . . . . . . . DLB-50

Hawthorne, Nathaniel 1804-1864
. . . DLB-1, 74, 183, 223, 269; DS-5; CDALB-2

    The Nathaniel Hawthorne Society . . . . . . . Y-00

    The Old Manse . . . . . . . . . . . . . . . . . DLB-223

Hawthorne, Sophia Peabody
1809-1871 . . . . . . . . . . . . . . . . . DLB-183, 239

Hay, John 1835-1905 . . . . . . . . . DLB-12, 47, 189

Hay, John 1915- . . . . . . . . . . . . . . . . . . DLB-275

Hayashi Fumiko 1903-1951 . . . . . . . . . . . DLB-180

Haycox, Ernest 1899-1950 . . . . . . . . . . . . DLB-206

Haycraft, Anna Margaret (see Ellis, Alice Thomas)

Hayden, Robert
1913-1980 . . . . . . . . . . DLB-5, 76; CDALB-1

Haydon, Benjamin Robert 1786-1846 . . . DLB-110

Hayes, John Michael 1919- . . . . . . . . . . . . DLB-26

Hayley, William 1745-1820 . . . . . . . . DLB-93, 142

Haym, Rudolf 1821-1901 . . . . . . . . . . . . . DLB-129

Hayman, Robert 1575-1629 . . . . . . . . . . . . DLB-99

Hayman, Ronald 1932- . . . . . . . . . . . . . . DLB-155

Hayne, Paul Hamilton
1830-1886 . . . . . . . . . . . . . DLB-3, 64, 79, 248

Hays, Mary 1760-1843 . . . . . . . . . . DLB-142, 158

Hayward, John 1905-1965 . . . . . . . . . . . . DLB-201

Haywood, Eliza 1693?-1756 . . . . . . . . . . . . DLB-39

    Dedication of *Lasselia* [excerpt]
    (1723) . . . . . . . . . . . . . . . . . . . . . . . DLB-39

    Preface to *The Disguis'd Prince*
    [excerpt] (1723) . . . . . . . . . . . . . . . . DLB-39

    *The Tea-Table* [excerpt] . . . . . . . . . . . . DLB-39

Willis P. Hazard [publishing house] . . . . . . DLB-49

Hazlitt, William 1778-1830 . . . . . . . . DLB-110, 158

Hazzard, Shirley 1931- . . . . . . . . . . . . . . . . Y-82

Head, Bessie
1937-1986 . . . . . . . . DLB-117, 225; CDWLB-3

Headley, Joel T. 1813-1897 . . DLB-30, 183; DS-13

Heaney, Seamus 1939- . . DLB-40; Y-95; CDBLB-8

    Nobel Lecture 1994: Crediting Poetry . . . . Y-95

Heard, Nathan C. 1936- . . . . . . . . . . . . . DLB-33

Hearn, Lafcadio 1850-1904 . . . . . . DLB-12, 78, 189

Hearn, Mary Anne (Marianne Farningham,
Eva Hope) 1834-1909 . . . . . . . . . . . DLB-240

Hearne, John 1926- . . . . . . . . . . . . . . . . DLB-117

Hearne, Samuel 1745-1792 . . . . . . . . . . . . DLB-99

Hearne, Thomas 1678?-1735 . . . . . . . . . . DLB-213

Hearst, William Randolph 1863-1951 . . . . DLB-25

Hearst, William Randolph, Jr.
1908-1993 . . . . . . . . . . . . . . . . . . . . DLB-127

Heartman, Charles Frederick 1883-1953 . DLB-187

Heath, Catherine 1924- . . . . . . . . . . . . . . DLB-14

Heath, James Ewell 1792-1862 . . . . . . . . DLB-248

Heath, Roy A. K. 1926- . . . . . . . . . . . . . DLB-117

Heath-Stubbs, John 1918- . . . . . . . . . . . . DLB-27

Heavysege, Charles 1816-1876 . . . . . . . . . DLB-99

Hebbel, Friedrich
1813-1863 . . . . . . . . . . . DLB-129; CDWLB-2

Hebel, Johann Peter 1760-1826 . . . . . . . . . DLB-90

Heber, Richard 1774-1833 . . . . . . . . . . . . DLB-184

Hébert, Anne 1916-2000 . . . . . . . . . . . . . . DLB-68

Hébert, Jacques 1923- . . . . . . . . . . . . . . . DLB-53

Hecht, Anthony 1923- . . . . . . . . . . . DLB-5, 169

Hecht, Ben 1894-1964 . . . . DLB-7, 9, 25, 26, 28, 86

Hecker, Isaac Thomas 1819-1888 . . . . DLB-1, 243

Hedge, Frederic Henry
1805-1890 . . . . . . . . . . . DLB-1, 59, 243; DS-5

Hefner, Hugh M. 1926- . . . . . . . . . . . . . DLB-137

Hegel, Georg Wilhelm Friedrich
1770-1831 . . . . . . . . . . . . . . . . . . . . . DLB-90

Heide, Robert 1939- . . . . . . . . . . . . . . . . DLB-249

Heidish, Marcy 1947- . . . . . . . . . . . . . . . . . Y-82

Heißenbüttel, Helmut 1921-1996 . . . . . . . . DLB-75

Heike monogatari . . . . . . . . . . . . . . . . . . DLB-203

Hein, Christoph 1944- . . . DLB-124; CDWLB-2

Hein, Piet 1905-1996 . . . . . . . . . . . . . . . . DLB-214

Heine, Heinrich 1797-1856 . . . DLB-90; CDWLB-2

Heinemann, Larry 1944- . . . . . . . . . . . . . . . DS-9

William Heinemann Limited . . . . . . . . . . DLB-112

Heinesen, William 1900-1991 . . . . . . . . . . DLB-214

Heinlein, Robert A. 1907-1988 . . . . . . . . . . DLB-8

Heinrich, Willi 1920- . . . . . . . . . . . . . . . . DLB-75

Heinrich Julius of Brunswick 1564-1613 . DLB-164

Heinrich von dem Türlîn
flourished circa 1230 . . . . . . . . . . . . DLB-138

Heinrich von Melk
flourished after 1160 . . . . . . . . . . . . DLB-148

Heinrich von Veldeke
circa 1145-circa 1190 . . . . . . . . . . . . DLB-138

Heinse, Wilhelm 1746-1803 . . . . . . . . . . . . DLB-94

Heinz, W. C. 1915- . . . . . . . . . . . . . . . . DLB-171

Heiskell, John 1872-1972 . . . . . . . . . . . . . DLB-127

Hejinian, Lyn 1941- . . . . . . . . . . . . . . . . DLB-165

Helder, Herberto 1930- . . . . . . . . . . . . . . DLB-287

*Heliand* circa 850 . . . . . . . . . . . . . . . . . . DLB-148

Heller, Joseph
1923-1999 . . . . . . DLB-2, 28, 227; Y-80, 99, 02

Excerpts from Joseph Heller's
USC Address, "The Literature
of Despair" . . . . . . . . . . . . . . . . . . . . Y-96

Remembering Joe Heller, by William
Price Fox . . . . . . . . . . . . . . . . . . . . . . Y-99

A Tribute to Joseph Heller . . . . . . . . . . . . . Y-99

Heller, Michael 1937- . . . . . . . . . . . . . . DLB-165

Hellman, Lillian 1906-1984 . . . . . DLB-7, 228; Y-84

Hellwig, Johann 1609-1674 . . . . . . . . . . . DLB-164

Helprin, Mark 1947- . . . . . . . . . . Y-85; CDALB-7

Helwig, David 1938- . . . . . . . . . . . . . . . . DLB-60

Hemans, Felicia 1793-1835 . . . . . . . . . . . . DLB-96

Hemenway, Abby Maria 1828-1890 . . . . DLB-243

Hemingway, Ernest 1899-1961
. . . . . . . . DLB-4, 9, 102, 210; Y-81, 87, 99;
                    DS-1, 15, 16; CDALB-4

A Centennial Celebration . . . . . . . . . . . . . Y-99

Come to Papa . . . . . . . . . . . . . . . . . . . . Y-99

The Ernest Hemingway Collection at
the John F. Kennedy Library . . . . . . . . Y-99

Ernest Hemingway Declines to
Introduce *War and Peace* . . . . . . . . . . Y-01

Ernest Hemingway's Reaction to
James Gould Cozzens . . . . . . . . . . . . . Y-98

Ernest Hemingway's Toronto Journalism
Revisited: With Three Previously
Unrecorded Stories . . . . . . . . . . . . . . Y-92

Falsifying Hemingway . . . . . . . . . . . . . . . Y-96

Hemingway Centenary Celebration
at the JFK Library . . . . . . . . . . . . . . . Y-99

The Hemingway/Fenton
Correspondence . . . . . . . . . . . . . . . . Y-02

Hemingway in the JFK . . . . . . . . . . . . . . Y-99

The Hemingway Letters Project
Finds an Editor . . . . . . . . . . . . . . . . . Y-02

Hemingway Salesmen's Dummies . . . . . . . Y-00

Hemingway: Twenty-Five Years Later . . . Y-85

A Literary Archaeologist Digs On:
A Brief Interview with Michael
Reynolds . . . . . . . . . . . . . . . . . . . . . Y-99

Not Immediately Discernible . . . but
Eventually Quite Clear: The *First
Light* and *Final Years* of
Hemingway's Centenary . . . . . . . . . . Y-99

Packaging Papa: *The Garden of Eden* . . . . . Y-86

Second International Hemingway
Colloquium: Cuba . . . . . . . . . . . . . . Y-98

Hémon, Louis 1880-1913 . . . . . . . . . . . . . DLB-92

Hempel, Amy 1951- . . . . . . . . . . . . . . . DLB-218

Hempel, Carl G. 1905-1997 . . . . . . . . . . . DLB-279

Hemphill, Paul 1936- . . . . . . . . . . . . . . . . Y-87

Hénault, Gilles 1920-1996 . . . . . . . . . . . . . DLB-88

Henchman, Daniel 1689-1761 . . . . . . . . . . DLB-24

Henderson, Alice Corbin 1881-1949 . . . . . DLB-54

Henderson, Archibald 1877-1963 . . . . . . . DLB-103

Henderson, David 1942- . . . . . . . . . . . . . DLB-41

Henderson, George Wylie 1904-1965 . . . . DLB-51

Henderson, Zenna 1917-1983 . . . . . . . . . . . DLB-8

Henighan, Tom 1934- . . . . . . . . . . . . . . DLB-251

Henisch, Peter 1943- . . . . . . . . . . . . . . . . DLB-85

Henley, Beth 1952- .................. Y-86
Henley, William Ernest 1849-1903 ....... DLB-19
Henniker, Florence 1855-1923 .......... DLB-135
Henning, Rachel 1826-1914 ............. DLB-230
Henningsen, Agnes 1868-1962 ......... DLB-214
Henry, Alexander 1739-1824 ............ DLB-99
Henry, Buck 1930- ................... DLB-26
Henry, Marguerite 1902-1997 .......... DLB-22
Henry, O. (see Porter, William Sydney)
Henry, Robert Selph 1889-1970 ......... DLB-17
Henry, Will (see Allen, Henry W.)
Henry VIII of England 1491-1547 ...... DLB-132
Henry of Ghent circa 1217-1229 - 1293 ... DLB-115
Henryson, Robert
 1420s or 1430s-circa 1505 .......... DLB-146
Henschke, Alfred (see Klabund)
Hensher, Philip 1965- .............. DLB-267
Hensley, Sophie Almon 1866-1946 ....... DLB-99
Henson, Lance 1944- ................. DLB-175
Henty, G. A. 1832-1902 ............. DLB-18, 141
 The Henty Society .................. Y-98
Hentz, Caroline Lee 1800-1856 ....... DLB-3, 248
Heraclitus
 flourished circa 500 B.C. .......... DLB-176
Herbert, Agnes circa 1880-1960 ........ DLB-174
Herbert, Alan Patrick 1890-1971 ..... DLB-10, 191
Herbert, Edward, Lord, of Cherbury
 1582-1648 .............. DLB-121, 151, 252
Herbert, Frank 1920-1986 ...... DLB-8; CDALB-7
Herbert, George 1593-1633 .. DLB-126; CDBLB-1
Herbert, Henry William 1807-1858 ..... DLB-3, 73
Herbert, John 1926- .................. DLB-53
Herbert, Mary Sidney, Countess of Pembroke
 (see Sidney, Mary)
Herbert, Xavier 1901-1984 ............ DLB-260
Herbert, Zbigniew
 1924-1998 ............. DLB-232; CDWLB-4
Herbst, Josephine 1892-1969 ............. DLB-9
Herburger, Gunter 1932- ......... DLB-75, 124
Herculano, Alexandre 1810-1877 ........ DLB-287
Hercules, Frank E. M. 1917-1996 ........ DLB-33
Herder, Johann Gottfried 1744-1803 ...... DLB-97
B. Herder Book Company ............. DLB-49
Heredia, José-María de 1842-1905 ....... DLB-217
Herford, Charles Harold 1853-1931 ..... DLB-149
Hergesheimer, Joseph 1880-1954 ...... DLB-9, 102
Heritage Press ...................... DLB-46
Hermann the Lame 1013-1054 ......... DLB-148
Hermes, Johann Timotheu 1738-1821 ..... DLB-97
Hermlin, Stephan 1915-1997 ........... DLB-69
Hernández, Alfonso C. 1938- ......... DLB-122
Hernández, Inés 1947- .............. DLB-122
Hernández, Miguel 1910-1942 .......... DLB-134
Hernton, Calvin C. 1932- ............ DLB-38
Herodotus circa 484 B.C.-circa 420 B.C.
 .................... DLB-176; CDWLB-1

Heron, Robert 1764-1807 .............. DLB-142
Herr, Michael 1940- ................. DLB-185
Herrera, Juan Felipe 1948- ........... DLB-122
E. R. Herrick and Company ............ DLB-49
Herrick, Robert 1591-1674 ............ DLB-126
Herrick, Robert 1868-1938 ........ DLB-9, 12, 78
Herrick, William 1915- .............. Y-83
Herrmann, John 1900-1959 ............. DLB-4
Hersey, John
 1914-1993 ....... DLB-6, 185, 278; CDALB-7
Hertel, François 1905-1985 ........... DLB-68
Hervé-Bazin, Jean Pierre Marie (see Bazin, Hervé)
Hervey, John, Lord 1696-1743 ......... DLB-101
Herwig, Georg 1817-1875 ............. DLB-133
Herzen, Alexander (Aleksandr Ivanovich
 Gersten) 1812-1870 ............... DLB-277
Herzog, Emile Salomon Wilhelm
 (see Maurois, André)
Hesiod eighth century B.C. ........... DLB-176
Hesse, Hermann 1877-1962 ... DLB-66; CDWLB-2
Hessus, Eobanus 1488-1540 ........... DLB-179
Heureka! (see Kertész, Imre and Nobel Prize
 in Literature: 2002) ................. Y-02
Hewat, Alexander circa 1743-circa 1824 ... DLB-30
Hewitt, John 1907-1987 ............... DLB-27
Hewlett, Maurice 1861-1923 ........ DLB-34, 156
Heyen, William 1940- ................. DLB-5
Heyer, Georgette 1902-1974 ........ DLB-77, 191
Heym, Stefan 1913-2001 ............... DLB-69
Heyse, Paul 1830-1914 ................ DLB-129
Heytesbury, William
 circa 1310-1372 or 1373 ............ DLB-115
Heyward, Dorothy 1890-1961 ........ DLB-7, 249
Heyward, DuBose 1885-1940 ... DLB-7, 9, 45, 249
Heywood, John 1497?-1580? .......... DLB-136
Heywood, Thomas 1573 or 1574-1641 .... DLB-62
Hibbs, Ben 1901-1975 ................ DLB-137
 "The Saturday Evening Post reaffirms
 a policy," Ben Hibb's Statement
 in The Saturday Evening Post
 (16 May 1942) ................ DLB-137
Hichens, Robert S. 1864-1950 .......... DLB-153
Hickey, Emily 1845-1924 .............. DLB-199
Hickman, William Albert 1877-1957 ..... DLB-92
Hicks, Granville 1901-1982 ........... DLB-246
Hidalgo, José Luis 1919-1947 ......... DLB-108
Hiebert, Paul 1892-1987 .............. DLB-68
Hieng, Andrej 1925- ................. DLB-181
Hierro, José 1922-2002 ............... DLB-108
Higgins, Aidan 1927- ................. DLB-14
Higgins, Colin 1941-1988 ............. DLB-26
Higgins, George V.
 1939-1999 ............ DLB-2; Y-81, 98–99
 Afterword [in response to Cozzen's
 Mens Rea (or Something)] ......... Y-97
 At End of Day: The Last George V.
 Higgins Novel ................... Y-99

The Books of George V. Higgins:
 A Checklist of Editions
 and Printings .................... Y-00
George V. Higgins in Class ........... Y-02
Tribute to Alfred A. Knopf ........... Y-84
Tributes to George V. Higgins ........ Y-99
"What You Lose on the Swings You Make
 Up on the Merry-Go-Round" ... Y-99
Higginson, Thomas Wentworth
 1823-1911 ................ DLB-1, 64, 243
Highwater, Jamake 1942?- ....... DLB-52; Y-85
Hijuelos, Oscar 1951- ............... DLB-145
Hildegard von Bingen 1098-1179 ....... DLB-148
Das Hildesbrandslied
 circa 820 .............. DLB-148; CDWLB-2
Hildesheimer, Wolfgang 1916-1991 .. DLB-69, 124
Hildreth, Richard 1807-1865 ... DLB-1, 30, 59, 235
Hill, Aaron 1685-1750 ................ DLB-84
Hill, Geoffrey 1932- ......... DLB-40; CDBLB-8
George M. Hill Company .............. DLB-49
Hill, "Sir" John 1714?-1775 ............. DLB-39
Lawrence Hill and Company, Publishers .. DLB-46
Hill, Leslie 1880-1960 ................ DLB-51
Hill, Reginald 1936- ................ DLB-276
Hill, Susan 1942- ................ DLB-14, 139
Hill, Walter 1942- ................... DLB-44
Hill and Wang ....................... DLB-46
Hillberry, Conrad 1928- ............. DLB-120
Hillerman, Tony 1925- ............... DLB-206
Hilliard, Gray and Company ........... DLB-49
Hills, Lee 1906-2000 ................. DLB-127
Hillyer, Robert 1895-1961 ............. DLB-54
Hilton, James 1900-1954 ........... DLB-34, 77
Hilton, Walter died 1396 ............. DLB-146
Hilton and Company ................. DLB-49
Himes, Chester 1909-1984 ... DLB-2, 76, 143, 226
Joseph Hindmarsh [publishing house] .... DLB-170
Hine, Daryl 1936- ................... DLB-60
Hingley, Ronald 1920- ............... DLB-155
Hinojosa-Smith, Rolando 1929- ........ DLB-82
Hinton, S. E. 1948- ................ CDALB-7
Hippel, Theodor Gottlieb von
 1741-1796 ........................ DLB-97
Hippocrates of Cos flourished circa
 425 B.C. ............. DLB-176; CDWLB-1
Hirabayashi Taiko 1905-1972 .......... DLB-180
Hirsch, E. D., Jr. 1928- .............. DLB-67
Hirsch, Edward 1950- ............... DLB-120
Hoagland, Edward 1932- ............... DLB-6
Hoagland, Everett H., III 1942- ....... DLB-41
Hoban, Russell 1925- ............ DLB-52; Y-90
Hobbes, Thomas 1588-1679 ... DLB-151, 252, 281
Hobby, Oveta 1905-1995 .............. DLB-127
Hobby, William 1878-1964 ............ DLB-127
Hobsbaum, Philip 1932- .............. DLB-40
Hobson, Laura Z. 1900- .............. DLB-28

Hobson, Sarah 1947- .............. DLB-204
Hoby, Thomas 1530-1566 ........... DLB-132
Hoccleve, Thomas
    circa 1368-circa 1437 ............ DLB-146
Hochhuth, Rolf 1931- .............. DLB-124
Hochman, Sandra 1936- ............. DLB-5
Hocken, Thomas Morland 1836-1910 ... DLB-184
Hocking, William Ernest 1873-1966 ..... DLB-270
Hodder and Stoughton, Limited ....... DLB-106
Hodgins, Jack 1938- ............... DLB-60
Hodgman, Helen 1945- .............. DLB-14
Hodgskin, Thomas 1787-1869 ........ DLB-158
Hodgson, Ralph 1871-1962 .......... DLB-19
Hodgson, William Hope
    1877-1918 ............ DLB-70, 153, 156, 178
Hoe, Robert, III 1839-1909 ......... DLB-187
Hoeg, Peter 1957- ................. DLB-214
Hoffenstein, Samuel 1890-1947 ...... DLB-11
Hoffman, Charles Fenno 1806-1884 ... DLB-3, 250
Hoffman, Daniel 1923- .............. DLB-5
    Tribute to Robert Graves .......... Y-85
Hoffmann, E. T. A.
    1776-1822 ............ DLB-90; CDWLB-2
Hoffman, Frank B. 1888-1958 ........ DLB-188
Hoffman, William 1925- ............ DLB-234
    Tribute to Paxton Davis ........... Y-94
Hoffmanswaldau, Christian Hoffman von
    1616-1679 ..................... DLB-168
Hofmann, Michael 1957- ............ DLB-40
Hofmannsthal, Hugo von
    1874-1929 ........ DLB-81, 118; CDWLB-2
Hofstadter, Richard 1916-1970 ....... DLB-17, 246
Hogan, Desmond 1950- ............. DLB-14
Hogan, Linda 1947- ................ DLB-175
Hogan and Thompson ............... DLB-49
Hogarth Press ............ DLB-112; DS-10
Hogg, James 1770-1835 ....... DLB-93, 116, 159
Hohberg, Wolfgang Helmhard Freiherr von
    1612-1688 ..................... DLB-168
von Hohenheim, Philippus Aureolus
    Theophrastus Bombastus (see Paracelsus)
Hohl, Ludwig 1904-1980 ............ DLB-56
Højholt, Per 1928- ................ DLB-214
Holan, Vladimir 1905-1980 .......... DLB-215
Holbrook, David 1923- ............. DLB-14, 40
Holcroft, Thomas 1745-1809 ..... DLB-39, 89, 158
    Preface to *Alwyn* (1780) ......... DLB-39
Holden, Jonathan 1941- ............ DLB-105
    "Contemporary Verse Story-telling" .. DLB-105
Holden, Molly 1927-1981 ........... DLB-40
Hölderlin, Friedrich
    1770-1843 ............ DLB-90; CDWLB-2
Holdstock, Robert 1948- ........... DLB-261
Holiday House ..................... DLB-46
Holinshed, Raphael died 1580 ....... DLB-167
Holland, J. G. 1819-1881 ........... DS-13
Holland, Norman N. 1927- .......... DLB-67

Hollander, John 1929- .............. DLB-5
Holley, Marietta 1836-1926 ......... DLB-11
Hollinghurst, Alan 1954- ........... DLB-207
Hollingsworth, Margaret 1940- ...... DLB-60
Hollo, Anselm 1934- ............... DLB-40
Holloway, Emory 1885-1977 ......... DLB-103
Holloway, John 1920- .............. DLB-27
Holloway House Publishing Company ... DLB-46
Holme, Constance 1880-1955 ........ DLB-34
Holmes, Abraham S. 1821?-1908 ..... DLB-99
Holmes, John Clellon 1926-1988 ..... DLB-16, 237
    "Four Essays on the Beat
    Generation" .................... DLB-16
Holmes, Mary Jane 1825-1907 ..... DLB-202, 221
Holmes, Oliver Wendell
    1809-1894 ....... DLB-1, 189, 235; CDALB-2
Holmes, Richard 1945- ............. DLB-155
Holmes, Thomas James 1874-1959 .... DLB-187
Holroyd, Michael 1935- ........... DLB-155; Y-99
Holst, Hermann E. von 1841-1904 ... DLB-47
Holt, John 1721-1784 ............... DLB-43
Henry Holt and Company ........... DLB-49, 284
Holt, Rinehart and Winston ......... DLB-46
Holtby, Winifred 1898-1935 ........ DLB-191
Holthusen, Hans Egon 1913-1997 ..... DLB-69
Hölty, Ludwig Christoph Heinrich
    1748-1776 ..................... DLB-94
Holub, Miroslav
    1923-1998 .......... DLB-232; CDWLB-4
Holz, Arno 1863-1929 .............. DLB-118
Home, Henry, Lord Kames
    (see Kames, Henry Home, Lord)
Home, John 1722-1808 .............. DLB-84
Home, William Douglas 1912- ....... DLB-13
Home Publishing Company .......... DLB-49
Homer circa eighth-seventh centuries B.C.
    ........................ DLB-176; CDWLB-1
Homer, Winslow 1836-1910 ......... DLB-188
Homes, Geoffrey (see Mainwaring, Daniel)
Honan, Park 1928- ................. DLB-111
Hone, William 1780-1842 .......... DLB-110, 158
Hongo, Garrett Kaoru 1951- ........ DLB-120
Honig, Edwin 1919- ................ DLB-5
Hood, Hugh 1928-2000 ............. DLB-53
Hood, Mary 1946- .................. DLB-234
Hood, Thomas 1799-1845 ........... DLB-96
Hook, Sidney 1902-1989 ........... DLB-279
Hook, Theodore 1788-1841 ......... DLB-116
Hooker, Jeremy 1941- .............. DLB-40
Hooker, Richard 1554-1600 ........ DLB-132
Hooker, Thomas 1586-1647 ......... DLB-24
hooks, bell 1952- .................. DLB-246
Hooper, Johnson Jones
    1815-1862 ............. DLB-3, 11, 248
Hope, Anthony 1863-1933 ......... DLB-153, 156
Hope, Christopher 1944- ........... DLB-225

Hope, Eva (see Hearn, Mary Anne)
Hope, Laurence (Adela Florence
    Cory Nicolson) 1865-1904 ........ DLB-240
Hopkins, Ellice 1836-1904 .......... DLB-190
Hopkins, Gerard Manley
    1844-1889 .......... DLB-35, 57; CDBLB-5
Hopkins, John ?-1570 ............... DLB-132
Hopkins, John H., and Son ......... DLB-46
Hopkins, Lemuel 1750-1801 ........ DLB-37
Hopkins, Pauline Elizabeth 1859-1930 ... DLB-50
Hopkins, Samuel 1721-1803 ......... DLB-31
Hopkinson, Francis 1737-1791 ...... DLB-31
Hopkinson, Nalo 1960- ............. DLB-251
Hopper, Nora (Mrs. Nora Chesson)
    1871-1906 ..................... DLB-240
Hoppin, Augustus 1828-1896 ....... DLB-188
Hora, Josef 1891-1945 ......... DLB-215; CDWLB-4
Horace 65 B.C.-8 B.C. ...... DLB-211; CDWLB-1
Horgan, Paul 1903-1995 ...... DLB-102, 212; Y-85
    Tribute to Alfred A. Knopf ........ Y-84
Horizon Press ..................... DLB-46
Hornby, C. H. St. John 1867-1946 ... DLB-201
Hornby, Nick 1957- ................ DLB-207
Horne, Frank 1899-1974 ............ DLB-51
Horne, Richard Henry (Hengist)
    1802 or 1803-1884 .............. DLB-32
Horne, Thomas 1608-1654 .......... DLB-281
Horney, Karen 1885-1952 .......... DLB-246
Hornung, E. W. 1866-1921 ......... DLB-70
Horovitz, Israel 1939- ............. DLB-7
Horta, Maria Teresa (see The Three Marias:
    A Landmark Case in Portuguese
    Literary History)
Horton, George Moses 1797?-1883? ... DLB-50
    George Moses Horton Society ...... Y-99
Horváth, Ödön von 1901-1938 ..... DLB-85, 124
Horwood, Harold 1923- ............ DLB-60
E. and E. Hosford [publishing house] ... DLB-49
Hoskens, Jane Fenn 1693-1770? ..... DLB-200
Hoskyns, John circa 1566-1638 ..... DLB-121, 281
Hosokawa Yūsai 1535-1610 ......... DLB-203
Hospers, John 1918- ................ DLB-279
Hostovský, Egon 1908-1973 ......... DLB-215
Hotchkiss and Company ............ DLB-49
Hough, Emerson 1857-1923 ........ DLB-9, 212
Houghton, Stanley 1881-1913 ....... DLB-10
Houghton Mifflin Company ......... DLB-49
*Hours at Home* ................... DS-13
Household, Geoffrey 1900-1988 ..... DLB-87
Housman, A. E. 1859-1936 ... DLB-19; CDBLB-5
Housman, Laurence 1865-1959 ...... DLB-10
Houston, Pam 1962- ............... DLB-244
Houwald, Ernst von 1778-1845 ..... DLB-90
Hovey, Richard 1864-1900 .......... DLB-54
Howard, Donald R. 1927-1987 ...... DLB-111
Howard, Maureen 1930- ............ Y-83

Howard, Richard 1929- ..............DLB-5
Howard, Roy W. 1883-1964..........DLB-29
Howard, Sidney 1891-1939....... DLB-7, 26, 249
Howard, Thomas, second Earl of Arundel
 1585-1646......................DLB-213
Howe, E. W. 1853-1937............DLB-12, 25
Howe, Henry 1816-1893..............DLB-30
Howe, Irving 1920-1993..............DLB-67
Howe, Joseph 1804-1873..............DLB-99
Howe, Julia Ward 1819-1910 ....DLB-1, 189, 235
Howe, Percival Presland 1886-1944 .....DLB-149
Howe, Susan 1937- ...............DLB-120
Howell, Clark, Sr. 1863-1936..........DLB-25
Howell, Evan P. 1839-1905..............DLB-23
Howell, James 1594?-1666............DLB-151
Howell, Soskin and Company..........DLB-46
Howell, Warren Richardson
 1912-1984......................DLB-140
Howells, William Dean 1837-1920
 ........ DLB-12, 64, 74, 79, 189; CDALB-3
 Introduction to Paul Laurence
  Dunbar's *Lyrics of Lowly Life*
  (1896).......................DLB-50
 The William Dean Howells Society .....Y-01
Howitt, Mary 1799-1888..........DLB-110, 199
Howitt, William 1792-1879 ............DLB-110
Hoyem, Andrew 1935- ..............DLB-5
Hoyers, Anna Ovena 1584-1655......DLB-164
Hoyle, Fred 1915-2001 ..............DLB-261
Hoyos, Angela de 1940- ............DLB-82
Henry Hoyt [publishing house] .........DLB-49
Hoyt, Palmer 1897-1979..............DLB-127
Hrabal, Bohumil 1914-1997..........DLB-232
Hrabanus Maurus 776?-856...........DLB-148
Hronský, Josef Cíger 1896-1960 ......DLB-215
Hrotsvit of Gandersheim
 circa 935-circa 1000..............DLB-148
Hubbard, Elbert 1856-1915............DLB-91
Hubbard, Kin 1868-1930..............DLB-11
Hubbard, William circa 1621-1704.....DLB-24
Huber, Therese 1764-1829.............DLB-90
Huch, Friedrich 1873-1913.............DLB-66
Huch, Ricarda 1864-1947.............DLB-66
Huddle, David 1942- ..............DLB-130
Hudgins, Andrew 1951- .........DLB-120, 282
Hudson, Henry Norman 1814-1886 ......DLB-64
Hudson, Stephen 1868?-1944 ..........DLB-197
Hudson, W. H. 1841-1922 ..... DLB-98, 153, 174
Hudson and Goodwin..................DLB-49
Huebsch, B. W., oral history............Y-99
B. W. Huebsch [publishing house]......DLB-46
Hueffer, Oliver Madox 1876-1931......DLB-197
Huet, Pierre Daniel
 Preface to *The History of Romances*
  (1715).......................DLB-39
Hugh of St. Victor circa 1096-1141 .....DLB-208
Hughes, David 1930- ..............DLB-14

Hughes, Dusty 1947- ..............DLB-233
Hughes, Hatcher 1881-1945 ..........DLB-249
Hughes, John 1677-1720..............DLB-84
Hughes, Langston 1902-1967 .....DLB-4, 7, 48,
 51, 86, 228; ; DS-15; CDALB-5
Hughes, Richard 1900-1976..........DLB-15, 161
Hughes, Ted 1930-1998 ..........DLB-40, 161
Hughes, Thomas 1822-1896 ........DLB-18, 163
Hugo, Richard 1923-1982............DLB-5, 206
Hugo, Victor 1802-1885 ...... DLB-119, 192, 217
Hugo Awards and Nebula Awards ........DLB-8
Huidobro, Vicente 1893-1948..........DLB-283
Hull, Richard 1896-1973 ............DLB-77
Hulme, T. E. 1883-1917 ..............DLB-19
Hulton, Anne ?-1779? ................DLB-200
Humboldt, Alexander von 1769-1859 .....DLB-90
Humboldt, Wilhelm von 1767-1835.......DLB-90
Hume, David 1711-1776..........DLB-104, 252
Hume, Fergus 1859-1932.............DLB-70
Hume, Sophia 1702-1774 ............DLB-200
Hume-Rothery, Mary Catherine
 1824-1885......................DLB-240
Humishuma (see Mourning Dove)
Hummer, T. R. 1950- ..............DLB-120
Humor
 American Humor: A Historical
  Survey.......................DLB-11
 American Humor Studies Association....Y-99
 The Comic Tradition Continued
  [in the British Novel] ..........DLB-15
 Humorous Book Illustration.........DLB-11
 International Society for Humor Studies.. Y-99
 Newspaper Syndication of American
  Humor........................DLB-11
 Selected Humorous Magazines
  (1820-1950)...................DLB-11
Humphrey, Duke of Gloucester
 1391-1447 .....................DLB-213
Humphrey, William
 1924-1997 ........... DLB-6, 212, 234, 278
Humphreys, David 1752-1818..........DLB-37
Humphreys, Emyr 1919- ............DLB-15
Bruce Humphries [publishing house] .....DLB-46
Huncke, Herbert 1915-1996 ..........DLB-16
Huneker, James Gibbons 1857-1921 ......DLB-71
Hunold, Christian Friedrich 1681-1721...DLB-168
Hunt, Irene 1907- ................DLB-52
Hunt, Leigh 1784-1859 ....... DLB-96, 110, 144
Hunt, Violet 1862-1942 ......... DLB-162, 197
Hunt, William Gibbes 1791-1833 ........DLB-73
Hunter, Evan 1926- ................Y-82
 Tribute to John D. MacDonald..........Y-86
Hunter, Jim 1939- .................DLB-14
Hunter, Kristin 1931- ...............DLB-33
 Tribute to Julian Mayfield.............Y-84
Hunter, Mollie 1922- ...............DLB-161
Hunter, N. C. 1908-1971 ..............DLB-10

Hunter-Duvar, John 1821-1899.........DLB-99
Huntington, Henry E. 1850-1927 .......DLB-140
 The Henry E. Huntington Library......Y-92
Huntington, Susan Mansfield 1791-1823..DLB-200
Hurd and Houghton ..................DLB-49
Hurst, Fannie 1889-1968..............DLB-86
Hurst and Blackett....................DLB-106
Hurst and Company ..................DLB-49
Hurston, Zora Neale
 1901?-1960 .........DLB-51, 86; CDALB-7
Husson, Jules-François-Félix (see Champfleury)
Huston, John 1906-1987 ..............DLB-26
Hutcheson, Francis 1694-1746.......DLB-31, 252
Hutchinson, Ron 1947- .............DLB-245
Hutchinson, R. C. 1907-1975 ..........DLB-191
Hutchinson, Thomas 1711-1780 ......DLB-30, 31
Hutchinson and Company
 (Publishers) Limited ..............DLB-112
Huth, Angela 1938- ................DLB-271
Hutton, Richard Holt 1826-1897.........DLB-57
von Hutten, Ulrich 1488-1523.........DLB-179
Huxley, Aldous 1894-1963
 ...... DLB-36, 100, 162, 195, 255; CDBLB-6
Huxley, Elspeth Josceline
 1907-1997 .................DLB-77, 204
Huxley, T. H. 1825-1895 ..............DLB-57
Huyghue, Douglas Smith 1816-1891......DLB-99
Huysmans, Joris-Karl 1848-1907 ........DLB-123
Hwang, David Henry 1957- .......DLB-212, 228
Hyde, Donald 1909-1966 ..............DLB-187
Hyde, Mary 1912- .................DLB-187
Hyman, Trina Schart 1939- ............DLB-61

# I

Iavorsky, Stefan 1658-1722 ............DLB-150
Iazykov, Nikolai Mikhailovich
 1803-1846......................DLB-205
Ibáñez, Armando P. 1949- ............DLB-209
Ibn Bajja circa 1077-1138 ..............DLB-115
Ibn Gabirol, Solomon
 circa 1021-circa 1058...............DLB-115
Ibuse Masuji 1898-1993................DLB-180
Ichijō Kanera (see Ichijō Kaneyoshi)
Ichijō Kaneyoshi (Ichijō Kanera)
 1402-1481......................DLB-203
Iffland, August Wilhelm 1759-1814......DLB-94
Ignatieff, Michael 1947- .............DLB-267
Ignatow, David 1914-1997..............DLB-5
Ike, Chukwuemeka 1931- ............DLB-157
Ikkyū Sōjun 1394-1481 ..............DLB-203
Iles, Francis (see Berkeley, Anthony)
Il'f, Il'ia (Il'ia Arnol'dovich Fainzil'berg)
 1897-1937......................DLB-272
Illich, Ivan 1926-2002 ................DLB-242
Illustration
 Children's Book Illustration in the
  Twentieth Century.............DLB-61

# Cumulative Index

Children's Illustrators, 1800-1880 . . . DLB-163
Early American Book Illustration . . . . DLB-49
The Iconography of Science-Fiction
 Art . . . . . . . . . . . . . . . . . . . . . . . . DLB-8
The Illustration of Early German
 Literary Manuscripts, circa
 1150-circa 1300 . . . . . . . . . . . . . DLB-148
Minor Illustrators, 1880-1914 . . . . . . DLB-141
Illyés, Gyula 1902-1983 . . . . DLB-215; CDWLB-4
Imbs, Bravig 1904-1946 . . . . . . . . . DLB-4; DS-15
Imbuga, Francis D. 1947- . . . . . . . . DLB-157
Immermann, Karl 1796-1840 . . . . . . . . . DLB-133
Inchbald, Elizabeth 1753-1821 . . . . . . . DLB-39, 89
Indiana University Press . . . . . . . . . . . . . . . . Y-02
Ingamells, Rex 1913-1955 . . . . . . . . . . . . DLB-260
Inge, William 1913-1973 . . . DLB-7, 249; CDALB-1
Ingelow, Jean 1820-1897 . . . . . . . . . DLB-35, 163
Ingersoll, Ralph 1900-1985 . . . . . . . . . . . DLB-127
The Ingersoll Prizes . . . . . . . . . . . . . . . . . . . Y-84
Ingoldsby, Thomas (see Barham, Richard Harris)
Ingraham, Joseph Holt 1809-1860 . . . . DLB-3, 248
Inman, John 1805-1850 . . . . . . . . . . . . . . . DLB-73
Innerhofer, Franz 1944- . . . . . . . . . . . . . . DLB-85
Innes, Michael (J. I. M. Stewart)
 1906-1994 . . . . . . . . . . . . . . . . . . . . DLB-276
Innis, Harold Adams 1894-1952 . . . . . . . . DLB-88
Innis, Mary Quayle 1899-1972 . . . . . . . . . DLB-88
Inō Sōgi 1421-1502 . . . . . . . . . . . . . . . . . DLB-203
Inoue Yasushi 1907-1991 . . . . . . . . . . . . DLB-182
"The Greatness of Southern Literature":
 League of the South Institute for the
 Study of Southern Culture and History . . . . . . . . Y-02
International Publishers Company . . . . . . . DLB-46
Internet (publishing and commerce)
 Author Websites . . . . . . . . . . . . . . . . . . Y-97
 The Book Trade and the Internet . . . . . . Y-00
 E-Books Turn the Corner . . . . . . . . . . . . Y-98
 The E-Researcher: Possibilities
  and Pitfalls . . . . . . . . . . . . . . . . . . . . Y-00
 Interviews on E-publishing . . . . . . . . . . . Y-00
 John Updike on the Internet . . . . . . . . . Y-97
 LitCheck Website . . . . . . . . . . . . . . . . . Y-01
 Virtual Books and Enemies of Books . . . . . Y-00
Interviews
 Adoff, Arnold . . . . . . . . . . . . . . . . . . . Y-01
 Aldridge, John W. . . . . . . . . . . . . . . . . Y-91
 Anastas, Benjamin . . . . . . . . . . . . . . . . Y-98
 Baker, Nicholson . . . . . . . . . . . . . . . . . Y-00
 Bank, Melissa . . . . . . . . . . . . . . . . . . . Y-98
 Bass, T. J. . . . . . . . . . . . . . . . . . . . . . . Y-80
 Bernstein, Harriet . . . . . . . . . . . . . . . . Y-82
 Betts, Doris . . . . . . . . . . . . . . . . . . . . . Y-82
 Bosworth, David . . . . . . . . . . . . . . . . . Y-82
 Bottoms, David . . . . . . . . . . . . . . . . . . Y-83
 Bowers, Fredson . . . . . . . . . . . . . . . . . Y-80
 Burnshaw, Stanley . . . . . . . . . . . . . . . . Y-97

Carpenter, Humphrey . . . . . . . . . . . . . Y-84, 99
Carr, Virginia Spencer . . . . . . . . . . . . . . . Y-00
Carver, Raymond . . . . . . . . . . . . . . . . . . Y-83
Cherry, Kelly . . . . . . . . . . . . . . . . . . . . . Y-83
Conroy, Jack . . . . . . . . . . . . . . . . . . . . . Y-81
Coppel, Alfred . . . . . . . . . . . . . . . . . . . . Y-83
Cowley, Malcolm . . . . . . . . . . . . . . . . . . Y-81
Davis, Paxton . . . . . . . . . . . . . . . . . . . . . Y-89
Devito, Carlo . . . . . . . . . . . . . . . . . . . . . Y-94
De Vries, Peter . . . . . . . . . . . . . . . . . . . . Y-82
Dickey, James . . . . . . . . . . . . . . . . . . . . . Y-82
Donald, David Herbert . . . . . . . . . . . . . . Y-87
Editors, Conversations with . . . . . . . . . . . Y-95
Ellroy, James . . . . . . . . . . . . . . . . . . . . . Y-91
Fancher, Betsy . . . . . . . . . . . . . . . . . . . . Y-83
Faust, Irvin . . . . . . . . . . . . . . . . . . . . . . Y-00
Fulton, Len . . . . . . . . . . . . . . . . . . . . . . Y-86
Furst, Alan . . . . . . . . . . . . . . . . . . . . . . Y-01
Garrett, George . . . . . . . . . . . . . . . . . . . Y-83
Gelfman, Jane . . . . . . . . . . . . . . . . . . . . Y-93
Goldwater, Walter . . . . . . . . . . . . . . . . . Y-93
Gores, Joe . . . . . . . . . . . . . . . . . . . . . . . Y-02
Greenfield, George . . . . . . . . . . . . . . . . . Y-91
Griffin, Bryan . . . . . . . . . . . . . . . . . . . . . Y-81
Groom, Winston . . . . . . . . . . . . . . . . . . Y-01
Guilds, John Caldwell . . . . . . . . . . . . . . . Y-92
Hamilton, Virginia . . . . . . . . . . . . . . . . . Y-01
Hardin, James . . . . . . . . . . . . . . . . . . . . Y-92
Harris, Mark . . . . . . . . . . . . . . . . . . . . . Y-80
Harrison, Jim . . . . . . . . . . . . . . . . . . . . Y-82
Hazzard, Shirley . . . . . . . . . . . . . . . . . . . Y-82
Herrick, William . . . . . . . . . . . . . . . . . . Y-01
Higgins, George V. . . . . . . . . . . . . . . . . . Y-98
Hoban, Russell . . . . . . . . . . . . . . . . . . . . Y-90
Holroyd, Michael . . . . . . . . . . . . . . . . . . Y-99
Horowitz, Glen . . . . . . . . . . . . . . . . . . . Y-90
Iggulden, John . . . . . . . . . . . . . . . . . . . . Y-01
Jakes, John . . . . . . . . . . . . . . . . . . . . . . Y-83
Jenkinson, Edward B. . . . . . . . . . . . . . . . Y-82
Jenks, Tom . . . . . . . . . . . . . . . . . . . . . . Y-86
Kaplan, Justin . . . . . . . . . . . . . . . . . . . . Y-86
King, Florence . . . . . . . . . . . . . . . . . . . . Y-85
Klopfer, Donald S. . . . . . . . . . . . . . . . . . Y-97
Krug, Judith . . . . . . . . . . . . . . . . . . . . . Y-82
Lamm, Donald . . . . . . . . . . . . . . . . . . . . Y-95
Laughlin, James . . . . . . . . . . . . . . . . . . . Y-96
Lawrence, Starling . . . . . . . . . . . . . . . . . Y-95
Lindsay, Jack . . . . . . . . . . . . . . . . . . . . . Y-84
Mailer, Norman . . . . . . . . . . . . . . . . . . . Y-97
Manchester, William . . . . . . . . . . . . . . . . Y-85
Max, D. T. . . . . . . . . . . . . . . . . . . . . . . . Y-94
McCormack, Thomas . . . . . . . . . . . . . . . Y-98
McNamara, Katherine . . . . . . . . . . . . . . Y-97
Mellen, Joan . . . . . . . . . . . . . . . . . . . . . Y-94

Menaker, Daniel . . . . . . . . . . . . . . . . . . . Y-97
Mooneyham, Lamarr . . . . . . . . . . . . . . . . Y-82
Murray, Les . . . . . . . . . . . . . . . . . . . . . . Y-01
Nosworth, David . . . . . . . . . . . . . . . . . . Y-82
O'Connor, Patrick . . . . . . . . . . . . . . . Y-84, 99
Ozick, Cynthia . . . . . . . . . . . . . . . . . . . . Y-83
Penner, Jonathan . . . . . . . . . . . . . . . . . . Y-83
Pennington, Lee . . . . . . . . . . . . . . . . . . . Y-82
Penzler, Otto . . . . . . . . . . . . . . . . . . . . . Y-96
Plimpton, George . . . . . . . . . . . . . . . . . . Y-99
Potok, Chaim . . . . . . . . . . . . . . . . . . . . . Y-84
Powell, Padgett . . . . . . . . . . . . . . . . . . . Y-01
Prescott, Peter S. . . . . . . . . . . . . . . . . . . Y-86
Rabe, David . . . . . . . . . . . . . . . . . . . . . . Y-91
Rechy, John . . . . . . . . . . . . . . . . . . . . . . Y-82
Reid, B. L. . . . . . . . . . . . . . . . . . . . . . . . Y-83
Reynolds, Michael . . . . . . . . . . . . . . . . Y-95, 99
Robinson, Derek . . . . . . . . . . . . . . . . . . Y-02
Rollyson, Carl . . . . . . . . . . . . . . . . . . . . Y-97
Rosset, Barney . . . . . . . . . . . . . . . . . . . . Y-02
Schlafly, Phyllis . . . . . . . . . . . . . . . . . . . . Y-82
Schroeder, Patricia . . . . . . . . . . . . . . . . . Y-99
Schulberg, Budd . . . . . . . . . . . . . . . . . Y-81, 01
Scribner, Charles, III . . . . . . . . . . . . . . . . Y-94
Sipper, Ralph . . . . . . . . . . . . . . . . . . . . . Y-94
Smith, Cork . . . . . . . . . . . . . . . . . . . . . . Y-95
Staley, Thomas F. . . . . . . . . . . . . . . . . . . Y-00
Styron, William . . . . . . . . . . . . . . . . . . . Y-80
Talese, Nan . . . . . . . . . . . . . . . . . . . . . . Y-94
Thornton, John . . . . . . . . . . . . . . . . . . . Y-94
Toth, Susan Allen . . . . . . . . . . . . . . . . . . Y-86
Tyler, Anne . . . . . . . . . . . . . . . . . . . . . . Y-82
Vaughan, Samuel . . . . . . . . . . . . . . . . . . Y-97
Von Ogtrop, Kristin . . . . . . . . . . . . . . . . Y-92
Wallenstein, Barry . . . . . . . . . . . . . . . . . Y-92
Weintraub, Stanley . . . . . . . . . . . . . . . . . Y-82
Williams, J. Chamberlain . . . . . . . . . . . . . Y-84
Into the Past: William Jovanovich's
 Reflections in Publishing . . . . . . . . . . . . . Y-02
The National Library of Ireland's
 New James Joyce Manuscripts . . . . . . . . . . Y-02
Irving, John 1942- . . . . . . . . . . DLB-6, 278; Y-82
Irving, Washington 1783-1859
 . . . . . . . . . . . . . . . DLB-3, 11, 30, 59, 73, 74,
  183, 186, 250; CDALB-2
Irwin, Grace 1907- . . . . . . . . . . . . . . . . DLB-68
Irwin, Will 1873-1948 . . . . . . . . . . . . . . DLB-25
Isaksson, Ulla 1916-2000 . . . . . . . . . . . . DLB-257
Iser, Wolfgang 1926- . . . . . . . . . . . . . . . DLB-242
Isherwood, Christopher
 1904-1986 . . . . . . . . . . . . . DLB-15, 195; Y-86
 The Christopher Isherwood Archive,
  The Huntington Library . . . . . . . . . . Y-99
Ishiguro, Kazuo
 1954- . . . . . . . . . . . . . . . . . . . . . . . DLB-194
Ishikawa Jun 1899-1987 . . . . . . . . . . . . . DLB-182

412

The Island Trees Case: A Symposium on
    School Library Censorship
    An Interview with Judith Krug
    An Interview with Phyllis Schlafly
    An Interview with Edward B. Jenkinson
    An Interview with Lamarr Mooneyham
    An Interview with Harriet Bernstein..... Y-82

Islas, Arturo
    1938-1991 .................... DLB-122

Issit, Debbie 1966- ............. DLB-233

Ivanišević, Drago 1907-1981 .......... DLB-181

Ivanov, Vsevolod Viacheslavovich
    1895-1963 .................... DLB-272

Ivaska, Astrīde 1926- .............. DLB-232

M. J. Ivers and Company .............. DLB-49

Iwaniuk, Wacław 1915- ............. DLB-215

Iwano Hōmei 1873-1920 ............. DLB-180

Iwaszkiewicz, Jarosław 1894-1980 ...... DLB-215

Iyayi, Festus 1947- ............... DLB-157

Izumi Kyōka 1873-1939 ............. DLB-180

# J

Jackmon, Marvin E. (see Marvin X)

Jacks, L. P. 1860-1955 .............. DLB-135

Jackson, Angela 1951- .............. DLB-41

Jackson, Charles 1903-1968 .......... DLB-234

Jackson, Helen Hunt
    1830-1885 ........... DLB-42, 47, 186, 189

Jackson, Holbrook 1874-1948 .......... DLB-98

Jackson, Laura Riding 1901-1991 ....... DLB-48

Jackson, Shirley
    1916-1965 .......... DLB-6, 234; CDALB-1

Jacob, Max 1876-1944 .............. DLB-258

Jacob, Naomi 1884?-1964 ............ DLB-191

Jacob, Piers Anthony Dillingham
    (see Anthony, Piers)

Jacob, Violet 1863-1946 ............. DLB-240

Jacobi, Friedrich Heinrich 1743-1819 ...... DLB-94

Jacobi, Johann Georg 1740-1841 ........ DLB-97

George W. Jacobs and Company ........ DLB-49

Jacobs, Harriet 1813-1897 ........... DLB-239

Jacobs, Joseph 1854-1916 ............ DLB-141

Jacobs, W. W. 1863-1943 ............ DLB-135

    The W. W. Jacobs Appreciation Society . . Y-98

Jacobsen, Jørgen-Frantz 1900-1938 ...... DLB-214

Jacobsen, Josephine 1908- .......... DLB-244

Jacobson, Dan 1929- ........ DLB-14, 207, 225

Jacobson, Howard 1942- ............ DLB-207

Jacques de Vitry circa 1160/1170-1240 ... DLB-208

Jæger, Frank 1926-1977 ............. DLB-214

William Jaggard [publishing house] ...... DLB-170

Jahier, Piero 1884-1966 ........... DLB-114, 264

Jahnn, Hans Henny 1894-1959 ...... DLB-56, 124

Jaimes, Freyre, Ricardo 1866?-1933..... DLB-283

Jakes, John 1932- ............. DLB-278; Y-83
    Tribute to John Gardner ............. Y-82
    Tribute to John D. MacDonald ........ Y-86

Jakobson, Roman 1896-1982 .......... DLB-242

James, Alice 1848-1892 ............. DLB-221

James, C. L. R. 1901-1989 ........... DLB-125

James, George P. R. 1801-1860 ........ DLB-116

James, Henry 1843-1916
    ...... DLB-12, 71, 74, 189; DS-13; CDALB-3
    "The Future of the Novel" (1899)..... DLB-18
    "The Novel in [Robert Browning's]
        'The Ring and the Book'"
        (1912) ..................... DLB-32

James, John circa 1633-1729 ........... DLB-24

James, M. R. 1862-1936 .......... DLB-156, 201

James, Naomi 1949- ............... DLB-204

James, P. D. (Phyllis Dorothy James White)
    1920- ...... DLB-87, 276; DS-17; CDBLB-8
    Tribute to Charles Scribner Jr. .......... Y-95

James, Thomas 1572?-1629 ........... DLB-213

U. P. James [publishing house] .......... DLB-49

James, Will 1892-1942 ................ DS-16

James, William 1842-1910 ........... DLB-270

James VI of Scotland, I of England
    1566-1625 ............... DLB-151, 172

    Ane Schort Treatise Conteining Some Revlis
        and Cautelis to Be Obseruit and
        Eschewit in Scottis Poesi (1584) ..... DLB-172

Jameson, Anna 1794-1860 ......... DLB-99, 166

Jameson, Fredric 1934- ............ DLB-67

Jameson, J. Franklin 1859-1937 ......... DLB-17

Jameson, Storm 1891-1986 ............ DLB-36

Jančar, Drago 1948- ................ DLB-181

Janés, Clara 1940- .................. DLB-134

Janevski, Slavko 1920- ..... DLB-181; CDWLB-4

Jansson, Tove 1914-2001 .............. DLB-257

Janvier, Thomas 1849-1913 ........... DLB-202

Japan
    "The Development of Meiji Japan"...DLB-180
    "Encounter with the West" ........ DLB-180

Japanese Literature
    Letter from Japan ................. Y-94, 98
    Medieval Travel Diaries ........... DLB-203
    Surveys: 1987-1995 ............... DLB-182

Jaramillo, Cleofas M. 1878-1956 ........ DLB-122

Jarman, Mark 1952- ............ DLB-120, 282

Jarrell, Randall
    1914-1965 ........... DLB-48, 52; CDALB-1

Jarrold and Sons .................... DLB-106

Jarry, Alfred 1873-1907 ........... DLB-192, 258

Jarves, James Jackson 1818-1888 ........ DLB-189

Jasmin, Claude 1930- ................ DLB-60

Jaunsudrabiņš, Jānis 1877-1962 ........ DLB-220

Jay, John 1745-1829 .................. DLB-31

Jean de Garlande (see John of Garland)

Jefferies, Richard 1848-1887 ........ DLB-98, 141

    The Richard Jefferies Society .......... Y-98

Jeffers, Lance 1919-1985 .............. DLB-41

Jeffers, Robinson
    1887-1962 .......... DLB-45, 212; CDALB-4

Jefferson, Thomas
    1743-1826 .......... DLB-31, 183; CDALB-2

Jégé 1866-1940 ..................... DLB-215

Jelinek, Elfriede 1946- .............. DLB-85

Jellicoe, Ann 1927- ............. DLB-13, 233

Jemison, Mary circa 1742-1833 ........ DLB-239

Jenkins, Dan 1929- ................. DLB-241

Jenkins, Elizabeth 1905- ............. DLB-155

Jenkins, Robin 1912- ............ DLB-14, 271

Jenkins, William Fitzgerald (see Leinster, Murray)

Herbert Jenkins Limited .............. DLB-112

Jennings, Elizabeth 1926- ............ DLB-27

Jens, Walter 1923- .................. DLB-69

Jensen, Johannes V. 1873-1950 ......... DLB-214

Jensen, Merrill 1905-1980 .............. DLB-17

Jensen, Thit 1876-1957 ................ DLB-214

Jephson, Robert 1736-1803 ............. DLB-89

Jerome, Jerome K. 1859-1927 .... DLB-10, 34, 135

    The Jerome K. Jerome Society ......... Y-98

Jerome, Judson 1927-1991 ............. DLB-105

    "Reflections: After a Tornado" ...... DLB-105

Jerrold, Douglas 1803-1857 ........ DLB-158, 159

Jersild, Per Christian 1935- ........... DLB-257

Jesse, F. Tennyson 1888-1958 ........... DLB-77

Jewel, John 1522-1571 ................ DLB-236

John P. Jewett and Company ........... DLB-49

Jewett, Sarah Orne 1849-1909 .... DLB-12, 74, 221

The Jewish Publication Society .......... DLB-49

Studies in American Jewish Literature ....... Y-02

Jewitt, John Rodgers 1783-1821 .......... DLB-99

Jewsbury, Geraldine 1812-1880 .......... DLB-21

Jewsbury, Maria Jane 1800-1833 ........ DLB-199

Jhabvala, Ruth Prawer 1927- ..... DLB-139, 194

Jiménez, Juan Ramón 1881-1958 ........ DLB-134

Jin, Ha 1956- ..................... DLB-244

Joans, Ted 1928- ................. DLB-16, 41

Jōha 1525-1602 .................... DLB-203

Johannis de Garlandia (see John of Garland)

John, Errol 1924-1988 ................ DLB-233

John, Eugenie (see Marlitt, E.)

John of Dumbleton
    circa 1310-circa 1349 ............ DLB-115

John of Garland (Jean de Garlande,
    Johannis de Garlandia)
    circa 1195-circa 1272 ............. DLB-208

Johns, Captain W. E. 1893-1968 ........ DLB-160

Johnson, Mrs. A. E. ca. 1858-1922 ...... DLB-221

Johnson, Amelia (see Johnson, Mrs. A. E.)

Johnson, B. S. 1933-1973 ........... DLB-14, 40

Johnson, Charles 1679-1748 ............ DLB-84

Johnson, Charles 1948- ........... DLB-33, 278

Johnson, Charles S. 1893-1956 ....... DLB-51, 91

Johnson, Denis 1949- ................ DLB-120

Johnson, Diane 1934- .................. Y-80

Johnson, Dorothy M. 1905-1984 ........ DLB-206

Johnson, E. Pauline (Tekahionwake)
    1861-1913 ...................... DLB-175

# Cumulative Index

Johnson, Edgar 1901-1995 . . . . . . . . . . . DLB-103
Johnson, Edward 1598-1672. . . . . . . . . . . DLB-24
Johnson, Eyvind 1900-1976 . . . . . . . . . DLB-259
Johnson, Fenton 1888-1958 . . . . . . . . DLB-45, 50
Johnson, Georgia Douglas
 1877?-1966. . . . . . . . . . . . . . . . DLB-51, 249
Johnson, Gerald W. 1890-1980 . . . . . . . . DLB-29
Johnson, Greg 1953- . . . . . . . . . . . . . . DLB-234
Johnson, Helene 1907-1995. . . . . . . . . . . . DLB-51
Jacob Johnson and Company . . . . . . . . . DLB-49
Johnson, James Weldon
 1871-1938 . . . . . . . . . . . DLB-51; CDALB-4
Johnson, John H. 1918- . . . . . . . . . . . . DLB-137
 "Backstage," Statement From the
  Initial Issue of *Ebony*
  (November 1945) . . . . . . . . . . . . DLB-137
Johnson, Joseph [publishing house]. . . . . . DLB-154
Johnson, Linton Kwesi 1952- . . . . . . . . DLB-157
Johnson, Lionel 1867-1902 . . . . . . . . . . . DLB-19
Johnson, Nunnally 1897-1977 . . . . . . . . . DLB-26
Johnson, Owen 1878-1952 . . . . . . . . . . . . . Y-87
Johnson, Pamela Hansford 1912-1981 . . . . DLB-15
Johnson, Pauline 1861-1913 . . . . . . . . . . DLB-92
Johnson, Ronald 1935-1998 . . . . . . . . . . DLB-169
Johnson, Samuel 1696-1772 . . . DLB-24; CDBLB-2
Johnson, Samuel
 1709-1784 . . . . . . . DLB-39, 95, 104, 142, 213
 *Rambler*, no. 4 (1750) [excerpt] . . . . . . DLB-39
 The BBC Four Samuel Johnson Prize
  for Non-fiction . . . . . . . . . . . . . . . . . Y-02
Johnson, Samuel 1822-1882 . . . . . . . . DLB-1, 243
Johnson, Susanna 1730-1810. . . . . . . . . . DLB-200
Johnson, Terry 1955- . . . . . . . . . . . . . . DLB-233
Johnson, Uwe 1934-1984 . . . . DLB-75; CDWLB-2
Benjamin Johnson [publishing house] . . . . DLB-49
Benjamin, Jacob, and Robert Johnson
 [publishing house] . . . . . . . . . . . . . . . DLB-49
Johnston, Annie Fellows 1863-1931 . . . . . DLB-42
Johnston, Basil H. 1929- . . . . . . . . . . . . DLB-60
Johnston, David Claypole 1798?-1865 . . . DLB-188
Johnston, Denis 1901-1984. . . . . . . . . . . . DLB-10
Johnston, Ellen 1835-1873 . . . . . . . . . . . DLB-199
Johnston, George 1912-1970 . . . . . . . . . DLB-260
Johnston, George 1913- . . . . . . . . . . . . . DLB-88
Johnston, Sir Harry 1858-1927. . . . . . . . DLB-174
Johnston, Jennifer 1930- . . . . . . . . . . . . DLB-14
Johnston, Mary 1870-1936 . . . . . . . . . . . . DLB-9
Johnston, Richard Malcolm 1822-1898 . . . DLB-74
Johnstone, Charles 1719?-1800? . . . . . . . DLB-39
Johst, Hanns 1890-1978 . . . . . . . . . . . . DLB-124
Jolas, Eugene 1894-1952. . . . . . . . . . . DLB-4, 45
Jones, Alice C. 1853-1933. . . . . . . . . . . . . DLB-92
Jones, Charles C., Jr. 1831-1893. . . . . . . . DLB-30
Jones, D. G. 1929- . . . . . . . . . . . . . . . . DLB-53
Jones, David
 1895-1974. . . . . . . . DLB-20, 100; CDBLB-7
Jones, Diana Wynne 1934- . . . . . . . . . DLB-161

Jones, Ebenezer 1820-1860. . . . . . . . . . . . DLB-32
Jones, Ernest 1819-1868 . . . . . . . . . . . . . DLB-32
Jones, Gayl 1949- . . . . . . . . . . . . . DLB-33, 278
Jones, George 1800-1870 . . . . . . . . . . . DLB-183
Jones, Glyn 1905-1995 . . . . . . . . . . . . . . DLB-15
Jones, Gwyn 1907- . . . . . . . . . . . . . DLB-15, 139
Jones, Henry Arthur 1851-1929 . . . . . . . . DLB-10
Jones, Hugh circa 1692-1760 . . . . . . . . . . DLB-24
Jones, James 1921-1977. . . . . . . DLB-2, 143; DS-17
 James Jones Papers in the Handy
  Writers' Colony Collection at
  the University of Illinois at
  Springfield . . . . . . . . . . . . . . . . . . . Y-98
 The James Jones Society . . . . . . . . . . . . Y-92
Jones, Jenkin Lloyd 1911- . . . . . . . . . . DLB-127
Jones, John Beauchamp 1810-1866. . . . . . DLB-202
Jones, Joseph, Major
 (see Thompson, William Tappan)
Jones, LeRoi (see Baraka, Amiri)
Jones, Lewis 1897-1939. . . . . . . . . . . . . DLB-15
Jones, Madison 1925- . . . . . . . . . . . . . DLB-152
Jones, Marie 1951- . . . . . . . . . . . . . . . DLB-233
Jones, Preston 1936-1979 . . . . . . . . . . . . DLB-7
Jones, Rodney 1950- . . . . . . . . . . . . . . DLB-120
Jones, Thom 1945- . . . . . . . . . . . . . . . DLB-244
Jones, Sir William 1746-1794 . . . . . . . . . DLB-109
Jones, William Alfred 1817-1900. . . . . . . . DLB-59
Jones's Publishing House . . . . . . . . . . . . DLB-49
Jong, Erica 1942- . . . . . . . . DLB-2, 5, 28, 152
Jonke, Gert F. 1946- . . . . . . . . . . . . . DLB-85
Jonson, Ben
 1572?-1637 . . . . . . . DLB-62, 121; CDBLB-1
Jordan, June 1936- . . . . . . . . . . . . . . DLB-38
Joseph, Jenny 1932- . . . . . . . . . . . . . . DLB-40
Joseph and George . . . . . . . . . . . . . . . . Y-99
Michael Joseph Limited . . . . . . . . . . . . DLB-112
Josephson, Matthew 1899-1978 . . . . . . . . . DLB-4
Josephus, Flavius 37-100 . . . . . . . . . . . . DLB-176
Josephy, Alvin M., Jr.
 Tribute to Alfred A. Knopf . . . . . . . . . . Y-84
Josiah Allen's Wife (see Holley, Marietta)
Josipovici, Gabriel 1940- . . . . . . . . . . . DLB-14
Josselyn, John ?-1675 . . . . . . . . . . . . . . DLB-24
Joudry, Patricia 1921-2000 . . . . . . . . . . . DLB-88
Jouve, Pierre Jean 1887-1976. . . . . . . . . DLB-258
Jovanovich, William 1920-2001 . . . . . . . . . Y-01
 Into the Past: William Jovanovich's
  Reflections on Publishing . . . . . . . . . . Y-02
 [Repsonse to Ken Auletta] . . . . . . . . . . Y-97
 *The Temper of the West*: William
  Jovanovich. . . . . . . . . . . . . . . . . . . Y-02
 Tribute to Charles Scribner Jr. . . . . . . . . Y-95
Jovine, Francesco 1902-1950 . . . . . . . . . DLB-264
Jovine, Giuseppe 1922- . . . . . . . . . . . . DLB-128
Joyaux, Philippe (see Sollers, Philippe)
Joyce, Adrien (see Eastman, Carol)

Joyce, James 1882-1941
 . . . . . . . . DLB-10, 19, 36, 162, 247; CDBLB-6
 Danis Rose and the Rendering of *Ulysses* . . Y-97
 James Joyce Centenary: Dublin, 1982 . . . . Y-82
 James Joyce Conference. . . . . . . . . . . . . Y-85
 A Joyce (Con)Text: Danis Rose and the
  Remaking of *Ulysses* . . . . . . . . . . . . Y-97
 The National Library of Ireland's
  New James Joyce Manuscripts. . . . . . . Y-02
 The New *Ulysses*. . . . . . . . . . . . . . . . Y-84
 Public Domain and the Violation of
  Texts . . . . . . . . . . . . . . . . . . . . . Y-97
 The Quinn Draft of James Joyce's
  Circe Manuscript. . . . . . . . . . . . . . . Y-00
 Stephen Joyce's Letter to the Editor of
  *The Irish Times* . . . . . . . . . . . . . . . Y-97
 *Ulysses*, Reader's Edition: First Reactions . . Y-97
 We See the Editor at Work . . . . . . . . . . Y-97
 Whose *Ulysses*? The Function of Editing . . Y-97
Jozsef, Attila 1905-1937. . . . . . DLB-215; CDWLB-4
Juarroz, Roberto 1925-1995 . . . . . . . . . DLB-283
Orange Judd Publishing Company. . . . . . DLB-49
Judd, Sylvester 1813-1853 . . . . . . . . . DLB-1, 243
*Judith* circa 930. . . . . . . . . . . . . . . . DLB-146
Julian of Norwich 1342-circa 1420 . . . . . DLB-1146
Julius Caesar
 100 B.C.-44 B.C. . . . . . . DLB-211; CDWLB-1
June, Jennie (see Croly, Jane Cunningham)
Jung, Franz 1888-1963 . . . . . . . . . . . . DLB-118
Jünger, Ernst 1895- . . . . . . . DLB-56; CDWLB-2
*Der jüngere Titurel* circa 1275 . . . . . . . . DLB-138
Jung-Stilling, Johann Heinrich 1740-1817. . . DLB-94
Junqueiro, Abílio Manuel Guerra
 1850-1923 . . . . . . . . . . . . . . . . . . DLB-287
Justice, Donald 1925- . . . . . . . . . . . . . . Y-83
Juvenal circa A.D. 60-circa A.D. 130
 . . . . . . . . . . . . . . . . . . DLB-211; CDWLB-1
The Juvenile Library
 (see M. J. Godwin and Company)

# K

Kacew, Romain (see Gary, Romain)
Kafka, Franz 1883-1924 . . . . . DLB-81; CDWLB-2
Kahn, Gus 1886-1941. . . . . . . . . . . . . . DLB-265
Kahn, Roger 1927- . . . . . . . . . . . . . . . DLB-171
Kaikō Takeshi 1939-1989. . . . . . . . . . . . DLB-182
Kaiser, Georg 1878-1945 . . . . DLB-124; CDWLB-2
*Kaiserchronik* circa 1147 . . . . . . . . . . . . DLB-148
Kaleb, Vjekoslav 1905- . . . . . . . . . . . . DLB-181
Kalechofsky, Roberta 1931- . . . . . . . . . DLB-28
Kaler, James Otis 1848-1912 . . . . . . . DLB-12, 42
Kalmar, Bert 1884-1947 . . . . . . . . . . . . DLB-265
Kames, Henry Home, Lord
 1696-1782. . . . . . . . . . . . . . . . DLB-31, 104
Kamo no Chōmei (Kamo no Nagaakira)
 1153 or 1155-1216. . . . . . . . . . . . . . DLB-203
Kamo no Nagaakira (see Kamo no Chōmei)
Kampmann, Christian 1939-1988 . . . . . . DLB-214

| | | |
|---|---|---|
| Kandel, Lenore 1932- ................DLB-16 | Keble, John 1792-1866...............DLB-32, 55 | Kenzheev, Bakhyt Shkurullaevich 1950- ........................DLB-285 |
| Kanin, Garson 1912-1999 ...............DLB-7 | Keckley, Elizabeth 1818?-1907..........DLB-239 | Keough, Hugh Edmund 1864-1912......DLB-171 |
| A Tribute (to Marc Connelly)..........Y-80 | Keeble, John 1944- .....................Y-83 | Keppler and Schwartzmann..............DLB-49 |
| Kant, Hermann 1926- ...............DLB-75 | Keeffe, Barrie 1945- ...............DLB-13, 245 | Ker, John, third Duke of Roxburghe 1740-1804 ......................DLB-213 |
| Kant, Immanuel 1724-1804 ............DLB-94 | Keeley, James 1867-1934 ...............DLB-25 | |
| Kantemir, Antiokh Dmitrievich 1708-1744.......................DLB-150 | W. B. Keen, Cooke and Company .......DLB-49 | Ker, N. R. 1908-1982 ................DLB-201 |
| | The Mystery of Carolyn Keene...........Y-02 | Kerlan, Irvin 1912-1963................DLB-187 |
| Kantor, MacKinlay 1904-1977........DLB-9, 102 | Keillor, Garrison 1942- .................Y-87 | Kermode, Frank 1919- ...............DLB-242 |
| Kanze Kōjirō Nobumitsu 1435-1516 .....DLB-203 | Keith, Marian (Mary Esther MacGregor) 1874?-1961 .....................DLB-92 | Kern, Jerome 1885-1945 ...............DLB-187 |
| Kanze Motokiyo (see Zeimi) | | Kernaghan, Eileen 1939- .............DLB-251 |
| Kaplan, Fred 1937- ..................DLB-111 | Keller, Gary D. 1943- ................DLB-82 | Kerner, Justinus 1786-1862 ..............DLB-90 |
| Kaplan, Johanna 1942- ................DLB-28 | Keller, Gottfried 1819-1890 ............DLB-129; CDWLB-2 | Kerouac, Jack 1922-1969 ...DLB-2, 16, 237; DS-3; CDALB-1 |
| Kaplan, Justin 1925- ...........DLB-111; Y-86 | | |
| Kaplinski, Jaan 1941- .................DLB-232 | Kelley, Edith Summers 1884-1956.........DLB-9 | Auction of Jack Kerouac's *On the Road* Scroll ................Y-01 |
| Kapnist, Vasilii Vasilevich 1758?-1823 ...DLB-150 | Kelley, Emma Dunham ?-? ............DLB-221 | |
| Karadžić, Vuk Stefanović 1787-1864.............DLB-147; CDWLB-4 | Kelley, William Melvin 1937- ...........DLB-33 | The Jack Kerouac Revival ............Y-95 |
| | Kellogg, Ansel Nash 1832-1886..........DLB-23 | "Re-meeting of Old Friends": The Jack Kerouac Conference ......Y-82 |
| Karamzin, Nikolai Mikhailovich 1766-1826 ......................DLB-150 | Kellogg, Steven 1941- .................DLB-61 | |
| | Kelly, George E. 1887-1974 ..........DLB-7, 249 | Statement of Correction to "The Jack Kerouac Revival"................Y-96 |
| Karinthy, Frigyes 1887-1938 ...........DLB-215 | Kelly, Hugh 1739-1777..................DLB-89 | |
| Karsch, Anna Louisa 1722-1791..........DLB-97 | Kelly, Piet and Company................DLB-49 | Kerouac, Jan 1952-1996................DLB-16 |
| Kasack, Hermann 1896-1966............DLB-69 | Kelly, Robert 1935- ...........DLB-5, 130, 165 | Charles H. Kerr and Company..........DLB-49 |
| Kasai Zenzō 1887-1927................DLB-180 | Kelman, James 1946- ................DLB-194 | Kerr, Orpheus C. (see Newell, Robert Henry) |
| Kaschnitz, Marie Luise 1901-1974........DLB-69 | Kelmscott Press.....................DLB-112 | Kersh, Gerald 1911-1968...............DLB-255 |
| Kassák, Lajos 1887-1967 ..............DLB-215 | Kelton, Elmer 1926- .................DLB-256 | Kertész, Imre .........................Y-02 |
| Kaštelan, Jure 1919-1990 ..............DLB-147 | Kemble, E. W. 1861-1933 ..............DLB-188 | Kesey, Ken 1935-2001........DLB-2, 16, 206; CDALB-6 |
| Kästner, Erich 1899-1974...............DLB-56 | Kemble, Fanny 1809-1893..............DLB-32 | |
| Kataev, Evgenii Petrovich (see Il'f, Il'ia and Petrov, Evgenii) | Kemelman, Harry 1908-1996 ...........DLB-28 | Kessel, Joseph 1898-1979................DLB-72 |
| | Kempe, Margery circa 1373-1438 .......DLB-146 | Kessel, Martin 1901-1990 ...............DLB-56 |
| Kataev, Valentin Petrovich 1897-1986....DLB-272 | Kempner, Friederike 1836-1904 ........DLB-129 | Kesten, Hermann 1900-1996............DLB-56 |
| Katenin, Pavel Aleksandrovich 1792-1853 ......................DLB-205 | Kempowski, Walter 1929- ..............DLB-75 | Keun, Irmgard 1905-1982 ...............DLB-69 |
| | Claude Kendall [publishing company].....DLB-46 | Key, Ellen 1849-1926 .................DLB-259 |
| Kattan, Naim 1928- .................DLB-53 | Kendall, Henry 1839-1882 .............DLB-230 | Key and Biddle .....................DLB-49 |
| Katz, Steve 1935- .....................Y-83 | Kendall, May 1861-1943 ..............DLB-240 | Keynes, Sir Geoffrey 1887-1982.........DLB-201 |
| Kauffman, Janet 1945- ............DLB-218; Y-86 | Kendell, George 1809-1867 .............DLB-43 | Keynes, John Maynard 1883-1946 ........DS-10 |
| Kauffmann, Samuel 1898-1971 .........DLB-127 | Kenedy, P. J., and Sons ................DLB-49 | Keyserling, Eduard von 1855-1918.......DLB-66 |
| Kaufman, Bob 1925-1986 ...........DLB-16, 41 | Kenkō circa 1283-circa 1352 ..........DLB-203 | Khan, Ismith 1925-2002 ..............DLB-125 |
| Kaufman, George S. 1889-1961...........DLB-7 | Kennan, George 1845-1924 ............DLB-189 | Kharitonov, Evgenii Vladimirovich 1941-1981......................DLB-285 |
| Kaufmann, Walter 1921-1980 ..........DLB-279 | Kennedy, A. L. 1965- ................DLB-271 | |
| Kavan, Anna (Helen Woods Ferguson Edmonds) 1901-1968 ............DLB-255 | Kennedy, Adrienne 1931- .............DLB-38 | Kharitonov, Mark Sergeevich 1937- ....DLB-285 |
| | Kennedy, John Pendleton 1795-1870 ...DLB-3, 248 | Khaytov, Nikolay 1919- ...............DLB-181 |
| Kavanagh, P. J. 1931- .................DLB-40 | Kennedy, Leo 1907-2000 ...............DLB-88 | Khemnitser, Ivan Ivanovich 1745-1784 ......................DLB-150 |
| Kavanagh, Patrick 1904-1967 ........DLB-15, 20 | Kennedy, Margaret 1896-1967 ...........DLB-36 | |
| Kaverin, Veniamin Aleksandrovich (Veniamin Aleksandrovich Zil'ber) 1902-1989 .....................DLB-272 | Kennedy, Patrick 1801-1873 ...........DLB-159 | Kheraskov, Mikhail Matveevich 1733-1807 ......................DLB-150 |
| | Kennedy, Richard S. 1920- ......DLB-111; Y-02 | |
| | Kennedy, William 1928- ........DLB-143; Y-85 | Khomiakov, Aleksei Stepanovich 1804-1860......................DLB-205 |
| Kawabata Yasunari 1899-1972.........DLB-180 | Kennedy, X. J. 1929- ...................DLB-5 | |
| Kay, Guy Gavriel 1954- ...............DLB-251 | Tribute to John Ciardi ...............Y-86 | Khristov, Boris 1945- .................DLB-181 |
| Kaye-Smith, Sheila 1887-1956 ..........DLB-36 | | Khvoshchinskaia, Nadezhda Dmitrievna 1824-1889 ......................DLB-238 |
| Kazin, Alfred 1915-1998 ...............DLB-67 | Kennelly, Brendan 1936- ..............DLB-40 | |
| Keane, John B. 1928- .................DLB-13 | Kenner, Hugh 1923- .................DLB-67 | Khvostov, Dmitrii Ivanovich 1757-1835.......................DLB-150 |
| Keary, Annie 1825-1879 ...............DLB-163 | Tribute to Cleanth Brooks ............Y-80 | |
| Keary, Eliza 1827-1918.................DLB-240 | Mitchell Kennerley [publishing house].....DLB-46 | Kibirov, Timur Iur'evich (Timur Iur'evich Zapoev) 1955- ...........DLB-285 |
| Keating, H. R. F. 1926- ................DLB-87 | Kenny, Maurice 1929- ................DLB-175 | |
| Keatley, Charlotte 1960- ..............DLB-245 | Kent, Frank R. 1877-1958 ..............DLB-29 | Kidd, Adam 1802?-1831 ...............DLB-99 |
| Keats, Ezra Jack 1916-1983 .............DLB-61 | | William Kidd [publishing house]........DLB-106 |
| Keats, John 1795-1821 ....DLB-96, 110; CDBLB-3 | Kenyon, Jane 1947-1995 .............DLB-120 | Kidder, Tracy 1945- .................DLB-185 |
| | | Kiely, Benedict 1919- .................DLB-15 |

# Cumulative Index

Kieran, John 1892-1981 . . . . . . . . . . . . .DLB-171
Kies, Marietta 1853-1899 . . . . . . . . . . . . .DLB-270
Kiggins and Kellogg . . . . . . . . . . . . . . . . . DLB-49
Kiley, Jed 1889-1962. . . . . . . . . . . . . . . . . . DLB-4
Kilgore, Bernard 1908-1967 . . . . . . . . . . DLB-127
Kilian, Crawford 1941- . . . . . . . . . . . . . DLB-251
Killens, John Oliver 1916-1987 . . . . . . . . . DLB-33
    Tribute to Julian Mayfield . . . . . . . . . . . . Y-84
Killigrew, Anne 1660-1685 . . . . . . . . . . . . DLB-131
Killigrew, Thomas 1612-1683 . . . . . . . . . . DLB-58
Kilmer, Joyce 1886-1918 . . . . . . . . . . . . . . DLB-45
Kilroy, Thomas 1934- . . . . . . . . . . . . . . . DLB-233
Kilwardby, Robert circa 1215-1279 . . . . . DLB-115
Kilworth, Garry 1941- . . . . . . . . . . . . . . DLB-261
Kim, Anatolii Andreevich 1939- . . . . . . . DLB-285
Kimball, Richard Burleigh 1816-1892 . . . DLB-202
Kincaid, Jamaica 1949-
    . . . . . . . . DLB-157, 227; CDALB-7; CDWLB-3
King, Charles 1844-1933 . . . . . . . . . . . . . DLB-186
King, Clarence 1842-1901 . . . . . . . . . . . . . DLB-12
King, Florence 1936- . . . . . . . . . . . . . . . . . . Y-85
King, Francis 1923- . . . . . . . . . . . . DLB-15, 139
King, Grace 1852-1932 . . . . . . . . . . . DLB-12, 78
King, Harriet Hamilton 1840-1920 . . . . . . DLB-199
King, Henry 1592-1669 . . . . . . . . . . . . . . DLB-126
Solomon King [publishing house] . . . . . . . DLB-49
King, Stephen 1947- . . . . . . . . . . . .DLB-143; Y-80
King, Susan Petigru 1824-1875 . . . . . . . . DLB-239
King, Thomas 1943- . . . . . . . . . . . . . . . .DLB-175
King, Woodie, Jr. 1937- . . . . . . . . . . . . . . DLB-38
Kinglake, Alexander William
    1809-1891 . . . . . . . . . . . . . . . . . DLB-55, 166
Kingsbury, Donald 1929- . . . . . . . . . . . DLB-251
Kingsley, Charles
    1819-1875 . . . . . . . . DLB-21, 32, 163, 178, 190
Kingsley, Henry 1830-1876 . . . . . . . DLB-21, 230
Kingsley, Mary Henrietta 1862-1900 . . . . .DLB-174
Kingsley, Sidney 1906-1995 . . . . . . . . . . . . DLB-7
Kingsmill, Hugh 1889-1949 . . . . . . . . . . . DLB-149
Kingsolver, Barbara
    1955- . . . . . . . . . . . . . DLB-206; CDALB-7
Kingston, Maxine Hong
    1940- . . . . . .DLB-173, 212; Y-80; CDALB-7
Kingston, William Henry Giles
    1814-1880 . . . . . . . . . . . . . . . . . . . . DLB-163
Kinnan, Mary Lewis 1763-1848 . . . . . . . . DLB-200
Kinnell, Galway 1927- . . . . . . . . . . .DLB-5; Y-87
Kinsella, Thomas 1928- . . . . . . . . . . . . . . DLB-27
Kipling, Rudyard 1865-1936
    . . . . . . . . . . DLB-19, 34, 141, 156; CDBLB-5
Kipphardt, Heinar 1922-1982 . . . . . . . . . DLB-124
Kirby, William 1817-1906 . . . . . . . . . . . . . DLB-99
Kircher, Athanasius 1602-1680 . . . . . . . . . DLB-164
Kireevsky, Ivan Vasil'evich 1806-1856 . . . DLB-198
Kireevsky, Petr Vasil'evich 1808-1856 . . . DLB-205
Kirk, Hans 1898-1962 . . . . . . . . . . . . . . . DLB-214

Kirk, John Foster 1824-1904 . . . . . . . . . . . DLB-79
Kirkconnell, Watson 1895-1977 . . . . . . . . DLB-68
Kirkland, Caroline M.
    1801-1864 . . . . . . .DLB-3, 73, 74, 250; DS-13
Kirkland, Joseph 1830-1893 . . . . . . . . . . . DLB-12
Francis Kirkman [publishing house] . . . . . .DLB-170
Kirkpatrick, Clayton 1915- . . . . . . . . . . DLB-127
Kirkup, James 1918- . . . . . . . . . . . . . . . DLB-27
Kirouac, Conrad (see Marie-Victorin, Frère)
Kirsch, Sarah 1935- . . . . . . . . . . . . . . . . . DLB-75
Kirst, Hans Hellmut 1914-1989 . . . . . . . . DLB-69
Kiš, Danilo 1935-1989 . . . . . DLB-181; CDWLB-4
Kita Morio 1927- . . . . . . . . . . . . . . . . . DLB-182
Kitcat, Mabel Greenhow 1859-1922 . . . . . DLB-135
Kitchin, C. H. B. 1895-1967 . . . . . . . . . . . DLB-77
Kittredge, William 1932- . . . . . . DLB-212, 244
Kiukhel'beker, Vil'gel'm Karlovich
    1797-1846 . . . . . . . . . . . . . . . . . . . . DLB-205
Kizer, Carolyn 1925- . . . . . . . . . . . DLB-5, 169
Klabund 1890-1928 . . . . . . . . . . . . . . . . . . DLB-66
Klaj, Johann 1616-1656 . . . . . . . . . . . . . . DLB-164
Klappert, Peter 1942- . . . . . . . . . . . . . . . . DLB-5
Klass, Philip (see Tenn, William)
Klein, A. M. 1909-1972 . . . . . . . . . . . . . . DLB-68
Kleist, Ewald von 1715-1759 . . . . . . . . . . . DLB-97
Kleist, Heinrich von
    1777-1811 . . . . . . . . . . . . DLB-90; CDWLB-2
Klíma, Ivan 1931- . . . . . . . DLB-232; CDWLB-4
Klimentev, Andrei Platonovic
    (see Platonov, Andrei Platonovich)
Klinger, Friedrich Maximilian
    1752-1831 . . . . . . . . . . . . . . . . . . . . . DLB-94
Kliushnikov, Viktor Petrovich
    1841-1892 . . . . . . . . . . . . . . . . . . . . DLB-238
Klopfer, Donald S.
    Impressions of William Faulkner . . . . . . . . Y-97
    Oral History Interview with Donald
        S. Klopfer . . . . . . . . . . . . . . . . . . . . Y-97
    Tribute to Alfred A. Knopf . . . . . . . . . . . . Y-84
Klopstock, Friedrich Gottlieb
    1724-1803 . . . . . . . . . . . . . . . . . . . . . DLB-97
Klopstock, Meta 1728-1758 . . . . . . . . . . . . DLB-97
Kluge, Alexander 1932- . . . . . . . . . . . . . DLB-75
Kluge, P. F. 1942- . . . . . . . . . . . . . . . . . . . Y-02
Knapp, Joseph Palmer 1864-1951 . . . . . . . DLB-91
Knapp, Samuel Lorenzo 1783-1838 . . . . . DLB-59
J. J. and P. Knapton [publishing house] . . DLB-154
Kniazhnin, Iakov Borisovich 1740-1791 . . DLB-150
Knickerbocker, Diedrich (see Irving, Washington)
Knigge, Adolph Franz Friedrich Ludwig,
    Freiherr von 1752-1796 . . . . . . . . . . . DLB-94
Charles Knight and Company . . . . . . . . . DLB-106
Knight, Damon 1922-2002 . . . . . . . . . . . . . DLB-8
Knight, Etheridge 1931-1992 . . . . . . . . . . DLB-41
Knight, John S. 1894-1981 . . . . . . . . . . . . DLB-29
Knight, Sarah Kemble 1666-1727 . . . . DLB-24, 200
Knight-Bruce, G. W. H. 1852-1896 . . . . . .DLB-174

Knister, Raymond 1899-1932 . . . . . . . . . . DLB-68
Knoblock, Edward 1874-1945 . . . . . . . . . DLB-10
Knopf, Alfred A. 1892-1984 . . . . . . . . . . . . . Y-84
    Knopf to Hammett: The Editoral
        Correspondence . . . . . . . . . . . . . . . . Y-00
Alfred A. Knopf [publishing house] . . . . . . DLB-46
Knorr von Rosenroth, Christian
    1636-1689 . . . . . . . . . . . . . . . . . . . . DLB-168
Knowles, John 1926- . . . . . . . . DLB-6; CDALB-6
Knox, Frank 1874-1944 . . . . . . . . . . . . . . DLB-29
Knox, John circa 1514-1572 . . . . . . . . . . . DLB-132
Knox, John Armoy 1850-1906 . . . . . . . . . DLB-23
Knox, Lucy 1845-1884 . . . . . . . . . . . . . . DLB-240
Knox, Ronald Arbuthnott 1888-1957 . . . . . DLB-77
Knox, Thomas Wallace 1835-1896 . . . . . DLB-189
Kobayashi Takiji 1903-1933 . . . . . . . . . . . DLB-180
Kober, Arthur 1900-1975 . . . . . . . . . . . . . DLB-11
Kobiakova, Aleksandra Petrovna
    1823-1892 . . . . . . . . . . . . . . . . . . . . DLB-238
Kocbek, Edvard 1904-1981 . . DLB-147; CDWLB-4
Koch, Howard 1902-1995 . . . . . . . . . . . . DLB-26
Koch, Kenneth 1925-2002 . . . . . . . . . . . . . DLB-5
Kōda Rohan 1867-1947 . . . . . . . . . . . . . DLB-180
Koehler, Ted 1894-1973 . . . . . . . . . . . . . DLB-265
Koenigsberg, Moses 1879-1945 . . . . . . . . DLB-25
Koeppen, Wolfgang 1906-1996 . . . . . . . . DLB-69
Koertge, Ronald 1940- . . . . . . . . . . . . . DLB-105
Koestler, Arthur 1905-1983 . . . . . . . Y-83; CDBLB-7
Kohn, John S. Van E. 1906-1976 . . . . . . . .DLB-187
Kokhanovskaia
    (see Sokhanskaia, Nadezhda Stepanova)
Kokoschka, Oskar 1886-1980 . . . . . . . . . DLB-124
Kolb, Annette 1870-1967 . . . . . . . . . . . . . DLB-66
Kolbenheyer, Erwin Guido
    1878-1962 . . . . . . . . . . . . . . . . . DLB-66, 124
Kolleritsch, Alfred 1931- . . . . . . . . . . . . DLB-85
Kolodny, Annette 1941- . . . . . . . . . . . . . DLB-67
Kol'tsov, Aleksei Vasil'evich 1809-1842 . . DLB-205
Komarov, Matvei circa 1730-1812 . . . . . . DLB-150
Komroff, Manuel 1890-1974 . . . . . . . . . . . DLB-4
Komunyakaa, Yusef 1947- . . . . . . . . . . DLB-120
Kondoleon, Harry 1955-1994 . . . . . . . . . DLB-266
Koneski, Blaže 1921-1993 . . . . DLB-181; CDWLB-4
Konigsburg, E. L. 1930- . . . . . . . . . . . . . DLB-52
Konparu Zenchiku 1405-1468? . . . . . . . . DLB-203
Konrád, György 1933- . . . . DLB-232; CDWLB-4
Konrad von Würzburg circa 1230-1287 . . DLB-138
Konstantinov, Aleko 1863-1897 . . . . . . . .DLB-147
Konwicki, Tadeusz 1926- . . . . . . . . . . . DLB-232
Kooser, Ted 1939- . . . . . . . . . . . . . . . . DLB-105
Kopit, Arthur 1937- . . . . . . . . . . . . . . . . . DLB-7
Kops, Bernard 1926?- . . . . . . . . . . . . . . . DLB-13
Kornbluth, C. M. 1923-1958 . . . . . . . . . . . DLB-8
Körner, Theodor 1791-1813 . . . . . . . . . . . DLB-90
Kornfeld, Paul 1889-1942 . . . . . . . . . . . . DLB-118

Korolenko, Vladimir Galaktionovich
  1853-1921 . . . . . . . . . . . . . . . . . . . . . DLB-277
Kosinski, Jerzy 1933-1991 . . . . . . . . . DLB-2; Y-82
Kosmač, Ciril 1910-1980 . . . . . . . . . . . . . DLB-181
Kosovel, Srečko 1904-1926 . . . . . . . . . . . DLB-147
Kostrov, Ermil Ivanovich 1755-1796 . . . . . DLB-150
Kotzebue, August von 1761-1819. . . . . . . . DLB-94
Kotzwinkle, William 1938- . . . . . . . . . . DLB-173
Kovačić, Ante 1854-1889. . . . . . . . . . . . . DLB-147
Kovalevskaia, Sof'ia Vasil'evna
  1850-1891 . . . . . . . . . . . . . . . . . . . . . DLB-277
Kovič, Kajetan 1931- . . . . . . . . . . . . . . . DLB-181
Kozlov, Ivan Ivanovich 1779-1840. . . . . . . DLB-205
Kraf, Elaine 1946- . . . . . . . . . . . . . . . . . . Y-81
Kramer, Jane 1938- . . . . . . . . . . . . . . . . DLB-185
Kramer, Larry 1935- . . . . . . . . . . . . . . . DLB-249
Kramer, Mark 1944- . . . . . . . . . . . . . . . DLB-185
Kranjčević, Silvije Strahimir 1865-1908. . . DLB-147
Krasko, Ivan 1876-1958. . . . . . . . . . . . . . DLB-215
Krasna, Norman 1909-1984. . . . . . . . . . . . DLB-26
Kraus, Hans Peter 1907-1988. . . . . . . . . . DLB-187
Kraus, Karl 1874-1936. . . . . . . . . . . . . . . DLB-118
Krause, Herbert 1905-1976 . . . . . . . . . . . DLB-256
Krauss, Ruth 1911-1993 . . . . . . . . . . . . . . DLB-52
Kreisel, Henry 1922-1991 . . . . . . . . . . . . . DLB-88
Krestovsky V.
  (see Khvoshchinskaia, Nadezhda Dmitrievna)
Krestovsky, Vsevolod Vladimirovich
  1839-1895 . . . . . . . . . . . . . . . . . . . . . DLB-238
Kreuder, Ernst 1903-1972 . . . . . . . . . . . . . DLB-69
Krėvė-Mickevičius, Vincas 1882-1954. . . . DLB-220
Kreymborg, Alfred 1883-1966. . . . . . . . DLB-4, 54
Krieger, Murray 1923- . . . . . . . . . . . . . . DLB-67
Krim, Seymour 1922-1989. . . . . . . . . . . . . DLB-16
Kripke, Saul 1940- . . . . . . . . . . . . . . . . DLB-279
Kristensen, Tom 1893-1974. . . . . . . . . . . DLB-214
Kristeva, Julia 1941- . . . . . . . . . . . . . . . DLB-242
Kritzer, Hyman W. 1918-2002 . . . . . . . . . . Y-02
Krivulin, Viktor Borisovich 1944-2001 . . . DLB-285
Krleža, Miroslav
  1893-1981 . . . . . . . . . . . DLB-147; CDWLB-4
Krock, Arthur 1886-1974. . . . . . . . . . . . . . DLB-29
Kroetsch, Robert 1927- . . . . . . . . . . . . . . DLB-53
Kropotkin, Petr Alekseevich 1842-1921. . . DLB-277
Kross, Jaan 1920- . . . . . . . . . . . . . . . . . DLB-232
Krúdy, Gyula 1878-1933 . . . . . . . . . . . . . DLB-215
Krutch, Joseph Wood
  1893-1970 . . . . . . . . . . . . . DLB-63, 206, 275
Krylov, Ivan Andreevich 1769-1844 . . . . . DLB-150
Krymov, Iurii Solomonovich
  (Iurii Solomonovich Beklemishev)
  1908-1941 . . . . . . . . . . . . . . . . . . . . . DLB-272
Kubin, Alfred 1877-1959 . . . . . . . . . . . . . . DLB-81
Kubrick, Stanley 1928-1999. . . . . . . . . . . . DLB-26
*Kudrun* circa 1230-1240 . . . . . . . . . . . . DLB-138
Kuffstein, Hans Ludwig von 1582-1656 . . DLB-164
Kuhlmann, Quirinus 1651-1689 . . . . . . . . DLB-168

Kuhn, Thomas S. 1922-1996. . . . . . . . . . DLB-279
Kuhnau, Johann 1660-1722 . . . . . . . . . . . DLB-168
Kukol'nik, Nestor Vasil'evich
  1809-1868 . . . . . . . . . . . . . . . . . . . . . DLB-205
Kukučín, Martin
  1860-1928 . . . . . . . . . . DLB-215; CDWLB-4
Kumin, Maxine 1925- . . . . . . . . . . . . . . . DLB-5
Kuncewicz, Maria 1895-1989 . . . . . . . . . DLB-215
Kundera, Milan 1929- . . . . DLB-232; CDWLB-4
Kunene, Mazisi 1930- . . . . . . . . . . . . . . DLB-117
Kunikida Doppo 1869-1908 . . . . . . . . . . DLB-180
Kunitz, Stanley 1905- . . . . . . . . . . . . . . . DLB-48
Kunjufu, Johari M. (see Amini, Johari M.)
Kunnert, Gunter 1929- . . . . . . . . . . . . . . DLB-75
Kunze, Reiner 1933- . . . . . . . . . . . . . . . . DLB-75
Kupferberg, Tuli 1923- . . . . . . . . . . . . . . DLB-16
Kuraev, Mikhail Nikolaevich 1939- . . . . DLB-285
Kurahashi Yumiko 1935- . . . . . . . . . . . . DLB-182
Kureishi, Hanif 1954- . . . . . . . . . . DLB-194, 245
Kürnberger, Ferdinand 1821-1879. . . . . . DLB-129
Kurz, Isolde 1853-1944 . . . . . . . . . . . . . . DLB-66
Kusenberg, Kurt 1904-1983 . . . . . . . . . . . DLB-69
Kushchevsky, Ivan Afanas'evich
  1847-1876. . . . . . . . . . . . . . . . . . . . . DLB-238
Kushner, Tony 1956- . . . . . . . . . . . . . . DLB-228
Kuttner, Henry 1915-1958. . . . . . . . . . . . . DLB-8
Kyd, Thomas 1558-1594. . . . . . . . . . . . . . DLB-62
Kyffin, Maurice circa 1560?-1598 . . . . . . . DLB-136
Kyger, Joanne 1934- . . . . . . . . . . . . . . . DLB-16
Kyne, Peter B. 1880-1957 . . . . . . . . . . . . . DLB-78
Kyōgoku Tamekane 1254-1332 . . . . . . . . DLB-203
Kyrklund, Willy 1921- . . . . . . . . . . . . . DLB-257

# L

L. E. L. (see Landon, Letitia Elizabeth)
Laberge, Albert 1871-1960 . . . . . . . . . . . . DLB-68
Laberge, Marie 1950- . . . . . . . . . . . . . . . DLB-60
Labiche, Eugène 1815-1888. . . . . . . . . . . DLB-192
Labrunie, Gerard (see Nerval, Gerard de)
La Bruyère, Jean de 1645-1696 . . . . . . . . DLB-268
La Calprenède 1609?-1663 . . . . . . . . . . . DLB-268
La Capria, Raffaele 1922- . . . . . . . . . . . DLB-196
Lacombe, Patrice
  (see Trullier-Lacombe, Joseph Patrice)
Lacretelle, Jacques de 1888-1985 . . . . . . . . DLB-65
Lacy, Ed 1911-1968. . . . . . . . . . . . . . . . . DLB-226
Lacy, Sam 1903- . . . . . . . . . . . . . . . . . . DLB-171
Ladd, Joseph Brown 1764-1786 . . . . . . . . DLB-37
La Farge, Oliver 1901-1963 . . . . . . . . . . . . DLB-9
Lafayette, Marie-Madeleine, comtesse de
  1634-1693 . . . . . . . . . . . . . . . . . . . . . DLB-268
Laffan, Mrs. R. S. de Courcy
  (see Adams, Bertha Leith)
Lafferty, R. A. 1914-2002 . . . . . . . . . . . . . . DLB-8
La Flesche, Francis 1857-1932 . . . . . . . . . DLB-175
La Fontaine, Jean de 1621-1695 . . . . . . . . DLB-268

Laforge, Jules 1860-1887 . . . . . . . . . . . . DLB-217
Lagerkvist, Pär 1891-1974 . . . . . . . . . . . DLB-259
Lagerlöf, Selma 1858-1940 . . . . . . . . . . . DLB-259
Lagorio, Gina 1922- . . . . . . . . . . . . . . . DLB-196
La Guma, Alex
  1925-1985 . . . . . . . DLB-117, 225; CDWLB-3
Lahaise, Guillaume (see Delahaye, Guy)
Lahontan, Louis-Armand de Lom d'Arce,
  Baron de 1666-1715?. . . . . . . . . . . . . . DLB-99
Laing, Kojo 1946- . . . . . . . . . . . . . . . . . DLB-157
Laird, Carobeth 1895-1983 . . . . . . . . . . . . . Y-82
Laird and Lee . . . . . . . . . . . . . . . . . . . . . DLB-49
Lake, Paul 1951- . . . . . . . . . . . . . . . . . . DLB-282
Lalić, Ivan V. 1931-1996 . . . . . . . . . . . . . DLB-181
Lalić, Mihailo 1914-1992 . . . . . . . . . . . . . DLB-181
Lalonde, Michèle 1937- . . . . . . . . . . . . . DLB-60
Lamantia, Philip 1927- . . . . . . . . . . . . . . DLB-16
Lamartine, Alphonse de 1790-1869 . . . . . DLB-217
Lamb, Lady Caroline 1785-1828 . . . . . . . DLB-116
Lamb, Charles
  1775-1834 . . . . . . DLB-93, 107, 163; CDBLB-3
Lamb, Mary 1764-1874 . . . . . . . . . . . . . . DLB-163
Lambert, Angela 1940- . . . . . . . . . . . . . DLB-271
Lambert, Betty 1933-1983 . . . . . . . . . . . . . DLB-60
Lamm, Donald
  Goodbye, Gutenberg? A Lecture at
  the New York Public Library,
  18 April 1995 . . . . . . . . . . . . . . . . . . . . Y-95
Lamming, George
  1927- . . . . . . . . . . . . . DLB-125; CDWLB-3
La Mothe Le Vayer, François de
  1588-1672 . . . . . . . . . . . . . . . . . . . . . DLB-268
L'Amour, Louis 1908-1988 . . . . . . DLB-206; Y-80
Lampman, Archibald 1861-1899 . . . . . . . . DLB-92
Lamson, Wolffe and Company . . . . . . . . . DLB-49
Lancer Books . . . . . . . . . . . . . . . . . . . . . . DLB-46
Lanchester, John 1962- . . . . . . . . . . . . . DLB-267
Lander, Peter (see Cunningham, Peter)
Landesman, Jay 1919- and
  Landesman, Fran 1927- . . . . . . . . . . . . DLB-16
Landolfi, Tommaso 1908-1979 . . . . . . . . DLB-177
Landon, Letitia Elizabeth 1802-1838 . . . . . DLB-96
Landor, Walter Savage 1775-1864 . . . DLB-93, 107
Landry, Napoléon-P. 1884-1956 . . . . . . . . DLB-92
Lane, Charles 1800-1870 . . . . . . DLB-1, 223; DS-5
Lane, F. C. 1885-1984 . . . . . . . . . . . . . . . DLB-241
Lane, Laurence W. 1890-1967 . . . . . . . . . DLB-91
Lane, M. Travis 1934- . . . . . . . . . . . . . . . DLB-60
Lane, Patrick 1939- . . . . . . . . . . . . . . . . . DLB-53
Lane, Pinkie Gordon 1923- . . . . . . . . . . . DLB-41
John Lane Company . . . . . . . . . . . . . . . . DLB-49
Laney, Al 1896-1988 . . . . . . . . . . . . . . DLB-4, 171
Lang, Andrew 1844-1912 . . . . . . DLB-98, 141, 184
Langer, Susanne K. 1895-1985 . . . . . . . . DLB-270
Langevin, André 1927- . . . . . . . . . . . . . . DLB-60
Langford, David 1953- . . . . . . . . . . . . . . DLB-261
Langgässer, Elisabeth 1899-1950 . . . . . . . . DLB-69

# Cumulative Index

Langhorne, John 1735-1779 .......... DLB-109
Langland, William circa 1330-circa 1400 . DLB-146
Langton, Anna 1804-1893 .............. DLB-99
Lanham, Edwin 1904-1979................. DLB-4
Lanier, Sidney 1842-1881........ DLB-64; DS-13
Lanyer, Aemilia 1569-1645............ DLB-121
Lapointe, Gatien 1931-1983 ............ DLB-88
Lapointe, Paul-Marie 1929- ............. DLB-88
Larcom, Lucy 1824-1893 ......... DLB-221, 243
Lardner, John 1912-1960 ................DLB-171
Lardner, Ring 1885-1933
........DLB-11, 25, 86, 171; DS-16; CDALB-4
    Lardner 100: Ring Lardner
        Centennial Symposium ............ Y-85
Lardner, Ring, Jr. 1915-2000 ........DLB-26, Y-00
Larkin, Philip 1922-1985 ..... DLB-27; CDBLB-8
    The Philip Larkin Society ............. Y-99
La Roche, Sophie von 1730-1807 ....... DLB-94
La Rochefoucauld, François duc de
    1613-1680...................... DLB-268
La Rocque, Gilbert 1943-1984 ......... DLB-60
Laroque de Roquebrune, Robert
    (see Roquebrune, Robert de)
Larrick, Nancy 1910- ................. DLB-61
Lars, Claudia 1899-1974................ DLB-283
Larsen, Nella 1893-1964.............. DLB-51
Larson, Clinton F. 1919-1994............ DLB-256
La Sale, Antoine de
    circa 1386-1460/1467.............. DLB-208
Lasch, Christopher 1932-1994 ......... DLB-246
Lasker-Schüler, Else 1869-1945 ..... DLB-66, 124
Lasnier, Rina 1915-1997............... DLB-88
Lassalle, Ferdinand 1825-1864 ......... DLB-129
Late-Medieval Castilian Theater ..... DLB-286
Latham, Robert 1912-1995............ DLB-201
Lathrop, Dorothy P. 1891-1980 ......... DLB-22
Lathrop, George Parsons 1851-1898 ..... DLB-71
Lathrop, John, Jr. 1772-1820............ DLB-37
Latimer, Hugh 1492?-1555............ DLB-136
Latimore, Jewel Christine McLawler
    (see Amini, Johari M.)
Latin Literature, The Uniqueness of .... DLB-211
La Tour du Pin, Patrice de 1911-1975 ... DLB-258
Latymer, William 1498-1583 .......... DLB-132
Laube, Heinrich 1806-1884 ........... DLB-133
Laud, William 1573-1645 ............. DLB-213
Laughlin, James 1914-1997...... DLB-48; Y-96, 97
    A Tribute [to Henry Miller]............ Y-80
    Tribute to Albert Erskine............... Y-93
    Tribute to Kenneth Rexroth ........... Y-82
    Tribute to Malcolm Cowley ........... Y-89
Laumer, Keith 1925-1993............... DLB-8
Lauremberg, Johann 1590-1658 ........ DLB-164
Laurence, Margaret 1926-1987......... DLB-53
Laurentius von Schnüffis 1633-1702..... DLB-168
Laurents, Arthur 1918- ............... DLB-26

Laurie, Annie (see Black, Winifred)
Laut, Agnes Christiana 1871-1936 ....... DLB-92
Lauterbach, Ann 1942- ............. DLB-193
Lautréamont, Isidore Lucien Ducasse,
    Comte de 1846-1870 ............. DLB-217
Lavater, Johann Kaspar 1741-1801....... DLB-97
Lavin, Mary 1912-1996 ............... DLB-15
Law, John (see Harkness, Margaret)
Lawes, Henry 1596-1662 ............. DLB-126
Lawless, Anthony (see MacDonald, Philip)
Lawless, Emily (The Hon. Emily Lawless)
    1845-1913 ................... DLB-240
Lawrence, D. H. 1885-1930
    ..... DLB-10, 19, 36, 98, 162, 195; CDBLB-6
    The D. H. Lawrence Society of
        North America .................. Y-00
Lawrence, David 1888-1973 ......... DLB-29
Lawrence, Jerome 1915- ............ DLB-228
Lawrence, Seymour 1926-1994 ......... Y-94
    Tribute to Richard Yates ............. Y-92
Lawrence, T. E. 1888-1935 ........... DLB-195
    The T. E. Lawrence Society ........... Y-98
Lawson, George 1598-1678 .......... DLB-213
Lawson, Henry 1867-1922 ........... DLB-230
Lawson, John ?-1711.................. DLB-24
Lawson, John Howard 1894-1977 ...... DLB-228
Lawson, Louisa Albury 1848-1920....... DLB-230
Lawson, Robert 1892-1957............. DLB-22
Lawson, Victor F. 1850-1925 .......... DLB-25
Layard, Austen Henry 1817-1894....... DLB-166
Layton, Irving 1912- ................. DLB-88
LaZamon flourished circa 1200 ....... DLB-146
Lazarević, Laza K. 1851-1890.......... DLB-147
Lazarus, George 1904-1997 .......... DLB-201
Lazhechnikov, Ivan Ivanovich
    1792-1869..................... DLB-198
Lea, Henry Charles 1825-1909 ......... DLB-47
Lea, Sydney 1942- ............ DLB-120, 282
Lea, Tom 1907-2001................... DLB-6
Leacock, John 1729-1802 ............. DLB-31
Leacock, Stephen 1869-1944 .......... DLB-92
Lead, Jane Ward 1623-1704 .......... DLB-131
Leadenhall Press................... DLB-106
"The Greatness of Southern Literature":
    League of the South Institute for the
    Study of Southern Culture and History
    ................................. Y-02
Leakey, Caroline Woolmer 1827-1881... DLB-230
Leapor, Mary 1722-1746............. DLB-109
Lear, Edward 1812-1888 ...... DLB-32, 163, 166
Leary, Timothy 1920-1996............. DLB-16
W. A. Leary and Company ........... DLB-49
Léautaud, Paul 1872-1956 ............ DLB-65
Leavis, F. R. 1895-1978............... DLB-242
Leavitt, David 1961- ............... DLB-130
Leavitt and Allen ................... DLB-49
Le Blond, Mrs. Aubrey 1861-1934.......DLB-174

le Carré, John (David John Moore Cornwell)
    1931- ............... DLB-87; CDBLB-8
    Tribute to Graham Greene ........... Y-91
    Tribute to George Greenfield ......... Y-00
Lécavelé, Roland (see Dorgeles, Roland)
Lechlitner, Ruth 1901- .............. DLB-48
Leclerc, Félix 1914-1988............... DLB-60
Le Clézio, J. M. G. 1940- ............ DLB-83
Leder, Rudolf (see Hermlin, Stephan)
Lederer, Charles 1910-1976 ........... DLB-26
Ledwidge, Francis 1887-1917 .......... DLB-20
Lee, Dennis 1939- ................... DLB-53
Lee, Don L. (see Madhubuti, Haki R.)
Lee, George W. 1894-1976............. DLB-51
Lee, Harper 1926- .......... DLB-6; CDALB-1
Lee, Harriet 1757-1851 and
    Lee, Sophia 1750-1824............. DLB-39
Lee, Laurie 1914-1997 ............... DLB-27
Lee, Leslie 1935- ................... DLB-266
Lee, Li-Young 1957- ................ DLB-165
Lee, Manfred B. 1905-1971 ............DLB-137
Lee, Nathaniel circa 1645-1692 ......... DLB-80
Lee, Robert E. 1918-1994............. DLB-228
Lee, Sir Sidney 1859-1926 ........ DLB-149, 184
    "Principles of Biography," in
        Elizabethan and Other Essays ...... DLB-149
Lee, Tanith 1947- ................. DLB-261
Lee, Vernon
    1856-1935 ........DLB-57, 153, 156, 174, 178
Lee and Shepard..................... DLB-49
Le Fanu, Joseph Sheridan
    1814-1873...........DLB-21, 70, 159, 178
Leffland, Ella 1931- .................... Y-84
le Fort, Gertrud von 1876-1971.......... DLB-66
Le Gallienne, Richard 1866-1947......... DLB-4
Legaré, Hugh Swinton
    1797-1843...............DLB-3, 59, 73, 248
Legaré, James Mathewes 1823-1859... DLB-3, 248
Léger, Antoine-J. 1880-1950 .......... DLB-88
Leggett, William 1801-1839........... DLB-250
Le Guin, Ursula K.
    1929- ......DLB-8, 52, 256, 275; CDALB-6
Lehman, Ernest 1920- ............... DLB-44
Lehmann, John 1907-1989 ..........DLB-27, 100
John Lehmann Limited................ DLB-112
Lehmann, Rosamond 1901-1990 ........ DLB-15
Lehmann, Wilhelm 1882-1968.......... DLB-56
Leiber, Fritz 1910-1992 .............. DLB-8
Leibniz, Gottfried Wilhelm 1646-1716 ... DLB-168
Leicester University Press ............ DLB-112
Leigh, Carolyn 1926-1983 ............ DLB-265
Leigh, W. R. 1866-1955 .............. DLB-188
Leinster, Murray 1896-1975 ............ DLB-8
Leiser, Bill 1898-1965................ DLB-241
Leisewitz, Johann Anton 1752-1806 ...... DLB-94
Leitch, Maurice 1933- ................ DLB-14

Leithauser, Brad 1943- .........DLB-120, 282

Leland, Charles G. 1824-1903...........DLB-11

Leland, John 1503?-1552..............DLB-136

Lemay, Pamphile 1837-1918 ...........DLB-99

Lemelin, Roger 1919-1992..............DLB-88

Lemercier, Louis-Jean-Népomucène
 1771-1840 ......................DLB-192

Le Moine, James MacPherson 1825-1912 ..DLB-99

Lemon, Mark 1809-1870 ..............DLB-163

Le Moyne, Jean 1913-1996 ..............DLB-88

Lemperly, Paul 1858-1939..............DLB-187

L'Engle, Madeleine 1918- ..............DLB-52

Lennart, Isobel 1915-1971 ..............DLB-44

Lennox, Charlotte 1729 or 1730-1804.....DLB-39

Lenox, James 1800-1880 ...............DLB-140

Lenski, Lois 1893-1974 ................DLB-22

Lentricchia, Frank 1940- ..............DLB-246

Lenz, Hermann 1913-1998 ..............DLB-69

Lenz, J. M. R. 1751-1792 ...............DLB-94

Lenz, Siegfried 1926- .................DLB-75

Leonard, Elmore 1925- ........ DLB-173, 226

Leonard, Hugh 1926- .................DLB-13

Leonard, William Ellery 1876-1944.......DLB-54

Leonov, Leonid Maksimovich
 1899-1994......................DLB-272

Leonowens, Anna 1834-1914 .......DLB-99, 166

Leont'ev, Konstantin Nikolaevich
 1831-1891 ......................DLB-277

Leopold, Aldo 1887-1948...............DLB-275

LePan, Douglas 1914-1998 ..............DLB-88

Lepik, Kalju 1920-1999 ................DLB-232

Leprohon, Rosanna Eleanor 1829-1879....DLB-99

Le Queux, William 1864-1927............DLB-70

Lermontov, Mikhail Iur'evich 1814-1841 .DLB-205

Lerner, Alan Jay 1918-1986............DLB-265

Lerner, Max 1902-1992................DLB-29

Lernet-Holenia, Alexander 1897-1976 ....DLB-85

Le Rossignol, James 1866-1969 ..........DLB-92

Lescarbot, Marc circa 1570-1642 .........DLB-99

LeSeur, William Dawson 1840-1917 ......DLB-92

LeSieg, Theo. (see Geisel, Theodor Seuss)

Leskov, Nikolai Semenovich 1831-1895 ..DLB-238

Leslie, Doris before 1902-1982 .........DLB-191

Leslie, Eliza 1787-1858 ................DLB-202

Leslie, Frank (Henry Carter)
 1821-1880 ....................DLB-43, 79

Frank Leslie [publishing house] .........DLB-49

Leśmian, Bolesław 1878-1937 ..........DLB-215

Lesperance, John 1835?-1891 ............DLB-99

Lessing, Bruno 1870-1940 ..............DLB-28

Lessing, Doris
 1919- .......DLB-15, 139; Y-85; CDBLB-8

Lessing, Gotthold Ephraim
 1729-1781 .............DLB-97; CDWLB-2

The Lessing Society .................Y-00

Lettau, Reinhard 1929-1996 ...........DLB-75

The Hemingway Letters Project Finds
 an Editor......................... Y-02

Lever, Charles 1806-1872 ..............DLB-21

Lever, Ralph ca. 1527-1585 ............DLB-236

Leverson, Ada 1862-1933 ............DLB-153

Levertov, Denise
 1923-1997 .........DLB-5, 165; CDALB-7

Levi, Peter 1931-2000 .................DLB-40

Levi, Primo 1919-1987.................DLB-177

Levien, Sonya 1888-1960...............DLB-44

Levin, Meyer 1905-1981 ........ DLB-9, 28; Y-81

Levin, Phillis 1954- ..................DLB-282

Levine, Norman 1923- ................DLB-88

Levine, Philip 1928- ...................DLB-5

Levis, Larry 1946- ..................DLB-120

Lévi-Strauss, Claude 1908- .........DLB-242

Levitov, Aleksandr Ivanovich
 1835?-1877 ....................DLB-277

Levy, Amy 1861-1889............DLB-156, 240

Levy, Benn Wolfe 1900-1973 ...... DLB-13; Y-81

Lewald, Fanny 1811-1889 ..............DLB-129

Lewes, George Henry 1817-1878.....DLB-55, 144

 "Criticism in Relation to Novels"
 (1863) .......................DLB-21

 *The Principles of Success in Literature*
 (1865) [excerpt]................DLB-57

Lewis, Agnes Smith 1843-1926 .........DLB-174

Lewis, Alfred H. 1857-1914 ........DLB-25, 186

Lewis, Alun 1915-1944 ........... DLB-20, 162

Lewis, C. Day (see Day Lewis, C.)

Lewis, C. I. 1883-1964................DLB-270

Lewis, C. S. 1898-1963
 ..........DLB-15, 100, 160, 255; CDBLB-7

 The New York C. S. Lewis Society......Y-99

Lewis, Charles B. 1842-1924 ............DLB-11

Lewis, David 1941-2001 ...............DLB-279

Lewis, Henry Clay 1825-1850.........DLB-3, 248

Lewis, Janet 1899-1999 ................ Y-87

 Tribute to Katherine Anne Porter....... Y-80

Lewis, Matthew Gregory
 1775-1818 .............. DLB-39, 158, 178

Lewis, Meriwether 1774-1809 .......DLB-183, 186

Lewis, Norman 1908- ...............DLB-204

Lewis, R. W. B. 1917- ................DLB-111

Lewis, Richard circa 1700-1734 .........DLB-24

Lewis, Sinclair
 1885-1951 ......DLB-9, 102; DS-1; CDALB-4

 Sinclair Lewis Centennial Conference.... Y-85

 The Sinclair Lewis Society ............Y-99

Lewis, Wilmarth Sheldon 1895-1979.....DLB-140

Lewis, Wyndham 1882-1957............DLB-15

 *Time and Western Man*
 [excerpt] (1927)................DLB-36

Lewisohn, Ludwig 1882-1955 ...DLB-4, 9, 28, 102

Leyendecker, J. C. 1874-1951 ..........DLB-188

Lezama Lima, José 1910-1976 ......DLB-113, 283

L'Heureux, John 1934- ............DLB-244

Libbey, Laura Jean 1862-1924.........DLB-221

Libedinsky, Iurii Nikolaevich
 1898-1959 ......................DLB-272

Library History Group .................. Y-01

E-Books' Second Act in Libraries........... Y-02

The Library of America................DLB-46

The Library of America: An Assessment
 After Two Decades.................. Y-02

Licensing Act of 1737..................DLB-84

Leonard Lichfield I [publishing house] ...DLB-170

Lichtenberg, Georg Christoph
 1742-1799 ......................DLB-94

The Liddle Collection .................Y-97

Lidman, Sara 1923- .................DLB-257

Lieb, Fred 1888-1980..................DLB-171

Liebling, A. J. 1904-1963 ............ DLB-4, 171

Lieutenant Murray (see Ballou, Maturin Murray)

Lighthall, William Douw 1857-1954 ......DLB-92

Lihn, Enrique 1929-1988...............DLB-283

Lilar, Françoise (see Mallet-Joris, Françoise)

Lili'uokalani, Queen 1838-1917.........DLB-221

Lillo, George 1691-1739.................DLB-84

Lilly, J. K., Jr. 1893-1966...............DLB-140

Lilly, Wait and Company ...............DLB-49

Lily, William circa 1468-1522 ..........DLB-132

Limited Editions Club ................DLB-46

Limón, Graciela 1938- ..............DLB-209

Lincoln and Edmands ..................DLB-49

Lindesay, Ethel Forence
 (see Richardson, Henry Handel)

Lindgren, Astrid 1907-2002 ..............DLB-257

Lindgren, Torgny 1938- ...............DLB-257

Lindsay, Alexander William, Twenty-fifth
 Earl of Crawford 1812-1880.........DLB-184

Lindsay, Sir David circa 1485-1555......DLB-132

Lindsay, David 1878-1945...............DLB-255

Lindsay, Jack 1900-1990 .................. Y-84

Lindsay, Lady (Caroline Blanche
 Elizabeth Fitzroy Lindsay)
 1844-1912 ......................DLB-199

Lindsay, Norman 1879-1969 ..........DLB-260

Lindsay, Vachel
 1879-1931 ..............DLB-54; CDALB-3

Linebarger, Paul Myron Anthony
 (see Smith, Cordwainer)

Link, Arthur S. 1920-1998 ............ DLB-17

Linn, Ed 1922-2000...................DLB-241

Linn, John Blair 1777-1804..............DLB-37

Lins, Osman 1924-1978 ...............DLB-145

Linton, Eliza Lynn 1822-1898 ..........DLB-18

Linton, William James 1812-1897 .......DLB-32

Barnaby Bernard Lintot
 [publishing house].................DLB-170

Lion Books ........................DLB-46

Lionni, Leo 1910-1999..................DLB-61

Lippard, George 1822-1854.............DLB-202

Lippincott, Sara Jane Clarke
 1823-1904......................DLB-43

419

# Cumulative Index

J. B. Lippincott Company............. DLB-49
Lippmann, Walter 1889-1974.......... DLB-29
Lipton, Lawrence 1898-1975 .......... DLB-16
Lisboa, Irene 1892-1958.............. DLB-287
Liscow, Christian Ludwig 1701-1760 ..... DLB-97
Lish, Gordon 1934- ................ DLB-130
    Tribute to Donald Barthelme.......... Y-89
    Tribute to James Dickey .............. Y-97
Lisle, Charles-Marie-René Leconte de 1818-1894.................... DLB-217
Lispector, Clarice 1925-1977........... DLB-113; CDWLB-3
LitCheck Website..................... Y-01
Literary Awards and Honors .......... Y-81-02
    Booker Prize.................. Y-86, 96-98
    The Drue Heinz Literature Prize ........ Y-82
    The Elmer Holmes Bobst Awards in Arts and Letters............... Y-87
    The Griffin Poetry Prize .............. Y-00
    Literary Prizes [British] ........ DLB-15, 207
    National Book Critics Circle Awards.................... Y-00-01
    The National Jewish Book Awards ...... Y-85
    Nobel Prize...................... Y-80-02
    Winning an Edgar ................... Y-98
*The Literary Chronicle and Weekly Review 1819-1828* ..................... DLB-110
Literary Periodicals:
    *Callaloo* ........................... Y-87
    Expatriates in Paris ................DS-15
    New Literary Periodicals: A Report for 1987 .............. Y-87
    A Report for 1988 ................. Y-88
    A Report for 1989 ................. Y-89
    A Report for 1990 ................. Y-90
    A Report for 1991 ................. Y-91
    A Report for 1992 ................. Y-92
    A Report for 1993 ................. Y-93
Literary Research Archives
    The Anthony Burgess Archive at the Harry Ransom Humanities Research Center ................ Y-98
    Archives of Charles Scribner's Sons..... DS-17
    Berg Collection of English and American Literature of the New York Public Library .......... Y-83
    The Bobbs-Merrill Archive at the Lilly Library, Indiana University .... Y-90
    Die Fürstliche Bibliothek Corvey........ Y-96
    Guide to the Archives of Publishers, Journals, and Literary Agents in North American Libraries .......... Y-93
    The Henry E. Huntington Library ...... Y-92
    The Humanities Research Center, University of Texas............... Y-82
    The John Carter Brown Library ........ Y-85
    Kent State Special Collections ......... Y-86
    The Lilly Library.................... Y-84
    The Modern Literary Manuscripts Collection in the Special

Collections of the Washington University Libraries ............. Y-87
A Publisher's Archives: G. P. Putnam .... Y-92
Special Collections at Boston University ..................... Y-99
The University of Virginia Libraries ..... Y-91
The William Charvat American Fiction Collection at the Ohio State University Libraries ............. Y-92
Literary Societies .................... Y-98-02
    The Margery Allingham Society ....... Y-98
    The American Studies Association of Norway ..................... Y-00
    The Arnold Bennett Society........... Y-98
    The Association for the Study of Literature and Environment (ASLE) ....................... Y-99
    Belgian Luxembourg American Studies Association ..................... Y-01
    The E. F. Benson Society............. Y-98
    The Elizabeth Bishop Society.......... Y-01
    The [Edgar Rice] Burroughs Bibliophiles .................... Y-98
    The Byron Society of America......... Y-00
    The Lewis Carroll Society of North America ................ Y-00
    The Willa Cather Pioneer Memorial and Education Foundation ......... Y-00
    New Chaucer Society................. Y-00
    The Wilkie Collins Society ............ Y-98
    The James Fenimore Cooper Society..... Y-01
    The Stephen Crane Society ........ Y-98, 01
    The E. E. Cummings Society.......... Y-01
    The James Dickey Society ............ Y-99
    John Dos Passos Newsletter........... Y-00
    The Priory Scholars [Sir Arthur Conan Doyle] of New York ............. Y-99
    The International Theodore Dreiser Society....................... Y-01
    The Friends of the Dymock Poets ...... Y-00
    The George Eliot Fellowship .......... Y-99
    The T. S. Eliot Society: Celebration and Scholarship, 1980-1999 ............. Y-99
    The Ralph Waldo Emerson Society ..... Y-99
    The William Faulkner Society ......... Y-99
    The C. S. Forester Society ............ Y-00
    The Hamlin Garland Society.......... Y-01
    The [Elizabeth] Gaskell Society ........ Y-98
    The Charlotte Perkins Gilman Society ... Y-99
    The Ellen Glasgow Society ............ Y-01
    Zane Grey's West Society ............. Y-00
    The Ivor Gurney Society ............. Y-98
    The Joel Chandler Harris Association .... Y-99
    The Nathaniel Hawthorne Society....... Y-00
    The [George Alfred] Henty Society ..... Y-98
    George Moses Horton Society.......... Y-99
    The William Dean Howells Society...... Y-01
    WW2 HMSO Paperbacks Society....... Y-98
    American Humor Studies Association .... Y-99

International Society for Humor Studies .. Y-99
The W. W. Jacobs Appreciation Society .. Y-98
The Richard Jefferies Society........... Y-98
The Jerome K. Jerome Society......... Y-98
The D. H. Lawrence Society of North America .................. Y-00
The T. E. Lawrence Society ........... Y-98
The [Gotthold] Lessing Society ........ Y-00
The New York C. S. Lewis Society ...... Y-99
The Sinclair Lewis Society............. Y-99
The Jack London Research Center ...... Y-00
The Jack London Society.............. Y-99
The Cormac McCarthy Society......... Y-99
The Melville Society ................. Y-01
The Arthur Miller Society ............ Y-01
The Milton Society of America ......... Y-00
International Marianne Moore Society ... Y-98
International Nabokov Society......... Y-99
The Vladimir Nabokov Society......... Y-01
The Flannery O'Connor Society ....... Y-99
The Wilfred Owen Association ........ Y-98
Penguin Collectors' Society ............ Y-98
The [E. A.] Poe Studies Association..... Y-99
The Katherine Anne Porter Society...... Y-01
The Beatrix Potter Society............. Y-98
The Ezra Pound Society .............. Y-01
The Powys Society................... Y-98
Proust Society of America ............ Y-00
The Dorothy L. Sayers Society ........ Y-98
The Bernard Shaw Society............ Y-99
The Society for the Study of Southern Literature............... Y-00
The Wallace Stevens Society........... Y-99
The Harriet Beecher Stowe Center ...... Y-00
The R. S. Surtees Society............. Y-98
The Thoreau Society................. Y-99
The Tilling [E. F. Benson] Society....... Y-98
The Trollope Societies................ Y-00
H. G. Wells Society .................. Y-98
The Western Literature Association ..... Y-99
The William Carlos Williams Society .... Y-99
The Henry Williamson Society ......... Y-98
The [Nero] Wolfe Pack ............... Y-99
The Thomas Wolfe Society............ Y-99
Worldwide Wodehouse Societies ....... Y-98
The W. B. Yeats Society of N.Y......... Y-99
The Charlotte M. Yonge Fellowship ..... Y-98
Literary Theory
    The Year in Literary Theory...... Y-92-Y-93
*Literature at Nurse, or Circulating Morals* (1885), by George Moore.................. DLB-18
Litt, Toby 1968- ................. DLB-267
Littell, Eliakim 1797-1870 .............. DLB-79
Littell, Robert S. 1831-1896 ............ DLB-79
Little, Brown and Company............ DLB-49

Little Magazines and Newspapers . . . . . . . . . DS-15
  Selected English-Language Little
    Magazines and Newspapers
    [France, 1920-1939] . . . . . . . . . . . . . DLB-4
The Little Magazines of the
  New Formalism . . . . . . . . . . . . . . . . . DLB-282
*The Little Review* 1914-1929 . . . . . . . . . . . . DS-15
Littlewood, Joan 1914-2002 . . . . . . . . . . . . DLB-13
Lively, Penelope 1933-  . . . . . . . DLB-14, 161, 207
Liverpool University Press . . . . . . . . . . . DLB-112
*The Lives of the Poets* (1753) . . . . . . . . . . . DLB-142
Livesay, Dorothy 1909-1996 . . . . . . . . . . . DLB-68
Livesay, Florence Randal 1874-1953 . . . . . . DLB-92
Livings, Henry 1929-1998 . . . . . . . . . . . . . DLB-13
Livingston, Anne Howe 1763-1841 . . . DLB-37, 200
Livingston, Jay 1915-2001 . . . . . . . . . . . . DLB-265
Livingston, Myra Cohn 1926-1996 . . . . . . . DLB-61
Livingston, William 1723-1790 . . . . . . . . . DLB-31
Livingstone, David 1813-1873 . . . . . . . . . DLB-166
Livingstone, Douglas 1932-1996 . . . . . . . . DLB-225
Livy 59 B.C.-A.D. 17 . . . . . . . DLB-211; CDWLB-1
Liyong, Taban lo (see Taban lo Liyong)
Lizárraga, Sylvia S. 1925-  . . . . . . . . . . . DLB-82
Llewellyn, Richard 1906-1983 . . . . . . . . . . DLB-15
Edward Lloyd [publishing house] . . . . . . . DLB-106
Lobel, Arnold 1933-  . . . . . . . . . . . . . . DLB-61
Lochridge, Betsy Hopkins (see Fancher, Betsy)
Locke, Alain 1886-1954 . . . . . . . . . . . . . . DLB-51
Locke, David Ross 1833-1888 . . . . . . . DLB-11, 23
Locke, John 1632-1704 . . . . . DLB-31, 101, 213, 252
Locke, Richard Adams 1800-1871 . . . . . . . DLB-43
Locker-Lampson, Frederick
  1821-1895 . . . . . . . . . . . . . . . . DLB-35, 184
Lockhart, John Gibson
  1794-1854 . . . . . . . . . . . . DLB-110, 116 144
Lockridge, Ross, Jr. 1914-1948 . . . . DLB-143; Y-80
*Locrine and Selimus* . . . . . . . . . . . . . . . . . DLB-62
Lodge, David 1935-  . . . . . . . . . . . DLB-14, 194
Lodge, George Cabot 1873-1909 . . . . . . . . DLB-54
Lodge, Henry Cabot 1850-1924 . . . . . . . . . DLB-47
Lodge, Thomas 1558-1625 . . . . . . . . . . . DLB-172
  *Defence of Poetry* (1579) [excerpt] . . . . . . DLB-172
Loeb, Harold 1891-1974 . . . . . . . . DLB-4; DS-15
Loeb, William 1905-1981 . . . . . . . . . . . . DLB-127
Loesser, Frank 1910-1969 . . . . . . . . . . . . DLB-265
Lofting, Hugh 1886-1947 . . . . . . . . . . . . DLB-160
Logan, Deborah Norris 1761-1839 . . . . . . DLB-200
Logan, James 1674-1751 . . . . . . . . . DLB-24, 140
Logan, John 1923-1987 . . . . . . . . . . . . . . . DLB-5
Logan, Martha Daniell 1704?-1779 . . . . . . DLB-200
Logan, William 1950-  . . . . . . . . . . . . . DLB-120
Logau, Friedrich von 1605-1655 . . . . . . . . DLB-164
Logue, Christopher 1926-  . . . . . . . . . . . DLB-27
Lohenstein, Daniel Casper von
  1635-1683 . . . . . . . . . . . . . . . . . . . DLB-168
Lo-Johansson, Ivar 1901-1990 . . . . . . . . . DLB-259

Lokert, George (or Lockhart)
  circa 1485-1547 . . . . . . . . . . . . . . . . DLB-281
Lomonosov, Mikhail Vasil'evich
  1711-1765 . . . . . . . . . . . . . . . . . . . DLB-150
London, Jack
  1876-1916 . . . . . DLB-8, 12, 78, 212; CDALB-3
  The Jack London Research Center . . . . . . Y-00
  The Jack London Society . . . . . . . . . . . . Y-99
*The London Magazine* 1820-1829 . . . . . . . DLB-110
Long, David 1948-  . . . . . . . . . . . . . . DLB-244
Long, H., and Brother . . . . . . . . . . . . . . . DLB-49
Long, Haniel 1888-1956 . . . . . . . . . . . . . DLB-45
Long, Ray 1878-1935 . . . . . . . . . . . . . . DLB-137
Longfellow, Henry Wadsworth
  1807-1882 . . . . . . . . DLB-1, 59, 235; CDALB-2
Longfellow, Samuel 1819-1892 . . . . . . . . . . DLB-1
Longford, Elizabeth 1906-2002 . . . . . . . . DLB-155
  Tribute to Alfred A. Knopf . . . . . . . . . . Y-84
Longinus circa first century . . . . . . . . . . . DLB-176
Longley, Michael 1939-  . . . . . . . . . . . . DLB-40
T. Longman [publishing house] . . . . . . . . DLB-154
Longmans, Green and Company . . . . . . . . DLB-49
Longmore, George 1793?-1867 . . . . . . . . . DLB-99
Longstreet, Augustus Baldwin
  1790-1870 . . . . . . . . . . . . DLB-3, 11, 74, 248
D. Longworth [publishing house] . . . . . . . DLB-49
Lonsdale, Frederick 1881-1954 . . . . . . . . . DLB-10
Loos, Anita 1893-1981 . . . . . DLB-11, 26, 228; Y-81
Lopate, Phillip 1943-  . . . . . . . . . . . . . . . Y-80
Lopes, Fernão 1380/1390?-1460? . . . . . . . DLB-287
Lopez, Barry 1945-  . . . . . . . . . . DLB-256, 275
López de Mendoza, Íñigo
  (see Santillana, Marqués de)
López, Diana (see Isabella, Ríos)
López, Josefina 1969-  . . . . . . . . . . . . . DLB-209
Loranger, Jean-Aubert 1896-1942 . . . . . . . . DLB-92
Lorca, Federico García 1898-1936 . . . . . . DLB-108
Lord, John Keast 1818-1872 . . . . . . . . . . . DLB-99
Lorde, Audre 1934-1992 . . . . . . . . . . . . . DLB-41
Lorimer, George Horace 1867-1937 . . . . . . DLB-91
A. K. Loring [publishing house] . . . . . . . . DLB-49
Loring and Mussey . . . . . . . . . . . . . . . . DLB-46
Lorris, Guillaume de (see *Roman de la Rose*)
Lossing, Benson J. 1813-1891 . . . . . . . . . . DLB-30
Lothar, Ernst 1890-1974 . . . . . . . . . . . . . DLB-81
D. Lothrop and Company . . . . . . . . . . . . DLB-49
Lothrop, Harriet M. 1844-1924 . . . . . . . . . DLB-42
Loti, Pierre 1850-1923 . . . . . . . . . . . . . . DLB-123
Lotichius Secundus, Petrus 1528-1560 . . . DLB-179
Lott, Emmeline ?-? . . . . . . . . . . . . . . . . DLB-166
Louisiana State University Press . . . . . . . . . Y-97
Lounsbury, Thomas R. 1838-1915 . . . . . . . DLB-71
Louÿs, Pierre 1870-1925 . . . . . . . . . . . . . DLB-123
Lovejoy, Arthur O. 1873-1962 . . . . . . . . . DLB-270
Lovelace, Earl 1935-  . . . . . . . DLB-125; CDWLB-3
Lovelace, Richard 1618-1657 . . . . . . . . . . DLB-131

John W. Lovell Company . . . . . . . . . . . . . DLB-49
Lovell, Coryell and Company . . . . . . . . . . DLB-49
Lover, Samuel 1797-1868 . . . . . . . . . DLB-159, 190
Lovesey, Peter 1936-  . . . . . . . . . . . . . . DLB-87
  Tribute to Georges Simenon . . . . . . . . . . Y-89
Lovinescu, Eugen
  1881-1943 . . . . . . . . . . . . . DLB-220; CDWLB-4
Lovingood, Sut
  (see Harris, George Washington)
Low, Samuel 1765-? . . . . . . . . . . . . . . . . DLB-37
Lowell, Amy 1874-1925 . . . . . . . . . . . DLB-54, 140
Lowell, James Russell 1819-1891
  . . . . . . DLB-1, 11, 64, 79, 189, 235; CDALB-2
Lowell, Robert
  1917-1977 . . . . . . . . . . . DLB-5, 169; CDALB-7
Lowenfels, Walter 1897-1976 . . . . . . . . . . . DLB-4
Lowndes, Marie Belloc 1868-1947 . . . . . . . DLB-70
Lowndes, William Thomas 1798-1843 . . . DLB-184
Humphrey Lownes [publishing house] . . . DLB-170
Lowry, Lois 1937-  . . . . . . . . . . . . . . . . DLB-52
Lowry, Malcolm 1909-1957 . . . . DLB-15; CDBLB-7
Lowther, Pat 1935-1975 . . . . . . . . . . . . . . DLB-53
Loy, Mina 1882-1966 . . . . . . . . . . . . . DLB-4, 54
Loynaz, Dulce María 1902-1997 . . . . . . . DLB-283
Lozeau, Albert 1878-1924 . . . . . . . . . . . . . DLB-92
Lubbock, Percy 1879-1965 . . . . . . . . . . . DLB-149
Lucan A.D. 39-A.D. 65 . . . . . . . . . . . . . . DLB-211
Lucas, E. V. 1868-1938 . . . . . . . . DLB-98, 149, 153
Fielding Lucas Jr. [publishing house] . . . . . . DLB-49
Luce, Clare Booth 1903-1987 . . . . . . . . . . DLB-228
Luce, Henry R. 1898-1967 . . . . . . . . . . . . DLB-91
John W. Luce and Company . . . . . . . . . . DLB-46
Lucena, Juan de ca. 1430-1501 . . . . . . . . . DLB-286
Lucian circa 120-180 . . . . . . . . . . . . . . . DLB-176
Lucie-Smith, Edward 1933-  . . . . . . . . . . DLB-40
Lucilius circa 180 B.C.-102/101 B.C. . . . . . DLB-211
Lucini, Gian Pietro 1867-1914 . . . . . . . . . DLB-114
Lucretius circa 94 B.C.-circa 49 B.C.
  . . . . . . . . . . . . . . . . . . . DLB-211; CDWLB-1
Luder, Peter circa 1415-1472 . . . . . . . . . . DLB-179
Ludlam, Charles 1943-1987 . . . . . . . . . . DLB-266
Ludlum, Robert 1927-2001 . . . . . . . . . . . . Y-82
*Ludus de Antichristo* circa 1160 . . . . . . . . . DLB-148
Ludvigson, Susan 1942-  . . . . . . . . . . . DLB-120
Ludwig, Jack 1922-  . . . . . . . . . . . . . . DLB-60
Ludwig, Otto 1813-1865 . . . . . . . . . . . . . DLB-129
*Ludwigslied* 881 or 882 . . . . . . . . . . . . . DLB-148
Luera, Yolanda 1953-  . . . . . . . . . . . . . DLB-122
Luft, Lya 1938-  . . . . . . . . . . . . . . . . . DLB-145
Lugansky, Kazak Vladimir
  (see Dal', Vladimir Ivanovich)
Lugn, Kristina 1948-  . . . . . . . . . . . . . DLB-257
Lugones, Leopoldo 1874-1938 . . . . . . . . . DLB-283
Lukács, Georg (see Lukács, György)
Lukács, György
  1885-1971 . . . . . . . . DLB-215, 242; CDWLB-4

Luke, Peter 1919- ............... DLB-13
Lummis, Charles F. 1859-1928........ DLB-186
Lundkvist, Artur 1906-1991......... DLB-259
Lunts, Lev Natanovich 1901-1924...... DLB-272
F. M. Lupton Company............. DLB-49
Lupus of Ferrières circa 805-circa 862 ... DLB-148
Lurie, Alison 1926- ................ DLB-2
Lussu, Emilio 1890-1975........... DLB-264
Lustig, Arnošt 1926- ............. DLB-232
Luther, Martin 1483-1546 ...DLB-179; CDWLB-2
Luzi, Mario 1914- ................ DLB-128
L'vov, Nikolai Aleksandrovich
  1751-1803..................... DLB-150
Lyall, Gavin 1932- ................ DLB-87
Lydgate, John circa 1370-1450 ......... DLB-146
Lyly, John circa 1554-1606........ DLB-62, 167
Lynch, Patricia 1898-1972 ........ DLB-160
Lynch, Richard flourished 1596-1601 ....DLB-172
Lynd, Robert 1879-1949........... DLB-98
Lyon, Matthew 1749-1822 ........... DLB-43
Lyotard, Jean-François 1924-1998 ...... DLB-242
Lyricists
  Additional Lyricists: 1920-1960..... DLB-265
Lysias circa 459 B.C.-circa 380 B.C....... DLB-176
Lytle, Andrew 1902-1995.......... DLB-6; Y-95
  Tribute to Caroline Gordon ......... Y-81
  Tribute to Katherine Anne Porter ....... Y-80
Lytton, Edward
  (see Bulwer-Lytton, Edward)
Lytton, Edward Robert Bulwer
  1831-1891..................... DLB-32

# M

Maass, Joachim 1901-1972 ............. DLB-69
Mabie, Hamilton Wright 1845-1916 ..... DLB-71
Mac A'Ghobhainn, Iain (see Smith, Iain Crichton)
MacArthur, Charles 1895-1956 .....DLB-7, 25, 44
Macaulay, Catherine 1731-1791 ........ DLB-104
Macaulay, David 1945- ............... DLB-61
Macaulay, Rose 1881-1958........... DLB-36
Macaulay, Thomas Babington
  1800-1859........... DLB-32, 55; CDBLB-4
Macaulay Company................ DLB-46
MacBeth, George 1932-1992 .......... DLB-40
Macbeth, Madge 1880-1965 .......... DLB-92
MacCaig, Norman 1910-1996 ........ DLB-27
MacDiarmid, Hugh
  1892-1978............. DLB-20; CDBLB-7
MacDonald, Cynthia 1928- ......... DLB-105
MacDonald, George 1824-1905 ... DLB-18, 163, 178
MacDonald, John D. 1916-1986..... DLB-8; Y-86
MacDonald, Philip 1899?-1980 ........ DLB-77
Macdonald, Ross (see Millar, Kenneth)
Macdonald, Sharman 1951- ........ DLB-245
MacDonald, Wilson 1880-1967 ....... DLB-92
Macdonald and Company (Publishers) .. DLB-112

MacEwen, Gwendolyn 1941-1987 ... DLB-53, 251
Macfadden, Bernarr 1868-1955 ..... DLB-25, 91
MacGregor, John 1825-1892 ......... DLB-166
MacGregor, Mary Esther (see Keith, Marian)
Machado, Antonio 1875-1939......... DLB-108
Machado, Manuel 1874-1947 ......... DLB-108
Machar, Agnes Maule 1837-1927 ....... DLB-92
Machaut, Guillaume de
  circa 1300-1377 ................ DLB-208
Machen, Arthur Llewelyn Jones
  1863-1947.............DLB-36, 156, 178
MacIlmaine, Roland fl. 1574........... DLB-281
MacInnes, Colin 1914-1976 ......... DLB-14
MacInnes, Helen 1907-1985 ......... DLB-87
Mac Intyre, Tom 1931- ........... DLB-245
Mačiulis, Jonas (see Maironis, Jonas)
Mack, Maynard 1909- ............. DLB-111
Mackall, Leonard L. 1879-1937 ....... DLB-140
MacKay, Isabel Ecclestone 1875-1928 .... DLB-92
MacKaye, Percy 1875-1956 .......... DLB-54
Macken, Walter 1915-1967 .......... DLB-13
Mackenzie, Alexander 1763-1820........ DLB-99
Mackenzie, Alexander Slidell
  1803-1848 .................... DLB-183
Mackenzie, Compton 1883-1972 .... DLB-34, 100
Mackenzie, Henry 1745-1831 ........... DLB-39
  *The Lounger*, no. 20 (1785) ......... DLB-39
Mackenzie, Kenneth (Seaforth Mackenzie)
  1913-1955 .................... DLB-260
Mackenzie, William 1758-1828......... DLB-187
Mackey, Nathaniel 1947- ........... DLB-169
Mackey, Shena 1944- ............. DLB-231
Mackey, William Wellington 1937- ..... DLB-38
Mackintosh, Elizabeth (see Tey, Josephine)
Mackintosh, Sir James 1765-1832........ DLB-158
Macklin, Charles 1699-1797 .......... DLB-89
Maclaren, Ian (see Watson, John)
MacLaverty, Bernard 1942- ........ DLB-267
MacLean, Alistair 1922-1987 ..........DLB-276
MacLean, Katherine Anne 1925- ....... DLB-8
Maclean, Norman 1902-1990......... DLB-206
MacLeish, Archibald 1892-1982
  ........DLB-4, 7, 45; Y-82; DS-15; CDALB-7
MacLennan, Hugh 1907-1990 ......... DLB-68
MacLeod, Alistair 1936- ........... DLB-60
Macleod, Fiona (see Sharp, William)
Macleod, Norman 1906-1985............ DLB-4
Mac Low, Jackson 1922- .......... DLB-193
Macmillan and Company............. DLB-106
The Macmillan Company ............. DLB-49
Macmillan's English Men of Letters,
  First Series (1878-1892) ........... DLB-144
MacNamara, Brinsley 1890-1963........ DLB-10
MacNeice, Louis 1907-1963 ....... DLB-10, 20
Macphail, Andrew 1864-1938 ......... DLB-92
Macpherson, James 1736-1796 ........ DLB-109

Macpherson, Jay 1931- ............. DLB-53
Macpherson, Jeanie 1884-1946.......... DLB-44
Macrae Smith Company............... DLB-46
MacRaye, Lucy Betty (see Webling, Lucy)
John Macrone [publishing house]........ DLB-106
MacShane, Frank 1927-1999........... DLB-111
Macy-Masius ...................... DLB-46
Madden, David 1933- ............... DLB-6
Madden, Sir Frederic 1801-1873........ DLB-184
Maddow, Ben 1909-1992............. DLB-44
Maddux, Rachel 1912-1983 .......DLB-234; Y-93
Madgett, Naomi Long 1923- ......... DLB-76
Madhubuti, Haki R. 1942- ..... DLB-5, 41; DS-8
Madison, James 1751-1836........... DLB-37
Madsen, Svend Åge 1939- .......... DLB-214
Madrigal, Alfonso Fernández de (El Tostado)
  ca. 1405-1455................... DLB-286
Maeterlinck, Maurice 1862-1949 ....... DLB-192
Mafūz, Najīb 1911- ................... Y-88
  Nobel Lecture 1988................. Y-88
The Little Magazines of the
  New Formalism ................ DLB-282
Magee, David 1905-1977 .............DLB-187
Maginn, William 1794-1842........DLB-110, 159
Magoffin, Susan Shelby 1827-1855...... DLB-239
Mahan, Alfred Thayer 1840-1914 ........ DLB-47
Maheux-Forcier, Louise 1929- ........ DLB-60
Mahin, John Lee 1902-1984 .......... DLB-44
Mahon, Derek 1941- ............... DLB-40
Maikov, Apollon Nikolaevich
  1821-1897 .....................DLB-277
Maikov, Vasilii Ivanovich 1728-1778 .... DLB-150
Mailer, Norman 1923-
  ........DLB-2, 16, 28, 185, 278; Y-80, 83, 97;
  DS-3; CDALB-6
  Tribute to Isaac Bashevis Singer ........ Y-91
  Tribute to Meyer Levin............... Y-81
Maillart, Ella 1903-1997.............. DLB-195
Maillet, Adrienne 1885-1963 ......... DLB-68
Maillet, Antonine 1929- ........... DLB-60
Maillu, David G. 1939- .............DLB-157
Maimonides, Moses 1138-1204 ........ DLB-115
Main Selections of the Book-of-the-Month
  Club, 1926-1945 ................. DLB-9
Mainwaring, Daniel 1902-1977.......... DLB-44
Mair, Charles 1838-1927 ............. DLB-99
Mair, John circa 1467-1550............ DLB-281
Maironis, Jonas 1862-1932.. DLB-220; CDWLB-4
Mais, Roger 1905-1955 .....DLB-125; CDWLB-3
Maitland, Sara 1950- ................DLB-271
Major, Andre 1942- ............... DLB-60
Major, Charles 1856-1913 ........... DLB-202
Major, Clarence 1936- ............. DLB-33
Major, Kevin 1949- ................ DLB-60
Major Books...................... DLB-46

Makanin, Vladimir Semenovich 1937- ....................DLB-285
Makarenko, Anton Semenovich 1888-1939 ......................DLB-272
Makemie, Francis circa 1658-1708........DLB-24
*The Making of Americans* Contract ...........Y-98
Maksimović, Desanka 1898-1993 ............DLB-147; CDWLB-4
Malamud, Bernard 1914-1986 ........DLB-2, 28, 152; Y-80, 86; CDALB-1
    Bernard Malamud Archive at the Harry Ransom Humanities Research Center..................Y-00
Mălăncioiu, Ileana 1940- ............DLB-232
Malaparte, Curzio (Kurt Erich Suckert) 1898-1957......DLB-264
Malerba, Luigi 1927- ...............DLB-196
Malet, Lucas 1852-1931.............DLB-153
Mallarmé, Stéphane 1842-1898 ........DLB-217
Malleson, Lucy Beatrice (see Gilbert, Anthony)
Mallet-Joris, Françoise (Françoise Lilar) 1930- ........................DLB-83
Mallock, W. H. 1849-1923 .........DLB-18, 57
    "Every Man His Own Poet; or, The Inspired Singer's Recipe Book" (1877)...................DLB-35
    "Le Style c'est l'homme" (1892) ......DLB-57
    *Memoirs of Life and Literature* (1920), [excerpt] .................DLB-57
Malone, Dumas 1892-1986 ............DLB-17
Malone, Edmond 1741-1812 ...........DLB-142
Malory, Sir Thomas circa 1400-1410 - 1471 ... DLB-146; CDBLB-1
Malpede, Karen 1945- ..............DLB-249
Malraux, André 1901-1976 ............DLB-72
Malthus, Thomas Robert 1766-1834 ................ DLB-107, 158
Maltz, Albert 1908-1985 .............DLB-102
Malzberg, Barry N. 1939- ..............DLB-8
Mamet, David 1947- ..................DLB-7
Mamin, Dmitrii Narkisovich 1852-1912 ..DLB-238
Manaka, Matsemela 1956- ...........DLB-157
Manchester University Press...........DLB-112
Mandel, Eli 1922-1992................DLB-53
Mandeville, Bernard 1670-1733 ........DLB-101
Mandeville, Sir John mid fourteenth century ...........DLB-146
Mandiargues, André Pieyre de 1909-1991 .....................DLB-83
Manea, Norman 1936- ..............DLB-232
Manfred, Frederick 1912-1994....DLB-6, 212, 227
Manfredi, Gianfranco 1948- ..........DLB-196
Mangan, Sherry 1904-1961 ............DLB-4
Manganelli, Giorgio 1922-1990........DLB-196
Manilius fl. first century A.D. .........DLB-211
Mankiewicz, Herman 1897-1953 .......DLB-26
Mankiewicz, Joseph L. 1909-1993 ......DLB-44
Mankowitz, Wolf 1924-1998 ..........DLB-15
Manley, Delariviëre 1672?-1724.......DLB-39, 80

Preface to *The Secret History, of Queen Zarah, and the Zarazians* (1705) .....DLB-39
Mann, Abby 1927- .................DLB-44
Mann, Charles 1929-1998................Y-98
Mann, Emily 1952- ................DLB-266
Mann, Heinrich 1871-1950 ........DLB-66, 118
Mann, Horace 1796-1859 ...........DLB-1, 235
Mann, Klaus 1906-1949..............DLB-56
Mann, Mary Peabody 1806-1887 .......DLB-239
Mann, Thomas 1875-1955....DLB-66; CDWLB-2
Mann, William D'Alton 1839-1920......DLB-137
Mannin, Ethel 1900-1984 ........DLB-191, 195
Manning, Emily (see Australie)
Manning, Frederic 1882-1935 ..........DLB-260
Manning, Laurence 1899-1972 ..........DLB-251
Manning, Marie 1873?-1945 ..........DLB-29
Manning and Loring ..................DLB-49
Mannyng, Robert flourished 1303-1338 ..DLB-146
Mano, D. Keith 1942- ................DLB-6
Manor Books.......................DLB-46
Manrique, Gómez 1412?-1490..........DLB-286
Manrique, Jorge ca. 1440-1479 ........DLB-286
Mansfield, Katherine 1888-1923 ........DLB-162
Mantel, Hilary 1952- ...............DLB-271
Manuel, Niklaus circa 1484-1530 .......DLB-179
Manzini, Gianna 1896-1974...........DLB-177
Mapanje, Jack 1944- ...............DLB-157
Maraini, Dacia 1936- ...............DLB-196
March, William (William Edward Campbell) 1893-1954 ...................DLB-9, 86
Marchand, Leslie A. 1900-1999........DLB-103
Marchant, Bessie 1862-1941 ..........DLB-160
Marchant, Tony 1959- .............DLB-245
Marchenko, Anastasiia Iakovlevna 1830-1880 .....................DLB-238
Marchessault, Jovette 1938- ...........DLB-60
Marcinkevičius, Justinas 1930- .......DLB-232
Marcus, Frank 1928- ...............DLB-13
Marcuse, Herbert 1898-1979 ..........DLB-242
Marden, Orison Swett 1850-1924 .......DLB-137
Marechera, Dambudzo 1952-1987.......DLB-157
Marek, Richard, Books ...............DLB-46
Mares, E. A. 1938- ................DLB-122
Margulies, Donald 1954- ...........DLB-228
Mariani, Paul 1940- ...............DLB-111
Marie de France flourished 1160-1178....DLB-208
Marie-Victorin, Frère (Conrad Kirouac) 1885-1944 ......................DLB-92
Marin, Biagio 1891-1985..............DLB-128
Marinetti, Filippo Tommaso 1876-1944 .................DLB-114, 264
Marinina, Aleksandra (Marina Anatol'evna Alekseeva) 1957- ..............DLB-285
Marinković, Ranko 1913- ..............DLB-147; CDWLB-4
Marion, Frances 1886-1973 ............DLB-44

Marius, Richard C. 1933-1999 ............Y-85
Markevich, Boleslav Mikhailovich 1822-1884...................DLB-238
Markfield, Wallace 1926-2002.........DLB-2, 28
Markham, Edwin 1852-1940 .....DLB-54, 186
Markle, Fletcher 1921-1991........DLB-68; Y-91
Marlatt, Daphne 1942- ................DLB-60
Marlitt, E. 1825-1887.................DLB-129
Marlowe, Christopher 1564-1593 .............DLB-62; CDBLB-1
Marlyn, John 1912- .................DLB-88
Marmion, Shakerley 1603-1639..........DLB-58
Der Marner before 1230-circa 1287......DLB-138
Marnham, Patrick 1943- ............DLB-204
The *Marprelate Tracts* 1588-1589 .......DLB-132
Marquand, John P. 1893-1960.........DLB-9, 102
Marques, Helena 1935- .............DLB-287
Marqués, René 1919-1979 .............DLB-113
Marquis, Don 1878-1937 ...........DLB-11, 25
Marriott, Anne 1913-1997 ..............DLB-68
Marryat, Frederick 1792-1848 .......DLB-21, 163
Marsh, Capen, Lyon and Webb .........DLB-49
Marsh, George Perkins 1801-1882 ................DLB-1, 64, 243
Marsh, James 1794-1842 .............DLB-1, 59
Marsh, Narcissus 1638-1713 ...........DLB-213
Marsh, Ngaio 1899-1982...............DLB-77
Marshall, Alan 1902-1984 .............DLB-260
Marshall, Edison 1894-1967 ..........DLB-102
Marshall, Edward 1932- .............DLB-16
Marshall, Emma 1828-1899............DLB-163
Marshall, James 1942-1992 ............DLB-61
Marshall, Joyce 1913- ................DLB-88
Marshall, Paule 1929-  DLB-33, 157, 227
Marshall, Tom 1938-1993.............DLB-60
Marsilius of Padua circa 1275-circa 1342..............DLB-115
Mars-Jones, Adam 1954- ............DLB-207
Marson, Una 1905-1965 .............DLB-157
Marston, John 1576-1634...........DLB-58, 172
Marston, Philip Bourke 1850-1887 .......DLB-35
Martens, Kurt 1870-1945...............DLB-66
Martial circa A.D. 40-circa A.D. 103 .................DLB-211; CDWLB-1
William S. Martien [publishing house] ....DLB-49
Martin, Abe (see Hubbard, Kin)
Martin, Catherine ca. 1847-1937 .......DLB-230
Martin, Charles 1942- ...........DLB-120, 282
Martin, Claire 1914- ................DLB-60
Martin, David 1915-1997..............DLB-260
Martin, Jay 1935- ..................DLB-111
Martin, Johann (see Laurentius von Schnüffis)
Martin, Thomas 1696-1771 ............DLB-213
Martin, Violet Florence (see Ross, Martin)
Martin du Gard, Roger 1881-1958 .......DLB-65

423

# Cumulative Index

Martineau, Harriet
    1802-1876.....DLB-21, 55, 159, 163, 166, 190

Martínez, Demetria 1960- ........... DLB-209

Martínez de Toledo, Alfonso
    1398?-1468..................... DLB-286

Martínez, Eliud 1935- .............. DLB-122

Martínez, Max 1943- ................ DLB-82

Martínez, Rubén 1962- .............. DLB-209

Martinson, Harry 1904-1978 .......... DLB-259

Martinson, Moa 1890-1964 ........... DLB-259

Martone, Michael 1955- ............. DLB-218

Martyn, Edward 1859-1923 ............ DLB-10

Marvell, Andrew
    1621-1678.............. DLB-131; CDBLB-2

Marvin X 1944- ..................... DLB-38

Marx, Karl 1818-1883 ................ DLB-129

Marzials, Theo 1850-1920 ............ DLB-35

Masefield, John
    1878-1967... DLB-10, 19, 153, 160; CDBLB-5

Masham, Damaris Cudworth, Lady
    1659-1708...................... DLB-252

Masino, Paola 1908-1989 ............ DLB-264

Mason, A. E. W. 1865-1948........... DLB-70

Mason, Bobbie Ann
    1940- .......... DLB-173; Y-87; CDALB-7

Mason, William 1725-1797 ........... DLB-142

Mason Brothers .................... DLB-49

*The Massachusetts Quarterly Review*
    1847-1850....................... DLB-1

Massey, Gerald 1828-1907 ............ DLB-32

Massey, Linton R. 1900-1974 ......... DLB-187

Massie, Allan 1938- ................ DLB-271

Massinger, Philip 1583-1640........ DLB-58

Masson, David 1822-1907 ............ DLB-144

Masters, Edgar Lee 1868-1950 . DLB-54; CDALB-3

Masters, Hilary 1928- ............... DLB-244

Mastronardi, Lucio 1930-1979 ........ DLB-177

Matevski, Mateja 1929- ... DLB-181; CDWLB-4

Mather, Cotton
    1663-1728....... DLB-24, 30, 140; CDALB-2

Mather, Increase 1639-1723 .......... DLB-24

Mather, Richard 1596-1669 ........... DLB-24

Matheson, Annie 1853-1924........... DLB-240

Matheson, Richard 1926- .......... DLB-8, 44

Matheus, John F. 1887- ............. DLB-51

Mathews, Cornelius 1817?-1889... DLB-3, 64, 250

Elkin Mathews [publishing house] ...... DLB-112

Mathews, John Joseph 1894-1979 ........DLB-175

Mathias, Roland 1915- .............. DLB-27

Mathis, June 1892-1927 ............. DLB-44

Mathis, Sharon Bell 1937- .......... DLB-33

Matković, Marijan 1915-1985......... DLB-181

Matoš, Antun Gustav 1873-1914 ...... DLB-147

Matsumoto Seichō 1909-1992 ........ DLB-182

The Matter of England 1240-1400 ..... DLB-146

The Matter of Rome early twelfth to late
    fifteenth century................ DLB-146

Matthew of Vendôme
    circa 1130-circa 1200 ............. DLB-208

Matthews, Brander 1852-1929 ..DLB-71, 78; DS-13

Matthews, Jack 1925- ................ DLB-6

Matthews, Victoria Earle 1861-1907 .... DLB-221

Matthews, William 1942-1997 .......... DLB-5

Matthiessen, F. O. 1902-1950........... DLB-63

Matthiessen, Peter 1927- ....... DLB-6, 173, 275

Maturin, Charles Robert 1780-1824......DLB-178

Maugham, W. Somerset 1874-1965
    ..... DLB-10, 36, 77, 100, 162, 195; CDBLB-6

Maupassant, Guy de 1850-1893........ DLB-123

Maupin, Armistead 1944- ............DLB-278

Mauriac, Claude 1914-1996 ........... DLB-83

Mauriac, François 1885-1970 .......... DLB-65

Maurice, Frederick Denison 1805-1872 ... DLB-55

Maurois, André 1885-1967............ DLB-65

Maury, James 1718-1769............... DLB-31

Mavor, Elizabeth 1927- .............. DLB-14

Mavor, Osborne Henry (see Bridie, James)

Maxwell, Gavin 1914-1969 ........... DLB-204

Maxwell, William
    1908-2000 ............ DLB-218, 278; Y-80

    Tribute to Nancy Hale............... Y-88

H. Maxwell [publishing house].......... DLB-49

John Maxwell [publishing house] ....... DLB-106

May, Elaine 1932- ................... DLB-44

May, Karl 1842-1912 ................ DLB-129

May, Thomas 1595/1596-1650 ......... DLB-58

Mayer, Bernadette 1945- ............ DLB-165

Mayer, Mercer 1943- ................ DLB-61

Mayer, O. B. 1818-1891 ............ DLB-3, 248

Mayes, Herbert R. 1900-1987.......... DLB-137

Mayes, Wendell 1919-1992 ........... DLB-26

Mayfield, Julian 1928-1984..........DLB-33; Y-84

Mayhew, Henry 1812-1887 ..... DLB-18, 55, 190

Mayhew, Jonathan 1720-1766........... DLB-31

Mayne, Ethel Colburn 1865-1941 ...... DLB-197

Mayne, Jasper 1604-1672 ............ DLB-126

Mayne, Seymour 1944- .............. DLB-60

Mayor, Flora Macdonald 1872-1932 ..... DLB-36

Mayröcker, Friederike 1924- .......... DLB-85

Mazrui, Ali A. 1933- ................ DLB-125

Mažuranić, Ivan 1814-1890 .......... DLB-147

Mazursky, Paul 1930- ................ DLB-44

McAlmon, Robert 1896-1956... DLB-4, 45; DS-15

    "A Night at Bricktop's" ............. Y-01

McArthur, Peter 1866-1924 ........... DLB-92

McAuley, James 1917-1976 ........... DLB-260

Robert M. McBride and Company ...... DLB-46

McCabe, Patrick 1955- .............. DLB-194

McCaffrey, Anne 1926- ............... DLB-8

McCann, Colum 1965- .............. DLB-267

McCarthy, Cormac 1933- ..... DLB-6, 143, 256

    The Cormac McCarthy Society........ Y-99

McCarthy, Mary 1912-1989.........DLB-2; Y-81

McCarthy, Shaun Lloyd (see Cory, Desmond)

McCay, Winsor 1871-1934 ............ DLB-22

McClane, Albert Jules 1922-1991........DLB-171

McClatchy, C. K. 1858-1936 .......... DLB-25

McClellan, George Marion 1860-1934.... DLB-50

    "The Negro as a Writer" ........... DLB-50

McCloskey, Robert 1914- ............ DLB-22

McClung, Nellie Letitia 1873-1951....... DLB-92

McClure, James 1939- ..............DLB-276

McClure, Joanna 1930- ............. DLB-16

McClure, Michael 1932- ............. DLB-16

McClure, Phillips and Company ....... DLB-46

McClure, S. S. 1857-1949 ............ DLB-91

A. C. McClurg and Company .......... DLB-49

McCluskey, John A., Jr. 1944- ........ DLB-33

McCollum, Michael A. 1946- .......... Y-87

McConnell, William C. 1917- ........ DLB-88

McCord, David 1897-1997 ............ DLB-61

McCord, Louisa S. 1810-1879 ......... DLB-248

McCorkle, Jill 1958- ...........DLB-234; Y-87

McCorkle, Samuel Eusebius 1746-1811 ... DLB-37

McCormick, Anne O'Hare 1880-1954.... DLB-29

McCormick, Kenneth Dale 1906-1997....... Y-97

McCormick, Robert R. 1880-1955 ...... DLB-29

McCourt, Edward 1907-1972 ......... DLB-88

McCoy, Horace 1897-1955 ............. DLB-9

McCrae, Hugh 1876-1958 ............ DLB-260

McCrae, John 1872-1918 ............. DLB-92

McCullagh, Joseph B. 1842-1896........ DLB-23

McCullers, Carson
    1917-1967...... DLB-2, 7, 173, 228; CDALB-1

McCulloch, Thomas 1776-1843 ......... DLB-99

McDonald, Forrest 1927- ............DLB-17

McDonald, Walter 1934- .......DLB-105, DS-9

    "Getting Started: Accepting the
    Regions You Own–or Which
    Own You"................. DLB-105

    Tribute to James Dickey ............. Y-97

McDougall, Colin 1917-1984 .......... DLB-68

McDowell, Katharine Sherwood Bonner
    1849-1883 ................. DLB-202, 239

Obolensky McDowell
    [publishing house] ................ DLB-46

McEwan, Ian 1948- ............. DLB-14, 194

McFadden, David 1940- ............. DLB-60

McFall, Frances Elizabeth Clarke
    (see Grand, Sarah)

McFarland, Ron 1942- ............. DLB-256

McFarlane, Leslie 1902-1977 .......... DLB-88

McFee, William 1881-1966............ DLB-153

McGahern, John 1934- ......... DLB-14, 231

McGee, Thomas D'Arcy 1825-1868 ..... DLB-99

McGeehan, W. O. 1879-1933........DLB-25, 171

McGill, Ralph 1898-1969 ............. DLB-29

McGinley, Phyllis 1905-1978 ....... DLB-11, 48

| | | |
|---|---|---|
| McGinniss, Joe 1942- ............... DLB-185 | Mead, Matthew 1924- ............... DLB-40 | Mergerle, Johann Ulrich (see Abraham ä Sancta Clara) |
| McGirt, James E. 1874-1930 ........... DLB-50 | Mead, Taylor ?- .................... DLB-16 | Mérimée, Prosper 1803-1870 ....... DLB-119, 192 |
| McGlashan and Gill ................ DLB-106 | Meany, Tom 1903-1964 .............. DLB-171 | Merivale, John Herman 1779-1844 ...... DLB-96 |
| McGough, Roger 1937- .............. DLB-40 | Mechthild von Magdeburg circa 1207-circa 1282 ............. DLB-138 | Meriwether, Louise 1923- ............ DLB-33 |
| McGrath, John 1935- ............... DLB-233 | Medieval Galician-Portuguese Poetry .... DLB-287 | Merlin Press ...................... DLB-112 |
| McGrath, Patrick 1950- ............. DLB-231 | Medill, Joseph 1823-1899 ............. DLB-43 | Merriam, Eve 1916-1992 .............. DLB-61 |
| McGraw-Hill ...................... DLB-46 | Medoff, Mark 1940- .................. DLB-7 | The Merriam Company ............. DLB-49 |
| McGuane, Thomas 1939- .... DLB-2, 212; Y-80 | Meek, Alexander Beaufort 1814-1865 .. DLB-3, 248 | Merril, Judith 1923-1997 ............. DLB-251 |
| Tribute to Seymour Lawrence ......... Y-94 | Meeke, Mary ?-1816? ................ DLB-116 | Tribute to Theodore Sturgeon ......... Y-85 |
| McGuckian, Medbh 1950- ............ DLB-40 | Mei, Lev Aleksandrovich 1822-1862 ..... DLB-277 | Merrill, James 1926-1995 ....... DLB-5, 165; Y-85 |
| McGuffey, William Holmes 1800-1873 .... DLB-42 | Meinke, Peter 1932- .................. DLB-5 | Merrill and Baker .................... DLB-49 |
| McGuinness, Frank 1953- ........... DLB-245 | Mejia Vallejo, Manuel 1923- ......... DLB-113 | The Mershon Company ............. DLB-49 |
| McHenry, James 1785-1845 ........... DLB-202 | Melanchthon, Philipp 1497-1560 ....... DLB-179 | Merton, Thomas 1915-1968 ....... DLB-48; Y-81 |
| McIlvanney, William 1936- ....... DLB-14, 207 | Melançon, Robert 1947- .............. DLB-60 | Merwin, W. S. 1927- ............. DLB-5, 169 |
| McIlwraith, Jean Newton 1859-1938 ...... DLB-92 | Mell, Max 1882-1971 .............. DLB-81, 124 | Julian Messner [publishing house] ........ DLB-46 |
| McIntosh, Maria Jane 1803-1878 .... DLB-239, 248 | Mellow, James R. 1926-1997 ......... DLB-111 | Mészöly, Miklós 1921- ............... DLB-232 |
| McIntyre, James 1827-1906 ........... DLB-99 | Mel'nikov, Pavel Ivanovich 1818-1883 ... DLB-238 | J. Metcalf [publishing house] ........... DLB-49 |
| McIntyre, O. O. 1884-1938 ............ DLB-25 | Meltzer, David 1937- ................. DLB-16 | Metcalf, John 1938- .................. DLB-60 |
| McKay, Claude 1889-1948 .... DLB-4, 45, 51, 117 | Meltzer, Milton 1915- ................ DLB-61 | The Methodist Book Concern .......... DLB-49 |
| The David McKay Company .......... DLB-49 | Melville, Elizabeth, Lady Culross circa 1585-1640 ................. DLB-172 | Methuen and Company .............. DLB-112 |
| McKean, William V. 1820-1903 ........ DLB-23 | Melville, Herman 1819-1891 ........ DLB-3, 74, 250; CDALB-2 | Meun, Jean de (see Roman de la Rose) |
| McKenna, Stephen 1888-1967 ........ DLB-197 | | Mew, Charlotte 1869-1928 ......... DLB-19, 135 |
| The McKenzie Trust .................... Y-96 | The Melville Society ................. Y-01 | Mewshaw, Michael 1943- ............... Y-80 |
| McKerrow, R. B. 1872-1940 .......... DLB-201 | Melville, James (Roy Peter Martin) 1931- ........ DLB-276 | Tribute to Albert Erskine ............ Y-93 |
| McKinley, Robin 1952- .............. DLB-52 | Mena, Juan de 1411-1456 ............. DLB-286 | Meyer, Conrad Ferdinand 1825-1898 .... DLB-129 |
| McKnight, Reginald 1956- ........... DLB-234 | Mena, María Cristina 1893-1965 .... DLB-209, 221 | Meyer, E. Y. 1946- .................. DLB-75 |
| McLachlan, Alexander 1818-1896 ........ DLB-99 | Menander 342-341 B.C.-circa 292-291 B.C. .................... DLB-176; CDWLB-1 | Meyer, Eugene 1875-1959 .............. DLB-29 |
| McLaren, Floris Clark 1904-1978 ....... DLB-68 | | Meyer, Michael 1921-2000 ............ DLB-155 |
| McLaverty, Michael 1907- ............ DLB-15 | Menantes (see Hunold, Christian Friedrich) | Meyers, Jeffrey 1939- ................ DLB-111 |
| McLean, Duncan 1964- .............. DLB-267 | Mencke, Johann Burckhard 1674-1732 ... DLB-168 | Meynell, Alice 1847-1922 .......... DLB-19, 98 |
| McLean, John R. 1848-1916 ........... DLB-23 | Mencken, H. L. 1880-1956 ........ DLB-11, 29, 63, 137, 222; CDALB-4 | Meynell, Viola 1885-1956 ............ DLB-153 |
| McLean, William L. 1852-1931 ......... DLB-25 | "Berlin, February, 1917" .............. Y-00 | Meyrink, Gustav 1868-1932 ........... DLB-81 |
| McLennan, William 1856-1904 .......... DLB-92 | From the Initial Issue of American Mercury (January 1924) ................. DLB-137 | Mézières, Philipe de circa 1327-1405 ..... DLB-208 |
| McLoughlin Brothers ................ DLB-49 | | Michael, Ib 1945- ................... DLB-214 |
| McLuhan, Marshall 1911-1980 .......... DLB-88 | Mencken and Nietzsche: An Unpublished Excerpt from H. L. Mencken's My Life as Author and Editor ....................... Y-93 | Michael, Livi 1960- ................. DLB-267 |
| McMaster, John Bach 1852-1932 ........ DLB-47 | | Michaëlis, Karen 1872-1950 ............ DLB-214 |
| McMurtry, Larry 1936- ...... DLB-2, 143, 256; Y-80, 87; CDALB-6 | | Michaels, Leonard 1933- ............ DLB-130 |
| | Mendelssohn, Moses 1729-1786 ......... DLB-97 | Michaux, Henri 1899-1984 ........... DLB-258 |
| McNally, Terrence 1939- .......... DLB-7, 249 | Mendes, Catulle 1841-1909 ........... DLB-217 | Micheaux, Oscar 1884-1951 ........... DLB-50 |
| McNeil, Florence 1937- .............. DLB-60 | Méndez M., Miguel 1930- ............ DLB-82 | Michel of Northgate, Dan circa 1265-circa 1340 .............. DLB-146 |
| McNeile, Herman Cyril 1888-1937 ...... DLB-77 | The Mercantile Library of New York ....... Y-96 | Micheline, Jack 1929-1998 ............. DLB-16 |
| McNickle, D'Arcy 1904-1977 ....... DLB-175, 212 | Mercer, Cecil William (see Yates, Dornford) | Michener, James A. 1907?-1997 ........... DLB-6 |
| McPhee, John 1931- ........... DLB-185, 275 | Mercer, David 1928-1980 ............. DLB-13 | Micklejohn, George circa 1717-1818 ...... DLB-31 |
| McPherson, James Alan 1943- ..... DLB-38, 244 | Mercer, John 1704-1768 .............. DLB-31 | Middle Hill Press ................... DLB-106 |
| McPherson, Sandra 1943- ............. Y-86 | Mercer, Johnny 1909-1976 ........... DLB-265 | Middleton, Christopher 1926- ......... DLB-40 |
| McTaggart, J. M. E. 1866-1925 ........ DLB-262 | Meredith, George 1828-1909 .... DLB-18, 35, 57, 159; CDBLB-4 | Middleton, Richard 1882-1911 ........ DLB-156 |
| McWhirter, George 1939- ............ DLB-60 | | Middleton, Stanley 1919- ............. DLB-14 |
| McWilliam, Candia 1955- ............ DLB-267 | Meredith, Louisa Anne 1812-1895 .. DLB-166, 230 | Middleton, Thomas 1580-1627 ........ DLB-58 |
| McWilliams, Carey 1905-1980 ......... DLB-137 | Meredith, Owen (see Lytton, Edward Robert Bulwer) | Miegel, Agnes 1879-1964 .............. DLB-56 |
| "The Nation's Future," Carey McWilliams's Editorial Policy in Nation .................... DLB-137 | | Mieželaitis, Eduardas 1919-1997 ........ DLB-220 |
| | Meredith, William 1919- ............... DLB-5 | Miguéis, José Rodrigues 1901-1980 ...... DLB-287 |
| Mda, Zakes 1948- ................. DLB-225 | Meres, Francis Palladis Tamia, Wits Treasurie (1598) [excerpt] .............. DLB-172 | Mihailović, Dragoslav 1930- .......... DLB-181 |
| Mead, George Herbert 1863-1931 ....... DLB-270 | | Mihalić, Slavko 1928- ............... DLB-181 |
| Mead, L. T. 1844-1914 .............. DLB-141 | | |

Mikhailov, A.
(see Sheller, Aleksandr Konstantinovich)

Mikhailov, Mikhail Larionovich
1829-1865 .................... DLB-238

Mikhailovsky, Nikolai Konstantinovich
1842-1904 .................... DLB-277

Miles, Josephine 1911-1985 ........... DLB-48

Miles, Susan (Ursula Wyllie Roberts)
1888-1975 .................... DLB-240

Miliković, Branko 1934-1961 ......... DLB-181

Milius, John 1944- ................. DLB-44

Mill, James 1773-1836 ........ DLB-107, 158, 262

Mill, John Stuart
1806-1873 ...... DLB-55, 190, 262; CDBLB-4

Thoughts on Poetry and Its Varieties
(1833) ..................... DLB-32

Andrew Millar [publishing house] ...... DLB-154

Millar, Kenneth
1915-1983 .......... DLB-2, 226; Y-83; DS-6

Millay, Edna St. Vincent
1892-1950 ........ DLB-45, 249; CDALB-4

Millen, Sarah Gertrude 1888-1968 ...... DLB-225

Miller, Andrew 1960- ............. DLB-267

Miller, Arthur 1915- .... DLB-7, 266; CDALB-1

The Arthur Miller Society ........... Y-01

Miller, Caroline 1903-1992 ............. DLB-9

Miller, Eugene Ethelbert 1950- ....... DLB-41

Tribute to Julian Mayfield .......... Y-84

Miller, Heather Ross 1939- ......... DLB-120

Miller, Henry
1891-1980 ...... DLB-4, 9; Y-80; CDALB-5

Miller, Hugh 1802-1856 ............. DLB-190

Miller, J. Hillis 1928- .............. DLB-67

Miller, Jason 1939- ................. DLB-7

Miller, Joaquin 1839-1913 .......... DLB-186

Miller, May 1899-1995 ............... DLB-41

Miller, Paul 1906-1991 .............. DLB-127

Miller, Perry 1905-1963 .......... DLB-17, 63

Miller, Sue 1943- .................. DLB-143

Miller, Vassar 1924-1998 ............ DLB-105

Miller, Walter M., Jr. 1923-1996 ....... DLB-8

Miller, Webb 1892-1940 .............. DLB-29

James Miller [publishing house] ....... DLB-49

Millett, Kate 1934- ................ DLB-246

Millhauser, Steven 1943- ............. DLB-2

Millican, Arthenia J. Bates 1920- ..... DLB-38

Milligan, Alice 1866-1953 ........... DLB-240

Mills, Magnus 1954- ................ DLB-267

Mills and Boon .................... DLB-112

Milman, Henry Hart 1796-1868 ....... DLB-96

Milne, A. A. 1882-1956 .... DLB-10, 77, 100, 160

Milner, Ron 1938- ................. DLB-38

William Milner [publishing house] ..... DLB-106

Milnes, Richard Monckton (Lord Houghton)
1809-1885 ............ DLB-32, 184

Milton, John
1608-1674 ..... DLB-131, 151, 281; CDBLB-2

The Milton Society of America ........ Y-00

Miłosz, Czesław 1911- ... DLB-215; CDWLB-4

Minakami Tsutomu 1919- ........... DLB-182

Minamoto no Sanetomo 1192-1219 ..... DLB-203

The Minerva Press .................. DLB-154

Minnesang circa 1150-1280 ........... DLB-138

The Music of Minnesang .......... DLB-138

Minns, Susan 1839-1938 ............. DLB-140

Minton, Balch and Company .......... DLB-46

Mirbeau, Octave 1848-1917 ...... DLB-123, 192

Mirk, John died after 1414? ......... DLB-146

Miron, Gaston 1928-1996 ............ DLB-60

A Mirror for Magistrates ............. DLB-167

Mishima Yukio 1925-1970 ........... DLB-182

Mistral, Gabriela 1889-1957 ......... DLB-283

Mitchel, Jonathan 1624-1668 ......... DLB-24

Mitchell, Adrian 1932- ............. DLB-40

Mitchell, Donald Grant
1822-1908 .......... DLB-1, 243; DS-13

Mitchell, Gladys 1901-1983 ......... DLB-77

Mitchell, James Leslie 1901-1935 ...... DLB-15

Mitchell, John (see Slater, Patrick)

Mitchell, John Ames 1845-1918 ....... DLB-79

Mitchell, Joseph 1908-1996 ....... DLB-185; Y-96

Mitchell, Julian 1935- ............. DLB-14

Mitchell, Ken 1940- ............... DLB-60

Mitchell, Langdon 1862-1935 .......... DLB-7

Mitchell, Loften 1919- ............. DLB-38

Mitchell, Margaret 1900-1949 .. DLB-9; CDALB-7

Mitchell, S. Weir 1829-1914 ......... DLB-202

Mitchell, W. J. T. 1942- ........... DLB-246

Mitchell, W. O. 1914-1998 .......... DLB-88

Mitchison, Naomi Margaret (Haldane)
1897-1999 ......... DLB-160, 191, 255

Mitford, Mary Russell 1787-1855 ... DLB-110, 116

Mitford, Nancy 1904-1973 ........... DLB-191

Mittelholzer, Edgar
1909-1965 .......... DLB-117; CDWLB-3

Mitterer, Erika 1906- .............. DLB-85

Mitterer, Felix 1948- .............. DLB-124

Mitternacht, Johann Sebastian
1613-1679 .................... DLB-168

Miyamoto Yuriko 1899-1951 ......... DLB-180

Mizener, Arthur 1907-1988 .......... DLB-103

Mo, Timothy 1950- ................ DLB-194

Moberg, Vilhelm 1898-1973 ......... DLB-259

Modern Age Books .................. DLB-46

Modern Language Association of America
The Modern Language Association of
America Celebrates Its Centennial ... Y-84

The Modern Library ................ DLB-46

Modiano, Patrick 1945- ............. DLB-83

Moffat, Yard and Company .......... DLB-46

Moffet, Thomas 1553-1604 .......... DLB-136

Mofolo, Thomas 1876-1948 .......... DLB-225

Mohr, Nicholasa 1938- ............. DLB-145

Moix, Ana María 1947- ............ DLB-134

Molesworth, Louisa 1839-1921 ....... DLB-135

Molière (Jean-Baptiste Poquelin)
1622-1673 .................... DLB-268

Möllhausen, Balduin 1825-1905 ...... DLB-129

Molnár, Ferenc 1878-1952 ... DLB-215; CDWLB-4

Molnár, Miklós (see Mészöly, Miklós)

Momaday, N. Scott
1934- ....... DLB-143, 175, 256; CDALB-7

Monkhouse, Allan 1858-1936 ......... DLB-10

Monro, Harold 1879-1932 ........... DLB-19

Monroe, Harriet 1860-1936 ........ DLB-54, 91

Monsarrat, Nicholas 1910-1979 ....... DLB-15

Montagu, Lady Mary Wortley
1689-1762 .................. DLB-95, 101

Montague, C. E. 1867-1928 .......... DLB-197

Montague, John 1929- .............. DLB-40

Montale, Eugenio 1896-1981 ......... DLB-114

Montalvo, Garci Rodríguez de
ca. 1450?-before 1505 ............ DLB-286

Montalvo, José 1946-1994 ........... DLB-209

Monterroso, Augusto 1921-2003 ...... DLB-145

Montesquiou, Robert de 1855-1921 .... DLB-217

Montgomerie, Alexander
circa 1550?-1598 ............... DLB-167

Montgomery, James 1771-1854 ..... DLB-93, 158

Montgomery, John 1919- ............ DLB-16

Montgomery, Lucy Maud
1874-1942 ............. DLB-92; DS-14

Montgomery, Marion 1925- ........... DLB-6

Montgomery, Robert Bruce (see Crispin, Edmund)

Montherlant, Henry de 1896-1972 ...... DLB-72

The Monthly Review 1749-1844 ......... DLB-110

Montigny, Louvigny de 1876-1955 ..... DLB-92

Montoya, José 1932- .............. DLB-122

Moodie, John Wedderburn Dunbar
1797-1869 .................... DLB-99

Moodie, Susanna 1803-1885 .......... DLB-99

Moody, Joshua circa 1633-1697 ........ DLB-24

Moody, William Vaughn 1869-1910 ... DLB-7, 54

Moorcock, Michael 1939- .... DLB-14, 231, 261

Moore, Alan 1953- ................ DLB-261

Moore, Brian 1921-1999 ............ DLB-251

Moore, Catherine L. 1911-1987 ........ DLB-8

Moore, Clement Clarke 1779-1863 ..... DLB-42

Moore, Dora Mavor 1888-1979 ........ DLB-92

Moore, G. E. 1873-1958 ............ DLB-262

Moore, George 1852-1933 .... DLB-10, 18, 57, 135

Literature at Nurse, or Circulating Morals
(1885) .................... DLB-18

Moore, Lorrie 1957- .............. DLB-234

Moore, Marianne
1887-1972 ....... DLB-45; DS-7; CDALB-5

International Marianne Moore Society ... Y-98

Moore, Mavor 1919- .............. DLB-88

Moore, Richard 1927- ............. DLB-105

"The No Self, the Little Self, and
the Poets" ................. DLB-105

Moore, T. Sturge 1870-1944 ............DLB-19
Moore, Thomas 1779-1852 .........DLB-96, 144
Moore, Ward 1903-1978 ................DLB-8
Moore, Wilstach, Keys and Company ....DLB-49
Moorehead, Alan 1901-1983 ............DLB-204
Moorhouse, Geoffrey 1931- .........DLB-204
The Moorland-Spingarn Research
    Center .........................DLB-76
Moorman, Mary C. 1905-1994 ........DLB-155
Mora, Pat 1942- ....................DLB-209
Moraga, Cherríe 1952- ..........DLB-82, 249
Morales, Alejandro 1944- ............DLB-82
Morales, Mario Roberto 1947- .......DLB-145
Morales, Rafael 1919- .............DLB-108
Morality Plays: *Mankind* circa 1450-1500
    and *Everyman* circa 1500 ........DLB-146
Morand, Paul (1888-1976) .............DLB-65
Morante, Elsa 1912-1985 ..............DLB-177
Morata, Olympia Fulvia 1526-1555 ......DLB-179
Moravia, Alberto 1907-1990 ..........DLB-177
Mordaunt, Elinor 1872-1942 ..........DLB-174
Mordovtsev, Daniil Lukich 1830-1905 ...DLB-238
More, Hannah
    1745-1833 .........DLB-107, 109, 116, 158
More, Henry 1614-1687 ........DLB-126, 252
More, Sir Thomas
    1477/1478-1535 ...........DLB-136, 281
Morejón, Nancy 1944- .............DLB-283
Morency, Pierre 1942- ...............DLB-60
Moreno, Dorinda 1939- .............DLB-122
Moretti, Marino 1885-1979 ........DLB-114, 264
Morgan, Berry 1919- .................DLB-6
Morgan, Charles 1894-1958 ........DLB-34, 100
Morgan, Edmund S. 1916- ............DLB-17
Morgan, Edwin 1920- ................DLB-27
Morgan, John Pierpont 1837-1913 .......DLB-140
Morgan, John Pierpont, Jr. 1867-1943 ....DLB-140
Morgan, Robert 1944- ...............DLB-120
Morgan, Sydney Owenson, Lady
    1776?-1859 ................DLB-116, 158
Morgner, Irmtraud 1933-1990 ...........DLB-75
Morhof, Daniel Georg 1639-1691 .......DLB-164
Mori Ōgai 1862-1922 ................DLB-180
Móricz, Zsigmond 1879-1942 ..........DLB-215
Morier, James Justinian
    1782 or 1783?-1849 ................DLB-116
Mörike, Eduard 1804-1875 ............DLB-133
Morin, Paul 1889-1963 ................DLB-92
Morison, Richard 1514?-1556 .........DLB-136
Morison, Samuel Eliot 1887-1976 .......DLB-17
Morison, Stanley 1889-1967 ..........DLB-201
Moritz, Karl Philipp 1756-1793 ........DLB-94
*Moriz von Craûn* circa 1220-1230 ......DLB-138
Morley, Christopher 1890-1957 .........DLB-9
Morley, John 1838-1923 ....... DLB-57, 144, 190
Morris, George Pope 1802-1864 .........DLB-73

Morris, James Humphrey (see Morris, Jan)
Morris, Jan 1926- ..................DLB-204
Morris, Lewis 1833-1907 ..............DLB-35
Morris, Margaret 1737-1816 ..........DLB-200
Morris, Richard B. 1904-1989 ..........DLB-17
Morris, William 1834-1896
    .... DLB-18, 35, 57, 156, 178, 184; CDBLB-4
Morris, Willie 1934-1999 ..............Y-80
    Tribute to Irwin Shaw ..............Y-84
    Tribute to James Dickey .............Y-97
Morris, Wright
    1910-1998 ......... DLB-2, 206, 218; Y-81
Morrison, Arthur 1863-1945 .... DLB-70, 135, 197
Morrison, Charles Clayton 1874-1966 .....DLB-91
Morrison, John 1904-1998 ............DLB-260
Morrison, Toni 1931-
    ........ DLB-6, 33, 143; Y-81, 93; CDALB-6
    Nobel Lecture 1993 ..................Y-93
Morrissy, Mary 1957- ................DLB-267
William Morrow and Company ........DLB-46
Morse, James Herbert 1841-1923 .......DLB-71
Morse, Jedidiah 1761-1826 .............DLB-37
Morse, John T., Jr. 1840-1937 ..........DLB-47
Morselli, Guido 1912-1973 ............DLB-177
*Morte Arthure*, the *Alliterative* and the
    *Stanzaic* circa 1350-1400 ............DLB-146
Mortimer, Favell Lee 1802-1878 ........DLB-163
Mortimer, John
    1923- ........DLB-13, 245, 271; CDBLB-8
Morton, Carlos 1942- ................DLB-122
Morton, H. V. 1892-1979 .............DLB-195
John P. Morton and Company ..........DLB-49
Morton, Nathaniel 1613-1685 ...........DLB-24
Morton, Sarah Wentworth 1759-1846 .....DLB-37
Morton, Thomas circa 1579-circa 1647 ....DLB-24
Moscherosch, Johann Michael
    1601-1669 .....................DLB-164
Humphrey Moseley
    [publishing house] ................DLB-170
Möser, Justus 1720-1794 ..............DLB-97
Mosley, Nicholas 1923- ..........DLB-14, 207
Moss, Arthur 1889-1969 ...............DLB-4
Moss, Howard 1922-1987 ...............DLB-5
Moss, Thylias 1954- ................DLB-120
Motion, Andrew 1952- ................DLB-40
Motley, John Lothrop
    1814-1877 ...........DLB-1, 30, 59, 235
Motley, Willard 1909-1965 ........DLB-76, 143
Mott, Lucretia 1793-1880 .............DLB-239
Benjamin Motte Jr.
    [publishing house] ................DLB-154
Motteux, Peter Anthony 1663-1718 ......DLB-80
Mottram, R. H. 1883-1971 .............DLB-36
Mount, Ferdinand 1939- ..............DLB-231
Mouré, Erin 1955- ...................DLB-60
Mourning Dove (Humishuma) between
    1882 and 1888?-1936 .........DLB-175, 221

Movies
    Fiction into Film, 1928-1975: A List
    of Movies Based on the Works
    of Authors in British Novelists,
    1930-1959 ....................DLB-15
    Movies from Books, 1920-1974 .......DLB-9
Mowat, Farley 1921- ................DLB-68
A. R. Mowbray and Company,
    Limited .......................DLB-106
Mowrer, Edgar Ansel 1892-1977 .........DLB-29
Mowrer, Paul Scott 1887-1971 ..........DLB-29
Edward Moxon [publishing house] ......DLB-106
Joseph Moxon [publishing house] .......DLB-170
Moyes, Patricia 1923-2000 .............DLB-276
Mphahlele, Es'kia (Ezekiel)
    1919- ............DLB-125, 225; CDWLB-3
Mrożek, Sławomir 1930- ... DLB-232; CDWLB-4
Mtshali, Oswald Mbuyiseni
    1940- ....................DLB-125, 225
*Mucedorus* ........................DLB-62
Mudford, William 1782-1848 ..........DLB-159
Mueller, Lisel 1924- ................DLB-105
Muhajir, El (see Marvin X)
Muhajir, Nazzam Al Fitnah (see Marvin X)
Mühlbach, Luise 1814-1873 ...........DLB-133
Muir, Edwin 1887-1959 ........DLB-20, 100, 191
Muir, Helen 1937- ..................DLB-14
Muir, John 1838-1914 ..........DLB-186, 275
Muir, Percy 1894-1979 ..............DLB-201
Mujū Ichien 1226-1312 ..............DLB-203
Mukherjee, Bharati 1940- .........DLB-60, 218
Mulcaster, Richard 1531 or 1532-1611 ...DLB-167
Muldoon, Paul 1951- ................DLB-40
Müller, Friedrich (see Müller, Maler)
Müller, Heiner 1929-1995 .............DLB-124
Müller, Maler 1749-1825 ..............DLB-94
Muller, Marcia 1944- ................DLB-226
Müller, Wilhelm 1794-1827 ............DLB-90
Mumford, Lewis 1895-1990 ............DLB-63
Munby, A. N. L. 1913-1974 ...........DLB-201
Munby, Arthur Joseph 1828-1910 ........DLB-35
Munday, Anthony 1560-1633 ....... DLB-62, 172
Mundt, Clara (see Mühlbach, Luise)
Mundt, Theodore 1808-1861 ..........DLB-133
Munford, Robert circa 1737-1783 ........DLB-31
Mungoshi, Charles 1947- ............DLB-157
Munk, Kaj 1898-1944 ................DLB-214
Munonye, John 1929- ................DLB-117
Munro, Alice 1931- ..................DLB-53
George Munro [publishing house] .......DLB-49
Munro, H. H.
    1870-1916 .........DLB-34, 162; CDBLB-5
Munro, Neil 1864-1930 ...............DLB-156
Norman L. Munro [publishing house] .....DLB-49
Munroe, Kirk 1850-1930 ..............DLB-42
Munroe and Francis .................DLB-49
James Munroe and Company ..........DLB-49

Joel Munsell [publishing house] ......... DLB-49
Munsey, Frank A. 1854-1925 ........ DLB-25, 91
Frank A. Munsey and Company ....... DLB-49
Murakami Haruki 1949- ............ DLB-182
Murav'ev, Mikhail Nikitich 1757-1807 ... DLB-150
Murdoch, Iris 1919-1999
........... DLB-14, 194, 233; CDBLB-8
Murdock, James
From *Sketches of Modern Philosophy* ....... DS-5
Murdoch, Rupert 1931- ............ DLB-127
Murfree, Mary N. 1850-1922 ........ DLB-12, 74
Murger, Henry 1822-1861 ............ DLB-119
Murger, Louis-Henri (see Murger, Henry)
Murner, Thomas 1475-1537 ............. DLB-179
Muro, Amado 1915-1971 ............ DLB-82
Murphy, Arthur 1727-1805 ........ DLB-89, 142
Murphy, Beatrice M. 1908-1992 ........ DLB-76
Murphy, Dervla 1931- ............ DLB-204
Murphy, Emily 1868-1933 ............ DLB-99
Murphy, Jack 1923-1980 ............ DLB-241
Murphy, John H., III 1916- ............ DLB-127
Murphy, Richard 1927-1993 ............ DLB-40
John Murphy and Company ........... DLB-49
Murray, Albert L. 1916- ............ DLB-38
Murray, Gilbert 1866-1957 ............. DLB-10
Murray, Jim 1919-1998 ............. DLB-241
John Murray [publishing house] ........ DLB-154
Murry, John Middleton 1889-1957 ...... DLB-149
"The Break-Up of the Novel"
(1922) ..................... DLB-36
Murry, John Middleton, Jr. (see Cowper, Richard)
Murray, Judith Sargent 1751-1820 .... DLB-37, 200
Murray, Pauli 1910-1985 ............. DLB-41
Musäus, Johann Karl August 1735-1787 ... DLB-97
Muschg, Adolf 1934- ................. DLB-75
Musil, Robert
1880-1942 ........ DLB-81, 124; CDWLB-2
*Muspilli* circa 790-circa 850 ............ DLB-148
Musset, Alfred de 1810-1857 ....... DLB-192, 217
Benjamin B. Mussey
and Company ................... DLB-49
Mutafchieva, Vera 1929- ............ DLB-181
Mutis, Alvaro 1923- ............ DLB-283
Mwangi, Meja 1948- ............ DLB-125
Myers, Frederic W. H. 1843-1901 ...... DLB-190
Myers, Gustavus 1872-1942 ............ DLB-47
Myers, L. H. 1881-1944 ............. DLB-15
Myers, Walter Dean 1937- ............ DLB-33
Myerson, Julie 1960- ............ DLB-267
Mykolaitis-Putinas,
Vincas 1893-1967 ................ DLB-220
Myles, Eileen 1949- ............ DLB-193
Myrdal, Jan 1927- ............ DLB-257
Mystery
1985: The Year of the Mystery:
A Symposium .................. Y-85
Comments from Other Writers ........ Y-85

The Second Annual New York Festival
of Mystery .................... Y-00
Why I Read Mysteries ................ Y-85
Why I Write Mysteries: Night and Day,
by Michael Collins .............. Y-85

# N

Na Prous Boneta circa 1296-1328 ...... DLB-208
Nabl, Franz 1883-1974 ............. DLB-81
Nabakov, Véra 1902-1991 ............ Y-91
Nabokov, Vladimir 1899-1977 .. DLB-2, 244, 278;
Y-80, 91; DS-3; CDALB-1
International Nabokov Society .......... Y-99
An Interview [On Nabokov], by
Fredson Bowers ................ Y-80
Nabokov Festival at Cornell ............ Y-83
The Vladimir Nabokov Archive in the
Berg Collection of the New York
Public Library: An Overview ....... Y-91
The Vladimir Nabokov Society ......... Y-01
Nádaši, Ladislav (see Jégé)
Naden, Constance 1858-1889 .......... DLB-199
Nadezhdin, Nikolai Ivanovich
1804-1856 .................... DLB-198
Nadson, Semen Iakovlevich 1862-1887 ...DLB-277
Naevius circa 265 B.C.-201 B.C. ....... DLB-211
Nafis and Cornish .................. DLB-49
Nagai Kafū 1879-1959 ............... DLB-180
Nagel, Ernest 1901-1985 .............DLB-279
Naipaul, Shiva 1945-1985 .........DLB-157; Y-85
Naipaul, V. S. 1932- ....... DLB-125, 204, 207;
Y-85, Y-01; CDBLB-8; CDWLB-3
Nobel Lecture 2001: "Two Worlds" ..... Y-01
Nakagami Kenji 1946-1992 ........... DLB-182
Nakano-in Masatada no Musume (see Nijō, Lady)
Nałkowska, Zofia 1884-1954 ......... DLB-215
Namora, Fernando 1919-1989 ........ DLB-287
Joseph Nancrede [publishing house] ..... DLB-49
Naranjo, Carmen 1930- ............. DLB-145
Narbikova, Valeriia Spartakovna
1958- .................... DLB-285
Narezhny, Vasilii Trofimovich
1780-1825 ................... DLB-198
Narrache, Jean (Emile Coderre)
1893-1970 ................... DLB-92
Nasby, Petroleum Vesuvius (see Locke, David Ross)
Eveleigh Nash [publishing house] ....... DLB-112
Nash, Ogden 1902-1971 ............. DLB-11
Nashe, Thomas 1567-1601? ............ DLB-167
Nason, Jerry 1910-1986 ............ DLB-241
Nasr, Seyyed Hossein 1933- ...........DLB-279
Nast, Condé 1873-1942 ............. DLB-91
Nast, Thomas 1840-1902 ............ DLB-188
Nastasijević, Momčilo 1894-1938 ....... DLB-147
Nathan, George Jean 1882-1958 ........ DLB-137
Nathan, Robert 1894-1985 ............ DLB-9
National Book Critics Circle Awards ..... Y-00-01
The National Jewish Book Awards ......... Y-85

Natsume Sōseki 1867-1916 ........... DLB-180
Naughton, Bill 1910-1992 ............ DLB-13
Navarro, Joe 1953- ................ DLB-209
Naylor, Gloria 1950- .................DLB-173
Nazor, Vladimir 1876-1949 ............DLB-147
Ndebele, Njabulo 1948- ........DLB-157, 225
Neagoe, Peter 1881-1960 ............. DLB-4
Neal, John 1793-1876 ....... DLB-1, 59, 243
Neal, Joseph C. 1807-1847 ............ DLB-11
Neal, Larry 1937-1981 ............... DLB-38
The Neale Publishing Company ........ DLB-49
Nebel, Frederick 1903-1967 ........... DLB-226
Nebrija, Antonio de 1442 or 1444-1522.. DLB-286
F. Tennyson Neely [publishing house] .... DLB-49
Negoițescu, Ion 1921-1993 ........... DLB-220
Negri, Ada 1870-1945 ................ DLB-114
Neihardt, John G. 1881-1973 ..... DLB-9, 54, 256
Neidhart von Reuental
circa 1185-circa 1240 ............. DLB-138
Neilson, John Shaw 1872-1942 ........ DLB-230
Nekrasov, Nikolai Alekseevich
1821-1877 .....................DLB-277
Neledinsky-Meletsky, Iurii Aleksandrovich
1752-1828 ..................... DLB-150
Nelligan, Emile 1879-1941 ............ DLB-92
Nelson, Alice Moore Dunbar 1875-1935 .. DLB-50
Nelson, Antonya 1961- ............. DLB-244
Nelson, Kent 1943- ................. DLB-234
Nelson, Richard K. 1941- ............DLB-275
Nelson, Thomas, and Sons [U.K.] ...... DLB-106
Nelson, Thomas, and Sons [U.S.] ........ DLB-49
Nelson, William 1908-1978 ............ DLB-103
Nelson, William Rockhill 1841-1915 ..... DLB-23
Nemerov, Howard 1920-1991 .....DLB-5, 6; Y-83
Németh, László 1901-1975 ........... DLB-215
Nepos circa 100 B.C.-post 27 B.C. ....... DLB-211
Nėris, Salomėja 1904-1945 .. DLB-220; CDWLB-4
Neruda, Pablo 1904-1973 ............. DLB-283
Nerval, Gérard de 1808-1855 ..........DLB-217
Nesbit, E. 1858-1924 .........DLB-141, 153, 178
Ness, Evaline 1911-1986 ............... DLB-61
Nestroy, Johann 1801-1862 ........... DLB-133
Nettleship, R. L. 1846-1892 ........... DLB-262
Neugeboren, Jay 1938- .............. DLB-28
Neukirch, Benjamin 1655-1729 ........ DLB-168
Neumann, Alfred 1895-1952 ........... DLB-56
Neumann, Ferenc (see Molnár, Ferenc)
Neumark, Georg 1621-1681 ........... DLB-164
Neumeister, Erdmann 1671-1756 ....... DLB-168
Nevins, Allan 1890-1971 ..........DLB-17; DS-17
Nevinson, Henry Woodd 1856-1941.... DLB-135
The New American Library ........... DLB-46
New Directions Publishing Corporation .. DLB-46
*The New Monthly Magazine* 1814-1884 .... DLB-110
*New York Times Book Review* ................ Y-82

| | | |
|---|---|---|
| John Newbery [publishing house] . . . . . . . DLB-154 | "The Practice of Biography," in *The English Sense of Humour and Other Essays* . . . . . . . . . . . . . . . . DLB-149 | Wole Soyinka . . . . . . . . . . . . . . . . . . . . . . Y-86 |
| Newbolt, Henry 1862-1938 . . . . . . . . . . . . DLB-19 | | Wisława Szymborska . . . . . . . . . . . . . . . . Y-96 |
| Newbound, Bernard Slade (see Slade, Bernard) | | Derek Walcott. . . . . . . . . . . . . . . . . . . . . Y-92 |
| Newby, Eric 1919- . . . . . . . . . . . . . . . DLB-204 | Nicolson, Nigel 1917- . . . . . . . . . . . . . . DLB-155 | Gao Xingjian. . . . . . . . . . . . . . . . . . . . . . Y-00 |
| Newby, P. H. 1918- . . . . . . . . . . . . . . . . DLB-15 | Niebuhr, Reinhold 1892-1971 . . . . . DLB-17; DS-17 | Nobre, António 1867-1900. . . . . . . . . . . . DLB-287 |
| Thomas Cautley Newby [publishing house] . . . . . . . . . . . . . . . DLB-106 | Niedecker, Lorine 1903-1970. . . . . . . . . . . DLB-48 | Nodier, Charles 1780-1844 . . . . . . . . . . . DLB-119 |
| | Nieman, Lucius W. 1857-1935. . . . . . . . . . DLB-25 | Noël, Marie (Marie Mélanie Rouget) 1883-1967 . . . . . . . . . . . . . . . . . . . . DLB-258 |
| Newcomb, Charles King 1820-1894 . . . DLB-1, 223 | Nietzsche, Friedrich 1844-1900 . . . . . . . . . . . DLB-129; CDWLB-2 | |
| Newell, Peter 1862-1924 . . . . . . . . . . . . . DLB-42 | | Noel, Roden 1834-1894. . . . . . . . . . . . . . . DLB-35 |
| Newell, Robert Henry 1836-1901 . . . . . . . DLB-11 | Mencken and Nietzsche: An Unpublished Excerpt from H. L. Mencken's *My Life as Author and Editor* . . . . . . . . . . . . . . Y-93 | Nogami Yaeko 1885-1985 . . . . . . . . . . . . DLB-180 |
| Newhouse, Samuel I. 1895-1979 . . . . . . . DLB-127 | | Nogo, Rajko Petrov 1945- . . . . . . . . . . . DLB-181 |
| Newman, Cecil Earl 1903-1976 . . . . . . . . DLB-127 | | Nolan, William F. 1928- . . . . . . . . . . . . . DLB-8 |
| Newman, David 1937- . . . . . . . . . . . . . . DLB-44 | Nievo, Stanislao 1928- . . . . . . . . . . . . . DLB-196 | Tribute to Raymond Chandler . . . . . . . . . Y-88 |
| Newman, Frances 1883-1928. . . . . . . . . . . . . Y-80 | Niggli, Josefina 1910-1983 . . . . . . . . . . . . . . Y-80 | Noland, C. F. M. 1810?-1858 . . . . . . . . . . DLB-11 |
| Newman, Francis William 1805-1897 . . . . DLB-190 | Nightingale, Florence 1820-1910 . . . . . . . DLB-166 | Noma Hiroshi 1915-1991 . . . . . . . . . . . . DLB-182 |
| Newman, John Henry 1801-1890 . . DLB-18, 32, 55 | Nijō, Lady (Nakano-in Masatada no Musume) 1258-after 1306 . . . . . . . . . . . . . . . DLB-203 | Nonesuch Press . . . . . . . . . . . . . . . . . . . DLB-112 |
| Mark Newman [publishing house]. . . . . . . DLB-49 | | Creative Nonfiction . . . . . . . . . . . . . . . . . . Y-02 |
| Newmarch, Rosa Harriet 1857-1940 . . . . . DLB-240 | Nijō Yoshimoto 1320-1388 . . . . . . . . . . . DLB-203 | Noon, Jeff 1957- . . . . . . . . . . . . . . . . . DLB-267 |
| George Newnes Limited . . . . . . . . . . . . . DLB-112 | Nikitin, Ivan Savvich 1824-1861 . . . . . . . . DLB-277 | Noonan, Robert Phillipe (see Tressell, Robert) |
| Newsome, Effie Lee 1885-1979 . . . . . . . . . DLB-76 | Nikitin, Nikolai Nikolaevich 1895-1963 . . DLB-272 | Noonday Press. . . . . . . . . . . . . . . . . . . . . DLB-46 |
| Newton, A. Edward 1864-1940 . . . . . . . . DLB-140 | Nikolev, Nikolai Petrovich 1758-1815. . . . DLB-150 | Noone, John 1936- . . . . . . . . . . . . . . . . DLB-14 |
| Newton, Sir Isaac 1642-1727 . . . . . . . . . . DLB-252 | Niles, Hezekiah 1777-1839 . . . . . . . . . . . . DLB-43 | Nora, Eugenio de 1923- . . . . . . . . . . . . DLB-134 |
| Nexø, Martin Andersen 1869-1954 . . . . . DLB-214 | Nims, John Frederick 1913-1999 . . . . . . . . DLB-5 | Nordan, Lewis 1939- . . . . . . . . . . . . . . DLB-234 |
| Nezval, Vítěslav 1900-1958 . . . . . . . . . . DLB-215; CDWLB-4 | Tribute to Nancy Hale . . . . . . . . . . . . . . Y-88 | Nordbrandt, Henrik 1945- . . . . . . . . . . . DLB-214 |
| | Nin, Anaïs 1903-1977. . . . . . . . . . . DLB-2, 4, 152 | Nordhoff, Charles 1887-1947. . . . . . . . . . . . DLB-9 |
| Ngugi wa Thiong'o 1938- . . . . . . . . . . . . DLB-125; CDWLB-3 | Niño, Raúl 1961- . . . . . . . . . . . . . . . . . DLB-209 | Norén, Lars 1944- . . . . . . . . . . . . . . . . DLB-257 |
| | Nissenson, Hugh 1933- . . . . . . . . . . . . . DLB-28 | Norfolk, Lawrence 1963- . . . . . . . . . . . DLB-267 |
| Niatum, Duane 1938- . . . . . . . . . . . . . . DLB-175 | Niven, Frederick John 1878-1944. . . . . . . . DLB-92 | Norman, Charles 1904-1996 . . . . . . . . . . DLB-111 |
| The *Nibelungenlied* and the *Klage* circa 1200 . . . . . . . . . . . . . . . . . . . . DLB-138 | Niven, Larry 1938- . . . . . . . . . . . . . . . . . DLB-8 | Norman, Marsha 1947- . . . . . . . DLB-266; Y-84 |
| | Nixon, Howard M. 1909-1983 . . . . . . . . . DLB-201 | Norris, Charles G. 1881-1945 . . . . . . . . . . . DLB-9 |
| Nichol, B. P. 1944-1988. . . . . . . . . . . . . . . DLB-53 | Nizan, Paul 1905-1940. . . . . . . . . . . . . . . DLB-72 | Norris, Frank 1870-1902 . . . . . . . DLB-12, 71, 186; CDALB-3 |
| Nicholas of Cusa 1401-1464 . . . . . . . . . . DLB-115 | Njegoš, Petar II Petrović 1813-1851 . . . . . . . . . . . DLB-147; CDWLB-4 | |
| Nichols, Ann 1891?-1966. . . . . . . . . . . . . DLB-249 | | Norris, John 1657-1712. . . . . . . . . . . . . . DLB-252 |
| Nichols, Beverly 1898-1983 . . . . . . . . . . . DLB-191 | Nkosi, Lewis 1936- . . . . . . . . . . . DLB-157, 225 | Norris, Leslie 1921- . . . . . . . . . . . DLB-27, 256 |
| Nichols, Dudley 1895-1960 . . . . . . . . . . . . DLB-26 | Noah, Mordecai M. 1785-1851 . . . . . . . . . DLB-250 | Norse, Harold 1916- . . . . . . . . . . . . . . . DLB-16 |
| Nichols, Grace 1950- . . . . . . . . . . . . . . DLB-157 | Noailles, Anna de 1876-1933 . . . . . . . . . . DLB-258 | Norte, Marisela 1955- . . . . . . . . . . . . . . DLB-209 |
| Nichols, John 1940- . . . . . . . . . . . . . . . . . . Y-82 | Nobel Peace Prize The Nobel Prize and Literary Politics . . . . Y-88 | North, Marianne 1830-1890 . . . . . . . . . . DLB-174 |
| Nichols, Mary Sargeant (Neal) Gove 1810-1884 . . . . . . . . . . . . . . . . DLB-1, 243 | | North Point Press . . . . . . . . . . . . . . . . . . DLB-46 |
| | Elie Wiesel . . . . . . . . . . . . . . . . . . . . Y-86 | Nortje, Arthur 1942-1970. . . . . . . . . DLB-125, 225 |
| Nichols, Peter 1927- . . . . . . . . . . DLB-13, 245 | Nobel Prize in Literature Joseph Brodsky . . . . . . . . . . . . . . . . . . . . Y-87 | Norton, Alice Mary (see Norton, Andre) |
| Nichols, Roy F. 1896-1973. . . . . . . . . . . . . DLB-17 | | Norton, Andre 1912- . . . . . . . . . . . . DLB-8, 52 |
| Nichols, Ruth 1948- . . . . . . . . . . . . . . . . DLB-60 | Camilo José Cela. . . . . . . . . . . . . . . . . Y-89 | Norton, Andrews 1786-1853 . . . . DLB-1, 235; DS-5 |
| Nicholson, Edward Williams Byron 1849-1912 . . . . . . . . . . . . . . . . . . . DLB-184 | Dario Fo . . . . . . . . . . . . . . . . . . . . . . Y-97 | Norton, Caroline 1808-1877 . . . . DLB-21, 159, 199 |
| | Gabriel García Márquez . . . . . . . . . . . . Y-82 | Norton, Charles Eliot 1827-1908 . . . DLB-1, 64, 235 |
| Nicholson, Geoff 1953- . . . . . . . . . . . . . DLB-271 | William Golding . . . . . . . . . . . . . . . . . Y-83 | Norton, John 1606-1663 . . . . . . . . . . . . . DLB-24 |
| Nicholson, Norman 1914- . . . . . . . . . . . . DLB-27 | Nadine Gordimer . . . . . . . . . . . . . . . . Y-91 | Norton, Mary 1903-1992. . . . . . . . . . . . . DLB-160 |
| Nicholson, William 1872-1949 . . . . . . . . . DLB-141 | Günter Grass. . . . . . . . . . . . . . . . . . . . Y-99 | Norton, Thomas 1532-1584 . . . . . . . . . . . DLB-62 |
| Ní Chuilleanáin, Eiléan 1942- . . . . . . . . DLB-40 | Seamus Heaney. . . . . . . . . . . . . . . . . . . Y-95 | W. W. Norton and Company . . . . . . . . . . DLB-46 |
| Nicol, Eric 1919- . . . . . . . . . . . . . . . . . DLB-68 | Imre Kertész . . . . . . . . . . . . . . . . . . . . Y-02 | Norwood, Robert 1874-1932 . . . . . . . . . . . DLB-92 |
| Nicolai, Friedrich 1733-1811 . . . . . . . . . . . DLB-97 | Najīb Mahfūz . . . . . . . . . . . . . . . . . . . Y-88 | Nosaka Akiyuki 1930- . . . . . . . . . . . . . DLB-182 |
| Nicolas de Clamanges circa 1363-1437 . . . DLB-208 | Toni Morrison . . . . . . . . . . . . . . . . . . . Y-93 | Nossack, Hans Erich 1901-1977 . . . . . . . . DLB-69 |
| Nicolay, John G. 1832-1901 and Hay, John 1838-1905 . . . . . . . . . . . DLB-47 | V. S. Naipaul. . . . . . . . . . . . . . . . . . . . Y-01 | Notker Balbulus circa 840-912. . . . . . . . . DLB-148 |
| | Kenzaburō Ōe . . . . . . . . . . . . . . . . . . Y-94 | Notker III of Saint Gall circa 950-1022 . . . DLB-148 |
| Nicole, Pierre 1625-1695 . . . . . . . . . . . . DLB-268 | Octavio Paz . . . . . . . . . . . . . . . . . . . . Y-90 | Notker von Zweifalten ?-1095 . . . . . . . . . DLB-148 |
| Nicolson, Adela Florence Cory (see Hope, Laurence) | José Saramago . . . . . . . . . . . . . . . . . . Y-98 | |
| | Jaroslav Seifert. . . . . . . . . . . . . . . . . . . Y-84 | |
| Nicolson, Harold 1886-1968 . . . . . . . DLB-100, 149 | Claude Simon . . . . . . . . . . . . . . . . . . . Y-85 | Nourse, Alan E. 1928- . . . . . . . . . . . . . . . DLB-8 |

Novak, Slobodan 1924- .......... DLB-181
Novak, Vjenceslav 1859-1905 ......... DLB-147
Novakovich, Josip 1956- ......... DLB-244
Novalis 1772-1801 .......... DLB-90; CDWLB-2
Novaro, Mario 1868-1944 ........... DLB-114
Novás Calvo, Lino 1903-1983 ........ DLB-145
Novelists
   *Library Journal* Statements and
      Questionnaires from First Novelists .... Y-87
Novels
   *The Columbia History of the American Novel*
      A Symposium on ............ Y-92
   The Great Modern Library Scam ....... Y-98
   The Proletarian Novel ............. DLB-9
   Novels for Grown-Ups ............... Y-97
   The Year in the Novel ..... Y-87–88, Y-90–93
Novels, British
   "The Break-Up of the Novel" (1922),
      by John Middleton Murry ....... DLB-36
   The Consolidation of Opinion: Critical
      Responses to the Modernists ..... DLB-36
   "Criticism in Relation to Novels"
      (1863), by G. H. Lewes ......... DLB-21
   "Experiment in the Novel" (1929)
      [excerpt], by John D. Beresford ... DLB-36
   "The Future of the Novel" (1899), by
      Henry James ................ DLB-18
   *The Gay Science* (1866), by E. S. Dallas
      [excerpt] .................... DLB-21
   A Haughty and Proud Generation
      (1922), by Ford Madox Hueffer .. DLB-36
   Literary Effects of World War II ..... DLB-15
   "Modern Novelists –Great and Small"
      (1855), by Margaret Oliphant .... DLB-21
   The Modernists (1932),
      by Joseph Warren Beach ........ DLB-36
   A Note on Technique (1926), by
      Elizabeth A. Drew [excerpts] ..... DLB-36
   Novel-Reading: *The Works of Charles
      Dickens; The Works of W. Makepeace
      Thackeray* (1879),
      by Anthony Trollope .......... DLB-21
   Novels with a Purpose (1864), by
      Justin M'Carthy ............... DLB-21
   "On Art in Fiction" (1838),
      by Edward Bulwer ........... DLB-21
   The Present State of the English Novel
      (1892), by George Saintsbury .... DLB-18
   Representative Men and Women:
      A Historical Perspective on
      the British Novel, 1930-1960 ..... DLB-15
   "The Revolt" (1937), by Mary Colum
      [excerpts] .................... DLB-36
   "Sensation Novels" (1863), by
      H. L. Manse ................ DLB-21
   Sex, Class, Politics, and Religion [in
      the British Novel, 1930-1959] .... DLB-15
   *Time and Western Man* (1927),
      by Wyndham Lewis [excerpts] ... DLB-36
Noventa, Giacomo 1898-1960 ........ DLB-114
Novikov, Nikolai Ivanovich 1744-1818 .. DLB-150
Novomeský, Laco 1904-1976 ......... DLB-215
Nowlan, Alden 1933-1983 ........... DLB-53

Noyes, Alfred 1880-1958 ............. DLB-20
Noyes, Crosby S. 1825-1908 .......... DLB-23
Noyes, Nicholas 1647-1717 ........... DLB-24
Noyes, Theodore W. 1858-1946 ....... DLB-29
Nozick, Robert 1938-2002 ........... DLB-279
N-Town Plays circa 1468 to early
   sixteenth century ................ DLB-146
Nugent, Frank 1908-1965 ............ DLB-44
Nušić, Branislav 1864-1938 ..DLB-147; CDWLB-4
David Nutt [publishing house] ......... DLB-106
Nwapa, Flora 1931-1993 ... DLB-125; CDWLB-3
Nye, Edgar Wilson (Bill)
   1850-1896 ............. DLB-11, 23, 186
Nye, Naomi Shihab 1952- ........... DLB-120
Nye, Robert 1939- .............. DLB-14, 271
Nyka-Niliūnas, Alfonsas 1919- ....... DLB-220

# O

Oakes, Urian circa 1631-1681 .......... DLB-24
Oakes Smith, Elizabeth
   1806-1893 ............. DLB-1, 239, 243
Oakley, Violet 1874-1961 ............ DLB-188
Oates, Joyce Carol 1938-
   ............. DLB-2, 5, 130; Y-81; CDALB-6
   Tribute to Michael M. Rea ......... Y-97
Ōba Minako 1930- ................ DLB-182
Ober, Frederick Albion 1849-1913 ...... DLB-189
Ober, William 1920-1993 ............. Y-93
Oberholtzer, Ellis Paxson 1868-1936 ..... DLB-47
The Obituary as Literary Form ........... Y-02
Obradović, Dositej 1740?-1811 ........ DLB-147
O'Brien, Charlotte Grace 1845-1909 .... DLB-240
O'Brien, Edna 1932- ... DLB-14, 231; CDBLB-8
O'Brien, Fitz-James 1828-1862 ......... DLB-74
O'Brien, Flann (see O'Nolan, Brian)
O'Brien, Kate 1897-1974 ............. DLB-15
O'Brien, Tim
   1946- .... DLB-152; Y-80; DS-9; CDALB-7
O'Casey, Sean 1880-1964 ..... DLB-10; CDBLB-6
Occom, Samson 1723-1792 ........... DLB-175
Occomy, Marita Bonner 1899-1971 ...... DLB-51
Ochs, Adolph S. 1858-1935 ........... DLB-25
Ochs-Oakes, George Washington
   1861-1931 .................... DLB-137
O'Connor, Flannery 1925-1964
   ........ DLB-2, 152; Y-80; DS-12; CDALB-1
   The Flannery O'Connor Society ........ Y-99
O'Connor, Frank 1903-1966 .......... DLB-162
O'Connor, Joseph 1963- ............. DLB-267
Octopus Publishing Group ............ DLB-112
Oda Sakunosuke 1913-1947 .......... DLB-182
Odell, Jonathan 1737-1818 ........ DLB-31, 99
O'Dell, Scott 1903-1989 .............. DLB-52
Odets, Clifford 1906-1963 ..........DLB-7, 26
Odhams Press Limited ............... DLB-112
Odio, Eunice 1922-1974 ............. DLB-283

Odoevsky, Aleksandr Ivanovich
   1802-1839 .................... DLB-205
Odoevsky, Vladimir Fedorovich
   1804 or 1803-1869 .............. DLB-198
O'Donnell, Peter 1920- .............. DLB-87
O'Donovan, Michael (see O'Connor, Frank)
O'Dowd, Bernard 1866-1953 ......... DLB-230
Ōe, Kenzaburō 1935- ..........DLB-182; Y-94
   Nobel Lecture 1994: Japan, the
      Ambiguous, and Myself .......... Y-94
O'Faolain, Julia 1932- ............ DLB-14, 231
O'Faolain, Sean 1900-1991 ........ DLB-15, 162
Off-Loop Theatres .................... DLB-7
Offord, Carl Ruthven 1910- ........... DLB-76
O'Flaherty, Liam 1896-1984 ...DLB-36, 162; Y-84
Ogarev, Nikolai Platonovich 1813-1877 ...DLB-277
J. S. Ogilvie and Company ............ DLB-49
Ogilvy, Eliza 1822-1912 .............. DLB-199
Ogot, Grace 1930- ................. DLB-125
O'Grady, Desmond 1935- ............ DLB-40
Ogunyemi, Wale 1939- .............DLB-157
O'Hagan, Howard 1902-1982 .......... DLB-68
O'Hara, Frank 1926-1966 ........DLB-5, 16, 193
O'Hara, John
   1905-1970 ....... DLB-9, 86; DS-2; CDALB-5
   John O'Hara's Pottsville Journalism ..... Y-88
O'Hegarty, P. S. 1879-1955 .......... DLB-201
Ohio State University
   The William Charvat American Fiction
      Collection at the Ohio State
      University Libraries ............... Y-92
Okara, Gabriel 1921- .....DLB-125; CDWLB-3
O'Keeffe, John 1747-1833 ............ DLB-89
Nicholas Okes [publishing house] ........DLB-170
Okigbo, Christopher
   1930-1967 ............DLB-125; CDWLB-3
Okot p'Bitek 1931-1982 .....DLB-125; CDWLB-3
Okpewho, Isidore 1941- .............DLB-157
Okri, Ben 1959- ................DLB-157, 231
Old Dogs / New Tricks? New Technologies,
   the Canon, and the Structure of
   the Profession ...................... Y-02
Old Franklin Publishing House ......... DLB-49
*Old German Genesis* and *Old German Exodus*
   circa 1050-circa 1130 ............. DLB-148
The *Old High German Isidor*
   circa 790-800 ................... DLB-148
Older, Fremont 1856-1935 ............ DLB-25
Oldham, John 1653-1683 ............ DLB-131
Oldman, C. B. 1894-1969 ............ DLB-201
Olds, Sharon 1942- ................ DLB-120
Olearius, Adam 1599-1671 ........... DLB-164
O'Leary, Ellen 1831-1889 ............ DLB-240
Olesha, Iurii Karlovich 1899-1960 .......DLB-272
Oliphant, Laurence 1829?-1888 ..... DLB-18, 166
Oliphant, Margaret 1828-1897 ...DLB-18, 159, 190
   "Modern Novelists–Great and Small"
      (1855) ...................... DLB-21

Oliveira, Carlos de 1921-1981 . . . . . . . . . DLB-287
Oliver, Chad 1928-1993 . . . . . . . . . . . . . . . DLB-8
Oliver, Mary 1935- . . . . . . . . . . . . . . DLB-5, 193
Ollier, Claude 1922- . . . . . . . . . . . . . . . . DLB-83
Olsen, Tillie 1912/1913-
    . . . . . . . . . . . . . DLB-28, 206; Y-80; CDALB-7
Olson, Charles 1910-1970 . . . . . . . . DLB-5, 16, 193
Olson, Elder 1909- . . . . . . . . . . . . . . . DLB-48, 63
Olson, Sigurd F. 1899-1982 . . . . . . . . . . . DLB-275
The Omega Workshops . . . . . . . . . . . . . . . . DS-10
Omotoso, Kole 1943- . . . . . . . . . . . . . . . DLB-125
Omulevsky, Innokentii Vasil'evich
    1836 [or 1837]-1883 . . . . . . . . . . . . . DLB-238
Ondaatje, Michael 1943- . . . . . . . . . . . . . DLB-60
O'Neill, Eugene 1888-1953 . . . . . DLB-7; CDALB-5
    Eugene O'Neill Memorial Theater
        Center . . . . . . . . . . . . . . . . . . . . . . . DLB-7
    Eugene O'Neill's Letters: A Review . . . . . Y-88
Onetti, Juan Carlos
    1909-1994 . . . . . . . . . . . . DLB-113; CDWLB-3
Onions, George Oliver 1872-1961 . . . . . . . DLB-153
Onofri, Arturo 1885-1928 . . . . . . . . . . . . DLB-114
O'Nolan, Brian 1911-1966 . . . . . . . . . . . . DLB-231
Opie, Amelia 1769-1853 . . . . . . . . . DLB-116, 159
Opitz, Martin 1597-1639 . . . . . . . . . . . . . DLB-164
Oppen, George 1908-1984 . . . . . . . . . . DLB-5, 165
Oppenheim, E. Phillips 1866-1946 . . . . . . . DLB-70
Oppenheim, James 1882-1932 . . . . . . . . . . DLB-28
Oppenheimer, Joel 1930-1988 . . . . . . . . DLB-5, 193
Optic, Oliver (see Adams, William Taylor)
Orczy, Emma, Baroness 1865-1947 . . . . . . . DLB-70
Oregon Shakespeare Festival . . . . . . . . . . . . . Y-00
Origo, Iris 1902-1988 . . . . . . . . . . . . . . . . DLB-155
O'Riordan, Kate 1960- . . . . . . . . . . . . . . DLB-267
Orlovitz, Gil 1918-1973 . . . . . . . . . . . . . DLB-2, 5
Orlovsky, Peter 1933- . . . . . . . . . . . . . . . DLB-16
Ormond, John 1923- . . . . . . . . . . . . . . . . DLB-27
Ornitz, Samuel 1890-1957 . . . . . . . . . . DLB-28, 44
O'Rourke, P. J. 1947- . . . . . . . . . . . . . . . DLB-185
Orozco, Olga 1920-1999 . . . . . . . . . . . . . DLB-283
Orten, Jiří 1919-1941 . . . . . . . . . . . . . . . DLB-215
Ortese, Anna Maria 1914- . . . . . . . . . . . . DLB-177
Ortiz, Simon J. 1941- . . . . . . . DLB-120, 175, 256
Ortnit and Wolfdietrich circa 1225-1250 . . . . DLB-138
Orton, Joe 1933-1967 . . . . . . . . DLB-13; CDBLB-8
Orwell, George (Eric Arthur Blair)
    1903-1950 . . . DLB-15, 98, 195, 255; CDBLB-7
    The Orwell Year . . . . . . . . . . . . . . . . . . . Y-84
    (Re-)Publishing Orwell . . . . . . . . . . . . . Y-86
Ory, Carlos Edmundo de 1923- . . . . . . . . DLB-134
Osbey, Brenda Marie 1957- . . . . . . . . . . . DLB-120
Osbon, B. S. 1827-1912 . . . . . . . . . . . . . . DLB-43
Osborn, Sarah 1714-1796 . . . . . . . . . . . . DLB-200
Osborne, John 1929-1994 . . . . DLB-13; CDBLB-7
Osgood, Frances Sargent 1811-1850 . . . . . DLB-250
Osgood, Herbert L. 1855-1918 . . . . . . . . . DLB-47

James R. Osgood and Company . . . . . . . . DLB-49
Osgood, McIlvaine and Company . . . . . . . DLB-112
O'Shaughnessy, Arthur 1844-1881 . . . . . . . DLB-35
Patrick O'Shea [publishing house] . . . . . . . DLB-49
Osipov, Nikolai Petrovich 1751-1799 . . . . . DLB-150
Oskison, John Milton 1879-1947 . . . . . . . DLB-175
Osler, Sir William 1849-1919 . . . . . . . . . DLB-184
Osofisan, Femi 1946- . . . . . DLB-125; CDWLB-3
Ostenso, Martha 1900-1963 . . . . . . . . . . . DLB-92
Ostrauskas, Kostas 1926- . . . . . . . . . . . . DLB-232
Ostriker, Alicia 1937- . . . . . . . . . . . . . . . DLB-120
Ostrovsky, Aleksandr Nikolaevich
    1823-1886 . . . . . . . . . . . . . . . . . . . DLB-277
Ostrovsky, Nikolai Alekseevich
    1904-1936 . . . . . . . . . . . . . . . . . . . DLB-272
Osundare, Niyi 1947- . . . . . DLB-157; CDWLB-3
Oswald, Eleazer 1755-1795 . . . . . . . . . . . . DLB-43
Oswald von Wolkenstein
    1376 or 1377-1445 . . . . . . . . . . . . . . DLB-179
Otero, Blas de 1916-1979 . . . . . . . . . . . . DLB-134
Otero, Miguel Antonio 1859-1944 . . . . . . . DLB-82
Otero, Nina 1881-1965 . . . . . . . . . . . . . . DLB-209
Otero Silva, Miguel 1908-1985 . . . . . . . . . DLB-145
Otfried von Weißenburg
    circa 800-circa 875? . . . . . . . . . . . . . DLB-148
Otis, Broaders and Company . . . . . . . . . . DLB-49
Otis, James (see Kaler, James Otis)
Otis, James, Jr. 1725-1783 . . . . . . . . . . . . . DLB-31
Ottaway, James 1911-2000 . . . . . . . . . . . DLB-127
Ottendorfer, Oswald 1826-1900 . . . . . . . . DLB-23
Ottieri, Ottiero 1924- . . . . . . . . . . . . . . . DLB-177
Otto-Peters, Louise 1819-1895 . . . . . . . . . DLB-129
Otway, Thomas 1652-1685 . . . . . . . . . . . . DLB-80
Ouellette, Fernand 1930- . . . . . . . . . . . . . DLB-60
Ouida 1839-1908 . . . . . . . . . . . . . . . DLB-18, 156
Outing Publishing Company . . . . . . . . . . DLB-46
Overbury, Sir Thomas
    circa 1581-1613 . . . . . . . . . . . . . . . . DLB-151
The Overlook Press . . . . . . . . . . . . . . . . . DLB-46
Ovid 43 B.C.-A.D. 17 . . . . . . DLB-211; CDWLB-1
Owen, Guy 1925- . . . . . . . . . . . . . . . . . . DLB-5
Owen, John 1564-1622 . . . . . . . . . . . . . . DLB-121
John Owen [publishing house] . . . . . . . . . DLB-49
Peter Owen Limited . . . . . . . . . . . . . . . . DLB-112
Owen, Robert 1771-1858 . . . . . . . . DLB-107, 158
Owen, Wilfred
    1893-1918 . . . . . . . DLB-20; DS-18; CDBLB-6
    A Centenary Celebration . . . . . . . . . . . Y-93
    The Wilfred Owen Association . . . . . . . Y-98
The Owl and the Nightingale
    circa 1189-1199 . . . . . . . . . . . . . . . . DLB-146
Owsley, Frank L. 1890-1956 . . . . . . . . . . . DLB-17
Oxford, Seventeenth Earl of, Edward
    de Vere 1550-1604 . . . . . . . . . . . . . . DLB-172
OyamO (Charles F. Gordon)
    1943- . . . . . . . . . . . . . . . . . . . . . . . DLB-266

Ozerov, Vladislav Aleksandrovich
    1769-1816 . . . . . . . . . . . . . . . . . . . DLB-150
Ozick, Cynthia 1928- . . . . . . . DLB-28, 152; Y-82
    First Strauss "Livings" Awarded
        to Cynthia Ozick and
        Raymond Carver
        An Interview with Cynthia Ozick . . . . Y-83
    Tribute to Michael M. Rea . . . . . . . . . . . Y-97

# P

Pace, Richard 1482?-1536 . . . . . . . . . . . . DLB-167
Pacey, Desmond 1917-1975 . . . . . . . . . . . DLB-88
Pack, Robert 1929- . . . . . . . . . . . . . . . . . DLB-5
Padell Publishing Company . . . . . . . . . . . DLB-46
Padgett, Ron 1942- . . . . . . . . . . . . . . . . . DLB-5
Padilla, Ernesto Chávez 1944- . . . . . . . . . DLB-122
L. C. Page and Company . . . . . . . . . . . . . DLB-49
Page, Louise 1955- . . . . . . . . . . . . . . . . DLB-233
Page, P. K. 1916- . . . . . . . . . . . . . . . . . . DLB-68
Page, Thomas Nelson
    1853-1922 . . . . . . . . . . . . . DLB-12, 78; DS-13
Page, Walter Hines 1855-1918 . . . . . . . DLB-71, 91
Paget, Francis Edward 1806-1882 . . . . . . . DLB-163
Paget, Violet (see Lee, Vernon)
Pagliarani, Elio 1927- . . . . . . . . . . . . . . . DLB-128
Pain, Barry 1864-1928 . . . . . . . . . . . . DLB-135, 197
Pain, Philip ?-circa 1666 . . . . . . . . . . . . . . DLB-24
Paine, Robert Treat, Jr. 1773-1811 . . . . . . . DLB-37
Paine, Thomas
    1737-1809 . . . . DLB-31, 43, 73, 158; CDALB-2
Painter, George D. 1914- . . . . . . . . . . . . DLB-155
Painter, William 1540?-1594 . . . . . . . . . . DLB-136
Palazzeschi, Aldo 1885-1974 . . . . . . . DLB-114, 264
Palei, Marina Anatol'evna 1955- . . . . . . . DLB-285
Palencia, Alfonso de 1424-1492 . . . . . . . . DLB-286
Paley, Grace 1922- . . . . . . . . . . . . . . DLB-28, 218
Paley, William 1743-1805 . . . . . . . . . . . . DLB-252
Palfrey, John Gorham 1796-1881 . . . DLB-1, 30, 235
Palgrave, Francis Turner 1824-1897 . . . . . . DLB-35
Palmer, Joe H. 1904-1952 . . . . . . . . . . . . DLB-171
Palmer, Michael 1943- . . . . . . . . . . . . . . DLB-169
Palmer, Nettie 1885-1964 . . . . . . . . . . . . DLB-260
Palmer, Vance 1885-1959 . . . . . . . . . . . . DLB-260
Paltock, Robert 1697-1767 . . . . . . . . . . . . DLB-39
Paludan, Jacob 1896-1975 . . . . . . . . . . . . DLB-214
Pan Books Limited . . . . . . . . . . . . . . . . . DLB-112
Panaev, Ivan Ivanovich 1812-1862 . . . . . . . DLB-198
Panaeva, Avdot'ia Iakovlevna
    1820-1893 . . . . . . . . . . . . . . . . . . . DLB-238
Panama, Norman 1914- and
    Frank, Melvin 1913-1988 . . . . . . . . . . DLB-26
Pancake, Breece D'J 1952-1979 . . . . . . . . DLB-130
Panduro, Leif 1923-1977 . . . . . . . . . . . . . DLB-214
Panero, Leopoldo 1909-1962 . . . . . . . . . . DLB-108
Pangborn, Edgar 1909-1976 . . . . . . . . . . . . DLB-8
Panizzi, Sir Anthony 1797-1879 . . . . . . . . DLB-184
Panneton, Philippe (see Ringuet)

# Cumulative Index

Panshin, Alexei 1940- ................. DLB-8
Pansy (see Alden, Isabella)
Pantheon Books ..................... DLB-46
Papadat-Bengescu, Hortensia
    1876-1955..................... DLB-220
Papantonio, Michael 1907-1976 ........ DLB-187
Paperback Library .................... DLB-46
Paperback Science Fiction............. DLB-8
Papini, Giovanni 1881-1956........... DLB-264
Paquet, Alfons 1881-1944.............. DLB-66
Paracelsus 1493-1541 ................DLB-179
Paradis, Suzanne 1936- ............... DLB-53
Páral, Vladimír, 1932- ............... DLB-232
Pardoe, Julia 1804-1862 .............. DLB-166
Paredes, Américo 1915-1999 ........... DLB-209
Pareja Diezcanseco, Alfredo 1908-1993 .. DLB-145
Parents' Magazine Press .............. DLB-46
Parfit, Derek 1942- .................. DLB-262
Parise, Goffredo 1929-1986 ...........DLB-177
Parish, Mitchell 1900-1993 ........... DLB-265
Parizeau, Alice 1930-1990............. DLB-60
Park, Ruth 1923?- .................... DLB-260
Parke, John 1754-1789 ................ DLB-31
Parker, Dan 1893-1967................. DLB-241
Parker, Dorothy 1893-1967 ...... DLB-11, 45, 86
Parker, Gilbert 1860-1932 ............ DLB-99
Parker, James 1714-1770 .............. DLB-43
Parker, John [publishing house] ........ DLB-106
Parker, Matthew 1504-1575 ............ DLB-213
Parker, Stewart 1941-1988 ............ DLB-245
Parker, Theodore 1810-1860 ... DLB-1, 235; DS-5
Parker, William Riley 1906-1968 ....... DLB-103
J. H. Parker [publishing house] ....... DLB-106
Parkes, Bessie Rayner (Madame Belloc)
    1829-1925 ..................... DLB-240
Parkman, Francis
    1823-1893 ........DLB-1, 30, 183, 186, 235
Parks, Gordon 1912- .................. DLB-33
Parks, Tim 1954- ..................... DLB-231
Parks, William 1698-1750.............. DLB-43
William Parks [publishing house]....... DLB-49
Parley, Peter (see Goodrich, Samuel Griswold)
Parmenides late sixth-fifth century B.C....DLB-176
Parnell, Thomas 1679-1718............. DLB-95
Parnicki, Teodor 1908-1988........... DLB-215
Parr, Catherine 1513?-1548 ........... DLB-136
Parra, Nicanor 1914- ................. DLB-283
Parrington, Vernon L. 1871-1929......DLB-17, 63
Parrish, Maxfield 1870-1966 .......... DLB-188
Parronchi, Alessandro 1914- .......... DLB-128
Parshchikov, Aleksei Maksimovich
    (Raiderman) 1954- ............. DLB-285
Parton, James 1822-1891 .............. DLB-30
Parton, Sara Payson Willis
    1811-1872................ DLB-43, 74, 239
S. W. Partridge and Company ......... DLB-106

Parun, Vesna 1922- ..... DLB-181; CDWLB-4
Pascal, Blaise 1623-1662.............DLB-268
Pasinetti, Pier Maria 1913- ..........DLB-177
    Tribute to Albert Erskine............. Y-93
Pasolini, Pier Paolo 1922-1975 ......DLB-128, 177
Pastan, Linda 1932- .................. DLB-5
Paston, George (Emily Morse Symonds)
    1860-1936 .................DLB-149, 197
The Paston Letters 1422-1509 .......... DLB-146
Pastorius, Francis Daniel
    1651-circa 1720 ................. DLB-24
Patchen, Kenneth 1911-1972 ........ DLB-16, 48
Pater, Walter 1839-1894...DLB-57, 156; CDBLB-4
    Aesthetic Poetry (1873) ........... DLB-35
    "Style" (1888) [excerpt] ........... DLB-57
Paterson, A. B. "Banjo" 1864-1941...... DLB-230
Paterson, Katherine 1932- ........... DLB-52
Patmore, Coventry 1823-1896 ....... DLB-35, 98
Paton, Alan 1903-1988.......... DLB-225; DS-17
Paton, Joseph Noel 1821-1901 .......... DLB-35
Paton Walsh, Jill 1937- .............. DLB-161
Patrick, Edwin Hill ("Ted") 1901-1964 .. DLB-137
Patrick, John 1906-1995 ............... DLB-7
Pattee, Fred Lewis 1863-1950.......... DLB-71
Patterson, Alicia 1906-1963 .......... DLB-127
Patterson, Eleanor Medill 1881-1948..... DLB-29
Patterson, Eugene 1923- ............. DLB-127
Patterson, Joseph Medill 1879-1946 ..... DLB-29
Pattillo, Henry 1726-1801.............. DLB-37
Paul, Elliot 1891-1958 ........... DLB-4; DS-15
Paul, Jean (see Richter, Johann Paul Friedrich)
Paul, Kegan, Trench, Trubner and
    Company Limited ............... DLB-106
Peter Paul Book Company............ DLB-49
Stanley Paul and Company Limited..... DLB-112
Paulding, James Kirke
    1778-1860................DLB-3, 59, 74, 250
Paulin, Tom 1949- .................... DLB-40
Pauper, Peter, Press ................. DLB-46
Paustovsky, Konstantin Georgievich
    1892-1968 .....................DLB-272
Pavese, Cesare 1908-1950 ........DLB-128, 177
Pavić, Milorad 1929- ..... DLB-181; CDWLB-4
Pavlov, Konstantin 1933- ............ DLB-181
Pavlov, Nikolai Filippovich 1803-1864 .... DLB-198
Pavlova, Karolina Karlovna 1807-1893 .... DLB-205
Pavlović, Miodrag
    1928- ............ DLB-181; CDWLB-4
Paxton, John 1911-1985 ............... DLB-44
Payn, James 1830-1898................. DLB-18
Payne, John 1842-1916................. DLB-35
Payne, John Howard 1791-1852......... DLB-37
Payson and Clarke .................... DLB-46
Paz, Octavio 1914-1998 ............. Y-90, 98
    Nobel Lecture 1990 ................. Y-90
Pazzi, Roberto 1946- ................ DLB-196

Pea, Enrico 1881-1958 .............. DLB-264
Peabody, Elizabeth Palmer
    1804-1894 .................. DLB-1, 223
    Preface to Record of a School:
      Exemplifying the General Principles
      of Spiritual Culture ................DS-5
Elizabeth Palmer Peabody
    [publishing house] ............... DLB-49
Peabody, Josephine Preston 1874-1922 .. DLB-249
Peabody, Oliver William Bourn
    1799-1848..................... DLB-59
Peace, Roger 1899-1968...............DLB-127
Peacham, Henry 1578-1644? .......... DLB-151
Peacham, Henry, the Elder
    1547-1634 ...............DLB-172, 236
Peachtree Publishers, Limited.......... DLB-46
Peacock, Molly 1947- ................ DLB-120
Peacock, Thomas Love 1785-1866... DLB-96, 116
Pead, Deuel ?-1727 .................... DLB-24
Peake, Mervyn 1911-1968 ..... DLB-15, 160, 255
Peale, Rembrandt 1778-1860 .......... DLB-183
Pear Tree Press ..................... DLB-112
Pearce, Philippa 1920- ............. DLB-161
H. B. Pearson [publishing house] ........ DLB-49
Pearson, Hesketh 1887-1964........... DLB-149
Peattie, Donald Culross 1898-1964 ....DLB-275
Pechersky, Andrei (see Mel'nikov, Pavel Ivanovich)
Peck, George W. 1840-1916......... DLB-23, 42
H. C. Peck and Theo. Bliss
    [publishing house] ............... DLB-49
Peck, Harry Thurston 1856-1914......DLB-71, 91
Peden, William 1913-1999 ............ DLB-234
    Tribute to William Goyen............. Y-83
Peele, George 1556-1596 ..........DLB-62, 167
Pegler, Westbrook 1894-1969 .........DLB-171
Péguy, Charles 1873-1914 ........... DLB-258
Peirce, Charles Sanders 1839-1914.......DLB-270
Pekić, Borislav 1930-1992 ...DLB-181; CDWLB-4
Pelevin, Viktor Olegovich 1962- ..... DLB-285
Pellegrini and Cudahy ................ DLB-46
Pelletier, Aimé (see Vac, Bertrand)
Pelletier, Francine 1959- ............ DLB-251
Pemberton, Sir Max 1863-1950 ......... DLB-70
de la Peña, Terri 1947- .............. DLB-209
Penfield, Edward 1866-1925 .......... DLB-188
Penguin Books [U.K.]................. DLB-112
    Fifty Penguin Years ................. Y-85
    Penguin Collectors' Society ........... Y-98
Penguin Books [U.S.] ................. DLB-46
Penn, William 1644-1718 .............. DLB-24
Penn Publishing Company............. DLB-49
Penna, Sandro 1906-1977 ............ DLB-114
Pennell, Joseph 1857-1926 ........... DLB-188
Penner, Jonathan 1940- ............... Y-83
Pennington, Lee 1939- ................ Y-82
Penton, Brian 1904-1951 ............. DLB-260

Pepper, Stephen C. 1891-1972 .........DLB-270
Pepys, Samuel
    1633-1703 ........DLB-101, 213; CDBLB-2
Percy, Thomas 1729-1811 ............DLB-104
Percy, Walker 1916-1990 .......DLB-2; Y-80, 90
    Tribute to Caroline Gordon ..........Y-81
Percy, William 1575-1648 .............DLB-172
Perec, Georges 1936-1982 .............DLB-83
Perelman, Bob 1947- ................DLB-193
Perelman, S. J. 1904-1979 ...........DLB-11, 44
Pérez de Guzmán, Fernán
    ca. 1377-ca. 1460 ...............DLB-286
Perez, Raymundo "Tigre" 1946- ......DLB-122
Peri Rossi, Cristina 1941- ...........DLB-145
Perkins, Eugene 1932- ...............DLB-41
Perkins, Maxwell
    The Claims of Business and Literature:
    An Undergraduate Essay ..........Y-01
Perkins, William 1558-1602 ...........DLB-281
Perkoff, Stuart Z. 1930-1974 ............DLB-16
Perley, Moses Henry 1804-1862 ........DLB-99
Permabooks ........................DLB-46
Perovsky, Aleksei Alekseevich
    (Antonii Pogorel'sky) 1787-1836 ......DLB-198
Perrault, Charles 1628-1703 ...........DLB-268
Perri, Henry 1561-1617 ...............DLB-236
Perrin, Alice 1867-1934 ..............DLB-156
Perry, Anne 1938- ..................DLB-276
Perry, Bliss 1860-1954 ................DLB-71
Perry, Eleanor 1915-1981 ..............DLB-44
Perry, Henry (see Perri, Henry)
Perry, Matthew 1794-1858 .............DLB-183
Perry, Sampson 1747-1823 .............DLB-158
Perse, Saint-John 1887-1975 ...........DLB-258
Persius A.D. 34-A.D. 62 ...............DLB-211
Perutz, Leo 1882-1957 .................DLB-81
Pesetsky, Bette 1932- ................DLB-130
Pessanha, Camilo 1867-1926 ..........DLB-287
Pessoa, Fernando 1888-1935 ..........DLB-287
Pestalozzi, Johann Heinrich 1746-1827 .....DLB-94
Peter, Laurence J. 1919-1990 ...........DLB-53
Peter of Spain circa 1205-1277 .........DLB-115
Peterkin, Julia 1880-1961 ..............DLB-9
Peters, Ellis (Edith Pargeter) 1913-1995 ...DLB-276
Peters, Lenrie 1932- ................DLB-117
Peters, Robert 1924- ................DLB-105
    "Foreword to Ludwig of Baviria" ......DLB-105
Petersham, Maud 1889-1971 and
    Petersham, Miska 1888-1960 ........DLB-22
Peterson, Charles Jacobs 1819-1887 .......DLB-79
Peterson, Len 1917- .................DLB-88
Peterson, Levi S. 1933- ..............DLB-206
Peterson, Louis 1922-1998 ............DLB-76
Peterson, T. B., and Brothers ..........DLB-49
Petitclair, Pierre 1813-1860 ............DLB-99
Petrescu, Camil 1894-1957 ............DLB-220

Petronius circa A.D. 20-A.D. 66
    ..................DLB-211; CDWLB-1
Petrov, Aleksandar 1938- ............DLB-181
Petrov, Evgenii (Evgenii Petrovich Kataev)
    1903-1942 .....................DLB-272
Petrov, Gavriil 1730-1801 .............DLB-150
Petrov, Valeri 1920- .................DLB-181
Petrov, Vasilii Petrovich 1736-1799 ......DLB-150
Petrović, Rastko
    1898-1949 ............DLB-147; CDWLB-4
Petrushevskaia, Liudmila Stefanovna
    1938- ........................DLB-285
Petruslied circa 854? .................DLB-148
Petry, Ann 1908-1997 .................DLB-76
Pettie, George circa 1548-1589 ........DLB-136
Peyton, K. M. 1929- .................DLB-161
Pfaffe Konrad flourished circa 1172......DLB-148
Pfaffe Lamprecht flourished circa 1150 ...DLB-148
Pfeiffer, Emily 1827-1890 ..............DLB-199
Pforzheimer, Carl H. 1879-1957 ........DLB-140
Phaedrus circa 18 B.C.-circa A.D. 50.....DLB-211
Phaer, Thomas 1510?-1560 ............DLB-167
Phaidon Press Limited................DLB-112
Pharr, Robert Deane 1916-1992 .........DLB-33
Phelps, Elizabeth Stuart 1815-1852 ......DLB-202
Phelps, Elizabeth Stuart 1844-1911 ...DLB-74, 221
Philander von der Linde
    (see Mencke, Johann Burckhard)
Philby, H. St. John B. 1885-1960 ........DLB-195
Philip, Marlene Nourbese 1947- .......DLB-157
Philippe, Charles-Louis 1874-1909........DLB-65
Philips, John 1676-1708 ................DLB-95
Philips, Katherine 1632-1664............DLB-131
Phillipps, Sir Thomas 1792-1872 .........DLB-184
Phillips, Caryl 1958- .................DLB-157
Phillips, David Graham 1867-1911 .....DLB-9, 12
Phillips, Jayne Anne 1952- ..............Y-80
    Tribute to Seymour Lawrence .........Y-94
Phillips, Robert 1938- ................DLB-105
    "Finding, Losing, Reclaiming: A Note
    on My Poems" .................DLB-105
    Tribute to William Goyen ............Y-83
Phillips, Stephen 1864-1915 ............DLB-10
Phillips, Ulrich B. 1877-1934 ............DLB-17
Phillips, Wendell 1811-1884 ............DLB-235
Phillips, Willard 1784-1873 .............DLB-59
Phillips, William 1907-2002 ............DLB-137
Phillips, Sampson and Company ........DLB-49
Phillpotts, Adelaide Eden (Adelaide Ross)
    1896-1993 .....................DLB-191
Phillpotts, Eden 1862-1960 .. DLB-10, 70, 135, 153
Philo circa 20-15 B.C.-circa A.D. 50 .....DLB-176
Philosophical Library..................DLB-46
Philosophy
    Eighteenth-Century Philosophical
    Background ...................DLB-31
    Philosophic Thought in Boston......DLB-235

Translators of the Twelfth Century:
    Literary Issues Raised and
    Impact Created................DLB-115
Elihu Phinney [publishing house] ........DLB-49
Phoenix, John (see Derby, George Horatio)
PHYLON (Fourth Quarter, 1950),
    The Negro in Literature:
    The Current Scene .................DLB-76
Physiologus circa 1070-circa 1150 .........DLB-148
Piccolo, Lucio 1903-1969..............DLB-114
Pickard, Tom 1946- .................DLB-40
William Pickering [publishing house] ....DLB-106
Pickthall, Marjorie 1883-1922 ...........DLB-92
Pictorial Printing Company............DLB-49
Piel, Gerard 1915- ..................DLB-137
    "An Announcement to Our Readers,"
    Gerard Piel's Statement in Scientific
    American (April 1948) ..........DLB-137
Pielmeier, John 1949- ................DLB-266
Piercy, Marge 1936- .............DLB-120, 227
Pierro, Albino 1916-1995...............DLB-128
Pignotti, Lamberto 1926- .............DLB-128
Pike, Albert 1809-1891 .................DLB-74
Pike, Zebulon Montgomery 1779-1813 ...DLB-183
Pillat, Ion 1891-1945 ..................DLB-220
Pil'niak, Boris Andreevich (Boris Andreevich
    Vogau) 1894-1938...................DLB-272
Pilon, Jean-Guy 1930- ................DLB-60
Pinar, Florencia fl. ca. late
    fifteenth century .................DLB-286
Pinckney, Eliza Lucas 1722-1793 ........DLB-200
Pinckney, Josephine 1895-1957 ...........DLB-6
Pindar circa 518 B.C.-circa 438 B.C.
    ..................... DLB-176; CDWLB-1
Pindar, Peter (see Wolcot, John)
Pineda, Cecile 1942- .................DLB-209
Pinero, Arthur Wing 1855-1934 .........DLB-10
Piñero, Miguel 1946-1988 ..............DLB-266
Pinget, Robert 1919-1997 ..............DLB-83
Pinkney, Edward Coote 1802-1828......DLB-248
Pinnacle Books .....................DLB-46
Piñon, Nélida 1935- .................DLB-145
Pinsky, Robert 1940- ..................Y-82
    Reappointed Poet Laureate............Y-98
Pinter, Harold 1930- .......DLB-13; CDBLB-8
    Writing for the Theatre ............DLB-13
Pinto, Fernão Mendes 1509/1511?-1583 ..DLB-287
Piontek, Heinz 1925- .................DLB-75
Piozzi, Hester Lynch [Thrale]
    1741-1821 .................DLB-104, 142
Piper, H. Beam 1904-1964...............DLB-8
Piper, Watty .......................DLB-22
Pirandello, Luigi 1867-1936.............DLB-264
Pirckheimer, Caritas 1467-1532.........DLB-179
Pirckheimer, Willibald 1470-1530 .......DLB-179
Pires, José Cardoso 1925-1998 .........DLB-287
Pisar, Samuel 1929- ...................Y-83

Pisarev, Dmitrii Ivanovich 1840-1868 . . . .DLB-277

Pisemsky, Aleksei Feofilaktovich
   1821-1881 . . . . . . . . . . . . . . . . . . . DLB-238

Pitkin, Timothy 1766-1847 . . . . . . . . . . . DLB-30

Pitter, Ruth 1897- . . . . . . . . . . . . . . . . DLB-20

Pix, Mary 1666-1709 . . . . . . . . . . . . . . DLB-80

Pixerécourt, René Charles Guilbert de
   1773-1844 . . . . . . . . . . . . . . . . . . . DLB-192

Pizarnik, Alejandra 1936-1972 . . . . . . . . DLB-283

Plaatje, Sol T. 1876-1932 . . . . . . . . DLB-125, 225

Plante, David 1940- . . . . . . . . . . . . . . . . . Y-83

Platen, August von 1796-1835 . . . . . . . . . DLB-90

Plantinga, Alvin 1932- . . . . . . . . . . . . . .DLB-279

Plath, Sylvia
   1932-1963 . . . . . . . . DLB-5, 6, 152; CDALB-1

Plato circa 428 B.C.-348-347 B.C.
   . . . . . . . . . . . . . . . . . . . .DLB-176; CDWLB-1

Plato, Ann 1824?-? . . . . . . . . . . . . . . . DLB-239

Platon 1737-1812 . . . . . . . . . . . . . . . . DLB-150

Platonov, Andrei Platonovich (Andrei
   Platonovich Klimentev) 1899-1951 . . DLB-272

Platt, Charles 1945- . . . . . . . . . . . . . . . DLB-261

Platt and Munk Company . . . . . . . . . . . DLB-46

Plautus circa 254 B.C.-184 B.C.
   . . . . . . . . . . . . . . . . . . DLB-211; CDWLB-1

Playboy Press . . . . . . . . . . . . . . . . . . . . DLB-46

John Playford [publishing house] . . . . . . . .DLB-170

Der Pleier flourished circa 1250 . . . . . . . . DLB-138

Pleijel, Agneta 1940- . . . . . . . . . . . . . . DLB-257

Plenzdorf, Ulrich 1934- . . . . . . . . . . . . . DLB-75

Pleshcheev, Aleksei Nikolaevich
   1825?-1893 . . . . . . . . . . . . . . . . . . .DLB-277

Plessen, Elizabeth 1944- . . . . . . . . . . . . DLB-75

Pletnev, Petr Aleksandrovich
   1792-1865 . . . . . . . . . . . . . . . . . . . . DLB-205

Pliekšāne, Elza Rozenberga (see Aspazija)

Pliekšāns, Jānis (see Rainis, Jānis)

Plievier, Theodor 1892-1955 . . . . . . . . . . DLB-69

Plimpton, George 1927- . . . . .DLB-185, 241; Y-99

Pliny the Elder A.D. 23/24-A.D. 79 . . . . . DLB-211

Pliny the Younger
   circa A.D. 61-A.D. 112 . . . . . . . . . . . . DLB-211

Plomer, William
   1903-1973 . . . . . . . . . . DLB-20, 162, 191, 225

Plotinus 204-270 . . . . . . . . . .DLB-176; CDWLB-1

Plowright, Teresa 1952- . . . . . . . . . . . . DLB-251

Plume, Thomas 1630-1704 . . . . . . . . . . . DLB-213

Plumly, Stanley 1939- . . . . . . . . . . . . DLB-5, 193

Plumpp, Sterling D. 1940- . . . . . . . . . . . DLB-41

Plunkett, James 1920- . . . . . . . . . . . . . . DLB-14

Plutarch
   circa 46-circa 120 . . . . . . .DLB-176; CDWLB-1

Plymell, Charles 1935- . . . . . . . . . . . . . DLB-16

Pocket Books . . . . . . . . . . . . . . . . . . . . DLB-46

Poe, Edgar Allan 1809-1849
   . . . . . . . . DLB-3, 59, 73, 74, 248; CDALB-2

   The Poe Studies Association . . . . . . . . . Y-99

Poe, James 1921-1980 . . . . . . . . . . . . . . DLB-44

The Poet Laureate of the United States . . . . . . Y-86

   Statements from Former Consultants
     in Poetry . . . . . . . . . . . . . . . . . . . . Y-86

Poetry
   Aesthetic Poetry (1873) . . . . . . . . . . . DLB-35

   A Century of Poetry, a Lifetime of
     Collecting: J. M. Edelstein's
     Collection of Twentieth-
     Century American Poetry . . . . . . . . . Y-02

   "Certain Gifts," by Betty Adcock . . . . DLB-105

   Contempo Caravan: Kites in a
     Windstorm . . . . . . . . . . . . . . . . . Y-85

   "Contemporary Verse Story-telling,"
     by Jonathan Holden . . . . . . . . . DLB-105

   "A Detail in a Poem," by Fred
     Chappell . . . . . . . . . . . . . . . . . . DLB-105

   "The English Renaissance of Art"
     (1908), by Oscar Wilde . . . . . . . . . DLB-35

   "Every Man His Own Poet; or,
     The Inspired Singer's Recipe
     Book" (1877), by
     H. W. Mallock . . . . . . . . . . . . . . . DLB-35

   "Eyes Across Centuries: Contemporary
     Poetry and 'That Vision Thing,'"
     by Philip Dacey . . . . . . . . . . . . . DLB-105

   A Field Guide to Recent Schools
     of American Poetry . . . . . . . . . . . . . Y-86

   "Finding, Losing, Reclaiming:
     A Note on My Poems,
     by Robert Phillips" . . . . . . . . . . DLB-105

   "The Fleshly School of Poetry and Other
     Phenomena of the Day" (1872) . . . DLB-35

   "The Fleshly School of Poetry:
     Mr. D. G. Rossetti" (1871) . . . . . . DLB-35

   The G. Ross Roy Scottish Poetry Collection
     at the University of South Carolina . . Y-89

   "Getting Started: Accepting the Regions
     You Own–or Which Own You,"
     by Walter McDonald . . . . . . . . . DLB-105

   "The Good, The Not So Good," by
     Stephen Dunn . . . . . . . . . . . . . . DLB-105

   The Griffin Poetry Prize . . . . . . . . . . . . Y-00

   The Hero as Poet. Dante; Shakspeare
     (1841), by Thomas Carlyle . . . . . . . DLB-32

   "Images and 'Images,'" by Charles
     Simic . . . . . . . . . . . . . . . . . . . DLB-105

   "Into the Mirror," by Peter Cooley . . DLB-105

   "Knots into Webs: Some Autobiographical
     Sources," by Dabney Stuart . . . . . DLB-105

   "L'Envoi" (1882), by Oscar Wilde . . . DLB-35

   "Living in Ruin," by Gerald Stern . . . DLB-105

   Looking for the Golden Mountain:
     Poetry Reviewing . . . . . . . . . . . . . . Y-89

   Lyric Poetry (French) . . . . . . . . . . . . DLB-268

   Medieval Galician-Portuguese
     Poetry . . . . . . . . . . . . . . . . . . . DLB-287

   "The No Self, the Little Self, and the
     Poets," by Richard Moore . . . . . . DLB-105

   On Some of the Characteristics of Modern
     Poetry and On the Lyrical Poems of
     Alfred Tennyson (1831) . . . . . . . . DLB-32

   The Pitt Poetry Series: Poetry Publishing
     Today . . . . . . . . . . . . . . . . . . . . Y-85

   "The Poetry File," by Edward
     Field . . . . . . . . . . . . . . . . . . . . DLB-105

   Poetry in Nineteenth-Century France:
     Cultural Background and Critical
     Commentary . . . . . . . . . . . . . . .DLB-217

   The Poetry of Jorge Luis Borges . . . . . . . Y-86

   "The Poet's Kaleidoscope: The Element
     of Surprise in the Making of the
     Poem" by Madeline DeFrees . . . . DLB-105

   The Pre-Raphaelite Controversy . . . . . DLB-35

   Protest Poetry in Castile . . . . . . . . . . DLB-286

   "Reflections: After a Tornado,"
     by Judson Jerome . . . . . . . . . . . DLB-105

   Statements from Former Consultants
     in Poetry . . . . . . . . . . . . . . . . . . . Y-86

   Statements on the Art of Poetry . . . . . . DLB-54

   The Study of Poetry (1880), by
     Matthew Arnold . . . . . . . . . . . . . DLB-35

   A Survey of Poetry Anthologies,
     1879-1960 . . . . . . . . . . . . . . . . . DLB-54

   Thoughts on Poetry and Its Varieties
     (1833), by John Stuart Mill . . . . . . DLB-32

   Under the Microscope (1872), by
     A. C. Swinburne . . . . . . . . . . . . . DLB-35

   The Unterberg Poetry Center of the
     92nd Street Y . . . . . . . . . . . . . . . . Y-98

   Victorian Poetry: Five Critical
     Views . . . . . . . . . . . . . . . . . . . DLBV-35

   Year in Poetry . . . . . . . . . . . . Y-83–92, 94–01

   Year's Work in American Poetry . . . . . . . Y-82

Poets
   The Lives of the Poets (1753) . . . . . . . . DLB-142

   Minor Poets of the Earlier
     Seventeenth Century . . . . . . . . . . DLB-121

   Other British Poets Who Fell
     in the Great War . . . . . . . . . . . . DLB-216

   Other Poets [French] . . . . . . . . . . . . .DLB-217

   Second-Generation Minor Poets of
     the Seventeenth Century . . . . . . . DLB-126

   Third-Generation Minor Poets of
     the Seventeenth Century . . . . . . . DLB-131

Pogodin, Mikhail Petrovich 1800-1875 . . . DLB-198

Pogorel'sky, Antonii
   (see Perovsky, Aleksei Alekseevich)

Pohl, Frederik 1919- . . . . . . . . . . . . . . . DLB-8

   Tribute to Isaac Asimov . . . . . . . . . . . . Y-92

   Tribute to Theodore Sturgeon . . . . . . . . Y-85

Poirier, Louis (see Gracq, Julien)

Poláček, Karel 1892-1945 . . . .DLB-215; CDWLB-4

Polanyi, Michael 1891-1976 . . . . . . . . . . DLB-100

Pole, Reginald 1500-1558 . . . . . . . . . . . DLB-132

Polevoi, Nikolai Alekseevich 1796-1846 . . DLB-198

Polezhaev, Aleksandr Ivanovich
   1804-1838 . . . . . . . . . . . . . . . . . . . DLB-205

Poliakoff, Stephen 1952- . . . . . . . . . . . DLB-13

Polidori, John William 1795-1821 . . . . . . DLB-116

Polite, Carlene Hatcher 1932- . . . . . . . . DLB-33

Pollard, Alfred W. 1859-1944 . . . . . . . . DLB-201

Pollard, Edward A. 1832-1872 . . . . . . . . DLB-30

Pollard, Graham 1903-1976 . . . . . . . . . DLB-201

Pollard, Percival 1869-1911 . . . . . . . . . . DLB-71

Pollard and Moss . . . . . . . . . . . . . . . . . DLB-49

Pollock, Sharon 1936- ..............DLB-60
Polonsky, Abraham 1910-1999 .........DLB-26
Polonsky, Iakov Petrovich 1819-1898....DLB-277
Polotsky, Simeon 1629-1680 ..........DLB-150
Polybius circa 200 B.C.-118 B.C........DLB-176
Pomialovsky, Nikolai Gerasimovich
  1835-1863 .....................DLB-238
Pomilio, Mario 1921-1990.............DLB-177
Ponce, Mary Helen 1938- ............DLB-122
Ponce-Montoya, Juanita 1949- .......DLB-122
Ponet, John 1516?-1556...............DLB-132
Ponge, Francis 1899-1988 ........DLB-258; Y-02
Poniatowska, Elena
  1933- .............DLB-113; CDWLB-3
Ponsard, François 1814-1867..........DLB-192
William Ponsonby [publishing house]....DLB-170
Pontiggia, Giuseppe 1934- ..........DLB-196
Pony Stories, Omnibus Essay on........DLB-160
Poole, Ernest 1880-1950 ...............DLB-9
Poole, Sophia 1804-1891 ..............DLB-166
Poore, Benjamin Perley 1820-1887 .......DLB-23
Popa, Vasko 1922-1991.....DLB-181; CDWLB-4
Pope, Abbie Hanscom 1858-1894 .......DLB-140
Pope, Alexander
  1688-1744 .....DLB-95, 101, 213; CDBLB-2
Popov, Aleksandr Serafimovich
  (see Serafimovich, Aleksandr Serafimovich)
Popov, Evgenii Anatol'evich 1946- ....DLB-285
Popov, Mikhail Ivanovich
  1742-circa 1790 .................DLB-150
Popović, Aleksandar 1929-1996.........DLB-181
Popper, Karl 1902-1994...............DLB-262
Popular Culture Association/
  American Culture Association........Y-99
Popular Library......................DLB-46
Poquelin, Jean-Baptiste (see Molière)
Porete, Marguerite ?-1310 .............DLB-208
Porlock, Martin (see MacDonald, Philip)
Porpoise Press .....................DLB-112
Porta, Antonio 1935-1989 ............DLB-128
Porter, Anna Maria 1780-1832......DLB-116, 159
Porter, Cole 1891-1964 ..............DLB-265
Porter, David 1780-1843 ..............DLB-183
Porter, Eleanor H. 1868-1920 ...........DLB-9
Porter, Gene Stratton (see Stratton-Porter, Gene)
Porter, Hal 1911-1984 ................DLB-260
Porter, Henry ?-?.....................DLB-62
Porter, Jane 1776-1850 ............DLB-116, 159
Porter, Katherine Anne 1890-1980
  ......DLB-4, 9, 102; Y-80; DS-12; CDALB-7
  The Katherine Anne Porter Society .....Y-01
Porter, Peter 1929- ..................DLB-40
Porter, William Sydney (O. Henry)
  1862-1910 ......DLB-12, 78, 79; CDALB-3
Porter, William T. 1809-1858 ....DLB-3, 43, 250
Porter and Coates ....................DLB-49
Portillo Trambley, Estela 1927-1998 .....DLB-209

Portis, Charles 1933- ................DLB-6
Medieval Galician-Portuguese Poetry ....DLB-287
Posey, Alexander 1873-1908 ...........DLB-175
Postans, Marianne circa 1810-1865 ......DLB-166
Postgate, Raymond 1896-1971..........DLB-276
Postl, Carl (see Sealsfield, Carl)
Poston, Ted 1906-1974 ................DLB-51
Potekhin, Aleksei Antipovich 1829-1908..DLB-238
Potok, Chaim 1929-2002...........DLB-28, 152
  A Conversation with Chaim Potok......Y-84
  Tribute to Bernard Malamud .........Y-86
Potter, Beatrix 1866-1943 .............DLB-141
  The Beatrix Potter Society .............Y-98
Potter, David M. 1910-1971.............DLB-17
Potter, Dennis 1935-1994 .............DLB-233
John E. Potter and Company...........DLB-49
Pottle, Frederick A. 1897-1987 .....DLB-103; Y-87
Poulin, Jacques 1937- ................DLB-60
Pound, Ezra 1885-1972
  .........DLB-4, 45, 63; DS-15; CDALB-4
  The Cost of the Cantos: William Bird
    to Ezra Pound...................Y-01
  The Ezra Pound Society .............Y-01
Poverman, C. E. 1944- ...............DLB-234
Povich, Shirley 1905-1998.............DLB-171
Powell, Anthony 1905-2000 ...DLB-15; CDBLB-7
  The Anthony Powell Society: Powell and
    the First Biennial Conference .......Y-01
Powell, Dawn 1897-1965
  Dawn Powell, Where Have You Been
    All Our Lives? ..................Y-97
Powell, John Wesley 1834-1902 ........DLB-186
Powell, Padgett 1952- ...............DLB-234
Powers, J. F. 1917-1999 ...............DLB-130
Powers, Jimmy 1903-1995 .............DLB-241
Pownall, David 1938- ................DLB-14
Powys, John Cowper 1872-1963 .....DLB-15, 255
Powys, Llewelyn 1884-1939 ............DLB-98
Powys, T. F. 1875-1953 ...........DLB-36, 162
  The Powys Society ..................Y-98
Poynter, Nelson 1903-1978 ............DLB-127
Prado, Pedro 1886-1952 ..............DLB-283
Prados, Emilio 1899-1962 .............DLB-134
Praed, Mrs. Caroline (see Praed, Rosa)
Praed, Rosa (Mrs. Caroline Praed)
  1851-1935 .....................DLB-230
Praed, Winthrop Mackworth 1802-1839...DLB-96
Praeger Publishers ....................DLB-46
Praetorius, Johannes 1630-1680.........DLB-168
Pratolini, Vasco 1913-1991 ............DLB-177
Pratt, E. J. 1882-1964.................DLB-92
Pratt, Samuel Jackson 1749-1814 ........DLB-39
Preciado Martin, Patricia 1939- ........DLB-209
Préfontaine, Yves 1937- ...............DLB-53
Prelutsky, Jack 1940- .................DLB-61
Prentice, George D. 1802-1870 ..........DLB-43

Prentice-Hall .......................DLB-46
Prescott, Orville 1906-1996...............Y-96
Prescott, William Hickling
  1796-1859 .............DLB-1, 30, 59, 235
Prešeren, Francè
  1800-1849 .........DLB-147; CDWLB-4
Presses (See also Publishing)
  Small Presses in Great Britain and
    Ireland, 1960-1985 ..............DLB-40
  Small Presses I: Jargon Society .........Y-84
  Small Presses II: The Spirit That Moves
    Us Press .....................Y-85
  Small Presses III: Pushcart Press ........Y-87
Preston, Margaret Junkin
  1820-1897 ...................DLB-239, 248
Preston, May Wilson 1873-1949 ........DLB-188
Preston, Thomas 1537-1598 .............DLB-62
Prévert, Jacques 1900-1977 ............DLB-258
Price, Anthony 1928- ................DLB-276
Price, Reynolds 1933- ........DLB-2, 218, 278
Price, Richard 1723-1791 ..............DLB-158
Price, Richard 1949- ..................Y-81
Prichard, Katharine Susannah
  1883-1969 .....................DLB-260
Prideaux, John 1578-1650 .............DLB-236
Priest, Christopher 1943- .....DLB-14, 207, 261
Priestley, J. B. 1894-1984
  ....DLB-10, 34, 77, 100, 139; Y-84; CDBLB-6
Priestley, Joseph 1733-1804 ...........DLB-252
Prigov, Dmitrii Aleksandrovich 1940- ..DLB-285
Prime, Benjamin Young 1733-1791 .......DLB-31
Primrose, Diana floruit circa 1630.......DLB-126
Prince, F. T. 1912- ..................DLB-20
Prince, Nancy Gardner 1799-?..........DLB-239
Prince, Thomas 1687-1758..........DLB-24, 140
Pringle, Thomas 1789-1834............DLB-225
Printz, Wolfgang Casper 1641-1717......DLB-168
Prior, Matthew 1664-1721 ..............DLB-95
Prisco, Michele 1920- ................DLB-177
Prishvin, Mikhail Mikhailovich
  1873-1954 .....................DLB-272
Pritchard, William H. 1932- ..........DLB-111
Pritchett, V. S. 1900-1997 .........DLB-15, 139
Probyn, May 1856 or 1857-1909........DLB-199
Procter, Adelaide Anne 1825-1864 ...DLB-32, 199
Procter, Bryan Waller 1787-1874 .....DLB-96, 144
Proctor, Robert 1868-1903 ............DLB-184
Prokopovich, Feofan 1681?-1736.........DLB-150
Prokosch, Frederic 1906-1989 ..........DLB-48
Pronzini, Bill 1943- .................DLB-226
Propertius circa 50 B.C.-post 16 B.C.
  ....................DLB-211; CDWLB-1
Propper, Dan 1937- ..................DLB-16
Prose, Francine 1947- ...............DLB-234
Protagoras circa 490 B.C.-420 B.C........DLB-176
Protest Poetry in Castile
  ca. 1445-ca. 1506.................DLB-286
Proud, Robert 1728-1813...............DLB-30

435

Proust, Marcel 1871-1922............ DLB-65
   Marcel Proust at 129 and the Proust
      Society of America............... Y-00
   Marcel Proust's *Remembrance of Things Past*:
      The Rediscovered Galley Proofs..... Y-00
Prutkov, Koz'ma Petrovich 1803-1863....DLB-277
Prynne, J. H. 1936-................ DLB-40
Przybyszewski, Stanislaw 1868-1927..... DLB-66
Pseudo-Dionysius the Areopagite floruit
   circa 500..................... DLB-115
Public Lending Right in America
   PLR and the Meaning of Literary
      Property...................... Y-83
   Statement by Sen. Charles
      McC. Mathias, Jr. PLR........... Y-83
   Statements on PLR by American Writers . Y-83
Public Lending Right in the United Kingdom
   The First Year in the United Kingdom ... Y-83
Publishers [listed by individual names]
   Publishers, Conversations with:
      An Interview with Charles Scribner III Y-94
      An Interview with Donald Lamm....... Y-95
      An Interview with James Laughlin...... Y-96
      An Interview with Patrick O'Connor.... Y-84
Publishing
   The Art and Mystery of Publishing:
      Interviews..................... Y-97
   Book Publishing Accounting: Some Basic
      Concepts...................... Y-98
   1873 Publishers' Catalogues......... DLB-49
   The Literary Scene 2002: Publishing, Book
      Reviewing, and Literary Journalism.. Y-02
   Main Trends in Twentieth-Century
      Book Clubs................... DLB-46
   Overview of U.S. Book Publishing,
      1910-1945.................... DLB-9
   The Pitt Poetry Series: Poetry Publishing
      Today........................ Y-85
   Publishing Fiction at LSU Press........ Y-87
   The Publishing Industry in 1998:
      *Sturm-und-drang.com*................ Y-98
   The Publishing Industry in 1999........ Y-99
   Publishers and Agents: The Columbia
      Connection.................... Y-87
   Responses to Ken Auletta............. Y-97
   Southern Writers Between the Wars... DLB-9
   The State of Publishing.............. Y-97
   Trends in Twentieth-Century
      Mass Market Publishing......... DLB-46
   The Year in Book Publishing.......... Y-86
Pückler-Muskau, Hermann von
   1785-1871.....................DLB-133
Pufendorf, Samuel von 1632-1694..... DLB-168
Pugh, Edwin William 1874-1930....... DLB-135
Pugin, A. Welby 1812-1852.......... DLB-55
Puig, Manuel 1932-1990.... DLB-113; CDWLB-3
Pulgar, Hernando del (Fernando del Pulgar)
   ca. 1436-ca. 1492.............. DLB-286
Pulitzer, Joseph 1847-1911............. DLB-23
Pulitzer, Joseph, Jr. 1885-1955......... DLB-29
Pulitzer Prizes for the Novel, 1917-1945.... DLB-9

Pulliam, Eugene 1889-1975.......... DLB-127
Purcell, Deirdre 1945-.............. DLB-267
Purchas, Samuel 1577?-1626.......... DLB-151
Purdy, Al 1918-2000................ DLB-88
Purdy, James 1923-............... DLB-2, 218
Purdy, Ken W. 1913-1972........... DLB-137
Pusey, Edward Bouverie 1800-1882..... DLB-55
Pushkin, Aleksandr Sergeevich
   1799-1837.................... DLB-205
Pushkin, Vasilii L'vovich
   1766-1830.................... DLB-205
Putnam, George Palmer
   1814-1872..............DLB-3, 79, 250, 254
G. P. Putnam [publishing house]...... DLB-254
G. P. Putnam's Sons [U.K.]......... DLB-106
G. P. Putnam's Sons [U.S.]......... DLB-49
   A Publisher's Archives: G. P. Putnam.... Y-92
Putnam, Hilary 1926-................DLB-279
Putnam, Samuel 1892-1950........ DLB-4; DS-15
Puttenham, George 1529?-1590........ DLB-281
Puzo, Mario 1920-1999.............. DLB-6
Pyle, Ernie 1900-1945................ DLB-29
Pyle, Howard 1853-1911.... DLB-42, 188; DS-13
Pyle, Robert Michael 1947-.............DLB-275
Pym, Barbara 1913-1980...... DLB-14, 207; Y-87
Pynchon, Thomas 1937-.............DLB-2, 173
Pyramid Books.................... DLB-46
Pyrnelle, Louise-Clarke 1850-1907...... DLB-42
Pythagoras circa 570 B.C.-?.............DLB-176

# Q

Quad, M. (see Lewis, Charles B.)
Quaritch, Bernard 1819-1899......... DLB-184
Quarles, Francis 1592-1644........... DLB-126
*The Quarterly Review* 1809-1967......... DLB-110
Quasimodo, Salvatore 1901-1968........ DLB-114
Queen, Ellery (see Dannay, Frederic, and
   Manfred B. Lee)
Queen, Frank 1822-1882............ DLB-241
The Queen City Publishing House...... DLB-49
Queirós, Eça de 1845-1900........... DLB-287
Queneau, Raymond 1903-1976..... DLB-72, 258
Quennell, Peter 1905-1993........ DLB-155, 195
Quental, Antero de 1842-1891......... DLB-287
Quesnel, Joseph 1746-1809........... DLB-99
Quiller-Couch, Sir Arthur Thomas
   1863-1944..............DLB-135, 153, 190
Quin, Ann 1936-1973............ DLB-14, 231
Quinault, Philippe 1635-1688..........DLB-268
Quincy, Samuel, of Georgia ?-?......... DLB-31
Quincy, Samuel, of Massachusetts
   1734-1789.................... DLB-31
Quine, W. V. 1908-2000.............DLB-279
Quinn, Anthony 1915-2001.......... DLB-122
Quinn, John 1870-1924............. DLB-187
Quiñónez, Naomi 1951-............ DLB-209

Quintana, Leroy V. 1944-............ DLB-82
Quintana, Miguel de 1671-1748
   A Forerunner of Chicano
      Literature.................... DLB-122
Quintilian
   circa A.D. 40-circa A.D. 96....... DLB-211
Quintus Curtius Rufus
   fl. A.D. 35................... DLB-211
Harlin Quist Books................. DLB-46
Quoirez, Françoise (see Sagan, Françoise)

# R

Raabe, Wilhelm 1831-1910........... DLB-129
Raban, Jonathan 1942-.............. DLB-204
Rabe, David 1940-........DLB-7, 228; Y-91
Raboni, Giovanni 1932-.............. DLB-128
Rachilde 1860-1953............. DLB-123, 192
Racin, Kočo 1908-1943..............DLB-147
Racine, Jean 1639-1699.............DLB-268
Rackham, Arthur 1867-1939.......... DLB-141
Radauskas, Henrikas
   1910-1970............ DLB-220; CDWLB-4
Radcliffe, Ann 1764-1823...........DLB-39, 178
Raddall, Thomas 1903-1994.......... DLB-68
Radford, Dollie 1858-1920........... DLB-240
Radichkov, Yordan 1929-............ DLB-181
Radiguet, Raymond 1903-1923........ DLB-65
Radishchev, Aleksandr Nikolaevich
   1749-1802.................... DLB-150
Radnóti, Miklós
   1909-1944.............DLB-215; CDWLB-4
Radványi, Netty Reiling (see Seghers, Anna)
Rahv, Philip 1908-1973..............DLB-137
Raich, Semen Egorovich 1792-1855..... DLB-205
Raičković, Stevan 1928-.............. DLB-181
Raiderman (see Parshchikov, Aleksei Maksimovich)
Raimund, Ferdinand Jakob 1790-1836.... DLB-90
Raine, Craig 1944-................. DLB-40
Raine, Kathleen 1908-............... DLB-20
Rainis, Jānis 1865-1929.... DLB-220; CDWLB-4
Rainolde, Richard
   circa 1530-1606............. DLB-136, 236
Rainolds, John 1549-1607............ DLB-281
Rakić, Milan 1876-1938.....DLB-147; CDWLB-4
Rakosi, Carl 1903-................. DLB-193
Ralegh, Sir Walter
   1554?-1618............ DLB-172; CDBLB-1
Raleigh, Walter
   *Style* (1897) [excerpt]............... DLB-57
Ralin, Radoy 1923-................ DLB-181
Ralph, Julian 1853-1903............. DLB-23
Ramat, Silvio 1939-................ DLB-128
Ramée, Marie Louise de la (see Ouida)
Ramírez, Sergío 1942-.............. DLB-145
Ramke, Bin 1947-................. DLB-120
Ramler, Karl Wilhelm 1725-1798....... DLB-97
Ramon Ribeyro, Julio 1929-1994....... DLB-145

| | | |
|---|---|---|
| Ramos, Manuel 1948- .............DLB-209 | Raworth, Tom 1938- ...............DLB-40 | Reich, Ebbe Kløvedal 1940- .........DLB-214 |
| Ramous, Mario 1924- ...............DLB-128 | Ray, David 1932- ..................DLB-5 | Reid, Alastair 1926- ................DLB-27 |
| Rampersad, Arnold 1941- ...........DLB-111 | Ray, Gordon Norton 1915-1986 ....DLB-103, 140 | Reid, B. L. 1918-1990 ...............DLB-111 |
| Ramsay, Allan 1684 or 1685-1758........DLB-95 | Ray, Henrietta Cordelia 1849-1916.......DLB-50 | Reid, Christopher 1949- .............DLB-40 |
| Ramsay, David 1749-1815..............DLB-30 | Raymond, Ernest 1888-1974 ..........DLB-191 | Reid, Forrest 1875-1947 .............DLB-153 |
| Ramsay, Martha Laurens 1759-1811.....DLB-200 | Raymond, Henry J. 1820-1869 .......DLB-43, 79 | Reid, Helen Rogers 1882-1970 .........DLB-29 |
| Ramsey, Frank P. 1903-1930..........DLB-262 | Raymond, René (see Chase, James Hadley) | Reid, James ?-? .....................DLB-31 |
| Ranck, Katherine Quintana 1942- .....DLB-122 | Razaf, Andy 1895-1973 ..............DLB-265 | Reid, Mayne 1818-1883............DLB-21, 163 |
| Rand, Avery and Company............DLB-49 | Rea, Michael 1927-1996...............Y-97 | Reid, Thomas 1710-1796 ..........DLB-31, 252 |
| Rand, Ayn 1905-1982 ... DLB-227, 279; CDALB-7 | Michael M. Rea and the Rea Award for the Short Story .................Y-97 | Reid, V. S. (Vic) 1913-1987 ...........DLB-125 |
| Rand McNally and Company ..........DLB-49 | Reach, Angus 1821-1856.............DLB-70 | Reid, Whitelaw 1837-1912.............DLB-23 |
| Randall, David Anton 1905-1975........DLB-140 | Read, Herbert 1893-1968 ..........DLB-20, 149 | Reilly and Lee Publishing Company......DLB-46 |
| Randall, Dudley 1914- ...............DLB-41 | Read, Martha Meredith................DLB-200 | Reimann, Brigitte 1933-1973 ...........DLB-75 |
| Randall, Henry S. 1811-1876...........DLB-30 | Read, Opie 1852-1939................DLB-23 | Reinmar der Alte circa 1165-circa 1205...DLB-138 |
| Randall, James G. 1881-1953...........DLB-17 | Read, Piers Paul 1941- ...............DLB-14 | Reinmar von Zweter circa 1200-circa 1250.............DLB-138 |
| The Randall Jarrell Symposium: A Small Collection of Randall Jarrells ........Y-86 | Reade, Charles 1814-1884.............DLB-21 | Reisch, Walter 1903-1983 .............DLB-44 |
| Excerpts From Papers Delivered at the Randall Jarrel Symposium ..........Y-86 | Reader's Digest Condensed Books ........DLB-46 | Reizei Family ......................DLB-203 |
| | Reading, Peter 1946- .................DLB-40 | Religion |
| Randall, John Herman, Jr. 1899-1980 ....DLB-279 | Reading Series in New York City ..........Y-96 | A Crisis of Culture: The Changing Role of Religion in the New Republic..................DLB-37 |
| Randolph, A. Philip 1889-1979 ..........DLB-91 | Reaney, James 1926- .................DLB-68 | Remarque, Erich Maria 1898-1970 ..........DLB-56; CDWLB-2 |
| Anson D. F. Randolph [publishing house].................DLB-49 | Rebhun, Paul 1500?-1546 ............DLB-179 | Remington, Frederic 1861-1909 ............DLB-12, 186, 188 |
| Randolph, Thomas 1605-1635 ......DLB-58, 126 | Rèbora, Clemente 1885-1957...........DLB-114 | Renaud, Jacques 1943- ...............DLB-60 |
| Random House .....................DLB-46 | Rebreanu, Liviu 1885-1944 ...........DLB-220 | Renault, Mary 1905-1983 ..............Y-83 |
| Rankin, Ian (Jack Harvey) 1960- .....DLB-267 | Rechy, John 1931- ........ DLB-122, 278; Y-82 | Rendell, Ruth (Barbara Vine) 1930- ............... DLB-87, 276 |
| Henry Ranlet [publishing house].........DLB-49 | Redding, J. Saunders 1906-1988 ......DLB-63, 76 | Rensselaer, Maria van Cortlandt van 1645-1689......................DLB-200 |
| Ransom, Harry 1908-1976.............DLB-187 | J. S. Redfield [publishing house]..........DLB-49 | Repplier, Agnes 1855-1950 ............DLB-221 |
| Ransom, John Crowe 1888-1974 ..........DLB-45, 63; CDALB-7 | Redgrove, Peter 1932- ................DLB-40 | Reshetnikov, Fedor Mikhailovich 1841-1871......................DLB-238 |
| Ransome, Arthur 1884-1967 ..........DLB-160 | Redmon, Anne 1943- .................Y-86 | Rettenbacher, Simon 1634-1706 ........DLB-168 |
| Raphael, Frederic 1931- ..............DLB-14 | Redmond, Eugene B. 1937- ............DLB-41 | Retz, Jean-François-Paul de Gondi, cardinal de 1613-1679................DLB-268 |
| Raphaelson, Samson 1896-1983 ........DLB-44 | Redol, Alves 1911-1969...............DLB-287 | Reuchlin, Johannes 1455-1522..........DLB-179 |
| Rare Book Dealers Bertram Rota and His Bookshop .......Y-91 | James Redpath [publishing house]........DLB-49 | Reuter, Christian 1665-after 1712 .......DLB-168 |
| An Interview with Glenn Horowitz......Y-90 | Reed, Henry 1808-1854................DLB-59 | Fleming H. Revell Company............DLB-49 |
| An Interview with Otto Penzler .......Y-96 | Reed, Henry 1914-1986...............DLB-27 | Reverdy, Pierre 1889-1960 ............DLB-258 |
| An Interview with Ralph Sipper .......Y-94 | Reed, Ishmael 1938- ........ DLB-2, 5, 33, 169, 227; DS-8 | Reuter, Fritz 1810-1874 ...............DLB-129 |
| New York City Bookshops in the 1930s and 1940s: The Recollections of Walter Goldwater...............Y-93 | Reed, Rex 1938- ...................DLB-185 | Reuter, Gabriele 1859-1941............DLB-66 |
| Rare Books Research in the American Antiquarian Book Trade ....................Y-97 | Reed, Sampson 1800-1880............DLB-1, 235 | Reventlow, Franziska Gräfin zu 1871-1918......................DLB-66 |
| | Reed, Talbot Baines 1852-1893.........DLB-141 | Review of Reviews Office .............DLB-112 |
| Two Hundred Years of Rare Books and Literary Collections at the University of South Carolina .......Y-00 | Reedy, William Marion 1862-1920 ......DLB-91 | Rexroth, Kenneth 1905-1982 ..... DLB-16, 48, 165, 212; Y-82; CDALB-1 |
| | Reese, Lizette Woodworth 1856-1935.....DLB-54 | |
| Rashi circa 1040-1105 ................DLB-208 | Reese, Thomas 1742-1796 .............DLB-37 | The Commercialization of the Image of Revolt....................DLB-16 |
| Raskin, Ellen 1928-1984 ..............DLB-52 | Reeve, Clara 1729-1807 ...............DLB-39 | |
| Rastell, John 1475?-1536 ......... DLB-136, 170 | Preface to The Old English Baron (1778) ......................DLB-39 | Rey, H. A. 1898-1977 ................DLB-22 |
| Rattigan, Terence 1911-1977 .......... DLB-13; CDBLB-7 | The Progress of Romance (1785) [excerpt] .....................DLB-39 | Reynal and Hitchcock ................DLB-46 |
| Raven, Simon 1927-2001 .............DLB-271 | Reeves, James 1909-1978..............DLB-161 | Reynolds, G. W. M. 1814-1879..........DLB-21 |
| Rawlings, Marjorie Kinnan 1896-1953 .........DLB-9, 22, 102; DS-17; CDALB-7 | Reeves, John 1926- ..................DLB-88 | Reynolds, John Hamilton 1794-1852......DLB-96 |
| | Reeves-Stevens, Garfield 1953- .......DLB-251 | Reynolds, Sir Joshua 1723-1792 ........DLB-104 |
| Rawlinson, Richard 1690-1755 .........DLB-213 | Régio, José (José Maria dos Reis Pereira) 1901-1969......................DLB-287 | Reynolds, Mack 1917-1983 .............DLB-8 |
| Rawlinson, Thomas 1681-1725 .........DLB-213 | Henry Regnery Company.............DLB-46 | |
| Rawls, John 1921-2002 ............... DLB-279 | Rehberg, Hans 1901-1963 ............DLB-124 | |
| | Rehfisch, Hans José 1891-1960 ........DLB-124 | Reznikoff, Charles 1894-1976 ........DLB-28, 45 |

# Cumulative Index          DLB 287

Rhetoric
    Continental European Rhetoricians,
        1400-1600, and Their Influence
        in Reaissance England ........ DLB-236

    A Finding Guide to Key Works on
        Microfilm ............... DLB-236

    Glossary of Terms and Definitions of
        Rhetoic and Logic ........... DLB-236

Rhett, Robert Barnwell 1800-1876 ....... DLB-43

Rhode, John 1884-1964 ............... DLB-77

Rhodes, Eugene Manlove 1869-1934 .... DLB-256

Rhodes, James Ford 1848-1927 ......... DLB-47

Rhodes, Richard 1937- ............ DLB-185

Rhys, Jean 1890-1979
    ..... DLB-36, 117, 162; CDBLB-7; CDWLB-3

Ribeiro, Bernadim
    fl. ca. 1475/1482-1526/1544 ........ DLB-287

Ricardo, David 1772-1823 ......... DLB-107, 158

Ricardou, Jean 1932- ............... DLB-83

Rice, Elmer 1892-1967 ............. DLB-4, 7

Rice, Grantland 1880-1954 ......... DLB-29, 171

Rich, Adrienne 1929- ..... DLB-5, 67; CDALB-7

Richard, Mark 1955- ............... DLB-234

Richard de Fournival
    1201-1259 or 1260 ............ DLB-208

Richards, David Adams 1950- ........ DLB-53

Richards, George circa 1760-1814 ....... DLB-37

Richards, I. A. 1893-1979 .............. DLB-27

Richards, Laura E. 1850-1943 .......... DLB-42

Richards, William Carey 1818-1892 ..... DLB-73

Grant Richards [publishing house] ...... DLB-112

Richardson, Charles F. 1851-1913 ....... DLB-71

Richardson, Dorothy M. 1873-1957 ..... DLB-36

    The Novels of Dorothy Richardson
        (1918), by May Sinclair ........ DLB-36

Richardson, Henry Handel
    (Ethel Florence Lindesay Robertson)
    1870-1946 .................. DLB-197, 230

Richardson, Jack 1935- ............... DLB-7

Richardson, John 1796-1852 ......... DLB-99

Richardson, Samuel
    1689-1761 ......... DLB-39, 154; CDBLB-2

    Introductory Letters from the Second
        Edition of *Pamela* (1741) ........ DLB-39

    Postscript to [the Third Edition of]
        *Clarissa* (1751) .............. DLB-39

    Preface to the First Edition of
        *Pamela* (1740) ................ DLB-39

    Preface to the Third Edition of
        *Clarissa* (1751) [excerpt] ....... DLB-39

    Preface to Volume 1 of *Clarissa*
        (1747) ....................... DLB-39

    Preface to Volume 3 of *Clarissa*
        (1748) ....................... DLB-39

Richardson, Willis 1889-1977 ........... DLB-51

Riche, Barnabe 1542-1617 ............. DLB-136

Richepin, Jean 1849-1926 ............ DLB-192

Richler, Mordecai 1931-2001 ........... DLB-53

Richter, Conrad 1890-1968 ......... DLB-9, 212

Richter, Hans Werner 1908-1993 ....... DLB-69

Richter, Johann Paul Friedrich
    1763-1825 .......... DLB-94; CDWLB-2

Joseph Rickerby [publishing house] ..... DLB-106

Rickword, Edgell 1898-1982 .......... DLB-20

Riddell, Charlotte 1832-1906 ......... DLB-156

Riddell, John (see Ford, Corey)

Ridge, John Rollin 1827-1867 ......... DLB-175

Ridge, Lola 1873-1941 ............ DLB-54

Ridge, William Pett 1859-1930 ........ DLB-135

Riding, Laura (see Jackson, Laura Riding)

Ridler, Anne 1912- ................ DLB-27

Ridruego, Dionisio 1912-1975 ......... DLB-108

Riel, Louis 1844-1885 ................ DLB-99

Riemer, Johannes 1648-1714 .......... DLB-168

Rifbjerg, Klaus 1931- ............ DLB-214

Riffaterre, Michael 1924- .............. DLB-67

A Conversation between William Riggan
    and Janette Turner Hospital ........... Y-02

Riggs, Lynn 1899-1954 ................ DLB-175

Riis, Jacob 1849-1914 ................ DLB-23

John C. Riker [publishing house] ........ DLB-49

Riley, James 1777-1840 ............ DLB-183

Riley, John 1938-1978 ............. DLB-40

Rilke, Rainer Maria
    1875-1926 .......... DLB-81; CDWLB-2

Rimanelli, Giose 1926- ............ DLB-177

Rimbaud, Jean-Nicolas-Arthur
    1854-1891 .................. DLB-217

Rinehart and Company .............. DLB-46

Ringuet 1895-1960 ................ DLB-68

Ringwood, Gwen Pharis 1910-1984 ...... DLB-88

Rinser, Luise 1911- ............ DLB-69

Ríos, Alberto 1952- ............ DLB-122

Ríos, Isabella 1948- ............ DLB-82

Ripley, Arthur 1895-1961 .............. DLB-44

Ripley, George 1802-1880 ..... DLB-1, 64, 73, 235

The Rising Glory of America:
    Three Poems .................. DLB-37

The Rising Glory of America: Written in 1771
    (1786), by Hugh Henry Brackenridge
    and Philip Freneau .............. DLB-37

Riskin, Robert 1897-1955 .............. DLB-26

Risse, Heinz 1898- ................ DLB-69

Rist, Johann 1607-1667 .............. DLB-164

Ristikivi, Karl 1912-1977 ............ DLB-220

Ritchie, Anna Mowatt 1819-1870 ..... DLB-3, 250

Ritchie, Anne Thackeray 1837-1919 ..... DLB-18

Ritchie, Thomas 1778-1854 .......... DLB-43

The Ritz Paris Hemingway Award ......... Y-85

    Mario Varga Llosa's Acceptance Speech .. Y-85

Rivard, Adjutor 1868-1945 ............ DLB-92

Rive, Richard 1931-1989 ........ DLB-125, 225

Rivera, José 1955- ............... DLB-249

Rivera, Marina 1942- ............ DLB-122

Rivera, Tomás 1935-1984 .......... DLB-82

Rivers, Conrad Kent 1933-1968 ......... DLB-41

Riverside Press .................... DLB-49

Rivington, James circa 1724-1802 ........ DLB-43

Charles Rivington [publishing house] .... DLB-154

Rivkin, Allen 1903-1990 ............. DLB-26

Roa Bastos, Augusto 1917- ......... DLB-113

Robbe-Grillet, Alain 1922- ......... DLB-83

Robbins, Tom 1936- .................. Y-80

Roberts, Charles G. D. 1860-1943 ...... DLB-92

Roberts, Dorothy 1906-1993 .......... DLB-88

Roberts, Elizabeth Madox
    1881-1941 ............. DLB-9, 54, 102

Roberts, John (see Swynnerton, Thomas)

Roberts, Keith 1935-2000 ............. DLB-261

Roberts, Kenneth 1885-1957 ........... DLB-9

Roberts, Michèle 1949- ............ DLB-231

Roberts, Theodore Goodridge
    1877-1953 .................. DLB-92

Roberts, Ursula Wyllie (see Miles, Susan)

Roberts, William 1767-1849 ......... DLB-142

James Roberts [publishing house] ...... DLB-154

Roberts Brothers ................. DLB-49

A. M. Robertson and Company ......... DLB-49

Robertson, Ethel Florence Lindesay
    (see Richardson, Henry Handel)

Robertson, William 1721-1793 ......... DLB-104

Robin, Leo 1895-1984 ............. DLB-265

Robins, Elizabeth 1862-1952 .......... DLB-197

Robinson, A. Mary F. (Madame James
    Darmesteter, Madame Mary
    Duclaux) 1857-1944 .............. DLB-240

Robinson, Casey 1903-1979 ............ DLB-44

Robinson, Derek ..................... Y-02

Robinson, Edwin Arlington
    1869-1935 ............ DLB-54; CDALB-3

    Review by Derek Robinson of George
        Greenfield's *Rich Dust* ............ Y-02

Robinson, Henry Crabb 1775-1867 ...... DLB-107

Robinson, James Harvey 1863-1936 ..... DLB-47

Robinson, Lennox 1886-1958 ......... DLB-10

Robinson, Mabel Louise 1874-1962 ...... DLB-22

Robinson, Marilynne 1943- ......... DLB-206

Robinson, Mary 1758-1800 .......... DLB-158

Robinson, Richard circa 1545-1607 ..... DLB-167

Robinson, Therese 1797-1870 ....... DLB-59, 133

Robison, Mary 1949- ............. DLB-130

Roblès, Emmanuel 1914-1995 ......... DLB-83

Roccatagliata Ceccardi, Ceccardo
    1871-1919 .................. DLB-114

Rocha, Adolfo Correira da (see Torga, Miguel)

Roche, Billy 1949- ................ DLB-233

Rochester, John Wilmot, Earl of
    1647-1680 .................. DLB-131

Rochon, Esther 1948- ............. DLB-251

Rock, Howard 1911-1976 .............. DLB-127

Rockwell, Norman Perceval 1894-1978 .. DLB-188

Rodgers, Carolyn M. 1945- ......... DLB-41

Rodgers, W. R. 1909-1969 ............ DLB-20

Rodney, Lester 1911- .............DLB-241

Rodríguez, Claudio 1934-1999 ........DLB-134

Rodríguez, Joe D. 1943- .............DLB-209

Rodríguez, Luis J. 1954- .............DLB-209

Rodriguez, Richard 1944- ........DLB-82, 256

Rodríguez Julia, Edgardo 1946- .......DLB-145

Roe, E. P. 1838-1888.................DLB-202

Roethke, Theodore
    1908-1963 ..........DLB-5, 206; CDALB-1

Rogers, Jane 1952- .................DLB-194

Rogers, Pattiann 1940- ..............DLB-105

Rogers, Samuel 1763-1855.............DLB-93

Rogers, Will 1879-1935................DLB-11

Rohmer, Sax 1883-1959 ..............DLB-70

Roiphe, Anne 1935- .................Y-80

Rojas, Arnold R. 1896-1988 ..........DLB-82

Rojas, Fernando de ca. 1475-1541 .......DLB-286

Rolfe, Frederick William
    1860-1913 ...................DLB-34, 156

Rolland, Romain 1866-1944 ...........DLB-65

Rolle, Richard circa 1290-1300 - 1340....DLB-146

Rölvaag, O. E. 1876-1931 ...........DLB-9, 212

Romains, Jules 1885-1972 .............DLB-65

A. Roman and Company................DLB-49

*Roman de la Rose:* Guillaume de Lorris
    1200/1205-circa 1230, Jean de
    Meun 1235-1240-circa 1305 ........DLB-208

Romano, Lalla 1906-2001 .............DLB-177

Romano, Octavio 1923- .............DLB-122

Rome, Harold 1908-1993 .............DLB-265

Romero, Leo 1950- ..................DLB-122

Romero, Lin 1947- ..................DLB-122

Romero, Orlando 1945- .............DLB-82

Rook, Clarence 1863-1915 ............DLB-135

Roosevelt, Theodore
    1858-1919 .............DLB-47, 186, 275

Root, Waverley 1903-1982 .............DLB-4

Root, William Pitt 1941- ............DLB-120

Roquebrune, Robert de 1889-1978 .......DLB-68

Rorty, Richard 1931- ...........DLB-246, 279

Rosa, João Guimarães 1908-1967.......DLB-113

Rosales, Luis 1910-1992 .............DLB-134

Roscoe, William 1753-1831 ...........DLB-163

Rose, Reginald 1920-2002 .............DLB-26

Rose, Wendy 1948- .................DLB-175

Rosegger, Peter 1843-1918 ...........DLB-129

Rosei, Peter 1946- .................DLB-85

Rosen, Norma 1925- .................DLB-28

Rosenbach, A. S. W. 1876-1952........DLB-140

Rosenbaum, Ron 1946- .............DLB-185

Rosenberg, Isaac 1890-1918.........DLB-20, 216

Rosenfeld, Isaac 1918-1956 ...........DLB-28

Rosenthal, Harold 1914-1999 .........DLB-241

    Jimmy, Red, and Others: Harold
    Rosenthal Remembers the Stars of
    the Press Box ...................Y-01

Rosenthal, M. L. 1917-1996..............DLB-5

Rosenwald, Lessing J. 1891-1979........DLB-187

Ross, Alexander 1591-1654............DLB-151

Ross, Harold 1892-1951 ..............DLB-137

Ross, Jerry 1926-1955 ................DLB-265

Ross, Leonard Q. (see Rosten, Leo)

Ross, Lillian 1927- ..................DLB-185

Ross, Martin 1862-1915...............DLB-135

Ross, Sinclair 1908-1996 ..............DLB-88

Ross, W. W. E. 1894-1966 .............DLB-88

Rosselli, Amelia 1930-1996 ...........DLB-128

Rossen, Robert 1908-1966.............DLB-26

Rosset, Barney......................Y-02

Rossetti, Christina 1830-1894 ...DLB-35, 163, 240

Rossetti, Dante Gabriel
    1828-1882 ............DLB-35; CDBLB-4

    The Stealthy School of
    Criticism (1871) ..............DLB-35

Rossner, Judith 1935- .................DLB-6

Rostand, Edmond 1868-1918 ..........DLB-192

Rosten, Leo 1908-1997 ................DLB-11

Rostenberg, Leona 1908- ............DLB-140

Rostopchina, Evdokiia Petrovna
    1811-1858 ....................DLB-205

Rostovsky, Dimitrii 1651-1709 ........DLB-150

Rota, Bertram 1903-1966..............DLB-201

    Bertram Rota and His Bookshop .......Y-91

Roth, Gerhard 1942- ............DLB-85, 124

Roth, Henry 1906?-1995...............DLB-28

Roth, Joseph 1894-1939................DLB-85

Roth, Philip
    1933- .....DLB-2, 28, 173; Y-82; CDALB-6

Rothenberg, Jerome 1931- .........DLB-5, 193

Rothschild Family ....................DLB-184

Rotimi, Ola 1938- ..................DLB-125

Rotrou, Jean 1609-1650 ..............DLB-268

Routhier, Adolphe-Basile 1839-1920 ......DLB-99

Routier, Simone 1901-1987 .............DLB-88

George Routledge and Sons............DLB-106

Roversi, Roberto 1923- ..............DLB-128

Rowe, Elizabeth Singer 1674-1737 .....DLB-39, 95

Rowe, Nicholas 1674-1718 .............DLB-84

Rowlands, Samuel circa 1570-1630 ......DLB-121

Rowlandson, Mary
    circa 1637-circa 1711 ...........DLB-24, 200

Rowley, William circa 1585-1626 .......DLB-58

Rowling, J. K.
    The Harry Potter Phenomenon ........Y-99

Rowse, A. L. 1903-1997...............DLB-155

Rowson, Susanna Haswell
    circa 1762-1824 ............... DLB-37, 200

Roy, Camille 1870-1943...............DLB-92

The G. Ross Roy Scottish Poetry Collection
    at the University of South Carolina .....Y-89

Roy, Gabrielle 1909-1983 .............DLB-68

Roy, Jules 1907-2000 .................DLB-83

The Royal Court Theatre and the English
    Stage Company...................DLB-13

The Royal Court Theatre and the New
    Drama.........................DLB-10

The Royal Shakespeare Company
    at the Swan .....................Y-88

Royall, Anne Newport 1769-1854 ....DLB-43, 248

Royce, Josiah 1855-1916 ..............DLB-270

The Roycroft Printing Shop ............DLB-49

Royde-Smith, Naomi 1875-1964 ........DLB-191

Royster, Vermont 1914-1996 ..........DLB-127

Richard Royston [publishing house] .....DLB-170

Różewicz, Tadeusz 1921- ............DLB-232

Ruark, Gibbons 1941- ...............DLB-120

Ruban, Vasilii Grigorevich 1742-1795....DLB-150

Rubens, Bernice 1928- ...........DLB-14, 207

Rubina, Dina Il'inichna 1953- ........DLB-285

Rubinshtein, Lev Semenovich 1947- ...DLB-285

Rudd and Carleton ...................DLB-49

Rudd, Steele (Arthur Hoey Davis) ......DLB-230

Rudkin, David 1936- .................DLB-13

Rudnick, Paul 1957- .................DLB-266

Rudolf von Ems circa 1200-circa 1254 ...DLB-138

Ruffin, Josephine St. Pierre 1842-1924 ....DLB-79

Ruganda, John 1941- ................DLB-157

Ruggles, Henry Joseph 1813-1906........DLB-64

Ruiz de Burton, María Amparo
    1832-1895 ..................DLB-209, 221

Rukeyser, Muriel 1913-1980...........DLB-48

Rule, Jane 1931- ....................DLB-60

Rulfo, Juan 1918-1986 ......DLB-113; CDWLB-3

Rumaker, Michael 1932- .............DLB-16

Rumens, Carol 1944- ................DLB-40

Rummo, Paul-Eerik 1942- ...........DLB-232

Runyon, Damon 1880-1946 ..... DLB-11, 86, 171

*Ruodlieb* circa 1050-1075...............DLB-148

Rush, Benjamin 1746-1813 .............DLB-37

Rush, Rebecca 1779-?.................DLB-200

Rushdie, Salman 1947- ...............DLB-194

Rusk, Ralph L. 1888-1962.............DLB-103

Ruskin, John
    1819-1900 .......DLB-55, 163, 190; CDBLB-4

Russ, Joanna 1937- ..................DLB-8

Russell, Benjamin 1761-1845 ..........DLB-43

Russell, Bertrand 1872-1970........DLB-100, 262

Russell, Charles Edward 1860-1941 ......DLB-25

Russell, Charles M. 1864-1926 .........DLB-188

Russell, Eric Frank 1905-1978 .........DLB-255

Russell, Fred 1906-2003...............DLB-241

Russell, George William (see AE)

Russell, Countess Mary Annette Beauchamp
    (see Arnim, Elizabeth von)

Russell, Willy 1947- ................DLB-233

B. B. Russell and Company............DLB-49

R. H. Russell and Son ................DLB-49

Rutebeuf flourished 1249-1277 ........DLB-208

# Cumulative Index

Rutherford, Mark 1831-1913 .......... DLB-18
Ruxton, George Frederick 1821-1848 ... DLB-186
R-va, Zeneida (see Gan, Elena Andreevna)
Ryan, James 1952- ................ DLB-267
Ryan, Michael 1946- ................... Y-82
Ryan, Oscar 1904- .................. DLB-68
Ryder, Jack 1871-1936 .............. DLB-241
Ryga, George 1932-1987 .............. DLB-60
Rylands, Enriqueta Augustina Tennant 1843-1908 .................. DLB-184
Rylands, John 1801-1888 ............. DLB-184
Ryle, Gilbert 1900-1976 .............. DLB-262
Ryleev, Kondratii Fedorovich 1795-1826 ..................... DLB-205
Rymer, Thomas 1643?-1713 ........... DLB-101
Ryskind, Morrie 1895-1985 ........... DLB-26
Rzhevsky, Aleksei Andreevich 1737-1804 ..................... DLB-150

# S

The Saalfield Publishing Company ..... DLB-46
Saba, Umberto 1883-1957 ............ DLB-114
Sábato, Ernesto 1911- .... DLB-145; CDWLB-3
Saberhagen, Fred 1930- .............. DLB-8
Sabin, Joseph 1821-1881 ............. DLB-187
Sacer, Gottfried Wilhelm 1635-1699 .... DLB-168
Sachs, Hans 1494-1576 ...... DLB-179; CDWLB-2
Sá-Carneiro, Mário de 1890-1916 ...... DLB-287
Sack, John 1930- ................... DLB-185
Sackler, Howard 1929-1982 ........... DLB-7
Sackville, Lady Margaret 1881-1963 .... DLB-240
Sackville, Thomas 1536-1608 and Norton, Thomas 1532-1584 ........ DLB-62
Sackville, Thomas 1536-1608 ......... DLB-132
Sackville-West, Edward 1901-1965 ..... DLB-191
Sackville-West, V. 1892-1962 ....... DLB-34, 195
Sá de Miranda, Francisco de 1481-1588? .................... DLB-287
Sadlier, Mary Anne 1820-1903 ......... DLB-99
D. and J. Sadlier and Company ......... DLB-49
Sadoff, Ira 1945- ................... DLB-120
Sadoveanu, Mihail 1880-1961 ......... DLB-220
Sadur, Nina Nikolaevna 1950- ........ DLB-285
Sáenz, Benjamin Alire 1954- .......... DLB-209
Saenz, Jaime 1921-1986 .......... DLB-145, 283
Saffin, John circa 1626-1710 .......... DLB-24
Sagan, Françoise 1935- .............. DLB-83
Sage, Robert 1899-1962 .............. DLB-4
Sagel, Jim 1947- ................... DLB-82
Sagendorph, Robb Hansell 1900-1970 ... DLB-137
Sahagún, Carlos 1938- .............. DLB-108
Sahkomaapii, Piitai (see Highwater, Jamake)
Sahl, Hans 1902-1993 ................ DLB-69
Said, Edward W. 1935- .............. DLB-67
Saigyō 1118-1190 ................... DLB-203
Saiko, George 1892-1962 ............. DLB-85

Sainte-Beuve, Charles-Augustin 1804-1869 ..................... DLB-217
Saint-Exupéry, Antoine de 1900-1944 .... DLB-72
St. John, J. Allen 1872-1957 .......... DLB-188
St John, Madeleine 1942- ............ DLB-267
St. Johns, Adela Rogers 1894-1988 ...... DLB-29
St. Omer, Garth 1931- .............. DLB-117
Saint Pierre, Michel de 1916-1987 ...... DLB-83
St. Dominic's Press ................. DLB-112
The St. John's College Robert Graves Trust .. Y-96
St. Martin's Press .................. DLB-46
St. Nicholas 1873-1881 ................ DS-13
Saintsbury, George 1845-1933 ....... DLB-57, 149
"Modern English Prose" (1876) ...... DLB-57
The Present State of the English Novel (1892), .................. DLB-18
Saiokuken Sōchō 1448-1532 .......... DLB-203
Saki (see Munro, H. H.)
Salaam, Kalamu ya 1947- ............ DLB-38
Šalamun, Tomaž 1941- ... DLB-181; CDWLB-4
Salas, Floyd 1931- ................. DLB-82
Sálaz-Marquez, Rubén 1935- ......... DLB-122
Salemson, Harold J. 1910-1988 ........ DLB-4
Salesbury, William 1520?-1584? ...... DLB-281
Salinas, Luis Omar 1937- ............ DLB-82
Salinas, Pedro 1891-1951 ............ DLB-134
Salinger, J. D. 1919- ........ DLB-2, 102, 173; CDALB-1
Salkey, Andrew 1928- .............. DLB-125
Sallust circa 86 B.C.-35 B.C. ............... DLB-211; CDWLB-1
Salt, Waldo 1914-1987 ............... DLB-44
Salter, James 1925- ................ DLB-130
Salter, Mary Jo 1954- ............... DLB-120
Saltus, Edgar 1855-1921 ............. DLB-202
Saltykov, Mikhail Evgrafovich 1826-1889 ..................... DLB-238
Salustri, Carlo Alberto (see Trilussa)
Salverson, Laura Goodman 1890-1970 .... DLB-92
Samain, Albert 1858-1900 ............ DLB-217
Sampson, Richard Henry (see Hull, Richard)
Samuels, Ernest 1903-1996 ........... DLB-111
Sanborn, Franklin Benjamin 1831-1917 .................... DLB-1, 223
Sánchez de Arévalo, Rodrigo 1404-1470 .................... DLB-286
Sánchez, Luis Rafael 1936- .......... DLB-145
Sánchez, Philomeno "Phil" 1917- .... DLB-122
Sánchez, Ricardo 1941-1995 .......... DLB-82
Sánchez, Saúl 1943- ................ DLB-209
Sanchez, Sonia 1934- .......... DLB-41; DS-8
Sand, George 1804-1876 .......... DLB-119, 192
Sandburg, Carl 1878-1967 ..DLB-17, 54; CDALB-3
Sanders, Edward 1939- .......... DLB-16, 244
Sanderson, Robert 1587-1663 ......... DLB-281
Sandoz, Mari 1896-1966 ........... DLB-9, 212

Sandwell, B. K. 1876-1954 ............ DLB-92
Sandy, Stephen 1934- ............... DLB-165
Sandys, George 1578-1644 ......... DLB-24, 121
Sangster, Charles 1822-1893 .......... DLB-99
Sanguineti, Edoardo 1930- .......... DLB-128
Sanjōnishi Sanetaka 1455-1537 ........ DLB-203
San Pedro, Diego de fl. ca. 1492 ...... DLB-286
Sansay, Leonora ?-after 1823 ......... DLB-200
Sansom, William 1912-1976 .......... DLB-139
Santayana, George 1863-1952 ...... DLB-54, 71, 246, 270; DS-13
Santiago, Danny 1911-1988 .......... DLB-122
Santillana, Marqués de (Íñigo López de Mendoza) 1398-1458 ................... DLB-286
Santmyer, Helen Hooven 1895-1986 ....... Y-84
Sanvitale, Francesca 1928- ......... DLB-196
Sapidus, Joannes 1490-1561 .......... DLB-179
Sapir, Edward 1884-1939 ............. DLB-92
Sapper (see McNeile, Herman Cyril)
Sappho circa 620 B.C.-circa 550 B.C. ..................... DLB-176; CDWLB-1
Saramago, José 1922- ........... DLB-287; Y-98
Nobel Lecture 1998: How Characters Became the Masters and the Author Their Apprentice ................ Y-98
Sarban (John W. Wall) 1910-1989 ...... DLB-255
Sardou, Victorien 1831-1908 .......... DLB-192
Sarduy, Severo 1937-1993 ............ DLB-113
Sargent, Pamela 1948- .............. DLB-8
Saro-Wiwa, Ken 1941- .............. DLB-157
Saroyan, Aram
Rites of Passage [on William Saroyan] .... Y-83
Saroyan, William 1908-1981 ..... DLB-7, 9, 86; Y-81; CDALB-7
Sarraute, Nathalie 1900-1999 .......... DLB-83
Sarrazin, Albertine 1937-1967 ......... DLB-83
Sarris, Greg 1952- ................. DLB-175
Sarton, May 1912-1995 .......... DLB-48; Y-81
Sartre, Jean-Paul 1905-1980 .......... DLB-72
Sassoon, Siegfried 1886-1967 .......... DLB-20, 191; DS-18
A Centenary Essay ................ Y-86
Tributes from Vivien F. Clarke and Michael Thorpe. ............... Y-86
Sata Ineko 1904- .................. DLB-180
Saturday Review Press ............... DLB-46
Saunders, James 1925- .............. DLB-13
Saunders, John Monk 1897-1940 ...... DLB-26
Saunders, Margaret Marshall 1861-1947 ..................... DLB-92
Saunders and Otley ................ DLB-106
Saussure, Ferdinand de 1857-1913 ...... DLB-242
Savage, James 1784-1873 ............. DLB-30
Savage, Marmion W. 1803?-1872 ....... DLB-21
Savage, Richard 1697?-1743 .......... DLB-95
Savard, Félix-Antoine 1896-1982 ...... DLB-68
Savery, Henry 1791-1842 ............ DLB-230

Saville, (Leonard) Malcolm 1901-1982 ...DLB-160
Savinio, Alberto 1891-1952 ............DLB-264
Sawyer, Robert J. 1960- ...............DLB-251
Sawyer, Ruth 1880-1970 ...............DLB-22
Sayers, Dorothy L.
    1893-1957 .... DLB-10, 36, 77, 100; CDBLB-6
    The Dorothy L. Sayers Society .........Y-98
Sayle, Charles Edward 1864-1924 .......DLB-184
Sayles, John Thomas 1950- ............DLB-44
Sbarbaro, Camillo 1888-1967 ..........DLB-114
Scalapino, Leslie 1947- ...............DLB-193
Scannell, Vernon 1922- ...............DLB-27
Scarry, Richard 1919-1994 ............DLB-61
Schaefer, Jack 1907-1991 .............DLB-212
Schaeffer, Albrecht 1885-1950 .........DLB-66
Schaeffer, Susan Fromberg 1941- ......DLB-28
Schaff, Philip 1819-1893 ..............DS-13
Schaper, Edzard 1908-1984 ...........DLB-69
Scharf, J. Thomas 1843-1898 ..........DLB-47
Schede, Paul Melissus 1539-1602 ......DLB-179
Scheffel, Joseph Viktor von 1826-1886 ...DLB-129
Scheffler, Johann 1624-1677 ..........DLB-164
Schelling, Friedrich Wilhelm Joseph von
    1775-1854 .......................DLB-90
Scherer, Wilhelm 1841-1886 ..........DLB-129
Scherfig, Hans 1905-1979 ............DLB-214
Schickele, René 1883-1940 ............DLB-66
Schiff, Dorothy 1903-1989 ............DLB-127
Schiller, Friedrich
    1759-1805 .........DLB-94; CDWLB-2
Schirmer, David 1623-1687 ..........DLB-164
Schlaf, Johannes 1862-1941 ..........DLB-118
Schlegel, August Wilhelm 1767-1845 ...DLB-94
Schlegel, Dorothea 1763-1839 .........DLB-90
Schlegel, Friedrich 1772-1829 .........DLB-90
Schleiermacher, Friedrich 1768-1834 ....DLB-90
Schlesinger, Arthur M., Jr. 1917- ......DLB-17
Schlumberger, Jean 1877-1968 .........DLB-65
Schmid, Eduard Hermann Wilhelm
    (see Edschmid, Kasimir)
Schmidt, Arno 1914-1979 .............DLB-69
Schmidt, Johann Kaspar (see Stirner, Max)
Schmidt, Michael 1947- ...............DLB-40
Schmidtbonn, Wilhelm August
    1876-1952 .......................DLB-118
Schmitz, Aron Hector (see Svevo, Italo)
Schmitz, James H. 1911-1981 .........DLB-8
Schnabel, Johann Gottfried 1692-1760 ...DLB-168
Schnackenberg, Gjertrud 1953- .......DLB-120
Schnitzler, Arthur
    1862-1931 ........DLB-81, 118; CDWLB-2
Schnurre, Wolfdietrich 1920-1989 ......DLB-69
Schocken Books ......................DLB-46
Scholartis Press ......................DLB-112
Scholderer, Victor 1880-1971 .........DLB-201

The Schomburg Center for Research
    in Black Culture ..................DLB-76
Schönbeck, Virgilio (see Giotti, Virgilio)
Schönherr, Karl 1867-1943 ...........DLB-118
Schoolcraft, Jane Johnston 1800-1841 ....DLB-175
School Stories, 1914-1960 .............DLB-160
Schopenhauer, Arthur 1788-1860 .......DLB-90
Schopenhauer, Johanna 1766-1838 .....DLB-90
Schorer, Mark 1908-1977 .............DLB-103
Schottelius, Justus Georg 1612-1676 ....DLB-164
Schouler, James 1839-1920 ...........DLB-47
Schoultz, Solveig von 1907-1996 .......DLB-259
Schrader, Paul 1946- .................DLB-44
Schreiner, Olive
    1855-1920 .........DLB-18, 156, 190, 225
Schroeder, Andreas 1946- ............DLB-53
Schubart, Christian Friedrich Daniel
    1739-1791 .......................DLB-97
Schubert, Gotthilf Heinrich 1780-1860 ...DLB-90
Schücking, Levin 1814-1883 ..........DLB-133
Schulberg, Budd 1914- .....DLB-6, 26, 28; Y-81
    Excerpts from USC Presentation
    [on F. Scott Fitzgerald] ............Y-96
F. J. Schulte and Company ............DLB-49
Schulz, Bruno 1892-1942 ....DLB-215; CDWLB-4
Schulze, Hans (see Praetorius, Johannes)
Schupp, Johann Balthasar 1610-1661 ....DLB-164
Schurz, Carl 1829-1906 ..............DLB-23
Schuyler, George S. 1895-1977 ........DLB-29, 51
Schuyler, James 1923-1991 ..........DLB-5, 169
Schwartz, Delmore 1913-1966 .......DLB-28, 48
Schwartz, Jonathan 1938- .............Y-82
Schwartz, Lynne Sharon 1939- ........DLB-218
Schwarz, Sibylle 1621-1638 ..........DLB-164
Schwerner, Armand 1927-1999 ........DLB-165
Schwob, Marcel 1867-1905 ...........DLB-123
Sciascia, Leonardo 1921-1989 .........DLB-177
Science Fiction and Fantasy
    Documents in British Fantasy and
    Science Fiction .................DLB-178
    Hugo Awards and Nebula Awards .....DLB-8
    The Iconography of Science-Fiction
    Art ...............................DLB-8
    The New Wave ......................DLB-8
    Paperback Science Fiction ...........DLB-8
    Science Fantasy ....................DLB-8
    Science-Fiction Fandom and
    Conventions ......................DLB-8
    Science-Fiction Fanzines: The Time
    Binders .........................DLB-8
    Science-Fiction Films ...............DLB-8
    Science Fiction Writers of America
    and the Nebula Award ............DLB-8
    Selected Science-Fiction Magazines and
    Anthologies .....................DLB-8
    A World Chronology of Important Science
    Fiction Works (1818-1979) ........DLB-8

The Year in Science Fiction
    and Fantasy ....................Y-00, 01
Scot, Reginald circa 1538-1599 ........DLB-136
Scotellaro, Rocco 1923-1953 ..........DLB-128
Scott, Alicia Anne (Lady John Scott)
    1810-1900 ......................DLB-240
Scott, Catharine Amy Dawson
    1865-1934 ......................DLB-240
Scott, Dennis 1939-1991 ..............DLB-125
Scott, Dixon 1881-1915 ..............DLB-98
Scott, Duncan Campbell 1862-1947 .....DLB-92
Scott, Evelyn 1893-1963 ............DLB-9, 48
Scott, F. R. 1899-1985 ...............DLB-88
Scott, Frederick George 1861-1944 .....DLB-92
Scott, Geoffrey 1884-1929 ...........DLB-149
Scott, Harvey W. 1838-1910 ..........DLB-23
Scott, Lady Jane (see Scott, Alicia Anne)
Scott, Paul 1920-1978 ...........DLB-14, 207
Scott, Sarah 1723-1795 ..............DLB-39
Scott, Tom 1918- ....................DLB-27
Scott, Sir Walter 1771-1832
    ......DLB-93, 107, 116, 144, 159; CDBLB-3
Scott, William Bell 1811-1890 .........DLB-32
Walter Scott Publishing Company
    Limited .........................DLB-112
William R. Scott [publishing house] ....DLB-46
Scott-Heron, Gil 1949- ...............DLB-41
Scribe, Eugene 1791-1861 ............DLB-192
Scribner, Arthur Hawley 1859-1932 ....DS-13, 16
Scribner, Charles 1854-1930 ........DS-13, 16
Scribner, Charles, Jr. 1921-1995 .......Y-95
    Reminiscences .....................DS-17
Charles Scribner's Sons ....DLB-49; DS-13, 16, 17
    Archives of Charles Scribner's Sons ....DS-17
*Scribner's Magazine* ..................DS-13
*Scribner's Monthly* ...................DS-13
Scripps, E. W. 1854-1926 .............DLB-25
Scudder, Horace Elisha 1838-1902 ....DLB-42, 71
Scudder, Vida Dutton 1861-1954 .....DLB-71
Scudéry, Madeleine de 1607-1701 .....DLB-268
Scupham, Peter 1933- ................DLB-40
Seabrook, William 1886-1945 .........DLB-4
Seabury, Samuel 1729-1796 ..........DLB-31
Seacole, Mary Jane Grant 1805-1881 ...DLB-166
*The Seafarer* circa 970 .................DLB-146
Sealsfield, Charles (Carl Postl)
    1793-1864 ...................DLB-133, 186
Searle, John R. 1932- ................DLB-279
Sears, Edward I. 1819?-1876 ..........DLB-79
Sears Publishing Company ............DLB-46
Seaton, George 1911-1979 ............DLB-44
Seaton, William Winston 1785-1866 .....DLB-43
Martin Secker [publishing house] .......DLB-112
Martin Secker, and Warburg Limited ....DLB-112
Sedgwick, Arthur George 1844-1915 ....DLB-64

# Cumulative Index

Sedgwick, Catharine Maria
1789-1867..........DLB-1, 74, 183, 239, 243

Sedgwick, Ellery 1872-1960............DLB-91

Sedgwick, Eve Kosofsky 1950-.......DLB-246

Sedley, Sir Charles 1639-1701.........DLB-131

Seeberg, Peter 1925-1999............DLB-214

Seeger, Alan 1888-1916..............DLB-45

Seers, Eugene (see Dantin, Louis)

Segal, Erich 1937-....................Y-86

Šegedin, Petar 1909-................DLB-181

Seghers, Anna 1900-1983....DLB-69; CDWLB-2

Seid, Ruth (see Sinclair, Jo)

Seidel, Frederick Lewis 1936-..........Y-84

Seidel, Ina 1885-1974................DLB-56

Seifert, Jaroslav
1901-1986.......DLB-215; Y-84; CDWLB-4

   Jaroslav Seifert Through the Eyes of
   the English-Speaking Reader........Y-84

   Three Poems by Jaroslav Seifert......Y-84

Seifullina, Lidiia Nikolaevna 1889-1954..DLB-272

Seigenthaler, John 1927-..............DLB-127

Seizin Press.......................DLB-112

Séjour, Victor 1817-1874..............DLB-50

Séjour Marcou et Ferrand, Juan Victor
(see Séjour, Victor)

Sekowski, Józef-Julian, Baron Brambeus
(see Senkovsky, Osip Ivanovich)

Selby, Bettina 1934-.................DLB-204

Selby, Hubert, Jr. 1928-...........DLB-2, 227

Selden, George 1929-1989.............DLB-52

Selden, John 1584-1654...............DLB-213

Selenić, Slobodan 1933-1995...........DLB-181

Self, Edwin F. 1920-.................DLB-137

Self, Will 1961-.....................DLB-207

Seligman, Edwin R. A. 1861-1939.......DLB-47

Selimović, Meša
1910-1982............DLB-181; CDWLB-4

Sellars, Wilfrid 1912-1989............DLB-279

Sellings, Arthur (Arthur Gordon Ley)
1911-1968........................DLB-261

Selous, Frederick Courteney 1851-1917...DLB-174

Seltzer, Chester E. (see Muro, Amado)

Thomas Seltzer [publishing house].......DLB-46

Selvon, Sam 1923-1994......DLB-125; CDWLB-3

Semmes, Raphael 1809-1877............DLB-189

Senancour, Etienne de 1770-1846.......DLB-119

Sena, Jorge de 1919-1978.............DLB-287

Sendak, Maurice 1928-................DLB-61

Seneca the Elder
circa 54 B.C.-circa A.D. 40.........DLB-211

Seneca the Younger
circa 1 B.C.-A.D. 65.....DLB-211; CDWLB-1

Senécal, Eva 1905-..................DLB-92

Sengstacke, John 1912-1997............DLB-127

Senior, Olive 1941-..................DLB-157

Senkovsky, Osip Ivanovich
(Józef-Julian Sekowski, Baron Brambeus)
1800-1858......................DLB-198

Šenoa, August 1838-1881....DLB-147; CDWLB-4

Sepamla, Sipho 1932-...........DLB-157, 225

Serafimovich, Aleksandr Serafimovich
(Aleksandr Serafimovich Popov)
1863-1949.......................DLB-272

Serao, Matilde 1856-1927.............DLB-264

Seredy, Kate 1899-1975................DLB-22

Sereni, Vittorio 1913-1983...........DLB-128

William Seres [publishing house]......DLB-170

Sergeev-Tsensky, Sergei Nikolaevich (Sergei
Nikolaevich Sergeev) 1875-1958.....DLB-272

Serling, Rod 1924-1975................DLB-26

Sernine, Daniel 1955-................DLB-251

Serote, Mongane Wally 1944-.....DLB-125, 225

Serraillier, Ian 1912-1994............DLB-161

Serrano, Nina 1934-.................DLB-122

Service, Robert 1874-1958............DLB-92

Sessler, Charles 1854-1935............DLB-187

Seth, Vikram 1952-.............DLB-120, 271

Seton, Elizabeth Ann 1774-1821........DLB-200

Seton, Ernest Thompson
1860-1942..................DLB-92; DS-13

Seton, John circa 1509-1567..........DLB-281

Setouchi Harumi 1922-...............DLB-182

Settle, Mary Lee 1918-................DLB-6

Seume, Johann Gottfried 1763-1810.....DLB-94

Seuse, Heinrich 1295?-1366...........DLB-179

Seuss, Dr. (see Geisel, Theodor Seuss)

Severin, Timothy 1940-...............DLB-204

Sévigné, Marie de Rabutin Chantal,
Madame de 1626-1696.............DLB-268

Sewall, Joseph 1688-1769..............DLB-24

Sewall, Richard B. 1908-.............DLB-111

Sewall, Samuel 1652-1730..............DLB-24

Sewell, Anna 1820-1878...............DLB-163

Sexton, Anne 1928-1974...DLB-5, 169; CDALB-1

Seymour-Smith, Martin 1928-1998......DLB-155

Sgorlon, Carlo 1930-.................DLB-196

Shaara, Michael 1929-1988.............Y-83

Shabel'skaia, Aleksandra Stanislavovna
1845-1921......................DLB-238

Shadwell, Thomas 1641?-1692..........DLB-80

Shaffer, Anthony 1926-...............DLB-13

Shaffer, Peter 1926-......DLB-13, 233; CDBLB-8

Shaftesbury, Anthony Ashley Cooper,
Third Earl of 1671-1713..........DLB-101

Shaginian, Marietta Sergeevna
1888-1982......................DLB-272

Shairp, Mordaunt 1887-1939............DLB-10

Shakespeare, Nicholas 1957-..........DLB-231

Shakespeare, William
1564-1616......DLB-62, 172, 263; CDBLB-1

   The New Variorum Shakespeare........Y-85

   Shakespeare and Montaigne: A Symposium
   by Jules Furthman................Y-02

   $6,166,000 for a *Book!* Observations on
   *The Shakespeare First Folio: The History
   of the Book*......................Y-01

   Taylor-Made Shakespeare? Or Is
   "Shall I Die?" the Long-Lost Text
   of Bottom's Dream?..............Y-85

   The Shakespeare Globe Trust..........Y-93

Shakespeare Head Press..............DLB-112

Shakhova, Elisaveta Nikitichna
1822-1899......................DLB-277

Shakhovskoi, Aleksandr Aleksandrovich
1777-1846......................DLB-150

Shange, Ntozake 1948-...........DLB-38, 249

Shapiro, Karl 1913-2000..............DLB-48

Sharon Publications..................DLB-46

Sharov, Vladimir Aleksandrovich
1952-..........................DLB-285

Sharp, Margery 1905-1991.............DLB-161

Sharp, William 1855-1905.............DLB-156

Sharpe, Tom 1928-..............DLB-14, 231

Shaw, Albert 1857-1947................DLB-91

Shaw, George Bernard
1856-1950........DLB-10, 57, 190; CDBLB-6

   The Bernard Shaw Society.............Y-99

   "Stage Censorship: The Rejected
   Statement" (1911) [excerpts].....DLB-10

Shaw, Henry Wheeler 1818-1885........DLB-11

Shaw, Irwin
1913-1984........DLB-6, 102; Y-84; CDALB-1

Shaw, Joseph T. 1874-1952............DLB-137

   "As I Was Saying," Joseph T. Shaw's
   Editorial Rationale in *Black Mask*
   (January 1927)..................DLB-137

Shaw, Mary 1854-1929................DLB-228

Shaw, Robert 1927-1978............DLB-13, 14

Shaw, Robert B. 1947-...............DLB-120

Shawn, Wallace 1943-................DLB-266

Shawn, William 1907-1992............DLB-137

Frank Shay [publishing house]..........DLB-46

Shchedrin, N. (see Saltykov, Mikhail Evgrafovich)

Shcherbakova, Galina Nikolaevna
1932-..........................DLB-285

Shcherbina, Nikolai Fedorovich
1821-1869......................DLB-277

Shea, John Gilmary 1824-1892..........DLB-30

Sheaffer, Louis 1912-1993............DLB-103

Sheahan, Henry Beston (see Beston, Henry)

Shearing, Joseph 1886-1952............DLB-70

Shebbeare, John 1709-1788............DLB-39

Sheckley, Robert 1928-................DLB-8

Shedd, William G. T. 1820-1894........DLB-64

Sheed, Wilfrid 1930-..................DLB-6

Sheed and Ward [U.S.]................DLB-46

Sheed and Ward Limited [U.K.].......DLB-112

Sheldon, Alice B. (see Tiptree, James, Jr.)

Sheldon, Edward 1886-1946.............DLB-7

Sheldon and Company.................DLB-49

Sheller, Aleksandr Konstantinovich
1838-1900......................DLB-238

Shelley, Mary Wollstonecraft 1797-1851
.........DLB-110, 116, 159, 178; CDBLB-3

Preface to *Frankenstein; or, The Modern Prometheus* (1818) ........ DLB-178

Shelley, Percy Bysshe 1792-1822 ...... DLB-96, 110, 158; CDBLB-3

Shelnutt, Eve 1941- ............... DLB-130

Shenshin (see Fet, Afanasii Afanas'evich)

Shenstone, William 1714-1763 ........... DLB-95

Shepard, Clark and Brown ............. DLB-49

Shepard, Ernest Howard 1879-1976 ...... DLB-160

Shepard, Sam 1943- ............. DLB-7, 212

Shepard, Thomas I, 1604 or 1605-1649 ... DLB-24

Shepard, Thomas, II, 1635-1677 ........ DLB-24

Shepherd, Luke flourished 1547-1554 .... DLB-136

Sherburne, Edward 1616-1702 .......... DLB-131

Sheridan, Frances 1724-1766 ......... DLB-39, 84

Sheridan, Richard Brinsley 1751-1816 ............. DLB-89; CDBLB-2

Sherman, Francis 1871-1926 ........... DLB-92

Sherman, Martin 1938- ............. DLB-228

Sherriff, R. C. 1896-1975 ....... DLB-10, 191, 233

Sherrod, Blackie 1919- ............... DLB-241

Sherry, Norman 1935- ................ DLB-155

    Tribute to Graham Greene ........... Y-91

Sherry, Richard 1506-1551 or 1555 ..... DLB-236

Sherwood, Mary Martha 1775-1851 ..... DLB-163

Sherwood, Robert E. 1896-1955 ... DLB-7, 26, 249

Shevyrev, Stepan Petrovich 1806-1864 ... DLB-205

Shiel, M. P. 1865-1947 ................ DLB-153

Shiels, George 1886-1949 .............. DLB-10

Shiga Naoya 1883-1971 ............... DLB-180

Shiina Rinzō 1911-1973 ............... DLB-182

Shikishi Naishinnō 1153?-1201 ......... DLB-203

Shillaber, Benjamin Penhallow 1814-1890 ............. DLB-1, 11, 235

Shimao Toshio 1917-1986 ............. DLB-182

Shimazaki Tōson 1872-1943 ........... DLB-180

Shimose, Pedro 1940- ................. DLB-283

Shine, Ted 1931- ..................... DLB-38

Shinkei 1406-1475 .................... DLB-203

Ship, Reuben 1915-1975 ............... DLB-88

Shirer, William L. 1904-1993 .......... DLB-4

Shirinsky-Shikhmatov, Sergii Aleksandrovich 1783-1837 .................... DLB-150

Shirley, James 1596-1666 .............. DLB-58

Shishkov, Aleksandr Semenovich 1753-1841 .................... DLB-150

Shockley, Ann Allen 1927- ............. DLB-33

Sholokhov, Mikhail Aleksandrovich 1905-1984 .................... DLB-272

Shōno Junzō 1921- ................... DLB-182

Shore, Arabella 1820?-1901 ............ DLB-199

Shore, Louisa 1824-1895 ............... DLB-199

Short, Luke (see Glidden, Frederick Dilley)

Peter Short [publishing house] ......... DLB-170

Shorter, Dora Sigerson 1866-1918 ....... DLB-240

Shorthouse, Joseph Henry 1834-1903 ..... DLB-18

Short Stories
    Michael M. Rea and the Rea Award for the Short Story ............... Y-97
    The Year in Short Stories ............. Y-87
    The Year in the Short Story ..... Y-88, 90–93

Shōtetsu 1381-1459 ................... DLB-203

Showalter, Elaine 1941- ............... DLB-67

Shulevitz, Uri 1935- .................. DLB-61

Shulman, Max 1919-1988 .............. DLB-11

Shute, Henry A. 1856-1943 ............. DLB-9

Shute, Nevil (Nevil Shute Norway) 1899-1960 .................... DLB-255

Shuttle, Penelope 1947- ........... DLB-14, 40

Shvarts, Evgenii L'vovich 1896-1958 .... DLB-272

Sibbes, Richard 1577-1635 ............. DLB-151

Sibiriak, D. (see Mamin, Dmitrii Narkisovich)

Siddal, Elizabeth Eleanor 1829-1862 ..... DLB-199

Sidgwick, Ethel 1877-1970 ............. DLB-197

Sidgwick, Henry 1838-1900 ............ DLB-262

Sidgwick and Jackson Limited .......... DLB-112

Sidney, Margaret (see Lothrop, Harriet M.)

Sidney, Mary 1561-1621 ............... DLB-167

Sidney, Sir Philip 1554-1586 .. DLB-167; CDBLB-1

    *An Apologie for Poetrie* (the Olney edition, 1595, of *Defence of Poesie*) ........ DLB-167

Sidney's Press ....................... DLB-49

Sierra, Rubén 1946- .................. DLB-122

Sierra Club Books .................... DLB-49

Siger of Brabant circa 1240-circa 1284 ... DLB-115

Sigourney, Lydia Huntley 1791-1865 ...... DLB-1, 42, 73, 183, 239, 243

Silkin, Jon 1930-1997 ................. DLB-27

Silko, Leslie Marmon 1948- ........... DLB-143, 175, 256, 275

Silliman, Benjamin 1779-1864 .......... DLB-183

Silliman, Ron 1946- .................. DLB-169

Silliphant, Stirling 1918-1996 .......... DLB-26

Sillitoe, Alan 1928- ..... DLB-14, 139; CDBLB-8
    Tribute to J. B. Priestly .............. Y-84

Silman, Roberta 1934- ................ DLB-28

Silone, Ignazio (Secondino Tranquilli) 1900-1978 .................... DLB-264

Silva, Beverly 1930- .................. DLB-122

Silva, José Asunció 1865-1896 ......... DLB-283

Silverberg, Robert 1935- ............... DLB-8

Silverman, Kaja 1947- ................ DLB-246

Silverman, Kenneth 1936- ............. DLB-111

Simak, Clifford D. 1904-1988 ........... DLB-8

Simcoe, Elizabeth 1762-1850 ........... DLB-99

Simcox, Edith Jemima 1844-1901 ....... DLB-190

Simcox, George Augustus 1841-1905 ..... DLB-35

Sime, Jessie Georgina 1868-1958 ........ DLB-92

Simenon, Georges 1903-1989 ..... DLB-72; Y-89

Simic, Charles 1938- ................. DLB-105
    "Images and 'Images'" ............... DLB-105

Simionescu, Mircea Horia 1928- ....... DLB-232

Simmel, Johannes Mario 1924- ........ DLB-69

Valentine Simmes [publishing house] .... DLB-170

Simmons, Ernest J. 1903-1972 ......... DLB-103

Simmons, Herbert Alfred 1930- ........ DLB-33

Simmons, James 1933- ................ DLB-40

Simms, William Gilmore 1806-1870 ....... DLB-3, 30, 59, 73, 248

Simms and M'Intyre ................. DLB-106

Simon, Claude 1913- ............. DLB-83; Y-85
    Nobel Lecture ...................... Y-85

Simon, Neil 1927- ................ DLB-7, 266

Simon and Schuster .................. DLB-46

Simons, Katherine Drayton Mayrant 1890-1969 .................... Y-83

Simović, Ljubomir 1935- .............. DLB-181

Simpkin and Marshall [publishing house] .................. DLB-154

Simpson, Helen 1897-1940 ............. DLB-77

Simpson, Louis 1923- .................. DLB-5

Simpson, N. F. 1919- .................. DLB-13

Sims, George 1923- .............. DLB-87; Y-99

Sims, George Robert 1847-1922 ... DLB-35, 70, 135

Sinán, Rogelio 1904-1994 ............. DLB-145

Sinclair, Andrew 1935- ................ DLB-14

Sinclair, Bertrand William 1881-1972 ..... DLB-92

Sinclair, Catherine 1800-1864 .......... DLB-163

Sinclair, Jo 1913-1995 ................ DLB-28

Sinclair, Lister 1921- .................. DLB-88

Sinclair, May 1863-1946 ........... DLB-36, 135
    The Novels of Dorothy Richardson (1918) ...................... DLB-36

Sinclair, Upton 1878-1968 ...... DLB-9; CDALB-5

Upton Sinclair [publishing house] ........ DLB-46

Singer, Isaac Bashevis 1904-1991
    ....... DLB-6, 28, 52, 278; Y-91; CDALB-1

Singer, Mark 1950- .................. DLB-185

Singmaster, Elsie 1879-1958 ............ DLB-9

Sinisgalli, Leonardo 1908-1981 .......... DLB-114

Siodmak, Curt 1902-2000 .............. DLB-44

Sîrbu, Ion D. 1919-1989 ............... DLB-232

Siringo, Charles A. 1855-1928 .......... DLB-186

Sissman, L. E. 1928-1976 ............... DLB-5

Sisson, C. H. 1914- ................... DLB-27

Sitwell, Edith 1887-1964 ...... DLB-20; CDBLB-7

Sitwell, Osbert 1892-1969 ......... DLB-100, 195

Skácel, Jan 1922-1989 ................ DLB-232

Skalbe, Kārlis 1879-1945 .............. DLB-220

Skármeta, Antonio 1940- .............. DLB-145; CDWLB-3

Skavronsky, A. (see Danilevsky, Grigorii Petrovich)

Skeat, Walter W. 1835-1912 ............ DLB-184

William Skeffington [publishing house] ... DLB-106

Skelton, John 1463-1529 .............. DLB-136

Skelton, Robin 1925-1997 .......... DLB-27, 53

Škėma, Antanas 1910-1961 ............ DLB-220

Skinner, Constance Lindsay 1877-1939 .................. DLB-92

Skinner, John Stuart 1788-1851 ........ DLB-73

Skipsey, Joseph 1832-1903 ............ DLB-35

Skou-Hansen, Tage 1925- ........... DLB-214

Škvorecký, Josef 1924- .... DLB-232; CDWLB-4

Slade, Bernard 1930- ................ DLB-53

Slamnig, Ivan 1930- ................ DLB-181

Slančeková, Božena (see Timrava)

Slataper, Scipio 1888-1915 ............ DLB-264

Slater, Patrick 1880-1951 .............. DLB-68

Slaveykov, Pencho 1866-1912 ......... DLB-147

Slaviček, Milivoj 1929- ............ DLB-181

Slavitt, David 1935- ............... DLB-5, 6

Sleigh, Burrows Willcocks Arthur 1821-1869 ..................... DLB-99

Sleptsov, Vasilii Alekseevich 1836-1878 ...DLB-277

Slesinger, Tess 1905-1945 ............ DLB-102

Slessor, Kenneth 1901-1971 ........... DLB-260

Slick, Sam (see Haliburton, Thomas Chandler)

Sloan, John 1871-1951 ............... DLB-188

Sloane, William, Associates ........... DLB-46

Slonimsky, Mikhail Leonidovich 1897-1972 ..................... DLB-272

Sluchevsky, Konstantin Konstantinovich 1837-1904 ......................DLB-277

Small, Maynard and Company ......... DLB-49

Smart, Christopher 1722-1771 ......... DLB-109

Smart, David A. 1892-1957 ............ DLB-137

Smart, Elizabeth 1913-1986 ........... DLB-88

Smart, J. J. C. 1920- ............... DLB-262

Smedley, Menella Bute 1820?-1877 ..... DLB-199

William Smellie [publishing house] ...... DLB-154

Smiles, Samuel 1812-1904 ............. DLB-55

Smiley, Jane 1949- ............... DLB-227, 234

Smith, A. J. M. 1902-1980 ............ DLB-88

Smith, Adam 1723-1790 ........ DLB-104, 252

Smith, Adam (George Jerome Waldo Goodman) 1930- ............... DLB-185

Smith, Alexander 1829-1867......... DLB-32, 55

"On the Writing of Essays" (1862) ... DLB-57

Smith, Amanda 1837-1915 ........... DLB-221

Smith, Betty 1896-1972................. Y-82

Smith, Carol Sturm 1938- .............. Y-81

Smith, Charles Henry 1826-1903 ...... DLB-11

Smith, Charlotte 1749-1806 ........ DLB-39, 109

Smith, Chet 1899-1973 ................DLB-171

Smith, Cordwainer 1913-1966 .......... DLB-8

Smith, Dave 1942- ................. DLB-5
  Tribute to James Dickey .............. Y-97
  Tribute to John Gardner ............. Y-82

Smith, Dodie 1896- ................. DLB-10

Smith, Doris Buchanan 1934- ......... DLB-52

Smith, E. E. 1890-1965................ DLB-8

Smith, Elihu Hubbard 1771-1798 ....... DLB-37

Smith, Elizabeth Oakes (Prince) (see Oakes Smith, Elizabeth)

Smith, Eunice 1757-1823.............. DLB-200

Smith, F. Hopkinson 1838-1915...........DS-13

Smith, George D. 1870-1920........... DLB-140

Smith, George O. 1911-1981 ........... DLB-8

Smith, Goldwin 1823-1910............. DLB-99

Smith, H. Allen 1907-1976 .......... DLB-11, 29

Smith, Harry B. 1860-1936............. DLB-187

Smith, Hazel Brannon 1914-1994....... DLB-127

Smith, Henry circa 1560-circa 1591 ..... DLB-136

Smith, Horatio (Horace) 1779-1849.................. DLB-96, 116

Smith, Iain Crichton 1928-1998 ..... DLB-40, 139

Smith, J. Allen 1860-1924 ............. DLB-47

Smith, James 1775-1839 .............. DLB-96

Smith, Jessie Willcox 1863-1935......... DLB-188

Smith, John 1580-1631 ............ DLB-24, 30

Smith, John 1618-1652 ............. DLB-252

Smith, Josiah 1704-1781 .............. DLB-24

Smith, Ken 1938- ................. DLB-40

Smith, Lee 1944- ............... DLB-143; Y-83

Smith, Logan Pearsall 1865-1946 ........ DLB-98

Smith, Margaret Bayard 1778-1844 ..... DLB-248

Smith, Mark 1935- .................... Y-82

Smith, Michael 1698-circa 1771 ........ DLB-31

Smith, Pauline 1882-1959............. DLB-225

Smith, Red 1905-1982 ............DLB-29, 171

Smith, Roswell 1829-1892 ............. DLB-79

Smith, Samuel Harrison 1772-1845....... DLB-43

Smith, Samuel Stanhope 1751-1819 ...... DLB-37

Smith, Sarah (see Stretton, Hesba)

Smith, Sarah Pogson 1774-1870 ........ DLB-200

Smith, Seba 1792-1868 .......... DLB-1, 11, 243

Smith, Stevie 1902-1971 .............. DLB-20

Smith, Sydney 1771-1845 ............DLB-107

Smith, Sydney Goodsir 1915-1975 ....... DLB-27

Smith, Sir Thomas 1513-1577.......... DLB-132

Smith, Wendell 1914-1972 ............DLB-171

Smith, William flourished 1595-1597 .... DLB-136

Smith, William 1727-1803 ............. DLB-31

  *A General Idea of the College of Mirania* (1753) [excerpts] ............... DLB-31

Smith, William 1728-1793 ............. DLB-30

Smith, William Gardner 1927-1974....... DLB-76

Smith, William Henry 1808-1872....... DLB-159

Smith, William Jay 1918- ............. DLB-5

Smith, Elder and Company ........... DLB-154

Harrison Smith and Robert Haas [publishing house] ............... DLB-46

J. Stilman Smith and Company ......... DLB-49

W. B. Smith and Company ........... DLB-49

W. H. Smith and Son ................ DLB-106

Leonard Smithers [publishing house] .... DLB-112

Smollett, Tobias 1721-1771 ......... DLB-39, 104; CDBLB-2

Dedication to *Ferdinand Count Fathom* (1753)..................... DLB-39

Preface to *Ferdinand Count Fathom* (1753).................... DLB-39

Preface to *Roderick Random* (1748)..... DLB-39

Smythe, Francis Sydney 1900-1949 ..... DLB-195

Snelling, William Joseph 1804-1848..... DLB-202

Snellings, Rolland (see Touré, Askia Muhammad)

Snodgrass, W. D. 1926- .............. DLB-5

Snow, C. P. 1905-1980 .... DLB-15, 77; DS-17; CDBLB-7

Snyder, Gary 1930- ........ DLB-5, 16, 165, 212, 237, 275

Sobiloff, Hy 1912-1970 ............... DLB-48

The Society for Textual Scholarship and *TEXT*...................... Y-87

The Society for the History of Authorship, Reading and Publishing............... Y-92

Söderberg, Hjalmar 1869-1941......... DLB-259

Södergran, Edith 1892-1923.......... DLB-259

Soffici, Ardengo 1879-1964......... DLB-114, 264

Sofola, 'Zulu 1938- .................DLB-157

Sokhanskaia, Nadezhda Stepanovna (Kokhanovskaia) 1823?-1884........DLB-277

Sokolov, Sasha (Aleksandr Vsevolodovich Sokolov) 1943- ............... DLB-285

Solano, Solita 1888-1975................ DLB-4

Soldati, Mario 1906-1999............DLB-177

Soledad (see Zamudio, Adela)

Šoljan, Antun 1932-1993 ............. DLB-181

Sollers, Philippe (Philippe Joyaux) 1936- ...................... DLB-83

Sollogub, Vladimir Aleksandrovich 1813-1882 ..................... DLB-198

Sollors, Werner 1943- ............... DBL-246

Solmi, Sergio 1899-1981 ............. DLB-114

Solomon, Carl 1928- ................ DLB-16

Solway, David 1941- ................ DLB-53

Solzhenitsyn, Aleksandr I. 1918- Solzhenitsyn and America ............ Y-85

Some Basic Notes on Three Modern Genres: Interview, Blurb, and Obituary ......... Y-02

Somerville, Edith Œnone 1858-1949 .... DLB-135

Somov, Orest Mikhailovich 1793-1833 .. DLB-198

Sønderby, Knud 1909-1966 .......... DLB-214

Song, Cathy 1955- ................. DLB-169

Sonnevi, Göran 1939- .............. DLB-257

Sono Ayako 1931- ................. DLB-182

Sontag, Susan 1933- ............... DLB-2, 67

Sophocles 497/496 B.C.-406/405 B.C. ................DLB-176; CDWLB-1

Šopov, Aco 1923-1982 ............... DLB-181

Sorel, Charles ca.1600-1674 ...........DLB-268

Sørensen, Villy 1929- .............. DLB-214

Sorensen, Virginia 1912-1991.......... DLB-206

Sorge, Reinhard Johannes 1892-1916.... DLB-118

Sorokin, Vladimir Georgievich 1955- ...................... DLB-285

Sorrentino, Gilbert 1929- ..... DLB-5, 173; Y-80

Sotheby, James 1682-1742 . . . . . . . . . . . . .DLB-213
Sotheby, John 1740-1807 . . . . . . . . . . . . . .DLB-213
Sotheby, Samuel 1771-1842 . . . . . . . . . . . .DLB-213
Sotheby, Samuel Leigh 1805-1861. . . . . . .DLB-213
Sotheby, William 1757-1833. . . . . . . .DLB-93, 213
Soto, Gary 1952- . . . . . . . . . . . . . . . . . . .DLB-82
Soueif, Ahdaf 1950- . . . . . . . . . . . . . . . .DLB-267
Souster, Raymond 1921- . . . . . . . . . . . . . .DLB-88
The *South English Legendary* circa
   thirteenth-fifteenth centuries . . . . . . . .DLB-146
Southerland, Ellease 1943- . . . . . . . . . . . . .DLB-33
Southern, Terry 1924-1995 . . . . . . . . . . . . . .DLB-2
Southern Illinois University Press . . . . . . . . . .Y-95
Southern Literature
   Fellowship of Southern Writers. . . . . . . . .Y-98
   The Fugitives and the Agrarians:
      The First Exhibition . . . . . . . . . . . . . .Y-85
   "The Greatness of Southern Literature":
      League of the South Institute for the
      Study of Southern Culture and
      History . . . . . . . . . . . . . . . . . . . . . . .Y-02
   The Society for the Study of
      Southern Literature. . . . . . . . . . . . . .Y-00
   Southern Writers Between the Wars. . . .DLB-9
Southerne, Thomas 1659-1746 . . . . . . . . . .DLB-80
Southey, Caroline Anne Bowles
   1786-1854 . . . . . . . . . . . . . . . . . . . . .DLB-116
Southey, Robert 1774-1843 . . . . . DLB-93, 107, 142
Southwell, Robert 1561?-1595. . . . . . . . . .DLB-167
Southworth, E. D. E. N. 1819-1899. . . . . .DLB-239
Sowande, Bode 1948- . . . . . . . . . . . . . . .DLB-157
Tace Sowle [publishing house]. . . . . . . . . .DLB-170
Soyfer, Jura 1912-1939. . . . . . . . . . . . . . .DLB-124
Soyinka, Wole
   1934- . . . . DLB-125; Y-86, Y-87; CDWLB-3
   Nobel Lecture 1986: This Past Must
      Address Its Present . . . . . . . . . . . . . . . Y-86
Spacks, Barry 1931- . . . . . . . . . . . . . . . .DLB-105
Spalding, Frances 1950- . . . . . . . . . . . . . .DLB-155
Spanish Travel Writers of the
   Late Middle Ages . . . . . . . . . . . . . . . .DLB-286
Spark, Muriel 1918- . . . .DLB-15, 139; CDBLB-7
Michael Sparke [publishing house]. . . . . . .DLB-170
Sparks, Jared 1789-1866. . . . . . . . .DLB-1, 30, 235
Sparshott, Francis 1926- . . . . . . . . . . . . . .DLB-60
Späth, Gerold 1939- . . . . . . . . . . . . . . . . .DLB-75
Spatola, Adriano 1941-1988. . . . . . . . . . . .DLB-128
Spaziani, Maria Luisa 1924- . . . . . . . . . . .DLB-128
*Specimens of Foreign Standard Literature*
   1838-1842 . . . . . . . . . . . . . . . . . . . . . .DLB-1
*The Spectator* 1828- . . . . . . . . . . . . . . . .DLB-110
Spedding, James 1808-1881 . . . . . . . . . . . .DLB-144
Spee von Langenfeld, Friedrich
   1591-1635 . . . . . . . . . . . . . . . . . . . . .DLB-164
Speght, Rachel 1597-after 1630 . . . . . . . . .DLB-126
Speke, John Hanning 1827-1864 . . . . . . . .DLB-166
Spellman, A. B. 1935- . . . . . . . . . . . . . . . .DLB-41
Spence, Catherine Helen 1825-1910 . . . . .DLB-230

Spence, Thomas 1750-1814 . . . . . . . . . . . .DLB-158
Spencer, Anne 1882-1975. . . . . . . . . .DLB-51, 54
Spencer, Charles, third Earl of Sunderland
   1674-1722 . . . . . . . . . . . . . . . . . . . . .DLB-213
Spencer, Elizabeth 1921- . . . . . . . . .DLB-6, 218
Spencer, George John, Second Earl Spencer
   1758-1834 . . . . . . . . . . . . . . . . . . . . .DLB-184
Spencer, Herbert 1820-1903 . . . . . . . . DLB-57, 262
   "The Philosophy of Style" (1852). . . . .DLB-57
Spencer, Scott 1945- . . . . . . . . . . . . . . . . . . Y-86
Spender, J. A. 1862-1942. . . . . . . . . . . . . .DLB-98
Spender, Stephen 1909-1995 . . DLB-20; CDBLB-7
Spener, Philipp Jakob 1635-1705 . . . . . . . .DLB-164
Spenser, Edmund
   circa 1552-1599. . . . . . . .DLB-167; CDBLB-1
   Envoy from *The Shepheardes Calender* . .DLB-167
   "The Generall Argument of the
      Whole Booke," from
      *The Shepheardes Calender* . . . . . . . . .DLB-167
   "A Letter of the Authors Expounding
      His Whole Intention in the Course
      of this Worke: Which for that It
      Giueth Great Light to the Reader,
      for the Better Vnderstanding
      Is Hereunto Annexed,"
      from *The Faerie Queene* (1590) . . . .DLB-167
   "To His Booke," from
      *The Shepheardes Calender* (1579) . . .DLB-167
   "To the Most Excellent and Learned
      Both Orator and Poete, Mayster
      Gabriell Haruey, His Verie Special
      and Singular Good Frend E. K.
      Commendeth the Good Lyking of
      This His Labour, and the Patronage
      of the New Poete," from
      *The Shepheardes Calender* . . . . . . . .DLB-167
Sperr, Martin 1944- . . . . . . . . . . . . . . . .DLB-124
Spewack, Bella Cowen 1899-1990. . . . . . .DLB-266
Spewack, Samuel 1899-1971 . . . . . . . . . . .DLB-266
Spicer, Jack 1925-1965. . . . . . . . . .DLB-5, 16, 193
Spielberg, Peter 1929- . . . . . . . . . . . . . . . . Y-81
Spielhagen, Friedrich 1829-1911 . . . . . . . .DLB-129
"*Spielmannsepen*" (circa 1152-circa 1500) . . .DLB-148
Spier, Peter 1927- . . . . . . . . . . . . . . . . . .DLB-61
Spillane, Mickey 1918- . . . . . . . . . . . . . .DLB-226
Spink, J. G. Taylor 1888-1962. . . . . . . . . .DLB-241
Spinrad, Norman 1940- . . . . . . . . . . . . . . .DLB-8
   Tribute to Isaac Asimov . . . . . . . . . . . . . . Y-92
Spires, Elizabeth 1952- . . . . . . . . . . . . . .DLB-120
Spitteler, Carl 1845-1924. . . . . . . . . . . . . .DLB-129
Spivak, Lawrence E. 1900- . . . . . . . . . . . .DLB-137
Spofford, Harriet Prescott
   1835-1921 . . . . . . . . . . . . . . . . .DLB-74, 221
Sports
   Jimmy, Red, and Others: Harold
      Rosenthal Remembers the Stars
      of the Press Box . . . . . . . . . . . . . . . .Y-01
   The Literature of Boxing in England
      through Arthur Conan Doyle. . . . . .Y-01
   Notable Twentieth-Century Books
      about Sports . . . . . . . . . . . . . . . . .DLB-241
Sprigge, Timothy L. S. 1932- . . . . . . . .DLB-262

Spring, Howard 1889-1965 . . . . . . . . . . . .DLB-191
Squibob (see Derby, George Horatio)
Squier, E. G. 1821-1888. . . . . . . . . . . . . .DLB-189
Stableford, Brian 1948- . . . . . . . . . . . . .DLB-261
Stacpoole, H. de Vere 1863-1951 . . . . . . .DLB-153
Staël, Germaine de 1766-1817 . . . . . .DLB-119, 192
Staël-Holstein, Anne-Louise Germaine de
   (see Staël, Germaine de)
Stafford, Jean 1915-1979 . . . . . . . . . .DLB-2, 173
Stafford, William 1914-1993 . . . . . . . .DLB-5, 206
Stallings, Laurence 1894-1968. . . . . . . . DLB-7, 44
Stallworthy, Jon 1935- . . . . . . . . . . . . . . .DLB-40
Stampp, Kenneth M. 1912- . . . . . . . . . . .DLB-17
Stănescu, Nichita 1933-1983 . . . . . . . . . . .DLB-232
Stanev, Emiliyan 1907-1979 . . . . . . . . . . .DLB-181
Stanford, Ann 1916- . . . . . . . . . . . . . . . . .DLB-5
Stangerup, Henrik 1937-1998 . . . . . . . . . .DLB-214
Stanihurst, Richard 1547-1618. . . . . . . . . .DLB-281
Stanitsky, N. (see Panaeva, Avdot'ia Iakovlevna)
Stankevich, Nikolai Vladimirovich
   1813-1840 . . . . . . . . . . . . . . . . . . . . .DLB-198
Stanković, Borisav ("Bora")
   1876-1927 . . . . . . . . . .DLB-147; CDWLB-4
Stanley, Henry M. 1841-1904 . . . . DLB-189; DS-13
Stanley, Thomas 1625-1678. . . . . . . . . . . .DLB-131
Stannard, Martin 1947- . . . . . . . . . . . . .DLB-155
William Stansby [publishing house]. . . . . . .DLB-170
Stanton, Elizabeth Cady 1815-1902. . . . . . .DLB-79
Stanton, Frank L. 1857-1927 . . . . . . . . . . .DLB-25
Stanton, Maura 1946- . . . . . . . . . . . . . .DLB-120
Stapledon, Olaf 1886-1950 . . . . . . . . .DLB-15, 255
Star Spangled Banner Office . . . . . . . . . . .DLB-49
Stark, Freya 1893-1993 . . . . . . . . . . . . . .DLB-195
Starkey, Thomas circa 1499-1538 . . . . . . .DLB-132
Starkie, Walter 1894-1976 . . . . . . . . . . . .DLB-195
Starkweather, David 1935- . . . . . . . . . . . . .DLB-7
Starrett, Vincent 1886-1974 . . . . . . . . . . . .DLB-187
Stationers' Company of London, The . . . .DLB-170
Statius circa A.D. 45-A.D. 96. . . . . . . . . . .DLB-211
Stead, Christina 1902-1983 . . . . . . . . . . . .DLB-260
Stead, Robert J. C. 1880-1959 . . . . . . . . . .DLB-92
Steadman, Mark 1930- . . . . . . . . . . . . . . .DLB-6
Stearns, Harold E. 1891-1943 . . . . . . .DLB-4; DS-15
Stebnitsky, M. (see Leskov, Nikolai Semenovich)
Stedman, Edmund Clarence 1833-1908 . . .DLB-64
Steegmuller, Francis 1906-1994 . . . . . . . . .DLB-111
Steel, Flora Annie 1847-1929 . . . . . . .DLB-153, 156
Steele, Max 1922- . . . . . . . . . . . . . . . . . . .Y-80
Steele, Richard
   1672-1729 . . . . . . . . . .DLB-84, 101; CDBLB-2
Steele, Timothy 1948- . . . . . . . . . . . . . . .DLB-120
Steele, Wilbur Daniel 1886-1970 . . . . . . . .DLB-86
Wallace Markfield's "Steeplechase". . . . . . . .Y-02
Steere, Richard circa 1643-1721. . . . . . . . .DLB-24
Stefanovski, Goran 1952- . . . . . . . . . . . .DLB-181

Stegner, Wallace
  1909-1993 .......... DLB-9, 206, 275; Y-93
Stehr, Hermann 1864-1940 ........... DLB-66
Steig, William 1907- ............... DLB-61
Stein, Gertrude 1874-1946
  ....... DLB-4, 54, 86, 228; DS-15; CDALB-4
Stein, Leo 1872-1947.................. DLB-4
Stein and Day Publishers ............. DLB-46
Steinbeck, John 1902-1968
  ........ DLB-7, 9, 212, 275; DS-2; CDALB-5
  John Steinbeck Research Center,
    San Jose State University............ Y-85
  The Steinbeck Centennial ............. Y-02
Steinem, Gloria 1934- ............... DLB-246
Steiner, George 1929- ............... DLB-67
Steinhoewel, Heinrich 1411/1412-1479....DLB-179
Steloff, Ida Frances 1887-1989.......... DLB-187
Stendhal 1783-1842.................... DLB-119
Stephen, Leslie 1832-1904 ......DLB-57, 144, 190
Stephen Family (Bloomsbury Group).......DS-10
Stephens, A. G. 1865-1933 ............. DLB-230
Stephens, Alexander H. 1812-1883........ DLB-47
Stephens, Alice Barber 1858-1932 ........ DLB-188
Stephens, Ann 1810-1886 ........ DLB-3, 73, 250
Stephens, Charles Asbury 1844?-1931 .... DLB-42
Stephens, James 1882?-1950.... DLB-19, 153, 162
Stephens, John Lloyd 1805-1852 ... DLB-183, 250
Stephens, Michael 1946- ............. DLB-234
Stephensen, P. R. 1901-1965 ........... DLB-260
Sterling, George 1869-1926 ............ DLB-54
Sterling, James 1701-1763 ............. DLB-24
Sterling, John 1806-1844............... DLB-116
Stern, Gerald 1925- ................. DLB-105
  "Living in Ruin".................... DLB-105
Stern, Gladys B. 1890-1973............. DLB-197
Stern, Madeleine B. 1912- ....... DLB-111, 140
Stern, Richard 1928- ............DLB-218; Y-87
Stern, Stewart 1922- ................ DLB-26
Sterne, Laurence 1713-1768 ... DLB-39; CDBLB-2
Sternheim, Carl 1878-1942 ........ DLB-56, 118
Sternhold, Thomas ?-1549 ............. DLB-132
Steuart, David 1747-1824 .............. DLB-213
Stevens, Henry 1819-1886 ............. DLB-140
Stevens, Wallace 1879-1955 ... DLB-54; CDALB-5
  The Wallace Stevens Society ........... Y-99
Stevenson, Anne 1933- ............... DLB-40
Stevenson, D. E. 1892-1973 ............ DLB-191
Stevenson, Lionel 1902-1973 ........... DLB-155
Stevenson, Robert Louis
  1850-1894 ........DLB-18, 57, 141, 156, 174;
                              DS-13; CDBLB-5
  "On Style in Literature:
    Its Technical Elements" (1885) ... DLB-57
Stewart, Donald Ogden
  1894-1980 .......... DLB-4, 11, 26; DS-15
Stewart, Douglas 1913-1985 ........... DLB-260
Stewart, Dugald 1753-1828............. DLB-31

Stewart, George, Jr. 1848-1906.......... DLB-99
Stewart, George R. 1895-1980 .......... DLB-8
Stewart, Harold 1916-1995.............. DLB-260
Stewart, J. I. M. (see Innes, Michael)
Stewart, Maria W. 1803?-1879........... DLB-239
Stewart, Randall 1896-1964 ............ DLB-103
Stewart, Sean 1965- ................. DLB-251
Stewart and Kidd Company............. DLB-46
Stickney, Trumbull 1874-1904 .......... DLB-54
Stieler, Caspar 1632-1707 ............. DLB-164
Stifter, Adalbert
  1805-1868 ........ DLB-133; CDWLB-2
Stiles, Ezra 1727-1795 ................ DLB-31
Still, James 1906-2001................DLB-9; Y-01
Stirling, S. M. 1953- ................ DLB-251
Stirner, Max 1806-1856 ............... DLB-129
Stith, William 1707-1755 .............. DLB-31
Stivens, Dal 1911-1997 ............... DLB-260
Elliot Stock [publishing house] ........ DLB-106
Stockton, Annis Boudinot 1736-1801 .... DLB-200
Stockton, Frank R. 1834-1902 ..DLB-42, 74; DS-13
Stockton, J. Roy 1892-1972............. DLB-241
Ashbel Stoddard [publishing house] ...... DLB-49
Stoddard, Charles Warren 1843-1909 ... DLB-186
Stoddard, Elizabeth 1823-1902.......... DLB-202
Stoddard, Richard Henry
  1825-1903 .......... DLB-3, 64, 250; DS-13
Stoddard, Solomon 1643-1729 .......... DLB-24
Stoker, Bram
  1847-1912........DLB-36, 70, 178; CDBLB-5
  On Writing Dracula, from the
    Introduction to Dracula (1897)....DLB-178
Frederick A. Stokes Company .......... DLB-49
Stokes, Thomas L. 1898-1958 .......... DLB-29
Stokesbury, Leon 1945- ............. DLB-120
Stolberg, Christian Graf zu 1748-1821 .... DLB-94
Stolberg, Friedrich Leopold Graf zu
  1750-1819....................... DLB-94
Stone, Lucy 1818-1893............. DLB-79, 239
Stone, Melville 1848-1929 ............ DLB-25
Stone, Robert 1937- ................ DLB-152
Stone, Ruth 1915- .................. DLB-105
Stone, Samuel 1602-1663 .............. DLB-24
Stone, William Leete 1792-1844........ DLB-202
Herbert S. Stone and Company ......... DLB-49
Stone and Kimball ................... DLB-49
Stoppard, Tom
  1937- ........ DLB-13, 233; Y-85; CDBLB-8
  Playwrights and Professors ......... DLB-13
Storey, Anthony 1928- .............. DLB-14
Storey, David 1933- ......DLB-13, 14, 207, 245
Storm, Theodor
  1817-1888........... DLB-129; CDWLB-2
Storni, Alfonsina 1892-1938........... DLB-283
Story, Thomas circa 1670-1742 ......... DLB-31
Story, William Wetmore 1819-1895... DLB-1, 235

Storytelling: A Contemporary Renaissance ... Y-84
Stoughton, William 1631-1701.......... DLB-24
Stow, John 1525-1605.................. DLB-132
Stow, Randolph 1935- ............... DLB-260
Stowe, Harriet Beecher 1811-1896..... DLB-1,12,
                  42, 74, 189, 239, 243; CDALB-3
  The Harriet Beecher Stowe Center ...... Y-00
Stowe, Leland 1899-1994 ............. DLB-29
Stoyanov, Dimitr Ivanov (see Elin Pelin)
Strabo 64/63 B.C.-circa A.D. 25.........DLB-176
Strachey, Lytton 1880-1932 ..... DLB-149; DS-10
  Preface to Eminent Victorians ........ DLB-149
William Strahan [publishing house] ..... DLB-154
Strahan and Company ................ DLB-106
Strand, Mark 1934- ................. DLB-5
The Strasbourg Oaths 842............ DLB-148
Stratemeyer, Edward 1862-1930 ........ DLB-42
Strati, Saverio 1924- .................DLB-177
Stratton and Barnard ................. DLB-49
Stratton-Porter, Gene
  1863-1924 .......... DLB-221; DS-14
Straub, Peter 1943- .................... Y-84
Strauß, Botho 1944- ................ DLB-124
Strauß, David Friedrich 1808-1874...... DLB-133
The Strawberry Hill Press ............ DLB-154
Strawson, P. F. 1919- ............... DLB-262
Streatfeild, Noel 1895-1986 .......... DLB-160
Street, Cecil John Charles (see Rhode, John)
Street, G. S. 1867-1936 ............... DLB-135
Street and Smith .................... DLB-49
Streeter, Edward 1891-1976 .......... DLB-11
Streeter, Thomas Winthrop 1883-1965 .. DLB-140
Stretton, Hesba 1832-1911 ...... DLB-163, 190
Stribling, T. S. 1881-1965................ DLB-9
Der Stricker circa 1190-circa 1250 ..... DLB-138
Strickland, Samuel 1804-1867.......... DLB-99
Strindberg, August 1849-1912 ........ DLB-259
Stringer, Arthur 1874-1950............ DLB-92
Stringer and Townsend ............... DLB-49
Strittmatter, Erwin 1912-1994 ......... DLB-69
Strniša, Gregor 1930-1987 ........... DLB-181
Strode, William 1630-1645............ DLB-126
Strong, L. A. G. 1896-1958 .......... DLB-191
Strother, David Hunter (Porte Crayon)
  1816-1888 ................. DLB-3, 248
Strouse, Jean 1945- ................ DLB-111
Stuart, Dabney 1937- ............... DLB-105
  "Knots into Webs: Some
    Autobiographical Sources" ..... DLB-105
Stuart, Jesse 1906-1984......DLB-9, 48, 102; Y-84
Lyle Stuart [publishing house] ......... DLB-46
Stuart, Ruth McEnery 1849?-1917...... DLB-202
Stubbs, Harry Clement (see Clement, Hal)
Stubenberg, Johann Wilhelm von
  1619-1663 ................... DLB-164
Studebaker, William V. 1947- ....... DLB-256

| | | |
|---|---|---|
| Studies in American Jewish Literature . . . . . . . Y-02 | Swedish Literature<br>The Literature of the Modern<br>Breakthrough . . . . . . . . . . . . . . . . DLB-259 | Taiheiki late fourteenth century . . . . . . . DLB-203 |
| Studio . . . . . . . . . . . . . . . . . . . . . . . . . . . . . DLB-112 | | Tait, J. Selwin, and Sons . . . . . . . . . . . . . . . DLB-49 |
| Stump, Al 1916-1995 . . . . . . . . . . . . . . . . . DLB-241 | | *Tait's Edinburgh Magazine* 1832-1861 . . . . . DLB-110 |
| Sturgeon, Theodore 1918-1985 . . . . . . DLB-8; Y-85 | Swenson, May 1919-1989 . . . . . . . . . . . . . . . DLB-5 | The Takarazaka Revue Company . . . . . . . . . Y-91 |
| Sturges, Preston 1898-1959 . . . . . . . . . . . . DLB-26 | Swerling, Jo 1897- . . . . . . . . . . . . . . . . . . . DLB-44 | Talander (see Bohse, August) |
| Styron, William<br>1925- . . . . . . . DLB-2, 143; Y-80; CDALB-6 | Swift, Graham 1949- . . . . . . . . . . . . . . . . DLB-194 | Talese, Gay 1932- . . . . . . . . . . . . . . . . . . DLB-185 |
| | Swift, Jonathan<br>1667-1745 . . . . . . . DLB-39, 95, 101; CDBLB-2 | Tribute to Irwin Shaw . . . . . . . . . . . . . . . Y-84 |
| Tribute to James Dickey . . . . . . . . . . . . . Y-97 | | Talev, Dimitr 1898-1966 . . . . . . . . . . . . . . DLB-181 |
| Suárez, Mario 1925- . . . . . . . . . . . . . . . . . DLB-82 | Swinburne, A. C.<br>1837-1909 . . . . . . . . . . DLB-35, 57; CDBLB-4 | Taliaferro, H. E. 1811-1875 . . . . . . . . . . . . DLB-202 |
| Such, Peter 1939- . . . . . . . . . . . . . . . . . . . DLB-60 | | Tallent, Elizabeth 1954- . . . . . . . . . . . . . . DLB-130 |
| Suckling, Sir John 1609-1641? . . . . . . DLB-58, 126 | Under the Microscope (1872) . . . . . . . . DLB-35 | TallMountain, Mary 1918-1994 . . . . . . . . . DLB-193 |
| Suckow, Ruth 1892-1960 . . . . . . . . . . DLB-9, 102 | Swineshead, Richard floruit circa 1350 . . . DLB-115 | Talvj 1797-1870 . . . . . . . . . . . . . . . . . DLB-59, 133 |
| Sudermann, Hermann 1857-1928 . . . . . . . DLB-118 | Swinnerton, Frank 1884-1982 . . . . . . . . . . DLB-34 | Tamási, Áron 1897-1966 . . . . . . . . . . . . . . DLB-215 |
| Sue, Eugène 1804-1857 . . . . . . . . . . . . . . DLB-119 | Swisshelm, Jane Grey 1815-1884 . . . . . . . . DLB-43 | Tammsaare, A. H.<br>1878-1940 . . . . . . . . . . DLB-220; CDWLB-4 |
| Sue, Marie-Joseph (see Sue, Eugène) | Swope, Herbert Bayard 1882-1958 . . . . . . . DLB-25 | |
| Suetonius circa A.D. 69-post A.D. 122 . . . DLB-211 | Swords, James ?-1844 . . . . . . . . . . . . . . . . DLB-73 | Tan, Amy 1952- . . . . . . . . . DLB-173; CDALB-7 |
| Suggs, Simon (see Hooper, Johnson Jones) | Swords, Thomas 1763-1843 . . . . . . . . . . . . DLB-73 | Tandori, Dezső 1938- . . . . . . . . . . . . . . . DLB-232 |
| Sui Sin Far (see Eaton, Edith Maude) | T. and J. Swords and Company . . . . . . . . . DLB-49 | Tanner, Thomas 1673/1674-1735 . . . . . . . DLB-213 |
| Suits, Gustav 1883-1956 . . . . DLB-220; CDWLB-4 | Swynnerton, Thomas (John Roberts)<br>circa 1500-1554 . . . . . . . . . . . . . . . . . DLB-281 | Tanizaki Jun'ichirō 1886-1965 . . . . . . . . . DLB-180 |
| Sukenick, Ronald 1932- . . . . . . . DLB-173; Y-81 | | Tapahonso, Luci 1953- . . . . . . . . . . . . . . DLB-175 |
| An Author's Response . . . . . . . . . . . . . . . Y-82 | Sykes, Ella C. ?-1939 . . . . . . . . . . . . . . . . DLB-174 | The Mark Taper Forum . . . . . . . . . . . . . . . DLB-7 |
| Sukhovo-Kobylin, Aleksandr Vasil'evich<br>1817-1903 . . . . . . . . . . . . . . . . . . . . . DLB-277 | Sylvester, Josuah 1562 or 1563-1618 . . . . . DLB-121 | Taradash, Daniel 1913- . . . . . . . . . . . . . . DLB-44 |
| | Symonds, Emily Morse (see Paston, George) | Tarasov-Rodionov, Aleksandr Ignat'evich<br>1885-1938 . . . . . . . . . . . . . . . . . . . . . DLB-272 |
| Suknaski, Andrew 1942- . . . . . . . . . . . . . . DLB-53 | Symonds, John Addington<br>1840-1893 . . . . . . . . . . . . . . . . DLB-57, 144 | |
| Sullivan, Alan 1868-1947 . . . . . . . . . . . . . . DLB-92 | | Tarbell, Ida M. 1857-1944 . . . . . . . . . . . . . . DLB-47 |
| Sullivan, C. Gardner 1886-1965 . . . . . . . . . DLB-26 | "Personal Style" (1890) . . . . . . . . . . . . . DLB-57 | Tardivel, Jules-Paul 1851-1905 . . . . . . . . . . DLB-99 |
| Sullivan, Frank 1892-1976 . . . . . . . . . . . . . DLB-11 | Symons, A. J. A. 1900-1941 . . . . . . . . . . . . DLB-149 | Targan, Barry 1932- . . . . . . . . . . . . . . . . DLB-130 |
| Sulte, Benjamin 1841-1923 . . . . . . . . . . . . . DLB-99 | Symons, Arthur 1865-1945 . . . . . DLB-19, 57, 149 | Tribute to John Gardner . . . . . . . . . . . . . Y-82 |
| Sulzberger, Arthur Hays 1891-1968 . . . . . DLB-127 | Symons, Julian 1912-1994 . . . . . DLB-87, 155; Y-92 | Tarkington, Booth 1869-1946 . . . . . . . . DLB-9, 102 |
| Sulzberger, Arthur Ochs 1926- . . . . . . . DLB-127 | Julian Symons at Eighty . . . . . . . . . . . . . Y-92 | Tashlin, Frank 1913-1972 . . . . . . . . . . . . . DLB-44 |
| Sulzer, Johann Georg 1720-1779 . . . . . . . . DLB-97 | Symons, Scott 1933- . . . . . . . . . . . . . . . . DLB-53 | Tasma (Jessie Couvreur) 1848-1897 . . . . . DLB-230 |
| Sumarokov, Aleksandr Petrovich<br>1717-1777 . . . . . . . . . . . . . . . . . . . . . DLB-150 | Synge, John Millington<br>1871-1909 . . . . . . . . . . DLB-10, 19; CDBLB-5 | Tate, Allen 1899-1979 . . . . . . DLB-4, 45, 63; DS-17 |
| | | Tate, James 1943- . . . . . . . . . . . . . . . DLB-5, 169 |
| Summers, Hollis 1916- . . . . . . . . . . . . . . . DLB-6 | Synge Summer School: J. M. Synge<br>and the Irish Theater, Rathdrum,<br>County Wiclow, Ireland . . . . . . . . . . . Y-93 | Tate, Nahum circa 1652-1715 . . . . . . . . . . DLB-80 |
| Sumner, Charles 1811-1874 . . . . . . . . . . . DLB-235 | | *Tatian* circa 830 . . . . . . . . . . . . . . . . . . . DLB-148 |
| Sumner, William Graham 1840-1910 . . . . DLB-270 | | Taufer, Veno 1933- . . . . . . . . . . . . . . . . DLB-181 |
| Henry A. Sumner<br>[publishing house] . . . . . . . . . . . . . . . . DLB-49 | Syrett, Netta 1865-1943 . . . . . . . . . DLB-135, 197 | Tauler, Johannes circa 1300-1361 . . . . . . . DLB-179 |
| | Szabó, Lőrinc 1900-1957 . . . . . . . . . . . . . DLB-215 | Tavares, Salette 1922-1994 . . . . . . . . . . . . DLB-287 |
| Sundman, Per Olof 1922-1992 . . . . . . . . . DLB-257 | Szabó, Magda 1917- . . . . . . . . . . . . . . . DLB-215 | Tavčar, Ivan 1851-1923 . . . . . . . . . . . . . . . DLB-147 |
| Supervielle, Jules 1884-1960 . . . . . . . . . . DLB-258 | Szymborska, Wisława<br>1923- . . . . . . . . DLB-232, Y-96; CDWLB-4 | Taverner, Richard ca. 1505-1575 . . . . . . . . DLB-236 |
| Surtees, Robert Smith 1803-1864 . . . . . . . . DLB-21 | | Taylor, Ann 1782-1866 . . . . . . . . . . . . . . DLB-163 |
| The R. S. Surtees Society . . . . . . . . . . . . Y-98 | Nobel Lecture 1996:<br>The Poet and the World . . . . . . . . . Y-96 | Taylor, Bayard 1825-1878 . . . . . . DLB-3, 189, 250 |
| Sutcliffe, Matthew 1550?-1629 . . . . . . . . . DLB-281 | | Taylor, Bert Leston 1866-1921 . . . . . . . . . . DLB-25 |
| Sutcliffe, William 1971- . . . . . . . . . . . . . DLB-271 | **T** | Taylor, Charles H. 1846-1921 . . . . . . . . . . . DLB-25 |
| Sutherland, Efua Theodora<br>1924-1996 . . . . . . . . . . . . . . . . . . . . DLB-117 | | Taylor, Edward circa 1642-1729 . . . . . . . . . DLB-24 |
| | Taban lo Liyong 1939?- . . . . . . . . . . . . . DLB-125 | Taylor, Elizabeth 1912-1975 . . . . . . . . . . . DLB-139 |
| Sutherland, John 1919-1956 . . . . . . . . . . . . DLB-68 | Tabori, George 1914- . . . . . . . . . . . . . . . DLB-245 | Taylor, Sir Henry 1800-1886 . . . . . . . . . . . DLB-32 |
| Sutro, Alfred 1863-1933 . . . . . . . . . . . . . . DLB-10 | Tabucchi, Antonio 1943- . . . . . . . . . . . . DLB-196 | Taylor, Henry 1942- . . . . . . . . . . . . . . . . DLB-5 |
| Svendsen, Hanne Marie 1933- . . . . . . . . DLB-214 | Taché, Joseph-Charles 1820-1894 . . . . . . . . DLB-99 | Who Owns American Literature . . . . . . . Y-94 |
| Svevo, Italo (Ettore Schmitz)<br>1861-1928 . . . . . . . . . . . . . . . . . . . . . DLB-264 | Tachihara Masaaki 1926-1980 . . . . . . . . . DLB-182 | |
| | Tacitus circa A.D. 55-circa A.D. 117<br>. . . . . . . . . . . . . . . . . . . . DLB-211; CDWLB-1 | Taylor, Jane 1783-1824 . . . . . . . . . . . . . . DLB-163 |
| Swados, Harvey 1920-1972 . . . . . . . . . . . . . DLB-2 | | Taylor, Jeremy circa 1613-1667 . . . . . . . . . DLB-151 |
| Swain, Charles 1801-1874 . . . . . . . . . . . . . DLB-32 | Tadijanović, Dragutin 1905- . . . . . . . . . DLB-181 | Taylor, John 1577 or 1578 - 1653 . . . . . . . DLB-121 |
| Swallow Press . . . . . . . . . . . . . . . . . . . . . DLB-46 | Tafdrup, Pia 1952- . . . . . . . . . . . . . . . . DLB-214 | Taylor, Mildred D. 1943- . . . . . . . . . . . . . DLB-52 |
| Swan Sonnenschein Limited . . . . . . . . . . DLB-106 | Tafolla, Carmen 1951- . . . . . . . . . . . . . . DLB-82 | Taylor, Peter 1917-1994 . . . DLB-218, 278; Y-81, 94 |
| Swanberg, W. A. 1907-1992 . . . . . . . . . . . DLB-103 | Taggard, Genevieve 1894-1948 . . . . . . . . . . DLB-45 | |
| | Taggart, John 1942- . . . . . . . . . . . . . . . DLB-193 | Taylor, Susie King 1848-1912 . . . . . . . . . . DLB-221 |
| | Tagger, Theodor (see Bruckner, Ferdinand) | |

Taylor, William Howland 1901-1966 ... DLB-241

William Taylor and Company .......... DLB-49

Teale, Edwin Way 1899-1980 ......... DLB-275

Teasdale, Sara 1884-1933 ............. DLB-45

Teillier, Jorge 1935-1996 ............ DLB-283

Telles, Lygia Fagundes 1924- ........ DLB-113

*The Temper of the West:* William Jovanovich .... Y-02

Temple, Sir William 1555?-1627 ...... DLB-281

Temple, Sir William 1628-1699 ....... DLB-101

Temple, William F. 1914-1989 ........ DLB-255

Temrizov, A. (see Marchenko, Anastasia Iakovlevna)

Tench, Watkin ca. 1758-1833 ......... DLB-230

*Tender Is the Night* (Documentary) ...... DLB-273

Tenn, William 1919- ................. DLB-8

Tennant, Emma 1937- ................. DLB-14

Tenney, Tabitha Gilman 1762-1837 ... DLB-37, 200

Tennyson, Alfred 1809-1892 .. DLB-32; CDBLB-4

   On Some of the Characteristics of
   Modern Poetry and On the Lyrical
   Poems of Alfred Tennyson
   (1831) ....................... DLB-32

Tennyson, Frederick 1807-1898 ........ DLB-32

Tenorio, Arthur 1924- ............... DLB-209

Tepl, Johannes von
   circa 1350-1414/1415 .............. DLB-179

Tepliakov, Viktor Grigor'evich
   1804-1842 ....................... DLB-205

Terence circa 184 B.C.-159 B.C. or after
   .................. DLB-211; CDWLB-1

Terhune, Albert Payson 1872-1942 ....... DLB-9

Terhune, Mary Virginia 1830-1922 ........ DS-13

Terpigorev, Sergei Nikolaevich (S. Atava)
   1841-1895 ....................... DLB-277

Terry, Megan 1932- ............. DLB-7, 249

Terson, Peter 1932- ................ DLB-13

Tesich, Steve 1943-1996 ............... Y-83

Tessa, Delio 1886-1939 ............. DLB-114

Testori, Giovanni 1923-1993 ....... DLB-128, 177

Texas
   The Year in Texas Literature .......... Y-98

Tey, Josephine 1896?-1952 ............. DLB-77

Thacher, James 1754-1844 ............. DLB-37

Thacher, John Boyd 1847-1909 ........ DLB-187

Thackeray, William Makepeace
   1811-1863 ... DLB-21, 55, 159, 163; CDBLB-4

Thames and Hudson Limited .......... DLB-112

Thanet, Octave (see French, Alice)

Thaxter, Celia Laighton 1835-1894 ..... DLB-239

Thayer, Caroline Matilda Warren
   1785-1844 ....................... DLB-200

Thayer, Douglas H. 1929- .......... DLB-256

Theater
   Black Theatre: A Forum [excerpts] ... DLB-38

   Community and Commentators:
   Black Theatre and Its Critics ..... DLB-38

   German Drama from Naturalism
   to Fascism: 1889-1933 ......... DLB-118

   A Look at the Contemporary Black
   Theatre Movement ............. DLB-38

The Lord Chamberlain's Office and
   Stage Censorship in England ..... DLB-10

New Forces at Work in the American
   Theatre: 1915-1925 .............. DLB-7

Off Broadway and Off-Off Broadway .. DLB-7

Oregon Shakespeare Festival .......... Y-00

Plays, Playwrights, and Playgoers .... DLB-84

Playwrights on the Theater .......... DLB-80

Playwrights and Professors .......... DLB-13

Producing *Dear Bunny, Dear Volodya:*
   *The Friendship and the Feud* ........... Y-97

Viewpoint: Politics and Performance,
   by David Edgar ................. DLB-13

Writing for the Theatre,
   by Harold Pinter ............... DLB-13

The Year in Drama ......... Y-82–85, 87–98

The Year in U.S. Drama ............. Y-00

Theater, English and Irish
   Anti-Theatrical Tracts ............ DLB-263

   The Chester Plays circa 1505-1532;
   revisions until 1575 ........... DLB-146

   Dangerous Years: London Theater,
   1939-1945 .................... DLB-10

   A Defense of Actors ............. DLB-263

   The Development of Lighting in the
   Staging of Drama, 1900-1945 .... DLB-10

   Education ....................... DLB-263

   The End of English Stage Censorship,
   1945-1968 .................... DLB-13

   Epigrams and Satires ............ DLB-263

   Eyewitnesses and Historians ....... DLB-263

   Fringe and Alternative Theater in
   Great Britain ................. DLB-13

   The Great War and the Theater,
   1914-1918 [Great Britain] ....... DLB-10

   Licensing Act of 1737 ............ DLB-84

   Morality Plays: *Mankind* circa 1450-1500
   and *Everyman* circa 1500 ....... DLB-146

   The New Variorum Shakespeare ....... Y-85

   N-Town Plays circa 1468 to early
   sixteenth century ........... DLB-146

   Politics and the Theater ......... DLB-263

   Practical Matters ............... DLB-263

   Prologues, Epilogues, Epistles to
   Readers, and Excerpts from
   Plays ........................ DLB-263

   The Publication of English
   Renaissance Plays ............. DLB-62

   Regulations for the Theater ....... DLB-263

   Sources for the Study of Tudor and
   Stuart Drama .................. DLB-62

   Stage Censorship: "The Rejected
   Statement" (1911), by Bernard
   Shaw [excerpts] ............... DLB-10

   Synge Summer School: J. M. Synge and
   the Irish Theater, Rathdrum,
   County Wiclow, Ireland .......... Y-93

   The Theater in Shakespeare's Time .. DLB-62

   The Theatre Guild ................ DLB-7

   The Townely Plays fifteenth and
   sixteenth centuries ........... DLB-146

   The Year in British Drama ......... Y-99–01

The Year in Drama: London ......... Y-90

The Year in London Theatre ......... Y-92

*A Yorkshire Tragedy* ................. DLB-58

Theaters
   The Abbey Theatre and Irish Drama,
   1900-1945 .................... DLB-10

   Actors Theatre of Louisville ......... DLB-7

   American Conservatory Theatre ...... DLB-7

   Arena Stage ..................... DLB-7

   Black Theaters and Theater
   Organizations in America,
   1961-1982: A Research List ..... DLB-38

   The Dallas Theater Center ......... DLB-7

   Eugene O'Neill Memorial Theater
   Center ...................... DLB-7

   The Goodman Theatre ............. DLB-7

   The Guthrie Theater ............. DLB-7

   The Mark Taper Forum ........... DLB-7

   The National Theatre and the Royal
   Shakespeare Company: The
   National Companies .......... DLB-13

   Off-Loop Theatres ................ DLB-7

   The Royal Court Theatre and the
   English Stage Company ........ DLB-13

   The Royal Court Theatre and the
   New Drama ................... DLB-10

   The Takarazaka Revue Company ....... Y-91

Thegan and the Astronomer
   flourished circa 850 ............. DLB-148

Thelwall, John 1764-1834 ......... DLB-93, 158

Theocritus circa 300 B.C.-260 B.C. .... DLB-176

Theodorescu, Ion N. (see Arghezi, Tudor)

Theodulf circa 760-circa 821 .......... DLB-148

Theophrastus circa 371 B.C.-287 B.C. .... DLB-176

Thériault, Yves 1915-1983 .......... DLB-88

Thério, Adrien 1925- ............. DLB-53

Theroux, Paul 1941- .... DLB-2, 218; CDALB-7

Thesiger, Wilfred 1910- ........... DLB-204

They All Came to Paris ............... DS-15

Thibaudeau, Colleen 1925- ......... DLB-88

Thielen, Benedict 1903-1965 ........ DLB-102

Thiong'o Ngugi wa (see Ngugi wa Thiong'o)

*This Quarter* 1925-1927, 1929-1932 ......... DS-15

Thoma, Ludwig 1867-1921 .......... DLB-66

Thoma, Richard 1902- .............. DLB-4

Thomas, Audrey 1935- ............. DLB-60

Thomas, D. M.
   1935- ............ DLB-40, 207; CDBLB-8

   The Plagiarism Controversy .......... Y-82

Thomas, Dylan
   1914-1953 ...... DLB-13, 20, 139; CDBLB-7

   The Dylan Thomas Celebration ........ Y-99

Thomas, Edward
   1878-1917 ............ DLB-19, 98, 156, 216

   The Friends of the Dymock Poets ....... Y-00

Thomas, Frederick William 1806-1866 .. DLB-202

Thomas, Gwyn 1913-1981 ......... DLB-15, 245

Thomas, Isaiah 1750-1831 ....... DLB-43, 73, 187

Thomas, Johann 1624-1679 . . . . . . . . . . .DLB-168
Thomas, John 1900-1932 . . . . . . . . . . . . . . .DLB-4
Thomas, Joyce Carol 1938-  . . . . . . . . . . .DLB-33
Thomas, Lewis 1913-1993 . . . . . . . . . . . . .DLB-275
Thomas, Lorenzo 1944-  . . . . . . . . . . . . .DLB-41
Thomas, R. S. 1915-2000 . . . . . .DLB-27; CDBLB-8
Isaiah Thomas [publishing house] . . . . . . .DLB-49
Thomasîn von Zerclære
    circa 1186-circa 1259 . . . . . . . . . . . . . .DLB-138
Thomason, George 1602?-1666 . . . . . . . .DLB-213
Thomasius, Christian 1655-1728 . . . . . . . .DLB-168
Thompson, Daniel Pierce 1795-1868 . . . . .DLB-202
Thompson, David 1770-1857 . . . . . . . . . . .DLB-99
Thompson, Dorothy 1893-1961 . . . . . . . . .DLB-29
Thompson, E. P. 1924-1993 . . . . . . . . . . . .DLB-242
Thompson, Flora 1876-1947 . . . . . . . . . . .DLB-240
Thompson, Francis
    1859-1907 . . . . . . . . . . .DLB-19; CDBLB-5
Thompson, George Selden (see Selden, George)
Thompson, Henry Yates 1838-1928 . . . . .DLB-184
Thompson, Hunter S. 1939-  . . . . . . . . .DLB-185
Thompson, Jim 1906-1977 . . . . . . . . . . . .DLB-226
Thompson, John 1938-1976 . . . . . . . . . . . .DLB-60
Thompson, John R. 1823-1873 . . . .DLB-3, 73, 248
Thompson, Lawrance 1906-1973 . . . . . . . .DLB-103
Thompson, Maurice 1844-1901 . . . . . .DLB-71, 74
Thompson, Ruth Plumly 1891-1976 . . . . .DLB-22
Thompson, Thomas Phillips 1843-1933 . . .DLB-99
Thompson, William 1775-1833 . . . . . . . . .DLB-158
Thompson, William Tappan
    1812-1882 . . . . . . . . . . . . . . . .DLB-3, 11, 248
Thomson, Cockburn
    "Modern Style" (1857) [excerpt] . . . . . .DLB-57
Thomson, Edward William 1849-1924 . . . .DLB-92
Thomson, James 1700-1748 . . . . . . . . . . . .DLB-95
Thomson, James 1834-1882 . . . . . . . . . . . .DLB-35
Thomson, Joseph 1858-1895 . . . . . . . . . . .DLB-174
Thomson, Mortimer 1831-1875 . . . . . . . . .DLB-11
Thomson, Rupert 1955-  . . . . . . . . . . . . .DLB-267
Thon, Melanie Rae 1957-  . . . . . . . . . . . .DLB-244
Thoreau, Henry David 1817-1862
    . . . . . .DLB-1, 183, 223, 270; DS-5; CDALB-2
    The Thoreau Society . . . . . . . . . . . . . . . . Y-99
    The Thoreauvian Pilgrimage: The
        Structure of an American Cult . . .DLB-223
Thorne, William 1568?-1630 . . . . . . . . . . .DLB-281
Thornton, John F.
    [Repsonse to Ken Auletta] . . . . . . . . . . . . Y-97
Thorpe, Adam 1956-  . . . . . . . . . . . .DLB-231
Thorpe, Thomas Bangs
    1815-1878 . . . . . . . . . . . . . . . .DLB-3, 11, 248
Thorup, Kirsten 1942-  . . . . . . . . . . . . .DLB-214
Thrale, Hester Lynch
    (see Piozzi, Hester Lynch [Thrale])
The Three Marias: A Landmark Case in
    Portuguese Literary History
    (Maria Isabel Barreno, 1939-  ;

Maria Teresa Horta, 1937-  ;
Maria Velho da Costa, 1938-  ) . . . . .DLB-287
Thubron, Colin 1939-  . . . . . . . . . .DLB-204, 231
Thucydides
    circa 455 B.C.-circa 395 B.C. . . . . . . .DLB-176
Thulstrup, Thure de 1848-1930 . . . . . . .DLB-188
Thümmel, Moritz August von
    1738-1817 . . . . . . . . . . . . . . . . . . . . . .DLB-97
Thurber, James
    1894-1961 . . . . .DLB-4, 11, 22, 102; CDALB-5
Thurman, Wallace 1902-1934 . . . . . . . . . .DLB-51
    "Negro Poets and Their Poetry" . . . . . DLB-50
Thwaite, Anthony 1930-  . . . . . . . . . . . .DLB-40
    The Booker Prize, Address  . . . . . . . . . . Y-86
Thwaites, Reuben Gold 1853-1913 . . . . . . .DLB-47
Tibullus circa 54 B.C.-circa 19 B.C. . . . . .DLB-211
Ticknor, George 1791-1871 . . .DLB-1, 59, 140, 235
Ticknor and Fields . . . . . . . . . . . . . . . . . . .DLB-49
Ticknor and Fields (revived) . . . . . . . . . . .DLB-46
Tieck, Ludwig 1773-1853 . . . . . .DLB-90; CDWLB-2
Tietjens, Eunice 1884-1944 . . . . . . . . . . . .DLB-54
Tikkanen, Märta 1935-  . . . . . . . . . . . .DLB-257
Tilghman, Christopher circa 1948 . . . . . . .DLB-244
Tilney, Edmund circa 1536-1610 . . . . . . . .DLB-136
Charles Tilt [publishing house] . . . . . . . . .DLB-106
J. E. Tilton and Company . . . . . . . . . . . . .DLB-49
Time-Life Books . . . . . . . . . . . . . . . . . . . . .DLB-46
Times Books . . . . . . . . . . . . . . . . . . . . . . . .DLB-46
Timothy, Peter circa 1725-1782 . . . . . . . . .DLB-43
Timrava 1867-1951 . . . . . . . . . . . . . . . . . .DLB-215
Timrod, Henry 1828-1867 . . . . . . . . . . .DLB-3, 248
Tindal, Henrietta 1818?-1879 . . . . . . . . . .DLB-199
Tinker, Chauncey Brewster 1876-1963 . . .DLB-140
Tinsley Brothers . . . . . . . . . . . . . . . . . . . .DLB-106
Tiptree, James, Jr. 1915-1987 . . . . . . . . . . . .DLB-8
Tišma, Aleksandar 1924-  . . . . . . . . . . .DLB-181
Titus, Edward William
    1870-1952 . . . . . . . . . . . . . . . . .DLB-4; DS-15
Tiutchev, Fedor Ivanovich 1803-1873 . . . .DLB-205
Tlali, Miriam 1933-  . . . . . . . . . .DLB-157, 225
Todd, Barbara Euphan 1890-1976 . . . . . . .DLB-160
Todorov, Tzvetan 1939-  . . . . . . . . . . . .DLB-242
Tofte, Robert
    1561 or 1562-1619 or 1620 . . . . . . . .DLB-172
Tóibín, Colm 1955-  . . . . . . . . . . . . . .DLB-271
Toklas, Alice B. 1877-1967 . . . . . . . .DLB-4; DS-15
Tokuda Shūsei 1872-1943 . . . . . . . . . . . . .DLB-180
Toland, John 1670-1722 . . . . . . . . . . . . . .DLB-252
Tolkien, J. R. R.
    1892-1973 . . . . . .DLB-15, 160, 255; CDBLB-6
Toller, Ernst 1893-1939 . . . . . . . . . . . . . . .DLB-124
Tollet, Elizabeth 1694-1754 . . . . . . . . . . . .DLB-95
Tolson, Melvin B. 1898-1966 . . . . . . . .DLB-48, 76
Tolstaya, Tatyana 1951-  . . . . . . . . . . . .DLB-285
Tolstoy, Aleksei Konstantinovich
    1817-1875 . . . . . . . . . . . . . . . . . . . . . .DLB-238
Tolstoy, Aleksei Nikolaevich 1883-1945 . . .DLB-272

Tolstoy, Leo 1828-1910 . . . . . . . . . . . . . . .DLB-238
Tomalin, Claire 1933-  . . . . . . . . . . . . .DLB-155
Tomasi di Lampedusa, Giuseppe
    1896-1957 . . . . . . . . . . . . . . . . . . . . . .DLB-177
Tomlinson, Charles 1927-  . . . . . . . . . . .DLB-40
Tomlinson, H. M. 1873-1958 . . .DLB-36, 100, 195
Abel Tompkins [publishing house] . . . . . . .DLB-49
Tompson, Benjamin 1642-1714 . . . . . . . . .DLB-24
Tomson, Graham R.
    (see Watson, Rosamund Marriott)
Ton'a 1289-1372 . . . . . . . . . . . . . . . . . . . .DLB-203
Tondelli, Pier Vittorio 1955-1991 . . . . . . .DLB-196
Tonks, Rosemary 1932-  . . . . . . . . .DLB-14, 207
Tonna, Charlotte Elizabeth 1790-1846 . . .DLB-163
Jacob Tonson the Elder
    [publishing house] . . . . . . . . . . . . . . .DLB-170
Toole, John Kennedy 1937-1969 . . . . . . . . . . Y-81
Toomer, Jean 1894-1967 . . .DLB-45, 51; CDALB-4
Tor Books . . . . . . . . . . . . . . . . . . . . . . . . . .DLB-46
Torberg, Friedrich 1908-1979 . . . . . . . . . .DLB-85
Torga, Miguel (Adolfo Correira da Rocha)
    1907-1995 . . . . . . . . . . . . . . . . . . . . . .DLB-287
Torrence, Ridgely 1874-1950 . . . . . . . .DLB-54, 249
Torres-Metzger, Joseph V. 1933-  . . . . . .DLB-122
El Tostado (see Madrigal, Alfonso Fernández de)
Toth, Susan Allen 1940-  . . . . . . . . . . . . . . Y-86
Richard Tottell [publishing house] . . . . . . .DLB-170
    "The Printer to the Reader,"
    (1557) . . . . . . . . . . . . . . . . . . . . . . . .DLB-167
Tough-Guy Literature . . . . . . . . . . . . . . . . .DLB-9
Touré, Askia Muhammad 1938-  . . . . . . .DLB-41
Tourgée, Albion W. 1838-1905 . . . . . . . . .DLB-79
Tournemir, Elizaveta Sailhas de (see Tur, Evgeniia)
Tourneur, Cyril circa 1580-1626 . . . . . . . .DLB-58
Tournier, Michel 1924-  . . . . . . . . . . . .DLB-83
Frank Tousey [publishing house] . . . . . . . .DLB-49
Tower Publications . . . . . . . . . . . . . . . . . . .DLB-46
Towne, Benjamin circa 1740-1793 . . . . . . .DLB-43
Towne, Robert 1936-  . . . . . . . . . . . . . .DLB-44
The Townely Plays fifteenth and sixteenth
    centuries . . . . . . . . . . . . . . . . . . . . . . .DLB-146
Townsend, Sue 1946-  . . . . . . . . . . . . .DLB-271
Townshend, Aurelian
    by 1583-circa 1651 . . . . . . . . . . . . . . .DLB-121
Toy, Barbara 1908-2001 . . . . . . . . . . . . . .DLB-204
Tozzi, Federigo 1883-1920 . . . . . . . . . . . .DLB-264
Tracy, Honor 1913-1989 . . . . . . . . . . . . . .DLB-15
Traherne, Thomas 1637?-1674 . . . . . . . . .DLB-131
Traill, Catharine Parr 1802-1899 . . . . . . . .DLB-99
Train, Arthur 1875-1945 . . . . . . . .DLB-86; DS-16
Tranquilli, Secondino (see Silone, Ignazio)
The Transatlantic Publishing Company . . .DLB-49
The Transatlantic Review 1924-1925 . . . . . . . . . DS-15
The Transcendental Club
    1836-1840 . . . . . . . . . . . . . .DLB-1; DLB-223
Transcendentalism . . . . . . .DLB-1; DLB-223; DS-5

"A Response from America," by
John A. Heraud...................DS-5

Publications and Social Movements....DLB-1

The Rise of Transcendentalism,
1815-1860......................DS-5

Transcendentalists, American..........DS-5

"What Is Transcendentalism? By a
Thinking Man," by James
Kinnard Jr......................DS-5

*transition* 1927-1938.....................DS-15

Translations (Vernacular) in the Crowns of
Castile and Aragon 1352-1515......DLB-286

Tranströmer, Tomas 1931-..........DLB-257

Travel Writing
American Travel Writing, 1776-1864
(checklist)....................DLB-183

British Travel Writing, 1940-1997
(checklist)....................DLB-204

Travel Writers of the Late
Middle Ages.................DLB-286

(1876-1909).....................DLB-174

(1837-1875).....................DLB-166

(1910-1939).....................DLB-195

Traven, B. 1882?/1890?-1969?.........DLB-9, 56

Travers, Ben 1886-1980..........DLB-10, 233

Travers, P. L. (Pamela Lyndon)
1899-1996......................DLB-160

Trediakovsky, Vasilii Kirillovich
1703-1769......................DLB-150

Treece, Henry 1911-1966.............DLB-160

Treitel, Jonathan 1959-..............DLB-267

Trejo, Ernesto 1950-1991.............DLB-122

Trelawny, Edward John
1792-1881...............DLB-110, 116, 144

Tremain, Rose 1943-..........DLB-14, 271

Tremblay, Michel 1942-..............DLB-60

Trent, William P. 1862-1939.........DLB-47, 71

Trescot, William Henry 1822-1898......DLB-30

Tressell, Robert (Robert Phillipe Noonan)
1870-1911......................DLB-197

Trevelyan, Sir George Otto
1838-1928......................DLB-144

Trevisa, John circa 1342-circa 1402.....DLB-146

Trevor, William 1928-.........DLB-14, 139

*Trierer Floyris* circa 1170-1180.........DLB-138

Trillin, Calvin 1935-..................DLB-185

Trilling, Lionel 1905-1975..........DLB-28, 63

Trilussa 1871-1950....................DLB-114

Trimmer, Sarah 1741-1810.............DLB-158

Triolet, Elsa 1896-1970.................DLB-72

Tripp, John 1927-......................DLB-40

Trocchi, Alexander 1925-1984..........DLB-15

Troisi, Dante 1920-1989..............DLB-196

Trollope, Anthony
1815-1882.......DLB-21, 57, 159; CDBLB-4

Novel-Reading: *The Works of Charles
Dickens; The Works of W. Makepeace
Thackeray* (1879)..............DLB-21

The Trollope Societies................Y-00

Trollope, Frances 1779-1863........DLB-21, 166

Trollope, Joanna 1943-.............DLB-207

Troop, Elizabeth 1931-..............DLB-14

Trotter, Catharine 1679-1749.......DLB-84, 252

Trotti, Lamar 1898-1952..............DLB-44

Trottier, Pierre 1925-................DLB-60

Trotzig, Birgitta 1929-..............DLB-257

Troupe, Quincy Thomas, Jr. 1943-......DLB-41

John F. Trow and Company...........DLB-49

Trowbridge, John Townsend 1827-1916..DLB-202

Trudel, Jean-Louis 1967-............DLB-251

Truillier-Lacombe, Joseph-Patrice
1807-1863......................DLB-99

Trumbo, Dalton 1905-1976.............DLB-26

Trumbull, Benjamin 1735-1820..........DLB-30

Trumbull, John 1750-1831..............DLB-31

Trumbull, John 1756-1843.............DLB-183

Truth, Sojourner 1797?-1883.........DLB-239

Tscherning, Andreas 1611-1659........DLB-164

Tsubouchi Shōyō 1859-1935...........DLB-180

Tuchman, Barbara W.
Tribute to Alfred A. Knopf...........Y-84

Tucholsky, Kurt 1890-1935............DLB-56

Tucker, Charlotte Maria
1821-1893..................DLB-163, 190

Tucker, George 1775-1861......DLB-3, 30, 248

Tucker, James 1808?-1866?...........DLB-230

Tucker, Nathaniel Beverley
1784-1851.....................DLB-3, 248

Tucker, St. George 1752-1827.........DLB-37

Tuckerman, Frederick Goddard
1821-1873......................DLB-243

Tuckerman, Henry Theodore 1813-1871..DLB-64

Tumas, Juozas (see Vaizgantas)

Tunis, John R. 1889-1975..........DLB-22, 171

Tunstall, Cuthbert 1474-1559.........DLB-132

Tunström, Göran 1937-2000..........DLB-257

Tuohy, Frank 1925-.............DLB-14, 139

Tupper, Martin F. 1810-1889..........DLB-32

Tur, Evgeniia 1815-1892.............DLB-238

Turbyfill, Mark 1896-1991............DLB-45

Turco, Lewis 1934-....................Y-84

Tribute to John Ciardi................Y-86

Turgenev, Aleksandr Ivanovich
1784-1845......................DLB-198

Turgenev, Ivan Sergeevich 1818-1883...DLB-238

Turnbull, Alexander H. 1868-1918.....DLB-184

Turnbull, Andrew 1921-1970..........DLB-103

Turnbull, Gael 1928-.................DLB-40

Turner, Arlin 1909-1980.............DLB-103

Turner, Charles (Tennyson) 1808-1879...DLB-32

Turner, Ethel 1872-1958.............DLB-230

Turner, Frederick 1943-..............DLB-40

Turner, Frederick Jackson
1861-1932....................DLB-17, 186

A Conversation between William Riggan
and Janette Turner Hospital.........Y-02

Turner, Joseph Addison 1826-1868.....DLB-79

Turpin, Waters Edward 1910-1968......DLB-51

Turrini, Peter 1944-.................DLB-124

Tutuola, Amos 1920-1997....DLB-125; CDWLB-3

Twain, Mark (see Clemens, Samuel Langhorne)

Tweedie, Ethel Brilliana circa 1860-1940..DLB-174

A Century of Poetry, a Lifetime of
Collecting: J. M. Edelstein's
Collection of Twentieth-
Century American Poetry..........YB-02

Twombly, Wells 1935-1977...........DLB-241

Twysden, Sir Roger 1597-1672........DLB-213

Tyler, Anne
1941-........DLB-6, 143; Y-82; CDALB-7

Tyler, Mary Palmer 1775-1866.........DLB-200

Tyler, Moses Coit 1835-1900........DLB-47, 64

Tyler, Royall 1757-1826..............DLB-37

Tylor, Edward Burnett 1832-1917......DLB-57

Tynan, Katharine 1861-1931......DLB-153, 240

Tyndale, William circa 1494-1536......DLB-132

# U

Uchida, Yoshika 1921-1992..........CDALB-7

Udall, Nicholas 1504-1556............DLB-62

Ugrêsić, Dubravka 1949-.............DLB-181

Uhland, Ludwig 1787-1862............DLB-90

Uhse, Bodo 1904-1963.................DLB-69

Ujević, Augustin ("Tin")
1891-1955......................DLB-147

Ulenhart, Niclas flourished circa 1600...DLB-164

Ulibarrí, Sabine R. 1919-.............DLB-82

Ulica, Jorge 1870-1926................DLB-82

Ulitskaya, Liudmila Evgen'evna
1943-.........................DLB-285

Ulivi, Ferruccio 1912-...............DLB-196

Ulizio, B. George 1889-1969..........DLB-140

Ulrich von Liechtenstein
circa 1200-circa 1275.............DLB-138

Ulrich von Zatzikhoven
before 1194-after 1214............DLB-138

Unaipon, David 1872-1967............DLB-230

Unamuno, Miguel de 1864-1936........DLB-108

Under, Marie 1883-1980....DLB-220; CDWLB-4

Underhill, Evelyn 1875-1941..........DLB-240

Ungaretti, Giuseppe 1888-1970........DLB-114

Unger, Friederike Helene 1741-1813.....DLB-94

United States Book Company..........DLB-49

Universal Publishing and Distributing
Corporation....................DLB-46

University of Colorado
Special Collections at the University of
Colorado at Boulder..............Y-98

Indiana University Press..............Y-02

The University of Iowa
Writers' Workshop Golden Jubilee......Y-86

University of Missouri Press............Y-01

University of South Carolina
The G. Ross Roy Scottish
Poetry Collection..................Y-89

Two Hundred Years of Rare Books and
    Literary Collections at the
    University of South Carolina . . . . . . . Y-00
The University of South Carolina Press . . . . . Y-94
University of Virginia
    The Book Arts Press at the University
        of Virginia. . . . . . . . . . . . . . . . . . . . Y-96
    The Electronic Text Center and the
        Electronic Archive of Early American
        Fiction at the University of Virginia
        Library . . . . . . . . . . . . . . . . . . . . . . Y-98
    University of Virginia Libraries . . . . . . . . Y-91
University of Wales Press . . . . . . . . . . . . . DLB-112
University Press of Florida . . . . . . . . . . . . . . Y-00
University Press of Kansas . . . . . . . . . . . . . . Y-98
University Press of Mississippi . . . . . . . . . . . Y-99
Uno Chiyo 1897-1996 . . . . . . . . . . . . . . . DLB-180
Unruh, Fritz von 1885-1970. . . . . . . . DLB-56, 118
Unsworth, Barry 1930- . . . . . . . . . . . . . . DLB-194
Unt, Mati 1944- . . . . . . . . . . . . . . . . . . . DLB-232
The Unterberg Poetry Center of the
    92nd Street Y. . . . . . . . . . . . . . . . . . . . . Y-98
T. Fisher Unwin [publishing house]. . . . . . DLB-106
Upchurch, Boyd B. (see Boyd, John)
Updike, John 1932-   . . . DLB-2, 5, 143, 218, 227;
                                Y-80, 82; DS-3; CDALB-6
    John Updike on the Internet . . . . . . . . . . Y-97
    Tribute to Alfred A. Knopf. . . . . . . . . . . . Y-84
    Tribute to John Ciardi . . . . . . . . . . . . . . Y-86
Upīts, Andrejs 1877-1970 . . . . . . . . . . . . . DLB-220
Upton, Bertha 1849-1912 . . . . . . . . . . . . . DLB-141
Upton, Charles 1948- . . . . . . . . . . . . . . . DLB-16
Upton, Florence K. 1873-1922 . . . . . . . . . DLB-141
Upward, Allen 1863-1926 . . . . . . . . . . . . . DLB-36
Urban, Milo 1904-1982 . . . . . . . . . . . . . . DLB-215
Ureña de Henríquez, Salomé
    1850-1897 . . . . . . . . . . . . . . . . . . . . DLB-283
Urfé, Honoré d' 1567-1625 . . . . . . . . . . . DLB-268
Urista, Alberto Baltazar (see Alurista)
Urquhart, Fred 1912-1995. . . . . . . . . . . . DLB-139
Urrea, Luis Alberto 1955- . . . . . . . . . . . . DLB-209
Urzidil, Johannes 1896-1970 . . . . . . . . . . . DLB-85
U.S.A. (Documentary) . . . . . . . . . . . . . . DLB-274
Usk, Thomas died 1388 . . . . . . . . . . . . . . DLB-146
Uslar Pietri, Arturo 1906-2001 . . . . . . . . DLB-113
Uspensky, Gleb Ivanovich 1843-1902 . . . DLB-277
Ussher, James 1581-1656 . . . . . . . . . . . . . DLB-213
Ustinov, Peter 1921- . . . . . . . . . . . . . . . . . DLB-13
Uttley, Alison 1884-1976 . . . . . . . . . . . . . DLB-160
Uz, Johann Peter 1720-1796 . . . . . . . . . . . DLB-97

# V

Vadianus, Joachim 1484-1551 . . . . . . . . . DLB-179
Vac, Bertrand (Aimé Pelletier) 1914- . . . . DLB-88
Vācietis, Ojārs 1933-1983 . . . . . . . . . . . . DLB-232
Vaculík, Ludvík 1926- . . . . . . . . . . . . . . DLB-232
Vaičiulaitis, Antanas 1906-1992 . . . . . . . . DLB-220

Vaičiūnaite, Judita 1937- . . . . . . . . . . . . . DLB-232
Vail, Laurence 1891-1968 . . . . . . . . . . . . . . DLB-4
Vail, Petr L'vovich 1949- . . . . . . . . . . . . . DLB-285
Vailland, Roger 1907-1965. . . . . . . . . . . . . DLB-83
Vaižgantas 1869-1933 . . . . . . . . . . . . . . . DLB-220
Vajda, Ernest 1887-1954 . . . . . . . . . . . . . . DLB-44
Valdés, Gina 1943- . . . . . . . . . . . . . . . . DLB-122
Valdez, Luis Miguel 1940- . . . . . . . . . . . DLB-122
Valduga, Patrizia 1953- . . . . . . . . . . . . . DLB-128
Vale Press . . . . . . . . . . . . . . . . . . . . . . . DLB-112
Valente, José Angel 1929-2000 . . . . . . . . . DLB-108
Valenzuela, Luisa 1938- . . . DLB-113; CDWLB-3
Valera, Diego de 1412-1488 . . . . . . . . . . DLB-286
Valeri, Diego 1887-1976. . . . . . . . . . . . . . DLB-128
Valerius Flaccus fl. circa A.D. 92. . . . . . . . DLB-211
Valerius Maximus fl. circa A.D. 31 . . . . . . DLB-211
Valéry, Paul 1871-1945 . . . . . . . . . . . . . . DLB-258
Valesio, Paolo 1939- . . . . . . . . . . . . . . . DLB-196
Valgardson, W. D. 1939- . . . . . . . . . . . . . DLB-60
Valle, Víctor Manuel 1950- . . . . . . . . . . . DLB-122
Valle-Inclán, Ramón del 1866-1936. . . . . . DLB-134
Vallejo, Armando 1949- . . . . . . . . . . . . . DLB-122
Vallès, Jules 1832-1885 . . . . . . . . . . . . . . DLB-123
Vallette, Marguerite Eymery (see Rachilde)
Valverde, José María 1926-1996 . . . . . . . . DLB-108
Van Allsburg, Chris 1949- . . . . . . . . . . . . DLB-61
Van Anda, Carr 1864-1945 . . . . . . . . . . . . DLB-25
Vanbrugh, Sir John 1664-1726. . . . . . . . . . DLB-80
Vance, Jack 1916?- . . . . . . . . . . . . . . . . . . DLB-8
Vančura, Vladislav
    1891-1942 . . . . . . . . . DLB-215; CDWLB-4
van der Post, Laurens 1906-1996 . . . . . . . DLB-204
Van Dine, S. S. (see Wright, Williard Huntington)
Van Doren, Mark 1894-1972. . . . . . . . . . . DLB-45
van Druten, John 1901-1957 . . . . . . . . . . . DLB-10
Van Duyn, Mona 1921- . . . . . . . . . . . . . . . DLB-5
    Tribute to James Dickey . . . . . . . . . . . . . Y-97
Van Dyke, Henry 1852-1933 . . . . . DLB-71; DS-13
Van Dyke, Henry 1928- . . . . . . . . . . . . . DLB-33
Van Dyke, John C. 1856-1932 . . . . . . . . . DLB-186
Vane, Sutton 1888-1963 . . . . . . . . . . . . . . DLB-10
Vanguard Press . . . . . . . . . . . . . . . . . . . . DLB-46
van Gulik, Robert Hans 1910-1967 . . . . . . . DS-17
van Itallie, Jean-Claude 1936- . . . . . . . . . . DLB-7
Van Loan, Charles E. 1876-1919 . . . . . . . DLB-171
Vann, Robert L. 1879-1940 . . . . . . . . . . . . DLB-29
Van Rensselaer, Mariana Griswold
    1851-1934 . . . . . . . . . . . . . . . . . . . . . DLB-47
Van Rensselaer, Mrs. Schuyler
    (see Van Rensselaer, Mariana Griswold)
Van Vechten, Carl 1880-1964 . . . . . . DLB-4, 9, 51
van Vogt, A. E. 1912-2000 . . . . . . . . DLB-8, 251
Vargas Llosa, Mario
    1936- . . . . . . . . . . . . DLB-145; CDWLB-3
    Acceptance Speech for the Ritz Paris
        Hemingway Award . . . . . . . . . . . . . Y-85

Varley, John 1947- . . . . . . . . . . . . . . . . . . Y-81
Varnhagen von Ense, Karl August
    1785-1858 . . . . . . . . . . . . . . . . . . . . . DLB-90
Varnhagen von Ense, Rahel
    1771-1833 . . . . . . . . . . . . . . . . . . . . . DLB-90
Varro 116 B.C.-27 B.C. . . . . . . . . . . . . . . DLB-211
Vasilenko, Svetlana Vladimirovna
    1956- . . . . . . . . . . . . . . . . . . . . . . . DLB-285
Vasiliu, George (see Bacovia, George)
Vásquez, Richard 1928- . . . . . . . . . . . . . DLB-209
Vásquez Montalbán, Manuel 1939- . . . . DLB-134
Vassa, Gustavus (see Equiano, Olaudah)
Vassalli, Sebastiano 1941- . . . . . . . . . DLB-128, 196
Vaugelas, Claude Favre de 1585-1650 . . . . DLB-268
Vaughan, Henry 1621-1695 . . . . . . . . . . . DLB-131
Vaughan, Thomas 1621-1666 . . . . . . . . . . DLB-131
Vaughn, Robert 1592?-1667 . . . . . . . . . . . DLB-213
Vaux, Thomas, Lord 1509-1556 . . . . . . . . DLB-132
Vazov, Ivan 1850-1921 . . . . . DLB-147; CDWLB-4
Véa, Alfredo, Jr. 1950- . . . . . . . . . . . . . . DLB-209
Veblen, Thorstein 1857-1929. . . . . . . . . . . DLB-246
Vega, Janine Pommy 1942- . . . . . . . . . . . . DLB-16
Veiller, Anthony 1903-1965 . . . . . . . . . . . . DLB-44
Velásquez-Trevino, Gloria 1949- . . . . . . . DLB-122
Veley, Margaret 1843-1887 . . . . . . . . . . . . DLB-199
Velleius Paterculus
    circa 20 B.C.-circa A.D. 30 . . . . . . . . . DLB-211
Veloz Maggiolo, Marcio 1936- . . . . . . . . . DLB-145
Vel'tman, Aleksandr Fomich
    1800-1870 . . . . . . . . . . . . . . . . . . . . DLB-198
Venegas, Daniel ?-? . . . . . . . . . . . . . . . . . DLB-82
Venevitinov, Dmitrii Vladimirovich
    1805-1827 . . . . . . . . . . . . . . . . . . . . DLB-205
Verde, Cesário 1855-1886 . . . . . . . . . . . . DLB-287
Vergil, Polydore circa 1470-1555 . . . . . . . . DLB-132
Veríssimo, Erico 1905-1975 . . . . . . . . . . . DLB-145
Verlaine, Paul 1844-1896 . . . . . . . . . . . . . DLB-217
Vernacular Translations in the Crowns of
    Castile and Aragon 1352-1515 . . . . . . DLB-286
Verne, Jules 1828-1905 . . . . . . . . . . . . . . DLB-123
Verplanck, Gulian C. 1786-1870 . . . . . . . . DLB-59
Very, Jones 1813-1880. . . . . . . DLB-1, 243; DS-5
Vian, Boris 1920-1959 . . . . . . . . . . . . . . . DLB-72
Viazemsky, Petr Andreevich
    1792-1878 . . . . . . . . . . . . . . . . . . . . DLB-205
Vicars, Thomas 1591-1638 . . . . . . . . . . . . DLB-236
Vicente, Gil 1465-1536/1540? . . . . . . . . . DLB-287
Vickers, Roy 1888?-1965. . . . . . . . . . . . . . DLB-77
Vickery, Sukey 1779-1821 . . . . . . . . . . . . DLB-200
Victoria 1819-1901 . . . . . . . . . . . . . . . . . . DLB-55
Victoria Press. . . . . . . . . . . . . . . . . . . . . DLB-106
Vidal, Gore 1925- . . . . . . DLB-6, 152; CDALB-7
Vidal, Mary Theresa 1815-1873 . . . . . . . . DLB-230
Vidmer, Richards 1898-1978 . . . . . . . . . . DLB-241
Viebig, Clara 1860-1952 . . . . . . . . . . . . . . DLB-66
Viereck, George Sylvester 1884-1962 . . . . . DLB-54
Viereck, Peter 1916- . . . . . . . . . . . . . . . . . DLB-5

Vietnam War (ended 1975)
  Resources for the Study of Vietnam War
    Literature.....................DLB-9
Viets, Roger 1738-1811................DLB-99
Vigil-Piñon, Evangelina 1949- ........DLB-122
Vigneault, Gilles 1928- ..............DLB-60
Vigny, Alfred de
  1797-1863..............DLB-119, 192, 217
Vigolo, Giorgio 1894-1983.............DLB-114
The Viking Press......................DLB-46
Vilde, Eduard 1865-1933...............DLB-220
Vilinskaia, Mariia Aleksandrovna
  (see Vovchok, Marko)
Villanueva, Alma Luz 1944- ...........DLB-122
Villanueva, Tino 1941- ...............DLB-82
Villard, Henry 1835-1900..............DLB-23
Villard, Oswald Garrison 1872-1949....DLB-25, 91
Villarreal, Edit 1944- ...............DLB-209
Villarreal, José Antonio 1924- .......DLB-82
Villaseñor, Victor 1940- .............DLB-209
Villedieu, Madame de (Marie-Catherine
  Desjardins) 1640?-1683..............DLB-268
Villegas de Magnón, Leonor
  1876-1955...........................DLB-122
Villehardouin, Geoffroi de
  circa 1150-1215.....................DLB-208
Villemaire, Yolande 1949- ............DLB-60
Villena, Enrique de ca. 1382/84-1432..DLB-286
Villena, Luis Antonio de 1951- .......DLB-134
Villiers, George, Second Duke
  of Buckingham 1628-1687.............DLB-80
Villiers de l'Isle-Adam, Jean-Marie
  Mathias Philippe-Auguste,
  Comte de 1838-1889..............DLB-123, 192
Villon, François 1431-circa 1463?.....DLB-208
Vine Press............................DLB-112
Viorst, Judith ?- ....................DLB-52
Vipont, Elfrida (Elfrida Vipont Foulds,
  Charles Vipont) 1902-1992...........DLB-160
Viramontes, Helena María 1954- .......DLB-122
Virgil 70 B.C.-19 B.C.......DLB-211; CDWLB-1
Vischer, Friedrich Theodor 1807-1887..DLB-133
Vitier, Cintio 1921- .................DLB-283
Vitruvius circa 85 B.C.-circa 15 B.C..DLB-211
Vitry, Philippe de 1291-1361..........DLB-208
Vittorini, Elio 1908-1966.............DLB-264
Vivanco, Luis Felipe 1907-1975........DLB-108
Vivian, E. Charles (Charles Henry Cannell,
  Charles Henry Vivian, Jack Mann,
  Barry Lynd) 1882-1947...............DLB-255
Viviani, Cesare 1947- ................DLB-128
Vivien, Renée 1877-1909...............DLB-217
Vizenor, Gerald 1934- ............DLB-175, 227
Vizetelly and Company.................DLB-106
Voaden, Herman 1903-1991..............DLB-88
Voß, Johann Heinrich 1751-1826........DLB-90
Vogau, Boris Andreevich
  (see Pil'niak, Boris Andreevich)
Voigt, Ellen Bryant 1943- ............DLB-120

Vojnović, Ivo 1857-1929.....DLB-147; CDWLB-4
Volkoff, Vladimir 1932- ..............DLB-83
P. F. Volland Company.................DLB-46
Vollbehr, Otto H. F.
  1872?-1945 or 1946..................DLB-187
Vologdin (see Zasodimsky, Pavel Vladimirovich)
Volponi, Paolo 1924-1994..............DLB-177
Vonarburg, Élisabeth 1947- ...........DLB-251
von der Grün, Max 1926- ..............DLB-75
Vonnegut, Kurt 1922-
  ........DLB-2, 8, 152; Y-80; DS-3; CDALB-6
  Tribute to Isaac Asimov.............Y-92
  Tribute to Richard Brautigan........Y-84
Voranc, Prežihov 1893-1950............DLB-147
Voronsky, Aleksandr Konstantinovich
  1884-1937...........................DLB-272
Vovchok, Marko 1833-1907..............DLB-238
Voynich, E. L. 1864-1960..............DLB-197
Vroman, Mary Elizabeth circa 1924-1967 . DLB-33

# W

Wace, Robert ("Maistre")
  circa 1100-circa 1175...............DLB-146
Wackenroder, Wilhelm Heinrich
  1773-1798...........................DLB-90
Wackernagel, Wilhelm 1806-1869........DLB-133
Waddell, Helen 1889-1965..............DLB-240
Waddington, Miriam 1917- .............DLB-68
Wade, Henry 1887-1969.................DLB-77
Wagenknecht, Edward 1900- ............DLB-103
Wägner, Elin 1882-1949................DLB-259
Wagner, Heinrich Leopold 1747-1779....DLB-94
Wagner, Henry R. 1862-1957............DLB-140
Wagner, Richard 1813-1883.............DLB-129
Wagoner, David 1926- .............DLB-5, 256
Wah, Fred 1939- ......................DLB-60
Waiblinger, Wilhelm 1804-1830.........DLB-90
Wain, John
  1925-1994......DLB-15, 27, 139, 155; CDBLB-8
  Tribute to J. B. Priestly...........Y-84
Wainwright, Jeffrey 1944- ............DLB-40
Waite, Peirce and Company.............DLB-49
Wakeman, Stephen H. 1859-1924.........DLB-187
Wakoski, Diane 1937- .................DLB-5
Walahfrid Strabo circa 808-849........DLB-148
Henry Z. Walck [publishing house].....DLB-46
Walcott, Derek
  1930- .......DLB-117; Y-81, 92; CDWLB-3
  Nobel Lecture 1992: The Antilles:
    Fragments of Epic Memory..........Y-92
Robert Waldegrave [publishing house]..DLB-170
Waldis, Burkhard circa 1490-1556?.....DLB-178
Waldman, Anne 1945- ..................DLB-16
Waldrop, Rosmarie 1935- ..............DLB-169
Walker, Alice 1900-1982...............DLB-201
Walker, Alice
  1944- ........DLB-6, 33, 143; CDALB-6

Walker, Annie Louisa (Mrs. Harry Coghill)
  circa 1836-1907.....................DLB-240
Walker, George F. 1947- ..............DLB-60
Walker, John Brisben 1847-1931........DLB-79
Walker, Joseph A. 1935- ..............DLB-38
Walker, Margaret 1915-1998........DLB-76, 152
Walker, Obadiah 1616-1699.............DLB-281
Walker, Ted 1934- ....................DLB-40
Walker, Evans and Cogswell Company...DLB-49
Wall, John F. (see Sarban)
Wallace, Alfred Russel 1823-1913......DLB-190
Wallace, Dewitt 1889-1981.............DLB-137
Wallace, Edgar 1875-1932..............DLB-70
Wallace, Lew 1827-1905................DLB-202
Wallace, Lila Acheson 1889-1984.......DLB-137
  "A Word of Thanks," From the Initial
    Issue of *Reader's Digest*
    (February 1922)...................DLB-137
Wallace, Naomi 1960- .................DLB-249
Wallace Markfield's "Steeplechase"....Y-02
Wallant, Edward Lewis
  1926-1962.................DLB-2, 28, 143
Waller, Edmund 1606-1687..............DLB-126
Walpole, Horace 1717-1797.....DLB-39, 104, 213
  Preface to the First Edition of
    *The Castle of Otranto* (1764)....DLB-39, 178
  Preface to the Second Edition of
    *The Castle of Otranto* (1765)....DLB-39, 178
Walpole, Hugh 1884-1941...............DLB-34
Walrond, Eric 1898-1966...............DLB-51
Walser, Martin 1927- .............DLB-75, 124
Walser, Robert 1878-1956..............DLB-66
Walsh, Ernest 1895-1926...............DLB-4, 45
Walsh, Robert 1784-1859...............DLB-59
Walters, Henry 1848-1931..............DLB-140
*Waltharius* circa 825................DLB-148
Walther von der Vogelweide
  circa 1170-circa 1230...............DLB-138
Walton, Izaak
  1593-1683...........DLB-151, 213; CDBLB-1
Wambaugh, Joseph 1937- ............DLB-6; Y-83
Wand, Alfred Rudolph 1828-1891........DLB-188
Waniek, Marilyn Nelson 1946- .........DLB-120
Wanley, Humphrey 1672-1726............DLB-213
War of the Words (and Pictures):
  The Creation of a Graphic Novel.....Y-02
Warburton, William 1698-1779..........DLB-104
Ward, Aileen 1919- ...................DLB-111
Ward, Artemus (see Browne, Charles Farrar)
Ward, Arthur Henry Sarsfield (see Rohmer, Sax)
Ward, Douglas Turner 1930- .......DLB-7, 38
Ward, Mrs. Humphry 1851-1920..........DLB-18
Ward, James 1843-1925.................DLB-262
Ward, Lynd 1905-1985..................DLB-22
Ward, Lock and Company................DLB-106
Ward, Nathaniel circa 1578-1652.......DLB-24
Ward, Theodore 1902-1983..............DLB-76

Wardle, Ralph 1909-1988 . . . . . . . . . . . . . .DLB-103
Ware, Henry, Jr. 1794-1843. . . . . . . . . . . . . .DLB-235
Ware, William 1797-1852. . . . . . . . . . .DLB-1, 235
Warfield, Catherine Ann 1816-1877 . . . . . . .DLB-248
Waring, Anna Letitia 1823-1910 . . . . . . . . . .DLB-240
Frederick Warne and Company [U.K.] . . . .DLB-106
Frederick Warne and Company [U.S.] . . . . .DLB-49
Warner, Anne 1869-1913 . . . . . . . . . . . . . . .DLB-202
Warner, Charles Dudley 1829-1900 . . . . . .DLB-64
Warner, Marina 1946- . . . . . . . . . . . . . . . .DLB-194
Warner, Rex 1905-1986 . . . . . . . . . . . . . . . . .DLB-15
Warner, Susan 1819-1885 . . . . DLB-3, 42, 239, 250
Warner, Sylvia Townsend
 1893-1978 . . . . . . . . . . . . . . . . . . . DLB-34, 139
Warner, William 1558-1609 . . . . . . . . . . . .DLB-172
Warner Books . . . . . . . . . . . . . . . . . . . . . . . . .DLB-46
Warr, Bertram 1917-1943 . . . . . . . . . . . . . . . .DLB-88
Warren, John Byrne Leicester (see De Tabley, Lord)
Warren, Lella 1899-1982. . . . . . . . . . . . . . . . . . . Y-83
Warren, Mercy Otis 1728-1814 . . . . . . .DLB-31, 200
Warren, Robert Penn 1905-1989
 . . . . . . . .DLB-2, 48, 152; Y-80, 89; CDALB-6
 Tribute to Katherine Anne Porter. . . . . . . Y-80
Warren, Samuel 1807-1877 . . . . . . . . . . . . . .DLB-190
Die Wartburgkrieg circa 1230-circa 1280 . . .DLB-138
Warton, Joseph 1722-1800. . . . . . . . .DLB-104, 109
Warton, Thomas 1728-1790 . . . . . . .DLB-104, 109
Warung, Price (William Astley)
 1855-1911 . . . . . . . . . . . . . . . . . . . . . . .DLB-230
Washington, George 1732-1799 . . . . . . . . . .DLB-31
Washington, Ned 1901-1976 . . . . . . . . . . . .DLB-265
Wassermann, Jakob 1873-1934 . . . . . . . . . . .DLB-66
Wasserstein, Wendy 1950- . . . . . . . . . . .DLB-228
Wasson, David Atwood 1823-1887 . . . .DLB-1, 223
Watanna, Onoto (see Eaton, Winnifred)
Waterhouse, Keith 1929- . . . . . . . . . .DLB-13, 15
Waterman, Andrew 1940- . . . . . . . . . . . .DLB-40
Waters, Frank 1902-1995 . . . . . . .DLB-212; Y-86
Waters, Michael 1949- . . . . . . . . . . . . .DLB-120
Watkins, Tobias 1780-1855 . . . . . . . . . . . . . . .DLB-73
Watkins, Vernon 1906-1967 . . . . . . . . . . . . . .DLB-20
Watmough, David 1926- . . . . . . . . . . . .DLB-53
Watson, Colin 1920-1983 . . . . . . . . . . . . . . .DLB-276
Watson, Ian 1943- . . . . . . . . . . . . . . . . .DLB-261
Watson, James Wreford (see Wreford, James)
Watson, John 1850-1907 . . . . . . . . . . . . . . .DLB-156
Watson, Rosamund Marriott
 (Graham R. Tomson) 1860-1911 . . . .DLB-240
Watson, Sheila 1909-1998 . . . . . . . . . . . . . . . .DLB-60
Watson, Thomas 1545?-1592 . . . . . . . . . . . .DLB-132
Watson, Wilfred 1911- . . . . . . . . . . . . . . .DLB-60
W. J. Watt and Company . . . . . . . . . . . . . . . .DLB-46
Watten, Barrett 1948- . . . . . . . . . . . . . .DLB-193
Watterson, Henry 1840-1921 . . . . . . . . . . . .DLB-25
Watts, Alan 1915-1973. . . . . . . . . . . . . . . . . . .DLB-16

Watts, Isaac 1674-1748. . . . . . . . . . . . . . . . . .DLB-95
Franklin Watts [publishing house] . . . . . . . .DLB-46
Waugh, Alec 1898-1981 . . . . . . . . . . . . . . .DLB-191
Waugh, Auberon 1939-2000 . . . DLB-14, 194; Y-00
Waugh, Evelyn
 1903-1966 . . . . . . DLB-15, 162, 195; CDBLB-6
Way and Williams. . . . . . . . . . . . . . . . . . . .DLB-49
Wayman, Tom 1945- . . . . . . . . . . . . . . . .DLB-53
Weatherly, Tom 1942- . . . . . . . . . . . . . . .DLB-41
Weaver, Gordon 1937- . . . . . . . . . . . . . .DLB-130
Weaver, Robert 1921- . . . . . . . . . . . . . . . .DLB-88
Webb, Beatrice 1858-1943 . . . . . . . . . . . . . .DLB-190
Webb, Francis 1925-1973 . . . . . . . . . . . . . . .DLB-260
Webb, Frank J. ?-? . . . . . . . . . . . . . . . . . . . . .DLB-50
Webb, James Watson 1802-1884. . . . . . . . .DLB-43
Webb, Mary 1881-1927. . . . . . . . . . . . . . . . .DLB-34
Webb, Phyllis 1927- . . . . . . . . . . . . . . . . .DLB-53
Webb, Sidney 1859-1947. . . . . . . . . . . . . . . .DLB-190
Webb, Walter Prescott 1888-1963. . . . . . . . .DLB-17
Webbe, William ?-1591 . . . . . . . . . . . . . . . . .DLB-132
Webber, Charles Wilkins 1819-1856? . . . .DLB-202
Webling, Lucy (Lucy Betty MacRaye)
 1877-1952 . . . . . . . . . . . . . . . . . . . . . . .DLB-240
Webling, Peggy (Arthur Weston)
 1871-1949 . . . . . . . . . . . . . . . . . . . . . . .DLB-240
Webster, Augusta 1837-1894 . . . . . . . .DLB-35, 240
Webster, John
 1579 or 1580-1634?. . . . . . DLB-58; CDBLB-1
 The Melbourne Manuscript . . . . . . . . . . Y-86
Webster, Noah
 1758-1843 . . . . . . DLB-1, 37, 42, 43, 73, 243
Webster, Paul Francis 1907-1984. . . . . . . .DLB-265
Charles L. Webster and Company . . . . . . .DLB-49
Weckherlin, Georg Rodolf 1584-1653. . . .DLB-164
Wedekind, Frank
 1864-1918 . . . . . . . . . . . DLB-118; CDWLB-2
Weeks, Edward Augustus, Jr. 1898-1989 . DLB-137
Weeks, Stephen B. 1865-1918 . . . . . . . . . . .DLB-187
Weems, Mason Locke 1759-1825 . . DLB-30, 37, 42
Weerth, Georg 1822-1856 . . . . . . . . . . . . . .DLB-129
Weidenfeld and Nicolson . . . . . . . . . . . . . .DLB-112
Weidman, Jerome 1913-1998 . . . . . . . . . . . .DLB-28
Weigl, Bruce 1949- . . . . . . . . . . . . . . . . .DLB-120
Weinbaum, Stanley Grauman 1902-1935 . . .DLB-8
Weiner, Andrew 1949- . . . . . . . . . . . . . .DLB-251
Weintraub, Stanley 1929- . . . . . . DLB-111; Y82
Weise, Christian 1642-1708 . . . . . . . . . . . . .DLB-168
Weisenborn, Gunther 1902-1969 . . . .DLB-69, 124
Weiss, John 1818-1879. . . . . . . . . . . . . . .DLB-1, 243
Weiss, Paul 1901-2002 . . . . . . . . . . . . . . . . .DLB-279
Weiss, Peter 1916-1982 . . . . . . . . . . . . .DLB-69, 124
Weiss, Theodore 1916- . . . . . . . . . . . . . . . .DLB-5
Weiß, Ernst 1882-1940 . . . . . . . . . . . . . . . . . .DLB-81
Weiße, Christian Felix 1726-1804 . . . . . . . . .DLB-97
Weitling, Wilhelm 1808-1871 . . . . . . . . . . .DLB-129
Welch, James 1940- . . . . . . . . . . . DLB-175, 256

Welch, Lew 1926-1971?. . . . . . . . . . . . . . . . . .DLB-16
Weldon, Fay 1931- . . . .DLB-14, 194; CDBLB-8
Wellek, René 1903-1995 . . . . . . . . . . . . . . . .DLB-63
Wells, Carolyn 1862-1942. . . . . . . . . . . . . . .DLB-11
Wells, Charles Jeremiah
 circa 1800-1879 . . . . . . . . . . . . . . . . . . .DLB-32
Wells, Gabriel 1862-1946 . . . . . . . . . . . . . .DLB-140
Wells, H. G.
 1866-1946 . . . DLB-34, 70, 156, 178; CDBLB-6
 H. G. Wells Society. . . . . . . . . . . . . . . . . . Y-98
 Preface to The Scientific Romances of
  H. G. Wells (1933). . . . . . . . . . . . . DLB-178
Wells, Helena 1758?-1824 . . . . . . . . . . . . . .DLB-200
Wells, Robert 1947- . . . . . . . . . . . . . . . .DLB-40
Wells-Barnett, Ida B. 1862-1931 . . . . .DLB-23, 221
Welsh, Irvine 1958- . . . . . . . . . . . . . . . .DLB-271
Welty, Eudora 1909-2001 . . . . . . DLB-2, 102, 143;
 Y-87, 01; DS-12; CDALB-1
 Eudora Welty: Eye of the Storyteller . . . . . Y-87
 Eudora Welty Newsletter . . . . . . . . . . . . . . . . . Y-99
 Eudora Welty's Funeral . . . . . . . . . . . . . Y-01
 Eudora Welty's Ninetieth Birthday . . . . . Y-99
 Eudora Welty Remembered in
  Two Exhibits . . . . . . . . . . . . . . . . . . Y-02
Wendell, Barrett 1855-1921. . . . . . . . . . . . . .DLB-71
Wentworth, Patricia 1878-1961 . . . . . . . . . .DLB-77
Wentworth, William Charles 1790-1872 . .DLB-230
Werder, Diederich von dem 1584-1657 . .DLB-164
Werfel, Franz 1890-1945 . . . . . . . . . . . . .DLB-81, 124
Werner, Zacharias 1768-1823 . . . . . . . . . . . .DLB-94
The Werner Company . . . . . . . . . . . . . . . . .DLB-49
Wersba, Barbara 1932- . . . . . . . . . . . . . .DLB-52
Wescott, Glenway
 1901-1987 . . . . . . . . . . . . DLB-4, 9, 102; DS-15
Wesker, Arnold 1932- . . . . . .DLB-13; CDBLB-8
Wesley, Charles 1707-1788. . . . . . . . . . . . . . .DLB-95
Wesley, John 1703-1791. . . . . . . . . . . . . . . .DLB-104
Wesley, Mary 1912-2002 . . . . . . . . . . . . . . .DLB-231
Wesley, Richard 1945- . . . . . . . . . . . . . . .DLB-38
A. Wessels and Company . . . . . . . . . . . . . . .DLB-46
Wessobrunner Gebet circa 787-815 . . . . . . . . .DLB-148
West, Anthony 1914-1988. . . . . . . . . . . . . . .DLB-15
 Tribute to Liam O'Flaherty . . . . . . . . . . . Y-84
West, Cheryl L. 1957- . . . . . . . . . . . . . .DLB-266
West, Cornel 1953- . . . . . . . . . . . . . . . .DLB-246
West, Dorothy 1907-1998 . . . . . . . . . . . . . . .DLB-76
West, Jessamyn 1902-1984 . . . . . . . . . .DLB-6; Y-84
West, Mae 1892-1980 . . . . . . . . . . . . . . . . . .DLB-44
West, Michelle Sagara 1963- . . . . . . . .DLB-251
West, Nathanael
 1903-1940 . . . . . . . . . .DLB-4, 9, 28; CDALB-5
West, Paul 1930- . . . . . . . . . . . . . . . . . . .DLB-14
West, Rebecca 1892-1983 . . . . . . . . .DLB-36; Y-83
West, Richard 1941- . . . . . . . . . . . . . . .DLB-185
West and Johnson . . . . . . . . . . . . . . . . . . . . .DLB-49
Westcott, Edward Noyes 1846-1898 . . . . .DLB-202

453

# Cumulative Index

The Western Literature Association........Y-99

*The Western Messenger*
1835-1841 ............DLB-1; DLB-223

Western Publishing Company .........DLB-46

Western Writers of America ............Y-99

*The Westminster Review* 1824-1914 .......DLB-110

Weston, Arthur (see Webling, Peggy)

Weston, Elizabeth Jane circa 1582-1612...DLB-172

Wetherald, Agnes Ethelwyn 1857-1940 ...DLB-99

Wetherell, Elizabeth (see Warner, Susan)

Wetherell, W. D. 1948- ............DLB-234

Wetzel, Friedrich Gottlob 1779-1819 .....DLB-90

Weyman, Stanley J. 1855-1928.....DLB-141, 156

Wezel, Johann Karl 1747-1819 .........DLB-94

Whalen, Philip 1923-2002 ............DLB-16

Whalley, George 1915-1983............DLB-88

Wharton, Edith 1862-1937
......DLB-4, 9, 12, 78, 189; DS-13; CDALB-3

Wharton, William 1920s?- ...............Y-80

Whately, Mary Louisa 1824-1889 ......DLB-166

Whately, Richard 1787-1863...........DLB-190

*Elements of Rhetoric* (1828;
revised, 1846) [excerpt] .........DLB-57

Wheatley, Dennis 1897-1977.........DLB-77, 255

Wheatley, Phillis
circa 1754-1784.......DLB-31, 50; CDALB-2

Wheeler, Anna Doyle 1785-1848? ......DLB-158

Wheeler, Charles Stearns 1816-1843 ..DLB-1, 223

Wheeler, Monroe 1900-1988 ............DLB-4

Wheelock, John Hall 1886-1978.........DLB-45

From John Hall Wheelock's
Oral Memoir......................Y-01

Wheelwright, J. B. 1897-1940...........DLB-45

Wheelwright, John circa 1592-1679 ......DLB-24

Whetstone, George 1550-1587 .........DLB-136

Whetstone, Colonel Pete (see Noland, C. F. M.)

Whewell, William 1794-1866 ..........DLB-262

Whichcote, Benjamin 1609?-1683 ......DLB-252

Whicher, Stephen E. 1915-1961 .........DLB-111

Whipple, Edwin Percy 1819-1886 .....DLB-1, 64

Whitaker, Alexander 1585-1617.........DLB-24

Whitaker, Daniel K. 1801-1881 .........DLB-73

Whitcher, Frances Miriam
1812-1852.................DLB-11, 202

White, Andrew 1579-1656 .............DLB-24

White, Andrew Dickson 1832-1918......DLB-47

White, E. B. 1899-1985 ...DLB-11, 22; CDALB-7

White, Edgar B. 1947- ................DLB-38

White, Edmund 1940- ..............DLB-227

White, Ethel Lina 1887-1944 ..........DLB-77

White, Hayden V. 1928- ...........DLB-246

White, Henry Kirke 1785-1806 .........DLB-96

White, Horace 1834-1916..............DLB-23

White, James 1928-1999...............DLB-261

White, Patrick 1912-1990............DLB-260

White, Phyllis Dorothy James (see James, P. D.)

White, Richard Grant 1821-1885........DLB-64

White, T. H. 1906-1964.........DLB-160, 255

White, Walter 1893-1955..............DLB-51

William White and Company ..........DLB-49

White, William Allen 1868-1944 .....DLB-9, 25

White, William Anthony Parker
(see Boucher, Anthony)

White, William Hale (see Rutherford, Mark)

Whitchurch, Victor L. 1868-1933.......DLB-70

Whitehead, Alfred North
1861-1947..............DLB-100, 262

Whitehead, James 1936- .............Y-81

Whitehead, William 1715-1785......DLB-84, 109

Whitfield, James Monroe 1822-1871 .....DLB-50

Whitfield, Raoul 1898-1945 ...........DLB-226

Whitgift, John circa 1533-1604.........DLB-132

Whiting, John 1917-1963 .............DLB-13

Whiting, Samuel 1597-1679 ...........DLB-24

Whitlock, Brand 1869-1934............DLB-12

Whitman, Albery Allson 1851-1901......DLB-50

Whitman, Alden 1913-1990 ...........Y-91

Whitman, Sarah Helen (Power)
1803-1878.................DLB-1, 243

Whitman, Walt
1819-1892 ... DLB-3, 64, 224, 250; CDALB-2

Albert Whitman and Company .........DLB-46

Whitman Publishing Company .........DLB-46

Whitney, Geoffrey 1548 or 1552?-1601..DLB-136

Whitney, Isabella flourished 1566-1573 ..DLB-136

Whitney, John Hay 1904-1982.........DLB-127

Whittemore, Reed 1919-1995............DLB-5

Whittier, John Greenleaf
1807-1892...........DLB-1, 243; CDALB-2

Whittlesey House...................DLB-46

Wickham, Anna (Edith Alice Mary Harper)
1884-1947.....................DLB-240

Wickram, Georg circa 1505-circa 1561 ...DLB-179

Wicomb, Zoë 1948- ................DLB-225

Wideman, John Edgar 1941- .....DLB-33, 143

Widener, Harry Elkins 1885-1912......DLB-140

Wiebe, Rudy 1934- .................DLB-60

Wiechert, Ernst 1887-1950 ............DLB-56

Wied, Martina 1882-1957..............DLB-85

Wiehe, Evelyn May Clowes (see Mordaunt, Elinor)

Wieland, Christoph Martin 1733-1813....DLB-97

Wienbarg, Ludolf 1802-1872 ..........DLB-133

Wieners, John 1934- ................DLB-16

Wier, Ester 1910- ..................DLB-52

Wiesel, Elie
1928- .........DLB-83; Y-86, 87; CDALB-7

Nobel Lecture 1986: Hope, Despair and
Memory......................Y-86

Wiggin, Kate Douglas 1856-1923 .......DLB-42

Wigglesworth, Michael 1631-1705 .......DLB-24

Wilberforce, William 1759-1833........DLB-158

Wilbrandt, Adolf 1837-1911 ..........DLB-129

Wilbur, Richard 1921- ..DLB-5, 169; CDALB-7

Tribute to Robert Penn Warren ........Y-89

Wild, Peter 1940- ..................DLB-5

Wilde, Lady Jane Francesca Elgee
1821?-1896....................DLB-199

Wilde, Oscar 1854-1900.......DLB-10, 19, 34, 57,
141, 156, 190; CDBLB-5

"The Critic as Artist" (1891) ........DLB-57

"The Decay of Lying" (1889) .......DLB-18

"The English Renaissance of
Art" (1908) ..................DLB-35

"L'Envoi" (1882) ................DLB-35

Oscar Wilde Conference at Hofstra
University ......................Y-00

Wilde, Richard Henry 1789-1847......DLB-3, 59

W. A. Wilde Company ................DLB-49

Wilder, Billy 1906- .................DLB-26

Wilder, Laura Ingalls 1867-1957.....DLB-22, 256

Wilder, Thornton
1897-1975.........DLB-4, 7, 9, 228; CDALB-7

Thornton Wilder Centenary at Yale.....Y-97

Wildgans, Anton 1881-1932...........DLB-118

Wiley, Bell Irvin 1906-1980.............DLB-17

John Wiley and Sons .................DLB-49

Wilhelm, Kate 1928- ................DLB-8

Wilkes, Charles 1798-1877 ............DLB-183

Wilkes, George 1817-1885 .............DLB-79

Wilkins, John 1614-1672 .............DLB-236

Wilkinson, Anne 1910-1961............DLB-88

Wilkinson, Eliza Yonge
1757-circa 1813....................DLB-200

Wilkinson, Sylvia 1940- ...............Y-86

Wilkinson, William Cleaver 1833-1920...DLB-71

Willard, Barbara 1909-1994 ...........DLB-161

Willard, Emma 1787-1870.............DLB-239

Willard, Frances E. 1839-1898 .........DLB-221

Willard, Nancy 1936- .............DLB-5, 52

Willard, Samuel 1640-1707.............DLB-24

L. Willard [publishing house]...........DLB-49

Willeford, Charles 1919-1988 ..........DLB-226

William of Auvergne 1190-1249 .......DLB-115

William of Conches
circa 1090-circa 1154 .............DLB-115

William of Ockham circa 1285-1347 ....DLB-115

William of Sherwood
1200/1205-1266/1271...............DLB-115

The William Charvat American Fiction
Collection at the Ohio State
University Libraries..................Y-92

Williams, Ben Ames 1889-1953 .......DLB-102

Williams, C. K. 1936- ................DLB-5

Williams, Chancellor 1905-1992 .......DLB-76

Williams, Charles 1886-1945 ...DLB-100, 153, 255

Williams, Denis 1923-1998 ...........DLB-117

Williams, Emlyn 1905-1987..........DLB-10, 77

Williams, Garth 1912-1996 ...........DLB-22

Williams, George Washington
1849-1891 .....................DLB-47

Williams, Heathcote 1941- ...........DLB-13

Williams, Helen Maria 1761-1827 . . . . . . .DLB-158
Williams, Hugo 1942- . . . . . . . . . . . . . . .DLB-40
Williams, Isaac 1802-1865 . . . . . . . . . . . . .DLB-32
Williams, Joan 1928- . . . . . . . . . . . . . . . . .DLB-6
Williams, Joe 1889-1972 . . . . . . . . . . . . .DLB-241
Williams, John A. 1925- . . . . . . . . . . .DLB-2, 33
Williams, John E. 1922-1994 . . . . . . . . . . .DLB-6
Williams, Jonathan 1929- . . . . . . . . . . . . . .DLB-5
Williams, Miller 1930- . . . . . . . . . . . . . . .DLB-105
Williams, Nigel 1948- . . . . . . . . . . . . . . .DLB-231
Williams, Raymond
 1921-1988 . . . . . . . . . . . .DLB-14, 231, 242
Williams, Roger circa 1603-1683 . . . . . . . .DLB-24
Williams, Rowland 1817-1870 . . . . . . . . .DLB-184
Williams, Samm-Art 1946- . . . . . . . . . . .DLB-38
Williams, Sherley Anne 1944-1999 . . . . . .DLB-41
Williams, T. Harry 1909-1979 . . . . . . . . . .DLB-17
Williams, Tennessee
 1911-1983 . . . . .DLB-7; Y-83; DS-4; CDALB-1
Williams, Terry Tempest 1955- . . .DLB-206, 275
Williams, Ursula Moray 1911- . . . . . . .DLB-160
Williams, Valentine 1883-1946 . . . . . . . . .DLB-77
Williams, William Appleman 1921- . . . . .DLB-17
Williams, William Carlos
 1883-1963 . . . . . .DLB-4, 16, 54, 86; CDALB-4
 The William Carlos Williams Society . . . .Y-99
Williams, Wirt 1921- . . . . . . . . . . . . . . . . .DLB-6
A. Williams and Company . . . . . . . . . . . . .DLB-49
Williams Brothers . . . . . . . . . . . . . . . . . . . .DLB-49
Williamson, Henry 1895-1977 . . . . . . . . . .DLB-191
 The Henry Williamson Society . . . . . . . . Y-98
Williamson, Jack 1908- . . . . . . . . . . . . . . .DLB-8
Willingham, Calder Baynard, Jr.
 1922-1995 . . . . . . . . . . . . . . . . . . .DLB-2, 44
Williram of Ebersberg circa 1020-1085 . . .DLB-148
Willis, John circa 1572-1625 . . . . . . . . . . .DLB-281
Willis, Nathaniel Parker 1806-1867
 . . . . . . . . DLB-3, 59, 73, 74, 183, 250; DS-13
Willkomm, Ernst 1810-1886 . . . . . . . . . .DLB-133
Wills, Garry 1934- . . . . . . . . . . . . . . . . .DLB-246
 Tribute to Kenneth Dale McCormick . . . . Y-97
Willson, Meredith 1902-1984 . . . . . . . . . .DLB-265
Willumsen, Dorrit 1940- . . . . . . . . . . . . .DLB-214
Wilmer, Clive 1945- . . . . . . . . . . . . . . . . .DLB-40
Wilson, A. N. 1950- . . . . . . . .DLB-14, 155, 194
Wilson, Angus 1913-1991 . . . . . .DLB-15, 139, 155
Wilson, Arthur 1595-1652 . . . . . . . . . . . . .DLB-58
Wilson, August 1945- . . . . . . . . . . . . . . .DLB-228
Wilson, Augusta Jane Evans 1835-1909 . . .DLB-42
Wilson, Colin 1931- . . . . . . . . . . . .DLB-14, 194
 Tribute to J. B. Priestly . . . . . . . . . . . . . .Y-84
Wilson, Edmund 1895-1972 . . . . . . . . . . .DLB-63
Wilson, Ethel 1888-1980 . . . . . . . . . . . . . .DLB-68
Wilson, F. P. 1889-1963 . . . . . . . . . . . . .DLB-201
Wilson, Harriet E.
 1827/1828?-1863? . . . . . . . .DLB-50, 239, 243

Wilson, Harry Leon 1867-1939 . . . . . . . . . .DLB-9
Wilson, John 1588-1667 . . . . . . . . . . . . . .DLB-24
Wilson, John 1785-1854 . . . . . . . . . . . . . .DLB-110
Wilson, John Anthony Burgess
 (see Burgess, Anthony)
Wilson, John Dover 1881-1969 . . . . . . . . .DLB-201
Wilson, Lanford 1937- . . . . . . . . . . . . . . .DLB-7
Wilson, Margaret 1882-1973 . . . . . . . . . . .DLB-9
Wilson, Michael 1914-1978 . . . . . . . . . . . .DLB-44
Wilson, Mona 1872-1954 . . . . . . . . . . . . .DLB-149
Wilson, Robert Charles 1953- . . . . . . . . .DLB-251
Wilson, Robert McLiam 1964- . . . . . . . . .DLB-267
Wilson, Robley 1930- . . . . . . . . . . . . . . .DLB-218
Wilson, Romer 1891-1930 . . . . . . . . . . . .DLB-191
Wilson, Thomas 1524-1581 . . . . . . . .DLB-132, 236
Wilson, Woodrow 1856-1924 . . . . . . . . . . .DLB-47
Effingham Wilson [publishing house] . . . . .DLB-154
Wimpfeling, Jakob 1450-1528 . . . . . . . . .DLB-179
Wimsatt, William K., Jr. 1907-1975 . . . . . .DLB-63
Winchell, Walter 1897-1972 . . . . . . . . . . . .DLB-29
J. Winchester [publishing house] . . . . . . . .DLB-49
Winckelmann, Johann Joachim
 1717-1768 . . . . . . . . . . . . . . . . . . . .DLB-97
Winckler, Paul 1630-1686 . . . . . . . . . . . .DLB-164
Wind, Herbert Warren 1916- . . . . . . . . .DLB-171
John Windet [publishing house] . . . . . . . . .DLB-170
Windham, Donald 1920- . . . . . . . . . . . . . .DLB-6
Wing, Donald Goddard 1904-1972 . . . . . .DLB-187
Wing, John M. 1844-1917 . . . . . . . . . . . .DLB-187
Allan Wingate [publishing house] . . . . . . .DLB-112
Winnemucca, Sarah 1844-1921 . . . . . . . .DLB-175
Winnifrith, Tom 1938- . . . . . . . . . . . . . .DLB-155
Winsloe, Christa 1888-1944 . . . . . . . . . . .DLB-124
Winslow, Anna Green 1759-1780 . . . . . . .DLB-200
Winsor, Justin 1831-1897 . . . . . . . . . . . . .DLB-47
John C. Winston Company . . . . . . . . . . . .DLB-49
Winters, Yvor 1900-1968 . . . . . . . . . . . . . .DLB-48
Winterson, Jeanette 1959- . . . . . . .DLB-207, 261
Winthrop, John 1588-1649 . . . . . . . . .DLB-24, 30
Winthrop, John, Jr. 1606-1676 . . . . . . . . . .DLB-24
Winthrop, Margaret Tyndal 1591-1647 . .DLB-200
Winthrop, Theodore 1828-1861 . . . . . . . .DLB-202
Wirt, William 1772-1834 . . . . . . . . . . . . . .DLB-37
Wise, John 1652-1725 . . . . . . . . . . . . . . . .DLB-24
Wise, Thomas James 1859-1937 . . . . . . . .DLB-184
Wiseman, Adele 1928-1992 . . . . . . . . . . . .DLB-88
Wishart and Company . . . . . . . . . . . . . . .DLB-112
Wisner, George 1812-1849 . . . . . . . . . . . . .DLB-43
Wister, Owen 1860-1938 . . . . . . . .DLB-9, 78, 186
Wister, Sarah 1761-1804 . . . . . . . . . . . . . .DLB-200
Wither, George 1588-1667 . . . . . . . . . . . .DLB-121
Witherspoon, John 1723-1794 . . . . . . . . . .DLB-31
 *The Works of the Rev. John Witherspoon*
  (1800-1801) [excerpts] . . . . . . . . . .DLB-31
Withrow, William Henry 1839-1908 . . . . .DLB-99

Witkacy (see Witkiewicz, Stanisław Ignacy)
Witkiewicz, Stanisław Ignacy
 1885-1939 . . . . . . . . . . .DLB-215; CDWLB-4
Wittenwiler, Heinrich before 1387-
 circa 1414? . . . . . . . . . . . . . . . . . . .DLB-179
Wittgenstein, Ludwig 1889-1951 . . . . . . .DLB-262
Wittig, Monique 1935- . . . . . . . . . . . . . .DLB-83
Wodehouse, P. G.
 1881-1975 . . . . . . . . . .DLB-34, 162; CDBLB-6
 Worldwide Wodehouse Societies . . . . . . .Y-98
Wohmann, Gabriele 1932- . . . . . . . . . . .DLB-75
Woiwode, Larry 1941- . . . . . . . . . . . . . . .DLB-6
 Tribute to John Gardner . . . . . . . . . . . . .Y-82
Wolcot, John 1738-1819 . . . . . . . . . . . . .DLB-109
Wolcott, Roger 1679-1767 . . . . . . . . . . . . .DLB-24
Wolf, Christa 1929- . . . . . . .DLB-75; CDWLB-2
Wolf, Friedrich 1888-1953 . . . . . . . . . . . .DLB-124
Wolfe, Gene 1931- . . . . . . . . . . . . . . . . . .DLB-8
Wolfe, Thomas 1900-1938 . . . . . DLB-9, 102, 229;
 Y-85; DS-2, DS-16; CDALB-5
 "All the Faults of Youth and Inexperience":
  A Reader's Report on
  Thomas Wolfe's *O Lost* . . . . . . . . . . .Y-01
 Emendations for *Look Homeward, Angel* . . . Y-00
 Eugene Gant's Projected Works . . . . . . . .Y-01
 Fire at the Old Kentucky Home
  [Thomas Wolfe Memorial] . . . . . . . . .Y-98
 Thomas Wolfe Centennial
  Celebration in Asheville . . . . . . . . . . .Y-00
 The Thomas Wolfe Collection at
  the University of North Carolina
  at Chapel Hill . . . . . . . . . . . . . . . . . . .Y-97
 The Thomas Wolfe Society . . . . . . . . .Y-97, 99
Wolfe, Tom 1931- . . . . . . . . . . . .DLB-152, 185
John Wolfe [publishing house] . . . . . . . . . .DLB-170
Reyner (Reginald) Wolfe
 [publishing house] . . . . . . . . . . . . . . .DLB-170
Wolfenstein, Martha 1869-1906 . . . . . . . .DLB-221
Wolff, David (see Maddow, Ben)
Wolff, Helen 1906-1994 . . . . . . . . . . . . . . .Y-94
Wolff, Tobias 1945- . . . . . . . . . . . . . . . .DLB-130
 Tribute to Michael M. Rea . . . . . . . . . . .Y-97
 Tribute to Raymond Carver . . . . . . . . . .Y-88
Wolfram von Eschenbach
 circa 1170-after 1220 . . . .DLB-138; CDWLB-2
 Wolfram von Eschenbach's *Parzival*:
  Prologue and Book 3 . . . . . . . . . .DLB-138
Wolker, Jiří 1900-1924 . . . . . . . . . . . . . .DLB-215
Wollstonecraft, Mary 1759-1797
 . . . . . . . . .DLB-39, 104, 158, 252; CDBLB-3
Women
 Women's Work, Women's Sphere:
  Selected Comments from Women
  Writers . . . . . . . . . . . . . . . . . . . . .DLB-200
Wondratschek, Wolf 1943- . . . . . . . . . . .DLB-75
Wong, Elizabeth 1958- . . . . . . . . . . . . . .DLB-266
Wood, Anthony à 1632-1695 . . . . . . . . . .DLB-213
Wood, Benjamin 1820-1900 . . . . . . . . . . . .DLB-23
Wood, Charles 1932-1980 . . . . . . . . . . . . .DLB-13

The Charles Wood Affair:
A Playwright Revived . . . . . . . . . . . . Y-83
Wood, Mrs. Henry 1814-1887 . . . . . . . . . DLB-18
Wood, Joanna E. 1867-1927 . . . . . . . . . . . DLB-92
Wood, Sally Sayward Barrell Keating
1759-1855 . . . . . . . . . . . . . . . . . . . . DLB-200
Wood, William ?-? . . . . . . . . . . . . . . . . . . . DLB-24
Samuel Wood [publishing house] . . . . . . . DLB-49
Woodberry, George Edward
1855-1930 . . . . . . . . . . . . . . . . . DLB-71, 103
Woodbridge, Benjamin 1622-1684 . . . . . . DLB-24
Woodbridge, Frederick J. E. 1867-1940 . . DLB-270
Woodcock, George 1912-1995 . . . . . . . . . DLB-88
Woodhull, Victoria C. 1838-1927 . . . . . . . DLB-79
Woodmason, Charles circa 1720-? . . . . . . . DLB-31
Woodress, James Leslie, Jr. 1916- . . . . . DLB-111
Woods, Margaret L. 1855-1945 . . . . . . . . DLB-240
Woodson, Carter G. 1875-1950 . . . . . . . . . DLB-17
Woodward, C. Vann 1908-1999 . . . . . . . . DLB-17
Woodward, Stanley 1895-1965 . . . . . . . . DLB-171
Woodworth, Samuel 1785-1842 . . . . . . . DLB-250
Wooler, Thomas 1785 or 1786-1853 . . . . DLB-158
Woolf, David (see Maddow, Ben)
Woolf, Douglas 1922-1992 . . . . . . . . . . . DLB-244
Woolf, Leonard 1880-1969 . . . . . DLB-100; DS-10
Woolf, Virginia 1882-1941
. . . . . . . . DLB-36, 100, 162; DS-10; CDBLB-6
"The New Biography," *New York Herald
Tribune*, 30 October 1927 . . . . . . . DLB-149
Woollcott, Alexander 1887-1943 . . . . . . . . DLB-29
Woolman, John 1720-1772 . . . . . . . . . . . . DLB-31
Woolner, Thomas 1825-1892 . . . . . . . . . . DLB-35
Woolrich, Cornell 1903-1968 . . . . . . . . . . DLB-226
Woolsey, Sarah Chauncy 1835-1905 . . . . . DLB-42
Woolson, Constance Fenimore
1840-1894 . . . . . . . . . . . DLB-12, 74, 189, 221
Worcester, Joseph Emerson
1784-1865 . . . . . . . . . . . . . . . . . . . DLB-1, 235
Wynkyn de Worde
[publishing house] . . . . . . . . . . . . . . DLB-170
Wordsworth, Christopher 1807-1885 . . . . DLB-166
Wordsworth, Dorothy 1771-1855 . . . . . . . DLB-107
Wordsworth, Elizabeth 1840-1932 . . . . . . . DLB-98
Wordsworth, William
1770-1850 . . . . . . . . . DLB-93, 107; CDBLB-3
Workman, Fanny Bullock 1859-1925 . . . . DLB-189
*World Literatue Today:* A Journal for the
New Millennium . . . . . . . . . . . . . . . . . Y-01
World Publishing Company . . . . . . . . . . . DLB-46
World War I (1914-1918) . . . . . . . . . . . . . . . DS-18
The Great War Exhibit and Symposium
at the University of South Carolina . . . Y-97
The Liddle Collection and First World
War Research . . . . . . . . . . . . . . . . . . . . Y-97
Other British Poets Who Fell
in the Great War . . . . . . . . . . . . . DLB-216
The Seventy-Fifth Anniversary of
the Armistice: The Wilfred Owen
Centenary and the Great War Exhibit
at the University of Virginia . . . . . . . . Y-93

World War II (1939–1945)
Literary Effects of World War II . . . . . DLB-15
World War II Writers Symposium
at the University of South Carolina,
12–14 April 1995 . . . . . . . . . . . . . . . . . Y-95
WW2 HMSO Paperbacks Society . . . . . Y-98
R. Worthington and Company . . . . . . . . . DLB-49
Wotton, Sir Henry 1568-1639 . . . . . . . . . DLB-121
Wouk, Herman 1915- . . . . . . . . Y-82; CDALB-7
Tribute to James Dickey . . . . . . . . . . . . Y-97
Wreford, James 1915- . . . . . . . . . . . . . . . DLB-88
Wren, Sir Christopher 1632-1723 . . . . . . DLB-213
Wren, Percival Christopher 1885-1941 . . DLB-153
Wrenn, John Henry 1841-1911 . . . . . . . . DLB-140
Wright, C. D. 1949- . . . . . . . . . . . . . . . . DLB-120
Wright, Charles 1935- . . . . . . . . . DLB-165; Y-82
Wright, Charles Stevenson 1932- . . . . . . DLB-33
Wright, Chauncey 1830-1875 . . . . . . . . . DLB-270
Wright, Frances 1795-1852 . . . . . . . . . . . . DLB-73
Wright, Harold Bell 1872-1944 . . . . . . . . . DLB-9
Wright, James 1927-1980
. . . . . . . . . . . . . . . . DLB-5, 169; CDALB-7
Wright, Jay 1935- . . . . . . . . . . . . . . . . . . DLB-41
Wright, Judith 1915-2000 . . . . . . . . . . . . DLB-260
Wright, Louis B. 1899-1984 . . . . . . . . . . . DLB-17
Wright, Richard
1908-1960 . . . . DLB-76, 102; DS-2; CDALB-5
Wright, Richard B. 1937- . . . . . . . . . . . . DLB-53
Wright, S. Fowler 1874-1965 . . . . . . . . . DLB-255
Wright, Sarah Elizabeth 1928- . . . . . . . . DLB-33
Wright, T. H.
"Style" (1877) [excerpt] . . . . . . . . . . . DLB-57
Wright, Willard Huntington
("S. S. Van Dine") 1888-1939 . . . . . . . DS-16
Wrigley, Robert 1951- . . . . . . . . . . . . . . DLB-256
*Writers' Forum* . . . . . . . . . . . . . . . . . . . . . . . Y-85
Writing
A Writing Life . . . . . . . . . . . . . . . . . . . . Y-02
On Learning to Write . . . . . . . . . . . . . . Y-88
The Profession of Authorship:
Scribblers for Bread . . . . . . . . . . . . . Y-89
A Writer Talking: A Collage . . . . . . . . . Y-00
Wroth, Lawrence C. 1884-1970 . . . . . . . DLB-187
Wroth, Lady Mary 1587-1653 . . . . . . . . DLB-121
Wurlitzer, Rudolph 1937- . . . . . . . . . . . . DLB-173
Wyatt, Sir Thomas circa 1503-1542 . . . . . DLB-132
Wycherley, William
1641-1715 . . . . . . . . . . . . DLB-80; CDBLB-2
Wyclif, John
circa 1335-31 December 1384 . . . . . . DLB-146
Wyeth, N. C. 1882-1945 . . . . . . DLB-188; DS-16
Wyle, Niklas von circa 1415-1479 . . . . . . DLB-179
Wylie, Elinor 1885-1928 . . . . . . . . . . . . DLB-9, 45
Wylie, Philip 1902-1971 . . . . . . . . . . . . . . DLB-9
Wyllie, John Cook 1908-1968 . . . . . . . . DLB-140
Wyman, Lillie Buffum Chace
1847-1929 . . . . . . . . . . . . . . . . . . . . . DLB-202
Wymark, Olwen 1934- . . . . . . . . . . . . . DLB-233
Wynd, Oswald Morris (see Black, Gavin)

Wyndham, John (John Wyndham Parkes
Lucas Beynon Harris) 1903-1969 . . . DLB-255
Wynne-Tyson, Esmé 1898-1972 . . . . . . . DLB-191

# X

Xenophon circa 430 B.C.-circa 356 B.C. . . . DLB-176

# Y

Yasuoka Shōtarō 1920- . . . . . . . . . . . . . DLB-182
Yates, Dornford 1885-1960 . . . . . . . . . DLB-77, 153
Yates, J. Michael 1938- . . . . . . . . . . . . . . DLB-60
Yates, Richard 1926-1992 . . . DLB-2, 234; Y-81, 92
Yau, John 1950- . . . . . . . . . . . . . . . . . . DLB-234
Yavorov, Peyo 1878-1914 . . . . . . . . . . . . DLB-147
Yearsley, Ann 1753-1806 . . . . . . . . . . . . DLB-109
Yeats, William Butler
1865-1939 . . . DLB-10, 19, 98, 156; CDBLB-5
The W. B. Yeats Society of N.Y. . . . . . . Y-99
Yellen, Jack 1892-1991 . . . . . . . . . . . . . . DLB-265
Yep, Laurence 1948- . . . . . . . . . . . . . . . . DLB-52
Yerby, Frank 1916-1991 . . . . . . . . . . . . . . DLB-76
Yezierska, Anzia
1880-1970 . . . . . . . . . . . . . . . . . DLB-28, 221
Yolen, Jane 1939- . . . . . . . . . . . . . . . . . . DLB-52
Yonge, Charlotte Mary
1823-1901 . . . . . . . . . . . . . . . . . . DLB-18, 163
The Charlotte M. Yonge Fellowship . . . . Y-98
The York Cycle circa 1376-circa 1569 . . . DLB-146
*A Yorkshire Tragedy* . . . . . . . . . . . . . . . . . DLB-58
Thomas Yoseloff [publishing house] . . . . . DLB-46
Youd, Sam (see Christopher, John)
Young, A. S. "Doc" 1919-1996 . . . . . . . . DLB-241
Young, Al 1939- . . . . . . . . . . . . . . . . . . . DLB-33
Young, Arthur 1741-1820 . . . . . . . . . . . . DLB-158
Young, Dick 1917 or 1918 - 1987 . . . . . . DLB-171
Young, Edward 1683-1765 . . . . . . . . . . . . DLB-95
Young, Frank A. "Fay" 1884-1957 . . . . . . DLB-241
Young, Francis Brett 1884-1954 . . . . . . . DLB-191
Young, Gavin 1928- . . . . . . . . . . . . . . . DLB-204
Young, Stark 1881-1963 . . . . . . . DLB-9, 102; DS-16
Young, Waldeman 1880-1938 . . . . . . . . . DLB-26
William Young [publishing house] . . . . . . DLB-49
Young Bear, Ray A. 1950- . . . . . . . . . . . DLB-175
Yourcenar, Marguerite 1903-1987 . . . DLB-72; Y-88
Yovkov, Yordan 1880-1937 . . DLB-147; CDWLB-4

# Z

Zachariä, Friedrich Wilhelm 1726-1777 . . . DLB-97
Zagajewski, Adam 1945- . . . . . . . . . . . . DLB-232
Zagoskin, Mikhail Nikolaevich
1789-1852 . . . . . . . . . . . . . . . . . . . . . DLB-198
Zajc, Dane 1929- . . . . . . . . . . . . . . . . . . DLB-181
Zālīte, Māra 1952- . . . . . . . . . . . . . . . . . DLB-232
Zamiatin, Evgenii Ivanovich
1884-1937 . . . . . . . . . . . . . . . . . . . . . DLB-272
Zamora, Bernice 1938- . . . . . . . . . . . . . . DLB-82
Zamudio, Adela (Soledad) 1854-1928 . . . DLB-283
Zand, Herbert 1923-1970 . . . . . . . . . . . . . DLB-85
Zangwill, Israel 1864-1926 . . . . . . DLB-10, 135, 197
Zanzotto, Andrea 1921- . . . . . . . . . . . . . DLB-128

Zapata Olivella, Manuel 1920- .........DLB-113

Zapoev, Timur Iur'evich
(see Kibirov, Timur Iur'evich)

Zasodimsky, Pavel Vladimirovich
1843-1912 ..................DLB-238

Zebra Books.....................DLB-46

Zebrowski, George 1945- .............DLB-8

Zech, Paul 1881-1946 ...............DLB-56

Zeidner, Lisa 1955- ................DLB-120

Zeidonis, Imants 1933- ..............DLB-232

Zeimi (Kanze Motokiyo) 1363-1443 .....DLB-203

Zelazny, Roger 1937-1995 .............DLB-8

Zenger, John Peter 1697-1746........DLB-24, 43

Zepheria........................DLB-172

Zesen, Philipp von 1619-1689.........DLB-164

Zhadovskaia, Iuliia Valerianovna
1824-1883 ..................DLB-277

Zhukova, Mar'ia Semenovna
1805-1855 ..................DLB-277

Zhukovsky, Vasilii Andreevich
1783-1852 ..................DLB-205

Zhvanetsky, Mikhail Mikhailovich
1934- ......................DLB-285

G. B. Zieber and Company ............DLB-49

Ziedonis, Imants 1933- ...........CDWLB-4

Zieroth, Dale 1946- ................DLB-60

Zigler und Kliphausen, Heinrich
Anshelm von 1663-1697 ..........DLB-168

Zil'ber, Veniamin Aleksandrovich
(see Kaverin, Veniamin Aleksandrovich)

Zimmer, Paul 1934- .................DLB-5

Zinberg, Len (see Lacy, Ed)

Zincgref, Julius Wilhelm 1591-1635 .....DLB-164

Zindel, Paul 1936- ........DLB-7, 52; CDALB-7

Zinnes, Harriet 1919- ...............DLB-193

Zinzendorf, Nikolaus Ludwig von
1700-1760....................DLB-168

Zitkala-Ša 1876-1938 ................DLB-175

Zīverts, Mārtiņš 1903-1990 ...........DLB-220

Zlatovratsky, Nikolai Nikolaevich
1845-1911 ..................DLB-238

Zola, Emile 1840-1902...............DLB-123

Zolla, Elémire 1926- ...............DLB-196

Zolotow, Charlotte 1915- ............DLB-52

Zoshchenko, Mikhail Mikhailovich
1895-1958 ..................DLB-272

Zschokke, Heinrich 1771-1848..........DLB-94

Zubly, John Joachim 1724-1781 .........DLB-31

Zu-Bolton, Ahmos, II 1936- ..........DLB-41

Zuckmayer, Carl 1896-1977 ........DLB-56, 124

Zukofsky, Louis 1904-1978 ..........DLB-5, 165

Zupan, Vitomil 1914-1987............DLB-181

Župančič, Oton 1878-1949...DLB-147; CDWLB-4

zur Mühlen, Hermynia 1883-1951 .......DLB-56

Zweig, Arnold 1887-1968..............DLB-66

Zweig, Stefan 1881-1942 ..........DLB-81, 118

Zwinger, Ann 1925- ................DLB-275

Zwingli, Huldrych 1484-1531 ..........DLB-338

ISBN 0-7876-6824-9

PQ
9027
.P67

2004